S0-CBM-667

# basic marketing

## A GLOBAL-MANAGERIAL APPROACH

ELEVENTH CANADIAN EDITION

Kenneth B. Wong
Queen's School of Business
Queen's University

Stanley J. Shapiro
Simon Fraser University
(Professor Emeritus)

William D. Perreault
University of North Carolina

E. Jerome McCarthy
Michigan State University

Toronto Montréal Boston Burr Ridge, IL Dubuque, IA Madison, WI New York
San Francisco St. Louis Bangkok Bogotá Caracas Kuala Lumpur Lisbon London
Madrid Mexico City Milan New Delhi Santiago Seoul Singapore Sydney Taipei

The McGraw·Hill Companies

BASIC MARKETING
A GLOBAL-MANAGERIAL APPROACH
*Eleventh Canadian Edition*



ISBN: 0-07-091666-7

1 2 3 4 5 6 7 8 9 10 VH 0 9 8 7 6 5

Printed and bound in the United States of America.



*Vice President and Editorial Director: Pat Ferrier*
*Senior Sponsoring Editor: James Buchanan*
*Developmental Editor: Sandra de Ruiter*
*Managing Editor: Kim Brewster*
*Sales Manager: Megan Farrell*
*Marketing Manager: Kim Verhaeghe*
*Manager, Editorial Services: Kelly Dickson*
*Supervising Editor: Joanne Murray*
*Copy Editor: Kelli Howey*
*Senior Production Coordinator: Jennifer Wilkie*
*Permissions Research: Alison Derry/Permissions Plus*
*Composition: Claire Milne/First Folio Resource Group, Inc.*
*Cover Design: Dianna Little*
*Printer: Von Hoffmann Press, Inc.*

National Library of Canada Cataloguing in Publication Data
Basic marketing : a global-managerial approach / Kenneth Wong ... [et al.]. -- 11th Canadian ed.

E. Jerome McCarthy listed first on 1st–7th Canadian eds.; 8th–9th Canadian eds. by Stanley J. Shapiro, William D. Perreault, E. Jerome McCarthy.
Includes bibliographical references and index.
ISBN 0-07-091666-7

1. Marketing--Management. I. Wong, Kenneth II. Shapiro, Stanley J. Basic marketing.

HF5415.13.B38 2004 658.8 C2004-901486-2

# DEDICATION

**To James and Sandra at McGraw-Hill Ryerson**

*I was blessed to be a part of your team.*

**To my RAs – Lesley, Nat, Patricia, Jared, Anne, Angie, Logan, and Carolyn**

*I was blessed to have you on my team.*

**To my Family – Marcel, Alice, Barb, James, Ben, Lauren, and Lesley**

*I am blessed.*

**KW**

**To Roberta**

*Partner "par excellence" in all the joint ventures of a lifetime.*
*Ours has been the ultimate strategic alliance.*

**SJS**

# About the Authors

## Kenneth B. Wong

Ken Wong is a faculty member at Queen's School of Business, where he has held both teaching and administrative positions.

In his last administrative assignment, he was a principal architect of the first full-time degree program in Canada to operate completely outside of government subsidy: a distinction that earned him the cover of *Canadian Business* in April 1994. (The new program, the MBA for Science & Technology, has itself been a cover feature: it was named Canada's Number One MBA in *Canadian Business'* annual ratings in five of its first seven years of operation, and was rated by *Business Week* as #2 among non–U.S. MBAs in the magazine's 2002 survey.)

As a teacher, Professor Wong has received numerous awards for his courses in strategic planning, marketing, and business strategy. In 1998 he won the *Financial Post*'s Leaders in Management Education award, a lifetime achievement award for his work in undergraduate, MBA, and executive development programs. Beyond Queen's, he has also taught in degree programs at Carleton University, Radcliffe College, and Harvard's Continuing Education Program, and in executive programs at York University, the University of Toronto, Dalhousie University, and the University of Alberta.

Professor Wong is a frequent speaker and facilitator for conferences and executive development programs around the world. His corporate clients have included Accelio; Accenture; Alcan; AT&T (Canada); BC Hydro; Bell Canada; Campbell's Soup (Canada); Canada Post; Cara; Carstar; Cartier Partners; Central Park Lodges; Coast Spas; COGECO; The Co-operators; Credit Union Central (Alberta); Credit Union Central (BC); Dalsa; Dillon Consulting; DuPont; Eagle Human Resources; Empire Financial Group; Equifax Canada; Falconbridge Mines; Farmer's Credit Canada (FCC); Frito-Lay; General Accident Insurance; General Mills; GlaxoSmithKline; Hummingbird; Humpty Dumpty; H.Y. Louie (London Drugs and IGA); IFIC; Interac; Jacques-Whitford; Jannsen-Ortho; The Johnson Group; Lombard Insurance; Mattel; McCain; Microsoft; Mountain Equipment Co-op; PBB Global Logistics; Red Lobster; RLG International; Rohm & Haas; Royal-SunAlliance; SaskTel; Scott Paper; Sonoco Products Company; Starbucks; St. Joseph's Printing; TD-Canada Trust; Telus; Texec; and 3M Canada. He has also served a variety of public agencies and associations, including Attorney General (Ontario); Canada Customs and Revenue Agency (CCRA); Canada Mortgage & Housing Corporation (CMHC); Canadian Advanced Technology Managers (CATM); Canadian Agricultural Marketing Association (CAMA); Canadian Association of Chemical Distributors (CACD); Canadian Council of Grocery Distributors; Canadian Poultry and Egg Processors (CPEPC); Canadian Professional Sales Association; Canadian Urban Transit Association; Communications Canada (CCMD); Credit Union Central of Saskatchewan; Electro Federation; Hostex; National Association of Printers & Lithographers; New Brunswick Department of Economic Development & Tourism; North American State & Provincial Lottery Association; North York Board of Education; Ontario Dairy Council; Province of Nova Scotia; and Saskatchewan Wheat Pool.

As a researcher, Professor Wong has worked with the Strategic Planning Institute (Cambridge, MA) and the Conference Board of Canada. He has written for *Marketing Magazine*, the *Financial Post*, and the *National Post*. His current research focuses on devices that assist organizations in becoming more market-oriented and in enhancing their marketing productivity.

Private corporations that have used Professor Wong as a marketing and strategic planning consultant include Acklands Grainger; Baxter Corporation; Bell Canada; Equifax; General Electric (U.S.); Hoffman-LaRoche; QL Systems; Rohm & Haas; Rx Plus; Sherritt-Gordon; Southmedic; Sprint Canada; Tremco Products; and Xerox. He has also served as a strategic adviser to the Ontario Ministry of Education and Training; on various local, provincial, and federal government task forces; and on the Community Editorial Board of the *Kingston Whig-Standard*. He often assists on judging panels, most recently for the 2003 Canadian "Best 50" competition (excellence in management), the 2003 Canadian Entrepreneur of the Year, and the 2001 Cassies (advertising).

He received his B.Comm and MBA degrees from Queen's University prior to a period of doctoral studies at the Harvard Business School. He is Chairman of the Board, PBB Global Logistics Inc. and a member of a number of other advisory boards and boards of directors. He is listed in the *Canadian Who's Who* and the *International Who's Who of Professionals*.

## Stanley J. Shapiro

Stanley J. Shapiro received his B.A. from Harvard and his MBA and Ph.D. degrees from the Wharton School of the University of Pennsylvania. His doctoral dissertation was a "politics of distribution" study focusing on the Ontario Hog Producers' Marketing Board. He then taught at Wharton for three years before moving to Montreal to join first an advertising agency and then a marketing research firm. In 1967, he became an associate professor at the McGill Graduate School of Business. He became a full professor in 1972 and between 1973 and 1978 he was Dean of the McGill Faculty of Management. In 1981, he became a Professor of Marketing at Simon Fraser University, where he was also Dean of Business Administration between 1987 and 1997. Dr. Shapiro has also been a Visiting Professor at Queen's University, Bentley College, and Royal Roads University. Dr. Shapiro is a Past Chair of the Canadian Federation of Deans of Management and Administrative Studies. During his career he has conducted numerous evaluations of BBA, MBA, and Ph.D. programs at other Canadian universities. He was also a member of a CIDA–sponsored task force that established close (and still continuing) federation links with comparable organizations of deans in South Asia. Dr. Shapiro is also a former editor of the *Journal of Macromarketing* and was an editorial board member of the *Journal of Marketing* for more than 30 years. He currently serves on the editorial boards of the *Journal of Macromarketing*, the *Journal of Global Marketing*, the *International Marketing Review*, and the *Journal of Business Ethics*. Dr. Shapiro is a past president of the Montreal chapter of the American Marketing Association and a former National Director of that organization. Also, he is both a Past Governor and a Distinguished Fellow of the Academy of Marketing Science. He has published extensively in subjects ranging from marketing history to the financial dimensions of marketing management. Much of his consulting has been public sector–related, including such major projects as the first marketing study ever conducted by Canada Post and active involvement in the Canadian government's Conserver Society initiatives. Between 1987 and 1993, Dr. Shapiro was also an elected School Trustee in Burnaby, British Columbia.

### William D. Perreault, Jr.

William D. Perreault, Jr. is currently Kenan Professor at the University of North Carolina Kenan-Flagler Business School. He has also taught at Stanford University, the University of Georgia, and North Carolina State University, and has been an invited speaker at more than 80 universities. During 1997 he was the Arthur Andersen Distinguished Visitor at Cambridge University. Dr. Perreault is the recipient of the two most prestigious awards in his field: the American Marketing Association Distinguished Educator Award and the Academy of Marketing Science Outstanding Educator Award. He also was selected for the Churchill Award, which honours career impact on marketing research. He was editor of the *Journal of Marketing Research* and has been on the review board of the *Journal of Marketing* and other journals. His research has also been published in many journals, and one *Journal of Marketing* article was recently voted one of the most influential articles on sales and sales management of the 20th century. The Decision Sciences Institute has recognized Dr. Perreault for innovations in marketing education, and at UNC he has received several awards for teaching excellence. His books include two other widely used texts: *Essentials of Marketing* and *The Marketing Game!* Dr. Perreault is a past president of the American Marketing Association Academic Council and was on the AMA Board. He was chair of an advisory committee to the U.S. Bureau of the Census, a trustee of the Marketing Science Institute, and on the Council of the Decision Sciences Institute. He is a Fellow of the Society for Marketing Advances. He has also worked as a consultant to organizations that range from GE and IBM to the Federal Trade Commission and the Venezuelan Ministry of Education. He is on the advisory board for Copernicus: The Marketing Investment Strategy Group.

### E. Jerome McCarthy

E. Jerome McCarthy received his Ph.D. from the University of Minnesota. He has taught at the Universities of Oregon, Notre Dame, and Michigan State. He was honoured with the American Marketing Association's Trailblazer Award in 1987, and he was voted one of the Top Five Leaders in Marketing Thought by marketing educators. He has been deeply involved in teaching and developing new teaching materials. Besides writing various articles and monographs, he is the author of textbooks on data processing and social issues in marketing. Dr. McCarthy is active in making presentations to business meetings and academic conferences. He has worked with groups of teachers throughout the country and has addressed international conferences in South America, Africa, and India. He was also a Ford Foundation Fellow in 1963–64, studying the role of marketing in global economic development. In 1959–60 he was a Ford Foundation Fellow at the Harvard Business School working on mathematical methods in marketing. Besides his academic interests, Dr. McCarthy has been involved in consulting for, and guiding the growth of, a number of businesses in the U.S. and overseas. He has worked with top managers from Bemis, Dow Chemical, Grupo Industrial Alfa, 3M, Steelcase, and many other companies. He is also active in executive education and is a director of several organizations. His primary interests, however, are in (1) converting students to marketing and marketing strategy planning, and (2) preparing teaching materials to help others do the same. This is why he has spent a large part of his career developing, revising, and improving marketing texts to reflect the most current thinking in the field.

# Brief Contents

# Contents

## Chapter Eleven
## Place: Channel Systems and Physical Distribution



## Chapter Twelve
## Retailers, Wholesalers, and Their Strategy Planning



## Chapter Thirteen
## Promotion—Introduction to Integrated Marketing Communications



## Chapter Fourteen
## Personal Selling



## Chapter Fifteen
## Advertising and Sales Promotion

# Preface

## *Basic Marketing* Is Designed to Satisfy Your Needs

This is a book about marketing and marketing strategy planning. It's also a book that "practises what it preaches." And, since the heart of marketing and marketing strategy is figuring out how to do a superior job of satisfying customers, it seems appropriate here to outline some of the important changes that we've made with instructors and students—our customers—in mind.

## Continuous Innovation and Improvement

The success of *Basic Marketing* is not the result of a single strength or one long-lasting innovation. Rather, the text's Four Ps framework, managerial orientation, and strategy-planning focus have proved to be pillars of a foundation that is remarkably robust for supporting new developments in the field and innovations in the text and package.

In developing this 11th Canadian edition, we've reorganized chapters, made hundreds of additions big and small, and improved the text and the supporting materials that accompany it. We've added new instructional and learning aids, new case studies, and improvements to our Online Learning Centre. The goal was simple: to make this the most user-friendly source of information possible.

## A Tradition of Innovation Rooted in the Fundamentals

When *Basic Marketing* was first published more than 40 years ago, it pioneered an innovative way of organizing marketing knowledge for introductory marketing courses. The managerially oriented "Four Ps" quickly became *the* language of marketing, and *Basic Marketing* became one of the most widely used business textbooks ever published. The reason was simple: it not only listed the various decisions marketing managers must make every day, but also provided a unifying theme or philosophy that integrated those decisions: a focus on the customer. Today, that philosophy is so deeply rooted in marketing thought and practice that it often goes without saying.

But not in this book. While *Basic Marketing* has undergone constant change to reflect the realities of the contemporary marketplace, its focus on customers as the heart of marketing action—and on students and instructors as the customers for marketing knowledge—has not wavered. As a result, readers of *Basic Marketing* learn tools and approaches that have withstood the test of time and remain vital to understanding the complexities that modern marketers face. It is gratifying that the Four Ps has proven to be an organizing structure that has worked well for thousands of students and instructors.

## A Book Designed for Both Instructors and Students

The preparation of the 11th edition went beyond the standard textbook review process. As most textbook authors do, we went to instructors to determine what they needed—both within and beyond the text—to improve the book as a teaching resource and learning aid. Then we went one step further: **we went to the students themselves**.

A team of students has critically reviewed every chapter of the text. The students came from Queen's Business School and the faculties of Arts & Science and Engineering. Their mission was not to identify *what* to cover, but to help us decide *how* to cover the material. They looked at the examples used, the photos and advertisements, the charts and graphs, even the language used to communicate the material.

We also asked them to comment on the value of each paragraph to their understanding of the concepts: in this way, we sought to reduce the chapter size, the required reading time, and the cost of the text. The revised manuscript was then submitted to a second round of instructor review to ensure that we had not compromised the book's instructional value along the way.

The result was a major change in the organization of material: almost every chapter received a new layout and sequence. We believe the result is another exciting innovation that will continue the tradition of focusing on our "customers" and, in doing so, generate not only marketing knowledge but also a sense of excitement and passion for the field.

## Critical Revisions, Updates and Rewrites = A New Order

The 11th edition organizes material into four parts: Marketing Fundamentals, The Marketing Environment, Marketing Policies and Decisions, and Managing the Marketing. Each of these parts has a theme unto itself and a set of learning objectives attached to it. The goal was to give students a better sense of the relevance and practical significance of the material being covered, thereby enhancing their motivation as they approach each chapter.

The material covered in earlier editions was then redistributed among these four parts to establish a more easily followed flow of thought. Our belief was that marketing should not be viewed as a series of independent chapters but rather as a continuous story. To assist in telling that story, each chapter received a new vignette and a new element, located at the start of each chapter, entitled "In This Chapter".

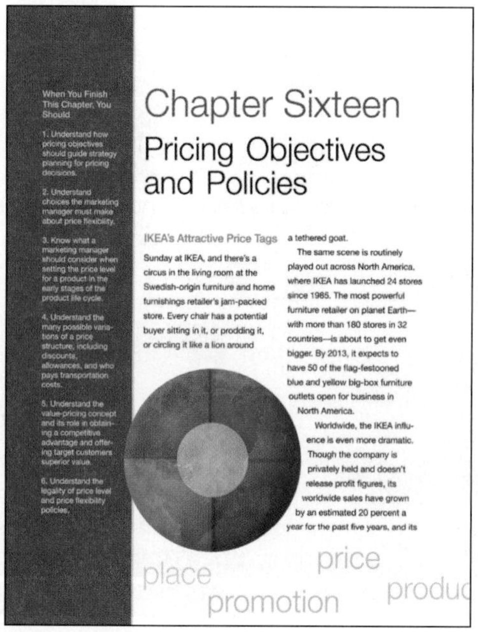

When You Finish This Chapter, You Should

1. Understand how pricing objectives should guide strategy planning for pricing decisions.
2. Understand choices the marketing manager must make about price flexibility.
3. Know what a marketing manager should consider when setting the price level for a product in the early stages of the product life cycle.
4. Understand the many possible variations of a price structure, including discounts, allowances, and who pays transportation costs.
5. Understand the value-pricing concept and its role in obtaining a competitive advantage and offering target customers superior value.
6. Understand the legality of price level and price flexibility policies.

Chapter Sixteen

Pricing Objectives and Policies

IKEA's Attractive Price Tags

Sunday at IKEA, and there's a circus in the living room at the Swedish-origin furniture and home furnishings retailer's jam-packed store. Every chair has a potential buyer sitting in it, or prodding it, or circling it like a lion around a tethered goat.

The same scene is routinely played out across North America, where IKEA has launched 24 stores since 1985. The most powerful furniture retailer on planet Earth—with more than 180 stores in 32 countries—is about to get even bigger. By 2013, it expects to have 50 of the flag-festooned blue and yellow big-box furniture outlets open for business in North America.

Worldwide, the IKEA influence is even more dramatic. Though the company is privately held and doesn't release profit figures, its worldwide sales have grown by an estimated 20 percent a year for the past five years, and its



This new introduction goes beyond alerting students to key learning objectives to provide the student with a **roadmap** to how the current chapter relates to earlier chapters, what will be covered in the chapter, and why it is laid out in that manner. New chapter summaries revisit those themes to reinforce the student takeaways.

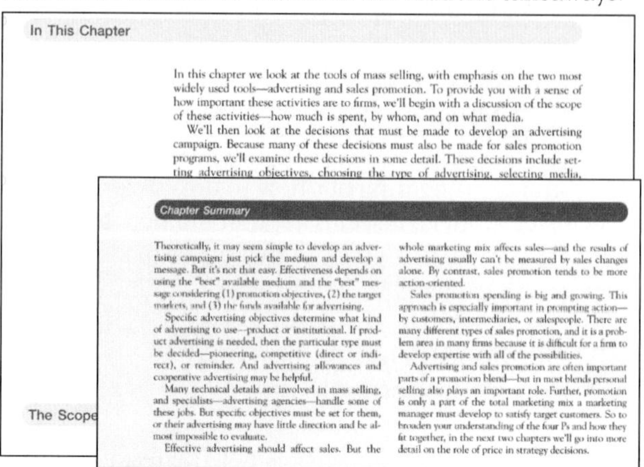

In This Chapter

In this chapter we look at the tools of mass selling, with emphasis on the two most widely used tools—advertising and sales promotion. To provide you with a sense of how important these activities are to firms, we'll begin with a discussion of the scope of these activities—how much is spent, by whom, and on what media.

We'll then look at the decisions that must be made to develop an advertising campaign. Because many of these decisions must also be made for sales promotion programs, we'll examine these decisions in some detail. These decisions include setting advertising objectives, choosing the type of advertising, selecting media,

The Scope

Chapter Summary

Theoretically, it may seem simple to develop an advertising campaign: just pick the medium and develop a message. But it's not that easy. Effectiveness depends on using the "best" available medium and the "best" message considering (1) promotion objectives, (2) the target markets, and (3) the funds available for advertising.

Specific advertising objectives determine what kind of advertising to use—product or institutional. If product advertising is needed, then the particular type must be decided—pioneering, competitive (direct or indirect), or reminder. And advertising allowances and cooperative advertising may be helpful.

Many technical details are involved in mass selling, and specialists—advertising agencies—handle some of these jobs. But specific objectives must be set for them, or their advertising may have little direction and be almost impossible to evaluate.

Effective advertising should affect sales. But the whole marketing mix affects sales—and the results of advertising usually can't be measured by sales changes alone. By contrast, sales promotion tends to be more action-oriented.

Sales promotion spending is big and growing. This approach is especially important in prompting action—by customers, intermediaries, or salespeople. There are many different types of sales promotion, and it is a problem area in many firms because it is difficult for a firm to develop expertise with all of the possibilities.

Advertising and sales promotion are often important parts of a promotion blend—but in most blends personal selling also plays an important role. Further, promotion is only a part of the total marketing mix a marketing manager must develop to satisfy target customers. So to broaden your understanding of the four Ps and how they fit together, in the next two chapters we'll go into more detail on the role of price in strategy decisions.

## Environment

The goal was to get the student "faster to marketing": to enable the students to begin looking at the world using marketing tools and concepts at an earlier stage in their course. For example, by moving the chapter on segmentation and positioning from Chapter 8 (10th edition) to Chapter 3 (11th edition), students start dealing with marketing issues anywhere from two to four weeks sooner in a typical course. As an added benefit, with these concepts in mind, students will also find it much easier to appreciate the relevance of material on marketing's external environment, consumer behaviour and demographics.

But we didn't stop our re-ordering process at the chapter level. We wrote each chapter so as to highlight the strategic issues in the chapter and to identify the key decisions to be made. This is especially apparent in Part 3 (Chapters 9–17) where each chapter identifies the key decisions and organizes the discussion of those decisions around a common approach—starting with the identification of objectives and ending with implementation and control. The result is that students should find it easier to understand "where the pieces fit." And, if working on projects or cases, students will be able to more quickly locate necessary background material.

## We Listened! The Return of What You Like

We were very careful to attend to reviewers' comments about what they liked and didn't want to see changed. As a result, we continued the practice—with updated materials—of using opening vignettes,

Marketing Demos,

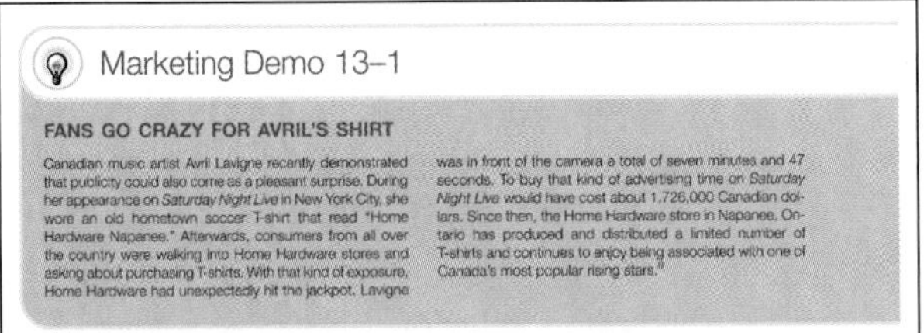

Marketing Demo 13–1

**FANS GO CRAZY FOR AVRIL'S SHIRT**

Canadian music artist Avril Lavigne recently demonstrated that publicity could also come as a pleasant surprise. During her appearance on *Saturday Night Live* in New York City, she wore an old hometown soccer T-shirt that read "Home Hardware Napanee." Afterwards, consumers from all over the country were walking into Home Hardware stores and asking about purchasing T-shirts. With that kind of exposure, Home Hardware had unexpectedly hit the jackpot. Lavigne was in front of the camera a total of seven minutes and 47 seconds. To buy that kind of advertising time on *Saturday Night Live* would have cost about 1,726,000 Canadian dollars. Since then, the Home Hardware store in Napanee, Ontario has produced and distributed a limited number of T-shirts and continues to enjoy being associated with one of Canada's most popular rising stars.[8]

Ethical Dimensions,

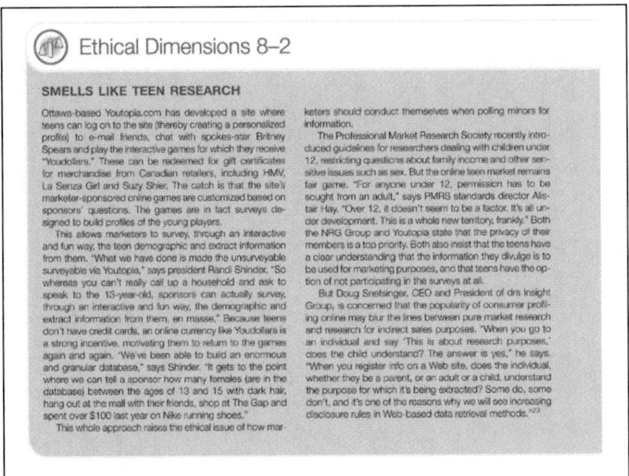

Ethical Dimensions 8–2

**SMELLS LIKE TEEN RESEARCH**

Ottawa-based Youtopia.com has developed a site where teens can log on to the site (thereby creating a personalized profile) to e-mail friends, chat with spokes-star Britney Spears and play the interactive games for which they receive "Youdollars." These can be redeemed for gift certificates for merchandise from Canadian retailers, including HMV, La Senza Girl and Suzy Shier. The catch is that the site's marketer-sponsored online games are customized based on sponsors' questions. The games are in fact surveys designed to build profiles of the young players.

This allows marketers to survey, through an interactive and fun way, the teen demographic and extract information from them. "What we have done is made the unsurveyable surveyable via Youtopia," says president Randi Shinder. "So whereas you can't really call up a household and ask to speak to the 13-year-old, sponsors can actually survey, through an interactive and fun way, the demographic and extract information from them, en masse." Because teens don't have credit cards, an online currency like Youdollars is a strong incentive, motivating them to return to the games again and again. "We've been able to build an enormous and granular database," says Shinder. "It gets to the point where we can tell a sponsor how many females (are in the database) between the ages of 13 and 15 with dark hair, hang out at the mall with their friends, shop at The Gap and spent over $100 last year on Nike running shoes."

This whole approach raises the ethical issue of how marketers should conduct themselves when polling minors for information.

The Professional Market Research Society recently introduced guidelines for researchers dealing with children under 12, restricting questions about family income and other sensitive issues such as sex. But the online teen market remains fair game. "For anyone under 12, permission has to be sought from an adult," says PMRS standards director Alistair Hay. "Over 12, it doesn't seem to be a factor. It's all under development. This is a whole new territory, frankly." Both the NRG Group and Youtopia state that the privacy of their members is a top priority. Both also insist that the teens have a clear understanding that the information they divulge is to be used for marketing purposes, and that teens have the option of not participating in the surveys at all.

But Doug Snetsinger, CEO and President of drs Insight Group, is concerned that the popularity of consumer profiling online may blur the lines between pure market research and research for indirect sales purposes. "When you go to an individual and say 'This is about research purposes,' does the child understand? The answer is yes," he says. "When you register info on a Web site, does the individual, whether they be a parent, or an adult or a child, understand the purpose for which it's being extracted? Some do, some don't, and it's one of the reasons why we will see increasing disclosure rules in Web-based data retrieval methods."[23]

extensive illustrations, end of chapter notes, Questions and Problems, and Computer-Aided Problems.

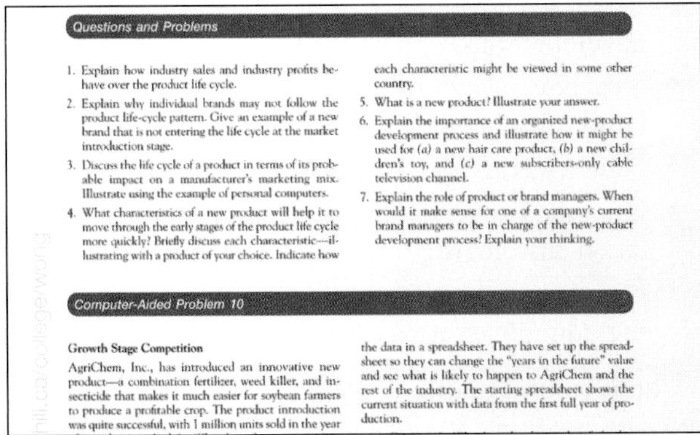

*Questions and Problems*

1. Explain how industry sales and industry profits behave over the product life cycle.
2. Explain why individual brands may not follow the product life-cycle pattern. Give an example of a new brand that is not entering the life cycle at the market introduction stage.
3. Discuss the life cycle of a product in terms of its probable impact on a manufacturer's marketing mix. Illustrate using the example of personal computers.
4. What characteristics of a new product will help it to move through the early stages of the product life cycle more quickly? Briefly discuss each characteristic—illustrating with a product of your choice. Indicate how each characteristic might be viewed in some other country.
5. What is a new product? Illustrate your answer.
6. Explain the importance of an organized new-product development process and illustrate how it might be used for *(a)* a new hair care product, *(b)* a new children's toy, and *(c)* a new subscribers-only cable television channel.
7. Explain the role of product or brand managers. When would it make sense for one of a company's current brand managers to be in charge of the new-product development process? Explain your thinking.

*Computer-Aided Problem 10*

**Growth Stage Competition**

AgriChem, Inc., has introduced an innovative new product—a combination fertilizer, weed killer, and insecticide that makes it much easier for soybean farmers to produce a profitable crop. The product introduction was quite successful, with 1 million units sold in the year the data in a spreadsheet. They have set up the spreadsheet so they can change the "years in the future" value and see what is likely to happen to AgriChem and the rest of the industry. The starting spreadsheet shows the current situation with data from the first full year of production.

In addition, Ramesh Venkat, of the Sobey School of Business, has authored an entirely new set of Internet Insites to provide up-to-date information on the latest e-commerce topics.

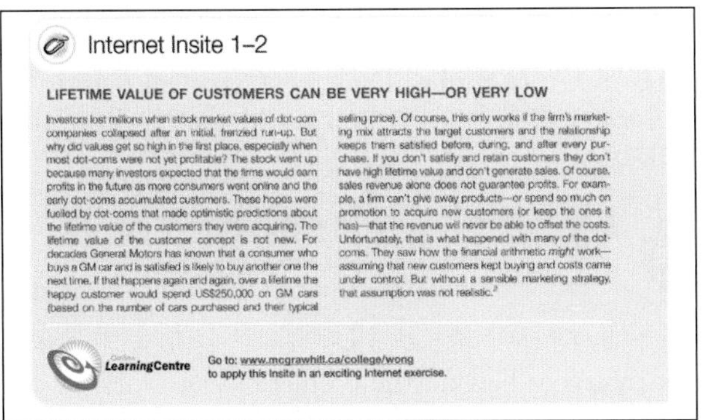

Internet Insite 1–2

**LIFETIME VALUE OF CUSTOMERS CAN BE VERY HIGH—OR VERY LOW**

Investors lost millions when stock market values of dot-com companies collapsed after an initial, frenzied run-up. But why did values get so high in the first place, especially when most dot-coms were not yet profitable? The stock went up because many investors expected that the firms would earn profits in the future as more consumers went online and the early dot-coms accumulated customers. These hopes were fuelled by dot-coms that made optimistic predictions about the lifetime value of the customers they were acquiring. The lifetime value of the customer concept is not new. For decades General Motors has known that a consumer who buys a GM car and is satisfied is likely to buy another one the next time. If that happens again and again, over a lifetime the happy customer would spend US$250,000 on GM cars (based on the number of cars purchased and their typical selling price). Of course, this only works if the firm's marketing mix attracts the target customers and the relationship keeps them satisfied before, during, and after every purchase. If you don't satisfy and retain customers they don't have high lifetime value and don't generate sales. Of course, sales revenue alone does not guarantee profits. For example, a firm can't give away products—or spend so much on promotion to acquire new customers (or keep the ones it has)—that the revenue will never be able to offset the costs. Unfortunately, that is what happened with many of the dot-coms. They saw how the financial arithmetic *might* work—assuming that new customers kept buying and costs came under control. But without a sensible marketing strategy, that assumption was not realistic.[2]

LearningCentre Go to: www.mcgrawhill.ca/college/wong to apply this Insite in an exciting Internet exercise.

Those familiar with the 10th and earlier editions will recognize the return of three Appendices that were omitted from the 10th edition:

- Marketing "YOU INC.": Preparing a Personal Marketing Plan
- Economics Fundamentals
- Marketing Arithmetic

These appendices are written at a level that enables students who lack prior courses in economics and accounting to feel comfortable with the vocabulary of business. This gives greater flexibility in the placement of an introductory marketing course within the academic calendar: *Basic Marketing* can be used as early as the first semester of the first year of studies. Also note that an appendix on Career Planning in Marketing can now be found on the Online Learning Centre.

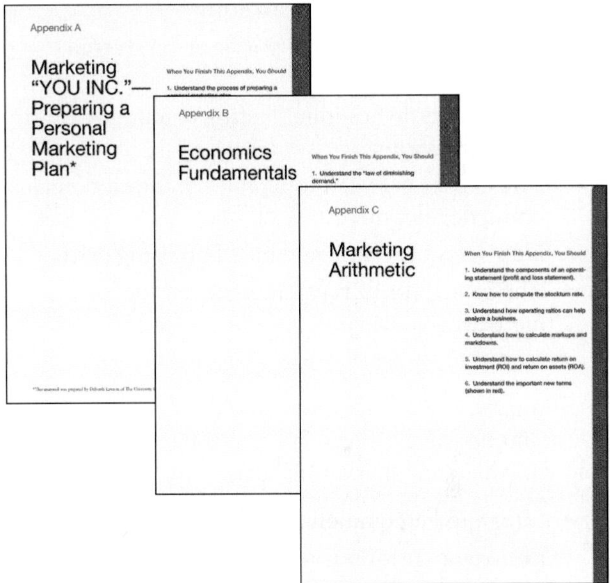

## What You Said—What We Did

We've heard from instructors that it is extremely challenging to keep cases current. Thus, in the 11th edition we've removed the cases from the book and will be offering a **new casebook with the text every year** with new and updated cases! It is the commitment of the publisher to provide this casebook free of charge, shrinkwrapped with each new copy of *Basic Marketing*. For this edition, substantial new case materials have been developed. More than 70 percent of the cases are new and revised—50 percent of those are new global cases, and 10 percent of those are new Canadian cases. If you prefer some of the classics, cases from the 10th edition can still be accessed through the Online Learning Centre. This should provide instructors with tremendous flexibility in choosing cases for discussion, assignment, or exam purposes.

## A Clear Focus on Contemporary Issues

This edition focuses special attention on changes taking place in today's dynamic markets. Throughout every chapter of the text we have integrated discussion and examples of major issues such as:

- Customer Relationship Management (CRM): developing and sustaining customer relationships and the costs and benefits of different approaches to customer acquisition and retention
- Customer Value: the importance of providing superior customer value as a means to achieve customer satisfaction and competitive advantage
- Integrated Marketing Communications (IMC): including the growing use and methods of direct marketing and public relations as a marketing tool, including "buzz" marketing
- The increasing channel power of large retail chains
- New technologies in marketing communication and distribution
- The debate between using sales promotion versus brand development
- New ways of setting and merchandising price
- The growth of B2B (business-to-business) marketing
- New privacy legislation

Similarly, we've also integrated new material on many important and fast-evolving topics. Look for the following dynamic marketing areas:

- Integrated e-commerce throughout
- More emphasis on how breakthroughs in technology are affecting marketing and why these changes are happening
- More on the process of marketing strategic planning
- New/updated IMC coverage
- New/updated coverage of relationship marketing
- Updated coverage of data management capabilities for CRM
- New/updated coverage of B2B and the use of technology
- New material on direct-response promotion and customer-initiated marketing communications
- New/updated coverage of sales and self-service technologies
- New/updated coverage of distribution channels (including the Internet and when it makes sense to use a website for direct distribution or dual distribution and when it doesn't)
- New coverage on the increasing channel power of large retail chains
- New/updated coverage of competitor analysis and creating competitive advantage
- New/updated coverage of using flexibility pricing and evaluating price sensitivity
- Increased coverage of five key themes: customer satisfaction, value, relationships, competition, and ethics.
- New/updated coverage of global demographics and population trends
- New/updated coverage of the differences between B2B and B2C marketing
- New/updated coverage of branding (to both B2B & B2C)
- New coverage of product risk management
- New/updated coverage of factors influencing product life cycles
- New/updated coverage of retail strategy and why it evolves
- Expanded coverage of retail and wholesale evolution
- New/updated coverage of direct marketing
- New coverage of permission marketing and pointcasting
- Expanded coverage of sales promotion and brand development
- New coverage of promotional campaigns that build "buzz" among consumers
- New coverage of pricing decisions
- Expanded coverage of traditional vs. Internet-based customers
- New/updated coverage of marketing control, including marketing cost analysis

Three external authors were commissioned to write pieces for use solely in the 11th edition. These contributions ensure that students receive practical insights from executives who deal with market changes every day.

- Bryan Pearson, President of Air Miles, on "Direct Marketing"
- Dan Tisch, President of Argyle Rowland Communications, on "Public Relations"
- Steven Cross, former Director, Canadian Centre for Ethics & Corporate Policy, on Marketing Ethics (in OLC)

## A Fresh Design—To Make Important Concepts Even Clearer

The 11th edition also sports a very new look. But it's a look that goes beyond the cosmetic. Our typestyle and paper quality enhance the readability of the book and the use of colour coding makes it easy to find material within the text. These changes, along with our usual practice of including key terms in the margins, make the 11th edition our easiest version ever to read.

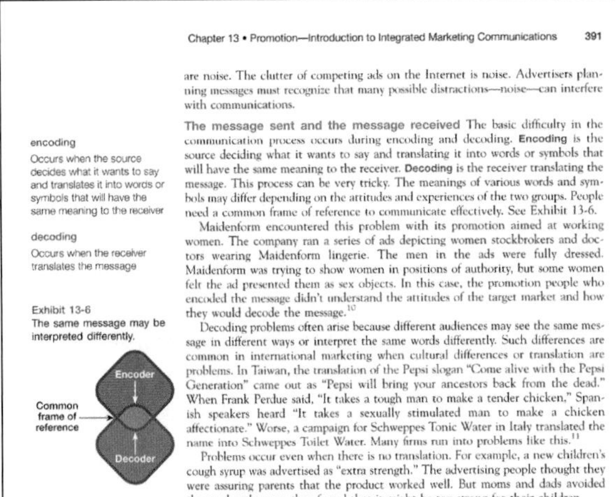
Chapter 13 • Promotion—Introduction to Integrated Marketing Communications 391

are noise. The clutter of competing ads on the Internet is noise. Advertisers planning messages must recognize that many possible distractions—noise—can interfere with communications.

**The message sent and the message received** The basic difficulty in the communication process occurs during encoding and decoding. **Encoding** is the source deciding what it wants to say and translating it into words or symbols that will have the same meaning to the receiver. **Decoding** is the receiver translating the message. This process can be very tricky. The meanings of various words and symbols may differ depending on the attitudes and experiences of the two groups. People need a common frame of reference to communicate effectively. See Exhibit 13-6.

**encoding** Occurs when the source decides what it wants to say and translates it into words or symbols that will have the same meaning to the receiver

**decoding** Occurs when the receiver translates the message

Maidenform encountered this problem with its promotion aimed at working women. The company ran a series of ads depicting women stockbrokers and doctors wearing Maidenform lingerie. The men in the ads were fully dressed. Maidenform was trying to show women in positions of authority, but some women felt the ad presented them as sex objects. In this case, the promotion people who encoded the message didn't understand the attitudes of the target market and how they would decode the message.[10]

Exhibit 13-6
**The same message may be interpreted differently.**



Decoding problems often arise because different audiences may see the same message in different ways or interpret the same words differently. Such differences are common in international marketing when cultural differences or translation are problems. In Taiwan, the translation of the Pepsi slogan "Come alive with the Pepsi Generation" came out as "Pepsi will bring your ancestors back from the dead." When Frank Perdue said, "It takes a tough man to make a tender chicken," Spanish speakers heard "It takes a sexually stimulated man to make a chicken affectionate." Worse, a campaign for Schweppes Tonic Water in Italy translated the name into Schweppes Toilet Water. Many firms run into problems like this.[11]

Problems occur even when there is no translation. For example, a new children's cough syrup was advertised as "extra strength." The advertising people thought they were assuring parents that the product worked well. But moms and dads avoided the product because they feared that it might be too strong for their children.

## Students Get "How-to-Do-It" Skill and Confidence

Really understanding marketing and how to plan marketing strategies can build self-confidence—and it can help prepare a student to take an active part in the business world. To move students in this direction, we've deliberately included a variety of frameworks, models, classification systems, cases, and "how-to-do-it" techniques that relate to our overall framework for marketing strategic planning.

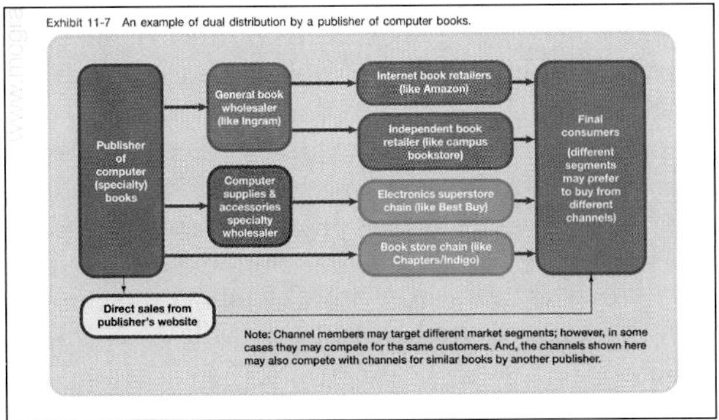
Exhibit 11-7 An example of dual distribution by a publisher of computer books.



Taken together, they should speed the development of "marketing sense" and enable the student to analyze marketing situations and develop marketing plans in a confident and meaningful way. They are practical and they work. In addition, because they are interesting and understandable, they motivate students to see marketing as the challenging and rewarding area it is.

## The Spirit of Nineteen Chapters—With an Emphasis on Marketing Strategic Planning

The 11th edition has several major changes from earlier editions. In fact, every chapter had a "change theme" attached to it—a statement of what we wanted to do better in this version.

**Part 1 (Marketing Fundamentals)** comprises Chapters 1–3. It seeks to establish what marketing is and is not. It provides a viewpoint that marketing is as much a way of thinking and managing as it is a collection of techniques.

**Chapter 1 (The Nature of Marketing)** discusses not only what marketing is but also, equally important, why it is relevant for students. We wanted students to get excited about marketing and motivated to learn about it, even if they were not considering a marketing career. To that end, the early sections of this chapter show how marketing touches the everyday, professional, and personal lives of students. Beyond buying and selling activities, we portray marketing as applicable to any exchange—whether of ideas, products, services, feelings, or friendships. This chapter also introduces five key themes that influence what marketers do and how they do it (and, as such, run through all remaining chapters): customer satisfaction, value, relationships, competitive advantage, and ethics and social responsibility.

**Chapter 2 (Marketing's Role within the Firm or Nonprofit Organization)** is about the "what and how" of marketing and how those decisions are made. Building on the discussion of major themes in Chapter 1, this chapter introduces the classic four Ps of marketing, with customers at the heart of all decisions. This is an important chapter, because it highlights the number-one source of many subsequent marketing problems: inappropriate attention to the selection of target markets and the need to align marketing actions with the behaviour of that group.

**Chapter 3 (Focusing Marketing Strategy with Segmentation and Positioning)** continues the theme of market selection and alignment by showing how segmentation and positioning assist in those tasks. However, before offering these concepts as "solutions," we first concentrate on getting to recognize the challenge and opportunity created by the "problem" of customer diversity. The goal is to help the student appreciate the opportunities created by customer diversity and to overcome the temptation to think in terms of "one size fits all."

**Part 2 (The Marketing Environment)** comprises Chapters 4–8. These chapters collectively lay out a number of factors that influence the behaviour of customers and therefore the types of marketing strategies and mixes required to reach them. In doing so, this part of the text builds directly on Part 1: if target-market selection and positioning are critical to marketing success, what types of factors do we need to consider in making those decisions?

**Chapter 4 (The Changing Marketing Environment)** presents the external factors that affect how marketing is performed. The perspective taken is that while many of these factors may be beyond management's direct control, we can plan and manage in anticipation of trends and other developments. Thus, we not only identify some developments but also discuss how organizations respond to those developments. This viewpoint is key to developing effective, action-oriented marketing plans, since the factors discussed are the usual headings found in the situation assessments section of most plans.

**Chapter 5 (Demographic Dimensions of Canadian and Global Consumer Markets)** presents demographic data and analysis. In addition to offering a new section on global demographics, this chapter also details the uses of data on where we live, what we buy, where and how we earn, and various ethnic dimensions. In this way, the chapter has been reworked so that students (1) can see the commercial implications of Canada's diversity, and (2) can see how Canada compares to the rest of the world.

**Chapter 6 (Behavioural Dimensions of the Consumer Market)** presents a variety of concepts central to understanding consumer behaviour. These concepts have been organized into two sections—"why people buy what they do" and "how people buy what they do." This distinction helps the student see the difference between factors that shape primary demand versus selective demand and adds a keener focus to material covered in Chapters 4 and 5.

**Chapter 7 (Business and Organizational Customers and Their Buying Behaviour)** is the organizational-buying equivalent of Chapter 6. Recognizing that most of the students using this book would not have considerable experience in buying or selling to an organization, we've restructured this chapter to follow the flow of Chapter 6 so that students can see the similarities in both the issues being considered and the frameworks used to explore them. We also added new materials on e-commerce and relationship marketing.

**Chapter 8 (Improving Decisions with Marketing Information)** covers the methods used to gather information on the factors detailed in Chapters 4 through 7. While we have retained and updated much of the material contained in earlier editions, we restructured that material to separate the "managerial process" of research (i.e., how we determine what we need to know) from the "technical performance" (i.e., how we find out) of research. The result is a smoother flow to the discussion and enhanced student understanding of how the various technologies and methodologies are interrelated.

**Part 3 (Marketing Policies and Decisions)** comprises Chapters 9–17. These are the key managerial decision areas. The 11th edition uses a common structure to the treatment of each area: in each chapter we'll identify the constituent decisions, the alternatives available, and the kinds of factors to consider in choosing among alternatives. This parallel structure should make it easier to organize teaching materials and for students to organize their notes.

**Chapter 9 (Elements of Product Planning for Goods and Services)** is an important chapter in shaping student thinking about sources of competitive advantage. Thus, instead of describing product policy as an inventory of elements, we focus on a product or service as a "bundle of capabilities" and show how all other product decisions take their cue from the customer whose bundle we seek to provide. We added a section up front called "What Is a Product?" The goal was to get students thinking about our "offering" as much more than a product per se ... or even a product with associated services. We wanted the student to think about a product as a "bundle of capabilities" built around solving a consumption problem—a model far better suited to today's technologies. Consistent with this line of thinking, we greatly expanded our discussion of branding to now cover the major branding decisions (for both B2B and B2C) and added new material on packaging and warranties.

**Chapter 10 (Product Management and New-Product Development)** covers two distinct but related topics. The first half of the chapter deals with managing products over their lifetime—the product life cycle (PLC) is the organizing theme for this discussion. This is a very strong chapter for examining industry trends and evolutionary patterns. However, in recognition that students might view this approach as an all-out endorsement of the PLC as a management decision-making tool, we added a section of "special considerations" in using the model. The second part of the chapter deals with new-product development. We've added sections on "minimizing risk" and "best practices," but our intention was less to teach methods than to show that product development is as much about managing ideas and people as it is about physical products or prototypes. To that end, we also added an Internet Insite on how some firms use the Internet to generate and evaluate new product ideas.

**Chapter 11 (Place: Channel Systems and Physical Distribution)** breaks with the tradition of having separate chapters for channels and physical distribution. This facilitated the introduction of the supply chain management concept and the growing need to manage strategies for the two areas together. The chapter may be broken down into three parts. The first (The Basics) section reviews how distribution practices and arrangements add value for customers and suppliers and, within that context, reviews how information technology can either augment or replace traditional distribution systems. The second section (Channel Decisions) proposes four key decisions as collectively representing a firm's channel strategy and includes a more in-depth discussion of channel relations. The third section (Physical Distribution) reviews the basics of PD but with emphasis on the use of PD to gain competitive advantage.

Chapter 12 (Retailers, Wholesalers, and Their Strategy Planning) augments the descriptions of alternative retail and wholesale formats with new material on retail careers and retail strategy. This chapter has several new elements, including a discussion of retail strategy and an expanded discussion of retail and wholesale evolution. The coverage of retailer strategy focuses on the "seven Ps" of a retail marketing mix and discusses the use of segmentation and positioning within the industry. It also reviews the basics of selecting a retail strategy and the impact of retailer size on competitiveness. This leads to a discussion of why retail strategy changes or evolves and the implications for those hoping for a career in these sectors.

Chapter 13 (Promotion: Introduction to Integrated Marketing Communications) breaks out into three component parts: (1) why we do IMC, (2) the consumer behaviours that we must accommodate to realize those objectives, and (3) how we actually do it, including discussion of how the role of communications changes over the product's life cycle and two new sections on direct marketing and Internet-based marketing.

Chapter 14 (Personal Selling) presents the alternative types of salesforces and the associated sales management tasks to be undertaken. The treatment of this material in the 11th edition is more prescriptive than in past years, recognizing that more and more students are opting for sales careers and thus wish to move beyond simple descriptions.

Chapter 15 (Advertising and Sales Promotion) expands the coverage of the key decisions to be made in managing advertising and sales promotion with new material on managing public relations and Internet-based communications (like permission marketing and pointcasting). In addition, to reflect contemporary issues, students will learn about the "advertising vs. sales promotion" debate and the rise of "contingency billing" in advertising.

Chapter 16 (Pricing Objectives and Policies) organizes the conceptual discussion of pricing around five key pricing decisions and shows how one might make those decisions differently depending upon market and competitive conditions.

Chapter 17 (Price Setting in the Business World) by contrast, is a more technical discussion that offers an overview and comparison of cost-, market- and competitive-based pricing methods.

Part 4 (Managing the Marketing Environment) comprises Chapters 18 and 19. Collectively, these chapters take the student through the major planning tasks: in organizing their thoughts and data (planning), presenting them in a written or verbal format (writing a plan), and monitoring and controlling the performance against plan.

Chapter 18 (Developing Innovative Marketing Plans) reminds students why certain information is helpful to include in a plan and provides templates and best practices for the construction of a plan. In this regard, it reminds students that planning and writing a plan are distinct activities.

Chapter 19 (Implementing and Controlling Marketing Plans: Evolution and Revolution) focuses on techniques that managers can use to monitor performance in order to make adjustments to their plans and offers suggestions for how information technology can be used to translate performance feedback into institutional learning.

## A Comprehensive and Integrated Teaching and Learning Package

*Basic Marketing* has always offered a wide array of instructional and learning support materials, and the 11th edition is no exception. You may want to use all of these materials, or none of them, but whatever you elect to use—and in whatever medium you like to work—the teaching and learning materials work well together. These include:

### Supporting the Teaching Process:

- **Instructor's Manual and Lecture Guide**—Provides lecture outlines, suggestions and ideas about teaching introductory marketing, and numerous teaching suggestions, chapter-by-chapter aids, case teaching notes, and answers to end-of-chapter exercises.
- **PowerPoint Slides**—A completely new and expanded archive of Microsoft® PowerPoint® Presentation lecture slides incorporating text figures and multimedia assets to support the professor.
- 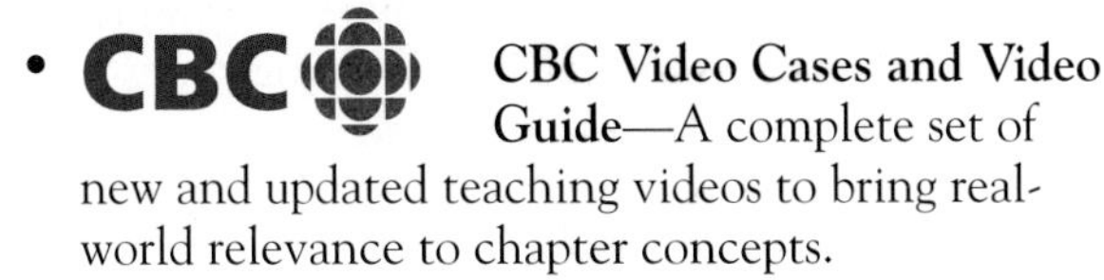

**CBC Video Cases and Video Guide**—A complete set of new and updated teaching videos to bring real-world relevance to chapter concepts.

- **Computerized Test Bank Using Brownstone Diploma**—More than 3,000 questions are supplied in true/false and multiple-choice formats in the easy-to-use Brownstone software.
- **Instructor's Resource CD**—Includes in electronic format all of the instructor resources available for *Basic Marketing*.
- 

**The *integrator***—This pioneering instructional resource from McGraw-Hill Ryerson is your roadmap to all the elements of your text's support package. Keyed to the chapters and topics of your McGraw-Hill Ryerson textbook, the ***integrator*** ties together all of the elements in your resource package, guiding you to where you'll find corresponding coverage in each of the related support package components!
- 

**Online Learning Centre**—Both students and faculty can access this website for a variety of support materials, including an interactive glossary, computer-aided problems, student quizzes with e-mail feature, video cases, learning objectives, and additional Appendices. Instructors adopting this text are also given password-protected access to additional support materials. Visit the site at www.mcgrawhill.ca/college/wong.
- **Superior Service**—Service takes on a whole new meaning with McGraw-Hill Ryerson and *Basic Marketing*. More than just bringing you the textbook, we have consistently raised the bar in terms of innovation and educational research—both in marketing and in education in general. These investments in learning and the education community have helped us to understand the needs of students and educators across the country, and allowed us to foster the growth of truly innovative, integrated learning.
- 

**Integrated Learning**—Your Integrated Learning Sales Specialist is a McGraw-Hill Ryerson representative who has the experience, product knowledge, training, and support to help you assess and integrate any of our products, technology, and services into your course for optimum teaching and learning performance. Whether it's using our test bank software, helping your students improve their grades, or putting your entire course online, your *i*-Learning Sales Specialist is there to help you do it. Contact your local *i*-Learning Sales Specialist today to learn how to maximize all of McGraw-Hill Ryerson's resources!
- 

***i*-Learning Services Program**—McGraw-Hill Ryerson offers a unique *i*Services package designed for Canadian faculty. Our mission is to equip providers of higher education with superior tools and resources required for excellence in teaching. For additional information, visit www.mcgrawhill.ca/highereducation/eservices.
- **Teaching, Technology & Learning Conference Series**—The educational environment has changed tremendously in recent years, and McGraw-Hill Ryerson continues to be committed to helping you acquire the skills you need to succeed in this new milieu. Our innovative Teaching, Technology & Learning Conference Series brings faculty together from across Canada with 3M Teaching Excellence award winners to share teaching and learning best practices in a collaborative and stimulating environment. Pre-conference workshops on general topics, such as teaching large classes and technology integration, will also be offered. We will also work with you at your own institution to customize workshops that best suit the needs of your faculty. **These include our Teaching Excellence and Accounting Innovation symposium series**.
- **Research Reports into Mobile Learning and Student Success**—These landmark reports, undertaken in conjunction with academic and private-sector advisory boards, are the result of research studies into the challenges professors face in helping students succeed and the opportunities that new technology presents to impact teaching and learning.
- **PageOut**—This unique point-and-click course website tool enables you to create a high-quality course website without knowing HTML coding. With PageOut you can post your syllabus online, assign McGraw-Hill Online Learning Centre or e-Book content, add links to important off-site resources, and maintain student results in the online gradebook. Visit www.mhhe.com/pageout or contact your *i*-Learning Sales Specialist for details.

- 

Bb Blackboard www.blackboard.com In addition, content cartridges are also available for course management systems, such as **WebCT** and **Blackboard,** to expand the reach of your course and open up distance-learning options.

**Supporting the Learning Process:**

- **Learning Aid**—The *Learning Aid* can be used alone or with instructor direction. Portions of the *Learning Aid* help students review what they have studied. For example, there is a list of important new terms, true/false questions (with answers) that cover important terms and concepts, and multiple-choice questions (with answers) illustrating the kinds of questions that may appear on examinations. In addition, the *Learning Aid* has cases, exercises, and problems—with clear instructions and worksheets for the student to complete. The *Learning Aid* exercises can be used as class work or homework—to drill on certain topics and to deepen understanding of others by motivating application and then discussion. In fact, reading *Basic Marketing* and working with the *Learning Aid* can be the basic activity of the course.

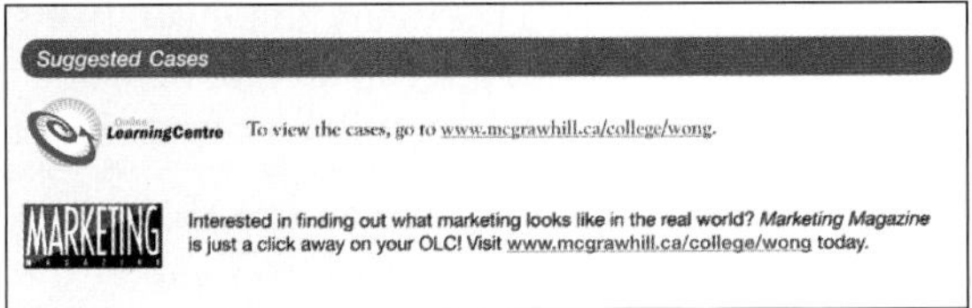


- **Online Learning Centre** —Both students and faculty can access this website for a variety of support materials, including an interactive glossary, computer-aided problems, student quizzes with e-mail feature, video cases, learning objectives, and additional Appendices. Accessing and using the material at this site will help students obtain a better understanding of what is in the text. Visit the site at www.mcgrawhill.ca/college/wong.

**The 11th edition adds even more resources for instructors and students.** The new chapter organization of material resulted in a sequencing that was closer to that used in the U.S. edition of *Basic Marketing*. As a result, Canadian adopters will be able to more seamlessly integrate a host of supplemental materials from the U.S. These include:

- a dedicated video for each chapter
- a student CD that provides an electronic glossary with hotlinks, copies of selected illustrations, PowerPoint slides, and a small number of chapter-keyed videos
- a computer simulation that unfolds chapter by chapter
- an "Applications" book of selected articles, keyed to each chapter

# Acknowledgements

The best part of writing a textbook is having an opportunity to thank those who made it possible. And in this instance the task is especially welcome because there are so many people to whom I am beholden.

I could never overstate the incredible level of support and championship effort demonstrated by the team at McGraw-Hill Ryerson. Far beyond the excellence they demonstrated in the performance of their responsibilities, their professionalism and understanding is what made this book possible: and I do not say this as a matter of protocol but rather true and sincere gratitude.

At a time when people are constantly challenging both the entrepreneurial spirit and integrity found in large corporations, James Buchanan, the Sponsoring Editor, showed that large organizations can be phenomenally agile and concerned with people and quality when they have the right leadership. James championed our new approach and removed every barrier that appeared along the way. He was our champion.

Sandra de Ruiter, the Developmental Editor on this project, oversaw the organization and development of the project from the initial Author Planning Day through manuscript handover. Her efforts in securing reviewer feedback and project scheduling went so far beyond the call of duty that I am at a loss for words in expressing my deep gratitude to her. Suffice it to say that I would "go to war" anytime and anyplace with her, secure that my every error and shortcoming was being covered.

While James and Sandra were at the helm, their team was the fuel that propelled this book to completion:

- Kim Brewster, Managing Editor, lent her considerable talents and knowledge of previous editions to act as an adviser and resource for the project: her efforts enabled us to build on the traditional strengths of *Basic Marketing*.
- Joanne Murray, Supervising Editor, coordinated the transition of the textbook from final manuscript to typeset pages and through to finished book: no small task when dealing with an author who missed more deadlines than he met.
- Greg Devitt, Designer, had the complex task of blending the interior designs of this edition with previous Canadian and U.S. editions: many of the ease-of-use enhancements to this edition's layout are attributable to him.
- Dianna Little, Art Director, designed and created the original cover design and, in doing so, gave expression to this edition's personality.
- Kim Verhaeghe, Marketing Manager, provided the market information and communications that made it possible for this book to achieve a true point of competitive differentiation.
- Megan Ferrell, Sales Manager, provided leads for supplement authors and reviewers and serves as an ongoing resource for the sales team: her contributions were and continue to be mission critical in this book realizing its vision.
- Alison Derry, Freelance Permissions Editor, researched photos and obtained permission for the text's photo program: I lost count of the number of times she showed incredible fortitude and creativity in securing the visual images that are so important to a book like this.
- Darren Hick, Developmental Editor, coordinated the creation and production of the text's ancillary supplements: a key role in our efforts to make this 11th edition the best teaching and learning resource available.
- Carole Harfst and Christine Lomas, Editorial Coordinators, organized the many administrative tasks associated with this project: an often unsung role that provided the foundation for the team's efforts.

I was blessed to be asked to author this edition at a time when I had immediate access to some of the finest young marketing minds in the world—my students at Queen's School of Business. As noted earlier, their reviews, constructive criticism, and ideas were a central part of this book's distinctiveness. We put a lot of faith in these talented individuals and they rewarded that trust with performance that went far beyond even my most optimistic expectations. Readers may wish to note their names—I am certain you will hear much more from them in the future. In order of appearance within the book:

- Lesley Tod—Chapter 3: Focusing Marketing Strategy with Segmentation and Positioning; Chapter 4: The Changing Marketing Environment.
- Nathaniel (Nat) Barnes—Chapter 5: Demographic Dimensions of Canadian and Global Consumer Markets.
- Carolyn Hudson—Chapter 6: Behavioural Dimensions of the Consumer Market; Chapter 11: Place—Channel Systems and Physical Distribution; Chapter 12: Retailers, Wholesalers, and Their Strategy Planning. Carolyn also edited the new Canadian case studies.

- Angie Chan—Chapter 8: Improving Decisions with Marketing Information; Chapter 14: Personal Selling.
- Anne Kozak—Chapter 9: Elements of Product Planning for Goods and Services; Chapter 10: Product Management and New-Product Development.
- Patricia Tay—Chapter 13: Promotion—Introduction to Integrated Marketing Communications; Chapter 15: Advertising and Sales Promotion.
- Logan Chambers—Chapter 16: Pricing Objectives and Policies; Chapter 17: Price Setting in the Business World.
- Jared Ginsberg—Chapter 18: Developing Innovative Marketing Plans; Chapter 19: Implementing and Controlling Marketing Plans: Evolution and Revolution.

The 11th edition also benefited from a number of alliances and partnerships. Exhibit A-1 lists the many contributors to this text. In particular, Ramesh Venkat of the Sobey School of Business at Saint Mary's University provided superlative material in the Internet Insites that are found throughout the book. In addition, I must thank

- Stan Sutter and his staff at *Marketing Magazine*, who contributed material for many of our vignettes and Marketing Demos;
- Statistics Canada, who continued their long tradition of providing accurate and timely data for our exhibits

While the 11th edition is an innovative version of *Basic Marketing*, it owes its pedigree and much of its substance to earlier authors. In this regard, I remain personally indebted to Stanley Shapiro who, along with his wife, Roberta, nurtured this text for many years; to Bill Perreault, the author of the U.S. 14th edition for his insights on how we could better utilize the global resources of McGraw-Hill, and, of course, to Eugene McCarthy for his original pioneering efforts.

I would be greatly remiss if I did not mention the contributions of my own school, Queen's School of Business, and my Dean, David Saunders, for their support and encouragement in this undertaking. As a student and now as a faculty member I owe much of my professional knowledge to the faculty and staff at Queen's.

And last, but certainly not least, I owe an enormous debt of gratitude to my family. To my parents—Marcel and Alice—for giving me all the tools I need to be happy. To my own family—Barb, James, Ben, Lauren, and Lesley—who gave up family time so that I could pursue this effort and toward whom, ultimately, anything I do is directed. From the bottom of my heart....

***Ken Wong***

***Kingston, Ontario***

***February 2004***

**Exhibit A-1** Academic Colleagues and Marketing Practitioners Making Significant Contributions

### Authors of Specially Commissioned Text Material

| | | |
|---|---|---|
| 1. | Ramesh Venkat<br>Author of Internet Insites found throughout the text | Saint Mary's University, Sobey School of Business |
| 2. | Deborah Lawton<br>Author of Appendix A. Marketing "YOU INC.": Preparing a Personal Marketing Plan | University College of the Cariboo |

### Case Authors or Supervisors (with affiliation at the time of case preparation)

| | | |
|---|---|---|
| 1. | Daniel Aronchick | Ryerson Polytechnic University |
| 2. | Carmel Augustyn | Ontario Agricultural College at the University of Guelph |
| 3. | Peter Banting | McMaster University |
| 4. | Ken Blawatt | Simon Fraser/ Visiting Professor at the University of the West Indies |
| 5. | Maurice Borts | McGill University/ Marketec Business Consultants Ltd |
| 6. | Brahm Canzer | John Abbott College and Concordia University |
| 7. | Judith Cumby | Memorial University |
| 8. | Stephan Fleming | Ontario Agricultural College at the University of Guelph |
| 9. | Jane Funk | University of Guelph |
| 10. | Thomas Funk | Ontario Agricultural College at the University of Guelph |
| 11. | Walter Good | University of Manitoba |
| 12. | Patricia Hannas | Hannas Seeds |
| 13. | Ken Hardy | University of Western Ontario |
| 14. | Mark Henderson | University of New Brunswick at Saint John |
| 15. | George Jacob | British Columbia Institute of Technology |
| 16. | Katy Kuzminski | Ontario Agricultural College at the University of Guelph |
| 17. | Martha Lawrence | Acadia University |
| 18. | David Litvack | University of Ottawa |
| 19. | Shelley MacDougall | Acadia University |
| 20. | Lindsay Meredith | Simon Fraser University |
| 21. | James Mintz | Health Canada |
| 22. | Philip Rosson | Dalhousie University |
| 23. | Julia Sagebien | Saint Mary's University |
| 24. | Joseph J. Schiele | Direct Selling Education Foundation of Canada |
| 25. | Colin Steen | Syngenta Crop Protection |
| 26. | Robert Tamilia | University of Quebec at Montreal |
| 27. | Christopher Vaughan | Saint Mary's University |
| 28. | Ramesh Venkat | Saint Mary's University |
| 29. | Charles Weinberg | University of British Columbia |

### Academic Reviewers of the Tenth Canadian Edition

| | |
|---|---|
| Kerry Jarvis | Seneca College of Applied Arts and Technology |
| John Pliniussen | Queen's University |
| Mary Louise Huebner | Seneca College of Applied Arts and Technology |
| Simon Pierre Sigué | Athabasca University |
| Dan Gardiner | University of British Columbia |
| Shirley Lichti | Wilfrid Laurier University |
| Heather Stevens | George Brown College |
| Jean-Paul Olivier | Red River College |
| Ronald Gallagher | New Brunswick Community College |
| Barry Wallace | George Brown College |
| Deborah Lawton | University College of the Cariboo |
| Vivian Vaupshas | McGill University |
| M. Carolyn Guichon | University of Calgary |
| Chris Fader | University of Waterloo |
| Darryl Innes | Malaspina University College |
| Scott Colwell | University of Guelph |
| Megan Mills | Okanagan University College |
| Maria Vincenten | Red River College |
| Brent McKenzie | University of Western Ontario |
| Michael J. O'Hanlon | Red Deer College |
| Joseph Chang | University of Regina |
| F. Alex Boultbee | Seneca College of Applied Arts and Technology |
| Charles Ireland | Centennial College |
| Hoa Trinh | University of Toronto |
| Gord Rein | Simon Fraser University |
| John Daly | Seneca College of Applied Arts and Technology |

When You Finish This Chapter, You Should

1. Know what marketing is and why you should learn about it.
2. Understand how marketing creates satisfied customers.
3. Understand how marketing serves customer differences.
4. Know what the marketing concept is—and how it affects how we manage a firm or nonprofit organization.
5. Understand what customer value is and why it is important to customer satisfaction.

# Chapter One

# The Nature of Marketing

## Marketing—What's In It for You?

Welcome to the world of marketing and to a book that will serve as your travel guide to that world. Your guidebook will describe marketing, highlight ideas and practices worthy of additional focus, identify some potentially dangerous situations, and present a range of skills and organizational processes that we believe *every* manager must know in order to prosper.

*Every manager?* This might seem to be a very bold statement. Certainly, it is not hard to accept this claim if you are planning a career in marketing, advertising, or sales. But what about everyone else? What's in it for them?

We believe there are both professional and personal rewards that everyone can gain from knowing more about marketing. Let's take a moment to review these so that you can better focus your energies in this course.

**Marketing can help you get the job you want.** In this sense, you are the product, your

place price promotion produ

wages are your price, and your employer is the customer. What should you consider to ensure you have the right "features" for employers? How will you communicate your features to your customer? What kind of "packaging" would make the greatest impression on that employer? You can gain tremendous insights into the answers to these questions by thinking like a marketer.

**Marketing can also help you perform better once you have that job.** Think of the kinds of activities performed in different functional areas and you can see a direct link to marketing.

- Financial advisers need to determine whether a company's stock represents a good investment: to make that assessment, they must be able to assess a company's capability to attract and retain customers and to develop, promote, and distribute competitively superior product.
- Corporate finance groups are responsible for securing the investment resources

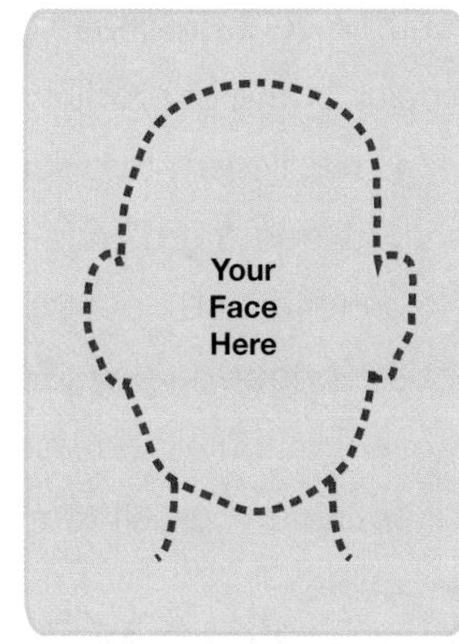


needed to finance the new ventures and long-term growth plans developed by marketers. In a sense, these managers are selling potential investors on the merits of investing in their business.
- Accounting professionals like CAs and GPAs not only keep an organization's records, but also serve as general business consultants or advisers; clients need to know whether their marketing expenditures and practices are appropriate to their size and industry.
- Operations and production staff need to align production capabilities with the volume and nature of the products and services being offered. Their activities are largely determined by decisions like whether they should make all products alike and reduce costs, or whether they should offer a broader assortment of products.
- Human resources people need to know the skills required of prospective employees and the compensation levels merited by employee contributions. Their activities are largely driven by the type of people needed to design, produce, and market the products the organization chooses to sell.
- Information technology (IT) departments are often charged with providing marketing and sales departments with the information they need to make decisions: IT needs to understand what marketing decisions are to be supported in order to determine what data to collect and analyze. IT groups also play a major role in conducting electronic business via devices like the Internet.
- Entrepreneurs usually operate in a setting where one or a small number of people

place price promotion product

do all of the jobs listed above (and more!).

**Marketing can make you a better leader.** Your marketing edge can go beyond the linkages with different functions. It can help you lead and influence others in your organization. Think of any idea or project you'd like the organization to undertake: it could be a new product or service, an idea for how the organization is structured or run, or a new way of evaluating performance. What could you say to get everyone to agree (i.e., to get "buy-in" or consensus)? Would you say the same things in the same way to all senior managers, peers, or subordinates? Because marketing deals with issues like these in introducing new products, your marketing lessons can provide frameworks you can use to plan your "internal marketing" campaign.

**Marketing can make you a better consumer.** Those who come to truly understand marketing will also recognize a large number of personal as well as professional benefits. As consumers you'll learn the various devices used to encourage your purchase of a particular brand of product or service. You'll learn to distinguish between "hard" and "soft" benefits and how they affect the price you pay for whatever you buy. Indeed, you'll position yourself to get better deals.

**Marketing can raise your role in your community.** Many important community services are provided by nonprofit organizations. These include charities and other groups that have formed to pursue special interests. For example, you might have membership at a local "Y" or have a brother or sister involved in a community sports league or performing arts group. Or maybe you belong to a group that is focused on influencing political direction. All of these organizations need funding to survive, and their ability to gain that funding depends greatly on how they communicate their objectives and programs to government, the general public, and intended clients. Your knowledge of marketing can help these organizations and in the process make your community a better place to be.

**Marketing can add to your social skills.** A knowledge of marketing will make you better informed and more confident in discussing business issues with others. You'll learn why companies structure advertisements and promotions as they do (e.g., why do companies run ads in a certain way); why companies continue to sell products/services you might never buy yourself; and ways to offer comments on the ethical issues discussed in so many media today.

You may even find that marketing techniques can make your interpersonal relationships more rewarding. In fact, one of the hottest topics in marketing today is *customer relationship marketing*, or CRM. CRM focuses on how to identify customers with whom we want to build a relationship and how to sustain the benefits to both suppliers and customers as the nature of the relationship changes. As you'll see, while the specifics are obviously different the general rules for great relationship management are not significantly different in the personal or professional arena.

In sum, marketing is far more than an inventory of decisions or set of procedures to be followed. Marketing is a fundamental skill and a valuable resource for leading an organization. Welcome aboard!

## In This Chapter

This chapter is the first of three that provide a broad overview of the field of marketing. We'll begin by making certain that everyone knows what we mean by the term "marketing" and how it relates to the kinds of decisions you'll learn to make in this book. In later chapters, we'll deal in greater detail with the mechanics of making those decisions. Here, our focus is on helping you to understand how marketing managers think about the role of marketing, how they approach decision-making in both firms and nonprofit organizations, and how they think about their broader social responsibilities. Think of this as the "why" of marketing—by the chapter's end you will be better able to understand why marketers do what they do.

## Marketing—What's It All About?

If asked to define marketing, most people—including some business managers—say that it means "selling" or "advertising." It's true that these are parts of marketing. But, as shown in the opening vignette, *marketing is much more than selling and advertising.*

To illustrate, imagine you're starting a business making and selling bicycles. At a basic level, a bike is a means of transportation—a way to get a person from one place to another. But consider the bikes shown below. While they all transport people, there are many important differences between them. Some are designed for children, while others are intended for older riders. Some transport people for work,

Who would buy each of these bicycles? Why? When? Where?

while others move them for play or competition. Some are intended for use on roads, while others are better suited to off-road use. Some could be bought in mass merchandise outlets like Canadian Tire, while others would be found only in specialty bike shops. Which bike would you make?

Now imagine your company makes the "best" bike of a certain type. What happens if the bike is too expensive for the intended buyer? As a consumer, would you spend $500 on a child's bicycle? What if your company doesn't know how or where to advertise to reach riders of the appropriate age? Do parents look to *Sports Illustrated* for information on children's bikes? What if the bikes are sold through a kind of retail store that those riders don't usually frequent? Would a competitive rider shop for a bike at Canadian Tire or Toys-R-Us?

It isn't hard to see how businesses can fail even when they make truly superior products. The product has to be priced appropriately, communicated appropriately, and distributed appropriately for the business to succeed. It is for this reason that companies consider and accomplish a long list of things before committing to make a product or provide a service. In our bike example, these things might include

1. Analyzing the needs of people who might buy a bike and deciding if they want more or different models.
2. Predicting what types of bikes—handlebar style, wheel type, weight, and materials—different customers will want and deciding which customers to try to satisfy.
3. Estimating how many of these people will be riding bikes over the next several years and how many bikes they'll buy.
4. Predicting exactly when these people will want to buy bicycles.
5. Determining where in the world these bike riders will be and how to get the firm's bikes to them.
6. Estimating what price they are willing to pay for their bikes and whether the firm can make a profit selling at that price.
7. Deciding which kinds of promotion should be used to tell potential customers about the company's bikes.
8. Estimating how many competing companies will be making bikes, how many bikes they'll produce, what kind, and at what prices.
9. Figuring out how to provide warranty service if a customer has a problem after buying a bike.

This example shows a broad set of marketing activities beyond just advertising and selling. In the next chapter we'll describe these decisions and what we mean above by "appropriately." For now, the important thing to remember is that marketing is about doing whatever it takes to create **customer satisfaction**—the extent to which a firm fulfills a customer's needs, desires, and expectations. When a business does this, it not only survives but also thrives. This is what marketing is all about.

**customer satisfaction**

The extent to which a firm fulfills a customer's needs, desires, and expectations



## How Marketing Creates Satisfied Customers

You may have heard the expression, "Make a better mousetrap and the world will beat a path to your door." In other words, if you have a good product, your business will be a success. But is a good product all that it takes to satisfy a customer?

Business history has countless examples of cases where great products failed or came very close to doing so. Sony introduced the world's first VCR using its Betamax format. While many people believed it was a technically superior product to VHS, most households today use a VHS product. Many people thought Apple computers were superior to IBM-type machines and yet Apple nearly went bankrupt. Federal Express introduced one of the first fax services in the 1980s and lost more than US$200 million when the public failed to adopt it.

History also has several examples of heavily marketed products that failed because of production problems. Cantel introduced Amigo, marketed as Canada's first pay-as-you-go cellular phone service, but discontinued it after operational problems appeared and consumers stopped buying and even returned their phones. Once these problems were resolved, the service was relaunched with great success. Coca-Cola, arguably one of the world's greatest marketers, averted a near–consumer revolt when they recalled New Coke after the public complained that it didn't taste as good as the original Coca-Cola. Indeed, many pop stars often have short-lived careers despite sophisticated and extensive marketing when people tire of their sound. And who hasn't heard of a heavily hyped blockbuster movie that failed to win over audiences or reviewers?

**production**
Actually making goods or performing services

**utility**
The power to provide consumers with goods that satisfy their needs and wants

The point is that **production**—actually making goods or performing services—and marketing must work closely together to create satisfied customers. Both are important parts of a total business system aimed at creating **utility**—the power to provide consumers with goods that satisfy their needs and wants.

Utility is an important concept. The pursuit of utility is the reason why people enter into buyer–seller exchanges: each party gives something up in order to acquire something else that leaves them more satisfied. As such, any successful organization must create utility or no customer will ever enter into an exchange with it (i.e., buy something). Let's take a moment to consider the five different types of economic utility that are targeted by marketing activities (see Exhibit 1-1).

**form utility**
Provided when someone produces something tangible

**task utility**
Provided when someone performs a task for someone else

Form utility and task utility focus on what the customer is buying. **Form utility** is provided when someone produces something tangible—for instance, a bicycle. **Task utility** is provided when someone performs a task for someone else—for instance, when a bank handles a financial transaction.

But just producing bicycles (creating a form) or handling bank accounts (performing a task) doesn't result in consumer satisfaction. It has to be the form or task that consumers want. Let's take our mousetrap example a step further. Some customers may want a disposable trap, while others may want to reuse it. Some may want a trap that allows for the mouse's release. And some customers don't want *any kind* of mousetrap. They may want someone else to provide a service and exterminate the mice for them. For these buyers, a mousetrap creates little utility regardless of how good a trap it may be. After all, customers aren't buying a mousetrap: they are buying freedom from mice!

**time utility**
Having the product available *when* the customer wants it

**place utility**
Having the product available *where* the customer wants it

But as our bicycle example showed, even when marketing and production combine to provide form or task utility consumers won't be satisfied unless time and place utility are also provided. **Time utility** means having the product available *when* the customer wants it. **Place utility** means having the product available *where* the customer wants it.



**Exhibit 1-1** Types of utility and how they are provided.

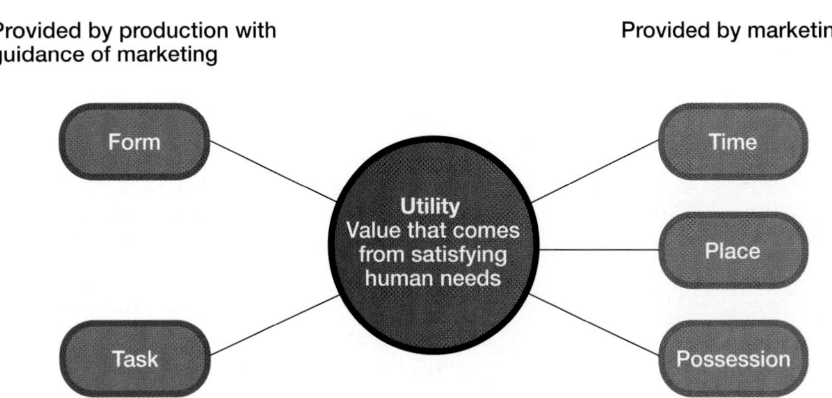

Companies spend an enormous amount of time deciding where and how to sell their products and in telling people where they can be purchased. Retailers fail or succeed based on whether they have the right assortment of products at the right locations. In fact, time and place utility are a major reason why some people prefer to shop using the Internet.

Time and place utility are even more important for services. Unlike products, a service can be neither shipped nor stored. As a result, much of the usefulness of any service depends on where and when the service is offered. For example, neighbourhood emergency-care health clinics have become very popular. People just walk in as soon as they feel sick, not a day later when their doctor can schedule an appointment.

## Internet Insite 1–1



### INTERMEDIARIES AND ONLINE MARKETING SYSTEMS

The Internet facilitates the exchange of goods and services among businesses or between businesses and individuals on a global scale. It creates time utility by enabling 24/7 operation of businesses. The Internet also creates place utility by connecting buyers and sellers from all over the world. A small firm in PEI called GreatHobbies.com is able to attract customers from many countries for its model aircraft products without incurring the traditional costs of establishing international operations. Customers find Great Hobbies through search engine listings and hobby sites. The location of the seller or the buyer is no longer a barrier to commerce. eBay, the popular online auction site, has millions of participants from all over the world selling and buying every conceivable product.

Larger firms as well as firms that have established a brand name have an easier time attracting traffic and customers to their website. For some consumers, the Internet can be a confusing place with too many choices; listing with popular portal sites and online malls may help in overcoming the clutter and gaining some exposure.

While the Internet allows buyers and sellers to connect directly with each other, it has led to the creation of new types of intermediaries who connect buyers and sellers. For businesses in a variety of fields, from electronics to hotels, VertMarkets (formerly VerticalNet) brings buyers and sellers together. VertMarkets operates more than 50 industry-specific portals (or "vortals"). Sellers can post catalogues, participate in bidding, and provide product information. VertMarkets lowers the search costs for buyers and lowers marketing and selling costs for sellers by bring the two parties together online.

Traditional retailers including Sears and Canadian Tire have their own online stores. Some retailers, such as the Body Shop, prefer to be located in an online shopping mall—for example, the one operated by Yahoo!, a leading portal site (see http://ca.store.yahoo.com/ca.html). If you go to Yahoo! Shopping, which caters to the U.S. market, several brand-name stores such as Macy's, JC Penney, and the Gap are listed (see http://shopping.yahoo.com). Yahoo! acts as a gateway (or portal) that sends traffic to various sites. eBay and Amazon (see zShops in Amazon.com) offer a venue for many small businesses to sell their wares. Canada Post offers an online mall featuring a good selection of smaller and regional retailers (http://goshopping.canadapost.ca).

The relatively low cost of setting up a storefront online or becoming part of an established online mall makes it easier for smaller firms to compete. A visit to http://ca.store.yahoo.com/ca.html or http://goshopping.canadapost.ca will reveal the presence of several lesser-known online retailers. For consumers, the Internet offers greater choice. Even those who live in remote regions of Canada now have access to the best products from all over the world.

For consumers, the Internet allows for fast and efficient information search, 24/7 access to shopping and services, and the ability to find great bargains. For businesses, the Internet offers the ability to monitor the competition, track consumer behaviour, and respond with real-time offers (e.g., a consumer who just bought a shirt can be given an online offer for a tie). Many economists believe that the access to information makes the Internet a more efficient marketplace, where firms that offer better products and services at acceptable prices will succeed in the long run. Consumers are no longer constrained to shopping in the neighbourhood mall—therefore all firms, offline and online, have to strive harder to please the consumer.

Go to: **www.mcgrawhill.ca/college/wong**
to apply this Insite in an exciting Internet exercise.

**possession utility**

Obtaining a good or service and having the right to use or consume it

Once we have the right product in the right place at the right time, we still need to transfer ownership. **Possession utility** means obtaining a good or service and having the right to use or consume it. Customers usually exchange money or something else of value for possession utility. Companies affect possession utility when they make decisions about, for example, prices, credit terms, and delivery schedules.

As you can see, utility is more than just a theoretical concept. Customer satisfaction—and business success—is ultimately sourced in the creation of utility. *It is for this reason that the value of any marketing activity can be determined on the basis of whether it creates or enhances some form of utility.* The challenge is that it takes different types of activities to create utility for different customers and for different products or services. Internet Insite 1-1 shows how the Internet can be used to service this diversity.

## Satisfying Customer Differences Lies at the Heart of Marketing

It would be relatively easy to provide form and task utility if everyone wanted the same product. Similarly, the creation of time and place utility would be simplified if everyone wanted that product at the same time and place. And decisions about how to create possession utility would be easier to make if all buyers had the same level of information about the product availability and usage and if they all had the same economic means. We would need only one form of product, only one way to acquire it, and so on.

In addition, since there would be nothing of difference among the products offered by competing firms, customers would have a much easier task in deciding which firm's product to buy. With no differences between competing goods, they would buy from the least expensive firm. In order to have the lowest price, a firm would need to have the lowest cost and thus marketing's role would simply be to perform the standard activities at the lowest possible cost.

But while selling standardized products in standardized ways would greatly reduce the cost and complexity of running a business, it is unlikely that all customers would be equally happy with their purchases. Different customers have different needs and preferences (recall the bike example at the start of the chapter), and there is little merit in being the lowest-cost producer of a product no one wants to buy.

At the same time, there usually are limits to how much customer difference we can accommodate. Just as standardization lowers costs and prices, customizing a product or service tends to increase costs and prices. For example, two items of clothing made of the same material and design will have very different costs and prices if one is mass-produced while the other is tailor-made to an individual's particular measurements. A major issue for marketers is determining how much customization a customer is willing and able to purchase: there is little merit in selling the best-fitting suit if the user finds the price too high.

## Putting It All Together—The Marketing Concept

**marketing concept**

A way of thinking about management that has an organization aiming *all* its efforts at satisfying its customers at a profit

Up to this point, we have talked about three key characteristics of marketing: its goal of creating satisfied customers; the need for marketing to be closely aligned with other functions (like production) in order to create that value; and the challenge of finding the right balance between customization and standardization. These three characteristics are brought together in the **marketing concept**—a way of thinking about management that has an organization aiming *all* its efforts at satisfying its customers at a profit (see Exhibit 1-2).

**production orientation**

When firms make whatever products they want to produce and *then* try to sell them

The value of the marketing concept is as an approach to managing and decision-making. While every organization must make marketing decisions, not every firm approaches those decisions in the same way. Some firms operate under a **production orientation**—making whatever products they want to produce and *then* trying to sell them. Most decisions in these firms are based on doing whatever is most conven-

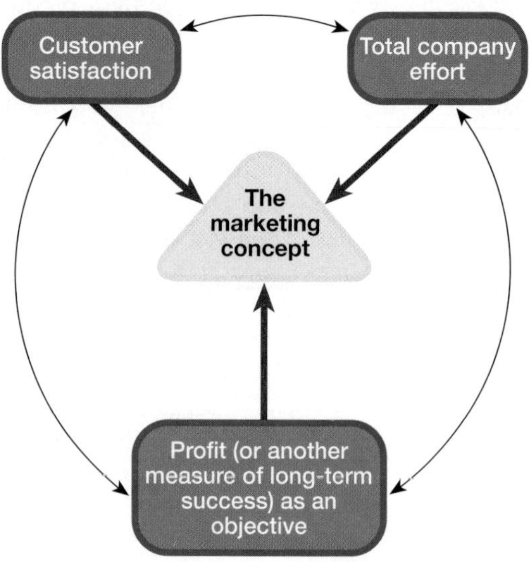


Exhibit 1-2 Organizations with a marketing orientation carry out the marketing concept.



**marketing orientation**
Identifying and channelling all of an organization's efforts into profitably satisfying the customer's needs

**market-oriented firm**
A firm that uses customers' needs to determine what is required to create customer satisfaction and then commits all of its efforts to those opportunities where it can profitably service those needs

ient for the company. The role of marketing in these firms is largely to convince or persuade the customer that the firm's product is superior, regardless of what the customer really needs. This is *not* the approach to marketing presented in this book.

Rather, this book promotes a **marketing orientation**—identifying and channelling all of the organization's efforts into profitably satisfying the customer's needs. This does not mean giving the customer everything they want regardless of cost, nor does it mean charging more than people can afford. Rather, a **market-oriented firm** uses customers' needs to determine what is required to create customer satisfaction and then commits all of the firm's efforts to those opportunities where it can profitably service those needs. Exhibit 1-3 provides some examples of how decisions are viewed in production-oriented versus marketing-oriented firms.

The marketing concept and marketing orientation was first accepted by consumer products companies such as General Electric and Procter & Gamble. Competition was intense in their markets—and trying to satisfy customers' needs more fully was a way to win in this competition. Widespread publicity about the success of the marketing concept at these companies helped spread the message to other firms.[1]

Today, most firms strive to be market-oriented and many would claim to follow the marketing concept. But do they really? We can answer this by considering three basic ideas that are included in the definition of the marketing concept: (1) customer satisfaction, (2) a total company effort, and (3) profit—not just sales—as an objective.

**Customer satisfaction** You may wonder why we give special attention to the notion to "give the customers what they need." In fact, you may see this as little more than stating the obvious. However, preserving customer satisfaction is far more easily said than done. People might not agree on what the customer needs or even on the customer's ability to know what he or she needs. Consider these examples:

- You go to a concert to hear your favourite rock band perform. How would you—the customer—feel if the band members decided they were tired of playing their hits and instead decided to play new, experimental music that night? Most would say, "That's not why I came!" but the band might argue they were maintaining their artistic integrity and that you were paying to see them, not to hear their hit songs. Who is right?
- You go to see your doctor because you want to try some new wonder drug you just heard about. Should the doctor give you what you want, even if she doesn't think the drug is effective? Would all doctors give you the same answer?

Exhibit 1-3 Some differences in outlook between adopters of the marketing concept and the typical production-oriented managers.

| Topic | Marketing Orientation | Production Orientation |
|---|---|---|
| **Attitudes toward customers** | Customer needs determine company plans. | They should be glad we exist, trying to cut costs and bringing out better products. |
| **An Internet website** | A new way to serve customers. | If we have a website customers will flock to us. |
| **Product offering** | Company makes what it can sell. | Company sells what it can make. |
| **Role of marketing research** | To determine customer needs and how well company is satisfying them. | To determine customer reaction, if used at all. |
| **Interest in innovation** | Focus on locating new opportunities. | Focus on technology and cost cutting. |
| **Importance of profit** | A critical objective. | A residual, what's left after all costs are covered. |
| **Role of packaging** | Designed for customer convenience and as a selling tool. | Seen merely as protection for the product. |
| **Inventory levels** | Set with customer requirements and costs in mind. | Set to make production more convenient. |
| **Focus of advertising** | Need-satisfying benefits of products and services. | Product features and how products are made. |
| **Role of salesforce** | Help the customer to buy if the product fits customer's needs, while coordinating with rest of firm. | Sell the customer, don't worry about coordination with other promotion efforts or rest of firm. |
| **Relationship with customer** | Customer satisfaction before and after sale leads to a profitable long-run relationship. | Relationship is seen as short-term—ends when a sale is made. |
| **Costs** | Eliminate costs that do not give value to customer. | Keep costs as low as possible. |



- You decide to start a business based on your favourite hobby, cooking. It would seem natural to want to cook in the style that you liked the most—say, spicy Cajun style. But suppose your customers preferred something less spicy and less exotic. Would you stop offering Cajun and start featuring steak and potatoes or roast chicken? Would you try to educate the market as to the wonders of Cajun food? Would you try to get a celebrity to endorse Cajun food in an effort to create a trend? Would your answer change if you had already invested your life savings in opening a Cajun restaurant?

As you can see, while it may be easy to accept the idea of customer satisfaction, it can be very hard to put that idea into practice. But someone in the organization must assume responsibility for clearly stating what the firm believes are the customers' needs, and those beliefs must be constantly challenged in order to ensure that the firm is properly grounded.

**Total company effort** One outcome of a clear statement of customer needs is that all parts of the organization work together and toward the same goals. Without a common reference point, departments could frequently find themselves in conflict due to their different responsibilities, objectives, and performance measurements. For example:

- A scientist responsible for research and development (R&D) may want to satisfy their intellectual curiosity by producing highly technical and advanced products.

Firms that adopt the marketing concept want consumers and others in the channel of distribution to know that they provide superior customer value.

In fact, their status within their profession may be set on the basis of their sophisticated uses of technology. But customers may want only basic features.

- Production managers are often evaluated on the basis of the cost of producing a product. They will naturally prefer to make a small assortment of products with few features because that approach lowers production costs. But customers may want to have a highly customized product.
- At the same time, a sales representative might want lots of features in order to appeal to a broad set of customers; however, the cost of those features might make the product so expensive to produce that no one can afford it.

As you can see, each department would do what was in its own best interests in the absence of some overall point of focus. In many instances, this would bring departments in direct conflict with one another. It is for this reason that every part of a market-oriented firm must adhere to the marketing concept and, as stated above, must understand what customer satisfaction means in their company.

**Profit objective** Firms must satisfy customers, or the customers won't continue to "vote" for the firm's survival and success with their money. But a firm does not have to sell to *all* customers or meet *all* customer needs. Depending upon the nature of a firm and its capabilities, it may cost more to satisfy some needs than any customers are willing to pay. For example, assume it takes 50 hours to hand-knit a child's sweater. If you have to pay $7 per hour to a knitter and another $50 for wool, the price of the sweater would have to be $400 just to cover your costs! Clearly, many people would be unwilling or unable to pay such a price and the firm would not survive.

Sometimes firms forget the profit objective and instead focus on sales. They believe that all sales are equally profitable. This is rarely the case. For example, who would you rather sell to if you were a computer store: someone who needed extensive technical support or someone who is self-sufficient? Note that the store has "hidden costs" beyond the cost of the computer and these costs must be recaptured through pricing. This is why many software firms now charge for technical assistance.

*Profit*—the difference between a firm's total revenues and total costs—is the bottom-line measure of a firm's ability to survive and grow. From a manager's perspective, it is also the balancing point that helps a firm determine which needs it will try to satisfy with its total effort. The next time you hear someone muse aloud "I wonder why no one makes a...," recall that making something that will sell is not the same as making something at a profit.

## Decision Making under the Marketing Concept

The real proof that a firm is following the marketing concept lies in how it approaches the various decisions it has to make. Let's look at three closely related concepts—value, relationships, and competition—to see how market-oriented firms approach their business decisions.

### The Marketing Concept and Customer Value

There are both benefits (what the customer receives) and costs (what the customer gives up) associated with every product or service. Combining these two perspectives leads us to the concept of **customer value**—the difference between the benefits a customer sees from a market offering and the costs of obtaining those benefits.

**customer value**
The difference between the benefits a customer sees from a market offering and the costs of obtaining those benefits

A manager who adopts the marketing concept sees customer satisfaction as the path to profits. In that regard, a consumer is likely to be more satisfied when the customer value is higher—when benefits exceed costs by a larger margin. On the other hand, a consumer who sees the costs as greater than the benefits (i.e., lower customer value) isn't likely to become a customer. From a manager's viewpoint, this would seem to suggest that we should simply give the customer the best possible product at the best possible price. But how do we know what "best" really means?

Consumers may associate different benefits and costs with the same product or service. For example, consider two students getting a mocha latte from Starbucks. One wants a quick pick-me-up to drink between classes. The other is using a trip to Starbucks as a way to break the ice and get to know a classmate. Would these two students be equally satisfied with the same product?

When we say the two students want different benefits from their coffee purchase, we are also saying that they have different needs. The first student wants rapid service so they won't be late; the second wants more leisurely service so they can talk. The first isn't concerned about seating areas, while the second sees seating comfort as essential.

In addition, these two students might even look at the costs differently. While they both pay the same price for their coffee, there might be other costs that the students consider as well. For example, how far it is to the Starbucks, and how much time and money will it take to get there? While both may want convenience, the first student would be unwilling (or unable) to pay the "costs" required if Starbucks is off-campus. By contrast, the socializing student may not see an off-campus location as a cost at all: for them, an off-campus location might make the occasion seem less ordinary.

As this example suggests, both benefits and costs can take many different forms—perhaps ranging from the economic to the emotional—and can vary from one situation to another. In short, what is best for one customer may not be best for all customers, or even for the same customer all of the time. This means that market-oriented managers must decide which customers to serve, and must look at things from that customer's point of view to determine which of the various benefits and costs are most important.

Our example also reminds us that customers look at both costs and benefits in making purchase decisions. Some people think that low price and high customer value are the same thing. But a product that doesn't meet a consumer's needs results in low customer value, even if the price is very low. At the same time, a high price may be more than acceptable when it obtains the desired benefits. Think again about our Starbucks example. You can get a cup of coffee for a much lower price, but Starbucks offers more than *just* a cup of coffee.

### The Marketing Concept and Competition

You can't afford to ignore competition. Consumers usually have choices about how they will meet their needs. As such, you could satisfy a customer and still lose their business to a competitor that satisfies them better. For example, suppose you were buying a cell phone and had to decide between two brands that met all your basic requirements. Both phones could be said to satisfy you. But suppose one of these sold for less money or had an additional feature for the same price. It isn't hard to guess which one would have the greatest value.

Given situations like these, some critics say that the marketing concept does not go far enough in today's highly competitive markets. They think of marketing as "warfare" for customers—and argue that a marketing manager should focus on competitors, not customers. That view, however, misses the point. Since customers, and not competitors, decide what is bought, an overemphasis on competitive moves as a basis for decision-making is the same as saying "the competition knows the customer better than we do." If that is true, the company's prospects for long-term survival are not very good.

In fact, often the best way to improve customer value and beat the competition is to be first to find and satisfy a need that others have not even considered. The competition between Pepsi and Coke illustrates this. Coke and Pepsi were spending millions of dollars on promotion—fighting head-to-head for the same cola customers. They put so much emphasis on the cola competition that they missed other opportunities. That gave firms like Snapple the chance to enter the market and steal away customers. Today, Snapple is a recognized global brand with sales around the world. For these customers, the desired benefits—and the greatest customer value—came from the variety of a fruit-flavoured drink, not from one more cola.

When the customer defines value—the specific benefits and costs they consider—they are telling marketers what they need to provide in order to be considered; whether one firm or another wins the customer's business will depend upon which one best satisfies those criteria. In this regard, customers tell us what to provide; competition dictates how much of it we have to give in order to win the business. In order to provide customer satisfaction, market-oriented managers must continually monitor their competitive standing on the factors used by customers, not competitors, to define value. See Internet Insite 1-2 for more on the lifetime value of customers.

### The Marketing Concept and Customer Relationships

It is one thing to make a sale; it is quite another to win a customer. Sales occur at a single point in time; satisfied customers buy again and again. You may require an elaborate and expensive program to convince the first-time customer that both the company and its products are sound; repeat customers already know the company is sound and may be willing to assume—without the time and expense of an introductory campaign—that any new products are also of high quality. In fact, one researcher found that it can cost six to eight times more to win a new customer than it does to resell to and service an existing customer!

Given the importance of profitability in the marketing concept, it isn't hard to see why market-oriented firms are constantly looking for ways to build a long-term relationship with each customer, and why firms today focus on customer loyalty.

## Internet Insite 1–2

### LIFETIME VALUE OF CUSTOMERS CAN BE VERY HIGH—OR VERY LOW

Investors lost millions when stock market values of dot-com companies collapsed after an initial, frenzied run-up. But why did values get so high in the first place, especially when most dot-coms were not yet profitable? The stock went up because many investors expected that the firms would earn profits in the future as more consumers went online and the early dot-coms accumulated customers. These hopes were fuelled by dot-coms that made optimistic predictions about the lifetime value of the customers they were acquiring. The lifetime value of the customer concept is not new. For decades General Motors has known that a consumer who buys a GM car and is satisfied is likely to buy another one the next time. If that happens again and again, over a lifetime the happy customer would spend US$250,000 on GM cars (based on the number of cars purchased and their typical selling price). Of course, this only works if the firm's marketing mix attracts the target customers and the relationship keeps them satisfied before, during, and after every purchase. If you don't satisfy and retain customers they don't have high lifetime value and don't generate sales. Of course, sales revenue alone does not guarantee profits. For example, a firm can't give away products—or spend so much on promotion to acquire new customers (or keep the ones it has)—that the revenue will never be able to offset the costs. Unfortunately, that is what happened with many of the dot-coms. They saw how the financial arithmetic *might* work—assuming that new customers kept buying and costs came under control. But without a sensible marketing strategy, that assumption was not realistic.[2]

Go to: www.mcgrawhill.ca/college/wong
to apply this Insite in an exciting Internet exercise.

But long-term relationships do not happen by themselves. Building mutually beneficial relationships with customers requires that everyone in an organization work together to provide customer value before *and after* each purchase. For example:

- If there is a problem with a customer's bill, the accounting people can't just leave it to the salesperson to straighten it out or, even worse, act like it's the customer's problem. Rather, it's the firm's problem. The long-term relationship with the customer—and the lifetime value of the customer's future purchases—is threatened if the accountant, the salesperson, and anyone else who might be involved don't work together quickly to make things right for the customer.
- A firm's advertising people can't just develop ads that try to convince a customer to buy once. If the firm doesn't deliver on the benefits promised in its ads, the customer is likely to go elsewhere the next time the need arises. The same ideas apply whether the issue is meeting promised delivery dates, resolving warranty problems, giving a customer help on how to use a product, or even making it easy for the customer to return a purchase made in error.

In other words, any time the customer value is reduced—because the benefits to the customer decrease or the costs increase—the relationship is weakened.[3]

The importance and methods of managing customer relationships will be a major theme throughout this book. For now, Exhibit 1-4 summarizes the important ideas we've been discussing. In a firm that has adopted the marketing concept everyone focuses on customer satisfaction: they offer superior customer value. That helps attract customers in the first place—and keeps them satisfied after they buy. Because customers are satisfied, they want to purchase from the firm again. The ongoing relationship with customers is profitable, so the firm is encouraged to continue to find new and better ways to offer superior customer value. In other words, when a firm adopts the marketing concept, it wins and so do its customers (see Marketing Demo 1-1 for an example of how one firm accomplishes this).

Exhibit 1-4 Satisfying customers with superior customer value to build profitable relationships.

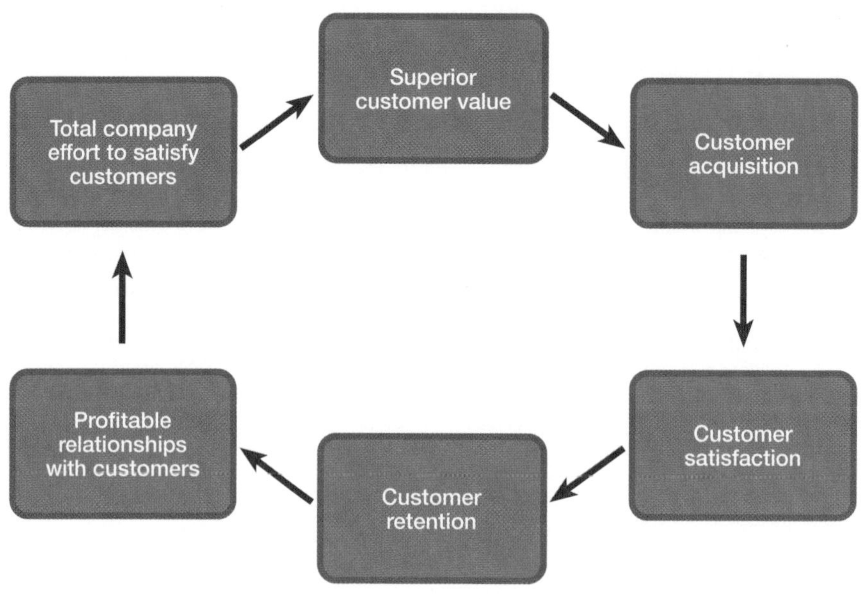

## Marketing Demo 1–1

### L.L.BEAN DELIVERS SUPERIOR VALUE

L.L.Bean is a firm that builds enduring relationships with its customers. It offers good customer value to consumers who are interested in enjoying the outdoors. L.L.Bean's quality products are well suited to a wide variety of outdoor needs—whether it's clothing for hikers or equipment for campers. The firm field-tests all its products to be certain they live up to the firm's "100% satisfaction" guarantee. Although L.L.Bean operates a retail store in Freeport, Maine, its website (www.llbean.com) and catalogues reach customers all over the world. Bean's computers track what each customer is buying, so new catalogues that feature specific types of goods are mailed only to the people who are most interested in those goods. To make ordering convenient, customers can call toll-free 24 hours a day—and they get whatever advice they need, because the salespeople are real experts on what they sell. L.L.Bean also makes it easy for consumers to return a product, and encourages them to complain about any problem. That way, L.L.Bean can solve the problem before it disrupts the relationship. L.L.Bean's prices are competitive with other outdoor sporting goods specialty stores, but the company retains its loyal customers because they like the benefits of the relationship.[4]

## The Marketing Concept in Nonprofit Organizations

The marketing concept is as important for nonprofit organizations as it is for business firms. However, prior to 1970 few people in nonprofits paid attention to the role of marketing. Now marketing is widely recognized as applicable to all sorts of public and private nonprofit organizations—ranging from government agencies, health care organizations, educational institutions, and religious groups to charities, political parties, and fine arts organizations. Some nonprofit organizations operate just like a business. For example, there may be no practical difference between the gift shop at a museum and a for-profit shop located across the street. And some unprofitable dot-com firms have now resurfaced as nonprofits. On the other hand, some nonprofits differ from business firms in a variety of ways. The major differences are discussed below.

### Support May Not Come from "Satisfied Customers"

As with any business, a nonprofit organization needs resources and support to survive and achieve its objectives. Yet support often does not come directly from those who receive the benefits the organization produces. For example, the World Wildlife Fund protects animals, but support comes from donors. Similarly, the United Way and other charities provide needed services to individuals who are unable to pay for them.

This raises the question of what nonprofits "sell" to supporters. Perhaps it is the good feelings that one derives from making a contribution. Perhaps it is an activity the supporter would like to do him- or herself but lacks the time or knowledge. As you can see, customer satisfaction is still central to the survival of a nonprofit, but the need being served may be very different from the activity performed.

It is important for nonprofits to focus on the exact need being satisfied. Just as most firms face competition for customers, most nonprofits face competition for the resources and support they need. The Armed Forces faces a big problem if it can't attract recruits because people feel their career prospects or patriotic spirit is best served elsewhere. A shelter for the homeless may fail if supporters decide to focus on some other cause, such as AIDS education. A community theatre group may find that the theatre is empty if potential patrons' support is intended to purchase entertainment as opposed to subsidizing the arts.

### It May Be Harder to Manage the Team

Some nonprofits face other challenges in organizing to adopt the marketing concept. Often no one individual has overall responsibility for marketing activities. A treasurer or accountant may keep the books, and someone may be in charge of "operations," but marketing may somehow seem less crucial, especially if no one understands what marketing is all about. Even when some leaders do the marketing thinking, they may have trouble getting unpaid volunteers with many different interests to all agree with the marketing strategy. Volunteers tend to do what they feel like doing!

### Profit Is Not Always the Objective

As with a business, a nonprofit must take in as much money as it spends or it won't survive. However, a nonprofit organization does not measure "profit" in the same way as a firm. And its key measures of long-term success are also different. The YMCA, colleges, symphony orchestras, and the post office, for example, all seek to achieve different objectives and need different measures of success.

Profit guides business decisions because it reflects both the costs and benefits of different activities. In a nonprofit organization, it is sometimes more difficult to be objective in evaluating the benefits of different activities relative to what they cost. However, if everyone in an organization agrees to *some* measure of long-run success, it helps serve as a guide to where the organization should focus its efforts.

### The Customer Remains Focal

We have been discussing some of the differences between nonprofit and business organizations. However, the marketing concept is helpful in any type of organization. Success is most likely when everyone pulls together to strive for common objectives that can be achieved with the available resources. Adopting the marketing concept helps to bring this kind of focus. After all, each organization is trying to satisfy some group of consumers in some way.[5]

A simple example shows how marketing thinking helped a small town reduce robberies. Initially, the chief of police asked the town manager for a larger budget, for more officers and patrol cars. Instead of a bigger budget, the town manager suggested a different approach. She put two officers in charge of a community watch program. They helped neighbours to organize and notify the police of any suspicious situations. They also set up a program to engrave ID numbers on belongings. And new signs warned thieves that a community watch was in effect. Break-ins all but stopped, without increasing the police budget. What the town *really* needed was more effective crime prevention—not just more police officers.

Throughout this book, we'll be discussing the marketing concept and related ideas as they apply in many different settings. Often we'll simply say "in a firm" or "in a business"—but remember that most of the ideas can be applied in *any* type of organization.



## The Marketing Concept, Social Responsibility, and Marketing Ethics

Sometimes when a firm focuses its efforts on satisfying some consumers—to achieve its objectives—there are negative effects on society. For example:

- Many people want the convenience of disposable products and products in easy-to-use, small-serving packages. But these convenience products and packaging can be damaging to the environment and an inefficient use of natural resources. Whose needs take priority?
- Hundreds of products, including fire extinguishers, cooling systems, and electronic circuit boards, use a chemical called CFCs. We now know that CFCs deplete the Earth's ozone layer. Yet when this was learned it was not possible to immediately stop producing and using all CFCs. For many products critical to society there was no feasible short-term substitute for CFCs. How is society best served in a case like this?

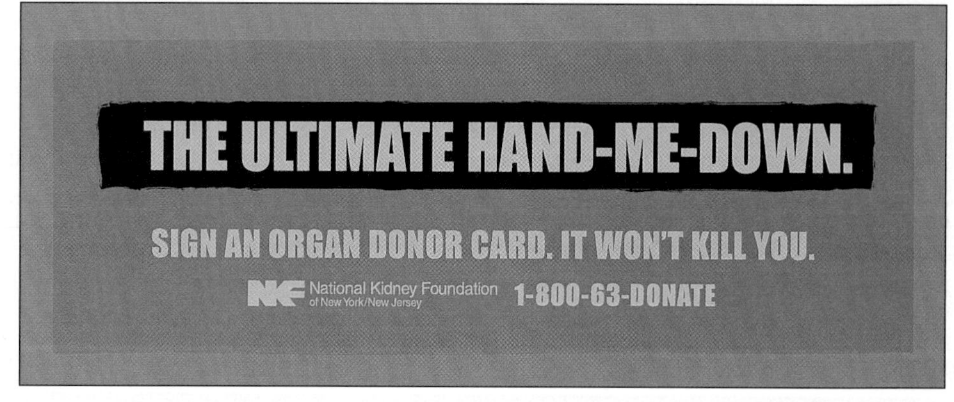


Marketing is now widely accepted by many nonprofit organizations, including the National Kidney Foundation, which wants to increase the number of organ donors.

These types of questions are not easy to answer. Many different people have a stake in the outcomes—and social consequences—of the choices made by marketing managers and consumers. This is why marketing managers are showing an increasing concern for **social responsibility**—a firm's obligation to improve its positive effects on society and reduce its negative effects.

**social responsibility**

A firm's obligation to improve its positive effects on society and reduce its negative effects

The issue of social responsibility in marketing goes beyond environmental concerns. It also raises other important questions for which there are no easy answers. Watch for special sections throughout the book called "Ethical Dimensions," where we'll focus on some of these issues.

Organizations that have adopted the marketing concept are concerned about **marketing ethics**—moral standards that guide marketing decisions and actions—as well as broader issues of social responsibility. It is simply not possible for a firm to be truly consumer-oriented and at the same time intentionally unethical.

**marketing ethics**

Moral standards that guide marketing decisions and actions

Individual managers in an organization may have different values. As a result, problems may arise when someone does not share the same marketing ethics as others in the organization. One person operating alone can damage a firm's reputation and even its survival. Because the marketing concept involves a companywide focus, it is a foundation for marketing ethics common to everyone in a firm—and helps to avoid such problems.

To be certain that standards for marketing ethics are as clear as possible, many organizations have developed their own written codes of ethics. Consistent with the marketing concept, these codes usually state—at least at a general level—the ethical standards that everyone in the firm should follow in dealing with customers and other people. Many professional societies have also adopted such codes. For example, the American Marketing Association's code of ethics sets specific ethical standards for many aspects of the management job in marketing (see Exhibit 1-5).[6]

Exhibit 1-5 American Marketing Association Code of Ethics.

**CODE OF ETHICS**

Members of the American Marketing Association (AMA) are committed to ethical professional conduct. They have joined together in subscribing to this Code of Ethics embracing the following topics:

**Responsibilities of the Marketer**

Marketers must accept responsibility for the consequences of their activities and make every effort to ensure that their decisions, recommendations, and actions function to identify, serve, and satisfy all relevant publics: customers, organizations and society.

Marketers' professional conduct must be guided by:

1. The basic rule of professional ethics: not knowingly to do harm;
2. The adherence to all applicable laws and regulations;
3. The accurate representation of their education, training and experience; and
4. The active support, practice and promotion of this Code of Ethics.

**Honesty and Fairness**

Marketers shall uphold and advance the integrity, honor, and dignity of the marketing profession by:

1. Being honest in serving consumers, clients, employees, suppliers, distributors and the public;
2. Not knowingly participating in conflict of interest without prior notice to all parties involved; and
3. Establishing equitable fee schedules including the payment or receipt of usual, customary and/or legal compensation for marketing exchanges.

**Rights and Duties of Parties in the Marketing Exchange Process**

Participants in the marketing exchange process should be able to expect that:

1. Products and services offered are safe and fit for their intended uses;
2. Communications about offered products and services are not deceptive;
3. All parties intend to discharge their obligations, financial and otherwise, in good faith; and
4. Appropriate internal methods exist for equitable adjustment and/or redress of grievances concerning purchases.

It is understood that the above would include, but is not limited to, the following responsibilities of the marketer:

**In the area of product development and**

Exhibit 1-5 American Marketing Association Code of Ethics (continued).

**management,**

- disclosure of all substantial risks associated with product or service usage;
- identification of any product component substitution that might materially change the product or impact on the buyer's purchase decision;
- identification of extra-cost added features.

**In the area of promotions,**

- avoidance of false and misleading advertising;
- rejection of high pressure manipulations, or misleading sales tactics;
- avoidance of sales promotions that use deception or manipulation.

**In the area of distribution,**

- not manipulating the availability of a product for purpose of exploitation;
- not using coercion in the marketing channel;
- not exerting undue influence over the reseller's choice to handle a product.

**In the area of pricing,**

- not engaging in price fixing;
- not practicing predatory pricing;
- disclosing the full price associated with any purchase.

**In the area of marketing research,**

- prohibiting selling or fund raising under the guise of conducting research;
- maintaining research integrity by avoiding misrepresentation and omission of pertinent research data;
- treating outside clients and suppliers fairly.

**Organizational Relationships**

Marketers should be aware of how their behavior may influence or impact on the behavior of others in organizational relationships. They should not demand, encourage or apply coercion to obtain unethical behavior in their relationships with others, such as employees, suppliers or customers.

1. Apply confidentiality and anonymity in professional relationships with regard to privileged information;
2. Meet their obligations and responsibilities in contracts and mutual agreements in a timely manner;
3. Avoid taking the work of others, in whole, or in part, and represent this work as their own or directly benefit from it without compensation or consent of the originator or owner;
4. Avoid manipulation to take advantage of situations to maximize personal welfare in a way that unfairly deprives or damages the organization or others.

Any AMA member found to be in violation of any provision of this Code of Ethics may have his or her Association membership suspended or revoked.



## Chapter Summary

This chapter has examined the nature of marketing and how it contributes to an organization's overall performance. We started with an overview of the large number of decisions that must be made by every organization in marketing a product or service. And we promoted a focus on customer satisfaction as the key to making those decisions wisely.

However, customers may differ in what they need and want. Thus we looked at what marketing can do to create satisfied customers, and some of the challenges presented by the fact that not all customers are satisfied by the same things.

The marketing concept is an approach to decision-making that embraces these ideas. We considered how market-oriented companies think about customer value, competition, and customer relationships. We also looked at the nature of marketing in nonprofit organizations to explore similarities and differences with for-profit firms. Finally, we looked at social responsibility and marketing ethics in market-oriented firms.

Later chapters will examine, in much more detail, specific marketing decisions and the factors that influence how those decisions are made. The key to remember in all of those discussions is that customer satisfaction is the ultimate measure of whether we make those decisions well.

## Key Concepts

customer satisfaction, p. 6
customer value, p. 13
form utility, p. 7
market-oriented firm, p. 10
marketing concept, p. 9
marketing ethics, p. 19
marketing orientation, p. 10
place utility, p. 7
possession utility, p. 9
production, p. 7
production orientation, p. 9
social responsibility, p. 19
task utility, p. 7
time utility, p. 7
utility, p. 7

## Questions and Problems

1. List your activities for the first two hours after you woke up this morning. Briefly indicate how marketing affected your activities.
2. It is fairly easy to see why people do not beat a path to a mousetrap manufacturer's door, but would they be similarly indifferent if a food processor developed a revolutionary new food product that would provide all the necessary nutrients in small pills for about $100 per year per person?
3. Briefly describe how the adoption of the marketing concept might affect the organization and operation of your college or university. How does it change for different customers such as students, academics, alumni, governments, and so on?
4. Online shopping makes it possible for individual consumers to get direct information from hundreds of companies they would not otherwise know about. Consumers can place an order for a purchase that is then shipped to them directly. Will growth of these services ultimately eliminate the need for retailers and wholesalers? Explain your thinking, with specific attention to what marketing functions are involved in these electronic purchases and who performs them.
5. Explain why a small producer might want a marketing research firm to take over some of its information-gathering activities.

## Computer-Aided Problem 1

### Revenue, Cost, and Profit Relationships

This problem introduces you to the computer-aided problem (CAP) software—which is on the CD that accompanies this text—and gets you started with the use of spreadsheet analysis for marketing decision making. This problem is simple; in fact, you could work it without the software. But by starting with a simple problem, you will learn how to use the program more quickly and see how it will help you with more complicated problems. Instructions for the software are available at the end of this text.

Sue Cline, the business manager at Magna University Student Bookstore, is developing plans for the next academic year. The bookstore is one of the university's nonprofit activities, but any "surplus" (profit) it earns is used to support the student activity centre.

Two popular products at the bookstore are the student academic calendar and notebooks with the school name. Sue Cline thinks that she can sell calendars to 90 percent of Magna's 3,000 students, so she has had 2,700 printed. The total cost, including artwork and printing, is $11,500. Last year the calendar sold for $5.00, but Sue is considering changing the price this year.

Sue thinks that the bookstore will be able to sell 6,000 notebooks if they are priced right. But she knows that many students will buy similar notebooks (without the school name) from stores in town if the bookstore price is too high.

Sue has entered the information about selling price, quantity, and costs for calendars and notebooks in the spreadsheet program so that it is easy to evaluate the effect of different decisions. The spreadsheet is also set up to calculate revenue and profit, based on

$$\text{Revenue} = (\text{Selling price}) \times (\text{Quantity sold})$$
$$\text{Profit} = (\text{Revenue}) - (\text{Total cost})$$

Use the program to answer the questions below. Record your answers on a separate sheet of paper.

a. *From the spreadsheet screen, how much revenue does Sue expect from calendars? How much revenue from notebooks? How much profit will the store earn from calendars? From notebooks?*

b. *If Sue increases the price of her calendars to $6.00 and still sells the same number, what is the expected revenue? The expected profit? (Hint: Change the price from $5.00 to $6.00 on the spreadsheet and the program will recompute revenue and profit.) On your sheet of paper, show the calculations that confirm the program has given you the correct values.*

c. *Sue is interested in getting an overview of how a change in the price of notebooks would affect revenue and profit, assuming that she sells all 6,000 notebooks she is thinking of ordering. Prepare a table—on your sheet of paper—with column headings for three variables: selling price, revenue, and profit. Show the value for revenue and profit for different possible selling prices for a notebook—starting at a minimum price of $1.60 and adding 8 cents to the price until you reach a maximum of $2.40. At what price will selling 6,000 notebooks contribute $5,400 to profit? At what price would notebook sales contribute only $1,080? (Hint: Use the What If analysis feature to compute the new values. Start by selecting "selling price" for notebooks as the value to change, with a minimum value of $1.60 and a maximum value of $2.40. Select the revenue and profit for notebooks as the values to display.)*

## Suggested Cases

To view the cases, go to www.mcgrawhill.ca/college/wong.

Interested in finding out what marketing looks like in the real world? *Marketing Magazine* is just a click away on your OLC! Visit www.mcgrawhill.ca/college/wong today.

# Chapter Two

# Marketing's Role within the Firm or Nonprofit Organization

When You Finish This Chapter, You Should

1. Understand what a marketing manager does.

2. Know what marketing strategy planning is—and why it will be the focus of this book.

3. Understand target marketing.

4. Be familiar with the four Ps in a marketing mix.

5. Know the difference between a marketing strategy, a marketing plan, and a marketing program.

## Dell Computer

As a freshman in college, Michael Dell started buying and reselling computers from his dorm room. At that time, the typical marketing mix for PCs emphasized distribution through specialized computer stores that sold to business users and some final consumers. Often the dealers' service quality didn't justify the high prices they charged, the features of the PCs they had in stock didn't match what customers wanted, and repairs were a hassle.

Dell decided there was a target market of price-conscious customers who would respond to a different marketing mix. He used direct-response advertising in computer

place price promotion produ

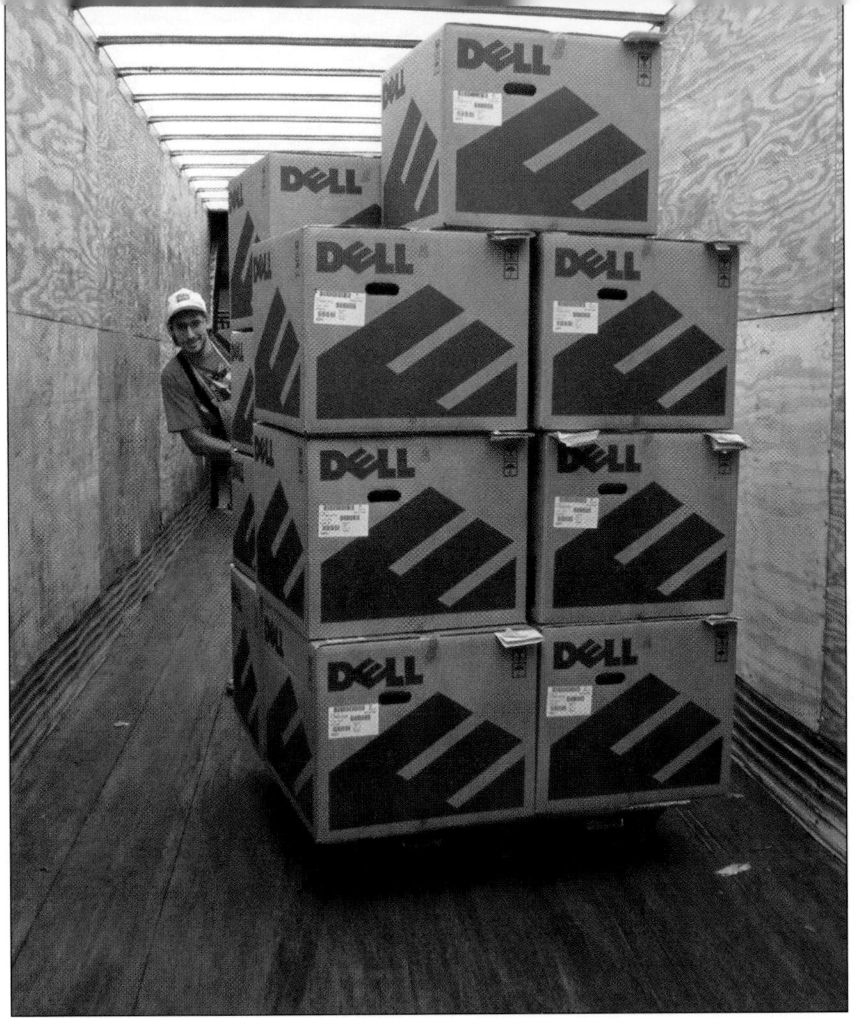


magazines—customers called a toll-free number to order a computer with the exact features they wanted. Dell built computers to match the specific orders that came in and used UPS to quickly ship orders directly to the customer. Prices were low, too; the direct channel meant there was no retailer markup and the build-to-order approach reduced inventory costs. This approach also kept Dell in constant contact with customers. Problems could be identified quickly and corrected. Dell also implemented the plan well—with constant improvements—to make good on its promise of reliable machines and superior service. For example, Dell pioneered a system of guaranteed on-site service within 24 hours. Dell also set up ongoing programs to train all employees to work together to please customers.

Of course, it's hard to satisfy everyone all of the time. For example, profits fell when Dell's laptop design didn't measure up; customers simply didn't see them as a good value. However, smart marketers learn from and fix mistakes. Dell quickly got its product line back on the bull's eye.

As sales grew, Dell put more money into advertising. Its ad agency crafted ads to position Dell in consumers' minds as an aggressive, value-oriented source of computers. At the same time, Dell added a direct salesforce to call on big government and corporate buyers, clients that expected in-person selling and a relationship, not just a telephone contact. When these important customers said they wanted Dell to offer high-power machines to run their corporate networks, Dell put money into R&D to create what they needed.

Dell also saw the prospect for international growth. Many firms moved into Europe by exporting, but Dell set up its own operations there. Dell

price

place

product

promotion

knew it would be tough to win over skeptical European buyers, who had never bought big-ticket items such as PCs on the phone. Yet, in less than five years, sales in Europe grew to 40 percent of Dell's total revenue and Dell pushed into Asian markets for more growth. That also posed challenges, so Dell's advertising manager invited major ad agencies to make presentations on how Dell could be more effective with its US$80-million global advertising campaign.

By the mid 1990s, other firms were trying to imitate Dell's direct-order approach. For example, IBM set up Ambra, a direct-sales division. However, the retailers who were selling the bulk of IBM's computers were not happy about facing price competition from their own supplier! So, IBM couldn't simply copy Dell's strategy: it was in conflict with the rest of IBM's marketing program.

As computer prices fell, many firms were worried about how to cope with slim profits. But Dell saw an opportunity for profitable growth by extending its direct model to a website (www.dell.com) that had recently generated about US$1.5 billion in sales each month! Moreover, online selling lowered expenses and reduced supply and inventory costs. For example, when a customer ordered a PC produced in one factory and a monitor produced in another, the two pieces were brought together enroute to the customer. This cost cutting proved to be especially important when the economy softened and demand for PCs fell off. Building on its strengths, Dell cut prices in what many competitors saw as an "irrational" price war. But the design of Dell's website and sales system allowed it to charge different prices to different segments to match demand with supply. For example, high-margin laptops were priced lower to educational customers—to stimulate demand—than to government buyers, who were less price-sensitive. Similarly, if the supply of 17-inch monitors fell short, Dell could use an online promotion for 19-inch monitors and shift demand. To create more profit opportunities from its existing customers, Dell also put more emphasis on selling extended-care service agreements.

Clearly, the growth of the PC market is tapering off. That means that Dell's future profits will depend even more heavily on careful strategy planning. But perhaps Dell can continue to find new ways to satisfy customers' PC-related needs—or even identify other new, high-growth opportunities to pursue.[1]



## In This Chapter

In Chapter 1 we looked at how marketers approach decision-making (i.e., the marketing concept) and the reasons behind that approach. In this chapter we'll see some of the major concepts and frameworks that guide marketers in making decisions—in moving from a way of "thinking" to a way of "doing."

We'll look at the marketing management process to identify the set of tasks that every marketing manager must perform. One of these tasks, *planning marketing strategies and tactics*, will be the focus for our discussion. We'll identify the elements that make up a marketing strategy and the types of decisions that must be made to translate the strategy from words into actions. We'll also present a process, *marketing strategy planning*, that managers use to ensure that individual decisions support the overall strategy and to stay abreast of changes in the marketplace.

## Making Marketing Decisions

The Dell case shows a number of decisions that Dell's marketing managers made as the business grew from a virtual garage shop to a multinational giant. It also shows how these decisions affect each other. For example, the low prices that many associate with Dell could not have materialized if Dell had chosen to use traditional distribution instead of selling direct. But how do firms make these decisions? How do they know when they have it "right"? This is the role of the marketing management process.

### The Marketing Management Process

**marketing management process**

The process of (1) *planning* marketing activities, (2) directing the *implementation* of the plans, and (3) *controlling* these plans

The **marketing management process** is the process of (1) *planning* marketing activities, (2) directing the *implementation* of the plans, and (3) *controlling* these plans. Planning, implementation, and control are basic jobs of all managers—but here we will emphasize what they mean to marketing managers.

As shown in Exhibit 2-1, the three tasks in the marketing management process are connected in a continuous cycle. In the planning job, managers set guidelines for implementing the job—and specify expected results. They use these expected results in the control job—to determine if everything has worked out as planned. The link from the control job to the planning job is especially important. This feedback often leads to changes in the plans—or to new plans.

Exhibit 2-1 The marketing management process.

But marketing managers cannot be satisfied just planning present activities. Markets are dynamic. Consumers' needs, competitors, and the environment keep changing. Consider Parker Brothers, a company that once seemed to have a "Monopoly" in family games. While it continued selling board games, firms like Sega, Nintendo, Sony, and Microsoft zoomed in with videogame competition. Should Parker Brothers have entered the videogame market?

**strategic (management) planning**
The managerial process of developing and maintaining a match between an organization's resources and its market opportunities

The process used to make that decision is called **strategic (management) planning**—the managerial process of developing and maintaining a match between an organization's resources and its market opportunities. This is a top-management job. It includes planning not only for marketing but also for production, finance, human resources, and other areas. Although marketing strategies are not whole-company plans, company plans should be market-oriented. And the marketing plan often sets the tone and direction for the whole company. So we will use *strategy planning* and *marketing strategy planning* to mean the same thing.[2]

## Planning a Marketing Strategy

**marketing strategy**
Specifies a target market and a related marketing mix; a big picture of what a firm will do in some market

Planning a marketing strategy involves finding attractive opportunities and developing profitable marketing strategies. But what is a "marketing strategy"? We have used these words rather casually so far. Now let's see what they really mean.

A **marketing strategy** specifies a target market and a related marketing mix. It is a big picture of what a firm will do in some market. Two interrelated parts are needed:

**target market**
A fairly homogeneous (similar) group of customers to which a company wishes to appeal

**marketing mix**
The controllable variables the company puts together to satisfy this target group

1. A **target market**—a fairly homogeneous (similar) group of customers to which a company wishes to appeal.
2. A **marketing mix**—the controllable variables the company puts together to satisfy this target group.

The importance of target customers in this process can be seen in Exhibit 2-2, where the customer—the "C"—is at the centre of the diagram. The customer is surrounded by a set of marketing decisions which, taken together, are called the marketing mix. A typical marketing mix includes some product, offered at a price, with some promotion to tell consumers about the product, and a way to reach the consumer's place. As you will see in later chapters, there are many alternative ways that this mix can be carried out. However, since it is the customer who decides what is bought, the customer is the ultimate judge of which alternatives are best suited to their needs.

The focus on the customer has a very important implication: targeting different customers leads to different marketing mixes. For example:

- Spin Master Toys is Canada's largest toymaker. Its products include Devil Sticks, the Air Hog line of motorized toys, and Flick Trix, a line of finger-sized bicycles with moving parts. While these products can be used by people of all ages, Spin Master concentrates its efforts on pre-teens and teens; all products are tested on this age group. Promotion includes special display cases and personal demonstrations at stores like Toys-R-Us to let the target group experience the fun. When Spin Master discovered that kids couldn't figure out how to fly Air Hogs they included a how-to video and had "flight technicians" on call 24 hours a day to help master tricky skills like climbs, loops, and hairpin turns.

Exhibit 2-2
A marketing strategy.

- The Learning Company's marketing strategy for its software aims at a specific group of target customers: young parents who have a computer at home and want their kids to learn while playing. The strategy calls for a variety of educational software products—like *Reader Rabbit* and *Where in the World Is Carmen Sandiego?* The firm's software is designed with entertaining graphics and sound, and it's tested on kids to be certain that it is easy to use. The software can be ordered from the firm's own website (www.learningco.com) or from other retailers. Promotion and direct-mail flyers to registered customers promote some of the firm's other products. Some firms sell less-expensive games for kids, but parents are loyal to The Learning Co. because it caters to their needs and offers first-class customer service—including a 90-day, no-questions-asked guarantee that assures the buyer of good customer value.[3]
- IBM sells a software product called Lotus Notes. However, its target customer is corporations and other institutional users. The emphasis is on selling communications capabilities that are accessible to everyone within an organization. A broad array of related products increases Notes' capabilities beyond e-mail. The design uses menus and simple commands to make that power available to anyone in the organization. Distribution is handled by a direct salesforce or packaged in original computer equipment: either way, the installation of the software is customized to each client's needs. Promotion uses the business media, trade shows, and limited television advertising.

All three of these companies succeed, but they use very different marketing mixes. While Spin Master and The Learning Company make products for use by children, the different benefits and the roles of parents result in different promotional mixes and distribution channels. While The Learning Company and IBM both make software, their different target markets call for differences in almost every area of the marketing mix. This is one of the things that makes marketing an exciting but complex field: there is no single way to do marketing that is best in all cases. Rather, the appropriateness of *everything* in marketing can be judged only through the customer's eyes. It is for this reason that one of the most important of all marketing ideas is *target marketing*.

**Step 1: Select a target market** No decision will have greater impact on marketing and a company's performance than the selection of a target market. It defines the size of the opportunity. Its characteristics, needs, and preferences shape the marketing mix and therefore the kinds of capabilities and resources organizations need to be successful. Thus, the starting point for every marketing strategy is the identification of *particular* target customers.

**target marketing**

Sees everyone as different and therefore requires a tailored marketing mix

**mass marketing**

Vaguely aims at everyone with the same marketing mix

There are two different approaches to the selection of a target market: target marketing and mass marketing. **Target marketing** sees everyone as different and therefore requires a tailored marketing mix. In contrast, **mass marketing**—the typical production-oriented approach—vaguely aims at everyone with the same marketing mix. Mass marketing assumes that everyone is the same—and it considers everyone to be a potential customer. It may help to think of target marketing as the "rifle approach" and mass marketing as the "shotgun approach." See Exhibit 2-3.

Because marketing mixes are built around characteristics of a target market, it is essential that target markets be composed of customers who are basically similar or homogeneous with respect to their needs and attitudes. Sometimes, people are so different that there can be many different target markets and many different marketing mixes required to serve all of them. For example, because people differ in their attitudes about hair care and their working and living conditions, many different brands of shampoo exist, as distinguished by their scent, texture, colour, ingredients, and so on. On the other hand, products like disposable diapers are sold

Exhibit 2-3
Production-oriented and marketing-oriented managers have different views of the market.

Production-oriented manager sees everyone as basically similar and practises "mass marketing"
Marketing-oriented manager sees everyone as different and practises "target marketing"

to a very large target market (worth more than $4 billion in North America alone!) of parents of young children who are homogeneous on many dimensions—including their attitudes about changing diapers. As a result, there are very few alternative brands available.

**Step 2: Develop a marketing mix for the target market** There are many possible ways to satisfy the needs of target customers. A product might have many different features. Customer-service levels before or after the sale can be adjusted. The package, brand name, and warranty can be changed. Various advertising media—newspapers, magazines, cable, the Internet—may be used. A company's own salesforce or other sales specialists can be used. The price can be changed, discounts can be given, and so on. With so many possible variables, it may be helpful to organize all these decisions by reducing the number of decisions down to four basic ones:

**product**
The need-satisfying offering of the firm

**price**
Everything the target group gives up to receive it

**place**
Making goods and services available in the right quantities and locations, when the customer wants them

**promotion**
Everything that is done to communicate the other three elements to the target group

- **Product:** Decisions about everything the target group receives
- **Price:** Decisions about everything the target group gives up to receive it
- **Place:** Decisions about everything that is done to get the product to the target group
- **Promotion:** Decisions about everything that is done to communicate the other three elements to the target group

Viewed in this way, we can think of the marketing mix as made up of these four major parts, often referred to as the "four Ps." Exhibit 2-4 emphasizes their relationship and their common focus on the customer—"C."

Exhibit 2-4
A marketing strategy showing the four Ps of a marketing mix.

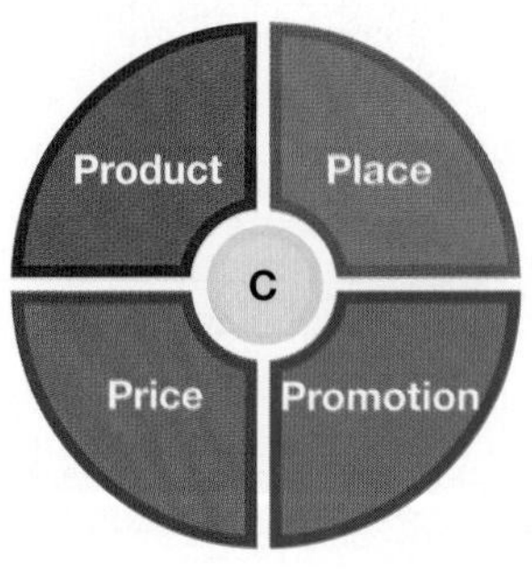
Product
Place
C
Price
Promotion

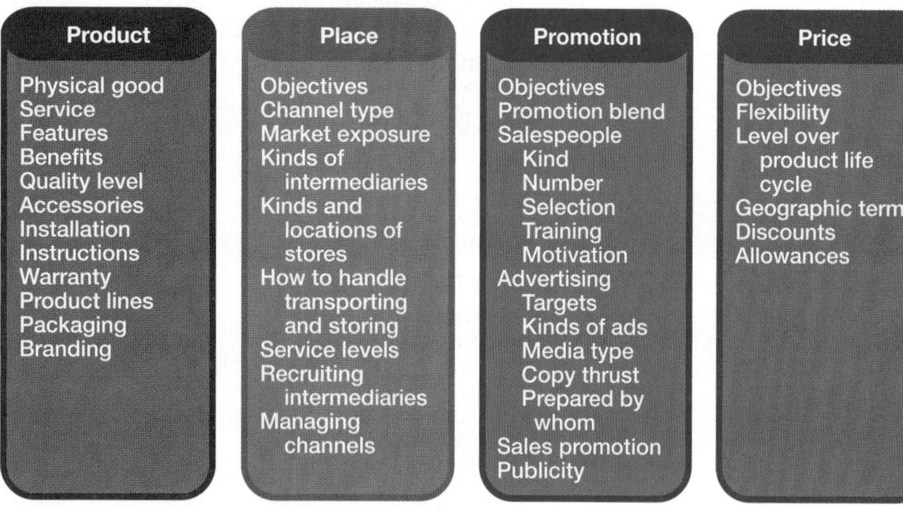

Product
Physical good
Service
Features
Benefits
Quality level
Accessories
Installation
Instructions
Warranty
Product lines
Packaging
Branding
Place
Objectives
Channel type
Market exposure
Kinds of intermediaries
Kinds and locations of stores
How to handle transporting and storing
Service levels
Recruiting intermediaries
Managing channels
Promotion
Objectives
Promotion blend
Salespeople
Kind
Number
Selection
Training
Motivation
Advertising
Targets
Kinds of ads
Media type
Copy thrust
Prepared by whom
Sales promotion
Publicity
Price
Objectives
Flexibility
Level over product life cycle
Geographic terms
Discounts
Allowances


Exhibit 2-5 Strategy decision areas organized by the four Ps.

Each of the four Ps is a set of decisions that every organization must make in order to carry out an exchange with its customers. Exhibit 2-5 shows some of the decisions usually grouped under each of the four Ps. These will be discussed in later chapters. For now, we'll just describe each P briefly and note where you can find more information about them in this book.

***Product*** This area is concerned with developing the right product for the target market; this offering may involve a physical good, a service, or a blend of both. Keep in mind that product is not limited to physical goods. For example, the product for H&R Block is a completed tax form. The product for a political party is the set of causes it will work to achieve. The important thing to remember is that your good and/or service should satisfy some customer's needs. We'll discuss product decisions in more detail in Chapter 9, where we'll explore topics like branding, packaging, and warranties. In Chapter 10 we will talk about developing and managing products from their launch to the end of their commercial life. We'll also look at some issues that arise when an organization has more than one product to sell.

***Place*** Place is concerned with all the decisions involved in getting the "right" product to the target market. Products reach a customer's place through a channel of distribution. A **channel of distribution** is any series of firms (or individuals) that participate in the flow of products from producer to final user or consumer.

**channel of distribution**

Any series of firms (or individuals) that participate in the flow of products from producer to final user or consumer

Sometimes a channel system is quite short. It may run directly from a producer to a final user or consumer. This is especially common in business markets and in the marketing of services. The channel is direct when a producer uses a website to handle orders by target customers, whether the customer is a final consumer or an organization. So, direct channels have become much more common since the development of the Internet.

On the other hand, often the channel system is much more complex—involving many different retailers and wholesalers (see Exhibit 2-6 for some examples). When a marketing manager has several different target markets, several different channels of distribution may be needed.

We'll discuss the advantages and disadvantages of direct and indirect distribution in Chapter 11; in Chapter 12, we'll look at the challenges faced by retailers and direct marketers, along with some of the issues involved in managing multiple channels of distribution and in making the logistical arrangements to move products and services from a firm to its customers.

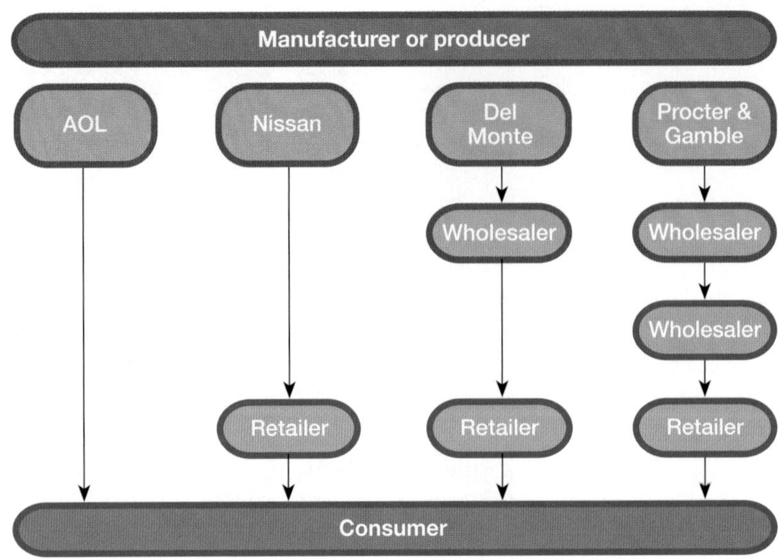


**Exhibit 2-6** Four examples of basic channels of distribution for consumer products.

***Promotion*** Promotion is concerned with telling the target market or others in the channel of distribution about the other elements in the marketing mix. Sometimes promotion is focused on acquiring new customers, and sometimes it's focused on retaining current customers. Promotion includes personal selling, mass selling, direct marketing, and sales promotion. As you will see in Chapter 13, it is the marketing manager's job to blend these methods of communication.

**Personal selling** involves direct spoken communication between sellers and potential customers. Personal selling lets the salesperson adapt the firm's marketing mix to each potential customer. But this individual attention comes at a price; personal selling can be very expensive, and often this personal effort has to be blended with mass selling and sales promotion. Chapter 14 identifies situations when the cost of personal selling is merited and discusses the issues involved in managing a salesforce as part of an integrated promotional program.

**Mass selling** is communicating with large numbers of customers at the same time. The main form of mass selling is **advertising**—any *paid* form of nonpersonal presentation of ideas, goods, or services by an identified sponsor. **Publicity or public relations**—any *unpaid* form of nonpersonal presentation of ideas, goods, or services—is another important form of mass selling. Mass selling may involve a wide variety of media, ranging from newspapers and billboards to the Internet.

**Direct marketing**—communicating with carefully selected individual customers to secure an immediate response—has been gaining popularity in recent years as marketers seek to develop more personal relationships with customers. Newer media, such as e-mail and cell phones, and more traditional media like mail, telephone, and fax provide several new ways of securing direct responses to marketing messages.

**Sales promotion** refers to those promotion activities—other than advertising, publicity, and personal selling—that stimulate interest, trial, or purchase by final customers or others in the channel. This can involve the use of coupons, point-of-purchase materials, samples, signs, novelties, and circulars. We'll look at the strengths and weaknesses of each of these promotional devices in Chapter 15.

***Price*** The management of price involves decisions about setting prices and adjusting prices over time. Managers responsible for price setting must consider the kind of competition in the target market, the cost of the whole marketing mix, and customer reaction to possible prices. Besides this, the manager must know current practices as to markups, discounts, and other terms of sale. If any of these factors

**personal selling**
Direct spoken communication between sellers and potential customers

**mass selling**
Communicating with large numbers of customers at the same time

**advertising**
Any *paid* form of nonpersonal presentation of ideas, goods, or services by an identified sponsor

**publicity or public relations**
Any *unpaid* form of nonpersonal presentation of ideas, goods, or services

**direct marketing**
Direct communication between a seller and an individual customer using a promotion method other than face-to-face personal selling.

**sales promotion**
Those promotion activities, other than advertising, publicity, and personal selling, that stimulate interest, trial, or purchase by final customers or others in the channel

change, managers must also decide whether to adjust their prices in order to retain existing customers and to attract new ones. Chapters 16 and 17 will focus on how managers cope with these factors in setting and adjusting prices over time.

### The Keys to an Effective Marketing Mix

As shown above, in its most basic form setting a marketing mix for a target market involves four sets of decisions. We decide which *product* will best satisfy the target customers. We decide which way to reach our target customers' *place*. We decide which tools of *promotion* best tell the target customers (and others in the channel) about the product that has been designed for them. And we decide on a *price* after estimating expected customer reaction to the total offering and the costs of getting it to them.

However, it is important to stress—and it cannot be overemphasized—that no one part of the marketing mix is more important than the others. When a marketing mix is being developed, all final decisions about the Ps should be made at the same time.

The arrangement of the four Ps around the customer (C) in a circle (refer to Exhibit 2-4) is intended to show that they are all equally important. It is also intended to show that they all are focused on the target customer. The needs of the target market virtually determine the nature of the appropriate marketing mix. So marketers must analyze their potential target markets with care. They need to know why people buy what they do; how and where they look for and process information; where and when they shop, and so on. We'll look at all of these topics in Chapters 3 to 8. Marketing Demo 2-1 shows a perfect example of a business that put these principles into practice with great success.

### The Marketing Plan: A Guide to Implementation and Control

As noted earlier, the marketing management process consists of three basic elements: planning, implementing, and controlling. As the Toddler University case described in Marketing Demo 2-1 illustrates, planning a marketing strategy focuses on selecting a target market and a marketing mix. It is a big picture of what a firm will do in some market. However, if the plan is to produce results it must also be *implemented*, or put into action.

## Marketing Demo 2–1

### MARKET-ORIENTED STRATEGY PLANNING AT TODDLER UNIVERSITY

The case of Jeff Silverman and Toddler University (TU), Inc., a shoe company he started, illustrates the strategy planning process. During high school and college, Silverman worked as a salesperson at local shoe stores. He also gained valuable experience during a year working for Nike. From these jobs he learned a lot about customers' needs and interests. He also realized that some parents were not satisfied when it came to finding shoes for their preschool children.

Silverman thought that there was a large, but hard to describe, mass market for general-purpose baby shoes—perhaps 60 or 70 percent of the potential for all kinds of baby shoes. Silverman did not focus on this market because it didn't make sense for his small company to compete head-on with many other firms where he had no particular advantage. However, he identified four other markets that were quite different. In the following description of these markets, note that useful marketing mixes come to mind immediately.

The *Traditionalists* seemed to be satisfied with a well-manufactured shoe that was available from "quality" stores where they could seek help in selecting the right size and fit. They didn't mind if the design was old-fashioned and didn't change. They wanted a well-known brand that had a reputation for quality, even if it was a bit more expensive.

Many of the *Economy-Oriented* parents were in the lower

income group. They wanted a basic shoe at a low price. They saw baby shoes as all pretty much the same—so a "name" brand didn't have much appeal. They were willing to shop around to see what was on sale at local discount, department, or shoe stores.

The *Fashion Conscious* were interested in dressing up baby in shoes that looked like smaller versions of the latest styles that they bought for themselves. Fit was important, but beyond that a colourful design is what got their attention. They were more likely to look for baby-size shoes at the shop where they bought their own athletic shoes.

The *Attentive Parents* wanted shoes that met a variety of needs. They wanted shoes to be fun and fashionable and functional. They didn't want just a good fit but also design and materials that were really right for baby play and learning to walk. These well-informed, upscale shoppers were likely to buy from a store that specialized in baby items. They were willing to pay a premium price if they found the right product.

Silverman thought that Stride Rite and Buster Brown were meeting the needs of the Traditionalists quite well. The Economy-Oriented and Fashion Conscious customers were satisfied with shoes from a variety of other companies, including Nike. But Silverman saw a way to get a toe up on the competition by targeting the Attentive Parents with a marketing mix that combined, in his words, "fit and function with fun and fashion." He developed a detailed marketing plan that attracted financial backers, and at age 24 his company came to life.

TU didn't have its own production facilities, so Silverman contracted with a producer in Taiwan to make shoes with his brand name and to his specs. And his specs were different—they improved the product for his target market. Unlike most rigid high-topped infant shoes, he designed softer shoes with more comfortable rubber soles. The shoes lasted longer because they are stitched rather than glued. An extra-wide opening made fitting easier on squirming feet. He also patented a special insert so parents could adjust the width. This change also helped win support from retailers. Since there are 11 sizes of children's shoes—and five widths—retailers usually need to stock 55 pairs of each model. TU's adjustable width reduced this stocking problem and made it more profitable for retailers to sell the line. It also made it possible for TU to resupply sold-out inventory faster than competitors. Silverman's product and place decisions worked together well to provide customer value and also to give him a competitive advantage.

For promotion, Silverman developed print ads with close-up photos of babies wearing his shoes and informative details about their special benefits. Creative packaging also helped promote the shoe and attract customers in the store. For example, he put one athletic-style shoe in a box that looked like a grey gym locker. Silverman also provided the stores with "shoe rides"—electric-powered rocking replicas of its shoes. The rides attracted kids to the shoe department, and since they were coin-operated they paid for themselves in a year.

TU priced most of its shoes at $35 to $40 a pair. This is a premium price, but with today's smaller families the Attentive Parents are willing to spend more on each child.

In just four years, TU's sales jumped from $100,000 to more than $40 million. To keep growth going, Silverman expanded distribution to reach new markets in Europe. To take advantage of TU's relationship with its satisfied target customers, he also added shoes for older kids to the Toddler University product assortment. Then Silverman made his biggest sale of all: he sold his company to Genesco, one of the biggest firms in the footwear business.[4]

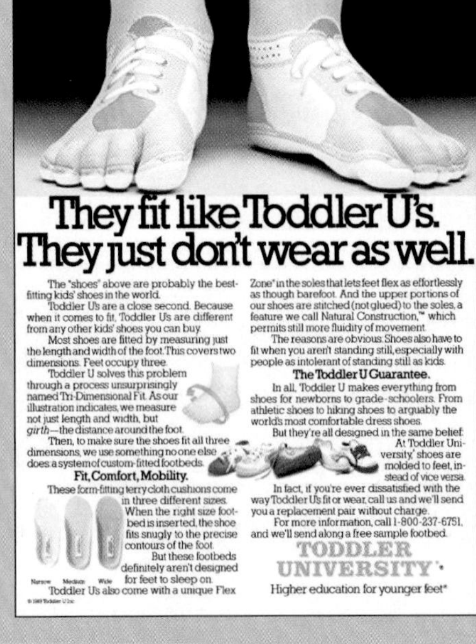


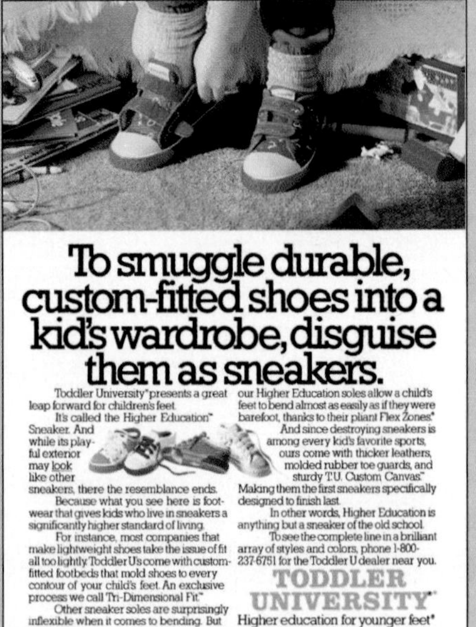


Toddler University's marketing strategy was successful because it developed a distinctive marketing mix that was precisely relevant to the needs of its target market.

**marketing plan**

A written statement of a marketing strategy and the time-related details for carrying out the strategy

Marketing plans are invaluable aids to translating a strategy from a set of intentions into actions. A **marketing plan** is a written statement of a marketing strategy *and* the time-related details for carrying out the strategy. It should spell out the following elements in detail:

1. What marketing mix will be offered, to whom (that is, the target market), and for how long;
2. What company resources (shown as costs) will be needed at what rate (month by month, perhaps);
3. What results are expected (sales and profits perhaps monthly or quarterly, customer satisfaction levels, and the like).
4. What control procedures and measures will be monitored to evaluate the plan's success. This might be something as simple as comparing actual sales to expected sales, with a warning flag to be raised whenever total sales fall below a certain level.

**tactical or operational decisions**

Short-run decisions about the specific activities required to implement a marketing plan

**Implementation** After a marketing plan is developed, a marketing manager knows *what* needs to be done. However, the manager will still need to make a number of **tactical or operational decisions**—short-run decisions about the specific activities required—in order bring the plan to life.

Operational decisions are made within the policies or guidelines that are developed during strategy planning. These guidelines outline the general nature of the four Ps the firm will use. As long as these operational decisions stay within the policy guidelines, managers are making no change in the basic strategy and can choose programs based on factors like cost and time requirement. If the controls show that operational decisions are not producing the desired results, however, the managers may have to re-evaluate the whole strategy—rather than just working harder at implementing it.

It's easier to see the difference between strategy decisions and operational decisions if we illustrate these ideas using the Toddler University example presented in Marketing Demo 2-1. Possible four-Ps or basic strategy policies are shown in the left-hand column in Exhibit 2-7, and examples of operational decisions are shown in the right-hand column.

**Control** Control is the third component of the management process. As described earlier, control provides the feedback on the various indicators—sales, market share, pricing, promotional activity, and the like—that may suggest to marketing managers there is a need to modify their marketing strategies. To maintain control,



Exhibit 2-7 Relation of strategy policies to operational decisions for a baby-shoe company.

| Marketing-Mix Decision Area | Strategy Policies | Likely Operational Decisions |
|---|---|---|
| **Product** | Carry as limited a line of colours, styles, and sizes as will satisfy the target market. | Add, change, or drop colours, styles, and/or sizes as customer tastes dictate. |
| **Place** | Distribute through selected "baby-products" retailers who will carry the full line and provide good in-store sales support and promotion. | In market areas where sales potential is not achieved, add new retail outlets and/or drop retailers whose performance is poor. |
| **Promotion** | Promote the benefits and value of the special design and how it meets customer needs. | When a retailer hires a new salesperson, send current training package with details on product line; increase use of local newspaper print ads during peak demand periods (before holidays, etc.). |
| **Price** | Maintain a "premium" price, but encourage retailers to make large-volume orders by offering discounts on quantity purchases. | Offer short-term introductory price "deals" to retailers when a new style is first introduced. |

a marketing manager uses a number of tools—like computer sales analyses, marketing research surveys, and accounting analyses of expenses and profits. Chapter 18 considers the important topic of controlling marketing plans and programs. In addition, as we talk about each of the marketing decision areas in other chapters, we will discuss some of the control problems. This will help you understand how control keeps the firm on course—or shows the need to plan a new course.

## From Marketing Plans to an Organization-wide Marketing Program

Most companies implement more than one marketing strategy—and related marketing plan—at the same time. They may have several products—some of them quite different—that are aimed at different target markets. The other elements of the marketing mix may vary too. Gillette's Right Guard deodorant, its Mach3 razor blades, and its Duracell Ultra batteries all have different marketing mixes. Yet the strategies for each must be implemented at the same time.[5]

**marketing program**

Program that blends all of the firm's marketing plans into one "big" plan

As shown in Exhibit 2-8, a **marketing program** blends all of the firm's marketing plans into one "big" plan. It looks for common requirements and developments across plans in order to uncover potential efficiencies. It also seeks to coordinate the timing of individual plans to ensure that they don't overtax the organization or compete with each other for consumer attention. Typically, the whole *marketing program* is an integrated part of the whole-company strategic plan we discussed earlier, and as such is the responsibility of the whole company.

Our focus in this book will be on planning one marketing strategy at a time, rather than planning—or implementing—a whole marketing program. This approach will let you develop a deeper understanding of how parts of a marketing mix work together. Once we master the development of marketing plans, in Chapter 19 we'll turn our attention to merging those plans into a marketing program.

## The Keys to Effective Marketing Strategy Planning

The "one-time" strategy decisions—the decisions that decide what business the company is in and the strategies it will follow—play a major role in the success or failure of a business. While superior implementation is needed for a plan to deliver the most performance possible, implementation cannot compensate for a bad strategy. In fact, because implementation means the ability to translate a plan into actions, the combination of a bad strategy with great implementation is the same as "doing the wrong things in the right way": a condition that would hasten the weakening of the firm.

As we have discussed throughout this chapter, strategy decisions are made after considering a large number of factors such as customer needs and preferences and competitors' practices. If these factors did not change over time then there would be little need to revise strategies and plans. Planning, beyond setting the initial strategy, would do little more than review performance and make some refinements to or updates of the operational decisions already being used. But these factors do change, and a once-winning strategy can quickly become obsolete if it is not revised. Marketing Demo 2-2 shows how managers at Timex have responded to the changes in their industry.

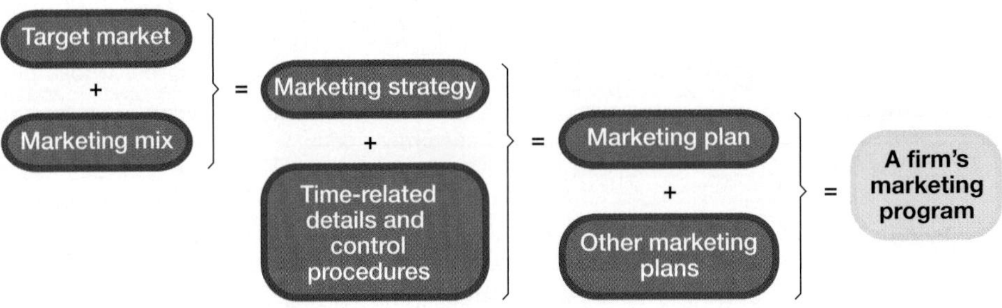


**Exhibit 2-8** Elements of a firm's marketing program.

# Marketing Demo 2–2

## TIME FOR NEW STRATEGIES IN THE WATCH INDUSTRY

The conventional watchmakers—both domestic and foreign—had always aimed at customers who thought of watches as high-priced, high-quality symbols to mark special events—like graduations or retirement. Advertising was concentrated around Christmas and graduation time and stressed a watch's symbolic appeal. Expensive jewellery stores were the main retail outlets.

This commonly accepted strategy of the major watch companies ignored people in the target market that just wanted to tell the time and were interested in a reliable, low-priced watch. So the U.S. Time Company developed a successful strategy around its Timex watches and became the world's largest watch company. Timex completely upset the watch industry—both foreign and domestic—not only by offering a good product (with a one-year repair or replace guarantee) at a lower price, but also by using new, lower-cost channels of distribution. Its watches were widely available in drugstores, discount houses, and nearly any other retail stores that would carry them.

Marketing managers at Timex soon faced a new challenge. Texas Instruments, a new competitor in the watch market, took the industry by storm with its low-cost but very accurate electronic watches—using the same channels Timex had originally developed. But other firms quickly developed a watch that used a more stylish liquid crystal display for the digital readout. Texas Instruments could not change quickly enough to keep up, and the other companies took away its customers. The competition became so intense that Texas Instruments stopped marketing watches altogether.

While Timex and others were focusing on lower-priced watches, Japan's Seiko captured a commanding share of the high-priced gift market for its stylish and accurate quartz watches by obtaining strong distribution. All of this forced many traditional watchmakers—like some of the once-famous Swiss brands—to close their factories.

Then Switzerland's Swatch launched its colourful, affordable plastic watches and changed what consumers see when they check the time. Swatch promoted its watches as fashion accessories and set them apart from those of other firms, whose ads squabbled about whose watches were most accurate and dependable. Swatch was also able to attract new retailers by focusing its distribution on upscale fashion and department stores. The total size of the watch market increased because many consumers bought several watches to match different fashions.

The economic downturn in the early 1990s brought more changes. Consumers were more cost-conscious and less interested in expensive watches like those made by Rolex, which were the "in" status symbol a few years earlier. The re-emergence of value-seeking customers prompted Timex to return to its famous advertising tagline of the 1960s: "It takes a licking and keeps on ticking." Its position as the inexpensive-but-durable choice has helped it strengthen its distribution and has given it a leg up in getting shelf space for new products, such as its Indiglo line of watches.

By the turn of the twenty-first century, the total market for watches was growing at only about 5 percent a year. To spark higher sales of its lines, Timex pushed to introduce more watches that combine time-telling and other needs. For example, its women's fitness watch includes a pulse timer and on-screen displays; its Internet Messenger Watch, for about $100 and a monthly service charge, can receive short text messages, like an alert from the wearer's stockbroker that it's time to sell. Of course, all the new features can make a watch more complicated to use, so Timex is refocusing on the need for simple convenience with its iControl technology, which it promotes with trendy ads and the tagline "Ridiculously easy to use." Competitors are on the move as well. For example, Casio has a watch with a global positioning system, and Swatch is considering a watch with a smart chip that will also make it a debit card. With such changes always underway, marketing strategies must constantly be updated and revised.[6]

To better meet the needs of a specific target market, Timex has developed a line of Rush sportwatches for women. It is also developing other watches to meet specific needs, such as its iControl watches that are very easy to program.

Dramatic shifts in strategy—like those described in Marketing Demo 2-2—may surprise conventional, production-oriented managers. But such changes should be expected. Managers who embrace the marketing concept realize that they cannot just define their line of business in terms of the products they currently produce or sell. Rather, they have to think about the basic consumer needs they serve, how

## Internet Insite 2–1

### ROLE OF THE INTERNET IN NONPROFIT ORGANIZATIONS



The Internet has become a vital part of marketing and fundraising activities in the nonprofit sector. Every major nonprofit organization now has a website. Many nonprofit organizations have suffered from lack of professional management. There is help available online for such organizations. The Internet Nonprofit Center (www.nonprofits.org), Internet Resources for Nonprofits (www.ucp-utica.org/uwlinks/directory.html), and Charity Village (www.charityvillage.com) are among several sites that offer useful information on a wide variety of topics from technology to fundraising and financial management. Charity Village, a Canadian supersite for nonprofit organizations, covers a wide range of topics, from jobs in the nonprofit sector to volunteering, giving, and educational programs.

Leading nonprofit organizations such as the Canadian Cancer Society (www.cancer.ca) offer the public the opportunity to get information, get support, and get involved through the website. Organizations like the Red Cross (www.redcross.ca), which offers disaster relief services, use the Internet to disseminate timely information. They can solicit help and donations specific to a current project. Nonprofits can reach their different stakeholders effectively through the Internet, and use the Web to achieve a variety of marketing and business goals.

Consumers find it easy to donate money online. At the same time, Consumer WebWatch, a site that monitors websites, suggests that consumers should verify the identity and activities of online charity sites before donating money. Donating money through intermediaries such as Network for Good (www.networkforgood.org), which acts as a clearinghouse for more than 850,000 charities, may be a safer bet for those who are security-conscious.

A survey by the technology firm Cisco showed a surprisingly high level of technology usage among non-profit organizations. About 86 percent of them use information technology to some extent, with e-mail topping the list of applications.[7] At the same time, some studies show that nonprofit organizations are not managing their websites well.[8] They are also underrepresented in job posting sites.[9] Sites that specialize in services to the nonprofit sector, such as http://idealist.org, do offer career services.

Direct marketing online, using e-mail to a targeted audience, seems to be the most effective online marketing tool. A survey in the U.S. found that 59 percent of respondents were likely to make a contribution in response to a direct-mail campaign from a nonprofit entity. While those with Internet access had similar attitudes toward giving when compared to those without Internet access, the former group was more aware of nonprofits that had a Web presence.[10] Given the growing number of Internet users and the convenience of donating or receiving information through the Internet, it makes sense for nonprofit organizations to make effective use of the Internet.

Some questions to ponder: 1) Keeping in mind limited resources, what are some ways in which a nonprofit organization can attract traffic to its website? 2) Think of your favourite charity. Can you propose features that should be included in its website?

Go to: www.mcgrawhill.ca/college/wong
to apply this Insite in an exciting Internet exercise.

those needs may change in the future, and how they can improve the value they offer to customers. If they are too nearsighted, they may fail to see what's coming until it's too late. Internet Insite 2-1 shows that what applies to for-profit businesses is no less valid for nonprofit organizations that are using devices like the Internet to stay abreast of, and respond to, changes in their various stakeholders.

Even when the need for change is recognized, managers cannot simply rely on traditional methods to make the adjustment. It may not be enough to simply do things better; we may need to be more creative and find better things to do. Domestic and foreign competition threatens those who can't provide superior customer value or find ways to build stronger relationships with customers. New markets, new customers, and new ways of doing things must be found if companies are to operate profitably in the future.

The Marketing Demos, examples, and concepts in this chapter highlight effective marketing thinking. Throughout the text, we will continue with this thrust—focusing on marketing frameworks and concepts that produce good results. Some of these are new and innovative, and others are well established. What they have in common is that they all work well when they are properly used. To that end, sometimes we will warn you about common marketing errors, so you can avoid them. We don't just give you laundry lists of different approaches and then leave it to you to guess what might work; rather, our focus will be on "best-practices" marketing.

There is an important reason for this approach. In too many firms, managers do a poor job planning and implementing marketing strategies and programs. And, as shown in Exhibit 2-9, this type of "death wish" marketing is both costly and ineffective. In fact, you can see that even the average marketing program isn't producing great results—and that accounts for the majority of firms!

Exhibit 2-9 was developed by experts at Copernicus, one of the world's premier marketing research and consulting firms. As these experts indicate in the chart, some managers are creating marketing programs that produce exceptional results for their companies. This book will help you do exactly that.



Exhibit 2-9 Distribution of different firms based on their marketing performance.

Death-wish marketing ⟵⟶ Best-practices marketing

| | (Well below average) 2% | (Below average) 14% | 68% (Average marketing program) | (Above average) 14% | (Well above average) 2% |
|---|---|---|---|---|---|
| **MARKETING PERFORMANCE:** | **TOTAL FAILURE** | **POOR** | **FAIR** | **GOOD** | **EXCEPTIONAL** |
| *Marketing share growth* | Precipitous decline | Significant decline | Modest Decline | Increase | Dramatic increase |
| *New-product success rate* | 0% | 5% | 10% | 25% | 40%+ |
| *Advertising ROI* | Negative | 0% | 1–4% | 5–10% | 20% |
| *Promotional programs* | Disaster | Unprofitable | Marginally unprofitable | Profitable | Very profitable |
| *Customer satisfaction* | 0–59% | 60–69% | 70–79% | 80–89% | 90–95% |
| *Customer acquisition programs* | Disturbing losses | Significant losses | Marginal losses | Break even | profitable |
| *Customer retention/loyalty* | 0–44% | 45–59% | 60–74% | 75–89% | 90–94% |

## Chapter Summary

The job of marketing management involves continuous planning, implementation, and control. The marketing manager must constantly study the environment, seeking attractive opportunities and planning new strategies. Possible target markets must be matched with marketing mixes the firm can offer. Then, attractive strategies—really, whole marketing plans—are chosen for implementation. Controls are needed to ensure that the plans are carried out successfully. If anything goes wrong along the way, continual feedback should cause the process to be started over again—with the marketing manager planning more attractive marketing strategies.

A marketing mix has four major decision areas, called the four Ps—product, place, promotion, and price. Most of this text is concerned with developing profitable marketing mixes for clearly defined target markets. So, after several chapters on the marketing strategy planning process and several on analyzing target markets, we will discuss each of the four Ps in greater detail.

While market-oriented strategy planning is helpful to marketers, it is also needed by accountants, production and personnel managers, and all other specialists. A market-oriented plan lets everybody in the firm know what ballpark they are playing in and what they are trying to accomplish.

We will use the term *marketing manager* for editorial convenience, but really when we talk about marketing strategy planning we are talking about the planning that a market-oriented manager should do when developing a firm's strategic plans. This kind of thinking should be undertaken, or at least understood, by everyone in the organization—even the entry-level salesperson, production supervisor, retail buyer, or personnel counsellor.



## Key Concepts

advertising, p. 32
channel of distribution, p. 31
direct marketing, p. 32
marketing management process, p. 27
marketing mix, p. 28
marketing plan, p. 35
marketing program, p. 36
marketing strategy, p. 28
mass marketing, p. 29
mass selling, p. 32
personal selling, p. 32
place, p. 30
price, p. 30
product, p. 30
promotion, p. 30
publicity or public relations, p. 32
sales promotion, p. 32
strategic (management) planning, p. 28
tactical or operational decisions, p. 35
target market, p. 28
target marketing, p. 29

## Questions and Problems

1. When a firm changes one or more elements in its marketing mix, does that mean it is also changing its strategy? (Hint: What is the difference between a "marketing strategy" and a "marketing mix"?)
2. Which of the following brands practise mass marketing? Target marketing? Why?
   - Bubblicious
   - Coca-Cola
   - The Discovery Channel
   - The Gap
   - IBM
   - *Marketing Magazine*
   - Nike
   - MuchMusic
   - Molson Canadian
   - Roots
   - Sears
   - Starbucks
3. Using any brand or retailer you wish, profile its marketing mix (that is, the four Ps) and comment on its appropriateness given who you believe is the target customer.
4. Why is the customer placed in the centre of the four Ps in the diagram of a marketing strategy in Exhibit 2-4? How does this help to explain the differences between how Apple and IBM sell computers?
5. If a company sells its products only from a website, which is accessible to customers from all over the world, does it still need to worry about having a specific target market? Explain your thinking.

6. Explain, in your own words, what each of the four Ps involves.
7. Evaluate this statement from the text: "A marketing strategy sets the details of implementation."
8. Distinguish between strategy decisions and operational decisions, illustrating a local retailer.
9. Distinguish between a strategy, a marketing plan, and a marketing program, illustrating your answer using a local retailer.
10. Outline a marketing strategy for each of the following new products: (a) a radically new design for a toothbrush, (b) a new fishing reel, (c) a new wonder drug, and (d) a new industrial stapling machine.
11. Provide a specific illustration of why marketing strategy planning is important for all businesspeople, not just for those in the marketing department.

## Computer-Aided Problem 2

### Target Marketing

Marko, Inc.'s managers are comparing the profitability of a target marketing strategy with a mass-marketing strategy. The spreadsheet gives information about both approaches.

The mass-marketing strategy is aiming at a much bigger market. But a smaller percentage of the consumers in the market will actually buy this product, because not everyone needs or can afford it. Moreover, because this marketing mix is not tailored to specific needs, Marko will get a smaller share of the business from those who do buy than it would with a more targeted marketing mix.

Just trying to reach the mass market will take more promotion and require more retail outlets in more locations—so promotion costs and distribution costs are higher than with the target-marketing strategy. On the other hand, the cost of producing each unit is higher with the target-marketing strategy, to build in a more satisfying set of features. But, because the more targeted marketing mix is trying to satisfy the needs of a specific target market, those customers will be willing to pay a higher price.

In the spreadsheet, "quantity sold" (by the firm) is equal to the number of people in the market who will actually buy one of the product, multiplied by the share of those purchases won by the firm's marketing mix. Thus, a change in the size of the market, the percentage of people who purchase, or the share captured by the firm will affect quantity sold; a change in quantity sold will affect total revenue, total cost, and profit.

a. *On a piece of paper, show the calculations that prove that the spreadsheet "total profit" value for the target-marketing strategy is correct. (Hint: Remember to multiply unit production cost and unit distribution cost by the quantity sold.) Which approach seems better, target marketing or mass marketing? Why?*
b. *If the target marketer could find a way to reduce distribution cost per unit by $.25, how much would profit increase?*
c. *If Marko, Inc. decided to use the target-marketing strategy and better marketing-mix decisions increased its share of purchases from 50 to 60 percent—without increasing costs—what would happen to total profit? What does this analysis suggest about the importance of marketing managers knowing enough about their target markets to be effective target marketers?*



## Suggested Cases

To view the cases, go to www.mcgrawhill.ca/college/wong.

Interested in finding out what marketing looks like in the real world? *Marketing Magazine* is just a click away on your OLC! Visit **www.mcgrawhill.ca/college/wong** today.

When You Finish This Chapter, You Should

1. Know about the different kinds of marketing opportunities.

2. Understand why opportunities in international markets should be considered.

3. Understand why marketing strategy planning involves a process of narrowing down from broad opportunities to a specific target market and marketing mix.

4. Know how to define a market and distinguish between generic markets and product-markets.

5. Know what market segmentation is and how to segment product-markets into submarkets.

6. Know three approaches to market-oriented strategy planning.

7. Know dimensions that may be useful for segmenting markets.

8. Know what positioning is and why it is useful.

# Chapter Three

# Focusing Marketing Strategy with Segmentation and Positioning

## Jones Soda Co.

Peter van Stolk doesn't look like your typical CEO. Fashionably bald and goateed, the marketing mind behind Jones Soda Co. has a penchant for ratty T-shirts and jeans, and peppers his conversations with "hey, dude" and "later." But Jones Soda isn't exactly your average company. Its purple, pink, and blue soft drinks boast names like Fufu Berry and Bug Juice. Its defiantly retro bottles bear ever-changing labels that feature bizarre photographs sent in by customers. And its targeted distribution strategy includes selling its wares in tattoo parlours and dance clubs. There's even a line of energy drinks called Whoop Ass.

place price promotion prod

The unconventional extends to Jones's office space. The firm's 43 employees romp around a bright orange and blue office. Inside there are flame-shaped neon lights in the windows, sleek steel lettering on the wall, and a hairdryer seat from a 1950s salon in the reception area. Twentysomething employees sporting casual clothing (and the occasional tattoo) charge the environment with energy and fun.

Coke may be the pause that refreshes, but it's Jones Soda that owns cool. By forging an emotional connection with young, hip consumers, van Stolk has created a tightly knit community of thirsty disciples who believe Jones is as much an attitude as a drink. Says van Stolk: "It's a fashion statement in a bottle." The financial statement isn't bad, either. In six years, van Stolk has carved out a niche in the $12-billion alternative-beverage market, transforming a barely there juice-distribution company into a cult classic. That loyalty boosted Jones's sales from

US$2.4 million in 1997 to US$19 million in 2000. And the growth continues: in the nine months ended September 30, 2001, Jones's revenue reached US$19.6 million, up 31 percent from a year earlier.

Jones Soda's young hipsters even pay a premium—some $1.50 a bottle—to pledge allegiance to Jones's brand of cool. In fact, Jones may be a textbook example of how to market outside the box, charge extra for attitude, and earn the loyalty of young, ever-moody consumers better known for rebellion than loyalty.

Still, van Stolk's biggest test lies ahead. To lay the groundwork for its ambitious expansion plans, the company has moved its headquarters from Vancouver to Seattle. It has launched a new health drink, Jones Juice, and a mass distribution strategy to broaden its demographic reach. Its five-year goal: $100 million in revenues. But as the company grows, it faces the task of staying hip in a market where the next big thing changes as quickly as West Coast weather.

It's not the first time van Stolk, 39, has set challenging goals. His history of entrepreneurial pole-vaulting dates from the age of 21, when he sold his sports car to go into business selling orange juice. Wanting to prove he could make it on his own, he set up business in Calgary distributing a fresh juice called Just Pik't.

In his first year, van Stolk made a paltry $12,000. Never one to give up, van Stolk reordered, and then began selling the new juice in Calgary's Co-op grocery chain. Says van Stolk: "I went from $12,000 to $240,000 in sales that year."

Van Stolk started with the premise that the world doesn't need another soda. "If you

place price promotion product

enter the market with the belief that the world needs your product, then you're opening yourself up to the constraints of your own vision, your own beliefs." He wanted to differentiate his product, and set out to "create a brand that people could relate to."

From the get-go, van Stolk's selling strategy was based on what he calls "grounding the brand," creating grassroots acceptance as opposed to simply positioning the product. That meant thinking and planning around consumers' wants and needs, and, more importantly, forging an emotional connection with its target market: 12- to 24-year-old trendsetters. For Jones that meant opening a dialogue with customers and placing its products where its buyers like to be: tattoo parlours; skate, surf, and snowboarding shops; and music stores.

Besides hitting his target market, van Stolk says his new soft drink garnered more attention in these alternative shops: "The average convenience store, like 7-Eleven and Mac's, carries an average of 650 choices. We weren't going to get noticed in that crowd, so we said, 'Let's go where no one's gone before.' "

That pioneering philosophy continues in Jones's interactive marketing strategy, which encourages consumers to submit photos and artwork for its bottle labels.

Jones Soda bottles have distinctive labels: black-and white backgrounds that give over major space to its consumers' pictures. Continually changing images allow Jones to stay fresh and to resonate with today's fashion-conscious youth. At the same time, people get excited about seeing their pictures on the label. "We receive 40,000 pictures a year," says Jennifer Cue, Jones's chief financial officer.

Taking the concept even further, Jones lets customers personalize their own bottles. Got a birthday party coming up? For US$35, Jones will put your face on a case of 12 bottles of your favourite soda.

Not only have such tactics built a strong relationship between Jones and its market, says Cue, they help keep the product current and give it edge. Today, some bottles with discontinued labels are collectibles, which are selling on the cyber-auction house eBay for up to US$10.

The concept is all about allowing customers to speak directly to Jones, says van Stolk: "They can get on our label, our cap and our website." By encouraging consumers to become part of the process, to define and shape all things Jones, they will develop an emotional bond with the company, he says. It's a tangible connection that creates unwavering brand loyalty.

Cathy Ace, a University of British Columbia marketing professor, says it's this alternative profile that has helped Jones stay alive in a market where Coke and Pepsi control 75 percent of sales. "The young like to be different. While Pepsi and Coke seem to represent youth, they represent the broadly acceptable face of youth," says Ace. "With rebellion being very much a part of youth, an alternative, a renegade drink, would appeal to a certain sub-segment."

U.S. soft-drink industry analyst Shane Glenn is bullish, too. "Jones is better positioned than any other company in the alternative-beverage category," he says. "Jones has the more exciting and innovative marketing scheme and it is beginning to experience critical mass. They're still growing, but the bottom line is becoming a bigger focus."

Meantime, van Stolk continues to build the brand. This year, Jones struck a deal with Chicago-based Archibald Candy, which will produce "gummy" candies in the shape and flavours of Jones Soda bottles. They are being distributed in about 300 candy stores in the U.S. and Canada, including Sweet Factory and Laura Secord. It could be the first in a line of brand extensions, says van Stolk.[1]

## In This Chapter

This chapter provides the last leg of our overview of marketing fundamentals. With an understanding of the overall marketing strategy process at a general level, we now can delve a little deeper into the methods used to carry out the analysis that underlies marketing plans.

We start by reviewing the types of opportunities that an organization can pursue. The goal is to give you a framework that you can use to systematically identify the alternative ways a business can grow. Next we'll revisit the strategic marketing planning process to show how these alternatives can be evaluated. In addition, we'll cover some techniques that help you uncover "breakthrough" opportunities that others might miss. We'll complete our review by looking at two key tools in the planning process—and two of the most important concepts in marketing—market segmentation and positioning.

## Types of Opportunities to Pursue

Some alert marketers, like Peter van Stolk of Jones Soda Co., seem able to spot attractive opportunities everywhere they look. Unfortunately, many opportunities seem obvious only after someone else identifies them. Marketers need a framework for thinking about the broad kinds of opportunities they may find. Exhibit 3-1 shows four broad possibilities: market penetration, market development, product development, and diversification. It is based on the notion that businesses sell something (products) to someone (markets). Thus, a business can grow by selling more of its existing products or by bringing out new products. It can also grow within its current markets or it can enter new markets. We will look at these possibilities separately, but some firms pursue more than one type of opportunity at the same time.

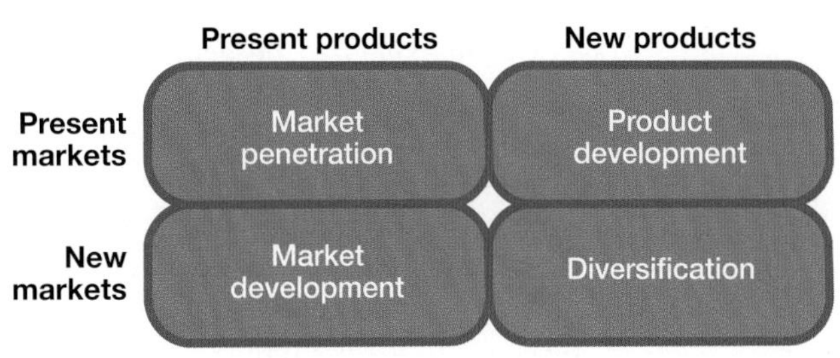


Exhibit 3-1 Four basic types of opportunities.

## Market Penetration

**market penetration**
Trying to increase sales of a firm's present products in its present markets, usually through a more aggressive marketing mix

**Market penetration** means trying to increase sales of a firm's present products in its present markets—usually through a more aggressive marketing mix. The firm may try to strengthen its relationships with customers to increase their rate of use or repeat purchases, or try to steal competitors' customers or attract current nonusers. Some companies are now using effective loyalty programs to reward and retain current customers and ultimately increase profits. Coleman got a 50-percent increase in sales of its outdoor equipment, including camping lanterns and stoves, by reaching its target market with special promotional displays at outdoor events such as concerts, fishing tournaments, and Nascar races. For example, about 250,000 auto-racing fans camp onsite at Nascar races each year, so a display at the campground is an effective way to reach customers when they have leisure time to browse through product displays and demos.[2]

New promotion appeals alone may not be effective. A firm may need to enable its website to process orders so that customers can buy products online. Or it may need to add more stores in certain areas for greater convenience. Short-term price cuts, coupons, or other incentive offers may help. But remember—any firm that cuts prices can expect an immediate response from its competitors, and could even find that while it wins a sale, it makes little profit on that sale. To be successful in pursuing an opportunity, a business must do effective analysis to understand why some people are buying now and to determine what will motivate them to change brands, buy more, or begin or resume buying.



## Market Development

**market development**
Trying to increase sales by selling current products in new markets

**Market development** means trying to increase sales by selling current products in new markets. For example, selling into new international markets is an example of market development. So are the efforts of firms advertising in different media to reach new target customers. Or, a firm may add channels of distribution or new stores in new areas, including overseas. For example, to reach new customers McDonald's opens outlets in airports, office buildings, zoos, and casinos, and it's rapidly expanding into international markets with outlets in places like Russia, Brazil, and China.[3]

Since the firm is selling basically the same product it always has, market development strategies often require very little incremental R&D, and often the product can be made in existing facilities. However, to be successful, firms must carefully research these new markets to ensure that customer needs and behaviour are similar to those of existing customers. Failure to do so can cause some serious marketing blunders. For example, many golfers in British Columbia play golf during January, when rainfall can be frequent and heavy. Some of these golfers cope with the wet conditions by wearing specially designed, ankle-covering, all-rubber golf boots: some B.C. golfers might use these boots 11 months a year! While golfers in, say, Eastern Canada might also be able to use these boots, the lower incidence of rain during their summer golf season and the absence of play during the winter months might make Easterners less inclined to buy this specialty product.

But markets can be defined in ways other than just geography. Marketers often search for new uses for a product by defining markets in terms of end-use applications. For example, Lipton provides recipes showing how to use its dry soup mixes to make chip dip. Velcro fasteners started out as a device for securing surgical gowns: Velcro later expanded into footwear, clothing, and outdoors gear. Baking soda is a classic example of a market development strategy: apart from its conventional use in baking, the product has applications as a refrigerator deodorant, carpet deodorizer, and tooth whitener.

General Mills encourages consumers to use products in new ways by including recipes in its advertising.

## Product Development

**product development**
Offering new or improved products for current markets

**Product development** means offering new or improved products for current markets. By identifying the present market's needs, a firm may see ways to modify its current offerings to better satisfy customers. For example, kids are the major consumers of ketchup. So Heinz set out to find a way to make ketchup more fun. Producing ketchup in gross green and funky purple colours—in an "EZ Squirt" dispenser moulded to fit little hands—increased sales so much that the factory had to run 24 hours a day, 7 days a week to keep up with demand! To increase consumption by adults Heinz next launched Kickers, a line of sharply flavoured ketchups. Coke and Pepsi are now available in an array of flavoured colas. Hellman's has several mayonnaise-based dressings available. Ski resorts have developed trails for hiking and biking to bring their winter ski customers back in the summer. Procter & Gamble added toothbrushes and tooth whitening products to its Crest line of toothpaste. Nike moved beyond shoes and sportswear to offer its athletic target market a running watch, digital audio player, and even a portable heart-rate monitor. And, of course, Intel boosts sales by developing newer and faster chips.[4] Successes like these again show the value of deep and lasting customer relationships.

### Diversification

**diversification**
Moving into totally different lines of business

**Diversification** means moving into totally different lines of business—perhaps entirely unfamiliar products, markets, or even levels in the production-marketing system. For example, most people associate the Canon brand name with cameras. However, Canon used its superior capability in developing photographic lenses to become one of the world's largest manufacturers of photocopy equipment.

Diversification presents the most challenging—and potentially rewarding—opportunities. It also usually presents the biggest risks. Marketers need to keep in mind that the products and customers that are very different from a firm's current base may look attractive, but are usually hard to evaluate. As a result, the landscape is littered with failed efforts at diversification.

Usually firms find attractive opportunities fairly close to markets they already know. This may allow them to capitalize on changes in their present markets, or more basic changes in the external environment. Moreover, many firms are finding that the easiest way to increase profits is to do a better job of hanging on to the customers they've already won, by meeting their needs so well that they wouldn't consider switching to another firm.

### The Special Case of International Opportunities

One avenue of market development merits special attention: international marketing. Beyond the obvious opportunity for growth there are several additional incentives for entering international markets, and the benefits of selling abroad are more accessible than ever before. It is vital that Canadian firms take advantage of this opportunity given the small size of the Canadian marketplace relative to the marketplaces of other nations such as the United States and Japan. In fact, in some industries, like computer software and hardware, Canadian firms will typically generate less than 10 percent of their sales in Canada.

International trade is increasing all around the world, and trade barriers are breaking down. In addition, advances in e-commerce, transportation, and communications are making it easier and cheaper for even small firms to reach international customers. The real question is whether a firm can effectively use its resources to meet these customers' needs at a profit.

If customers in other countries are interested in the products a firm offers—or could offer—serving them may improve economies of scale. Lower costs (and prices) may give a firm a competitive advantage both in its home markets and abroad. Black & Decker, for example, uses electric motors in many of its tools and appliances. By selling overseas as well as in Canada and the U.S., it gets economies of scale and the cost per motor is very low.

Marketing managers who are interested only in the "convenient" customers in their own backyards may be rudely surprised to find that an aggressive, low-cost foreign producer is willing to pursue those customers even if doing so is not convenient. Many companies expecting to avoid the struggles of international competition have learned this lesson the hard way.

A company facing tough competition, thin profit margins, and slow sales growth at home may get a fresh start in another country where demand for its product is just beginning to grow. A marketing manager may be able to transfer marketing or technological know-how, or some other competitive advantage that the firm has already developed. In addition, unfavourable trends in the domestic environment, or favourable trends in other countries, may make international marketing particularly attractive. For example, population growth in Canada has slowed and income is levelling off. In other places in the world, such as in China and India, population and income are increasing rapidly. Managers for Canadian firms can no longer rely on the constant market growth that drove domestic sales for so many years. For many firms, growth—and perhaps even survival—will come only by aiming at more distant customers.

## Identifying and Evaluating Opportunities

The exercise of considering new products and new market opportunities is likely to produce a lengthy list of alternative opportunities for a business to pursue. Strategic market planning tries to match those opportunities to the firm's resources (what it can do) and its objectives (what top management wants to do). This is an important evaluation to perform because an opportunity that is attractive for one firm may not be attractive for another. As the Jones Soda case suggests, attractive opportunities for a particular firm are those that the firm has some chance of doing something about given its resources and objectives.

**breakthrough opportunities**

Opportunities that help innovators develop hard-to-copy marketing strategies that will be profitable in the long term

Throughout this book, we will emphasize finding **breakthrough opportunities**—opportunities that help innovators develop hard-to-copy marketing strategies that will be profitable in the long term. This is important because there are always imitators trying to "share" the innovator's profits if they can. It's hard to continuously provide superior value to target customers if competitors can easily copy your marketing mix.

**competitive advantage**

A marketing mix that the target market sees as better than a competitor's mix

Even if a manager can't find a breakthrough opportunity, the firm should try to obtain a competitive advantage to increase its chances for profit or survival. **Competitive advantage** means that a firm has a marketing mix that the target market sees as better than a competitor's mix.

What makes one firm's marketing mix better than another's? There are three basic types of advantage: lower cost, higher quality, and customer focus. The sources of these advantages can be almost anything: cutting production costs, innovative R&D, more effective purchasing of needed components, or financing for a new distribution facility. Similarly, a strong salesforce, a well-known brand name, or good dealers may give a company a competitive advantage in pursuing an opportunity. Whatever the source, an advantage succeeds only if it allows the firm to provide superior value (the ratio of the firm's quality to price) and satisfy customers better than some competitor.

Sometimes a firm can achieve breakthrough opportunities and competitive advantage by simply fine-tuning its current marketing mix(es) or developing closer relationships with its customers. Other times it may need new facilities, new people in new world markets, and totally new ways of solving problems. But every firm

Attractive new opportunities are often fairly close to markets the firm already knows.

needs some competitive advantage so that marketers have something unique to sell, and success doesn't just hinge on offering lower and lower prices.[5]

From Chapter 2, you know that a marketing strategy requires decisions about the specific customers the firm will target and the marketing mix the firm will develop to appeal to that target market. We can organize the many marketing-mix decisions (refer to Exhibit 2-4) in terms of the four Ps—product, place, promotion, and price. Thus, the "final" strategy decisions are represented by the target market surrounded by the four Ps. However, the idea isn't just to develop *some* strategy. After all, there are hundreds or even thousands of combinations of marketing-mix decisions and target markets (i.e., strategies) that a firm might try. Rather, the challenge is to zero in on the best strategy. This is the objective of the marketing strategy planning process.

## Overview of the Marketing Strategy Planning Process

As Exhibit 3-2 suggests, it is useful to think of strategic market planning as a narrowing-down process aimed at selecting the best target market and marketing mix. Let's briefly review the general logic of this process.

The process starts with a broad look at a market—paying special attention to customer needs, the firm's objectives and resources, and competitors. This helps to identify new and unique opportunities that might be overlooked if the focus is narrowed too quickly. Chapters 4 and 5 will provide some tools that can be used in that review. Because a key objective of marketing is to satisfy the needs of a particular group of customers, we want to be especially alert for customers with unmet needs or needs that are not being satisfied as well as they might be.

Exhibit 3-2 Overview of the marketing strategy planning process.

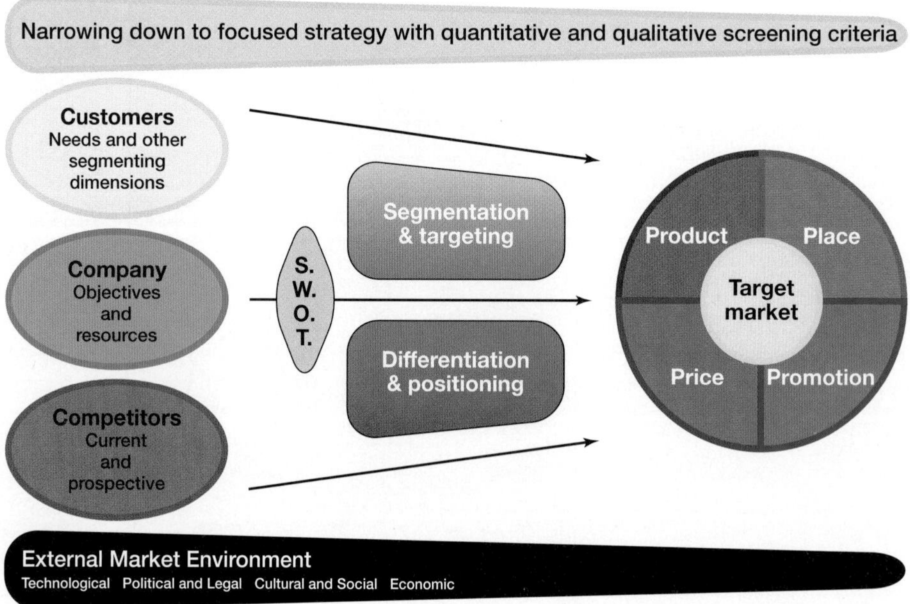

Consumer needs may be unmet because customers don't all have the same needs—nor do they always want these needs met in the same way. Part of the reason for such dissimilarities is that people with certain attitudes or interests have different preferences for how they spend their time, what shows they watch, and the like. For example, suppose you were selling a backpack. Would a thrill-seeking teenager living in an urban centre respond favourably to the marketing mix designed around a mother of four who lives in a small town and has a passion for the outdoors? As you can imagine, the teenager would have several unmet needs if the

## Internet Insite 3–1

### TARGET MARKETING ONLINE

Anyone who has surfed the Web for a while will realize that every conceivable demographic and lifestyle group has a site (or few hundred) that it can call its home (or homepage!). The variety of consumers and the variety of sites online present a great marketing opportunity and a challenge at the same time.

On the Internet, marketers can target their advertising to a very specific demographic or lifestyle group. For instance, marketers no longer see women as a single target market. There are different types of women who have different interests, lifestyles, and consumption habits. The Internet allows marketers to make these fine distinctions. A marketer interested in reaching professional women can go to iVillage or Women.com. A financial services company targeting women can advertise on these sites or sponsor a newsletter on the Women's Financial Network (www.wfn.com). Pregnant women and new mothers can be reached via BabyCenter (www.babycenter.com) and dozens of other such sites. Other demographic groups such as pre-teens and teens also have many destination sites.

Yahoo!, the popular portal and media site, has extended its brand by creating Yahooligans! (www.yahooligans.com), a gateway to the Internet designed for kids. Marketers like Kellogg's and the Cartoon Network use Yahooligans! to reach their target market. Gaming sites are also popular advertising locations for companies targeting a young audience. Visit sites like CIO.com and Orbitz (www.orbitz.com) to see examples of how advertising is related to the site's target audience.

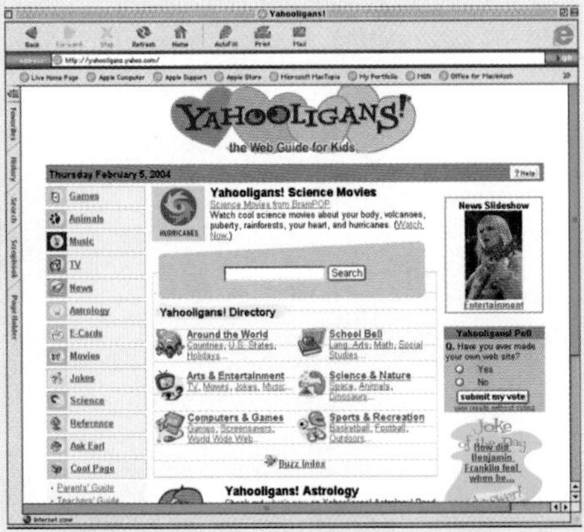


Lifestyle sites focused on music, sports, outdoor activities, healthy living, and so on allow marketers to target their advertising messages at well-defined audiences. In this respect, the Internet is more "targetable" than traditional media like television or print, which offer limited choice and can be very expensive.

The choice offered by the Internet is a double-edged sword. A keyword search on Google often will produce thousands of sites. Given the choice that consumers have online for information, shopping, community, and entertainment, some marketers believe that the Web is already too fragmented. With some exceptions, like Yahoo!, there are very few heavy hitters who draw visitors by the millions. Marketers who use the Internet for target marketing must choose their sites carefully, keeping in mind the size and nature of the audience.

Banner advertising on websites is only one way of implementing a target marketing program. There are other alternatives. For instance, context-sensitive advertising on Google and other search engines or portals enables advertisers to reach consumers who are currently seeking a product or information on a product. For instance, a marketer of cat food can have its name shown every time a consumer searches using the keywords "cat food." Such real-time targeting is not possible in traditional media such as television and print.

Larger advertisers have many options, for example the creation of microsites, which are permanent or temporary websites that focus on a single product or service. Such sites are often used by large companies with multiple products when they wish to focus attention on specific brands or products. Procter & Gamble's Always and Tampax brands are used to sponsor a site for teenaged girls called Beinggirl.com. P&G has sites for each of its major brands, including Crest, Tide, and Oil of Olay. BMW has microsites in several languages for its Mini brand (see the Canadian version at www.mini.ca).

The Web allows firms to track consumer purchase history and behaviour. Amazon.com tracks the shopping behaviour of its customers and makes recommendations based on previous purchases. By tailoring the recommendations to individual behaviour and preferences, Amazon.com's target marketing is more likely to be effective compared to a mass advertising campaign.

The Internet has other advantages when it comes to market segmentation and target marketing. Unlike television, which is a passive medium, the Web demands greater participation from consumers. Surfers make choices on where to go and what to read. Web browsing is often goal-driven (e.g., read news, get product information). Being so cognitively engaged means that consumers may actually pay some attention to advertisements that are relevant to what they are doing online. At the same time, the growing number of sites and advertising clutter online do present a challenge to marketers.

Here are some questions to ponder: If you were in charge of marketing for a consumer product firm (such as shampoo, pet food, or brand-name clothes), would you use the Internet to reach your target market or are mass media preferable? What are some ways of reaching the appropriate target market on the Internet if you are a smaller firm with a limited advertising budget?

Go to: www.mcgrawhill.ca/college/wong
to apply this Insite in an exciting Internet exercise.



family-oriented backpack were the only one available. Now think back to a time when backpacks were used primarily for camping and trekking. What unmet needs might students have? skateboarders? shoppers?

**Market segmentation and targeting** With so many possible differences between consumers, is it possible to systematically review the major opportunities? It is, because in spite of the many possible differences there often are subgroups (segments) of consumers who are similar and could be satisfied with the same marketing mix. Thus, we try to identify and understand these different subgroups with **market segmentation**. We will explain general approaches for segmenting markets later in this chapter. Then, in Chapters 5 to 7, we investigate the many interesting aspects of customer behaviour. For now, however, you should know that truly understanding customers is at the heart of using market segmentation to zoom in on a specific target market. In other words, segmentation helps a manager decide to serve some segment(s)—subgroups of customers—and not others.

**market segmentation**
A technique used to identify and understand different subgroups

Internet Insite 3-1 shows how the Internet can be used to assist marketers in designing and delivering tailored marketing programs to different groups of customers.

## Marketing Demo 3–1

### AUDI'S SUPERIOR MARKETING MIX

In Norway, many auto buyers are particularly concerned about safety in the snow. So, Audi offers a permanent four-wheel-drive system, called Quattro, that helps the car to hold the road. Audi ads emphasize this differentiation. Rather than show the car, however, the ads feature things that are very sticky (like bubblegum!) and the only text is the headline "Sticks like Quattro" and the Audi brand name. Of course, handling is not Audi's only strength, but it is an important one in helping to position Audi as better than competing brands within this target market. In contrast, consider General Motors' decision to discontinue the 100-year-old Oldsmobile line. In spite of repeated efforts, marketers for Oldsmobile were no longer able to develop a differentiated position in the crowded North American auto market. And when target customers don't see an advantage with a firm's marketing mix, they simply move on.[6]

**Differentiation and positioning** A marketing mix must meet the needs of target customers, but a firm isn't likely to obtain a competitive advantage if it *just* meets needs in the same way as some other firm. So, in evaluating possible strategies the marketing manager should think about whether there is a way to differentiate or make distinctive a product's marketing mix. **Differentiation** means that the marketing mix is distinct from and better than what is available from a competitor. As suggested above, differentiation often requires that the firm tailor all of the elements of its marketing mix to the specific needs of a distinctive target market. Sometimes the difference is based mainly on one important element of the marketing mix—say, an improved product or faster delivery. Differentiation is more obvious to target customers, though, when there is a consistent theme integrated across the four-Ps decision areas. Indeed, imagine how differentiated a marketing mix would be if it focused on a less-traditional customer with peculiar needs that everyone else either ignored or lumped in with all other customers: imagine, too, which marketing mix would be most favoured by the customer! This is the thinking behind **positioning**—where the central idea is to narrow down all possible marketing mixes to one that is differentiated to meet target customers' needs in a superior way. Marketing Demo 3-1 shows how one company, Audi, uses this approach to its advantage.

**differentiation**

When the marketing mix is distinct from and better than what is available from a competitor

**positioning**

When the central idea is to narrow down all possible marketing mixes to one that is differentiated to meet target customers' needs in a superior way

**Making the final choice** Usually, the range of opportunities—and strategy possibilities—is larger than a firm can pursue. Each alternative has its own advantages and disadvantages. Trends in the external market environment may make a potential opportunity more or less attractive. These complications can make it difficult to identify the best target market and marketing mix. However, developing a set of specific qualitative and quantitative screening criteria can help a manager define which markets the firm wants to compete in and what products it will use to compete with. It can also help eliminate potential strategies that are not well suited for the firm. We will cover screening criteria in more detail in Chapter 4. For now, you should realize that the criteria you select in a specific situation grow out of an analysis of the company's objectives and resources.

A useful aid for identifying relevant screening criteria and for zeroing in on a feasible strategy is **S.W.O.T. analysis**—which identifies and lists the firm's strengths and weaknesses, and its opportunities and threats. The name S.W.O.T. is simply an abbreviation for the first letters of the words strengths, weaknesses, opportunities, and threats. A good S.W.O.T. analysis helps the manager focus on a strategy that takes advantage of the firm's opportunities and builds on its strengths while minimizing its weaknesses and dealing with threats to its success. Marketing Demo 3-2 shows how one entrepreneur used this approach to successfully compete against giants like Procter & Gamble and Unilever.

**S.W.O.T. analysis**

A strategy that identifies and lists the firm's strengths and weaknesses, and its opportunities and threats

## Marketing Demo 3–2

### A S.W.O.T.-BASED ADVANTAGE

The marketing strategy developed by Amilya Antonetti illustrates the basic ideas behind a S.W.O.T. analysis. Her son was allergic to the chemicals in standard detergents, and her research showed that many other children had the same problem. So to pursue this opportunity she developed a line of hypoallergenic cleaning products and started SoapWorks. Unlike the big companies, she didn't have established relationships with grocery chains or money for national TV ads. To get around these weaknesses, she used inexpensive radio ads in local markets and touted SoapWorks as a company created for moms by a mom who cared about kids. She had a credible claim that the big corporations couldn't make. Her ads also helped her get shelf space because they urged other mothers to ask for SoapWorks products and to tell friends about stores that carried them. This wasn't the fastest possible way to introduce a new product line, but her cash-strapped strategy played to her unique strengths with her specific target market.[7]

## Finding the Breakthrough Opportunity

A marketing manager who really understands a target market may see breakthrough opportunities. But a target market's real needs—and the breakthrough opportunities that can come from serving those needs—are not always obvious. This is because many potential breakthrough markets are made up of people who currently satisfy their needs using a different technology or kind of product than those being considered by the manager. For example, when Palm first launched its Palm Pilot personal digital assistant (PDA), there were no competing PDAs available. Consumers used appointment books, scheduling systems, and a variety of other devices to keep track of their meetings and special events. They also used address books to keep track of contacts, and so on. Palm's breakthrough came when it recognized that there was a market of consumers who wanted all of these capabilities in a single product and with the speed and convenience of computer technology.

But how does one uncover these opportunities for products that don't currently exist? Since products gain value only through the customer satisfaction they generate, the place to start is with a deeper understanding of "the market."

### Defining the Market

The term *definition* usually makes one think of a phrase to be memorized and recited on command. While this can apply to a "market definition," in this instance the goal is more one of narrowing down the set of customers we wish to pursue. In this sense, a **market** is a group of potential customers with similar needs who are willing to exchange something of value with sellers offering various goods and/or services—that is, ways of satisfying those needs.

**market**

A group of potential customers with similar needs who are willing to exchange something of value with sellers offering various goods and/or services

To understand why this narrowing-down process is important, consider the case of a cell phone. On one hand, we might define the market as people who want a wireless phone. But soon that market would be filled. If we continue to think of the cell unit as a wireless phone there are a limited set of enhancements that might be added to the phone: clearer display, better signal, nicer appearance, and so on. *But* if we define the market as a "personal information device" we might add cameras, voice recording, access to e-mail or Internet, SMS messaging, paging ... the possi-

The Olympus pocket camera competes directly with other 35-mm cameras, but it may also compete in a broader product-market against Vivitar's digital camera for kids or even Sony's innovative Mavica, which stores digital pictures on a 3-inch CD-R.

bilities become endless. And so too do the number of alternative "phones" one could imagine making.

Marketing-oriented managers develop marketing mixes for *specific* target markets. Getting the firm to focus on specific target markets is vital: it is hard to focus on something that cannot be described or defined. As shown in Exhibit 3-3, deciding on a specific target market involves a narrowing-down process—to get beyond production-oriented mass market thinking.

**generic market**
A market with broadly similar needs

**product-market**
A market with very similar needs and sellers offering various close-substitute ways of satisfying those needs

To understand the narrowing-down process, it's useful to think of two basic types of markets. A **generic market** is a market with broadly similar needs—and sellers offering various, often diverse, ways of satisfying those needs. In contrast, a **product-market** is a market with very similar needs and sellers offering various close-substitute ways of satisfying those needs.[8]

A generic-market description looks at markets broadly and from a customer's viewpoint. Status seekers, for example, have several very different ways to satisfy their status needs. A status seeker might buy a Mont Blanc pen, Oakley sunglasses, or an Armani suit. Any one of these very different products may satisfy this status need, and other needs as well. Sellers in this generic status-seeker market have to focus on the need(s) the customers want satisfied, not on how one seller's product (pen, sunglasses, or suit) is better than that of another producer.

It is sometimes hard to understand and define generic markets because, as our status-seeker example shows, quite different product types may compete with each other. But if customers see all these products as substitutes—as competitors in the same generic market—then marketers must deal with this complication.

Suppose, however, that one of our status seekers decides to satisfy this status need with a new, expensive suit. Then, in this product-market, Versace, Armani, Ralph Lauren, and other similar designers may compete with each other for the status seeker's dollars. In this product-market concerned with suits *and* status, consumers compare similar products—suits, but not all possible suits—to satisfy their need for status.

You may wonder why we go through this lengthy and somewhat complicated process. Why not just start with the product we are planning to sell? Certainly it would be easier. But would it be as effective?

Some production-oriented managers get into trouble because they ignore the tough part of defining markets. To make the narrowing-down process easier, they just describe their markets in terms of *products* they sell. For example, producers and



**Exhibit 3-3** Narrowing down to target markets.

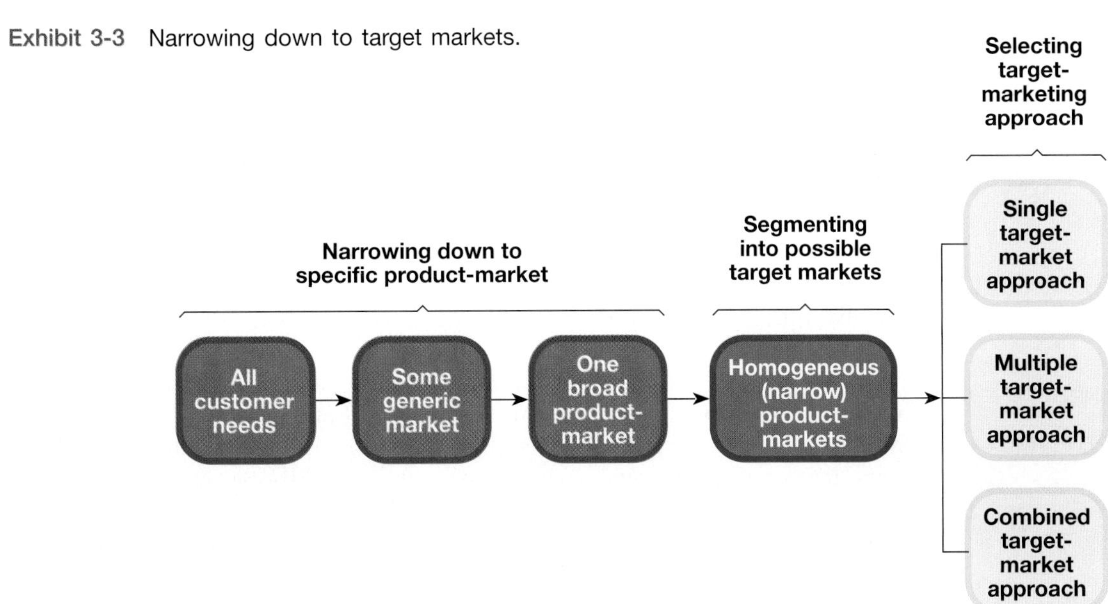

retailers of greeting cards might define their market as the "greeting card market." But this production-oriented approach ignores the real need being served: the customer isn't buying a card, but rather a means of expression. Viewed this way, we might ask, "Is a greeting card always the best way to express yourself?" If not, there may be several opportunities being missed.

Hallmark isn't missing these opportunities. Instead, Hallmark aims at the "personal expression market." Hallmark stores offer all kinds of products that can be sent as "memory makers"—to express one person's feelings toward another. And as opportunities related to these needs change, Hallmark changes too. For example, at the Hallmark website (www.hallmark.com) it is easy to get shopping suggestions from an online "gift assistant," to order flowers, or to personalize an electronic greeting card to send over the Internet.[9]

But defining the target market isn't done solely to identify opportunities. Once an opportunity is selected, a market definition becomes an important tool in selecting a marketing mix. Recall our opening vignette, Jones Soda. The success of the line is not in having a good-tasting soda, but rather in using that soda as a means of satisfying a much broader need: the need for self-expression by North American youths. Now, consider what that market definition suggests about the appropriateness of Jones's marketing mix. Would you make a soda product coloured purple, pink, or blue? Would you call it Fufu Berry, Bug Juice, or Whoop Ass? Coca-Cola and Pepsi probably wouldn't, but Jones Soda should—and does.

## Defining and Naming Product-Markets and Generic Markets

The Hallmark and Jones Soda examples demonstrate that product-related terms do not by themselves adequately describe a market and do not provide a strong foundation for the design of a marketing mix. A more complete description or definition of the opportunity would include:

1. What is offered: the type of product or service provided
2. Why it is valued: the customer (user) needs met, benefits offered, or problems solved
3. For whom: the type of customers who have this need or want this benefit
4. Where: the geographic area where these customers can be found

*Product type* describes the goods and/or services that customers want. Sometimes the product type is strictly a physical good or strictly a service. But sometimes it is a combination of product and service: for example, a caterer provides both a product (a meal) and a service (planning a menu and serving the meal).

*Customer (user) needs* refer to the needs the product type satisfies for the customer. At a very basic level, product types usually provide functional benefits such as nourishing, protecting, warming, cooling, transporting, cleaning, holding, saving time, and so forth. Although we need to identify such "basic" needs first, in advanced economies we usually go on to emotional needs—such as needs for fun, excitement, pleasing appearance, or status. Correctly defining the need(s) relevant to a market is crucial and requires a good understanding of customers. We discuss these topics more fully in Chapters 6 and 7. For example, suppose we had three shirts that were the same in terms of material and design. Suppose one of these was plain, one had the name of a resort area, and the third had a well-publicized designer logo on it. While all of these shirts satisfy the same basic physical need, the shirt with the resort name or logo might also provide other, more emotional needs. As with value-adding services, marketers are always looking for ways to extend the set of needs served by their products and services as a way of creating value for customers.

*Customer type* refers to the final consumer or user of a product type. Here we want to choose a name that describes all present (possible) types of customers. To define customer type, marketers should identify the final consumer or user of the

Exhibit 3-4 Relationship between generic and product-market definitions.

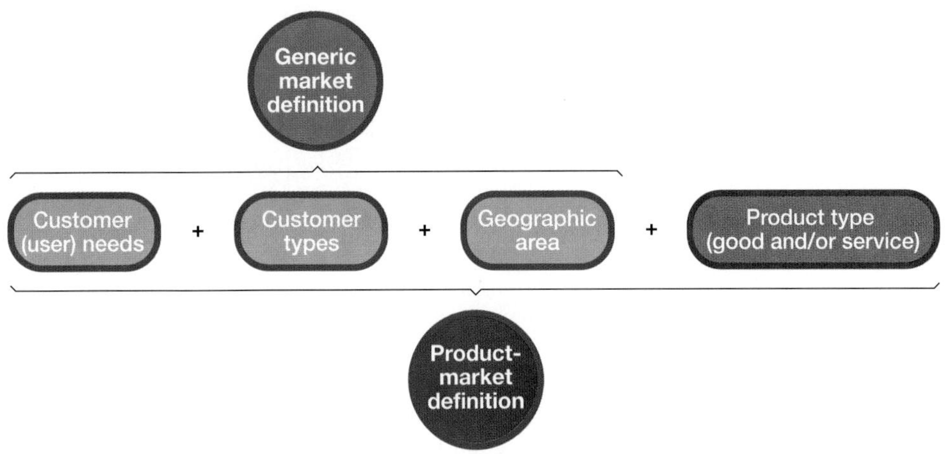




product type rather than the buyer, if they are different. For instance, textbooks are usually selected for use in the classroom by teachers and professors. However, students must also be considered in a customer-type definition, as they are often the end-user.

The *geographic area* is where a firm competes—or plans to compete—for customers. Naming the geographic area may seem trivial, but understanding geographic boundaries of a market can suggest new opportunities. A firm aiming at only the Canadian market, for example, may want to expand into world markets.

We refer to these four-part descriptions as product-market "names" because most managers label their markets when they think, write, or talk about them. Such a four-part definition can be clumsy, however, so we often use a nickname—for example, "golden oldies" for well-to-do Canadian retirees interested in winter cruises. And the nickname should refer to people, not products—because, as we emphasize throughout this book, people make markets!

In keeping with the notion of market definition as a narrowing-down process (recall Exhibit 3-3), it is helpful to distinguish between a generic-market definition and a product-market definition. A generic-market description *doesn't include any product-type terms*. It consists of only three parts of the product-market definition—without the product type. For example, you may recall that in our status-seeker market example, very different product types were competitors. This emphasizes that any product type that satisfies the customer's needs can compete in a generic market. Generic-market definitions help us avoid being bound to traditional methods of serving customers. For example, the innovative Amazon.com owes its success to the fact that it serves the same basic needs as a bookstore without being bound by the requirements of a bricks-and-mortar location. Exhibit 3-4 shows the relationship between generic-market and product-market definitions.

## Market Segmentation

Market segmentation is the two-step process of (1) *naming* broad product-markets and (2) *segmenting* these broad product-markets in order to select target markets and develop suitable marketing mixes. We name broad product-markets to identify the kinds of opportunities we might pursue. Once identified, we segment the customers in those markets to determine the best way to serve them.

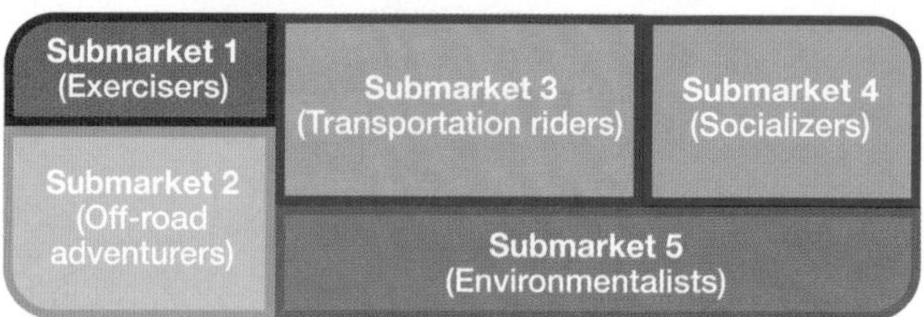


Exhibit 3-5 A market grid diagram showing submarkets.

Some managers make the mistake of ignoring the naming stage. Instead, they might try to find one or two demographic characteristics to segment the market. For example, they might segment based on age and gender, identifying, say, elderly women as a target segment.

But in doing so, these managers make the same mistake that production-oriented managers make when they define a market solely on the basis of the product type (see earlier discussion): they miss opportunities and develop a weak understanding of what customers really want. Customer behaviour is usually too complex to be explained in terms of just one or two demographic characteristics. Returning to our earlier example, not all elderly women buy the same products or brands. At the same time, in some cases, younger and older women may buy exactly the same products or brands. A small number of demographic characteristics rarely does an adequate job of explaining customer preference.

### Stage 1—Naming Broad Target Markets

Naming (or defining) a broad product-market begins by "disaggregating" or breaking apart all possible needs into some generic markets. These generic markets are then further disaggregated into broad product-markets, and finally assessed as to whether the firm would be able to operate profitably in them (refer to Exhibit 3-3).

The naming step involves brainstorming about very different solutions to various generic needs and selecting some broad areas—broad product-markets—where the firm has some resources and experience. This means that a car manufacturer would probably ignore all the possible opportunities in food and clothing markets and focus on the generic market, "transporting people in the world," and probably on the broad product-market, "cars, trucks, and utility vehicles for transporting people in the world."

Usually it is possible—and advisable—to further refine this broad product-market. For example, the customer looking for family transportation is unlikely to be happy with the same vehicle required by a Formula One racecar driver. So, marketers disaggregate the broad product-market into submarkets. Each one of these submarkets represents smaller, more homogeneous product-markets. Exhibit 3-5, for example, represents the broad product-market of bicycle riders. The boxes show different submarkets. One submarket might focus on people who want basic transportation, another on people who want exercise, and so on.

### Stage 2—Segmenting

**segmenting**

An aggregating process of clustering people with similar needs into a market segment.

Marketing-oriented managers think of **segmenting** as an aggregating process—clustering people with similar needs into a "market segment." A market segment is a (relatively) homogeneous group of customers who will respond to a marketing mix in a similar way. These similarities enable marketers to pursue multiple individual customers (within a segment) using a single marketing mix.

This part of the market segmentation process (refer to Exhibit 3-3) takes a different approach from the naming part. Here we look for similarities rather than basic

Exhibit 3-6 Every individual has his or her own position in a market; those with similar positions can be aggregated into potential target markets.

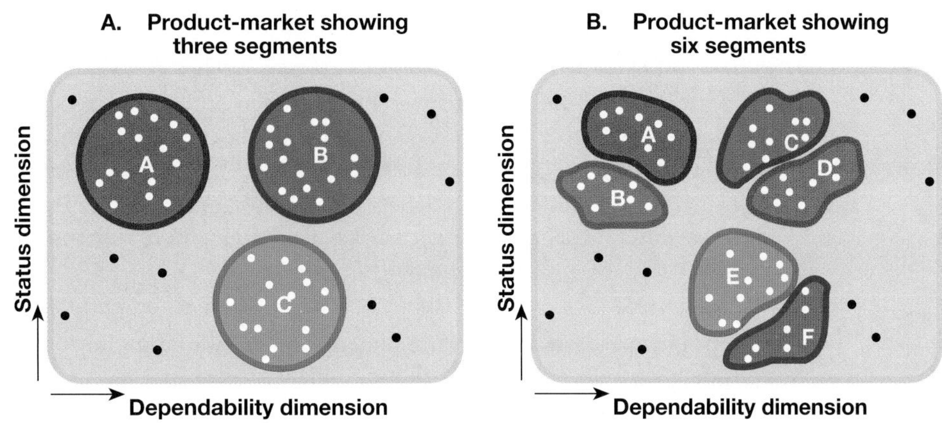


differences in needs. Segmenters start with the idea that each person is one of a kind but that it may be possible to aggregate some similar people into a product-market.

One way to understand how segmentation creates value is to think about the selling of jeans. Since every person's body is in some way different, tailor-made jeans would provide the ultimate in accommodating individual needs. However, the cost would be significant. At the other extreme, we could reduce costs by manufacturing jeans in "one size fits all" sizing; however, the quality of fit would likely leave something lacking. As an alternative, we might group together all people according to their waist size and design a jean using the other measurements (hips, legs, etc.) typical of people with that size waist. The resulting off-the-rack product would be superior in fit to a one-size-fits-all offering, slightly inferior in fit to tailor-made, but closer to one-size-fits-all in pricing. Thus, relative to one-size-fits-all (a mass-marketing approach), the customer gets much better quality at an only slightly higher price: a formula for better value.

Exhibit 3-6A offers a graphical view of segmentation. Consider a product-market in which customers' needs differ on two important segmenting dimensions: the need for status and the need for dependability. In Exhibit 3-6A, each dot shows a person's position on the two dimensions. While each person's position is unique, many of these people are similar in terms of how much status and dependability they want. So a segmenter may aggregate them into three (an arbitrary number) relatively homogeneous submarkets—A, B, and C. Group A might be called "status-oriented" and Group C "dependability-oriented." Members of Group B want both and might be called the "demanders," since they seem to want both status and dependability. Armed with this information, a segmenter could now develop a specific marketing mix for each homogeneous segment it wishes to target.

While segmentation is clearly a powerful concept, the identification of segments and the assignment of individual customers to any one segment is not always clear-cut. Look again at Exhibit 3-6A; remember that we talked about three segments, but this was an arbitrary number. As Exhibit 3-6B shows, there may really be six segments. (What do you think—does this broad product-market consist of three segments or six?) In addition, some potential customers just don't fit neatly into market segments. For example, not everyone in Exhibit 3-6B was put into one of the groups. Forcing them into one of the groups would have made these segments more heterogeneous and harder to please. Further, forming additional segments for them probably wouldn't be profitable. They are too few and not very similar in terms of the two dimensions. These people are simply too unique to be catered to and may have to be ignored—unless they are willing to pay a high price for special treatment.

The number of segments that should be formed depends more on judgment than on some scientific rule. But the following guidelines can help. Ideally, "good" market segments meet the following criteria:

1. *Homogeneous (similar) within*—The customers in a market segment should be as similar as possible with respect to their likely responses to marketing-mix variables and their segmenting dimensions.
2. *Heterogeneous (different) between*—The customers in different segments should be as different as possible with respect to their likely responses to marketing-mix variables and their segmenting dimensions.
3. *Substantial*—The segment should be big enough to be profitable.
4. *Operational*—The segmenting dimensions should be useful for identifying customers and deciding on marketing-mix variables.

It is especially important that segmenting dimensions be *operational*—so that a company can easily and accurately identify and reach its targeted customers. This leads marketers to include demographic dimensions such as age, sex, income, location, and family size. In fact, it is difficult to make some place and promotion decisions without such information. Segmenting dimensions that have no practical operational use should be avoided. For example, you may find a personality trait such as moodiness among the traits of heavy buyers of a product, but how could you use this fact? Salespeople can't give a personality test to each buyer. Similarly, advertising couldn't make much use of this information, since there isn't likely to be a TV show or print vehicle focused on moody people. So although moodiness might be related in some way to previous purchases, it would not be a useful dimension for segmenting.

## Moving from Segmentation to Target Marketing

Once you accept the idea that broad product-markets may have submarkets, you can see that target marketers usually have a choice among many possible target markets. There are three basic ways to develop market-oriented strategies in a broad product-market.

Exhibit 3-7 Target marketers have specific aims.

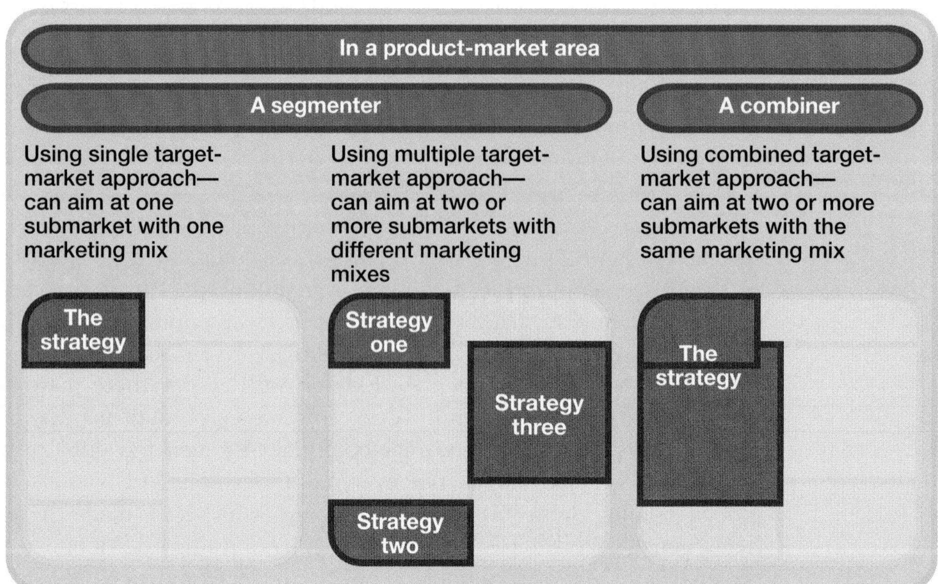

**single target market approach** Segmenting the market and choosing one of the homogeneous segments as the firm's target market

**multiple target market approach** Segmenting the market and choosing two or more segments, then treating each as a separate target market needing a different marketing mix

**combined target market approach** Combining two or more submarkets into one larger target market as a basis for one strategy

1. The **single target market approach**—Segmenting the market and choosing one of the homogeneous segments as the firm's target market.
2. The **multiple target market approach**—Segmenting the market and choosing two or more segments, then treating each as a separate target market needing a different marketing mix.
3. The **combined target market approach**—Combining two or more submarkets into one larger target market as a basis for one strategy.

Note that all three approaches involve target marketing. As shown in Exhibit 3-7, they all aim at specific, clearly defined target markets. For convenience, we call people who follow the first two approaches the "segmenters" and people who use the third approach the "combiners."

**Combiners** *Combiners* try to increase the size of their target markets by combining two or more segments. Combiners look at various submarkets for similarities rather than differences and then try to extend or modify their basic offering to appeal to these "combined" customers with just one marketing mix (see Exhibit 3-7). For example, combiners may try a new package, more service, a new brand, or a new flavour. But even if they make product or other marketing-mix changes, they don't try to satisfy unique, smaller submarkets. Instead, combiners try to improve the general appeal of their marketing mix to appeal to a bigger "combined" target market.

A combined target market approach may help achieve some economies of scale. It may also require less investment than developing different marketing mixes for different segments—making it especially attractive for firms with limited resources.

It is tempting to aim at larger combined markets instead of using different marketing mixes for smaller segmented markets. But combiners must be careful not to aggregate too far. As they enlarge the target market, individual differences within each submarket may begin to outweigh the similarities. This makes it harder to develop marketing mixes that can effectively reach and satisfy potential customers within each of the submarkets.

In addition, a combiner faces the continual risk that innovative segmenters will chip away at the various segments of the combined target market by offering more attractive marketing mixes to more homogeneous submarkets. IBM saw this happen very quickly when it first came out with its personal computers. As the market became increasingly attractive, Apple took the segment that wanted an easy-to-use computer. Toshiba took travellers who wanted laptop convenience. Compaq got those who wanted the fastest machines. Dell attracted customers who wanted reliability at a low price.

**Segmenters** *Segmenters* aim at one or more homogeneous segments and try to develop a different marketing mix for each. Segmenters usually adjust their mar-



Exhibit 3-8 There may be different demand curves in different market segments.

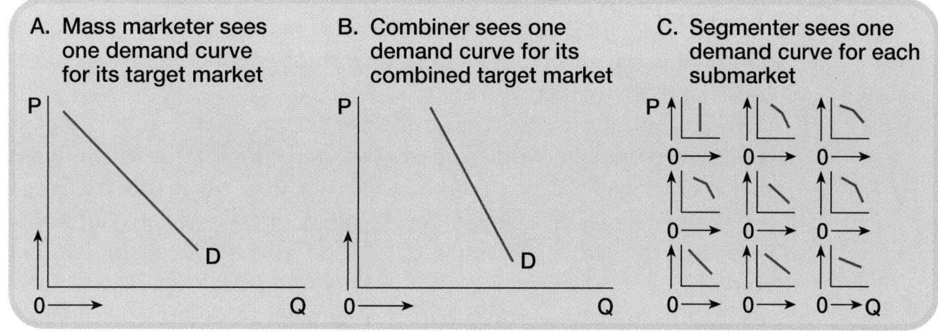

iVillage.com's website focuses on women to do a better job in meeting their specific needs.

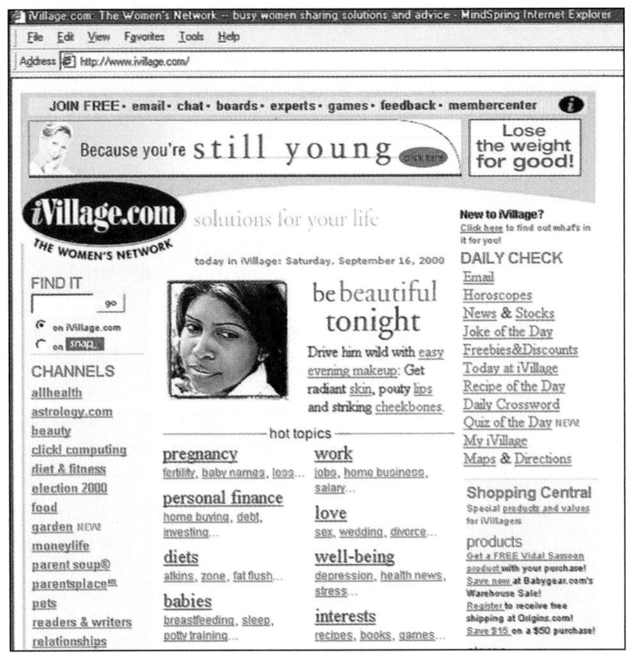


keting mixes for each target market, perhaps making basic changes in the product itself, because they want to satisfy each segment very well.

Instead of assuming that the whole market consists of a fairly similar set of customers (like the mass marketer does) or merging various submarkets together (like the combiner), segmenters believe customers in each segment have different needs and may even have demand curves reflecting how much they are willing to buy at different prices (see Exhibit 3-8). Thus, aiming at one of these smaller markets makes it possible to provide superior value and satisfy them better. This then provides greater profit potential for the firm.

For example, the Department of Economic Development and Tourism in New Brunswick used segmentation to increase tourism in the province. Instead of spending money trying to attract tourists from everywhere in the world, it identified groups of customers based on geographic proximity (e.g., Quebec, Northeastern United States) or specific interests that fit with the province's natural capacities (e.g., beaches, ecotourism, salmon fishing). By developing tourism products that emphasized the appropriate attractions and using the appropriate media, the province became one of the fastest-growing tourism centres in Canada.

Note that segmenters are not settling for smaller sales potential or lower profits. Instead, they hope to increase sales by winning a much larger share of the business in the market(s) they target. A segmenter that truly satisfies the target market can often build such a close relationship with customers that it faces no real competition. A segmenter that offers a marketing mix precisely matched to the needs of the target market can often charge a higher price that produces higher profits.

Which approach should a firm use? This depends on the firm's resources, the nature of competition, and—most important—the similarity of customer needs, attitudes, and buying behaviour.

In general, it's usually safer to be a segmenter—that is, to try to satisfy some customers very well instead of many just *fairly* well. That's why many firms use the single or multiple target market approach instead of the combined target market approach. Procter & Gamble, for example, offers many products that seem to compete directly with each other (e.g., Tide versus Cheer, or Pantene Pro-V versus Herbal Essences). However, P&G offers tailor-made marketing mixes to each submarket that is large—and profitable—enough to deserve a separate marketing mix.

Though extremely effective, this approach may not be possible for a smaller company with more limited resources. A smaller company may have to use the single target market approach—focusing all its efforts at the one submarket niche where it sees the best opportunity.[10]

In practice, cost considerations probably encourage more aggregating—to obtain economies of scale—while demand considerations suggest less aggregating—to satisfy needs more exactly.

*Profit* is the balancing point between the sales effectiveness of segmenting and the cost efficiencies of combining customers. Ultimately, calculations must be made of the profit available under the different approaches. These calculations compare the higher sales and costs that are often found in segmenting to the lower sales but lower costs of combining. This determines how unique a marketing mix the firm can afford to offer to a particular group.

## Which Dimensions Are Used to Segment Markets?

As noted earlier, identifying the number of segments in a market requires a great deal of judgment. Much depends on the dimensions used to classify customers into segments. For example, in Exhibits 3-6A and 3-6B we used the dimensions "dependability" and "status." If we replaced one of these with, for example, "ease of use," we might find that customers fall into entirely different groupings.

Market segmentation forces a marketing manager to decide which product-market dimensions best explain what people will buy. By considering the demographics and other characteristics of customers in the segment, managers gain insights that help guide marketing-mix planning. Exhibit 3-9 shows the basic kinds of dimensions we'll be talking about in Chapters 5 and 6—and their probable effects on the four Ps. As noted earlier, we want to describe any potential product-market in terms of all three types of customer-related dimensions—plus a product-type description—because these dimensions help us develop better marketing mixes.

Customers can be described by many specific dimensions. For example, in the snack-food market, health-food enthusiasts are interested in nutrition, dieters worry about calories, and economical shoppers with lots of kids may want volume to "fill them up." Exhibit 3-10 shows some dimensions that are useful for segmenting consumer markets. A few are behavioural dimensions, others are geographic and demographic. Exhibit 3-11 shows some additional dimensions for segmenting markets when the customers are businesses, government agencies, or other types of organizations. Regardless of whether customers are final consumers or organizations, segmenting a broad product-market may require using several different dimensions at the same time.[11]



**Exhibit 3-9** Relation of potential target market dimensions to marketing strategy decision areas.

| Potential Target-Market Dimensions | Effects on Strategy Decision Areas |
|---|---|
| 1. Behavioural needs, attitudes, and how present and potential goods and services fit into customers' consumption patterns. | Affects *Product* (features, packaging, product-line assortment, branding) and *Promotion* (what potential customers need and want to know about the firm's offering, and what appeals should be used). |
| 2. Urgency to get need satisfied and desire and willingness to seek information, compare, and shop. | Affects *Place* (how directly products are distributed from producer to customer, how extensively they are made available, and the level of service needed) and *Price* (how much potential customers are willing to pay). |
| 3. Geographic location and other demographic characteristics of potential customers. | Affects size of *Target Markets* (economic potential), *Place* (where products should be made available), and *Promotion* (where and to whom to target advertising and personal selling). |

**qualifying dimensions**
Dimensions that are relevant to including a customer type in a product-market

**determining dimensions**
Dimensions that actually affect the customer's purchase of a specific product or brand in a product-market

With so many dimensions to choose from, it may be helpful to think about two different types of dimensions. **Qualifying dimensions** are those relevant to including a customer type in a product-market. They help us to estimate the size of the product-market, which in turn helps us to determine how much we might be able to spend to win customers. The qualifying dimensions also help identify the "core features" that must be offered to everyone in a product-market. **Determining dimensions** are those that actually affect the customer's purchase of a specific product or brand in a product-market. These help us decide the marketing mix to use.

A prospective car buyer, for example, has to have enough money—or credit—to buy a car and insure it. Our buyer also needs a driver's licence. This still doesn't guarantee a purchase. He or she must have a real need—like a job that requires "wheels," or kids who have to be carpooled. This need may motivate the purchase of *some* car. But these qualifying dimensions don't determine what brand or model of car the person might buy. That depends on more specific interests—such as the kind of safety rating, performance, or appearance the customer wants. Determining dimensions related to these needs affect the specific car the customer purchases. If safety is a determining dimension for a customer, a Volvo wagon that offers side



Exhibit 3-10 Possible segmenting dimensions and typical breakdowns for consumer markets.

| | |
|---|---|
| **Behavioural** | |
| Needs | Economic, functional, physiological, psychological, social, and more detailed needs. |
| Benefits sought | Situation-specific, but to satisfy specific or general needs. |
| Thoughts | Favourable or unfavourable attitudes, interests, opinions, beliefs. |
| Rate of use | Heavy, medium, light, nonusers. |
| Purchase relationship | Positive and ongoing, intermittent, no relationship, bad relationship. |
| Brand familiarity | Insistence, preference, recognition, nonrecognition, rejection. |
| Kind of shopping | Convenience, comparison shopping, specialty, none (unsought product). |
| Type of problem-solving | Routinized response, limited, extensive. |
| Information required | Low, medium, high. |
| **Geographic** | |
| Region of world, country | North America (Canada, United States), Europe (France, Italy, Germany), and so on. |
| Region in country | (Examples in Canada): The North, the West Coast, the Prairies, Central Canada, the Atlantic Region. |
| Size of city | No city; population under 5,000; 5,000–19,999; 20,000–49,999; 50,000–99,999; 100,000–249,999; 250,000–499,999; 500,000–999,999; 1,000,000–3,999,999; 4,000,000 or over. |
| **Demographic** | |
| Income | Under $5,000; $5,000–9,999; $10,000–14,999; $15,000–19,999; $20,000–29,999; $30,000–39,999; $40,000–59,999; $60,000 and over. |
| Sex | Male, female. |
| Age | Infant; under 6; 6–11; 12–17; 18–24; 25–34; 35–49; 50–64; 65 or over. |
| Family size | 1, 2, 3–4, 5 or more. |
| Family life cycle | Young, single; young, married, no children; young, married, youngest child under 6; young, married, youngest child over 6; older, married, with children; older, married, no children under 18; older, single; other variations for single parents, divorced, etc. |
| Occupation | Professional and technical; managers, officials, and proprietors; clerical sales; craftspeople, managers; operatives; farmers; retired; students; homemakers; unemployed. |
| Education | Grade school or less; some high school; high school graduate; some postsecondary; post-secondary graduate. |
| Ethnicity | Asian, Black, Native, White, Multiracial. |
| Social class | Lower-lower, upper-lower, lower-middle, upper-middle, lower-upper, upper-upper. |

Note: Terms used in this exhibit are explained in detail later in the text.

**Exhibit 3-11** Possible segmenting dimensions for business/organizational markets.

| | |
|---|---|
| Kind of relationship | Weak loyalty → strong loyalty to vendor<br>Single source → multiple vendors<br>"Arm's length" dealings → close partnership<br>No reciprocity → complete reciprocity |
| Type of customer | Manufacturer, service producer, government agency, military, nonprofit, wholesaler or retailer (when end user), and so on. |
| Demographics | Geographic location (region of world, country, region within country, urban → rural)<br>Size (number of employees, sales volume)<br>Primary business or industry (North American Industry Classification System)<br>Number of facilities |
| How customer will use product | Installations, components, accessories, raw materials, supplies, professional services |
| Type of buying situation | Decentralized → centralized<br>Buyer → multiple buying influence<br>Straight rebuy → modified rebuy → new-task buying |
| Purchasing methods | Vendor analysis, purchasing specifications, Internet bids, negotiated contracts, long-term contracts, e-commerce websites |

Note: Terms used in this exhibit are explained in detail later in the text.

impact protection, airbags, and all-wheel drive might be the customer's first choice. By contrast, if sporty looks is a determining dimension, a Tiburon or street-customized Honda Civic would more probably be selected.

How specific the determining dimensions are depends on whether you are concerned with a general product type or a specific brand (see Exhibit 3-12). The more specific you want to be, the more particular the determining dimensions may be. In a particular case, the determining dimensions may seem minor. But they are important because they *are* the determining dimensions.

For example, marketers at Kellogg's undertook an extensive study of breakfast eating habits. They discovered that customers are often pressed for time in the morning when trying to get to work or school and don't have time for a sit-down breakfast.

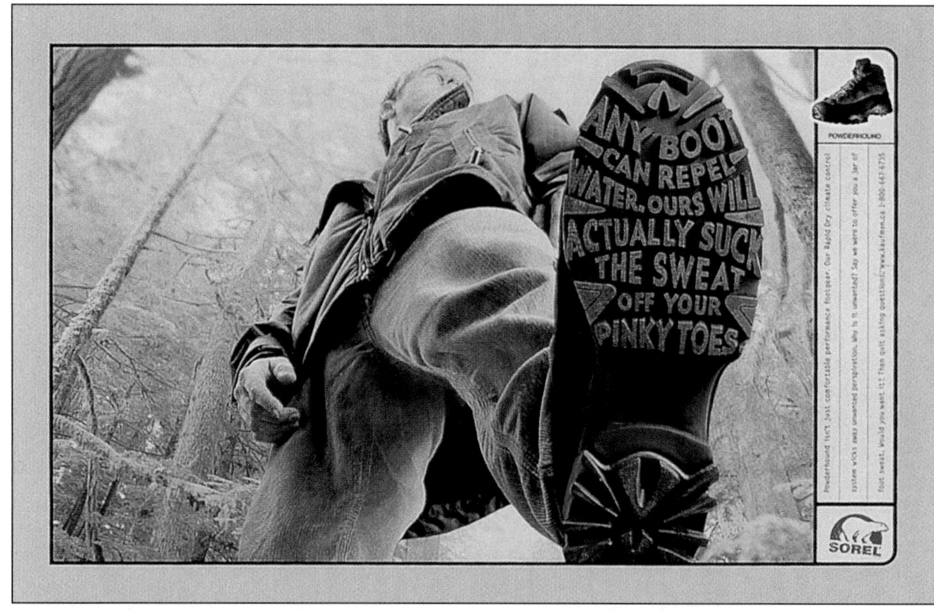


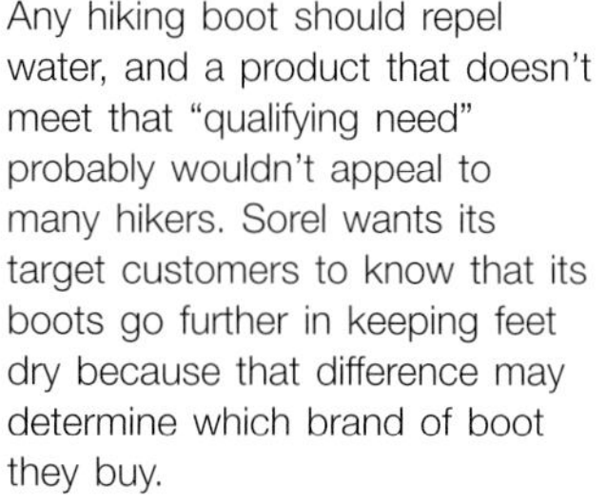
Any hiking boot should repel water, and a product that doesn't meet that "qualifying need" probably wouldn't appeal to many hikers. Sorel wants its target customers to know that its boots go further in keeping feet dry because that difference may determine which brand of boot they buy.

Exhibit 3-12 Finding the relevant segmenting dimensions.

| All potential dimensions | Qualifying dimensions | Determining dimensions (product type) | Determining dimensions (brand-specific) |
|---|---|---|---|
| Dimensions generally relevant to purchasing behaviour | Dimensions relevant to including a customer type in the product-market | Dimensions that affect the customer's purchase of a specific type of product | Dimensions that affect the customer's choice of a specific brand |

Segmenting dimensions become more specific to reasons why the target segment chooses to buy a particular brand of the product



Kellogg's figured out that for many of these target customers the real determining dimension in picking a breakfast food is whether it can be eaten "on the go." This discovery led them to the development of their Nutrigrain cereal bars—a satisfying morning snack that can easily be eaten on the way to work or school. This new-product launch was so successful that Kellogg's inspired an entire new category of breakfast foods.[12]

The Kellogg's example shows that a marketing manager should seek new ways to serve existing customers and strengthen the relationship with them. Too often firms let their strategies get stagnant after they've established a base of customers and a set of marketing-mix decisions. For example, special business services—like voice mail—related to determining the needs of upscale executives might initially help a motel win this business. However, the motel will lose its competitive edge if other motels start to offer the same benefits. Then, the determining dimensions change. To retain its customers, the motel must find new and better ways to meet needs. For example, the motel might make it easier for travelling executives by providing high-speed Internet access for their use during a stay.[13] See Ethical Dimensions 3-1 for a perspective on the issues involved in selecting segmenting dimensions.

## Ethical Dimensions 3–1

### ISSUES IN SELECTING SEGMENTING DIMENSIONS

Marketing managers sometimes face ethical decisions when selecting segmenting dimensions. Problems may arise if a firm targets customers who are somehow at a disadvantage in dealing with the firm or who are unlikely to see the negative effects of their own choices. For example, some people criticize shoe companies for targeting poor, inner-city kids who see expensive athletic shoes as an important status symbol. Many firms, including producers of infant formula, have been criticized for targeting consumers in less-developed nations. Encyclopedia publishers have been criticized for aggressive selling to less-educated parents who don't realize that the "pennies a day" credit terms are more than they can afford. Some nutritionists criticize companies that market soft drinks, candy, and snack foods to children.

Sometimes a marketing manager must decide whether a firm should serve customers it really doesn't want to serve. For example, banks sometimes offer marketing mixes that are attractive to wealthy customers but that basically drive off low-income consumers.

People often disagree about what segmenting dimensions are ethical in a given situation. A marketing manager needs to consider not only his or her own views but also the views of other groups in society. Even when there is no clear "right" answer, negative publicity may be very damaging. This is what Amazon.com encountered when it was revealed that it was charging some regular customers higher prices than new customers at its site.[14]

## Segmenting Business Markets

While we can apply the above approach to segmenting markets when the customers (or final users) are business organizations rather than individual consumers, there are some important differences. The first difference is in selecting the broad product-market. Business organizations usually make purchases to meet basic functional needs. But their needs are derived from the needs of their consumers—that is, the business (or nonprofit organization) market makes purchases that help it produce finished goods or services desired by its customers. Such firms may buy physical goods and do the work themselves, or they may pay someone else to provide the service.

Second, in some instances a single business account represents such a large dollar volume in sales that it might justify a marketing mix dedicated solely to it. In these cases, a firm might have distinct marketing mixes for each major account as well as for segments comprising smaller accounts.

The third major difference in segmenting industrial markets is that we use different segmenting dimensions (see Exhibit 3-13). We'll discuss these in more detail in Chapter 7.

## Segmenting International Markets

Success in international marketing requires even more attention to segmenting. There are more than 228 nations with their own unique cultures, and they differ greatly in language, customs (including business ethics), beliefs, religions, race, and income-distribution patterns. (We'll discuss some of these differences in Chapters 5 and 6.) These additional differences can complicate the segmenting process. Even worse, critical data are often less available—and less dependable—as firms move into international markets. This is one reason why some firms insist that local operations and decisions be handled by local representatives. They, at least, have a feel for their markets.

The process of segmenting international markets may require more dimensions, but it is essentially the same as for domestic markets with some additional steps. First, marketers segment by country or region—looking at demographic, cultural, and other characteristics, including stage of economic development. This may help them find regional or national submarkets that are fairly similar. Then—depending on whether the firm is aiming at final consumers or business markets—they apply the same basic approaches discussed earlier.

## More Sophisticated Techniques May Help in Segmenting

Marketing researchers and managers often turn to computer-aided methods for help with the job of segmenting. These techniques include commercial services that show general characteristics of the population and statistical techniques that can help sort

Exhibit 3-13 Lifestyle dimensions (and some related demographic dimensions).

| Dimension | Examples | | |
|---|---|---|---|
| Activities | Work | Vacation | Community |
| | Hobbies | Entertainment | Shopping |
| | Social events | Club membership | Sports |
| Interests | Family | Community | Food |
| | Home | Recreation | Media |
| | Job | Fashion | Achievements |
| Opinions | Themselves | Business | Products |
| | Social issues | Economics | Future |
| | Politics | Education | Culture |
| Demographics | Income | Geographic area | Occupation |
| | Age | City size | Family size |
| | Family life cycle | Dwelling | Education |

out a company's own data. A detailed review of the possibilities is beyond the scope of this book, but it can be said that most of these involve a form of psychographic or lifestyle analysis. We'll look at two of the more popular models to give you an idea of what they present before discussing how the models are developed:

- VALS 2: VALS stands for values, attitudes, and lifestyles. SRI International developed this approach to describe a firm's target market in terms of a set of typical VALS 2 lifestyle groups (segments). An advantage of this approach is that SRI has developed very detailed information about the various VALS 2 groups. The VALS 2 approach has been used to profile consumers in the United Kingdom, Germany, Japan, Canada, and the United States.
- Goldfarb: The Goldfarb organization has developed the best-known made-in-Canada approach to lifestyle segmentation. The Goldfarb segments are based on a sample of 1,400 adult Canadians, who responded to approximately 200 questions. These questions dealt with attitudes toward life, goals, values, stands on moral issues, and life satisfaction. An individual was assigned to a segment on the basis of his or her "dominant" attitudinal and behavioural characteristics. Using this information, the dominant characteristics are the primary factors that influence the behaviour of individuals in a given segment.

These psychographics, or lifestyle analyses, involve analyzing a person's activities, interests, and opinions—sometimes referred to as AIOs. Exhibit 3-13 identifies a number of variables for each of the AIO dimensions, along with some demographics used to add detail to the lifestyle profile of a target market.

Lifestyle analysis assumes that marketers can plan more effective strategies if they know more about their target markets. For example, lifestyles help marketers paint a more human portrait of the target market, which can be especially helpful in providing for advertising themes. Marketing Demo 3-3 illustrates how BC Transit segmented its market in terms of demographics, the purpose of the trip, and psychographics.

**Cluster analysis** Clustering techniques try to group customers with similar characteristics into homogeneous segments. Clustering searches sets of data to find similar patterns in customer information. It is sometimes said that clustering approaches use computers to do what previously was done with much intuition and judgment.



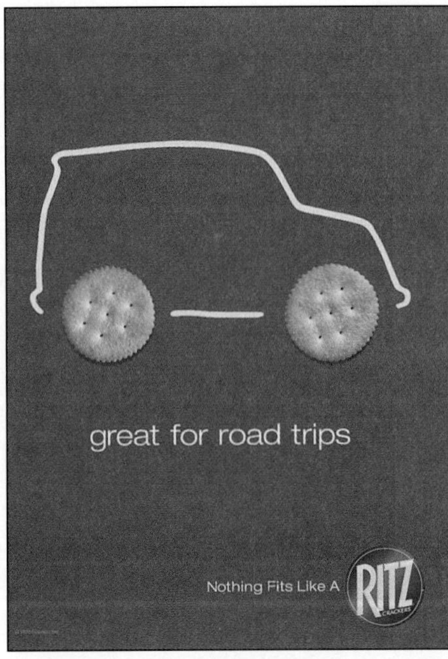


This ad for Ritz crackers focuses on the needs satisfied by the product rather than on the product characteristics themselves.

The data to be clustered might include such dimensions as demographic characteristics, the importance of different needs, attitudes toward the product, and past buying behaviour. Computerized statistical programs are used to search all the data for homogeneous groups of people. When such groups are found, marketers study the dimensions of the people in the groups to see why the computer clustered them together. The results sometimes suggest new, or at least better, marketing strategies.[15]

## Marketing Demo 3–3

### MARKET SEGMENTATION AT BC TRANSIT

BC Transit has identified two ways to increase ridership in its target market—maintain a highly satisfied customer base with few customer dropouts, or develop new ridership among the nonuser segment. BC Transit set out to identify its target market by using the nature and purpose of the trip and demographic data to segment the market into identifiable groups. It was able to identify nine segments.

1 *Educational/school-based trips.* This applies to three groups: ages 5–17, who require transit to public schools; ages 14–18, who require service to school and who will use transit for other purposes; and those requiring transit to postsecondary institutions.

2 *Commuter/work-based trips.* This is the largest segment, generating the greatest number of trips. This segment consists of the urban- and suburban-based commuters who require service from 6:30 am to 9:00 am and from 4:00 pm to 6:00 pm.

3 *Seniors, ages 65+.* This segment is the fastest-growing segment, with an increasing demand for convenient service.

4 *Accessible.* This encompasses the disabled community, who need specialized service.

5 *Tourist.* The Lower Mainland is a growing tourist destination. As a result, there is considerable demand for transit service to tourist attractions and destinations. This demand is fairly constant from year to year but fluctuates on a seasonal basis.

6 *Sport/special event.* Transit needs for the large crowds that occur throughout the year.

7 *Shoppers.* This segment requires service generally during midday to and from the major shopping/urban centres.

8 *Leisure/recreation.* Routing and frequency demands vary considerably, but service is generally required during the midday, afternoon, and evening periods.

9 *Medical/dental/banking.* Demand for service is generally heaviest during midday for this segment, and service is generally to the urban centres.

BC Transit has also used psychographics to understand more precisely the motivations people have for using public transit and to discover strategies for building ridership. This analysis revealed six clusters of transit user (or non-user) types.

1 *Captives.* This group contained 23 percent of the total sample and represented 67 percent of total transit volume. These are individuals who have no private vehicle and, therefore, have no alternative to public transit (other than carpooling). This group tends to be female, non-ethnic, and of low socioeconomic status.

2 *Transit advocates.* This group, making up 14 percent of the total sample, represented 16 percent of total transit volume. Transit advocates are sensitive to the stress and cost of driving. They consistently rate transit positively in all areas and use transit frequently.

3 *Critical transit users.* This group accounted for 11 percent of the sample and 8 percent of total transit volume. These individuals tend to be high-income women who use transit a moderate amount but who negatively evaluate the service.

4 *Grudging transit users.* This group contained 15 percent of the total sample but accounted for only 7 percent of total transit volume. Its members tend to be young, mobile, high socioeconomic status, non-ethnic men. People in this group tend to use their cars to run errands and feel that the convenience of a car is important.

5 *Car lovers.* This group included 22 percent of the total sample but accounted for only 2 percent of total transit volume. Its members tend to be ethnic, unfamiliar with transit, and concerned about the safety of the transit system. They are possible converts to transit.

6 *Committed non-users.* This group contained 15 percent of the sample but made only 1 percent of all transit trips. Its members are disproportionately retired men. All aspects of transit service are unimportant to this group. Transit is entirely irrelevant to them.

SOURCE: Bruce Campbell, Ph.D., Campbell, Goodell, Traynor Consultants. Courtesy of BC Transit.

A cluster analysis of the toothpaste market, for example, might show that some people buy toothpaste because it tastes good (the sensory segment), while others are concerned with the effect of clean teeth and fresh breath on their social image (the sociables). Still others worry about decay or tartar (the worriers), and some are just interested in the best value for their money (the value seekers). Each of these market segments calls for a different marketing mix—although some of the four Ps may be similar.

A variation of the clustering approach is based on customer relationship management methods. With customer relationship management (CRM), the seller fine-tunes the marketing effort with information from a detailed customer database. This usually includes data on a customer's past purchases as well as other segmenting information. For example, an auto-repair garage that keeps a database of customer oil changes can send a reminder postcard when it's time for the next oil change. Similarly, a florist that keeps a database of customers who have ordered flowers for Mother's Day or Valentine's Day can call them in advance with a special offer. Firms that operate over the Internet may have a special advantage with these database-focused approaches. They are able to communicate with customers via a website or e-mail, which means that the whole effort is not only targeted but also very inexpensive. Further, it's fast and easy for a customer to reply.[16]

However, in order for a technique like CRM to be successful, a company must ensure that its overall strategy and capabilities are aligned to meet the objectives of CRM.

## Differentiation and Positioning

As we've emphasized throughout this chapter, the reason for focusing on a specific target market is so you can fine-tune the whole marketing mix to provide some group of potential customers with superior value. By *differentiating* the marketing mix to do a better job meeting customers' needs, the firm builds a competitive advantage. In other words, target customers view the firm's position in the market as uniquely suited to their preferences and needs. Further, because everyone in the firm is clear about what position it wants to achieve with customers, the product, promotion, and other marketing-mix decisions can be blended better to achieve the desired objectives.

Firms often use promotion to help "position" how a marketing mix meets target customers' specific needs. For example, Bic ads along the roadside in Thailand highlight an ultra-close shave. Volvo reminds customers of the safety aspects of its brand of vehicles.

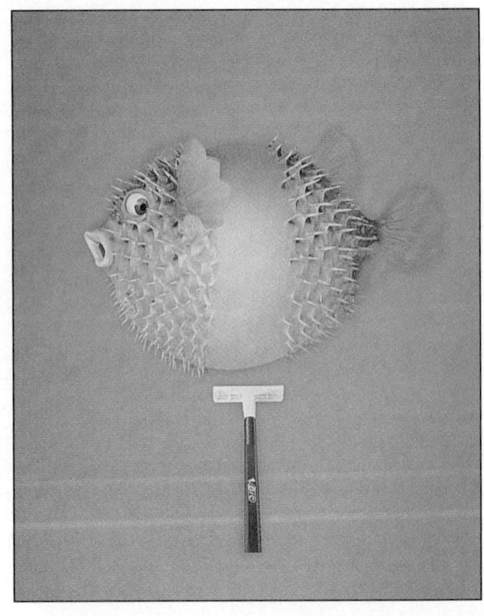

Although the marketing manager may want customers to see the firm's offering as unique, that is not always possible. "Me-too" imitators may come along and copy the firm's strategy. Further, even if a firm's marketing mix is different, consumers may not know or care. Even so, in looking for opportunities it's important for the marketing manager to know how customers *do* view the firm's offering. It's also important for the marketing manager to have a clear idea about how he or she would like the customer to perceive the firm's product or service. This is where another important concept, *positioning*, comes in.

## Positioning

Positioning refers to how customers think about proposed and/or present brands in a market *relative to competing brands*. A marketing manager needs a realistic view of how customers think about offerings in the market. Without that, it's hard to differentiate. At the same time, the manager should know how he or she *wants* target customers to think about the firm's marketing mix. Positioning issues are especially important when competitors in a market appear to be very similar.

Once you know what customers think, then you can decide whether to leave the product (and marketing mix) alone or reposition it. This may mean *physical changes* in the product or simply *image changes based on promotion*. For example, most cola drinkers can't pick out their favourite brand in a blind test—so physical changes might not be necessary (and might not even work) to reposition a cola. Yet, ads that portray Pepsi drinkers in funny situations help position the "Joy of Pepsi." Conversely, 7-Up reminds us that it is the "uncola" with no caffeine—"Never had it and never will."

Figuring out what customers really think about competing products isn't easy, but there are approaches that help. Most of them require some formal marketing research. The results are usually plotted on graphs to help show how consumers view the competing products. Usually, the products' positions are related to two or three product features that are important to the target customers.

Managers make the graphs for positioning decisions by asking consumers to make judgments about different brands—including their "ideal" brand—and then use computer programs to summarize the ratings and plot the results. The details of positioning techniques—sometimes called "perceptual mapping"—are beyond the scope of this text, but Exhibit 3-14 shows some possibilities.[17]



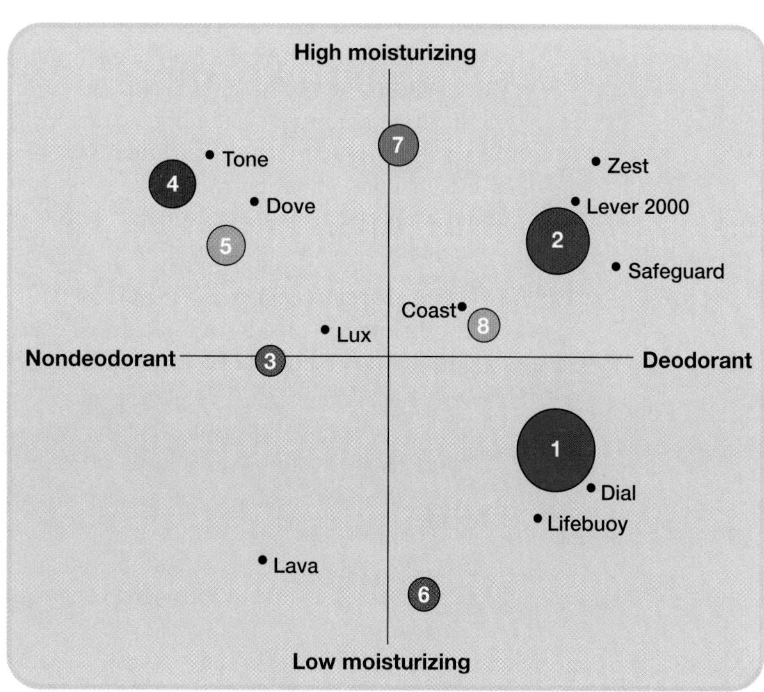


**Exhibit 3-14** "Product space" diagram representing consumers' perceptions for different brands of bar soap.

Exhibit 3-14 shows the "product space" for different brands of bar soap using two dimensions—the extent to which consumers think the soaps moisturize and deodorize their skin. For example, consumers see Dial as quite low on moisturizing but high on deodorizing. Lifebuoy and Dial are close together—implying that consumers think of them as similar on these characteristics. Dove is viewed as different and is farther away on the graph. Remember that positioning maps are based on *customers' perceptions*—the actual characteristics of the products (as determined by a chemical test) might be different!

The circles in Exhibit 3-14 show different sets (submarkets) of consumers clustered near their ideal soap preferences. Groups of respondents with a similar ideal product are circled to show apparent customer concentrations. In this graph, the size of the circles suggests the size of the segments for the different ideals.

Ideal clusters 1 and 2 are the largest and are close to two popular brands—Dial and Lever 2000. It appears that customers in cluster 1 want more moisturizing than they see in Dial and Lifebuoy. However, exactly what these brands should do about this isn't clear. Perhaps both of these brands should leave their physical products alone—but emphasize moisturizing more in their promotion to make a stronger appeal to those who want moisturizers. A marketing manager talking about this approach might simply refer to it as "positioning the brand as a good moisturizer." Of course, whether the effort is successful depends on whether the whole marketing mix delivers on the promise of the positioning communication.

Note that ideal cluster 7 is not near any of the present brands. This may suggest an opportunity for introducing a new product—a strong moisturizer with some deodorizers. A firm that chooses to follow this approach would be making a segmenting effort.

A positioning analysis helps managers understand how customers see their market. It is a visual aid to understanding a product-market. The first time such an analysis is done, managers may be shocked to see how much customers' perceptions of a market differ from their own. For this reason alone, positioning analysis may be crucial. But, a positioning analysis usually focuses on specific product features and brands that are close competitors in the product-market. Thus, it is a product-oriented approach. Important *customer*-related dimensions—including needs and attitudes—may be overlooked.

### Creating a Positioning Statement

When the initial positioning analysis is complete, marketers can then decide which target market to pursue. This decision must be based on the company's skills and resources and the attractiveness of each market segment. Once a manager has made this decision, he or she must begin the vital process of crafting a positioning statement. A positioning statement is not an advertising slogan or tagline—it is an internal document used to outline how a product or brand will be perceived in the minds of consumers. Furthermore, it must be unique to the product or service to differentiate from its competitors.

In general, a positioning statement should answer the following three questions:[18]

1. *When should customers use the product?* For example, Coca-Cola wants consumers to consider its soft drink every time they are thirsty. Kit Kat wants customers to think of its chocolate bar each time they want to "Take a break."
2. *Why should the product be chosen over other alternatives?* In essence, what is the unique selling proposition that the product has to offer? Volvo offers safety, Ivory soap offers purity, Subway offers a healthier fast-food alternative.
3. *What does the consumer gain by choosing the product?* In almost all cases, the purchase of a product or service satisfies a particular end-goal for the customer. A classic example is that the manufacturer of nails does not actually sell nails, it sells holes. Michelin provides you with safe tires so you can protect yourself

and your family, Palm helps you organize your professional life so you can spend your time on more useful activities.

### Positioning and the Unique Selling Proposition

**unique selling proposition**
tells its target audience why they should choose the given product over others in the market

As in all of the examples above, each company identified a **unique selling proposition** that tells its target audience why they should choose the given product over others in the market. These propositions determine the overall theme of the positioning statement. In general, there are six alternatives bases that can be used to express a value proposition:

- *Product/service attributes:* In this case, positioning is based on a specific aspect that is most valued by the target market. For example, Crest offers users superior cavity protection.
- *Overall value:* Value is determined by customers based on the relationship between quality and price. Wal-Mart consistently competes on this dimension with its "Everyday low price" guarantee.
- *Class of user:* Marketers often position their product based on the personality of their target market. In this case, the product offers a particular lifestyle, image, or attitude—such as Nike, which wants buyers to think of themselves as winners and not just average competitors.
- *Product class:* Usually there is an entrenched standard or technology that a company is trying to challenge. For example, the manufacturers of margarine often try to convince consumers of its benefits over butter.
- *End-use application:* This type of positioning is based on the user's situation. Consider Gatorade, which is positioned as an athletic drink aimed to quench users' thirst.
- *Specific competitor:* Competition-based positioning tries to target an area of dissatisfaction with a competing brand. This tactic is most often used with packaged goods such as laundry detergent or toilet paper.

As in naming generic markets and product-markets, marketers should keep in mind that premature emphasis on product features as the basis of a selling proposition is dangerous. As our bar soap example shows, starting with a product-oriented definition of a market and how bar soaps compete against other bar soaps can make a firm miss more basic shifts in markets. For example, bars might be losing popularity to liquid soaps. Or other products, like bath oils or body shampoos for use in the shower, may be part of the relevant competition. Managers wouldn't see these shifts if they looked only at alternative bar soap brands—the focus is just too narrow.

It's also important to choose a positioning basis that reflects how customers—not managers—think about the products in question. How consumers look at a product isn't just a matter of chance. Let's return to our bar soap example. While many consumers do think about soap in terms of moisturizing and deodorizing, other needs shouldn't be overlooked. For example, some consumers are especially concerned about wiping out germs. Marketers for Dial soap recognized this need and developed ads that positioned Dial as the choice for these target customers.

As we emphasize throughout the text, you must understand potential needs and attitudes when planning marketing strategies. If customers treat different products as substitutes, then a firm has to position itself against those products too. Customers won't always be conscious of all the detailed ways that a firm's marketing mix might be different, but careful positioning can help highlight a unifying theme or benefits that relate to the determining dimensions of the target market. Thus, it's usually best to rely on positioning approaches when they are part of a broader analysis. This helps ensure that the entire marketing mix is positioned for competitive advantage.

## Chapter Summary

Firms need creative strategy planning to survive in our increasingly competitive markets. In this chapter, we discussed how to find attractive target-market opportunities. We started by considering four basic types of opportunities—market penetration, market development, product development, and diversification—with special emphasis on opportunities in international markets. We also saw that carefully defining generic markets and product-markets can help find new opportunities. We stressed the shortcomings of a too-narrow, product-oriented view of markets.

We also discussed market segmentation—the process of naming and then segmenting broad product-markets to find potentially attractive target markets. Some people try to segment markets by starting with the mass market and then dividing it into smaller submarkets based on a few dimensions. But this can lead to poor results. Instead, market segmentation should first focus on a broad product-market and then group similar customers into homogeneous submarkets. The more similar the potential customers are, the larger the submarkets can be. Four criteria for evaluating possible product-market segments were presented.

Once a broad product-market is segmented, marketing managers can use one of three approaches to market-oriented strategy planning: (1) the single target market approach, (2) the multiple target market approach, and (3) the combined target market approach. In general, we encouraged marketers to be segmenters rather than combiners.

We also discussed some computer-aided approaches—clustering techniques, CRM, and positioning.

In summary, good marketers should be experts on markets and segmenting dimensions. By creatively segmenting markets, they may spot opportunities—even breakthrough opportunities—and help their firms succeed against aggressive competitors offering similar products. Segmenting is basic to target marketing; the more you practise segmenting, the more meaningful market segments you will see.



## Key Concepts

breakthrough opportunities, p. 49
combined target market approach, p. 61
competitive advantage, p. 49
determining dimensions, p. 64
differentiation, p. 53
diversification, p. 48
generic market, p. 55
market, p. 54
market development, p. 46
market penetration, p. 46
market segmentation, p. 52
multiple target market approach, p. 61
positioning, p. 53
product development, p. 47
product-market, p. 55
qualifying dimensions, p. 64
S.W.O.T. analysis, p. 53
segmenting, p. 58
single target market approach, p. 61
unique selling proposition, p. 73

## Questions and Problems

1. Distinguish between an attractive opportunity and a breakthrough opportunity. Give an example.
2. Explain how new opportunities may be seen by defining a firm's markets more precisely. Illustrate for a situation where you believe there is an opportunity—namely, an unsatisfied market segment—even if it is not very large.
3. In your own words, explain why we suggest that you think of marketing strategy planning as a narrowing-down process.
4. Distinguish between a generic market and a product-market. Illustrate your answer.
5. Explain the major differences among the four basic types of opportunities discussed in the text and cite examples for two of these types of opportunities.
6. Explain why a firm may want to pursue a market-penetration opportunity before pursuing one involving product development or diversification.
7. In your own words, explain several reasons why marketing managers should consider international markets when evaluating possible opportunities.

8. Give an example of a foreign-made product (other than an automobile) that you personally have purchased. Give some reasons why you purchased that product. Do you think that there was a good opportunity for a domestic firm to get your business? Explain why or why not.
9. Explain what market segmentation is.
10. List the types of potential segmenting dimensions and explain which you would try to apply first, second, and third in a particular situation. If the nature of the situation would affect your answer, explain how.
11. Explain why segmentation efforts based on attempts to divide the mass market using a few demographic dimensions may be very disappointing.
12. Illustrate the concept that segmenting is an aggregating process by referring to the admissions policies of your own school and a nearby college or university.
13. Review the types of segmenting dimensions listed in Exhibits 3-10 and 3-11, and select the ones you think should be combined to fully explain the market segment you personally would be in if you were planning to buy a new watch today. List several dimensions and try to develop a shorthand name, like "fashion-oriented," to describe your own personal market segment. Then try to estimate what proportion of the total watch market would be accounted for by your market segment. Next, explain if there are any offerings that come close to meeting the needs of your market. If not, what sort of a marketing mix is needed? Would it be economically attractive for anyone to try to satisfy your market segment? Why or why not?
14. Identify the determining dimension or dimensions that explain why you bought the specific brand you did in your most recent purchase of *(a)* a soft drink, *(b)* shampoo, *(c)* a shirt or blouse, and *(d)* a larger, more expensive item, such as a bicycle, camera, or boat. Try to express the determining dimension(s) in terms of your own personal characteristics rather than the product's characteristics. Estimate what share of the market would probably be motivated by the same determining dimension(s).
15. Consider the market for off-campus apartments in your city. Identify some submarkets that have different needs and determining dimensions. Then evaluate how well the needs in these market segments are being met in your geographic area. Is there an obvious breakthrough opportunity waiting for someone?
16. Explain how positioning analysis can help a marketing manager identify target market opportunities.

## Computer-Aided Problem 3

### Segmenting Customers

The marketing manager for Audiotronics Software Company is seeking new market opportunities. He is focusing on the voice-recognition market and has narrowed down to three segments: the Fearful Typists, the Power Users, and the Professional Specialists. The Fearful Typists don't know much about computers—they just want a fast way to create e-mail messages, letters, and simple reports without errors. They don't need a lot of special features. They want simple instructions and a program that's easy to learn. The Power Users know a lot about computers, use them often, and want a voice-recognition program with many special features. All computer programs seem easy to them, so they aren't worried about learning to use the various features. The Professional Specialists have jobs that require a lot of writing. They don't know much about computers but are willing to learn. They want special features needed for their work—but only if they aren't too hard to learn and use.

The marketing manager prepared a table summarizing the importance of each of three key needs in the three segments (see below).

**Importance of Need (1=not important; 10=very important)**

| Market Segment | Features | Easy to Use | Easy to Learn |
|---|---|---|---|
| Fearful Typists | 3 | 8 | 9 |
| Power Users | 9 | 2 | 2 |
| Professional Specialists | 7 | 5 | 6 |

Audiotronics' sales staff conducted interviews with seven potential customers who were asked to rate how important each of these three needs were in their work. The manager prepared a spreadsheet to help him cluster (aggregate) each person into one of the segments along with other similar people. Each person's ratings were entered in the spreadsheet, and the clustering procedure computed a similarity score indicating how similar (a low score) or dissimilar (a high score) the person is to the typical person in each of the segments. The manager could then "aggregate" potential customers into the segment that is most similar (that is, the one with the *lowest* similarity score).

a. *The ratings for a potential customer appear on the first spreadsheet. Into which segment would you aggregate this person?*

b. *The responses for seven potential customers who were*

*interviewed are listed in the table below. Enter the ratings for a customer in the spreadsheet and then write down the similarity score for each segment. Repeat the process for each customer. Based on your analysis, indicate the segment into which you would aggregate each customer. Indicate the size (number of customers) of each segment.*

c. *In the interview, each potential customer was also asked what type of computer he or she would be using. The responses are shown in the table along with the ratings. Group the responses based on the customer's segment. If you were targeting the Fearful Typists segment, what type of computer would you focus on when developing your software?*

d. *Based on your analysis, which customer would you say is least like any of the segments? Briefly explain the reason for your choice.*

**Importance of Need (1=not important; 10=very important)**

| Potential Customer | Features | Easy to Use | Easy to Learn | Type of Computer |
|---|---|---|---|---|
| A. | 8 | 1 | 2 | Dell laptop |
| B. | 6 | 6 | 5 | IBM desktop |
| C. | 4 | 9 | 8 | Apple |
| D. | 2 | 6 | 7 | Apple |
| E. | 5 | 6 | 5 | IBM desktop |
| F. | 8 | 3 | 1 | Dell laptop |
| G. | 4 | 6 | 8 | Apple |

## Suggested Cases

To view the cases, go to www.mcgrawhill.ca/college/wong.

Interested in finding out what marketing looks like in the real world? *Marketing Magazine* is just a click away on your OLC! Visit www.mcgrawhill.ca/college/wong today.

When You Finish This Chapter, You Should

1. Know the variables that shape the environment of marketing strategy planning.

2. Understand why company objectives are important in guiding marketing strategy planning.

3. See how the resources of a firm affect the search for opportunities.

4. Know how the different kinds of competitive situations affect strategy planning.

5. Understand how the economic and technological environments can affect strategy planning.

6. Know why you could be sent to prison if you ignore the political and legal environment.

7. Understand how to screen and evaluate marketing strategy opportunities.

# Chapter Four

# The Changing Marketing Environment

## Smart Car

As oversized SUVs and minivans roll out of assembly plants in North America, Europeans are turning their attention to the latest innovation from DaimlerChrysler. At 2.5 metres long, the Smart car is every city driver's dream—ideal for tooling around crowded streets, fuel efficient, and a dream to park. Three of them, nose to the curb, can fit in a single parallel-parking space.[1] Some European parking garages even give Smart owners 50 percent off the regular hourly rate.[2] Other attractions are the affordable price tag and the money consumers save on owning the most fuel-efficient car in the industry.

Launched in 1998 by Micro Compact Car (MCC), a wholly owned subsidiary of Daimler-

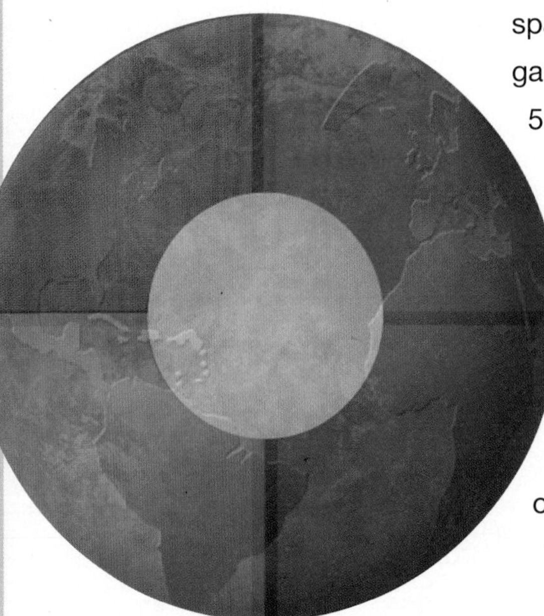

place price promotion prod

Chrysler, the Smart is rapidly picking up speed in Europe and Japan by addressing the concerns of environmentally conscious consumers in urban centres around the world.

In 1994, when rising fuel prices, pollution, and urban congestion found their way to the top of the consumer's agenda, auto manufacturer Mercedes-Benz and watch-maker Swatch decided to do something about it. The idea was to create an eco-friendly vehicle, designed specifically for the crowded cities of Europe.

Hans Jurg Schar, former head of sales and marketing for MCC, calls the two-seater "two-thirds product and one-third philosophy."[3] This philosophy is rooted in the concept of personal mobility and based on a single observation: that when commuting to work, only one car in five had someone in the passenger seat, and only one in ten had someone in the back. The Smart gives consumers the ease of mobility while putting their environmental conscience to rest—all at an extremely affordable price.

The wish to build a "green" car dictated design: Keep it small, simple, and light. The car is essentially an egg-shaped welded frame of steel, more than 40 percent of it high-strength. Hanging on the frame are plastic panels with moulded-in colour—so there's no need for paint booths with their volatile emissions. The parts of the steel body that remain visible aren't painted. Instead, they're powder-coated, so there's no wastewater or solvent to dispose of.[4] Remarkably, the entire car assembly process takes only 7.5 hours, 25 percent fewer than required by the world's best automakers.[5]

The company's strong emphasis on respecting natural resources through the production process to the final product has caused industry leaders to take note. Recently, MCC won accolades for its low-ozone-destroying emissions, fuel efficiency, and assertion that 85 percent of its materials are recyclable. Kieren Ring, Executive Director of the Institute of Transport Management, says that "As companies and their employees become even more aware of their responsibility towards the environment, Smart is setting the standard that other companies will have to follow. That their environmental initiatives are undertaken as company policy and not as compliance to legislation makes the company even more unique."[6]

To lend leverage to the remarkable design of the product, the marketing department is geared not only to market the vehicle as a new car concept, but also to create new markets, using unconventional channels and sales processes.[7] When the company launched in Great Britain, marketers set out to directly strike a chord with their target audience. By placing the cars in the middle of London's underground, MCC was able to get the attention of consumers who understood both the problems of urban congestion and the freedom of personal mobility.

place price promotion product




www.mcgrawhill.ca/college/wong

While slow to start, the Smart is gaining ground across Europe, especially in places like Italy and Germany where negotiating the crowded streets of Rome and Berlin practically requires a special licence. Although revenue growth has been slightly less than projections, sales growth for 2001 was nearly 14 percent—impressive considering the increasingly competitive global auto market. The Smart's small size has also scored big with the Japanese government, making it the first import to qualify for extensive tax breaks for mini-vehicles, a move that boosted overseas sales for 2001 by 12 times.

"Customers are increasingly viewing the Smart city-coupe and cabrio as an attractive alternative in ecological and economical terms," says Philipp Shiemer, current director of marketing and sales.[8] The company also recently expanded its current line of models—appropriately titled Pulse, Pure, and Passion—to include a hip roadster. And if owners get bored of their current model, for US$750 and one hour of their time they can change the body colour by simply exchanging one set of exterior panels for another to suit their tastes.

MCC is also testing the waters for a full-blown entry into the ultra-competitive North American market. In April 2002 it made a deal with eMotion Mobility, a small U.S. venture, that will bring the cars to the streets of Atlanta, Georgia. eMotion Mobility will begin importing Smarts as "gliders," cars without engines. A small plant in Hinesville, Georgia, will add electric power. In time, 2,500 Smarts will be parked and plugged in at various stops on Atlanta's MARTA (the metropolitan transportation system): use MARTA to cover distance, and rent a Smart by the hour to get to your meeting, the restaurant, or Grandma's house. If eMotion works, the company will bring the program and fleets of Smarts to California, then the U.S. Northeast.[9]

While the future for Smart in North America is unknown, MCC has been able to create a strong niche as a second or third car for commuters who are fed up with the madness of city traffic and who want to save their large sedan for weekend road trips.[10] Whatever the case, industry analysts will likely agree that this innovative car is an affordable, well-designed response to consumer concerns.

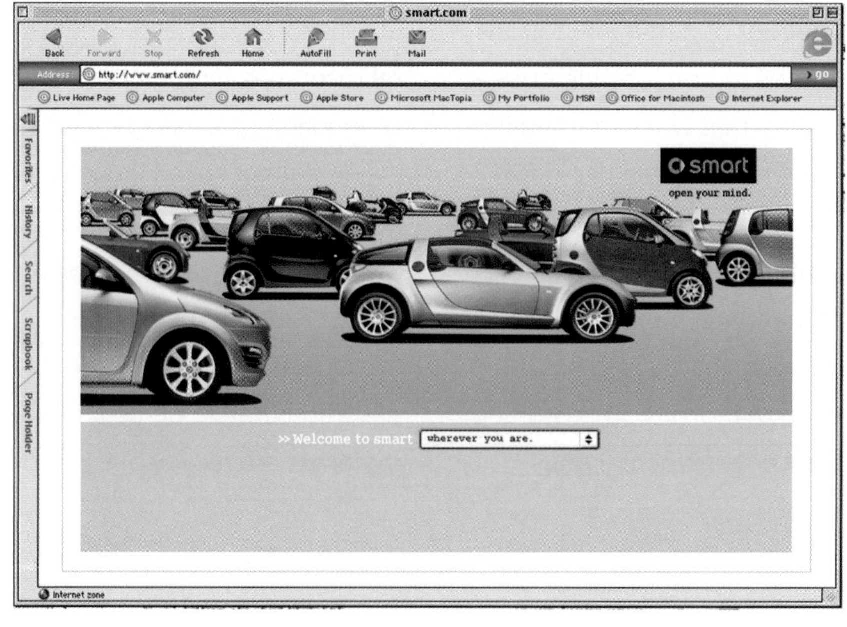

## In This Chapter

This chapter is the first of four that explore the world in which marketers operate. We begin by identifying the various "environments" or forces that shape that world: competitive, economic, technological, political, legal, and cultural/social. In each of these areas we'll highlight some key developments and trends. Next, we'll show how companies take these environments into account in evaluating alternative opportunities. Finally, we'll discuss some of the challenges faced by firms competing in a variety of different product-markets to see how managers compare alternatives based in very different businesses.

## The Marketing Environment



You saw in the last chapter that finding target-market opportunities is the key to effective marketing management. You also saw that developing a competitive advantage and a strategy that offers customers superior value takes an understanding of the capabilities of your own company and of your competitors. This chapter takes this thinking further. Markets don't exist in a vacuum: they are ever-changing as the world around us changes. As the Smart car case shows, a marketing manager must analyze customer needs and choose marketing strategy variables that can accommodate such changes.

A large number of forces shape the marketing environment. To help organize your thinking, it's useful to classify the various forces as falling into either (1) the direct market environment or (2) the external market environment. The direct environment of any generic market or product-market includes customers, the company, and competitors. The external market environment is broader and includes:

1. Competitive environment
2. Economic environment
3. Technological environment
4. Political environment
5. Legal environment
6. Cultural/social environment

These environments are sometimes referred to as "uncontrollable variables," because marketing managers cannot change or shape environmental factors the way they can the elements of a marketing mix. Rather, they can either react to changes as they occur or, better yet, forecast changes and plan in advance for how they will respond to them.

### The Internal Environment

As a teenager, you probably could identify a number of activities you wanted to pursue. However, if you were like most teens, your ability to undertake those activities was determined at least in part by the opinions and economic means of your parents. In much the same way, managers may identify a large number of opportunities they would like to pursue. However, their ability to pursue them will depend upon the policies and resources of their company.

Much of what a company encourages its managers to do is driven by the firm's objectives and its available resources. The two are closely interrelated, since objectives essentially define what management believes are the highest-priority uses of available resources.

**Issues in setting objectives** Objectives should not be set arbitrarily or based on some pie-in-the-sky wishlist. Rather, they should be set through a process that forces top management to look at the whole business, relate its present objectives and resources to the external environment, and then decide what the firm wants to accomplish in the future.

It would be convenient if a company could set one objective—such as making a profit—and let that serve as the guide. However, this would give little direction to managers. Profit could be made by selling a few units at a high price or many units at a low price: imagine how different the marketing mix could be if one route were preferred over another.

There are three basic objectives that most companies would accept and that could guide managers' actions:

1. Engage in specific activities that will perform a socially and economically useful function.
2. Develop an organization to carry on the business and implement its strategies.
3. Earn enough profit to survive.[11]

These objectives may seem little more than "do-gooder" sentiments. If a firm's activities appear to be contrary to the consumer good, the firm can be wiped out almost overnight by political or legal action—or by consumers' own negative responses. Businesses can't exist without the approval of consumers and the ability to implement their strategies. And there is little motivation to satisfy customers if profits cannot be secured. However, even in these areas, there is room for debate.

In our list above, the point about performing a "function" makes no mention of how broad a function we should perform. As noted in the last chapter, focusing on too narrow a function may blind the firm to new opportunities. Too broad a function may make it hard for the firm to find homogeneous customers to serve.

The point about "profit" does not mention whether our time frame is the long run or the short run. Firms that place too much emphasis on the short run may fail to make the investments needed for long-term success. Conversely, a company may go bankrupt if it ignores the short run completely. Thousands of new dot-com firms went belly-up after a year or two of losses because they could not cover their short-run expenses. Therefore, companies should set a *target* rate of profit that represents the balance between the two that they—and their investors—are willing to accept.

It isn't hard to see that while our three general objectives provide guidelines, a firm must be much more precise in the objectives it expects managers to achieve. While this may seem obvious, top executives often don't state their objectives clearly enough. In these cases, different managers may hold unspoken and conflicting assumptions about what the company wants—a common problem in large companies and in nonprofit organizations. This makes it hard for the company to focus its total efforts on anything, let alone customers.

**mission statement**
Statement that sets out an organization's basic purpose for being

Many firms try to avoid this problem by developing a **mission statement**, which sets out the organization's basic purpose for being. For example, the mission of the Kingston General Hospital (www.kgh.on.ca) is "We learn, we discover, we care for patients and each other." As illustrated by this example, a good mission statement should focus on a few key goals rather than embracing everything. It should also supply guidelines when managers face difficult decisions. For example, if an administrator of the hospital is trying to decide whether to invest in new MRI technology it should be clear that these services are within the scope of the hospital's stated mission. On the other hand, if another possible opportunity were to purchase an entertainment system for the hospital cafeteria, it would appear to be beyond the stated mission. Of course, a mission statement may need to be revised as new market needs arise or as the marketing environment changes, but this would be a fundamental change and not one that is made casually.[12]

A mission statement is important, but it is not a substitute for more specific objectives that provide guidance in screening possible opportunities. For example, top management might set objectives such as "Earn a 25-percent annual return on investment," "Become the market-share leader in each of our product-markets," and "Introduce at least three innovative and successful products in the next two years."

Of course, when there are a number of specific objectives stated by top management it is critical that they be compatible. If they're not, frustration and even failure may result. For example, a top-management objective of a 25-percent annual return on investment may seem reasonable taken by itself. And the objective of introducing new products is reasonable. However, if the costs of developing and introducing the new products cannot be recouped within one year, the return on investment objective may be impossible.[13]

In addition, top management must be careful to avoid the "more is better" trap. For example, some top managers want a large market share because they believe this ensures greater profitability. But many large firms with big market shares have gone bankrupt (Eaton's is an example). These firms sought large market shares, but earned little profit. Increasingly, managers are shifting their objectives toward *profitable* sales growth rather than just larger market share as they realize that the two don't necessarily go together.[14]

You can see why the marketing manager should be involved in setting company objectives. Company objectives guide managers as they search for and evaluate opportunities—and, later, plan marketing strategies. Particular *marketing* objectives should be set within the framework of larger company objectives. As shown in Exhibit 4-1, firms need a hierarchy of objectives that moves from company objectives to marketing-department objectives. For each marketing strategy, firms also need objectives for each of the four Ps—as well as more detailed objectives. For example, in the promotion area we need objectives for advertising, sales promotion, and personal selling.

Toyota provides a good example. One of its company objectives is to achieve high customer satisfaction. So, the R&D people design vehicles to meet specific reliability objectives. Similarly, the production people work to cut manufacturing defects. The marketing department, in turn, sets specific customer satisfaction objectives for every product. That leads to specific promotion objectives to ensure that the sales and advertising people don't promise more than the company can deliver. Dealers' service people, in turn, work to fix any problem the first time it's reported.

Finally, both company objectives and marketing objectives should be realistic and



**Exhibit 4-1** A hierarchy of objectives.

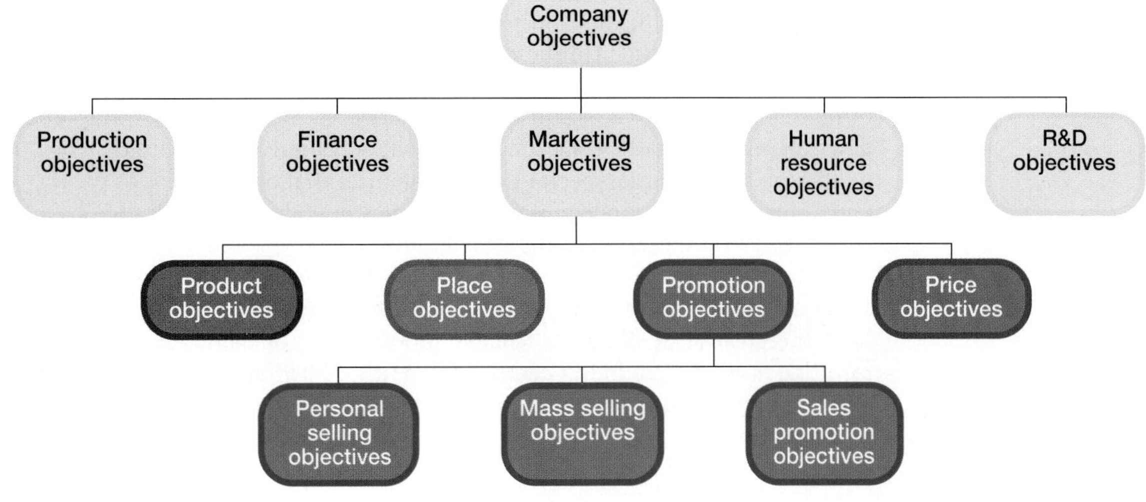

achievable. While there are some managers who believe that objectives should force managers to "stretch," overly ambitious objectives are useless if the firm lacks the resources to achieve them. In these cases, frustration—not performance—is the eventual outcome. How would you feel if you lacked artistic ability but were told you had to paint a museum-quality picture?

**Types of company resources** There is an old cliché to the effect that you increase the chance of success when you pursue an opportunity that lets you build on a strength; that is, where you can take full advantage of the resources you already have. When we speak here of resources we do not focus exclusively on financial resources. Every firm has non-financial resources—hopefully some unique ones—that set it apart. Breakthrough opportunities—or at least some competitive advantage—come from making use of these strengths while avoiding direct competition with firms having similar strengths.

To find its strengths, a firm must evaluate its functional areas (production, research and engineering, marketing, and finance) as well as its present products and markets. The expertise and knowledge of the firm's human resources can also be an important asset. By analyzing successes or failures in relation to the firm's resources, management can discover why the firm was successful—or why it failed—in the past.

For example, in the 1970s Harley-Davidson's motorcycle business was suffering, and it was losing customers to Japanese competitors. Studying the Japanese firms helped Harley identify ways to produce higher-quality motorcycles at lower cost. With these resource-use problems resolved, Harley was again on the road to achieving its objectives. As its sales and reputation grew, the company's close relationship with Harley owners became a resource that helped Harley introduce a profitable line of accessories. The Harley-Davidson case highlights both manufacturing quality and relationships with existing customers as resources. Other resources that should be considered as part of an evaluation of strengths and weaknesses are discussed in the following sections.[15]

This is not to say that financial resources aren't important. Indeed, some opportunities require large amounts of capital just to get started. Before a firm makes its first sale, it may require money for R&D, production facilities, marketing research, or advertising. Even a really good opportunity may not be profitable for years; so, lack of financial strength is often a barrier to entry into an otherwise attractive market.

In some instances, company size can be a major resource. For many businesses, the cost of producing and selling each unit decreases as the quantity increases. Therefore, smaller firms can be at a great cost disadvantage if they try to win business from larger competitors. As a result, they will avoid opportunities that might bring them head-to-head against larger, lower-cost competitors. On the other hand, new—or smaller—firms sometimes have the advantage of flexibility. They are not handicapped with large, special-purpose facilities that are obsolete or poorly located. Large steel producers once enjoyed economies of scale, but today they have trouble competing with producers using smaller, more flexible plants.

Interestingly, some firms are finding that sometimes the best resource is an arrangement that does away with the need for a resource at all. For example, they have the greatest flexibility to change products by not having any in-house manufacturing at all. Outsourcing certain capabilities, like manufacturing or distribution, allows a firm to focus on its core competencies, which can help a firm achieve and sustain a competitive advantage.

**Marketing as a company resource** Our marketing strategy planning framework (refer to Exhibit 3-1) helps in analyzing current marketing resources. In the product area, for example, a familiar brand can be a big strength. For example, clothing manufacturers like Roots Canada and Ralph Lauren used their brand names to enter the home-decorating market. A new idea or process may also be protected by a patent. A patent owner in Canada has a 20-year monopoly to develop and use its product, process, or material. If one firm has a strong patent, competitors may be limited to second-rate offerings—and their efforts may be doomed to failure.[16]

Good relations with established retailers—or control of good locations within retail outlets—can be important resources in reaching some target markets. When marketing managers at Microsoft decided to introduce the Xbox game console, Microsoft software and computer accessories had already proved profitable for retailers, like Future Shop, that could reach the target market. So, these retailers were willing to give the new product shelf space even if they were already carrying competing products from Nintendo or Sony.[17]

Similarly, existing computer systems that effectively share information in the channel, speed delivery of orders, and control inventory can be a big advantage. For example, P&G and Wal-Mart are linked through an electronic data interchange (EDI) system that automatically informs P&G of product sales, inventory levels, and the like; this process greatly reduces the costs of both parties. Perhaps even more significantly, when P&G adds a new type of detergent or other product the new product has a built-in competitive advantage since the systems to manage distribution are already in place.

Promotion and price resources must also be considered. Investor's Group already has a skilled salesforce for selling its line of mutual funds. Marketing managers know these sales reps can handle new products and customers. And low-cost facilities, like those used by Wal-Mart and Costco, may enable a firm to undercut competitors' prices.

Finally, thorough understanding of a target market can give a company an edge. As Marketing Demo 4-1 illustrates, Tim Hortons has developed an exceedingly effective marketing mix by building on its knowledge of customer needs.

## The Competitive Environment

**competitive environment**

Affects the number and types of competitors the marketing manager must face and how they may behave

The **competitive environment** affects the number and types of competitors the marketing manager must face and how they may behave. Although marketing managers usually can't control these factors, they can choose strategies that avoid head-on competition. And where competition is inevitable they can plan for it.

Economists describe four basic kinds of market (competitive) situations: pure competition, oligopoly, monopolistic competition, and monopoly. Understanding the differences among these market situations is helpful in analyzing the competitive environment, and our discussion assumes some familiarity with these concepts. (For a review, visit the OLC at www.mcgrawhill.ca/college/wong.)

The economist's traditional view is that most product-markets head toward pure competition, or oligopoly, over the long run. In these situations, companies must compete against competitors offering very similar products. Because customers see the different available products (marketing mixes) as close substitutes, managers just compete with lower and lower prices, and profit margins shrink. Sometimes managers do this much too quickly, without really thinking through the question of how they might add more value to the marketing mix. It's crucial to remember that the marketing mix that offers customers the best value is not necessarily the one with the lowest price.

Avoiding pure competition is sensible and certainly fits with our emphasis on target marketing and the need to find a competitive advantage on which to differentiate the firm's marketing mix. This is why effective target marketing is fundamentally different from effective decision making in other areas of business. Accounting, production, and financial managers for competing firms can learn about

## Marketing Demo 4–1

### CANADA'S BEST-OILED MARKETING MACHINE?

One of every three cups of coffee sold in Canada comes from Tim Hortons. It's worth pausing a moment, just to let that small fact resonate. Here's another: Oakville, Ont.'s TDL Group—the licensing company for all Tim Hortons franchises—sells over *three million* donuts each and every day.

Generations of competitors have come and gone, trying to replicate Hortons' perfect blend of slick marketing and home-spun advertising: that quirky man who floods the ice; the boys overseas wishing for nothing more than a few tins of Tim's coffee to remind them of home. The little donut shop opened up 36 years ago by a hockey player and a Hamilton ex-cop has deeply embedded itself into our cultural consciousness. Even when TDL was purchased by the dreaded Americans—Dublin, Ohio-based Wendy's International—in 1995, Tim's status as an all-Canadian icon wasn't tarnished a bit: if anything, it's shined even brighter.

According to Toronto's Kostuch Publications' annual ranking of Canada's top 100 foodservice companies, TDL outearned its closest competitor by more than $1.26 billion last year, with $1.603 billion in revenues. Compare this to The Second Cup Ltd. of Toronto—17th on the list—with earnings of $340 million. Hortons accounts for 13% of Canada's quick-service sector. Sometime next year, it's expected to surpass McDonald's Restaurants in total revenues.

Studies commissioned by Hortons reveal a consistent 50% of respondents favouring Tim Hortons over other quick-service coffee providers. The next closest brand is at 4%.

Whatever its budget, Hortons' advertising aims to reflect what people already believe about the product. "You can advertise and advertise," says Doug Poad, vice-president and director of planning at Toronto's Enterprise Creative Selling, Hortons' ad agency, "but advertising is a lot more relevant to people when they actually see the stores on the street."

Indeed, a key element of Tim's astonishing success is the use of market share to pile up more market share.

"Our method of development has always been to try to reach a critical mass in a given marketplace," says Patti Jameson, director of corporate communications. "We're able to more effectively use our regional market strategy, building as we go on brand awareness."

"You're trying to educate people as to what your brand is all about," says Jameson. "In our case, getting people to come into Tim Hortons first thing in the morning for coffee and breakfast, then training them to come in several times during the rest of the day."

To that end, Hortons routinely upgrades and refurbishes its outlets, adding double drive-throughs and establishing satellite outlets in settings like hospitals and retail stores—bringing the restaurant to the consumer instead of the other way around.

Is it any wonder we've always got time for Tim Hortons?[18]

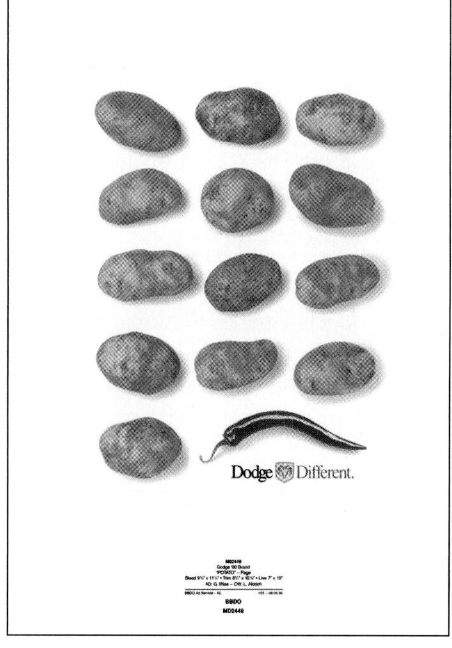


Dodge would like to avoid head-on competition with other auto producers, but that is difficult if potential customers view competing autos as very similar.

and use the same standardized approaches—and they will work well in each case. By contrast, marketing managers can't just adopt the same "good" marketing strategy being used by other firms. That just leads to head-on competition and a downward spiral in prices and profits. So target marketers try to offer a marketing mix that is better suited to customers' needs than competitors' offerings.

Most marketing managers would like to have such a strong marketing mix that customers see it as uniquely able to meet their needs. This competitor-free ideal guides the search for breakthrough opportunities. Yet monopoly situations, in which one firm completely controls a broad product-market, are rare in market-directed economies. Further, governments commonly regulate monopolies. For example, in many parts of the world prices set by utility companies must be approved by a government agency. Although most marketing managers can't expect to operate with complete control in an unregulated monopoly, they can move away from head-on competition.

In monopolistic competition, a number of different firms offer marketing mixes that at least some customers see as different. Each competitor tries to get control (a monopoly) in its "own" target market. But competition still exists, because some customers see the various alternatives as substitutes. Marketing managers sometimes try to differentiate very similar products by relying on other elements of the marketing mix.

For example, Clorox bleach uses the same basic chemicals as other bleaches. But marketing managers for Clorox may help to set it apart from other bleaches by offering an improved pouring spout, by producing ads that demonstrate its stain-killing power, or by getting it better shelf positions in supermarkets. Yet such approaches may not work, especially if competitors can easily imitate each new idea. Efforts to promote real, but subtle, differences may not do any good either. If potential customers view the different offerings as essentially similar, the market will become more and more competitive—and firms will have to rely on lower costs to obtain a competitive advantage.

Sometimes, despite the best efforts of marketing managers, the profitability of all competitors may be weakening. For example, buyers might pool their purchases and demand volume discounts. Or suppliers of necessary ingredients might raise their prices, making the product more expensive to produce. In instances like these, price (and marketing) wars can break out. Since the profitability of all competitors suffers during these wars, many businesses will avoid these industries.

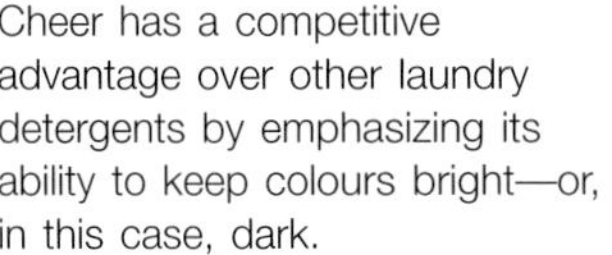
Cheer has a competitive advantage over other laundry detergents by emphasizing its ability to keep colours bright—or, in this case, dark.

Similarly, a firm may find that it cannot avoid highly competitive situations. Attracted by a firm's profitability, other firms might choose to follow its lead. For example, Rubbermaid was one of the first companies to introduce sturdy, low-cost plastic housewares—now it is a respected brand name, but faces competition from hundreds of other firms. Since most of these new entrants lack Rubbermaid's R&D and reputation, they choose to compete on price; unable to differentiate themselves, many of them fail. Unfortunately for Rubbermaid, new firms enter the market to replace those that have failed, possibly because they don't see more attractive alternatives. Rubbermaid, on the other hand, has expanded into new product-markets like office accessories and lawn and garden equipment.

**Competitor analysis** The best way for a marketing manager to avoid head-on competition is to find new or better ways to satisfy customers' needs and provide value. The search for a breakthrough opportunity—or some sort of competitive advantage—requires an understanding not only of customers but also of competitors. That's why marketing managers turn to **competitor analysis**—an organized approach for evaluating the strengths and weaknesses of current or potential competitors' marketing strategies. A complete discussion of the possible approaches for competitor analysis is beyond the scope of a first marketing course, but we will briefly cover an approach that works well in many different market situations.

**competitor analysis**
An organized approach for evaluating the strengths and weaknesses of current or potential competitors' marketing strategies

The basic approach to competitor analysis is simple. You compare the strengths and weaknesses of your current (or planned) target market and marketing mix with what competitors are currently doing or are likely to do in response to your strategy.

The initial step in competitor analysis is to identify potential competitors. It's useful to start broadly and from the viewpoint of target customers. Companies may offer quite different products to meet the same needs, but they are competitors if customers see them as offering close substitutes. For example, disposable diapers, cloth diapers, and diaper rental services all compete in the same generic market concerned with baby care. Identifying a broad set of potential competitors helps marketing managers understand the different ways customers are currently meeting needs and sometimes points to new opportunities. For example, even parents who usually prefer the economy of cloth diapers may be interested in the convenience of disposables when they travel.

Usually, however, marketing managers quickly narrow the focus of their analysis to a set of **competitive rivals**—firms that will be the closest competitors. Rivals offering similar products are usually easy to identify. However, with a really new and different product concept there may not be a current competitor with a similar product. In that case, the closest competitor may be a firm that is currently serving similar needs with a different type of product. Although such firms may not appear to be close competitors, they are likely to fight back—perhaps with a directly competitive product—if another firm starts to take away customers.

**competitive rivals**
Firms that will be the closest competitors

In addition to understanding current competitors, marketing managers must consider how long it might take for competitors to appear. It's easy to make the mistake of assuming that there won't be competitors—or of discounting how aggressive competition may become. But a successful strategy attracts copycats who jump in for a share of the profit. Sometimes a creative imitator figures out a way to provide customers with superior value. Then, sales may disappear before the pioneer even knows what's happened.

Finding a sustainable competitive advantage requires special attention to competitor strengths and weaknesses. For example, it is very difficult to dislodge a firm that is already a market leader simply by attacking with a similar strategy. The leader can usually defend its position by quickly copying the best parts of what a new competitor is trying to do. On the other hand, an established competitor may not be able to defend quickly if it is attacked where it is weak. For example, Right Guard deodorant built its strong position with an aerosol spray dispenser. But many consumers don't like the messy aerosol cloud; that weakness provided Old Spice with an opportunity for a deodorant in a pump dispenser. Right Guard did not quickly fight back with its own pump, because that could have hurt sales of its established product.[19]

**competitive barriers**
Conditions that may make it difficult, or even impossible, for a firm to compete in a market

In a competitor analysis, you also consider **competitive barriers**—the conditions that may make it difficult, or even impossible, for a firm to compete in a market. Such barriers may limit your own plans or, alternatively, block competitors' responses to an innovative strategy.

For example, Exhibit 4-2 summarizes a competitor analysis in the Japanese market for disposable diapers. P&G was about to replace its original Pampers, which were selling poorly, with a new version that offered improved fit and better absorbency. Kao and Uni-Charm, the two leading Japanese producers, both had better distribution networks. Kao also had a better computer system to handle reorders. This was crucial because most Japanese grocery stores and drugstores are very small—about 150 square feet. Shelf space is limited, and frequent restocking by wholesalers is critical. So getting cooperation in the channel was a potential competitive barrier for P&G. Uni-Charm further reduced P&G's access to customers when it took advantage of its relationship with retailers to introduce a second, lower-priced brand. To help overcome resistance in the channel, P&G improved the product, changed the packaging to take up less shelf space, and offered wholesalers and retailers better markups.[20]

Where can you find the information for a competitor analysis? Although most firms try to keep the specifics of their plans secret, much public information may be available. For example, many firms routinely monitor competitors' local newspapers. In one such case, an article discussed a change in the competitor's sales organization. An alert marketing manager realized that the change was made to strengthen

Exhibit 4-2 Competitor analysis (summary): disposable diaper competition in Japan.

| | P&G's Current and Planned Strategy | Kao's Strengths (+) and Weaknesses (−) | Uni-Charm's Strengths (+) and Weaknesses (−) |
|---|---|---|---|
| **Target Market(s)** | Upscale, modern parents who can afford disposable diapers | Same as for P&G | Same as for P&G, but also budget-conscious segment that includes cloth diaper users (+) |
| **Product** | Improved fit and absorbency (+); brand-name imagery weak in Japan (−) | Brand familiarity (+), but no longer the best performance (−) | Two brands—for different market segments—and more convenient package with handles (+) |
| **Place** | Distribution through independent wholesalers to both food stores and drugstores (+), but handled by fewer retailers (−) | Close relations with and control over wholesalers who carry only Kao products (+); computerized inventory reorder system (+) | Distribution through 80% of food stores in best locations (+); shelf space for two brands (+) |
| **Promotion** | Heaviest spending on daytime TV, heavy sales promotion, including free samples (+); small salesforce (−) | Large efficient salesforce (+); lowest advertising spending (−) and out-of-date ad claims (−) | Advertising spending high (+); effective ads that appeal to Japanese mothers (+) |
| **Price** | High retail price (−), but lower unit price for larger quantities (+) | Highest retail price (−), but also best margins for wholesalers and retailers (+) | Lowest available retail price (+); price of premium brand comparable to P&G (−) |
| **(Potential) Competitive Barriers** | Patent protection (+), limits in access to retail shelf space (−) | Inferior product (−), excellent logistics support system (+) | Economies of scale and lower costs (+); loyal customers (+) |
| **Likely Response(s)** | Improve wholesaler and retailer margins; faster deliveries in channel; change package to require less shelf space | Press retailers to increase in-store promotion; change advertising and/or improve product | Increase short-term sales promotions; but if P&G takes customers, cut price on premium brand |

## Ethical Dimensions 4–1

### ETHICAL ISSUES MAY ARISE

The search for information about competitors sometimes raises ethical issues. For example, it's not unusual for people to change jobs and move to a competing firm in the same industry. Such people may have a great deal of information about their previous employer—now their competitor—but is it ethical for them to use it? Similarly, some firms have been criticized for going too far—like waiting at a landfill for a competitor's trash to find copies of confidential company reports. In a high-tech version of this practice, computer hackers use the Internet to break into a competitor's computer network. In minutes, hackers can steal information that has taken years to collect.

Beyond the moral issues, spying on competitors to obtain trade secrets is illegal. Damage awards can be huge. The courts ordered competing firms to pay Procter & Gamble about $125 million in damages for stealing secrets about its Duncan Hines soft cookies. For example, a Frito-Lay employee once posed as a potential customer to attend a confidential sales presentation.[21]



the competitor's ability to take business from one of her firm's key target markets. This early warning provided time to make adjustments. Other sources of competitor information include trade publications, alert sales reps, intermediaries, and other industry experts. In business markets, customers may be quick to explain what competing suppliers are offering. However, firms need to be careful about how such information is acquired; see Ethical Dimensions 4-1.

The Internet is a powerful way to get information about competitors (see Internet Insite 4-1). A firm that puts all of its marketing information on a website for customers also makes it readily available to competitors. Similarly, computer programs make it easy to search through thousands of online publications and databases for any mention of a competitor. It's also increasingly common to specify what you want and instruct a software robot to send you a copy as soon as it's available. This is an incredibly powerful source of information that didn't even exist a few years ago.

## Internet Insite 4–1

### COMPETITIVE INTELLIGENCE ONLINE

Competitive intelligence (CI) is defined as the use of publicly available information on competitors and competition to gain an advantage.[22] Business intelligence is a broader term that encompasses use of competitive and non-competitive information (e.g., economy, suppliers, channel, and customers) in strategic decision making. The Internet is a goldmine when it comes to gathering information needed to evaluate market opportunities.

When conducting competitive and economic analyses using online information, there are a few important considerations:

- *Commercial vs. free sources*: In addition to commercial sources, there are literally hundreds of free sources that offer information on countries, industries, and companies. There are also government-operated websites (such as Industry Canada or the U.S. SEC site) that offer reliable information. Free private websites can provide quick access to information, but the user should check to see if the information is reliable—sometimes, you do get what you pay for.
- *Quality control*: The user should see if the source is credible, if data are supported by references, if the document is dated, and if the information is regularly updated. Generally, commercial sources will have fairly good quality control. If market conditions are rapidly changing (e.g., the change in the information technology industry between 2000 and 2002), information that is even one year old may not be very useful.
- *Searchability and access*: The effectiveness of the search engine in a site can determine the site's usage level. Powerful search engines that can retrieve information based on multiple keywords and Boolean searches make the site more useful. The site must be available and accessible with very little downtime.

Hoover's Online provides company profile information (history, products, financials, key officers, competitors, etc.) on more than 12 million companies worldwide (see below for a portion of a sample report from Hoover's Online). Dun & Bradstreet's database covers more than 80 million businesses worldwide.

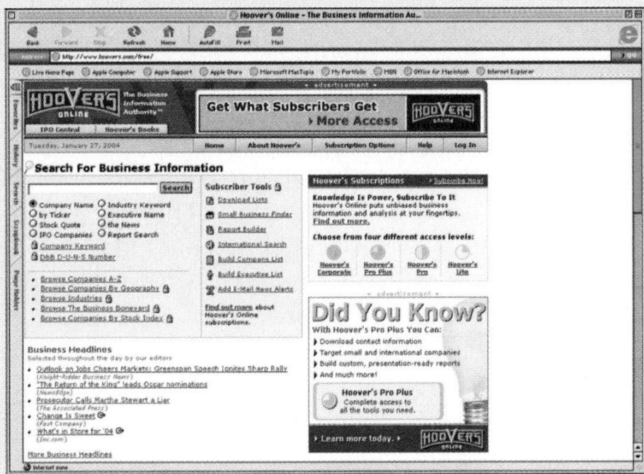


In addition to relying on commercial, free, and government websites for industry, economic, and competitive information, one can always visit the competitor's website for information. Most public companies post their annual reports (usually in the Investors or Investor Relations section) and news on new products, acquisitions, or market plans (usually in the Press Releases or Media section of the site). These can be valuable sources for understanding the competitor's strategic intent and direction.

Just as you can go to a competitor's site, they can come to your site, and they can also learn about your company through the commercial and non-commercial business information sites. There is little one can do to prevent this. Companies can, however, be selective regarding the type of information disclosed in their own websites.

Some useful commercial sites for competitive and business intelligence online:

- Dun & Bradstreet (www.dnb.com)
- LexisNexis (www.lexis-nexis.com)
- Hoover's Online (www.hoovers.com)
- Dialog (www.dialog.com)
- HighBeam Research (www.highbeam.com)

Some useful non-commercial sites for competitive and business intelligence online:

**Canadian Sites**

- Strategis—Industry Canada (www.strategis.ic.gc.ca)
- Strategis Competitive Intelligence E-Monitor (http://strategis.ic.gc.ca/sc_mangb/cip/engdoc/ciem_hpg.html)
- Links to Competitive Intelligence Sites (http://strategis.ic.gc.ca/sc_mangb/cip/engdoc/cilinks.html)
- SEDAR (www.sedar.com)
- Statistics Canada (www.statscan.ca)

**Other Sites**

- SEC (www.sec.gov)—see EDGAR database for detailed information on public companies in the U.S.
- CIA World Factbook (www.cia.gov/cia/publications/factbook/index.html) for market and economic information on foreign countries.
- ThomasRegister (www.thomasregister.com) for product and brand information on Canadian and U.S. firms.
- Society of Competitive Intelligence Professionals (www.scip.org).

Refer to Internet Insite 8-2 for other good sources of secondary information that can be used in accessing market opportunities and environments. Financial or business sections of Canadian online newspapers as well as publications such as *The Economist* (www.economist.com) and *The Wall Street Journal* (www.wsj.com) (subscription required for both) are excellent sources of company information.

Software vendors like DataMirror (www.datamirror .com) and MicroStrategy (www.microstrategy.com) offer solutions to gather and disseminate business intelligence information on intranets (closed networks for employees). Now, information can be made available to everyone in the organization who needs it, not only to the privileged few.

Business intelligence also includes monitoring what is written and said about your company. On the Internet, companies like eWatch (www.ewatch.com) monitor newsgroups, bulletin boards, online newspapers, and content sites and report what is written about a company. If incorrect information or rumours are being spread, the company can respond quickly. Companies also use services like eWatch to monitor what is being written and said about major competitors.

Competitive intelligence involves ongoing information gathering and analysis. CI does not have to be restricted to secondary sources. It can include interviews, surveys, and observations. The use of various online sources makes it easier to gather business intelligence. At the end of the day, there is still a lot of human judgment involved in the interpretation of the data. The easy access to information means that there is no excuse for making major marketing or business decisions without evaluating relevant information.

Go to: www.mcgrawhill.ca/college/wong
to apply this Insite in an exciting Internet exercise.

**economic and technological environments**

Affect the way that firms—and the whole economy—use resources

## The Economic Environment

The **economic and technological environments** affect the way that firms—and the whole economy—use resources. We will treat the economic and technological environments separately to emphasize that the technological environment provides a *base* for the economic environment. Technical skills and equipment affect the way companies convert an economy's resources into output. The economic environment, on the other hand, is affected by the way all of the parts of a macro-economic system interact. This then affects such things as national income, economic growth, and inflation. The economic environment may vary from one country to another, but economies around the world are linked. Let's look at some of the indicators that managers use in assessing the economic environment.

**Consumer spending** Consumer spending represents about two-thirds of Canada's economy's activity. Thus, anything that influences consumers' ability or willingness to buy—employment rates, wages, and so on—must be closely monitored. If these indicators show weakness, then consumer spending is limited to what they can draw from their savings or buy on credit. In addition, if consumers see weaknesses in these indicators then they may worry about their financial future and postpone purchases. This is why managers often monitor the savings rate and the amount of credit owed by Canadians.

It is also the reason why we closely watch overall economic conditions. The economic environment can, and does, change quite rapidly. Even a well-planned marketing strategy may fail if a country or region goes through a rapid business decline. As consumers' incomes drop, they must shift their spending patterns; they may simply have to do without some products. In late 2001, Argentina was struck with an economic crisis, and many companies went out of business. Those that did not had big losses. In a few months, the buying power of the Argentine peso was devalued nearly 30 percent.[23] As a result, consumers could not afford to buy many of the products they once enjoyed. You can imagine what effect this had on local businesses. Of course, economic changes are not always this dramatic.

A weak economy (like the one in Canada and many other parts of the world in the early 1990s) also undermines consumer confidence, even among families whose income is not affected. When consumer confidence is low people delay making purchases, especially of big-ticket items. Similarly, firms cut back on their own purchases. Many companies aren't strong enough to survive such bad times.

**Interest rates and inflation** Changes in the economy are often accompanied by changes in the interest rate—the charge for borrowing money. Interest rates directly affect the total price borrowers must pay for products. So the interest rate affects when, and if, they will buy. This is an especially important factor in some business markets, but it also affects consumer purchases of homes, cars, furniture, computers, and other items usually bought on credit.

Interest rates usually increase during periods of inflation, and inflation is a fact of life in many economies. In some Latin American countries inflation has exceeded 400 percent a year in recent years. In contrast, recent Canadian levels—2 to 4 percent—seem low. Still, inflation must be considered in strategy planning. When costs are rising rapidly and there are no more cost-cutting measures to take, a marketing manager may have to increase prices. But the decisions of individual marketing managers to raise prices add to macro-level inflation. That can lead to government policies that reduce income, employment, *and* consumer spending.

**International trade** In the past, marketing managers often focused their attention on the economy of their home country. It's no longer that simple. The economies of the world are connected—and changes in one economy quickly affect others. One reason for this is that the amount of international trade is increasing—and it is affected by changes in and between economies.

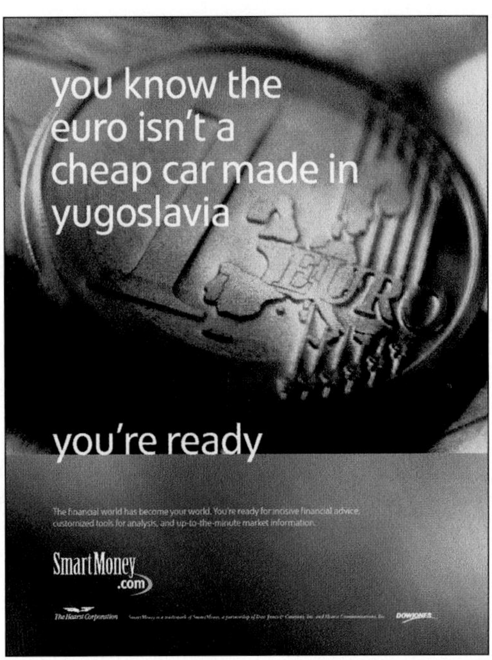


Managers who compete in global markets need to be aware of how changes in the global economy will impact their strategies and opportunities.

All countries trade to some extent—we live in an interdependent world. Trade expands as a country develops and industrializes. In fact, the largest changes in world trade are usually seen in developing economies. Over the last 20 years, for example, exports from Hong Kong, Taiwan, and Singapore have risen dramatically.

Even so, the largest traders are highly developed nations. The United States, Japan, Canada, and the countries of the European Union together account for more than half of all world trade. However, each country has its own pattern of trade. Exhibit 4-3 makes clear the impact of international trade for Canada. For example, despite Team Canada export initiatives to increase trade with other countries, the U.S. market is three times as important to Canada as the rest of the world combined. As you can imagine, it is hard to be in business in Canada and not pay close attention to economic conditions in the United States. In addition, the continued importance to the Canadian economy of resource and automotive exports is also highlighted.

**exchange rate**
How much one country's money is worth in another country's currency

**The exchange rate** Changes in the **exchange rate**—how much one country's money is worth in another country's currency—have an important effect on international trade. When the loonie is strong, it's worth more in foreign countries. This sounds good—but it makes Canadian products more expensive overseas and foreign products cheaper in Canada. Then, firms like Magna International, a Canadian auto-parts manufacturer, and some natural resource–based businesses lose foreign customers to producers from other countries.

**Tariffs and quotas** Taxes and restrictions at national or regional borders greatly reduce the free flow of goods and services between the marketing systems of different countries. Tariffs—taxes on imported products—vary depending on whether a country is trying to raise revenue or limit trade. Restrictive tariffs often block all movement. But even revenue-producing tariffs cause red tape, discourage the free movement of products, and increase the prices consumers pay.

Quotas set the specific quantities of products that can move into or out of a country. Tremendous marketing opportunities may exist in a unified Europe, for example, but import quotas (or export controls directed against a specific country) could discourage outsiders from entering.

Trade restrictions can be a major source of conflict. For example, Canada charged the United States with unfair trading practices when a tariff was placed on

Exhibit 4-3A Canada's largest trading partners, 2001 (millions of dollars).

| Canadian Exports By Country | | | Canadian Imports By Country | | |
|---|---|---|---|---|---|
| United States | 350,734.5 | (87.2%) | United States | 218,295.5 | (63.6%) |
| Japan | 8,164.3 | (2.03%) | Japan | 14,647.4 | (4.3%) |
| European Union (15) | 18,256.7 | (4.5%) | European Union | 38,356.2 | (11.2%) |
| Developing countries | 21,569.8 | (5.4%) | Developing countries | 55,444.0 | (16.2%) |
| Other countries | 3,500 | (0.9%) | Other countries | 16,121.13 | (4.7%) |
| **Total** | **402,295.6** | | **Total** | **343,002.8** | |

**Source:** "Provincial Pocket Facts," Statistics Canada, <www.dfait-maeci.gc.ca/eet/menu-e.ap>.

Exhibit 4-3B Canada's exports and imports, 2001 (millions of dollars).

| | Exports | | Imports | |
|---|---|---|---|---|
| Motor vehicles and parts | 82,141 | (20.4%) | 59,153 | (17.2%) |
| Mineral fuels and parts | 56,776 | (14.1%) | 19,220 | (5.6%) |
| Machinery | 34,692 | (8.6%) | 61,884 | (18.0%) |
| Electrical machinery and equipment | 22,083 | (5.5%) | 40,273 | (11.7%) |
| Wood | 19,048 | (4.7%) | — | |
| Optical/photo equipment | — | | 12,184 | (3.6%) |
| Other | 187,872 | (46.7%) | 150,578 | (43.9%) |
| **Total** | **402,295** | | **343,003** | |

**Source:** "Canada's Merchandise Exports," Statistics Canada, Trade and Economic Analysis Division, <www.dfait-maeci.gc.ca/eet>, June 7, 2002.



Canadian softwood lumber shipments. American timber interests had charged that Canadian provinces were unfairly subsidizing their lumber companies, in part by charging low stumpage prices for government-owned trees. Needless to say, Canadian forest products firms disagreed. As this book goes to press, there remain considerable differences of opinion on both sides of the border as to the kind of trade arrangements governing softwood lumber that should be put into place.

There are still many obstacles to free trade among nations, and trade wars among nations are likely to continue. Even so, the trend is toward fewer restrictions on international trade. Perhaps the most visible evidence of this was the creation in 1995 of the World Trade Organization (WTO)—the only international body dealing with the rules of trade between nations. At its heart are the WTO agreements, which are the legal ground rules for international commerce and for trade policy. The agreements have three main objectives: (1) to help trade flow as freely as possible, (2) to provide an impartial means of settling disputes, and (3) to facilitate further negotiation. In general, the WTO agreements try to encourage competition and discourage protectionism; they also seek to provide more predictable policies.

You can see that the marketing manager must watch the economic environment carefully. In contrast to the cultural and social environment, economic conditions change continuously. And they can move rapidly—up or down—requiring immediate strategy changes.[24]

## The Technological Environment

Technology is the application of science to convert an economy's resources to output. Technology affects marketing in two basic ways: with new products and with new processes (ways of doing things). For example, we are moving from an industrial society to an information society. Advances in information technology make it possible for people in different parts of the world to communicate face-to-face using satellite video-conferencing and to transmit complex design drawings over the Internet. Websites enable sophisticated e-commerce exchanges between remote firms, and EDI—electronic data interchange—links manufacturers with suppliers, distributors, and customers.[25] These process changes are accompanied by an exciting explosion of high-tech products—from genome-based medicines to micro-lasers in factories to cars that contact the police if they are stolen.

New technologies have created important new industries: fifteen years ago, Amazon.com and eBay.com didn't exist. Now, they are two of the best-known brands in the world and have subsidiaries focused on the Canadian market (Amazon.ca and eBay.ca, respectively). With such big opportunities at stake, you can also see why there is such a rapid transfer of technology from one part of the world to another. But technology transfer is not automatic. Someone—perhaps you—has to see the opportunity.

Many of the big advances in business have come from the early recognition of new ways to do things. There is perhaps no better example of this than the Internet and the World Wide Web. The idea of the Internet—linking computers around the world in a network—is not new; it's been around for years. Further, we say that the Internet is a "system," but it might be more accurate to just think of it as a collection of consistent hardware and software standards. Even so, the Internet expands the network concept to include any computer, anywhere. Further, the World Wide Web makes the exchange of information on the Internet easy. As a result, this new technology is radically changing just about every aspect of marketing. We'll be discussing these changes in more detail throughout the text, so for now we'll just briefly illustrate the impact.

Consider the arena of promotion. The invention of television changed marketing because it suddenly made it possible for a sponsor to broadcast a vivid message to millions of people at the same time. Now, the Internet makes it possible for that sponsor to select any of millions of messages and to simultaneously "narrowcast" any of them to millions of different individuals. It is just as easy for customers to request the information in the first place, or to respond electronically once they have it. Thus, the Internet's capability radically changes our ideas about how companies communicate with customers, and vice versa. And it doesn't stop with the Internet. New communications technologies like Wi-Fi (which provides high-speed, wireless Internet access from a laptop), Bluetooth (which lets different devices share information), and .NET (which offers the potential to access databases anytime, anywhere, on any device) will provide marketers with a dizzying array of new promotional tools.

Similarly, the Internet is creating totally different approaches to pricing. Airlines are now running online auctions of seats that might otherwise go unsold. If you sell every seat to the highest bidder, you are really pricing precisely to match supply and demand. To check out an online auction, go to eBay.ca.

In hindsight, new approaches such as these seem obvious—given that the technology is available. But they are not obvious up front, unless you're really looking for them. Marketers should help their companies see such opportunities by trying to understand present markets—and what is keeping their companies from being more successful. Then, as new technological developments come along, marketers will be alert to possible uses of those technologies and see how opportunities can be turned into profits.[26]

The rapid pace of technological change opens up new opportunities, but it also poses challenges for marketers (for some examples, see Ethical Dimensions 4-2). For some firms, success hinges on how quickly new ideas can be brought to market. But it's easy for a firm to immediately jump into production mode in the flush of excitement that comes from a new idea or R&D discovery. That makes it more important than ever for marketing thinking to guide the production process—starting at the

## Ethical Dimensions 4–2

### TECHNOLOGY AND ETHICAL ISSUES

Marketers must also help their firms decide what technological developments are ethically acceptable. For example, many firms use a system to identify incoming callers. Before the phone is even answered the computer shows who is calling along with detailed information—ranging from what purchases the customer has made in the past to the income level of people who live in the caller's neighbourhood. This can be a powerful marketing tool, but many people feel that it's an invasion of privacy. Similarly, many firms track information about who "hits" the company website and what site they came from. The firm can then sell this information to whoever wants to use it to send promotional e-mail. Yet uninvited e-mail is just another form of invasion of privacy.

With the growing concern about environmental pollution and the quality of life, some attractive technological developments may be rejected because of their long-run effects on the environment. Aseptic drink boxes, for example, are convenient but difficult to recycle. In a case like this, what's good for the firm and some customers may not be good for the cultural and social environment or acceptable in the political and legal environment. Being close to the market should give marketers a better feel for current trends and help firms avoid serious mistakes.[27]



beginning with decisions about what customers will really value and where development efforts should be focused.

### The Political Environment

**political environment**
Affects opportunities at a local or international level

The attitudes and reactions of people, social critics, and governments all affect the **political environment**. The political environment can also have a dramatic effect on opportunities at a local or international level. Some business managers have become very successful by studying the political environment and developing strategies that take advantage of opportunities related to changing political dimensions.

Strong sentiments of nationalism—an emphasis on a country's interests before everything else—affect how marketing systems work. They can affect how marketing managers work as well. Nationalistic feelings can reduce sales—or even block all marketing activity—in some international markets. For many years, Japan has made it difficult for outside firms to do business there—in spite of the fact that Japanese producers of cars, TVs, digital cameras, and other products have established profitable markets in Canada, the United States, and Europe. Japan is under pressure to change, but the changes are coming slowly.

Nationalistic feelings can determine whether a firm can enter a market, because businesses often must get permission to operate. In some political environments, this is only a formality. In others, a lot of red tape and personal influence are involved, and bribes are sometimes expected. This raises ethical issues for marketing managers—and legal issues too, since it's illegal for Canadian and American firms to offer such bribes. Clearly, that can make it difficult for a Canadian firm to compete with a company from a country that doesn't have similar laws.

Important dimensions of the political environment are likely to be similar among nations that have banded together to have common regional economic boundaries. The move toward the economic unification of Europe and free trade among the nations of North and South America are outstanding examples of this sort of regional grouping.

**Free trade** The North American Free Trade Agreement (NAFTA) has been successful in developing new investment opportunities for Canadians by decreasing the trade barriers that exist between Canada, the United States, and Mexico. The easing of trade restrictions has allowed exporters in all three countries to open up new markets.

The successes of NAFTA, however, have been countered with concerns such as the "level playing field" issue. Wages in Mexico are much lower than in Canada or the United States. That being so, Mexico, it is argued, will be able to draw labour-intensive jobs away from its two NAFTA partners. Also, Mexico's less-restrictive environmental laws may encourage many firms to relocate there from the north. Mexico's fragile economic and political system also worries investors. The very sharp decline in the value of the peso some years ago made both existing and proposed Mexican investments far less attractive.

Mexico's problems notwithstanding, efforts are being made to expand NAFTA to include countries in Central and South America through the FTAA—Free Trade Area of the Americas. A western-hemisphere free trade agreement may still be a long way off, but the United States is fiercely driving such an initiative to promote the purchase of American goods in the western hemisphere.

In the past, each country in the European Union (EU) had its own unique trade rules and regulations. These differences—and nationalistic squabbles—made it difficult and expensive to move products from one country to the others. Now, the member countries of the EU are trying to reduce conflicting laws, taxes, and other obstacles to trade within Europe. Trucks loaded with products now spill across borders of the European continent and Britain. The increased efficiency is reducing costs (and the prices European consumers pay) and creating new jobs. Even bigger changes may come if Britain decides to join other key member countries that have moved to the *euro*, a new unified money system for the EU. With the currencies of countries in the euro-zone phased out, transactions no longer involve the extra uncertainty and cost of converting payments from one currency to another. These changes make Europe the largest unified market in the world, but marketers should still expect to encounter some differences among European countries.

Of course, removal of some economic and political barriers—whether across North and South America or Europe—will not eliminate the need to adjust strategies to reach submarkets of consumers. Centuries of cultural differences will not disappear overnight, and may never disappear. Yet these co-operative arrangements will give firms operating in regions easier access to larger markets, and the countries involved will have a more powerful voice in protecting their own interests.

**consumerism**

A social movement that seeks to increase the rights and powers of consumers in relation to sellers and the government

**Consumerism** **Consumerism** is a social movement that seeks to increase the rights and powers of consumers in relation to sellers and the government. Canadian con-

Adero wants marketers to keep in mind that a website that can attract prospects from all over the world won't be successful in turning them into customers if it ignores nationalism and cultural differences.

sumerism became an important movement in the late 1960s. One reason for this increased consumer consciousness was the establishment in 1968 of Consumer and Corporate Affairs Canada (CCAC), whereby one department became responsible for administering a number of existing consumer protection laws and a wide variety of new programs designed to further the Canadian consumer's interests.

CCAC moved aggressively in the area of consumer protection. Additional laws were passed and existing legislation was more vigorously enforced. Great emphasis was placed on educating and informing consumers. Complaints received by CCAC were studied to determine the serious problem areas that required corrective action. At the provincial level, consumer-protection bureaus and agencies were also greatly strengthened.

While consumerism now has a much lower profile, it remains an important feature of the Canadian marketing scene. Government efforts focus on consumer education and awareness. The Web is now being used by the Office of Consumer Affairs to help create that awareness (see their website at **http://consumerinformation.ca**). Specialized groups with a limited focus, such as the Automobile Protection Association with its annual publication *Lemon-Aid*, are also busy educating and informing consumers. Newspapers and television programs regularly promote "smart shopping," often by helping dissatisfied customers obtain a fair deal from local merchants.

**Environmentalism** Although consumerism has received less attention in recent years, the 1990s brought with them a renewed interest in the environment. Environmentalism was first recognized by some as an important cause in the 1960s. However, widespread uneasiness over what we buy, how we use products, and how we then dispose of consumer waste surfaced only in the late 1980s. Campaigns sponsored by environmental groups, various levels of government, and even businesses now urge Canadians to reduce, to reuse, and to recycle.

Environmental issues are currently receiving far more attention than more traditional consumer-protection issues. Recent attention has turned to the Kyoto Protocol, an aggressive international agreement aimed at reducing harmful greenhouse gases. With 3.3 percent of the world's carbon emissions coming from Canada, Jean Chrétien's December 10, 2002 decision to make Canada the 100th country to ratify the agreement was an important one. By signing this pact, Canada agrees to reduce carbon emissions by 6 percent below 1990 levels by 2012. Unfortunately, this move has caused a serious rift among Canadian regions, as the agreement has significant economic implications for oil-producing provinces like Alberta. Furthermore, with major players such as Russia, China, and the United States holding out, the ultimate effectiveness of the agreement remains unclear.[28] What is clear, however, is that both consumers and manufacturers are looking for environmentally friendly ways of doing things. You can expect to hear a great deal about "sustainable marketing" and "green consumers" over the next few years.

**Increased ethical climate** Since the bankruptcy in December 2001 of Enron, a U.S.–based multi-billion dollar energy-trading company, companies have operated in a heightened ethical climate. The downfall of Enron, once America's seventh largest company, caused creditors, customers, and the general public to question the integrity of major corporations across Canada and the United States. Further to the increased public scrutiny and loss of investor confidence, new laws and regulations were passed to clean up the auditing process and ultimately alter the shape of the business environment. In response to such acts, major corporations have begun to review their accounting and corporate governance practices to once again instill trust in their stakeholders. Now more than ever, marketers must be conscious of the public perception of their company and must work hard to retain the trust and confidence of their consumers.[29]

## The Legal Environment

**legal environment**

Sets the basic rules for how a business can operate in society

Changes in the economic and political environments often lead to changes in the **legal environment** and in the ways existing laws are enforced. The legal environment sets the basic rules for how a business can operate in society. Legislation may severely limit some choices, but changes in laws and how they are interpreted also create new opportunities. We, of course, will focus on how the law has evolved in Canada. However, don't forget that laws and their enforcement vary from one country to the next. For example, Canada has not been nearly as aggressive as the United States either in regulating trade practices or in prohibiting proposed mergers.

**The Competition Act** Canada's Combines Investigation Act was passed to prevent anticompetitive behaviour. Until it was amended in 1975, difficulties in prosecuting those charged kept it from being effective legislation. Offences had to be treated as violations of criminal law and, therefore, to win a case the government had to prove guilt "beyond any reasonable doubt." Difficulties in establishing that degree of proof discouraged prosecution. So did a requirement that competition had to be completely or virtually eliminated before the courts could act. These requirements greatly reduced the likelihood that any firm brought to court would be found guilty.

In December 1975, dissatisfaction with the Combines Investigation Act led Parliament to pass Bill C-2, the first part of which became a two-stage revision of the existing legislation. The second series of major changes, dealing primarily with mergers and acquisitions, was not passed until ten years later. The resulting legislation, incorporating both sets of changes, became the Competition Act of 1986.

Bill C-2 tightened legislation so that it would more effectively regulate then-current marketing practices and make it easier for the government to win cases brought to court. To achieve the latter objective, both the "burden of proof" and the "effective destruction of competition" requirements were somewhat relaxed. To some extent, enforcement has become both easier and more effective. Individuals and organizations—both large and small—have been convicted of deceptive price advertising, price fixing, and other anti-competitive behaviour.

**Consumer privacy** As new technologies make it possible to collect and analyze more data about Canadians, there is a growing concern as to whether their rights to privacy are being eroded. In much the same way that the environmental movement shaped manufacturing practices, privacy concerns will shape how organizations collect and use data.[30] Broadly sweeping privacy laws already exist in Canada, the United States, Australia, and Hong Kong, to name a few. In fact, some companies—like RBC Financial Group, the largest financial institution in Canada—have a corporate privacy code and a corporate privacy officer.

In Canada, a privacy commissioner was established under the Canadian Human Rights Act in 1977. Today, many provinces and territories have established their own privacy laws governing the use of government data. These include Quebec (1982); Ontario (1988); Saskatchewan (1992); British Columbia (1993); Nova Scotia (1994); Alberta (1995); Yukon (1996); Northwest Territories (1997); Manitoba (1998); Nunavut (1999); New Brunswick (2001); and Newfoundland & Labrador (2002). As you can see, the incidence of such laws has been growing at a rapid rate in recent years.

On April 13, 2000, Parliament passed progressive privacy legislation that had a significant effect on direct-marketing practices across the country. According to the Privacy Commission's website, Bill C-6, the Personal Information Protection and Electronic Documents Act, "sets out ground rules for how private sector organizations may collect, use or disclose personal information in the course of commercial activities." Under the Act, which went into effect on January 1, 2001, organizations must obtain an individual's consent when they collect, use, or disclose personal information. The Act also gives consumers the right to access their information, while forcing businesses to ensure the accuracy of collected data and limiting the amount of data that can be collected. Although there are exceptions to the new regulations, there are major implications for telemarketing firms, which employ more than 270,000 Canadians[31] and whose business relies on the collection of private information.[32] See Ethical Dimensions 4-3 for the Organisation for Economic Co-operation and Development's Code of Fair Information Practices.

**Other federal legislation** Other laws and regulations are also designed to protect the consumer's interests. See Exhibit 4-4 for more detailed information on the current structure and scope of the Competition Bureau (now a part of Industry Canada, the organization with which Consumer and Corporate Affairs Canada has been merged). Here, we will mention only a few of the many relevant federal laws and regulations. Other laws affecting the four Ps will be discussed in the chapters describing the practices to which they apply.

The Food and Drugs Act regulates the sale of food, drugs, cosmetics, and medical devices. This legislation deals with quality standards, packaging, labelling, and advertising, as well as with the manufacturing practices and selling policies of food and drug manufacturers. Certain forms of misrepresentation in food labelling, packaging, selling, and advertising are specifically outlawed by the Food and Drugs Act. Many federal units establish product standards and grades. There are also laws concerning the labelling of wool, furs, precious metals, and flammable fabrics.

**Provincial and local regulations** Provincial and local laws also affect marketing. There are regulations for starting up a business (licences, examinations, and even tax payments); in some communities, there are ordinances prohibiting certain

## Ethical Dimensions 4–3

### THE OECD CODE OF FAIR INFORMATION PRACTICES

1. Collection Limitation: Limited to the collection of personal data; data should be obtained by lawful and fair means and, where appropriate, with the knowledge and consent of the data subject
2. Data Quality: Personal data should be relevant to the purpose for which it is used and, to the extent necessary for those purposes, should be accurate, complete, and kept up-to-date
3. Purpose Specification: The purposes for which personal data are collected should be specified not later than at the time of data collection, and subsequent use limited to the fulfillment of those purposes or such others as are not incompatible with those purposes and are as specified on each occasion of change of purpose
4. Use Limitation: Personal data should not be disclosed, made available or otherwise used for purposes other than those specified except (a) with the consent of the data subject, or (b) by the authority of law
5. Security Safeguards: Personal data should be protected with reasonable security standards against such risks as loss of unauthorized access, destruction, use, modification, or disclosure of data
6. Openness: There should be a general policy of openness about developments, practices and policies with respect to personal data. Means should be readily available of establishing the existence and nature of personal data and the main purpose of their use, as well as the identity and residence of the data controller.
7. Individual Participation: An individual should have the right
   a. To obtain confirmation of data the controller has relating to them
   b. To have communicated to him, data relating to him (1) within a reasonable time (2) at a charge, if any, that is not excessive (3) in a form that is readily intelligible to him
   c. To be given reasons if a request made under subparagraphs (a) and (b) is denied, and to be able to challenge that denial,
   d. To challenge data relating to him and, if the challenge is successful, to have data erased, rectified, completed or amended
8. Accountability: A data controller should be accountable for complying with measures which give effect to the principles stated above.

Exhibit 4-4 Organizational structure of the federal Competition Bureau.

The Bureau employs 296 people in the National Capital Region and 86 in seven regional offices. As the organizational chart below shows, the Bureau comprises six branches.

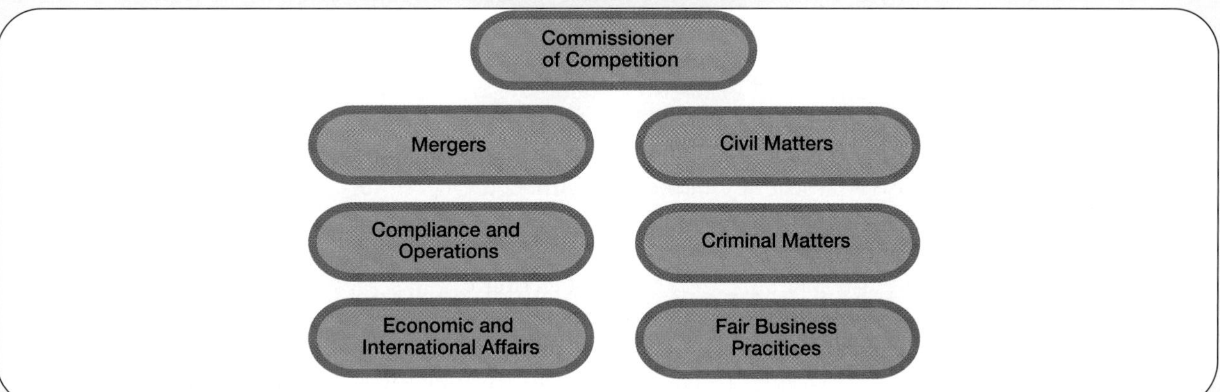


**The Commissioner of Competition** is head of the Competition Bureau and is responsible for the administration and enforcement of the *Competition Act*, the *Consumer Packaging and Labelling Act*, the *Precious Metals Marking Act* and the *Textile Labelling Act*.

**Mergers Branch** reviews merger transactions. Mergers in which the parties have combined sales or assets in excess of $400 million, and in which the value of the transaction exceeds $35 million, require advance filing with the Prenotification Unit of the Mergers Branch.

**Compliance and Operations Branch** develops the Bureau's compliance program, enforcement policy, public education initiatives and communications programs. It also handles planning, administration and informatics activities.

**Economics and International Affairs Branch** coordinates international cooperation and policy development in many fora on international competition policy, and liaises with foreign authorities and other government departments and agencies. The Branch provides economic advice and analysis to the enforcement branches on specific cases, on enforcement policy issues and on legislative changes and regulatory interventions. The Branch also assists other government departments and agencies by providing competition policy advice and recommendations.

**Civil Matters Branch** reviews anti-competitive behaviours, such as abuse of dominant position, and restraints imposed by suppliers on customers, such as refusal to supply, exclusive dealing and tied selling. The Branch is also responsible for the Bureau's interventions before federal and provincial regulatory boards and tribunals.

**Criminal Matters Branch** reviews criminal offences relating to anti-competitive behaviours. These include conspiracies that have an undue impact on competition, bid rigging, price discrimination, predatory pricing and price maintenance. The Branch is also responsible for the Amendments Unit, which ensures that the provisions of the *Competition Act* and labelling legislation remain relevant.

**Fair Business Practices Branch** administers and enforces the misleading representations and deceptive marketing practices provisions of the *Competition Act*. These provisions include deceptive telemarketing, ordinary price claims and promotional contests. The Branch is also responsible for administering and enforcing the *Consumer Packaging and Labelling Act*, the *Precious Metals Marking Act* and the *Textile Labelling Act*. The Branch's work is carried out by staff in a network of offices located in the Atlantic Region, Quebec Region, the National Capital Region, Ontario Region, Prairie Region and Pacific Region.

activities, such as door-to-door selling. Provinces have also attempted to set the store hours for various types of retailers. For example, it wasn't until the early 1990s that Ontario finally legalized Sunday shopping. The sale and advertising of alcoholic beverages are also provincially controlled.

Individual provinces have passed laws that regulate the granting of credit and otherwise call for truth in lending. Those who make purchases from door-to-door salespeople are often provided with a cooling-off period during which they may cancel a contract. The provinces also exercise their regulatory authority over car dealers, travel agents, and many other types of businesses that deal with large numbers of consumers spending considerable amounts of money.

Perhaps the most significant development on the provincial scene has been the passing of trade practices legislation. Such legislation protects the consumer from unconscionable and deceptive practices. Though the laws passed by different provinces aren't identical, they all attempt to deal with the same set of problems.

**The legislative environment in Quebec** Like every other jurisdiction in Canada, Quebec has passed a number of laws to protect its consumers. Quebec's Consumer Protection Act is modelled after, but goes far beyond, trade practices legislation previously passed in British Columbia, Ontario, and Alberta. One unique feature of the Quebec statute is its virtual ban on all advertising directed toward children.

Some laws are intended to ensure the pre-eminence of the French language in every aspect of Quebec life. Although Quebec regulations introduced in 1993 allow for a somewhat greater use of other languages, the primacy of French remains unchanged.

**A final comment on the legal environment** Traditional thinking about buyer–seller relations has been "let the buyer beware"—but now it seems to be shifting to "let the *seller* beware." The emphasis now is on protecting consumers directly, rather than indirectly through laws designed to preserve competition. Much of the impact of consumer protection legislation tends to fall on manufacturers. They're the producers of the product, and they are expected to stand behind what they make. The courts are placing an ever-greater degree of responsibility on manufacturers. Some firms have even been held liable for injuries caused by the user's own carelessness. When this happens, it very definitely becomes a "let the seller beware" world. Therefore, manufacturers should use product elements, such as packaging and warning labels, to actively make sure consumers are fully informed.

Marketers must also stay alert to how legislation is being interpreted and enforced. Often, good legal assistance is required to keep up to date. Managers must accept the political and legal environments as important parts of the context within which businesses must function.

## The Cultural and Social Environment

**cultural and social environment**
Affects how and why people live and behave as they do

The **cultural and social environment** affects how and why people live and behave as they do—which affects customer buying behaviour and eventually the economic, political, and legal environments. Many variables make up the cultural and social environment. Some examples are the languages people speak, the type of education they have, their religious beliefs, what type of food they eat, the style of clothing and housing they have, and how they view work, marriage, and family.

A marketing manager can't afford to take the cultural and social environment for granted. Although changes tend to come slowly, they can have far-reaching effects. A marketing manager who sees the changes early may be able to identify big opportunities. Further, within any broad society different subgroups of people may be affected by the cultural and social environment in different ways. In most countries, the trend toward multiculturalism is making such differences even more important to marketers. They require special attention when segmenting markets. In fact, dealing with these differences is often one of the greatest challenges managers face when planning strategies, especially for international markets.

We will discuss details of how the cultural and social environment relates to buying behaviour in Chapters 5 through 7; here, we will just use an example to illustrate its impact on marketing strategy planning.

**How different are Canada and the U.S.?** Is there a distinct Canadian culture? If so, how do cultural differences and so-called national characteristics help determine the way Canadians live, work, and consume? It's easy to ask such questions, but difficult to answer them in a way that is helpful to marketers. All we can do now is indicate some of the cultural similarities and differences that must be taken into consideration.

Seymour Lipset has provided important insights into how Canadians differ from Americans. He sees distinct differences that find their roots in the American Revolution. From this event the two countries emerged: one victorious and independent of its British ties, the other content to maintain its links to England.

Canadians appear to have more tolerance for "elites," Lipset believes. We also place less importance on equality. Americans are more religious, more patriotic, and more committed to higher education. Americans don't favour large welfare programs or an active role for government in the economy.

National identity is a very important issue for Canadians, and we look endlessly for qualities that make us distinct. Unfortunately, as Lipset says, we often define ourselves by how we differ from Americans. If they're brash risk-takers, then we're solid, reliable, and decent. Canadians are more class-aware, law-abiding, and group-oriented.[33]

Whether we're really the "kinder, gentler" nation may not be easily established. Lipset argues that the two countries differ on the principles that organize them. Nevertheless, similarities in values, living patterns, work roles, family relationships, and consumer behaviour are much more obvious than the differences that might exist between Americans and Anglo-Canadians.

**Important differences within Canada** One of the Canadian market's most important characteristics is its distinctive regional differences. Incomes, consumption patterns, lifestyles, dialects, and attitudes vary from province to province. There are, for example, considerable differences between what consumers in Atlantic Canada purchase and what's bought in British Columbia. Some of these differences are as significant as those existing between French Canadians and their English-speaking counterparts.

Cultural differences similar to those found among the regions are also common within major urban areas. Large ethnic communities are to be found in Toronto, Montreal, and Vancouver. Food stores, newsstands, travel agencies, credit unions, and restaurants cater specifically to culturally defined markets. The size and importance of Canada's ethnic and French Canadian markets are discussed at some length in Chapter 5.

**Changing women's roles** The shifting roles of women in society illustrate the importance of the cultural and social environment on marketing strategy planning. Fifty years ago, many people in North America believed that a woman's primary role in society was as a wife and mother. As a result, women had less opportunity for higher education and were completely shut out of many of the most interesting jobs. Obviously, there have been big changes in that stereotyped thinking. With better job opportunities, more women are delaying marriage, and once married they are likely to stay in the workforce and have fewer children.

Still, the flood of women into the job market boosted economic growth and changed Canadian society in many other ways. Many in-home jobs that used to be done primarily by women—ranging from family shopping to preparing meals to doing volunteer work—still need to be done by someone. Husbands and children now do some of these jobs, a situation that has changed the target market for many products. Or, a working woman may face a crushing "poverty of time" and look for help elsewhere, creating opportunities for producers of frozen meals, child care centres, dry cleaners, financial services, and the like.

The changing role of women has created real marketing opportunities, as well as a real challenge. For example, a marketing mix targeted at women may require a careful balancing act. Advertisements showing a woman at the office may attract some customers but alienate stay-at-home mothers. Conversely, advertising that shows a woman cheerfully doing housework may be criticized by some for reinforcing old stereotypes.

Exhibit 4-5 A framework for analyzing the external environment.

1. **Competitive forces**
   a. Who are our major brand, product, generic, and total budget competitors? What are their characteristics in terms of size, growth, profitability, strategies, and target markets?
   b. What are our competitors' key strengths and weaknesses?
   c. What are our competitors' key marketing capabilities in terms of products, distribution, promotion, and pricing?
   d. What response can we expect from our competitors if environmental conditions change or if we change our marketing strategy?
   e. Is this competitive set likely to change in the future? If so, how? Who are our new competitors likely to be?
2. **Economic forces**
   a. What are the general economic conditions of the country, region, province, and local area in which our firm operates?
   b. Overall, are our customers optimistic or pessimistic about the economy?
   c. What is the buying power of customers in our target market(s)?
   d. What are the current spending patterns of customers in our target market(s)? Are customers buying less or more of our product and why?
3. **Political forces**
   a. Have recent elections changed the political landscape within our domestic or foreign markets? What type of industry regulations do newly elected officials favor?
   b. What are we currently doing to maintain good relations with elected political officials? Have these activities been effective? Why or why not?
4. **Legal and regulatory forces**
   a. What changes in international, federal, provincial, or local laws and regulations are being proposed that would affect our marketing activities?
   b. Do recent court decisions suggest that we should modify our marketing activities?
   c. Do the recent rulings of federal, provincial, local and self-regulatory agencies suggest that we should modify our marketing activities?
   d. What effect will changes in global trade agreements (e.g. NAFTA and WTO) have on our international marketing opportunities?
5. **Technological forces**
   a. What impact has changing technology had on our customers?
   b. What technological changes will affect the way we operate or manufacture our products?
   c. What technological changes will affect the way we conduct marketing activities, such as distribution or promotion?
   d. Are there any current technologies that we are not using to their fullest potential in making our marketing activities more effective and efficient?
   e. Do any technological advances threaten to make our product(s) obsolete? Does new technology have the potential to satisfy previously unmet or unknown customer needs?
6. **Sociocultural forces**
   a. How are society's demographics and values changing? What effect will these changes have on our product(s)? pricing? distribution? promotion? people?
   b. What problems or opportunities are being created by changes in the diversity of our customers and employees?
   c. What is the general attitude of society about our industry, company, and product(s)? Could we take actions to improve this attitude?
   d. What consumer or environmental groups could intervene in the operations of our industry or company?
   e. What ethical issues should we address?



Most changes in basic cultural values and social attitudes come slowly. An individual company can't hope to encourage big changes in the short run. Instead, it should identify current attitudes and work within these constraints as it seeks new and better opportunities.[34] Exhibit 4-5 provides a systematic approach to gathering the necessary information. By doing so, it directs corporate efforts at what might be called either *environmental monitoring* or *environmental scanning*. Most of the questions being asked require managers to focus on what's going on in the uncontrollable environment that's really important to the corporation and the product-markets it has targeted. However, we have not yet discussed customer buying power and spending patterns. These very important factors, ones that do in fact complete the environmental picture, are examined in detail in the next chapter.

## Evaluating Opportunities

In Chapter 3 we presented an overview of "strategic marketing planning" and the "marketing strategy planning process." As noted, these processes are designed to help narrow the list of opportunities a business *could* pursue to a smaller list of those it *should* pursue given its resources and objectives. In this section we look at a collection of tools that help you carry out that process and make use of the environmental information you collect.

### Screening

A progressive firm constantly looks for new opportunities. Usually, a firm can't pursue all available opportunities, so it helps to screen out obvious mismatches so other opportunities can be analyzed more carefully.

After you analyze the firm's resources (for strengths and weaknesses), the environmental trends the firm faces, and the objectives of top management, you merge them all into a set of product-market screening criteria. These criteria should include both quantitative and qualitative components. The quantitative components summarize the firm's objectives: sales, profit, and return on investment (ROI) targets. (Note: ROI analysis is discussed briefly in Appendix B.) The qualitative components summarize what kinds of businesses the firm wants to be in, what businesses it wants to exclude, what weaknesses it should avoid, and what resources (strengths) and trends it should build on.[35]

Screening criteria summarize in one place what the firm wants to accomplish—in quantitative terms—as well as roughly how and where it wants to accomplish it. Developing screening criteria is difficult. When a manager can explain the specific criteria that are relevant to selecting (or screening out) an opportunity, others can understand the manager's logic. Thus, marketing decisions are not just made or accepted based on intuition and gut feel. On the other hand, if the criteria are constantly changing when the focus moves from one opportunity to another then the decision making is not consistent. Finally, the criteria should be realistic—that is, they should be achievable. Opportunities that pass the screening process should be able to be turned into strategies that the firm can implement with the resources it has. Exhibit 4-6 shows some product-market screening criteria for a small retail and wholesale distributor.

In order to "grade" each alternative on the criteria, you will need to forecast the probable results of implementing a marketing strategy. That is, you will need to estimate expected results on measures like sales, profits, and return on investment (ROI). For a rough screening, you need to estimate only the likely results of implementing each opportunity over a logical planning period. If a product's life is likely to be three years, for example, a good strategy may not produce profitable results for 6 to 12 months. But evaluated over the projected three-year life, the product may look like a winner. When evaluating the potential of possible opportunities (product-market strategies), it is important to evaluate similar things—that is, *whole* plans.

Opportunities that pass the screening criteria should be evaluated in more detail before being accepted as *the* product-market strategic plans for implementation. Usually, a firm has more opportunities than resources and has to choose among them to match its opportunities to its resources and objectives. The total-profit approach and ROI analysis can help firms select among possible plans.

**Total-profit approach** In this approach, management forecasts potential sales and costs during the life of the plan to estimate likely profitability. Managers may evaluate the prospects for each plan over a five-year planning period, using monthly and/or annual sales and cost estimates. This is shown graphically in Exhibit 4-7.

Note that managers can evaluate different marketing plans at the same time.

Exhibit 4-6 An example of product-market screening criteria for a small retail and wholesale distributor ($10 million annual sales).

1. **Quantitative criteria**
   a. Increase sales by $1,500,000 per year for the next five years.
   b. Earn ROI of at least 25 percent before taxes on new ventures.
   c. Break even within one year on new ventures.
   d. Opportunity must be large enough to justify interest (to help meet objectives) but small enough so company can handle with the resources available.
   e. Several opportunities should be pursued to reach the objectives—to spread the risks.
2. **Qualitative criteria**
   a. Nature of business preferred.
      (1) Should take advantage of our online Internet order system and website promotion.
      (2) New goods and services for present customers to strengthen relationships and revenue.
      (3) "Quality" products that do not cannibalize sales of current products.
      (4) Competition should be weak and opportunity should be hard to copy for several years.
      (5) There should be strongly felt (even unsatisfied) needs—to reduce promotion costs and permit "high" prices.
   b. Constraints.
      (1) Nature of businesses to exclude.
         (a) Manufacturing.
         (b) Any requiring large fixed capital investments.
         (c) Any requiring many support people who must be "good" all the time and would require much supervision.
      (2) Geographic.
         (a) United States, Mexico, and Canada only.
      (3) General.
         (a) Make use of current strengths.
         (b) Attractiveness of market should be reinforced by more than one of the following basic trends: technological, demographic, social, economic, political.
         (c) Market should not be bucking any basic trends.



Exhibit 4-7 compares a much-improved product and product concept (Product A) with a "me-too" product (Product B) for the same target market. In the short run, the me-too product will make a profit sooner and might look like the better choice—if managers consider only one year's results. The improved product, on the other hand, will take a good deal of pioneering, but over its five-year life will be much more profitable.

**ROI analysis** Besides evaluating the profit potential of possible plans, firms may also calculate the return on investment (ROI) of resources needed to implement plans. One plan may require a heavy investment in advertising and channel development, for example, while another relies primarily on lower price.

ROI analyses can be useful for selecting among possible plans because equally profitable plans may require vastly different resources and offer different rates of return on investment. Some firms are very concerned with ROI, especially those that borrow money for working capital. There is little point in borrowing to implement strategies that won't return enough to meet the cost of borrowing.

Exhibit 4-7
Expected sales and cost curves of two strategies over five-year planning periods.

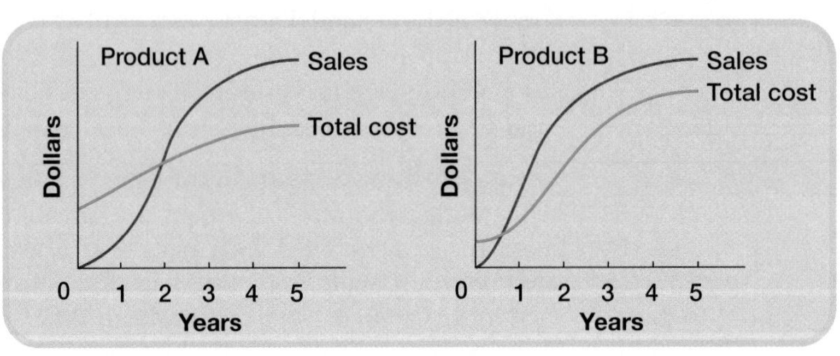

Exhibit 4-8
Strategic planning grid for General Electric.

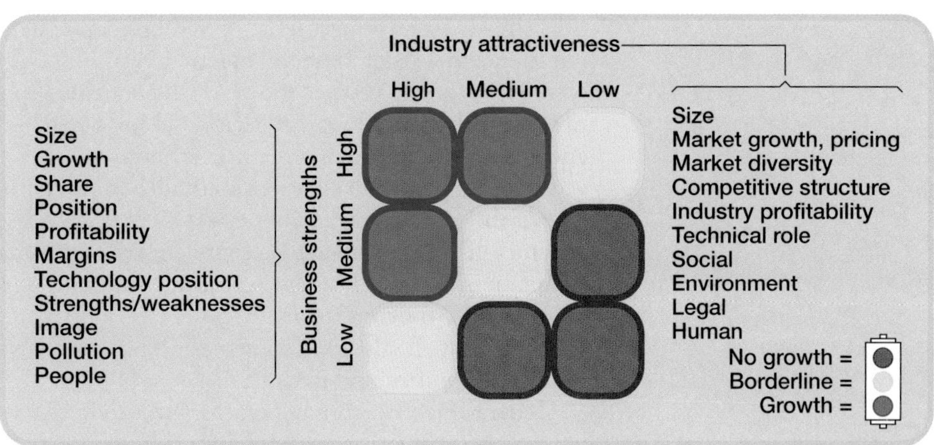


## Strategic-Planning Grids

When a firm has many possibilities to evaluate, it usually has to compare quite different ones. This problem is easier to handle with graphical approaches—such as the nine-box strategic planning grid developed by General Electric and used by many other companies. Such grids can help evaluate a firm's whole portfolio of strategic plans or businesses.

General Electric's strategic planning grid—see Exhibit 4-8—forces company managers to make three-part judgments (high, medium, and low) about the business strengths and industry attractiveness of all proposed or existing product-market plans. As you can see from Exhibit 4-8, this approach helps a manager organize information about the company's marketing environments (discussed earlier in this chapter) along with information about its strategy and translate it into relevant screening criteria.

The industry attractiveness dimension helps managers answer questions like: How profitable would an "average" firm competing in the product-market be? Does this product-market plan look like a good idea? Are there any factors tied to the competitive, economic, political, and other environments that will create downward pressure on profits? To answer that question, managers have to judge such factors (screening criteria) as the size of the market and its growth rate, the nature of competition, the plan's potential environmental or social impact, and how laws might affect it.

Note that an opportunity may be attractive for *some* company—but not well suited to the strengths (and weaknesses) of a particular firm. This is why we presented industry attractiveness as representing the prospects for an "average" firm. This is also why the GE grid requires an assessment of the opportunity on a second dimension: business (or competitive) strengths.

The business-strengths dimension focuses on the ability of the company to pursue a product-market plan effectively. To make judgments along this dimension, a manager evaluates whether the firm has people with the right talents and skills to implement the plan, whether the plan is consistent with the firm's image and profit objectives, and whether the firm could establish a profitable market share given its technical capability, costs, and size. Here again, these factors suggest screening criteria specific to this firm and market situation.

In a sense, the business-strengths measure is an evaluation of whether the firm will perform above, below, or the same as an "average" firm in that product-market. Thus, opportunities that fall into the green boxes in the upper-left corner of the grid are its best growth opportunities: the average firm will have strong profits, and this business will perform even higher than that! The red boxes in the lower-right corner of the grid, on the other hand, suggest a no-growth policy: average profits in these product-markets will be low and the business is expected to perform below that already low average. Existing red businesses may continue to generate earnings, but they no longer deserve much investment. Yellow businesses are borderline cases—they can go either way. GE may continue to support an existing yellow business but will probably reject a proposal for a new one. It simply wouldn't look good enough on the relevant screening criteria.

GE's "stoplight" evaluation method is a subjective, multiple-factor approach. It avoids the traps and possible errors of trying to use oversimplified, single-number criteria—like ROI or market share. Instead, top managers review detailed written summaries of many different screening criteria that help them make summary judgments; then, they can make a collective judgment. This approach generally leads to agreement. It also helps everyone understand why the company supports some new opportunities and not others.[36]

General Electric considers factors that reflect its objectives. Another firm might modify the evaluation to emphasize other factors—depending on its objectives and the type of product-market plans it is considering. While different firms focus on different screening criteria, using many factors helps ensure that managers consider all of the company's concerns when evaluating alternative opportunities.

## Multiproduct Firms Have a Difficult Strategy Planning Job

Multiproduct firms, like General Electric, obviously have a more difficult strategic planning job than firms with only a few products or product lines aimed at the same or similar target markets. Multiproduct firms have to develop strategic plans for very different businesses, and they have to balance plans and resources so the whole company reaches its objectives. This means they must analyze alternatives using approaches similar to the General Electric strategic planning grid and approve only plans that make sense for the whole company—even if it means getting needed resources by milking some businesses and eliminating others.

Details on how to manage a complicated multiproduct firm are beyond our scope. But to appreciate the challenge, consider the following scenario. Your parents have a limited amount of money available to help pay for your university tuition. You and your twin brother are about to graduate from high school and could both use the money. How should it be divided? In this situation, most would say evenly. But what if you plan on eventually doing a graduate degree, while your brother is more interested in sampling the social scene? Would you, the more studious twin, be more entitled? Could your parents justify financing your tuition at the expense of that of



His great grandfather was a Honda Civic.

Can it be possible for a robot to inherit style? Power? Intelligence? Assuming the robot is the revolutionary new Honda P3, the reply is "yes." After all, Mr. P3 comes from a long line of Honda products which share those traits. With a design based on extensive knowledge of human movement, P3 walks, climbs stairs and turns corners with ease. He carries loads. He pushes carts. He makes U-turns. All while maintaining a remarkable sense of balance and strength. P3 is merely one illustration of the many innovative ideas now taking shape at Honda. We're also hard at work on new technology for jet engines. Solar cars. Community-shared vehicles. Ideas that, like P3, are designed to work in harmony with humans. And, ultimately, will help us create new dimensions in mobility. So, in other words, it seems P3 is just like his great grandpa, after all.

HONDA
Thinking.

Large multiproduct firms, like Honda, evaluate and pursue a varied portfolio of strategic opportunities all around the world.

your brother the socialite? Would your socially inclined twin feel slighted if they did? This is precisely the challenge facing multiproduct firms.

**strategic business unit (SBU)**
An organizational unit (within a larger company) that focuses on some product-markets and is treated as a separate profit centre

One approach to managing this situation is to assign each opportunity to a **strategic business unit**. A strategic business unit (SBU) is an organizational unit (within a larger company) that focuses on some product-markets and is treated as a separate profit centre. By forming SBUs, a company formally acknowledges its very different activities. One SBU at Sara Lee, for example, produces baked goods for consumers and restaurants—another produces and markets Hanes brand T-shirts and underwear. Some SBUs grow rapidly and require a great deal of attention and resources. Others produce only average profits and should be *milked*—that is, allowed to generate cash for the businesses with more potential. Product lines with poor market position, low profits, and poor growth prospects should be dropped or sold.

**portfolio management**
Treats alternative products, divisions, or strategic business units (SBUs) as though they were stock investments, to be bought and sold using financial criteria

A slightly more sophisticated alternative is **portfolio management**—which treats alternative products, divisions, or strategic business units (SBUs) as though they were stock investments, to be bought and sold using financial criteria. Such managers make trade-offs among very different opportunities. They treat the various alternatives as investments that should be supported, milked, or sold off depending on profitability and return on investment (ROI). In effect, they evaluate each alternative just like a stock-market trader evaluates a stock.[37]

This approach makes some sense if alternatives are really quite different. Top managers often believe they can't become very familiar with the prospects for all of their alternatives, so they fall back on the easy-to-compare quantitative criteria. And, because the short run is much clearer than the long run, they place heavy emphasis on *current* profitability and return on investment. This puts great pressure on the operating managers to deliver *in the short run*—perhaps even neglecting the long run.

Neglecting the long run is risky—and this is the main weakness of the portfolio approach. This weakness can be overcome by enhancing the portfolio-management approach with market-oriented strategic plans. They make it possible for managers to more accurately evaluate the alternatives' short-run and long-run prospects.

## Evaluating Opportunities in International Markets

The approaches we've discussed so far apply to international markets just as they do to domestic ones. But in international markets it is often harder to fully understand the marketing-environment variables. This may make it harder to see the risks involved in particular opportunities. Some countries are politically unstable; their governments and constitutions come and go. An investment that is safe under one government might become a takeover target under another. Further, the possibility of foreign-exchange controls—and tax-rate changes—can reduce the chance of getting profits and capital back to the home country.

To reduce the risk of missing some basic variable that may help screen out a risky opportunity, marketing managers sometimes need a detailed analysis of the market environment they are considering entering. Such an analysis can reveal facts about an unfamiliar market that a manager in a distant country might otherwise overlook. Further, a local citizen who knows the marketing environment may be able to identify an "obvious" problem ignored even in a careful analysis. Thus, it is very useful for the analysis to include inputs from locals—perhaps cooperative intermediaries.[38]

The farther you go from familiar territory, the greater the risk of making big mistakes. But not all products, or marketing mixes, involve the same risk. Think of the risks as running along a "continuum of environmental sensitivity"; see Exhibit 4-9.

Some products are relatively insensitive to the economic and cultural environment they're placed in. These products may be accepted as-is—or they may require just a little adaptation to make them suitable for local use. Most industrial products are near the insensitive end of this continuum.

Exhibit 4-9
Continuum of environmental sensitivity.

| Insensitive | | Sensitive |
|---|---|---|
| Industrial products | Basic commodity-type consumer products | Consumer products that are linked to cultural variables |

At the other end of the continuum, we find highly sensitive products that may be difficult or impossible to adapt to all international situations. Consumer products closely linked to other social or cultural variables are at this end. For example, some of the scanty women's clothing popular in Western countries would be totally inappropriate in Arab countries where women are expected to cover even their faces. Similarly, some cultures view dieting as unhealthy; this explains why products like Diet Pepsi that are popular in the United States and Canada have done poorly there. "Faddy" type consumer products are also at this end of the continuum. It's sometimes difficult to understand why such products are well accepted in a home market. This, in turn, makes it even more difficult to predict how they might be received in a different environment.

This continuum helps explain why many of the early successes in international marketing were basic commodities such as gasoline, soap, transportation vehicles, mining equipment, and agricultural machinery. It also helps explain why some consumer-products firms have been successful with basically the same promotion and products in different parts of the globe.

Yet some managers don't understand the reason for these successes. They think they can develop a global marketing mix for just about *any* product. They fail to see that firms producing and/or selling products near the sensitive end of the continuum should carefully analyze how their products will be seen and used in new environments—and plan their strategies accordingly.[39]

If the risks of an international opportunity are hard to judge, it may be wise to look first for opportunities that involve exporting. This gives managers a chance to build experience, know-how, and confidence over time. Then the firm will be in a better position to judge the prospects and risks of taking further steps.



## Chapter Summary

Businesses need innovative strategy planning to survive in our increasingly competitive markets. In this chapter, we discussed the variables that shape the environment of marketing strategy planning and how they may affect opportunities. First, we looked at how the firm's own resources and objectives may help guide or limit the search for opportunities. We went on to look at the need to understand competition and how to do a competitive analysis. Then, we shifted our focus to the external market environments. They are important because changes in these environments present new opportunities, as well as problems that a marketing manager must deal with in marketing strategy planning.

The economic environment—including chances of recessions or inflation—also affects the choice of strategies. And the marketer must try to anticipate, understand, and deal with these changes—as well as changes in the technology underlying the economic environment.

The marketing manager must also be aware of legal restrictions and be sensitive to changing political climates. The acceptance of consumerism has already forced many changes.

The cultural and social environment affects how people behave and what marketing strategies will be successful.

Developing good marketing strategies within all these environments isn't easy. You can see that marketing management is a challenging job that requires integration of information from many disciplines.

Eventually, managers need procedures for screening

and evaluating opportunities. We explained an approach for developing qualitative and quantitative screening criteria—from an analysis of the strengths and weaknesses of the company's resources, the environmental trends it faces, and top management's objectives. We also discussed ways for evaluating and managing quite different opportunities—using the GE strategic planning grid, SBUs, and portfolio management.

In the rest of the book, we turn our attention to a discussion of how to turn opportunities into profitable marketing plans and programs.

## Key Concepts

competitive barriers, p. 89
competitive environment, p. 85
competitive rivals, p. 88
competitor analysis, p. 88
consumerism, p. 97
cultural and social environment, p. 102
economic and technological environment, p. 92
exchange rate, p. 93
legal environment, p. 99
mission statement, p. 82
political environment, p. 96
portfolio management, p. 109
strategic business units, p. 109

## Questions and Problems

1. Do you think it makes sense for a firm to base its mission statement on the type of product it produces? For example, would it be good for a division that produces electric motors to have as its mission: "We want to make the best (from our customers' point of view) electric motors available anywhere in the world"?
2. Explain how a firm's objectives may affect its search for opportunities.
3. Specifically, how would various company objectives affect the development of a marketing mix for a new type of Internet browser software? If this company were just being formed by a former programmer with limited financial resources, list the objectives the programmer might have. Then discuss how they would affect the development of the programmer's marketing strategy.
4. Explain how a firm's resources may limit its search for opportunities. Cite a specific example for a specific resource.
5. Discuss how a company's financial strength may have a bearing on the kinds of products it produces. Will it have an impact on the other three Ps as well? If so, how? Use an example in your answer.
6. In your own words, explain how a marketing manager might use a competitor analysis to avoid situations that involve head-on competition.
7. The owner of a small hardware store—the only one in a medium-sized town in the mountains—has just learned that a large home-improvement chain plans to open a new store nearby. How difficult will it be for the owner to plan for this new competitive threat? Explain your answer.
8. Discuss the probable impact on your hometown if a major breakthrough in air transportation allowed foreign producers to ship into any Canadian market for about the same transportation cost that domestic producers incur.
9. Will the elimination of trade barriers between countries in Europe eliminate the need to consider submarkets of European consumers? Why or why not?
10. Which way does the Canadian political and legal environment seem to be moving with respect to business-related affairs?
11. Why is it necessary to have so many laws regulating business? Why hasn't Parliament just passed one set of laws to take care of business problems?
12. What and whom is the Canadian government attempting to protect in its effort to preserve and regulate competition?
13. Are consumer protection laws really new? Discuss the evolution of consumer protection. Is more such legislation likely?
14. Explain the components of product-market screening criteria that can be used to evaluate opportunities.
15. Explain the differences between the total-profit approach and the return-on-investment approach to evaluating alternative plans.

16. Explain General Electric's strategic planning grid approach to evaluating opportunities.

17. Distinguish between the operation of a strategic business unit and a firm that only pays lip service to adopting the marketing concept.

## Computer-Aided Problem 4

### Competitor Analysis

Mediquip, Inc. produces medical equipment and uses its own salesforce to sell the equipment to hospitals. Recently, several hospitals have asked Mediquip to develop a laser-beam "scalpel" for eye surgery. Mediquip has the needed resources, and 200 hospitals will probably buy the equipment. But Mediquip managers have heard that Laser Technologies—another quality producer—is thinking of competing for the same business. Mediquip has other good opportunities it could pursue, so it wants to see if it would have a competitive advantage over Laser Tech.

Mediquip and Laser Tech are similar in many ways, but there are important differences. Laser Technologies already produces key parts that are needed for the new laser product, so its production costs would be lower. It would cost Mediquip more to design the product—and getting parts from outside suppliers would result in higher production costs.

On the other hand, Mediquip has marketing strengths. It already has a good reputation with hospitals—and its salesforce calls on only hospitals. Mediquip thinks that each of its current sales reps could spend some time selling the new product and that it could adjust sales territories so only four more sales reps would be needed for good coverage in the market. In contrast, Laser Tech's sales reps call on only industrial customers, so it would have to add 14 reps to cover the hospitals.

Hospitals have budget pressures—so the supplier with the lowest price is likely to get a larger share of the business. But Mediquip knows that either supplier's price will be set high enough to cover the added costs of designing, producing, and selling the new product, and leave something for profit.

Mediquip gathers information about its own likely costs and can estimate Laser Tech's costs from industry studies and Laser Tech's annual report. Mediquip has set up a spreadsheet to evaluate the proposed new product.

a. *The initial spreadsheet results are based on the assumption that Mediquip and Laser Tech will split the business 50/50. If Mediquip can win at least 50 percent of the market, does Mediquip have a competitive advantage over Laser Tech? Explain.*

b. *Because of economies of scale, both suppliers' average cost per machine will vary depending on the quantity sold. If Mediquip had only 45 percent of the market and Laser Tech 55 percent, how would their costs (average total cost per machine) compare? What if Mediquip had 55 percent of the market and Laser Tech only 45 percent? What conclusion do you draw from these analyses?*

c. *It is possible that Laser Tech may not enter the market. If Mediquip has 100 percent of the market, and quantity purchases from its suppliers will reduce the cost of producing one unit to $6,500, what price would cover all its costs and contribute $1,125 to profit for every machine sold? What does this suggest about the desirability of finding your own unsatisfied target markets? Explain.*

## Suggested Cases

To view the cases, go to www.mcgrawhill.ca/college/wong.

Interested in finding out what marketing looks like in the real world? *Marketing Magazine* is just a click away on your OLC! Visit www.mcgrawhill.ca/college/wong today.

# Chapter Five

# Demographic Dimensions of Canadian and Global Consumer Markets

When You Finish This Chapter, You Should

1. Know about population and income trends in global markets and how they affect marketers.

2. Understand how population growth is shifting in different areas and for different age groups.

3. Know about the distribution of income in Canada.

4. Know how consumer spending is related to family life cycle and other demographic dimensions.

5. Know why ethnic markets are important—and why increasingly they are the focus of multicultural marketing strategies.

## Building Better Relationships

One of the first things you notice about the Rona Home and Garden Warehouse on Grandview Highway in East Vancouver are the large blue banners with the Chinese characters. They hang directly under the English signs that announce the products in each aisle. Walk a bit further and you'll see pictures of paint cans, tiles, and toilets; you might even notice that there is an unusual amount of product displayed throughout.

The big box hardware store opened in May 1996. At the time it was owned by Revy, a Western Canadian chain, but, since its purchase by the

place

price

promotion

prod

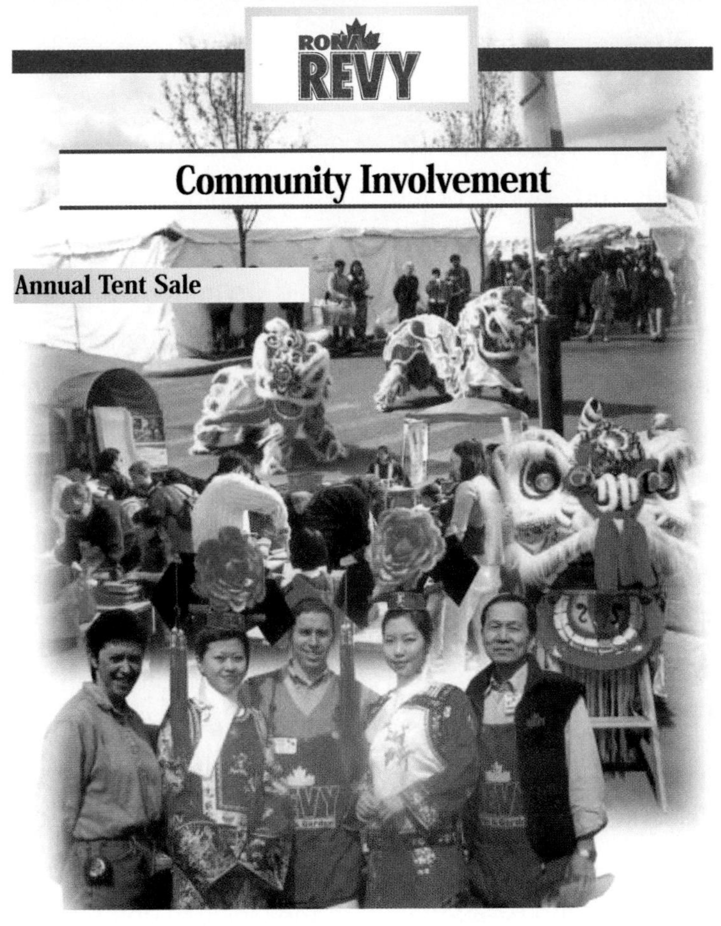


Boucherville, Que.–based Rona two years ago, it has gradually morphed from Revy to Rona-Revy to plain Rona.

But, back to 1996. Russ Jones, a 17-year veteran of Revy, was put in charge as store manager. Sales were slow, the store was underperforming and Jones took a careful look at his neighbourhood. Statistics Canada figures bore out what he saw: 40 percent of his customers were Asian. "We are just a few minutes away from Commercial Drive, which is pretty much the melting pot of Canada," he says. "It is the most multi-diverse ethnic background neighbourhood in Canada."

Jones quickly decided a cookie-cutter approach to selling hardware wasn't going to cut it. He recruited locally and pretty soon had a staff that could handle 27 different languages and dialects.

"We hired the people in the community who reflected the community, and that's been the most successful thing we've done," he says. "We really promote to our employees that you speak in whatever language our customer is comfortable in." The store also offers a translation service: "If you walk up to an employee in aisle six and you don't speak English, we will call a translator for you."

Jones and Bou Yeap, who is now in charge of commercial and export sales, and who speaks eight different Asian dialects, began interviewing customers at the cash registers. They were looking for Asian homeowners who lived in the neighbourhood and were willing to participate in focus groups. "We asked them a number of questions: 'What's important to you as a customer? Are you aware that we do translation services? What products would you like to see us carry that we don't carry?' All questions relating to how do we get more of your business."

What he found was that Asians shop differently. The older, more traditional Chinese couldn't read the boxes; so they'd tear them open.

"We've stepped up the way we merchandise products in the store and we've put a lot more products out on display," he says. "We've got 50,000 items here and it's very challenging to put one of everything on display."

Jones also found that Asian customers wanted different products. The Grandview store is possibly the only big box that carries clothesline poles for hanging out laundry. High-end range hoods designed for wok cooking also fly off the shelves.

Jones says the focus groups had other surprises. Asians liked the Chinese signs at the end of each aisle, but didn't want any more. "It was really strongly suggested by them not to do overkill with the Chinese; they felt that it could have a negative connotation." Jones instead settled on pictures, figuring it would also benefit the many other nationalities in the area.

On a national level, Rona recently launched a $60-million marketing campaign created by BCP in Montreal. The campaign aims to make the still little-recognized Rona brand better known in English Canada after its acquisition binge, which has included the purchase of Cashway three years ago, the 2001 acquisition of the Revy, Revelstoke and Lansing banners, and now the April purchase of the British-owned Réno-Dépôt.

Mark Hindman, the Toronto-based director of marketing for Rona, says there has been advertising in Chinese, Portuguese and Italian on ethnic radio stations in the Greater Toronto Area and there are plans to add television this year. Hindman says they take the English scripts and translate them. "We don't do a different strategy; we'd be all over the place," he says. "We are trying to figure out whether to convert the (national) campaign over to television or do something new. Maybe there's a news broadcast and we say 'Brought to you by Rona.' Maybe we do more endorsements or sponsorships."

Hindman says they've done live radio broadcasting in Italian from the Woodbridge store and multicultural station OMNI 1 was involved in a store opening in Mississauga. "It is effective. People understand we're not trying to be one-size-fits-all, that we are trying to talk to other communities," he says.

Though the Grandview Rona does run some print advertising in local Chinese-language papers such as the *World Journal* and *Sing Tao*, Jones finds Asians do business largely through word of mouth and networking. So Jones and Yeap are involved in the Chinese community, the store celebrates Chinese New Year, and for the past two years they have held a tent event in the parking lot that welcomes local businesses and serves up plenty of Asian-style food, bubble tea and entertainment.

The focus on the Asian customers has helped to turn around lacklustre sales, and while Jones won't give sales figures, he does say that the numbers have translated into "multiple years of double-digit growth." The store also now not only serves the local Asian population, but draws in customers as far away as

Richmond and the southern corridor of Vancouver.

In March, the Grandview store won an outstanding retailer award from *Hardware Merchandising* magazine in Toronto (which, like *Marketing*, is owned by Rogers Publishing). Robert Gerlsbeck, editor, says the judges were impressed by the rebound in sales in the late '90s in an otherwise tough economy. Gerlsbeck says they were also impressed with the commercial and export sales side of the business that has been growing steadily since 1999.

"I've never heard of a big box doing export; it's very unusual," he says. "Big boxes are trying to drive as many homeowners through their stores as possible, and in most cases big box stores, as a fluke, are very happy if some contractors come in." The commercial and export sales business Gerlsbeck refers to sprang from the knowledge Jones and Yeap discovered about their Asian customers. They found that while the majority of Asians were Chinese, there was a big demand in Japan and Korea for North American–style housing in rural areas. "Some of our customers were buying in larger quantities, and as we got to know them we found that some were shipping to Japan and China," says Jones. "We'll package up a whole house and send it over there, right down to the flooring and the light and plumbing fixtures."

The store now has an on-site facility that handles containers for export, with a dedicated sales team led by Yeap. Sales are now 5 percent of gross and climbing.

Jones may be store manager, but he says he also is given a lot of autonomy and support from the company. "We are the only store in the company that has Chinese banners," he says. "We requested these items and they brought them in for us. They want to help us achieve success. If I owned this operation, this is what I would do to get the business."[1]



## In This Chapter

This chapter looks at the demographics of the global and Canadian marketplace—who lives where, how they live, and how much they earn and spend. We'll discuss the current situation and draw your attention to some of the most important trends shaping customer behaviour. We'll also consider some patterns of spending across different demographic groups. And because Canada is one of the most ethnically diverse nations in the world, we'll also look in more depth at the impact of ethnic origins on buyer behaviour.

Since people can't buy what they can't hear about and find, this chapter will help you learn where to focus your marketing efforts in order to reach as many people in your target market as possible—and, once you do, you'll know a little more about how to build relationships with them.

## Why Study Demographics?

As shown in the opening vignette, target marketers believe that the *customer* should be the focus of all business and marketing activity. They develop unique marketing strategies by finding unsatisfied customers and offering them superior value with more attractive marketing mixes. They want to work in less-competitive markets and, in order to make differentiation easier to achieve, they want to find those customers who are willing to pay a higher price to get higher quality or more features. But finding these attractive opportunities takes real knowledge of potential customers and what they want. This means finding those market dimensions that make a difference—in terms of population, income, needs, attitudes, and buying behaviour.

Marketers need to answer three important questions about any potential market:

1. What are its relevant segmenting dimensions?
2. How big is it?
3. Where is it?

**demographics**
Information and trends about the size, location, and characteristics of target markets

Finding an answer to the first question requires management judgment, perhaps aided by analysis of existing data and new findings from marketing research. To help build your judgment regarding buying behaviour, this chapter and the next two will discuss what we know about various kinds of customers and their buying behaviour. In this chapter we focus on **demographics**—information and trends about the size, location, and characteristics of target markets. Keep in mind that we aren't trying to make generalizations about average customers or how the mass market behaves—but rather how *some* people in *some* markets behave. You should expect to find differences: in fact, if you find yourself saying "not everyone is that way" then you are well on the way to becoming a first-class marketer.

## The Global Market

A potential customer is someone with not only a willingness but also an ability to spend. So it makes sense to start with a broad view of how population, income, and

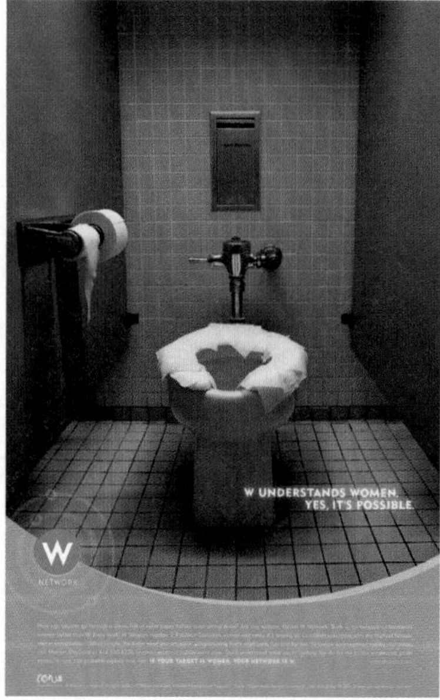


An often-used demographic distinction is gender. Sometimes, ads targeted at one gender might not make much sense to the other.

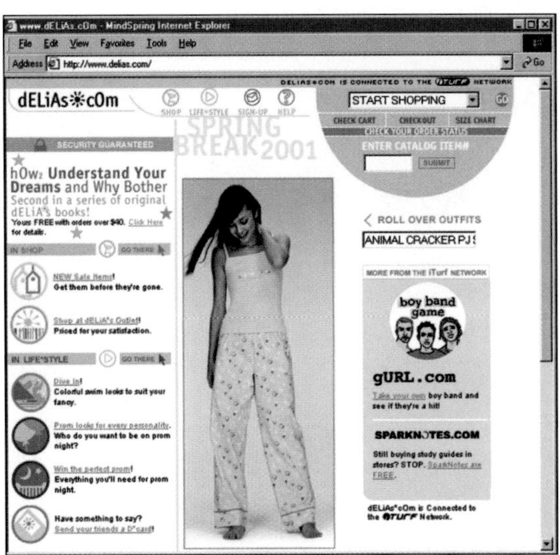

Marketers who are interested in the rapidly growing teen market often find that teens have many common interests, values, and needs—whether they are shopping online or in-store.

other key demographic dimensions vary for different countries around the world. This will help you see why so many firms pursue opportunities in international markets. And our examples will illustrate why companies must be careful in targeting which international markets to enter.

### Which Markets Are Growing?

Crowded Canadian cities like Toronto or Vancouver may seem to offer great potential, but Canada's population makes up far less than 1 percent of the total world population—which is now more than 6 billion. This means that a firm could "own" the entire Canadian marketplace and still be half the size of a firm that sells to only 2 percent of the global market! It is no small wonder that Canadian firms attach so much importance to export sales. But it isn't enough to know "there is a big world out there." That much is obvious. We need to know *where* those 6 billion people live and, equally important, whether there are any significant trends in their geographic distribution.

Thirty years ago, global population growth was more than 2 percent per year. Now it's down to just 1.3 percent. But these are averages for all countries. Some are growing faster than this, while others show a much lower rate of increase. Exhibit 5-1 summarizes current data for representative countries from different regions around the world.

In general, less-developed countries experience the fastest rate of growth. India (with a population of more than 1 billion) and China (with a population of almost 1.3 billion) are getting even larger. You can see why so many firms from all over the world want to reach consumers in these countries now that trade barriers are relaxing. The populations of Pakistan, Nicaragua, Nigeria, and Saudi Arabia are expected to double in 25 years or fewer. It will take about seven times as long for the population of Canada to double, and population growth is even slower in Japan and the European countries.[2]

However, these numbers can be misleading. The population in some countries is spread over a very large area. Population density is important to marketers. If the population is very spread out, as it is in Canada or many of the African countries, it is difficult and expensive for marketers to adjust time and place discrepancies between producers and consumers. This is especially a problem in countries without efficient highway and rail systems. Similarly, a widely spread population may make promotion more difficult, especially if there are language differences or communication systems are poor. Of course, even in countries with low population density, like Canada, major cities may be packed with people.

**Exhibit 5-1** Demographic dimensions for representative countries.

| Country | 2000 Population (000s) | 1990–2000 Annual Percent Population Growth | 2000 Years for Population to Double | 2000 Population Density (people/square mile) | 1999 Percent of Population in Urban Areas | 1999 GNP (millions of $U.S.) | 1999 GNP per Capita | 1999 GDP (millions of $U.S.) | 1999 Illiteracy Percent |
|---|---|---|---|---|---|---|---|---|---|
| Algeria | 31,194 | 2.1 | 29 | 34 | 60 | 46,455 | 1,550 | 47,015 | 33 |
| Argentina | 36,955 | 1.2 | 62 | 35 | 90 | 277,882 | 7,600 | 281,942 | 3 |
| Australia | 19,165 | 1.2 | 110 | 6 | 85 | 380,791 | 20,050 | 389,691 | 0 |
| Bangladesh | 129,194 | 1.6 | 38 | 2,305 | 24 | 46,960 | 370 | 45,779 | 59 |
| Brazil | 172,860 | 1.3 | 45 | 52 | 81 | 742,819 | 4,420 | 760,345 | 15 |
| Cameroon | 15,422 | 2.7 | 27 | 84 | 48 | 8,509 | 580 | 8,781 | 25 |
| Canada | 31,278 | 1.2 | 178 | 8 | 77 | 591,354 | 19,320 | 612,049 | 0 |
| Chile | 15,154 | 1.4 | 54 | 52 | 85 | 71,145 | 4,740 | 71,093 | 4 |
| China | 1,261,832 | 1.0 | 79 | 342 | 32 | 980,246 | 780 | 991,203 | 17 |
| Colombia | 39,686 | 1.9 | 34 | 91 | 73 | 93,558 | 2,250 | 88,596 | 9 |
| Croatia | 4,282 | −0.5 | no | 211 | 57 | 20,932 | 4,650 | 21,752 | 2 |
| Cuba | 11,142 | 0.6 | 103 | 260 | 75 | — | — | — | 3 |
| Ecuador | 12,920 | 2.2 | 33 | 116 | 64 | 16,231 | 1,310 | 18,713 | 9 |
| Egypt | 68,360 | 2.0 | 35 | 177 | 45 | 87,530 | 1,400 | 92,413 | 45 |
| Ethiopia | 64,117 | 2.8 | 29 | 150 | 17 | 6,578 | 100 | 6,534 | 63 |
| Finland | 5,167 | 0.4 | 433 | 40 | 67 | 122,874 | 23,780 | 126,130 | 0 |
| France | 59,330 | 0.4 | 204 | 279 | 75 | 1,427,160 | 23,480 | 1,410,260 | 0 |
| Germany | 82,797 | 0.4 | no | 596 | 87 | 2,079,230 | 25,350 | 2,081,200 | 0 |
| Ghana | 19,534 | 2.4 | 29 | 212 | 38 | 7,396 | 390 | 7,606 | 30 |
| Greece | 10,602 | 0.4 | no | 208 | 60 | 124,010 | 11,770 | 123,934 | 3 |
| Haiti | 6,868 | 1.3 | 40 | 599 | 35 | 3,163 | 410 | 3,871 | 51 |
| Hungary | 10,139 | −0.2 | no | 279 | 64 | 46,810 | 4,650 | 48,355 | 1 |
| Iceland | 276 | 0.8 | 81 | 7 | 92 | 8,109 | 29,280 | 8,483 | 0 |
| India | 1,014,004 | 1.8 | 39 | 789 | 28 | 442,233 | 450 | 459,765 | 44 |
| Indonesia | 224,784 | 1.8 | 44 | 289 | 40 | 119,544 | 580 | 140,964 | 14 |
| Iran | 65,620 | 1.6 | 48 | 107 | 61 | 110,535 | 1,760 | 101,073 | 24 |
| Iraq | 22,676 | 2.2 | 25 | 137 | 74 | — | — | — | 45 |
| Ireland | 3,797 | 0.8 | 116 | 140 | 59 | 71,405 | 19,160 | 84,861 | 0 |
| Israel | 5,842 | 2.6 | 45 | 766 | 91 | 104,081 | 17,450 | 125,031 | 4 |
| Italy | 57,634 | 0.2 | no | 497 | 67 | 1,135,990 | 19,710 | 1,149,960 | 2 |
| Jamaica | 2,653 | 0.7 | 45 | 615 | 56 | 6,042 | 2,330 | 6,134 | 14 |
| Japan | 126,550 | 0.2 | 462 | 870 | 79 | 4,078,920 | 32,230 | 4,395,080 | 0 |
| Kenya | 30,340 | 2.4 | 33 | 135 | 32 | 10,601 | 360 | 10,603 | 19 |
| Kuwait | 1,974 | −0.8 | 32 | 318 | 97 | 32,270 | 19,020 | 29,572 | 18 |
| Libya | 5,115 | 2.1 | 28 | 8 | 87 | — | — | — | 21 |
| Madagascar | 15,506 | 3.0 | 24 | 66 | 29 | 3,716 | 250 | 3,733 | 34 |
| Malaysia | 21,793 | 2.2 | 34 | 183 | 57 | 77,278 | 3,400 | 74,634 | 13 |

| Country | 2000 Population (000s) | 1990–2000 Annual Percent Population Growth | 2000 Years for Population to Double | 2000 Population Density (people/ square mile) | 1999 Percent of Population in Urban Areas | 1999 GNP (millions of $U.S.) | 1999 GNP per Capita | 1999 GDP (millions of $U.S.) | 1999 Illiteracy Percent |
|---|---|---|---|---|---|---|---|---|---|
| Mexico | 100,350 | 1.7 | 36 | 132 | 74 | 428,794 | 4,400 | 474,951 | 9 |
| Morocco | 30,122 | 2.0 | 41 | 167 | 55 | 33,816 | 1,200 | 35,238 | 52 |
| Mozambique | 19,105 | 2.9 | 32 | 62 | 39 | 3,889 | 230 | 4,169 | 57 |
| Nepal | 24,702 | 2.5 | 28 | 421 | 12 | 5,091 | 220 | 4,904 | 60 |
| Netherlands | 15,892 | 0.6 | 193 | 1,010 | 89 | 384,325 | 24,320 | 384,766 | 0 |
| Nicaragua | 4,813 | 2.8 | 23 | 101 | 56 | 2,110 | 430 | 2,302 | 32 |
| Nigeria | 123,338 | 2.9 | 24 | 346 | 43 | 37,882 | 310 | 43,286 | 37 |
| North Korea | 21,688 | 0.8 | 48 | 466 | 60 | — | — | — | 1 |
| Norway | 4,481 | 0.5 | 217 | 36 | 75 | 146,430 | 32,880 | 145,449 | 0 |
| Pakistan | 141,554 | 2.2 | 25 | 490 | 36 | 63,971 | 470 | 59,880 | 55 |
| Panama | 2,808 | 1.6 | 41 | 98 | 56 | 8,624 | 3,070 | 9,606 | 8 |
| Peru | 27,013 | 2.1 | 32 | 55 | 72 | 60,319 | 2,390 | 57,318 | 10 |
| Philippines | 81,160 | 2.2 | 31 | 693 | 58 | 77,966 | 1,020 | 75,350 | 5 |
| Poland | 38,646 | 0.1 | no | 310 | 65 | 153,065 | 3,960 | 154,146 | 0 |
| Romania | 22,411 | −0.2 | no | 244 | 56 | 34,188 | 1,520 | 33,750 | 2 |
| Russia | 146,001 | −0.1 | no | 22 | 77 | 332,536 | 2,270 | 375,345 | 1 |
| Saudi Arabia | 22,024 | 3.3 | 23 | 26 | 85 | 143,361 | 6,910 | 128,892 | 24 |
| Singapore | 4,152 | 3.2 | 84 | 16,714 | 100 | 95,429 | 29,610 | 84,945 | 8 |
| Somalia | 7,253 | 0.8 | 24 | 29 | 27 | — | — | — | — |
| South Africa | 43,421 | 1.3 | 55 | 92 | 52 | 133,216 | 3,160 | 131,127 | 15 |
| South Korea | 47,471 | 1.0 | 82 | 1,234 | 81 | 397,910 | 8,490 | 406,940 | 2 |
| Spain | 39,997 | 0.2 | 6,931 | 202 | 77 | 551,560 | 14,000 | 562,245 | 2 |
| Sri Lanka | 19,239 | 1.1 | 60 | 757 | 23 | 15,176 | 810 | 15,707 | 9 |
| Sudan | 35,080 | 2.8 | 32 | 30 | 35 | 8,300 | 290 | 10,695 | 43 |
| Sweden | 8,873 | 0.4 | no | 51 | 83 | 221,764 | 25,040 | 226,388 | 0 |
| Switzerland | 7,262 | 0.6 | 315 | 448 | 68 | 273,061 | 38,350 | 260,299 | 0 |
| Syria | 16,306 | 2.7 | 25 | 231 | 54 | 15,172 | 970 | 19,380 | 26 |
| Tanzania | 35,306 | 3.0 | 24 | 97 | 32 | 8,027 | 240 | 8,777 | 25 |
| Thailand | 61,231 | 1.1 | 70 | 313 | 21 | 121,019 | 1,960 | 123,887 | 5 |
| Turkey | 65,667 | 1.6 | 46 | 218 | 74 | 186,289 | 2,900 | 188,374 | 15 |
| Uganda | 23,318 | 3.1 | 24 | 251 | 14 | 6,786 | 320 | 6,349 | 34 |
| Ukraine | 49,153 | −0.5 | no | 212 | 68 | 42,713 | 850 | 42,415 | 0 |
| United Kingdom | 59,508 | 0.3 | 546 | 632 | 89 | 1,338,080 | 22,640 | 1,373,610 | 0 |
| United States | 281,422 | 1.0 | 120 | 77 | 77 | 8,350,960 | 30,600 | 8,708,870 | 0 |
| Venezuela | 23,543 | 2.0 | 34 | 69 | 87 | 86,963 | 3,670 | 103,918 | 8 |
| Vietnam | 78,774 | 1.7 | 48 | 615 | 20 | 28,157 | 370 | 28,567 | 7 |
| Zimbabwe | 11,343 | 1.2 | 69 | 75 | 35 | 6,131 | 520 | 5,716 | 12 |

In countries like the Philippines and Venezuela, where consumers have less purchasing power and shops are small, Colgate is gaining widespread acceptance by providing products in economical sizes.



The extent to which a country's population is clustered around urban areas varies significantly. In the United Kingdom, Argentina, Australia, Israel, and Singapore, for example, more than 85 percent of people live in urban areas (refer to Exhibit 5-1). By contrast, in Ethiopia, Nepal, and Uganda fewer than 17 percent of the people live in major urban areas. Nonetheless, there is a worldwide trend of people concentrated in major urban centres.

The worldwide trend toward urbanization has prompted increased interest in international markets. For many firms, the concentration of people in major cities simplifies place and promotion strategy decisions—especially for major cities in the wealthiest nations. Affluent, big-city consumers often have similar lifestyles and needs. Thus, many of the products successful in Toronto, New York, or Paris are likely to be successful in Caracas and Tokyo. The spread of the Internet, satellite TV, and other communication technologies will accelerate this trend.

### Which Markets Have Wealth?

Many of the world's consumers—whether crowded in cities or widely spread in rural areas—live in deplorable conditions. These people have little hope of escaping the crush of poverty. They certainly have needs—but they don't have the income to do anything about the needs. Profitable markets require income as well as people. The amount of money people can spend affects the products they are likely to buy. When considering international markets, income is often one of the most important demographic dimensions.

**gross national product (GNP)**
The total market value of goods and services produced by a country's economy in a year

**gross domestic product (GDP)**
The total market value of goods and services produced by a country's economy in a year, including foreign income

There are a variety of different measures of national income. One widely used measure is **gross national product (GNP)**—the total market value of goods and services produced by a country's economy in a year. **Gross domestic product (GDP)** is a similar measure that often is used to describe Canada's economy. The difference between the two measures is that GNP for a nation does not include income earned by foreigners who own resources in that nation; by contrast, the GDP does include foreign income. The measure you use can make a difference, especially when comparing countries with different patterns of international investment. For example, Bombardier has a factory in Germany. The GDP measure for Germany would include the profits from that factory because they were earned in that country. However, Bombardier is not a German firm, and most of its profit will ultimately flow out of Germany. Thus, the German GNP would not include those profits. You should see that using GDP income measures could give the impression that people in less-developed countries have more income than they really do. For that reason, we'll focus on comparisons that are based on GNP.

Exhibit 5-1 gives an estimate of GNP and GDP for each country listed. You can see that the more developed industrial nations—including the U.S., Japan, and Germany—have the biggest share of the world's GNP. This is why so much trade takes place among these countries—and why many firms see them as the more important markets.[3]

But while GNP tells us about the income of a whole nation, it doesn't tell us about the income levels of individual consumers. Countries with a large population spread their available income over more people. GNP per person is a useful figure because it gives some idea of the income level of people in a country. Exhibit 5-1 shows, for example, that GNP per capita in Canada is fairly high—about US$19,320. The U.S., Japan, Norway, Switzerland, and Singapore are among those countries with the highest GNP per capita. In general, markets like these offer the best potential for products that are targeted at consumers with higher income levels.

This does not mean that one should ignore countries with low GNP per capita. Many managers see great potential—and less competition—where GNP per capita is low. These people have needs, and many are eager to improve themselves. But they may not be able to raise their living standards without outside help. This presents a challenge and an opportunity to the developed nations—and to their business firms. Some companies are trying to help the people of less-developed countries. Corporations such as Pillsbury, Monsanto, and Coca-Cola have developed nutritious foods that can be sold cheaply—but still profitably—in poorer countries.[4]

The large number of countries with low GNP per capita is a stark reminder that much of the world's population lives in extreme poverty. Even among countries with the largest overall GNPs you see some sign of this. In India, for example, GNP per person is only $450 a year. Many countries are in the early stages of economic development. Most of their people work on farms—and live barely within the money economy. At the extreme, in Ethiopia GNP per person per year is only about US$100. To put this in perspective, 60 percent of the world's population—in 61 countries—receive only 6 percent of the world's total income, or about $2 a day. See Ethical Dimensions 5-1 for more on marketing to third-world consumers.

## WHAT DO THIRD-WORLD CONSUMERS REALLY NEED?

Marketing managers from developed nations sometimes face an ethical dilemma about whether their products help or hurt consumers in less-developed nations. For example, a United Nations report criticized Coke and Pepsi for expanding their soft-drink sales in the Philippines. The study concluded that consumers had shifted to soft drinks from local beverages—such as a mixture of lime juice and coconut water—that provided needed vitamins.

In another much publicized case, producers of infant formula were criticized for giving free samples to hospitals. Nestlé and other big suppliers in this market say that they gave the free samples only to children who were in need—and at the request of the hospitals. But critics argued that the practice encouraged new mothers to give up breastfeeding. Away from the hospital, mothers would rely on unsanitary water supplies. Such improper use of the formula could lead to malnutrition and other illnesses. So, Nestlé and the others pledged to stop giving away free samples. Although that step stopped some misuse, now the formula is not available to many people who really need it. For example, more than a million babies have been infected with AIDS from breastfeeding. To help fight this staggering epidemic, Nestlé is willing to donate formula, but not unless the World Health Organization agrees that it is not a violation of its pledge. In cases like these, a marketing manager may need to weigh the benefits and risks of trying to serve Third World markets.

### How Literate Are These Markets?

The ability of a country's people to read and write has a direct influence on the development of its economy—and on marketing strategy planning. The degree of literacy affects the way information is delivered—which in marketing means promotion. Unfortunately, only about three-fourths of the world's population can read and write. Data on illiteracy rates are inexact, because different countries use different measures. Even so, you may be surprised by the high illiteracy rates for some of the countries in Exhibit 5-1.

Illiteracy sometimes causes difficulties with product labels and instructions, for which we normally use words. This was one issue in the infant formula conflict. In an even more extreme case, some producers of baby food found that consumers misinterpreted a baby's picture on their packages. Illiterate natives believed that the product was just that—a ground-up baby! Many companies meet this lack of literacy with instructions that use pictures, symbols, colours, and other nonverbal means of communication to reach the masses.

In a world of electronic commerce and communication, technological literacy must also be considered. Internet Insite 5-1 discusses how technological literacy impacts upon the global marketplace.

## Internet Insite 5–1

### THE INTERNET AND THE GLOBAL MARKETPLACE

Many Internet firms failed during 2000–01, causing some to wonder if the Internet was just a fad. One look at the number of people using the Internet and spending money online worldwide suggests that the Internet has already made great economic impact.

There were an estimated 655 million Internet users at the end of 2002. Internet usage in the previous year grew at 30 percent or higher in Asia, Latin America, and Europe, while North American usage growth during the year was about 10 percent. The United States has the largest number of Internet users, with China taking the second spot.[5]

In the U.S., nearly 64 percent of the population has Internet access, with the average age slightly above 46 years and an even male–female split.[6] In Canada, more than two-thirds of all households have Internet access, and online shopping in 2002 was estimated at well over $2 billion.[7] In the early years of the World Wide Web, the typical Internet user was a male in his 20s, with a university education and a technical or professional job. Now the Internet demographics in Canada, the U.S., and most other countries are starting to resemble the mainstream population. That means marketers can use the Internet to reach a cross-section of the population, from teens to retirees.

Internet users worldwide browse the Web for information, use e-mail and text messaging, shop online, and access news and entertainment. A study by the United Nations Conference on Trade and Development (UNCTAD) projects that 18 percent of all commerce by firms and individuals globally will be conducted via the Internet by 2006.

The growth of e-commerce in the developing world has been very slow, according to UNCTAD. The U.S. still accounts for about 46 percent of online commerce, but Europe and Japan are catching up fast. According to eMarketer, a research firm, worldwide business-to-business and business-to-consumer e-commerce in 2003 is expected to reach $1.4 trillion, and will hit a staggering $2.7 trillion by 2004.[8]

The total number of Internet users worldwide is increasing. The online demographics are starting to resemble the mainstream demographics in many countries. Commercial activity online is growing, although at a slower pace than what was predicted by research firms in the late 1990s. The Internet has already become an integral part of business activity, with more than 80 percent of small and medium-sized enterprise (SMEs) in Canada using the Internet.

Internet marketing is not just about selling products online; not all firms can sell products or services online, but even those who do not can use the Internet for marketing and communication as well as building stronger customer relationships. Not using the Internet effectively will be a competitive disadvantage. It is therefore surprising that many Canadian firms do not seem to have a strategy for using the Internet.[9] Those that do will leave the rest behind.

Go to: www.mcgrawhill.ca/college/wong
to apply this Insite in an exciting Internet exercise.

### Sources of Further Information

Marketers can learn a great deal about possible opportunities in different countries by studying available demographic data and trends. The examples we considered here give you a feel, but much more useful data are available. For example, the United Nations Statistics Division compiles demographic information from many international sources, much of it available for free on their website (http://unstats.un.org). *The World Factbook* is prepared by the Central Intelligence Agency (CIA) for the use of U.S. government officials, but it is available to everyone. It gives facts and statistics on each country in the world. This book can be accessed at the CIA's website (www.odci.gov/cia/publications/factbook). The World Bank publishes *The World Development Indicators*, another excellent source for statistics on individual countries. It is available at the World Bank's website (www.worldbank.org/data/wdi).

After finding some countries or regions of possible interest (and eliminating unattractive ones), much more segmenting may be required. To illustrate how useful demographic dimensions can be in this effort, we will consider specific characteristics of the Canadian market in some detail. For additional data on the Canadian market, go to the Statistics Canada website (www.statcan.ca). Similar ideas apply to other markets around the world.

## Population Trends in the Canadian Consumer Market

Canada is the world's second largest country by land area, some 36 times larger than the state of California, but our population is only 90 percent that of California. Toronto and Vancouver, two of our largest cities, are among the most ethnically diverse in North America and probably in the world: Toronto, with 44 percent of its population born on foreign soil, ranks higher in ethnic diversity than Miami, home to huge Cuban and Caribbean communities. In fact, when it comes to ethnic diversity, Toronto and Vancouver outdistance Sydney, Los Angeles, and New York, which are known for their large ethnic communities.

To say that Canada has an interesting, if not unique, demographic profile would be an understatement. But the significance of this profile goes beyond being trivia for social conversation. Where and how Canadians live creates distinctive challenges for Canadian marketers. To see these, let's look deeper into some prominent features and major trends in where and how Canadians live.

### Where We Live

As shown in Exhibit 5-2, the population of Canada in 2001 was about 31,413,000.[10] But a deeper analysis shows some interesting facts—and marketing implications—about our nation.

**Concentrated population** More than three-fifths of Canadian residents live in Quebec and Ontario. Given those provincial populations, it is not surprising to find that these two provinces also account for the majority of consumer income and expenditure and the lion's share of the industrial market (see Exhibit 5-8 later in the chapter).

A strong position in these markets is a must for any national marketing strategy. At the same time, their very size can make Quebec and Ontario brutally competitive markets. Also, two very different linguistic and cultural traditions may necessitate distinct marketing approaches. Because central Canada is so large, some firms pay limited attention to the smaller markets in British Columbia, the Prairies, and Atlantic Canada. Yet these regions offer real opportunities to an alert marketer who is looking for areas with fewer competitors, or who is selling a product of particular interest to people in one of those regions.

Exhibit 5-2 Population of Canada by province, 1982 and 2002 (in thousands).

| | 1982 | | 2002 | | Percentage Change |
|---|---|---|---|---|---|
| | Total | Percent | Total | Percent | 1982–2002 |
| Canada | 24,658 | 100 | 31,413 | 100 | 27.4 |
| Newfoundland & Labrador | 569 | 2.3 | 531 | 1.7 | -6.7 |
| Prince Edward Island | 123 | 0.5 | 139 | 0.4 | 13.0 |
| Nova Scotia | 853 | 3.5 | 944 | 3.0 | 10.7 |
| New Brunswick | 700 | 2.8 | 756 | 2.4 | 8.0 |
| Quebec | 6,463 | 26.2 | 7,455 | 23.7 | 15.3 |
| Ontario | 8,736 | 35.4 | 12,068 | 38.4 | 38.1 |
| Manitoba | 1,038 | 4.2 | 1,150 | 3.7 | 10.8 |
| Saskatchewan | 982 | 4.0 | 1,011 | 3.2 | 3.0 |
| Alberta | 2,326 | 9.4 | 3,113 | 9.9 | 33.8 |
| British Columbia | 2,798 | 11.3 | 4,141 | 13.2 | 48.0 |
| Yukon Territory | 24 | 0.1 | 29 | 0.1 | 20.8 |
| Northwest Territories | 48 | 0.2 | 41 | 0.1 | -14.6 |
| Nunavut | — | — | 28 | 0.1 | — |



**Uneven population growth** The population of Canada more than doubled between 1946 and 1990. But—and this point is valuable to marketers—the population did *not* double everywhere. Exhibit 5-2 also shows that the national growth rate of 27.4 percent for the years 1982 to 2002 was exceeded in only three provinces: British Columbia, Ontario, and Alberta.

These different rates of growth are especially important to marketers. Sudden growth in one area may create a demand for many new shopping centres—while retailers in slow-growing or declining areas face tougher competition for a smaller number of customers. In growing areas, demand may increase so rapidly that profits may be good even in poorly planned facilities.

**Slower rates of population growth** Despite the large increases in the number of people living in Canada, the *rate* of population growth in Canada has slowed dramatically—to less than 1 percent a year during the last decade.[11] Thus, many Canadian marketers are turning to international markets—the United States, Europe, and Asia—where future population growth, and sales revenue, continue to grow.

In Canada, most of our future growth is expected to come from immigration. In fact, even now the total Canadian population would start to decline if immigration stopped. As of 2001, 18.4 percent of the population was born outside of Canada.[12]

## How We Live—What's Changing?

The nature of Canada is changing even as this book is being written. Indeed, one could write *several* books on how different Canada's demographic profile is today in comparison to earlier years. However, there are eight trends that most would agree have special significance:

1. Lower birthrate
2. Changing age distribution
3. Changing household composition
4. Increased number of non-traditional households
5. Increased number of single-person households

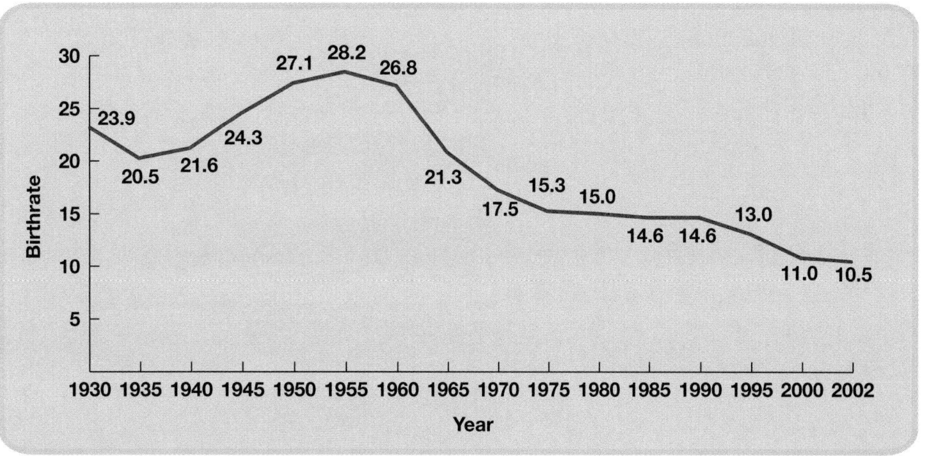


Exhibit 5-3 Changes in the Canadian birthrate, 1930–2002.

6. Population shift to urban centres
7. Rise of the megalopolis
8. Higher rates of geographic mobility

**birthrate**
The number of babies born per 1,000 people

**Trend 1: Lower birthrate** The Canadian **birthrate**—the number of babies born per 1,000 people—fluctuated greatly in the last 50 years: Exhibit 5-3 shows a clear pattern. A post–Second World War baby boom began as returning soldiers started families, and it lasted about 15 years into the early 1960s. In the 1970s the situation changed to a "baby bust" as more women stayed in the workforce and couples waited longer to have children. When you see the dip in the birthrate—and think about the declining market for baby products—you can understand why Johnson & Johnson promotes its baby shampoo to adults who want a gentle product. You can also understand why Johnson & Johnson looks for opportunities in Asia and Latin America, where the birthrate is higher.

With fewer children, parents can spend more money on each child. For example, expensive bikes, videogame consoles, MP3 players, and designer clothes for children have all sold well in recent years because parents can indulge one or two children more easily than a houseful.[13]

**Trend 2: Changing age distribution** The fall in the Canadian birthrate helps explain why the median age is rising. In 2001, that median age was 37.6 years, up from 35.2 in 1996 and 26.3 in 1961.[14] Stated another way, the percentage of the population in different age groups is changing. Exhibit 5-4 shows the number of people in different age groups in 1996 and 2001—and how the size of these groups will look in 2006. Note the big changes that can occur in only 10 years, especially in the 45–64 age group. Also note that, as both the absolute and relative size of older groupings increased, the number of Canadian teens (10–19) declined by half a million between 1981 and 1991 and has remained more or less unchanged to date. Such changes have had quite an impact on many industries, as teenagers consume more, per capita, than do either adults or children.

The major reason for the changing age distribution is that the post–Second World War baby boom produced about one-fourth of the present Canadian population. This large group crowded into the schools in the 1950s and 1960s—and then into the job market in the 1970s. In the 1980s, they swelled the middle-aged group. And early in the 21st century, they will reach retirement—still a dominant group in the total population. According to one population expert, "It's like a goat passing through a boa constrictor."

Some of the effects of this big market are very apparent. For example, recording-

**Exhibit 5-4**
Population distribution by age groups over a 10-year period.

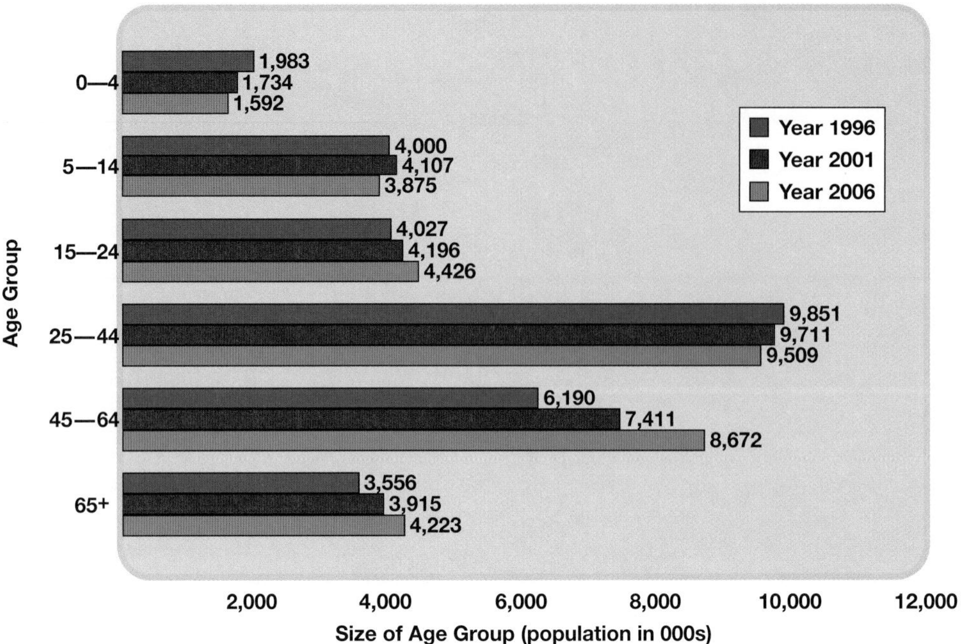


industry sales exploded—to the beat of rock and roll music and the Beatles—as members of the baby boom group moved into their record-buying teens. Soon after, colleges added facilities and faculty to handle the surge—then had to cope with excess capacity and loss of revenue when the student-age population dwindled. To relieve financial strain many colleges now add special courses and programs for adults to attract the now-aging baby boomer students. On the other hand, the fitness industry and food producers that offer low-calorie foods are reaping the benefit of a middle-aged "bulge" in the population.

Medical advances are helping people live longer and are also adding to the proportion of senior citizens in the population. The over-65 age group will continue to grow, both absolutely and in percentage terms, for decades to come. These dramatic changes are creating new opportunities for such industries as tourism, health care,

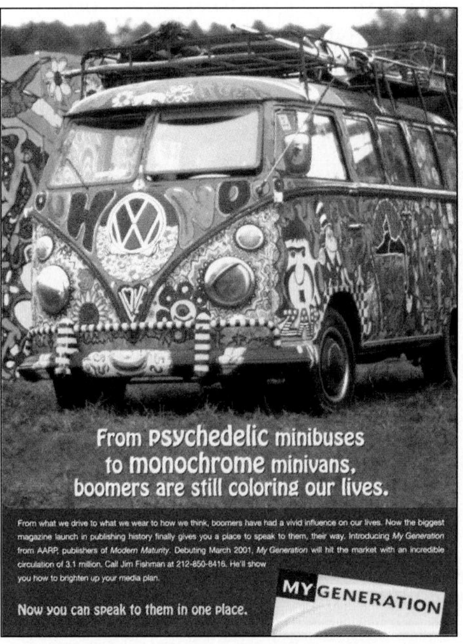


Highly targeted advertising media such as magazines and cable TV are proving especially effective at targeting messages to specific groups.

and financial services.[15] Marketing Demo 5-1 describes some of the myths and realities involved when targeting the mature market.

**Trend 3: Changing household composition** The portrait of the "typical" Canadian household—a married couple with two children living in the suburbs—has never been true, and it is even less true today. Although most Canadians eventually marry, they are marrying later, living for years in common-law relationships, delaying childbearing, having fewer children, and more likely to get divorced. More than 20 percent of all marriages are remarriages, and this is resulting in a growing number of "his," "her," and "our" children.

The number of families in Canada climbed 8 percent, to 8.4 million, between 1996 and 2001. Of these, 70.6 percent were married couples, 13.8 percent were living common law, and 15.7 percent were lone-parent families. In total, about 63.5 percent of all Canadian families had at least one child living at home.[16]

Single-parent families more than doubled in importance between 1971 and 2001, rising to more than 15.7 percent of all families.[17] By 2001, almost one in every five Canadian children lived in a single-parent family. More than 80 percent of lone-parent families are headed by women. More than two-thirds of these female single parents are in the labour force, the vast majority working full time. This increase in single-parent families follows from a doubling of the divorce rate in the past three decades, up to 37.7 percent in 2000.[18]

## Marketing Demo 5–1

### STRAIGHT TALK ON MARKETING TO WOMEN OVER 50

The first tip for marketing to women over 50 is that they hate to be categorized. Of course, all women dislike being labelled, but women over 50 hate it even more because they get categorized as "old" and, therefore, different from other women.

A woman of 50 or 60 could be in so many places in her life: if a mother, her children could still be in grade school or have careers and children of their own. She could be divorced, widowed or have chosen never to marry. She may be self-employed, working for someone else, or staying at home taking care of her family. Or perhaps the kids have grown up and she's retired, so she is enjoying life playing golf and bridge with friends.

Another thing we know about these women—regardless of their psychographic makeup—is that they have no tolerance for sexist and degrading marketing.

These same intolerant women are members of one of the most affluent spending groups in the country. They are the most influential category of buyers for big-ticket items and financial investments due to their high disposable income.

Many are the yuppies from the '80s who love the freedom to choose and are empowered by it. They want what they want, and they want it now. Unlike women in their 30s, the over-50 woman votes with her feet. Offend her, and she'll walk away, taking her healthy chequing account with her. She will walk out of a store and she will boycott its products; she won't say why, or complain too much about it—she'll just take her spending dollars and go somewhere else.

The over-50 are a generation who care about their physical appearance. They're health conscious and active. They eat healthily because they want to stay as youthful and healthy for as long as they can. They're a generation of women with role models like Susan Sarandon, Lauren Hutton and Sophia Loren.

Lots of women who are over 50 don't have arthritis or incontinence problems. They still think about sex and they still want people to think about having sex with them.

So don't talk to these women like they're grandmothers. Women are having children later in life than in previous generations, and so many of them aren't. Those that are are not your sterotypical cheek-pinching, lemonade-drinking blue hairs anymore. They're hip, they're intelligent and they're beautiful.

Don't expect 50-somethings to believe everything they're told about a product. Women over 50 have been around long enough to have tried many products and have had many experiences with marketing campaigns. Although they do rely on advertising to find out what is available in the marketplace, they follow up with research and word-of-mouth before the actual purchase. Many have lost faith and trust to the point where they are suspicious of companies that develop the products, the agencies that market them and the people who sell them.

Because they no longer trust the process, a staggering number of these women—recent research says as many as 70%—rely on recommendations from friends and family.

Source: Leslie Danis, *Marketing Magazine,* August 28, 2000.

This changing profile of Canadian households will likely lead to shifts in consumption patterns. For example, older parents tend to have more financial resources: with fewer children to support, the result could be a larger market for premium quality, child-related products. In addition, with more single-parent families, child care services will be in greater demand. Finally, the rise in common-law relationships, divorces, and "blended" families will mean more complex legal needs in the area of family law.

**Trend 4: Increased number of non-traditional households** Just over 2 million unmarried individuals were living together in Canada in 2001. About 45 percent of those living common law have children at home.[19] To reach this market, banks have changed their policies about loans to unmarried couples for homes and cars. Also, insurance companies are designing coverage oriented toward unmarried couples.

**Trend 5: Increased number of single-person households** The number of households in Canada greatly exceeds the number of families. This is because there were nearly 3 million individuals living alone in 2001. In fact, the proportion of one-person households has risen from about one-fifth of all households in 1981 to more than one-quarter in 2001.[20] These households include both young adults, who leave home when they finish school, and divorced singles. However, the aging of the population—more specifically, an increase in the number of widows—was largely responsible for the growth in this category.

In Canada's urban areas, the percentage of single-person households is even higher. These people need smaller apartments, smaller cars, smaller food packages, and in some cases less expensive household furnishings because they don't have very much money. Other singles have ample discretionary income, and join an attractive target market for luxury goods and services. So while non-traditional households may still be in the minority, marketers will be paying close attention to them.

**Trend 6: Population shift to urban centres** We have become an urban and suburban society. Since the Second World War, there has been a continuous flight to the suburbs by middle-income consumers. Retailers moved too, following their customers. Lower-income consumers—often with varied ethnic backgrounds—moved in, changing the nature of markets in the centre of the city.

Industries too have been fleeing the cities, moving many jobs closer to the suburbs. Today's urban economic system is not as dependent on central cities. A growing population must go somewhere—and the suburbs can combine pleasant neighbourhoods with easy transportation to higher-paying jobs nearby or in the city.

Purchase patterns are different in the suburbs. For example, a big-city resident may not need or own a car. But with no mass transportation, living carless in the suburbs is difficult. And in some areas, it almost seems that an SUV or a minivan—to carpool kids and haul lawn supplies or pets—is a necessity.

However, it seems that some families have given up on the suburban dream. The movement back to the city is most evident among older—and sometimes wealthier—families. They feel crowded by suburbia's expansion. These older families are creating a market for luxury condominiums and high-rise apartments close to downtown and its shopping, recreation, and office facilities. Some young people are also moving into downtown areas, fixing up old homes that still offer convenience and charm at a reasonable price. They are big buyers in the market for "do it yourself" home repair products like paint, insulation, and flooring. They also spend much of their extra money on the city's cultural events and interesting restaurants.

These continuing shifts—to and from urban and suburban areas—mean that the usual practice of reporting population by city and county boundaries can result in misleading descriptions of markets. Marketers are more interested in the size of homogeneous *marketing areas* than in the number of people within political boundaries. This is why Statistics Canada developed a separate population classification, the **Census Metropolitan Area** (CMA). The CMA is the "main labour market area" of a continuous built-up area having a population of 100,000 or more. It's a zone in which a significant number of people are able to commute on a daily basis to their workplaces in the main built-up area.[21]

**Census Metropolitan Area (CMA)**
The "main labour market area" of a continuous built-up area having a population of 100,000 or more

CMAs are usually known by the name of their largest city. In 2001, the 25 largest CMAs in Canada had a combined population of over 19 million, which represents about 60 percent of the 2001 Canadian total. Exhibit 5-5 lists Canada's largest urban areas. These CMAs are major target markets, with Toronto, Montreal, and Vancouver accounting for 10.1 million, or nearly one-third of the corresponding Canadian total. Note that although many CMAs such as Vancouver and Oshawa have experienced high growth rates, others such as Chicoutimi-Jonquière and Sudbury are facing small or even negative population growth.

**Trend 7: The rise of the megalopolis** Twelve of Canada's largest 25 CMAs fall within Canada's "megalopolis," a strip of land with less than 2 percent of the country's total land mass but with more than 40 percent of its population. This strip of land runs for approximately 1,200 kilometres, from Quebec City in the east to



**Exhibit 5-5** Total populations of Census Metropolitan Areas, 1981 and 2001 (in thousands).

| | 1981 | 2001 | Percentage Change 1981–2001 |
|---|---|---|---|
| Toronto (Ontario) | 3,130.4 | 4,682.9 | 49.6 |
| Montreal (Quebec) | 2,862.3 | 3,426.4 | 19.7 |
| Vancouver (British Columbia) | 1,268.2 | 1,987.0 | 56.7 |
| Ottawa–Hull (Ontario–Quebec) | 743.8 | 1,063.7 | 43.0 |
| Calgary (Alberta) | 626.0 | 951.4 | 52.0 |
| Edmonton (Alberta) | 740.9 | 937.8 | 26.6 |
| Quebec (Quebec) | 583.8 | 682.8 | 17.0 |
| Winnipeg (Manitoba) | 592.1 | 671.3 | 13.4 |
| Hamilton (Ontario) | 542.1 | 662.4 | 22.2 |
| London (Ontario) | 326.8 | 432.5 | 32.3 |
| Kitchener (Ontario) | 287.8 | 414.3 | 43.9 |
| St. Catharines–Niagara (Ontario) | 342.7 | 377.0 | 10.0 |
| Halifax (Nova Scotia) | 277.7 | 359.2 | 29.3 |
| Victoria (British Columbia) | 241.5 | 311.9 | 29.2 |
| Windsor (Ontario) | 250.9 | 307.9 | 22.7 |
| Oshawa (Ontario) | 186.5 | 296.3 | 58.9 |
| Saskatoon (Saskatchewan) | 175.1 | 225.9 | 29.0 |
| Regina (Saskatchewan) | 173.2 | 192.8 | 11.3 |
| St. John's (Newfoundland) | 154.8 | 172.9 | 11.7 |
| Greater Sudbury (Ontario) | 156.1 | 155.6 | –0.3 |
| Chicoutimi–Jonquière (Quebec) | 158.2 | 154.9 | –2.1 |
| Sherbrooke (Quebec) | 125.2 | 153.8 | 22.9 |
| Trois-Rivières (Quebec) | 125.3 | 137.5 | 9.7 |
| Saint John (New Brunswick) | 121.0 | 122.7 | 1.4 |
| Thunder Bay (Ontario) | 122.0 | 122.0 | 0.0 |

Windsor in the west, passing through such cities as Montreal, Ottawa, Toronto, and London.

**metropolitan areas**
Urban areas attractive to marketers because of their large, concentrated populations

Some national marketers sell only in **metropolitan areas** because of their large, concentrated populations. They know that having so many customers packed into a small area can simplify the marketing effort. They can use fewer intermediaries and still offer products conveniently. One or two local advertising media—a city newspaper or TV station—can reach most residents. If a salesforce is needed, it will incur less travel time and expense because people are closer together.

Metro areas are also attractive markets because they offer greater sales potential than their large population alone suggests. Consumers in these areas have more money to spend because wages tend to be higher. In addition, professionals—with higher salaries—are concentrated there. But, remember that competition for consumer dollars is usually stiff in a CMA.

**Trend 8: Higher rates of geographic mobility** Of course, no population shift is necessarily permanent. People move, stay awhile, and then move again. In fact, the 2001 Census, the latest available source, classified 41.9 percent of the Canadian population as movers over the previous five years, and about half that group moved to a new community.[22]

Often people who move in the same city trade up to a bigger or better house or neighbourhood. They tend to be younger and better educated people on the way up in their careers. Their income is rising, and they have money to spend. Buying a new house may spark many other purchases too. The old sofa may look shabby in the new house. And the bigger yard may require a new lawn mower—or even a yard service.

Many long-distance moves are prompted by the search for a better lifestyle. Many affluent retirees, for example, move to find a more comfortable life. Young people also hop from place to place, attracted by better job opportunities. This applies to graduates moving to high-paying, new-economy jobs as well as recent immigrants whose only choice may be a low-wage service job.

Regardless of why someone moves, many market-oriented decisions have to be made fairly quickly afterward. People must find new sources of food, clothing, medical and dental care, and household products. Once they make these basic buying decisions, they may not change for a long time. Alert marketers try to locate these potential customers early—to inform them of offerings before they make their purchase decisions. Retail chains, national brands, and franchised services available in different areas have a competitive advantage with mobiles. The customer who moves to a new town may find the familiar Loblaws sign down the street and never even try its local competitors.[23]



## Income Dimensions of the Canadian Market

So far, we have been concerned mainly with the *number* of different types of people. But is Canada's wealth and spending power distributed in the same way? How does it vary by region? by gender? by age? Should marketers pay more attention to certain types of Canadians?

### What We Earn

Average family income in 2000 was a little over $68,000.[24] After adjusting for inflation, as measured by changes in the consumer price index, this figure represents the seventh year of growth since the recession in the early 1990s drove family income down from a 1989 peak.[25]

There is heated debate about what will happen to consumer incomes—and income distribution—in the future. Some business analysts believe that the lack of significant *real* income growth signals worse things to come. They think that

Canada's middle-class standard of living is threatened by a decline in the manufacturing sector of the economy. These analysts argue that in industries with traditionally high wages, firms are replacing workers with technology—to be able to compete with low-cost foreign producers. At the same time, new jobs are coming from growth of the lower-paying service industries. But other analysts are not so pessimistic. They agree that the percentage of the workforce earning middle-income wages has declined recently—but they think this is a temporary shift, not a long-term trend, and that over time the efficiencies that come from new information technologies will "lift" the whole economy.

What happens to income levels will be critical to you—and to Canadian consumers in general. It is easy for both consumers and marketing managers to be lulled by the promise of a constantly increasing standard of living. Both consumer thinking—and marketing strategy—will have to adjust if growth does not resume.

### Who Earns What—Major Trends

How much the "average" Canadian earns is a key indicator of our standard of living. But the distribution of income across consumer groups tells us much more about who marketers should target. In this regard, there are three trends you should know about:

1. Wealth is concentrated in a small portion of the population
2. There are considerable variations in income levels by region
3. Increasing amounts of income are earned by two-income families

**Trend 1: Concentration of wealth** As a general rule, as a consumer's income rises he or she dedicates a lower percentage of income to essentials (we'll discuss this in more depth in the next section). Consequently, the rising income levels of the 1970s onward provided Canadians with more discretionary income—money that could be spent on luxuries, savings, and investments. Many products previously thought of as luxuries could now be sold to mass markets. In this way, the standard of living improved even more because large markets can lead to economies of scale.

However, as can be seen in Exhibit 5-6, which divides all families into five equal-sized groups based on their income, there is a sizable gap between the highest- and lowest-earning Canadians. Moreover, the highest-earning quartile (the top 20 percent) of families received more than 40 percent of total family income. This gave them extra buying power, especially for luxury items. By contrast, the lowest-earning quintile received only about 6.5 percent of total income.[26]

#### Trend 2: Regional variations

Exhibit 5-7 shows the percentage of total personal income and per capita personal income by province and territory. It is significant to note that the top four provinces together account for almost 87 percent of the nation's total income. As may be expected, these provinces represent primary markets for many consumer products.

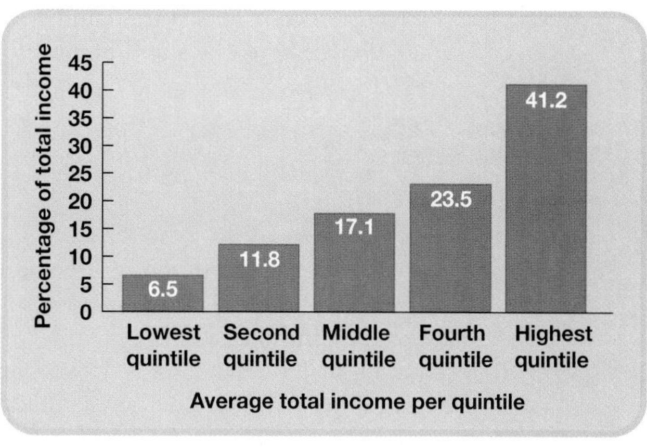


Exhibit 5-6
Percentage of family income going to different groups, 2000.

**Exhibit 5-7** Personal income geographic distribution, 2001.

| | Personal income (millions of dollars) | Percentage of national total | Personal income per capita (dollars) |
|---|---|---|---|
| Canada | 872,657 | 100 | 28,051 |
| Newfoundland & Labrador | 11,528 | 1.32 | 21,596 |
| Prince Edward Island | 3,141 | 0.36 | 22,613 |
| Nova Scotia | 23,212 | 2.66 | 24,618 |
| New Brunswick | 18,138 | 2.08 | 23,992 |
| Quebec | 194,417 | 22.28 | 26,210 |
| Ontario | 359,927 | 41.24 | 30,259 |
| Manitoba | 29,562 | 3.39 | 25,726 |
| Saskatchewan | 23,650 | 2.71 | 23,255 |
| Alberta | 95,194 | 10.91 | 31,119 |
| British Columbia | 110,258 | 12.63 | 26,882 |
| Yukon Territory | 1,007 | 0.12 | 33,344 |
| Northwest Territories | 1,540 | 0.18 | 37,379 |
| Nunavut | 789 | 0.09 | 28,078 |



However, there are major differences even among these top four regions: while the average Canadian per capita income is just above $28,000, two of the provinces with per capita incomes below the Canadian average—Quebec and British Columbia—represent almost 35 percent of Canada's total income.

**Trend 3: Two-income families** Between 1976 and 1996, increased female participation in the workforce accounted for two-thirds of all employment growth in Canada. By 1999, 55 percent of all women aged 15 and over worked outside the home. That year, 46 percent of all paid workers in Canada were women.

However, women still earn significantly less than men. In 1997, women working full-time in the paid workforce made 73 percent of the average earnings of their male counterparts. This ratio was up from 68 percent in 1990 and from about 64 percent in the early 1980s. Gender differences for managers and professionals doing roughly comparable work are somewhat smaller, but they still exist.[27]

In families where the wife works, family spending power is significantly increased. That is why average family income is as high as it is. But many families believe they need this additional income just to make ends meet. Working women spend more for food and are prime target markets for more expensive, and often already prepared, types of food. Families with working wives also spend more on clothing, alcohol, and tobacco, home furnishings and equipment, and cars. In short, when the wife works, it affects the family's spending habits. This fact must be considered when analyzing markets and planning marketing strategies.

## Drivers of Consumer Spending

Our focus in the discussion of income was *family income* as opposed to individual or personal income. This is because consumer budget studies show that most consumers spend their incomes as part of family or household units and pool their incomes when planning major expenditures. In keeping with this theme, most of our discussion on expenditures will examine how families or households spend their income.

Purchases of luxuries, like overseas tourist travel, come from discretionary income

## How Spending Varies with Income

**disposable income**
Income remaining after paying taxes

The amount anyone can spend is largely defined by his or her **disposable income**—income left after paying taxes. Some families don't spend all of their disposable income—they save or invest part of it. Some families may spend more than their disposable income by drawing on savings, selling assets, or buying on credit. However, since disposable income determines the ability to save and to obtain credit, it is a major determinant in the amount of spending by a family.

**discretionary income**
What is left of disposable income after paying for necessities

Most families spend a good portion of their income on such "necessities" as food, rent or house payments, car and home furnishings payments, and insurance. A family's purchase of luxuries comes from **discretionary income**—what is left of disposable income after paying for necessities.

Discretionary income is a difficult concept because the definition of "necessities" varies from family to family and over time. It depends on what they think is necessary for their lifestyle. A cable TV service might be purchased out of discretionary income by a lower-income family but be considered a necessity by a higher-income family. But if many people in a lower-income neighbourhood subscribe to cable TV, it might become a "necessity" for the others—and severely reduce the discretionary income available for other purchases.

The majority of Canadian families do not have enough discretionary income to afford the lifestyles they see on TV and in other mass media. On the other hand, some young adults and older people without family responsibilities have a lot of discretionary income. They may be especially attractive markets for electronic gear, digital cameras, new cars, foreign travel, cell phone services, and various kinds of recreation—tennis, skiing, boating, concerts, and fine restaurants.

It may seem obvious that a wealthy family will spend more money than a poor one—and that the money will be spent on different things. But how it's spent and how such spending varies for different target markets are important questions for marketers. Exhibit 5-8 shows the differences in how households in the upper and lower quintiles of income spend their money. The amount spent on major categories such as food, housing, clothing, transportation, and so on does vary by income level.

Exhibit 5-8 Household expenditures of upper and lower quintile in Canada, 2000.

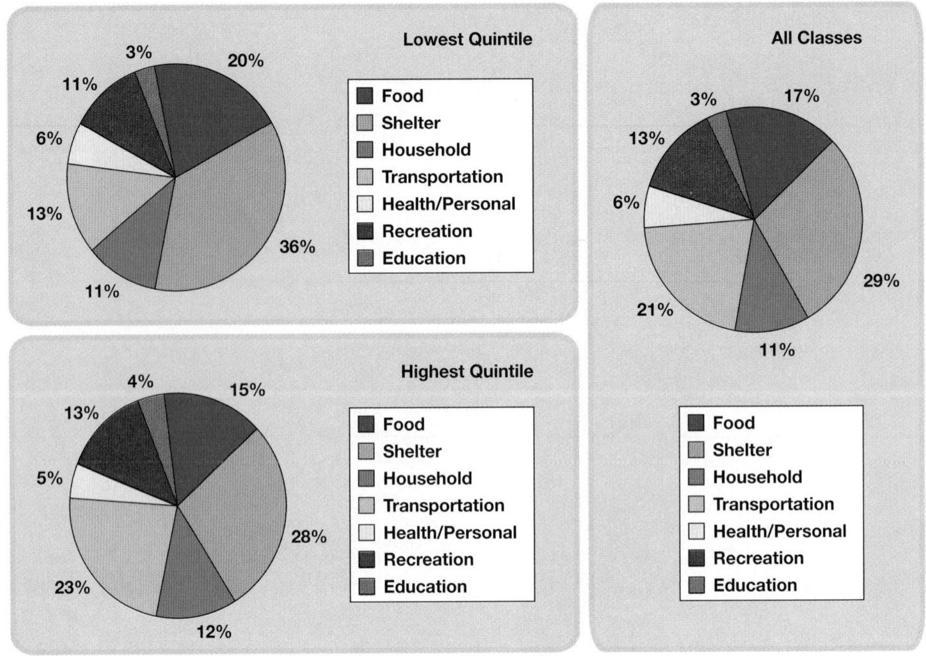


And the relationships are logical when you realize that many of the purchases in these categories are "necessities."

## How Spending Varies with Family Life Cycle

Income has a direct bearing on spending patterns, but many other demographic dimensions are also useful in understanding consumer buying. Marital status, age, and the age of any children in the family have an especially important effect on how people spend their income. Put together, these dimensions tell us about the life-cycle stage of a family. Exhibit 5-9 shows a summary of stages in the family life cycle. In the discussion below, we will focus on the traditional flow from one stage to the next—as shown in the middle of the diagram. However, as shown at the top and bottom of the exhibit, divorce does interrupt the flow for many people; after a divorce, they may re-cycle through earlier stages.[28]

Singles and young couples seem to be more willing to try new products and brands—and they are careful, price-conscious shoppers. Younger people often earn less than older consumers, but they spend a greater proportion of their income on discretionary items because they don't have the major expenses of home ownership, education, and family rearing. Although many young people are waiting longer to marry, most do tie the knot eventually. These younger families—especially those with no children—are still accumulating durable goods, such as automobiles and home furnishings. They spend less on food. Only as children arrive and grow does family spending shift to soft goods and services, such as education, medical, and personal care. This usually happens when the family head reaches the 35–44 age group. To meet expenses, people in this age group often make more purchases on credit, and they save less of their income.

Divorce—increasingly a fact of Canadian life—disrupts the family life-cycle pattern. Divorced parents don't spend like other singles. The mother usually has custody of the children, and the father may pay child support. The mother and children typically have much less income than two-parent families. Such families spend a larger percentage of their income on housing, child care, and other necessities—with little left for discretionary purchases. If a single parent remarries, the family life cycle may start over again.[29]

Exhibit 5-9 Stages in the modern family life cycle.

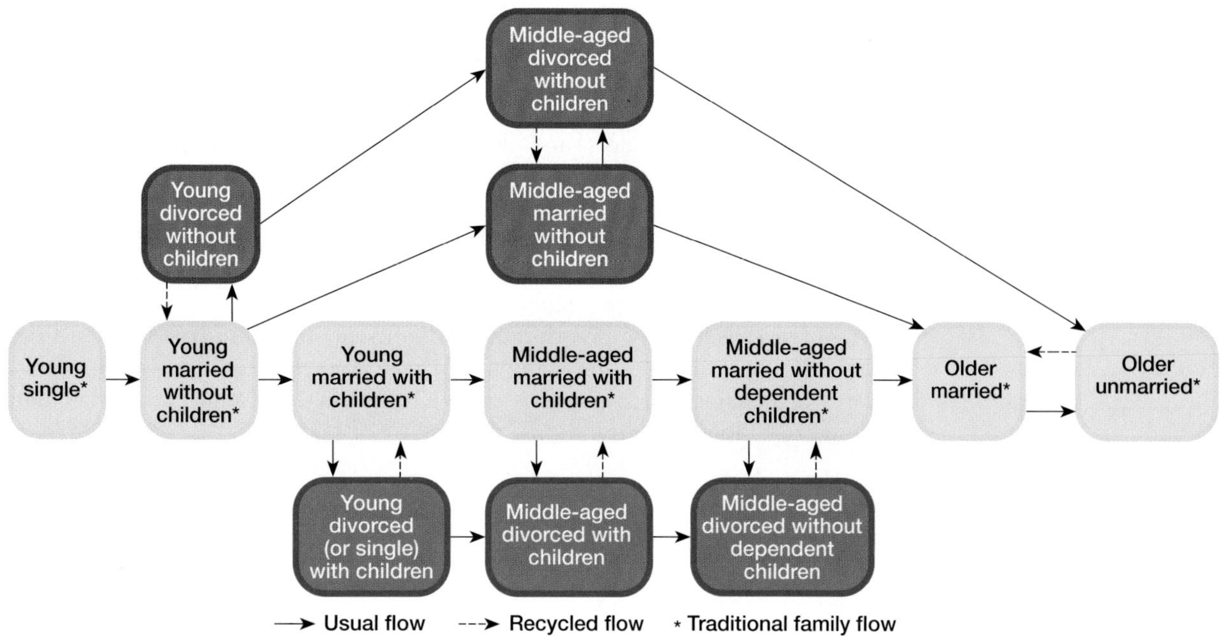


Once children become teenagers, further shifts in spending occur. Teenagers eat more, want to wear expensive clothes, and develop recreation interests and education needs that are hard on the family budget. The parents—or, increasingly, the single parent—may be forced to reallocate expenditures to cover these expenses—spending less on durable goods, such as appliances, automobiles, household goods, and housing. The fast-rising expense of postsecondary education can create a major financial crisis.

For many firms, teens are an important and attractive market. The amount of money involved may surprise you. Further, in today's families with a single parent or with two wage earners, teens play an increasingly important role in shopping and shaping family purchases. With teens spending more money, they are a target for many firms. For example, Siemens added an MP3 player to its wireless phone to help it win teen preference away from Nokia. Similarly, MasterCard is targeting teens with its credit card promotions, and Bausch & Lomb's contact-lens sales hit record levels when the firm refocused its marketing efforts on teens.[30]

Another important category is the empty nesters—people whose children are grown and who are now able to spend their money in other ways. Usually these people are in the 50–64 age group. But this is an elusive group because some people marry later and are still raising a family at this age. And in recent years lots of empty nesters have been surprised when adult singles move back in to avoid the major costs of housing.

Empty nesters are an attractive market for many items. They have paid for their homes, and the big expenses of raising a family are behind them. They are more interested in travel, small sports cars, and other things they couldn't afford before. Much depends on their income, of course. But this is a high-income period for many, especially white-collar workers.[31]

Finally, marketers should not neglect the senior citizens—people over age 65. The number of people over 65 is increasing rapidly because of modern medicine, improved sanitary conditions, and better nutrition. This group now makes up almost 13 percent of the population and, with the aging baby boomers, will soon become an even more significant proportion of the population. And senior citizens are more prosperous than ever before—their income is lower than during their peak earning years, but most do have money to spend.[32]

Older people also have very different needs. Many firms already cater to senior citizens—and more will be serving this market. For example, some companies have developed housing and "life care" centres designed to appeal to older people. Casio makes a calculator with large, easy-to-read numbers. Some travel agents find that senior citizens are an eager market for expensive tours and cruises. Other companies offer diet supplements and drug products—often in special easy-to-open packages. And senior-citizen discounts at drugstores are more than just a courtesy—the elderly make up the biggest market for medicines. Keep in mind, however, that older people are not all the same. With a group this large, generalities and stereotypes can be dangerous. Different senior-citizen target markets have different needs—and require different marketing strategies.[33]

As noted earlier, these descriptions of life-cycle stages are based on traditional lifestyles. Clearly, families following alternative lifestyles could show very different patterns of behaviour. However, as shown in Marketing Demo 5-2, most families continue to follow these traditional patterns.



## Ethnic Dimensions of the Canadian Market

Ethnic groups deserve special attention when markets are being analyzed. One basic reason is that people from different ethnic groups may be influenced by very different cultural variables. They may have quite different needs, as well as their own ways of thinking. Canada has long been a multicultural market; rather than disappearing in a melting pot, some important cultural and ethnic dimensions are being preserved and highlighted. This creates both opportunities and challenges for marketers.

### Canada's Ethnic Mix

When completing their 2001 Census forms, the latest available source of such data, 7.6 million Canadians (about 25 percent of the total population) indicated that they were members of a single or mixed ethnic heritage other than Canadian, English, or French. Until Canada introduced a colour-blind immigration policy in 1966, most immigrants were European Caucasians. This is no longer the case. When they completed their 2001 Census forms, nearly 4 million Canadians identified themselves as members of a visible minority. They represented 13.4 percent of the population, up from 11.2 percent in 1996 and 6.3 percent in 1986.[34]

Nearly 80 percent of Canada's entire ethnic population (and seven out of ten visible minorities) lives in Toronto, Vancouver, or Montreal. Recent projections indicate that the Chinese, East Indian, and Polish communities will enjoy especially strong growth, both in numbers and in their share of total purchasing power.[35]

Although ethnic origin is important to marketers, so is mother tongue (the language first spoken at home and still understood). Though not all members of an ethnic community regularly use or even understand their heritage language, obviously those born elsewhere would, and often so do the children of these first-generation immigrants. The 2001 Census, the latest available source at time of publication, showed a marked increase in the percentage of the population who reported their mother tongue as a nonofficial language—from 13.8 percent in 1986 to 18 percent in 2001.[36]

In 2001 the three main mother tongues other than English and French were Chinese (reported by 853,745 people), Italian (469,485), and German (438,080).[37] But even though 5.3 million people reported a mother tongue other than English or French in 2001, only 3.1 million of these people spoke a nonofficial language most often at home. Chinese was by far the most frequent of these home languages, followed by Italian, Punjabi, and Portuguese.[38]

## Marketing Demo 5–2

### J. WALTER THOMPSON'S LIFESTAGES

**SINGLES: 28% OF CANADIAN ADULTS**

**At home singles—59% male**

- 44% are in school.
- 42% have full-time employment.
- Are a group in transition who tend to live for today.
- Are a difficult audience to reach.

*Spend on entertainment and leisure products.*

**Starting out singles—65% male**

- Are financially independent, establishing credit cards and consolidating loans.
- A time of intense experimentation and indulgence.
- Reality and responsibility force rapid maturation.

*Spend on entertainment and furnishings for new residences.*

**Mature singles—59% males**

- Are a growing group, as Canadians wait longer to marry, more never marry, and divorces are more common.
- Live leisure-oriented lifestyles.

*Spend on their homes/apartments.*

**Left alone singles—76% female, older than mature singles**

- Are surprisingly healthy and relatively happy, with a positive self-image.
- Concerned about health.
- Not very status-conscious, non aspiring.

*Spend on necessities, small self-indulgences.*

**COUPLES: 26% OF CANADIAN ADULTS**

**Young couples**

- Are the happiest of all groups.
- High in self-esteem, with their lives revolving around spouse and work.

*Spend on gift buying and purchase of home furnishings (fed by two cheques).*

**Empty Nesters**

- Are relatively carefree.
- Materially well off.
- Enjoy their kids in a different way, no longer making sacrifices.

*Spend on trips, classes, eating out, gifts for grandchildren and convenience-oriented appliances.*

**PARENTS: 47% OF CANADIAN ADULTS**

**Young Parents**

- With children under 12, are driven by the needs of young children, which is a shift from being focussed on themselves.
- Most are juggling parenthood and careers.
- Concerned about the environment and value for money.

*Spend on children and home entertainment.*

**Mature parents—the Boomers**

- With more people waiting to have kids, this group is getting older.
- Are blessed with children moving into adolescence, so kids are their biggest worry.
- Fears include drugs/environment.
- More time for new hobbies, entertainment.

*Spend on their children, new leisure activities.*

**Single parents—80% are women**

- Are worriers and price shoppers.
- The most dominated by their children.
- Tend to have low self-images.

*Spend on the essentials, since they have difficulty making ends meet.*[39]

Every individual whose "language of comfort" is other than English or French does not present a mother-tongue marketing opportunity. Such individuals have to constitute enough of a marketing segment to be profitably cultivated. There has to be an economical way of reaching them, either in the communities in which they live or through mother-tongue media. In many cases, this can be—and has been—done. Many of those using a given mother tongue tend to live in the same communities, read the same newspapers, and enjoy the same mother-tongue radio and television shows.

### Marketing to the Ethnic Market

A marketer needs to study ethnic dimensions very carefully, because they can be subtle and fast-changing. This is also an area where stereotyped thinking is the most

## Marketing Demo 5–3

### HOW DOES FRENCH CANADIAN CONSUMPTION DIFFER?

On the whole, French Canadian consumers differ from their English-speaking counterparts. The following are just a few examples of the many reported differences in product use and preferences by French Canadians:

**Diet**

- Less likely to drink tea or diet cola or eat cookies and eggs on a daily basis
- Strong preference for instant coffee
- Higher proportion of wine and beer drinkers and smokers

**Personal Care**

- More importance placed on personal grooming and fashion
- Use less lip-gloss, foundation makeup, and perfume

**Sports and Leisure**

- Fewer golfers, joggers, and gardeners
- More cyclists, skiers, woodworkers, and live-theatre fans
- Travel less, and make fewer long-distance phone calls

**Finances**

- Widespread popularity of *caisses populaires* (credit unions)
- Dropping number of credit card holders

**Psychographics**

- More willing to pay premium prices for convenience and premium brands
- Cautious as to the use of new products, postponing trials until the product has proven itself
- Show more brand loyalty, but will buy a substitute if it is on special

Note: Marketers must be careful when considering these differences. It is clear that francophones show different consumption patterns, but what is not obvious is whether this is a matter of culture. Does ethnic background account for this variation, or are there other demographic factors that must be taken into consideration?[40]



common—and misleading. The greatest challenge is to get beyond the "them versus us" mentality and the urge to categorize ethnic Canadians, or a given ethnic community, as one homogeneous group. Every black person is not from the Caribbean, for example. A person of Chinese origin could be from Taiwan or Singapore, not just Hong Kong or mainland China. Not all ethnic Canadians are new to this country and speak with an accent, or speak only a language other than English.

To target visible minorities, businesses have two options: include visible minorities in "mainstream" campaigns, or target specific ethnic groups in their mother tongue. Many ethnic Canadians want to be included in mainstream advertising. According to the Canadian Advertising Foundation, one in five Canadians says that he or she is more likely to buy a product from a firm that makes a point of including visible minorities in its ads. Among visible minorities, that number jumps to nearly one in two (46 percent). Marketers forget that some ethnic groups are well established, with second-, third-, and even eighth-generation families; they consider themselves part of the mainstream and don't want to be reached other than through the mass media. And while new immigrants have strong ties to their cultural heritage, they also seek to assimilate with Canadian society.[41]

**The French Canadian consumer** French Canadians can be defined in many ways. The position most often taken is that a French Canadian consumer is anyone whose mother tongue is French or who tends to speak French rather than English at home.[42] However, marketers must realize that a large number of French Canadians are truly bilingual. They watch English-language television and read English-language publications. A significant number of French Canadians who aren't fully bilingual on occasion still prefer to listen to English radio, watch English TV, or read English-language publications. Marketers must carefully study French Canadians' media preferences. They cannot rely exclusively on census discussions of mother tongue or language most often spoken at home. French Canadian consumers also display many differences in their consumption patterns, compared with their English-speaking counterparts. Marketing Demo 5-3 describes a number of these differences.

**Where is the French Canadian market?** Is the French Canadian market essentially Quebec, or should it be defined more broadly? For marketing purposes, Quebec and the French Canadian market are not identical. One approach defines the French Canadian market as including Quebec, eight adjacent counties in Ontario, and seven counties in the northern part of New Brunswick. For the 15 counties taken together, the mother tongue of more than half the population is French. Of the 6.8 million Canadians in 2001 reporting French as their mother tongue, more than 90 percent lived in this region.[43]

**The "other" Quebec market** Some 591,000 individuals who in 2001 reported English as their mother tongue (often classified as anglophones) live in Quebec. In addition, Quebec has an even larger number of "allophone" residents (732,200), who reported some third language as their mother tongue. Although approximately 30,000 English-speaking consumers have left Quebec in the past five years, the number of Quebec residents with a mother tongue other than French is still larger than the total population of Manitoba or Saskatchewan. This "other" Quebec market is also a lot less expensive to reach since more than 80 percent of these consumers live in and around Montreal.[44]

## A Final Word

In Chapter 3 we discussed the key role of segmentation. We also noted that one of the most commonly employed bases of segmentation is demographic characteristics. This is why companies often need separate strategies for these ethnically or racially defined markets. Many of these strategies may require only changes in place and promotion. For example, many stores in Markham and Vancouver have Asian languages on their store signs and advertise in community papers or on TV specialty channels. But sometimes companies have more difficulty developing strategies and segmenting ethnic submarkets. For example, Asian Canadians have emigrated from China, Japan, the Philippines, India, Korea, Vietnam, Laos, and Cambodia. Many come from very different backgrounds with no common language, religion, or culture. That adds to the marketing challenge; it means marketers must really understand the basic needs that motivate specific target markets to think and act as they do. This is important with any consumer market—regardless of people's ethnic or racial background or where in the world they live. We'll deal with that important issue in more detail in the next chapter.[45]



## Chapter Summary

In this chapter, we studied population, income, and other demographic dimensions of consumer markets. Getting the facts straight on how about 6 billion people are spread over the world is important to marketing managers. We learned that the potential of a given market cannot be determined by population figures alone. Geographic location, income, stage in life cycle, ethnic background, and other factors are important too. We talked about some of the ways these dimensions—and changes in them—affect marketing strategy planning.

We also noted the growth of urban areas in countries around the world. The high concentration of population

## Chapter Summary continued

and spending power in large metropolitan areas of Canada has already made them attractive target markets. However, competition in these markets is often tough.

One of the outstanding characteristics of Canadian consumers is their mobility. Managers must pay attention to changes in markets. High mobility makes even relatively new data suspect. Data can only aid a manager's judgment—not replace it.

Canadian consumers are among the most affluent in the world. They have more discretionary income and can afford a wide variety of products that people in other parts of the world view as luxuries. However, in Canada as in most other societies income is distributed unevenly among different groups. Consumers at the top income levels have a disproportionately large share of the total buying power.

The kind of data discussed in this chapter can be very useful for estimating the market potential within possible target markets. But, unfortunately, it is not very helpful in explaining specific customer behaviour—why people buy *specific* products and *specific* brands. Yet such detailed forecasts are important to marketing managers. Better forecasts can come from a better understanding of consumer behaviour—the subject of the next chapter.

## Key Concepts

birthrate, p. 127
Census Metropolitan Area (CMA), p. 131
demographics, p. 118
discretionary income, p. 135
disposable income, p. 135
gross domestic product (GDP), p. 122
gross national product (GNP), p. 122
metropolitan areas, p. 132

## Questions and Problems

1. Drawing on data in this chapter, do you think that Romania would be an attractive market for a firm that produces home appliances? What about Finland? Discuss your reasons.
2. Discuss the value of gross national product and gross national product per capita as measures of market potential in international consumer markets. Refer to specific data in your answer.
3 Discuss how the worldwide trend toward urbanization is affecting opportunities for international marketing.
4. Discuss how slower population growth will affect businesses in your local community.
5. Discuss how the age distribution of Canadians is affecting marketing strategy planning in Canada.
6. Name three specific examples of firms that developed a marketing mix to appeal to senior citizens. Name three examples of firms that developed a marketing mix to appeal to teenagers.
7. Some demographic characteristics are more important than others in determining market potential. For each of the following characteristics, identify two products for which this characteristic is most important: *(a)* size of geographic area, *(b)* population, *(c)* income, *(d)* stage of life cycle.
8. Name three specific examples (specific products or brands—not just product categories) and explain how demand in Canada will differ by geographic location *and* urban–rural location.
9. Explain how the increasing mobility of Canada consumers—as well as the development of big metropolitan areas—should affect marketing strategy planning in the future. Be sure to consider the impact on the four Ps.
10. Explain why mobile consumers can be an attractive market.
11. Explain how the distribution of income in Canada has affected marketing planning thus far—and its likely impact in the future.
12. Why are marketing managers paying more attention to ethnic dimensions of consumer markets in Canada?

## Computer-Aided Problem 5

### Demographic Analysis

Stylco, Inc. is a producer of specialty clothing. To differentiate its designs and appeal to its target market, Stylco uses authentic African prints. Originally, it just focused on designs targeted at adults in the 35–44 age range. However, in the late 1990s, when sales to these middle-aged adults started to level off, Stylco added a more conservative line of clothes for older consumers. Most buyers of the conservative styles are in the 45–59 age group.

Stylco has focused on distributing its products through select fashion boutiques in metropolitan market areas with the highest concentrations of black consumers. This approach has reduced Stylco's personal selling expense; as a result, however, only a percentage of the total black population is served by current Stylco retailers. For example, about half of the consumers in the 35–44 age group are in the market areas served by Stylco retailers.

Naomi Davis, Stylco's marketing manager, recently read an article about the "greying of North America." She is wondering how shifts in the age distribution might affect her market and sales.

To get a long-run view of these trends, she looked at census data on black consumers by age group. She also looked up estimates of the expected percentage rate of change in the size of each group through the year 2005. By multiplying these rates by the size her target markets were in 2000, she can estimate how large they are likely to be in 2005. Further, from analysis of past sales data she knows that the number of units the firm sells is directly proportional to the size of each age group. Specifically, the ratio of units sold to target market size has been about 5 units per 1,000 people (that is, a ratio of .005). Finally, she determined the firm's average unit profit for each of the lines. To see how changes in population are likely to affect Stylco units sold and future profits from each line, Davis programmed all of these data, and the relationships discussed above, into a spreadsheet.

a. *Briefly compare the profit data for 2000 and estimated profit for 2005 as it appears on the initial spreadsheet. What is the basic reason for the expected shift? What are the implications of these and other data in the spreadsheet for Stylco's marketing strategy planning?*

b. *The rate of growth or decline for different age groups tends to vary from one geographic region to another. Davis thinks that in the market areas that Stylco serves the size of the 35–44 age group may decrease by as much as 10 to 12 percent by 2005. However, the Census Bureau estimates that the decline of the black 35–44 age group for the whole country will only be about 21.7 percent. If the decline in the target market size for Davis' market areas turns out to be 21.7 percent rather than the 210.1 she has assumed, what is the potential effect on profits from the young adult line? on overall profits?*

c. *Because more firms are paying attention to fast-growing ethnic markets, Davis thinks competition may increase in lines targeted at affluent black consumers in the 45–59 age group. Because of price competition, the line targeted at this group already earns a lower average profit per unit. Further, she thinks that her "ratio of units sold to market size" may decrease as more firms compete for this business. Use the what-if analysis to prepare a table showing how the percentage of profit from this group, as well as total profit, might change as the ratio of units sold to market size varies between a minimum of .001 and a maximum of .010. Explain the implications to the firm.*



## Suggested Cases

To view the cases, go to www.mcgrawhill.ca/college/wong.

Interested in finding out what marketing looks like in the real world? *Marketing Magazine* is just a click away on your OLC! Visit www.mcgrawhill.ca/college/wong today.

When You Finish This Chapter, You Should

1. Understand the economic-buyer model of buyer behaviour.

2. Understand how psychological variables affect an individual's buying behaviour.

3. Understand how social influences affect an individual's and a household's buying behaviour.

4. See why the purchase situation has an effect on consumer behaviour.

5. Know how consumers use problem-solving processes.

6. Have some feel for how a consumer handles all the behavioural variables and incoming stimuli.

# Chapter Six

# Behavioural Dimensions of the Consumer Market

## Skip the Chevy—Buy Yourself a Beemer

Canadians have developed a taste for the finer things in life, pushing up sales for luxury items including Belgian chocolate, imported beer, and cars priced in the six figures.

Luxury sales, while still comprising just a fraction of the overall retail market, have skyrocketed in a variety of shopping categories and are significantly outstripping the pace of sales for mainstream retail goods.

The way consumers are managing to trade up on the luxury scale is by shopping more at discount outlets for some of their needs, while pampering themselves with the savings.

The major casualty has been the middle ground, a new marketing study has found.

Growth in the past five years has been particularly torrid. For example:

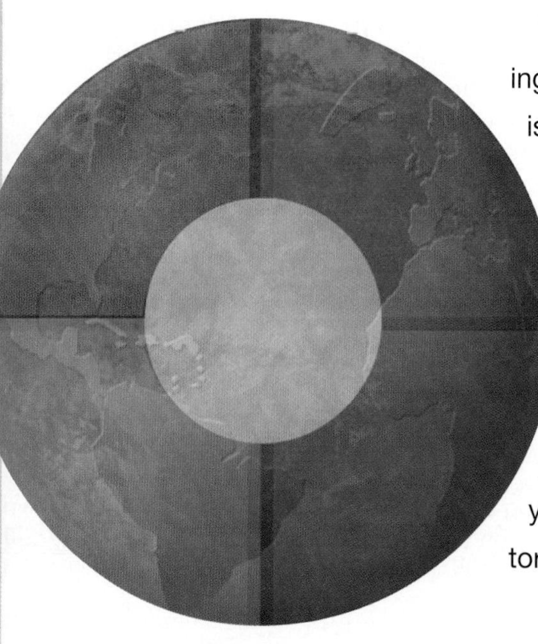

place

price

promotion

prod

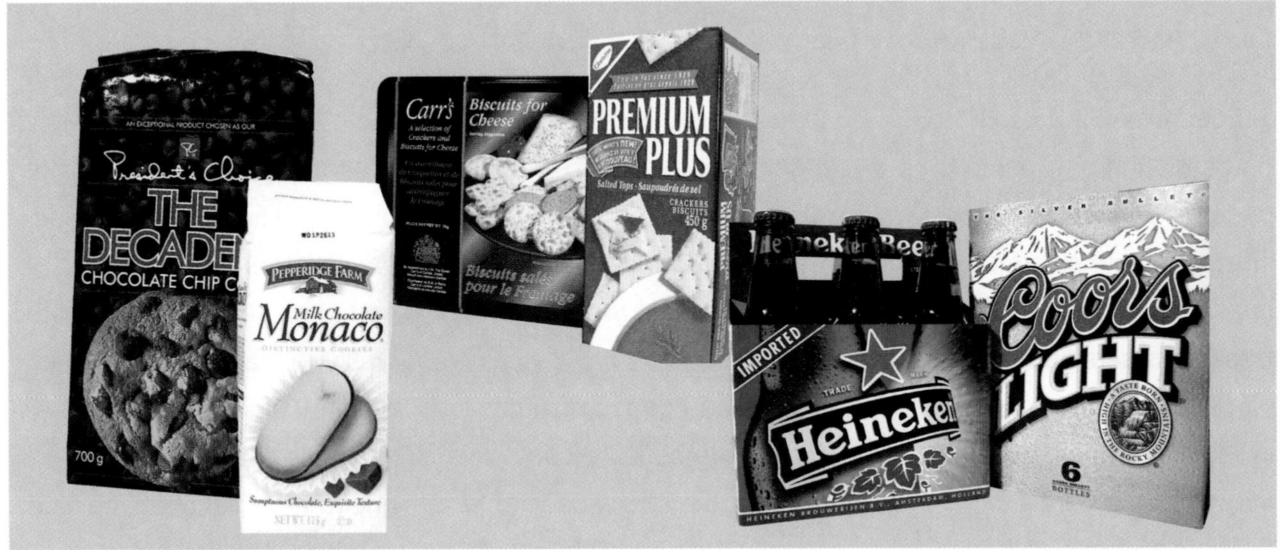


- The market for super-premium beer—imports and craft brews priced at 20 percent to 29 percent above regular beer—has grown 114 percent, or 16 percent per annum in the last five years, while the overall beer market has grown at about 1 percent a year.
- While Canadian auto sales grew 4 percent a year between 1997 and 2002, sales of Mercedes and Jaguar vehicles leapt 20 percent per annum; BMW sales grew 18 percent.
- Sales of high-end chocolate selling for $10 a pound or more are growing at 10 percent to 15 percent a year, while the mass market confection has seen average sales increases of 2 percent to 4 percent.

A Boston Consulting Group study notes that middle-market consumers are embracing luxury goods more now than they have in the past 20 years. Canadians with a household income of $50,000 to $105,000 have seen their level of disposable income rise about 10 percent to 15 percent since 1980, fuelling a trend towards buying pricier, higher-quality goods, the report notes.

The results seem surprising given the meteoric ascent of discount giant Wal-Mart into the country's biggest department store in less than a decade. Specialty stores aimed at consumers who want cheap and cheerful fashion fixes, such as Payless Shoe Source and Old Navy, have experienced similar success.

"Both trends are happening at the same time and are reinforcing each other," said Peter Stanger, vice-president of Boston Consulting. "The same middle-market consumers choose a couple of categories that are really important to them and they trade up in terms of the brand or the quality. They trade down in other categories that aren't important to them. That way they can save their money and spend it on the things that they really want."

Economic and cultural shifts in the last two decades have fuelled the trend, Mr. Stanger notes. The level of home equity has increased while mortgage costs have declined since 1980, while the participation of women in the workforce aged 25 to 54

place price promotion product

jumped from 52 percent to 81 percent during the same period. Average household size is also shrinking, as families with more than three members comprised 42 percent of the population in 2000 compared with 55 percent in 1977.

The phenomenon is also happening in the grocery industry, Mr. Stanger said, with sales of affordable luxuries such as fresh pasta and quality cheeses doubling or tripling that of dried, processed or frozen fare. In the last year, items including boxed pasta, canned tomato sauce, frozen vegetables and processed cheese slices have seen growth of minus-3 percent to 3 percent. Sales of fresh pasta and sauce, wet-packed fresh vegetables such as baby carrots and specialty cheese, meanwhile, jumped 8 percent to 15 percent in the same period.

"Branded goods manufacturers have benefited from this because they have been able to grow their premium categories significantly," Mr. Stanger noted.

The shift has prompted retailers who traditionally did the lion's share of business in the mid-price bracket to incorporate more expensive items into certain categories, such as home electronics and appliances. "It used to be a commonly held belief in the retail industry that you couldn't sell a washing machine for more than $1,000," said Mr. Stanger, who noted that sales of $1,400 front-loading washers at Sears Canada now comprise 40 percent of overall washing machine sales. The majority of washing machines available in the market are priced at about $600, he said.

While targeting value-minded customers through a program of promotional sales and a line of goods sold at "everyday low prices," Sears Canada is also trying to appeal to customers buying on the lower end of the price spectrum. "It's a question of getting the categories right," Mr. Stanger said. "Consumers are spending money on premium goods in several categories."[1]



## In This Chapter

There is no single question more at the heart of marketing than "Will customers buy this?" And, in virtually every instance, the answer would be a resounding "it depends." This chapter considers some of the things it depends upon and why this simple question often requires very complex answers.

The material covered in this chapter will provide you with a deeper understanding of the value of segmentation and positioning, and will equip you with some ideas about how customers could be classified for the purpose of target marketing. Always remember that there is very little about how one markets a product or service that can be said to be "good" or "bad" all of the time: everything in marketing can be evaluated only in the context of its appropriateness for the target market.

We'll begin by exploring some of the insights gained from economics, psychology, and sociology. This will provide us with a better understanding of the influences that shape buyer behaviour. Armed with that foundation, we'll then look at how

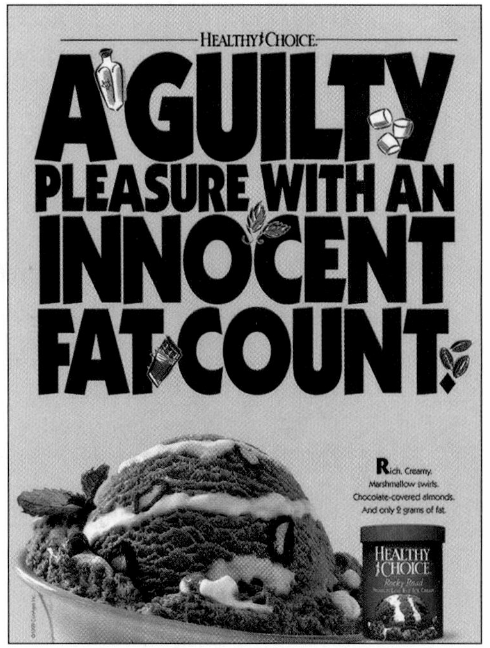


Economic needs affect many buying decisions, but for some purchases the behavioural influences on a consumer are more important.

these influences come together in the *consumer problem-solving process*. As you'll see, each stage of the problem-solving process offers marketers a unique opportunity to interact with the consumer. Finally, we'll look at how the process can vary among customers, across purchase situations, and in international markets.

## Consumer Behaviour—Why Do People Buy What They Buy?

It would be easy to develop effective marketing if all consumers responded to the same marketing mix in the same way. And yet the fact that they do not is what makes marketing an exciting field and provides tremendous career opportunities for those who can crack the code.

Specific consumer behaviours vary a great deal for different products and from one target market to the next. In fact, the same consumer might behave in seemingly inconsistent ways depending upon what they are buying. For example, ravers seem to show a particular attraction toward "underground" events, and yet they also show a distinct preference for branded products from companies like Diesel.

In today's global markets, the variations are countless, making it impractical to try to catalogue all of the detailed possibilities for every different market situation. But there are general behavioural principles—frameworks—that marketing managers can apply to learn more about their specific target markets.

### Economics-based Insights into Behaviour

**economic buyers**

People who know the facts and logically compare choices in terms of cost and value received to get the greatest satisfaction from spending their time and money

Most economists assume that consumers are **economic buyers**—people who know the facts and logically compare choices in terms of cost and value received to get the greatest satisfaction from spending their time and money. A logical extension of the economic-buyer theory led us to look at consumer income patterns in Chapter 5. This approach is valuable because consumers must at least have income to be in a market. Further, most consumers don't have enough income to buy everything they want; that's why economics is sometimes called the "dismal science."

As economic buyers, consumers decide what to buy based on their economic

**economic needs**
Making the best use of a consumer's time and money

needs. **Economic needs** are concerned with making the best use of a consumer's time and money—as the consumer judges it. Some consumers look for the lowest price. Others will pay extra for convenience. Still others may weigh price and quality for the best value. Some of the most commonly referred economic needs are:

1. Economy of purchase or use.
2. Convenience.
3. Efficiency in operation or use.
4. Dependability in use.
5. Improvement of earnings.

Clearly, marketing managers must be alert to new ways to appeal to economic needs. Most consumers appreciate firms that offer them improved value for the money they spend. But improved value does not just mean offering lower and lower prices. Many consumers face a "poverty of time." Carefully planned place decisions can make it easier and faster for customers to make a purchase. Products can be designed to work better, require less service, or last longer. Promotion can inform consumers about their choices or explain product benefits in terms of measurable factors like operating costs, the length of the guarantee, or the time a product will save.

The economic value that a purchase offers a customer is an important factor in many purchase decisions. But a product that one person sees as a good value—and is eager to buy—may be of little interest to someone else. For example, while some teens "crave" Marilyn Manson CDs, this is a sentiment that few parents—and even other teens—would seem to share. So we can't expect to understand buying behaviour without taking a broader view of why consumers focus on some needs more than others.

While there are many behavioural dimensions that could shape the nature and relative importance of the customer's needs, they can be broadly grouped into three main types: psychological variables, social influences, and the purchase situation. As shown in Exhibit 6-1, these influences lead consumers to focus energies on satisfying a particular need. How to satisfy that need is sometimes referred to as a "consumption problem," and thus buyer behaviour can be viewed as a problem-solving process. We'll discuss these topics in the next few pages. Then we'll expand the model to include the consumer problem-solving process.



**Exhibit 6-1** A model of buyer behaviour.

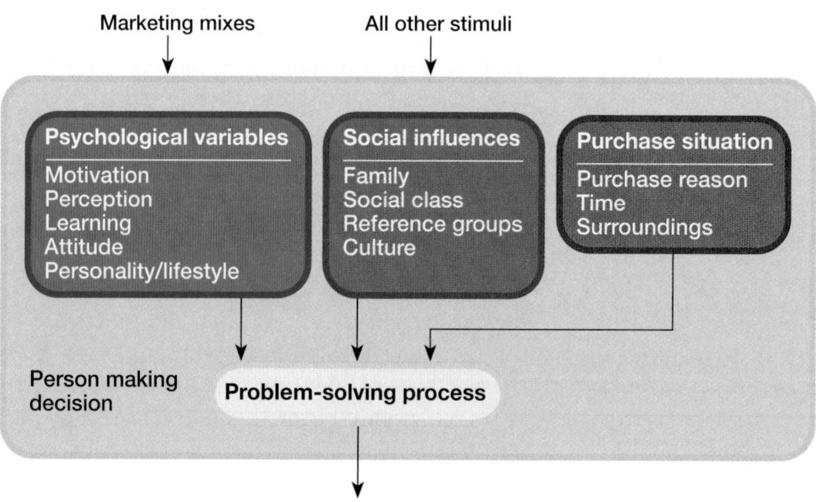

## Psychological Influences within an Individual

Much of what we know about these *psychological (intrapersonal) variables* draws from ideas originally developed in the field of psychology. Here we will discuss some variables of special interest to marketers—including motivation, perception, learning, attitudes and beliefs, personality, and psychographics.

**needs**

The basic forces that motivate a person to do something

**wants**

"Needs" that are learned during a person's life

**drive**

A strong stimulus that encourages action to reduce a need

**Motivation** Everybody is motivated by needs and wants. **Needs** are the basic forces that motivate a person to do something. Some needs involve a person's physical well-being, others the individual's self-view and relationship with others. Needs are more basic than wants. **Wants** are "needs" that are learned during a person's life. For example, everyone needs water or some kind of liquid, but some people also have learned to want Clearly Canadian's raspberry-flavoured sparkling water on the rocks.

When a need is not satisfied, it may lead to a drive. The need for liquid, for example, leads to a thirst drive. A **drive** is a strong stimulus that encourages action to reduce a need. Drives are internal—they are the reasons behind certain behaviour patterns. In marketing, a product purchase results from a drive to satisfy some need.

Some critics imply that marketers can somehow manipulate consumers to buy products against their will. But marketing managers can't create internal drives. Most marketing managers realize that trying to get consumers to act against their will is a waste of time. Instead, a good marketing manager studies what consumer drives, needs, and wants already exist and how they can be satisfied better. For example, while the hunger *need* might lead to a *drive* for food, it is much less likely (and much more expensive to change) that a vegetarian *wants* a meal containing meat.

We're all a bundle of needs and wants. Exhibit 6-2 lists some important needs that might motivate a person to some action. This list, of course, is not complete. But thinking about such needs can help you see what *benefits* consumers might seek from a marketing mix. Furthermore, the more needs that a single product can satisfy, the more benefits it will create for the customer (see Marketing Demo 6-1).

Exhibit 6-2 Possible needs motivating a person to action.

| Types of Needs | Specific Examples | | | |
|---|---|---|---|---|
| **Physiological needs** | Hunger<br>Sex<br>Rest | Thirst<br>Body elimination | Activity<br>Self-preservation | Sleep<br>Warmth/coolness |
| **Psychological needs** | Aggression<br>Family preservation<br>Nurturing<br>Playing/relaxing<br>Self-identification | Curiosity<br>Imitation<br>Order<br>Power<br>Tenderness | Being responsible<br>Independence<br>Personal fulfillment<br>Pride | Dominance<br>Love<br>Playing/compeition<br>Self-expression |
| **Desire for...** | Acceptance<br>Affiliation<br>Comfort<br>Esteem<br>Knowledge<br>Respect<br>Status | Achievement<br>Appreciation<br>Leisure<br>Fame<br>Prestige<br>Retaliation<br>Sympathy | Acquisition<br>Beauty<br>Distance/"space"<br>Happiness<br>Pleasure<br>Self-satisfaction<br>Variety | Affection<br>Companionship<br>Distinctiveness<br>Identification<br>Recognition<br>Sociability<br>Fun |
| **Freedom from...** | Fear<br>Pain<br>Harm | Depression<br>Stress<br>Ridicule | Discomfort<br>Loss<br>Sadness | Anxiety<br>Illness<br>Pressure |

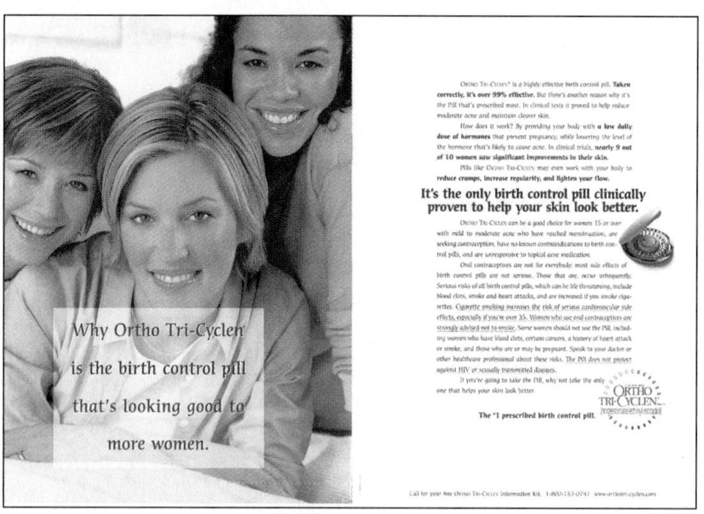


Some products fill more than one need at the same time.

**physiological needs**
Biological needs including food, drink, rest, and sex

**safety needs**
Needs for protection and physical well-being (health, food, medicine, and exercise)

**social needs**
Needs that involve a person's interaction with others (love, friendship, status, and esteem)

**personal needs**
An individual's need for personal satisfaction unrelated to what others think or do

With so many needs to satisfy, how does a consumer decide which one(s) to focus on? Some psychologists argue that a person may simultaneously have several reasons for buying. Maslow is well known for his five-level hierarchy of needs. We will discuss a similar four-level hierarchy that is easier to apply to consumer behaviour. Exhibit 6-3 illustrates these four levels along with an advertising slogan showing how a company has tried to appeal to each need. The lowest-level needs are physiological. Then come safety, social, and personal needs.

**Physiological needs** are concerned with biological needs—food, drink, rest, and sex. **Safety needs** are concerned with protection and physical well-being (perhaps involving health, food, medicine, and exercise). **Social needs** are concerned with love, friendship, status, and esteem—things that involve a person's interaction with others. **Personal needs**, on the other hand, are concerned with an individual's need for personal satisfaction, unrelated to what others think or do. Examples include self-esteem, accomplishment, fun, freedom, and relaxation.

Motivation theory suggests that we never reach a state of complete satisfaction. As soon as we get our lower-level needs reasonably satisfied, those at higher levels become more dominant. This explains why marketing efforts targeted at affluent consumers in advanced economies often focus on higher-level needs. It also explains

## Marketing Demo 6–1

### THE LOWLY PEELER

A particular product may satisfy more than one need simultaneously. Since most consumers try to fill a *set* of needs rather than just one need or another in sequence, marketers that satisfy bundles of needs at the same time have a higher likelihood of succeeding, even when the product in question is the lowly vegetable peeler. At first glance, a vegetable peeler would seem to satisfy a basic need—to peel something. But the *act* of peeling something involves a series or bundle of needs.

Marketing managers for OXO International realized that many people, especially young children and senior citizens, have trouble gripping the handle of a typical peeler. OXO redesigned the peeler with a bigger handle that addressed this physical need. OXO also coated the handle with dishwasher-safe rubber. This makes cleanup more convenient—and the sharp peeler is safer to use when the grip is wet. The attractively designed grip also appeals to consumers who get personal satisfaction from cooking and who want to impress their guests. Even though OXO priced the peeler much higher than most kitchen utensils, it has sold very well because it appeals to people with a variety of needs.[2]

Exhibit 6-3 The PSSP hierarchy of needs.

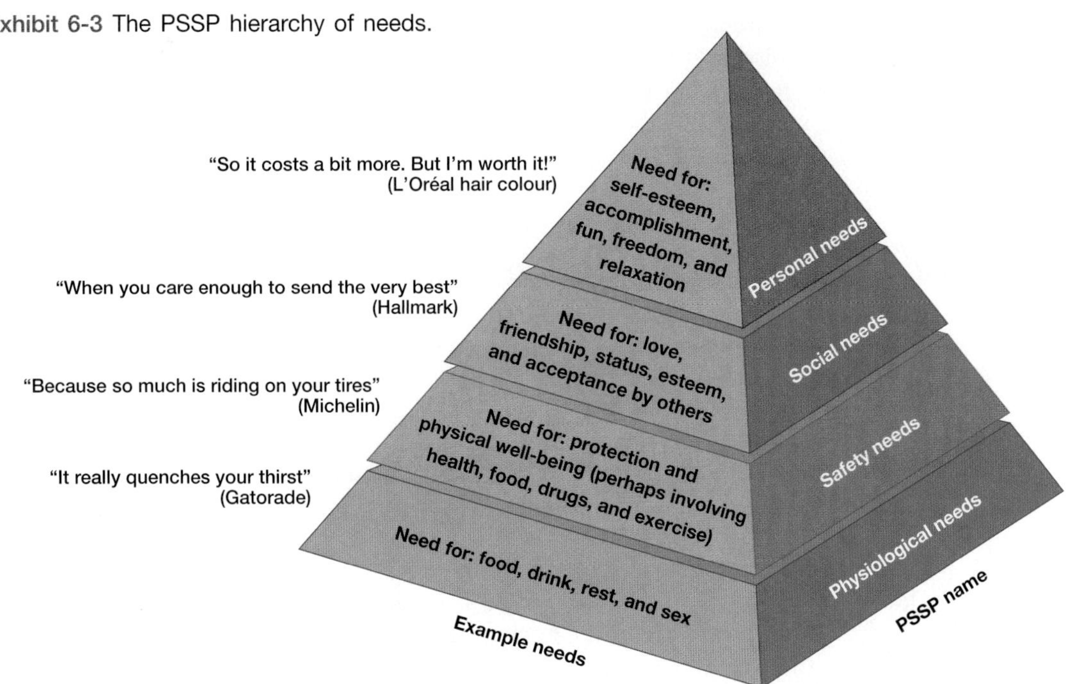
"So it costs a bit more. But I'm worth it!" (L'Oréal hair colour)
"When you care enough to send the very best" (Hallmark)
"Because so much is riding on your tires" (Michelin)
"It really quenches your thirst" (Gatorade)
Need for: self-esteem, accomplishment, fun, freedom, and relaxation
Need for: love, friendship, status, esteem, and acceptance by others
Need for: protection and physical well-being (perhaps involving health, food, drugs, and exercise)
Need for: food, drink, rest, and sex
Example needs
Personal needs
Social needs
Safety needs
Physiological needs
PSSP name

why these approaches may be useless in parts of the world where consumers' basic needs are not being met.

**perception**
How we gather and interpret information from the world around us

**selective exposure**
Our eyes and minds seek out and notice only information that interests us or is relevant to our life in some way

**selective perception**
We screen out or modify ideas, messages, and information that conflict with previously learned attitudes and beliefs

**selective retention**
We remember only what we want to remember

**Perception** Consumers select varying ways to meet their needs sometimes because of differences in **perception**—how we gather and interpret information from the world around us. We are constantly bombarded by stimuli—ads, products, stores—yet we may not hear or see anything. This is because we apply the following selective processes:

1. **Selective exposure**—our eyes and minds seek out and notice only information that interests us or is relevant to our life in some way.
2. **Selective perception**—we screen out or modify ideas, messages, and information that conflict with previously learned attitudes and beliefs.
3. **Selective retention**—we remember only what we want to remember.

These selective processes help explain why some people are not affected by some advertising—even offensive advertising. They just don't see or remember it!

***Perception—marketing implications*** Our needs affect these selective processes. And current needs receive more attention. For example, you may have seen numerous ads for laser eye surgery. If you do not have glasses or contact lenses, you probably never pay much attention to them. If you do need corrective lenses, you may. One way that Lasik Vision tries to make certain that people who use corrective lenses attend to their ads is by placing them in places—like stock market listings—where even the best of eyes might feel challenged.

looking for better ROI?
$700
LASIK VISION
1-888-673-EYES

Marketers are interested in these selective processes because they affect how target consumers get and retain information. In other words, marketers are interested in how consumers *learn*. After all, consumers cannot act on a message they don't remember, and they cannot remember a message that they never notice.

**learning**
A change in a person's thought processes caused by prior experience

**Learning** **Learning** is a change in a person's thought processes caused by prior experience. Learning is often based on direct experience: A little girl tastes her first cone of Ben & Jerry's Concession Obsession flavour ice cream, and learning occurs! Learning may also be based on indirect experience or associations. If you watch an ad that shows other people enjoying Ben & Jerry's Chocolate Fudge Brownie low-fat frozen yogurt, you might conclude that you'd like it too.

Consumer learning may result from things that marketers do, or it may result from stimuli that have nothing to do with marketing. Many needs are culturally (or socially) learned. The need for food, for instance, may lead to many specific food wants. Many Japanese enjoy sushi (raw fish), and their children learn to like it. Fewer Canadians, however, have learned to enjoy it. Either way, almost all consumer behaviour is learned.[3]

**cues**
Products, signs, ads, and other stimuli in the environment

**response**
An effort to satisfy a drive

**positive reinforcement**
Occurs when a response is followed by satisfaction

Experts describe a number of steps in the learning process. We've already discussed the idea of a drive as a strong stimulus that encourages action. Depending on the **cues**—products, signs, ads, and other stimuli in the environment—an individual chooses some specific response. A **response** is an effort to satisfy a drive. The specific response chosen depends on the cues and the person's past experience.

**Positive reinforcement** of the learning process occurs when the response is followed by satisfaction—that is, reduction of the drive. Reinforcement strengthens the relationship between the cue and the response. And it may lead to a similar response the next time the drive occurs. Repeated reinforcement leads to development of a habit—making the individual's decision process routine. Exhibit 6-4 shows the relationships of the important variables in the learning process.



***Learning—marketing implications*** Marketers' interest in the learning process can be illustrated by the actions of a thirsty person. The thirst *drive* could be satisfied in a variety of ways. But if the person happened to walk past a vending machine and saw a Mountain Dew sign—a *cue*—then he might satisfy the drive with a *response*—buying a Mountain Dew. If the experience is satisfactory, positive *reinforcement* will occur, and our friend may be quicker to satisfy this drive in the same way in the future. This emphasizes the importance of developing good products that live up to the promises of the firm's advertising. People can learn to like or dislike Mountain Dew—reinforcement and learning work both ways. Unless marketers satisfy their customers, they must constantly try to attract new ones to replace the dissatisfied ones who don't come back. Good experiences can lead to positive attitudes about a firm's product. Bad experiences can lead to negative attitudes that even good promotion won't be able to change. In fact, the subject of attitudes, an extremely important one to marketers, is discussed more fully below.

Sometimes marketers try to identify cues or images that have positive associations from some other situation and relate them to their marketing mix. Many people associate the smell of lemons with a fresh, natural cleanliness. So, companies often add lemon scent to household cleaning products—Clorox bleach and Pledge furniture polish, for example—because it has these associations. Similarly, some shampoos and deodorants are formulated to be clear and packaged in clear bottles because some consumers associate that look with being natural and pure.

**Exhibit 6-4** The learning process.

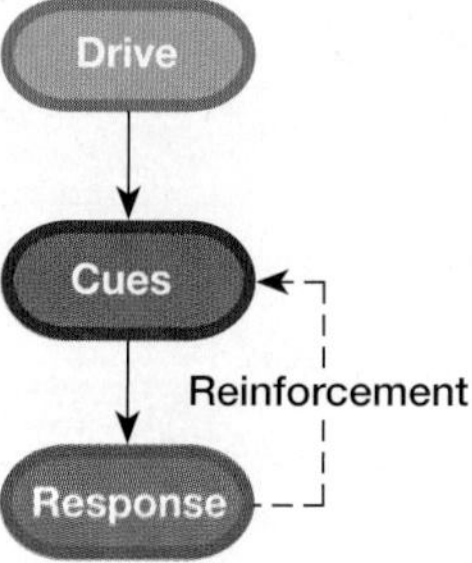

**attitude**
A person's point of view toward something

**Attitudes and beliefs** An **attitude** is a person's point of view toward something. The "something" may be a product, an advertisement, a salesperson, a firm, or an idea. Attitudes are an important topic for marketers because attitudes affect the selective processes, learning, and eventually the buying decisions people make.

**belief**
A person's opinion about something

Because attitudes are usually thought of as involving liking or disliking, they have some action implications. Beliefs are not so action-oriented. A **belief** is a person's opinion about something. Beliefs may help shape a consumer's attitudes but don't necessarily involve any liking or disliking. It is possible to have a belief—say, that Listerine has a medicinal taste—without really caring what it tastes like. On the other hand, beliefs about a product may have a positive or negative effect in shaping consumers' attitudes. For example, a person with allergies is unlikely to switch to a new medicine like Claritin unless she believes it will be more effective than what she has used in the past.

In an attempt to relate attitude more closely to purchase behaviour, some marketers stretched the attitude concept to include consumer "preferences" or "intention to buy." Managers who must forecast how much of their brand customers will buy are particularly interested in the intention to buy. Forecasts would be easier if attitudes were good predictors of intentions to buy. Unfortunately, the relationships usually are not that simple. A person may have positive attitudes toward Jacuzzi whirlpool bathtubs but no intention of buying one.

***Attitudes and beliefs—marketing implications*** Research on consumer attitudes and beliefs can sometimes help a marketing manager get a better picture of markets. For example, consumers with very positive attitudes toward a new product idea might provide a good opportunity—especially if they have negative attitudes about competitors' offerings. Or they may have beliefs that would discourage them from buying a product.

Marketing managers for Purina Dog Chow faced this challenge. Research showed that one segment of consumers thought that Purina was a great dog food, but they

Marketing managers for new Olay Daily Facials (and other Olay skin care products) wanted to take advantage of the familiar Oil of Olay brand name, but realized that many consumers didn't have a positive association between "oil" and beauty. So, the brand name was updated to just Olay and the logo of a woman's figure was changed slightly to appeal to younger women.

didn't buy it all of the time. They believed that their dogs would get bored with it—after all, people don't like eating the same thing all the time. But dogs are not people. Vets have found dogs benefit from a good, consistent diet. So, Purina developed an ad campaign to convince these dog owners that what they believed was not true. Each ad gives a dog's-eye-view reaction to being fed a different dog food. In one ad, after taking a few bites, the dog looks into the camera with a pained expression and walks away. He returns with a packet of antacid, which he drops in his water bowl. Advertising research and sales results both showed that the soft-sell ad hit the bull's-eye in convincing occasional customers that switching foods was not good. Many bought Purina more regularly, and Dog Chow sales increased by $36 million. Consumer beliefs—right or wrong—can have a significant impact on whether a strategy succeeds.[4]

Purina's efforts were successful in changing beliefs; however, as shown in Marketing Demo 6-2, some other firms have not has as positive an experience. But marketers generally try to understand the attitudes of their potential customers and work with them. We'll discuss this idea again when we review the way consumers evaluate product alternatives. For now, we want to emphasize that it's more economical to work with consumer attitudes than to try to change them. Attitudes tend to be enduring. Changing present attitudes—especially negative ones—is sometimes necessary. But that's probably the most difficult job marketers face.[5]

**expectation**

An outcome or event that a person anticipates or looks forward to

Attitudes and beliefs sometimes combine to form an **expectation**—an outcome or event that a person anticipates or looks forward to. Consumer expectations often focus on the benefits or value that the consumer expects from a firm's marketing mix. This is an important issue for marketers because a consumer is likely to be dissatisfied if his or her expectations are not met. For example, when Dryel home dry-cleaning kits were introduced, ads portrayed Dryel as an alternative to expensive dry-cleaner services. Many consumers who tried it were disappointed because it failed to get out some stains and clothing still needed to be pressed.[6]

A key point here is that consumers may evaluate a product not just on how well it performs, but on how it performs *relative to their expectations*. A product that otherwise might get high marks from a satisfied consumer may be a disappointment if there's a gap between what the consumer gets and what the consumer expects. Different elements of the marketing mix—down to the packaging of a product can generate consumer expectations. The examples in Ethical Dimensions 6-1 offer a good demonstration of how consumer expectations do not always coincide with

Companies that sell soy-based products are developing new marketing mixes to help overcome negative attitudes that some consumers have about the taste of soy. For example, White Wave Silk is now packaged like milk and promotion focuses on the health benefits. In the same vein, CardioLink's name and trade ads help position its soy powder as healthy for the heart.

what the marketer intended. Furthermore, promotion that overpromises what the rest of the marketing mix can really deliver leads to problems in this area. Finding the right balance, however, can be difficult. Consider the challenge faced by marketing managers for Van Heusen shirts. A few years ago Van Heusen came up with a new way to treat its shirts so that they look better when they come out of the wash than previous wash-and-wear shirts. Van Heusen promotes these shirts as "wrinkle-free," and the label shows an iron stuffed in a garbage can. Most people agree that the new shirt is an improvement. Even so, consumers who buy a shirt expecting it to look as crisp as if it had just been ironed are disappointed. For them, the improvement is not enough.[7]

## Marketing Demo 6–2

### UN-FIT BEHAVIOUR

Despite Procter & Gamble's best efforts, it couldn't convince consumers they needed a special product to wash their veggies.

When P&G hit the market with its new Swiffer, WetJet, Febreze and Dryel products, there was a fair amount of corporate bumph about how P&G is bringing innovative new products to consumers faster than ever before. That's certainly true, but one product you won't hear too much boasting about these days is Fit fruit and vegetable wash.

Fit was touted as being more effective at removing dirt, wax and pesticide residue from fresh fruits and vegetables than running them under plain tap water. But Fit didn't wash with consumers because it was too time-consuming and complex to use. You had to dilute one capful of Fit in the excruciatingly precise measurement of 1.89 litres or one-half gallon U.S. of water. Step 2 demanded a two- to three-minute commitment to rubbing or swishing, and Step 3, rinsing the food under running water. The latter is what most people did before Fit was invented and continue to do for free.

P&G Canada president Tim Penner says the company was unable to change consumers' food preparation behaviour. That's the funny thing about people: While they're used to being manipulated by marketers, they don't always do what they're told, despite millions of dollars in marketing persuasion.

Not every new product is going to hit the jackpot, but what makes P&G, or any other marketer, think it can orchestrate how we live pieces of our lives in ways that will pad their bottom lines? It's one thing to convince people to switch from one brand of tissue to another, but herding consumer behaviour in the direction of your product can be a monumental task.

But not impossible. One of the most obvious examples is the degree to which many new mothers turned their backs on the primal human behaviour of breastfeeding to embrace manufactured infant formulas some 30 years ago. A more recent example of successful behaviour manipulation is the way people have replaced cold, hard cash with Interac cards, and how many prefer online banking to a face-to-face teller experience.

But if people like online banking, why are many consumers uncomfortable with the notion of online grocery shopping? Why have people embraced cellphones, but won't give up their familiar home plug-in telephones?

One research analyst explains that financial institutions were able to withstand the initial negative reaction to virtual banking, and they've been able to prove it works. "They have been able to deliver on the value proposition that it is faster, it is secure and it will make your life easier," he says. "They had enough money to start it off so even if our subscription rate was low, they kept pushing and showing it works."

Chris Bandak, director of consumer research at Comquest Research in Toronto, says marketing research can sometimes be deceiving. "You really need to get a true measure of whether people are willing to take the effort to find the product, buy it and then use it. A lot of times, unless the questions are asked in the right way, you will get answers that may lead you to believe that you can change the behaviours, when in practice it doesn't happen."

Fit went through five years of research and testing before it debuted in April 2000, but just 14 months later P&G said it would discontinue Fit in the U.S. market. Penner says P&G has withdrawn a great deal of marketing support for the brand in Canada and has offered "make goods" to retailers.

Perhaps Fit would have been a bigger hit in the green-conscious early 1990s. It certainly made me question the safety of our produce, but I also questioned the logic of replacing one type of residue (pesticide) with another (Fit).

Sometimes, fear has to be a factor if consumers are going to change behaviour dramatically. In other words, Fit may have presented a solution to a problem that consumers didn't think existed. In any case, the marketer's job isn't to shepherd people towards their products, but to invent products and services that meet consumers' needs.[8]

## Ethical Dimensions 6–1

### WHEN IS A WORD MORE THAN A WORD?

Part of the marketing job is to inform and persuade consumers about a firm's offering. An ethical issue sometimes arises, however, if consumers have *inaccurate* beliefs. For example, many consumers are confused about what foods are really healthy. Marketers for a number of food companies have been criticized for packaging and promotion that take advantage of inaccurate consumer perceptions about the meaning of the words *lite* or *low-fat*. A firm's "lite" donuts may have less fat or fewer calories than its other donuts—but that doesn't mean that the donut is low in fat or calories. Similarly, promotion of a "children's cold formula" may play off parents' fears that adult medicines are too strong—even though the basic ingredients in the children's formula are the same and only the dosage is different. And when Tiger Woods' happy smile appears in the American Express ad it's easy to forget that he's paid for his endorsement.

Marketers must also be careful about promotion that might encourage false beliefs, even if the advertising is not explicitly misleading. For example, ads for Unilever's Axe male deodorant body spray are designed to lead the consumer to believe that the product will increase a person's desirability to the opposite sex. Axe has been sold in more than 60 countries worldwide and had an extremely successful introduction into Canada and the United States, despite the fact that there was not a pre-existing consumer need for this type of product.[9] Similarly, ads for Ultra Slim-Fast low-fat beverage don't claim that anyone who buys the product will lose all the weight they want or look like the slim models who appear in the ads—but some critics argue that the advertising gives that impression.[10]



**Internet**

**Internet Exercise** Check out the Axe website (www.theaxeeffect.com). Do you find this type of advertising offensive or humorous? How do you think Unilever's target market (18-year-old men) would perceive this advertising? Do you think that this website promotes false consumer beliefs or expectations?

**Personality** Many researchers study how personality affects people's behaviour, but the results have generally been disappointing to marketers. A trait like neatness can be associated with users of certain types of products—like cleaning materials. But marketing managers have not found a way to use personality in marketing strategy planning.[11] As a result, they've stopped focusing on personality measures borrowed from psychologists and instead developed lifestyle analysis.

**Exhibit 6-5** Lifestyle dimensions and some related demographic dimensions.

| Dimension | Examples | | |
|---|---|---|---|
| Activities | Work<br>Hobbies<br>Social events | Vacation<br>Entertainment<br>Club membership | Surfing Web<br>Shopping<br>Sports |
| Interests | Family<br>Home<br>Job | Community<br>Recreation<br>Fashion | Food<br>Media<br>Achievements |
| Opinions | Themselves<br>Social issues<br>Politics | Business<br>Economics<br>Education | Products<br>Future<br>Culture |
| Demographics | Income<br>Age<br>Family life cycle | Geographic area<br>Ethnicity<br>Dwelling | Occupation<br>Family size<br>Education |

**The original Betty, 1936**

**1965**

**1972**

**1980**

**1986**

**Betty Crocker 2000**

General Mills has changed Betty Crocker's appearance as consumer attitudes and lifestyles have changed. The face of the newest Betty Crocker reflects her multicultural background.

**psychographics (lifestyle analysis)**

The analysis of a person's day-to-day pattern of living as expressed in that person's activities, interests, and opinions

**Psychographics** **Psychographics** or **lifestyle analysis** is the analysis of a person's day-to-day pattern of living as expressed in that person's activities, interests, and opinions—sometimes referred to as AIOs. (As you may recall, we introduced this topic in Chapter 3 when we looked at alternative ways to segment a market.) Exhibit 6-5 shows a number of variables for each of the AIO dimensions—along with some demographics used to add detail to the lifestyle profile of a target market.

Lifestyle analysis assumes that marketers can plan more effective strategies if they know more about their target markets. Understanding the lifestyle of target customers has been especially helpful in providing ideas for advertising themes. Let's see how it adds to a typical demographic description. It may not help Mercury marketing managers much to know that an average member of the target market for a Mountaineer SUV is 34.8 years old, married, lives in a three-bedroom home, and has 2.3 children. Lifestyles help marketers paint a more human portrait of the target market. For example, lifestyle analysis might show that the 34.8-year-old is also a community-oriented consumer with traditional values who especially enjoys spectator sports and spends much time in other family activities. An ad might show the Mountaineer being used by a happy family at a ball game so the target market could really identify with the ad. And the ad might be placed on a TSN show whose viewers match the target lifestyle profile.[12]

## Social Influences on Consumer Behaviour

We've been discussing some of the ways needs, attitudes, and other psychological variables influence the buying process. Now we'll see that these variables—and the buying process—are usually affected by relations with other people too. We'll look at how the individual interacts with family, social class, and other groups that may have influence.

Relationships with other family members influence many aspects of consumer behaviour. We saw specific examples of this in Chapter 5 when we considered the effects of the family life cycle on family spending patterns. Family members may also share many attitudes and values, consider each other's opinions, and divide various buying tasks. In years past, most marketers in North America targeted the wife as the family purchasing agent. Now, as sex-role stereotypes have changed and with night and weekend shopping more popular, men and older children may take more responsibility for shopping and decision making. In other countries, family roles vary. For example, in Norway women still do most of the family shopping.

Although only one family member may go to the store and make a specific purchase, when planning marketing strategy it's important to know who else may be involved. Other family members may have influenced the decision or really decided what to buy. Still others may use the product.

You don't have to watch much Saturday morning TV to see that Kellogg's knows this. Cartoon characters like Tony the Tiger tell kids about the goodies found in certain cereal packages and urge them to remind Dad or Mom to pick up that brand at the store. Similarly, the box for Post's Oreo O's cereal looks like the wrapper on the cookies, to get kids' attention in the store. Kids also influence grown-up purchases—to the tune of $250 billion a year. Surveys show that kids often have a big say in a family's choice of products such as apparel, cars, vacations, electronics, and health and beauty aids.

Spouses may jointly agree on many important purchases, but sometimes they may have strong personal preferences. However, such individual preferences may change if the other partner has different priorities. One might want to take a family vacation to Disneyland, while the other wants a new Sony DVD player and large-screen TV. The actual outcome in such a situation is unpredictable. The preferences of one spouse might change because of affection for the other or because of the other's power and influence.

Buying responsibility and influence vary greatly depending on the product and the family. A marketer trying to plan a strategy will find it helpful to research the specific target market. Remember, many buying decisions are made jointly, and thinking only about who actually buys the product can misdirect the marketing strategy.[13]

**social class**

A group of people who have approximately equal social position as viewed by others in the society

**Social class affects attitudes, values, and buying** Up to now, we have been concerned with the individual and the way individuals relate to their families. Now let's consider how society looks at an individual, and perhaps the family, in terms of social class. A **social class** is a group of people who have approximately equal social position as viewed by others in the society. Almost every society has some social class structure. The Canadian class system is far less rigid than in most coun-

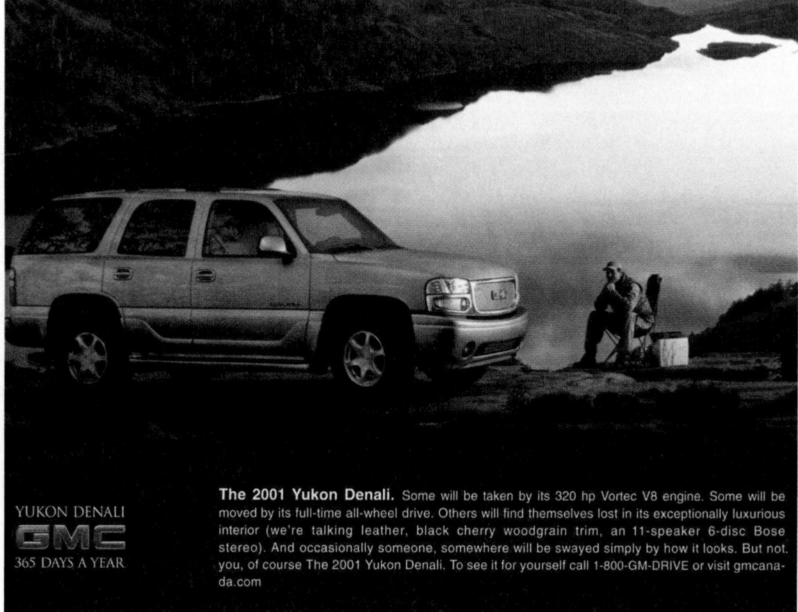


Which ad do you think would be most effective in selling to Canada's upper-middle class?

tries. People start out in the same social class as their parents, but they can move to a different social class depending on their education and the work they do.

Marketers want to know what buyers in various social classes are like. Simple approaches for measuring social class groupings are based on a person's occupation, education, and type and location of housing. By using marketing research surveys or studying available census data, marketers can get a feel for the social class of a target market. Note that income level is not included in this list. There is some general relationship between income level and social class, but the income levels of people within the same social class can vary greatly; people with the same amount of income may be in different social classes.

Dividing a nation's population into distinctly labelled social classes is no easy task. Would-be marketers needn't concern themselves with the specifics of the various ways this has been done in Canada or the United States. The most recent Canadian effort places primary reliance on occupation and education. These data, from the early 1990s, divide the Canadian consumer public into four major but further-divisible social strata: the upper classes (11 percent of the total and divisible in turn into very small upper-upper and lower-upper classes and a considerably larger upper-middle class); the middle class (28 percent of the total); the working



**Exhibit 6-6** Characteristics and attitudes of middle and lower classes.

| Middle Classes | Lower Classes |
|---|---|
| Plan and save for the future | Live for the present |
| Analyze alternatives | "Feel" what is "best" |
| Understand how the world works | Have simplistic ideas about how things work |
| Feel they have opportunities | Feel controlled by the world |
| Willing to take risks | Play it safe |
| Confident about decision making | Want help with decision making |
| Want long-run quality or value | Want short-run satisfaction |

**Exhibit 6-7** Consumption behaviour of Canada's upper-middle class.

1. Seek out genuine educational experiences for self and children (drama, piano, ballet, Suzuki violin lessons, museums, international student exchanges).
2. Admire those who can speak many languages and often try to learn languages themselves.
3. Believe in high culture (ballet, theatre, opera, art galleries, museums).
4. Participate in sports often associated with prestige and serenity, and those that deliver vigorous exercise (sailing, gliding, horseback riding, golf, tennis, squash, cycling).
5. In clothing, prefer organic materials (cotton, wool, silk, leather) and resist wearing synthetics, such as polyester.
6. Preferred colours tend to be navy blue and pastels. Like preppy Ralph Lauren fashions.
7. More willing to experiment with new dishes (foreign and exotic foods, haute cuisine, ethnic restaurants, and the foreign food and ingredients counters at specialty stores).
8. Generally, are more confident shoppers and decision makers than other classes and more skilful at evaluating products.

class (41 percent); and a lower class (20 percent of the total and divided in turn into upper-lower and lower-lower classes of approximately equal size).[14]

The seven Canadian social classes differ in terms of typical occupational and educational profiles, social and geographic horizons, consumption patterns, and personal values. Detailed comparisons reveal no truth to the old saying, "A rich man is simply a poor man with money." Given the same income as middle-class people, persons belonging to the lower classes handle themselves and their money very differently. The various classes shop at different stores. They prefer different treatment from salespeople. They buy different brands of products, even when prices are about the same. And they have different spending and saving attitudes. Some of these differences are shown in Exhibit 6-6.

The upper-middle class (about 9 percent of the Canadian population) consists of successful professionals, owners of small businesses, and managers of large corporations. These people are concerned about their quality of life. They view their purchases as symbols of success, so they want quality products. They also want to be seen as socially responsible. They support the arts and are community-minded. They are ambitious for their children and, in general, are more future-oriented than lower-class groups. Exhibit 6-7 provides additional information on the upper-middle class's consumption behaviour. The information from this and similar descriptions of the other Canadian social classes can be of great value to marketers.

**reference group**
The people to whom an individual looks when forming attitudes about a particular topic

**Reference groups** A **reference group** is the people to whom an individual looks when forming attitudes about a particular topic. People normally have several reference groups for different topics. Some they meet face-to-face, others they just wish to imitate. In either case, they may take values from these reference groups and make buying decisions based on what the group might accept.

We're always making comparisons between ourselves and others. So reference groups are more important when others will be able to "see" which product or brand we're using. Influence is stronger for products that relate to status in the group. For one group, owning an expensive fur coat may be a status symbol. In contrast, a group of animal lovers might view it as a sign of bad judgment. In either case, a consumer's decision to buy or not buy a fur coat might depend on the opinions of others in that consumer's reference group.[15]

**opinion leader**
A person who influences others

**Opinion leaders** An **opinion leader** is a person who influences others. Opinion leaders aren't necessarily wealthier or better educated. And opinion leaders on one subject aren't necessarily opinion leaders on another. For example, you may have a friend who is ahead of the curve in knowing about computer products, but you might

Reference-group influence is usually more important when others will be able to see which product a consumer is using, but Jockey wants young people to view its underwear as in fashion and encourages them to "Let 'em know you're Jockey."

not want that friend's opinion about new clothing styles and cosmetics. On the other hand, sometimes a leader in one area earns respect in another. For example, George Foreman, former heavyweight champion of the world, has become a household name representing his line of Foreman grills. Each social class and age group tends to have its own opinion leaders. Some marketing mixes aim especially at these people since their opinions affect others, and research shows that they are involved in many product-related discussions with "followers." Favourable word-of-mouth publicity from opinion leaders can really help a marketing mix. But the opposite is also true—if opinion leaders aren't satisfied, they're likely to talk about it and influence others.[16]

**culture**
The whole set of beliefs, attitudes, and ways of doing things of a reasonably homogeneous set of people

**Culture** **Culture** is the whole set of beliefs, attitudes, and ways of doing things of a reasonably homogeneous set of people. In Chapters 4 and 5, we looked at the broad impact of culture when we discussed ethnic and international marketing opportunities.

People within major cultural groupings tend to be more similar in outlook and behaviour. But sometimes it is useful to think of subcultures within such groupings. For example, within the North American culture there are various religious and ethnic subcultures. Also, different cultural forces tend to prevail in different regions of the continent.

Failure to consider cultural differences, even subtle ones, can result in problems. To promote their product and get people to try it, marketers for Pepto-Bismol often provide free samples at festivals and street fairs. Their idea is that people tend to overindulge at such events. However, when they distributed sample packets at a festival in San Francisco's Chinatown, they insulted many of the people they wanted to influence. Booths with Chinese delicacies lined the streets, and many of the participants interpreted the sample packets (which featured the word "Nauseous" in large letters) as suggesting that Chinese delicacies were nauseating. The possibility of this misinterpretation may seem obvious in hindsight, but if it had been that obvious in advance the whole promotion would have been handled differently.[17]

Planning strategies that consider cultural differences in international markets can be even harder—and such cultures usually vary more. Each foreign market may need to be treated as a separate market with its own submarkets. Ignoring cultural differences—or assuming that they are not important—almost guarantees failure in international markets.

For example, when marketing managers for Procter & Gamble first tried to sell the North American version of Cheer detergent to Japanese consumers, they promoted it as an effective all-temperature laundry detergent. But many Japanese wash clothes in cold tap water or leftover bath water, so they don't care about all-temperature washing. In addition, Cheer didn't make suds when it was used with the fabric softeners popular with Japanese consumers. When P&G's marketing managers discovered these problems, they changed Cheer so it wouldn't be affected by the fabric softeners. They also changed Cheer ads to promise superior cleaning in cold water. Cheer became one of P&G's best-selling products in Japan.[18]

From a target marketing point of view, a marketing manager probably wants to aim at people within one culture or subculture. A firm developing strategies for two cultures often needs two different marketing plans.[19] Because cultural forces tend to change slowly, marketers can often get good help from someone who already has a good understanding of the culture of the target customers.

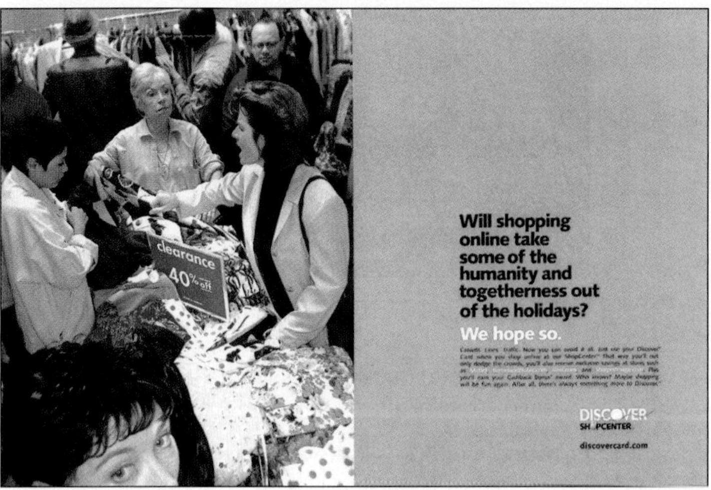

clearance
40% off
Will shopping
online take
some of the
humanity and
togetherness out
of the holidays?
We hope so.
discovercard.com


The nature of the purchase situation and the problem-solving processes that consumers use are typically different when they are shopping on the Internet rather than at a store.



### The Effect of Purchase Situation

Needs, benefits sought, attitudes, motivation, and even how a consumer selects certain products all vary depending on the purchase situation. So different purchase situations may require different marketing mixes—even when the same target market is involved. Let's briefly consider some of the ways that the purchase situation can vary.

*Why* a consumer makes a purchase can affect buying behaviour. For example, a student buying a pen to take notes might pick up an inexpensive Bic. But the same student might choose a Cross pen as a gift for a friend.

Time influences a purchase situation. *When* consumers make a purchase—and the time they have available for shopping—will influence their behaviour. A leisurely dinner or socializing with friends at a Starbucks induces different behaviour than grabbing a quick cup of Tim Hortons coffee on the way to work.

The urgency of the need is another time-related factor. A sports buff who needs a VCR in time for the Super Bowl—that evening—might spend an hour driving across town in heavy traffic to get the right unit. In a different circumstance, the same person might order the VCR online from a website and figure that the extra time for it to be shipped is well worth the money saved.

On the other hand, how long something takes may be relative. Our online shopper might be frustrated by a web page that takes two minutes to load and abandon his virtual shopping cart after the VCR is already selected. This happens all the time online. On the other hand, you don't often see a consumer walk away from a shopping cart because of a two-minute wait in a checkout line at a store.

Surroundings can affect buying behaviour. The excitement at an auction may stimulate impulse buying. Checking out an auction online might lead to a different response. Surroundings may discourage buying too. For example, some people don't like to stand in a checkout line where others can see what they're buying—even if the other shoppers are complete strangers.[20]

## Satisfying Needs: The Consumer Problem-Solving Process

The variables discussed affect *what* products a consumer finally decides to purchase. Marketing managers also need to understand *how* buyers use a problem-solving process to select particular products. For example, once the decision is made to buy CD-Rs, the customer must still decide whether to buy Fujifilm, Kodak, or some other brand of CD.

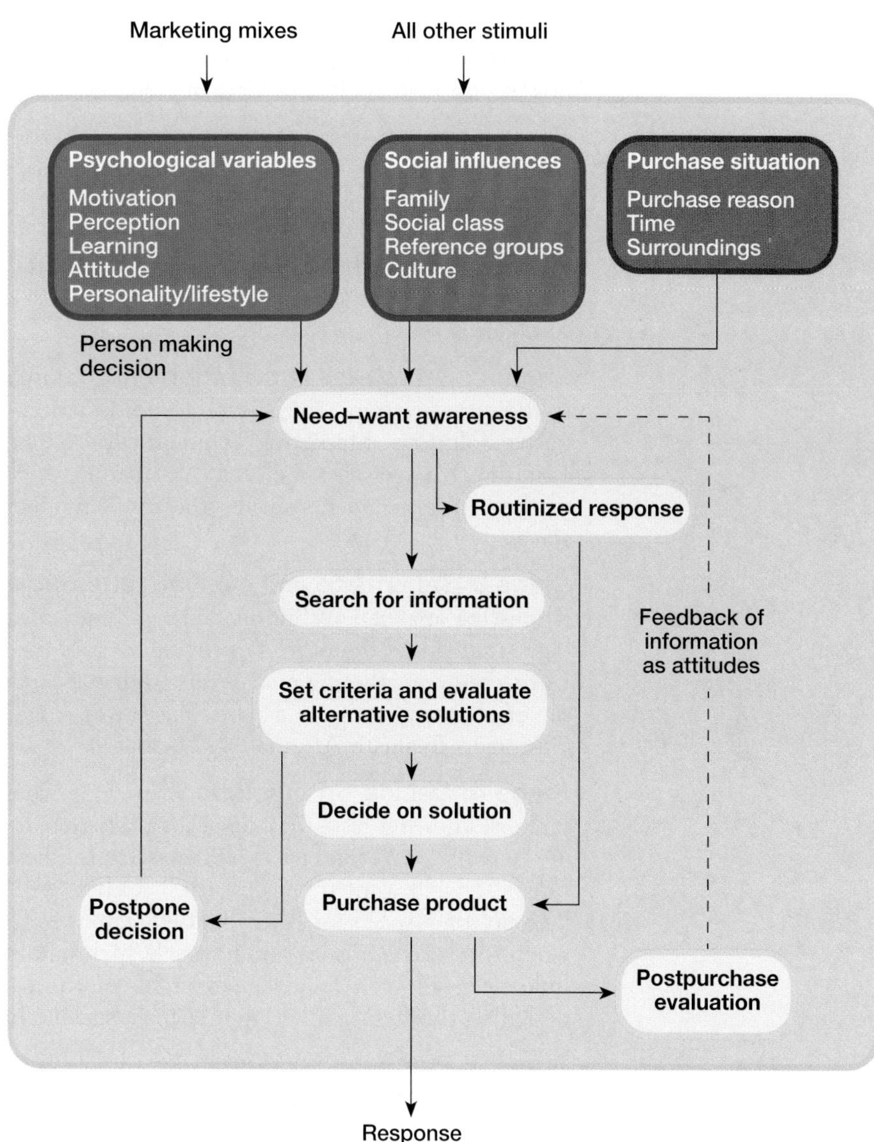


Exhibit 6-8 An expanded model of the consumer decision-making process.



Most consumers seem to use the following six-step problem-solving process:

1. Becoming aware of—or interested in—the problem.
2. Recalling and gathering information about possible solutions.
3. Evaluating alternative solutions—perhaps trying some out.
4. Deciding on the appropriate solution.
5. Purchasing the product.
6. Evaluating the decision.[21]

Exhibit 6-8 presents an expanded version of the buyer behaviour model shown in Exhibit 6-1. This exhibit shows the consumer beginning the problem-solving process and as a consequence the whole set of variables we've been reviewing. That is, they become aware of—or interested in—solving a consumption problem as a result of psychological, social, and situational influences.

### The Model in Detail

Each of the six stages of the problem-solving process has a distinct implication for how a firm markets its products or services.

**Stage 1: Need–want awareness** Before any decision-making can occur, the buyer must become aware of their need or want, the necessity of satisfying it, and the association between a firm's product and that need or want. Marketers can remind customers of their needs (e.g. "It's time to think about getting the garden ready for spring"), heighten awareness of why the need is important (e.g. "Doesn't your family deserve more?"), or build associations (e.g. Michelin's tagline "Because so much is riding on your tires").

**Stage 2: Search for information** Once consumers decide to seek out a solution to their need or want, they search for information on the qualities and costs of alternative solutions. Marketing communications play a central role at this stage by ensuring that messages are seen, understood, and remembered: the absence of any of these three elements means the firm's product will not be considered at later stages.

**Stage 3: Set criteria and evaluate alternatives** Once information is collected, it must be analyzed. While marketing communication focuses on getting the message attended to, the other Ps provide most of the source of content of the message. In this sense, marketing must ensure that the product, price, and place are the right set of characteristics for a particular buyer. This is discussed further under "How Customers Evaluate Alternatives" below.

**Stage 4: Decide on a solution** Knowing what a buyer wants to buy is not the same as knowing how they determine whether a particular product has what they are looking for. Some buyers will look for the best performance on a single characteristic (e.g. "I want the fastest car"). Others will trade off characteristics (e.g. "I'll give up some speed for better fuel efficiency"). The variations can be even greater when the purchase is for family use: Which family member will decide? How much influence will each family member have? Knowing these variations is critical in designing the right marketing mix for a specific buyer.

**Stage 5: Purchase product** Once the decision to buy a product is made, someone must still perform the physical act of purchasing it. A consumer might go a store fully intending to buy a specific brand but might change their mind at the last minute. This can happen for a variety of reasons: a competing brand may be featured or on sale at the store; the intended brand may be out of stock or hard to find; retail staff might promote another brand, and so on. Effective marketers anticipate these problems so that the firm does not lose sales it should receive.

**Stage 6: Post-purchase evaluation** A marketer's job is not done even after a purchase is made. The product still has to be used, and a consumer's experience in using the product will determine whether, on the next occasion, they buy the same brand again or whether they seek out a new source of supply. A buyer may have second thoughts after making a purchase decision. The buyer may have chosen from among several attractive alternatives—weighing the pros and cons and finally making a decision. Later doubts, however, may lead to **dissonance**—tension caused by uncertainty about the rightness of a decision. Dissonance may lead a buyer to search for additional information to confirm the wisdom of the decision and so reduce tension. Without this confirmation, the adopter might buy something else next time or not comment positively about the product to others.[22] This is the reason why so many firms now maintain contact with buyers after the purchase, provide online or telephone-based technical support, and may contact buyers with surveys to determine whether expectations were met.

**dissonance**
Tension caused by uncertainty about the rightness of a decision

Exhibit 6-9 Problem-solving continuum.

| Low involvement<br>Frequently purchased<br>Inexpensive<br>Little risk<br>Little information needed | Routinized response behaviour | Limited problem solving | Extensive problem solving | High involvement<br>Infrequently purchased<br>Expensive<br>High risk<br>Much information desired |
|---|---|---|---|---|

## The Model in Practice

While Exhibit 6-8 suggests a relatively orderly process for collecting, analyzing, and acting upon information, it is by no means a simple process. For example, when consumers evaluate information about purchase alternatives, they may weigh differences in brands and in the stores where the products may be available. This can be a very complicated evaluation procedure given the impact of purchase situations on buyer behaviour. Moreover, depending on their choice of criteria, consumers may make seemingly irrational decisions. For example, when convenient service is crucial, a buyer may pay list price for an unexciting car from a very convenient dealer.

There are countless numbers of ways in which these factors might interact to influence purchase behaviour. This is one of the reasons why sellers are so interested in the information-processing capabilities of e-commerce (see Internet Insite 6-1). Fortunately, there are some frameworks that can help marketers take these factors into account in designing marketing programs.

When consumers evaluate information about purchase alternatives, they may weigh a product type in relation not only to other types of products but also to differences in brands within a product type *and* the stores where the products may be available. This can be a very complicated evaluation procedure, and, depending on their choice of criteria, consumers may make seemingly irrational decisions. If convenient service is crucial, for example, a buyer might pay list price for an unexciting car from a very convenient dealer. It is for this reason that marketers think about three different ways in which the problem-solving process is used, each reflecting a different level of behaviour.

**Three levels of problem solving** The basic problem-solving process shows the steps consumers may go through trying to find a way to satisfy their needs—but it doesn't show how long this process will take or how much thought a consumer will give to each step. Individuals who have had a lot of experience solving certain problems can move quickly through some of the steps or almost directly to a decision.

It is helpful, therefore, to recognize three levels of problem solving: extensive problem solving, limited problem solving, and routinized response behaviour (see Exhibit 6-9). These problem-solving approaches are used for any kind of product. Consumers use **extensive problem solving** for a completely new or important need—when they put much effort into deciding how to satisfy it. For example, a music lover who wants to download music might decide to buy an MP3 player—but not have any idea what model to buy. After talking with friends to find out about their experiences with different models, she might do an Internet search to see if highly recommended models were still available, to get the details about features, and even to look for published product reviews. She might also compare prices listed by firms selling the players over the Internet. After thinking about her needs some more, she might want to visit a local dealer to listen to a Sony unit with an optional memory card to hold more tracks. And if she likes the sound—and the store has a good extended service guarantee at the right price—she'll buy it. This is not exactly an impulse purchase! Internet Insite 6-2 highlights the impact of the Internet on how consumers can conduct extensive problem solving in new and exciting ways.

**extensive problem solving**
When consumers put effort into deciding how to satisfy a completely new or important need

**limited problem solving**
Used when consumers are willing to put *some* effort into deciding the best way to satisfy a need

Consumers use **limited problem solving** when they're willing to put *some* effort into deciding the best way to satisfy a need. Limited problem solving is typical when a consumer has some previous experience in solving a problem but isn't certain which choice is best at the current time. If our music lover also wanted some new compact discs for her car CD player, she would already know what type of music she enjoys. She might go to a familiar store and evaluate what new CDs they had in stock for her favourite types of music.

**routinized response behaviour**
Used by consumers when they regularly select a particular way of satisfying a need when it occurs

Consumers use **routinized response behaviour** when they regularly select a particular way of satisfying a need when it occurs. Routinized response behaviour is typical when a consumer has considerable experience in how to meet a need and has no need for additional information. For example, our music lover might routinely buy the latest recording by her favourite band as soon as it's available.

Most marketing managers would like their target consumers to buy their products in this routinized way. Some firms provide special services for frequent buyers, encourage repeat business with discounts, or do other things to build a good relationship so that the customer purchases from them in a routinized way.

**low-involvement purchases**
Purchases that have little importance or relevance for the customer

Routinized response behaviour is also typical for **low-involvement purchases**—purchases that have little importance or relevance for the customer. Let's face it, buying a box of salt is probably not one of the burning issues in your life.[23]

The reason problem solving becomes simpler with time is that people learn from experience—both positive and negative things. As consumers approach the problem-solving process, they bring attitudes formed by previous experiences and social training. Each new problem-solving process may then contribute to or modify this attitude set. Since there is little that can go wrong in buying something like salt, the likelihood of satisfaction is high and thus routinized response sets in quickly. Just the opposite would be true for an infrequently purchased, expensive, and complex product like a car.

## Internet Insite 6–1

### TRACKING CONSUMER BEHAVIOUR

Understanding who buys the product, why they buy, how they use the product, and what influences their decision to buy or not are questions at the crux of consumer behaviour research. Consumer research has often been limited to the occasional survey or focus-group study in many organizations. Some firms have consumer panels, which allow for ongoing and longitudinal tracking of shopping behaviour and attitudes. While the importance of understanding consumers and their motivations has long been understood by marketers, very few firms in the past knew all they needed to know about their customers. Time, cost, difficulty of tracking consumers, and low response rates to surveys were some contributing reasons.

The Web offers marketers enhanced capability for tracking consumer behaviour that is unparallelled in the bricks-and-mortar world. Marketers now have the opportunity to get closer to their consumers.

Each time a consumer makes a purchase in an online store, there is a purchase transaction recorded in the company's computer system. Each customer can be identified by a unique customer account number as well as by name, address, and credit card number. The ability to track purchase history and make offers or customize the advertising is unique to the Web.

Amazon.com offers customers customized recommendations for books and other products based on their previous purchase history as well as the purchase histories of other customers with similar buying behaviour. Every time an Amazon.com customer logs in to that site, he or she is greeted with these personalized recommendations. A technology called "collaborative filtering" is used to make such recommendations. The Web makes it cost-effective to customize and target advertising based on actual behaviour.

Most large websites track visitors. The pages viewed, repeat visits, products purchased, duration of visits, frequency of visits, consumer response to an ad (or a link in a site), and many other variables can be measured and tracked. Sane Solutions' NetTracker (www.sane.com) and WebTrends by NetIQ (www.netiq.com) are two of the many software products that can track consumer behaviour online (see the exhibit below). These programs can also monitor click-throughs (the percentage of viewers who click on an ad or a link) and track the path the visitor takes during a browsing session. In addition to using such software, websites will often use a cookie file, which is a small text file stored in the user's computer that can contain information relating to web surfing or shopping preferences. Cookie files allow websites to recognize someone as a repeat visitor, and the site can then be customized for this person based on their past preferences.

Many online stores conduct exit customer satisfaction surveys after a customer has completed a purchase transaction. BizRate (www.bizrate.com) provides a satisfaction and complaint measurements service. For instance, after you pay for your purchase at stores such as 1800flowers.com or Buy.com, a small window may pop up with a request to complete a short survey. Feedback from customers is then compiled by BizRate and detailed results, including industry comparisons, are provided to the company. Consumers can see the average ratings of various online stores at the BizRate site. Companies can, of course, conduct their own satisfaction surveys online, but using an independent third party like BizRate lends the process greater credibility.

Through the use of behavioural tracking (provided by WebTrends and others) and attitudinal tracking (provided by BizRate and others), marketers should be able to gain a better understanding of consumer preferences both at the aggregate and individual levels, which can lead to increased consumer retention. Customer relationship management (CRM) programs are based on gathering and analyzing such behavioural and attitudinal data and then translating the results into effective marketing programs.

While the ability to track consumers sounds great, many companies do not effectively manage and use such information. Sites that attract a lot of visitors can end up with a volume of data. Data mining techniques need to be employed to understand trends and patterns. The resources needed to do this may be a barrier for smaller firms.

When consumers hear that they are being tracked or monitored by websites, it immediately raises concerns regarding privacy. Marketers would argue that using cookie files and tracking software enables them to better understand consumer needs. They can segment the market more effectively and respond to individual needs. At the same time, to protect consumer privacy the best practice on the Internet is to have a written privacy policy on the site. This policy document should unambiguously explain how the data are used and with whom they are shared. Some firms also give the consumer the right to not provide consent for certain types of use of such data. Such policies can go a long way in building consumer trust.

Some questions to ponder: Given what you know about tracking consumer behaviour online, what guidelines would you recommend for the use of such information? How can marketers use the information obtained through various tracking tools on the Web?

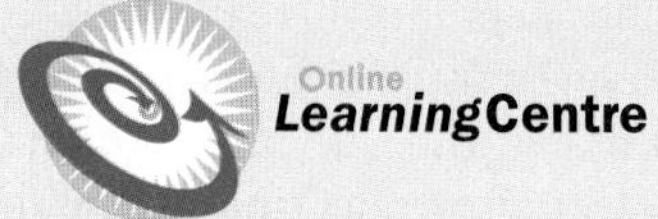


Go to: **www.mcgrawhill.ca/college/wong**
to apply this Insite in an exciting Internet exercise.

**How customers evaluate alternatives** On the basis of studies of how consumers seek out and evaluate product information, researchers suggest that marketing managers use an evaluative grid showing features common to different products (or marketing mixes). For example, Exhibit 6-10 shows some of the features common to three different cars a consumer might consider.

The grid encourages marketing managers to view each product as a bundle of features or attributes. The pluses and minuses in Exhibit 6-10 indicate one consumer's attitude toward each feature of each car. If members of the target market don't rate a feature of the marketing manager's brand with pluses, it may indicate a problem. The manager might want to change the product to improve that feature or perhaps

**Exhibit 6-10** Grid of evaluative criteria for three car brands.

| Brands | Common features | | | |
|---|---|---|---|---|
| | Gas mileage | Ease of service | Comfortable interior | Styling |
| Nissan | [−] | + | + | − |
| Saab | + | [−] | + | + |
| Toyota | + | + | [+] | [−] |

Note: Pluses and minuses indicate a consumer's evaluation of a feature for a brand.

use more promotion to emphasize an already acceptable feature. The consumer in Exhibit 6-10 has a minus under gas mileage for the Nissan. If the Nissan really gets better gas mileage than the other cars, promotion might focus on mileage to improve consumer attitudes toward this feature and toward the whole product.

Some consumers will reject a product if they see *one* feature as substandard—regardless of how favourably they regard the product's other features. The consumer in Exhibit 6-10 might avoid the Saab, which he saw as less than satisfactory on ease of service, even if it were superior in all other aspects. In other instances, a consumer's overall attitude toward the product might be such that a few good features could make up for some shortcomings. The comfortable interior of the Toyota (Exhibit 6-10) might make up for less exciting styling—especially if the consumer viewed comfort as really important.

Of course, most consumers don't use a grid like this. However, constructing such a grid helps managers think about what evaluative criteria target consumers consider really important, what consumers' attitudes are toward their product (or marketing mix) on each criteria, and how consumers combine the criteria to reach a final decision. Having a better understanding of the process should help a manager develop a better marketing mix.[24]

**adoption process**

The steps individuals go through on the way to accepting or rejecting a new idea

**The special case of new concepts** When consumers face a really new concept, they may not feel that their previous experience provides enough relevant information to make a decision. These situations involve the **adoption process**—the steps individuals go through on the way to accepting or rejecting a new idea. Although the adoption process is similar to the problem-solving process, learning plays a clearer role and promotion's contribution to a marketing mix is more visible.

## Internet Insite 6–2

### THE EMPOWERED CONSUMER

How often have you purchased a product without knowing all you needed to know about the alternatives (brands) available to you? Have there been occasions when you were not able to compare prices at different stores (perhaps you didn't have the time) and ended up paying a higher price? In the bricks-and-mortar world, a world of imperfect information, where stores selling comparable products are located far from each other, consumers are often forced to make less than optimal decisions. That is not the case online. Marketers, beware the empowered consumer.

Consumers can go to BizRate's comparison shopping site (or mySimon, NexTag, Price.com, Epinions.com, or dozens of other comparison shopping sites) and, with a few mouse clicks, find out information on different brands, prices, ratings of stores, and more (see the exhibit below). A comparison of prices for a Nikon Coolpix 5700 digital camera showed a $200 price difference across stores. BizRate also provides consumer ratings on store service and delivery for those who do not want to make a decision solely based on price. Epinions takes the notion of consumer feedback further by posting ratings and detailed product reviews by consumers for other consumers. Sites like these allow consumers to share their experiences, good or bad, with other consumers. Such word-of-mouth communication is perceived to be more credible than paid advertising.

A study by ForeSee Results (www.foreseeresults.com) revealed that almost three-quarters (73 percent) of online consumers used a shopping search engine to compare prices, and a significant number used search engines to compare products (54 percent) as well as find stores that sell those products (45 percent).[25] The use of the Internet as an information source is stronger for big-ticket items like cars, electronics, travel, and appliances. When consumers walk into a store these days, chances are they have already done their homework and are better informed than at any time in the past.

The Internet influences not only prepurchase behaviour, but also postpurchase behaviour. Consumers who are not satisfied with a product or service can take their complaint directly to the company's website or post their views on sites such as Epinions.com or Complaints.com. Alternatively, Better Business Bureau Online's dispute resolution system can be used (www.bbb.org/complaint.asp). BizRate allows consumers to rate stores on various attributes based on their experience.

While the Internet has had an impact on consumer decision-making and complaint behaviour, it also presents consumers some challenges. The variety of products and stores online may lead to information overload. At the same time, the ability to shop 24/7 and the ability to shop across borders means that stores cannot take their local customers for granted.

Greater choice, easy comparisons, and growing price competition among stores has led to lower consumer loyalty. Only 18 percent of consumers who bought airline tickets online were loyal toward Web-based travel agencies, and more than 70 percent of those who book tickets online use multiple sites before making a purchase.[26] Diminishing loyalty is a concern in other categories as well. The Internet is used primarily as an information source, with actual purchasing often done in bricks-and-mortar stores (called *multichannel shopping*). Such multichannel shoppers are especially prone to be less brand loyal. A study by Jupiter Research (www.jup.com) projects that by 2006 consumers who are not loyal to brands but make decisions based on price will account for 64 percent of online shoppers, while 19 percent of online shoppers will be brand-loyal.[27] Consumer loyalty has to be earned; it cannot be taken for granted.

Proactive Internet marketers have moved away from price competition to personalized marketing (e.g., Amazon.com's personalized product recommendations, Dell's customized computers, tailor-made clothing at IC3D). By tailoring the marketing efforts to each individual's taste, these firms offer consumers a superior value proposition that in turn increases customer retention rates and profitability. These firms have demonstrated that building customer loyalty takes effort, but it can still be done. While dissatisfied customers defect and can spread negative word-of-mouth online, satisfied customers purchase repeatedly and can be great targets for cross-selling opportunities. Even reasonably satisfied customers can defect on the Internet because switching costs are minimal. Firms must focus on understanding customer needs (sometimes at the individual level) and find ways of delivering superior value in order to succeed in this hyper-competitive environment.

Some questions to ponder: How can online stores ensure a high degree of customer satisfaction and loyalty? Will comparison-shopping search engines lead to more consumer decisions based on price (and therefore lower prices), or will brand differentiation still matter?

Go to: **www.mcgrawhill.ca/college/wong**
to apply this Insite in an exciting Internet exercise.

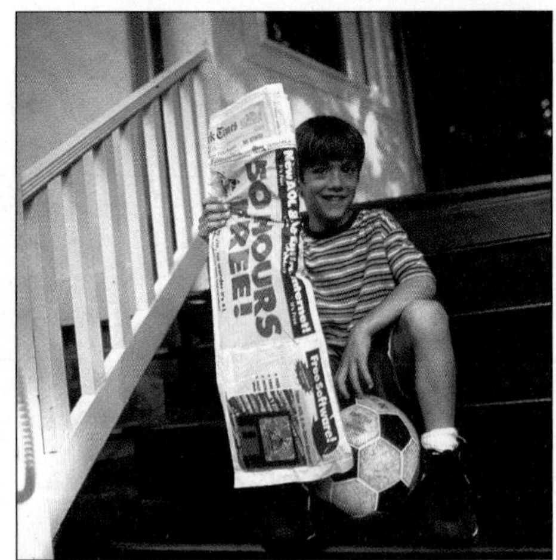


Marketers often want to make it easier for consumers to adopt a product. Colgate offers free samples to encourage consumers in Colombia to try its Protex Fresh soap bars; AOL gives away free discs in dozens of ways, including with newspapers.



In the adoption process, an individual moves through some fairly definite steps:

1. *Awareness*—the potential customer comes to know about the product but lacks details. The consumer may not even know how it works or what it will do.
2. *Interest*—if the consumer becomes interested, he or she will gather general information and facts about the product.
3. *Evaluation*—a consumer begins to give the product a mental trial, applying it to his or her personal situation.
4. *Trial*—the consumer may buy the product to experiment with it in use. A product that is either too expensive to try or isn't available for trial may never be adopted.
5. *Decision*—the consumer decides on either adoption or rejection. A satisfactory evaluation and trial may lead to adoption of the product and regular use. According to psychological learning theory, reinforcement leads to adoption.
6. *Confirmation*—the adopter continues to rethink the decision and searches for support for the decision—that is, further reinforcement.[28]

PepsiCo had to work with the adoption process when it introduced Pepsi One, a low-calorie cola. Many consumers are interested in staying trim, but diet sodas have an image of bad taste. In light of that, Pepsi's initial ads didn't directly say that Pepsi One was a diet drink. Rather, they used the slogan "True Cola Taste. One Calorie." But that confused a lot of consumers who couldn't tell what made it different from Diet Pepsi. As a result, consumer interest was not as great as Pepsi had expected. Because awareness and interest were low among consumers, retailers didn't devote much shelf space to Pepsi One, so it often wasn't even there for a consumer to evaluate. Even after a year on the market, trial was low.

To help more consumers through the adoption process, Pepsi made changes. To build awareness and interest, new ads explained that Pepsi One was using a new sweetener, recently approved by the government, which tasted better than the sweetener used in other diet drinks. The ads showed consumers drinking Pepsi One and not being able to taste the difference from a regular cola; they used the tagline

**Internet**

**Internet Exercise** To make it easier for consumers to visualize how certain fashions will look, the Lands' End website (www.landsend.com) has an interactive "virtual model" feature. Go to the Lands' End website, click on "My Model," and check out this feature. Do you think that it makes it easier to evaluate a potential purchase?

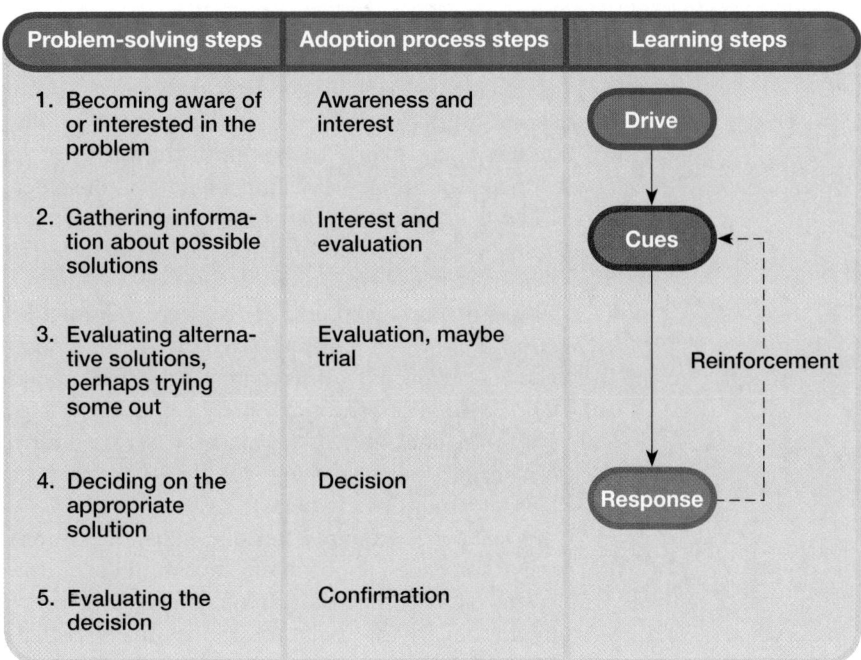

Problem-solving steps
Adoption process steps
Learning steps
1. Becoming aware of or interested in the problem
Awareness and interest
Drive
2. Gathering information about possible solutions
Interest and evaluation
Cues
3. Evaluating alternative solutions, perhaps trying some out
Evaluation, maybe trial
Reinforcement
4. Deciding on the appropriate solution
Decision
Response
5. Evaluating the decision
Confirmation


Exhibit 6-11 Relation of problem-solving process, adoption process, and learning (given a problem).

"Too good to be one calorie, but it is." Pepsi also changed the packaging graphics to put more emphasis on the sweetener at the point of purchase. To generate more trial, Pepsi pushed to get Pepsi One promoted on special end-aisle displays and stepped up its sampling program with taste-testing booths on campuses, in office cafeterias, and at movie theatres. Of course, consumers will decide to regularly buy Pepsi One only if they are satisfied with the taste.[29]

Exhibit 6-11 shows the interrelation of the problem-solving process, the adoption process, and learning. It is important to see this interrelation and to understand that promotion can modify or accelerate it. Also note that the potential buyers' problem-solving behaviour should affect how firms design their distribution systems. Similarly, customers' attitudes may determine how price sensitive they are and what price the firm should charge. Knowing how target markets handle these processes helps companies with their marketing strategy planning.

**Consumer behaviour in international markets** You're a consumer, so you probably have very good intuition about the many influences on consumer behaviour that we've been discussing. For many different purchase situations you also intuitively know from experience which variables are most important. That's good, but it's also a potential trap—especially when developing marketing mixes for consumers in international markets. The less a marketing manager knows about the *specific* social and intrapersonal variables that shape the behaviour of target customers, the more likely it is that relying on intuition will be misleading. We all have a tendency to try to explain things we don't understand by generalizing from what we do know. Yet when it comes to consumer behaviour, many of the specifics do not generalize from one culture to another.

Cadbury's effort to develop a Japanese market for its Dairy Milk Chocolate candy bar illustrates the point. Cadbury marketing managers conducted marketing research to find out more about candy preferences among Japanese consumers. The consumers said that they didn't like the high milk-fat content of Cadbury's bar. Cadbury's managers, however, reasoned that this reaction must be from lack of opportunity to become accustomed to the candy. After all, in most other countries it's the rich taste of the candy that turns consumers into "chocoholics." When Cadbury introduced the bar in Japan, it was a real flop. Taste preferences in other countries simply didn't generalize to Japan. It also wasn't just a matter of opportunity. The whole diet in Japan is different enough that eating the candy was unpleasant. By contrast, Dannon was successful because it took similar research findings to heart and dramatically modified its yogurt dairy desserts until they satisfied Japanese tastes.

Sometimes important influences on consumer behaviour are more subtle. When P&G first introduced disposable diapers in Japan, interest was limited. Research suggested that price and health concerns were a sticking point, as was product fit. The diapers leaked because the design was too large for most Japanese babies. From the Western vantage point, these were reasonable problems to work on. However, another powerful cultural force was also at work. At that time, most Japanese mothers were expected to dedicate themselves to caring for their babies. Many women who could afford the convenience of disposable diapers felt guilty using them. Japanese firms that entered the market later used ads to emphasize that disposables were *best for the baby*. That appeal relieved the mother's guilt. Even so, it took time for basic attitudes to change.

Our diaper example can also serve as a reminder to watch out for oversimplifying stereotypes. Consumers in a foreign culture may be bound by some similar cultural forces, but that doesn't mean that they are all the same. Further, changes in the underlying social forces may make outdated views irrelevant.

Many Westerners believe that the typical Japanese executive works very long hours and devotes very little time to family life. That stereotype has been highlighted in the Western media. It's still partly true. Yet in today's Japan, many young Japanese executives want a more balanced family life; they don't want to continue the almost total dedication to business accepted by the previous generation. A marketer who didn't recognize this change probably wouldn't fully understand these people, their needs, or the buying behaviour in their families.

Developing a marketing mix that really satisfies the needs of a target market takes a real understanding of consumer behaviour and the varied forces that shape it. That holds whether the target market is local or halfway around the world. So when planning strategies for international markets, it's best to involve locals who have a better chance of understanding the experience, attitudes, and interests of your customers. Many companies, even very sophisticated ones, have faltered because they failed to heed that simple advice.[30]

E*Trade ads often rely on humour in North America and abroad. For example, this Swedish ad says, "Here is a service for all of you that inherited money. Or brains." However, because humour may not work in the same way in different cultures, E*Trade often uses locally produced ads and in some countries, like France, a more serious approach is taken.

## Chapter Summary

In this chapter, we analyzed the individual consumer as a problem solver who is influenced by psychological variables, social influences, and the purchase situation. All of these variables are related, and our model of buyer behaviour helps integrate them into one process. Marketing strategy planning requires a good grasp of this material. Assuming that everyone behaves the way you do—or even like your family or friends do—can lead to expensive marketing errors. This is precisely why we focus so much attention on the concept of segmentation.

Consumer buying behaviour results from the consumer's efforts to satisfy needs and wants. We discussed some reasons why consumers buy and saw that consumer behaviour can't be fully explained by only a list of needs.

We presented a buyer behaviour model to help you interpret and integrate the present findings—as well as any new data you might get from marketing research. As of now, the behavioural sciences can offer only insights and theories, which the marketing manager must blend with intuition and judgment to develop marketing strategies.

Companies may have to use marketing research to answer specific questions. But if a firm has neither the money nor the time for research, then marketing managers have to rely on available descriptions of present behaviour and guesstimates about future behaviour. Popular magazines and leading newspapers often reflect the public's shifting attitudes. And many studies of the changing consumer are published regularly in the business and trade press. This material—coupled with the information in this book—will help your marketing strategy planning.

Remember that consumers—with all their needs and attitudes—may be elusive, but they aren't invisible. Research has provided more data and understanding of consumer behaviour than business managers generally use. Applying this information may help you find your breakthrough opportunity.

## Key Concepts

adoption process, p. 168
attitude, p. 153
belief, p. 153
cues, p. 152
culture, p. 161
dissonance, p. 164
drive, p. 149
economic buyers, p. 147
economic needs, p. 148
expectation, p. 154
extensive problem solving, p. 165
learning, p. 152
limited problem solving, p. 166
low-involvement purchases, p. 166
needs, p. 149
opinion leader, p. 160
perception, p. 151
personal needs, p. 150
physiological needs, p. 150
positive reinforcement, p. 152
psychographics, p. 157
reference group, p. 160
response, p. 152
routinized response behaviour, p. 166
safety needs, p. 150
selective exposure, p. 151
selective perception, p. 151
selective retention, p. 151
social class, p. 158
social needs, p. 150
wants, p. 149

## Questions and Problems

1. In your own words, explain economic needs and how they relate to the economic-buyer model of consumer behaviour. Give an example of a purchase you recently made that is consistent with the economic-buyer model. Give another that is not explained by the economic-buyer model. Explain your thinking.
2. Explain what is meant by a hierarchy of needs and provide examples of one or more products that enable you to satisfy each of the four levels of need.

## Questions and Problems continued

3. Cut out (or copy) two recent advertisements: one full-page colour ad from a magazine and one large display ad from a newspaper. In each case, indicate which needs the ads are appealing to.

4. Explain how an understanding of consumers' learning processes might affect marketing strategy planning. Give an example.

5. Briefly describe your own *beliefs* about the potential value of wearing automobile seat belts, your *attitude* toward seat belts, and your *intention* about using a seat belt the next time you're in a car.

6. Give an example of a recent purchase experience in which you were dissatisfied because a firm's marketing mix did not meet your expectations. Indicate how the purchase fell short of your expectations—and also explain whether your expectations were formed based on the firm's promotion or on something else.

7. Explain psychographics and lifestyle analysis. Explain how they might be useful for planning marketing strategies to reach college students, as opposed to average consumers.

8. A supermarket chain is planning to open a number of new stores. Give some examples that indicate how the four Ps might be different for stores located in Vancouver, Calgary, Montreal, and Moncton.

9. How should the social class structure affect the planning of a new restaurant in a large city? How might the four Ps be adjusted?

10. What social class would you associate with each of the following phrases or items? In each case, choose one class if you can. If you can't choose one class but rather feel that several classes are equally likely, then so indicate. In those cases where you feel that all classes are equally interested or characterized by a particular item, choose all five classes.

    *a.* A gun rack in a pickup truck.
    *b.* *The National Enquirer.*
    *c.* *The New Yorker* magazine.
    *d.* *Working Woman* magazine.
    *e.* People watching soap operas.
    *f.* Jaguar automobile.
    *g.* Men who drink beer after dinner.
    *h.* Families who vacation at a Disney theme park.
    *i.* Families who distrust banks (keep money in socks or mattresses).
    *j.* Owners of pit bulls.

11. Illustrate how the reference group concept may apply in practice by explaining how you personally are influenced by some reference group for some product. What are the implications of such behaviour for marketing managers?

12. Give two examples of recent purchases where the specific purchase situation influenced your purchase decision. Briefly explain how your decision was affected.

13. Give an example of a recent purchase in which you used extensive problem solving. What sources of information did you use in making the decision?

14. On the basis of the data and analysis presented in Chapters 5 and 6, what kind of buying behaviour would you expect to find for the following products: (*a*) a haircut, (*b*) a dishwasher detergent, (*c*) a printer for a personal computer, (*d*) a tennis racket, (*e*) a dress belt, (*f*) a telephone answering machine, (*g*) life insurance, (*h*) an ice cream cone, and (*i*) a new chequing account? Set up a chart for your answer with products along the left-hand margin as the row headings and the following factors as headings for the columns: (*a*) how consumers would shop for these products, (*b*) how far they would travel to buy the product, (*c*) whether they would buy by brand, (*d*) whether they would compare with other products, and (*e*) any other factors they should consider. Insert short answers—words or phrases are satisfactory—in the various boxes. Be prepared to discuss how the answers you put in the chart would affect each product's marketing mix.

## Computer-Aided Problem 6

### Selective Processes

Submag, Inc., uses direct-mail promotion to sell magazine subscriptions. Magazine publishers pay Submag $3.12 for each new subscription. Submag's costs include the expenses of printing, addressing, and mailing each direct-mail advertisement plus the cost of using a mailing list. There are many suppliers of mailing lists, and the cost and quality of different lists vary.

Submag's marketing manager, Shandra Debose, is trying to choose between two possible mailing lists. One list has been generated from phone directories. It is less expensive than the other list, but the supplier acknowledges that about 10 percent of the names are out-of-date (addresses where people have moved away). A competing supplier offers a list of active members of professional associations. This list costs 4 cents per name more than the phone list, but only 8 percent of the addresses are out-of-date.

In addition to concerns about out-of-date names, not every consumer who receives a mailing buys a subscription. For example, *selective exposure* is a problem. Some target customers never see the offer—they just toss out junk mail without even opening the envelope. Industry studies show that this wastes about 10 percent of each mailing—although the precise percentage varies from one mailing list to another.

*Selective perception* influences some consumers who do open the mailing. Some are simply not interested. Others don't want to deal with a subscription service. Although the price is good, these consumers worry that they'll never get the magazines. Submag's previous experience is that selective perception causes more than half of those who read the offer to reject it.

Of those who perceive the message as intended, many are interested. But selective retention can be a problem. Some people set the information aside and then forget to send in the subscription order.

Submag can mail about 25,000 pieces per week. Shandra Debose has set up a spreadsheet to help her study effects of the various relationships discussed above and to choose between the two mailing lists.

a. *If you were Debose, which of the two lists would you buy based on the initial spreadsheet? Why?*

b. *For the most profitable list, what is the minimum number of items that Submag will have to mail to earn a profit of at least $3,500?*

c. *For an additional cost of $.01 per mailing, Submag can include a reply card that will reduce the percentage of consumers who forget to send in an order (Percentage Lost—Selective Retention) to 45 percent. If Submag mails 25,000 items, is it worth the additional cost to include the reply card? Explain your logic.*

## Suggested Cases

To view the cases, go to www.mcgrawhill.ca/college/wong.

# Chapter Seven

# Business and Organizational Customers and Their Buying Behaviour

**When You Finish This Chapter, You Should**

1. Know who business and organizational customers are.

2. See why multiple influence is common in business and organizational purchase decisions.

3. Understand the problem-solving behaviour of organizational buyers.

4. Understand the different types of buyer–seller relationships and their benefits and limitations.

5. Know the basic e-commerce methods used in organizational buying.

6. Know about the number and distribution of manufacturers and why they are an important customer group.

7. Know how buying by service firms, retailers, wholesalers, and governments is similar to and different from buying by manufacturers.

## The Unique Partnership of MetoKote and John Deere

MetoKote Corp. specializes in protective coatings, like powder-coat and liquid paint, that other manufacturers need for the parts and equipment they make. For example, the familiar green finish you see on John Deere agricultural or construction equipment has probably come from MetoKote. In fact, John Deere and MetoKote have a close buyer–seller relationship. While purchasing managers at Deere use Internet portals to identify suppliers and get competitive bids for many items they need, it's different with MetoKote. Deere isn't going to switch to some other supplier just because an Internet

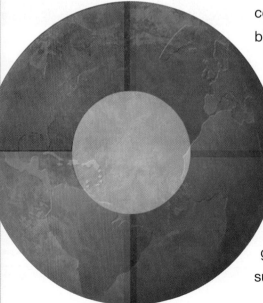

place price promotion prod

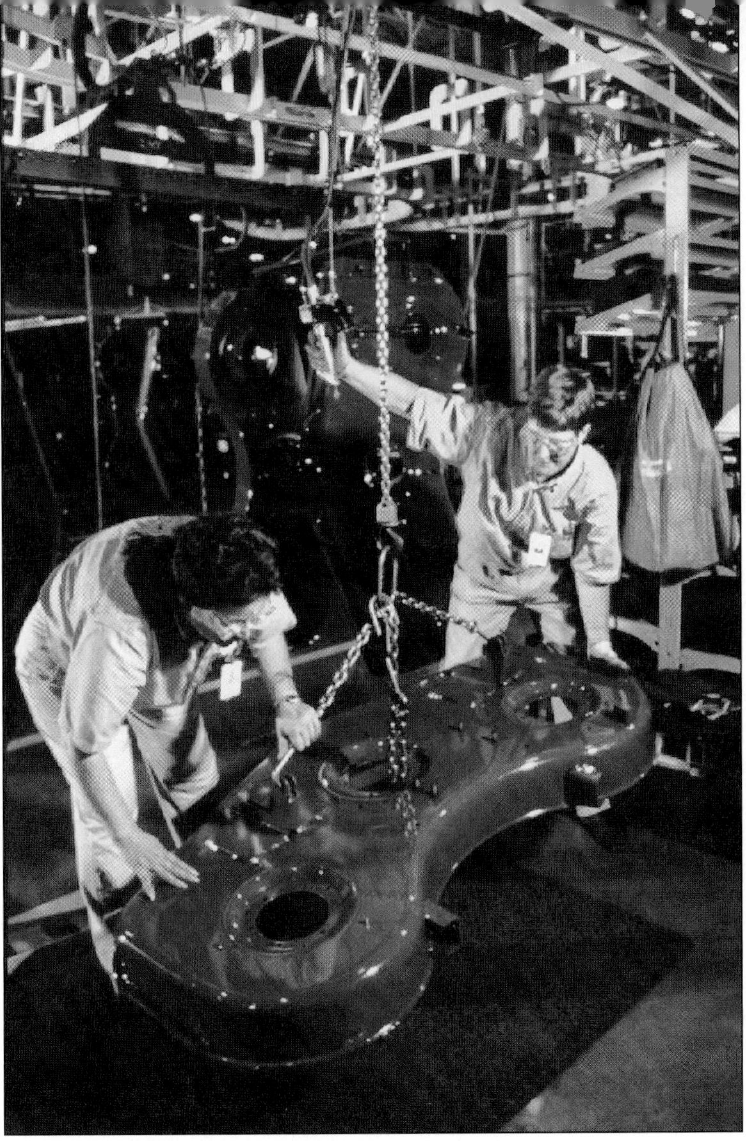

search identifies some cheaper coating. MetoKote doesn't just supply Deere with coatings; it handles the whole coating job for Deere. In fact, it has built facilities right next to some Deere plants. When it's time for a part to be coated, a conveyer belt moves it out of the JD plant and into the MetoKote facility. Four hours later it's back—and it's green.

The decision to purchase coating services this way wasn't made casually, and many people were involved. JD's production people favoured this arrangement. They let MetoKote's experts keep up with all of the environmental regulations and new technologies for coatings, so Deere can worry about doing what it does best. Deere's finance people liked the idea that a Deere plant could be smaller and less costly to build and maintain if it didn't need space for big spray booths. Because MetoKote does not have to ship the parts to Deere after they are coated, there are fewer scratches and dents—which impresses the quality people. And the purchasing people don't have to worry about parts being there when they're needed. Of course, this was not a simple sale for MetoKote—many people cooperate and share information on an ongoing basis to make it work for both firms.

John Deere needs high-quality protective finishes because the buyers for its customers want durable, long-lasting equipment. Like Deere, they want good value from their suppliers. That means that marketers at Deere need to think about the quality of Deere service as well as the quality of Deere equipment. For example, when a huge commercial farm in California or Brazil needs a repair part, it can't afford delays. Deere






www.mcgrawhill.ca/college/wong

helps these clients, and the dealers who sell its parts and equipment, with information technology. At any hour an equipment customer can check Deere's website (**www.deere.com**) to see which dealers have a needed part in inventory, to check the price, and to place an order for fast delivery. But helping its customers earn better profits in their own operations doesn't stop there. For example, some Deere farm equipment includes global positioning devices that track exactly where the equipment goes. That makes it possible for the owner to use JD's Vantage-Point Network to collect, store, and interpret detailed data generated by their farming operations online, right down to the creation of maps of fields that need to be ploughed, seeded, or cut. It is benefits like this that make Deere the supplier of choice for many business customers.[1]

## In This Chapter

In this chapter we shift our attention from individuals and households to look at organizational buying. We begin by discussing the significance of organizational buying and by providing an overview of *who buys*, *what they buy*, and *how they buy*. With those basics in place, we then consider three special topics in organizational buying: managing relationships, the role of e-commerce, and selling to governments. The chapter concludes by providing some further sources of information on industry trends.

## Organizational Buying: An Overview

When we hear the term *customer*, most of us think about individual final consumers. But many marketing managers aim at customers who are not final consumers. In fact, more purchases are made by businesses and other organizations than by final consumers. The reason is simple. Before a consumer can buy a product or service, someone has to provide it; in order to provide it, the business must buy the necessary components. In short, almost everything a consumer buys must first be bought by a business or organization.

And yet, for most people, the idea of a career in business-to-business marketing is not top-of-mind. They see the field as largely comprised of selling commodity-like components and void of many of the more glamorous activities associated with consumer marketing. How wrong they are!

In addition to buying components, businesses and organizations today are the largest market for high-technology and information-technology products. In addition, they are large buyers of services—everything from janitorial services to consulting services. Some of you may even find work through service providers like advertising agencies or market research agencies, which provide many of the marketing capabilities that organizations need to manage their affairs.

And marketing to businesses is anything but dull. As you will see in this chapter, the buying behaviour of these business customers can be very different from the buying behaviour of final consumers—and, because each order can be so large,

Exhibit 7-1 Business versus consumer buying.

**The following is a summary of the characteristics of business to business markets when compared to consumer markets:**

| Characteristic | Business to Business Market | Consumer Market |
|---|---|---|
| Sales volume | Greater | Smaller |
| Purchase volume | Larger | Smaller |
| Number of buyers | Fewer | Many |
| Size of individual buyers | Larger | Smaller |
| Location of buyers | Geographically concentrated | Diffuse |
| Buyer–seller relationship | Closer | More impersonal |
| Nature of channel | More direct | More indirect |
| Nature of buying | More professional | More personal |
| Nature of buying influence | Multiple | Single |
| Type of negotiations | More complex | Simpler |
| Use of reciprocity | Yes | No |
| Use of leasing | Greater | Smaller |
| Primary promotional method | Personal selling | Advertising |

these differences must be accommodated. Exhibit 7-1 provides a brief comparison. (Don't worry if the terms seem foreign at this time, we'll discuss them throughout the chapter.)

## Who They Are

**business and organizational customers**
Any buyers who buy for resale or to produce other goods and services

**Business and organizational customers** are any buyers who buy for resale or to produce other goods and services. Exhibit 7-2 shows the different types of customers in these markets. As you can see, not all of the organizational customers in these markets are business firms. Even so, to distinguish them from the final consumer market, managers sometimes refer to them collectively as the "business-to-business" market, or simply the *B2B market*.

Many characteristics of buying behaviour are common across these varied types of organizations. That's why the different kinds of organizational customers are sometimes loosely called "business buyers," "intermediate buyers," or "industrial buyers." As we discuss organizational buying, we will intermix examples of buying by many different types of organizations. Later in the chapter, however, we will highlight some of the specific characteristics of the different customer groups. As you will see, a knowledge of organizational behaviour can be a powerful tool in identifying B2B target markets.

While Exhibit 7-2 shows the types of organizations that buy, as you might expect, marketers are particularly concerned with *who* makes purchase decisions within these organizations. Organizational buying shows two major differences from consumer buying in this regard: professional buyers and multiple buying influences.

**Professional buyers** Many organizations, especially large ones, rely on specialists to ensure that purchases are handled sensibly. These specialists have different titles in different firms (such as purchasing agent, procurement officer, or buyer), but basically they are all **purchasing managers**—buying specialists for their employers. In large organizations, they usually specialize by product area and are real experts.

**purchasing managers**
Buying specialists for their employers

Some people think purchasing is handled by clerks who sit in cubicles and do the paperwork to place orders. That view is out-of-date. Today, most firms look to their purchasing departments to help cut costs and provide competitive advantage.

Exhibit 7-2
Examples of different types of business and organizational customers.

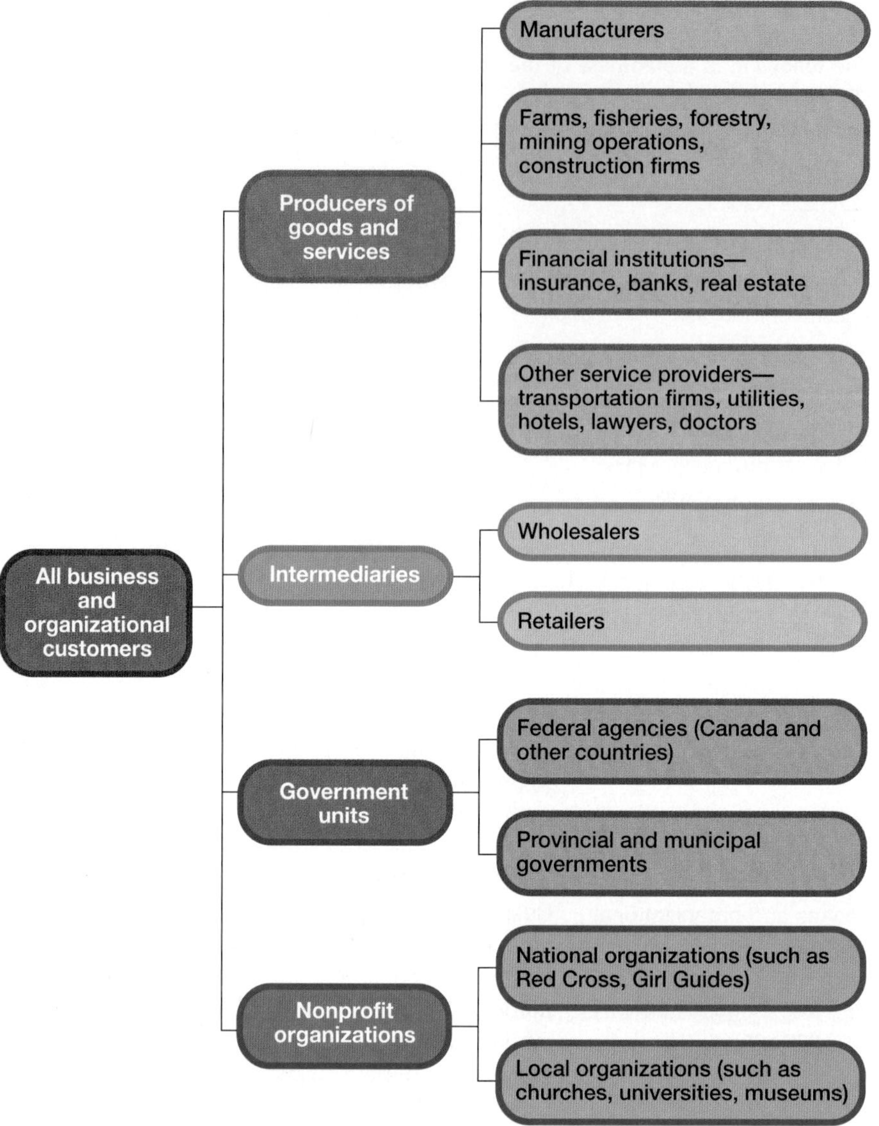




In this environment, purchasing people have a lot of clout. And there are good job opportunities in purchasing for capable business graduates.

Salespeople often have to see a purchasing manager first—before they contact any other employee. These buyers hold important positions and take a dim view of sales reps who try to go around them. Rather than being "sold," these buyers want salespeople to provide accurate information that will help them buy wisely. They like information on new goods and services, and tips on potential price changes, supply shortages, and other changes in market conditions. Sometimes all it takes for a sales rep to keep a buyer up to date is to send an occasional e-mail. But a buyer can tell when a sales rep has the customer firm's interests at heart.

Although purchasing managers usually coordinate relationships with suppliers, other people may also play important roles in influencing the purchase decision.[2]

**Multiple buying influences** Multiple buying influence means that several people—perhaps even top management—share in making a purchase decision. An example shows how the different buying influences work. Suppose Electrolux, the Swedish firm that produces vacuum cleaners, wants to buy a machine to stamp out the various metal parts it needs. Different vendors are eager for the business. But even before the vendors can reach the decision-makers, they may have to be rated as "qualified" by a screening person or committee (*gatekeepers*). Once qualified, they may need to reach several people (*influencers*) who help to evaluate the choices. A finance manager worries about the high cost and suggests leasing the machine. The quality control people want a machine that will do a more accurate job—although it's more expensive. The production manager is interested in speed of operation. The production line workers and their supervisors want the machine that is easiest to use so that workers can continue to rotate jobs.

While it may be relatively simple to identify who could be involved as an influencer in any one decision, it is unlikely that each of those people have the same amount or type of influence. One way that marketers can think and plan around these influences is in terms of the role (or, in some cases, roles) an individual plays in the buying process. Exhibit 7-3 shows the various roles that make up a buying centre and identifies where these roles are played in the buying process.

**initiators**

Those who act as a catalyst for the buying process

**Initiators** are those people who act as a catalyst for the buying process. As such, marketing campaigns often target initiators to remind them of the importance of the need and to build an association between them and that type of problem. For example, a computer software company selling tools for managing customer databases might advertise to marketing managers to inform them of the kinds of analysis that their software performs.

**influencers (gatekeepers)**

Those who define the specifications for what is bought and for gathering information on the alternative ways of meeting those specifications

**Influencers (gatekeepers)** help to define the specifications for what is bought and for gathering information on the alternative ways of meeting those specifications. Once contacted by the initiator, gatekeepers may call upon their existing knowledge or supplement that knowledge through a detailed information search. Because these people essentially provide the buying centre with a list of suppliers to consider, it is vital that marketers communicate to initiators the association between their products and certain needs or buying criteria; otherwise, their products will never be considered.

Significantly, gatekeepers and initiators may not be the same person. For example, once a marketing manager knows they want to develop a customer database to track patterns in buying behaviour, they might ask their information technology department or market research group to more precisely articulate their needs and to provide a listing of alternative, qualified suppliers. Therefore, communications that stimulate interest among initiators may not be as effective in winning over gatekeepers.

**deciders**

Those who evaluate the alternatives that are identified by gatekeepers

**Deciders** evaluate the alternatives that are identified by gatekeepers. Their goal is to reach a final decision about what to buy. In some instances there is only one decider, while in other cases there may be an ad hoc or full-time committee responsible for this activity. As a general rule, the more expensive the purchase or the more important the need being served, the more likely it is that a committee-like team will be involved. In these cases, marketing and sales must understand and accommodate the peculiar predispositions and preferences of *each* member of the committee if it hopes to win the account.

Exhibit 7-3
Roles played in the buying process.

| Stage of Buying Process | Role |
|---|---|
| 1. Need awareness | Initiator |
| 2. Search for information | Influencers/gatekeepers |
| 3. Set criteria and evaluate alternative solutions | Deciders |
| 4. Purchase the product | Buyers |
| 5. Use and postpurchase evaluation of the product | Users |

**buyers**
Those who make the actual purchase of the product or service

**users**
Those who actually use the product or service being bought

**Buyers** make the actual purchase of the product or service. They may be acting simultaneously as deciders or they may be acting upon the instructions of deciders. In either case, it is these people who ultimately negotiate prices, delivery, and other terms and serve as liaison with the chosen supplier.

**Users** are the people who actually use the product or service being bought. While we might expect that their preferences are the most important in deciding what to buy, other factors may be equally or more important. Therefore, just as the user of a consumer product (for example, a child) may not exert significant influence over what is bought by the buyer (for example, a parent), users in organizations sometimes, but not always, also play one or more of the above roles. Marketers must know this or risk communicating the wrong information about their product or service to influencers and gatekeepers.

Returning to our Electrolux example, the salesperson may have to talk to every member of the buying centre. Given the different responsibilities and interests of different members, the salesperson may need to stress different topics for each. This not only complicates the promotion job but also lengthens it. Approval of a routine order may take anywhere from a day to several months. On very important purchases—a new computer system, a new building, or major equipment—the selling period may take a year or more.[3]

## What They Buy

When they make purchase decisions, organizational buyers typically focus on economic factors. They are usually less emotional in their buying than final consumers. Buyers try to consider the total cost of selecting a supplier and a particular product, not just the initial price of the product. In this sense, their principal concern is for the total "cost in use" of the product. As shown in Exhibit 7-4, cost-in-use refers to not only the price paid but also any other costs incurred in buying the product, taking possession of the product, or using the product. Calculations like these are critical in the marketing of products at premium prices. Without these calculations, customers can be expected to ask "Why are you more expensive?"

For example, a hospital that needs a new type of X-ray equipment might look at both the original cost and the ongoing costs, at how it would affect doctor productivity, and of course at the quality of the images it produces. The hospital might also consider the seller's reliability and general cooperativeness; its ability to provide speedy maintenance and repair, steady supply under all conditions, and reliable and fast delivery; and any past and present relationships (including previous favours and cooperation in meeting special requests).

The matter of dependability deserves special emphasis. An organization may not be able to function if purchases don't arrive when they're expected. Dependable product quality is important, too. For example, a faulty wire might cause a large piece of equipment to break down, and the costs of finding and correcting the problem could be completely out of proportion to the cost of the wire.

Exhibit 7-4 Typical components of total cost-in-use.

| Acquisition Costs | + | Possession Costs | + | Usage Costs | = | Total Cost-in-Use |
|---|---|---|---|---|---|---|
| Price | | Interest | | Field defects | | |
| Paperwork | | Storage | | Training | | |
| Shopping time | | Quality control | | User labour | | |
| Expediting | | Taxes and insurance | | Product longevity | | |
| Mistakes in order | | Shrinkage and obsolescence | | Replacement | | |
| Prepurchase product evaluation | | General internal handling | | Disposal | | |

Business customers focus on economic needs when they make purchase decisions, so Microsoft wants top decision makers to realize that its reliable server software eliminates downtime costs because it is up and running 99.999 percent of the time.

**purchasing specifications**
A written description of what the firm wants to buy

To ensure that standards are met, organizational buyers often buy on the basis of a set of **purchasing specifications**—a written description of what the firm wants to buy. When quality is highly standardized, as is often the case with manufactured items, the specification may simply consist of a brand name or part number. With products like agricultural commodities, where there is more variation, the specification may include information about the grade of the product. Often, however, the purchase requirements are more complicated; then, the specifications may set out detailed information about the performance standards the product must meet. Purchase specifications for services tend to be detailed because services tend to be less standardized and usually are not performed until after they're purchased.

**ISO 9000**
A way for a supplier to document its quality procedures according to internationally recognized standards

Organizational customers considering a new supplier or one from overseas may be concerned about product quality. However, this is becoming less of an obstacle because of ISO 9000. **ISO 9000** is a way for a supplier to document its quality procedures according to internationally recognized standards.

ISO 9000 assures a customer that the supplier has effective quality checks in place, without the customer having to conduct its own costly and time-consuming audit. Some customers won't buy from any supplier that doesn't have it. To get ISO 9000–certified, a company basically must prove to outside auditors that it documents in detail how the company operates and who is responsible for quality every step of the way.[4]

## How They Buy

Just as different consumers might buy in different ways, so too might different businesses. Even "trivial" differences in buying behaviour may be important, because success often hinges on fine-tuning the marketing mix.

Sellers often approach each organizational customer directly, usually through a sales representative. This gives the seller more chance to adjust the marketing mix for each individual customer. A seller may even develop a unique strategy for each individual customer. This approach carries target marketing to its extreme. But sellers often need unique strategies to compete for large-volume purchases.

In such situations, the individual sales rep takes much responsibility for strategic planning. The sales rep often coordinates the entire relationship between the supplier and the customer. This may involve working with many people—including top management—in both firms. One of the sales rep's key functions is to identify who

Exhibit 7-5
Organizational buying processes.

| Characteristics | Type of Process | | |
|---|---|---|---|
| | New-Task Buying | Modified Rebuy | Straight Rebuy |
| Time Required | Much | Medium | Little |
| Multiple Influence | Much | Some | Little |
| Review of Suppliers | Much | Some | None |
| Information Needed | Much | Some | Little |



plays what role(s) in the buying process and how their opinions are brought together to make purchase decisions. Therefore, it helps to know about how organizations solve problems in general and how they perform vendor analysis.

**Organizational buying as problem solving** In Chapter 6, we discussed problem solving by consumers and how it might vary from extensive problem solving to routine buying. In organizational markets, we can adapt these concepts slightly and work with three similar buying processes: a new-task buying process, a modified rebuy process, or a straight rebuy.[5] (See Exhibit 7-5.)

**new-task buying**
Occurs when an organization has a new need and the customer wants a great deal of information

**straight rebuy**
A routine repurchase that may have been made many times before

**modified rebuy**
The in-between process where some review of the buying situation is done

**New-task buying** occurs when an organization has a new need and the customer wants a great deal of information. New-task buying can involve setting product specifications, evaluating sources of supply, and establishing an order routine that can be followed in the future if results are satisfactory. Multiple buying influence is typical in new-task buying.

A **straight rebuy** is a routine repurchase that may have been made many times before. Buyers probably don't bother looking for new information or new sources of supply. Most of a company's small or recurring purchases are of this type—but they take only a small part of an organized buyer's time. Important purchases may be made this way too—but only after the firm has decided what procedure will be "routine."

The **modified rebuy** is the in-between process where some review of the buying situation is done—though not as much as in new-task buying. Sometimes a competitor will get lazy enjoying a straight-rebuy situation. An alert marketer can turn these situations into opportunities by providing more information or a better marketing mix.

Customers in a new-task buying situation are likely to seek information from a variety of sources (see Exhibit 7-6). Keep in mind that many of the impersonal sources are readily available in electronic form online as well as in other formats. How much information a customer collects depends on the importance of the purchase and the level of uncertainty about what choice might be best. The time and

Exhibit 7-6
Major sources of information used by organizational buyers.

| | Marketing sources | Nonmarketing sources |
|---|---|---|
| Personal sources | • Salespeople<br>• Others from supplier firms<br>• Trade shows | • Buying centre members<br>• Outside business associates<br>• Consultants and outside experts |
| Impersonal sources | • Advertising in trade publications<br>• Sales literature<br>• Sales catalogues<br>• Web page | • Rating services<br>• Trade associations<br>• News publications<br>• Product directories<br>• Internet news pointcasts |

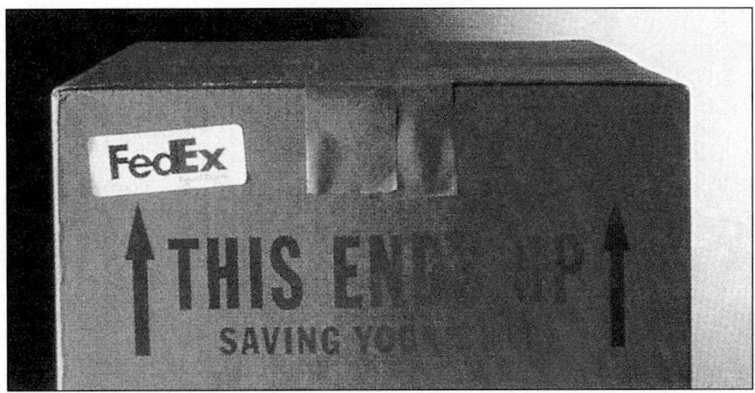


Organizational customers want reliable suppliers who will deliver on their promises and not reflect badly on the buyer's decisions.

expense of searching for information may not be justified for a minor purchase, but a major purchase often involves real detective work by the buyer.

Of course, the flip side of the new-task buying situation is that a seller's promotion has much more chance to have an impact. At the very least, the marketer needs to be certain that his or her firm will turn up in the buyer's search. In this regard, a good website is a crucial piece of insurance. Later we will talk more about the role of e-commerce at this stage, but for now you should see that even a simple website is likely to turn up in a buyer's Internet search.[6]

**vendor analysis**

A formal rating of suppliers on all relevant areas of performance

**Vendor analysis** Considering all of the economic factors and influences relevant to a purchase decision is sometimes complex. A supplier or product that is best in one way may not be best in others. To try to deal with these situations, many firms use **vendor analysis**—a formal rating of suppliers on all relevant areas of performance. The purpose isn't just to get a low price from the supplier on a given part or service. Rather, the goal is to lower the *total costs* associated with purchases (recall Exhibit 7-4). Analysis might show that the best vendor is the one that helps the customer reduce costs of excess inventory, retooling of equipment, or defective parts.[7]

Vendor analysis tries to focus on economic factors, but purchasing in organizations may also involve many of the same behavioural dimensions we discussed in Chapter 6. Purchasing managers and others involved in buying decisions are human, and they want friendly relationships with suppliers.

The purchasing people in some firms are eager to imitate progressive competitors or even to be the first to try new products. Such "innovators" deserve special attention when new products are being introduced.

The different people involved in purchase decisions are also human with respect to protecting their own interests and their own position in the company. That's one reason people from different departments may have different priorities in trying to influence what is purchased. Similarly, purchasing managers may want to avoid taking risks that might reflect badly on their decisions. They have to buy a wide variety of products and make decisions involving many factors beyond their control. If a new source delivers late or quality is poor, you can guess who will be blamed. Marketers who can help the buyer avoid risk have a definite appeal. In fact, this may make the difference between a successful and unsuccessful marketing mix.

A seller's marketing mix should satisfy *both* the needs of the customer company as well as the needs of individuals who influence the purchase (for more on this topic, see Ethical Dimensions 7-1). Therefore, sellers need to find an overlapping area where both can be satisfied (see Exhibit 7-7 for a summary of this idea).

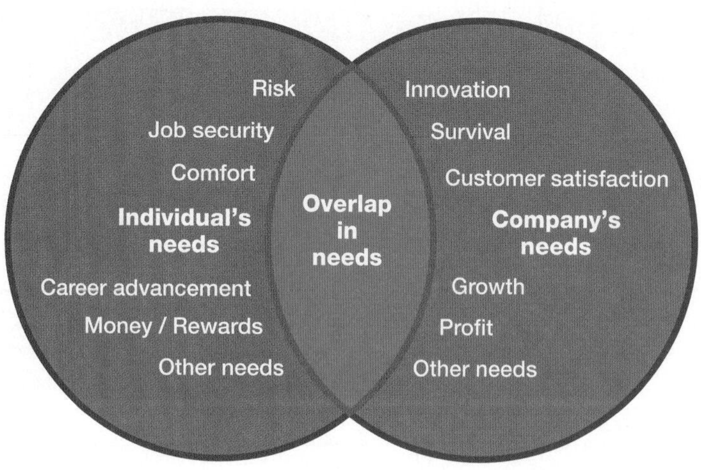


Exhibit 7-7
Overlapping needs of individual influences and the customer organization.



## Managing Buyer–Seller Relationships

Once a buying firm gets beyond the early stages of a new-task buying decision, it needs to make important decisions about how it is going to deal with one or more suppliers to meet its needs. At one extreme, a buyer might want to rely on competition among all available vendors to get the best price on each and every order it places. At the other extreme, it might just routinely buy from one vendor with whom it already has a good relationship. In practice, there are many important and common variations between these extremes. To better understand the variations—and why firms rely on different approaches in different situations—let's take a closer look at the benefits and limitations of different types of buyer–seller relationships. That will also help you to see why new e-commerce developments in business markets have become so important.

### Benefits of Close Relationships

There are often significant benefits of a close working relationship between a supplier and a customer firm. And such relationships are becoming common. Many

## Ethical Dimensions 7–1

### CONFLICTS MAY ARISE

Although organizational buyers are influenced by their own needs, most are serious professionals who are careful to avoid a conflict between their own self-interest and company outcomes. Marketers must be careful here. A salesperson who offers one of his company pens to a prospect may view the giveaway as part of the promotion effort—but the customer firm may have a policy against any employee accepting *any* gift from a supplier.

Most organizational buyers do their work ethically—and expect marketers to work the same way. Yet there have been highly publicized abuses. For example, some buyers may give contracts to suppliers who offer them vacation trips and other personal favours. Abuses of this sort have prompted many organizations to set up policies that prohibit a buyer from accepting anything from a potential supplier.[8]

Marketers need to take concerns about conflict of interest very seriously. Part of the promotion job is to persuade various individuals who may influence an organization's purchase. Yet the whole marketing effort may be tainted if it even appears that a marketer has encouraged a person who influences a decision to put personal gain ahead of company interest.

firms are reducing the number of suppliers with whom they work—expecting more in return from the suppliers that remain. The best relationships involve real partnerships where there's mutual trust and a long-term outlook.

Closely tied firms can often share tasks at lower total cost than would be possible working at arm's length. Costs are sometimes reduced simply by reducing uncertainty and risk. A supplier is often able to reduce its selling price if a customer commits to larger orders or orders over a longer period of time. A large sales volume may produce economies of scale and reduce selling costs. The customer benefits from lower cost and also is assured a dependable source of supply.

A firm that works closely with a supplier can resolve joint problems. For example, it may cost both the supplier and the customer more to resolve the problems of a defective product after it is delivered than it would have cost to prevent the problem. But without the customer's help it may be impossible for the supplier to identify a solution to the problem. As the head of purchasing at Motorola puts it, "Every time we make an error it takes people at both ends to correct it."

The partnership between AlliedSignal and Betz Laboratories shows the benefits of a good relationship. A while back, Betz was just one of several suppliers that sold Allied chemicals to keep the water in its plants from gunking up pipes and rusting machinery. But Betz didn't stop at selling commodity powders. Teams of Betz experts and engineers from Allied studied each plant to find places where water was being wasted. In less than a year a team in one plant found $2.5 million in potential cost reductions. For example, by adding a few valves to recycle the water in a cooling tower, Betz was able to save 300 gallons of water a minute, which resulted in savings of more than $100,000 a year and reduced environmental impact. Because of ideas like this, Allied's overall use of water-treatment chemicals decreased. However, Betz sales to Allied doubled because it became Allied's sole supplier.[9]

### Risks of Close Relationships

Although close relationships can produce benefits, they are not always best. A long-term commitment to a partner may reduce flexibility. When competition drives down prices and spurs innovation, the customer may be better off letting suppliers compete for the business. It may not be worth the customer's investment to build a relationship for purchases that are not particularly important or that are made frequently.

It may at first appear that a seller would *always* prefer to have a closer relationship with a customer, but that is not so. Some customers may place orders that are too small or require so much special attention that the relationship would never be profitable for the seller. Also, in situations where a customer doesn't want a relationship, trying to build one may cost more than it's worth. Further, many small suppliers have made the mistake of relying too heavily on relationships with too few customers. One failed relationship may bankrupt the business.[10]

### Alternative Forms of Buyer–Seller Relationships

Relationships are not "all or nothing" arrangements. Firms may have a close relationship in some ways and not in others. Thus, it's useful to know about five key dimensions that help characterize most buyer–seller relationships: cooperation, information sharing, operational linkages, legal bonds, and relationship-specific adaptations. Purchasing managers for the buying firm and salespeople for the supplier usually coordinate the different dimensions of a relationship. However, as shown in Exhibit 7-8, close relationships often involve direct contacts among a number of people from other areas in both firms.[11]

**Cooperation** In cooperative relationships, the buyer and seller work together to achieve both mutual and individual objectives. This doesn't mean that the buyer

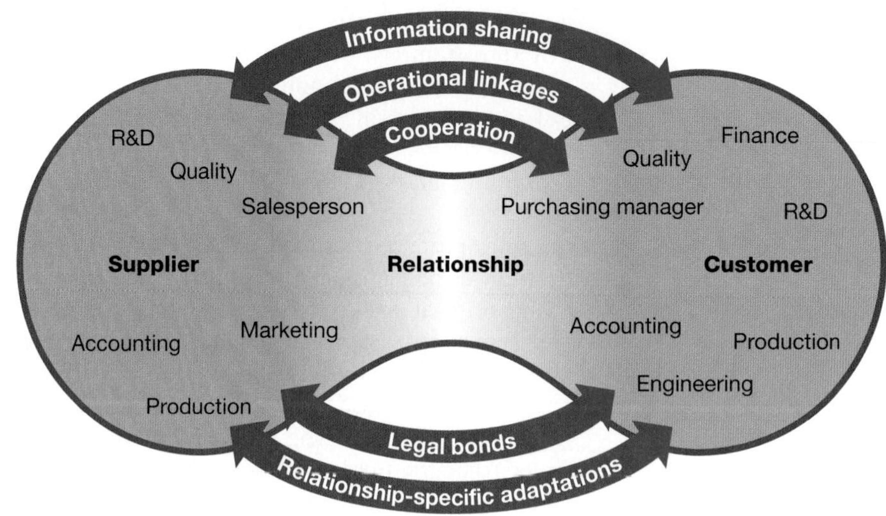


Exhibit 7-8
The dimensions of relationships in business markets.

(or seller) will always do what the other wants. Rather, the two firms treat problems that arise as a joint responsibility.

National Semiconductor (NS) and Siltec, a supplier of silicon wafers, have found clever ways to cooperate and cut costs. For example, workers at the NS plant used to throw away the expensive plastic cassettes that Siltec uses to ship the silicon wafers. Now Siltec and NS cooperate to recycle the cassettes. This helps the environment and also saves more than $300,000 a year; Siltec passes along most of that to NS as lower prices.[12]

**Sharing information** Some relationships involve open sharing of information that is useful to both the buyer and seller. This might include the exchange of proprietary cost data, discussion of demand forecasts, and joint work on new product designs. Information might be shared through information systems or over the Internet. This is often a key facet of relationships that involve e-commerce.

Many firms share information by providing relationship partners with access to password-protected websites. One big advantage of this approach is that it is fast and easy to update the information. A customer can trust that information is the same information used by someone inside the company. In addition, it provides easy "click-here" self-service access for customers who might have very different computer systems in their own firms. It also saves time. A customer can check detailed product specs or the status of a job on the production line without having to wait for a sales rep or someone else to answer the question.

Information sharing can lead to better decisions, reduced uncertainty about the future, and better planning. However, firms don't want to share information if there's a risk that a partner might misuse it. For example, some suppliers claim that General Motors' former purchasing chief showed blueprints of their secret technology to competing suppliers. Such violations of trust in a relationship are an ethical matter and should be taken seriously. However, as a practical matter, it makes sense to know a partner well before revealing all.

**Operational linkages** Operational linkages are direct ties between the internal operations of the buyer and seller firms. These linkages usually involve formal arrangements and ongoing coordination of activities between the firms. Shared activities are especially important when neither firm working on its own can perform a function as well as the two firms can working together. John Deere's relationship with MetoKote, described at the start of this chapter, involves operational linkages.

**just-in-time delivery**
Reliably getting products to a customer's location just before the customer needs them

Operational linkages are often required to reduce total inventory costs. Business customers want to maintain an adequate inventory—certainly enough to prevent stock-outs or keep production lines moving. On the other hand, keeping too much inventory is expensive. Providing a customer with inventory when it's needed may require that a supplier be able to provide **just-in-time delivery**—reliably getting products there *just* before the customer needs them. We'll discuss just-in-time systems in more detail in Chapter 12. For now, it's enough to see that just-in-time relationships between buyers and sellers usually require operational linkages (as well as information sharing). For example, Wal-Mart might want a producer of socks to pack cartons so that when they are unloaded at a Wal-Mart distribution facility all of the cartons for a certain store or district are grouped together. This makes it easier and faster for forklifts to "cross dock" the pallets and load them onto an outbound truck. This also reduces Wal-Mart's costs because the cartons need to be handled only one time. However, it means that the supplier's production and packing of socks in different colours and sizes must be closely linked to the precise store in the Wal-Mart chain that places each order.

Operational linkages may also involve the routine activities of individuals who almost become part of the customer's operations. Design engineers, salespeople, and service representatives may participate in developing solutions to ongoing problems, conduct regular maintenance checks on equipment, or monitor inventory and coordinate orders. At the DaimlerChrysler design centre, for example, 30 offices are set aside for full-time use by people employed by suppliers.

Linkages may be customized to a particular relationship, or they may be standardized and operate the same way across many exchange partners. For example, in the channel of distribution for grocery products many different producers are standardizing their distribution procedures and coordinating with retail chains to make it faster and cheaper to replenish grocery-store shelves.

When a customer's operations are dependent on those of a supplier, it may be difficult or expensive to switch to another supplier. So, buyers sometimes avoid a relationship that would result in these "switching costs."

**Legal bonds** Many purchases in business markets are simple transactions. The seller's basic responsibility is to transfer title to goods or perform services, and the buyer's basic responsibility is to pay the agreed price. However, in some buyer–seller relationships the responsibilities of the parties are spelled out in a detailed legal contract. An agreement may apply only for a short period, but long-term contracts are also common.

For example, a customer might ask a supplier to guarantee a 6-percent price reduction for a particular part for each of the next three years and pledge to virtually eliminate defects. In return, the customer might offer to double its orders and help the supplier boost productivity. This might sound attractive to the supplier but also require new people or facilities. The supplier may not be willing to make these long-term commitments unless the buyer is willing to sign a contract for promised purchases. The contract might spell out what would happen if deliveries are late or if quality is below specification.

**negotiated contract buying**
Agreeing to a contract that allows for changes in the purchase arrangements

Sometimes, the buyer and seller know roughly what is needed but can't fix all the details in advance. For example, specifications or total requirements may change over time. Then the relationship may involve **negotiated contract buying**, which means agreeing to a contract that allows for changes in the purchase arrangements. In such cases, the general project and basic price is described but with provision for changes and price adjustments up or down. Or a supplier may be asked to accept a contract that provides some type of incentive—such as full coverage of costs plus a fixed fee or full costs plus a profit percentage tied to costs.

When a contract provides a formal plan for the future of a relationship, some types of risk are reduced. But a firm may not want to be legally locked in when the future is unclear. Alternatively, some managers figure that even a detailed contract isn't a good substitute for regular, good-faith reviews to make sure that neither party gets hurt by changing business conditions.

Harley-Davidson used this approach when it moved toward closer relationships with a smaller number of suppliers. Purchasing executives tossed out detailed contracts and replaced them with a short statement of principles to guide relationships between Harley and its suppliers. This "operate on a handshake" approach is typical of relationships with Japanese firms. Many other firms have adopted it. It's great when it works, and a disaster when it doesn't.

**Adaptive relationships** Relationship-specific adaptations involve changes in a firm's product or procedures that are unique to the needs or capabilities of a relationship partner. Industrial suppliers often custom-design a new product for just one customer; this may require investments in R&D or new manufacturing technologies. Donnelly Corp. is an extreme example. It had been supplying Honda with mirrors for the interiors of its cars. Honda's purchasing people liked Donnelly's collaborative style, so they urged Donnelly to supply exterior mirrors as well. Donnelly had never been in that business—so it had to build a factory to get started.

Buying firms may also adapt to a particular supplier; a computer maker may design around Intel's Pentium chip, and independent photo processors say "We use Kodak paper for the good look" in their advertising. However, buyers are often hesitant about making big investments that increase dependence on a specific supplier. Typically, they do it only when there isn't a good alternative—perhaps because only one or a few suppliers are available to meet a need—or if the benefits of the investment are clear before it's made. On the other hand, sometimes a buyer will invest in a relationship because the seller has already demonstrated a willingness to do so.[13]

A seller may have more incentive to propose new ideas that save the customer money when the firms have a mutual investment in a long-term relationship. The customer firm usually rewards the seller with more orders or a larger share of its business, and this encourages future suggestions and loyalty by the supplier. In contrast, buyers who use a competitive bid system exclusively—either by choice or necessity, as in some government and institutional purchasing—may not be offered much beyond basic goods and services. They are interested primarily in price. Marketing

## Marketing Demo 7–1

### MAKING ADAPTATIONS

The relationship between Flex-N-Gate and Toyota illustrates relationship-specific adaptations. Flex-N-Gate had a contract to supply some of the rear bumpers Toyota needed for its U.S. facilities. After a while, however, Toyota's quality control people were unhappy about the number of minor defects in the bumpers. Further, Flex-N-Gate's deliveries were not as dependable as Toyota's production people required. Rather than just end the relationship, Toyota and Flex-N-Gate both made investments to improve it. Toyota sent a team of experts who spent a lot of time figuring out the reasons for the problems and then showing Flex-N-Gate how to build better bumpers faster and cheaper. Following the advice of Toyota's experts, Shahid Khan (Flex-N-Gate's owner) reorganized equipment in his factory. He also had to retrain his employees to do their jobs in new ways. The changes were so complicated that two of Khan's six production supervisors quit in frustration. But the trouble was worth the effort. Productivity went up 60 percent, the number of defects dropped by 80 percent, and Flex-N-Gate got a larger share of Toyota's business. Toyota got something it wanted, too: a committed supplier that could meet its standards and a big price reduction on bumpers.[14]

TOYOTA

Demo 7-1 shows how two firms adapted their relationship to bring significant cost savings to a buyer and significant profits to the seller.

### Potential Problems in Managing Relationships

Although a marketing manager may want to work in a cooperative partnership, that may be impossible with large customers who have the power to dictate how the relationship will work. For example, Duall/Wind, a plastics producer, was a supplier of small parts for Polaroid instant cameras. But when Duall/Wind wanted to raise its prices to cover increasing costs, Polaroid balked. Polaroid's purchasing manager demanded that Duall/Wind show a breakdown of all its costs, from materials to labour to profit. As Duall/Wind's president said, "I had a tough time getting through my head that Polaroid wanted to come right in here and have us divulge all that." But Polaroid is a big account—and it got the information it wanted. Polaroid buyers agreed to a price increase only after they were confident that Duall/Wind was doing everything possible to control costs.[15]

Even if a marketing manager develops the best marketing mix possible and cultivates a close relationship with the customer, the customer may not give *all* of its business to one supplier. Buyers often look for several dependable sources of supply to protect themselves from unpredictable events such as strikes, fires, or floods in one of their suppliers' plants. A good marketing mix is still likely to win a larger share of the total business—which can prove to be very important. From a buyer's point of view, it may not seem like a big deal to give a particular supplier a 30-percent share of the orders rather than a 20-percent share. But for the seller that's a 50-percent increase in sales![16]

### The Special Case of Reciprocity

**reciprocity**
Trading sales for sales

We've emphasized that most buyer–seller relationships are based on reducing the customer's total procurement costs. However, for completeness we should mention that some relationships are based on reciprocity. **Reciprocity** means trading sales for sales—that is, "if you buy from me, I'll buy from you." If a company's customers also can supply products that the firm buys, then the sales departments of both buyer and seller may try to trade sales for sales. Purchasing managers generally resist reciprocity but often face pressure from their sales departments.

When prices and quality are otherwise competitive, an outside supplier seldom can break a reciprocity relationship. The supplier can only hope to become an alternate source of supply and wait for the competitor to let its quality slip or prices rise.

Reciprocity is often a bigger factor in other countries than it is in North America. In Japan, for example, reciprocity is very common.[17]

## Internet E-commerce and B2B Marketing

We've been discussing some of the differences in how customer firms and their suppliers relate to each other. How a customer uses e-commerce is also related to these differences.

The Internet and new types of B2B e-commerce websites have quickly and dramatically changed the way in which many purchase decisions are made and how a firm relates to its suppliers. In general, the Web is making it possible for all types of information to flow back and forth between buyers and sellers much more quickly and efficiently. This lowers the cost of the search for market information and, in many cases, the cost of transactions. For example, online order systems can cut out paper-shuffling bottlenecks, speed the delivery of purchases, and reduce inventory costs. We'll discuss distribution service–related issues in more detail in Chapter 11.

### Types of Internet Resources

There are several different types of basic e-commerce website resources that many buyers use. Each of these plays a specific role and each has distinctive strengths. To see these more clearly, we'll consider them separately. However, it is not uncommon to see two or more of these on one website (or a linked set of websites).

**Community sites** Like online trade magazines (or online trade associations), community sites offer information and communications of interest for specific industries. A website may focus on a single "community," or feature different sections for many different industries. For example, www.vertmarkets.com has many separate communities for different industries, ranging from food processing and solid-waste management to health care and utilities. Community sites were among the first on the Web because many just put in digital form information that was already being distributed in other ways. Initially they relied on advertising revenue to operate, but now some of them are trying to earn commissions based on sales referrals.

**Catalogue sites** Catalogue sites, as the name implies, offer digital product catalogues, usually for a number of different sellers. For example, www.plasticsnet.com focuses on polymers and resins used in the plastics industry. The basic benefit of catalogue sites is that they make it easy for industrial buyers to search for a product and do one-stop shopping. For example, Grainger's http://orderzone.com features a vast array of supply items that are used across many different industries. Some catalogue sites are trying to upgrade their software and service to make it easier for a buyer to place an order, track delivery status, and update inventory information. Others are trying to improve the quality of the information available. For example, rather than just give a basic description of an electric motor a site might also provide a link so the buyer can download detailed engineering drawings and electrical details.

**Exchanges** Exchanges operate much like a stock exchange (for example, the Toronto Stock Exchange) by bringing buyers and sellers together, usually anonymously, to agree on prices for commodities such as energy (see, for example, www.theinterchange.com) or telecommunications capacity. Exchanges are sometimes independent intermediaries, or they may be backed by major firms in the industry. Either way, an exchange must maintain a neutral role and not favour either buyers or sellers if it expects return visits.

**Procurement hubs** Procurement hub sites direct suppliers to particular companies (or industries) in one place. Some large companies have created procurement hubs to handle purchasing for all of their own divisions. In some industries, recognized leaders have banded together to create procurement hubs. The big three automakers in the U.S. are doing this. These hubs are becoming an important, buyer-driven force in e-commerce. They make it easier for a larger number of suppliers to find out about the purchasing needs of customers in target industries. As a result, the number of suppliers competing for a buyer's business increases, and this tends to drive down selling prices or provide benefits to the buyer with respect to other terms of the sale. On the other hand, procurement hubs are a way for a seller to find out about and pursue sales opportunities with new customers (or new markets) without a lot of additional selling expense.

**competitive bids**

The terms of sale offered by different suppliers in response to purchase specifications posted by the buyer

Most procurement hubs incorporate some sort of interactive system to get competitive bids. **Competitive bids** are the terms of sale offered by different suppliers in response to the purchase specifications posted by the buyer. Usually, the focus is on the supplier's price. Firms have used the competitive bidding process for a long time. However, before the Internet it was usually too slow and too inconvenient to go through several rounds of bids. Now, however, the Internet makes it fast and easy for the customer firm to run what is sometimes called a *reverse auction*. Vendors are invited (via e-mail or at the procurement hub) to place a bid for a purchase with a given specification. Usually the bidding still focuses on price, but sometimes other terms of sales (like warranty period or delivery time) are considered as well. Each bid, and who made it, is typically visible to all potential bidders via the website. That way, other bidders can decide whether or not to offer the customer a lower price. Depending on the preferences of the customer, the bidding can be limited by a specific deadline.

**Auction sites** Auction sites tend to be more seller-driven and are especially popular for items such as used equipment and vehicles, surplus inventory, and perishable products (such as unsold advertising space or produce) that are unique and available for sale only once. For example, www.avbid.net runs auctions related to aircraft parts and services. At these auctions the seller lists and describes what's for sale, and potential buyers place their bids (what they would pay) at a website. Auctions use a variety of formats, but in general the highest bidder (prior to the deadline) purchases the product. Some auction sites also handle reverse auctions for the benefit of buyers.

**Collaboration hubs** Collaboration hubs go beyond matching buyers and sellers for a one-time transaction and instead are designed to help firms work together. The collaboration might involve design, manufacturing, and distribution. Many of these sites focus on the needs of smaller firms, usually within a vertical industry. For instance, Citadon (www.citadon.com) provides a single online workplace for construction contractors to collaborate with architects, store blueprints, work through building permit requirements, and purchase building materials.

### Some Difficulties in Internet-based Relationships

As the examples above suggest, some B2B e-commerce websites are specialized for firms at different levels of production and distribution within a particular industry.



Exhibit 7-9 Examples of different B2B e-commerce sites used by organizational buyers and sellers.

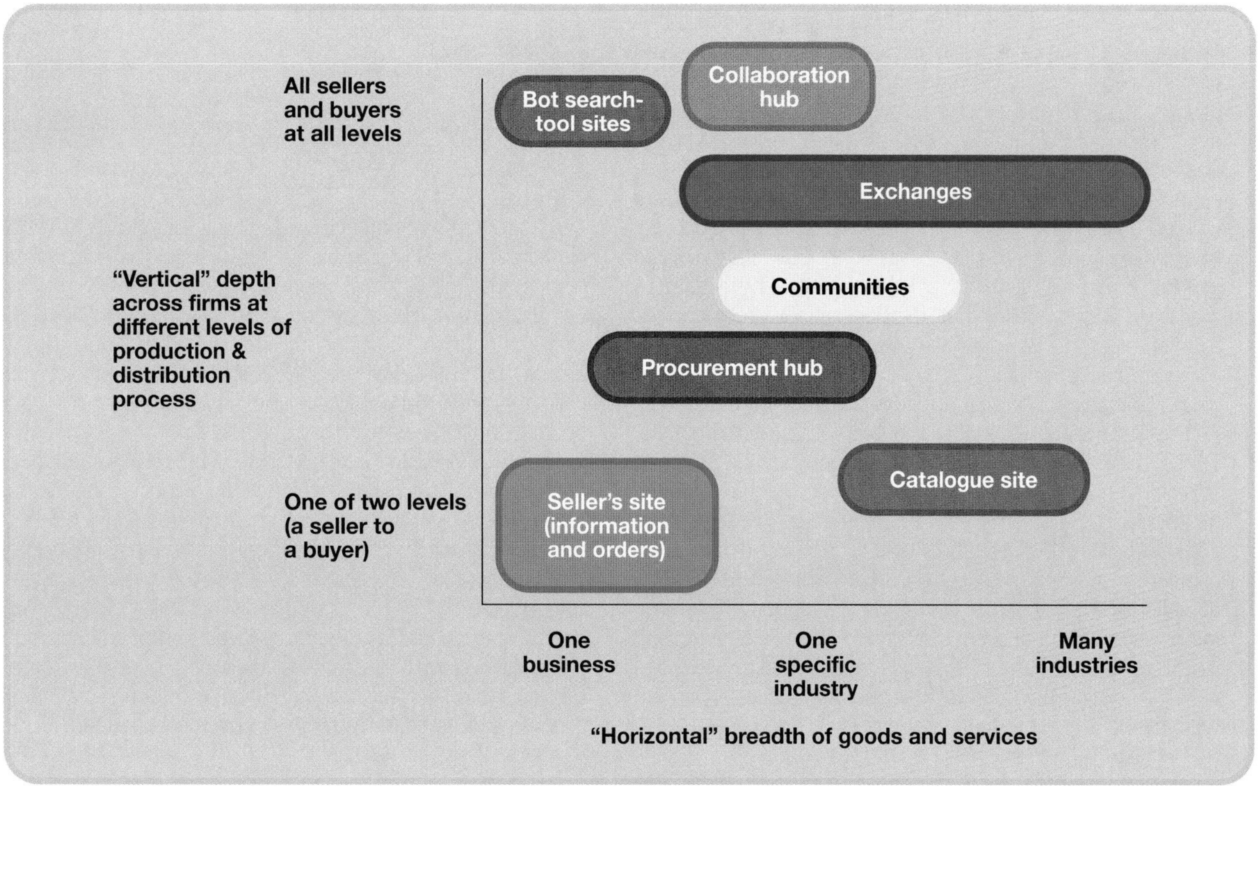

# Internet Insite 7–1

## THE BUSINESS OF E-BUSINESS

The Internet and its user-friendly incarnation, the World Wide Web, have had a bigger impact on businesses than on consumers. E-Marketer, which aggregates data from other research firms, estimated that worldwide B2B e-commerce revenues (i.e., the value of transactions among businesses or organizations) will exceed $1.4 trillion by the end of 2003.[18] To put this figure in perspective, the total business-to-consumer e-commerce (i.e., value of purchases made by individuals and households) worldwide was projected at only $38 billion for the last quarter of 2002 (the busiest shopping season).[19]

E-commerce offers several benefits for businesses, including lower transaction costs, fewer errors in order processing, ability to track customers, ability to source on a global basis, and speed.[20] To take advantage of the growing B2B e-commerce, many new intermediaries emerged on the Internet to facilitate transactions between buyers and sellers. These online marketplaces, or e-marketplaces, often specialized in one vertical industry. Examples include Chemdex for chemicals, e-Steel for steel, PaperExchange for paper products, and VertMarkets, which offers e-marketplaces for more than 50 sectors. None of these have been spectacular successes, and some (for example Chemdex and e-Steel) have already closed. Let us explore some of the reasons.

E-marketplaces that facilitated buyer–seller matching and transactions did not fully address the needs of businesses. Businesses typically seek long-term relationships with suppliers and may often need to collaborate with suppliers (e.g., automobile companies involve their suppliers in new product design). They do not make major purchase decisions solely on the basis of price (or cost savings). These e-marketplaces did not facilitate relationship building and collaboration, which did not please buyers. In addition, businesses realized that it is easier to buy standardized indirect materials (such as office supplies) online without worrying about quality, but mission-critical products are a different story. Businesses have been reluctant to trust e-marketplaces for purchase of direct materials and technical products with complex specifications.

Suppliers were also not too thrilled with e-marketplaces. These sites led to price-based competition among suppliers by promoting auctions, which led to lower margins for suppliers. Suppliers were also interested in building relationships with buyers. It is not surprising that many e-marketplaces failed to get a critical mass of buyers and suppliers to participate. A survey by the research firm Giga Information Group and consulting firm Booz Allen Hamilton revealed that more than 50 percent of businesses were dissatisfied with online marketplaces and only about 10 percent were moderately or extremely satisfied.[21]

Public exchanges backed by leading companies have a better track record than exchanges created by independent third parties. Covisint (www.covisint.com), which was created by GM, Ford, and DaimlerChrysler, facilitates the exchange of information between OEM manufacturers and the supplier community. Covisint has focused its efforts on providing the Automotive Industry Operating System that establishes a common infrastructure for the automotive industry to "Connect, Communicate, and Collaborate." This evolutionary system is based on two key components: Covisint Connect, a data-messaging service that provides a single connection for a company's computers to exchange data with the computers of its partners, and Covisint Communicate, portal services that provide a turnkey approach to supplier portals that is easy to implement and easy to use (see the exhibit below).

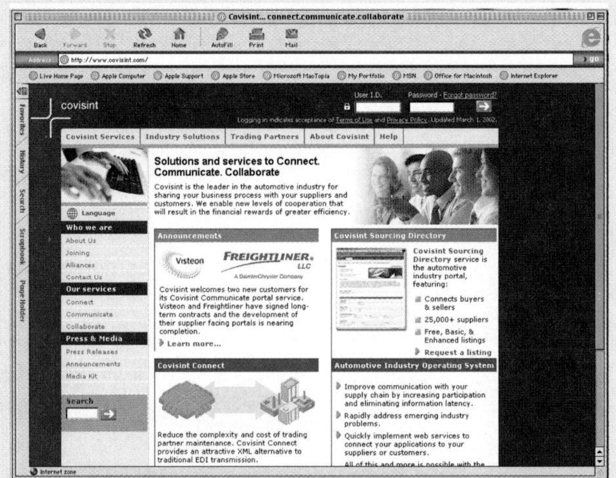


The retail industry has a similar consortium called GlobalNetXchange (www.gnx.com), which includes major retail chains such as Sears, Federated Department Stores, and Carrefour as well as major consumer product firms like P&G, Unilever, Johnson & Johnson, and Colgate-Palmolive. GNX claims that it facilitates "supply chain and procurement solutions that streamline core business processes and reduce costs along the entire supply chain."

GNX has learned from the failure of other e-marketplaces and realized that B2B transactions require negotiation, rather than fixed catalogue prices. This site allows sellers to submit bids or proposals in response to requests for quotes (RFQs) posted by buyers, and then it allows the two parties to negotiate online. Large retailers work collaboratively with suppliers to ensure low inventory levels and optimal product mix. GNX offers collaborative solutions where buyers can quickly share inventory levels and sales forecasts with suppliers to ensure effective supply chain management.

Some larger companies, such as IBM, have created private exchanges where only invited suppliers participate. This facilitates relationship building and allows suppliers to focus on differentiated services, rather than on price. Private exchanges can exclude competitors and can protect sensitive information.

From e-commerce (buying and selling products online), businesses are now moving to e-business (streamlining and achieving efficiency in business processes using Internet-enabled technologies). Collaborative product development using virtual teams (e.g., team members located in different countries), exchange of information with suppliers or partners (through extranets), information sharing within the organization (through enterprise portals), and managing customer relationships are some areas where e-business applications can be seen. The consumer side of e-commerce (often referred to as B2C e-commerce) is mainly focused on buying and selling. Businesses, on the other hand, have realized that e-commerce offers some benefits but e-business could potentially have a bigger impact.

Some questions to ponder: Why is the size of B2B e-commerce many times larger than B2C e-commerce? Why are competitors like GM and Ford or Sears and Federated Department Stores (which owns Macy's and Bloomingdales) joining forces to participate in e-marketplaces?

Go to: www.mcgrawhill.ca/college/wong to apply this Insite in an exciting Internet exercise.

For example, one of these "vertical" sites that specializes in the plastics industry might be of interest to firms that make the basic chemicals from which plastics are formed, firms that create plastic injection moulding equipment, and firms that use that equipment to make finished goods. On the other hand, some websites are designed to serve a broad ("horizontal") cross-section of firms from different industries. For example, a horizontal site might serve manufacturers regardless of whether they produce bearings, truck frames, or construction equipment (see Exhibit 7-9).

While these different types of sites offer many benefits to businesses, they have not been without problems (see Internet Insite 7-1). For example, one consequence of these differences in vertical versus horizontal focus is that there are many sites with potentially overlapping coverage. While some industries are not covered well, in other industries many sites compete to be the central market. As a result, this is an arena in which there are still many ongoing changes. Hundreds, or perhaps thousands, of B2B websites that were established just a few years ago have already disappeared, and consolidation is still underway. In some industries there are so many sites that instead of simplifying the buying and selling process they have made it unnecessarily complicated. For example, a seller who posts an auction on the wrong site may get few bids, or no bids, from firms that might be serious buyers. Those buyers, in turn, might waste time checking other sites not included in the sellers' efforts.

Because of such problems, purchasing managers often turn to special software packages to help with their search effort. For example, if a purchasing manager can specify a certain model of a product the search "bot" (short for *robot*) looks at all of the websites on the Internet to find everywhere that the product is mentioned. Some bots take things further and assemble price comparisons or e-mail distribution lists.

Bots are also helping purchasing people who have trouble figuring out exactly how to describe what they want. By searching for descriptions of products in a broad product category, it is often possible to develop a better understanding not only of what alternatives exist but also of what specs are best for the particular need.

You can see that there are many different B2B e-commerce sites that are helping sellers find interested buyers, and vice versa. Until recently, much of the attention was on providing information to drive down the purchase price for specific transactions. Yet as we've said from the start, business customers are usually interested in the total cost of working with a supplier and the value of a supplier's marketing mix—not just in the product price. When everything else is the same, a buyer would obviously prefer low prices. But "everything else" is not always the same. We considered many examples of this earlier when we reviewed why a buyer might prefer closer relationships with fewer sellers. So it is important to see that Internet tools that focus primarily on lowering purchase prices do not necessarily lower total purchasing costs or apply to all types of purchases.

On the other hand, great strides are being made in developing websites and Internet-based software tools that help both buyers and sellers work together in more efficient and effective relationships. National Semiconductor's website is a good

## Marketing Demo 7–2

### NATIONAL SEMICONDUCTOR'S WEBSITE

# Linking Buyers, Products, and Distributors

**NATIONAL SEMICONDUCTOR DESIGNED its Web site to serve several key audiences. Purchasers from large customers who buy directly from the company's salespeople have private extranets with tailored information. National's other customers buy through distributors, but they can use National's site to research products and link directly to distributors' sites to buy. National also allows engineers and purchasing agents to look at information in ways that suit their individual needs.**

**www.national.com**

**National's LARGEST CUSTOMERS log on to private extranets that show their purchasing history and the shipping status of products they have ordered.**

**ENGINEERS click to look at lists of products in different categories.**

**PURCHASERS can create and save a list of products needed for a project...**

**Each product has a page with detailed information...**

**...and then check the inventory of different distributors and link directly to their individual sites.**

**...and links to distributors' individual pages.**

**On the DISTRIBUTOR's page, buyers can purchase a product with a credit card.**

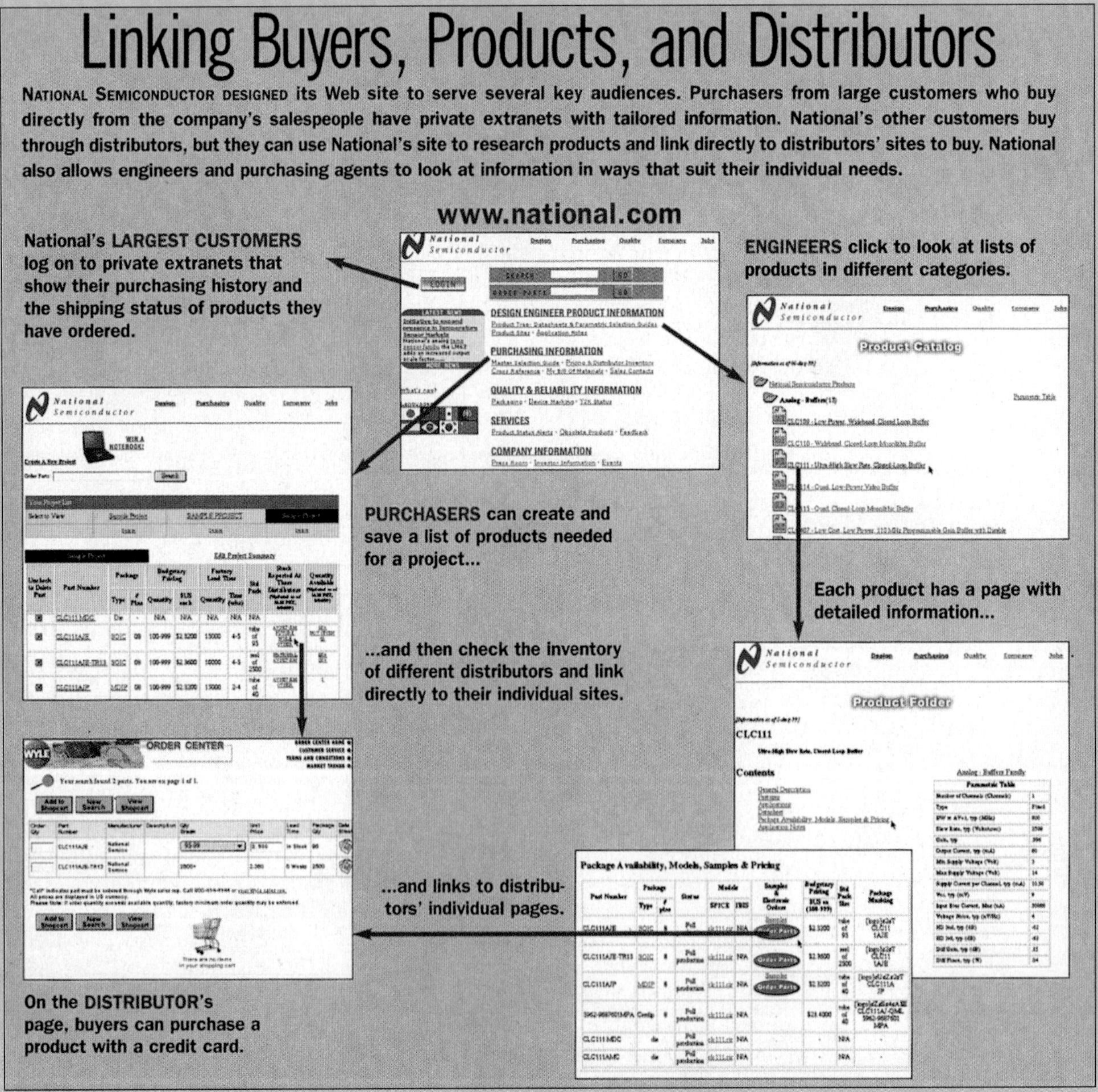

## Ethical Dimensions 7–2

### RIGGED SPECS ARE AN ETHICAL CONCERN

At the extreme, a government customer who wants a specific brand or supplier may try to write the description so that no other supplier can meet all the specs. The buyer may have good reasons for such preferences—a more reliable product, prompt delivery, or better service after the sale. This kind of loyalty sounds great, but marketers must be sensitive to the ethical issues involved. Laws that require government customers to get bids are intended to increase competition among suppliers, not reduce it. Specs that are written primarily to defeat the purpose of these laws may be viewed as illegal bid rigging.

example (see Marketing Demo 7-2). It is designed to create easy links between its customers, products, and distributors. Its large customers get special services, like access to a secure website that shows specific purchase histories and production or shipping status of their orders. Smaller customers can get all the product information they need and then link directly to the order page for the distributor that serves them. This system does not go as far as some, but it does illustrate how shared information and cooperation over the Internet is helping to create better relationships in business markets.[22]

### Automated Buying

We've been discussing ways in which buyers and sellers use the Web. But e-commerce computer systems now *automatically* handle a large portion of routine order placing. Buyers program decision rules that tell the computer how to order and leave the details of following through to the machine. For example, when an order comes in that requires certain materials or parts, the computer system automatically orders them from the appropriate suppliers, the delivery date is set, and production is scheduled.

When economic conditions change, buyers modify the computer instructions. When nothing unusual happens, however, the computer system continues to routinely rebuy as needs develop—electronically sending purchase orders to the regular supplier.

Obviously, it's a big sale to be selected as the major supplier that routinely receives all of a customer's electronic orders for the products you sell. Often this type of customer will be more impressed by an attractive marketing mix for a whole *line* of products than just a lower price for a particular order. Further, it may be too expensive and too much trouble to change the whole buying system just because somebody is offering a low price on a particular day.

In this sort of routine order situation, it's very important to be one of the regular sources of supply. For straight rebuys, the buyer (or computer) may place an order without even considering other potential sources. However, if a buyer believes that there are several suppliers who could meet the specs, the buyer may request competitive bids. If different suppliers' quality, dependability, and delivery schedules all meet the specs, the buyer will select the low-price bid. But a creative marketer needs to look carefully at the purchaser's specs—and the need—to see if other elements of the marketing mix could provide a competitive advantage. For more on selling according to specs, see Ethical Dimensions 7-2.

Sellers' sales reps (and perhaps whole teams of people) regularly call on these customers, but not to sell a particular item. Rather, they want to maintain relations, become a preferred source, or point out new developments that might cause the buyer to re-evaluate the present straight-rebuy procedure and give more business to the sales rep's company.

## The Government Market

Governments in Canada are a very large and concentrated market. On the federal level, for example, much of the buying is done through Public Works and Government Services Canada, a department that purchases billions of dollars' worth of goods and services a year for itself and for other federal departments and agencies. The Department of National Defence is generally Canada's largest single customer. Other major purchasers include the Canadian Commercial Corporation (a Crown corporation that helps foreign governments purchase goods made in Canada) and Transport Canada. Collectively, provincial and local governments are even more important markets than the federal government.

The range of goods and services purchased by governments is vast, and includes everything from advertising services to appliances. Governments run not only schools, police departments, and military organizations, but also supermarkets, public utilities, research laboratories, offices, hospitals, and liquor stores. And it's expected that government expenditures for these operations will continue to grow. Such opportunities must not be ignored by an aggressive marketing manager.

### Government Buying Methods

Most goods and services are purchased through contracts awarded after a requisition is received from the department that needs these items. Any Canadian business supplying such goods and services is eligible to bid. The only requirements are a desire to sell and evidence of the ability to supply under the terms and conditions of the contract. Any size firm can bid—the overall size of government expenditures is no indication of the size of individual contracts. Despite the overall amount spent by government, firms of all sizes can and do bid for such business, since many thousands of contracts are for relatively small amounts.

Although bidding procedures vary slightly among departments and levels of government, similar practices are followed. Potential suppliers are invited to tender on a particular contract. The government department in question has drawn up its list

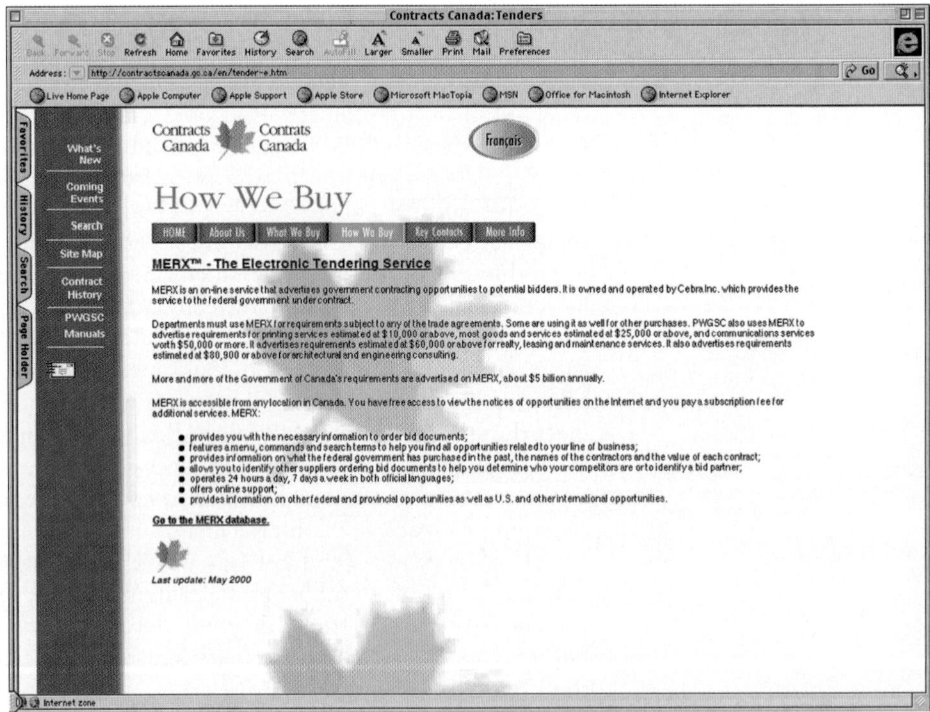

of specifications carefully, to clarify what any supplier must bid on and to simplify the selection procedure. The contract is then awarded to the firm submitting the lowest bid that also meets the specifications of the tender call.

Writing specifications isn't easy, and buyers usually appreciate help from knowledgeable salespeople. Salespeople want to have input on the specifications so that their product can be considered or even have an advantage. One company may get the business even with a bid that is not the lowest because the lower bids don't meet minimum specifications.

Not all government purchases are made this way. Many branded or standardized items are routinely purchased through standing-offer arrangements. These offers are issued to suppliers for specific time periods. The suppliers, in turn, agree to supply the goods or services at prearranged prices and delivery conditions. Pharmaceutical supplies, tires and tubes, and petroleum and oil are often bought this way. Invitations to tender on major construction contracts are both advertised and mailed to likely bidders.

Contracts may be negotiated for items that are not branded or easily described, or for products that require research and development, or in cases where there is no effective competition. Depending on the government unit involved, the contract may be subject to audit and renegotiation, especially if the contractor makes a larger profit than expected.

Negotiation is often necessary when there are many intangible factors. Unfortunately, this is exactly where favouritism and influence can slip in. Nevertheless, negotiation is an important buying method in government sales—so, a marketing mix should emphasize more than just low price.

### Learning What Governments Want

Since almost all government contracts are advertised, a prospective supplier can focus on particular government agencies or departments. Firms can now easily learn about potential government target markets using the assistance available from online government sources. Contracts Canada is an interdepartmental initiative to improve buyer awareness and simplify access to federal government purchasing. Its primary responsibility is to make it easier for Canadian suppliers to do business with the federal government. Contracts Canada also serves as a focal point for supplier and buyer inquiries. Information on past government purchases and forthcoming "opportunities to bid" is available through Merx, the government's electronic tendering service (**www.merx.cebra.com**). Additional information on the specifics of bidding and tendering is available from Contracts Canada's own website (**www.contractscanada.gc.ca**).

Various provincial and local governments also offer assistance. Industry-oriented magazines and trade associations provide information on how to reach schools, hospitals, highway departments, parks boards, and so on. Of course, marketers interested in selling to provincial and local governments must be aware of any "province first" procurement policies. Most of the provinces tend to favour local suppliers at the expense of firms manufacturing elsewhere. Although a provincial preference in purchasing may make political sense, it poses real problems for firms trying to sell nationally in what is already a very small internal common market.

### Dealing with Foreign Governments

Government agencies around the world spend a great deal of money, and they are important target customers for some firms. But selling to government units in foreign countries can be a real challenge. In many cases, a firm must get permission from the government in its own country to sell to a foreign government. Moreover, most government contracts favour domestic suppliers if they are available. Even if such favouritism is not explicit, public sentiment may make it very difficult for a foreign competitor to get a contract. Or the government bureaucracy may simply bury a foreign supplier in so much red tape that there's no way to win.

## More Information on Industry Trends

What products an industrial customer needs to buy depends on the business it is in. It follows that sales of a product are often concentrated among customers in similar businesses. For example, apparel manufacturers are the main customers for buttons. Marketing managers who can relate their own sales to their customers' type of business can focus their efforts.

Detailed information is often available to help a marketing manager learn more about customers in different lines of business. The federal government regularly collects and publishes data by Standard Industrial Classification (SIC) codes—groups of firms in similar lines of business. The number of establishments, as well as sales volumes and number of employees are given for each SIC code, broken down by geographic area. A number of other countries collect similar data but use somewhat different classification systems. That's why Canada, the United States, and some other countries are trying to coordinate their data collection efforts by also using the North American Industry Classification System (NAICS, pronounced "nakes"), an internationally accepted variation of the SIC system. In many other countries, however, data on business customers remains incomplete or inaccurate.

The NAICS is a relatively new development. It was adopted as a standard in 1997, to be phased in over time. The phase-in will make it easier to use the new system because in the past data were reported using Standard Industrial Classification (SIC) codes. Many of the codes are similar; check the website at www.naics.com for details. However, the move to the new system should help business marketers. The NAICS system is suited for identifying new or fast-changing industries—and, for marketers, that spells opportunity. NAICS is also more detailed than SIC and works better for services such as financial institutions, health-care providers, and firms in the entertainment business. The general logic of NAICS is similar to that of SIC. So, let's take a closer look at how NAICS codes work.



Exhibit 7-10 Illustrative NAICS code breakdown by apparel manufacturers.

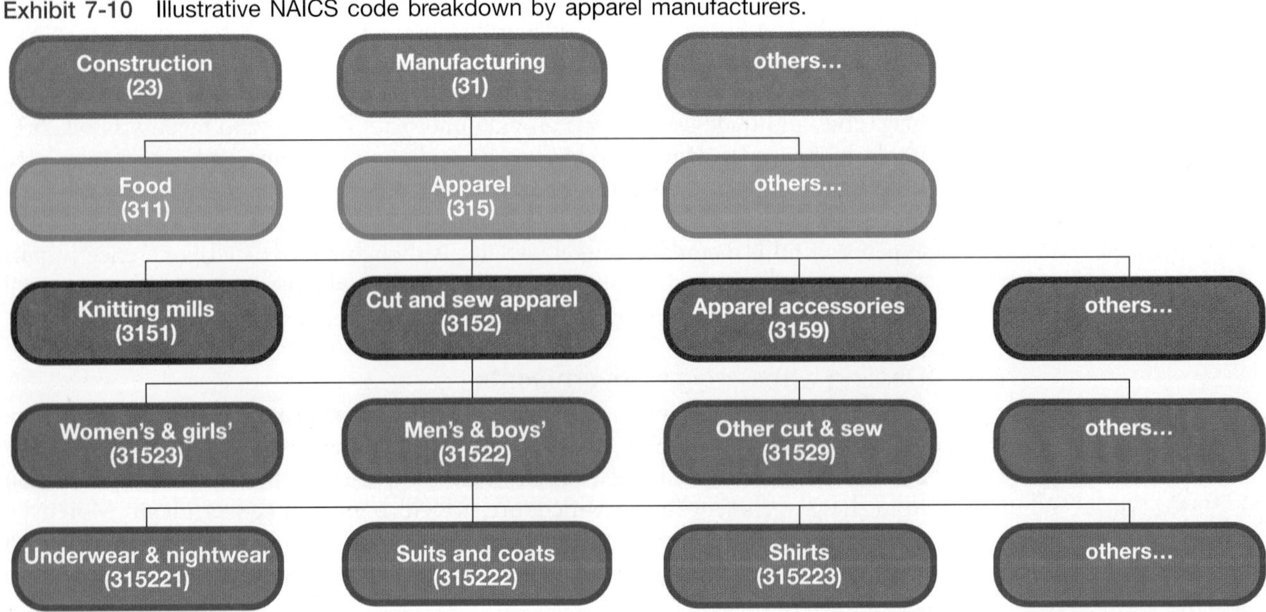

The NAICS code breakdowns start with broad industry categories such as construction (23), manufacturing (31), wholesale trade (42), finance and insurance (52), and so on. Within each two-digit industry breakdown, much more detailed data may be available for three-digit industries (that is, subindustries of the two-digit industries). For example, within the two-digit manufacturing industry (code 31) there are manufacturers of food (311), beverages and tobacco (312), and others, including apparel manufacturers (315). Then each three-digit group of firms is further subdivided into more detailed four-, five-, and six-digit classifications. For instance, within the three-digit (315) apparel manufacturers there are four-digit subgroups for knitting mills (3151), cut and sew firms (3152), and producers of apparel accessories (3159). Exhibit 7-10 illustrates that breakdowns are more detailed as you move to codes with more digits. However, detailed data (say, broken down at the four-digit level) isn't available for all industries in every geographic area. The government does not provide detail when only one or two plants are located in an area.

Many firms find their *current* customers' NAICS (or SIC) codes and then look at NAICS-coded lists for similar companies that may need the same goods and services. Other companies look at which NAICS categories are growing or declining to discover new opportunities. If companies aiming at business target markets in North America know exactly who they are aiming at, readily available data organized by NAICS (or SIC) codes can be valuable. Most trade associations and private organizations that gather data on business markets also use these codes.

The NAICS codes are an improvement over the old approach, but they are not perfect. Some companies have sales in several categories but are listed in only one—the code with the largest sales. In addition, some businesses don't fit any of the categories very well. So although a lot of good information is available, the codes must be used carefully.[23]



## Chapter Summary

In this chapter, we considered the number, size, location, and buying behaviour of various types of organizational customers to try to identify logical dimensions for segmenting markets and developing marketing mixes. We looked at who makes and influences organizational buying decisions, and how multiple influences may make the marketing job more difficult. We also saw that the nature of the buyer and the buying situation are relevant and that the problem-solving models of buyer behaviour introduced in Chapter 6 apply here with modifications.

Buying behaviour—and marketing opportunities—may change when there's a close relationship between a supplier and a customer. However, close relationships are not an all-or-nothing thing. There are different ways that a supplier can build a closer relationship with its customers. We identified key dimensions of relationships and their benefits and limitations.

We also looked at how buyers use e-commerce in the buying process. Some capabilities, like interactive competitive bidding, have already had a major impact. And much progress is underway toward fostering more efficient relationships.

The chapter focuses on aspects of buying behaviour that often apply to different types of organizational customers. However, we discussed some key differences in the manufacturer, services, intermediary, and government markets.

A clear understanding of organizational buying habits, needs, and attitudes can aid marketing strategy planning. And since there are fewer organizational customers than final consumers, it may even be possible for some marketing managers (and their salespeople) to develop a unique strategy for each potential customer.

This chapter offers some general principles that are useful in strategy planning—but the nature of the products being offered may require adjustments in the plans. Different product classes are discussed in Chapter 9. Variations by product may provide additional segmenting dimensions to help a marketing manager fine-tune a marketing strategy.

## Key Concepts

business and organizational customers, p. 179
buyers, p. 182
competitive bids, p. 192
deciders, p. 181
influencers (gatekeepers), p. 181
initiators, p. 181
ISO 9000, p. 183
just-in-time delivery, p. 189
modified rebuy, p. 184
negotiated contract buying, p. 189
new-task buying, p. 184
purchasing managers, p. 179
purchasing specifications, p. 183
reciprocity, p. 191
straight rebuy, p. 184
users, p. 182
vendor analysis, p. 185

## Questions and Problems



1. In your own words, explain how the buying behaviour of business customers in different countries may have been a factor in speeding the spread of international marketing.
2. Compare and contrast the buying behaviour of final consumers and organizational buyers. In what ways are they most similar and in what ways are they most different?
3. Briefly discuss why a marketing manager should think about who is likely to be involved in the buying centre for a particular purchase. Is the buying centre idea useful in consumer buying? Explain your answer.
4. If a nonprofit hospital were planning to buy expensive MRI scanning equipment (to detect tumours), who might be involved in the buying centre? Explain your answer and describe the types of influence that different people might have.
5. Describe the situations that would lead to the use of the three different buying processes for a particular product—lightweight bumpers for a pickup truck.
6. Why would an organizational buyer want to get competitive bids? What are some of the situations when competitive bidding can't be used?
7. How likely would each of the following be to use competitive bids: *(a)* a small town that needed a road resurfaced, *(b)* a scouting organization that needed a printer to print its scouting handbook, *(c)* a hardware retailer that wants to add a new lawn mower line, *(d)* a grocery-store chain that wants to install new checkout scanners, and *(e)* a sorority that wants to buy a computer to keep track of member dues? Explain your answers.
8. Discuss the advantages and disadvantages of just-in-time supply relationships from an organizational buyer's point of view. Are the advantages and disadvantages merely reversed from the seller's point of view?
9. Explain why a customer might be willing to work more cooperatively with a small number of suppliers rather than pitting suppliers in a competition against each other. Give an example that illustrates your points.
10. Would a tool manufacturer need a different marketing strategy for a big retail chain like Home Depot than for a single owner-operated hardware store? Discuss your answer.
11. How do you think a furniture manufacturer's buying habits and practices would be affected by the specific type of product to be purchased? Consider fabric for upholstered furniture, a lathe for the production line, cardboard for shipping cartons, and lubricants for production machinery.
12. Discuss the importance of target marketing when analyzing organizational markets. How easy is it to isolate homogeneous market segments in these markets?
13. Explain how NAICS codes might be helpful in evaluating and understanding business markets. Give an example.
14. Considering the nature of retail buying, outline the basic ingredients of promotion to retail buyers. Does it make any difference what kinds of products are involved? Are any other factors relevant?
15. The government market is obviously an extremely large one, yet it is often slighted or even ignored by many firms. Red tape is certainly one reason, but there are others. Discuss the situation and be sure to include the possibility of segmenting in your analysis.

## Computer-Aided Problem 7

### Vendor Analysis

CompuTech, Inc., makes circuit boards for microcomputers. It is evaluating two possible suppliers of electronic memory chips.

The chips do the same job. Although manufacturing quality has been improving, some chips are always defective. Both suppliers will replace defective chips. But the only practical way to test for a defective chip is to assemble a circuit board and "burn it in"—run it and see if it works. When one chip on a board is defective at that point, it costs $2.00 for the extra labour time to replace it. Supplier 1 guarantees a chip-failure rate of not more than 1 per 100 (that is, a defect rate of 1 percent). The second supplier's 2-percent defective rate is higher, but its price is lower.

Supplier 1 has been able to improve its quality because it uses a heavier plastic case to hold the chip. The only disadvantage of the heavier case is that it requires CompuTech to use a connector that is somewhat more expensive.

Transportation costs are added to the price quoted by either supplier, but Supplier 2 is farther away so transportation costs are higher. And because of the distance, delays in supplies reaching CompuTech are sometimes a problem. To ensure that a sufficient supply is on hand to keep production going, CompuTech must maintain a backup inventory—and this increases inventory costs. CompuTech figures inventory costs—the expenses of finance and storage—as a percentage of the total order cost.

To make its vendor analysis easier, CompuTech's purchasing agent has entered data about the two suppliers on a spreadsheet. He based his estimates on the quantity he thinks he will need over a full year.

a. *Based on the results shown in the initial spreadsheet, which supplier do you think CompuTech should select? Why?*
b. *CompuTech estimates it will need 100,000 chips a year if sales go as expected. But if sales are slow, fewer chips will be needed. This isn't an issue with Supplier 2; its price is the same at any quantity. However, Supplier 1's price per chip will be $1.95 if CompuTech buys less than 90,000 during the year. If CompuTech needs only 84,500 chips, which supplier would be more economical? Why?*
c. *If the actual purchase quantity will be 84,500 and Supplier 1's price is $1.95, what is the highest price at which Supplier 2 will still be the lower-cost vendor for CompuTech? (Hint: You can enter various prices for Supplier 2 in the spreadsheet—or use the analysis feature to vary Supplier 2's price and display the total costs for both vendors.)*

## Suggested Cases

To view the cases, go to www.mcgrawhill.ca/college/wong.

Interested in finding out what marketing looks like in the real world? *Marketing Magazine* is just a click away on your OLC! Visit www.mcgrawhill.ca/college/wong today.

When You Finish This Chapter, You Should

1. Know about marketing information systems.

2. Understand the scientific approach to marketing research.

3. Know how to define and solve marketing problems.

4. Know about getting secondary and primary data.

5. Understand the role of questioning, observing, and using experimental methods in marketing research.

# Chapter Eight

# Improving Decisions with Marketing Information

## LensCrafters

With more than 850 stores, LensCrafters has quickly become one of the largest chains of eyewear stores in the United States, Canada, and Puerto Rico.

A key to LensCrafters' success is that its managers use marketing research to better understand target-market needs and to plan strategies. It's also easy for managers to get—and share—marketing information. That's because the company has its own intranet, and the information on it is constantly updated.

When LensCrafters was first evaluating the eye-care market, a situation analysis revealed that there was a big opportunity. For example, library research revealed that 57 percent of people aged 18 or older wear eyeglasses, contact lenses, or both. Many also get

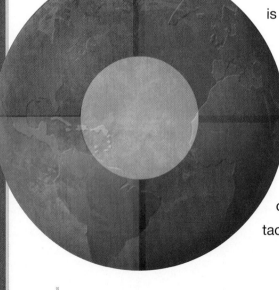

price

prod

sunglasses. Similarly, government statistics showed that demographic trends were favourable to long-run growth in the $10 billion a year eye-care market.

Subsequent LensCrafters research provided guidance for turning this opportunity into a marketing strategy. Focus group interviews and consumer surveys confirmed that most consumers viewed shopping for glasses as very inconvenient. Frame selections were too small, opticians' shops were typically closed when customers were off work and had time to shop, and the whole process usually required long waits and repeat trips. So LensCrafters put the labs that make the glasses right in its stores and kept the stores open nights and weekends. Ads tout LensCrafters' high-quality, one-hour service. With LensCrafters' new, patented Accu-Fit Measuring System, customers are assured of a perfect-fitting pair of glasses.

To be sure that service quality lives up to the advertising promises, LensCrafters sends a customer satisfaction survey to every customer. Surveys are analyzed by store and used to find out what's going on where. LensCrafters even ties satisfaction results to employee bonuses.

To make it convenient for more consumers to shop at LensCrafters, the chain has been aggressively opening new stores. The firm's website (**www.lenscrafters.com**) offers a store locator. Because the size and growth rate of various age groups in a geographic market drive demand for vision products, LensCrafters analyzes demographic data to locate new stores where profit potential is greatest. And each store carries a very large selection of frame styles, lenses, and sunglasses tailored to the age, gender, and ethnic makeup of the local market.

Managers at LensCrafters also routinely analyze sales

data that are available in the firm's marketing information system. By breaking down sales by product, store, and time period, they can spot buying trends early and plan for them.

Research also guides promotion decisions. For example, LensCrafters uses direct-mail advertising targeted to customers in segments where interest in its convenient eyeglass service is highest.

LensCrafters' new advertising and positioning is also based on research. The campaign is designed to encourage consumers to think of LensCrafters as "my personal vision place." The ads speak to the importance and value of vision care and foster LensCrafters' identity as the consumer's first choice for quality eye care and quality eyewear. The research shows that this message appeals to consumers and sets LensCrafters apart from competitors—who mainly rely on price-oriented messages about discounts and price points.[1]

The LensCrafters case shows that successful marketing strategies require information about potential target markets and their likely responses to marketing mixes as well as about competition and other marketing environment variables. Managers also need information for implementation and control. Without good information, managers are left to guess—and in today's fast-changing markets, that invites failure.



## In This Chapter

This chapter examines the tools used to acquire and interpret the information needed by managers to make marketing decisions. First we look at the management of the overall marketing information system (MIS). Our focus is to see how information from a variety of sources is brought together to support marketing decisions. We then look at the major sources of information contained in the MIS.

Marketing research is described and a five-step procedure for carrying out research studies is presented. Next we review the key sources of secondary or published information. We conclude by looking at the most commonly used methods for collecting data from consumers, including focus groups, various types of surveys, observation, experimentation, and syndicated data.

The chapter is quite technical. While we have provided a larger number of Marketing Demos and examples to illustrate the processes, you may find it helpful to start by writing out three or four questions you think a manager might want answered. As you go through the chapter, stop after each section and consider whether that technique would help find the answers you're looking for.

## Managing Marketing Information Systems

The successful planning of marketing strategies requires information—information about potential target markets, their likely responses to marketing mixes, competitors' actions, and other marketing environment variables. Information is also needed for implementation and control. For example, LensCrafters' customer satisfaction surveys play a key role in maintaining their service quality. Without good marketing information, managers would have to use intuition or guesses: in today's fast-changing and competitive markets, this invites failure.

The linkage between good information and good decision-making may seem obvious. Indeed, one could wonder how companies can make marketing mistakes given the amount of data that now seems available. But not all data are of the same quality and, even when data are available, managers may not have immediate access to them. Marketing information systems (MIS) play a key role in ensuring that good information is not only available but also accessible in an easy to use manner.

## What Is a Marketing Information System?

**marketing information system (MIS)**
An organized way of continually gathering, accessing, and analyzing the information that marketing managers need to make decisions

A **marketing information system (MIS)** is an organized way of continually gathering, accessing, and analyzing the information that marketing managers need to make decisions. We won't cover all of the technical details of planning for an MIS; that's beyond the scope of this course. But you should understand what an MIS is so you know some of the possibilities. So, we'll be discussing the elements of a complete MIS as shown in Exhibit 8-1.

## MIS Information Sources

**secondary data**
Information that has already been collected and published

**primary data**
Information collected to solve a current problem

Some of the data that management needs can be found in a business's accounting documentation and sales orders. These *internal* data sources would include sales, costs, spending levels, and so on. Some *external* data, such as competitors' sales, industry trends, and general economic and demographic data may be available from public sources as **secondary data**—information that has already been collected and published. Still other information needs can be met only through a dedicated marketing research study that generates **primary data**—information collected to solve a current problem. We'll say more about the sources of these data later in the chapter.

## How MIS Works

**data warehouse**
A place where databases are stored so that they are available when needed

An MIS organizes incoming information into a **data warehouse**—a place where databases are stored so that they are available when needed. You can think of a data warehouse as a sort of electronic library, where all of the information is indexed extremely well. Firms with an MIS often have information technology specialists who help managers get specialized reports and output from the warehouse. However, to get better decisions, most MIS systems now provide marketing



Exhibit 8-1
Elements of a complete marketing information system.

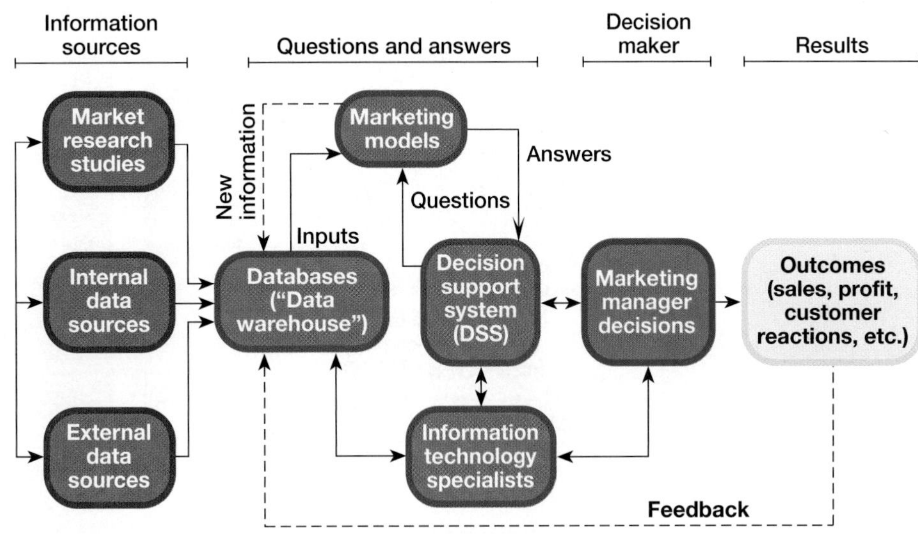

**decision support system (DSS)**

A computer program that makes it easy for a marketing manager to get and use information *as he or she is making decisions*

**search engine**

A computer program that helps a marketing manager find information that is needed

managers with a decision support system. A **decision support system (DSS)** is a computer program that makes it easy for a marketing manager to get and use information *as he or she is making decisions*.

A decision support system usually involves some sort of **search engine**—a computer program that helps a marketing manager find information that is needed. Often, the manager provides a word or phrase to guide the search. For example, a manager who wants sales data for the previous week or day might search for any database or computer file that references the term *unit sales* as well as the relevant data. The search engine would identify any files where that term appeared. If there were many, the manager could narrow the search further (say, by specifying the product of interest), or the manager could briefly review the files to find the most appropriate one.

When the search is focused on numerical data, simply finding the information may not go far enough. Thus, a DSS typically helps change raw data—like product sales for the previous day—into *more useful information*. For example, it may draw graphs to show relationships in data—perhaps comparing yesterday's sales to the sales on the same day in the last four weeks. The MIS that managers at Frito-Lay use illustrates the possibilities.

All of Frito-Lay's salespeople are equipped with hand-held computers. Throughout the day they input sales information at the stores they visit. In the evening they send all the data over telephone lines to a central computer, where it is analyzed. Within 24 hours marketing managers at headquarters and in regional offices get reports and graphs that summarize how sales went the day before—broken down by brands and locations. The information system even allows a manager to zoom in and take a closer look at a problem in Toronto or a sales success in Vancouver.[2]

Some decision support systems go even further. They allow the manager to see how answers to questions might change in various situations. For example, a manager at Kraft Foods may want to estimate how much sales will increase if the firm uses a certain type of promotion in a specific market area. The DSS will ask the manager for a *personal* judgment about how much business could be won from each competitor in that market. Then, using this input and drawing on data in the database about how the promotion had worked in other markets, the system will make a sales estimate using a marketing model. A **marketing model** is a statement of relationships among marketing variables.

**marketing model**

A statement of relationships among marketing variables

How does an intranet affect and change the way companies gather, analyze, and share marketing information?



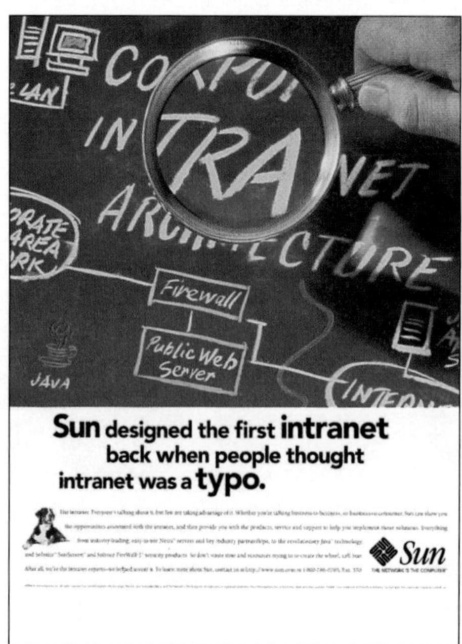

In short, the decision support system puts managers online so they can study available data and make better marketing decisions—faster.[3]

### How Technology Is Changing MIS

**intranet**
A system for linking computers within a company

Basic MIS concepts are not very different today than they were 20 years ago. However, recent developments in information technology are having a *radical* impact on what information is available to marketing managers and how quickly. A big difference today is how easy it is to set up and use an MIS. A short time ago, connecting remote computers or exchanging data over networks was very difficult. Now, many firms, even very small ones, have their own **intranet**—a system for linking computers within a company. (An intranet works like the Internet; however, to maintain security, access to sites on an intranet is usually limited to employees.) Even a manager with little computer experience can quickly learn to use an MIS to access information from or publish new information to the website. As a result, managers everywhere have access to much more information. It's instantly available, and often just a mouse-click away.

### Marketing's Role in MIS

Computers are getting easier to use, but setting up and supporting an MIS still requires technical skill. In fact, converting an existing MIS to take advantage of Internet capabilities can be a real challenge. So, in some companies, an MIS is set up by a person or group that provides *all* departments in the firm with information technology support. Or it may be set up by marketing specialists.

These specialists are important, but the marketing manager should play an important role, too. Marketing managers may not know in advance exactly what questions they will have or when. But they do know what data they've routinely used or needed in the past. They can also foresee what types of data might be useful. They should communicate these needs to the specialists so the information will be there when they want it and in the form they want it. While this may seem logical, a major stumbling block in many companies is that many managers are used to doing it the old way—and they don't think through what information they need.

For example, one sales manager thought he was progressive when he asked his assistant for a report listing each sales rep's sales for the previous month and the current month. The assistant quickly found the relevant information on the firm's intranet, put it into an Excel spreadsheet, and printed out the report. Later, however, she was surprised to see the sales manager working on the list with a calculator. He was figuring the percentage change in sales for the month and ranking the reps from largest increase in sales to smallest. The spreadsheet software could have done all of that—instantly—but the sales manager got what he *asked for*, not what he really needed. An MIS can provide information—but only the marketing manager knows what problem needs solving. It's the job of the manager—not the computer or the MIS specialist—to ask for the right information in the right form. See Marketing Demo 8-1 for a look at how some marketing managers are finding information.

## Marketing Research

**marketing research**
Procedures to develop and analyze new information

MIS systems tend to focus on recurring information needs. Routinely analyzing such information can be valuable to marketing managers, but it shouldn't be their only source of information for decision making. They must try to satisfy ever-changing needs in dynamic markets. So **marketing research**—procedures to develop and analyze new information—is needed to supplement data already available and accessible through the MIS. Indeed, one of the important jobs of a marketing researcher is to get the "facts" that are not currently available in the MIS.

### Who Does the Research?

Many large companies have a separate marketing research department to plan and carry out research projects. These departments often use outside specialists—including interviewing and tabulating services—to handle technical assignments. Further, they may call in specialized marketing consultants and marketing research organizations to take charge of a research project.

Small companies (those with less than $4 million or $5 million in sales) usually don't have separate marketing research departments. They often depend on their salespeople or managers to conduct what research they do.

Some nonprofit organizations have begun to use marketing research—usually with the help of outside specialists. For example, many politicians rely on research firms to conduct surveys of voter attitudes.[4]

## Marketing Demo 8–1

### MARKETERS ARE INCREASINGLY TURNING TO THEIR CUSTOMER INFORMATION BANKS FOR RESEARCH

In the past five to 10 years, there's been a growing realization that database mining could be a goldmine of information for companies, and market researchers are taking full advantage by working together with database marketers.

Stephen Popeil, senior vice-president, research and development at Goldfarb Consultants in Toronto, says there has been an increased realization that the database complements market research. "Market research can help you understand the full market, and database marketing can certainly help you understand where your strengths and weaknesses are in your current customer base," says Popeil.

Companies that previously had a fixed marketing budget devoted solely to market research are now directing some of it to database marketing because it's a new area to them and they're willing to spend the money to develop the expertise. But market research suppliers aren't worried about companies relying on them any less.

Ken Mison, senior VP of The Commitments Management Group at Market Facts in Toronto, says his clients "need as much information from survey research as they ever have."

Toronto-based Foster Parent Plan of Canada (FPP), which recently began combining market and database research, bears this out. By matching survey research conducted by Market Facts to its in-house database, the not-for-profit organization has been able to tag foster parents for commitment levels. "The early indications are that it's being quite predictive of whether or not a foster parent will continue their support or leave," says Mison. "It gives them a chance not only to look ahead and see what kind of risk they face, but also to try and take actions that will build and retain the support of a foster parent."

In order to generate and target customer profiles using the two disciplines, FPP started with survey research to determine commitment levels from a representative sample. Because the analysis consumes a lot of data, Mison says you need fairly large samples, preferably 2,000 to 5,000 people.

The survey results were then married to the information that FPP holds about the individuals who had been interviewed, and the combined data was analysed for predictors of commitment. "We can tell if a person is committed (their previously observed behavioural patterns are unlikely to change) or uncommitted (considering other options) based on these observed behaviours," says Mison. Once the predictors of commitment were established, FPP had a tagged database of foster parents.

Jordan Levitin, former president of the Professional Market Research Society (PMRS) and VP of custom and analytical services at Ipsos-NPD in Toronto, believes that a proper marketing information team now needs both market researchers and direct marketers. Market research suppliers agree that the two disciplines function better as a set. "Without any market research, and understanding of the full market, you can only grow your current customer base," says Popeil.

Richard Boire, a partner in the Boire Filler Group in Pickering, Ont., believes the two disciplines are equally important. "The database beats market research in the targeting, but the disadvantage is that you can't get inside the consumers' heads," he says. The most common reasons for marketers to combine the two disciplines are for measuring levels of consumer commitment, creating customer loyalty programs, developing new products, offers and creative, and bringing in new customers.[5]

Green ketchup? Who would ever dream of such a product? Heinz didn't—but when it targeted the youth market, market research revealed that kids did.



Regardless of who does the actual research, good marketing research requires cooperation between researchers and marketing managers. See Ethical Dimensions 8-1 for more on some issues in marketing research.

Marketing managers must be able to explain what their problems are and what kinds of information they need. They should be able to communicate with specialists in the specialists' language. Marketing managers may only be "consumers" of research, but they should be informed consumers—able to explain exactly what they want from the research. They should also know about some of the basic decisions made during the research process so they know the limitations of the findings.

For this reason, our discussion of marketing research will emphasize not mechanics but rather how to plan and evaluate the work of marketing researchers.[6] The most widely adopted framework for these activities is the scientific method.

## Market Research Using the Scientific Method

The scientific method—combined with the strategy planning framework we discussed in Chapter 3—can help marketing managers make better decisions.

**scientific method**

A decision-making approach that focuses on being objective and orderly in *testing* ideas before accepting them

**hypotheses**

Educated guesses about the relationships between things or about what will happen in the future

The **scientific method** is a decision-making approach that focuses on being objective and orderly in *testing* ideas before accepting them. With the scientific method, managers don't just *assume* that their intuition is correct. Instead, they use their intuition and observations to develop **hypotheses**—educated guesses about the relationships between things or about what will happen in the future. Then they test their hypotheses before making final decisions.

A manager who relies only on intuition might introduce a new product without testing consumer response. But a manager who uses the scientific method might say, "I think (hypothesize) that consumers currently using the most popular brand will prefer our new product. Let's run some consumer tests. If at least 60 percent of the consumers prefer our product, we can introduce it in a regional test market. If it doesn't pass the consumer test there, we can make some changes and try again."

The scientific method forces an orderly research process. Some managers don't carefully specify what information they need. They blindly move ahead—hoping that research will provide "the answer." Other managers may have a clearly defined problem or question but lose their way after that. These hit-or-miss approaches waste both time and money.

## Ethical Dimensions 8–1

### ISSUES IN MARKETING RESEARCH

The basic reason for doing marketing research is to get information that people can trust in making decisions. But as you will see in this chapter, research often involves many hidden details. A person who wants to misuse marketing research to pursue a personal agenda can often do so.

Perhaps the most common ethical issues concern decisions to withhold certain information from the research. For example, a manager might selectively share only those results that support his or her point of view. Others involved in a decision might never know they are getting only partial truths. Or during a set of interviews, a researcher may discover that consumers are interpreting a poorly worded question many different ways. If the researcher doesn't admit the problem, an unknowing manager may rely on meaningless results.

Another problem involves more blatant abuses. It is unethical for a firm to contact consumers under the pretense of doing research when the real purpose is to sell something. For example, some political organizations have been criticized for surveying consumers to find out their attitudes about various political candidates and issues. Then, armed with that information, someone else calls back to solicit donations. Legitimate marketing researchers are very concerned about such abuses. If the problem were to become widespread, consumers might not be willing to participate in any research.

The relationship between the researcher and the manager sometimes creates an ethical conflict, especially when the research is done by an outside firm. Managers must be careful not to send a signal that the only acceptable results from a research project are ones that confirm their existing point of view. Researchers are supposed to be objective, but that objectivity may be swayed if future contracts depend on getting the "right" results.[7]

**Data Collection**

Misrepresentation of the data collection process stems from two principal sources. The first is representing as research a marketing activity other than research. The second is the abuse of respondents' rights during the data collection process under the rationale of providing better quality research.

Consumers expect to be sold and to be surveyed and they expect to be able to tell the difference without great difficulty. When a selling or marketing activity uses the forms and language of survey research in order to mask the real nature of the activity being performed, it violates the public trust. Some classic examples of this type of practice are:

- The use of survey techniques for selling purposes. In this case, a person answers a few questions only to find him- or herself suddenly eligible to buy a specific product or service. The misuse of the survey approach as a disguise for sales canvassing is a widespread practice that shows no signs of abating.
- The use of survey techniques to obtain names and addresses of prospects for direct marketing. These efforts are usually conducted by mail. Questionnaires about products or brands are sent to households, and response is encouraged by the offer of free product samples to respondents. The listing firms compile the information by implying to the prospective customer that he or she has been interviewed in a market study.

These practices give legitimate research a bad name in the eyes of consumers. Other practices that abuse the rights of respondents and present ethical dilemmas to the researcher are:

- Disguising the purpose of a particular measurement such as a draw or free product choice question.
- Deceiving the prospective respondent as to the true duration of the interview.
- Misrepresenting the compensation in order to gain co-operation.
- Not mentioning to the respondent that a follow-up interview will be made.
- Using projective tests and unobtrusive measures to circumvent the need for a respondent's consent.
- Using hidden tape recorders to record personal interviews (or recording phone conversations without the permission of the respondent).
- Conducting simulated product tests in which the identical product is tried by the respondent except for variations in characteristics such as colour that have no influence on the quality of a product.[8]

Zero-Knowledge Systems, the Canadian company featured here, positions itself as the "consumer's advocate on privacy." What are some of the main concerns Canadian consumers have about submitting their personal information online? How can companies address these issues?

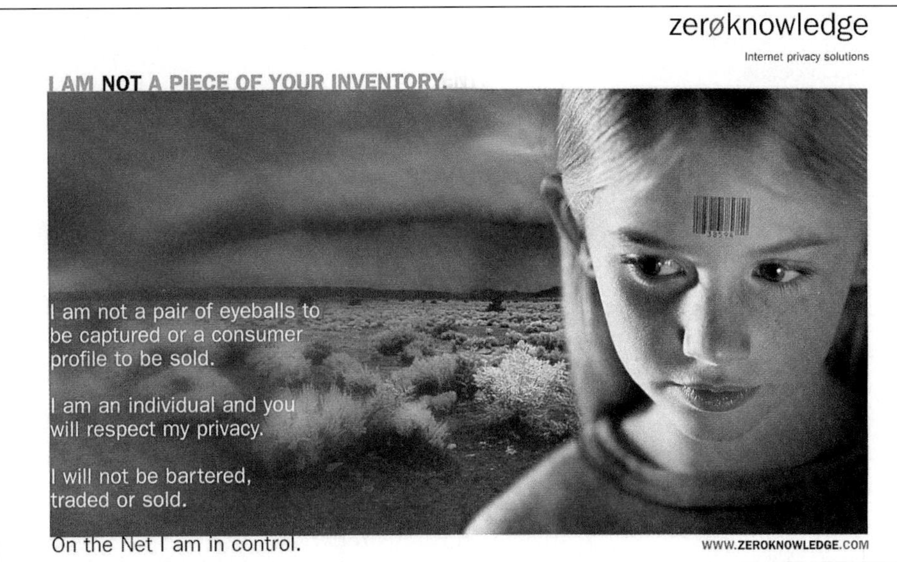

zerøknowledge
Internet privacy solutions
I AM NOT A PIECE OF YOUR INVENTORY.
I am not a pair of eyeballs to be captured or a consumer profile to be sold.
I am an individual and you will respect my privacy.
I will not be bartered, traded or sold.
On the Net I am in control.
WWW.ZEROKNOWLEDGE.COM


## Five-Step Approach to Marketing Research

**marketing research process**
A five-step application of the scientific method

The **marketing research process** is a five-step application of the scientific method that includes:

1. Defining the problem.
2. Analyzing the situation.
3. Getting problem-specific data.
4. Interpreting the data.
5. Solving the problem.

Exhibit 8-2 shows the five steps in the process. Note that the process may lead to a solution before all of the steps are completed. Or, as the feedback arrows show, researchers may return to an earlier step if needed. For example, the interpreting step may point to a new question—or reveal the need for additional information—before a final decision can be made.

**Step 1: Defining the problem** Defining the problem may seem simple. However, it is often the most difficult step in the marketing research process since it is easy to confuse symptoms with the problem. Suppose a firm's MIS shows that the company's sales are decreasing in certain territories while expenses are remaining the same—resulting in a decline in profits. The problem could be "How do we reverse the sales decline?" or the real problem could be "What is causing the declining sales?" It's hard to see how one could determine how to improve sales without first knowing the factors causing that performance.

It's easy to fall into the trap of mistaking symptoms for the problem. When this happens, the research objectives are not clear, and researchers may ignore relevant questions—while analyzing unimportant questions in expensive detail.

Sometimes the research objectives are very clear. A manager wants to know if the targeted households have tried a new product and what percentage of them bought it a second time. But research objectives aren't always so simple. The manager might also want to know why some didn't buy, or whether they had even heard of the product. Companies rarely have enough time and money to study everything. A manager must narrow the research objectives. One good way is to develop a list of research questions that includes all the possible problem areas. Then the manager can consider the items on the list more completely—in the situation-analysis step—before narrowing down to final research objectives.

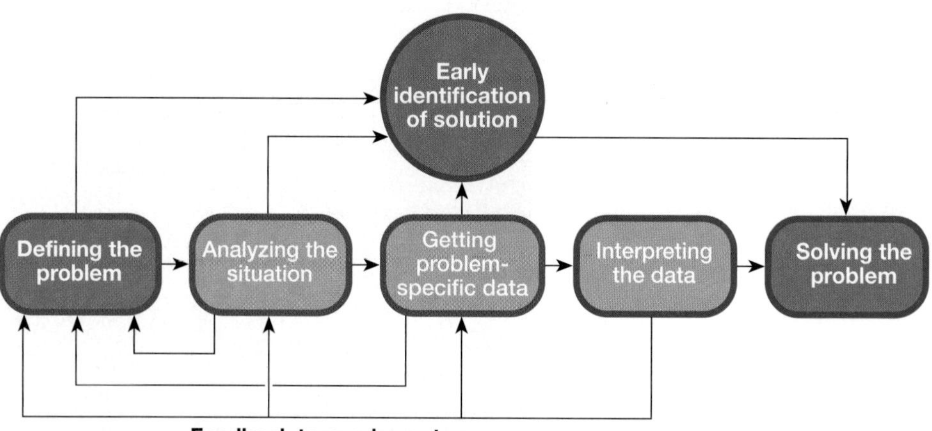


Exhibit 8-2 Five-step approach to the marketing research process.



The strategy planning framework introduced in Chapter 3 can be useful here. It can help the researcher identify the real problem area and what information is needed. Do we really know enough about our target markets to work out all of the four Ps? Do we know enough to decide what celebrity to use in an ad, or how to handle a price war in New York City or Tokyo? If not, we may want to do research rather than rely on intuition.

The importance of understanding the problem—and then trying to solve it—can be seen in the introduction of Fab One Shot, a laundry product developed to clean, soften, and reduce static cling all in one step. Marketing managers were sure that Fab One Shot was going to appeal to heavy users—especially working women with large families. Research showed that 80 percent of these women used three different laundry products for the family wash, but they were looking for more convenience.

When marketing managers found that other firms were testing similar products, they rushed Fab One Shot into distribution. To encourage first-time purchases, they offered introductory price discounts, coupons, and rebates. And they supported the sales promotion with heavy advertising on TV programs that research showed the heavy users watched.

However, research never addressed the problem of how the heavy-user target market would react. After the introductory price-off deals were dropped, sales dropped off too. While the product was convenient, heavy users weren't willing to pay the price—about 25 cents for each washload. For the heavy users, price was a qualifying dimension. And these consumers didn't like Fab's premeasured packets, because they had no control over how much detergent they could put in. The competing firms recognized these problems at the research stage and decided not to introduce their products.

After the fact, it was clear that Fab One Shot was most popular with college students, singles, and people living in small apartments. They didn't use much, so the convenience benefit offset the higher price. But the company never targeted those segments. It just assumed that it would be profitable to target the big market of heavy users.[9]

The moral of this story is that our strategy planning framework is useful for guiding the problem definition step—as well as the whole marketing-research process. First, a marketing manager should understand the target market and what needs the firm can satisfy. Then, the manager can focus on lower-level problems—namely, how sensitive the target market is to a change in one or more of the marketing-mix ingredients. Without such a framework, marketing researchers can waste time—and money—working on the wrong problem.

**situation analysis**
An informal study of what information is already available in the problem area

**Step 2: Analyzing the situation** When the marketing manager thinks the real problem has begun to surface, a situation analysis is useful. A **situation analysis** is an informal study of what information is *already* available in the problem area. It can help define the problem and specify what additional information, if any, is needed.

The situation analysis usually involves informal talks with informed people. Informed people can be others in the firm, a few good intermediaries who have close contact with customers, or others knowledgeable about the industry. In industrial markets—where relationships with customers are close—researchers may even call the customers themselves.

There are a variety of other information sources that can be used at this stage. As shown in Exhibit 8-3, secondary data (information that has already been collected and published) and primary data (information specifically collected to solve a current problem) could be used. However, secondary data are used whenever possible. This is done to ensure that researchers do not rush to gather primary data when much relevant secondary information is already available—at little or no cost!

The virtue of a good situation analysis is that it can be very informative but takes little time. And it's inexpensive compared with more formal research efforts—like a large-scale survey. Situation analysis can help focus further research or even eliminate the need for it entirely. The situation analyst is really trying to determine the exact nature of the situation and the problem.

At the end of the situation analysis, you can see which research questions—from the list developed during the problem definition step—remain unanswered. Then you have to decide exactly what information you need to answer those questions and how to get it.

**research proposal**
A plan that specifies what information will be obtained and how

This may require discussion between technical experts and the marketing manager. Often companies use a written **research proposal**—a plan that specifies what information will be obtained and how—to be sure no misunderstandings occur later. The research plan may include information about costs, what data will be collected, how it will be collected, who will analyze it and how, and how long the process will



Exhibit 8-3 Sources of primary and secondary data.

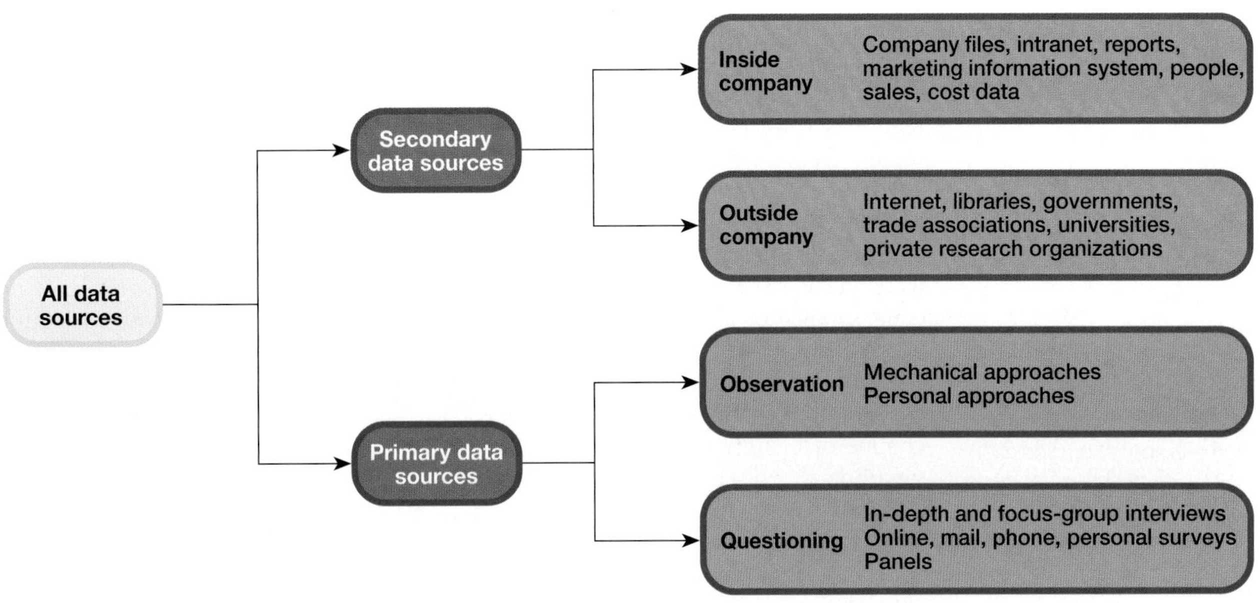

Specialized research firms like Intelligence Data (www.intelligencedata.com) can help a marketing manager solve a problem by offering relevant existing information. What are some of the benefits of using this service?

take. Then the marketing manager must decide if the time and costs involved are worthwhile. It's foolish to pay $100,000 for information to solve a $50,000 problem!

**Step 3: Getting problem-specific data** The next step is to plan a formal research project to gather primary data. There are different methods for collecting primary data; these are reviewed in more detail later in this chapter in the section on data collection. At this time, the important thing to know is that no single approach can meet all research needs.

The selection of a primary data collection method depends on the nature of the problem and how much time and money are available. In most primary data collection, the researcher tries to learn what customers think about some topic or how they behave under some conditions. There are two basic methods for obtaining information about customers: questioning and *observing*. Questioning can range from qualitative to quantitative research. And many kinds of observing are possible.

As you will see, these techniques have different strengths and weaknesses and vary in the amount of time, expertise, and money required to use them. This is why it is so important that the research proposals be developed *prior* to undertaking a research study.

**Sampling** One of the most important issues a manager must address is the nature of the people who will be the subjects of the research study. It's usually impossible for marketing managers to collect all the information they want about everyone in a **population**—the total group they are interested in. Marketing researchers typically study only a **sample**, a part of the relevant population. How well a sample *represents* the total population affects the results. Results from a sample that is not representative may not give a true picture.

**population**
The total group marketers are interested in

**sample**
A part of the relevant population

For example, the manager of a clothing retail store might want a phone survey to learn what consumers think about the store's selection. If interviewers make all of the calls during the day, the sample will not be representative. Consumers who work outside the home during the day or attend classes at school won't have an equal chance of being included. Those interviewed might say the store's selection is "satisfactory," yet it would be a mistake to assume that *all* consumers are satisfied.

You can see that getting a representative sample is very important. One method of doing so is **random sampling**, where each member of the population has the same chance of being included in the sample. Great care must be used to ensure that sampling is really random, not just haphazard. One example of random sampling is calling every tenth number in a telephone directory. Another is randomizing the last four digits of a phone number.

**random sampling**
Each member of a population has the same chance of being included in the sample

If a random sample is chosen from a population, it will tend to have the same characteristics of and be representative of the population. "Tend to" is important

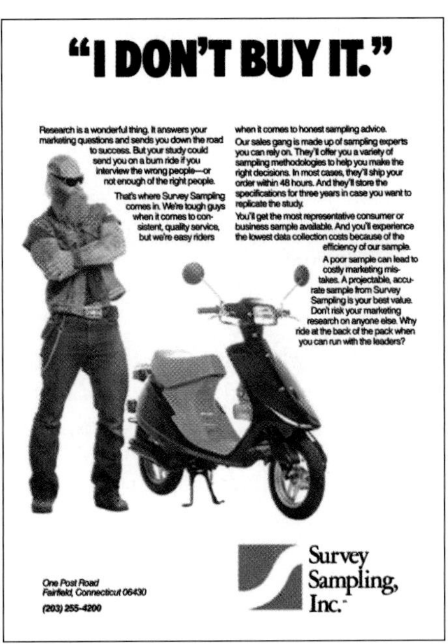

Survey Sampling, Inc. and Simmons Custom Research help marketing researchers develop samples that are really representative of the target market. Why is this so important?

because it is only a tendency—the sample is not exactly the same as the population.

Much marketing research is based on nonrandom sampling because of the high cost and difficulty of obtaining a truly random sample. Sometimes nonrandom samples give very good results—especially in industrial markets, where the number of customers may be relatively small and fairly similar. But results from nonrandom samples must be interpreted, and used, with care.

**Step 4: Interpreting the data** After someone collects the data, they have to be analyzed to decide what they all mean. In quantitative research, this step usually involves statistics. **Statistical packages**—easy-to-use computer programs that analyze data—have made this step easier. As we noted earlier, some firms provide *decision-support systems* so managers can use a statistical package to interpret data themselves. More often, however, technical specialists are involved at the interpretation step.

**statistical packages**

Easy-to-use computer programs that analyze data

Cross-tabulation is one of the most frequently used approaches for analyzing and interpreting marketing research data. It shows the relationship of answers to two different questions. Exhibit 8-4 is an example. The cross-tab analysis showed that customers who had moved in the last year were much more likely than non-movers to have adopted "Caller ID" on their phones at home.

There are many other approaches for statistical analysis—the best one depends on the situation. The details of statistical analysis are beyond the scope of this book. But a good manager should know enough to understand what a research project can and can't do.[10]

**Exhibit 8-4** Cross-tabulation breakdown of responses to a phone company consumer survey.

| | | Have You Moved in the Last Year? | | |
|---|---|---|---|---|
| | Answers: | No | Yes | Total |
| Do you have Caller ID on your phone at home? | *Yes* | 10.2% | 23.4% | 15.5% |
| | *No* | 89.8 | 76.6 | 84.5 |
| | *Total* | 100.0% | 100.0% | 100.0% |

Interpretation: 15.5 percent of people in the survey said that they had Caller ID on their phone at home. However, the percentage was much higher (23.4%) among people who had moved in the last year, and lower (10.2%) among people who had not moved.

***Evaluating the accuracy of research*** An estimate from a sample, even a representative one, usually varies somewhat from the true value for a total population. Managers sometimes forget this. They assume that survey results are exact. Instead, when interpreting sample estimates, managers should think of them as *suggesting* the approximate value.

If random selection is used to develop the sample, researchers can use various methods to help determine the likely accuracy of the sample value. This is done in terms of **confidence intervals**—the range on either side of an estimate that is likely to contain the true value for the whole population. Some managers are surprised to learn how wide that range can be.

**confidence intervals**
The range on either side of an estimate that is likely to contain the true value for the whole population

Consider a wholesaler who has 1,000 retail customers and wants to learn how many of these retailers carry a product from a competing supplier. If the wholesaler randomly samples 100 retailers and 20 say yes, then the sample estimate is 20 percent. But with that information the wholesaler can be only 95 percent confident that the percentage of all retailers is in the confidence interval between 12 and 28 percent.[11]

The larger the sample size, the greater the accuracy of estimates from a random sample. With a larger sample, a few unusual responses are less likely to make a big difference.

***Why estimates may be wrong*** We have already discussed the impact of sampling decisions on the quality of research. But even if the sampling is carefully planned, it is also important to evaluate the quality of the research data itself.

Managers and researchers should be sure that research data really measures what they are supposed to measure. Many of the variables marketing managers are interested in are difficult to measure accurately. Questionnaires may let us assign numbers to consumer responses, but that still doesn't mean that the result is precise. An interviewer might ask "How much did you spend on soft drinks last week?" A respondent may be perfectly willing to cooperate—and be part of the representative sample—but just not be able to remember.

**validity**
The extent to which data measure what they are intended to measure

**Validity** concerns the extent to which data measure what they are intended to measure. Validity problems are important in marketing research because many people will try to answer even when they don't know what they're talking about. Further, a poorly worded question can mean different things to different people and



SPSS and StatSoft are statistical packages that make it easy to summarize and graph marketing research data.

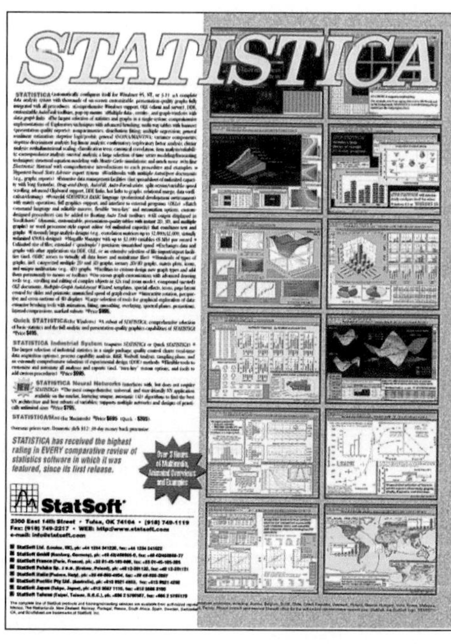

invalidate the results. Often, one or more pretests of a research project are required to evaluate the quality of the questions and measures and to ensure that potential problems have been identified. Managers must be sure that they pay only for research results that are representative and valid.

Besides sampling and validity problems, a marketing manager must consider whether the analysis of the data supports the *conclusions* drawn in the interpretation step. Sometimes technical specialists pick the right statistical procedure—their calculations are exact—but they misinterpret the data because they don't understand the management problem. In one survey, car buyers were asked to rank five cars in order from "most preferred" to "least preferred." One car was ranked first by slightly more respondents than any other car, so the researcher reported it as the "most liked car." That interpretation, however, ignored the fact that 70 percent of the respondents ranked the car *last!*

Interpretation problems like this can be subtle but crucial. Some people draw misleading conclusions on purpose to get the results they want. Marketing managers must decide whether *all* of the results support the interpretation and are relevant to their problem.

***Marketers shouldn't leave interpretation to others*** Marketing research involves many technical details. But you can see that the marketing researcher and the marketing manager must work together to be sure that they really do solve the problem facing the firm. If the whole research process has been a joint effort, then the interpretation step can move quickly to decision making—and solving the problem.

When done correctly, marketing research can be seamlessly integrated into marketing decisions and even advertising, as shown by the example of Toyota Canada's use of market research. Toyota Canada is one of the first advertisers to take advantage of *Time* Canada's ability to micro-target advertising to specific subscribers, further refining the ability to aim particular ads at the consumers most likely to buy. Depending on which vehicle research indicated the subscriber was more likely to buy, the magazine would carry an ad for either Toyota's Camry or Corolla. Market research allows Toyota to be more relevant to different target markets, while achieving reach and frequency.[12]

**Step 5: Solving the problem** In the problem-solution step, managers use the research results to make marketing decisions. Some researchers, and some managers, are fascinated by the interesting tidbits of information that come from the research process. They are excited if the research reveals something they didn't know before. But if research doesn't have action implications, it has little value and suggests poor planning by the researcher and the manager.

When the research process is finished, the marketing manager should be able to apply the findings in marketing strategy planning—the choice of a target market or the mix of the four Ps. If the research doesn't provide information to help guide these decisions, the company has wasted research time and money.

We emphasize this step because it is the reason for and logical conclusion to the whole research process. This final step must be anticipated at each of the earlier steps. See Marketing Demo 8-2 for a look at some special considerations for marketing research in Canada.

## International Marketing Research

Marketing research on overseas markets is often a major contributor toward international marketing success. Conversely, export failures are often due to a lack of home office management expertise concerning customer interests, needs, and other segmenting dimensions as well as environmental factors such as competitors' prices and products. Effective marketing research can help to overcome these problems.

Whether a firm is small and entering overseas markets for the first time or already large and well established internationally, there are often advantages to working with local market research firms. These research suppliers know the local situation and are less likely to make mistakes based on misunderstanding the customs, language, or circumstances of the customers they study.

Many large research firms have a network of local offices around the world to help with such efforts. Similarly, multinational or local advertising agencies and intermediaries can often provide leads on identifying the best research suppliers.

When a firm is doing similar research projects in different markets around the world, it makes sense for the marketing manager to coordinate the efforts. If the manager doesn't establish some basic guidelines at the outset, the different research projects may all vary so much that the results can't be compared from one market area to another. Such comparisons give a home office manager a better chance of understanding how the markets are similar and how they differ.

Multinational companies with operations in various countries often attempt to centralize some market research functions. One reason why is to reduce costs or achieve research economies of scale. The centralized approach also improves the firm's ability to transfer experience and know-how from one market area or project to another. For example, one of Eastman Kodak's international divisions appointed a market research specialist in each subsidiary company throughout the Asian region. The specialists report to local marketing managers but also receive research direction from expert research managers in the head office in the United States.

There is even greater opportunity and need to standardize and coordinate elements of a marketing information system in an international marketing operation. Computer databases and information systems are most useful when they are designed to include the same variables organized consistently over time. Without this, it is impossible for the manager to go into much depth in comparing and contrasting data from different markets.[13] See Marketing Demo 8-3 for some tips on conducting international marketing research.

## Marketing Demo 8–2

### A CANADIAN PERSPECTIVE TO MARKETING RESEARCH

Canada is one of the most multicultural countries in the world, and marketing researchers here are discovering the importance of researching and understanding different cultures in order to effectively market to different market segments. Tropicana—Canada's best-selling orange juice—used professional research to help understand its target market instead of simply translating its current marketing materials. What the research showed was that the Chinese community held the orange in high esteem as a harbinger of good luck and prosperity. After analyzing the research, Tropicana developed a successful ad campaign to share information about the brand with the Chinese community in Toronto and Vancouver. Increased awareness and customer loyalty built quickly.

When Molson's Joe states his belief in "diversity, not assimilation!" in the popular Canadian beer ads, he touches on a theme close to the fabric of our national identity. Because we pride ourselves on living in a multicultural, immigrant-friendly country, Canadians tend to puff their chests and smugly point out the diverse ethnic groups in our major metropolitan centres. For marketers, this diversity presents several opportunities, if handled correctly.

Research groups have developed some interesting and effective strategies to avoid the pitfalls of specialized ethnic-targeted marketing. The most obvious one, of course, is communicating in the group's language of origin, either on the phone or on questionnaires.

"The Chinese community has been the most heavily researched group in the past few years," says Wanda Gill, director of media and ethnic research at ACNielsen DJC Research in Toronto. "There is often some kind of language barrier, but if we so define a survey, we can speak to them in Mandarin or Cantonese, depending on client needs. This builds up a comfort level, offering them a choice."[14]

There are a large number of international marketing research firms that offer specialized services to marketing managers. Give an example where a company is better off hiring an international marketing research firm over conducting its own in-house research.

### How Much Information Do You Need?

We have been talking about the benefits of good marketing information, but dependable information can be expensive. A big company may spend millions developing an information system. A large-scale survey can cost from $20,000 to $100,000—or even more. The continuing research available from companies such as Information Resources Inc. can cost a company well over $100,000 a year. And a market test for 6 to 12 months may cost $200,000 to $500,000 per test market!

Companies that are willing and able to pay the cost often find that marketing information pays for itself. They are more likely to select the right target market and marketing mix—or they might see a potential problem before it becomes a costly crisis.

The high cost of good information must be balanced against its probable value to management. Managers never get all the information they would like to have. Very detailed surveys or experiments may be "too good" or "too expensive" or "too late" if all the company needs is a rough sampling of retailer attitudes toward a new pricing plan by tomorrow. Money is wasted if research shows that a manager's guesses are wrong and the manager ignores the facts.

Marketing managers must take risks because of incomplete information. That's part of their job and always will be. But they must weigh the cost of getting more data against its likely value. If the risk is not too great, the cost of getting more information may be greater than the potential loss from a poor decision. A decision to expand into a new territory with the present marketing mix, for example, might be made with more confidence after a $25,000 survey. But just sending a sales rep into the territory for a few weeks to try to sell potential customers would be a lot cheaper. And, if successful, the answer is in and so are some sales.[15]

## Finding Secondary Data

Secondary data can also come either from inside the company or from such sources as government agencies, libraries, business periodicals, and trade associations. Much

# Marketing Demo 8–3

## INTERNATIONAL MARKETING RESEARCH TIPS

Researching a faraway market before launching a product or service can seem overwhelmingly complex, expensive, and time-consuming. However, the benefits of getting it right greatly outweigh any perceptions about its difficulty.

Consider Sunglass Hut, the East Coast–based retail chain of sunglasses and related accessories. The retailers undertook extensive focus group and consumer-intercept research in the United Kingdom before opening stores there, so that it understood what demand—if any—there would be for sunglasses in a mostly cloudy climate. As a result, this chain positioned itself as not just the destination for all sunglass needs, but as an eyecare store, where sunglasses protect the eye from UV damage in any type of weather. Had Sunglass Hut maintained its *North American* positioning in the U.K, its revenues and market share would be significantly lower.

Pilkington Barnes Hind, a joint venture between a U.S. contact lens brand and a U.K.-based glass manufacturer, which recently was acquired by Chicago-based ophthalmic and medical products company Wesley Jessen, is another example of the dividends of diligent homework. Pilkington Barnes Hind learned that certain niche markets in Europe can be highly lucrative—particularly Germany, where dark-eyed, dark-haired Turkish women often seek to change their eye color to blue. Had the company not done its homework in its European markets before developing its national marketing strategies, this profitable market easily could have been overlooked and underserved.

Another successful U.S. transplant that did its homework well is book retailer Borders, which recently opened a store in Central London to the rapid detriment of local chains. Executives from this store's headquarters came to the United Kingdom to study the rents in prime locations, the propositions of indigenous competitors, the European consumer's appetite for books, music and atmosphere, and they decided this was the market for them. Their research highlighted the glaring gap in the European market for a book and music destination where one can linger and enjoy good refreshments in an unhurried, relaxing atmosphere. And—surprise, surprise—it's working fantastically.

So, what are the tricks to doing your homework about an international market before spending millions there, potentially making high-profile mistakes?

1. Profile your target customers and clients not just from census data or published statistical reports but by observing them first-hand. How does that European shopper behave in the experience you plan to stage for them? How are your customer's tastes different from those at home?
2. Interview these target segments to assess how well they match your pre-conceived ideal. It may be that little refinement is needed to the range of products and services you offer in the United States. Alternatively, a major product or packaging redesign might be necessary. (The case of Hansen Soft Drinks, a California-based "all natural" carbonated drink maker, in Europe is an interesting one—consumers in Europe found the white plastic screw-on top conveyed cheapness.)
3. Hire local researchers who know the costs and methods that are workable in local markets. Generally, consumers don't like being approached while doing their Saturday-moming shopping in Europe, as the hassles of public transportation, crowds and carrying heavy bags distract even the most enthusiastic respondent.

   As local research experts know the costs of each type of research, you'd be well-advised to heed their warnings about the most cost-effective method that gets the quality of results you need.
4. Use a variety of methods—not just one—to get a well-rounded picture of these markets. Often, U.S. companies rely solely on quantitative methods in Europe and miss the forest for the trees as a result. The best approach is a combination of qualitative and quantitative methods that provides a picture not just of preferences and strength of beliefs, but also the anecdotes. These often are profoundly useful in the PR and advertising messages about the benefits expected—in words usually different from those of U.S. consumers.
5. Look at the findings while asking yourself, "So what does this imply I need to do differently from what I do in the United States?" Research tables are dull reading at the best of times, and missing the important information that is implication for your future marketing activities abroad. By asking, "What do I do as a result?" after looking at the raw data, you'll find yourself talking in terms of actions rather than data.

Though research alone won't answer all your questions about that European market, it certainly helps inform your decisions about how much—and where—your investment is needed, whether that's in price adjustments, product redesign or reformulation, promotional methods or new distribution channels.

Now all you need is some time in the market—your success is sure to follow.[16]

of the inside information is available from the company's own MIS. Often, however, relevant data haven't been included in that system but are still available from the company's files or from special reports. Obviously, this is the place to start the search for secondary data. After that, the marketing researcher must examine both print-based and online external sources of secondary data.

**Internet**

**Internet Exercise** Assume that your boss has asked you to do a customer satisfaction survey. As part of a situation analysis, you want to get ideas about what others have done in this area. Go to the website for the Yahoo! search engine (www.yahoo.ca). In the dialogue box type 'customer satisfaction survey' (include the single quote marks) and click on search. Look at some of the websites identified. How helpful is this? How could it be improved?

### Using the Internet to Gather Secondary Data

There are a number of good tools for searching on the Internet and reference books that explain the details of the different tools. However, the basic idea is simple. And, usually, the best way to start is to use a search engine.

Most popular Internet browsers, like Netscape Navigator and Microsoft Internet Explorer, have a menu selection or button to activate an Internet search. In addition, there are hundreds of more specialized search engines. In general, a user specifies words or a phrase to find and the search engine produces a list of hyperlinks to websites where that search string is found. Usually all you do is type in the search string, click on search, wait while the reference list of links is assembled, and then click on the hyperlink of interest.

One of the most popular and useful search engines is Yahoo! Canada; it is especially good at searching for Web pages. Another very useful search engine is Altavista Canada; it does a good job of classifying online documents that include the search string. Google is a search engine that is particularly useful for locating specific people or businesses. The Northern Light search engine is very good at identifying published articles on the search topic. Keep in mind, however, that these are just a few of the popular search engines. If you want to get an idea of how many are available—and how they differ—go to Yahoo! Canada and do a search on the term "search engine."

Most computerized database and index services are now available on the Internet. Some of these are provided by libraries and private firms. For instance, for a

What are some of the benefits the Internet can offer to companies searching for marketing research and information?

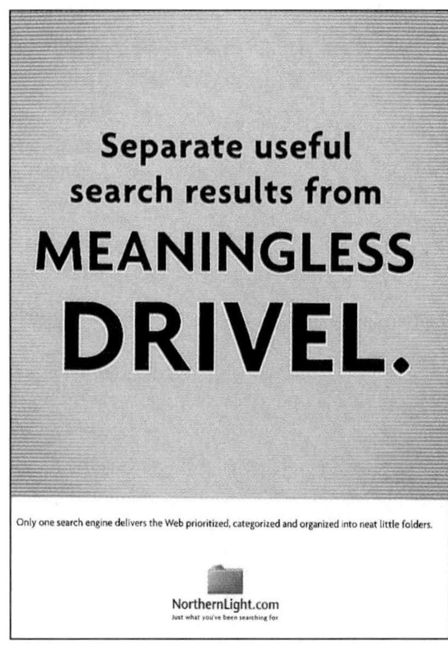
Separate useful
search results from
MEANINGLESS
DRIVEL.
Only one search engine delivers the Web prioritized, categorized and organized into neat little folders.
NorthernLight.com
Just what you've been searching for.

ARE YOU STILL BUYING MARKETING RESEARCH
DONE THE OLD-FASHIONED WAY?
Do it better on the Internet with the company that pioneered online marketing research.
Our panel of more than one million consumers from all across the Internet is the largest of its kind. It produces robust samples of any demographic or lifestyle you choose. You'll get richer, more actionable information quicker than you can say dot com.
Join the Research Revolution!™ Contact the world's most experienced Internet marketing research company for studies online, on time, on target and on budget.
www.greenfield.com 888.291.9997
Greenfield Online
Leading the Research Revolution®

fee a user can access the Dow Jones Interactive news retrieval system to search the full text of hundreds of publications, including newspapers from around the world. ProQuest Direct is another valuable research tool. It provides access to one of the world's largest collections of information, including summaries of articles from more than 5,000 publications. Many articles are available in full-text, full-image format. See Internet Insite 8-1 for more key resources for conducting secondary research using the Internet.

### Using Libraries to Find Secondary Data

While the Internet has revolutionized the gathering of potentially relevant marketing data, a number of important source documents are still available only in a print format or through the purchase of a CD-ROM. This is especially true of materials published before 1995 and for some very comprehensive industrial directories.

## Internet Insite 8–1

### KEY INTERNET SOURCES FOR SECONDARY RESEARCH

**A. Online Databases**

1. ABI/Inform (Proquest) (www.proquest.com)
   Provides access to the full text of more than 600 core business journals in advertising, marketing, sales, and many other areas. Mainly American but good Canadian and international content. Searchable through most Canadian college and university online library services.
2. LexisNexis (www.lexis-nexis.com)
   Full-text database of business, legal, and news publications. American, with strong Canadian and international coverage. Start by searching the CANADA Library.
3. CBCA: Canadian Business & Current Affairs (www.micromedia.ca/Products_Services/NEWS.htm)
   The essential Canadian Index. Covers Canadian newspapers, scholarly journals, popular magazines, and trade journals from 1982 to the present. These first three sites are fee-for-service databases best accessed (most economically) either electronically or by visiting your college or university library.
4. Canadian Corporate Newsnet (www.cdn-news.com)
   Up-to-the-minute news on thousands of Canadian companies. By setting up a "search profile," you can have information of particular interest sent to your e-mail address.
5. Canada Newswire (www.newswire.ca)
   The largest news release database in Canada. Searchable by keyword, date, organization name, stock symbol, industry, and so on.

**B. Canadian Government Sources**

1. Government of Canada (www.canada.gc.ca)
   Provides hotlink access to all departments, agencies, and branches of the federal government, and to the provinces as well.
2. Industry Canada Strategis (www.strategis.ic.gc.ca)
   More than 600,000 pages, some of which will almost certainly be relevant to the topic you are researching. See Canadian Company Capabilities for information on more than 50,000 Canadian businesses (http://strategis.ic.gc.ca/sc_coinf/ccc/engdoc/homepage.html).
3. Statistics Canada (www.statcan.ca)
   Canada's official statistical agency. Collects and publishes demographic, economic, and all sorts of other data on Canada and Canadians.
4. Department of Foreign Affairs and International Trade (www.dfait-maeci.gc.ca)
   Very useful when deciding whether, where, or how to export. Detailed country and regional information is available on this site.
5. Business Development Bank of Canada (www.bdc.ca)
   Has a major focus on launching and growing a new business, and exporting.

**C. Important American Sites**

1. FedWorld (www.fedworld.gov)
   Your point of entry into the U.S. federal government and all of its agencies.
2. STAT-USA/Internet (www.stat-usa.gov)
   For American economic, trade, and business information. The American equivalent of Strategis but much more "fee for service."
3. U.S. Census Bureau (www.census.gov)
   The place to obtain U.S. Census data and much more.
4. U.S. Office of Trade and Economic Analysis (www.ita.doc.gov/tradestats)
   Detailed U.S. foreign trade data by product and by country.
5. U.S. Statistical Resources on the Web (www.lib.umich.edu/govdocs/stats.html)
   A final stop to make certain you haven't missed anything at the other U.S. sites.

**D. Key Business Publications**

1. *Marketing Magazine* Online (www.marketingmag.ca)
   An incredibly important source of information on Canadian marketing practice.
2. *The Financial Post* (www.nationalpost.ca/financialpost/index.html)
   A very important source, although finance, not marketing, is its main concern.
3. *The Globe and Mail Report on Business Magazine* (www.robmagazine.com)
   Another essential stop when monitoring the Canadian business scene. This site provides links to *The Globe and Mail* newspaper.
4. Finance—Canada.com (http://finance.canada.com)
   Breaking business news with many external links.
5. Editor and Publisher's Interactive On-line Newspaper Database (www.mediainfo.com)
   Close to 2,500 (and climbing) online newspaper entries from all over the world.

**E. Sites Providing International Information**

1. globalEDGE (http://globaledge.msu.edu)
   The place to start when searching for information on any country outside North America in which Canadians might wish to do business.
2. One Stop Internet Shop for Business (http://europa.eu.int/business/en)
   Useful resource site for firms interested in doing business in Europe. European Union (EU) standards and business regulations are described.
3. World Trade Organization (www.wto.org)
   The best place to start a search for information on regional and world trade.
4. The World Bank (www.worldbank.org)
   Important economic data, with links to all the other international agencies.
5. CIA—The World Factbook (www.cia.gov/cia/publications/factbook/index.html)
6. NAFTA Secretariat (www.nafta-sec-alena.org/DefaultSite/index.html)
   A must-see site for companies interested in trading in the U.S. or Mexico.

**F. Some Specialized Sites of Possible Interest**

1. Business Research in Information and Technology (BRINT) (www.brint.com)
2. Entrepreneur.com (www.entrepreneur.com)
   Offers resources for start-up firms.
3. International Institute for Sustainable Development (http://iisd1.iisd.ca). See also http://iisd1.iisd.ca/business. This site focuses on sustainable development issues.
4. Ethics Resource Center (www.ethics.org)

**G. Sales Leads and Company Information (Competitive Intelligence)**

1. Dun & Bradstreet (www.dnb.com and www.zapdata.com)
2. Hoover's Online (www.hoovers.com)
3. Public Companies—SEC filings for U.S. companies (www.sec.gov/edgar.shtml) and securities filings for Canadian companies (www.sedar.com/homepage_en.htm). See Company Profiles in the SEDAR site for detailed information on Canadian public companies.

The above are but a few of the many sites on the Web that may provide you with secondary data on products, marketing practices, and potential markets. Many other useful sites are identified in the other Internet Insites prepared by Dr. Ramesh Venkat for this text. In addition, the OLC for this text (www.mcgrawhill.ca/college/wong) will hotlink you to hundreds of sites relevant to the topics you are studying. Also, don't forget that most college and university libraries have available through their websites links to specialized megasites on all sorts of topics. This material, often listed under "Internet Resources," can usually be accessed by everyone, not just by students at the university.[17]

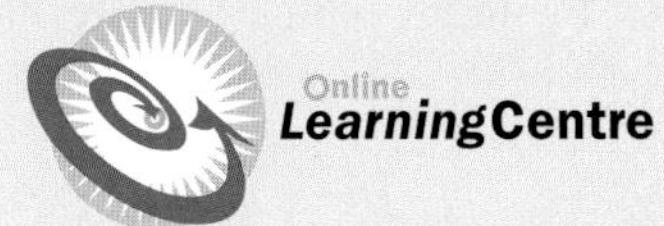


Go to: www.mcgrawhill.ca/college/wong
to apply this Insite in an exciting Internet exercise.

In other situations, material available for purchase online is still obtainable free of charge at a university or regional Statistics Canada library.

Another important reason to visit libraries is to make use of the expertise of the reference librarians who work in them. These information specialists will know what is available in print format only and what is available online. A librarian's assistance in showing marketing researchers how they can most effectively search data banks and other online sources will also prove invaluable. Of course, prospective market researchers would be well advised to familiarize themselves with government, private, and international data resources and to develop search expertise while still at university or college.

**Government sources** Governments and international organizations are among the best sources of social, economic, and demographic data. Statistics Canada publishes a great deal of relevant information. Government data are especially useful in estimating the size of markets. In the next chapter—and throughout the book—you will get a feel for the types of data Statistics Canada provides. Provincial and regional governments have units that provide useful information on traffic flows, building permits, school enrolments, and the like. Almost all government data are available at low cost. Much of this information is also available through the Internet and on computer disk.

For leads to more detailed documents, sometimes it makes sense to use summary publications. In Canada, a useful place to start is the *Market Research Handbook*, which is published every other year by Statistics Canada. For the American market, one of the most useful summaries is the *Statistical Abstract of the United States*. Like an almanac, it is issued every year; it contains 1,500 summary tables from more than 200 published sources. Detailed footnotes guide readers to more specific information on various topics.

**Private sources** Many private research organizations—as well as advertising agencies, newspapers, and magazines—regularly compile and publish data. A good business library is valuable for sources such as the *Financial Post, Marketing Magazine, The Globe and Mail Report on Business, Journal of Global Marketing*, and the publications of the Conference Board of Canada. Some advertising agencies make their information available at little or no cost to their clients and to buyers of ad space or time. Often a company's suppliers can also provide useful information.

**International sources** The *United Nations Statistical Yearbook* is one of the finest summaries of worldwide data. Also, most countries with advanced economies have government agencies that help researchers get the data they need. Eurostat, the statistical office for the European Union countries, offers many useful publications packed with both national and regional data. Other useful sources of international information include the World Bank and the Organisation for Economic Co-operation and Development (OECD).

Until fairly recently, finding comparable data on less developed economies was not nearly as easy. There were problems with gaining access to such information, as it might be found in only the very largest or most specialized of Canadian libraries. There were also problems associated with timeliness, and with the accuracy of such data. The accessibility problem (but not the problems of timeliness and accuracy) has in large part been overcome by the development of Internet sites providing whatever economic and demographic data are available on most of the world's nations. These sites link to others that contain handbooks on how to do business in different countries that have been prepared by large banks or international accounting firms.

## Collecting Primary Data

There are two basic methods for obtaining information about customers: *questioning* and *observing*. Questioning can range from qualitative to quantitative research. And many kinds of observing are possible.

Exhibit 8-5 Qualitative versus quantitative research.

| | QUALITATIVE RESEARCH | QUANTITATIVE RESEARCH |
|---|---|---|
| **Types of questions** | Probing | Limited probing |
| **Sample size** | Small | Large |
| **Amount of information from each respondent** | Substantial | Varies |
| **Type of analysis** | Subjective, interpretive | Statistical, summation |
| **Hardware** | Tape recorders, projection devices, video recorders, pictures, discussion guides | Questionnaires, computers, printouts |
| **Degree of replicability** | Low | High |
| **Researcher training** | Psychology, sociology, social psychology, consumer behaviour, marketing, marketing research | Statistics, decision models, decision support systems, computer programming, marketing, marketing research |
| **Type of research** | Exploratory | Descriptive or casual |

## Questioning

As you can imagine, there are many ways to ask the same question. But the distinction between questioning methods has less to do with the wording of the question than with the types of answers we receive. In this sense, the biggest distinction lies in whether we seek qualitative or quantitative data. Exhibit 8-5 shows the major differences between the two.

qualitative research

seeks in-depth, open-ended responses, not yes or no answers

**Qualitative research** **Qualitative research** seeks in-depth, open-ended responses, not yes or no answers. The researcher tries to get people to share their thoughts on a topic—without giving them many directions or guidelines about what to say.

A researcher might ask different consumers, "What do you think about when you decide where to shop for food?" One person may talk about convenient location, another about service, and others about the quality of the fresh produce. The real advantage of this approach is *depth*. Each person can be asked follow-up questions so the researcher really understands what *that* respondent is thinking. The depth of the qualitative approach gets at the details—even if the researcher needs a lot of judgment to summarize it all.

focus-group interview

Involves interviewing 6 to 10 people in an informal group setting

There are a number of ways that qualitative information can be collected (see Marketing Demo 8-4). However, the most widely used form of qualitative questioning in marketing research is the **focus-group interview**, which involves interviewing 6 to 10 people in an informal group setting. The focus group also uses open-ended questions, but here the interviewer wants to get group interaction—to stimulate thinking and get immediate reactions. Focus groups can be conducted quickly and at relatively low cost—an average of about $3,500 each. This is part of their appeal.

A skilled focus-group leader can learn a lot from this approach. A typical session may last an hour, so participants can cover a lot of ground. Sessions are often videotaped (or broadcast over the Internet or by satellite), so different managers can form their own impressions of what happened. Some research firms create electronic focus groups in which participants log on to a specified website and with others participate in a chat session; each person types in comments that are shared on the computer screen of each of the other participants. What they type is the record of the session.[18]

Regardless of how a focus group is conducted, conclusions reached from a session usually vary depending on who watches it. A typical problem—and serious limitation—with qualitative research is that it's hard to measure the results objectively.

The results seem to depend so much on the viewpoint of the researcher and on the opinions of a specific group of focus-group participants. People willing to participate in a focus group—especially those who talk the most—may not be representative of the broader target market. See Marketing Demo 8-5 for the story of how one restaurant franchise put its focus-group research to use.

Some researchers use qualitative research to prepare for quantitative research. For example, the Jacksonville Symphony Orchestra wanted to broaden its base of support and increase ticket sales. It hired a marketing-research firm to conduct focus-group interviews. These interviews helped the marketing managers refine their ideas about what these target "customers" liked and did not like about the orchestra. The ideas were then tested with a larger, more representative sample. Interviewers telephoned 500 people and asked them how interested they would be in various orchestra programs, event locations, and guest artists. Then they planned their promotion and the orchestra's program for the year based on the research. Ticket sales nearly doubled.[19]

As this example suggests, qualitative research can provide good ideas—hypotheses. But we need other approaches—perhaps based on more representative samples and objective measures—to *test* the hypotheses.



**quantitative research**

Research that seeks structured responses that can be summarized in numbers, like percentages, averages, or other statistics

**Quantitative research** When researchers use identical questions and response alternatives, they can summarize the information quantitatively. Samples can be larger and more representative, and various statistics can be used to draw conclusions. For these reasons, most survey research is **quantitative research**—which seeks structured responses that can be summarized in numbers, like percentages, averages, or other statistics. For example, a marketing researcher might calculate what percentage of respondents have tried a new product and then figure an average score for how satisfied they were.

Survey questionnaires usually provide fixed responses (e.g., multiple choice) to questions to simplify analysis of the replies. This multiple-choice approach makes it easier and faster for respondents to reply. Simple fill-in-a-number questions are also widely used in quantitative research. Fixed responses are also more convenient for computer analysis, which is how most surveys are analyzed.

## Marketing Demo 8–4

### GETTING INTO FOCUS

Research firms are constantly looking for new ways to find out about customers. Here's a sampling of some recent studies using qualitative research:

*Video verite*: In developing an ad campaign for Levi's, Toronto research firm Insignia Marketing Research gave video cameras to teenagers and asked them to film their friends. Marketers watched the videos, transfixed by this window into the teenage world.

*Reversion to childhood*: To design an ad campaign for McDonald's Arch Deluxe burger, a Minneapolis agency asked its focus group to mould figures with Play-doh to express their feelings about the burgers. The primal, childhood images became the basis for ads.

*Best-friend interviews*: Used by Canada's YTV cable channel to gauge the opinions of young teenagers, who are often aloof and obstinate. Kids are asked to bring their best friends, who usually inspire them to speak more frankly.

*The police board*: In designing new Ontario licence plates, police from various regions were assembled in a dark parking lot and asked to read various designs from a distance.

*Name association*: On behalf of a coffee chain, Angus Reid gave consumers names of Toronto neighbourhoods and asked them to come up with a relevant type of coffee. The Beaches neighbourhood, for example, was mocha java.[20]

One common approach to measuring consumers' attitudes and opinions is to have respondents indicate how much they agree or disagree with a questionnaire statement. A researcher interested in what target consumers think about frozen pizzas, for example, might include a statement like "I add extra toppings when I prepare frozen pizza." The respondent might check off a response such as (1) strongly disagree, (2) disagree, (3) agree, or (4) strongly agree.

Another approach is to have respondents rate a product, feature, or store. For example, a questionnaire might ask consumers to rate the taste of a pizza as *excellent, good, fair*, or *poor*.

Survey data can be collected by a variety of media. The major alternatives are mail, online, telephone, and personal interview. These media have particular strengths and weaknesses, so let's look at each one in more detail.

## Marketing Demo 8–5

### TACOTIME

TacoTime's head office is in a two-storey building of indeterminate colour tucked behind an auto parts store on Calgary's busiest commercial strip. It's a modest place, but TacoTime president Ken Pattenden's plans for his company are anything but. His vision is to make TacoTime "the dominant Mexican restaurant chain in Canada."

Pattenden is betting on a two-part marketing strategy the company is launching this year. The first, and most important element, is to rebrand TacoTime as a provider of authentic Mexican food, rather than simply fast food. The second initiative is a move into the growing fast casual dining segment with a line of restaurants under the Cantina banner.

Pattenden calls the rebranding, which will be backed by a $2-million ad campaign this year, "the biggest and most important strategic change in the history of the franchise." Since TacoTime's founding, it has positioned itself firmly in the Quick Service Restaurant (QSR) segment of the restaurant industry, operating small food court outlets and drive-throughs in strip malls. When Pattenden, a former shopping centre and real estate developer, bought the company from his father-in-law Jim Penny in 1993, he expanded from 80 outlets to 112 stretching from Victoria to Thunder Bay, but kept the focus on providing inexpensive fast food.

However, Pattenden realized three years ago that it was increasingly difficult for TacoTime to compete in the "99¢ value meal market" against heavyweights like Burger King, McDonald's and Wendy's, and he began looking at ways to reposition his company. About the same time, he started refurbishing many of the chain's aging outlets, hiring Maxim Design Group of Calgary to give them a more Mexican adobe and earth tones look. "Many of our stores were nondescript both in design and location," says Pattenden. "It was a real leap of faith when you walked by one to assume it offered Mexican food."

His marketing epiphany came after a series of customer focus groups held in the spring and summer of 2000. When participants were asked what came to mind when they thought of Mexico, food shared top billing with sunshine, beaches and tequila. "That blew us away," says Brian Carnwath, TacoTime's marketing vice-president. "There was a huge market out there for authentic Mexican food we didn't know existed."

With virtually no Mexican restaurant chains other than Taco Bell operating in Western Canada—where, unlike elsewhere in North America, Taco Bell is a fairly minor player—Pattenden and Carnwath saw not so much a marketing niche as a marketing chasm waiting to be filled.

The focus groups also told them that when food is served on a plate rather than wrapped in wax paper, it's more likely to be perceived as authentic and desirable. To test that finding, TacoTime took its existing Casita Platter and began to promote it heavily in store, picturing it on huge, colourful posters. Prior to the campaign, Carnwath says the average TacoTime outlet would sell one or two Casita Platters a day compared to its signature tacos, fajitas and burritos, but after the posters went up "we averaged 15 platters a day, and at some units it was as high as 50."

With that proof in hand, the executives decided to rebrand and reposition TacoTime as a Mexican restaurant serving authentic food.[21]

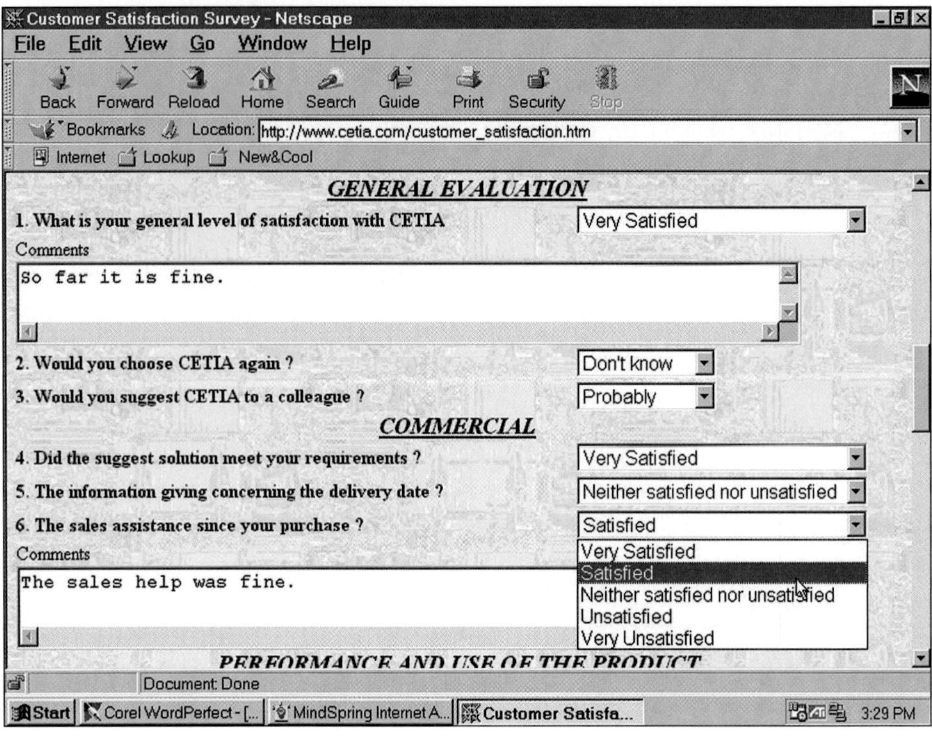


CETIA is a European manufacturer of minicomputers. When it delivers a product, it asks the customer to complete this interactive customer satisfaction survey, which is located at CETIA's website. The survey uses a combination of fixed-response questions and open-ended comments.



***Mail and online surveys*** A questionnaire distributed by mail, e-mail, or online is useful when extensive questioning is necessary. Respondents can complete the questions at their convenience and they may be more willing to provide personal information—since a questionnaire can be completed anonymously. But the questions must be simple and easy to follow since no interviewer is there to help. If the respondent is likely to be a computer user, it may be possible to send the questionnaire on a disk (or put it on a website) and include a help feature with additional directions for people who need them.

Speed is both a positive and negative aspect of questionnaires. Distributing questionnaires by e-mail, or at a website, provides almost instantaneous delivery—and the responses come back in computer form. Surveys sent by regular mail usually take a lot longer; pencil-and-paper responses also need to be computerized. In business markets, the time to deliver questionnaires can sometimes be reduced by faxing them. However, regardless of how quickly a questionnaire is distributed, people may take a long time to respond. For example, with a mail survey it often takes a month or more to get the data back, which is too slow for some decisions.

**response rate**

The percentage of people contacted who complete a questionnaire

Time issues aside, two major problems with questionnaires are tied to the number and nature of the people who agree to complete them. The **response rate**—the percentage of people contacted who complete the questionnaire—can be low and respondents may not be representative. For example, there can be a concern as to whether people who complete computer-based or online questionnaires are representative of the overall population: not everyone has Internet access and online respondents may be younger, better educated, or different in other ways that affect how they answer. In addition, in markets where illiteracy is a problem it may not be possible to get any response at all.

As shown in Marketing Demo 8-6, incentives can be used to encourage participation, although some managers believe the use of such incentives can also introduce bias. Therefore, whether using an incentive or not most survey researchers perform a statistical test on the sample of respondents to ensure that the sample is representative.

## Marketing Demo 8–6

### USING INCENTIVES TO INCREASE RESPONSE RATES

Incentives are very useful to add when distributing a survey, as they are able to increase the desire to respond. As one of its major New Year's resolutions at the start of 2002, CBC Radio's challenge was to develop a marketing strategy and direct mail piece to attract new listeners and gain share with occasional listeners who would benefit from being reminded of the variety of great programming CBC Radio has to offer. Using current audience research, three key markets were identified for growth—Toronto, Vancouver, and Calgary. In order to gather feedback on their new campaign, CBC enlisted agencies Cormark MacPhee Communications and OverCat Communications to facilitate a direct mail and office tower promotion using a market-specific DM piece consisting of a Best of CBC Radio CD sampler. The CD sampler, which included a program booklet, regional schedules and an *incentive-based response card*, featured a selection of CBC network programming and highlighted regional shows from the target markets. In total, 185,000 CDs were distributed. To date, CBC has received approximately 16,000 response cards, and the mail keeps on coming in. "The response has been extraordinary," says Aladin Jarrah, CBC Radio's senior manager of communications. "Based on norms for this type of promotion, we had anticipated a return of about 4,000 cards. To be sitting at 16,000 responses at this point indicates that the design and concept of the sampler hit the nail right on the head. Clearly the strategy has worked: People saw the ad campaign elements and reacted to the direct mail piece—the synergy of the components has yielded impressive results."[22]

In spite of these limitations, the convenience and economy of self-administered surveys makes them popular for collecting primary data.

***Telephone surveys*** Telephone interviews are popular. They are effective for getting quick answers to simple questions. Telephone interviews allow the interviewer to probe and really learn what the respondent is thinking. In addition, with computer-aided telephone interviewing answers are immediately recorded on a computer, resulting in fast data analysis. On the other hand, some consumers find calls intrusive—and about a third refuse to answer any questions. Moreover, the telephone is usually not a very good contact method if the interviewer is trying to get confidential personal information—such as details of family income. Respondents are not certain who is calling or how such personal information might be used.

Online surveys provide fast feedback, often at a lower cost. But how can managers ensure that the sample used is representative?

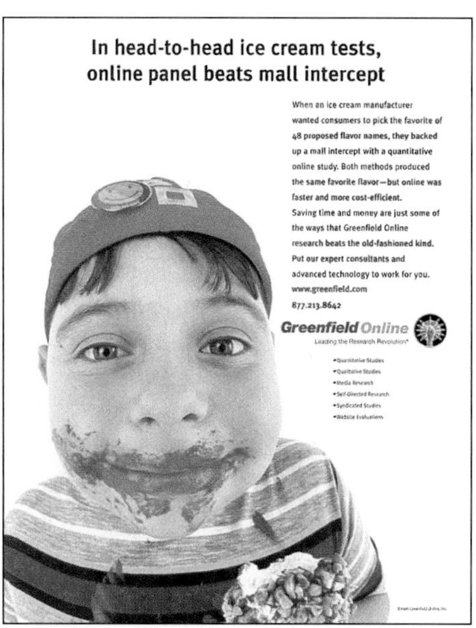

Internet

**Internet Exercise** Perseus Development Corporation sells software that allows a user to create online questionnaires that can be distributed by e-mail or used on the Internet. To see samples of online questions, go to the Perseus website (www.perseus.com) and then click on "Sample Surveys." Do you think that it's more convenient for a consumer to complete a survey online or with pencil and paper?

***Personal-interview surveys*** A personal-interview survey is usually much more expensive per interview than surveys by e-mail, mail, or telephone. But it's easier to get and keep the respondent's attention when the interviewer is right there. The interviewer can also help explain complicated directions and perhaps get better responses. For these reasons, personal interviews are commonly used for research on business customers. To reduce the cost of locating consumer respondents, interviews are sometimes done at a store or shopping mall. This is called a "mall-intercept interview" because the interviewer stops a shopper and asks for responses to the survey.

Researchers have to be careful that having an interviewer involved doesn't affect the respondent's answers. Sometimes people won't give an answer they consider embarrassing. Or they may try to impress or please the interviewer. Further, in some cultures people don't want to give any information. For example, many people in Africa, Latin America, and Eastern Europe are reluctant to be interviewed. This is also a problem in many low-income, inner-city areas in Canada, where even Statistics Canada interviewers have trouble getting cooperation.

***Online research*** While the medium is still in its infancy, firms are beginning to use the Internet to collect data that would otherwise be gathered using surveys or focus groups. (See Ethical Dimensions 8-2 for a perspective on the ethical issues involved in undertaking Internet research involving minors.) Internet Insite 8-2 discusses the current state of this practice. Given the speed with which online data can move from collection to analysis, this is a particularly exciting application of Internet technology, especially if linked to "bots" that execute specific actions in response to survey data.

### Observation

When questioning has its limitations, observing may be more accurate or economical. Observation—as a method of collecting data—focuses on a well-defined problem. Here we are not talking about the casual observations that may stimulate ideas in the early steps of a research project. With the observation method, researchers try to see or record what the subject does naturally. They don't want the observing to *influence* the subject's behaviour.

A museum director wanted to know which of the many exhibits was most popular. A survey didn't help. Visitors seemed to want to please the interviewer and usually said that all of the exhibits were interesting. Putting observers near exhibits—to record how long visitors spent at each one—didn't help either. The curious visitors stood around to see what the observer was recording, and that messed up the measures. Finally, the museum floors were waxed to a glossy shine. Several weeks later, the floors around the exhibits were inspected. It was easy to tell which exhibits were most popular—based on how much wax had worn off the floor!

In some situations, consumers are recorded on videotape. Later, researchers can study the tape by running the film at very slow speed or actually analyzing each frame. Researchers use this technique to study the routes consumers follow through a grocery store or how they select products in a department store. Similarly, firms that have online shopping services on the Internet can use software to "watch" how consumers use the website, how much time they spend at each display, and the like.

Similarly, many franchise companies use the observation method to check how well a franchisee is performing. KFC hires people to go to different KFC stores and act like normal customers. Then these "secret shoppers" report back to KFC on how they were treated, the quality of the service and food, and the cleanliness of the store.

**Ways of observing** Observation methods go beyond "watching" consumers in the act of buying or using products and services. Observation methods are common in advertising research. For example, Nielsen Media Research (www.nielsenmedia.com) uses a device called the "people meter" that adapts the observation method to television audience research. This machine is attached to the TV set in the homes of selected families. It records when the set is on and what station is tuned in.

Computerized scanners at retail checkout counters, a major breakthrough in observing, help researchers collect very specific, and useful, information. Often this type of data feeds directly into a firm's MIS. Managers of a large chain of stores can see exactly what products have sold each day and how much money each department in each store has earned. But the scanner also has wider applications for marketing research.

**consumer panels**
Groups of consumers who provide information on a continuing basis

Information Resources, Inc. (www.infores.com) and ACNielsen (acnielsen.com) use **consumer panels**—groups of consumers who provide information on a continuing basis. Whenever a panel member shops for groceries, he or she gives an ID number to the clerk, who keys in the number. Then the scanner records every

## Ethical Dimensions 8–2

### SMELLS LIKE TEEN RESEARCH

Ottawa-based Youtopia.com has developed a site where teens can log on to the site (thereby creating a personalized profile) to e-mail friends, chat with spokes-star Britney Spears and play the interactive games for which they receive "Youdollars." These can be redeemed for gift certificates for merchandise from Canadian retailers, including HMV, La Senza Girl and Suzy Shier. The catch is that the site's marketer-sponsored online games are customized based on sponsors' questions. The games are in fact surveys designed to build profiles of the young players.

This allows marketers to survey, through an interactive and fun way, the teen demographic and extract information from them. "What we have done is made the unsurveyable surveyable via Youtopia," says president Randi Shinder. "So whereas you can't really call up a household and ask to speak to the 13-year-old, sponsors can actually survey, through an interactive and fun way, the demographic and extract information from them, en masse." Because teens don't have credit cards, an online currency like Youdollars is a strong incentive, motivating them to return to the games again and again. "We've been able to build an enormous and granular database," says Shinder. "It gets to the point where we can tell a sponsor how many females (are in the database) between the ages of 13 and 15 with dark hair, hang out at the mall with their friends, shop at The Gap and spent over $100 last year on Nike running shoes."

This whole approach raises the ethical issue of how marketers should conduct themselves when polling minors for information.

The Professional Market Research Society recently introduced guidelines for researchers dealing with children under 12, restricting questions about family income and other sensitive issues such as sex. But the online teen market remains fair game. "For anyone under 12, permission has to be sought from an adult," says PMRS standards director Alistair Hay. "Over 12, it doesn't seem to be a factor. It's all under development. This is a whole new territory, frankly." Both the NRG Group and Youtopia state that the privacy of their members is a top priority. Both also insist that the teens have a clear understanding that the information they divulge is to be used for marketing purposes, and that teens have the option of not participating in the surveys at all.

But Doug Snetsinger, CEO and President of drs Insight Group, is concerned that the popularity of consumer profiling online may blur the lines between pure market research and research for indirect sales purposes. "When you go to an individual and say 'This is about research purposes,' does the child understand? The answer is yes," he says. "When you register info on a Web site, does the individual, whether they be a parent, or an adult or a child, understand the purpose for which it's being extracted? Some do, some don't, and it's one of the reasons why we will see increasing disclosure rules in Web-based data retrieval methods."[23]

# Internet Insite 8–2

## PRIMARY RESEARCH ONLINE

Students know that the Internet is a great source of information. The availability of content sites, online databases (free and subscription-based), current news, and full-text journal articles on the Internet has made secondary research incredibly efficient. There is another side to doing research online that the general public doesn't get to see often. The Internet is proving to be a cost-effective medium for conducting primary research as well.

Two commonly used primary research techniques are surveys and focus groups. Surveys are traditionally administered face-to-face, over the telephone, or mailed to the respondents. In each method, there are costs incurred in data gathering and data entry. Response rates for telephone or mail surveys can be 10 percent or less.

Web-based surveys offer an alternative and present several distinct advantages over the traditional methods. First, the cost of printing and distributing questionnaires can be eliminated. Second, there is no need for data entry since completed responses can go directly into a database—that eliminates data-entry errors and lowers costs. Third, respondents may find it easy to fill out an online survey as it can be done at a time of their convenience.

There are many Web-based survey software products on the market today. Market research companies also offer Web-based survey services. Two Canadian firms, SurveySite (www.surveysite.com) and Clear Picture (www.clearpicture.com), can be contracted to conduct surveys. Perseus (www.perseus.com) offers a popular Web-based survey software, which can be used by researchers (see the exhibit below).

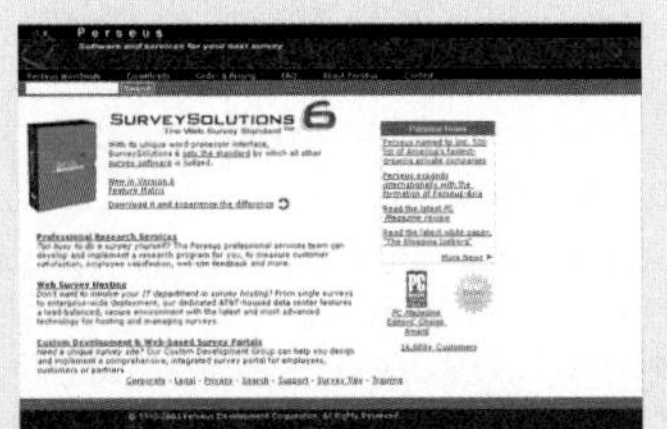

There are some caveats when it comes to online surveying. First, the questionnaire should not be too long. Second, the target of the survey should be reachable through the Internet and must have computer access. For instance, a study on why people without university degrees are not using the Internet cannot be conducted online since the target population is not well represented online. Third, respondents will not know that there is an online survey posted on some website. They need to be contacted—via phone, e-mail, or a letter. Lastly, except in the case of face-to-face surveys, one never really knows if the respondent really is who he or she claims to be. Soliciting prior approval through a phone call or e-mail or in some cases using a password to allow access to the Web survey can provide some confirmation regarding the respondent. Online surveys can be done anonymously without capturing or revealing the identity of the respondent.

In practice, we see shorter and instant surveys being used by marketers. Exit surveys when a consumer is leaving a website and pop-up surveys, where a small window with a short questionnaire pops up when the consumer is browsing a Web page, are frequently used now. These types of instant surveys and polls allow marketers to gather feedback on an ongoing basis at low cost.

Another form of primary data collection is the focus-group technique. This is considered to be a qualitative research method where a small group of people (usually around 10) participate in a group discussion with a moderator who asks questions and guides the discussion. The discussion is taped and later analyzed by experts. Participants are usually recruited for a small fee. While less established than online survey products, online focus-group solutions offer an interesting alternative. How does an online focus group work?

Participants will log in to a Web-based chat session. The moderator will ask questions and participants will respond. Unlike face-to-face focus groups, here all questions and responses are typed. Some online focus group applications include a "whiteboard," which is space above the chat screen where product demonstrations (through streaming video), pictures, Web pages, or drawings can be shown.

Obviously, body language, facial expression, tone of voice, and other nuances in communication cannot be captured in a chat environment. Computer-based video conferencing, which is already a reality, may be the next step to make online focus groups more realistic. The low cost, ability to attract participants from all over the world, convenience, and real-time creation of the focus group transcript are some of the advantages of online focus groups.

In the final analysis, the Internet offers market researchers one more way of reaching current and potential consumers. It offers some advantages, but at the same time it must be used appropriately. The target population must have Internet access and the research topic must be one that is conducive to online research. Sound principles of research methodology (in terms of representativeness of the sample, validity, and reliability of measures and ethics) must be followed regardless of whether the research is done online or offline.

Some questions to ponder: Do you think consumers are more likely to participate in online surveys or focus groups compared to the traditional methods? Why? Can you think of some topics that do not lend themselves to online primary research?

Go to: www.mcgrawhill.ca/college/wong
to apply this Insite in an exciting Internet exercise.

Data from electronic scanners helps retailers decide what brands they will sell and helps their suppliers plan so that products arrive at the store in time to prevent stock-outs.



purchase—including brands, sizes, prices, and any coupons used. In a variation of this approach, consumers use a hand-held scanner to record purchases once they get home. For a fee, clients can evaluate actual customer purchase patterns and answer questions about the effectiveness of their discount coupons. Did the coupons draw new customers, or did current customers simply use them to stock up? If consumers switched from another brand, did they go back to their old brand the next time? The answers to such questions are important in planning marketing strategies—and scanners can help marketing managers get the answers.

Some members of the consumer panel are also tied in to a special TV cable system. With this system, a company can direct advertisements to some houses and not others. Then researchers can evaluate the effect of the ads by comparing the purchases of consumers who saw the ads with the purchases of those who didn't.

The use of scanners to "observe" what customers actually do is changing consumer research methods. Companies can turn to firms like Information Resources as a *single source* of complete information about customers' attitudes, shopping behaviour, and media habits.

Data captured by electronic scanners is equally important to e-commerce in business-to-business markets. Increasingly, firms mark their shipping cartons and packages with computer-readable bar codes that make it fast and easy to track inventory, shipments, orders, and the like. As information about product sales or shipments becomes available, it is instantly included in the MIS and accessible over the Internet. That way, a manager can access any detailed piece of information or do an analysis to summarize trends and patterns. Here, as with scanner data on consumers, the information available is so detailed that the possibilities are limited more by imagination—and money—than by technology.[24]

## Experimental Methods

**experimental method**

Method where researchers compare the responses of two (or more) groups that are similar except on the characteristic being tested

A marketing manager can get a different kind of information—with either questioning or observing—using the **experimental method**. With the experimental method, researchers compare the responses of two (or more) groups that are similar except on the characteristic being tested. Researchers want to learn if the specific characteristic—which varies among groups—causes differences in some response among the groups. For example, a researcher might be interested in comparing responses of consumers who had seen an ad for a new product with consumers who had not seen the ad. The "response" might be an observed behaviour—like the purchase of a product—or the answer to a specific question—like "How interested are you in this new product?" (see Exhibit 8-6).

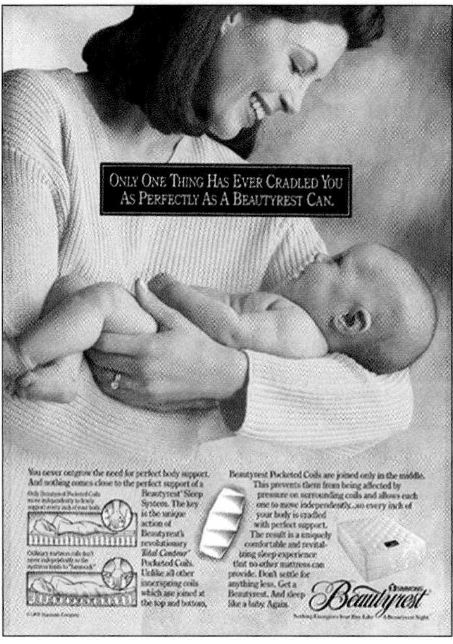


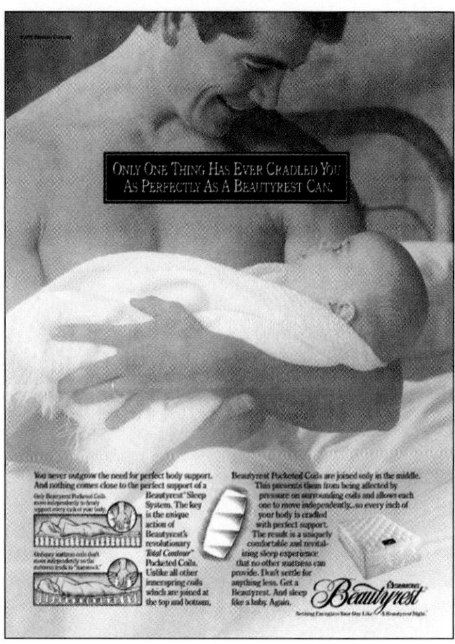


Simmons' ad agency used an experiment to improve a new print ad for the Beautyrest mattress. Groups of consumers saw two different ads. The ads were the same, except that one featured a father holding a baby and the other featured a mother. The ad with the father earned higher recall scores. Why do you think this was the case?

Marketing managers for Mars—the company that makes Snickers candy bars—used the experimental method to help solve a problem. They wanted to know if making their candy bar bigger would increase sales enough to offset the higher cost. To decide, they conducted a marketing experiment in which the company carefully varied the sizes of candy bars sold in *different* markets. Otherwise, the marketing mix stayed the same. Then researchers tracked sales in each market area to see the effect of the different sizes. They saw a big difference immediately: The added sales more than offset the cost of a bigger candy bar.

Test-marketing of new products is another type of marketing experiment. In a typical approach, a company tries variations on its planned marketing mix in a few geographic market areas. The results of the tests help to identify problems or refine the marketing mix—before the decision is made to go to broader distribution. For example, banks used test markets in two Ontario centres—Kingston and St. Catharines—to explore consumer and merchant reactions to pre-loaded cash cards.

**Exhibit 8-6** Illustration of experimental method in comparing effectiveness of two ads.

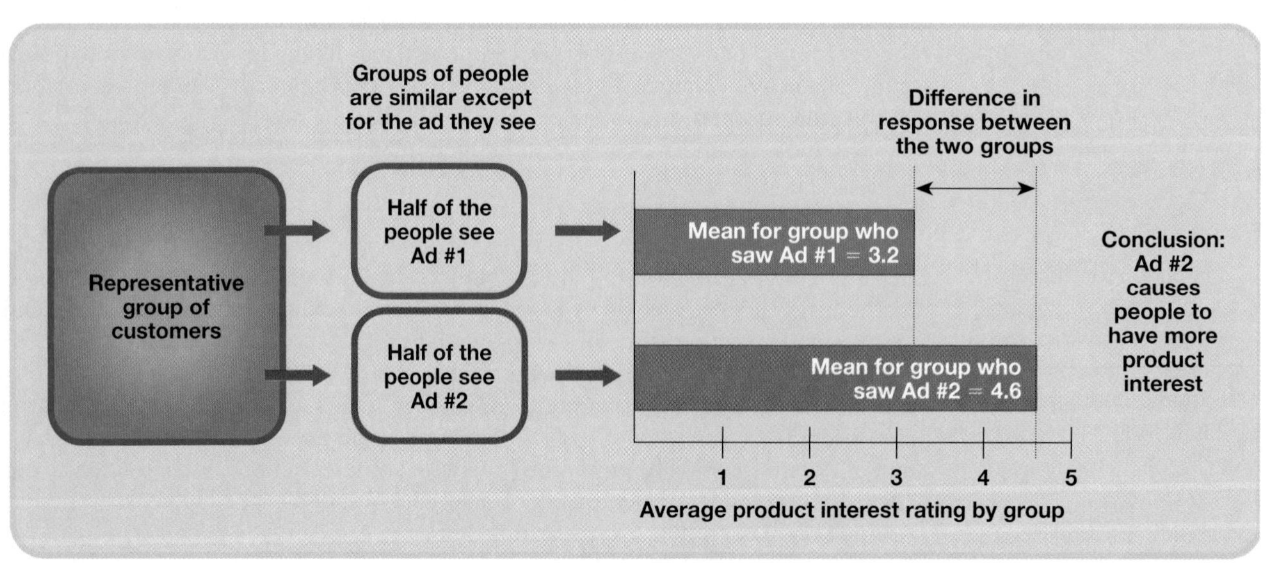

However, alert competitors may disrupt such tests—perhaps by increasing promotion or offering retailers extra discounts. To avoid these problems, small firms might conduct some of their tests in foreign markets. For example, because of the Canadian public's enthusiastic response to its Swiffer Sweeper floor cleaning product, U.S. consumer products giant Procter & Gamble used Canada as a test market for its new Swiffer WetJet—a battery-operated cleaning appliance—before deciding on a global strategy.[25]

Researchers don't use the experimental method as often as surveys and focus groups. Many managers don't understand the valuable information they can get from this method. Further, they don't like the idea of some researcher "experimenting" with their business.[26]

### Syndicated Data

Some private research firms specialize in collecting data and supplying it to managers in many different client firms. Often the marketing manager subscribes to the research service and gets regular updates.

Marketing managers from many different firms may have to make the same kinds of decisions and may need the same type of data. The most economical approach in a situation like this is for one specialist firm to collect the data and distribute it to the different users, who share the cost. This is how Information Resources, Inc., and ACNielsen operate.

Many other firms collect and distribute specialized types of data. For example, Synovate (**www.synovate.com**) sells access to its surveys on home appliances and electronics, retail banking and insurance, and other product categories. Simmons Market Research Bureau (**www.smrb.com**) does extensive research on consumer media habits and then sells its data to many advertising agencies and producers of consumer products who want to find out about their particular target markets. Many different auto producers use J. D. Power's (**www.jdpa.com**) surveys of customer satisfaction, often as the basis for advertising claims. Subscription data services are available for numerous different industries—ranging from food service to prescription drugs to microelectronic devices.[27]



## Chapter Summary


Marketing managers face difficult decisions in selecting target markets and managing marketing mixes. And managers rarely have all the information they would like to have. This problem is usually worse for managers who work with international markets. But they don't have to rely only on intuition. They can usually obtain good information to improve the quality of their decisions.

Computers and computer networks like the Internet are helping marketing managers become full-fledged members of the information age. Both large and small firms are setting up intranets and marketing information systems (MIS) to be certain that routinely needed data are available and accessible quickly.

Marketing managers deal with rapidly changing environments. Available data are not always adequate to answer the detailed questions that arise. Then a marketing research project may be required to gather new information.

Marketing research should be guided by the scientific method. The scientific approach to solving marketing problems involves five steps: defining the problem, analyzing the situation, obtaining data, interpreting data, and solving the problem. This objective and organized approach helps to keep research on target—reducing the risk of doing costly research that isn't necessary or doesn't solve the problem.

Our strategy-planning framework can be helpful in finding the real problem. By finding and focusing on the real problem, the researcher and marketing manager may be able to move quickly to a useful solution—without the cost and risks of gathering primary data in a formal research project. With imagination, they may even be able to find the answers in their MIS or in other readily available secondary data.

## Key Concepts

confidence intervals, p. 218
consumer panels, p. 233
data warehouse, p. 207
decision support system (DSS), p. 208
experimental method, p. 235
focus-group interview, p. 227
hypotheses, p. 211
intranet, p. 209
marketing information system (MIS), p. 207
marketing model, p. 208
marketing research, p. 209
marketing research process, p. 213
population, p. 216
primary data, p. 207
qualitative research, p. 227
quantitative research, p. 228
random sampling, p. 216
research proposal, p. 215
response rate, p. 230
sample, p. 216
scientific method, p. 211
search engine, p. 208
secondary data, p. 207
situation analysis, p. 215
statistical packages, p. 217
validity, p. 218

## Questions and Problems

1. Discuss the concept of a marketing information system and why it is important for marketing managers to be involved in planning the system.
2. In your own words, explain why a decision support system (DSS) can add to the value of a marketing information system. Give an example of how a decision support system might help.
3. If a firm's intranet and marketing decision support system do not include a search engine, would they still be useful to a marketing manager? Why?
4. Discuss how output from a marketing information system (MIS) might differ from the output of a typical marketing research department.
5. Discuss some of the likely problems facing the marketing manager in a small firm that has just purchased a personal computer with a cable modem to search the Internet for information on competitors' marketing plans.
6. Explain the key characteristics of the scientific method and show why these are important to managers concerned with research.
7. How is the situation analysis different from the data collection step? Can both these steps be done at the same time to obtain answers sooner? Is this wise?
8. Distinguish between primary data and secondary data and illustrate your answer.
9. With so much secondary information now available free or at low cost over the Internet, why would a firm ever want to spend the money to do primary research?
10. If a firm were interested in estimating the distribution of income in the province of Manitoba, how could it proceed? Be specific.
11. If a firm were interested in estimating lumber production in New Brunswick, how could it proceed? Be specific.
12. Go to the library (or get on the Internet) and find (in some government publication or website) three marketing-oriented "facts" on international markets that you did not know existed or were available. Record on one page and show sources.
13. Explain why a company might want to do focus-group interviews rather than individual interviews with the same people.
14. Distinguish between qualitative and quantitative approaches to research—and give some of the key advantages and limitations of each approach.
15. Define response rate and discuss why a marketing manager might be concerned about the response rate achieved in a particular survey. Give an example.
16. Prepare a table that summarizes some of the key advantages and limitations of mail, e-mail, telephone, and personal-interview approaches for administering questionnaires.
17. Would a firm want to subscribe to a shared-cost data service if the same data were going to be available to competitors? Discuss your reasoning.
18. Explain how you might use different types of research (focus groups, observation, survey, and experiment) to forecast market reaction to a new kind of disposable diaper, which is to receive no promotion other than what the retailer will give it. Further, assume that the new diaper's name will not be associated with other known products. The product will be offered at competitive prices.
19. Marketing research involves expense—sometimes considerable expense. Why does the text recommend the use of marketing research even though a highly experienced marketing executive is available?
20. A marketing manager is considering opportunities to export her firm's current consumer products to several

## Questions and Problems continued

different countries. She is interested in getting secondary data that will help her narrow down choices to countries that offer the best potential. The manager then plans to do more detailed primary research with consumers in those markets. What suggestions would you give her about how to proceed?

21. Discuss the concept that some information may be too expensive to obtain in relation to its value. Illustrate.

## Computer-Aided Problem 8

**Marketing Research**

Texmac, Inc., has an idea for a new type of weaving machine that could replace the machines now used by many textile manufacturers. Texmac has done a telephone survey to estimate how many of the old-style machines are now in use. Respondents using the present machines were also asked if they would buy the improved machine at a price of $10,000.

Texmac researchers identified a population of about 5,000 textile factories as potential customers. A sample of these were surveyed, and Texmac received 500 responses. Researchers think the total potential market is about 10 times larger than the sample of respondents. Two hundred twenty of the respondents indicated that their firms used old machines like the one the new machine was intended to replace. Forty percent of those firms said that they would be interested in buying the new Texmac machine.

Texmac thinks the sample respondents are representative of the total population, but the marketing manager realizes that estimates based on a sample may not be exact when applied to the whole population. He wants to see how sampling error would affect profit estimates. Data for this problem appear in the spreadsheet. Quantity estimates for the whole market are computed from the sample estimates. These quantity estimates are used in computing likely sales, costs, and profit contribution.

a. *An article in a trade magazine reports that there are about 5,200 textile factories that use the old-style machine. If the total market is really 5,200 customers—not 5,000 as Texmac originally thought—how does that affect the total quantity estimate and profit contribution?*

b. *Some of the people who responded to the survey didn't know much about different types of machines. If the actual number of old machines in the market is really 200 per 500 firms—not 220 as estimated from survey responses—how much would this affect the expected profit contribution (for 5,200 factories)?*

c. *The marketing manager knows that the percentage of textile factories that would actually buy the new machine might be different from the 40 percent who said they would in the survey. He estimates that the proportion that will replace the old machine might be as low as 36 and as high as 44 percent—depending on business conditions. Use the analysis feature to prepare a table that shows how expected quantity and profit contribution change when the sample percentage varies between a minimum of 36 and a maximum of 44 percent. What does this analysis suggest about the use of estimates from marketing research samples? (Note: Use 5,200 for the number of potential customers and use 220 as the estimate of the number of old machines in the sample.)*



## Suggested Cases

To view the cases, go to www.mcgrawhill.ca/college/wong.

Interested in finding out what marketing looks like in the real world? *Marketing Magazine* is just a click away on your OLC! Visit www.mcgrawhill.ca/college/wong today.

# Chapter Nine
# Elements of Product Planning for Goods and Services

When You Finish This Chapter, You Should

1. Understand what "product" really means.

2. Know the key differences between goods and services.

3. Know the differences among the various consumer and business product classes.

4. Understand how the product classes can help a marketing manager plan marketing strategies.

5. Understand what branding is and how to use it in strategy planning.

6. Understand the importance of packaging in strategy planning.

7. Understand the role of warranties in strategy planning.

## Kodak's Advantix

For decades, 35mm cameras have been the photographic standard. The technical quality of the films is excellent. They capture subtle colours and offer sharp resolution. And there's a lot of choice among cameras for serious photographers who study all of the details. Unfortunately, this isn't enough to satisfy most amateur photographers. For them, one camera seems pretty much like another. Their snapshots often come out botched because of errors loading the film or the wrong light. Sometimes the shape of the picture just doesn't fit the subject. Or if there's one great picture and someone wants a reprint, the negative can't be found. These problems have been around for a long time. So to address them—and to get new sales of films and cameras—Kodak and its four global

place price promotion prod

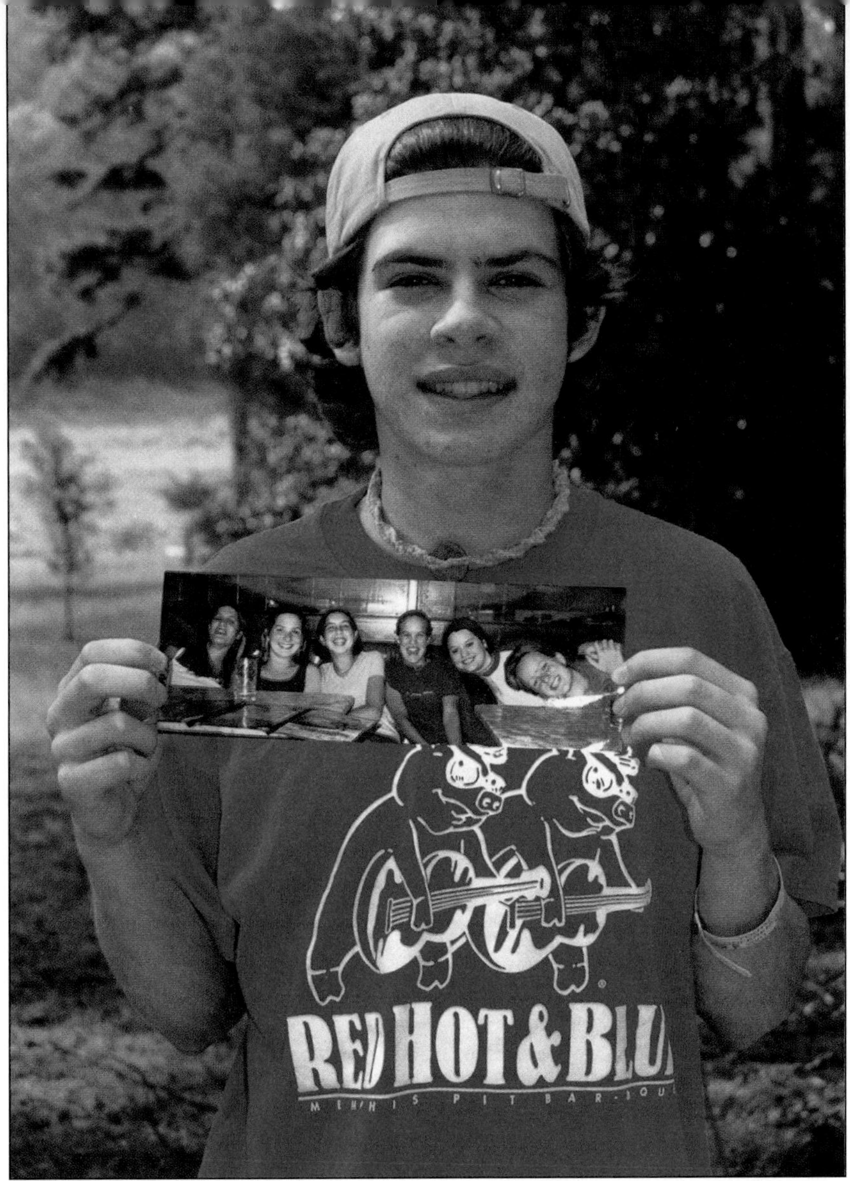

rivals agreed on a new photo standard, the Advanced Photo System (APS).

When Kodak was ready to introduce its new Advantix-brand APS film and cameras in 1996, it looked like a winning idea. A new cartridge made it easy to load the film. Photos could be shot in any of three sizes, including an extrawide format. The film adjusted for differences in light, and developed film came back protected in the cartridge. Reprints were easy to order too, because a numbered proof sheet came with each set of prints. Customers liked these benefits. What they really wanted was good snapshots, so Advantix seemed worth the 15-percent-higher price.

However, in its rush to beat rivals to market Kodak ran into production problems. It could not get enough cameras to retailers. So the big ad campaign to build familiarity with the Advantix brand of film and cameras was wasted. Worse, because of a confusing package, many people bought Advantix film expecting it to work in a 35mm camera; it wouldn't. Initially, getting Advantix pictures developed was also a hassle. Retailers were slow to put money into new equipment to develop Advantix film; they waited to see if customers wanted it. And it added to consumer confusion that Fuji, Minolta, and other firms each had their own brand names for APS products.

By 1998, these problems were smoothing out. But sales were slow because too few consumers knew about Advantix. So Kodak relaunched the product. Kodak stuck with the Advantix name but used a new package design. Ads directly pitted Advantix against the problems

place price promotion product


www.mcgrawhill.ca/college/wong

with 35mm pictures, even though that risked eating into Kodak's 35mm sales. Camera giveaway promotions on the Kodak website (www.kodak.com) stirred interest too. And price-off discounts on three-roll packages got consumers to take more pictures. As demand grew, retailers also gave Advantix more attention. For example, Wal-Mart put Kodak's $50 camera on special display. And many photo labs offered consumers a money-back guarantee on any Advantix prints that were not completely satisfactory.

For many customers in the target market, Kodak's Advantix line offers new benefits that they couldn't get before. But it involves new products that are basically incremental to what Kodak was already selling and what customers were already buying. Digital cameras and pictures are a more revolutionary type of new product. Consumers who adopt them will change their picture-taking behaviour, and, as Kodak knows, they'll certainly change their film-buying and film-processing behaviour too. It won't happen overnight, but digital cameras will make traditional cameras obsolete. And in the process the competition that Kodak faces has already changed, in some cases dramatically. Take, for example, HP's DeskJet-brand colour printers. If you buy a digital camera, the odds are that you'll print out the pictures on a DeskJet, not on a Kodak printer. So just as Kodak is fighting for shelf space against low-price Fuji and dealer brands in the mature market for 35mm film, it is fighting new and very different competitors in the fast-growing market related to digital photography.[1]



## In This Chapter

This is the first in a series of chapters that take an in-depth look at the specific marketing decisions made in organizations. We begin by identifying the elements that make up a "product." The Kodak case highlights some important topics we'll discuss in this chapter and the next. Here we'll look at how customers see a firm's product. Then we'll talk about product classes to help you better understand how marketing strategy planning changes to accommodate their different characteristics. Marketers use product classes as a shorthand way of describing how buyers think about the product in question and how those products will be bought and used.

A consistent theme throughout the chapter is the idea of a product as a bundle of elements centred on satisfying the customer. Thus, we'll consider how branding, packaging, and warranties can contribute to customer value and satisfaction. As shown in Exhibit 9-1, there are many strategy decisions related to the product area beyond "What should we make?"

## What Is a Product?

It may seem silly to ask "What is a product?" However, if you step back and look at the question from different perspectives, you'll see that the answer isn't as simple as we might expect. To a producer, a product is a collection of resources

Exhibit 9-1
Strategy planning for product.

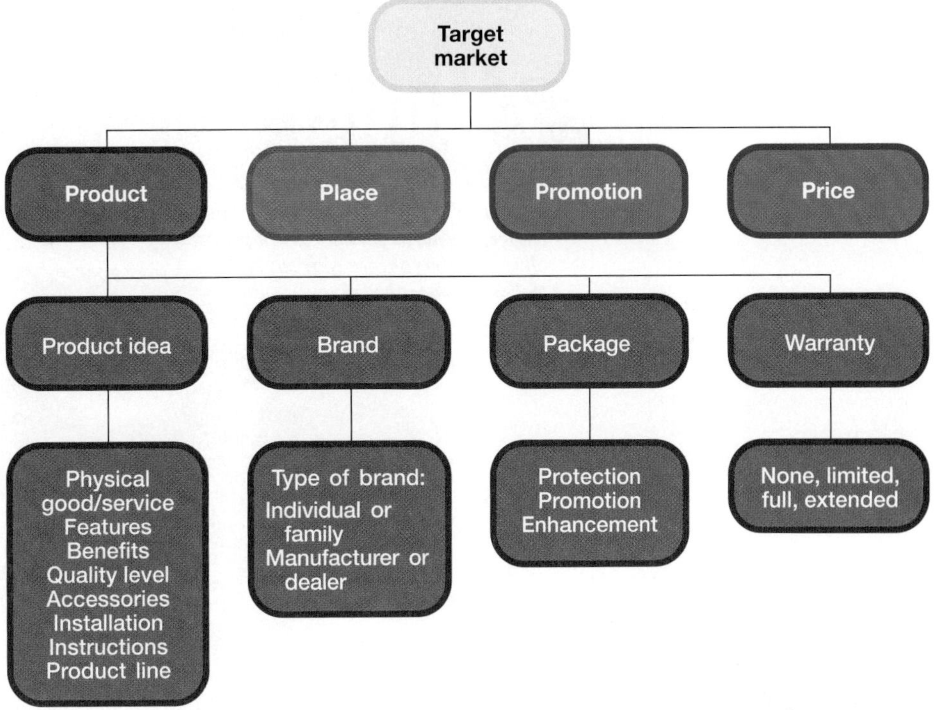


combined into a market offering. For example, a car maker might think of its car as a certain number of nuts and bolts, some sheet metal, an engine, and four wheels. By contrast, when producers and intermediaries buy a product, they're interested in the profit they can make from its purchase—through use or resale. But what about the customer? How do they see a "product"? Isn't the product simply the physical item or service they buy?

Throughout this book we have stressed the idea of customer satisfaction as the goal of marketing decisions and that satisfaction is created when we serve customer needs. In keeping with that thinking, a **product** is a need-satisfying offering of a firm. Thinking about a product as means of providing potential customer satisfaction or benefits is very important in being truly market-oriented. Many business managers in product-oriented firms get wrapped up in the technical details involved in producing a product. But most customers think about a product in terms of the total satisfaction it provides.

**product**
A need-satisfying offering of a firm

Why is it important to think this way? Consider the examples below. Is each pair the same product?

1. You are comparing two laptop computers. One has a 30-day warranty, the other a two-year warranty.
2. You are about to buy a satellite dish for your home entertainment system. One is sold as a kit to be assembled and installed by you, the other comes fully assembled with installation.
3. You are about to buy a bottle of wine. One bottle has a screw cap. The other has a more traditional cork cap.
4. You want to fly to the Caribbean for a vacation. One flight is no-frills with three stops along the way. The other is a full-service direct flight.
5. You want to buy golf equipment for a very good golfer. One set of balls has been designed by Tiger Woods. The other set carries no endorsement or brand name.

In each example, the items being compared are of the same product type but clearly each would be preferred under different circumstances. That is, neither one

Consumers don't buy "products" or "services," they buy the *benefits* provided by those products or services.

of each pair of items is necessarily better than the other. Indeed, you can probably identify circumstances under which you could purchase either and be perfectly satisfied. (Recall that this is why our concept of product-market definition—see Chapter 3—referred not only to a product but also to the need being served.)

### The Total Product

The main point of these examples is to demonstrate that customers don't buy products, they buy a means of having their needs satisfied. Since satisfaction may require something beyond the physical product, we need to think of a "total" product offering that is really a combination of excellent service, a physical good with the right features, useful instructions, a convenient package, a trustworthy warranty, and perhaps even a familiar name that has satisfied the consumer in the past, to name but a few.

Exhibit 9-2 presents these ideas. At the core of a total product is the customer's desire to satisfy a need. This is the "consumption problem." It's the product offering, its extended features and associated services—in short, everything the buyer receives when making a purchase constitutes a "solution" to that problem. Thus, marketers can choose to solve as much or as little of the customer's problem by providing different bundles of need satisfiers. Let's look at some important implications of looking at a product in this way.

### Total Product Quality and Customer Needs

**quality**
A total product's ability to satisfy a customer's needs or requirements

Many people think of *quality* in terms of technical quality or whether the product performs to expectations. Marketers take a much broader view, in keeping with our broader view of what a product is. From a marketing perspective, **quality** means a total product's ability to satisfy a customer's needs or requirements. This definition focuses on the customer—and how the customer thinks a product will fit some purpose. For example, the "best" satellite TV service may not be the one with the highest number of channels but the one that includes a local channel that a consumer wants to watch. Similarly, a heavier, stronger, and more durable tent may not have the best quality if you plan to carry it on your back as you trek up a mountainside.

When viewed in this way, product quality is a combination of everything the buyer receives when making a purchase. Whether they actually buy one offering or

Exhibit 9-2
The total product offering is everything the buyer associates with a purchase.

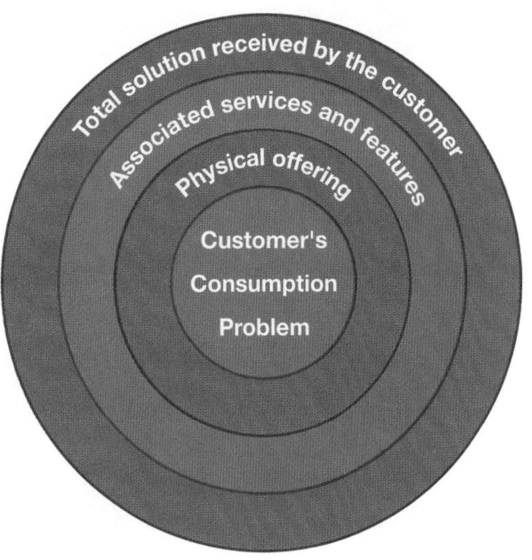
Total solution received by the customer
Associated services and features
Physical offering
Customer's
Consumption
Problem

**relative quality**

How products measure up against the criteria used by consumers in making a purchase decision

another depends upon **relative quality**—how products measure up against the criteria used by consumers in making a purchase decision. As you can imagine, relative quality has a major impact on the firm's ability to position and differentiate itself (see Chapter 3).

## Differences between Goods and Services

Because a good is a physical thing, it can be seen and touched. You can try on a pair of Timberland shoes, thumb through the latest issue of *Canadian Geographic* magazine, or smell Colombian coffee as it brews. A good is a *tangible* item. When you buy it you own it, and it's usually pretty easy to see exactly what you'll get.

**service**

A deed performed by one party for another

On the other hand, a **service** is a deed performed by one party for another. When you provide a customer with a service, the customer can't keep it. Rather, a service is experienced, used, or consumed. You go see a DreamWorks Pictures movie, but afterward all you have is a memory. You ride on a ski lift in Mont Tremblant, but you don't own the equipment. Services are not physical—they are *intangible*. You can't "hold" a service, and it may be hard to know exactly what you'll get when you buy it.

Most products are a combination of tangible and intangible elements. Shell gas and the credit card used to buy it are tangible—the credit the card grants is not. A Domino's pizza is tangible, but the fast home delivery is not.

Vos bagages sont assez grands pour voyager seuls.
SERVICE BAGAGES A DOMICILE
24H PORTE A PORTE
0 803 845 845*
95F le 1er bagage, 60F les suivants. Délai à compter du jour de l'enlèvement à 17h, hors samedis, dimanches et fêtes. *Renseignements et commandes 7j/7 de 7h à 22h. 1,09F/min.
Soumis à conditions. Prix au 25/09/98.
À NOUS DE VOUS FAIRE PRÉFÉRER LE TRAIN.
SNCF

To better satisfy its customers' needs and make travelling more enjoyable, this French railroad company's service includes door-to-door delivery of the passenger's luggage. The ad says, "Your luggage is old enough to travel by itself. It's up to us to ensure you'd rather go by train."

Providing consistent, high-quality service is a challenge, so many firms are using technology to make it easier and quicker for customers to get the services they want by themselves.

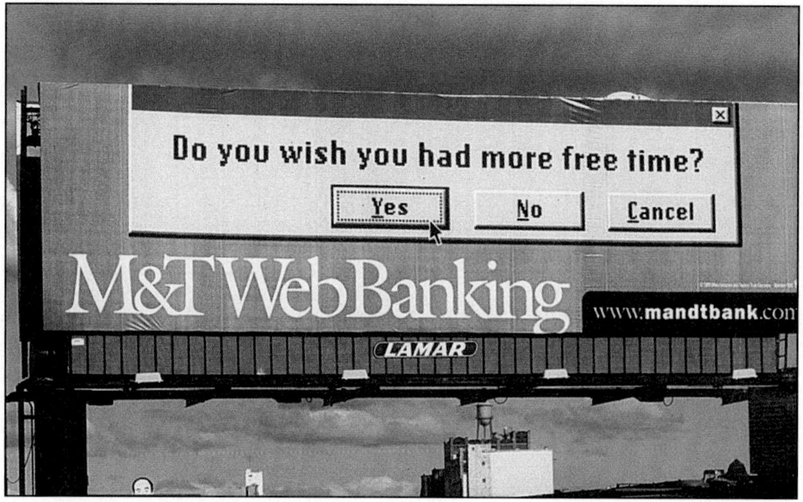




**Production and consumption are inseparable** Goods are usually produced in a factory and then sold. A Panasonic TV may be stored in a warehouse or store waiting for a buyer. By contrast, services are often sold first, then produced. And they're produced and consumed in the same time frame. Thus, goods producers may be far away from the customer, but service providers often work in the customer's presence.

Because of this characteristic, much of the customer's initial assessment of service quality is based on their interactions with the service staff—how they look, talk, and conduct themselves in front of customers. As a result, marketing managers should play a major role in shaping how service staff are selected and trained.

**Services are highly perishable** Services are perishable—they can't be stored. This makes it harder to balance supply and demand. An example explains the problem.

Bell Canada sells long-distance telephone services. Even when demand is high—during peak business hours or on Mother's Day—customers expect the service to be available. They don't want to hear "Sorry, all lines are busy." So, Bell Canada must have enough equipment and employees to deal with peak demand times. But when customers aren't making many calls, Bell's facilities are idle. Bell might be able to save money with less capacity (equipment and people), but then it will sometimes have to face dissatisfied customers.

**Services cannot be stored or transported** It's often difficult to have economies of scale when the product emphasis is on service. Services can't be produced in large, economical quantities and then transported to customers. In addition, *services often have to be produced in the presence of the customer*. So service

Exhibit 9-3
Examples of possible blends of physical goods and services in a product.

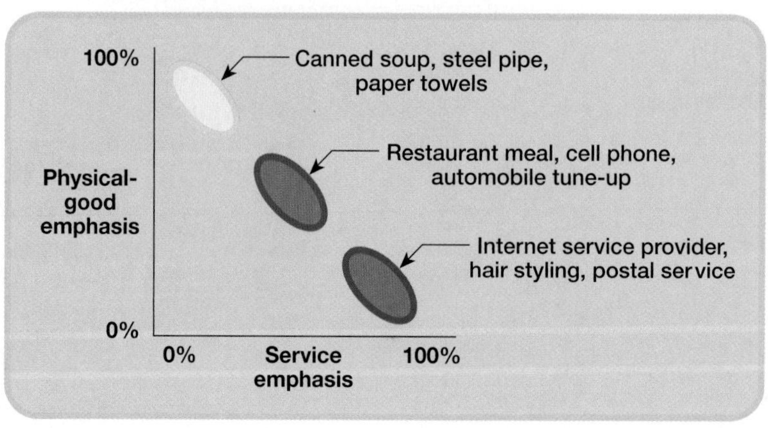

suppliers often need duplicate equipment and staff at places where the service is actually provided. Merrill Lynch sells investment advice along with financial products worldwide. That advice could, perhaps, be produced more economically in a single building in New York City and made available only on its website. But Merrill Lynch has offices all over the world. Many customers want a personal touch from the stockbroker telling them how to invest their money.[2]

**Products = goods + services** You already know that a product may be a physical *good* or a *service* or a *blend* of both. Yet, it's too easy to slip into a limited, physical-product point of view. We want to think of a product in terms of the needs it satisfies. If a firm's objective is to satisfy customer needs, service can be part of its product—or service alone may *be* the product—and must be provided as part of a total marketing mix.

Exhibit 9-3 shows this bigger view of "product." It shows that a product can range from a 100-percent emphasis on physical goods—for commodities like steel pipe—to a 100-percent emphasis on service, like high-speed Internet access from Cogeco. Regardless of the emphasis involved, the marketing manager must consider most of the same elements in planning products and marketing mixes. Given this, we usually won't make a distinction between goods and services but will call all of them *products*. Sometimes, however, understanding the differences in goods and services can help fine-tune marketing strategy planning.

**Serving complex needs may require a product line** Providing the right product—when and where and how the customer wants it—is a challenge, whether the product is primarily a service, primarily a good, or (as is usually the case) a blend of both. Marketing managers must think about the "whole" product they provide, and then make sure that all of the elements fit together and work with the rest of the marketing strategy. Sometimes a single product isn't enough to meet the needs of target customers, which may necessitate assortments of different products.

**product assortment**

The set of all product lines and individual products that a firm sells

**product line**

A set of individual products that are closely related

A **product assortment** is the set of all product lines and individual products that a firm sells. A **product line** is a set of individual products that are closely related. The seller may see the products in a line as related because they're produced and/or operate in a similar way, sold to the same target market, sold through the same types of outlets, or priced at about the same level. President's Choice, for example, focuses on the need for everyday household items and has many product lines in its product assortment—including coffee, tea, meat, desserts, snacks, housewares, financial

At companies like 3M, managers must develop marketing plans for individual products that are consistent with the marketing program for the whole product assortment.

Some items in Bridgestone's line of tire products sell as consumer products, others sell as business products, and some are both. However, when different target markets are involved the rest of the marketing mix may also need to be different.

services, and frozen dinners. John Deere might focus on the need to cut and bale hay—its product line features tractors, mowers, balers, and so on. By contrast, Hertz has one product line—different types of vehicles to rent.

**individual product**

A particular product within a product line

An **individual product** is a particular product within a product line. It usually is differentiated by brand, level of service offered, price, or some other characteristic. For example, each size and flavour of a brand of soup is an individual product. Intermediaries usually think of each separate product as a stock-keeping unit (SKU) and assign it a unique SKU number

Each individual product and target market may require a separate strategy. For example, President's Choice's strategy for selling tea is different from its strategy for selling financial services. We'll focus mainly on developing one marketing strategy at a time. But remember that a marketing manager may have to plan *several* strategies to develop an effective marketing program for a whole company.



## Using Product Classes to Plan Marketing Strategies

You don't have to treat *every* product as unique when planning strategies. Some product classes require similar marketing mixes. These product classes are a useful starting point for developing marketing mixes for new products and evaluating present mixes. However, the term "product class" is a little misleading: marketers use

**Exhibit 9-4**
Product classes.

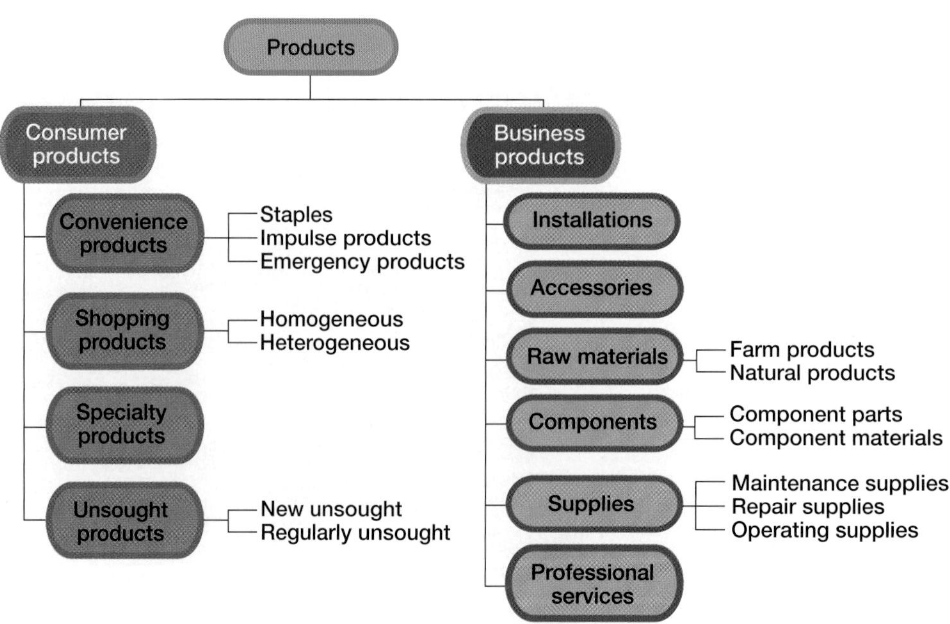

product classes as a shorthand way of describing how buyers think about the product in question and how those products will be bought and used.

All products fit into one of two broad groups based on the type of customer that will use them. **Consumer products** are products meant for the final consumer. **Business products** are products meant for use in producing other products. The same product—like Bertolli Olive Oil—*might* be in both groups. Consumers buy it to use in their own kitchens, but food-processing companies and restaurants buy it in large quantities as an ingredient in the products they sell. Selling the same product to both final consumers and business customers requires (at least) two different strategies. Exhibit 9-4 summarizes the different types of products.

**consumer products**
Products meant for the final consumer

**business products**
Products meant for use in producing other products

## Consumer Product Classes

There are product classes within each group. Consumer product classes are based on *how consumers think about and shop for products*. Business product classes are based on *how buyers think about products and how they'll be used.*

Consumer product classes divide into four groups: (1) convenience, (2) shopping, (3) specialty, and (4) unsought. *Each class is based on the way people buy products.* See Exhibit 9-5 for a summary of how these product classes relate to marketing mixes.[3]

**convenience products**
Products a consumer needs but isn't willing to spend much time or effort shopping for

### Convenience products

**Convenience products** are products a consumer needs but isn't willing to spend much time or effort shopping for. These products are bought often, require little service or selling, don't cost much, and may even be

**Exhibit 9-5** Consumer product classes and marketing-mix planning.

| Consumer Product Class | Marketing-Mix Considerations | Consumer Behaviour |
|---|---|---|
| Convenience products | | |
| Staples | Maximum exposure with widespread, low-cost distribution; mass selling by producer; usually low price; branding is important. | Routinized (habitual), low effort, frequent purchases; low involvement. |
| Impulse | Widespread distribution with display at point of purchase | Unplanned purchases bought quickly. |
| Emergency | Need widespread distribution near probable point of need; price sensitivity low. | Purchase made with time pressure when a need is great. |
| Shopping products | | |
| Homogeneous | Need enough exposure to facilitate price comparison; price sensitivity high. | Customers see little difference among alternatives, seek lowest price. |
| Heterogeneous | Need distribution near similar products; promotion (including personal selling) to highlight product advantages; less price sensitivity. | Extensive problem solving; consumer may need help in making a decision (salesperson, website, etc.). |
| Specialty products | Price sensitivity is likely to be low; limited distribution may be acceptable, but should be treated as a convenience or shopping product (in whichever category product would typically be included) to reach persons not yet sold on its specialty product status. | Willing to expend effort to get specific product, even if not necessary; strong preferences make it an important purchase; Internet becoming important information source. |
| Unsought products | | |
| New unsought | Must be available in places where similar (or related) products are sought; needs attention-getting promotion. | Need for product not strongly felt; unaware of benefits or not yet gone through adoption process. |
| Regularly unsought | Requires very aggressive promotion, usually personal selling. | Aware of product but not interested; attitude toward product may even be negative. |

bought by habit. A convenience product may be a staple, impulse product, or emergency product.

**staples**
Products that are bought often, routinely, and without much thought

**Staples** are products that are bought often, routinely, and without much thought—like breakfast cereal, canned soup, and most other packaged foods used almost every day in almost every household.

**impulse products**
Products that are bought quickly—as unplanned purchases—because of a strongly felt need

**Impulse products** are products that are bought quickly—as *unplanned* purchases—because of a strongly felt need. True impulse products are items that the customer hadn't planned to buy, decides to buy on sight, may have bought the same way many times before, and wants right now. If the buyer doesn't see an impulse product at the right time, the sale may be lost.[4]

**emergency products**
Products that are purchased immediately when the need is great

**Emergency products** are products that are purchased immediately when the need is great. The customer doesn't have time to shop around when a traffic accident occurs, a thunderstorm begins, or an impromptu party starts. The price of the ambulance service, raincoat, or ice cubes won't be important.

**shopping products**
Products that a customer feels are worth the time and effort to compare with competing products

### Shopping products

**Shopping products** are products that a customer feels are worth the time and effort to compare with competing products. Shopping products can be divided into two types, depending on what customers are comparing: (1) homogeneous or (2) heterogeneous shopping products.

**homogeneous shopping products**
Shopping products the customer sees as basically the same and wants at the lowest price

**Homogeneous shopping products** are shopping products the customer sees as basically the same and wants at the lowest price. Some consumers believe that certain sizes and types of computers, television sets, washing machines, and even cars are very similar. So they shop for the best price. For some products, the Internet has become a way to do that quickly.

Firms may try to emphasize and promote their product differences to avoid head-to-head price competition. For example, Bell Sympatico says that with its dial-up Internet service you get fewer busy signals and lost connections. But if consumers don't think the differences are real or important in terms of the value they seek, they'll just look at price.

**heterogeneous shopping products**
Shopping products the customer sees as different and wants to inspect for quality and suitability

**Heterogeneous shopping products** are shopping products the customer sees as different and wants to inspect for quality and suitability. Furniture, clothing, and membership in a spa are good examples. Often the consumer expects help from a knowledgeable salesperson. Quality and style matter more than price. In fact, once the customer finds the right product, price may not matter at all—as long as it's reasonable. For example, you may have asked a friend to recommend a good dentist without even asking what the dentist charges.

Branding may be less important for heterogeneous shopping products. The more consumers compare price and quality, the less they rely on brand names or labels. Some retailers carry competing brands so consumers won't go to a competitor to compare items.

**specialty products**
Consumer products that the customer really wants and makes a special effort to find

### Specialty products

**Specialty products** are consumer products that the customer really wants and makes a special effort to find. Shopping for a specialty product doesn't mean comparing—the buyer wants that special product and is willing to search for it. It's the customer's *willingness to search*—not the extent of searching—that makes it a specialty product.

*Any* branded product that consumers insist on by name is a specialty product. Marketing managers want customers to see their products as specialty products and ask for them over and over again. Building that kind of relationship isn't easy. It means satisfying the customer every time. However, that's easier and a lot less costly than trying to win back dissatisfied customers or attract new customers who are not seeking the product at all.

**unsought products**
Products that potential customers don't yet want or know they can buy

### Unsought products

**Unsought products** are products that potential customers don't yet want or know they can buy. So they don't search for them at all. In fact, consumers probably won't buy these products if they see them—unless promotion can show their value.

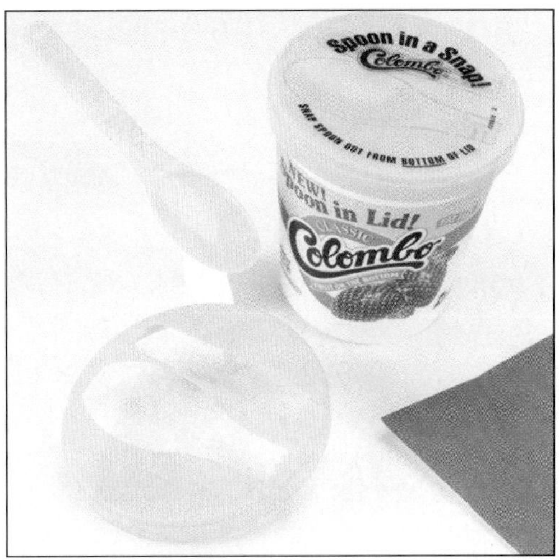

These products are popular now, but initially they were new unsought products.

**new unsought products**
Products offering really new ideas that potential customers don't know about yet

**regularly unsought products**
Products that stay unsought but not unbought forever

There are two types of unsought products. **New unsought products** are products offering really new ideas that potential customers don't know about yet. Informative promotion can help convince customers to accept the product, ending its unsought status. Astro yogurt, fax machines, and Microsoft's Web browser are all popular items now, but initially they were new unsought products.

**Regularly unsought products** are products—like gravestones, life insurance, and encyclopedias—that stay unsought but not unbought forever. There may be a need, but potential customers aren't motivated to satisfy it. For this kind of product, personal selling is *very* important.

Many nonprofit organizations try to "sell" their unsought products. For example, Canadian Blood Services regularly holds blood drives to remind prospective donors of how important it is to give blood.

**Classifications can be misleading** We've been looking at product classes one at a time. But the same product might be seen in different ways by different target markets at the same time. For example, a product viewed as a staple by most consumers in Canada, the United States, or some similar affluent country might be seen as a heterogeneous shopping product by consumers in another country. The price might be much higher when considered as a proportion of the consumer's budget, and the available choices might be very different. Similarly, a convenient place to shop often means very different things in different countries. In Japan, for example, retail stores tend to be much smaller and carry smaller selections of products.

## Business Product Classes

In Chapter 7 we looked at the similarities and differences between business and organizational buying and consumer or household buying. (These differences were summarized in Exhibit 7-1.) As might be expected, these distinctive characteristics make it hard to use the consumer product classes to reflect business products. But it is important we develop an alternative framework, since business firms use a system of buying related to these product classes.

### Common Characteristics

Before looking at differences between these classes of business products, we should note that there are some important commonalities shared by all business products.

Businesses buy the goods and services they need to produce products for their own customers, so the demand for GE's special plastic resins, used to make lightweight and impact-resistant body panels, is derived from consumer demand for VW's unique car.



**derived demand**
The demand for business products derives from the demand for final consumer products

**Derived demand** The big difference in the business products market is **derived demand**—the demand for business products derives from the demand for final consumer products. For example, car manufacturers buy about one-fifth of all steel products. But if demand for cars drops, they'll buy less steel. Then even the steel supplier with the best marketing mix is likely to lose sales.[5]

**Inelastic demand at the industry level** Total *industry* demand for business products is fairly inelastic. Business firms must buy what they need to produce their own products. Even if the cost of basic silicon doubles, for example, Intel needs it to make computer chips. The increased cost of the silicon won't have much effect on the price of the final computer or on the number of computers consumers demand. Sharp business buyers try to buy as economically as possible. So the demand facing *individual sellers* may be extremely elastic—if similar products are available at a lower price.

**Impact of tax treatments** How a firm's accountants—and the tax laws—treat a purchase is also important to business customers.

**expense item**
A product whose total cost is treated as a business expense in the year it's purchased

**capital item**
A long-lasting product that can be used and depreciated for many years

An **expense item** is a product whose total cost is treated as a business expense in the year it's purchased. A **capital item** is a long-lasting product that can be used and depreciated for many years. Often it's very expensive. Customers pay for the capital item when they buy it, but for tax purposes the cost is spread over a number of years. This may reduce the cash available for other purchases.

## Business Product Classes

*Business product classes are based on how buyers see products and how the products will be used.* The classes of business products are (1) installations, (2) accessories, (3) raw materials, (4) components, (5) supplies, and (6) professional services. Exhibit 9-6 relates these product classes to marketing-mix planning.

**installations**
Important capital items

**Installations** **Installations**—such as buildings, land rights, and major equipment—are important capital items. One-of-a-kind installations—like office buildings and custom-made machines—generally require special negotiations for each sale. Standardized major equipment is treated more routinely. Even so, negotiations for installations often involve top management and can stretch over months or even years.

Installations are a boom-or-bust business. When sales are high, businesses want to expand capacity rapidly. And if the potential return on a new investment is very attractive, firms may accept any reasonable price. But during a downswing, buyers have little or no need for new installations and sales fall off sharply.[6]

Exhibit 9-6 Business product classes and marketing-mix planning.

| Business Product Classes | Marketing-Mix Considerations | Buying Behaviour |
|---|---|---|
| Installations | Usually requires skilful personal selling by producer, including technical contacts, and/or understanding of applications; leasing and specialized support services may be required. | Multiple buying influence (including top management) and new-task buying are common; infrequent purchase, long decision period, and boom-or-bust demand are typical. |
| Accessory equipment | Need fairly widespread distribution and numerous contacts by experienced and sometimes technically trained personnel; price competition is often intense, but quality is important. | Purchasing and operating personnel typically make decisions; shorter decision period than for installations; Internet sourcing. |
| Raw materials | Grading is important, and transportation and storing can be crucial because of seasonal production and/or perishable products; markets tend to be very competitive. | Long-term contract may be required to ensure supply; online auctions. |
| Component parts and materials | Product quality and delivery reliability are usually extremely important; negotiation and technical selling typical on less-standardized items; replacement after market may require different strategies. | Multiple buying influence is common; online competitive bids used to encourage competitive pricing. |
| Maintenance, repair, and operating (MRO) supplies | Typically require widespread distribution or fast delivery (repair items); arrangements with appropriate intermediaries may be crucial. | Often handled as straight rebuys, except important operating supplies may be treated much more seriously and involve multiple buying influence. |
| Professional services | Services customized to buyer's need; personal selling very important; inelastic demand often supports high prices. | Customer may compare outside service with what internal people could provide; needs may be very specialized. |



Suppliers sometimes include special services with an installation at no extra cost. A firm that sells (or leases) equipment to dentists, for example, may install it and help the dentist learn to use it.

**accessories**
Short-lived capital items

**Accessory equipment** **Accessories** are short-lived capital items—tools and equipment used in production or office activities—like Canon's small copy machines, Rockwell's portable drills, and Steelcase's filing cabinets.

Since these products cost less and last a shorter time than installations, multiple buying influence is less important. Operating people and purchasing agents, rather than top managers, may make the purchase decision. As with installations, some customers may wish to lease or rent—to expense the cost.

Accessories are more standardized than installations. And they're usually needed by more customers. For example, IBM sells its robotics systems, which can cost more than $2 million, as custom installations to large manufacturers. But IBM's Thinkpad computers are accessory equipment for just about every type of modern business all around the world.

**raw materials**
Unprocessed expense items that are moved to the next production process with little handling

**Raw materials** **Raw materials** are unprocessed expense items—such as logs, iron ore, wheat, and cotton—that are moved to the next production process with little handling. Unlike installations and accessories, *raw materials become part of a physical good and are expense items.*

**farm products**
Products grown by farmers

**natural products**
Products that occur in nature

We can break raw materials into two types: (1) farm products and (2) natural products. **Farm products** are grown by farmers—examples are oranges, wheat, sugar cane, cattle, poultry, eggs, and milk. **Natural products** are products that occur in nature—such as fish and game, timber and maple syrup, and copper, zinc, iron ore, oil, and coal.

The need for grading is one of the important differences between raw materials and other business products. Nature produces what it will—and someone must sort and grade raw materials to satisfy various market segments. Top-graded fruits and vegetables may find their way into the consumer products market. Lower grades, which are treated as business products, are used in juices, sauces, and soups.

Most buyers of raw materials want ample supplies in the right grades for specific uses—fresh vegetables for Green Giant's production lines or logs for Weyerhaeuser's paper mills. To ensure steady quantities, raw-materials customers often sign long-term contracts, sometimes at guaranteed prices.

**components**
Processed expense items that become part of a finished product

**Components** **Components** are processed expense items that become part of a finished product. Component *parts* are finished (or nearly finished) items that are ready for assembly into the final product.

ATI's graphics cards included in personal computers, TRW's air bags in cars, and Briggs and Stratton's engines for lawn mowers are examples. Component *materials* are items such as wire, plastic, textiles, or cement. They have already been processed but must be processed further before becoming part of the final product. Since components become part of the firm's own product, quality is extremely important.

Components are often produced in large quantity to meet standard specifications. However, some components are custom-made. Then teamwork between the buyer and seller may be needed to arrive at the right specifications. So a buyer may find it attractive to develop a close partnership with a dependable supplier. And top management may be involved if the price is high or the component is extremely important to the final product. In contrast, standardized component materials are more likely to be purchased online using a competitive bidding system.

Since component parts go into finished products, a replacement market often develops. This *aftermarket* can be both large and very profitable. Car tires and batteries are two examples of components originally sold in the OEM *(original equipment market)* that become consumer products in the aftermarket. The target markets are different—and different marketing mixes are usually necessary.[7]

**supplies**
Expense items that do not become part of a finished product

**Supplies** **Supplies** are expense items that do not become part of a finished product. Buyers may treat these items less seriously. When a firm cuts its budget, orders for supplies may be the first to go. Supplies can be divided into three types:

The ability to arrange a lease or good financial terms is often important in the purchase of a business aircraft or other capital installation. By contrast, component parts become part of a firm's product and are paid for when the expense occurs.

Business customers usually want a convenient and low-cost way to buy standard equipment and supplies, so many are now turning to vendors who sell over the Internet.

Paper.
Equipment.
Supplies.
All available from here.
www.printnation.com
888.806.2246
printnation.com
Equipment and Supplies Auctions, Leasing,
Financing, Industry News, Resources and More.
No Minimums. Free Shipping. We're Always Open.


(1) maintenance, (2) repair, and (3) operating supplies—giving them their common name: MRO supplies.

Maintenance and small operating supplies are like convenience products. The item will be ordered because it is needed—but buyers won't spend much time on it. Branding may become important because it makes buying easier for such "nuisance" purchases. Breadth of assortment and the seller's dependability are also important. Intermediaries usually handle the many supply items, and now they are often purchased via online catalogue sites.[8]

If operating supplies are needed regularly, and in large amounts, they receive special treatment. Many companies buy coal and fuel oil in railroad-car quantities. Usually there are several sources for such commodity products—and large volumes may be purchased at global exchanges on the Internet.

**professional services**
Specialized services that support a firm's operations

**Professional services** **Professional services** are specialized services that support a firm's operations. They are usually expense items. Engineering or management consulting services can improve the plant layout or the company's efficiency. Information technology services can maintain a company's networks and websites. Design services can suggest a new look for products or promotion materials. Advertising agencies can help promote the firm's products. And food services can improve morale.

Here the *service* part of the product is emphasized. Goods may be supplied—as coffee and doughnuts are with food service—but the customer is primarily interested in the service.

Managers compare the cost of buying professional services outside the firm ("outsourcing") to the cost of having company people do them. For special skills needed only occasionally, an outsider can be the best source. Further, during the last decade, many firms have tried to cut costs by downsizing the number of people that they employ; in many cases, work that was previously done by an employee is now provided as a service by an independent supplier. Clearly, the number of service specialists is growing in our complex economy.



## Branding Basics

There are so many brands—and we're so used to seeing them—that we take them for granted. But branding is an important decision area and, in some cases, is an important part of product quality.

The earliest and most aggressive brand promoters in North America were the patent medicine companies. They were joined by the food manufacturers, who grew in size after the American Civil War. Some of the brands started in the 1860s and 1870s (and still going strong) are Quaker Oats, Pillsbury's Best Flour, and Ivory Soap. Today, familiar brands exist for most product categories, ranging from crayons (Crayola) to real estate services (ReMax). But before we look at what makes for a great brand, let's clarify some key terms.

**branding**

The use of a name, term, symbol, or design (or a combination of these) to identify a product

**brand name**

A word, letter, or group of words or letters

**trademark**

Only those words, symbols, or marks that are legally registered for use by a single company

**service mark**

The same as a trademark except that it refers to a service offering

## Brand Terminology

**Branding** means the use of a name, term, symbol, or design—or a combination of these—to identify a product. It includes the use of brand names, trademarks, and practically all other means of product identification. Brand name has a narrower meaning. A **brand name** is a word, letter, or a group of words or letters. Examples include Canadian Tire, WD-40, 3M Post-its, and Ford Trucks.

Trademark is a legal term. A **trademark** includes only those words, symbols, or marks that are legally registered for use by a single company. A **service mark** is the same as a trademark except that it refers to a service offering.

The word *Buick* can be used to explain these differences. The Buick car is branded under the brand name Buick (whether it's spoken or printed in any manner). When "Buick" is printed in a certain kind of script, however, it becomes a trademark. A trademark need not be attached to the product. It need not even be a word—it can be a symbol. Exhibit 9-7 shows some common trademarks.

These differences may seem technical. But they are very important in defining the legal rights of firms.

## The Impact of Branding on Product Quality

Well-recognized brands make shopping easier. Think of trying to buy groceries, for example, if you had to evaluate the advantages and disadvantages of each of 25,000 items every time you went to a supermarket. Instead you probably look for certain brands because you feel confident that your purchase will consistently lead to satisfying certain needs. The continued reinforcement of that expectation leads consumers to become loyal to a brand.

Brand promotion has advantages for branders as well as customers. A good brand reduces the marketer's selling time and effort. And sometimes a firm's brand name is the only element in its marketing mix that a competitor can't copy.

Good brands can improve the company's image—speeding acceptance of new products marketed under the same name. For example, many consumers quickly tried Starbucks' coffee-flavoured Frappuccino beverage when it appeared on grocery-



Exhibit 9-7 Recognized trademarks and symbols help in promotion.

store shelves because they already knew they liked Starbucks' coffee.[9] In addition, many believe that good brands have a positive effect on the value of the company's shares and can even make it easier to recruit talented staff. These benefits make it easier for the firm to invest in creating great products and services.

Successful brand promotion can even increase the set of needs met by a product. For example, the inclusion of a designer name on a piece of clothing, handbag, sunglasses, and similar items serves the need for status recognition for consumers.

### The Brand Challenge

However, these benefits do not occur simply because we attach a brand name or mark to a product. These benefits are the result of both the consistent performance of the product and a well-tuned promotional effort. The goal is to build an association or level of familiarity between a brand and a certain outcome. Internet Insite 9-1 shows how the Internet can be used to assist in these efforts.

**brand familiarity**
How well customers recognize and accept a company's brand

**Achieving brand familiarity** Brand acceptance must be earned with a good product and regular promotion. **Brand familiarity** means how well customers recognize and accept a company's brand. The degree of brand familiarity affects the planning for the rest of the marketing mix—especially where the product should be offered and what promotion is needed.

Five levels of brand familiarity are useful for strategy planning: (1) rejection, (2) nonrecognition, (3) recognition, (4) preference, and (5) insistence.

**brand rejection**
When potential customers won't buy a brand unless its image is changed

Some brands have been tried and found wanting. **Brand rejection** means that potential customers won't buy a brand unless its image is changed. Rejection may suggest a change in the product or perhaps only a shift to target customers who have

## Internet Insite 9–1

### BUILDING BRANDS ON THE WEB

Brands represent quality and evoke certain emotions. Branding strategies focus on establishing a brand promise as well as creating positive and favourable associations in the minds of consumers. An ongoing debate in the advertising community is the suitability of the Internet for building brands. There are some experts who think that the Internet is a great medium for direct selling, but not for building brands. Allen Rosenshine, Chairman and CEO of BBDO, one of the largest advertising agencies, is skeptical of the Internet's impact on branding. He wrote in an essay, "We also must recognize the current limitations of the Internet in delivering a truly creative product that touches people with sight, sound, motion and emotion without which brands cannot be communicated effectively."[10]

Does this mean only television (the medium with sound and motion) can be effective in brand advertising and the Internet has no role in branding? Let us explore the role that the Internet can play in building brands. You can then be the judge.

Television can create emotions, but at the same time advertising messages last a few seconds. There are too many ads and too many channels competing for attention. The brand website, on the other hand, can be a space where the marketer can engage the consumer with interesting visuals, content, and interactive experience. Top websites can be quite "sticky," with visitors spending 10 or more minutes on the site on average. That is a lot of time compared to a 30- or 60-second television commercial. Also, consider the fact that television viewership is declining, while the Internet as a primary source of news and entertainment is increasing.

Brand building on the Internet can take many forms. Banner advertising is a small part of it. Brand sites with interactive tools, content, offers, and even the ability to customize a product are increasingly deployed. Every major automobile brand has a site. Customization (see Saturn's site at www.saturn.com), brand comparisons, and a 360-degree view of the product (see Toyota's site at www.toyota.ca) are some of the features you will see on these sites. Payment calculators, application for financing, and booking a test-drive appointment are other features that consumers will find useful. Consumer electronics firms like Panasonic (www.panasonic.ca) and Sony (www.sony.ca) offer in-depth brand information. Product locators, brand comparisons, and store locators are often part of such sites.

The traditional view of branding suggests that awareness, associations, and emotions created through exposure to commercials play a key role. That may still be true, but marketers have a new weapon at their disposal. Once television creates the awareness and the initial interest, the Web can provide content, customization, and interactive experience. The Web can engage the consumer for a longer period of time, thereby creating a stronger connection between the consumer and the brand.

Packaged foods and soft drinks, two categories that are widely advertised on television, are not products that are usually bought online. However, brands like Kraft Foods (www.kraftfoods.com) are leading destination sites on the Internet. These top sites can attract a million or more visitors per month. Unlike television ads, which are thrust on the consumer, a visit to a website is a voluntary act. Consumers go there for recipes, games, contests, and information exchange. Whatever the reason, consumers end up spending time in a branded environment, which does seem to increase brand recall and brand choice.

There are a few different options available on the Internet when it comes to branding. The banner ads of various sizes and shapes can convey very limited information, but can be useful when placed in the right spot (e.g., car ad placed next to an article on new hybrid cars). Rich-media ads, which involve sound and animation, are catching on. With increasing use of high-bandwidth connections (through cable modems and DSL), we are likely to see Internet ads that look more like television ads, but with the addition of interactive capability. Advertisers are depending less on such ads and more on brand websites, where they can provide information, interactivity, and even fun.

If you think that the Web is not suitable for advertising frequently purchased consumer brands, think again. Consumer brand sites for Tide (www.tide.com), Oil of Olay (www.oilofolay.com), Clairol (www.clairol.com), and Crest (www.crest.com) (all by Procter & Gamble) offer not just product information, but also a variety of interactive experiences. Oil of Olay offers a personalized skin analyzer and a personalized beauty imaging system, along with expert advice on skin care. Cover Girl is full of interactive tools that allow consumers to get a personalized beauty consultation. Vanilla Coke, which has been Coca-Cola's recent success story, offers a mystery game with prizes that has attracted a lot of young consumers. The fact that they spent a lot of time on the Vanilla Coke site (www.vanillacoke.com) certainly hasn't hurt the brand sales.

Becel (www.becelcanada.com), a margarine brand, has turned its site into a destination for all people seeking a healthy lifestyle (see the exhibit below). Through interactive meal planners, recipes, an electronic newsletter on health topics, articles on health-related topics (including how to quit smoking), and a separate section for health professionals, the site attempts to transform a low-involvement product into a high-involvement product. Kraft has a similar strategy with its online *Food & Family* magazine, healthy living articles, interactive meal planner, and more. Kraft boasts five of the top ten food and beverage sites (see Kraft-brand sites at www.kraft.com).[11] Barbie.com, a site filled with interactive games, averages more than 4 million visitors per month—not surprisingly, Mattel vice-president Christina DeRosa says, "4 million girls going to the site and staying for 15 minutes, coupled with approving parents—that's bound to mean increased profits over long-term."[12]

Claritin (www.claritin.com) offers a great deal of information about allergies and allergy relief and even sends weekly e-mail alerts with weather and pollen forecasts. Kraft offers features that make nutritious meal planning easier. Tide's site is positioned as the Fabric Care Network, which raises the importance of a frequently purchased product. Tide's site is not just informational, but also attempts to offer a fun experience. The successful brand sites link the brand with something that is important to consumers, thereby increasing the importance of the brand and the site.

Many marketers target kids online with games and entertainment (e.g., Disney.com and Barbie.com). Disney and Barbie get extensive feedback from kids to ensure the design and colours on the site appeal to the target audience.[13] A website's traffic and repeat-visit rate are good indicators of the site's effectiveness.

When you survey a variety of consumer-durable and non-durable brand websites, the importance given to Web marketing becomes evident. The role of the Internet in brand building vis-à-vis television also becomes clear. Television can create emotions, convey one or two short messages, and—through repeated exposure—create brand awareness. The Internet can engage the consumer in an interactive experience with the brand, allow the marketer to fully exploit the position strategy (e.g., see Becel and its focus on healthy living), and offer personalized communication (as opposed to one message for all consumers). In many cases, television drives consumers to the website, which in turn engages and entices consumers. For most major purchases, such as cars, consumer electronics, computers, and travel, consumers go online for information even if the actual purchase happens offline.

Building brands and maintaining a strong customer–brand relationship is not just about flashy ads. Delivering superior value and keeping the brand promise are important to a successful branding campaign.

It's your turn now to judge the role of the Internet in brand building. Visit some of the sites discussed here. What role do you think the Internet can play in brand building?

Go to: **www.mcgrawhill.ca/college/wong**
to apply this Insite in an exciting Internet exercise.

a better image of the brand. Overcoming a negative image is difficult and can be very expensive.

Brand rejection is a big concern for service-oriented businesses because it's hard to control the quality of service. A business traveller who gets a dirty room in a Hilton Hotel in Caracas, Venezuela might not return to a Hilton anywhere. Yet it's difficult for Hilton to ensure that every maid does a good job every time.

**brand nonrecognition**
When final consumers don't recognize a brand at all

Some products are seen as basically the same. **Brand nonrecognition** means final consumers don't recognize a brand at all—even though intermediaries may use the brand name for identification and inventory control. Examples include school supplies, inexpensive dinnerware, many of the items that you'd find in a hardware store, and thousands of dot-coms on the Internet.

**brand recognition**
When customers remember a brand

**Brand recognition** means that customers remember the brand. This may not seem like much, but it can be a big advantage if there are many "nothing" brands on the market. Even if consumers can't recall the brand without help, they may be reminded when they see it in a store among other less familiar brands.

**brand preference**
When target customers usually choose the brand over other brands

Most branders would like to win **brand preference**—which means that target customers usually choose the brand over other brands, perhaps because of habit or favourable past experience.

**brand insistence (brand loyalty)**
When customers insist on a firm's branded product and are willing to search for it

**Brand insistence** or **brand loyalty** means customers insist on a firm's branded product and are willing to search for it. This is an objective of many target marketers.

**Protecting Canadian trademarks and brand names** If a company is to spend resources to create a distinctive identity in the marketplace, it must be prepared to defend that distinctive identity from imitation. The law protects the owners of trademarks and brand names. Ownership of brand names and trademarks is generally established by distinctiveness and continued use.

Since the basic right is found in "use," a Canadian firm need not register its trademark under the Trademarks Act. But when a trademark is so registered, the registering firm is legally protected against any other company using a trademark that might be confused with its own. In contrast, the holder of an unregistered trademark couldn't sue a firm merely for using a similar trademark. The owner of an unregistered trademark would have to prove that some other firm was deliberately using that name to confuse consumers by "passing off" its products as those of the trademark holder.

Canadian and U.S. laws differ in the types of trademark protection they provide. There's less chance of a Canadian trade name being ruled "generic" or a common descriptive term—and therefore no longer protectable by its original owner. For example, Bayer Aspirin is still a protected trademark in Canada, even though "aspirin" has become a generic term in the United States.[14]

A brand can be a real asset to a company. Every firm should try to ensure that its brand doesn't become the generic term for its kind of product. When this happens, the brand name or trademark falls into the public domain, and the owner loses all rights to it. This happened in the United States with the names cellophane, aspirin, shredded wheat, and kerosene. Teflon, Scotch Tape, and Xerox also came close to becoming common descriptive terms there. And Miller Brewing Company tried, unsuccessfully, in the U.S. courts to protect its Lite beer by suing other brewers who wanted to use the word light.[15]

Even when products are properly registered, counterfeiters may make unauthorized copies. Many well-known brands—ranging from Levi's jeans to Rolex watches to Zantax ulcer medicine—face this problem. Counterfeiting is especially common in developing nations. In China, most videotapes and CDs are bootleg copies. Counterfeiting is big business in some countries, so efforts to stop it may meet with limited success. There are also differences in cultural values. In South Korea, for example, many people don't see counterfeiting as unethical.[16]

## Brand Decisions

There are four major brand decisions: (1) whether to brand at all, (2) the name of the brand, (3) the type of brand to use, and (4) whether the manufacturer or dealer should sponsor the brand. While these decisions will be discussed in order, note that in reality they are usually made at the same time as opposed to in specific sequence.

### Decision 1: Whether to Brand

As you will see later in this and other chapters, it costs a great deal to create and support a brand. Is it worth it? The answer depends on a large number of factors. Certainly, we can all recall brand names in areas like cars, soup, and clothing. But can you recall a brand name for file folders, bed frames, electric extension cords, or nails? As these examples suggest, it's not always easy to establish a respected brand. More importantly, one should never automatically assume that branding is right for a particular product-market.

The following conditions are favourable to successful branding:

1. The product is easy to identify by brand or trademark.
2. The product quality is the best value for the price and the quality is easy to maintain.
3. Dependable and widespread availability is possible. When customers start using a brand, they want to be able to continue using it.
4. Demand is strong enough that the market price can be high enough to make the branding effort profitable.
5. There are economies of scale. If the branding is really successful, costs should drop and profits should increase.
6. Favourable shelf locations or display space in stores will help. This is something retailers can control when they brand their own products. Producers must use aggressive salespeople to get favourable positions.

In general, these conditions are less common in less-developed economies, and that may explain why efforts to build brands in less-developed nations often fail.

### Decision 2: The Brand Name

A good brand name can help build brand familiarity. It can help tell something important about the company or its product. Exhibit 9-8 lists some characteristics of a good brand name. Some successful brand names seem to break all these rules, but many of them got started when there was less competition.

Companies that compete in international markets face a special problem in selecting brand names. A name that conveys a positive image in one language may be meaningless in another. Or, worse, it may have unintended meanings. GM's Nova car is a classic example. GM stuck with the Nova name when it introduced the car in South America. It seemed like a sensible decision, because *nova* is the Spanish word for star. However, Nova also sounds the same as the Spanish words for "no go." Consumers weren't interested in a no-go car, and sales didn't pick up until GM changed the name.[17]

**brand equity**

The value of a brand's overall strength in the market

Because it's costly to build brand recognition, some firms prefer to acquire established brands rather than try to build their own. The value of a brand to its current owner or to a firm that wants to buy it is sometimes called **brand equity**—the value of a brand's overall strength in the market. For example, brand equity is likely to be higher if many satisfied customers insist on buying the brand and if retailers are eager to stock it. That almost guarantees ongoing profits.

Traditional financial statements don't show brand equity or the future profit potential of having close relationships with a large base of satisfied customers. Per-

Exhibit 9-8 Characteristics of a good brand name.

- Short and simple
- Easy to spell and read
- Easy to recognize and remember
- Easy to pronounce
- Can be pronounced in only one way
- Can be pronounced in all languages (for international markets)
- Suggestive of product benefits
- Adaptable to packaging/labelling needs
- No undesirable imagery
- Always timely (does not become outdated)
- Adaptable to any advertising medium
- Legally available for use (not in use by another firm)

haps they should. Having that information would prompt a lot of narrow-thinking finance managers to view marketing efforts as an investment, not just as an expense.

The financial value of the Yahoo! brand name illustrates this point. In 1994, Yahoo! was just a tiny start-up trying to make it with a directory site on the Internet. Most people had never heard the name, and for that matter few even knew what the Internet was or why you'd need a directory site. As interest in the Internet grew, Yahoo! promoted its brand name, not just on the Internet but also in traditional media like TV and magazines. It was often the only website name that newcomers to the Web knew, so for many it was a good place from which to start their surfing. When they found the Yahoo! site useful, they'd tell their friends—and that generated more familiarity with the name and more hits on the site. Within a few years—even before the Internet really took off—Yahoo! was attracting 30 million different people a month and 95 million page views a day. Since Yahoo!'s original marketing plan was to make money by charging fees to advertisers eager to reach the hordes of people who visit Yahoo!'s Web pages, the familiarity of its brand translated directly into ad revenues. Because it attracted traffic and ad revenue, it could offer users more specialized content, better search capability, free e-mail, community offerings, and e-commerce. And now, in less than a decade, it's become one of the best-known brands in not only cyberspace but also the world.[18] See Marketing Demo 9-1 for a discussion of what happens when a company has to deal with negative brand recognition.

## Marketing Demo 9–1

### HOW TO BLOW OUT A RELATIONSHIP WITH CUSTOMERS

There are few brand names that are more familiar to North American consumers than Firestone and Ford Explorer. Yet in the aftermath of tread separations on tires that resulted in many rollovers and tragic deaths, the reputations of these once lofty brand names are seriously tarnished. There are millions of consumers who say that they will never again buy any tire with the Firestone name on it. The Firestone brand may not survive. The plant where many of the unsafe tires were produced has already been shut down. What automaker would buy from that plant and risk its own image and sales? Tire retailers who sell replacement tires in the consumer market face similar reactions. It's easier for them to just sell tires by Michelin, a brand that positions itself on safety benefits.

In part to protect its customers, Ford recalled millions of Firestone tires, including many designs that Firestone says are not a problem. Who should pay the cost? Unlike most of the components used in building a car, the tires are covered by a Firestone warranty, not by Ford's warranty. Responsibility is clearer in government recalls, but staff shortages at the National Highway Traffic Safety Administration contributed to delays in figuring out who was really at fault.

The long-standing relationship between Ford and Firestone is severed. Imagine how you would feel if you were Bill Ford, chairman of Ford—Firestone Tire Co. founder Harvey Firestone was his great-grandfather. That aside, questions about rollovers have eroded the brand equity of the Explorer, one of the best sellers in Ford's whole product line. Rebuilding profits won't be easy. With all the bad publicity customers are very concerned about rollover hazards. Even if a complete redesign would help reassure them, that's not an option. The new-product development process for a big change in the Explorer will take years.[19]

## Decision 3: What Type of Brand to Use

**family brand**
Using the same brand name for several products

Branders of more than one product must decide whether they are going to use a **family brand**—the same brand name for several products—or individual brands for each product. Examples of family brands are Dare food products and Fisher-Price toys.

**Family brands** The use of the same brand for many products makes sense if all are similar in type and quality. The main benefit is that the goodwill attached to one or two products may help the others. Money spent to promote the brand name benefits more than one product, which cuts promotion costs for each product. For example, P&G recently introduced a line of electric toothbrushes and tooth-whitening products under the Crest name. Family brands can also be used at the corporate level for the same purpose. For example, firms like Nokia and Caterpillar stress corporate qualities they feel apply to all of their products.

However, there are some disadvantages to using family brands. When all products carry the same name, a major problem with any one member of the family can taint the entire line. Similarly, if a customer is dissatisfied with an individual product known by a family brand, they may choose to avoid all other products in the line. For example, suppose you rented a car and found it unsatisfactory: would you rent a truck from that firm on another occasion?

**licensed brand**
A well-known brand that sellers pay a fee to use

A special kind of family brand is a **licensed brand**—a well-known brand that sellers pay a fee to use. For example, the familiar Sunkist brand name has been licensed to many companies for use on more than 400 products in 30 countries.[20]

**individual brands**
Separate brand names for each product

**Individual brands** A company uses **individual brands**—separate brand names for each product—when it's important for the products to each have a separate identity, as when products vary in quality or type.

If the products are really different, such as Elmer's glue and Borden's ice cream, individual brands can avoid confusion. Some firms use individual brands with similar products to make segmentation and positioning efforts easier. Unilever, for example, markets Aim, Close-Up, and Pepsodent toothpastes, but each involves different positioning efforts.

Sometimes firms use individual brands to encourage competition within the company. Each brand is managed by a different group within the firm. They argue that if anyone is going to take business away from their firm, it ought to be their own brand. However, many firms that once used this approach have reorganized. Faced with slower market growth, they found they had plenty of competitive pressure from

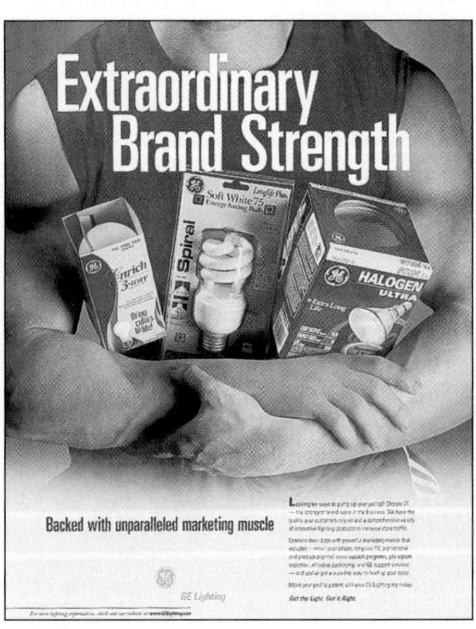


As these trade ads suggest, both Del Monte and GE want retailers to remember that many consumers already know and trust their brand names.

other firms. The internal competition just made it more difficult to coordinate different marketing strategies.[21]

**co-branding**

Combining both family and individual brand names

**Co-branding** A third option is to combine both family and individual brand names—**co-branding**. This is an attempt to gain both the efficiencies of family branding and the more contained and dedicated identity that comes from individual branding. For example, Levi's Dockers uses the association with Levi-Strauss to communicate quality and the distinction of Dockers to set this line of clothing apart from, say, blue jeans or women's wear. Other examples would include Sears's Kenmore Appliances and Sears's Craftsman Tools; Nintendo Gameboy and Nintendo Gamecube; and 3M Post-its and 3M Scotch brand tapes.

**generic products**

Products that have no brand at all other than identification of their contents and the manufacturer or intermediary

**Generic products** Products that some consumers see as commodities may be difficult or expensive to brand. Some manufacturers and intermediaries have responded to this problem with **generic products**—products that have no brand at all other than identification of their contents and the manufacturer or intermediary. Generic products are usually offered in plain packages at lower prices. They are quite common in less-developed nations.[22]

### Decision 4: Manufacturer Brands versus Dealer Brands

**manufacturer brands (national brands)**

Brands created by producers

**Manufacturer brands** are brands created by producers. These are sometimes called *national brands* because the brand is promoted all across the country or in large regions. Note, however, that many manufacturer brands are now distributed globally. Such brands include Nabisco, Campbell's, Whirlpool, Ford, and IBM. Many creators of service-oriented firms—like McDonald's, Orkin Pest Control, and Midas Muffler—promote their brands this way too.

**dealer brands (private brands)**

Brands created by intermediaries

**Dealer brands**, also called **private brands**, are brands created by intermediaries. Examples of dealer brands include the brands of Loblaw's, Home Hardware, Radio Shack, Wal-Mart, and The Bay. Some of these are advertised and distributed more widely than many national brands. For example, national TV ads have helped Cherokee Clothing (by Zellers) and Canyon River Blues (by Sears) compete with Levi's and Wrangler.

From the intermediary's perspective, the major advantage of selling a popular manufacturer brand is that the product is already presold to some target customers. Such products may bring in new customers and can encourage higher turnover with reduced selling cost. The major disadvantage is that manufacturers normally offer lower gross margins than the intermediary might be able to earn with a dealer brand. In addition, the manufacturer maintains control of the brand and may withdraw it from an intermediary at any time. Customers loyal to the brand rather than to the retailer or wholesaler may go elsewhere if the brand is not available.

Dealer branders take on more responsibility. They must promote their own product. They must be able to arrange a dependable source of supply and usually have to buy in fairly large quantities. This increases their risk and cost of carrying inventory. However, these problems are easier to overcome if the intermediary deals in a large sales volume, as is the case with many large retail chains.

**battle of the brands**

Competition between dealer brands and manufacturer brands

**The battle of the brands** The **battle of the brands**, the competition between dealer brands and manufacturer brands, is just a question of whose brands will be more popular and who will be in control.

At one time, manufacturer brands were much more popular than dealer brands. Now sales of both kinds of brands are about equal—but sales of dealer brands are expected to continue growing. Intermediaries have some advantages in this battle. With the number of large wholesalers and retail chains growing, they are better able to arrange reliable sources of supply at low cost. They can also control the point of sale and give the dealer brand special shelf position or promotion.

Consumers benefit from the battle. Competition has already narrowed price differences between manufacturer brands and well-known dealer brands. And big

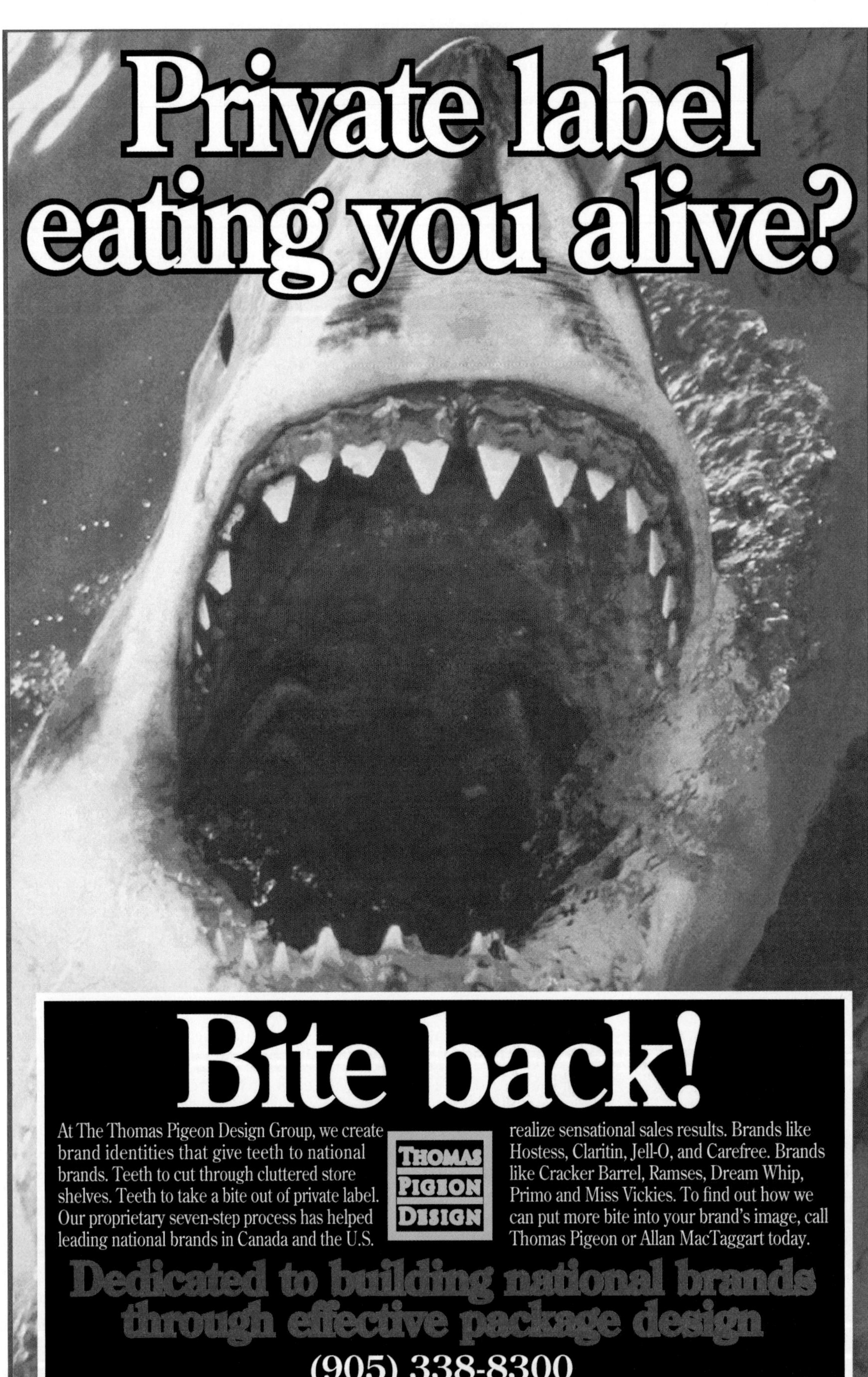

Private label eating you alive?
Bite back!
At The Thomas Pigeon Design Group, we create brand identities that give teeth to national brands. Teeth to cut through cluttered store shelves. Teeth to take a bite out of private label. Our proprietary seven-step process has helped leading national brands in Canada and the U.S. realize sensational sales results. Brands like Hostess, Claritin, Jell-O, and Carefree. Brands like Cracker Barrel, Ramses, Dream Whip, Primo and Miss Vickies. To find out how we can put more bite into your brand's image, call Thomas Pigeon or Allan MacTaggart today.
THOMAS PIGEON DESIGN
Dedicated to building national brands through effective package design
(905) 338-8300

retailers like Zellers are constantly pushing manufacturers to lower prices—because national brands at low prices bring in even more customers than store brands.[23]

## The Strategic Importance of Packaging

**packaging**
Involves promoting, protecting, and enhancing the product

**Packaging** involves promoting, protecting, and enhancing the product. Consistent with the notion of a total product, packaging can add tremendous value for a customer and seller (see Exhibit 9-9). It can make a product more convenient to use or store. It can prevent spoiling or damage. Good packaging makes products easier to identify and promotes the brand at the point of purchase and even in use.

### Packaging and Product Quality

A new package can make *the* important difference in a new marketing strategy—by meeting customers' needs better. Sometimes a new package makes the product easier to use. For example, Quaker State oil comes with a twist-off top and pouring spout to make it more convenient for customers at self-service gas stations. Similarly, many products now come in resealable plastic bags or with special spouts that allow for more precise application. Would you rather squeeze ketchup or shake it from a bottle?

Packaging also affects product safety. Most drug and food products now have special seals to prevent product tampering. Sellers of frequently handled products (like mouthwash) or products handled by young children (like peanut butter) benefited by adopting more break-resistant bottles.

Packaging can also be a means of ensuring quality control. For example, some products use dispensing mechanisms that either control or aid in controlling the amount of product used per application. This is an important capability, since for many products the application of too much or too little can lead to less than satisfactory results.

In fact, packaging can provide a source of customer satisfaction long after the product is consumed. For example, El Classico spaghetti sauce is sold in wide-mouth mason jars that many consumers reuse for other purposes.

**Exhibit 9-9** Some ways packaging benefits consumers and marketers.

| Opportunity to Add Value | Some Decision Factors | Examples |
|---|---|---|
| Promotion | Link product to promotion | The bunny on the Energizer battery package is a reminder that it "keeps going and going." |
| | Branding at point of purchase or consumption | Coke's logo greets almost everyone each time the refrigerator is opened. |
| | Product information | Kraft's nutrition label helps consumers decide which cheese to buy, and a UPC reduces checkout time and errors. |
| Protection | For shipping and storing | Sony's MP3 player is kept safe by Styrofoam inserts. |
| | From spoiling | Tylenol's safety seal prevents tampering. |
| | From shoplifting | Cardboard hang-tag on Gillette razor blades is too large to hide in hand. |
| Enhance product | The environment | Tide detergent bottle can be recycled. |
| | Convenience in use | Squeezable tube of Yoplait Go-Gurt is easy to eat on the go and in new situations. |
| | Added product functions | Plastic tub is useful for refrigerator leftovers after the Cool Whip is gone. |

### Packaging Can Support Promotional Activity

Packaging can tie the product to the rest of the marketing strategy. Packaging for Energizer batteries features the pink bunny seen in attention-getting TV ads and reminds consumers that the batteries are durable. A good package sometimes gives a firm more promotion effect than it could get with advertising. Customers see the package in stores, when they're actually buying.

### Packaging Can Lower Distribution Costs

Better protective packaging is very important to manufacturers and wholesalers. They sometimes have to pay the cost of goods damaged in shipment. Retailers need protective packaging too. It can reduce storing costs by cutting breakage, spoilage, and theft. Good packages save space and are easier to handle and display.[24]

**universal product code (UPC)**
Identifies each product with marks readable by electronic scanners

Packaging may also be a key factor in whether new technologies can be used in retailing. For example, to speed handling of fast-selling products, government and industry representatives have developed a **universal product code (UPC)** that identifies each product with marks readable by electronic scanners. A computer then matches each code to the product and its price. Supermarkets and other high-volume retailers have been eager to use these codes. They speed the check-out process and reduce the need to mark the price on every item. They also reduce errors by cashiers and make it easy to control inventory and track sales of specific products.[25]

### Socially Responsible Packaging

Some consumers say that some package designs are misleading—perhaps on purpose. Who hasn't been surprised by a candy bar half the size of the package? Others feel that the great variety of packages makes it hard to compare values. And some are concerned about whether the packages are biodegradable or can be recycled.

The task of adopting "greener" packaging isn't simple. In addition to establishing costs and benefits, simply coordinating solutions among producers, governments, and citizen organizations is an enormous task. To help Canadians identify better packaging and products, an "Ecologo" has been adopted.

## Ethical Dimensions 9–1

### ETHICAL DECISIONS REMAIN

Although various laws provide guidance on many packaging issues, many areas still require marketing managers to make ethical choices. For example, some firms have been criticized for designing packages that conceal a downsized product, giving consumers less for the money. Similarly, some retailers design packages and labels for their private-label products that look just like—and are easily confused with—manufacturer brands. Are efforts such as these unethical, or are they simply an attempt to make packaging a more effective part of a marketing mix? Different people will answer differently.

Some marketing managers promote environmentally friendly packaging on some products while simultaneously increasing the use of problematic packages on others. Empty packages now litter our streets, and some plastic packages will lie in a city dump for decades. But some consumers like the convenience that accompanies these problems. Is it unethical for a marketing manager to give consumers with different preferences a choice? Some critics argue that it is; others praise firms that give consumers a choice.

Many critics feel that labelling information is too often incomplete or misleading. Do consumers really understand the nutritional information required by law? Further, some consumers want information that is difficult—perhaps even impossible—to provide. For example, how can a label accurately describe a product's taste or texture? But the ethical issues focus on how far a marketing manager should go in putting potentially negative information on a package. For example, should Häagen-Dazs affix a label that says, "This product will clog your arteries"? That sounds extreme, but what type of information is appropriate?[26]

Food-label requirements help some consumers make healthier purchases, but many consumers don't understand or use the information.

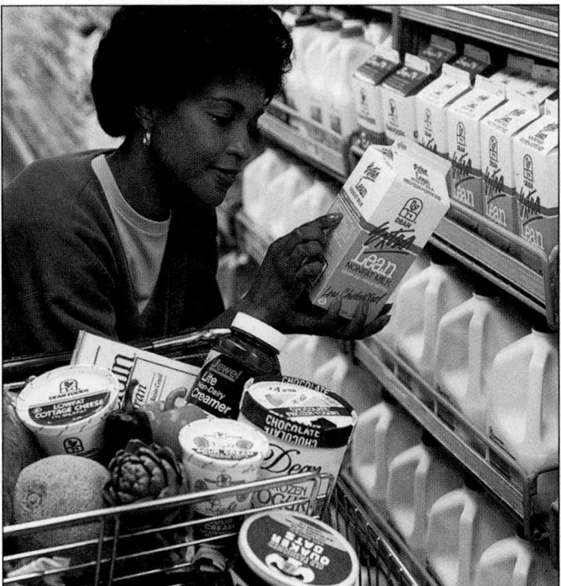

GRADE A • PASTEURIZED • HOMOGENIZED

**Nutrition Facts**
Serving Size 1 cup (240mL)
Servings Per Container 4

| **Amount Per Serving** | |
|---|---|
| **Calories** 80 | Calories from Fat 0 |
| | **% Daily Value*** |
| **Total Fat** 0g | 0% |
| Saturated Fat 0g | 0% |
| **Cholesterol** 5mg | 2% |
| **Sodium** 110mg | 5% |
| **Total Carbohydrate** 11g | 4% |
| Dietary Fiber 0g | 0% |
| Sugars 11g | |
| **Protein** 8g | 16% |

Vitamin A 10% • Vitamin C 2%
Calcium 25% • Iron 0% • Vitamin D 25%

*Percent Daily Values are based on a 2,000 calorie diet. Your daily values may be higher or lower depending on your calorie needs:

| | Calories: | 2,000 | 2,500 |
|---|---|---|---|
| Total Fat | Less than | 65g | 80g |
| Sat.Fat | Less than | 20g | 25g |
| Cholesterol | Less than | 300mg | 300mg |
| Sodium | Less than | 2,400mg | 2,400mg |
| Total Carbohydrate | | 300g | 375g |
| Dietary Fiber | | 25g | 30g |
| Protein | | 50g | 65g |

Calories per gram:
Fat 9 • Carbohydrate 4 • Protein 4

INGREDIENTS: SKIM MILK, VITAMIN A PALMITATE, AND VITAMIN $D_3$.

**Federal laws** The Hazardous Products Act gives Industry Canada the authority either to ban or to regulate the sale, distribution, and labelling of hazardous products. Since 1971, all products considered potentially hazardous (such as cleaning substances, chemicals, and aerosol products) have had to carry on their labels an appropriate symbol that reveals both the possible danger and the necessary precautions. The symbols chosen indicate whether the product is poisonous, flammable, explosive, or corrosive.

The Consumer Packaging and Labelling Act calls for bilingual labels and for the standardization of package sizes and shapes. It also requires that all food products be labelled in metric terms as well as in traditional measures. When reference is made on a label or package to the number of servings being provided, the average size of these servings must also be indicated. The term "best before" must appear in both official languages along with a date reflecting the product's durability.

Labelling requirements for certain specified products are also set forth in the National Trademark and True Labelling Act, the Textile Labelling Act, and the Precious Metals Marking Act. The Textile Care Labelling Program provides for all garments and other textiles to be labelled with washing or dry-cleaning instructions. Similarly, the CANTAG program now being widely used provides customers with performance, capacity, and energy consumption data on major appliances. See Ethical Dimensions 9-1 for a discussion of how marketers handle ethical issues that are not covered by legislation.

**unit pricing**
Placing the price per 100 grams (or some other standard measure) on or near the product

**Unit pricing** Some retailers, especially large supermarket chains, make it easier for consumers to compare packages with different weights or volumes. They use **unit pricing**—which involves placing the price per 100 grams (or some other standard measure) on or near the product. This makes price comparisons easier.[27]

## Warranties and Product Quality

**warranty**
Explains what the seller promises about its product

A **warranty** explains what the seller promises about its product. Since customer satisfaction depends on customer expectations being met, deciding on warranty policies can have significant impact on a brand's ability to gain and hold customers.

A marketing manager should decide whether to offer a specific warranty, what the warranty will cover, and how it will be communicated to target customers. In this area, the legal environment—as well as customer needs and competitive offerings—must be considered.

### Legal Issues

Both the common law and sale-of-goods legislation say that producers must stand behind their products, even if they don't offer a specific warranty. A written warranty provided by the seller may promise more than the common law provides; however, it may actually reduce the responsibility a producer would have under common law.

Provincial and federal laws attempt to see that any warranty offered is fair to the consumer, easy to understand, and precise as to what is and what isn't covered. Before this increased government concern, some firms simply said their products were "fully warranted" or "absolutely guaranteed" without either specifying a time period or spelling out the meaning of the guarantee.

On the federal level, protection against misleading warranties is provided by the Competition Act. Specifically prohibited are warranties that seem unlikely to be carried out, warranties where excessive labour or handling charges are used to cover the manufacturer's cost of allegedly replacing defective parts "free of charge," and warranties that reduce a purchaser's usual rights under common law.[28]

### Warranty Policies and the Marketing Mix

Some firms use warranties to improve the appeal of their marketing mix. They design more quality into their goods or services and offer refunds or replacement—not just repair—if there is a problem. Xerox uses this approach with its copy machines. Its three-year warranty says that a customer who is not satisfied with a copier—for any reason—can trade it for another model. This type of warranty sends a strong signal. A buyer doesn't have to worry about whether the copier will work as expected, or whether service calls will be prompt, or even whether the Xerox salesperson or dealer has recommended the appropriate model.

In a competitive market, a product warranty or a service guarantee can be a very important part of the marketing mix.

Automakers have traditionally altered warranties in response to the level of customer demand. They have changed not only the duration of the warranty but also the types of situations covered. For example, most automakers now offer some form of roadside assistance to provide towing services, battery boosts, and the like. In this way, they are no longer simply selling cars but rather a more complete solution to transportation needs.

### Service Guarantees

Customer-service guarantees are becoming more common as a way to attract and keep customers. Pizza Hut guarantees a luncheon pizza in five minutes or it's free. General Motors set up a fast-oil-change guarantee to compete with fast-lube specialists who were taking customers away from dealers. If the dealer doesn't get the job done in a time of 29 minutes or less, the next oil change is free. The Hampton Inn motel chain guarantees "100% satisfaction." All employees—even the cleaning crews—are empowered to offer an unhappy customer a discount or refund on the spot.

There's more risk in offering a service guarantee than a warranty on a physical product. An apathetic employee or a service breakdown can create a big expense. However, without the guarantee dissatisfied customers may just go away angry, without ever complaining. When customers collect on a guarantee, the company can clearly identify the problem. Then the problem can be addressed.

### Warranty Support Can Be Costly

The cost of warranty support ultimately must be covered by the price that consumers pay. This has led some firms to offer warranty choices. The basic price for a product may include a warranty that covers a short time period or that covers parts but not labour. Consumers who want more or better protection pay extra for an extended warranty or a service contract.[29]

## Chapter Summary

In this chapter, we looked at the concept of "product" very broadly. A product may not be a physical good at all. It may be a service, or it may be some combination of goods and services—like a meal at a restaurant. Most important, we saw that a firm's product is *what satisfies the needs of its target market*.

We introduced consumer-product and business-product classes and showed their effect on planning marketing mixes. Consumer product classes are based on consumers' buying behaviour. Business product classes are based on how buyers see the products and how they are used. Knowing these product classes—and learning how marketers handle specific products within these classes—will help you develop your marketing sense.

The fact that different people may see the same product in different product classes helps explain why seeming competitors may succeed with very different marketing mixes.

Branding and packaging can create new and more satisfying products. Packaging offers special opportunities to promote the product and inform customers. Variations in packaging can make a product attractive to different target markets. A specific package may have to be developed for each strategy.

Customers see brands as a guarantee of quality, and this leads to repeat purchasing. For marketers, such routine buying means lower promotion costs and higher sales.

Should companies stress branding? The decision depends on whether the costs of brand promotion and honouring the brand guarantee can be more than covered by a higher price or more rapid turnover, or both. The cost of branding may reduce pressure on the other three Ps.

Branding gives marketing managers a choice. They can add brands and use individual or family brands. In the end, however, customers express their approval or disapproval of the whole product (including the brand). The degree of brand familiarity is a measure of the marketing manager's ability to carve out a separate market. And brand familiarity affects place, price, and promotion decisions.

Warranties are also important in strategy planning. A warranty need not be strong—it just has to be clearly stated. But some customers find strong warranties attractive.

Product is concerned with much more than physical goods and services. To succeed in our increasingly competitive markets, the marketing manager must also be concerned about packaging, branding, and warranties.



## Key Concepts

## Key Concepts (continued)

individual brand, p. 262
individual product, p. 248
installations, p. 252
licensed brand, p. 262
manufacturer brand, p. 263
natural products, p. 253
new unsought products, p. 251
packaging, p. 265
product, p. 243
product assortment, p. 247
product line, p. 247
professional services, p. 255
quality, p. 244
raw materials, p. 253
regularly unsought products, p. 251
relative quality, p. 245
service, p. 245
service mark, p. 256
shopping products, p. 250
specialty products, p. 250
staples, p. 250
supplies, p. 254
trademark, p. 256
unit pricing, p. 267
universal product code (UPC), p. 266
unsought products, p. 250
warranty, p. 267

## Questions and Problems



1. Define, in your own words, what a product is.
2. Discuss several ways in which physical goods are different from pure services. Give an example of a good and then an example of a service that illustrates each of the differences.
3. What kinds of consumer products are the following: *(a)* watches, *(b)* automobiles, and *(c)* toothpastes? Explain your reasoning.
4. Consumer services tend to be intangible, and goods tend to be tangible. Use an example to explain how the lack of a physical good in a pure service might affect efforts to promote the service.
5. How would the marketing mix for a staple convenience product differ from the one for a homogeneous shopping product? How would the mix for a specialty product differ from the mix for a heterogeneous shopping product? Use examples.
6. Cite two examples of business products that require a substantial amount of service in order to be useful.
7. Explain why a new law office might want to lease furniture rather than buy it.
8. For the kinds of business products described in this chapter, complete the following table (use one or a few well-chosen words).
   a. *Kind of distribution facility(ies) needed and functions they will provide.*
   b. *Calibre of salespeople required.*
   c. *Kind of advertising required.*

| Products | 1 | 2 | 3 |
|---|---|---|---|
| Installations | | | |
| Buildings and land rights | | | |
| Major equipment | | | |
| Standard | | | |
| Custom-made | | | |
| Accessories | | | |
| Raw materials | | | |
| Farm products | | | |
| Natural products | | | |
| Components | | | |
| Supplies | | | |
| Maintenance and small operating supplies | | | |
| Operating supplies | | | |
| Professional services | | | |

9. Is there any difference between a brand name and a trademark? If so, why is this difference important?
10. Is a well-known brand valuable only to the owner of the brand?
11. List five brand names and indicate what product is associated with the brand name. Evaluate the strengths and weaknesses of the brand name.
12. Explain family brands. Should Toys"R"Us carry its own dealer brands to compete with some of the popular manufacturer brands it carries? Explain your reasons.
13. In the past, Sears emphasized its own dealer brands. Now it is carrying more well-known manufacturer brands. What are the benefits to Sears of carrying more manufacturer brands?

14. What does the degree of brand familiarity imply about previous and future promotion efforts? How does the degree of brand familiarity affect the place and price variables?
15. You operate a small hardware store with an emphasis on manufacturer brands and have barely been breaking even. Evaluate the proposal of a large wholesaler who offers a full line of dealer-branded hardware items at substantially lower prices. Specify any assumptions necessary to obtain a definite answer.
16. Give an example where packaging costs probably (*a*) lower total distribution costs and (*b*) raise total distribution costs.
17. Is it more difficult to support a warranty for a service than for a physical good? Explain your reasons.

## *Computer-Aided Problem 9*

### Branding Decision

Wholesteen Dairy, Inc. produces and sells Wholesteen-brand condensed milk to grocery retailers. The overall market for condensed milk is fairly flat, and there's sharp competition among dairies for retailers' business. Wholesteen's regular price to retailers is $8.88 a case (24 cans). FoodWorld—a fast-growing supermarket chain and Wholesteen's largest customer—buys 20,000 cases of Wholesteen's condensed milk a year. That's 20 percent of Wholesteen's total sales volume of 100,000 cases per year.

FoodWorld is proposing that Wholesteen produce private-label condensed milk to be sold with the FoodWorld brand name. FoodWorld proposes to buy the same total quantity as it does now, but it wants half (10,000 cases) with the Wholesteen brand and half with the FoodWorld brand. FoodWorld wants Wholesteen to reduce costs by using a lower-quality can for the FoodWorld brand. That change will cost Wholesteen $.01 less per can than it costs for the cans that Wholesteen uses for its own brand. FoodWorld will also provide preprinted labels with its brand name—which will save Wholesteen an additional $.02 a can.

Wholesteen spends $70,000 a year on promotion to increase familiarity with the Wholesteen brand. In addition, Wholesteen gives retailers an allowance of $.25 per case for their local advertising, which features the Wholesteen brand. FoodWorld has agreed to give up the advertising allowance for its own brand, but it is willing to pay only $7.40 a case for the milk that will be sold with the FoodWorld brand name. It will continue under the old terms for the rest of its purchases.

Sue Glick, Wholesteen's marketing manager, is considering the FoodWorld proposal. She has entered cost and revenue data on a spreadsheet so she can see more clearly how the proposal might affect revenue and profits.

a. *Based on the data in the initial spreadsheet, how will Wholesteen profits be affected if Glick accepts the FoodWorld proposal?*
b. *Glick is worried that FoodWorld will find another producer for the FoodWorld private-label milk if Wholesteen rejects the proposal. This would immediately reduce Wholesteen's annual sales by 10,000 cases; FoodWorld might even stop buying from Wholesteen altogether. What would happen to profits in these two situations?*
c. *FoodWorld is rapidly opening new stores and sells milk in every store. The FoodWorld buyer says that next year's purchases could be up to 25,000 cases of Wholesteen's condensed milk. But Sue Glick knows that FoodWorld may stop buying the Wholesteen brand and want all 25,000 cases to carry the FoodWorld private-label brand. How will this affect profit? (Hint: Enter the new quantities in the "proposal" column of the spreadsheet.)*
d. *What should Wholesteen do? Why?*



## *Suggested Cases*

To view the cases, go to www.mcgrawhill.ca/college/wong

Interested in finding out what marketing looks like in the real world? *Marketing Magazine* is just a click away on your OLC! Visit **www.mcgrawhill.ca/college/wong**.

# Chapter Ten
# Product Management and New-Product Development

When You Finish This Chapter, You Should

1. Understand how product life cycles affect strategy planning.

2. Know what is involved in designing new products and what "new products" really are.

3. Understand the new-product development process.

4. See why product liability must be considered in screening new products.

5. Understand the need for product or brand managers.

## The Evolution of the PDA Market

In today's markets, a few years can bring a lot of changes. When Palm introduced its first personal digital assistant (PDA) in the mid 1990s, it was a really new-product concept—even in the eyes of its target market of gadget-loving, on-the-go executives. It didn't do anything radical, but it did a few important things really well. It could store thousands of names and addresses, track expenses, schedule meetings and priorities, and program calculations. And it was easy to use, which helped Palm sell a million units in just the first two years. As sales growth accelerated, Palm introduced new

place price promotion prod

models with more features—like its connected organizer that could "beam" data to another Palm or a computer and even connect to e-mail anywhere anytime.

During those early years, Palm had little direct competition. Customers around the world bought 13 million PDAs in five years, and 75 percent of them were Palms. Business customers were not very price-sensitive, so without much competition Palm also enjoyed great profit margins.

Palm's marketing plan for its new m500 series (www.palm.com) was to improve graphics and power and add modular features like a digital camera and digital notepad for handwritten e-mail. While these were not big changes for the PDA market, they probably looked revolutionary to the marketing managers for DayTimer's pen-and-paper organizers, Timex's DataLink watches, HP's programmable calculators, IBM's Thinkpad laptops, and Motorola's digital pagers. The marketing managers for these products may not have seen the changes to the new m500 or the original PDA as a competitor. Yet when a firm finds a better way to meet customer needs, it disrupts old ways of doing things. And PDAs were taking business from other categories, even digital cameras.

But Palm wasn't immune to the forces of competition either. Its profits, and the growth of the PDA market, attracted rivals. Casio, IBM, Sharp, Psion, HP, and others jumped into the fray. For example, just as Palm was hoping to get growth from sales to students and other price-sensitive consumers, Handspring made big inroads with colourful, low-priced models. Similarly, Compaq's iPaq and other brands chipped away at the high end of the market with units using Microsoft's new Pocket PC operating system. Many users who wanted feature-packed PDAs with more power and better screens thought the

price
place
product
promotion

Pocket PC had benefits that Palm's system missed. As a weak economy eroded demand, price competition on high-end PDAs wiped out Palm's profit margins. It also didn't help that Palm's new-product development process hit delays. When its new model didn't come out on schedule, even loyal customers looked elsewhere.

Given the fast changes in this market environment, it's hard to know what will happen in the future or how marketing strategies may change. Soon a PDA may just be a promotional giveaway with a subscription to some service—like wireless video teleconferencing over the Internet. Or the really big market may be kids—if PDA makers build in more interactive gaming features.[1]



## In This Chapter

In this chapter we focus on developing new products and managing them over time. We begin by examining the "typical" life of a product-market. Our goal is to provide a sense of the various challenges marketing managers have to address as a product moves from introduction through decline. Those challenges should give you some insights into desirable qualities of new products. We conclude the chapter by presenting a process that offers an organized method for identifying product ideas and evaluating the presence of those qualities.

## Marketing as Things Change

Up to this point we have stressed the need to align marketing with its various environments. In brief, we have promoted the development of a marketing mix that is focused on the customer and sensitive to changes in technology, competitive practices, and the like. But suppose you developed the perfect marketing mix only to find that your customer or competition had changed: would your mix still be perfect? In other words, what happens when one or more of these environments change?

The various innovations cited in the Palm story typify the kinds of changes that occur in every product-market over time. Sometimes the main driver of change is the emergence of new technology. In the same way, cellular phones are replacing short-wave radios and CBs and making it possible for people to communicate from places where it was previously impossible. Cellular linkups over the Internet are coming on strong. Cassette tapes replaced vinyl records, and now CDs, digital minidiscs, and even VHS tapes are challenged by DVD and MP3 digital files on miniature electronic memory cards. Switchboard operators in many firms were replaced with answering machines, and then answering machines lost ground to voicemail services. "Video messaging" over the Internet is now beginning to replace voicemail.

In other instances the driver of change could be new competition that finds an innovative variation on the existing product-market offerings—Wal-Mart did it in retailing, and Apple did it in personal computing. In still other instances, changes in customer characteristics, tastes, or preferences can be the driving force for change. Some of the change in customer characteristics is inevitable: for example, the migration of buyers from first-time to repeat purchasers occurs in any successful market. On other occasions it may be stimulated by external factors. For example, growing public interest in the environment brought about major changes in the packaging and printing business and the maturation of post-war baby boomers led to the design and introduction of new versions of existing products or services.

Whatever the causes, marketing managers must find a way of adapting marketing programs to the "new" environments created by changes in technology, markets, and competition. Fortunately, concepts like the product life cycle can help prepare us for these changes by informing us of the typical events in the lifetime of every product-market.

## An Overview of the Product Life Cycle

Just as we expect a human to have different characteristics at different stages in life, so too do we expect product-markets to experience a kind of evolutionary process. In some instances, the process can unfold over several years. In other areas, such as high-technology products, the process can take as little as a few months.

Why is this important? Imagine yourself as a doctor examining a 20-year-old and a senior citizen to see if they are in good health. Would you expect them to have similar scores on health tests? Would you interpret their aches and pains the same way? Would you encourage them to undertake an equally strenuous exercise regimen? Just as a doctor would alter her expectations and prescriptions for patients at different life stages, marketers must temper their expectations and actions as products move through their life cycle.

As you will see, customers' attitudes and needs change over the product life cycle. In fact, the product may be aimed at entirely different target markets at different stages. The nature of competition also changes, shifting toward pure competition or oligopoly.

In addition, total sales of a product by all competitors in the industry vary in each of its four stages. They move from very low (in the market introduction stage), to high (at market maturity), and then back to low in the sales decline stage. More important, the profit picture changes, too. These general relationships can be seen in Exhibit 10-1. Note that sales and profits do not move together over time. Industry profits decline, while industry sales are still rising.[2]

Naturally, marketers must respond to these changes. Those who choose to simply react to, as opposed to plan for, such changes may find their marketing programs out of synch with their target markets.

**product life cycle**
The stages a new-product idea goes through from beginning to end

The **product life cycle** describes the stages a new-product idea goes through from beginning to end. The product life cycle is divided into four main stages: (1) market introduction, (2) market growth, (3) market maturity, and (4) sales decline. Note that we talk about a new-product idea as opposed to any one brand or prod-

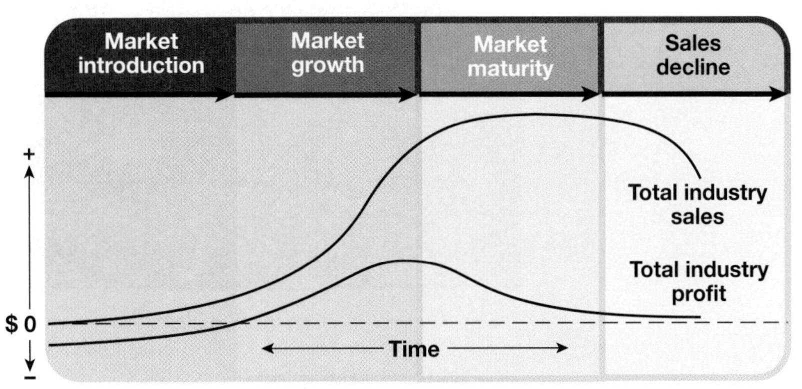


Exhibit 10-1
Typical life cycle of a new-product concept.

uct offering: the product life cycle is concerned with new types (or categories) of product in the market, not just what happens to an individual brand.

## Stage 1—Market Introduction

**market introduction**

The product life cycle stage when sales usually are low as a new idea is first introduced to a market

In the **market introduction** stage, sales usually are low as a new idea is first introduced to a market. Customers aren't looking for the product. They don't even know about it. Companies may need to spend considerable amounts on informative promotion in order to tell potential customers about the benefits and uses of the new-product concept.

But promotion alone isn't enough. Even though a firm promotes its new product, it takes time for customers to learn that the product is available and where they can find it. They may need to learn how to use the new product. In the case of organizational buying, time may be needed to allow for a more thorough evaluation of the new offering. Not surprisingly, sellers must spend a large amount of money on promotion, product, and place development to overcome these problems. However, with sales remaining low until these programs take effect, this means that most companies experience losses during the introduction stage.

## Stage 2—Market Growth

**market growth**

The product life cycle stage when industry sales grow fast and industry profits rise but then start falling

In the **market growth** stage, industry sales grow fast, and industry profits rise but then start falling. The innovator begins to make big profits as more and more customers buy. But competitors see the opportunity and enter the market. Some just copy the most successful product or try to improve it to compete better. Others try to refine their offerings to do a better job of appealing to some target markets. The new entries result in much greater product variety. However, for the innovator the result is a loss of monopoly position: suddenly it is no longer enough to have the new product, they must have it in a form that offers competitive advantage.

This can be the time of biggest profits for the industry. But it is also when industry profits begin to decline as competition increases and, in response to the availability of product variations and greater customer experience in using the prod-

The challenge of maintaining differentiation in mature markets often requires that we augment the core product to provide new kinds of benefits and to get new users to try our product. How do you think this promotion achieves both goals?

uct, the market begins to fragment into submarkets or segments (see Chapter 3 for a discussion of the implications of segmentation).

Some firms make big strategic planning mistakes at this stage by not understanding the product life cycle. They see the big sales and profit opportunities of the early market growth stage but ignore the competition that will soon follow. As a result, they continue to sell on a "one size fits all" approach while competitors focus on customizing products for particular market segments. By the time they realize their mistake, it may be too late. This happened with many dot-coms during the late 1990s. Marketing managers who pay attention to competitor analysis are less likely to encounter this problem.

### Stage 3—Market Maturity

**market maturity**

The product life cycle stage when industry sales level off as the pool of potential users is exhausted

During the **market maturity** stage, industry sales level off as the pool of potential users is exhausted. At the same time, aggressive competitors have usually entered the race for profits. And, in contrast to the growth stage (where every competitor could grow by cultivating new users), firms seeking to grow under these conditions have little choice but to steal customers away from competitors. Consequently, industry profits go down throughout the market maturity stage because promotion costs rise, and because some competitors cut prices to attract business. Less efficient firms can't compete with this pressure, and drop out of the market. This process is often termed "the industry shakeout."

New firms may still enter the market at this stage, increasing competition even more. Note that late entries skip the early life-cycle stages, including the profitable market-growth stage. And they must try to take a share of the saturated market from established firms, which is difficult and expensive. Satisfied customers who are happy with their current relationship typically won't be interested in switching to a new brand unless it offers a significantly lower price or substantially better quality.

Persuasive promotion becomes more important during the market maturity stage. Products may differ only slightly if at all. Most competitors have discovered the most effective appeals, or quickly copied the leaders. The various products become almost the same in the minds of potential consumers.

In Canada, the markets for most cars, boats, television sets, and many household appliances are in market maturity. This stage may continue for many years, until a basically new product idea comes along—even though individual brands or models come and go. For example, high-definition digital TV (HDTV) is coming on now, and over time it will make obsolete not only the old-style TVs but also the broadcast systems on which they rely.[3]

### Stage 4—Sales Decline

**sales decline**

The product life cycle stage when new products replace the old

During the **sales decline** stage, new products replace the old. Price competition from dying products becomes more vigorous, but firms with strong brands may make profits until the end because they successfully differentiated their products. In addition, they may keep some sales by appealing to the most loyal customers or to those who are slow to try new ideas. These buyers may switch later, smoothing the sales decline.

## Planning for Different Stages of the Product Life Cycle

The stages of the product life cycle tell us a great deal about the environment facing a business at different points in time. Since a marketing mix is a response to that environment, it also tells us a great deal about the kinds of marketing policies and programs that will be needed. Exhibit 10-2 shows the relationship of the product life cycle to the marketing-mix variables. The technical terms in this fig-

Exhibit 10-2
Typical changes in marketing variables over the product life cycle.

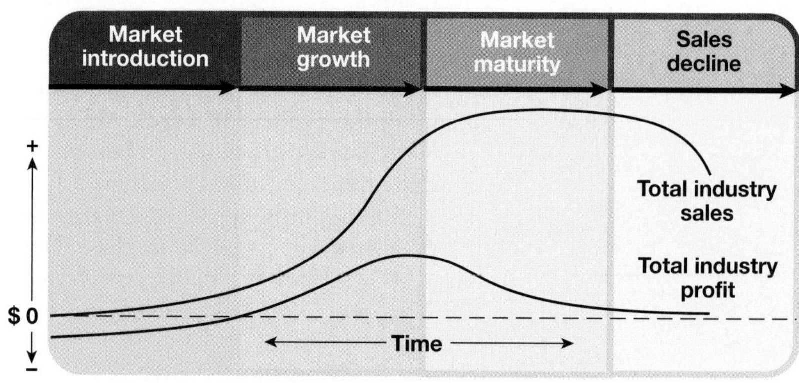


| | Market introduction | Market growth | Market maturity | Sales decline |
|---|---|---|---|---|
| **Competitive situation** | Monopoly or monopolistic competition | Monopolistic competition or oligopoly | Monopolistic competition or oligopoly heading toward pure competition → | → |
| **Product** | One or few | Variety—try to find best product<br>Build brand familiarity | All "same"<br>Battle of brands | Some drop out |
| **Place** | Build channels<br>Maybe selective distribution → | | Move toward more intensive distribution → | |
| **Promotion** | Build primary demand<br>Pioneering-informing | Build selective demand →<br>Informing/Persuading → Persuading/Reminding (frantically competitive) | | |
| **Price** | Skimming or penetration | Meet competition (especially in oligopoly) →<br>or<br>Price dealing and price cutting → | | |



ure are discussed later in the book: for now, the important thing to know is that companies need to adjust to these changing conditions. Here are some of the issues that arise.

## Managing Market Introduction

Perhaps the most significant thing about market introduction is the large number of activities and resources required to develop a new product. Even if the product is unique, this doesn't mean that everyone will immediately come running to the producer's door. As we discussed in the last section, there are many reasons why a new product might receive a less than enthusiastic welcome by customers.

But not all customers will see the product the same way. Some may see it as having a significant advantage; others may not. Some may see it as compatible with their values; others may not. Some will see it as complex to adopt; others may not. And so on. As a result, managers must be careful to try to identify which accounts or segments of the market are most likely to give the product a warm reception. These "initiators" or "early adopters" are vital to the product's success: if the product cannot convert these buyers, the likelihood of its being purchased by less enthusiastic buyers is very small. (Internet Insite 10-1 shows how firms are using information technology not only to uncover customer reactions but also to speed up the entire new-product development process and reduce time-to-market.)

# Internet Insite 10–1

## VIRTUAL NEW-PRODUCT DEVELOPMENT

In many industries and product categories the rate of obsolescence has increased, which means product life cycles are shorter now. Consumer electronics, cell phones and PDAs, computers and software are some categories where competing firms try to outwit each other with rapid introduction of new technology. Such competition forces firms to find ways to reduce time-to-market (i.e., the time it takes from idea generation to commercialization). Products must be developed quickly and brought to market faster than before. Here is where the Internet is increasingly playing a vital role.

Large multinationals such as Hewlett Packard, AT&T, Ford, and Microsoft have employees in many countries who contribute to new-product development efforts. The Internet connects members of the product development team who may be physically located in different countries. Members of the design team can share virtual models of the product, data, and computer design tools and work collaboratively.

New-product development is a cross-functional activity that includes design engineers, manufacturing specialists, marketers, and many others. The Internet not only improves intra-company communication among such a diverse group, but also can be used to improve communication with suppliers and partners during the product development phase. Automobile companies, for instance, depend on many suppliers for components. New-car design, therefore, should include design engineers from supply firms. Suppliers can provide input on what is feasible and what is not. Collaborative product development (CPD) tools and groupware applications are used to coordinate design information and processes within and among different groups, such as engineers, manufacturing specialists, partners, and sourcing and procurement agents.

These tools can create collaborative teams with engineers in different buildings, cities, or countries. CPD tools allow for visualization, where images of the product in development can be seen by everyone and real-time modifications can be made.[4] A survey of design engineers found that 28 percent of engineers use the Internet to collaborate with other engineering colleagues, and 28 percent share design and test data with other engineers.[5]

The Internet also allows firms to include the consumer in the product development activity. Software firms often release beta versions of the software to get feedback for end users. Expert users will identify bugs and limitations, which can be rectified before the final release. By obtaining consumer feedback at this early stage, firms can save money and can offer consumers a better product in the end. Many companies use the Internet to test new concepts before committing resources to further development of the product.

Polaroid is one such company that has designed a successful product based on consumer input. The company asked several hundred consumers to visit a private online research site and indicate their ideal i-Zone and the features they most valued. The overwhelming consumer response was that they saw i-Zone as a fashion accessory and wanted cool styles. This was very different from the design engineers' initial conception of the product, which was very technical and expensive. The Internet allowed Polaroid to avoid a costly mistake. Instead, in i-Zone Polaroid has a successful new product

The case of i-Zone amplifies the importance of seeking customer feedback at the idea-generation stage. Other firms like Microsoft and Netscape use customer feedback to improve products that are already in development. The famous Netscape browser has greatly benefited from feedback from expert users of its beta releases. Software companies release products that may still have a few flaws to get feedback from users who may use the product in a variety of settings. In addition to consumer research, the Web also allows firms to learn about new-product launches by competitors and new-technology development in related fields. Patents filed by competitors are available online (see www.uspto.gov), which can be valuable competitive intelligence. Industry leaders can turn this around and use the Web to send market signals on where the industry may be headed.

Many companies also use the Internet as part of the market launch campaign. While mass media, such as television, are more effective in creating product awareness, the Internet can be a vital part of the media mix at this stage. For instance, Citibank uses popular portals in its advertising campaign for new services. Apple, Microsoft, Toyota, BMW, and many other firms use their websites to provide information and educate consumers about new products. Pepsi and Coca-Cola used specially designed websites to complement their television campaigns for their Pepsi Vanilla (www.pepsivanilla.com) and Vanilla Coke (www.vanillacoke.com), respectively.

In addition to using the Web to create awareness, many companies use the Web to offer customer support, which is critical for new-product success. If the technology in a new product is very new, customer support assumes greater importance. Companies like Cisco and Gables Engineering (a firm that makes products for the aviation industry) use the Web to offer customer support.

From initial idea generation to product design, test marketing and market launch, the Internet can play a vital role in the new-product development process. When time-to-market is critical and the cost of failure very high, it does make sense to incorporate Internet-based technologies and tools.

Here are some questions to ponder: Are there any risks in seeking consumer input in the early stages of product development? How can firms prevent disclosure of too much information to competitors while continuing to engage consumers in the new-product development process?

Go to: **www.mcgrawhill.ca/college/wong** to apply this Insite in an exciting Internet exercise.

In addition, to build a base of customers the firm will have to build channels of distribution. This may not seem like a difficult task, but retailers and wholesalers must be convinced that carrying the new, untested product offers the potential for higher profits. In order to convince them to take the risk, the firm may need to offer special incentives to trade. Moreover, if the product is very different from anything else available, the seller and intermediary may need to work together to find the best way to merchandise the offering. Needless to say, all of these activities can dramatically increase marketing costs.

Promotion is needed to build demand for the whole idea, not just to sell a specific brand. In some instances, promotions may involve special activities to generate consumer trial. For example, the firm may use samples and in-store demonstrations to provide customers with a low-cost means of trying the product. They might sponsor events or conduct clinics and other forums to educate customers. Some firms also run cross-promotions with more established products that seem to be selling to the same target customer. In many business markets, especially in the high-technology arena, promotion may also involve intensive public-relations activity aimed at securing the recommendation of product reviewers.

Prices at this stage can range from very high to very low. Because promotion activity is expensive, it may lead the marketing manager to try to "skim" the market, charging a relatively high price to help pay for the introductory costs and to finance ongoing research in product development. Pricing under a skim approach may seem to limit the number of potential buyers. However, the greater margin it extracts can more than compensate for the loss of sales.

Alternatively, a manager might charge a low initial price in an effort to develop loyal customers early and keep competitors out. This is called "penetration" pricing. We'll discuss the reasons for adopting a skim versus penetration strategy in more detail in Chapter 17. At this point, the important thing to understand is that the correct strategy depends on how quickly the new idea will be accepted by customers, how quickly competitors will follow with their own products, and whether the firm is flexible enough to change its strategy as the life cycle moves on.

**Why pioneers might encourage competitive entry** Sometimes it's not in the best interests of the market pioneer for competitors to stay out of the market. This may seem odd. But building customer interest in a really new product idea—and obtaining distribution to make the product available—can be too big a job for a single company, especially a small one with limited resources. Two or more companies investing in promotion to build demand may help to stimulate the growth of the whole product-market. Similarly, a new product that is unique may languish if it is not compatible with other products that customers rely on. This is what recently happened with Digital Video Express (Divx) video disks. When Divx came out, many consumer-electronics makers, retailers, and film studios were struggling to launch DVD-format products. Divx had a number of advantages over DVD, but it was not compatible with many of the ordinary DVD players that were already on the market. Video-rental stores didn't want to stock movies for both DVD and Divx, and consumers didn't want to get stuck with Divx players if movies were not available. So, as DVD started to sizzle, Divx fizzled.[6]

**Timing the launch is critical** Not all new-product ideas catch on. But the success that eludes a firm with its initial strategy can sometimes be achieved by modifying the strategy. Videodisc players illustrate this point. They were a flop during their initial introduction in the home-entertainment market. Consumers didn't see any advantage over cheaper videotape players. But then new opportunities developed. For example, the business market for these systems grew because firms used them for sales presentations and for in-store selling. Customers could shop for products by viewing pictures at a video kiosk. Of course, change marches on. CD-ROM took over much of this market when computer manufacturers added a

CD drive as a standard feature. And now DVD has the advantage, because it can handle even more video on one disk.[7]

Also relevant is how quickly the firm can change its strategy as the life cycle moves on. Some firms are very flexible. They can compete effectively with larger, less adaptable competitors by adjusting their strategies more frequently.

## Managing Mature Products

There is a major shift that occurs as a product moves into the mature stage of its life cycle. By this time, most everyone who is a potential buyer of the product has bought it at least once. Those who remain, the "laggards," tend to be both relatively disinterested in the product and price-sensitive.

As the pool of first-time buyers disappears, competition is directed at repeat buyers. Marketing programs must be prepared for changes that can occur in buyers' preferences once they become more experienced users. Moreover, because overall industry demand may no longer be growing, the battle for market share heats up. Suddenly, one competitor's growth is another competitor's loss.

As competitive activity becomes more intense, prices start to fall and marketing spending may increase dramatically: as a result, overall industry profits start to decline. Top managers must realize this, or they will continue to expect the attractive profits of the market growth stage—profits that are no longer possible. They may set impossible goals for the marketing department, causing marketing managers to think about deceptive advertising or some other desperate attempt to reach impossible objectives.

In this stage of increased competitive activity, firms that lack competitive advantage may find their very existence threatened. The firm can no longer expect to benefit from a growth in overall demand. As the pie stops growing, each competitor must stake out a claim if it wishes to hold on to its piece. This is a time of great turbulence—but also a time when marketing can make some of its most important contributions to the organization.

It should be noted that at this stage even a small advantage can make a big difference—and some firms do very well by carefully managing their maturing products. They are able to capitalize on a slightly better product or perhaps lower production and/or marketing costs. Or they are simply more successful at promotion—allowing them to differentiate their more or less homogeneous product from competitors. For example, graham crackers were competing in a mature market and sales were flat. Nabisco used the same ingredients to create bite-sized Teddy Grahams and then promoted them heavily. These changes captured new sales and profits for Nabisco. However, competing firms quickly copied this idea with their own brands.[8]

As the pool of first-time buyers dries up, sales growth depends on the amount of product used per buyer: this can increase by increasing the number of usage occasions or the amount used per occasion. For example, cheese processors have run campaigns suggesting consumers "take their cheese out of the fridge more often." However, it may come to pass that the firm will need to look to new product-markets as their source of growth. We discussed this in Chapter 3 when we covered product development (improving a product or developing an innovative new product for the same market) and market development (marketing the product to a new market). For example, it might find a market in a country where the life cycle is not so far along, or it might try to serve a new need. Or the firm can withdraw the product before it completes the cycle and refocus on better opportunities (see Exhibit 10-3). Some examples of each will show that, even at maturity, marketing success involves a constant exercise of innovation.

**Product improvement** When a firm's product has won loyal customers it can be successful for a long time, even in a mature or declining market. However, continued improvements may be needed to keep customers satisfied, especially if their

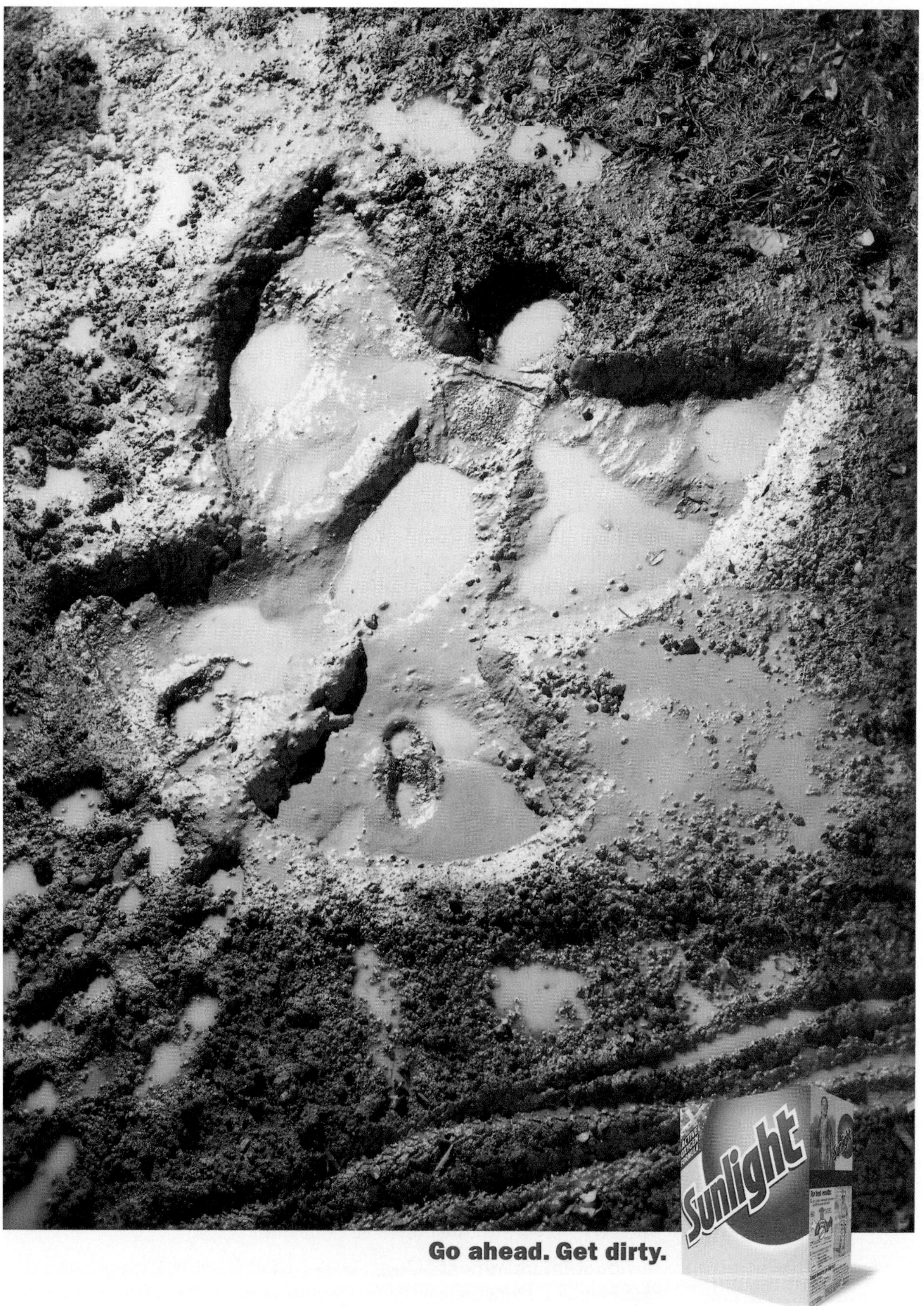


This ad is from a campaign that won the Gold Medal at the 1999 Cassies (Canadian Advertising Success Stories). In a very mature and competitive market, Sunlight was able to dramatically increase its sales without resorting to heavy price promotion: in fact, it had a small price increase.

Exhibit 10-3
Examples of three marketing strategy choices for a firm in a mature product-market.

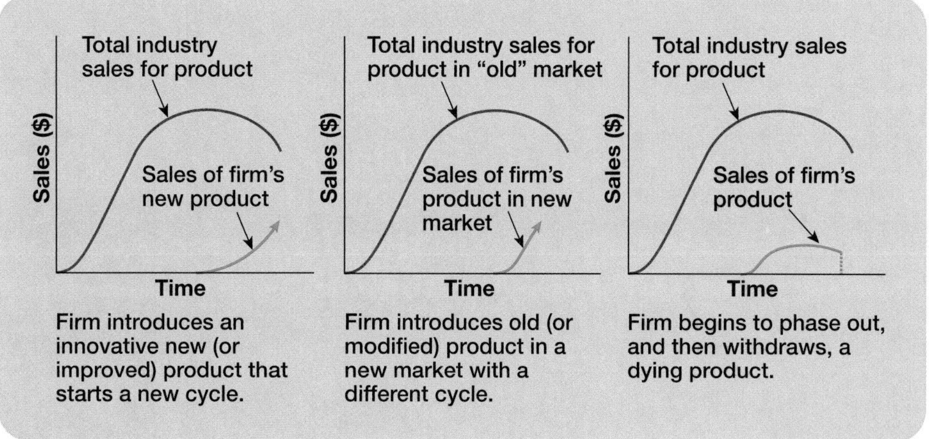


needs shift. An outstanding example is Procter & Gamble's Tide. Introduced in 1947, this powdered detergent gave consumers a much cleaner wash than they were able to get before because it did away with soap film. Tide led to a whole new generation of powdered laundry products that cleaned better with fewer suds. The demands on Tide continue to change because of new washing machines and fabrics—so the powdered Tide sold today is much different than the one sold in 1947. In fact, powdered Tide has had at least 55 (sometimes subtle) modifications.

Do product modifications—like those made with powdered Tide—create a wholly new product that should have its own product life cycle? Or are they technical adjustments of the original product idea? We will take the latter position—focusing on the product idea rather than changes in features. This means that some of these Tide changes were made in the market maturity stage. But this type of product improvement can help to extend the product life cycle.

On the other hand, a firm that develops an innovative new product may move to a new product life cycle. For example, by 1985 new liquid detergents like Wisk were moving into the growth stage, and sales of powdered detergents were declining. To share in the growth-stage profits for liquid detergents and to offset the loss of customers from powdered Tide, Procter & Gamble introduced Liquid Tide. Then, in 1997, P&G introduced Tide HE High Efficiency Laundry Detergent. It was the first detergent designed specifically to work with a new type of washing machine

A new product idea gives birth to lots of new products, so the idea is important.

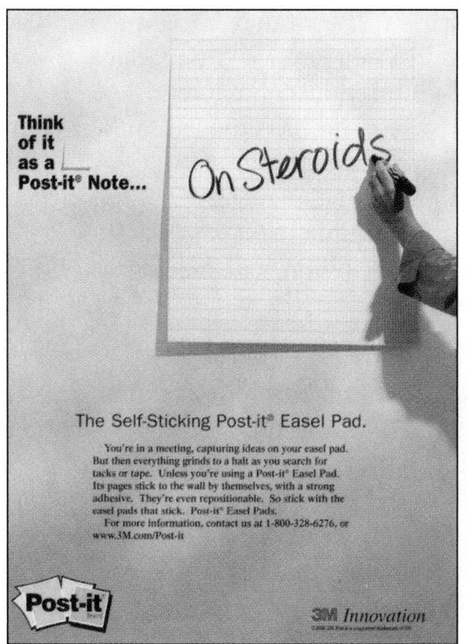


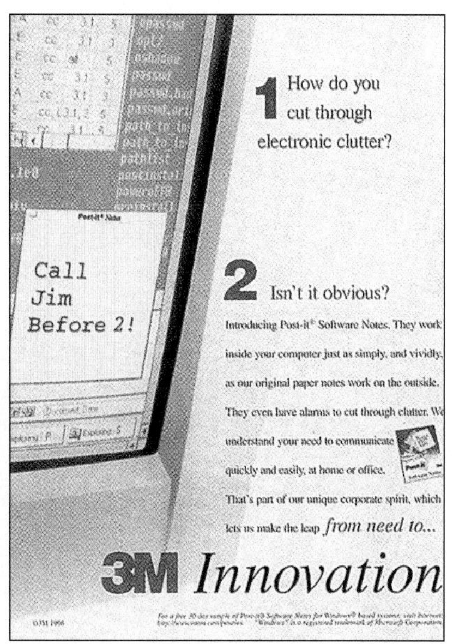

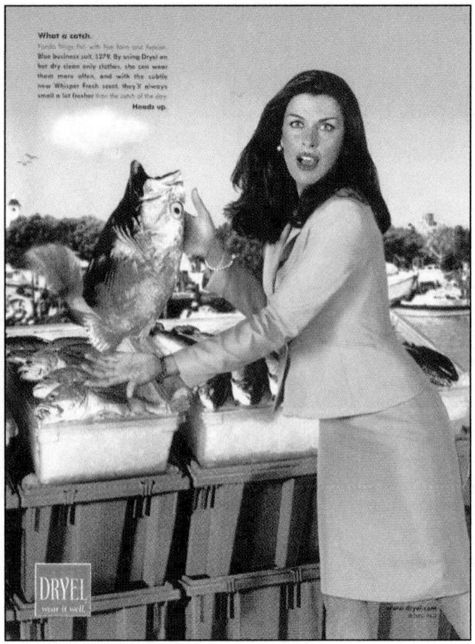


Tide detergent has been improved many times over the years, and now has a new WearCare formula that helps protect cotton threads from damage. By contrast, Dryel is a completely new type of product, and being able to dry clean delicate clothes at home is a new idea.



that is just now starting to appear in stores. These environmentally friendly front loaders use up to 40 percent less water per wash and more than 50 percent less electricity than regular washers. Regular detergents don't work in these washers because they do too much sudsing, but Tide HE is designed to be a low-suds solution. Although P&G used the familiar Tide brand name on both Liquid Tide and Tide HE, they appear to be different product concepts that compete in different product-markets. Traditional liquid detergent is probably now entering the market maturity stage, and Tide HE is probably just starting the growth stage.

Even though regular powdered detergents in general appear to be in the decline stage, traditional powdered Tide continues to sell well because it still does the job for some consumers. But sales growth is likely to come from liquid detergents and the new low-suds detergents.[9]

**Pursuing new markets** We already highlighted the fact that the same product may be in different life-cycle stages in different markets. That means that a firm may have to pursue very different strategies for a product at the same time in different markets.

In a mature market, a firm may be fighting to keep or increase its market share. But if the firm finds a new use for the product, it may need to try to stimulate overall demand. DuPont's Teflon fluorocarbon resin is a good example. It was developed more than 50 years ago and has enjoyed sales growth as a nonstick coating for cookware, as an insulation for aircraft wiring, and as a lining for chemically resistant equipment. But marketing managers for Teflon are not waiting to be stuck with declining profits in those mature markets. They are constantly developing strategies for new markets where Teflon will meet needs. For example, Teflon is now selling well as a special coating for the wires used in high-speed communications between computers.[10]

**Phasing-out strategies** Not all strategies have to be exciting growth strategies. If prospects are poor in some product-market, a phase-out strategy may be needed. The need for phasing out becomes more obvious as the sales decline stage arrives. But even in market maturity, it may be clear that a particular product is not going to be profitable enough to reach the company's objectives using the current strategy. Then the wisest move may be to develop a strategy that helps the firm phase out of the product-market—perhaps over several years.

Marketing plans are implemented as ongoing strategies. Salespeople make calls, inventory moves in the channel, advertising is scheduled for several months into the future, and so on. So the firm usually experiences losses if managers end a plan too abruptly. Because of this, it's sometimes better to phase out the product gradually. Managers order materials more selectively so production can end with a minimum of unused inventory and they shift salespeople to other jobs. They may cancel advertising and other promotion efforts more quickly since there's no point in promoting for the long run. These various actions obviously affect morale within the company—and they may cause intermediaries to pull back, too. So the company may have to offer price inducements in the channels. Employees should be told that a phase-out strategy is being implemented—and hopefully they can be shifted to other jobs as the plan is completed.

Obviously, there are some difficult implementation problems here. But phase-out is also a strategy—and it must be market-oriented to cut losses. In fact, it is possible to milk a dying product for some time if competitors move out more quickly. This situation occurs when there is still ongoing (though declining) demand and some customers are willing to pay attractive prices to get their old favourite.

## Important Considerations in Using Product Life Cycles

With so much that's known about how life cycles unfold, one could wonder how marketers could ever make a mistake. However, just as a person's age is not a perfect indicator of their physical state or their interests, life cycles represent general tendencies. Before applying the product life cycle in a planning exercise, there are some important qualifications that should be noted.

### Individual Brands May Not Follow the Pattern

Firms wishing to determine the life-cycle stage of their products may be tempted to review their sales history. However, it is important to remember that product life cycles describe industry sales and profits for a *product idea* within a particular product-market. The sales and profits of an individual product or brand may not, and often do not, follow the life-cycle pattern. They may vary up and down throughout the life cycle—sometimes moving in the opposite direction of industry sales and profits. Further, a product idea may be in a different life-cycle stage in different markets.

One reason is that a given firm may introduce or withdraw a specific product during any stage of the product life cycle. A "me-too" brand introduced during the market growth stage, for example, may never get any sales at all and suffer a quick death. Or it may reach its peak and start to decline even before the market maturity stage begins. Market leaders may enjoy high profits during the market maturity stage—even though industry profits are declining. Weaker products, on the other hand, may not earn a profit during any stage of the product life cycle. Sometimes the innovator brand loses so much in the introduction stage that it has to drop out just as others are reaping big profits in the growth stage.

A second reason why individual brands may not seem to follow a life cycle is that much of how we see product life cycles depends on how broadly we define a product-market. For example, about 91 percent of all Canadian households own microwave ovens.[11] Although microwave ovens appear to be at the market maturity stage here, in many other countries they're still early in the growth stage. Even in European countries like Switzerland, Denmark, Italy, and Spain, fewer than 20 percent of all households own microwave ovens. As this example suggests, a firm with a mature product can sometimes turn back the clock by focusing on new growth opportunities in international markets.

Marketing managers for Kellogg and Nabisco have found many opportunities for new growth in international markets.



How broadly we define the needs of customers in a product-market also affects who we see as competitors. For example, consider the set of consumer needs related to storing and preparing foods. Wax paper sales started to decline when Dow introduced Saran Wrap. Then sales of Saran Wrap (and other similar products) fell sharply when small plastic storage bags became popular. However, sales picked up again by the end of the decade. The product didn't change, but customers' needs did. Saran Wrap filled a new need—a wrap that would work well in microwave cooking. In the last few years, resealable bags like those from Ziploc have taken over because they can be used in both the freezer and the microwave.

If a market is defined broadly, there may be many competitors—and the market may appear to be in market maturity. On the other hand, if we focus on a narrow submarket—and a particular way of satisfying specific needs—then we may see much shorter product life cycles as improved product ideas come along to replace the old.

Strategy planners who naively expect sales of an individual product to follow the general product life-cycle pattern are likely to be rudely surprised. In fact, it might be more sensible to think in terms of "product-market life cycles" rather than product life cycles—but we will use the term *product life cycle* because it is commonly accepted and widely used.

## Product Life Cycles Vary in Length

How long a whole product life cycle takes—and the length of each stage—varies a lot across products. The cycle may vary from 90 days—in the case of toys like the Ghostbusters line—to possibly 100 years for gas-powered cars.

The product life-cycle concept does not tell a manager precisely *how long* the cycle will last. But a manager can often make a good guess based on the life cycle for similar products. Sometimes marketing research can help too. However, it is more important to expect and plan for the different stages than to know the precise length of each cycle.

**Fast-moving products** A new-product idea will move through the early stages of the life cycle more quickly when it has certain characteristics. For example, the greater the comparative advantage of a new product over those already on the market, the more rapidly its sales will grow. Sales growth is also faster when the product is easy to use and if its advantages are easy to communicate. If the product can be tried on a limited basis—without a lot of risk to the customer—it can usually be introduced more quickly. Finally, if the product is compatible with the values and experiences of target customers, they are likely to buy it more quickly.

The fast adoption of the Netscape Navigator Web browser is a good example. Netscape offered real benefits. The Internet had been around for a while, but it was used by very few people because it was hard to access. Compared to existing ways for computers to communicate on the Internet, Navigator was easy to use and it worked as well with pictures as data. It also offered a simple way to customize to the user's preferences. Free online downloads of the software made it easy for consumers to try the product. And Navigator worked like other Windows software that users already knew, so it was easy to install and learn—and it was compatible with their computers and how they were working. Most of the initial growth, however, was in the U.S. In less-developed countries where personal computers were less common and where there were fewer computer networks, Navigator did not initially have the same comparative advantages.[12]

### Product Life Cycles Are Getting Shorter

Although the life of different products varies, in general product life cycles are getting shorter. This is partly due to rapidly changing technology. One new invention may make possible many new products that replace old ones. Tiny electronic microchips led to hundreds of new products—from Texas Instruments calculators and Pulsar digital watches in the early days to microchip-controlled heart valves, colour fax machines, and wireless Internet devices such as the Palm now.

Some markets move quickly to market maturity—if there are fast copiers. In the highly competitive grocery products industry, cycles are down to 12 to 18 months for really new ideas. Simple variations on a new idea may have even shorter life cycles. Competitors sometimes copy flavour or packaging changes in a matter of weeks or months.

Patents for a new product may not be much protection in slowing down competitors. Competitors can often find ways to copy the product idea without violating a specific patent. Worse, some firms find out that an unethical competitor simply disregarded the patent protection. Patent violations by foreign competitors are very common. A product's life may be over before a case can get through patent-court bottlenecks. By then, the copycat competitor may even be out of business. These problems are even more severe in international cases because different governments, rules, and court systems are involved. The patent system, in Canada and internationally, needs significant improvement if it is to really protect firms that develop innovative ideas.[13]

Although life cycles are moving faster in the advanced economies, keep in mind that many advances bypass most consumers in less-developed economies. These consumers struggle at the subsistence level, without an effective macro-marketing system to stimulate innovation. However, some of the innovations and economies of scale made possible in the advanced societies do trickle down to benefit these consumers. Inexpensive antibiotics and drought-resistant plants, for example, are making a life-or-death difference.

### The Special Case of Fashions and Fads

**fashion**
The currently accepted or popular style

The sales of some products are influenced by **fashion**—the currently accepted or popular style. Fashion-related products tend to have short life cycles. What is currently popular can shift rapidly. A certain colour or style of clothing—baggy jeans, miniskirts, or four-inch-wide ties—may be in fashion one season and outdated the next. Marketing managers who work with fashions often have to make really fast product changes.

How fast is fast enough? Zara, a women's fashion retailer based in Spain, takes only about two weeks to go from a new fashion concept to having items on the racks of its stores. Zara's market-watching designers get a constant flow of new fashion ideas from music videos, what celebrities are wearing, fashion shows, and magazines—even trendy restaurants and bars. Zara quickly produces just enough of a design to test the waters and then sends it out for overnight delivery to some of its 449 stores around the world. Stores track consumer preferences every day through point-of-sale computers. Designers may not even wait for online summaries at the end of the day. They are in constant touch with store managers by phone to get an early take on what's selling and where. If an item is hot, more is produced and shipped. Otherwise it's dropped. Stores get deliveries several times a week. With this system items are rarely on the shelves of Zara stores for more than a week or two. As a result, there is almost no inventory—which helps Zara keep prices down relative to many of its fashion competitors.[14]

It's not really clear why a particular fashion becomes popular. Most present fashions are adaptations or revivals of previously popular styles. Designers are always looking for styles that will satisfy fashion innovators who crave distinctiveness. And lower-cost copies of the popular items may catch on with other groups and survive for a while. Yet the speed of change usually increases the cost of producing and marketing products. Companies sustain losses due to trial and error in finding acceptable styles, then producing them on a limited basis because of uncertainty about the length of the cycle. These increased costs are not always charged directly to the consumer, since some firms lose their investment and go out of business. But in total, fashion changes cost consumers money. Fashion changes are a luxury that most people in less-developed countries simply can't afford.

**fad**

An idea that is fashionable only to certain groups who are enthusiastic about it

A **fad** is an idea that is fashionable only to certain groups who are enthusiastic about it. But these groups are so fickle that a fad is even more short-lived than a regular fashion. Many toys—whether it's a Hasbro Planet of the Apes plastic figure or a Toymax Paintball pack—are fads but do well during a short-lived cycle. Some teenagers' music tastes are fads.[15]

### The Risks and Benefits of Being the Innovator

The increasing speed of the product life cycle means that firms must be developing new products all the time. Further, they must try to have marketing mixes that will make the most of the market growth stage—when profits are highest.

During the growth stage, competitors are likely to rapidly introduce product improvements. Fast changes in marketing strategy may be required here because profits don't necessarily go to the innovator. Sometimes fast copiers of the basic idea will share in the market growth stage. Sony, a pioneer in developing videocassette recorders, was one of the first firms to put VCRs on the market and enjoyed the benefits of a monopoly. Seeing these profits, other firms quickly followed. These new competitors, armed with a lower cost and lower priced technology called VHS, drove down prices. These new, lower prices increased the affordability of VCRs and thus increased demand.

But as sales of VCRs continued to grow, Sony doggedly stuck to its Beta-format VCRs in spite of the fact that most consumers were buying VHS-format machines offered by competitors. In part, this was due to the need to recover the large investment Sony made in developing and promoting the Beta format and to Sony's belief that Beta had a higher reproduction quality than VHS. It wasn't until a decade later that Sony finally "surrendered" and offered a VHS-format machine. However, by then the booming growth in VCR sales had ebbed, and competitors controlled 90 percent of the market.

Although Sony was slow to see its mistake, its lost opportunities were minor compared to North American producers who sat on the sidelines and watched as foreign producers captured the whole VCR market. Copiers can be even faster than the innovator in adapting to the market's needs. Marketers must be flexible, but they also must fully understand the needs and attitudes of their target markets.[16]

A certain colour or style may be in fashion one season and outdated the next.

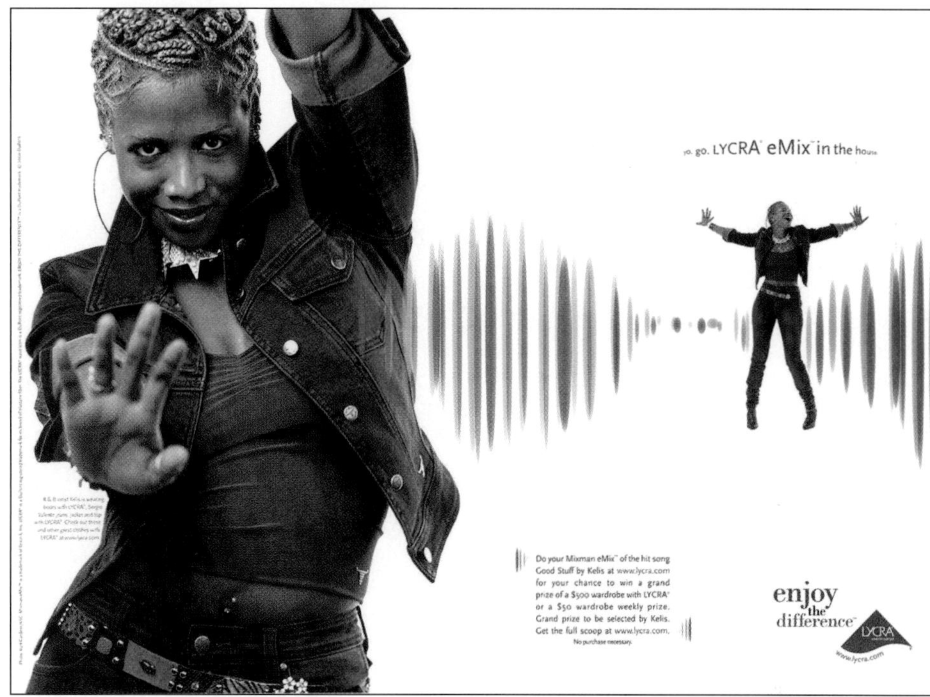




## New-Product Planning

As you can see from our discussion of product life cycles, competition is strong and dynamic in most markets. So it is essential for a firm to keep developing new products, as well as modifying its current products, to meet changing customer needs and competitors' actions. Not having an active new-product development process means that—consciously or subconsciously—the firm has decided to milk its current products and go out of business. New-product planning is not an optional matter. It has to be done just to survive in today's dynamic markets.

### What Is a "New" Product?

In discussing the introductory stage of product life cycles, we focused on the types of really new product innovations that tend to disrupt old ways of doing things. However, each year firms introduce many products that are basically refinements of existing products. So a **new product** is one that is new *in any way* for the company concerned.

**new product**
One that is new *in any way* for the company concerned

A product can become "new" in many ways. A fresh idea can be turned into a new product and start a new-product life cycle. For example, Alza Corporation's time-release skin patches are replacing pills and injections for some medications.

Variations on an existing product idea can also make a product new. Oral B changed its conventional toothbrush to include a strip of coloured bristles that fade as you brush; that way you know when it's time for a new brush. Colgate redesigned the toothbrush with a soft handle and angled bristles to do a better job removing tartar. Even small changes in an existing product can make it new.[17]

A firm can call its product new for only a limited time. Twelve months is the limit according to Industry Canada. To be called new, a product must be entirely new or changed in a "functionally significant or substantial respect." While 12 months may seem a very short time for production-oriented managers, it may be reasonable given the fast pace of change for many products. See Ethical Dimensions 10-1 for a discussion of some of the ethical issues related to new-product planning.

## Ethical Dimensions 10–1

### ETHICAL ISSUES IN NEW-PRODUCT PLANNING

New-product decisions—and decisions to abandon old products—often involve ethical considerations. For example, some firms (including firms that develop drugs to treat AIDS) have been criticized for holding back important new-product innovations until patents run out, or sales slow down, on their existing products.

At the same time, others have been criticized for "planned obsolescence"—releasing new products that the company plans to soon replace with improved new versions. Similarly, wholesalers and intermediaries complain that producers too often keep their new-product introduction plans a secret and leave intermediaries with dated inventory that they can sell only at a loss.

Companies also face ethical dilemmas when they decide to stop supplying a product or the service and replacement parts to keep it useful. An old model of a Cuisinart food processor, for example, might be in perfect shape except for a crack in the plastic mixing bowl. It's sensible for the company to improve the design if the crack is a frequent problem, but if consumers can't get a replacement part for the model they already own, they're left holding the bag.

Criticisms are also levelled at firms that constantly release minor variations of products that already saturate markets. Consider what happened with disposable diapers. Marketing managers thought that they were serving some customers' needs better when they offered diapers in boys' and girls' versions and in a variety of sizes, shapes, and colours. But many retailers felt that the new products were simply a ploy to get more shelf space. Further, some consumers complained that the bewildering array of choices made it impossible to make an informed decision. Of course, some people would level the same criticism at Huggies Little Swimmers Disposable Swimpants. But unlike other disposables, this new product doesn't swell in the water. They have been a success because they seem to fill a different need.

So, different marketing managers might have very different reactions to such criticisms. However, the fact remains that product management decisions often have a significant effect, one way or another, on customers and intermediaries. A marketing manager who is not sensitive to this fact may find that a too-casual decision leads to a negative backlash that affects the firm's strategy or reputation.[18]



### Managing the Risks in New-Product Planning

Identifying and developing new-product ideas—and effective strategies to go with them—is often the key to a firm's success and survival. But this isn't easy. New-product development demands effort, time, and talent—and still the risks and costs of failure are high. Experts estimate that consumer packaged-goods companies spend at least $20 million to introduce a new brand—and 70 to 80 percent of these new brands flop. Each year there are more than 20,000 new consumer packaged goods in Canada and the U.S.[19] So, about 16,000 failed. That's a big expense—and a waste. In the service sector, the front-end cost of a failed effort may not be as high, but it can have a devastating long-term effect if dissatisfied consumers turn elsewhere for help.[20]

A new product may fail for many reasons. Most often, companies fail to offer a unique benefit or underestimate the competition. Sometimes the idea is good but the company has design problems—or the product costs much more to produce than was expected. Some companies rush to get a product on the market without developing a complete marketing plan.[21]

But moving too slowly can be a problem too. With the fast pace of change for many products, speedy entry into the market can be a key to competitive advantage. Marketing managers at Xerox learned this the hard way. Japanese competitors were taking market share with innovative new models of copiers. It turned out that the competitors were developing new models twice as fast as Xerox, and at half the cost. For Xerox to compete, it had to slash its five-year product development cycle. Many other companies—ranging from manufacturers like Chrysler Corporation and Hewlett-Packard to Internet service firms like E*Trade and Yahoo—are working to speed up the new-product development process.[22]

Exhibit 10-4 New-product development process.

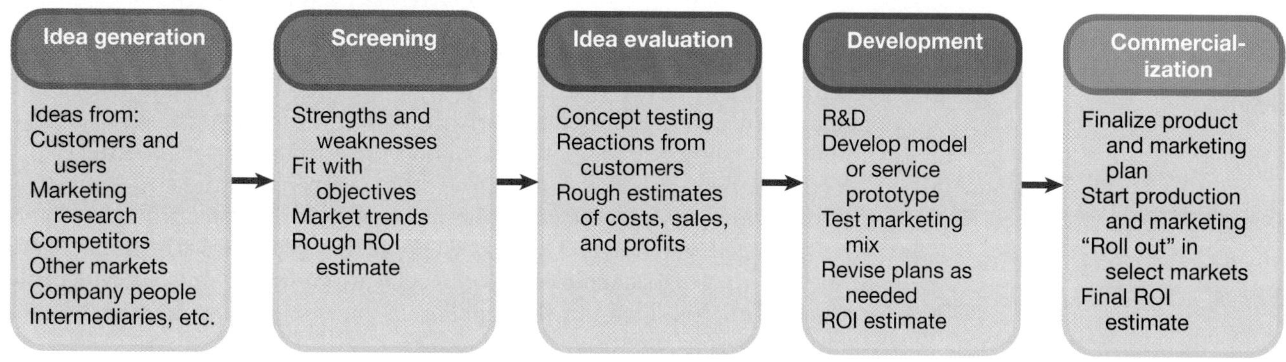


## The New-Product Development Process

To move quickly and also avoid expensive new-product failures, many companies follow an organized new-product development process. The following pages describe such a process, which moves logically through five steps: (1) idea generation, (2) screening, (3) idea evaluation, (4) development (of product and marketing mix), and (5) commercialization.[23] See Exhibit 10-4.

The general process is similar for both consumer and business markets—and for both goods and services. There are some significant differences, but we will emphasize the similarities in the following discussion.

An important element in this new-product development process is continued evaluation of a new idea's likely profitability and return on investment. In fact, the hypothesis-testing approach discussed in Chapter 8 works well for new-product development. The hypothesis tested is that the new idea will *not* be profitable. This puts the burden on the new idea—to prove itself or be rejected. Such a process may seem harsh, but experience shows that most new ideas have some flaw that can lead to problems and even substantial losses. Marketers try to discover those flaws early, and either find a remedy or reject the idea completely. Applying this process requires much analysis of the idea, both within and outside the firm, *before* the company spends money to develop and market a product. This is a major departure from the usual production-oriented approach—in which a company develops a product first and then asks sales to "get rid of it."

Of course, the actual new-product success rate varies among industries and companies. But many companies *are* improving the way they develop new products. It's important to see that if a firm doesn't use an organized process like this, it may bring many bad or weak ideas to market—at a big loss.

**Step 1: Idea generation** New ideas can come from a company's own sales or production staff, intermediaries, competitors, consumer surveys, or other sources such as trade associations, advertising agencies, or government agencies. By analyzing new and different views of the company's markets and studying present consumer behaviour, a marketing manager can spot opportunities that have not yet occurred to competitors or even to potential customers. For example, ideas for new service concepts may come directly from analysis of consumer complaints.

No one firm can always be first with the best new ideas. So in their search for ideas, companies should pay attention to what current or potential competitors are doing. Microsoft, for example, had to play catch-up with its Internet Explorer browser—and other changes to Windows—when Netscape Navigator became an instant hit. Some firms use what's called reverse engineering. For example, new-product specialists at Ford Motor Company buy other firms' cars as soon as they're available. Then they take the cars apart to look for new ideas or improvements. British Airways talks to travel agents to learn about new services offered by competitors. Many other companies use similar approaches.[24]

Many firms now "shop" in international markets for new ideas. Jamaica Broilers, a poultry producer in the Caribbean, moved into fish farming; it learned that many of the techniques it was using to breed chickens were also successful on fish farms in Israel. In the same vein, food companies in the United States and Europe are experimenting with an innovation recently introduced in Japan—a clear, odourless, natural film for wrapping food. Consumers don't have to unwrap it; when they put the product in boiling water or a microwave, the wrapper vanishes.[25]

Research shows that many new ideas in business markets come from customers who identify a need they have. Then they approach a supplier with the idea and perhaps even with a particular design or specification. These customers become the lead users of the product, but the supplier can pursue the opportunity in other markets.[26]

But finding new product ideas can't be left to chance. Companies need a formal procedure for seeking new ideas. The checkpoints discussed below, as well as the hierarchy of needs and other behavioural elements discussed earlier, should be reviewed regularly to ensure a continual flow of new, and sound, ideas. And companies do need a continual flow so they can spot an opportunity early—while there's still time to do something about it. Although later steps eliminate many ideas, a company must have some that succeed.



**Step 2: Screening** Screening involves evaluating the new ideas with the type of S.W.O.T analysis described in Chapter 3 and the product-market screening criteria described in Chapter 4. Recall that these criteria include the combined output of a resource (strengths and weaknesses) analysis, a long-run trends analysis, and a thorough understanding of the company's objectives (refer to Exhibit 3-1 and Exhibit 4-5). Further, a good new idea should eventually lead to a product (and marketing mix) that will give the firm a competitive advantage—hopefully, a lasting one.

Opportunities with better growth potential are likely to be more attractive. We discussed this idea earlier when we introduced the GE planning grid (refer to Exhibit 4-7). Now, however, you know that the life-cycle stage at which a firm's new product enters the market has a direct bearing on its prospects for growth. Clearly, screening should consider how the strategy for a new product will hold up over the whole product life cycle. In other words, screening should consider how attractive the new product will be in both the short and long terms.

Getting by the initial screening criteria doesn't guarantee success for the new idea. But it does show that the new idea is at least in the right ballpark *for this firm*. If many ideas pass the screening criteria, a firm must set priorities to determine which ones go on to the next step in the process. This can be done by comparing the ROI (return on investment) for each idea—assuming the firm is ROI-oriented. The most attractive alternatives are pursued first.

However, screening should not be based solely on the sales or even the profit outlook for the product. Successful new products impact on all of society and there can be significant risks and costs for those who take this responsibility lightly. To that end, screening should consider issues like consumer welfare, product safety, and product liability.

Exhibit 10-5
Types of new-product opportunity.

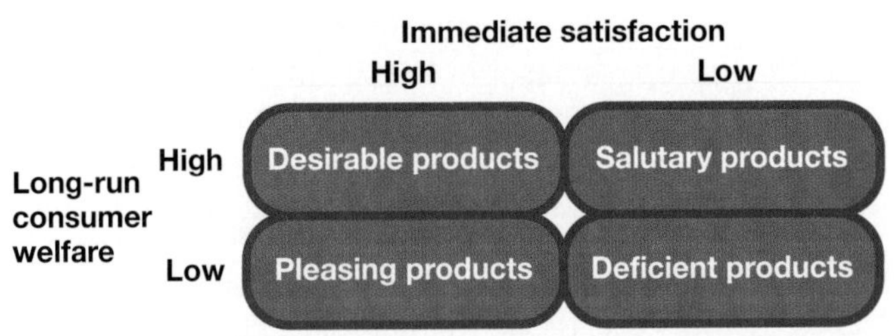

Products that can be regenerated or remanufactured provide both immediate satisfaction and long-run consumer welfare.

***Considering consumer welfare*** Screening should also consider how a new product will affect consumers over time. Ideally, the product should increase consumer welfare, not just satisfy a whim. Exhibit 10-5 shows different kinds of new-product opportunities. Obviously, a socially responsible firm tries to find desirable opportunities rather than deficient ones. This may not be as easy as it sounds, however. Some consumers want pleasing products instead of desirable ones. They emphasize immediate satisfaction and give little thought to their own long-term welfare. And some competitors willingly offer what consumers want in the short run. Generating socially responsible new-product ideas is a challenge for new-product planners, but consumer groups are helping firms to become more aware.

***Considering safety*** Real acceptance of the marketing concept certainly leads to safe products. But consumers still buy some risky products and services for the thrills and excitement they provide—for example, bicycles, skis, hang gliders, and bungee jumps. Even so, companies can usually add safety features—and some potential customers want them.

The Hazardous Products Act gives Industry Canada the authority either to ban outright or to regulate the sale, distribution, labelling, and advertising of potentially dangerous products. This act re-emphasizes the need for business people to become more safety-oriented.

Product safety complicates strategy planning because not all customers—even those who want better safety features—are willing to pay more for safer products. Some features cost a lot to add and increase prices considerably. These safety concerns must be considered at the screening step because a firm can later be held liable for unsafe products.

**product liability**

The legal obligation of sellers to pay damages to individuals who are injured by defective or unsafe products

***Product liability*** **Product liability** means the legal obligation of sellers to pay damages to individuals who are injured by defective or unsafe products. Product liability is a serious matter. Liability settlements may exceed not only a company's insurance coverage but also its total assets!

Some experts predict that this could happen to Dow-Corning because of its liability for faulty silicone breast implants. Firestone and Ford became the subject of much negative publicity and potentially face lawsuits as a result of problems with the tires on some Ford cars and trucks.

The courts have been enforcing a very strict product-liability standard. Producers may be held responsible for injuries related to their products, no matter how the items are used or how well they are designed. Riddell (whose football helmets protect the pros) was hit with a $12-million judgment in a case involving a high-school football player who broke his neck. The jury concluded that Riddell should have put a sticker on the helmet to warn players of the danger of butting into opponents! Cases and settlements like this are common.

Product liability is a serious ethical and legal matter. Many countries are attempting to change their laws so that they will be fair to both firms and consumers. But until product-liability questions are resolved, marketing managers must be even more sensitive when screening new-product ideas.[27]

**Step 3: Idea evaluation** When an idea moves past the screening step, it is evaluated more carefully. Note that an actual product has not yet been developed—and this can handicap the firm in getting feedback from customers. For help in idea evaluation, firms use **concept testing**—getting reactions from customers about how well a new-product idea fits their needs. Concept testing uses market research—ranging from informal focus groups to formal surveys of potential customers.

**concept testing**

Getting reactions from customers about how well a new-product idea fits their needs

Companies can often estimate likely costs, revenue, and profitability at this stage. And market research can help identify the size of potential markets. Even informal focus groups are useful—especially if they show that potential users are not excited about the new idea. If results are discouraging, it may be best to kill the idea at this stage. Remember, in this hypothesis-testing process, we're looking for any evidence that an idea is *not* a good opportunity for this firm and should be rejected.

Product planners must think about wholesaler and retailer customers as well as final consumers. Intermediaries may have special concerns about handling a proposed product. A Utah ice-cream maker was considering a new line of ice-cream novelty products—and he had visions of a hot market in California. But he had to drop his idea when he learned that grocery-store chains wanted payments of $20,000 each just to stock his frozen novelties in their freezers. Without the payment, they didn't want to risk using profitable freezer space on an unproven product. This is not an unusual case. At the idea evaluation stage, companies often find that other members of the distribution channel won't cooperate.[28]

Idea evaluation is often more precise in business markets. Potential customers are more informed—and their needs focus on the economic reasons for buying rather than emotional factors. Further, given the derived nature of demand in business markets, most needs are already being satisfied in some way. So, new products just substitute for existing ones. This means that product planners can compare the cost



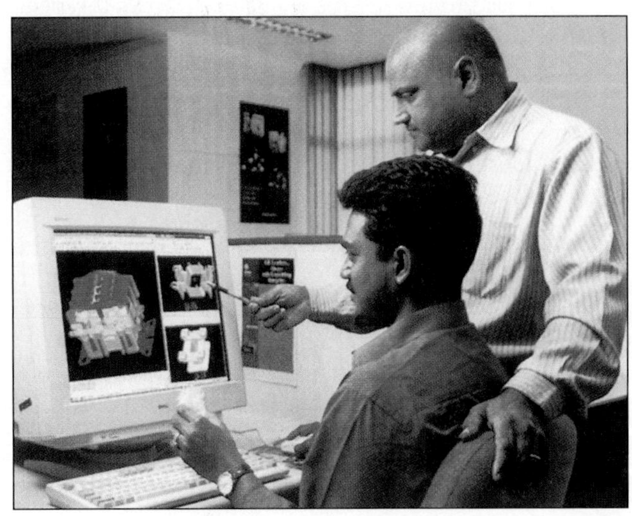

GE developed a software system so that its new-product design engineers in different parts of the world could collaborate over the Internet in real time—which helps GE bring concepts to market more quickly.

advantages and limitations of a new product with those currently being used. And by interviewing well-informed people, they can determine the range of product requirements and decide whether there is an opportunity.

For example, you've probably noticed that most new-car designs have switched to low-profile headlights. They allow sleeker styling and better gas mileage. Yet these lights were initially used only on high-priced cars. That's because the GE development team worked with engineers at Ford when they were first developing the bulbs for these headlights. Together they determined that the switch to the new bulb and headlight assembly would add about $200 to the price of a car. That meant that the bulb was initially limited to luxury cars—until economies of scale brought down the costs.[29]

Whatever research methods are used, the idea evaluation step should gather enough information to help decide whether there is an opportunity, whether it fits with the firm's resources, *and* whether there is a basis for developing a competitive advantage. With such information, the firm can estimate likely ROI in the various market segments and decide whether to continue the new-product development process.[30]

**Step 4: Development** Product ideas that survive the screening and idea evaluation steps must now be analyzed further. Usually, this involves some research and development (R&D) and engineering to design and develop the physical part of the product. In the case of a new service offering, the firm will work out the details of what training, equipment, staff, and so on will be needed to deliver on the idea. Input from the earlier efforts helps guide this technical work.

New computer-aided design (CAD) systems are sparking a revolution in design work. Designers can develop lifelike 3-D colour drawings of packages and products. Then the computer allows the manager to look at the product from different angles and views, just as with a real product. Changes can be made almost instantly. They can be sent by e-mail to managers all over the world for immediate review. They can even be put on a website for marketing research with remote customers. Then, once the designs are finalized, they feed directly into computer-controlled manufacturing systems. Companies like Motorola and Timex have found that these systems cut their new-product development time in half—giving them a leg up on many competitors. Most firms are now using variations on these systems.

Even so, it is still good to test models and early versions of the product in the market. This process may have several cycles. A manufacturer may build a model of a physical product or produce limited quantities; a service firm may try to train a small group of service providers. Product tests with customers may lead to revisions—*before* the firm commits to full-scale efforts to produce the good or service.

With actual goods or services, potential customers can react to how well the product meets their needs. Using small focus groups, panels, and larger surveys, marketers can get reactions to specific features and to the whole product idea. Sometimes that reaction kills the idea. For example, Coca-Cola Foods believed it had a great idea with Minute Maid Squeeze-Fresh, frozen orange juice concentrate in a squeeze bottle. Coca-Cola thought consumers would prefer to mix one glass at a time rather than find space for another litre-sized jug in the refrigerator. When actually tested, however, Squeeze-Fresh bombed. Consumers loved the idea but hated the product. It was messy to use, and no one could tell how much concentrate to squeeze in the glass.[31]

In other cases, testing can lead to revision of product specifications for different markets. For example, AMR Corporation had plans for a new reservation system to help travel agents, hotels, and airlines provide better customer service. But tests revealed too many problems, and plans for the service had to be revised. Sometimes a complex series of revisions may be required. Months or even years of research may be necessary to focus on precisely what different market segments will find acceptable. For example, Gillette's Mach3 razor blade took more than a decade and $750 million in development and tooling costs, plus another $300 million for introductory promotion.[32]

Firms often use full-scale market testing to get reactions in real market conditions or to test product variations and variations in the marketing mix. For example, a firm may test alternative brands, prices, or advertising copy in different cities. Note that the firm is testing the whole marketing mix, not just the product. For example, a hotel chain might test a new service offering at one location to see how it goes over.

Test-marketing can be risky because it may give information to competitors. In fact, a company in Chicago—Marketing Intelligence Services—monitors products in test markets and then sells the information to competing firms. Similar firms monitor markets in other countries.

But *not* testing is dangerous too. Frito-Lay was so sure it understood consumers' snack preferences that it introduced a three-item cracker line without market testing. Even with network-TV ad support, MaxSnax met with overwhelming consumer indifference. By the time Frito-Lay pulled the product from store shelves, it had lost $52 million. Market tests can be very expensive. Yet they can uncover problems that otherwise might go undetected and destroy the whole strategy.[33]

If a company follows the new-product development process carefully, the market test will provide a lot more information to the firm than to its competitors. Of course, the company must test specific variables rather than just vaguely testing whether a new idea will "sell." After the market test, the firm can estimate likely ROI for various strategies to determine whether the idea moves on to commercialization.

Some companies don't do market tests because they just aren't practical. In fashion markets, for example, speed is extremely important, and products are usually just tried in market. And durable products—which have high fixed production costs and

## Marketing Demo 10–1

### KELLOGG MARKETS "TASTY" SOY CEREAL

Kellogg Canada has entered the soy product category with Vive, a soy cereal. The long-awaited entry, which is already on shelf, is a mix of flakes and granola clusters with cinnamon. A two-thirds cup of cereal contains 4.4 grams of soy protein. The product, packaged in a sky-blue box with the impression of a handprint on it, is aimed at men and women 35 to 45 years old. Recent health reports cite soy as helping reduce the risk of heart disease and cancer and helping to decrease menopause

"This is the next generation in functional foods nutritional development," says Mark Childs, vice-president of marketing for Toronto-based Kellogg Canada, noting it was 10 years ago that Kellogg first entered the functional foods category by introducing Bran Buds with psyllium. "There's baggage that comes with soy from a taste perception, and I think we have the ability to change that. From a food point of view, you don't know that you're eating soy."

The product is the biggest new cereal launch for Kellogg Canada since it introduced Vector in 1999, a product aimed at active, health-conscious consumers. Both products were developed in Kellogg's Battle Creek, Mich.–based global development facility, and both were introduced in Canada first.

"I think Canadians are more health-conscious than other populations," says Childs. "The profile of today's cereal category is skewed more to a blend of healthier benefits and taste expectations."

To support the launch, a 30-second TV ad, "Live," debuts this month through Toronto-based J. Walter Thompson. The ad, featuring Iggy Pop's "Lust for Life," shows images of people enjoying life, such as a woman driving her car with her dog in the passenger seat, and a man practising martial arts outside, accompanied by a voiceover saying "live life large" and "live long and prosper."

Other support includes print advertising, sampling, direct to home and in-store, as well as event-based promotions. From a PR perspective, Kellogg is also telling key Canadian nutritionists, such as soy "guru" Leslie Beck, about the product.[34]

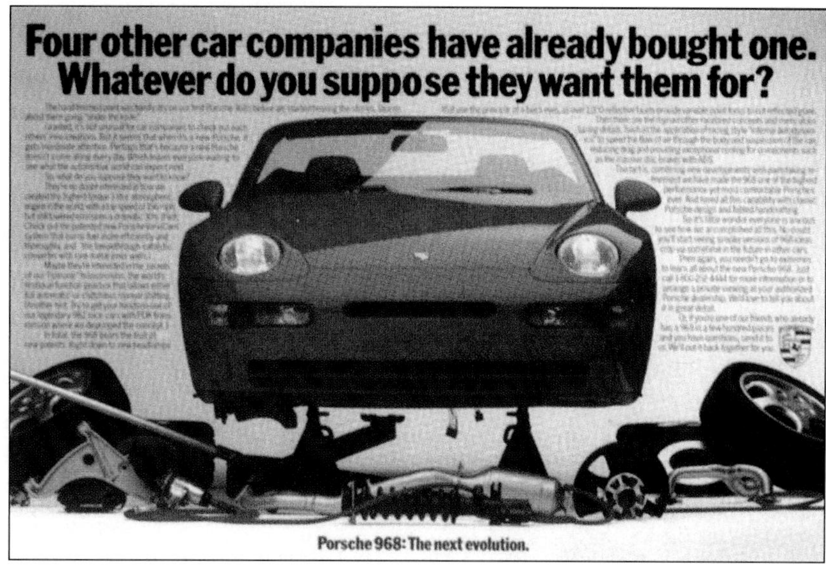


Firms often take apart competitors' products to look for ideas that they can apply or adapt in their own products.

long production lead times—may have to go directly to market. In these cases, it is especially important that the early steps be done carefully to reduce the chances for failure.[35] See Marketing Demo 10-1 for a look at how Kellogg's introduced a new product to the market.

**Step 5: Commercialization** A product idea that survives this far can finally be placed on the market. First, the new-product people decide exactly which product form or line to sell. Then they complete the marketing mix—really a whole strategic plan. And top management has to approve an ROI estimate for the plan before it is implemented. Finally, the product idea emerges from the new-product development process—but success requires the cooperation of the whole company.

Putting a product on the market is expensive. Manufacturing or service facilities have to be set up. Goods have to be produced to fill the channels of distribution, or people must be hired and trained to provide services. Further, introductory promotion is costly—especially if the company is entering a very competitive market.

Because of the size of the job, some firms introduce their products city by city or region by region—in a gradual "rollout"—until they have complete market coverage. Sprint used this approach in introducing its broadband wireless service that included a rooftop transmission device. Detroit, Phoenix, and San Francisco were targeted first. Rollouts also permit more market testing—although that is not their purpose. Rather, the purpose is to do a good job implementing the marketing plan. But marketing managers also need to pay close attention to control—to ensure that the implementation effort is working and that the strategy is on target.

## New-Product Development: Best Practices

We've been discussing the steps in a logical new-product development process. However, as shown in Exhibit 10-6, many factors can influence the success of the effort.

**Top-level support** Companies that are particularly successful at developing new goods and services seem to have one trait in common: enthusiastic top-management support for new-product development. New products tend to upset old routines that managers of established products often try in subtle but effective ways to maintain. So, someone with top-level support—and authority to get things done—needs to be responsible for new-product development.[36]

**A product champion** In addition, rather than leaving new-product development to someone in engineering, R&D, or sales who happens to be interested in taking

Exhibit 10-6 New-product development success factors.

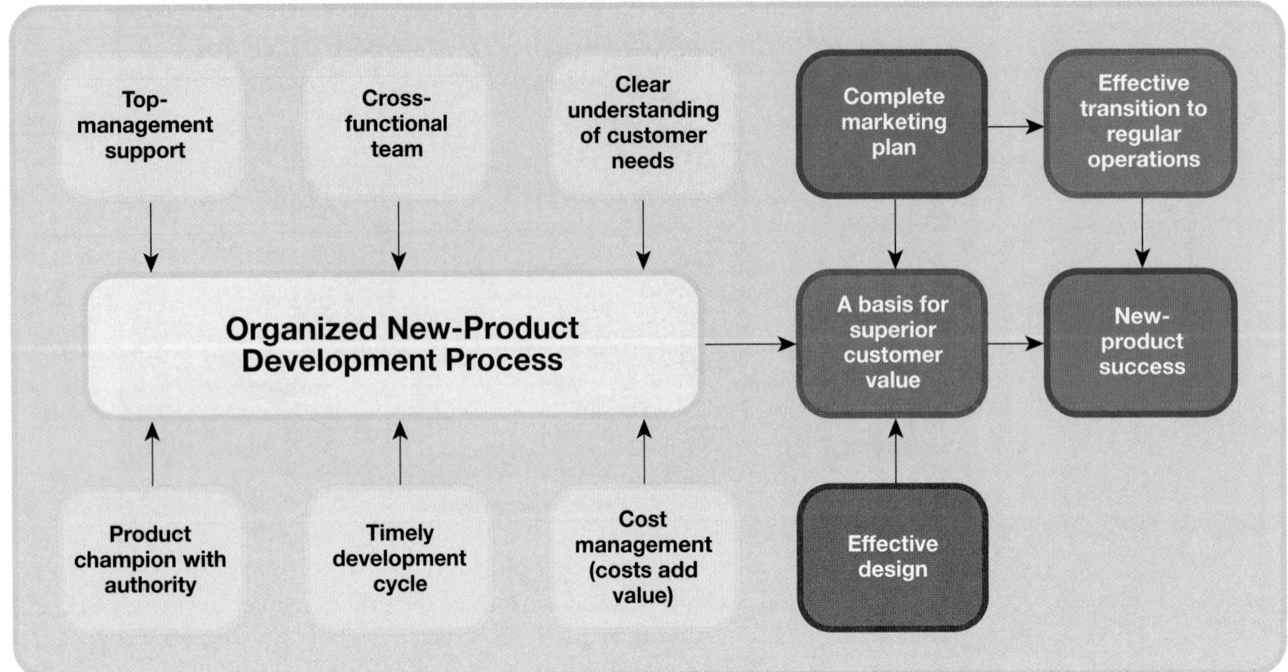




the initiative, successful companies put someone in charge. It may be a person, department, or team. But it's not a casual thing. It's a major responsibility of the job.

A new-product development department or team (committee) from different departments may help ensure that new ideas are carefully evaluated and profitable ones are quickly brought to market. It's important to choose the right people for the job. Overly conservative managers may kill too many, or even all, new ideas. Or, committees may create bureaucratic delays leading to late introduction and giving competitors a head start. A delay of even a few months can make the difference between a product's success or failure.

**Research and development** Many new-product ideas come from scientific discoveries and new technologies. That is why firms often assign specialists to study the technological environment in search of new ways to meet customers' needs. Many firms have their own R&D group that works on developing new products and new-product ideas. Even service firms have technical specialists who help in development work. For example, a bank thinking about offering customers a new set of investment alternatives must be certain that it can deliver on its promises. We've touched on this earlier, but the relationship between marketing and R&D warrants special emphasis.

The R&D effort is usually handled by scientists, engineers, and other specialists who have technical training and skills. Their work can make an important contribution to a firm's competitive advantage—especially if it competes in high-tech markets. However, technical creativity by itself is not enough. The R&D effort must be guided by the type of market-oriented new-product development process we've been discussing.

From the idea-generation stage to the commercialization stage, the R&D specialists, the operations people, and the marketing people must work together to evaluate the feasibility of new ideas. They may meet in person or communicate using e-mail, intranet sites, teleconferencing, or some other technology. There are many ways to share ideas. So, it isn't sensible for a marketing manager to develop elaborate marketing plans for goods or services that the firm simply can't produce—or produce profitably. It also doesn't make sense for R&D people to develop a technology or product that does not have potential for the firm and its markets. Clearly, a balancing act is involved here. But the critical point is the basic one we've been emphasizing throughout the whole book: marketing-oriented firms seek to satisfy customer needs at a profit with an integrated, whole-company effort.

**An integrated effort** Developing new products should be a total-company effort. The whole process—involving people in management, research, production, promotion, packaging, and branding—must move in steps from early exploration of ideas to development of the product and marketing mix. Even with a careful development process, many new products do fail—usually because a company skips some steps in the process. Because speed can be important, it's always tempting to skip needed steps when some part of the process seems to indicate that the company has a "really good idea." But the process moves in steps—gathering different kinds of information along the way. By skipping steps, a firm may miss an important aspect that could make a whole strategy less profitable or actually cause it to fail.

Eventually, the new product is no longer new—it becomes just another product. In some firms, at this point the new-product people turn the product over to the regular operating people and go on to developing other new ideas. In other firms, the person who was the new-product champion continues with the product, perhaps taking on the broader responsibility for turning it into a successful business. See Marketing Demo 10-2 for an example of how an established company put a new spin on an established product.

**Role of product managers** When a firm has only one or a few related products, everyone is interested in them. But when many new products are being developed, someone should be put in charge of new-product planning to be sure it is not neglected. Similarly, when a firm has products in several different product categories, management may decide to put someone in charge of each category, or each brand, to be sure that attention to these products is not lost in the rush of everyday business. **Product managers** or **brand managers** manage specific products—often taking over the jobs formerly handled by an advertising manager. That gives a clue to what is often their major responsibility—promotion—since the products have already been developed by the new-product people. However, some

**product (brand) managers**
Managers of specific products

## Marketing Demo 10–2

### HEINZ KICKERS TARGET ADULT TASTE BUDS

Heinz Canada is launching a line of flavoured ketchup to cater to adult tastes. Called "Ketchup Kickers," the products promise "bolder flavours" and come in three varieties: Roasted Garlic, Hot & Spicy, and Sweet Basil and Oregano. Heinz is also introducing an organic version of its ketchup made from 100-percent certified organic tomatoes and a barbecue cookbook to promote its products.

"Our research indicated that adults have an unmet need for flavour and variety in everyday foods," stated Susan Yorke, general manager, ketchup, condiments and sauces, Heinz Canada, in a release. "Today's busy, time-pressed consumers have discovered how other condiments, like the variety of sauces and marinades available today, can quickly and easily change the personality of a dish from boring to bold."

The flavoured ketchup comes in high-gloss packaging, with a 575-mL bottle selling for between $2.99 and $3.99. The new product will be supported nationally through advertising, along with in-store elements such as displays with litre bottles of ketchup to build consumer awareness and encourage trial.

In addition, the Heinz Barbecue Cookbook will be sold at bookstores across Canada. The book offers 57 meal ideas using many Heinz products such as its chili sauce, tomato juice, vinegar and Worcestershire sauce, along with Ketchup Kickers.[37]

brand managers start at the new-product development stage and carry on from there.

Product managers are especially common in large companies that produce many kinds of products. Several product managers may serve under a marketing manager. Sometimes these product managers are responsible for the profitable operation of a particular product's whole marketing effort. Then they have to coordinate their efforts with others—including the sales manager, advertising agencies, production and research people, and even channel members. This is likely to lead to difficulties if product managers have no control over the marketing strategy for other related brands or authority over other functional areas whose efforts they are expected to direct and coordinate.

To avoid these problems, in some companies the product manager serves mainly as a "product champion"—concerned with planning and getting the promotion effort implemented. A higher-level marketing manager with more authority coordinates the efforts and integrates the marketing strategies for different products into an overall plan.

The activities of product managers vary a lot depending on their experience and aggressiveness and the company's organizational philosophy. Today, companies are emphasizing marketing *experience*—because this important job takes more than academic training and enthusiasm. But it is clear that someone must be responsible for developing and implementing product-related plans—especially when a company has many products.[38] See Marketing Demo 10-3 for a look at 3M's corporate focus on innovation.

## Marketing Demo 10–3

### 3M STICKS TO ITS FOCUS ON INNOVATION

Minnesota Mining & Manufacturing (3M) is fast and successful in spinning out new products. This isn't just by chance. 3M's top executive set an objective that 30 percent of sales should come from products that didn't exist four years ago. You see the emphasis on innovation in even the quickest visit to 3M's website (www.3m.com). For example, current 3M innovations include radiant light film (for uses ranging from graphical signage to glittery toys), elastomers (which seal in aggressive chemicals in high-temperature settings), and electrostatic fibers (that filter dust out of heating vents). You can see why 3M says, "We are always new."

3M motivates innovation by staying close to customers, rewarding new-product champions, and sharing ideas among divisions. Teams from marketing, operations, and R&D screen new-product concepts for the ones with the highest profit potential. Then everyone works to bring the best ones to market fast. 3M's Scotch-Brite Never Rust Wool Soap Pads show how this approach can succeed. Consumers told 3M marketing researchers that they wanted an improved soap pad. Ordinary steel wool pads leave rust stains on sinks and tiny metal splinters in dishpan hands. 3M screens new products for their environmental impact, so the R&D people developed a pad using plastic fibres from recycled plastic bottles. Experts from 3M's abrasives division figured out how to coat the fibers with fine abrasives and biodegradable soap. Further marketing research refined the shape of the pads, and test markets evaluated details of the marketing plan. For example, tests confirmed that consumers liked the colourful package made from recycled paper and would pay more for Never Rust pads than they did for Brillo.

The managers varied the marketing plan for different countries. In mature markets such as the U.S. and Brazil, where steel wool pads already had a large consumer base, the objective was to capture share. In Japan, where steel wool is not commonly used, the objective was to pioneer the market and attract new customers. In a firm renowned for innovation, the launch of Never Rust pads was one of 3M's most profitable ever.

3M is also serious about how its innovations affect consumer welfare. When managers learned that traces of a chemical in 3M's Scotchgard fabric protector might persist in the environment, they didn't wait for scientists to do more tests. They voluntarily pulled the popular product off the market—before they even knew if R&D could find a substitute chemical.[39]

Consumer packaged goods companies, like Nabisco, usually assign brand managers who are responsible for individual products. However, when there are a number of products in the same product category there is often a higher-level manager who ensures that the marketing program for the whole category is effective.



## Chapter Summary

In highly competitive markets, it is no longer very profitable to just sell me-too products. And yet, without careful management, products can easily fall into a "commodity-like" strategy as markets, competition, and technologies change.

We reviewed the product life cycle to give you a sense of what to expect over the lifetime of a product. The product life cycle shows that a firm needs different marketing mixes—and even strategies—as a product moves through its cycle. This is an important point because profits change during the life cycle—with most of the profits going to the innovators or fast copiers.

This means that it is not enough to innovative only some of the time. New products are so important to business survival that firms need some organized process for developing them. The failure rate of new products is high—but it is lower for better-managed firms that recognize product development and management as vital processes. We discuss new-product planning process and emphasize some of the characteristics of processes that tend to be especially effective. Of particular note to those with a career interest in marketing, some firms appoint product managers to manage both individual products and new-product teams to ensure that the process is carried out successfully.

## Key Concepts

concept testing, p. 294
fad, p. 288
fashion, p. 287
market growth, p. 276
market introduction, p. 276
market maturity, p. 277
new product, p. 289
product (brand) managers, p. 299
product liability, p. 293
product life cycle, p. 275
sales decline, p. 277

## Questions and Problems

1. Explain how industry sales and industry profits behave over the product life cycle.
2. Explain why individual brands may not follow the product life-cycle pattern. Give an example of a new brand that is not entering the life cycle at the market introduction stage.
3. Discuss the life cycle of a product in terms of its probable impact on a manufacturer's marketing mix. Illustrate using the example of personal computers.
4. What characteristics of a new product will help it to move through the early stages of the product life cycle more quickly? Briefly discuss each characteristic—illustrating with a product of your choice. Indicate how each characteristic might be viewed in some other country.
5. What is a new product? Illustrate your answer.
6. Explain the importance of an organized new-product development process and illustrate how it might be used for *(a)* a new hair care product, *(b)* a new children's toy, and *(c)* a new subscribers-only cable television channel.
7. Explain the role of product or brand managers. When would it make sense for one of a company's current brand managers to be in charge of the new-product development process? Explain your thinking.



## Computer-Aided Problem 10

### Growth Stage Competition

AgriChem, Inc., has introduced an innovative new product—a combination fertilizer, weed killer, and insecticide that makes it much easier for soybean farmers to produce a profitable crop. The product introduction was quite successful, with 1 million units sold in the year of introduction. And AgriChem's profits are increasing. Total market demand is expected to grow at a rate of 200,000 units a year for the next five years. Even so, AgriChem's marketing managers are concerned about what will happen to sales and profits during this period.

Based on past experience with similar situations, they expect one new competitor to enter the market during each of the next five years. They think this competitive pressure will drive prices down about 6 percent a year. Further, although the total market is growing, they know that new competitors will chip away at AgriChem's market share—even with the 10 percent a year increase planned for the promotion budget. In spite of the competitive pressure, the marketing managers are sure that familiarity with AgriChem's brand will help it hold a large share of the total market and give AgriChem greater economies of scale than competitors. In fact, they expect that the ratio of profit to dollar sales for AgriChem should be about 10 percent higher than for competitors.

AgriChem's marketing managers have decided the best way to get a handle on the situation is to organize the data in a spreadsheet. They have set up the spreadsheet so they can change the "years in the future" value and see what is likely to happen to AgriChem and the rest of the industry. The starting spreadsheet shows the current situation with data from the first full year of production.

a. *Compare AgriChem's market share and profit for this year with what is expected next year—given the marketing managers' current assumptions. What are they expecting? (Hint: Set number of years in the future to 1.)*

b. *Prepare a table showing AgriChem's expected profit, and the expected industry revenue and profit, for the current year and the next five years. Briefly explain what happens to industry sales and profits and why. (Hint: Do an analysis to vary the number of years in the future value in the spreadsheet from a minimum of 0—the current year—to a maximum of 5. Display the three values requested.)*

c. *If market demand grows faster than expected—say, at 280,000 units a year—what will happen to AgriChem's profits and the expected industry revenues and profits over the next five years? What are the implications of this analysis?*

## Suggested Cases

To view the cases, go to www.mcgrawhill.ca/college/wong.

Interested in finding out what marketing looks like in the real world? *Marketing Magazine* is just a click away on your OLC! Visit **www.mcgrawhill.ca/college/wong** today.

# Chapter Eleven

# Place: Channel Systems and Physical Distribution

When You Finish This Chapter, You Should

1. Understand what product classes suggest about place objectives.

2. Understand why some firms use direct channel systems while others rely on intermediaries and indirect systems.

3. Understand how and why marketing specialists develop to make channel systems more effective.

4. Understand how to develop cooperative relationships and avoid conflict in channel systems.

5. Know how channel members in vertical marketing systems shift and share functions to meet customer needs.

6. Understand the differences between intensive, selective, and exclusive distribution.

7. Understand the physical distribution concept and how it affects decisions about customer service levels, costs, and the use of new technology.

## The Cola Wars Branch Out

If you want a Coca-Cola, there's usually one close by—no matter where you might be in the world. And that's no accident. An executive for the best-known brand name in the world stated the objective simply: "Make Coca-Cola available within an arm's reach of desire." To achieve that objective, Coke works with many different channels of distribution. But that's just the start. Think about what it takes for a bottle, can, or cup of Coke to be there whenever you're ready. In warehouses and distribution centres, on trucks, in gyms and sports arenas, and in thousands of other retail outlets Coke handles, stores, and transports more than 250 billion servings of soft drink a year. Getting all that product to consumers could be a logistical nightmare, but Coke does it effec-

place price promotion prod

tively and at a low cost.

Fast information about what the market needs helps keep Coke's distribution on target. In North America, computer systems show Coke managers exactly what's selling in each market; that allows Coke to plan inventories and deliveries. Coke also operates a 24-hour-a-day communications centre to respond to the two million requests it gets from channel members each year. Orders are processed instantly—so sales to consumers at the end of the channel aren't lost because of stock-outs. And Coke products move efficiently through the channel. In Cincinnati, for example, Coke built the beverage industry's first fully automated distribution centre. Forklifts were replaced with automatically guided vehicles that speed up the product flow and reduce labour costs.

Coke's strategies in international markets rely on many of the same ideas. But the stage of market development varies in different countries, so Coke's emphasis varies as well. To increase sales in France, for example, Coke must first make more product available at retail stores; so, Coke is installing thousands of soft-drink coolers in French supermarkets. In Great Britain, Coke is using multipacks because it wants to have more inventory at the point of consumption—in consumers' homes. In Japan, by contrast, single-unit vending machine sales are very important—so Coke uses an army of truck drivers to constantly restock its 870,000 machines, more per capita than anywhere else in the world. Coke is even testing vending machines that raise the price when it's hot or when few cans are left. In less-developed areas, the place system is not always so sophisticated. In China, for example, the Communist Party won't let Coke control all of the details, but a local manager struck a deal. For some cash, the Communist Party keeps inventories in some of its local offices. Then retired party members use bicycle-

price

place

product

promotion





www.mcgrawhill.ca/college/wong

powered pushcarts to sell the Coke inventory at densely populated housing projects.

Coke is also working to increase fountain-drink sales in domestic and international markets. As part of that effort, Coke equips restaurants and food outlets with Coke dispensers. Once a Coke dispenser is installed, the retailer usually doesn't have room for a competitor's dispenser. And when a consumer wants a fountain drink, Coke isn't just "the real thing," it's the only thing. The number of fountain outlets has grown so rapidly that one Coke account rep serves as many as a thousand customers in a geographic area. That means that the little guys could get lost in the shuffle. However, to give them the service they need at a reasonable cost, Coke recently initiated Coke.net, a password-protected Web portal where fountain customers can access account managers online, track syrup orders, request equipment repairs, or download marketing support materials.

Of course, Pepsi is a tough competitor and isn't taking all of this sitting down. Like Coke, Pepsi focuses on three main channels of distribution: retail (grocery and convenience stores), food service (fountain pop sales through restaurant chains), and of course vending machines. In recent years it has added more non-cola products, and its edgy ads for Mountain Dew and other products are helping it gain market share—which means it gets more shelf space and more Pepsi stocked at the point of purchase. Coke is pushing on new fronts as well. The competition is becoming even more intense; it's not just the "cola wars" anymore, but rather the wars for cola, juice, water, sports drinks, tea, and many other beverages. And who wins customers and profits in this broader competition will depend on overall marketing programs—but clearly place has an important role to play.[1]



## In This Chapter

In this chapter, we'll deal with the many important strategy decisions that a marketing manager must make concerning place. We start by identifying the various activities that must be performed to move a product from producer to consumer. Once identified, you'll learn the various types of distribution arrangements that can be made to perform these activities and see why specialists from outside the firm are often involved. With all of those people involved and receiving a share of the product's revenues, there is great potential for tensions to arise; we'll also discuss how to manage relations among channel members to reduce conflict and improve cooperation.

Our review of place decisions will also touch on the area of physical distribution, or logistics. We'll look at factors influencing distribution service levels and costs and examine how new technology is being used to reduce costs and gain competitive advantage.

In the next chapter, we'll take a closer look at the many different types of retailing and wholesaling firms. We'll also consider their role in channels as well as the strategy decisions they make to satisfy their own customers.

## Place—Why It Matters

**place**
Making goods and services available in the right quantities and locations—when the customer wants them

For many students, **place**—making the right quantities of goods and services available where and when customers want them—is one of the least glamorous parts of marketing. Indeed, most people who are new to marketing see distributions as a simple transaction: a manufacturer contracts with *somebody* to carry its products. But both the nature of place-related decisions and their strategic importance go far beyond just that. Exhibit 11-1 gives an overview of the many types of decisions that fall under the heading of "place." We'll be discussing these decisions throughout the chapter.

Place decisions affect both sales and profitability. Since customers cannot buy what they cannot find, offering a good product at a reasonable price is not enough for a successful marketing strategy. And when Coke pursues different target markets and those markets have different needs, a number of place variations may be required. In fact, in the case of Coke, the needs are so different that they have to use more than one channel of distribution. Each of those channels has different costs and arrangements, which can mean very different levels of profitability depending upon where the product is bought.

**channel of distribution**
Any series of firms or individuals that participate in the flow of products from producer to final user or consumer

Additionally, place decisions can dramatically change the nature and basis of competition in a product-market. In particular, the design of **channels of distribution**—any series of firms or individuals that participate in the flow of products from producer to final user or consumer—can be *the* key source of competitive advantage. This is especially important in business today because many firms are trying to use new information technologies, including websites and aspects of e-commerce, to reach customers directly. Some of the greatest business success stories of recent times have their foundations in using technological innovations to sell directly to customers (e.g., ING Direct, Dell, Amazon.com/Amazon.ca), complement more traditional retail outlets (e.g., the major banks, IBM, Indigo Books and Music), or provide cost savings that translate into greater value for consumers (e.g., Wal-Mart, Costco, Future Shop, and Grand & Toy).

Exhibit 11-1
Strategy decision areas in place.

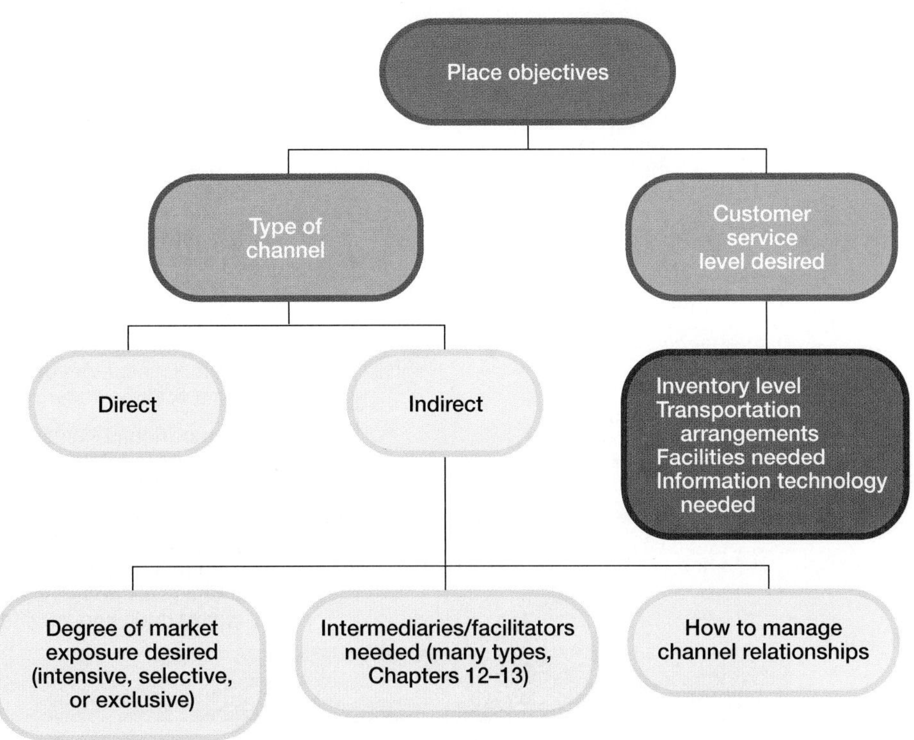

Finally, place decisions can affect the effectiveness of other parts of the marketing mix. Some of these may seem obvious. For example, the cost of distribution is reflected in price; certain product and service qualities like installation, technical advice, and returns may need to be arranged at the point of purchase. But even promotion is tied to distribution decisions. In part, this is because we may need to involve other channel members in promotional activities (e.g., coupons, rebates, display, and catalogues). However, promotion can also be affected by the image or associations consumers make between a product's qualities and where it is sold. For example, what challenges would you face in promoting a diamond engagement ring if the decision were made to sell it at a discount store versus at a jeweller? How would that affect the ring's price?

## What's Involved in Managing Place?



Effective marketing means delivering the goods and services that consumers want and need. It means getting products to them at the right time, in the right place, and at a price they're willing to pay. It means keeping consumers satisfied after the sale, and bringing them back to purchase again when they are ready. Let's look at the outcomes that place decisions must create to make this happen.

### The Task—To Overcome Separations and Discrepancies

As we saw in Chapter 1, marketing assists producers and consumers to conduct exchange by creating time, place, possession, form, and task utility. As Exhibit 11-2 shows, the potential to create these utilities is due to the spatial separation,

Exhibit 11–2 Marketing facilitates production and consumption.

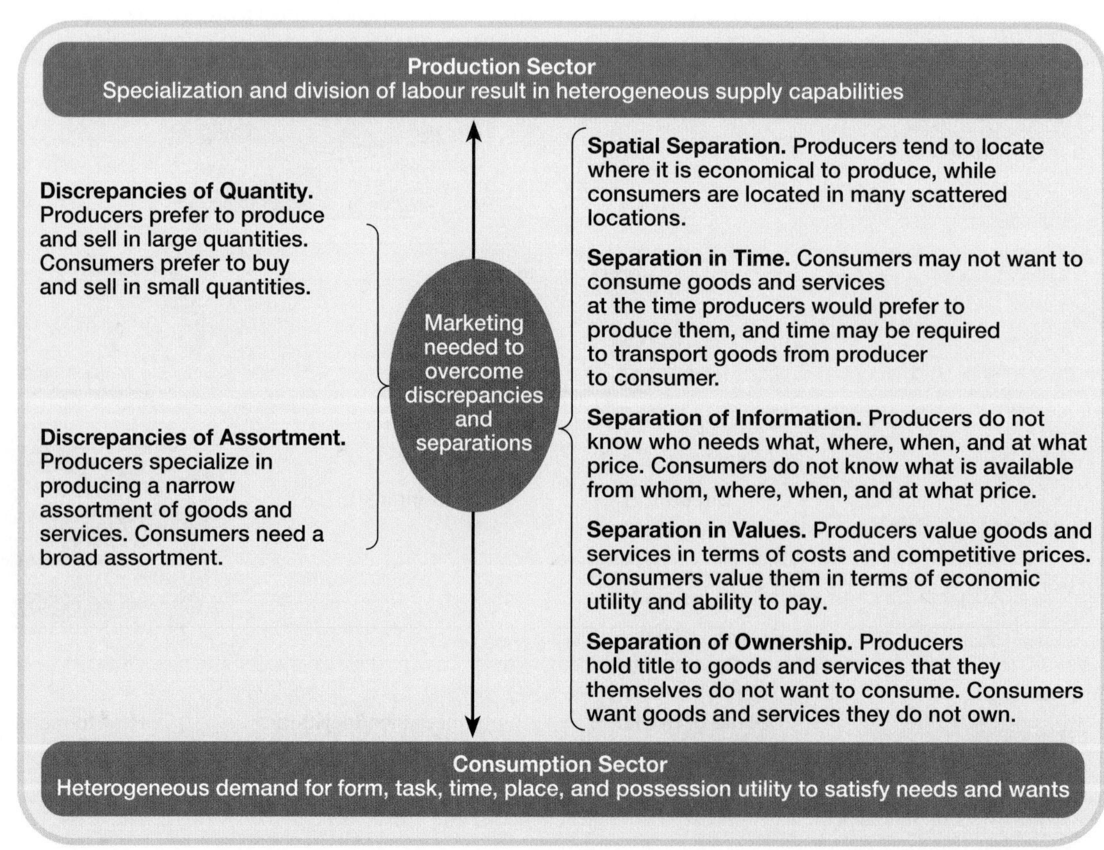

Office Depot, a large office supplies chain, accumulates products from many producers at its distribution centre (shown here) and then breaks bulk to provide the convenient assortments that consumers expect to find at individual Office Depot stores.

separation in time, separation of information and values, and separation of ownership that exist between producers and consumers.

"Discrepancies of quantity" and "discrepancies of assortment" often make it more difficult to create utilities. For example, each producer specializes in producing and selling large amounts of a narrow assortment of goods and services, but each consumer wants only small quantities of a wide assortment of goods and services.[2] Understanding these discrepancies provides insights as to the roles, costs, and potential rewards connected with place, and in doing so may provide you with some ideas for new businesses.

**discrepancy of quantity**
The difference between the quantity of products it is economical for a producer to make and the quantity final users or consumers normally want

**Discrepancies of quantity and assortment** **Discrepancy of quantity** means the difference between the quantity of products it is economical for a producer to make and the quantity final users or consumers normally want. For example, most manufacturers of golf balls produce large quantities—perhaps 200,000 to 500,000 in a given time period. The average golfer, however, wants only a few balls at a time. Adjusting for this discrepancy usually requires intermediaries—wholesalers and retailers.

**discrepancy of assortment**
The difference between the lines a typical producer makes and the assortment final consumers or users want

Producers typically specialize by product—and therefore another discrepancy develops. **Discrepancy of assortment** means the difference between the lines a typical producer makes and the assortment final consumers or users want. Most golfers, for example, need more than golf balls. They want golf shoes, gloves, clubs, a bag, and, of course, a golf course to play on. And they usually don't want to shop for each item separately. So, again, there is a need for wholesalers and retailers to adjust these discrepancies.

**regrouping activities**
Adjusting the quantities and/or assortments of products handled at each level in a channel of distribution

**Regrouping activities overcome discrepancies** **Regrouping activities** adjust the quantities and/or assortments of products handled at each level in a channel of distribution. There are four regrouping activities: accumulating, bulk-breaking, sorting, and assorting. When one or more of these activities is needed, a marketing specialist may develop to fill this need.

**accumulating**
Collecting products from many small producers

**Accumulating** involves collecting products from many small producers. Many intermediaries who operate from websites focus on accumulating. Specialized sites for everything from Chinese art to Dutch flower bulbs bring together the output of many producers. Much of the coffee that comes from Colombia is grown on small farms in the mountains. Accumulating the small crops into larger quantities is a way of getting the lowest transporting rate and making it more convenient for distant food-processing companies to buy and handle it. Accumulating is especially important in less-developed countries and in other situations, like agricultural markets, where there are many small producers.

Accumulating is also important with professional services, because they often involve the combined work of a number of individuals, each who is a specialized producer. A hospital makes it easier for patients by accumulating the services of a number of health care specialists, many who may not actually work for the hospital.

**bulk-breaking**
Dividing larger quantities into smaller quantities as products get closer to the final market

**Bulk-breaking** involves dividing larger quantities into smaller quantities as products get closer to the final market. For example, few people would consume enough chocolate bars in a week to justify placing an order with a manufacturer like Mars or Cadbury. In fact, even a corner store might sell only a box or two of any type of bar in a week. So a wholesaler might buy a large number of boxes from Mars and then resell the boxes in smaller quantities to a retailer, who in turn sells individual bars to consumers.

**sorting**
Separating products into grades and qualities desired by different target markets

**Sorting** means separating products into grades and qualities desired by different target markets. For example, an investment firm might offer its customers a chance to buy shares in a mutual fund made up only of stocks for certain types of companies—high-growth firms, ones that pay regular dividends, or ones that have good environmental track records. Similarly, a wholesaler that specializes in serving convenience stores may focus on smaller packages of frequently used products, whereas a wholesaler working with restaurants and hotels might handle only very large institutional sizes. Sorting is also a very important process for raw materials. Nature produces what it will—and then the products must be sorted to meet the needs of different target markets.

**assorting**
Putting together a variety of products to give a target market what it wants

**Assorting** means putting together a variety of products to give a target market what it wants. This usually is done by those closest to the final consumer or user—retailers or wholesalers that try to supply a wide assortment of products for the convenience of their customers; a grocery store is a good example. But some assortments involve very different products. A wholesaler selling Yazoo tractors and mowers to golf courses might also carry Pennington grass seed, Scott fertilizer, and even golf ball washers or irrigation systems—for the convenience of its customers.

## The Response—The Universal Functions of Marketing

The purpose of a marketing system is to overcome these separations and discrepancies. The "universal functions of marketing" help do this. Technologies such as the Internet are simply a medium through which these functions are performed. Indeed, one way to evaluate the potential of any e-commerce business is by considering the range of "universal functions" it performs and the significance of the savings generated by performing each function electronically. (You may even discover some potential business opportunities as you read this chapter!)

**universal functions of marketing**
Buying, selling, transporting, storing, standardization and grading, financing, risk taking, and market information

The **universal functions of marketing** are buying, selling, transporting, storing, standardization and grading, financing, risk taking, and market information. They must be performed in all marketing systems. How these functions are performed (and by who) may differ, but the functions must always be performed by someone in some way.

1. **Buying**: looking for and evaluating goods and services.
2. **Selling**: promoting the product.
3. **Transporting**: moving goods from one place to another.
4. **Storing**: holding goods until customers need them.
5. **Standardization and grading**: sorting products according to size and quality. This makes buying and selling easier by reducing the need for inspection and sampling.
6. **Financing**: providing the necessary cash and credit to produce, transport, store, promote, sell, and buy products.

7. **Risk taking**: bearing the uncertainties that are part of the marketing process, including sales performance, damage, theft, obsolescence.
8. **Market information**: collecting, analyzing, and distributing all the information needed to plan, carry out, and control marketing activities.

While it may seem mechanical and theoretical to split distribution into these activities, it is important to do so. As you will see in the next section, these activities can be performed by various parties and in different ways. Whoever performs the activities gets paid to do so. As such, marketers are always looking for ways to reduce the cost and improve the quality of each component activity. So it should not be surprising to learn that firms look at performance and cost in these activity areas when they are deciding among alternative distribution channels or individual distributors.

## The Decision—Who Performs the Functions?

While the universal functions must always be performed, they need not always be performed by the seller or end buyer. In a market-directed system like ours, marketing functions are often performed by a variety of marketing specialists (see Exhibit 11-3). These specialists arise in response to a search for more effective and efficient ways to overcome these discrepancies and separations.[3]

However, it is important to remember that specialists should develop to adjust discrepancies only if they must be adjusted. There is no point in having intermediaries just because that's the way it's been done in the past. Sometimes a breakthrough opportunity can come from finding a better way to reduce discrepancies—perhaps eliminating some steps in the channel. For example, many small manufacturers of business products can now reach more customers in distant markets with a website than it was previously possible for them to reach with independent manufacturers' reps who sold on commission but otherwise left distribution to the firm. If it costs the firm less to establish an order-taking website and advertise it by e-mail, at an industry community site, or in a trade magazine, the cost advantage can translate to lower prices and a marketing mix that is a better value for some target segments.[4]

Exhibit 11–3
Model of a marketing-directed macro-marketing system.

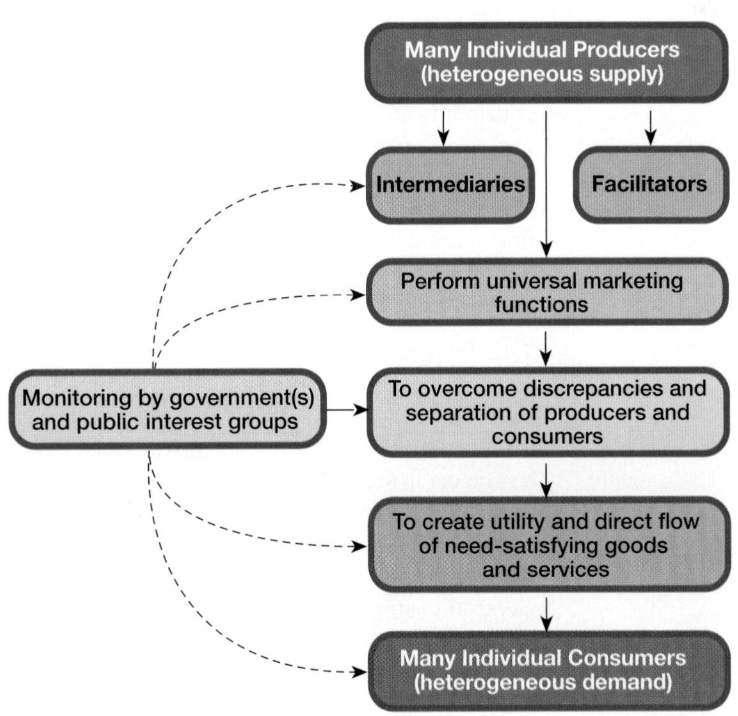

Exhibit 11-4

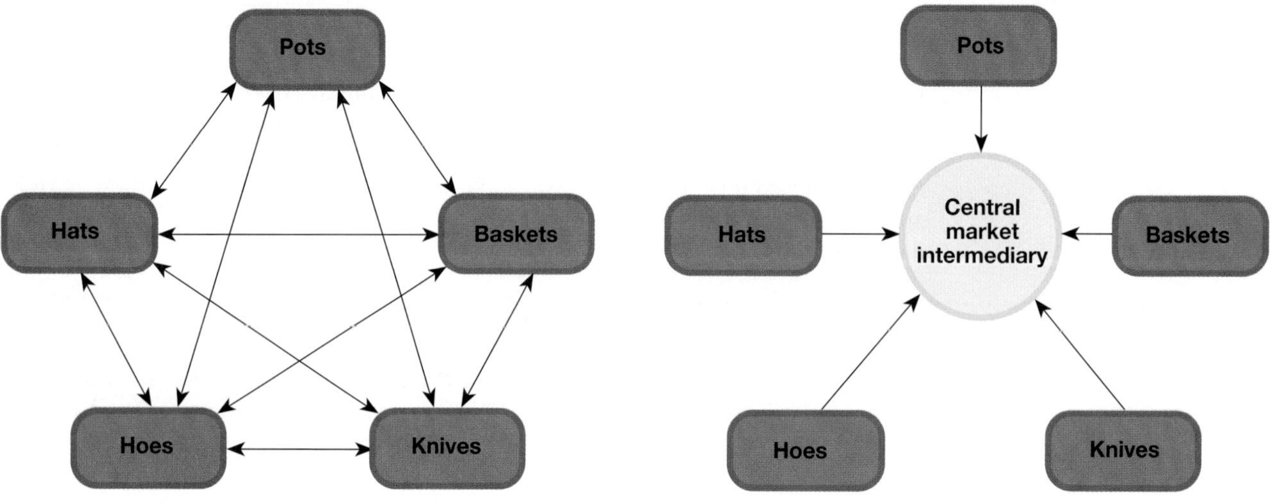




**intermediary**
Someone who specializes in trade rather than production

**facilitators**
Those who provide one or more of the marketing functions other than buying or selling

**The use of intermediaries and facilitators** An **intermediary** is someone who specializes in trade rather than production. Retailers and wholesalers are the most common type of intermediary. They provide a valuable service by creating a central exchange that reduces the number of transactions required in total (see Exhibit 11-4).

**Facilitators** provide one or more of the marketing functions other than buying or selling. These include advertising agencies, marketing research firms, independent product-testing laboratories, public warehouses, transporting firms, communications companies, and financial institutions (including banks).

Through specialization and economies of scale, marketing intermediaries and facilitators are often able to perform the marketing functions better—and at a lower cost—than producers or consumers can (imagine the cost—and resulting prices—if every food manufacturer needed to have its own retail store, advertising agency, and so on). This allows producers and consumers to spend more time on production and consumption. (You might recall that we discussed this concept in Chapter 7, in explaining why business customers outsourced activities to third parties.)

Some marketing specialists perform all the functions. Others specialize in only one or two. Marketing-research firms, for example, specialize only in the market information function. The important point to remember is this: responsibility for performing the marketing functions can be shifted and shared in a variety of ways, but no function can be completely eliminated.

**The impact of innovation and rapid change** Sometimes the discrepancies between buyers and sellers are adjusted badly—especially when consumer wants and attitudes shift rapidly. When cellular phones suddenly became popular, an opportunity developed for a new specialist. Cellular phone dealers came on the scene to help customers figure out what type of cellular phone and service would meet their needs. After all, the traditional phone companies didn't initially offer these services.

However, it cost the sellers of cellular services about $300 per customer to sell through dealers. As the market grew and the competition for customers heated up, electronics stores wanted a piece of the action, and they were willing to take a smaller markup. Now that the market is much more established, many cellular service providers are finding it cheaper to sell from a website or use their own salespeople.[5]

To reach its place objectives, Sprint sells PCS phones and its wireless services through 12,000 outlets, including retail chains like Staples and its own Sprint PCS Centres.

As the cellular service example shows, the nature of the separations and discrepancies change over time (recall our discussion of the PLC in Chapter 10), and marketers must adjust to them. However, marketers also must be careful in choosing when and how to adjust. Changing in ways that are not compatible with buyer behaviour or changing too many things too quickly can lead to customer confusion—or, worse, can introduce inconsistency into the marketing mix. For example, suppose a firm traditionally relied upon—and paid—its distributors to educate customers on product installation, use, and maintenance. Selling direct over the Internet might show cost savings, but promotional spending might have to increase in order to sustain the customer-education program. This is why it is so important to consider the *total* cost of marketing—not just the economics of an individual decision—when making any marketing decision, especially when it affects distribution.



## Setting Place Objectives—The Key to Effective Decisions

**coverage**
The amount of the target market that is reached by the channels of distribution

**promotional intensity**
How much effort is expended by the other members of the channel in order to promote, sell, and service the product

**distribution cost**
The amount that is paid to members of the distribution channel in order to achieve the desired levels of coverage and promotional intensity

Before we look at specific place-related decisions and the alternatives to be compared in making those decisions, it is important to remember that there is no single practice that is appropriate for all situations. Rather, decisions must be consistent with a firm's objectives—what they hope to achieve.

Place objectives centre on three main characteristics: coverage, promotional intensity, and cost. **Coverage** is the amount of the target market that is reached by the channels of distribution. **Promotional intensity** refers to how much effort is expended by the other members of the channel in order to promote, sell, and service the product. **Distribution cost** refers to the amount that is paid to members of the distribution channel in order to achieve the desired levels of coverage and promotional intensity. As a general rule, it is very rare for a firm to be able to have high levels of coverage and promotional intensity while also enjoying low cost.

The reason for this is the tradeoff between coverage and promotional intensity as seen from the distributor's position. A distributor may spend considerable time and effort to aggressively promote a firm's product. However, if that product has wide coverage, the distributor may be reluctant to make those expenditures for fear that other distributors might "piggyback" on its efforts and thereby avoid the promotional costs. These cost savings enable the non-promoting distributor to have lower prices for the same item. By contrast, if only one distributor in an area is allowed to carry the product—that is, coverage is low—then it is in their best interests to aggressively promote the product. Thus, a firm that has a high degree of coverage and also wants a high level of promotional intensity will likely have to "buy" those efforts from other channel members.

### Using Product Classes to Help Define Objectives

Given these tradeoffs, what is the right balance of coverage, promotional intensity, and distribution cost to pursue? As shown in Chapter 9, different consumer and business-product classes require different marketing-mix considerations. (You may want to review Exhibits 9-3 and 9-4, as they set up the framework for making place decisions.) In particular, the product classes help us decide how much market exposure we'll need in each geographic area.

The use of product classes can tell us a great deal about the right place objectives to pursue. However, no marketing decision is automatic. A product may be sold both to final consumers and business customers, and each type of customer may want to purchase in different ways. Further, several different product classes may be involved if different market segments view a product in different ways. Thus, just as there is no automatic classification for a specific product, we can't automatically decide the one best place arrangement.

However, since people in a particular target market should have similar attitudes, knowing how they classify the product can help us choose the right balance of objectives to meet their needs. If different target segments view a product in different ways, marketing managers may need to develop several strategies, each with its own place arrangements.

### Objectives Will Change over the Life Cycle

The marketing manager must also consider place objectives in relation to the product life cycle. Place decisions often have long-run effects. They're usually harder to change than product, price, and promotion decisions. Many firms expecting to quickly establish websites for direct online sales, for example, found that it took several years and millions of dollars to work out the kinks. It can take even longer to develop effective working relationships with others in the channel. Legal contracts with channel partners may also limit changes. And it's hard to move retail stores and wholesale facilities once leases are signed and customer shopping patterns are settled. Yet as products mature, they typically need broader distribution to reach different target customers.

Most pet-food companies focus on distribution through grocery stores, but Science Diet–brand premium pet foods reach consumers in North America, Japan, and Italy through a different channel—veterinary offices and pet stores. Because Science Diet has developed cooperative relationships with other members of this channel, Science Diet products often get special promotion support at the point of purchase.

The distribution of premium pet foods followed this pattern. A decade ago, supermarkets wouldn't carry specialized pet foods because there wasn't much demand. So, marketing managers for Science Diet products concentrated on getting distribution through pet shops and veterinary offices. These pet professionals were already focused on Science Diet's target market. Science Diet's sales in this channel grew rapidly. What's more, profit margins on the specialty foods were much higher than on traditional fare. Seeing that this market was growing, Purina, Kal Kan, and other producers developed new products and worked with their supermarket channels to set up special "nutrition centres" on the pet-food aisle. P&G bought Iams and pushed for distribution in pet superstores, at mass-merchandisers, and online. Perhaps the competition among channels was inevitable. But Science Diet is still doing well in its own channel. It's also using the same approach to expand into other countries. In pet stores in Japan and Italy, for example, Science Diet attracts new customers with special displays, samples, and free literature.[6]

## Place Decision 1—Directness

One of the most basic place decisions producers must make is whether to handle the whole distribution themselves—perhaps by relying on direct-to-customer e-commerce selling—or use wholesalers, retailers, and other specialists (refer to Exhibit 11-1).

Traditionally, direct distribution often was associated with narrow market coverage, since sales reps dealt with clients one-on-one. The Internet has changed that for many firms. Website-based e-commerce systems give many firms direct access to prospects and customers whom it would have been difficult or impossible to reach in the past. Even very small, specialized firms may be able to establish a Web page and draw customers from all over the world. Of course, there are limitations. If a customer wants a salesperson to demonstrate a product, then a "virtual store" may not be adequate. However, the concept of distribution over the Internet is still evolving. Some firms now use live-camera "feeds" while talking with the customer over an Internet video phone. Other innovations are being tested.

Many business products are sold direct-to-customer. Rolm, for example, sells its computerized voicemail systems direct. Alcan sells aluminum to General Motors direct. And Honda sells its motors direct to lawn mower producers. This is understandable because in business markets there are fewer transactions and orders are larger. In addition, customers may be concentrated in a small geographic area, making distribution easier. Further, once relationships are established e-commerce systems can provide an efficient way to handle orders, replenish inventory, and manage routine information needs (such as delivery schedules).

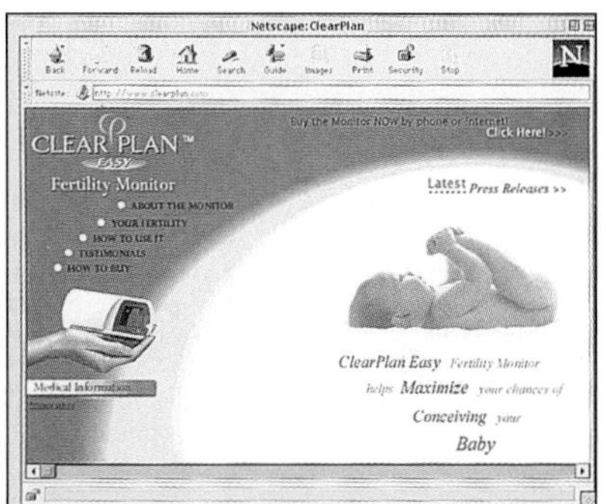


In Canada and many other developed nations, Unilever relies primarily on indirect distribution through a variety of wholesalers and retailers. However, in Spain it delivers frozen foods directly to consumers' homes, and in Vietnam a mobile store brings products to local consumers. And now some products are sold direct to consumers from a website.

Service firms often use direct channels. If the service must be produced in the presence of customers, there may be little need for intermediaries. An insurance firm like Sun Life, for example, must deal directly with its customers. However, many firms that produce physical goods turn to intermediary specialists to help provide the services customers expect as part of the product. Maytag may hope that its authorized dealers don't get many repair calls, but the service is available when customers need it. Here the intermediary produces the service.[7]

While most consumer products are sold through intermediaries, some consumer products are sold direct to consumers' homes. Tupperware, Mary Kay, and Avon cosmetics, Electrolux vacuum cleaners, and Amway household products are examples. Most of these firms rely on direct selling, which involves a personal sales contact between a representative of the company and an individual consumer. However, most of these "salespeople" are *not* company employees. Rather, they usually work as independent intermediaries, and the companies that they sell for refer to them as "dealers," "distributors," "agents," or some similar term. So, in a strict technical sense this is not really direct producer-to-consumer distribution. That does not mean, however, that this approach is unimportant. It has grown both in Canada and in international markets. In fact, many firms are finding that it's the best way to crack open international markets. Some of the distribution arrangements might surprise you. For example, Mattel has teamed up with Avon's door-to-door representatives to sell its Barbie dolls in China.[8]

**direct marketing**

Direct communication between a seller and an individual customer using a promotion method other than face-to-face personal selling

An increasing number of firms now rely on **direct marketing**—direct communication between a seller and an individual customer using a promotion method other than face-to-face personal selling. Sometimes direct marketing promotion is coupled with direct distribution from a producer to consumers. Park Seed Company, for example, sells the seeds it grows directly to consumers with a mail catalogue. However, many firms that use direct marketing promotion distribute their products through intermediaries. So the term *direct marketing* is primarily concerned with the promotion area, not place decisions. We'll talk about direct marketing promotion in more detail in Chapter 13.[9]

## Advantages of Direct Distribution

Perhaps the biggest advantage of direct distribution is control over the marketing job. Direct distribution may enable a firm to serve target customers at a lower cost or do the work more effectively than intermediaries. Further, working with independent intermediaries with different objectives can be troublesome.

If a firm is in direct contact with its customers, it is more aware of changes in customer attitudes. It is in a better position to adjust its marketing mix quickly because there is no need to convince other channel members to help. If a product needs an aggressive selling effort or special technical service, the marketing manager can ensure that salespeople receive the necessary training and motivation. In contrast, intermediaries often carry the products of several competing producers so they might not give any one item the special emphasis its producer wants.

Market access is a third reason why some firms turn to direct distribution. A firm may have to go direct if suitable intermediaries are not available or will not cooperate. For example, Apple is again opening its own stores in hopes of getting more in-store promotional emphasis on what's different about its iMac computers.[10]

Intermediaries who have the best contacts with the target market may be hesitant to add unproven vendors or new products, especially really new products that don't fit well with their current business. Many new products die because the producer can't find willing intermediaries and doesn't have the financial resources to handle direct distribution.

Statistics Canada publishes detailed data concerning wholesalers and retailers, including breakdowns by kind of business, product line, and geographic territory. Similar information is available for the United States and many other countries,

When Snapple bought SoBe's main wholesaler, other goods wholesalers were not available and SoBe was left with limited distribution. So marketers for SoBe sold directly to retailers. Getting retailer cooperation and good shelf space was easier when SoBe provided its own coolers.

including most of those in the European Union. Most of these data are available online. They can be very valuable in strategy planning—especially to learn whether potential channel members are serving a target market. You can also learn what sales volumes current intermediaries are achieving.

### Advantages of Indirect Distribution

While direct distribution has significant advantages, there are occasions where indirect channels of distribution can serve customer needs better and at lower cost. Indeed, even when a producer wants to handle the entire distribution job, sometimes it's simply not possible. Customers often have established buying patterns. For example, Square D, a producer of electrical supplies, may want to sell directly to big electrical contractors. But if contractors like to make all of their purchases in one convenient stop—at a local electrical wholesaler—the only practical way to reach them is through a wholesaler.

Similarly, consumers may be spread throughout many geographic areas and often prefer to shop for certain products at specific places. For example, a consumer may see London Drugs or Shoppers Drug Mart as *the* place to shop for convenience items. Moreover, if retailers that serve target customers make most of their purchases from specific wholesalers, the producer may have to work with those wholesalers in order to get on retailers' shelves. This is why most consumer products use indirect channels.[11]

There are also financial reasons for using indirect distribution. Direct distribution usually requires a significant investment in facilities, people, and information technology. A new company, one that has limited financial resources, or one that wants to retain flexibility may want to avoid that investment by working with an established intermediary.

Intermediaries may further reduce a producer's investment and need for working capital by buying the producer's output and carrying it in inventory until it's sold. If customers want a good "right now," there must be an inventory available to make the sale. And if customers are spread over a large area, it will probably be necessary to have widespread distribution.

Some intermediaries play a critical role by providing credit to customers at the end of the channel. This financing function may be very important to small-business customers; it provides their working capital. Even if the producer could afford to provide credit, an intermediary who knows local customers can help reduce credit risks. As sales via the Internet grow, sellers are looking for faster and better ways to check the credit ratings of distant customers. It's an unhappy day when the marketing manager learns that a customer who was shipped goods based on an online order can't pay the invoice.

## Place Decision 2—Managing Channel Relations

Intermediaries and specialists can help make either direct or indirect channels more efficient, but there may be problems getting the different firms in a channel to work together well. How well they work together depends on the type of relationship they have. This should be carefully considered, since marketing managers usually have choices about what type of channel system to join or develop.

Ideally, all of the members of a channel system should have a *shared product-market commitment*—with all members focusing on the same target market at the end of the channel and sharing the various marketing functions in appropriate ways. When members of a channel do this, they are better able to compete effectively for the customer's business.

This simple idea is very important. Unfortunately, many marketing managers overlook it because it's not the way their firms have traditionally handled relationships with others in the channel.

### The Source of the Problem

**traditional channel systems**
Systems where the various channel members buy and sell from each other but make little or no effort to cooperate

In **traditional channel systems**, the various channel members make little or no effort to cooperate with each other. They buy and sell from each other—and that's the extent of their relationship. Each channel member does only what it considers to be in its own best interests; it doesn't worry much about the effect of its policies on other members of the channel. This is shortsighted, but it's easy to see how it can happen. The objectives of the various channel members may be different. For example, General Electric wants a wholesaler of electrical building supplies to sell GE products. But an independent wholesaler who carries an assortment of products from different producers may not care whose products get sold. The wholesaler just wants happy customers and a good profit margin.

### Types of Channel Conflict

Specialization has the potential to make a channel more efficient—but not if the specialists are so independent that the channel doesn't work smoothly. Because members of traditional channel systems often have different objectives—and different ideas about how things should be done—conflict is common.

There are two basic types of conflict in channels of distribution. Vertical conflicts occur between firms at different levels in the channel of distribution. For example, a producer and a retailer may disagree about how much shelf space or promotion effort the retailer should give the producer's product. Or conflict may arise if a producer that wants to reduce its excess inventory pushes a wholesaler to carry more inventory than the wholesaler really needs.

In the early 1990s there was vertical conflict between the big recording companies—including Sony, Warner Music, and Capitol-EMI—and retail outlets that wanted to sell used CDs as well as new releases. Retailers were responding to consumers who liked the low cost of used CDs, but the record companies argued that the used CDs ate into their sales and deprived artists of royalties. When Wherehouse Entertainment (one of the largest American retail music chains) started to sell used CDs—at about half the price of new ones—several recording companies said that they would halt cooperative advertising payments to any retailer that sold used CDs. Garth Brooks, the best-selling artist at the time, underscored the conflict and the recording companies' point of view. He said that he would not release his new CDs to any stores that were selling used CDs.[12]

The emergence of the Internet as a means of direct distribution has given rise to vertical conflicts in many industries. The success of Dell (see the opening vignette in Chapter 2) encouraged many companies to see whether they could bypass intermediaries to reduce costs and prices. Internet Insite 11-1 discusses this issue and how some companies have resolved it.

## Internet Insite 11–1

### INTERNET AND CHANNEL CONFLICTS

Two companies with somewhat similar pasts have taken different routes to using the Internet. Avon (www.avon.com) and Mary Kay (www.marykay.com) cosmetics are known for personal selling of cosmetic products. Mary Kay uses the Web to connect consumers with local sales representatives, but has not ventured into direct online sales. Avon continues to use and recruit sales representatives, but also sells many of its products directly to consumers via its website.

Avon's case is not unique. The airline industry had an early taste of direct selling and figured that the 10-percent commission that travel agents are paid could be saved by bypassing the travel agents. By the first quarter of 2000, Southwest Airlines was reporting that 25 percent of its revenues were coming from direct sales of tickets from its website.[13]

The insurance industry is also likely to see a growth in direct selling. Currently insurance agents account for almost all of insurance sales, earning at least 10 percent on each sale. Several leading insurance firms now offer at least some services online, bypassing their agents.

Leading manufacturing firms such as Hewlett-Packard (www.hp.com) now use the direct distribution model in addition to their previously existing channels. HP sells products from its websites, but also continues to use resellers. Snap-on (www.snapon.com) is a manufacturer whose success was based on a vast network of dealers, who earned a living selling Snap-on's tools and shop equipment. Now Snap-on sells more than 14,000 products online directly to end users while continuing to use the dealer network. Clearly, there is room for channel conflict here. A survey of 50 top manufacturing firms by Forrester Research (see exhibit) in 2000 revealed that channel conflict was a leading concern for manufacturers that were selling online. Firms that would not have entertained the idea of direct distribution are now doing just that, thanks to the Internet.

Why are so many firms venturing into Internet retailing and risking channel conflict? Reasons include the ability to reach consumers directly, to lower costs by eliminating commissions to intermediaries, or even to learn more about consumers by directly interacting with them. Studies show that today's consumers want the ability to find information, buy,

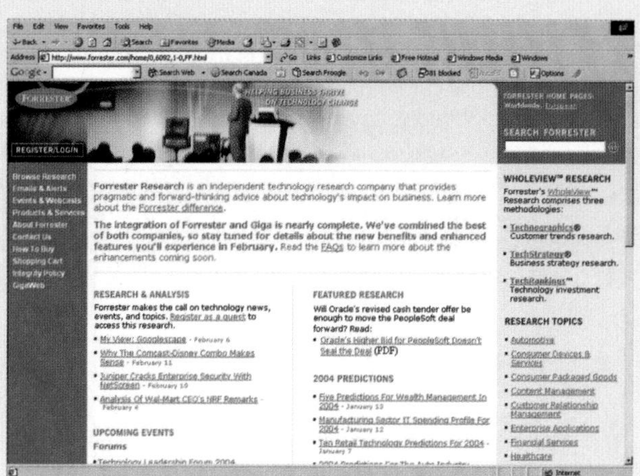


and get service in multiple channels—which means that firms cannot afford *not* to operate in the Internet channel.[14]

Avon found that the cost of processing orders online is 30 cents per order, compared to $1.50 per order for paper orders.[15] That was a strong incentive for the company's Web strategy. Avon started with about 400 products online, but now offers thousands of products. Avon adopted a hybrid channel model, which enables the company to get orders in three different ways: (a) Avon's representatives can continue to sell to their customers face-to-face, (b) representatives can sell online, and (c) Avon itself can sell its products online via www.avon.com to customers who prefer not to buy from "Avon ladies." When selling face-to-face, sales representatives can earn as much as 50 percent in commission, whereas if they make the sale through Avon's website they can make only 20 percent.[16] If a consumer buys directly from Avon without the representative's help, then the representative makes nothing.

How can Avon convince its sales representatives to be loyal to the firm, while the firm is selling directly to consumers and bypassing the sales reps? Mary Stevens, a full-time Avon representative for nine years, is among many at Avon who are concerned about their future. Stevens says, "If you have your eyes open, you've got to be concerned. Mary Kay isn't my competition. Avon is."[17] Like Southwest, HP, and

Snap-on, Avon cannot afford to alienate channel members, since it still continues to use the traditional channels.

In many industries channel conflict is a reality and the focus now is on managing the channel conflict. Providing certain products exclusively for the channel and not selling these products directly online, not undercutting the channel member's price, ensuring that each channel targets a different segment, and enabling the channel members to add value are some of the possible ways in which channel conflicts can be minimized or managed. On the other hand, offering too many concessions to channel members to appease them will lower the profitability of the Internet channel for the manufacturer. There are some difficult tradeoffs to be made here.

Companies in the same industry sometimes do pursue different strategies with respect to Internet retailing. We saw this with Avon and Mary Kay. In other industries, direct distribution is simply not in the cards for now. Brand-name apparel manufacturers have generally stayed away from direct online distribution. Levis Strauss flirted with Internet selling for a while and gave up because the business model was not viable. Tommy Hilfiger uses its site for brand advertising and offers consumers a retail store locator. Automobiles, home appliances, and most consumer electronics are other categories sold through dealers and retailers. That trend is likely to continue. In some of these cases, consumers want to touch, feel, and try the product. In other cases, direct selling is not economical.

Direct distribution requires a different set of capabilities that most manufacturers and service providers do not possess. Instead of shipping truckloads of goods to retailers or resellers, they have to receive individual orders and ship them to individual customers. Individual customers (as opposed to retail customers) often require more customer support. Firms have to handle returns and settle disputes. For some firms, developing capabilities in these areas may take the attention away from product innovation and other core business activities.

Disintermediation is unlikely in many industries because the channel members play an important role. Intermediaries in some industries need to reinvent themselves to survive. If the intermediary or channel member is not adding value and simply adding cost, then we are likely to see the elimination of intermediaries or disintermediation. Intermediaries need to add value in new ways and offer services that manufacturers cannot easily offer.

Some questions to ponder: When would direct selling online make sense for a manufacturing firm? Can you offer some suggestions for managing and minimizing channel conflict when a firm sells directly online and uses resellers?

Go to: www.mcgrawhill.ca/college/wong to apply this Insite in an exciting Internet exercise.



Horizontal conflicts occur between firms at the same level in the channel of distribution. For example, managers of a furniture store that keeps a complete line of furniture on display aren't happy to find out that a store down the street is offering customers lower prices on special orders of the same items. The discounter is getting a free ride from the competing store's investment in inventory. And nothing gets an independent retailer more charged up than finding out that a chain store is selling some product for less than the wholesale price the independent pays.

Traditional channel systems are still typical, and very important, in some industries. The members of these channels have their independence, but they may pay for it too. As we will see, such channels are declining in importance—with good reason.[18]

## Cooperative Channel Relationships

Potential channel conflicts should be anticipated and, if possible, resolved. Usually the best way to do that is to get everyone in the channel working together in a cooperative relationship that is focused on the same basic objective—satisfying the customer at the end of the channel. This leads us away from traditional channels to cooperative channel relationships and the "channel captain" concept.

**channel captain**

A manager who helps direct the activities of a whole channel and tries to avoid or solve channel conflicts

**Channel captains** Each channel system should act as a unit, where each member of the channel collaborates to serve customers at the end of the channel. In this view, cooperation is everyone's responsibility. However, some firms are in a better position to take the lead in the relationship and in coordinating the whole channel effort. This situation calls for a **channel captain**—a manager who helps direct the

A channel captain can improve the performance of the whole channel—by developing strategies that help everyone in the channel do a better job of meeting the needs of target customers at the end of the channel.

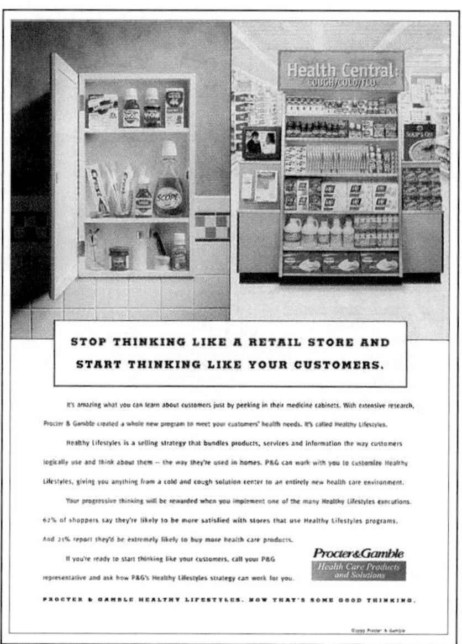

activities of a whole channel and tries to avoid or solve channel conflicts. See Marketing Demo 11-1 for a look at how Kimberly-Clark acts as a channel captain.

For example, when Harley-Davidson saw an opportunity to expand sales of its popular fashion accessories, it was difficult for motorcycle dealers to devote enough space to all of the different styles and sizes. Harley considered selling the items directly from its own website, but that would take sales away from dealers who were working hard to help Harley sell both cycles and fashions. So Harley's president asked a group of dealers and Harley managers to work together to come up with a plan they all liked. The result was a website that sells Harley products through the dealer that is closest to the customer.[19]

The concept of a single channel captain is logical. But some channels, including most traditional ones, don't have a recognized captain. The various firms don't act as a system. The reason may be lack of leadership or the fact that members of

## Marketing Demo 11–1

### KIMBERLY-CLARK BOOSTS BOTTOM LINE FOR DISPOSABLE DIAPERS

It's a messy problem when a busy parent makes a special trip to a Costco store to buy Huggies disposable diapers and they're out of stock. It can be costly, too. The average retailer's loss from out-of-stocks on high-volume items, like diapers, is about 11 percent of annual sales. So what should a Costco manager do to avoid the problem? Nothing. That job is handled by Kimberly-Clark (KC), the firm that makes Huggies. Costco has a system that it calls "vendor-managed inventory" in which key suppliers take over responsibility for managing a set of products, often a whole product category. Every day an analyst at KC's headquarters studies Costco's online data that details Huggies' sales and inventory at every Costco store. The analyst studies how much is sold of each item in each store in the average week. If inventory is getting low, a new order is placed and shipping is scheduled. It's also important not to order too much or too early. KC absorbs all of the inventory and delivery costs required to keep Huggies on the shelves at Costco. When KC does this job well, it makes more money and so does Costco. Costco is a powerful customer, but KC is the channel captain for this category. Costco could do the job itself, but it handles such a wide assortment of products that it would be costly to do all the work required in every high-volume category. Many large retailers use similar approaches. Smaller retailers, however, may find that vendors are not as eager to provide this kind of extra support. The benefits justify the costs when the vendor is more selective about where the service is provided.[20]

the system don't understand their interrelationship. Many managers—more concerned with individual firms immediately above and below them—seem unaware that they are part of a channel.

But like it or not, firms are interrelated, even if poorly, by their policies. So it makes sense to try to avoid channel conflicts by planning for channel relations. The channel captain arranges for the necessary functions to be performed in the most effective way.

**Producers as channel captains** As shown in Marketing Demo 11-2, producers frequently take the lead in channel relations. Intermediaries often wait to see what the producer intends to do and wants them to do. After marketing managers for Goodyear set price, promotion, and place policies, wholesalers and retailers decide whether their roles will be profitable and whether they want to join in the channel effort.

Exhibit 11-5A shows this type of producer-led channel system. Here the producer has selected the target market and developed the product, set the price structure, done some consumer and channel promotion, and developed the place setup. Intermediaries are then expected to finish the promotion job in their respective places. Of course, in a retailer-dominated channel system the marketing jobs would be handled in a different way.

**Intermediaries as channel captains** Sometimes large wholesalers or retailers do take the lead. These intermediaries analyze the types of products their customers want and then seek out producers that can provide these products at reasonable prices. With the growth of powerful retail chains, like Zellers and Toys"R"Us, this is becoming more common in Canada and the United States. It is already typical in many foreign markets. In Japan, for example, very large wholesalers (trading companies) are often the channel captains.

## Marketing Demo 11–2

### GOODYEAR

The situation faced by Goodyear is a good example. The Goodyear brand was sold almost exclusively through its own stores and its 2,500 independent tire dealers. But sales were falling. There were many reasons. France's Michelin and Japan's Bridgestone had aggressively expanded distribution in North America. The 850 Sears autocentres were selling one-tenth of all replacement tires. Moreover, many consumers were shopping at discount outlets and warehouse clubs. Goodyear decided it had no choice but to expand distribution beyond its independent dealer network. One of the first changes was to sell Goodyear tires to Sears, Penske autocentres, and other big retail chains. To better reach the discount shoppers, Goodyear converted many of its company-owned autocentres to no-frills, quick-serve stores operated under the Just Tires name. However, to reduce the conflict that these changes caused with its independent dealers, Goodyear introduced new lines of premium tires—like the innovative Aquatred line and specialized lines for sports cars and four-wheel drive vehicles. These were tires that appealed to the dealers' target market. Goodyear also increased advertising and promotion support to pull more customers into the dealers' stores, and offered training on how to build sales of related services. Goodyear also created the Gemini brand name to help promote service by Goodyear dealers. Because of this channel leadership, Goodyear's sales increased and so did the sales of its dealers.[21]

Exhibit 11-5 How channel functions may be shifted and shared in different channel systems.

A. How strategy decisions are handled in a producer-led channel

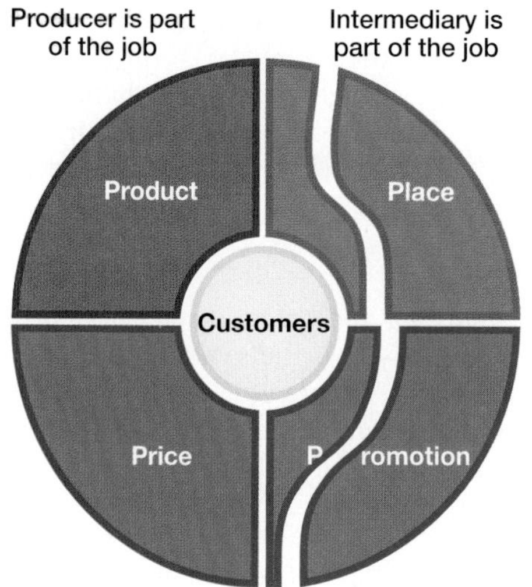


B. How strategy decisions are handled in a retailer-led channel

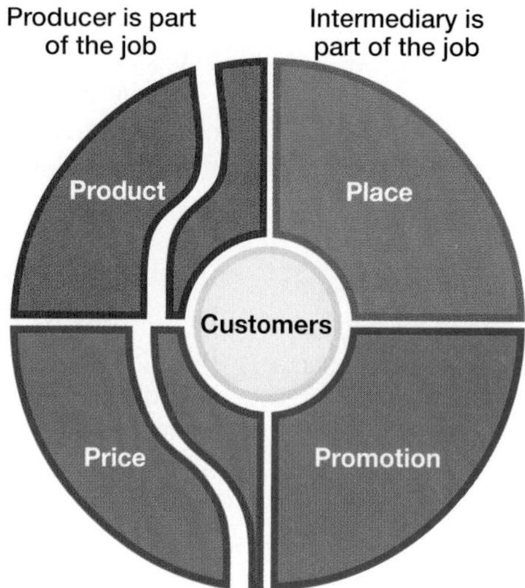


Channel captains who are intermediaries often develop their own dealer brands. Large retailers like Sears, Wal-Mart, and Costco in effect act like producers. They specify the whole marketing mix for a product and merely delegate production to a factory. Exhibit 11-5B shows how marketing strategy might be handled in this sort of retailer-led channel system.

Some strong intermediaries use their power to control channel relationships. Wal-Mart, the largest retail chain, is constantly looking for ways to cut its own costs—and sometimes that means cutting costs in the channel. Buyers for Wal-Mart look at the value added by a wholesaler. If they think Wal-Mart can be more effi-

The growing number of retailer-led channel systems is prompting growth of private-label dealer brands in a wide variety of product categories.

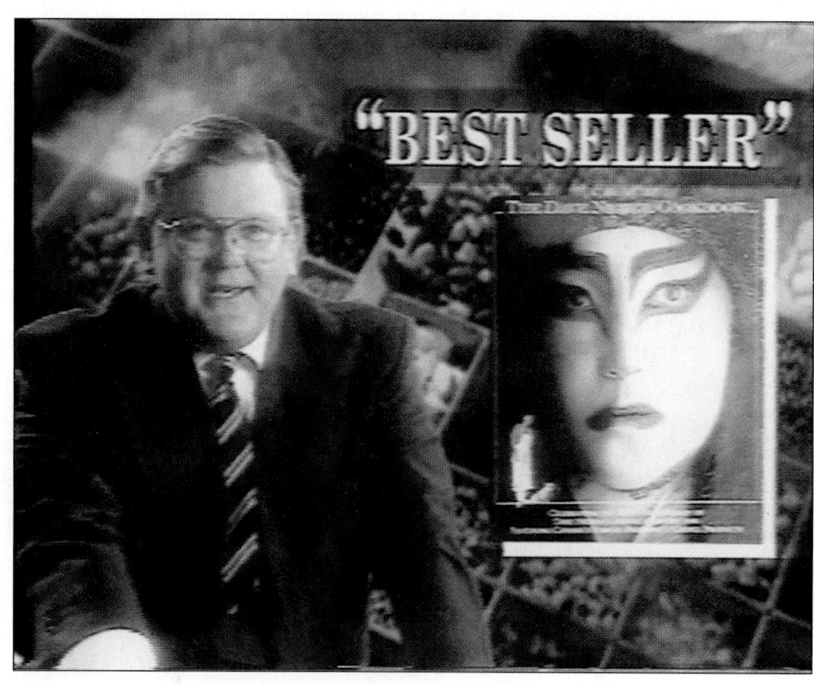

cient without the wholesaler, they tell the producer that the chain will only buy direct—usually at a lower price than was paid to the wholesaler.

Intermediaries are closer to the final user or consumer and are in an ideal position to assume the channel captain role. Intermediaries, especially large retailers, may even dominate the marketing systems of the future.[22]

Many marketing managers accept the view that a coordinated channel system can help everyone in the channel. These managers are moving their firms away from traditional channel systems and instead developing or joining vertical market systems.

**vertical marketing systems**
Systems in which the whole channel focuses on the same target market at the end of the channel

## Vertical Marketing Systems

In contrast to traditional channel systems are **vertical marketing systems**—channel systems in which the whole channel focuses on the same target market at the end of the channel. Such systems make sense, and are growing, because if the final customer doesn't buy the product the whole channel suffers. There are three types of vertical marketing systems—corporate, administered, and contractual. Exhibit 11-6 summarizes some characteristics of these systems and compares them with traditional systems.

Smoothly operating channel systems are more efficient and successful. In the consumer-products field, vertical systems have a healthy majority of retail sales and should continue to increase their share in the future. Vertical marketing systems are becoming the major competitive units in the Canadian distribution system, and are growing rapidly in other parts of the world as well.[23]

**corporate channel systems**
Systems that have corporate ownership all along the channel

**vertical integration**
The practice of acquiring firms at different levels of channel activity

**Corporate channel systems** Some corporations develop their own vertical marketing systems by internal expansion or by buying other firms. With **corporate channel systems**—corporate ownership all along the channel—we might say the firm is going "direct." But actually the firm may be handling manufacturing, wholesaling, *and* retailing—so it's more accurate to think of the firm as a vertical marketing system.

Corporate channel systems may develop by **vertical integration**—acquiring firms at different levels of channel activity. Bridgestone, for example, has rubber plantations in Liberia, tire plants in Ohio, and wholesale and retail outlets all over the world. Sherwin-Williams produces paint, but it also operates 2,000 retail outlets. In England, most of the quaint local pubs are actually owned and operated by the large breweries.



Exhibit 11-6
Characteristics of traditional and vertical marketing systems.

| Characteristics | Type of channel | | | |
|---|---|---|---|---|
| | | Vertical Marketing Systems | | |
| | Traditional | Administered | Contractual | Corporate |
| Amount of cooperation | Little or none | Some to good | Fairly good to good | Complete |
| Control maintained by | None | Economic power and leadership | Contracts | Ownership by one company |
| Examples | Typical channel of "independents" | General Electric, Miller Beer, O.M. Scott & Sons (lawn products) | McDonald's Holiday Inn, IGA, Home Hardware, Super Valu, Coca-Cola, Chevrolet | Florsheim Shoes, Sherwin-Williams |

## Marketing Demo 11–3

### BRINGING FASHION TO FOOD

Loblaw Companies Ltd., the jewel in the George Weston Ltd. empire, can claim many successes during the 1990s, but its lasting legacy will be that it shifted the balance of power on grocery store shelves from national brands to private labels.

Although Loblaw's President's Choice brand was born in 1984, it was in the '90s that it reached its full potential, under the hand of Dave Nichol when he was president of Loblaw International Merchants.

"I think Loblaw's greatest achievement was to bring fashion to food and to do it in a profitable and very appealing manner," says Wendy Evans, president of Evans & Co., a Toronto retail consultancy.

Realizing there were significant profits to be made through its in-house labels, Loblaw confiscated more shelf space for its own brands, among them No Name (created in 1978), Green (1989) and Too Good To Be True! (1991). In the '90s, national brands were no longer guaranteed prime real estate in national supermarkets.

Loblaw's raised the bar for food retailing across Canada. Loblaw turned President's Choice into a private-label superstar that is now stocked by supermarkets in the U.S. and as far away as Israel. The Decadent became one of Canada's best-selling cookies, while offerings such as Memories of Bangkok Spicy Thai Sauce tapped into a consumer desire for the exotic combined with premium quality and convenience.

Nichol, the face behind the PC label, kicked off the decade with a series of cheaply produced TV spots, in which he starred. Loblaw's competitors eventually clued in and by the middle of the decade the Great Atlantic & Pacific Co. of Canada Ltd. had upgraded and revamped its Master's Choice line, and Oshawa Group debuted its Our Compliments brand.

Loblaw is widely credited as being an innovative retailer, but it is also an adapter of successful concepts perfected by other marketers, particularly British supermarket giant Sainsbury's. Loblaw's genius is knowing what and when to adapt.

Loblaw borrowed the idea of premium private-label products from Sainsbury's. For instance, the superb *President's Choice Magazine*, launched last year, is modeled on a successful publication put out by the British grocer. There already was a Sainsbury's Bank when Loblaw launched PC Financial in February 1998, a joint undertaking with the Canadian Imperial Bank of Commerce. And by the time Loblaw began offering ready-made meals through in-store Movenpick Take Me! Marché kiosks in 1997, the home meal replacement trend had been going strong in the U.S. for three years.

During the '90s, Loblaw perfected the so-called main-street-in-a-box retail community that puts such services as dry cleaning, photocopy shops, jewelry stores, banking services and a fitness club under the same roof. The grocer's newest format is the farmer's market, with an emphasis on fresh produce, meats, and bakery products.

Loblaw, which was unsuccessful in a bid for Quebec's Steinberg chain 10 years ago, finally clinched the Quebec market late last year when it acquired Provigo Inc. Loblaw Companies exits the 1990s as Canada's largest grocery retailer, accounting for over 30% of total grocery sales. It reported sales of $14.2 billion for the 40 weeks ended Oct. 9, 1999.

"They have raised the bar for food retailing throughout North America," says Evans. "I think there are few retailers who can do it better than them."[24]

Corporate channel systems are not always started by producers. A retailer might integrate into wholesaling and perhaps even manufacturing. Marketing Demo 11-3 shows how Loblaws carried this out.

Vertical integration has potential advantages—stability of operations, assurance of materials and supplies, better control of distribution, better quality control, larger research facilities, greater buying power, and lower executive overhead. Provided that the discrepancies of quantity and assortment are not too great at each level in a channel—that is, that the firms fit together well—vertical integration can be efficient and profitable.

**Administered and contractual systems** However, many firms that have tried vertical integration have found it difficult to achieve these efficiencies. Some managers think it's hard to be really good at running manufacturing, wholesaling, and retailing businesses that are very different from each other. Instead, they try to be more efficient at what they do best and focus on ways to get cooperation in the channel for the other activities.

**administered channel systems**
Systems in which the channel members informally agree to cooperate with each other

**contractual channel systems**
Systems in which the channel members agree by contract to cooperate with each other

Firms can often gain the advantages of vertical integration without building an expensive corporate channel. A firm can develop administered or contractual channel systems instead. In **administered channel systems**, the channel members informally agree to cooperate with each other. They can agree to routinize ordering, share inventory and sales information over computer networks, standardize accounting, and coordinate promotion efforts. In **contractual channel systems**, the channel members agree by contract to cooperate with each other.

With both of these systems, the members achieve some of the advantages of corporate integration while retaining some of the flexibility of a traditional channel system. In fact, the opportunities to reduce costs and provide customers with superior value are growing in these systems as new information technologies help channel partners share data to make products flow more efficiently through the channel.

An appliance producer may develop an informal arrangement with the independent wholesalers in its administered channel system. It agrees to keep production and inventory levels in the system balanced—using sales data from the wholesalers. Every week, its managers do a thorough analysis of up to 130,000 major appliances located in the many warehouses operated by its 87 wholesalers. Because of this analysis, both the producer and the wholesalers can be sure that they have enough inventory but not the expense of too much. And the producer has better information to plan its manufacturing and marketing efforts.

Intermediaries in many industries—like groceries, drugs, hardware, and books—develop and coordinate similar systems. Computerized checkout systems can be used to track sales. The information is sent to the wholesaler's computer, which enters orders automatically when needed. Shipping cartons with computer-readable bar codes track the status of shipments and reduce errors. This reduces buying and selling costs, inventory investment, and customer frustration with out-of-stock items throughout the channel.

**Alliances—A short-term alternative** Firms that cooperate to build vertical marketing systems typically share a longer-term commitment. Sometimes, however, what a firm wants is a short-term collaboration to help it be more efficient in accomplishing a specific objective. This may lead to an alliance, a partnership (usually informal) among firms in which they agree to work together to achieve an objective. An alliance often involves two firms, but sometimes it involves a whole network of firms that spin a web to catch more customers. The firms may be at the same level in the channel or at different levels. For example, a number of firms in the computer business have formed alliances to promote a market for the Linux operating system. Some of these firms produce hardware and some produce software; some focus on distribution and some are even competitors (at least in a few of their product-markets). Nevertheless, by forming a temporary alliance they increase their chances of reaching potential customers at the end of the channel. Without the alliance, it would be difficult for any one of these firms to compete with Microsoft or Intel.[25]



## Place Decision 3—Market Exposure

**ideal market exposure**
Making a product available widely enough to satisfy target customers' needs but not exceed them

You may think that all marketing managers want their products to have maximum exposure to potential customers. This isn't true. Some product classes require much less market exposure than others. **Ideal market exposure** makes a product available widely enough to satisfy target customers' needs but not exceed them. Too much exposure only increases the total cost of marketing.

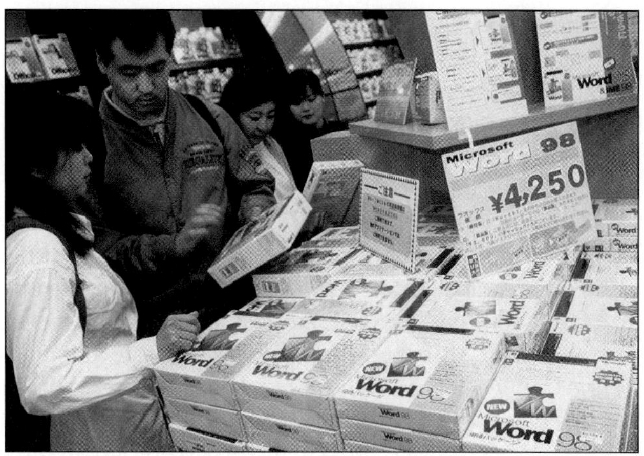


As the percentage of people and firms adopting personal computers has increased, Microsoft has moved to more intensive distribution of its products worldwide.

**intensive distribution**

Selling a product through all responsible and suitable wholesalers or retailers that will stock and/or sell the product

**selective distribution**

Selling through only those intermediaries who will give the product special attention

**exclusive distribution**

Selling through only one intermediary in a particular geographic area

**Intensive distribution** is selling a product through all responsible and suitable wholesalers or retailers that will stock and/or sell the product. **Selective distribution** is selling through only those intermediaries who will give the product special attention. **Exclusive distribution** is selling through only one intermediary in a particular geographic area. As we move from intensive to exclusive distribution, we give up exposure in return for some other advantage—including, but not limited to, lower cost.

In practice, this means that Trident chewing gum is handled through intensive distribution by thousands of Canadian retail outlets. Rolls Royce automobiles, on the other hand, are handled through exclusive distribution by only a limited number of intermediaries across the country.

## Intensive Distribution

Intensive distribution is commonly needed for convenience products and business supplies—such as laser-printer cartridges, ring binders, and copier paper—used by all offices. Customers want such products nearby. Coke must sell through an intensive channel of distribution as well, to ensure that its product is within arm's reach of desire of its consumers, whenever they might happen to be thirsty.

The seller's intent is important here. Intensive distribution refers to the desire to sell through *all* responsible and suitable outlets. What this means depends on customer habits and preferences. If target customers normally buy a certain product at a certain type of outlet, ideally you would specify this type of outlet in your place policies. If customers preferred to buy Sharp portable TVs only at electronics stores, you would try to sell through all electronics stores to achieve intensive distribution. Today, however, many customers buy small portable TVs at a variety of convenient outlets—including Costco, a local London Drugs, over the phone from the Sharper Image catalogue, or perhaps from a website on the Internet. This means that an intensive distribution policy requires use of all these outlets, and more than one channel, to reach one target market.

Rayovac batteries were not selling well against Duracell and Energizer, even though the performance of the different batteries was very similar. Part of that may have been due to the heavier advertising for the Duracell and Energizer brands. But consumers usually don't go shopping for batteries—83 percent of the time they're purchased on impulse. So to get a larger share of the purchases, Rayovac had to be in more stores. It offered retailers a marketing mix with less advertising and a lower price. In a period of three years, the brand moved from being available in 36,000 stores to 82,000 stores—and that was enough to give sales a big charge.[26]

### Selective Distribution

Selective distribution covers the broad area of market exposure between intensive and exclusive distribution. It may be suitable for all categories of products. Only the better intermediaries are used here. Companies usually use selective distribution to gain some of the advantages of exclusive distribution—while still achieving fairly widespread market coverage.

A selective policy might be used to avoid selling to wholesalers or retailers who (1) place orders that are too small to justify making calls or providing service, (2) have a reputation for making too many returns or requesting too much service, (3) have a poor credit rating, or (4) are not in a position to do a satisfactory job.

Selective distribution is becoming more popular than intensive distribution as firms see that they don't need 100-percent coverage of a market to justify or support national advertising. Often the majority of sales come from relatively few customers—and the others buy too little compared to the cost of working with them; that is, they are unprofitable to serve. This is called the 80/20 rule—80 percent of a company's sales often come from only 20 percent of its customers until it becomes more selective in choosing customers.

Esprit—a producer of colourful, trendy clothing—was selling through about 4,000 department stores and specialty shops nationwide. But Esprit found that about half of the stores generated most of the sales. Sales analysis also showed that sales in Esprit's own stores were about 400 percent better than sales in other sales outlets.



Esprit increased profits through a more selective channel of distribution by opening up more of its own stores.

As a result, Esprit cut back to about 2,000 outlets and opened more of its own stores and a website—and profits increased.[27]

When producers use selective distribution, fewer sales contacts have to be made—and fewer wholesalers are needed. A producer may be able to contact selected retailers directly. Hanes sells men's underwear this way.

Selective distribution can produce greater profits not only for the producer but also for all channel members—because of the closer cooperation among them. Wholesalers and retailers are more willing to promote products aggressively if they know they're going to obtain the majority of sales through their own efforts. They may carry more stock and wider lines, do more promotion, and provide more service—all of which lead to more sales.

In the early part of the life cycle of a new unsought good, a producer's marketing manager may have to use selective distribution to encourage enough intermediaries to handle the product. The manager wants to get the product out of the unsought category as soon as possible—but can't if it lacks distribution. Well-known intermediaries may have the power to get such a product introduced but sometimes on their own terms—which often include limiting the number of competing wholesalers and retailers. The producer may be happy with such an arrangement at first but dislike it later when more retailers want to carry the product.

**Exclusive distribution** Exclusive distribution is just an extreme case of selective distribution—the firm selects only one intermediary in each geographic area. Besides the various advantages of selective distribution, producers may want to use exclusive distribution to help control prices and the service offered in a channel.

Retailers of shopping products and specialty products often try to get exclusive distribution rights in their territories. Fast-food franchises often have exclusive distribution—and that's one reason why they're popular. Owners of McDonald's franchises pay a share of sales and follow McDonald's strategy to keep the exclusive right to a market.

### Legal Aspects of Market Exposure

Marketing managers must operate within the law, and any consideration of place must raise the question of the legality of limiting market exposure.

As long as there is no abuse of a dominant position, exclusive distribution as such isn't illegal in Canada. Indeed, "vertical" exclusive distribution contracts between a manufacturer and an intermediary have never been successfully challenged in the courts. "Horizontal" arrangements among competing retailers, wholesalers, and/or manufacturers operating at the same level would almost certainly be judged a violation of the Competition Act. However, it would have to be proven that such agreements had "unduly lessened competition."

The Competition Tribunal has the authority to review vertical agreements and to act against those judged as having an adverse effect on competition. The 1975 amendments to the Combines Act (now called the Competition Act) also specified that "unduly lessening competition" meant lessening it to any extent judged detrimental to the public interest. (Previously, it had to be shown that competition would be completely or virtually eliminated.) However, the same amendments allowed temporary exclusive dealing arrangements to permit the introduction of a new product or where there is some technological justification for such a policy.

The Competition Tribunal can also bar *consignment selling* when such a policy is being used to (1) fix the price at which a dealer sells the products so supplied or (2) discriminate among those receiving the product for resale. Until this change was made, a supplier could control the selling price by dealing only on consignment and by specifying the commission level built into the ultimate price. Alternatively, a supplier could allow a favoured customer on consignment a larger commission than other customers.

**refusal to supply**
Applies when a firm or individual is unable to obtain, on the usual terms, adequate supplies of an article or service not generally in short supply

The Tribunal can also help someone who has been injured by a **refusal to supply**. This applies when a firm or individual is unable to obtain, on the usual terms, adequate supplies of an article or service not generally in short supply. This amendment doesn't make refusal to supply an offence in itself. However, a complaint concerning such practices can be brought to the Competition Tribunal. If the complaint is upheld, the Tribunal can order that one or more suppliers accept that customer on usual trade terms.

## Place Decision 4—Channel Complexity

Trying to achieve the desired degree of market exposure can lead to complex channels of distribution. Firms may need different channels to reach different segments of a broad product-market or to be sure they reach each segment. Sometimes this results in competition between different channels.

Consider the different channels used by a company that publishes computer books (see Exhibit 11-7). This publisher sells through a general book wholesaler who in turn sells to Internet book retailers and independent book retailers. The publisher may have some direct sales of its best-selling books to a large chain or even to consumers who order directly from its website. However, it might also sell through a computer-supplies wholesaler that serves electronics superstores like Future Shop. This can cause problems because different wholesalers and retailers want different markups. It also increases competition, including price competition. And the competition among different intermediaries may result in conflicts between the intermediaries and the publisher.



**dual distribution**
Occurs when a producer uses several competing channels to reach the same target market, perhaps using several intermediaries in addition to selling directly

### Dual Distribution

**Dual distribution** occurs when a producer uses several competing channels to reach the same target market—perhaps using several intermediaries in addition to selling

Exhibit 11-7 An example of dual distribution by a publisher of computer books.

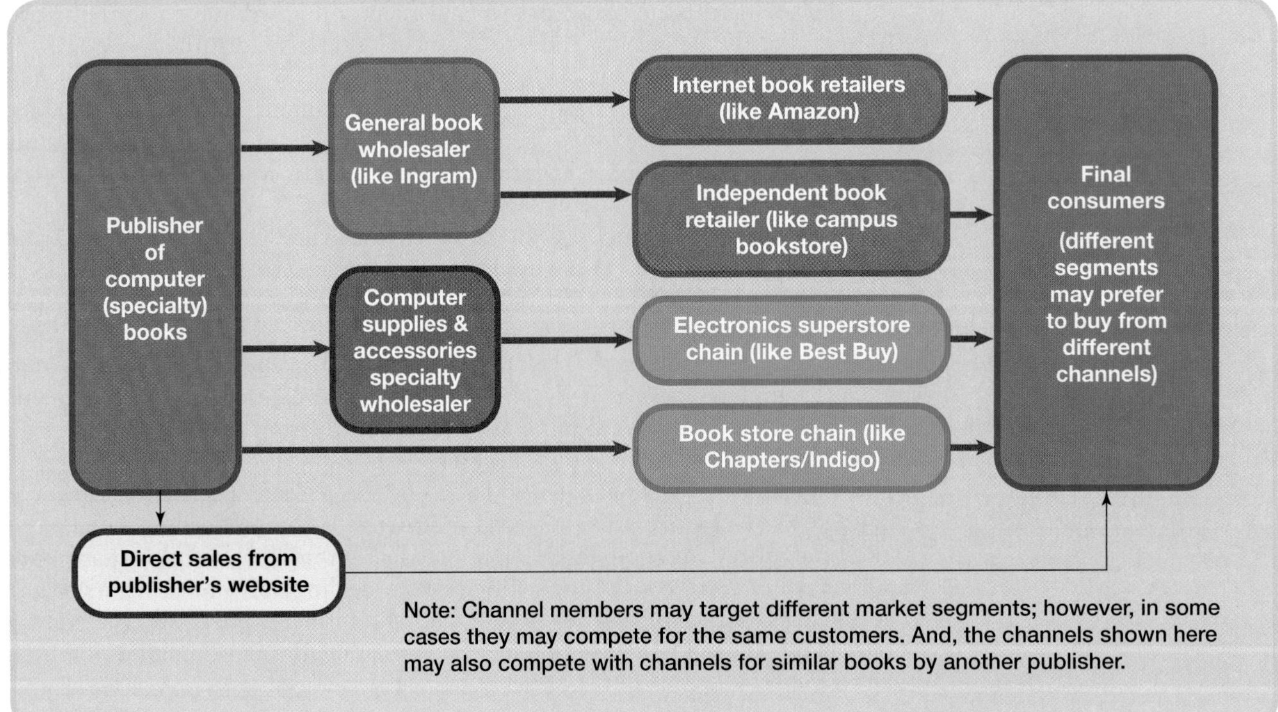

Some special models of the Beetle could only be ordered online direct from VW's website. However, the customer was then directed to a VW dealer who completed the transaction—an arrangement that avoids conflict between VW and its dealers.

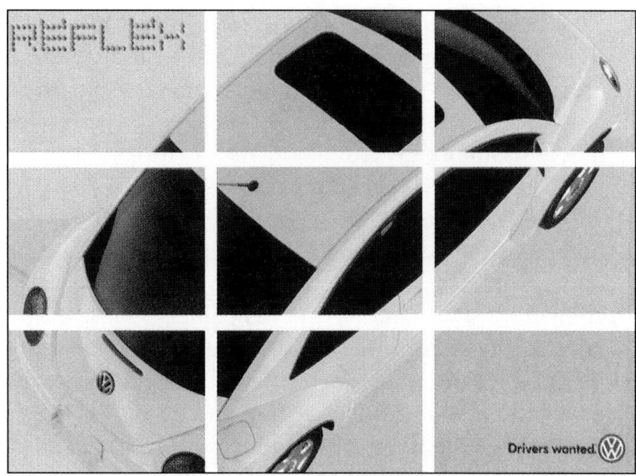


directly. Dual distribution is becoming more common. Big retail chains want to deal directly with producers. They want large quantities and low prices. The producer sells directly to retail chains and relies on wholesalers to sell to smaller accounts. Some established intermediaries resent this because they don't appreciate *any* competition—especially price competition set up by their own suppliers.

Other times, producers are forced to use dual distribution because their present channels are doing a poor job or aren't reaching some potential customers. For example, Reebok International had been relying on local sporting goods stores to sell its shoes to high-school and college athletic teams. But Reebok wasn't getting much of the business. When it set up its own team-sales department to sell directly to the schools, it got a 30,000-unit increase in sales. Of course, some of the stores weren't happy about their supplier also selling to their potential customers. However, they did get the message that Reebok wanted someone to reach that target market.[28] See Ethical Dimensions 11-1 for more on the ethics of decision making for channel issues.

## Ethical Dimensions 11–1

### DECISON MAKING FOR CHANNEL ISSUES

A shared product-market commitment guides co-operative relationships among channel members as long as the channel system is competitive. However, if customers' place requirements change, the current channel system may lose its effectiveness. The changes required to serve customer needs may hurt one or more members of the channel. The most difficult ethical dilemmas in the channels area arise in situations like this—because not everyone can win.

For example, wholesalers and the independent retailers they serve in a channel of distribution may trust a producer channel captain to develop marketing strategies that will work for the whole channel. However, the producer may conclude that everyone in the channel will ultimately fail if it continues exclusive distribution. It may decide that consumers—and its own business—would be best served by a change (say, dropping current intermediaries and selling direct to big retail chains). A move of this sort, if implemented immediately, may not give current intermediaries a chance to make adjustments of their own. The more dependent they are on the producer, the more severe the impact will likely be. It's not easy to determine the best or most ethical solution in these situations. However, marketing managers must think carefully about the implications of strategy changes in the place area, because they can have very severe consequences for other channel members. In channels, as in any business dealings, relationships of trust must be treated with care.[29]

### The Special Case of Reverse Channels

**reverse channels**
Channels used to retrieve products that customers no longer want

Most firms focus on getting products to their customers. But some marketing managers must also plan for **reverse channels**—channels used to retrieve products that customers no longer want. The need for reverse channels may arise in a variety of different situations. Toy companies, automobile firms, drug companies, and others sometimes have to recall products because of safety problems. A producer that makes an error in completing an order may have to take returns from intermediaries or other business customers. If a Viewsonic computer monitor breaks while it's still under warranty, someone needs to get it to the authorized repair centre. Soft-drink companies may need to recycle empty bottles. And of course, at some point or another, most consumers buy something in error and want to return it. For example, this is quite common with online purchases where consumers can't see, touch, or try the actual product before purchasing it.[30]

Another problem arises from products that are damaged in shipping or discontinued. Most manufacturers take them back. For example, until recently P&G had a reclamation centre that took back thousands of products, ranging from damaged boxes of Tide to leaking bottles of Crisco Oil. A grocery-products trade group says that the cost of such returns, in total, may be as much as $4 billion a year. This has prompted P&G to change its policies. Now, P&G has adopted a no-returns policy and instead gives retailers a payment for damaged items. The system is designed to reduce the cost of returns to both P&G and retailers. Ultimately, that cost must be paid by consumers. Some retailers don't like P&G's policy, but it is important to see that it is a specific plan and part of an overall strategy.

When marketing managers don't plan for reverse channels, the firm's customers may be left to solve "their" problem. That usually doesn't make sense. So a complete plan for place may need to consider an efficient way to return products—with policies that different channel members agree on. It may also require specialists who were not involved in getting the product to the consumer. But if that's what it takes to satisfy customers, it should be part of marketing strategy planning.[31]

## Issues in Distribution Customer Service and Logistics

**logistics (physical distribution)**
The transporting, storing, and handling of goods to match target customers' needs with a firm's marketing mix

Choosing the right channel of distribution is crucial in getting products to the target market's place. But as the Coke case shows, that alone is usually not enough to ensure that products are available at the right time and in the right quantities. Whenever the product includes a physical good, place requires logistics decisions. **Logistics** is the transporting, storing, and handling of goods to match target customers' needs with a firm's marketing mix—both within individual firms and along a channel of distribution. **Physical distribution (PD)** is another common name for logistics.

PD provides time and place utility and makes possession utility possible. A marketing manager may have to make many decisions to ensure that the physical distribution system provides utility and meets customers' needs with an acceptable service level and cost.

Logistics costs are very important to both firms and consumers. While these costs vary from firm to firm, for many physical goods firms spend half or more of their total marketing dollars on physical distribution activities. The total amount of money involved is so large that even small improvements in this area can have a big effect on a whole macro-marketing system and consumers' quality of life.

For example, during the past decade many supermarket chains and producers that supply them collaborated to create a system called Efficient Consumer Response (ECR) that cut grocers' costs, and prices, by about 11 percent. That translates to savings of about $3 billion a year for Canadian consumers! The basic idea of ECR involves paperless, computerized links between grocers and their suppliers, which leads to more effective merchandise assortments and continuous replenishment of shelves based on what actually sells each day. Although the ECR movement started in the U.S. and Canada, it quickly spread across Europe and in other regions. Now, 50 consumer packaged goods companies have banded together to create Transora, a Web portal (www.transora.com), to bring more e-commerce benefits to the ECR concept. Obviously, far-reaching innovations like these don't transform everything overnight, but you can see that more effective approaches in the distribution area have the potential to save firms, and their customers, massive amounts of money.[32]

## The Physical Distribution Concept

Just as marketing decision making is guided by the marketing concept, decisions about logistics are guided by the physical distribution (PD) concept—the idea that all transporting, storing, and product-handling activities of a business and a whole channel system should be coordinated as one system that seeks to minimize the cost of distribution for a given customer service level. Both lower costs and better service help to increase customer value. It may be hard to see this as a startling development. But until just a few years ago, even the most progressive companies treated physical distribution functions as separate and unrelated activities.

Within a firm, responsibility for different distribution activities was spread among various departments—production, shipping, sales, warehousing, and others. No one person was responsible for coordinating storing and shipping decisions or seeing how they related to customer service levels. Some firms even failed to calculate the costs for these activities, so they never knew the total cost of physical distribution. If it was unusual for distribution to be coordinated within a firm, it was even rarer for different firms in the channel to collaborate. Each just did its own thing.[33]

Unfortunately, in too many firms old-fashioned ways persist—with a focus on individual functional activities rather than the whole physical distribution system. Trying to reduce the cost of individual functional activities may actually increase total distribution costs—not only for the firm, but also for the whole channel. It may also lead to the wrong customer service level. Well-run firms now avoid these problems by paying attention to the physical distribution concept.

## Finding the Right Customer Service Levels

From the beginning, we've emphasized that marketing strategy planning is based on meeting customers' needs. Planning for logistics and place is no exception. So let's start by looking at logistics through a customer's eyes.

PD is, and should be, a part of marketing that is "invisible" to most consumers. Customers don't care how a product was moved or stored or what some channel member had to do to provide it. Rather, customers think in terms of the physical distribution **customer service level**—how rapidly and dependably a firm can deliver what its customers want. Marketing managers need to understand the customer's point of view.

**customer service level**
How rapidly and dependably a firm can deliver what its customers want

What does this really mean? It means that Toyota wants to have enough windshields delivered to make cars that day—not late (so production stops) or early (so there are a lot of extras to move around or store). In turn, it means that the Toyota dealer wants the car when it's due so that salespeople are not left making excuses to the customer who ordered it. It means that business executives who rent cars from Hertz want them to be ready when they get off their planes. It means that when you order a blue shirt at the Lands' End website you receive blue, not pink. It means you want your Lay's Baked Potato Chips to be whole when you buy a bag at the snack bar—not crushed into crumbs from rough handling in a warehouse.

With the physical distribution concept, firms work together to decide what aspects of service are most important to customers at the end of the channel and what specific service level to provide. Then they focus on finding the least expensive way to achieve the target level of service.

Exhibit 11-8
Examples of factors that affect PD service levels.

- Advance information on product availability
- Time to enter and process orders
- Backorder procedures
- Where inventory is stored
- Accuracy in filling orders
- Damage in shipping, storing, and handing
- Online status information
- Advance information on delays
- Time needed to deliver an order
- Reliability in meeting delivery date
- Complying with customer's instructions
- Defect-free deliveries
- How needed adjustments are handled
- Procedures for handling returns

Exhibit 11-8 shows a variety of factors that may influence the customer service level (at each level in the channel). The most important aspects of customer service depend on target-market needs. Xerox might focus on how long it takes to deliver copy machine repair parts once it receives an order. When a copier breaks down, customers want the repair "yesterday." The service level might be stated as "we will deliver 90 percent of all emergency repair parts within 8 business hours and the remainder within 24 hours." Such a service level might require that almost all such parts be kept in inventory, that the most commonly needed parts be available on the service truck, that order processing be very fast and accurate, and that parts not available locally be sent by airfreight. If Xerox doesn't make the part, it would need to be sent directly from Xerox's supplier. Obviously, supplying this service level will affect the total cost of the PD system. But it may also beat competitors who don't provide this service level. Marketing Demo 11-4 shows how Clorox uses PD to establish a major competitive advantage.

### The Cost–Service Tradeoff

Most customers would prefer very good service at a very low price. But that combination is hard to provide because it usually costs more to provide higher levels of service. So most physical distribution decisions involve tradeoffs between costs, the customer service level, and sales.

If you want a new Compaq computer and the Best Buy store where you would like to buy it doesn't have it on hand, you're likely to buy it elsewhere; or, if that

## Marketing Demo 11–4

### MAINTAINING A COMPETITIVE ADVANTAGE

Increasing service levels may be very profitable in highly competitive situations where a firm has little else to differentiate its marketing mix. Marketing managers at Clorox, for example, must do everything they can to develop and keep strong partnerships with Clorox intermediaries (supermarket chains, convenience stores, mass merchandisers, warehouse clubs, and wholesalers) and other business customers (ranging from white-tablecloth restaurants to fast-service chains). Many other firms sell products with precisely the same ingredients as Clorox and are constantly trying to get orders from Clorox's 100,000 business customers worldwide. Yet Clorox's objective is to "maintain the highest standards for customer service" in the product-markets it serves because that helps it obtain a competitive advantage.

For example, when the bleach buyer for a major retail chain went on vacation, the fill-in person was not familiar with the computerized reorder procedures. As a result, the chain's central distribution centre almost ran out of Clorox liquid bleach. But Clorox's distribution people identified the problem themselves—because of a computer system that allowed Clorox to access the chain's inventory records and sales data for Clorox products. Clorox rearranged production to get a shipment out fast enough to prevent the chain, and Clorox, from losing sales at individual stores. In the future when some other bleach supplier tries to tell buyers for the chain that "bleach is bleach," they'll remember the distribution service Clorox provides.[34]

Exhibit 11-9
Tradeoffs among physical distribution costs, consumer service levels, and sales.

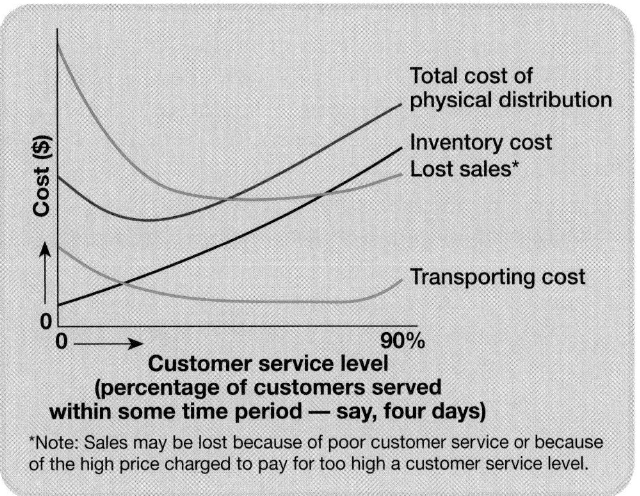




model of Compaq is hard to get, you might just switch to some other brand. Perhaps the Best Buy store could keep your business by guaranteeing two-day delivery of your computer—by using airfreight from Compaq's factory. In this case, the manager is trading the cost of storing inventory for the extra cost of speedy delivery—assuming that the computer is available in inventory somewhere in the channel. In this example, missing one sale may not seem that important, but it all adds up. In fact, using Compaq to illustrate this point is quite purposeful. A few years ago, Compaq lost more than $500 million in sales because its computers weren't available when and where customers were ready to buy them. With that kind of lesson in lost sales, you can see why Compaq worked hard to improve on the tradeoff it was making.

Exhibit 11-9 illustrates tradeoff relationships like those highlighted in the Compaq example. For example, faster but more expensive transportation may reduce the need for a costly inventory of computers. There is also a tradeoff between the service level and sales. If the service level is too low—if products are not available on a timely and dependable basis—customers will buy elsewhere, and sales will be lost. Alternatively, the supplier may hope that a higher service level will attract more customers or motivate them to pay a higher price. But if the service level is higher than customers want or are willing to pay for, sales will be lost to competitors who have figured out what kind of service customers value.

The important point is that many tradeoffs must be made in the PD area. The tradeoffs can be complicated. The lowest-cost approach may not be best, if customers aren't satisfied. A higher service level may make a better strategy. Further, if different channel members or target markets want different customer service levels, several different strategies may be needed.[35]

**total-cost approach**
Evaluating each possible PD system and identifying all of the costs of each alternative

It is for this reason that, in selecting a PD system, a growing number of firms use the **total-cost approach**—evaluating each possible PD system and identifying all of the costs of each alternative. This approach uses the tools of economics and cost accounting to assign costs that otherwise might be ignored, such as inventory carrying costs, lost sales, and the like. For example, a manager might start comparing transportation charges via rail versus air and lean toward the use of rail owing to its lower cost. However, under the total-cost approach, we might find that shipping by air reduces warehousing and other costs by far more than its price premium over rail travel.

**supply chain**
The complete set of firms and facilities and logistics activities that are involved in procuring materials, transforming them into intermediate or finished products, and distributing them to customers

## The Growing Role of Information Technology

Coordinating all of the elements of PD has always been a challenge—even in a single firm. Imagine what is required to coordinate PD for an entire **supply chain**—the complete set of firms and facilities and logistics activities that are involved in procuring materials, transforming them into intermediate or finished products, and distributing them to customers. Keeping track of inventory levels, when to order, and where goods are when they move is complicated. The Internet is becoming more and more important in finding solutions to these challenges.

Many firms now continuously update their marketing information systems—so they can immediately find out what products have sold, the level of the current inventory, and when goods being transported will arrive. And coordination of physical distribution decisions throughout channels of distribution continues to improve as more firms are able to have their computers "talk to each other" directly and as managers can get information from a website whenever they need it.

**electronic data interchange (EDI)**
An approach that puts information in a standardized format easily shared between different computer systems

Until recently, differences in computer systems from one firm to another hampered the flow of information. Many firms attacked this problem by adopting **electronic data interchange (EDI)**—an approach that puts information in a standardized format that can be easily shared between different computer systems. In many firms, purchase orders, shipping reports, and other paper documents were replaced with computerized EDI. With EDI, a customer transmits its order information directly to the supplier's computer. The supplier's computer immediately processes the order and schedules production, order assembly, and transportation. Inventory information is automatically updated, and status reports are available instantly. The supplier might then use EDI to send the updated information to the transportation provider's computer. This type of system is now very common. In fact, almost all international transportation firms rely on EDI links with their customers.

EDI systems were originally developed and popularized before the Internet and the World Wide Web gained widespread use. Most traditional EDI systems are expensive to develop, rely on proprietary computer networks, and use specialized software to exchange data securely. Alternatives to this approach that rely on the Internet are gaining in popularity. However, there are still some obstacles. While it's easy for firms to share many types of information that use the standard HTML Web-page format, HTML is not well suited for exchanging numerical data (like SKU numbers, sales volumes, purchase quantities, and the like) between software programs on different computers. However, a new standard format, called XML, is gaining popularity and fostering easier EDI-type data exchanges over the Internet.[36]

This improved information flow and coordination affects other PD activities too. Instantaneous order processing using an EDI system on the Internet, for example, can have the same effect on the customer service level as faster, more expensive transportation. And knowing what a customer has sold or has in stock can improve a supplier's own production planning and reduce both inventory costs and stockouts in the whole channel.

Better coordination of PD activities is a key reason for the success of Pepperidge Farm's line of premium cookies. It was making the wrong products and delivering them too slowly to the wrong market. Poor information was the problem. Delivery-truck drivers took orders from retailers, assembled them manually at regional offices, and then mailed them to Pepperidge Farm's bakeries. Now the company has instant networked data-sharing for sales, delivery, inventory, and production. Many of the company's 2,200 drivers use hand-held computers to record the inventory at each stop along their routes. They use the Internet to transmit the information into a computer at the bakeries—so that cookies in short supply will be produced. The right assortment of fresh cookies is quickly shipped to local markets, and delivery trucks are loaded with what retailers need that day. Pepperidge Farm now moves cookies from its bakeries to store shelves in about three days; most cookie producers take about 10 days. That means fresher cookies for consumers and helps to support Pepperidge Farm's high-quality positioning and premium price.[37]

In summary, using computers to share information and coordinate activities is helping some firms and channels compete successfully for customers and increase their own profits.

## Chapter Summary

In this chapter, we discussed the role of place and noted that place decisions are especially important because they may be difficult and expensive to change.

Marketing specialists, and channel systems, develop to adjust discrepancies of quantity and assortment. Their regrouping activities are basic in any economic system. And adjusting discrepancies provides opportunities for creative marketers.

Channel planning requires firms to make a number of decisions. We began that discussion by first identifying three key distribution objectives: coverage, promotional intensity, and distribution cost. A key point was that these objectives were conflicting in nature and thus marketers must prioritize them before setting distribution policies.

We considered four key place-related decisions: directness, method of relationship management, market exposure, and complexity. Direct and indirect distribution each have strengths and weaknesses; we discussed some of the customer and product characteristics that might lead a manager to prefer one over the other.

Similarly, we reviewed the factors to be considered in deciding whether the ideal level of market exposure was intensive, selective, or exclusive. In addition, we cited some of the legal issues in limiting market exposure. In our discussion of channel relationships, we focused on the importance of planning channel systems—along with the role of a channel captain and the use of vertical marketing systems. Finally, we identified some of the factors leading to and issues arising from channel complexity.

The chapter concluded with an overview of some key issues in managing physical distribution and logistics. We outlined the key parts of the physical-distribution concept and saw how it impacts on decisions about customer service, logistical arrangements, and the use of technology.

## Key Concepts

accumulating, p. 309
administered channel systems, p. 326
assorting, p. 310
bulk-breaking, p. 310
channel captain, p. 320
channels of distribution, p. 307
contractual channel systems, p. 326
corporate channel systems, p. 324
coverage, p. 313
customer service level, p. 333
direct marketing, p. 316
discrepancy of assortment, p. 309
discrepancy of quantity, p. 309
distribution cost, p. 313
dual distribution, p. 330
electronic data interchange (EDI), p. 336
exclusive distribution, p. 327
facilitators, p. 312
ideal market exposure, p. 326
intensive distribution, p. 327
intermediary, p. 312
logistics/physical distribution (PD), p. 332
place, p. 307
promotional intensity, p. 313
refusal to supply, p. 330
regrouping activities, p. 309
reverse channels, p. 332
selective distribution, p. 327
sorting, p. 310
supply chains, p. 335
total-cost approach, p. 335
traditional channel systems, p. 318
universal functions of marketing, p. 310
vertical integration, p. 324
vertical marketing systems, p. 324

## Questions and Problems

1. Give two examples of service firms that work with other channel specialists to sell their products to final consumers. What marketing functions is the specialist providing in each case?
2. Discuss some reasons why a firm that produces installations might use direct distribution in its domestic market but use intermediaries to reach overseas customers.
3. Explain discrepancies of quantity and assortment using the clothing business as an example. How does the application of these concepts change when selling steel to the automobile industry? What impact does this have on the number and kinds of marketing specialists required?
4. Explain the four regrouping activities with an example from the building-supply industry (nails, paint,

flooring, plumbing fixtures, etc.). Do you think that many specialists develop in this industry, or do producers handle the job themselves? What kinds of marketing channels would you expect to find in this industry, and what functions would various channel members provide?

5. Insurance agents are intermediaries who help other members of the channel by providing information and handling the selling function. Does it make sense for an insurance agent to specialize and work exclusively with one insurance provider? Why or why not?

6. Discuss the place objectives and distribution arrangements that are appropriate for the following products (indicate any special assumptions you have to make to obtain an answer):
   a. A postal scale for products weighing up to 2 kilograms.
   b. Children's toys: (1) radio-controlled model airplanes costing $80 or more, (2) small rubber balls.
   c. Heavy-duty, rechargeable, battery-powered nut tighteners for factory production lines.
   d. Fibreglass fabric used in making roofing shingles.

7. Give an example of a producer that uses two or more different channels of distribution. Briefly discuss what problems this might cause.

8. Explain how a channel captain can help traditional independent firms compete with a corporate (integrated) channel system.

9. Find an example of vertical integration within your city. Are there any particular advantages to this vertical integration? If so, what are they? If there are no such advantages, how do you explain the integration?

10. What would happen if retailer-organized channels (either formally integrated or administered) dominated consumer product marketing?

11. How does the nature of the product relate to the degree of market exposure desired?

12. Why would intermediaries want to be exclusive distributors for a product? Why would producers want exclusive distribution? Would intermediaries be equally anxious to get exclusive distribution for any type of product? Why or why not? Explain with reference to the following products: candy bars, batteries, golf clubs, golf balls, steak knives, televisions, and industrial woodworking machinery.

13. Explain the present legal status of exclusive distribution. Describe a situation where exclusive distribution is almost sure to be legal. Describe the nature and size of competitors and the industry, as well as the nature of the exclusive arrangement. Would this exclusive arrangement be of any value to the producer or intermediary?

14. Discuss the promotion a new producer of grocery products would need in order to develop appropriate channels and move products through those channels. Would the nature of this job change for a new producer of dresses? How about for a new, small producer of installations?

15. Explain how adjusting the customer service level could improve a marketing mix.

16. What aspects of customer service would be most important for a producer that sells fabric to a firm that manufactures furniture?

17. Discuss the tradeoffs involved in PD costs, service levels, and sales.

18. Explain the total-cost approach and why it might cause conflicts between some members of a supply chain. Might conflicts also occur between departments within the producing firm?



## *Computer-Aided Problem 11a*

### Intensive versus Selective Distribution

Hydropump, Inc. produces and sells high-quality pumps to business customers. Its marketing research shows a growing market for a similar type of pump aimed at final consumers—for use with Jacuzzi-style tubs in home remodelling jobs. Hydropump will have to develop new channels of distribution to reach this target market because most consumers rely on a retailer for advice about the combination of tub, pump, heater, and related plumbing fixtures they need. Hydropump's marketing manager, Robert Black, is trying to decide between intensive and selective distribution. With intensive distribution, he would try to sell through all the retailers of plumbing supplies, bathroom fixtures, and hot tubs that will carry the pump. He estimates that about 5,600 suitable retailers would be willing to carry a new pump. With selective distribution, he would focus on about 280 of the best hot-tub dealers (2 or 3 in the 100 largest metropolitan areas).

Intensive distribution would require Hydropump to do more mass selling—primarily advertising in home-renovation magazines—to help stimulate consumer familiarity with the brand and convince retailers that Hydropump equipment will sell. The price to the retailer might have to be lower too (to permit a bigger markup) so they will be motivated to sell Hydropump rather than some other brand offering a smaller markup.

With intensive distribution, each Hydropump sales rep could probably handle about 300 retailers effectively. With selective distribution, each sales rep could handle only about 70 retailers because more merchandising help would be necessary. Managing the smaller salesforce and fewer retailers with the selective approach would require less manager overhead cost.

Going to all suitable and available retailers would make the pump available through about 20 times as many retailers and have the potential of reaching more customers. However, many customers shop at more than one retailer before making a final choice—so selective distribution would reach almost as many potential customers. Further, if Hydropump is using selective distribution, it would get more in-store sales attention for its pump and a larger share of pump purchases at each retailer.

Black has decided to use a spreadsheet to analyze the benefits and costs of intensive versus selective distribution.

a. *Based on the initial spreadsheet, which approach seems to be the most sensible for Hydropump? Why?*
b. *A consultant points out that even selective distribution needs national promotion. If Black has to increase advertising and spend a total of $100,000 on mass selling to be able to recruit the retailers he wants for selective distribution, would selective or intensive distribution be more profitable?*
c. *With intensive distribution, how large a share (percentage) of the retailers' total unit sales would Hydropump have to capture to sell enough pumps to earn $200,000 profit?*

## Computer-Aided Problem 11b

### Total Distribution Cost

Proto Company has been producing various items made of plastic. It recently added a line of plain plastic cards that other firms (such as banks and retail stores) will imprint to produce credit cards. Proto offers its customers the plastic cards in different colours, but they all sell for $40 per box of 1,000. Tom Phillips, Proto's product manager for this line, is considering two possible physical distribution systems. He estimates that if Proto uses airfreight, transportation costs will be $7.50 a box, and its cost of carrying inventory will be 5 percent of total annual sales dollars. Alternatively, Proto could ship by rail for $2 a box. But rail transport will require renting space at four regional warehouses, at $26,000 a year each. Inventory carrying cost with this system will be 10 percent of total annual sales dollars. Phillips prepared a spreadsheet to compare the costs of the two alternative physical distribution systems.

a. *If Proto Company expects to sell 20,000 boxes a year, what are the total physical distribution costs for each of the systems?*
b. *If Phillips can negotiate cheaper warehouse space for the rail option so that each warehouse costs only $20,000 per year, which physical distribution system has the lowest overall cost?*
c. *Proto's finance manager predicts that interest rates are likely to be lower during the next marketing-plan year and suggests that Tom Phillips use inventory carrying costs of 4 percent for airfreight and 7.5 percent for railroads (with warehouse cost at $20,000 each). If interest rates are in fact lower, which alternative would you suggest? Why?*

## Suggested Cases

Online **LearningCentre** To view the cases, go to www.mcgrawhill.ca/college/wong.

Interested in finding out what marketing looks like in the real world? *Marketing Magazine* is just a click away on your OLC! Visit **www.mcgrawhill.ca/college/wong** today.

When You Finish This Chapter, You Should

1. Understand how retailers plan their marketing strategies.

2. Know about the many kinds of retailers that work with producers and wholesalers as members of channel systems.

3. Understand the differences among the conventional and non-conventional retailers—including Internet merchants and others who accept the mass-merchandising concept.

4. Understand scrambled merchandising and the "wheel of retailing."

5. See why size or belonging to a chain can be important to a retailer.

6. Know what progressive wholesalers are doing to modernize their operations and marketing strategies.

7. Know the various kinds of merchant wholesalers and agent intermediaries and the strategies that they use.

8. Understand why retailing and wholesaling have developed in different ways in different countries.

9. See why the Internet is impacting both retailing and wholesaling.

# Chapter Twelve

# Retailers, Wholesalers, and Their Strategy Planning

## The Best Bet from Your Bottom Dollar

In only a decade, the lowly dollar store has moved from the fringe of retailing to become a destination for a growing number of shoppers, and a force to be reckoned with among rival merchants.

The numbers bear out the phenomenon. Last year, dollar stores' sales rose 12.6 percent to $140 million from the previous year after climbing 13.9 percent in 2001, according to researcher ACNielsen. Last year's lift was more than twice the overall 6-percent growth in Canadian retailing that year, Statistics Canada figures show. It was also double the gains in the grocery sector and still above the 10-percent sales increase enjoyed by popular discounters such as Wal-Mart, the Nielsen data indicate.

While a lot of mom-and-pop dollar stores remain, they are being squeezed out by

place price promotion produ

sophisticated chains that are introducing updated merchandising practices to this modern version of the five-and-dime. Dollarama and the franchised Buck or Two stores, the latter under the Denninghouse Inc. umbrella, are the country's largest dollar-store chains, each with more than 320 outlets and targeting 500 over the next three to five years.

The dollar stores have become so respectable that they are now in some better malls. Moreover, a number of shopping centres feature two dollar stores, often an older, cramped one and a newer, relatively polished store with wider aisles, brighter lighting, and nicer finishings.

And the stores appeal to a broader mix of consumers than ever before. Customers range from the budget-conscious to the well-heeled who shop at the stores before throwing a party or heading off to the cottage, he said.

And while the chains are building bigger and brighter stores, that's not their only drawing power. The merchandising is getting sharper, enabling the stores to carry items that hitherto were unthinkable at only $1.

Product sourcing is largely responsible for the wider array of merchandise. The larger chains import directly from overseas, trimming costs by cutting out the intermediary and giving the retailers more control over the quality of the goods.

The chains are creating their own packaging and private labels, borrowing a page from Loblaw's in-store President's Choice and No Name brands. Among the Dollarama labels are Duramax hardware goods and Celebration party supplies.

place price promotion product

In addition, dollar stores are always hunting for special deals from manufacturers trying to unload excess or end-of-the-line inventory, Typical "opportunity buys" include ceramic dinnerware pieces for $1 each and a $1 girls' kit filled with a sponge, body gel, hair brush, and accessories—something that could easily sell for $7 at the local drugstore.

As the dollar stores fine-tune their operations, the competition is zeroing in on their territory.

The dollar store is even setting the retailing agenda. Loblaw Cos. Ltd. and Great Atlantic & Pacific Tea Co. are testing dollar-store aisles in their discount divisions. They are tapping into the same suppliers as the dollar stores, pitching similar products. The mighty Wal-Mart Stores Inc., the ultimate trendsetter in the sector, is piloting dollar-store merchandise at some of its U.S. stores; its Canadian division is currently considering a similar program, a spokesman said.

Despite the added competition, dollar stores are forging on, drafting their own expansion plans and arguing that consumers still want the convenience of the specialty outlet.[1]



## In This Chapter

The opening vignette shows that retailers are often a vital link in a channel system—and in the whole marketing process—helping both their suppliers and customers. Their role can be as straightforward as providing a storefront location or as complex as being the channel captain specifying the type of products that a manufacturer should produce. As might be expected, the nature of their operations can vary considerably. However, one constant is that retailers and wholesalers, like other businesses, must select their target markets and marketing mixes carefully.

In Chapter 11, we discussed the functions that wholesalers and retailers perform as intermediaries in channel systems. In this chapter, we'll focus on the major decision areas that retailers and wholesalers consider in developing their own strategies.

In addition, we'll discuss how retailers and wholesalers, and their strategies, are evolving. It's important to understand this evolution. As shown in the dollar-store example, retailers that start as mom-and-pop operations can easily become victims as their industry matures and more sophisticated organizations enter. And the pace of change is accelerating. Some traditional approaches are being modified and newer approaches, like selling from websites, are prompting marketers to come up with new and better ways to meet the needs of customers at the end of the channel. If you understand the evolution, you will be better prepared for changes that come in the future.

Whether these more-sophisticated operations are better cannot be assumed. Different types of retailers and wholesalers meet different needs in the marketplace. As we emphasized from the start, not all customers have the same needs. Seeing the different ways that retailers and wholesalers have modified their strategies will make it clear that it is the whole strategy—not just one aspect of it—that ultimately is a success or failure. This may seem obvious, but apparently it's not to everyone.

A few years ago, some people were proclaiming that marketers needed to throw out all of the thinking that anyone had ever done about retailing and wholesaling because the Internet had changed everything. It is certainly true that the Internet has fostered dramatic innovations and that many benefits (for firms and for consumers) are yet to be realized. But that doesn't mean that the Internet changes customers' basic needs, or wants, or for that matter the role that any sort of specialized intermediary (whether in a bricks-and-mortar facility, online, or both) plays in the place system.

Unfortunately, people who forget the lessons of the past are condemned to repeat them. Many creative people who had exciting ideas for online retailing innovations failed precisely because they didn't learn that. Many fell into the trap of thinking that all customers were the same—or that customers would be satisfied just because some aspect of a firm's marketing mix met some needs really well, even if it ignored other needs. Yet it doesn't matter if an online retailer has an incredible assortment if there's no way for buyers to get live customer service when they can't get the order page to work. It doesn't matter if a seller posts a low price if the products are not actually available to ship or if shipping costs make the real price exorbitant. And it isn't convenient to return a green shirt that looked blue on the website, even if the website is conveniently available 24/7.

So in general, in this chapter we will concentrate on strategy decisions that apply to *all* retailers and wholesalers. But we will also highlight the differences that are most significant in terms of the ongoing evolution. We'll start with a closer look at retailing, and then cover wholesaling.



## The Nature of Retailing and Retailing Strategy

**retailing**
All of the activities involved in the sale of products to final consumers

**Retailing** covers all of the activities involved in the sale of products to final consumers. Retailers range from large chains of specialized stores—like Toys"R"Us or Sleep Country Canada—to individual merchants like the woman who sells baskets from an open stall in the central market in Ibadan, Nigeria. Some retailers operate from stores and others operate without a store—by selling online, on TV, with a printed catalogue, from vending machines, or even in consumers' homes. Most retailers focus on selling physical goods produced by someone else. But in the case of service retailing—like drycleaning, fast food, tourist attractions, online bank accounts, or one-hour photo processing, for example—the retailer is also the producer. Because they serve individual consumers, even the largest retailers face the challenge of handling small transactions. And the total number of transactions with consumers is much greater than at other channel levels.

Retailing is a very competitive business, with annual sales close to $250 billion—that's $250,000,000,000 a year that Canadian consumers spend on goods and services.[2] Thousands of these retailers go out of business each year. The nature of retailing and its rate of change are generally related to the stage and speed of a country's economic development. In Canada, retailing is more varied and more dynamic than in most other countries. By studying the Canadian system and how it is changing you will better understand where retailing is headed in other parts of the world.

### Retailer Strategy

Retailers interact directly with final consumers—so strategy planning is critical to their survival. If a retailer loses a customer to a competitor, the retailer is the one who suffers. Producers and wholesalers still make *their* sale regardless of which retailer sells the product.

Like all businesses, a key factor driving retailer strategy is the target market. Different consumers prefer different kinds of retailers, but many retailers either don't

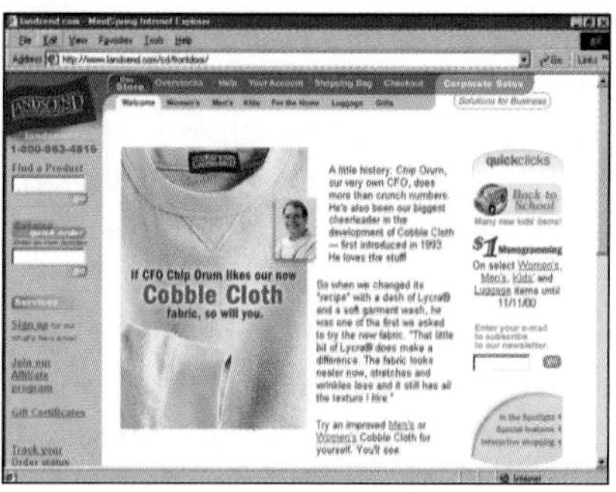

It's best to think of a retailer's product as its whole offering—including its assortment of goods and services, advice from salespeople, the convenience of shopping, and the hours it is available.



know or don't care why. All too often, beginning retailers just rent a store and assume customers will show up. Sometimes they offer too much service for their target customer, and sometimes too little. For example, would the customer buying a new car be happy with the level of customer service provided by dollar stores? As a result, a large number of new retailing ventures fail during the first year.

Even an established retailer can quickly lose its customers if they find a better way to meet their needs. For example, the Eaton's chain, a long-established Canadian retailing stalwart, went bankrupt in 2000. The faltering Woolworth chain in Canada was sold to Wal-Mart, and The Hudson's Bay Company purchased Kmart's money-losing Canadian stores. The Bay closed some 40 of these outlets while merging the rest of Kmart with the Zellers chain it also owns. To avoid a similar fate, a retailer should have a clear strategy. Retailers need to carefully identify possible target markets and try to understand why these people buy where they do; this helps retailers tune their marketing mix to the needs of specific target markets.[3]

A second key element in retail strategy is product assortment. Most retailers in developed nations sell more than one kind of product. So their product assortment (including brands carried) can be critical to their success. Yet it's best to take a broader view in thinking about the product strategy decisions for a retailer's marketing mix. The retailer's *whole* offering—assortment of goods and services, advice from salesclerks, convenience, and the like—is its product.

## The Retail Offering

As discussed in Chapter 6, different consumers have different needs—and needs vary from one purchase situation to another. Which retailer's product offers the best customer value depends on the needs that a customer wants to satisfy. Whatever the effect of other consumer needs, economic needs are usually very important in shaping the choice of a retailer. Social and individual needs may also come into play.

Features of a retailer's offering that relate to economic needs include:

- *Convenience* (location, available hours, parking, finding needed products, fast checkout).
- *Product selection* (width and depth of assortment, quality).
- *Special services* (special orders, home delivery, gift wrap, entertainment).
- *Fairness in dealings* (honesty, correcting problems, return privileges, purchase risks).
- *Helpful information* (courteous sales help, displays, demonstrations, product information).
- *Prices* (value, credit, special discounts, taxes or extra charges).

Some features that relate to social and emotional factors include:

- *Social image* (status, prestige, "fitting in" with other shoppers).
- *Shopping atmosphere* (comfort, safety, excitement, relaxation, sounds, smells).

A retailer should consciously make decisions that set policies on *all* of these factors. Each of them can impact a customer's view of the costs and benefits of choosing that retailer. And in combination they differentiate one retailer's offering and strategy from another. In short, it is the selection of which needs to service that underlies the particular marketing mix of a retail firm.

### The Seven Ps of Retail Marketing Mixes

Like all firms, the basic marketing mix for a retailer is comprised of the four Ps. However, the nature of retailing requires that we elaborate on the product dimension. As suggested in the discussion of economic and non-economic factors considered by the retail customer, the product is much more than whatever item is purchased. Consumers are also buying (and paying for) services received before, during, and after shopping and the physical layout of the store, to name but a few.

To keep this perspective top of mind, it is helpful to think of seven Ps that can be used to satisfy the emotional, social, and economic needs of a target market(s). These are the principal ways in which retailers can differentiate themselves from one another:

- **Product:** What the firm is offering.
- **Personnel:** Type and quality of assistance available.
- **Personalized services:** Return policies, ability to customize, hours, other extras.
- **Price:** Value relative to quality.
- **Place:** Store location, parking facilities, exterior elements.
- **Physical facilities:** Store layout, washrooms, interior elements.
- **Promotion:** Advertising, sales promotion including price features, in-store display.

### Segmentation and Positioning in Retailing

As in other businesses, segmentation and positioning decisions are important to retailers. And ignoring either economic or social and emotional values in those decisions can lead to serious errors in a retailer's strategy planning.

Consider, for example, how the shopping atmosphere may have an emotional effect on a consumer's view of a retailer. How merchandise is displayed, what decorations, colours, and finishes are used, and even the temperature, sounds, and smell of a store all contribute to its "atmospherics" and store image. The right combination may attract more target customers and encourage them to spend more. Tiffany's, for example, offers luxury surroundings and inventive displays to attract upscale consumers. But Tiffany's may also appeal to consumers who get an ego boost from Tiffany's prestige image and very attentive staff. Of course, interesting surroundings are usually costly, and the prices that consumers pay must cover that expense. An online jewellery retailer avoids those costs but offers a completely different shopping experience and deals with a different set of needs. So a retailer's atmosphere and image may be a plus or a minus, depending on the target market. And there's no single right answer about which target market is best. Like Tiffany's, Dollar General has been very profitable. But it has a budget image and atmosphere that appeals to working-class customers, many of whom prefer to shop where they don't feel out of place.[4]

### Selecting a Strategy

Retailers are not simply outlets through which producers can access their final consumers. Retail operations are also competitive businesses that must be strategically managed to achieve both short-term customer satisfaction and long-term customer loyalty. In North America, the recognition that stores are products in themselves (and not just a collection of producers' products) has led many retailers to question whether their suppliers (i.e., their wholesalers and producers) should be in charge of the channels of distribution. This, in turn, has encouraged established retailers to use the strategic market planning process to become much more aggressive in managing their own businesses.[5]

Often, the motive among small retailers for getting into retailing is "to be my own boss."[6] The approach taken is to set up a store that carries products that the new entrepreneur likes or that provides services he or she personally needs. This production-oriented approach is one of the key reasons why about three-quarters of all new retailing ventures fail during their first year. Small retailers must also use the strategic marketing planning process.[7]

As indicated in Exhibit 12-1, there are several key components that must work together to form an effective retail management program. The company's long-term objectives—generally a combination of diverse goals such as customer loyalty and maximum profits—must be set and kept in balance. These objectives, along with the needs and expectations of the firm's target market(s) and the realities of the marketing environment, must be taken into account in selecting the strategic marketing, human resource, and financial and technological elements that become the firm's business plan.

Besides achieving the retailer's long-term objectives, the resulting plan must also meet the short-term objectives of providing day-to-day customer satisfaction and



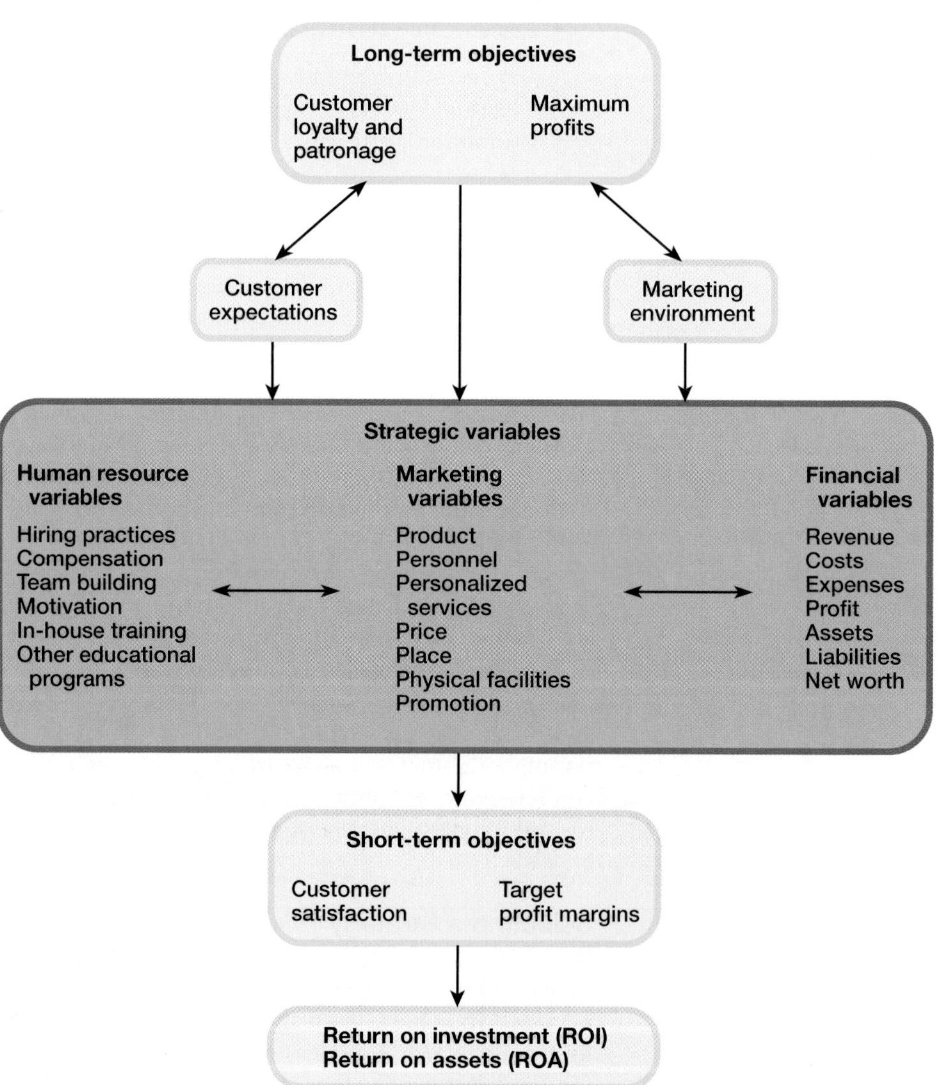


**Exhibit 12-1** Components of a strategic retail management program.

reaching annual profit margin targets, both of which are necessary to ensure year-to-year survival.

Short-term profit performance is the basis for the ROI and ROA measures used to establish how effectively the operation is using its resources. In turn, these measures help the retailer obtain loans and other financial support for investment in the operation. Continuous upgrading of assets is necessary to keep on top of customer expectations, to adjust to competitive and environmental changes, and thus to continue to achieve the operation's long-term goals.

All of the components in a strategic retail management program are interrelated, more so than a simple model can indicate. In other words, retail management is an ongoing, dynamic process. Changes in consumer expectations and the marketing environment are not unusual. Such changes can require frequent plan modifications during any given year. However, alert retail managers anticipate major changes and include contingency options in their annual business plans. Managers who fail to anticipate changes run the risk of making plan modifications that appear to be the right thing to do in the short run but have a negative impact on the firm's long-term objectives.

## The Impact of Retailer Size

A final key characteristic of a retail strategy is whether it operates as an independent or aligns itself with other retailers as part of a chain.

As discussed in Chapter 11, manufacturers deal with retailers and other intermediaries because of the efficiency they bring to the distribution channel. Given the relationship between business size and costs, many manufacturers believe these efficiencies are greater when they deal with larger retail chains. Producers can obtain large orders and maximize the number of consumers their products reach while making relatively few sales calls on retail headquarters. The chains benefit because their large orders qualify for maximum volume discounts. As a result of this mutually beneficial relationship between producers and large retailers, chains dominate the Canadian retail landscape.

However, there is also a cost to achieving this efficiency, which comes in the form of the increased buying and negotiation power of those retailers that represent large portions of a producer's business. As a rule, the more concentrated your sales are in a small number of accounts, the more dependent you are and, therefore, the more difficult it is to resist demands for price and other concessions. For example, the Loblaw's chain sells more than 30 percent of the grocery products sold in Canada. Imagine how difficult it would be to negotiate with a client if you knew that the loss of the sale would effectively shut you out of 30 percent of the market!

There are several different types of chains to which producers can sell. Most of Canada's major retail firms are *corporate chains*. Statistics Canada defines a **corporate chain** as "an organization operating four or more retail outlets in the same kind of business, under the same legal ownership." Corporate retail chains usually deal directly with producer-marketers. They sometimes charge producers fees for initially agreeing to carry their products. These chains are major marketers who make their own product, price, place, and promotion decisions.[8]

**corporate chain**
An organization operating four or more retail outlets in the same kind of business, under the same legal ownership

One might wonder how a smaller, independent retailer could hope to compete against the buying efficiency and buying power of corporate chains. Cooperative chains, voluntary chains, and franchise operations represent an attempt to provide smaller operators with some of the advantages of chains while retaining their independence.

**cooperative chains**
Retailer-sponsored groups, formed by independent retailers, that run their own buying organizations and conduct joint promotion efforts

**Cooperative chains** are retailer-sponsored groups, formed by independent retailers, that run their own buying organizations and conduct joint promotion efforts. Sales of cooperative chains are rising as they are learning how to compete with corporate chains. Examples of co-op chains include Associated Grocers, Certified Grocers, and Home Hardware.

**voluntary chains**

Wholesaler-sponsored groups that work with independent retailers

**Voluntary chains** are wholesaler-sponsored groups that work with independent retailers. Some are linked by contracts stating common operating procedures and requiring the use of common storefront designs, store names, and joint promotion efforts. Examples include IGA and SuperValu.

*Franchise operations* are another means for retailers to group together to compete with chains and offer efficient product distribution to producers. In a **franchise operation** the franchiser develops a good marketing strategy, which the retail franchise holders then carry out in their own units. Franchises can also pursue economies of scale by centralizing administrative, research, and other activities on behalf of their franchisees: the result can be considerable savings for the franchisee. The largest and best-established retail franchise operation in Canada is Canadian Tire. Each franchise holder benefits from the relationship with the franchiser and its experience, buying power, and image. In return, the franchise holder usually signs a contract to pay fees and commissions, and to strictly follow franchise rules designed to continue the successful strategy.[9]

**franchise operation**

The franchiser develops a good marketing strategy, which the retail franchise holders then carry out in their own units



## Types of Retailers and Their Strategies

Given the many factors that influence a retailer's strategy, it should not be surprising that retailers have an almost unlimited number of ways in which to alter their offerings—their marketing mixes—to appeal to a target market. Because of all the variations, it's oversimplified to classify retailers and their strategies on the basis of a single characteristic—such as merchandise, services, sales volume, or even whether they operate in cyberspace. But a good place to start is by considering basic types of retailers and some differences in their strategies.

Let's look first at conventional retailers. Then we'll see how other retailers successfully modify conventional offerings to better meet the needs of *some* consumers. Think about *why* the changes take place. That will help you identify opportunities and plan better marketing strategies.

### Conventional Retailers

A hundred and fifty years ago, general stores—which carried anything they could sell in reasonable volume—were the main retailers in North America. Now, most conventional retailers are **single-line** or **limited-line stores**—stores that specialize in certain lines of related products rather than a wide assortment. Many stores specialize not only in a single line, such as clothing, but also in a *limited line* within the broader line. Within the clothing line, a retailer might carry *only* shoes, formal wear, men's casual wear, or even neckties, but offer depth in that limited line.

**single-line** or **limited-line stores**

Stores that specialize in certain lines of related products rather than a wide assortment

The main advantage of such retailers is that they can satisfy some target markets better. Perhaps some are just more conveniently located near their customers. But for most it's because they adjust to suit specific customers. They try to build a long-term relationship with their customers and earn a position as *the* place to shop for a certain type of product. But single-line and limited-line stores face the costly problem of having to stock some slow-moving items in order to satisfy the store's target market. Many of these stores are small, with high expenses relative to sales. So they try to keep their prices up by avoiding competition on identical products.

Conventional retailers like this have been around for a long time and are still found in every community. Many now face stiff competition from other types of retailers. Even so, they are a durable lot and clearly satisfy some people's needs. In fact, in most countries conventional retailers still handle the vast majority of all retailing sales.

In spite of consumer interest in Western products and new retailing formats, most retailing in Asia is still handled by small, limited-line stores, like the independently owned Filipino store on the left and the Japanese electronics store on the right.

However, this situation is changing fast. Nowhere is the change clearer than in North America. Conventional retailers are being squeezed by retailers who modify their mixes in the various ways suggested in Exhibit 12-2. Let's look more closely at how retailers are making modifications to the marketing mix of conventional retailers.

## Specialty Shops and Department Stores

Specialty shops and department stores expand on the product assortment and service levels offered by conventional retailers. However, these changes come at a cost to the retailer and thus consumers usually pay higher prices. The premise underlying the success of this modification to the conventional store is that consumers will pay more because they sufficiently value the benefits offered by these formats. Therefore, not all products lend themselves to this form of retailing.

**Exhibit 12-2** Types of retailers and the nature of their offerings.

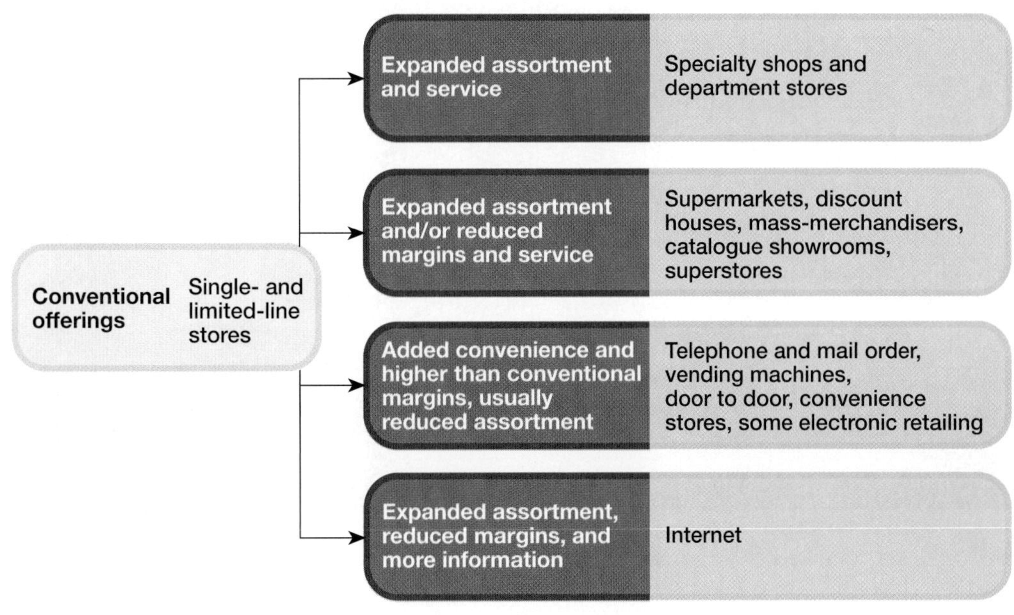

**specialty shop**
A type of conventional limited-line store

A **specialty shop**—a type of conventional limited-line store—is usually small and has a distinct personality. Specialty shops sell special types of shopping products—such as high-quality sporting goods, exclusive clothing, cameras, or even antiques. They aim at a carefully defined target market by offering a unique product assortment, knowledgeable salesclerks, and better service. As such, they are particularly well-suited to the sale of more complicated products or infrequently purchased products where customers are less willing to rely solely on their own judgment in making a purchase selection.

The specialty shop's major advantage is that it caters to certain types of customers, who the management and salespeople come to know well. This simplifies buying, speeds turnover, and cuts costs due to obsolescence and style changes. Specialty shops probably will continue to be a part of the retailing scene as long as customers have varied tastes and the money to satisfy them.[10]

**department stores**
Larger stores that are organized into many separate departments and offer many product lines

**Department stores** are larger stores that are organized into many separate departments and offer many product lines. Each department is like a separate limited-line store and handles a wide variety of shopping products—such as men's wear or housewares. Ideally, each department offers the benefits of specialty-store shopping. In addition, because the customer shops in many departments, consumers can meet several shopping needs with a single store visit and have the assurance that all departments operate under the same set of policies in areas like credit, merchandise return, and delivery.

Department stores are still a major force in big cities. However, the number of department stores, the average sales per store, and their share of retail business has declined continuously since the 1970s. Well-run limited-line stores compete with good service and often carry the same brands. In Canada and many other countries, mass-merchandising retailers have posed an even bigger threat; we'll discuss them next.[11]

Although U.S. supermarkets were the first mass-merchandisers, the mass-merchandising concept has now been introduced by many retailers. Single-line mass-merchandisers like Office Depot offer selections and prices that make it difficult for traditional retailers to compete.

## Mass-Merchandisers

So far we've been describing retailers primarily in terms of their product assortment. This reflects traditional thinking about retailing. We could talk about supermarkets, discount houses, or online retailers in these terms too. But then we would miss some important differences—just as some conventional retailers did when mass-merchandising retailers first appeared.

Conventional retailers think that demand in their area is fixed—and they have a "buy low and sell high" philosophy. Many modern retailers reject these ideas. They accept the **mass-merchandising concept**—which says that retailers should offer low prices to get faster turnover and greater sales volumes—by appealing to larger markets. The key premise is that costs will fall as volume increases; this, in turn, enables the mass-merchandiser to pass on to consumers the cost savings in the form of lower prices or additional services.

**mass-merchandising concept**
The idea that retailers should offer low prices to get faster turnover and greater sales volumes.

The mass-merchandising concept applies to many types of retailers—including both those that operate stores and those that sell online. But to understand mass-merchandising better, let's look at its evolution from the development of supermarkets and discounters to modern mass-merchandisers like Wal-Mart in North America, Tesco in the United Kingdom, and Amazon.com on the Internet.

From a world view, most food stores are relatively small single- or limited-line operations, a situation that makes shopping for food inconvenient and expensive. Many Italians, for example, still go to one shop for pasta, another for meat, and yet another for milk. Although this approach seems outdated, keep in mind that many of the world's consumers don't have access to **supermarkets**—large stores specializing in groceries with self-service and wide assortments.

**supermarkets**
Large stores specializing in groceries, with self-service and wide assortments

The basic idea for supermarkets developed in the U.S. during the early Depression years. Some innovators believed they could increase sales by charging lower prices. They introduced self-service to cut costs but provided a broad product

assortment in large bare-bones stores. Success and profits came from large-volume sales—not from high traditional markups.[12]

To outsell competitors, supermarkets try to differentiate their offerings. Some have better produce, others have lower prices, some offer a deli or a cleaner store, and so forth. But there are many things they all have to offer—like milk and eggs and cereal. In fact, an average family gets about 80 percent of its needs from only about 150 SKUs (individual stockkeeping units). Unfortunately from the retailer's perspective, those particular 150 SKUs vary from family to family. In the end, a consumer makes a single choice in deciding to shop at a certain supermarket. But to come out on top in *that* choice, the supermarket must offer consumers many thousands of choices and at the same time keep costs low.[13]

Modern supermarkets are planned for maximum efficiency. Scanners at checkout counters make it possible to carefully analyze the sales and profit of each item and allocate more shelf space to faster-moving and higher-profit items. This helps sell more products, faster. It also reduces the investment in inventory, makes stocking easier, and minimizes the cost of handling products. Survival depends on such efficiency. Net profits in supermarkets usually run a thin 1 percent of sales or less!

**catalogue showroom retailers**

Retailers that sell several lines out of a catalogue and display showroom

**Catalogue showroom retailers** sell several lines out of a catalogue and display showroom with backup inventories. Instead of having all merchandise on the floor of a retail store, they reduce the amount of floor space by showing only a small number of items and having a catalogue that displays the full range of products available. By reducing the amount of retail space and the cost of maintaining it, costs were reduced and prices could be lowered.

Before 1940, most catalogue sellers were wholesalers who also sold at discounted prices to friends and members of groups—such as labour unions or church groups. In the 1970s, however, these operations expanded rapidly by aiming at final consumers and offering attractive catalogues and improved facilities. Catalogue showroom retailers—like Service Merchandise in the U.S. and Consumers Distributing in Canada—offer price savings and deliver almost all the items in their catalogues from backroom warehouses. They emphasize well-known manufacturer brands of jewellery, gifts, luggage, and small appliances but offer few services.[14]

Early catalogue retailers didn't bother conventional retailers because they weren't well publicized and accounted for only a small portion of total retail sales. If those catalogue retailers had moved ahead aggressively, the current retailing scene might be different. But instead, discount houses developed and now most catalogue showroom retailers have gone out of business (including Consumers Distributing, which went bankrupt in October 1996).

Right after the Second World War, some retailers moved beyond offering discounts to selected customers. These *discount houses* offered "hard goods" (cameras, TVs, appliances) at substantial price cuts to customers who would go to the discounter's low-rent store, pay cash, and take care of any service or repair problems themselves. These retailers sold at 20 to 30 percent off the list price being charged by conventional retailers.

In the early 1950s, with war shortages finally over, manufacturer brands became more available. The discount houses were able to get any brands they wanted and offer wider assortments. At this stage, many discounters turned respectable—moving to better locations and offering more services and guarantees. It was from these origins that today's mass-merchandisers developed.

**mass-merchandisers**

Large, self-service stores with many departments that emphasize "soft goods" and staples with lower margins for faster turnover

**Mass-merchandisers** are large, self-service stores with many departments that emphasize "soft goods" (housewares, clothing, and fabrics) and staples (like health and beauty aids) but still follow the discount house's emphasis on lower margins to get faster turnover. Mass-merchandisers—like Wal-Mart and Zellers—have checkout counters in the front of the store and little sales help on the floor. Today the average mass-merchandiser has nearly 60,000 square feet of floor space, but many new stores are 100,000 square feet or more.

Mass-merchandisers grew rapidly, and they've become the primary non-food place to shop for many frequently purchased consumer products. By itself, Wal-Mart handles a whopping 20 percent or more of the total national sales for whole categories of products. Even if you don't shop at Wal-Mart, Sam Walton (who started the company) has had a big impact on your life. He pioneered the use of high-tech systems to create electronic links with suppliers and take inefficiencies out of retailing logistics. That brought down costs *and* prices and attracted more customers, which gave Wal-Mart even more influence in pressuring manufacturers to lower prices. Other retailers are still scrambling to catch up. It was competition from Wal-Mart on staples such as health and beauty aids and household cleaning products that prompted firms in the supermarket supply chain to start the Efficient Consumer Response movement. Many catalogue showroom retailers didn't adjust fast enough and went bust. Many conventional retailers are adjusting their strategies just to survive. And it's Wal-Mart's phenomenal growth and success that motivates many new online retailers to think that their innovations can do the same thing. But this dynamic change is what marketing is all about—and it is providing consumers with superior value.

Although these mass-merchandisers are the driving force in much of retailing in North America today, they've expanded so rapidly in many areas that they're no longer just taking customers from conventional retailers but instead are locked in head-to-head competition with each other. So their growth rate in North America has slowed substantially and, for future growth, they're expanding internationally.[15] (See Marketing Demo 12-1 for more on the perceived Wal-Mart threat to Canadian retailers.)

**supercentres (hypermarkets)**
Very large stores that try to carry not only food and drug items but also all goods and services that the consumer purchases routinely

Some supermarkets and mass-merchandisers have moved toward becoming **supercentres (hypermarkets)**—very large stores that try to carry not only food and drug

## Marketing Demo 12–1

### WAL-MART WATCH

You can almost, but not quite, hear a bit of exasperation in Andrew Pelletier's voice when he says: "We've said it many times—Wal-Mart Canada has no plans for groceries at the present time!" Pelletier, the director of public affairs for Wal-Mart, headquartered in Mississauga, Ont., has clearly been asked the question many times before.

Despite such assurance, Canadian grocers have been agonizing over Wal-Mart's possible introduction of its massively successful U.S. Supercenter concept into Canada almost since the day Wal-Mart first entered this country with the purchase of the old Woolco chain.

After all, it was the threat that Wal-Mart posed to grocers in the U.S., along with warehouse club stores, that caused the Food Marketing Institute of Washington, D.C., to endorse the first Efficient Consumer Response (ECR) initiative in the early 1990s. In those days, traditional grocery outlets found themselves far less efficient and effective than they thought they were. Wal-Mart, a hard goods retailer, was outsmarting grocers at their own game. Wal-Mart was able to operate at margins that were half those required by grocers. Wal-Mart was negotiating better deals from suppliers, and its technology was more advanced than that of the grocery industry.

The ECR initiative was developed to cut the traditional grocery distribution system's costs and redundancies, making it more competitive with the likes of Wal-Mart. Canadian grocers adopted ECR within 18 months of its introduction in the U.S. At the time, it was to help the Canadian industry compete more successfully against the growing warehouse club store phenomenon here, but even then, Wal-Mart was in the back of many Canadian grocers' minds. And when Wal-Mart arrived in Canada with such a bang, by buying 122 Woolco stores in 1994, the Canadian grocery industry threw itself almost totally into ECR.

Since 1995, rumours of the imminent arrival of Wal-Mart's Supercenter concept have pervaded the Canadian grocery industry. The rumour mill has been so active that, at times, Supercenters were said to be appearing here about every three or four months—near Toronto today, in Niagara Falls tomorrow, next week in the lower mainland of B.C., and so on.[16]

items but also all goods and services that the consumer purchases routinely. These superstores look a lot like a combination of the supermarkets, drugstores, and mass-merchandisers from which they have evolved, but the concept is different. A supercentre is trying to meet all the customer's routine needs at a low price.

Supercentres average more than 150,000 square feet and carry about 50,000 items. In addition to foods, a supercentre carries personal-care products, medicine, some apparel, toys, some lawn and garden products, gasoline, and services such as drycleaning, travel reservations, bill paying, and banking. Growth in the number of supercentres seems to be slowing. Their assortment in one place is convenient, but many time-pressured consumers think that the crowds, lines, and "wandering around" time in the store are not. In response, some grocery chains like Loblaw's and Safeway now offer "stores within the store": under the same roof as their grocery operations, additional small stores with separate display areas and checkout counters carry specific products like video rentals, candles, and flowers.

The warehouse club is another retailing format that quickly gained popularity. Sam's Club and Costco are two of the largest. Consumers usually pay an annual membership fee to shop in these large, no-frills facilities. Among the 3,500 items per store, they carry food, appliances, yard tools, tires, and other items that many consumers see as homogeneous shopping items and want at the lowest possible price. The rapid growth of these clubs has also been fuelled by sales to small-business customers. That's why some people refer to these outlets as wholesale clubs. However, when half or more of a company's sales are to final consumers, it is classified as a retailer, not a wholesaler.[17]

Since 1980 some retailers—focusing on single product lines—have adopted the mass-merchandisers' approach with great success. Toys"R"Us pioneered this trend. Similarly, London Drugs, IKEA, Home Depot, Future Shop, and Office Depot attract large numbers of customers with their large assortment and low prices in a specific product category. These stores are called "category killers," because it's so hard for less-specialized retailers to compete.[18] Increasingly, these so-called big-box stores are locating in a single shopping centre: in a sense, these "power centres" are the mass-merchandise equivalent of early department stores.

It's reasonable to think about the move to 24-hour-a-day online selling—by the established retailers, new firms that never relied on stores, or both—as a next step in the evolution of mass-merchandising. But we'll have a more complete basis for evaluating the strengths and limitations of selling and shopping on the Web if we first look at some retailers that have targeted consumers who want more convenience, even if the price is higher.

## Convenience-based Formats

**convenience (food) stores**

A convenience-oriented variation on the conventional limited-line food stores

**Convenience (food) stores** are a convenience-oriented variation on the conventional limited-line food stores. Instead of expanding their assortment, however, convenience stores limit their stock to pickup or fill-in items like bread, milk, and eat-on-the-go snacks. Stores such as 7-Eleven and Mac's Milk aim to fill consumers' needs between major shopping trips to a supermarket, and many of them are competing with fast-food outlets. They offer convenience, not assortment, and often charge prices 10 to 20 percent higher than nearby supermarkets. However, as many gas stations have been converted to convenience stores and other retailers have expanded their hours intense competition is driving down convenience-store prices and profits.[19]

**automatic vending**

Selling and delivering products through vending machines

**Automatic vending**—selling and delivering products through vending machines—is becoming more popular because more and more consumers appreciate their convenience. The major disadvantage with automatic vending is the higher retail prices that must be charged for producers' branded items. Since machines are expensive to buy, stock, and repair relative to the volume they sell, the vending industry

Many retailers are looking for ways to make shopping faster and more convenient. Systems using miniature electronic devices can identify the customer, initiate the service, and accept payment; the customer doesn't need to carry a credit card and can bypass lineups to pay.

must charge higher prices. However, as costs come down—and as consumers' desire for convenience rises—we will see more growth in this method of retailing. Automated teller machines are examples of how technology is changing automatic vending.[20] Indeed, many believe that ATMs will soon offer services far beyond those traditionally associated with a bank.

**door-to-door selling**

A selling approach where a salesperson goes directly to the consumer's home

In **door-to-door selling**, a salesperson goes directly to the consumer's home. Variations on this approach are still important for firms like Amway and Mary Kay. It meets some consumers' need for convenient personal attention. It is also growing in popularity in some international markets, like China, where it provides salespeople with a good income. Door-to-door selling is on the decline in Canada because more adults are working outside the home and it's getting harder to find someone at home during the day. However, some firms continue to use this method of distribution.

**telephone and direct-mail retailing**

Allow consumers to shop at home, placing orders by mail or a toll-free telephone call and charging the purchase to a credit card

On the other hand, time-pressured dual-career families are a prime target market for **telephone and direct-mail retailing**, which allow consumers to shop at home, placing orders by mail or a toll-free telephone call and charging the purchase to a credit card. Typically, catalogues and ads on TV let customers see the offerings, and purchases are delivered by a commercial courier company. Some consumers really like the convenience of this type of retailing—especially for products not available in local stores.

This approach reduces costs by using computer mailing lists to help target specific customers and by using warehouse-type buildings and limited sales help. And shoplifting—a big expense for most retailers—isn't a problem. After-tax profits for successful mail-order retailers average about 7 percent of sales—more than twice the profit margins for most other types of retailers. However, with increasing competition and slower sales growth, these margins have been eroding. As we will discuss, however, the Internet is opening up new growth opportunities for many of these firms.[21]

The Shopping Channel, Home Shopping Network, and others are succeeding by devoting cable TV channels to home shopping. Some experts think that the coming explosion in the number of available cable channels and interactive cable services will make sales from this approach grow even faster. In addition, The Shopping Channel has opened a major website on the Internet. However, selling on the Internet is turning into something much more than just a variation of selling on TV or from a catalogue.[22]

## Retailing on the Internet

Until now, as we've talked about the evolution of retailers and the varied ways they have innovated to respond to consumer demand and meet needs, we've not devoted much attention to retailing on the Internet. It's reasonable to ask why. As we said earlier, Wal-Mart and other mass-merchandisers now sell on the Web, so one could view that development as just another aspect of how low-margin mass-merchandisers are trying to appeal to a large target market with wide (or deep) assortments of products at discount prices. Or one might view the Internet as just another way to add convenient in-home shopping, with an electronic catalogue and ordering on a remote computer. After all, that's the way most people saw earlier pre-Internet dial-up systems such as Prodigy—a joint venture between Sears and IBM that fizzled because it was too complicated.

Both of these views make some sense, yet they are incomplete and probably misleading. The fact is that almost *all* types of retailers are now establishing a presence on the Internet. It has the potential over time to dramatically reshape many aspects of retail selling. So rather than just treat it as a new way that some types of retailers are incrementally varying their old strategies, let's look at it in terms of what it is likely to become—something that is *really* different.

Despite all the attention, Internet retailing is still in the early growth stages. On the one hand, Internet usage continues to rise and consumer e-commerce sales have grown at an exceptionally fast rate. In 1997, consumers spent about US$2.7 billion on the Internet. To put that number in perspective, it took about 3 percent of Wal-Mart's stores to rack up the same sales. By 2001 that number leaped to about US$144 billion. But don't confuse growth or the "big bang" that the Internet may have on retailing and consumer shopping behaviour with the reality of its immediate economic impact on the retail system. So far, all of that spending is less than 5 percent of total retailing sales dollars. Further, the numbers are as high as they are because a lot of expensive computer equipment has been sold that way. So in absolute dollars, retailing on the Internet is in its infancy. However, it has the potential to continue to grow. Taking these two vantage points in combination, it's useful to consider what's different about it today and how it will evolve; see Exhibit 12-3.



**Exhibit 12-3** Some illustrative differences between online and in-store shopping.

| Characteristics | Online Shopping | In-Store Shopping |
|---|---|---|
| Customer characteristics | Younger, better educated, more upscale | Cross-section; depends on store |
| Day-of-week emphasis | Higher percentage of purchases during weekdays | Higher percentage of purchases on the weekend |
| Customer service | Weak but improving | Varies, but usually better than online |
| Products purchased | More emphasis on one-time purchases | More emphasis on routine purchases |
| Availability of product | Not available for inspection or immediate use | Usually available for inspection and immediate use |
| Comparative information about products | Much more extensive, but sometimes poorly organized | Often weak (for example, limited to what is on packages) |
| Entertainment value | A media experience | Often a social experience |
| Charges | Product prices often lower, but shipping and handling costly | Product prices and taxes higher, but usually no delivery expense |
| Shopping hours and preparation | Completely flexible if online access is available | Depends on store and available transportation |

**Moving information versus moving goods** Stripped to its essence, the Internet dramatically lowers the cost of communication while making it happen faster. So, it can radically alter activities that depend on the flow of information. The Internet has produced the biggest gains in businesses where better information results in more efficient restructuring of tasks. As we discussed in Chapter 7, that's what happens in much online B2B e-commerce. On the other hand, place decisions for consumer markets need to deal with the challenge of handling truckloads of products and getting them to the consumer's place. Much of the investment in Internet retailing systems has been directed toward moving information (like orders), not physical goods. It takes, for example, about US$15 million to US$25 million to build a world-class website for consumer e-commerce. But it costs about US$150 million to build a distribution centre and systems to support a large-scale consumer Web operation. Therefore, much of the attention so far has been on the "front door" of the Internet store, and not on the back end of retailing operations where more of the big costs accumulate.

The investment and innovations will come into balance over time, just as they have with other retailing innovations. But demand is what will shape investments in new supply capabilities. So far, the basic patterns of consumer demand have not changed that much. There are, of course, exceptions. For example, more consumer financial services companies are selling on the Web than are retailers in any other industry—but that is an information-intensive service business, rather than one that adjusts physical discrepancies.

**The good and the bad—The consumer's view** As we noted earlier, traditional thinking about retailing looks at product assortments from the perspective of location and shopping convenience. On the Internet, by contrast, a consumer can get to a very wide assortment, perhaps from different sellers, by clicking from one website to another. The assortment moves toward being unlimited. However, the Internet may not be the best retail channel for all products. Let's consider the positives and negatives of using the Internet from the consumer's point of view to better understand where the Internet is likely to have its greatest impact.

***Convenience*** If the Internet makes it very convenient to shop, it is very inconvenient in other ways. You have to plan ahead. You can't touch or inspect a product. When you buy something from the Internet, you've actually just ordered it. You don't have it to hold. Someone has to deliver it, and that involves delays and costs.

Surfing around the Internet is convenient for people who are comfortable with computers, but many consumers are not. At present, people who actually shop on the Web are better educated, younger, and more well-to-do. Of course, access to and use of the Internet is evolving quickly. Cable operators and telephone companies are in a race to provide more consumers with faster access. Other firms and new technologies are being developed all the time. WebTV already makes it easy, but it is just the start. Costs will continue to come down, and within a decade most North American homes will have routine access to the Internet.

***Product interaction and information*** On the Internet, a consumer can't touch a product or really inspect it. For many products consumers want to be able to do that—or at least they're used to doing it. On the other hand, when a consumer is in a retail store it's often hard to get any information (not to mention good information!). At a website it's often possible to get much more information with just a mouse-click, even though only the product and a brief description are presented on the initial page.

It's also possible to access a much broader array of information. Ziff-Davis Publishing, for example, has a comprehensive website (www.ziffdavis.com) with product reviews, feature comparisons, performance tests, and other data on every computer-related product imaginable. Similar sites are being developed for everything from automobiles to vitamins. Better information will make many consumers better shoppers, even if they buy in a store rather than online (as many Web surfers currently do). That reduces the risk of not getting what they thought they were buying and the hassles of returning a product if there's a problem.

More powerful computers are also opening up many more possibilities for multimedia information—not just pictures, but full-motion product-demo videos and audio explanations. The Internet is also quickly turning into a medium for video conferencing; many computers come with a videocam as an inexpensive accessory. So it is likely that in the near future consumers will be able to get not only computer-provided help during a visit to a website but also help from a real person. Many failed dot-com retailers figured out too late that their website operations could cut some types of costs, but failing to provide human customer service support was a big mistake. As shown in Marketing Demo 12-2, they ignored the lessons learned by mass-merchandisers in their early days when they tried to do the same thing.

**Comparison shopping** If you know what you want, and it's one thing, you can usually find it fast on the Internet. You can look for "Oakley sunglasses" with a search engine and get a list of sellers and see pictures of every style made. It's quick and easy. If you don't know exactly what you're looking for, however, you may get too much information, or the wrong information. It's hard to narrow a search when you don't know what you're looking for. Clearly, for the appeal of Internet retailing to spread there will need to be better "virtual malls"—databases with lots of information that can be viewed lots of ways—to make it easier to get information you want and avoid the clutter that is, at best, irrelevant. Retailers like Amazon and Wal-Mart have constantly revised and improved their websites to address this issue, but more progress will be needed.

The Internet makes it easy to do comparison shopping and to compare prices from different sellers. That already is putting price pressure on Internet sellers, in part because few have figured out how else to differentiate what they offer. Even

## Marketing Demo 12–2

### WHY ETOYS.COM IS ETOYS.GONE

eToys was founded in 1997 with the dream of becoming the premier site on the Internet for the kids' product market. Many investors shared its vision of unlimited growth; at one time its stock-market value was 35 percent greater than its long-established profitable competitor, Toys"R"Us. eToys did deliver in producing one of the slickest e-commerce websites. Parents could search for toys by age group or theme or product. Kids could create and send "gift wish lists." But eToys failed to consider some basic marketing ideas. For example, toys are a mature category, so a user-friendly website doesn't increase total consumer demand. eToys also underestimated how competitors would react to its plan to take most of their customers—which is what it would have taken to even cover eToys' costs. Wal-Mart copied some of eToys' best ideas but also had the buying clout to create its own brands and sell toys cheaper. Toys"R"Us teamed up with Amazon. Worse, eToys assumed that once it got customers to its site—by spending huge amounts on advertising—those customers would be loyal. When 5 percent of its orders didn't go out on time during the 1999 holiday season, customers bolted. Every parent who let a kid down told everyone they knew. When eToys tried to improve its distribution systems, costs spiraled out of control because of the hassles of handling breakable toys that come in all sorts of sizes and shapes. In the end, the total costs of efforts were so high that it would have taken four or five years of constantly improving sales just to break even on operations—to say nothing about making up millions in losses. You can build a better mousetrap, but if it doesn't meet customer needs at a profit you're in trouble.[23]

Many established retailers, like Canadian Tire, are trying to figure out how to combine "clicks and mortar" to meet consumers' needs better than would be possible with only an online website or only a store.

when the consumer is able to locate the appropriate retail Internet site, the design and ease of use of the site will have a significant impact on buyer behaviour. It has been estimated that fewer than 5 percent of all "shopping carts" that are initiated on the Internet are ever "checked out." The reason: consumers are never more than a mouse-click away from going to a competing site if they find yours is too cumbersome to use or too slow to access.

### The Special Case of Scrambled Merchandising

**scrambled merchandising**

A retailer carrying any product line it thinks it can sell profitably

Sometimes it is not easy to classify a store as being of any one type. This is because many retail outlets are moving toward **scrambled merchandising**—carrying any product line they think they can sell profitably. Scrambled merchandising is a form of mass merchandising but with elements of convenience-based formats mixed in. A key premise is that one-stop shopping is valued by customers and that store location is a major factor in being the favoured one-stop. This is the approach being taken by Loblaw's when it expands beyond grocery items, and by Wal-Mart when it expands *into* grocery items.

For example, one of Canada's most successful retailers is British Columbia's London Drugs: in addition to being a major reseller of pharmaceuticals and health and beauty products, London Drugs also is one of Canada's largest resellers of computer hardware and software, camera equipment, and photofinishing. London Drugs also sells grocery items, a limited line of furniture, small appliances, and hardware items—to name but a few! Read Marketing Demo 12-3 to see how London Drugs takes advantage of the various opportunities of scrambled merchandising.

## Retail Evolution and Change

We've talked about many different types of retailers and how they evolved. Earlier, we noted that no single characteristic provided a good basis for classifying all retailers. Now it helps to see the three-dimensional view of retailing presented in Exhibit 12-4. It positions different types of retailers in terms of three consumer-oriented dimensions: (1) width of assortment desired, (2) depth of assortment desired, and (3) a price/service combination. Price and service are combined because they are often indirectly related. Services are costly to provide. So a retailer that wants to emphasize low prices usually has to cut some services—and retailers with a lot of services must charge prices that cover the added costs.

We can position most existing retailers within this three-dimensional market diagram. Exhibit 12-4, for example, suggests the *why* of vending machines. Some people—shown in the front upper left-hand corner—have a strong need for a specific item and are not interested in width of assortment, depth of assortment, or price. Note where Internet retailers are placed in the diagram. Does that position make sense to you? How does this exhibit explain the phenomenon discussed in Internet Insite 12-1: the growing use of multiple retail channels?

## Marketing Demo 12–3



### AIR DRUGSTORE

Although London Drugs plans to enter Saskatchewan this year, for now it only operates in B.C. and Alberta. But don't let that give you the impression that it's small-time. It is owned by H.Y. Louie Co., a holding company in Burnaby that since its founding in 1903 by Hok Yat Louie, a Chinese immigrant with a small general store, has grown to become what *Business in Vancouver* magazine estimates is B.C.'s second-largest private company, trailing only The Jim Pattison Group. H.Y. Louie's holdings include the IGA supermarkets in B.C. as well as London Drugs. The latter is a big regional player, with about 6,500 employees and an ad budget of $5 million to $10 million.

With 54 stores scattered across two provinces, and business to attend to all over North America, it means a lot of time spent checking into reservation counters, waiting for delayed flights, missing connections, eating airline food, and overnighting in hotels. Multiply that by all the other managers and staff who have to get somewhere by air, and it adds up to a lot of unproductive time and missed opportunities.

Wynne Powell, president and chief operating officer of London Drugs, travels up to 160,000 miles a year.

About five years ago, Powell, an accountant, crunched the numbers and found a "compelling business rationale" for using charter jets. After numerous occasions of not being able to book an aircraft, he decided that it made good corporate sense to buy one. The first Learjet 45, which carries nine passengers, was purchased for $15 million in 1999 and began chartering in May 2000 under the name London Air Services.

London Drugs bought a second Learjet 45 and expects delivery of a $25-million Challenger 604 in March 2002. It also has a Bombardier Continental on order with an expected delivery date of December 2005.

If you're wondering what a drugstore knows about running a small airline, the answer is that it doesn't have any particular expertise in this area. But it does know about competing in an array of fields, since it already operates across 11 product categories, including pharmaceutical products, cameras, microwaves, computers, and home entertainment equipment.

"It is an airline company, but what is not unique and I hope you experience it when you go into London Drugs is our dedication to the customer," says Powell. "It's a customer-driven organization, as London Drugs is. The customer is the boss."

While London Air Services is distinct from London Drugs, the latter is the airline's biggest customer, taking up about 35 to 40 percent of total flying time. London Drugs runs print ads in the Vancouver Board of Trade's monthly publication, the *Globe and Mail*, and various Hollywood publications that include the tag line, "A business tool that flies," Aside from those, it does little in the way of advertising. Business is predicated on word of mouth and repeat business.

While Americans have been using corporate charters for years as part of their business culture, the problem is that Canada is a "small-c conservative country," says Gage. "Many of the top executives of companies choose not to use this type of transportation. They see it as something that is perhaps ostentatious or something that is of not particular value to them. And that, I think, is the business culture that is typically Canadian."

Powell is working to change that perception, and he says Air Canada is making it easy. "If you go to Calgary for five people and you need to get there tomorrow and you can't get on WestJet, you go Air Canada. Last time I checked, it was $1,100 per person to go to Calgary. The charter to go to Calgary and bring you back that night is approximately $5,400," he says. "American companies for years have used these kind of tools, take them for granted being a necessary part of the business tools. So what we've being trying to do with London Air is to educate our fellow business and colleagues about the efficiency of using corporate aircraft."

He calls his investment in planes "an entrepreneurial leap of faith." And, while starting an airline in B.C.'s battered economy may seem like risky business, he is flying high on the economic future of the province.[24]

Exhibit 12-4 A three-dimensional view of the market for retail facilities and the probable position of some present offerings.

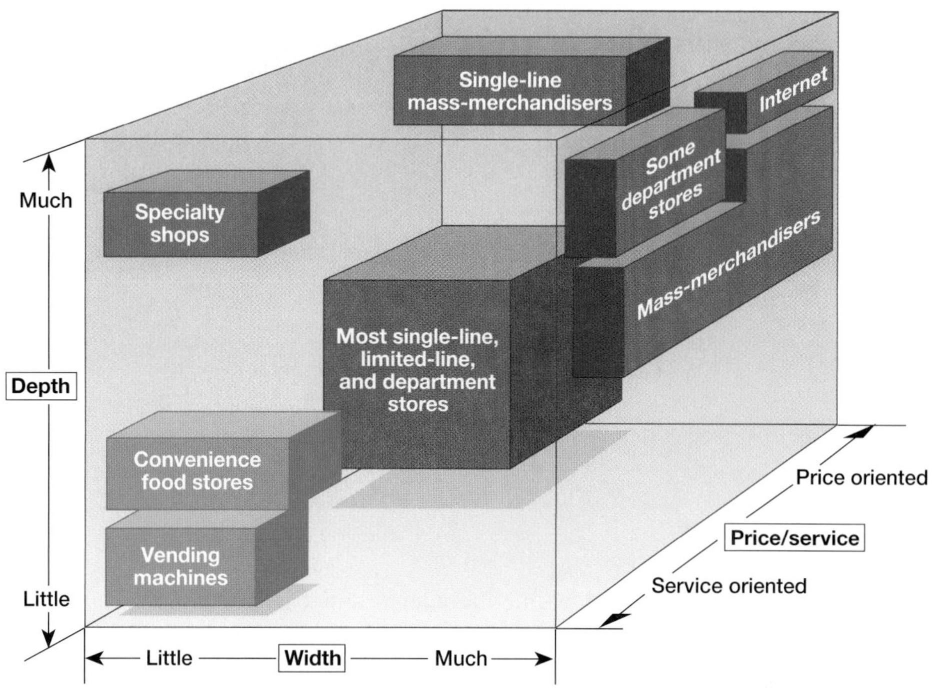


**wheel of retailing theory**

The idea that new types of retailers enter the market as low-status, low-margin, low-price operators and then evolve into more conventional retailers offering more services with higher operating costs and higher prices

## Why Retailers Evolve and Change

Just as the product life cycle seeks to identify the changes experienced over time in a product-market, there have been several attempts to show the pattern of evolution in retailing. The **wheel of retailing theory** says that new types of retailers enter the market as low-status, low-margin, low-price operators and then—if successful—evolve into more conventional retailers offering more services with higher operating costs and higher prices. Then they're threatened by new low-status, low-margin,

Some manufacturers have always had outlet stores near their factories, but outlet malls are emerging as a new retailing format that is popular with some consumers.

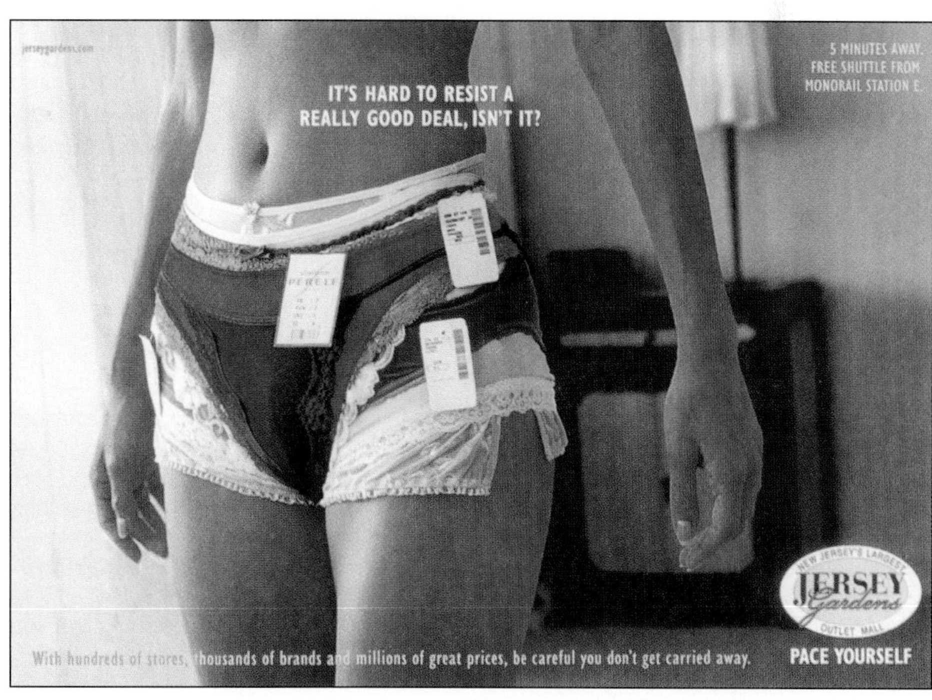

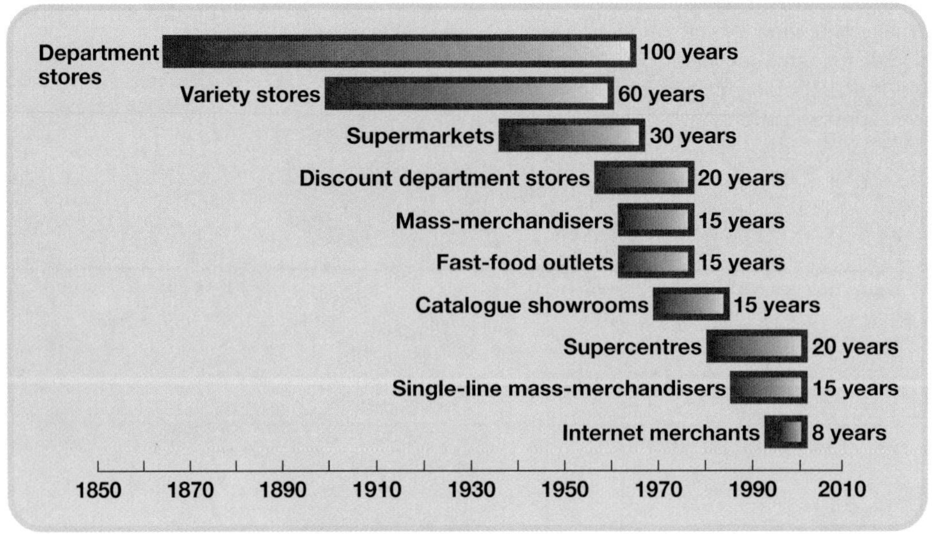


Exhibit 12-5 Retailer life cycles: timing and years to mature market.

low-price retailers—and the wheel turns again. Department stores, supermarkets, and mass-merchandisers all went through this cycle.

The wheel of retailing theory, however, doesn't explain all major retailing developments. Vending machines entered as high-cost, high-margin operations. Convenience food stores are high-priced. Suburban shopping centres don't emphasize low price. Current retailers that are adding websites are likely to face competitors who cut operating expenses even deeper.

As these examples suggest, many retail formats develop in response to changing consumer needs. Over time, they are modified by the strategies of existing competitors and the entry of new competitors. We can apply the product life cycle concept to understand this process better. A retailer with a new idea may have big profits—for a while. But if it's a really good idea, the retailer can count on speedy imitation and a squeeze on profits. Other retailers will copy the new format or scramble their product mix to sell products that offer them higher margins or faster turnover. That puts pressure on the original firm to change or lose its market. (Other pressures marketers face include issues of ethics; see Ethical Dimensions 12-1.)

Some conventional retailers are in decline as these life and death cycles continue. Recent innovators, like the Internet merchants, are still in the market growth stage (see Exhibit 12-5). Some retailing formats that are mature in North America are only now beginning to grow in other countries.

## Internet Insite 12–1

### MULTI-CHANNEL RETAILING

Consumers increasingly use multiple channels to shop for products and services. The Internet is often used for information search, but the actual purchase may be made in a local store. This is especially the case with expensive purchases such as cars and consumer electronics. Many consumers use Internet banking as their primary method of banking, but still do occasionally visit the local branch for certain transactions.

Studies show that if a firm sells its products through multiple channels, the buyer conversion rate tends to increase (i.e., the percentage of potential buyers who become actual buyers). A survey by Shop.org found that the average buyer conversion rate for Internet-only retailers was a mere 3 percent, compared to more than 6 percent for firms that had retail stores as well as Web stores.

A survey of 48,000 consumers by Shop.org found that

across several product categories, 73 percent of store purchases were preceded by some degree of product information search on the Internet. Thirty-four percent of consumers shop in three channels—stores, Internet, and catalogue.[25] The survey found significant levels of cross-channel shopping (store, online, and catalogue), meaning consumers like to shop in more than one channel with the same retailer. Consumers who shop with a retailer through multiple channels also seem to be more loyal to the retailer, with 45 percent of those who shop in a particular online store also preferring the same bricks-and-mortar store brand.

There is also some evidence that those who shop in multiple channels may spend more money. A survey by DoubleClick, an Internet advertising and research firm, found that 56 percent of the 1,270 adult consumers that were surveyed used a combination of shopping sources. For consumers who used multiple channels, the average spending was 39 percent more than those who visited only one channel—$909 for multi-channel shoppers, compared to $654 for single-channel consumers.[26] This survey focused on the spending patterns during the 2002 holiday season.

What are the challenges in multi-channel retailing? When consumers shop with the same store brand in multiple channels, they expect the same level of customer service, consistency in product assortment, consistency in price (or sometimes lower prices online), ability to find products easily, and a consistent return/refund policy. A customer may buy a sweater or a jacket online at Sears.ca and return it to a local Sears store for exchange or refund if it's not suitable. Another customer may want to browse through the Futureshop.ca website looking for a suitable camcorder and then buy a specific brand at a local store. In other words, consumers today want a seamless experience across channels.

In order for retailers to satisfy the demands placed by such consumers, they must fully integrate their online and offline operations. That is not an easy task. According to Peter Stanger, vice-president of Boston Consulting Group, "For multi-channel retailers, it is now more important than ever to ensure that the online businesses are integrated with the store and catalog businesses. It is by effectively analyzing the customer information across these channels that multi-channel retailers can realize a significant increase in share of wallet."[27]

Providing consumers a consistently high quality and seamless experience across different channels requires several things. First is appropriate information technology to ensure that the same customer database and inventory systems are accessible to service personnel in all channels.[28] No matter what channel the customer uses, the retailer must be able to recognize the customer and provide consistency in product offerings and service. Second is a very good understanding of customer needs in different channels and the ability to be responsive to such needs. One cannot assume that the preferences of those who buy online and in bricks-and-mortar stores are the same. Third is ensuring that the brand image and brand message are consistent in all channels. If managed properly, the Web can reinforce or redefine the image of a traditional bricks-and- mortar store. Nordstrom, known for its customer service, has created a simple site that ensures a stress-free shopping experience. You can see the prominence given to service in that site (www.nordstrom.com), which strengthens the brand image. Fourth is ongoing analysis of customer data in different channels, which can lead to better segmentation, customization, and overall improved marketing effort. Lastly, the retailer should be able to exploit the strengths of each channel. The Web can be effective in delivering product information and offering convenience. The physical channel may offer the ability to try the product and interact with sales personnel.

A bricks-and-mortar retailer serves thousands of customers from one location. Online, the same retailer has to take an order from an individual customer, process the order, package one or more products, and deliver to that individual customer. Returns, complaints, and service requests must be handled efficiently. For traditional retailers, developing the order-fulfillment capabilities for online operation can be a challenge—sometimes requiring changes in business processes and other times requiring huge investments.

Another risk in the multi-channel retailing approach is the possible cannibalization of sales. Consumers may choose the online channel because it is more convenient (especially once they trust the retailer). Retailers must see if adding a new channel brings additional revenues and profits.

In Canada, some retailers have responded to this challenge better than others. Canadian Tire (www.canadiantire.ca) and Future Shop (www.futureshop.ca) offer a wide range of products online, with a fair degree of consistency with their physical stores. Both stores allow for online purchases to be returned or exchanged in physical stores. Canadian Tire has integrated its print catalogue with its website (see the exhibit above) and so has Sears Canada (www.sears.ca). The Bay (www.hbc.com), on the other hand, offers a very limited selection online, which makes it difficult to do product research online and then buy in a local store.

Canadian apparel e-tailer JustWhiteShirts (www.justwhiteshirts.com) is now a multi-channel retailer. They offer catalogue (phone) shopping, a website with international operations, and bricks-and-mortar stores in the Toronto area. JustWhiteShirts started as a catalogue company and then made a name for itself as global online apparel company. Now the addition of a store in Toronto reflects the trend toward multiple channels. This is a case of a dot-com becoming a "clicks-and-mortar" operation. On their website, you can find directions to their store and order a print catalogue.

Sears, a pioneer in the catalogue business, has pursued the multiple-channel strategy for many years. For online purchases, they offer home delivery as well as delivery at a local store for customer pickup. Sears found that 21 percent of shoppers who came into stores to pick up products ordered online ended up buying additional items during the trip to the store.[29]

Some bricks-and-mortar retailers have found the transition to the online world difficult. Some of them have entered into alliances as a means to operate in multiple channels. The most prominent example is that of Toys"R"Us, whose online operation is handled by Amazon.com. This gives Toys"R"Us an online presence and the ability to generate a new revenue stream without having to acquire all the capabilities needed to be a successful e-tailer.

Emerging trends include shopping via handheld devices (PDAs, cell phones), which is referred to as *mobile commerce* or m-commerce. Some do not see this as an entirely new channel and are skeptical about whether consumers will shop using hand-held devices. For certain products and services, m-commerce may make sense. Content and entertainment services hold immediate promise for the m-commerce delivery channel. The promise of m-commerce is yet to be fulfilled.

The Internet has changed the retailing landscape forever. Very few large retailers can survive without some degree of integration of the Internet into their existing business model. Retailers that figure out how to exploit each channel while developing synergies across channels are the ones likely to succeed.

Some questions for you to ponder: If some customers are more prone to shopping in multiple channels than others, how can marketers take advantage of this behaviour? What are the essentials for providing a consistent and seamless experience across all channels?

Go to: www.mcgrawhill.ca/college/wong
to apply this Insite in an exciting Internet exercise.



## Retailing: The International Perspective

Historically, new retailing approaches that have succeeded in one developed country have quickly spread to others. Self-service approaches that started with supermarkets in North America are now found in many retail operations around the world. Similarly, mass-merchandising and superstore concepts were pioneered in Australia and Europe and then brought to North America.[30]

On the other hand, retailing in less developed nations has typically involved small shops selling very small quantities, often to a small number of consumers. A lack of personal financial resources has been a contributing factor to this situation. Consumers in these countries often haven't had the incomes to support mass

## Ethical Dimensions 12–1

### QUESTIONABLE MARKETING PRACTICES

Most retailers face intense competitive pressure. The desperation that comes with such pressure has pushed some retailers toward questionable marketing practices.

Critics argue, for example, that retailers too often advertise special sale items to bring price-sensitive shoppers into the store or to a website but then don't stock enough product to meet demand. Other retailers are criticized for pushing consumers to trade up to more expensive items. What is ethical and unethical in situations like these, however, is subject to debate.

Retailers can't always anticipate demand perfectly, and deliveries may not arrive on time. Similarly, trading up may be a sensible part of a strategy, if it's done honestly and with the consumer's best interests at heart. The difficulty arises from the consumer's ability to detect a retailer's motive. This is one reason why many retailers offer "rainchecks" on sale items or state the quantity of sale items they have available.

Some mass-merchandiser chains, like Tesco in the U.K., are looking for growth by opening small stores—which will put even more pressure on conventional retailers.

distribution. As well, the governments of some countries in Asia, Europe, and South America have severely limited the evolution of retailing through laws designed to protect small shopkeepers by keeping out large stores. Also, religious beliefs or societal norms have prevented retailers from opening on weekends or evenings, and this makes them less convenient for customers.[31]

Changes are taking place, however. Using sophisticated strategic management skills and enhanced technological capacity to run large, highly efficient operations, mega-retailers are beginning to expand throughout the world. These mega-retailers include U.S.–based operations such as Wal-Mart and Toys"R"Us, and European companies such as Benetton, Makro, and Marks & Spencer. These companies are seeking new markets because their home bases are saturated with competition. At home, they are sharing stagnant consumer markets with an increasing number of firms attempting to copy their success. They need to enter new markets to grow.[32]

The new markets that the mega-retailers are targeting include emerging economies such as Mexico, Southeast Asia, and China. In these countries, the use of credit to make purchases is beginning to gain acceptance. Furthermore, much of the population is younger than 18 and will move into their prime spending years over the next two decades. Will mega-retailers be able to establish long-term operations in these markets? This will depend on how successfully they adapt their marketing mixes to new cultures. It will also depend on their ability to build the physical distribution networks needed to stock and maintain their store shelves. Also, and as proof that the economic environment is always important, foreign retailers have had to adjust in recent years both to a peso crisis in Mexico and to major financial problems throughout Southeast Asia.

## Global Retailing Comes to Canada

Many American chains have been attracted to Canada in recent years by our low exchange rate and the North American Free Trade Agreement. Some, such as Toys"R"Us, Business Depot, Winners, and the Gap, have done quite well. Wal-Mart, in particular, has rapidly become a very major player in the Canadian department-store sector. Other American big-box warehouse stores have also successfully invaded Canada. There are now some 57 American and 20 non-American retailers operating in Canada. Foreign-controlled space now amounts to almost 70 million square feet, or approximately 17 percent of the total Canadian market, excluding food and automotive. There are now about 2 square feet of American retail space for every person in Canada.[33]

But the defensive marketing actions taken by established Canadian retailers have surprised some American firms. For example, Home Depot entered Canada in February 1994 by acquiring 75 percent of Aikenhead's Home Improvement Warehouse.

By June 1995, Home Depot had decided to scale back its operations in Canada because of the unexpectedly strong response of Canadian do-it-yourself chains such as Revelstoke Home Centres Ltd. In the mid and late 1990s, Canadian Tire also more than held its own against foreign-owned entrants into Canada.

### Canadian Retailing Goes Global

Can Canadian retail organizations successfully perform on a larger stage? Can they compete with the best? Canadian retailers have been criticized for not being aggressive enough in the global marketplace. There is concern that the resulting lack of managerial experience and sophistication will ultimately increase Canadian firms' vulnerability to takeover by foreign-based retailers. Others have argued that our domestic focus has been the reason that Canadian retailers have recently looked abroad for senior managers with both American and international experience.

Some attempts at expansion into the United States by major Canadian retailers have failed (for example, Canadian Tire). However, generalities about a lack of Canadian retail aggressiveness may be unwarranted. There are at least 21 Canadian retailers currently operating in the United States out of a total of 46 that have entered—a 46-percent survival rate. A further eight Canadian retailers are operating internationally in locations other than the United States. The American market is an extremely challenging one. Some of the Canadian retailers operating in the United States are performing well, while others are struggling. Future Shop is but one of many Canadian chains that at one time experienced serious losses. But other firms, such as Club Monaco and Roots, are succeeding both in the United States and in other international markets.[34]

## Wholesaling

It's hard to define what a wholesaler is because there are so many different wholesalers doing different jobs. Some of their activities may even seem like manufacturing. As a result, some wholesalers describe themselves as "manufacturer and dealer." Some like to identify themselves with such general terms as *merchant, jobber, dealer,* or *distributor*. And others just take the name commonly used in their trade—without really thinking about what it means.

To avoid a long technical discussion on the nature of wholesaling, we'll use the Statistics Canada definition:

> **Wholesalers** are primarily engaged in buying merchandise for resale to retailers; to industrial, commercial, institutional, and professional users; to other wholesalers; for export; to farmers for use in farm production; or acting as agents in such transactions.

Mixed-activity businesses (such as firms engaged in both wholesaling and retailing, contracting, service trades, manufacturing, and so on) are considered to be in wholesale trade whenever they derive the largest portion of their gross margin from their wholesaling activity.[35]

Wholesaling activities are just variations of the basic marketing functions we discussed in Chapter 1—gathering and providing information, buying and selling, grading, storing, transporting, financing, and risk taking. You can understand wholesalers' strategies better if you look at them as members of channels. They add value by doing jobs for their customers and for their suppliers. In Chapter 11, we considered some of the ways they provide value when we discussed why a producer might want to use indirect distribution and include an intermediary in the channel. Now we'll develop these ideas in more detail.

### The Changing Face of Wholesaling

In earlier years, wholesalers dominated distribution channels in Canada and most other countries. The many small producers and small retailers needed their services.

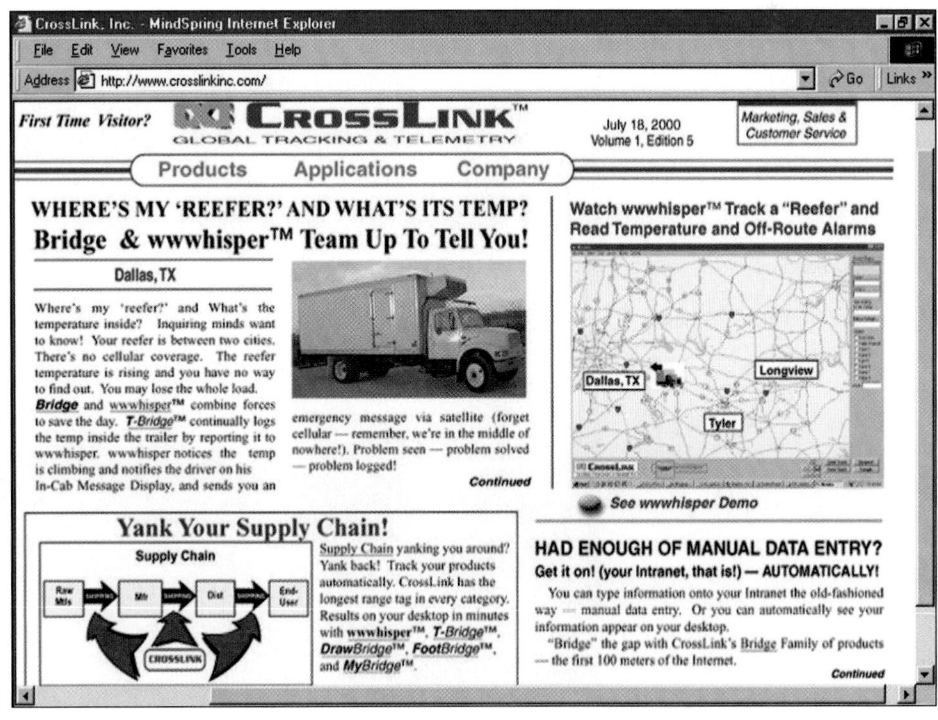


Many modern wholesalers are adopting new technologies to become more effective. For example, CrossLink's satellite communication system tracks the temperature of refrigerated deliveries and notifies the central office if there is any risk that products will be spoiled.

This situation still exists in many countries, especially those with less-developed economies. However, in the developed nations, as producers became larger many bypassed the wholesalers. Similarly, large retail chains often take control of functions that had been handled by wholesalers. Now e-commerce is making it easier for producers and consumers to "connect" without having a wholesaler in the middle of the exchange. In light of these changes, many people have predicted a gloomy future for wholesalers.

There certainly is reason to expect the worst for some types of wholesalers. With all the changes taking place, one could assume that wholesaling won't adapt fast enough. In the 1970s and 1980s that seemed to be the pattern. Now, however, rapid changes are underway. Even big changes are not always visible to consumers because they're hidden in the channel. But many wholesalers are adapting rapidly and finding new ways to add value in the channel. For example, some of the biggest B2B e-commerce sites on the Internet are wholesaler operations.

Partly due to new management and new strategies, many wholesalers are enjoying significant growth. Progressive wholesalers are becoming more concerned with their customers and with channel systems. Many are using technology to offer better service. Others develop voluntary chains that bind them more closely to their customers.

Modern wholesalers no longer require all customers to pay for all the services they offer simply because certain customers use them. Many offer a basic service at minimum cost—then charge additional fees for any special services required.

Most modern wholesalers have streamlined their operations to cut unnecessary costs and improve profits. In fact, wholesalers pioneered many of the recent logistics innovations we discussed in Chapter 11. They use computers to track inventory and reorder only when it's really needed. Computerized sales analysis helps them identify and drop unprofitable products and customers. This sometimes leads to a selective distribution policy—when it's unprofitable to build relationships with too many small customers. Then they can fine-tune how they add value for their profitable customers.

Many wholesalers are also modernizing their warehouses and physical handling facilities. They mark products with bar codes that can be read with hand-held scan-

McKesson is a leading distributor of drugs, and effective use of technology has been a key reason for its success. The space-age gizmo on this man's arm combines a scanner, computer, and two-way radio and is used to speed up order assembly and delivery from McKesson's distribution centre.

ners—so inventory, shipping, and sales records can be easily and instantly updated. Computerized order-picking systems speed the job of assembling orders. New storing facilities are carefully located to minimize the costs of both incoming freight and deliveries. Delivery vehicles travel to customers in a computer-selected sequence that reduces the number of kilometres travelled. And wholesalers that serve manufacturers are rising to the challenge of just-in-time delivery.

Not all wholesalers are progressive, and some less efficient ones will fail. Efficiency and low cost, however, are not all that's needed for success. Some wholesalers will disappear as the functions they provided in the past are shifted and shared in different ways in the channel. Cost-conscious buyers for Wal-Mart, Lowe's, and other chains are refusing to deal with some of the intermediaries that represent small producers. They want to negotiate directly with the producer—not just accept the wholesaler's price. Similarly, more producers see advantages in having closer direct relationships with fewer suppliers—and they're weeding out weaker vendors. Efficient delivery services like UPS and Federal Express are also making it easy and inexpensive for many producers to ship directly to their customers—even ones in foreign markets. The Internet is putting pressure on wholesalers whose primary role is providing information to bring buyers and sellers together.[36] (Other pressures wholesalers face include issues of ethics; see Ethical Dimensions 12-2.)

To survive, each wholesaler must develop a good marketing strategy. Profit margins are not large in wholesaling—typically ranging from less than 1 percent to 2 percent. And they've declined as the competitive squeeze has tightened.

The wholesalers that do survive will need to be efficient, but that doesn't mean they'll all have low costs. Some wholesalers' higher operating expenses result from the strategies they select—including the special services they offer to *some* customers.

### Different Types of Wholesalers

Exhibit 12-6 gives a big-picture view of the major types of wholesalers we'll be discussing and some of the functions that they perform. There are lots more specialized types, but our discussion will give you a sense of the diversity. Note that a major difference between merchant and agent wholesalers is whether they own the products they sell. Before discussing these wholesalers, we'll briefly consider producers who handle their own wholesaling activities.

## Ethical Dimensions 12–2

### A QUESTION OF ETHICS, OR GOOD BUSINESS PRACTICE?

The many changes in wholesaling are squeezing some wholesalers out of business. Some critics—including many of the wounded wholesalers—argue that it's unethical for powerful suppliers or customers to simply cut out wholesalers who spend money and time, perhaps decades, developing markets. Contracts between channel members and laws sometimes define what is or is not legal. But the ethical issues are often more ambiguous.

For example, as part of a broader effort to improve profits, Amana notified Cooper Distributing Co. that it intended to cancel their distribution agreement in 10 days. Cooper had been handling Amana appliances for 30 years, and Amana products represented 85 percent of Cooper's sales. Amana's explanation to Cooper? "It's not because you're doing a bad job: We just think we can do it better."

Situations like this arise often. They may be cold-hearted, but are they unethical? We argue that it isn't fair to cut off the relationship with such short notice. But most wholesalers realize that their business is always at risk—if they don't perform channel functions better or cheaper than what their suppliers or customers can do themselves.[37]

Exhibit 12-6 Types of wholesalers.

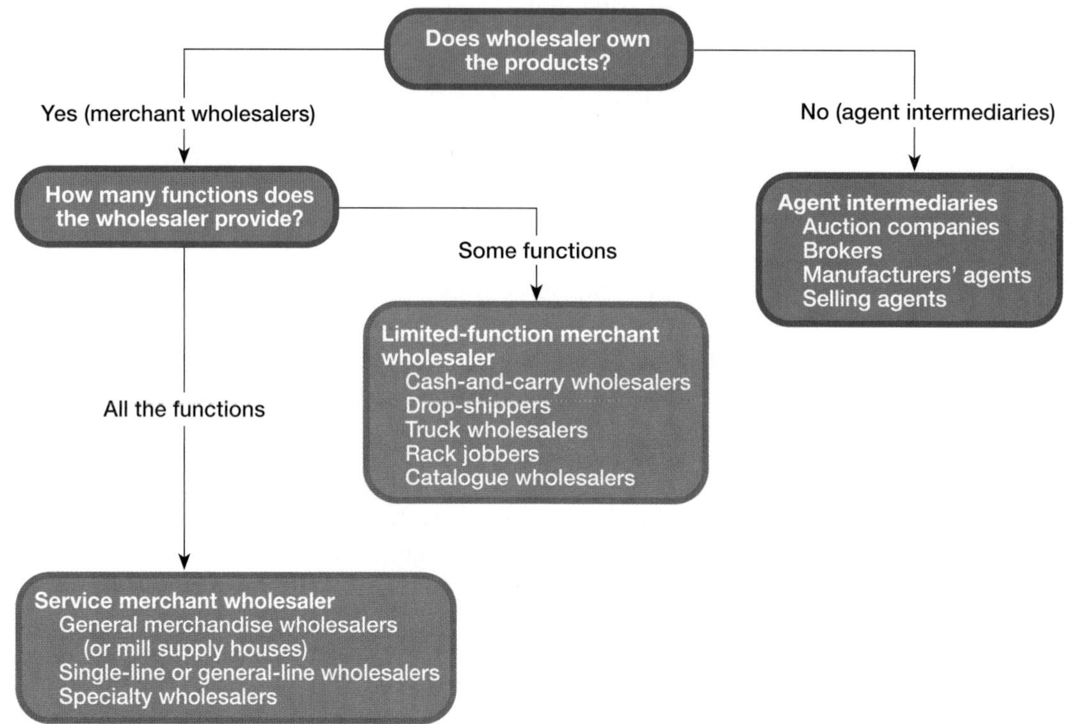




**manufacturers' sales branches**
Warehouses that producers set up at separate locations away from their factories

Manufacturers who just take over some wholesaling activities are not considered wholesalers. However, when they set up **manufacturers' sales branches**—warehouses that producers set up at separate locations away from their factories—these establishments basically operate as wholesalers. These manufacturer-owned branch operations are usually placed in the best market areas. This also helps explain why their operating costs, as a percentage of sales, are often lower. Another reason is that coordination is easier within a single firm. Manufacturers can more quickly set up efficient network systems for sharing information and logistics functions with their own branch operations than with independent wholesalers.[38]

Merchant wholesalers in Africa are often smaller, carry narrower product lines, and deal with fewer customers than their counterparts in North America.

**merchant wholesalers**

Wholesalers that own (take title to) the products they sell

**Merchant wholesalers** **Merchant wholesalers** own (take title to) the products they sell. They often specialize in certain types of products or customers. For example, Fastenal is a wholesaler that specializes in distributing threaded fasteners used by a variety of manufacturers. It owns (takes title to) the fasteners for some period before selling to its customers. If you think all merchant wholesalers are fading away, Fastenal is proof that they can serve a needed role. In the last decade Fastenal's profits have grown at about the same pace as Microsoft's.

Most wholesaling establishments in North America are merchant wholesalers. Such wholesalers are even more common in other countries. Japan is an extreme example. In its unusual multi-tiered distribution system, products are often bought and sold by a series of merchant wholesalers on their way to the business user or retailer.[39]

**service wholesalers**

Merchant wholesalers who provide all of the wholesaling functions

**general merchandise wholesalers**

Service wholesalers who carry a wide variety of nonperishable items

**single-line (or general-line) wholesalers**

Service wholesalers who carry a narrower line of merchandise than general merchandise wholesalers

**specialty wholesalers**

Service wholesalers who carry a very narrow range of products and offer more information and service than other service wholesalers

**Service wholesalers** **Service wholesalers** are merchant wholesalers who provide all of the wholesaling functions. Within this basic group are three types: (1) general merchandise, (2) single-line, and (3) specialty.

**General merchandise** wholesalers are service wholesalers who carry a wide variety of non-perishable items such as hardware, electrical supplies, plumbing supplies, furniture, drugs, cosmetics, and automobile equipment. With their broad line of convenience and shopping products they serve hardware stores, drugstores, and small department stores. *Mill supply houses* operate in a similar way, but they carry a broad variety of accessories and supplies to serve the needs of manufacturers.

**Single-line (or general-line) wholesalers** are service wholesalers who carry a narrower line of merchandise than general merchandise wholesalers. For example, they might carry only food, apparel, or certain types of industrial tools or supplies. In consumer products, they serve the single- and limited-line stores. In business products, they cover a wider geographic area and offer more specialized service.

**Specialty wholesalers** are service wholesalers who carry a very narrow range of products and offer more information and service than other service wholesalers. A consumer products specialty wholesaler might carry only health foods or oriental foods instead of a full line of groceries. Some limited-line and specialty wholesalers are growing by helping independent retailer-customers find better ways to compete with mass-merchandisers. But in general, many consumer-products wholesalers have been hit hard by the growth of retail chains that set up their own distribution centres and deal directly with producers.

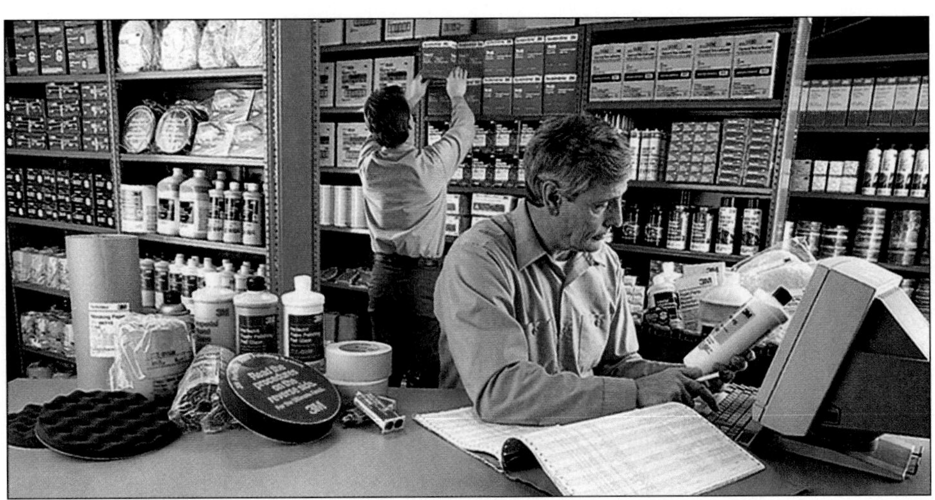

3M produces 1,600 products that are used by autobody repair shops in North America, Europe, Japan, and other countries. To reach this target market, 3M works with hundreds of specialty wholesalers.

A specialty wholesaler of business products might limit itself to fields requiring special technical knowledge or service. Richardson Electronics is an interesting example. It specializes in distributing replacement parts, such as electron tubes, for old equipment that many manufacturers still use on the factory floor. Richardson describes itself as "on the trailing edge of technology," but its unique products, expertise, and service are valuable to its target customers. Many of its customers operate in countries where new technologies are not yet common, but Richardson gives them easy access to information from its website (www.rell.com) and makes its products available quickly by stocking them in locations around the world.[40]

**limited-function wholesalers**
Wholesalers that provide only *some* wholesaling functions

### Limited-function wholesalers

**Limited-function wholesalers** provide only *some* wholesaling functions. In the following paragraphs, we briefly discuss the main features of these wholesalers. Although less numerous in some countries, these wholesalers are very important for some products.

**cash-and-carry wholesalers**
Wholesalers that operate like service wholesalers, except the customer must pay cash

**Cash-and-carry wholesalers** operate like service wholesalers—except that the customer must pay cash. Some retailers, such as small auto-repair shops, are too small to be served profitably by a service wholesaler. So service wholesalers set a minimum charge—or just refuse to grant credit to a small business that may have trouble paying its bills. Or the wholesaler may set up a cash-and-carry department to supply the small retailer for cash on the counter. The wholesaler can operate at lower cost because the retailers take over many wholesaling functions. And using cash-and-carry outlets may enable the small retailer to stay in business. These cash-and-carry operators are especially common in less-developed nations, where very small retailers handle the bulk of retail transactions. In Canada, big warehouse clubs are taking some of this business.

**drop-shippers**
Wholesalers that own the products they sell but do not actually handle, stock, or deliver them

**Drop-shippers** own (take title to) the products they sell—but they do not actually handle, stock, or deliver them. These wholesalers are mainly involved in selling. They get orders and pass them on to producers. Then the producer ships the order directly to the customer. Drop-shippers commonly sell bulky products (like lumber) for which additional handling would be expensive and possibly damaging. Some drop-shippers are already feeling the squeeze from buyers and sellers connecting directly via the Internet. But the progressive ones are fighting back by setting up their own websites and getting fees for referrals.

**truck wholesalers**
Wholesalers that specialize in delivering products they stock in their own trucks

**Truck wholesalers** specialize in delivering products that they stock in their own trucks. By handling perishable products in general demand—tobacco, candy, potato chips, and salad dressings—truck wholesalers may provide almost the same functions as full-service wholesalers. Their big advantage is that they promptly deliver perishable products that regular wholesalers prefer not to carry. A 7-Eleven store that runs out of potato chips on a busy Friday night doesn't want to be out of stock all weekend! They help retailers keep a tight rein on inventory, and they seem to meet a need.

**rack jobbers**
Wholesalers that specialize in hard-to-handle assortments of products that a retailer doesn't want to manage, usually displayed on their own wire racks

**Rack jobbers** specialize in hard-to-handle assortments of products that a retailer doesn't want to manage—and rack jobbers usually display the products on their own wire racks. For example, a grocery store or mass-merchandiser might rely on a rack jobber to decide which paperback books or magazines it sells. The wholesaler knows which titles sell in the local area and applies that knowledge in many stores. Historically, rack jobbers were paid cash for what sold or was delivered. Now that they are working with big chains, they've joined other wholesalers in waiting until the "accounts receivables" are paid at the end of the month.

**catalogue wholesalers**
Wholesalers that sell out of catalogues distributed widely to smaller industrial customers or retailers who might not be called on by other intermediaries

**Catalogue wholesalers** sell out of catalogues that may be distributed widely to smaller industrial customers or retailers who might not be called on by other intermediaries. Customers place orders at a website or by mail, e-mail, fax, or telephone. These wholesalers sell lines such as hardware, jewellery, sporting goods, and computers. For example, Inmac uses a printed catalogue and a website (www.inmac.com) to sell a complete line of computer accessories. Inmac's catalogues are printed in six languages and distributed to business customers in the U.S., Canada, and Europe. Many of these customers don't have a local wholesaler, but they can place orders from anywhere in the world. Most catalogue wholesalers quickly adapted to the Internet; it fits what they were already doing and makes it easier. But they're facing more competition too; the Internet allows customers to compare prices from more sources of supply.[41]

**agent intermediaries**
Wholesalers who do *not* own the products they sell

**Agent intermediaries** **Agent intermediaries** are wholesalers who do not own the products they sell. Their main purpose is to help in buying and selling. Agent intermediaries normally specialize by customer type and by product or product line. But they usually provide even fewer functions than the limited-function wholesalers. They operate at relatively low cost—sometimes 2 to 6 percent of their selling price, or less in the case of website-based agents who simply bring buyers and sellers together. Worldwide, the role of agent intermediary is rapidly being transformed by the Internet. Those who didn't get on board this fast-moving train were left behind.

Agent intermediaries are common in international trade. Many markets have only a few well-financed merchant wholesalers. The best many producers can do is get local representation through agents and then arrange financing through banks that specialize in international trade.

Agent intermediaries are usually experts on local business customs and rules concerning imported products in their respective countries. Sometimes a marketing manager can't work through a foreign government's red tape without the help of a local agent.

**manufacturers' agent**
Agent who sells similar products for several non-competing producers, for a commission on what is actually sold

A **manufacturers' agent** sells similar products for several non-competing producers, for a commission on what is actually sold. Such agents work almost as members of each company's salesforce, but they're really independent intermediaries. More than half of all agent intermediaries are manufacturers' agents.

Their big plus is that they already call on some customers and can add another product line at relatively low cost—and at no cost to the producer until something

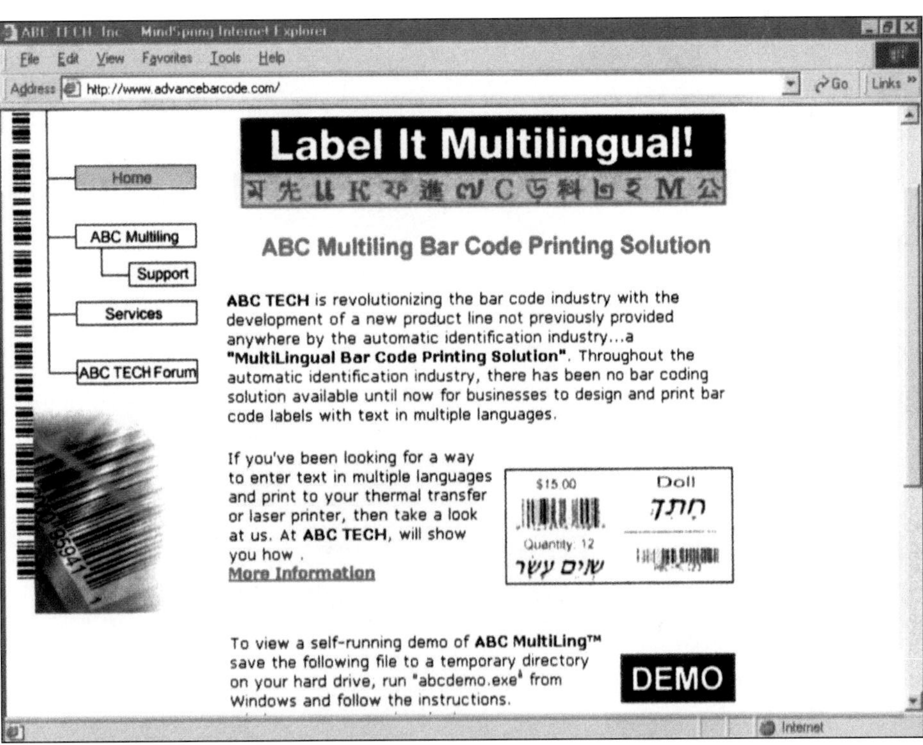


Innovative wholesalers are using multilingual bar codes to reduce costs and errors in overseas markets.

sells! If an area's sales potential is low, a company may use a manufacturers' agent because the agent can do the job at low cost. Small producers often use agents everywhere because their sales volume is too small to justify their own salesforce.

Agents can be especially useful for introducing new products. For this service, they may earn a 10- to 15-percent commission. (In contrast, their commission on large-volume established products may be quite low—perhaps only 2 percent.) A 10- to 15-percent commission rate may seem small for a new product with low sales. Once a product sells well, however, a producer may think the rate is high and begin using its own sales reps. Agents are well aware of this possibility. That's why most try to work for many producers and avoid being dependent on only one line.

**export or import agents**
Manufacturers' agents who specialize in international trade

Manufacturers' agents may cover a very narrow geographic area, such as a city or state. However, they are also very important in international marketing, and an agent may take on responsibility for a whole country. **Export or import agents** are basically manufacturers' agents who specialize in international trade. These agent intermediaries operate in every country and help international firms adjust to unfamiliar market conditions in foreign markets.

Manufacturers' reps will continue to play an important role in businesses that need an agent to perform order-getting tasks. But manufacturers' reps everywhere are feeling pressure when it comes to routine business contacts. More producers are turning to telephone selling, websites, e-mail, teleconferencing, and faxes to contact customers directly. This hits these agents where it hurts.[42]

**brokers**
Agents who bring buyers and sellers together

**export and import brokers**
Agents who operate like other brokers, but specialize in bringing together buyers and sellers from different countries

**Brokers** bring buyers and sellers together. Brokers usually have a *temporary* relationship with the buyer and seller while a particular deal is negotiated. They are especially useful when buyers and sellers don't come into the market very often. The broker's product is information about what buyers need and what supplies are available. They may also aid in buyer–seller negotiation. If the transaction is completed, they earn a commission from whichever party hired them. **Export and import brokers** operate like other brokers, but they specialize in bringing together buyers and sellers from different countries. Smart brokers quickly saw new opportunities to expand their reach by using the Internet. As the Internet causes consolidation, it will also provide more value. A smaller number of cyberbrokers will cut costs and dominate the business with larger databases of buyers and sellers.

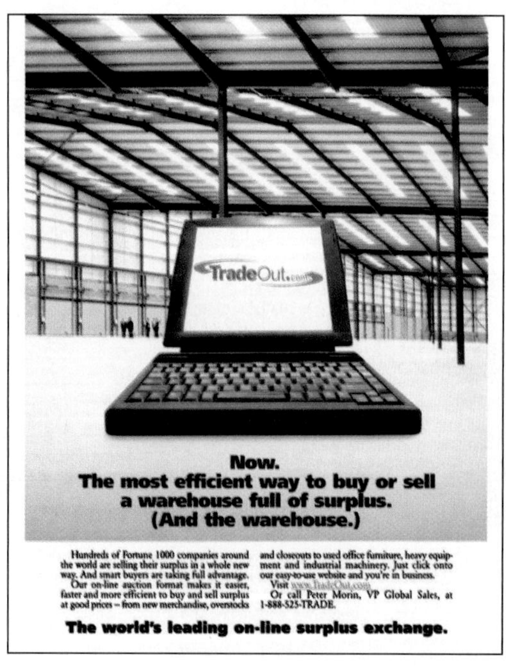


A few years ago wholesale brokers typically focused on a few specialized product categories, but now online brokers are finding markets for almost every sort of product.

**selling agents**

Agents that take over the whole marketing job of producers, not just the selling function

**combination export manager**

A blend of manufacturers' agent and selling agent who handles the entire export function for several producers of similar but non-competing lines

**auction companies**

Companies that provide a place where buyers and sellers can come together and bid to complete a transaction

**Selling agents** take over the whole marketing job of producers—not just the selling function. A selling agent may handle the entire output of one or more producers—even competing producers—with almost complete control of pricing, selling, and advertising. In effect, the agent becomes each producer's marketing manager.

Financial trouble is one of the main reasons a producer calls in a selling agent. The selling agent may provide working capital but may also take over the affairs of the business. But selling agents also work internationally. A **combination export manager** is a blend of manufacturers' agent and selling agent—handling the entire export function for several producers of similar but non-competing lines.

**Auction companies** provide a place where buyers and sellers can come together and bid to complete a transaction. There aren't many auction companies. Traditionally they have been important in certain lines—such as livestock, fur, tobacco, and used cars. For these products, demand and supply conditions change rapidly—and the product must be seen to be evaluated. The auction company brings buyers and sellers together. Buyers inspect the products—then demand and supply interact to determine the price.

A good example of an online auction company that put the bid process on the Internet is eBay. The problem with sites like these is that "what you see is what you get." A person may purchase a computer printer on eBay for five dollars; however, after shipping costs are added and the product arrives, the printer may or may not work. Some other websites offer new or used products through auctions on their own sites. The Sharper Image is one such company with its own online auction (www.sharperimage.com). The fact that an auction is backed up by a company may add credibility with customers. The Internet has spurred growth of all sorts of auction companies in lines of business where auctions have previously not been common.[43]

## What's in the Future for Retailers and Wholesalers?

A common theme in this chapter—and of the two before it—is that channels of distribution are in the midst of dynamic changes. There have been dramatic improvements due to more efficient ways to coordinate logistics. The Internet, as the backbone for e-commerce, is another force for change. But before all this, the evolution of retailing and wholesaling was ongoing. Intermediaries that find new and better ways to add value prosper. They find target segments that they serve very well by differentiating their services and doing something better than producers or customers can do without them.

It can't be overemphasized that such changes are ongoing. Clearly, we have just seen the tip of the iceberg when it comes to the impact that the Internet (and related technologies that will evolve in the future) will have on place. There is an explosion in the number and variety of firms that are trying to figure out how to have a presence on the Web. Many of them are reshaping competition in the product-markets in which they compete.

On the other hand, the adoption process that is underway is typical of other innovations. Much of the initial change has simply been an adjustment to what was done in the past. The catalogue becomes electronic. E-mail supplements toll-free phone orders. A retailer opens a new website instead of a new store. The technology is revolutionary and exciting, but much of what firms are doing with it so far is evolutionary. In time, revolutionary change will come and bring greater rewards to the innovators.

Imagine, for example, what it would take for you—and everyone you know—to do most of your routine shopping on the Internet. What new marketing functions would be needed, and who would provide them? What would the channel system look like? What new kind of intermediary will develop and what will it do? Let's consider one scenario.

After you surf the Internet and put products in your virtual shopping basket at one or more websites, what should happen next? Perhaps the seller would start by assembling your items in a carton with a bar code for your personal name, address, and account. Then that carton and cartons for all of the other orders that come into that website would be quickly taken in large economical batches to an intermediary. The computer-controlled sorting system going into the intermediary's facility would scan each carton's bar code and route it to the sorting area for a truck that serves you and each of your neighbours. After a night of accumulating all the cartons that are directed to you from different sellers, the intermediary would place the cartons on a delivery vehicle in the right sequence so they can be efficiently unloaded as the truck passes each customer on its route. Of course, you're not home. With money you've saved by not running all over town burning gas you're off on a vacation; you have time to take off because day after day you're not waiting in traffic and checkout lines. Although you're not home, you have a special cabinet—with a lock activated by a bar code printed on the package—mounted to the side of your house where the delivery person leaves your purchases.[44]

This little drama may seem far-fetched today. But it, or something like it, probably isn't far off. Specialist-intermediaries will develop to make distribution *after* an Internet purchase more efficient, just as intermediaries developed to make distribution more efficient *prior* to purchases in retail stores. What is described above isn't very different from what UPS does, one package at a time, when it makes deliveries from manufacturers to retailers. But the cost per package is much higher than it would be if everybody got deliveries every day. It's like the difference between the cost of a special delivery and regular mail.

If the after-purchase distribution problem is handled, who will the seller be? Will the Internet merchants of tomorrow be an evolved form of the retailers of today? Or will current-day wholesalers be in a better position to catch that prize? Some wholesalers are already working with very large assortments. Or, in a world where you can conveniently surf from one specialized seller to another, will the breadth of assortment from any one seller be irrelevant? That could put producers in a stronger position. Perhaps none of these traditional forms of business will lead the way, but rather it will be a firm that is born on the Internet to meet customers' needs in a completely new and unique way. The answers to these questions will take time, but they are taking shape even as you read. Already, new intermediaries are coming on the scene.

We can only speculate about where e-commerce will lead. But perhaps it's good to speculate a little. The way markets work in the future will depend on people like you, and the creative innovations that you speculate about, study, analyze, and ultimately turn into profitable marketing strategies. The competition will be tough, but hopefully you're now on your way to being up to the challenge.

## Chapter Summary

Modern retailing is scrambled—and we'll probably see more changes in the future. In such a dynamic environment, a producer's marketing manager must choose very carefully among the available kinds of retailers. And retailers must plan their marketing mixes with their target customers' needs in mind—while at the same time becoming part of an effective channel system.

We described many types of retailers—and we saw that each has its advantages and disadvantages. We also saw that modern retailers have discarded conventional practices. The old "buy low and sell high" philosophy is no longer a safe guide. Lower margins with faster turnover is the modern philosophy as more retailers move into mass-merchandising. But even this is no guarantee of success as retailers' life cycles move on.

Growth of chains and scrambled merchandising will continue as retailing evolves to meet changing consumer demands. But important breakthroughs are possible—perhaps with the Internet—and consumers probably will continue to move away from conventional retailers.

Wholesalers can provide functions for those both above and below them in a channel of distribution. These services are closely related to the basic marketing functions. There are many types of wholesalers. Some provide all the wholesaling functions, while others specialize in only a few. Eliminating wholesalers does not eliminate the need for the functions they now provide, but technology is helping firms to perform these functions in more efficient ways.

Merchant wholesalers are the most numerous and account for the majority of wholesale sales. Their distinguishing characteristic is that they take title to (own) products. Agent intermediaries, on the other hand, act more like sales representatives for sellers or buyers—and they do not take title.

Despite dire predictions, wholesalers continue to exist. The more progressive ones are adapting to a changing environment. But some less progressive wholesalers will fail. The Internet is already taking its toll. On the other hand, new types of intermediaries are evolving. Some are creating new ways of helping producers and their customers achieve their objectives by finding new ways to add value.

## Key Concepts

## Questions and Problems

1. What sort of a "product" are specialty shops offering? What are the prospects for organizing a chain of specialty shops?
2. Distinguish among discount houses, price-cutting by conventional retailers, and mass-merchandising. Forecast the future of low-price selling in food, clothing, and appliances. How will the Internet affect that future?
3. Discuss a few changes in the marketing environment that you think help to explain why telephone, mail-order, and Internet retailing have been growing so rapidly.
4. What are some advantages and disadvantages to using the Internet for shopping?
5. Apply the wheel of retailing theory to your local community. What changes seem likely? Will established retailers see the need for change, or will entirely new firms have to develop?
6. What advantages does a retail chain have over a retailer who operates with a single store? Does a small retailer have any advantages in competing against a chain? Explain your answer.
7. Many producers are now seeking new opportunities in international markets. Are the opportunities for international expansion equally good for retailers? Explain your answer.
8. Discuss how computer systems affect wholesalers' and retailers' operations.
9. Consider the evolution of wholesaling in relation to the evolution of retailing. List several changes that are similar, and several that are fundamentally different.
10. Do wholesalers and retailers need to worry about new-product planning just as a producer needs to have an organized new-product development process? Explain your answer.
11. How do you think a retailer of Maytag washing machines would react if Maytag set up a website, sold direct to consumers, and shipped direct from its distribution centre? Explain your thinking.
12. What risks do merchant wholesalers assume by taking title to goods? Is the size of this risk about constant for all merchant wholesalers?
13. Why would a manufacturer set up its own sales branches if established wholesalers were already available?
14. What is an agent intermediary's marketing mix?
15. Why do you think that many merchant intermediaries handle competing products from different producers, while manufacturers' agents usually handle only non-competing products from different producers?
16. What alternatives does a producer have if it is trying to expand distribution in a foreign market and finds that the best existing merchant intermediaries won't handle imported products?
17. Discuss the future growth and nature of wholesaling if chains, scrambled merchandising, and the Internet continue to become more important. How will wholesalers have to adjust their mixes? Will wholesalers be eliminated? If not, what wholesaling functions will be most important? Are there any particular lines of trade where wholesalers may have increasing difficulty?



## Computer-Aided Problem 12

### Selecting Channel Intermediaries

Art Glass Productions, a producer of decorative glass gift items, wants to expand into a new territory. Managers at Art Glass know that unit sales in the new territory will be affected by consumer response to the products. But sales will also be affected by which combination of wholesalers and retailers Art Glass selects. There is a choice between two wholesalers. One wholesaler, Giftware Distributing, is a merchant wholesaler that specializes in gift items; it sells to gift shops, department stores, and some mass-merchandisers. The other wholesaler, Margaret Degan & Associates, is a manufacturers' agent that calls on many of the gift shops in the territory.

Art Glass makes a variety of glass items, but the cost of making an item is usually about the same—$5.20 a unit. The items would sell to Giftware Distributing at $12.00 each—and in turn the merchant wholesaler's price to retailers would be $14.00—leaving Giftware with a $2.00 markup to cover costs and profit. Giftware Distributing is the only reputable merchant wholesaler in the territory, and it has agreed to carry the line only if Art Glass is willing to advertise in a trade magazine aimed at retail buyers for gift items. These ads will cost $8,000 a year.

As a manufacturers' agent, Margaret Degan would cover all of her own expenses and would earn 8 percent of the $14.00 price per unit charged the gift shops. Individual orders would be shipped directly to the retail gift shops by Art Glass, using United Parcel Service (UPS). Art Glass would pay the UPS charges at an average cost of $2.00 per item. In contrast, Giftware Distributing would anticipate demand and place larger orders in advance. This would reduce the shipping costs, which Art Glass would pay, to about $.60 a unit.

Art Glass' marketing manager thinks that Degan would only be able to sell about 75 percent as many items as Giftware Distributing—since she doesn't have time to call on all of the smaller shops and doesn't call on any department stores. On the other hand, the merchant wholesaler's demand for $8,000 worth of supporting advertising requires a significant outlay.

The marketing manager at Art Glass decided to use a spreadsheet to determine how large sales would have to be to make it more profitable to work with Giftware and to see how the different channel arrangements would contribute to profits at different sales levels.

a. *Given the estimated unit sales and other values shown on the initial spreadsheet, which type of wholesaler would contribute the most profit to Art Glass Productions?*
b. *If sales in the new territory are slower than expected, so that the merchant wholesaler was able to sell only 3,000 units—or the agent 2,250 units—which wholesaler would contribute the most to Art Glass' profits? (Note: Assume that the merchant wholesaler buys only what it can sell; that is, it doesn't carry extra inventory beyond what is needed to meet demand.)*
c. *Prepare a table showing how the two wholesalers' contributions to profit compare as the quantity sold varies from 3,500 units to 4,500 units for the merchant wholesaler and 75 percent of these numbers for the manufacturers' agent. Discuss these results. (Note: Use the analysis feature to vary the quantity sold by the merchant wholesaler, and the program will compute 75 percent of that quantity as the estimate of what the agent will sell.)*

## Suggested Cases

To view the cases, go to www.mcgrawhill.ca/college/wong.

Interested in finding out what marketing looks like in the real world? *Marketing Magazine* is just a click away on your OLC! Visit www.mcgrawhill.ca/college/wong today.

When You Finish This Chapter, You Should

1. Know the advantages and disadvantages of the promotion methods a marketing manager can use in strategy planning.

2. Understand the integrated marketing communications concept and why most firms use a blend of different promotion methods.

3. Understand the importance of promotion objectives.

4. Know how the communication process affects promotion planning.

5. Understand how new customer-initiated interactive communication is different.

6. Understand how direct-response promotion is helping marketers develop more targeted promotion blends.

7. Know how typical promotion plans are blended to get an extra push from intermediaries and help from customers in pulling products through the channel.

8. Understand how promotion blends typically vary over the adoption curve and product life cycle.

9. Understand how to determine how much to spend on promotion efforts.

# Chapter Thirteen

# Promotion—Introduction to Integrated Marketing Communications

## The Joy of Free Time

Summer is the busiest time of year in the beer industry. Breaking through the clutter and connecting with the target audience is a challenge, especially since the numerous competitors are forced to engage in an aggressive battle for market share. The weapon of choice: Innovative and creative marketing campaigns that will hopefully win over some, seemingly loyal, beer drinkers.

With such stiff competition and market saturation, there is continuous pressure on beer companies to up the ante on their promotions efforts. So, during the summer of 2001, Blue Light set out to exe-

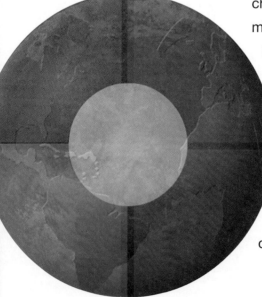

place price promotion produ

cute an integrated marketing strategy that was different, communicated the core brand messages, and gave consumers something to talk about. Thus, the Blue Light "Free Your Time" campaign was born.

The integrated campaign featured a PR program, online strategy, TV creative, special events, and unique outdoor media. These promotion techniques all conveyed a similar and consistent message: As the champion of free time, Blue Light sets out to help people escape the daily grind and find more time to spend with friends.

The new Blue Light TV advertising was unveiled during the highly watched Oscars in March 2001. Set to the tune "Time Has Come Today," they introduced the notion that Blue Light celebrates free time.

A week after the introduction of the ads, a petition was launched to obtain a new long weekend in June for Ontarians. Research commissioned by Blue Light through Ipsos-Reid of Toronto showed Canadians feel they have a marked lack of free time in their lives. Blue Light decided to take advantage of this knowledge. Through public relations and an interactive campaign, people were driven to freeyourtime.ca to sign the online petition, which was submitted to the Ontario government in June. An appealing viral e-mail campaign was used to help spread word of the petition. Consumers were encouraged to refer the site to their friends and families, in hopes of incurring a snowball effect.

To extend the campaign to the street, where the target could be reached more effectively, an innovative outdoor campaign was launched. Images of Fred Flintstone blowing his horn at the end of

place price promotion product

the day were the inspiration for this unique campaign. With the goal to deliver talk value, a team of talented marketers created the Blue Light Weekend Countdown Clock. Located at the corner of Toronto's Bay and Front Streets, the 14-by-44-foot structure signalled the end of the "daily grind" every Friday at 5 p.m. with its chrome horns. It was in operation from Victoria Day in May until Labour Day in September.

In addition to actually counting down the time, the Countdown Clock provided listings for events throughout Ontario as well as suggestions on how weekends could be celebrated. Feedback was extremely positive. The design of the clock commanded a lot of attention, and its position provided perfect sightlines for the thousands of commuters in downtown Toronto.

With the "Free Your Time" campaign, Blue Light was successful in breaking through and connecting with the target by communicating a consistent message. And despite that Blue Light failed to establish a new long-weekend holiday in June for Ontario residents, the "Free Your Time" campaign continues to thrive today. Recently, Blue Light has had its sights set on an even bigger goal, achieving a long-weekend holiday in June for all of Canada.[1]



## In This Chapter

Suppose you wish to introduce a new product. You might want to develop an advertising campaign to announce its availability. This seemingly simple act actually involves a large number of interrelated decisions: the target market, the message to be used, the media that will carry the ad, when they'll carry the ad, the amount of money you're willing to spend, and more.

But would that campaign be enough? Might it make sense to involve public relations efforts to generate coverage in the news? Would it make sense to have a direct-mail program that gave customers a sample of the product? Should we provide a promotional effort, like a coupon or special introductory pricing, to get consumers to try the new product? Do we need a trade program of sales reps calling on distributors and retailers to convince them to carry the product? These are the sorts of issues addressed in managing an integrated communications campaign.

In subsequent chapters we'll look at the component decisions involved in managing the major types of promotional activity. In this chapter we consider the factors that affect the mix of methods used. We'll start by providing a brief overview of the various promotional methods—personal selling, advertising, publicity, and sales promotion—and who has the responsibility for their management.

But effective communication is not just about what we do to reach customers. Rather, effective communication is about the response we get from customers who receive our communication. Thus, we'll discuss the basics of the communications process in an effort to establish what a good communications program should do. With that background in place, we'll consider the other factors that must be considered in developing promotional objectives and an integrated communications program to support them.

## An Overview of Integrated Marketing Communications

**promotion**
Communicating information between a seller and a potential buyer or others in the channel to influence attitudes and behaviour

**Promotion** is communicating information between a seller and a potential buyer or others in the channel to influence attitudes and behaviour. The marketing manager's main promotion job is to tell target customers that the right product is available at the right place at the right price.

A marketing manager can choose from several promotion methods—personal selling, mass selling, and sales promotion (see Exhibit 13-1). Further, because the different promotion methods have different strengths and limitations, a marketing manager usually uses them in combination. And, as with other marketing-mix decisions, it is critical that the marketer manage and coordinate the different promotion methods as an integrated whole, not as separate and unrelated parts.

**integrated marketing communications**
The intentional coordination of every communication from a firm to a target customer to convey a consistent and complete message

The goal is to effectively blend all of the firm's promotion efforts to produce **integrated marketing communications**—the intentional coordination of every communication from a firm to a target customer to convey a consistent and complete message. The Blue Light case at the start of this chapter is a good example of integrated marketing communications. Different promotion methods handle different parts of the job. Yet the methods are coordinated so that the sum is greater than the parts. The separate messages are complementary, but also consistent.

It seems obvious that a firm's different communications to a target market should be consistent. However, when a number of different people are working on different promotion elements, they are likely to see the same big picture only if a marketing manager ensures that it happens. Getting consistency is harder when different firms in the distribution channel handle different aspects of the promotion effort. Different channel members may have conflicting objectives—especially if they don't have a common focus on the customer at the end of the channel.

### Types of Promotion Methods

Many people think that promotion money gets spent primarily on advertising—because advertising is all around them. The many ads you see on the Web, in magazines and newspapers, and on TV are impressive—and costly. But all the special sales promotions—coupons, sweepstakes, trade shows, sporting events sponsored by firms, and the like—add up to even more money. Similarly, salesclerks complete most retail sales. And behind the scenes, much personal selling goes on in the channels and in other business markets. In total, firms spend less money on advertising than on personal selling or sales promotion.

**personal selling**
Direct spoken communication between sellers and potential customers

**Personal selling** involves direct spoken communication between sellers and potential customers. Face-to-face selling provides immediate feedback—which helps



**Exhibit 13-1**
Basic promotion methods and strategy planning.

salespeople to adapt to the circumstances surrounding each customer. Although some personal selling is included in most marketing mixes, it can be very expensive because each salesperson can call on only a limited number of customers at one time. So it's often desirable to combine personal selling with mass selling and sales promotion.

**mass selling**
Communicating with large numbers of potential customers at the same time

**advertising**
Any paid form of non-personal presentation of ideas, goods, or services by an identified sponsor

**Mass selling** is communicating with large numbers of potential customers at the same time. Because all customers receive essentially the same message in the same way, it is less flexible than personal selling. However, when the target market is large and scattered, mass selling may be the only cost-effective way of reaching target customers. **Advertising**, the main form of mass selling, is any paid form of non-personal presentation of ideas, goods, or services by an identified sponsor. It includes the use of traditional media like magazines, newspapers, radio and TV, signs, and direct mail, as well as new media such as the Internet (see Internet Insite 13-1). While advertising must be paid for, another form of mass selling—publicity—is "free."

## Internet Insite 13–1



### INTEGRATING THE INTERNET INTO THE MARKETING COMMUNICATIONS MIX

Mass media such as television and newspapers offer advertisers the ability to reach a vast audience. Television can reach millions of people at the same time. A TV spot during a popular primetime show or sporting event can reach tens of millions of consumers. At the same time, mass media advertising takes the one-size-fits-all approach, with the same message for everyone. The one-to-many nature of mass media (i.e., one advertiser sends the same message to everyone) leaves no room for customization or immediate feedback from consumers. If you missed a primetime show or didn't read yesterday's newspaper, the chance for ad exposure is lost forever.

The Internet as a communication medium has some unique characteristics. The Internet is a many-to-many medium, which not only allows marketers to send out messages, but also enables consumers to interact with marketers. Consumers can send feedback through the company's website, as well as through other brand or product rating sites such as Epinions and BizRate. Brand websites, which are essentially in-depth and often interactive advertisements, have a longer shelf life compared to mass media ads. Marketers on the Internet also have the ability to study individual preferences and tailor their Web pages to suit each individual consumer through the use of tracking methods (refer to Internet Insite 6-1). Unlike television ads, which are thrust upon consumers, consumers choose to go to brand websites, which means they are likely to be more attentive while there.

Ability to customize and offer in-depth information using multimedia (pictures, text, audio, and video), interactivity, and two-way communication are unique advantages offered by the Internet as a communication medium. The Internet does not offer the same reach that television does. The number of people logged in to a site at a given time does not come to close to the audience that top-rated TV programs can draw, and that is true even for the most popular sites like Yahoo!

Recent studies show that the Internet is displacing traditional media. A study by GartnerG2 (www.gartnerg2.com) in 2002 found that there was a 20-percent decline in both television and newspaper audience because of increased Internet activity.[2] The survey also found a decline in magazine readership by 15 percent, attributable to increased time spent on the Internet. Another study at UCLA found that Internet users watch 4.5 fewer hours of television weekly than do non-Internet users. Internet users who have had Internet access for five or more years had the highest percentage decline in television viewing time.[3] Younger people (12–24 years) are more likely to give up television in favour of the Internet.[4] Older consumers are more likely to view television as more indispensable than the Internet.

These numbers should make advertisers sit up and take notice. Large advertisers like Procter & Gamble, Kraft Foods, and Pepsi Cola now use the Internet as an integral part of their communications mix, while continuing to use television for reaching a large audience. Major brands often use similar themes and images in both television and the Internet. Pepsi, for instance, uses pop star Beyoncé on its website as well as in television ads. The continuity between television and the Web leads to a reinforcement of the brand image.

Many brands use television ads to create awareness and draw consumers to the website. The Web can provide more detailed information and can engage the consumer with interactive features. Automobile ads in magazines invariably carry the website address or URL. Visit some of the automobile websites (www.bmw.com, www.mbusa.com, www.toyota.ca, www.saturn.ca) and see how the Web is used to present in-depth information and guide the consumer decision-making process.

Nike demonstrated how television and the Web could be integrated. In a campaign designed to create awareness and enhance branding for Air Cross Trainer II, Nike used three prominent athletes in TV spots, with each spot ending with the athlete placed in a precarious position and the tagline "Continued at whatever.nike.com." On the site, viewers could choose different endings and complete the experience. A typical 30-second experience of viewing a TV spot was transformed to a more involving experience lasting several minutes.

Coca-Cola has gone a step further and created a site called CokeMusic.com, where one can listen to music by up-and-coming bands. The site has proven to be a big hit with teenagers, with more than a million page views per day. There are interactive games and contests, which have led to the average visit time exceeding 25 minutes.[5] The music and games are presented in a branded environment, which builds a stronger connection between Coke and its primary target market (i.e., teenagers). On television, Coca-Cola ads run for 30 seconds and serve as a reminder. On the Internet, there is a much more intense and involving experience. Television cannot buy that kind of involvement, especially from a teenaged audience. Dale Douthat, creative director of Interactive Services for Bandy Carroll Hellige (www.bch.com) summed up the power of the Internet as follows: "It's the only place where you can immediately create a dialogue with users."[6] Coca-Cola and other advertisers have realized that a strong online presence is critical.

Internet advertising is no longer static. It can be dynamic with Flash animation and streaming video. DoubleClick, a leading Internet advertising company, reported that during the first quarter of 2003 nearly 28 percent of all advertising campaigns managed by this company involved rich media, which includes Flash and video. A Jupiter Research report in 2003 found that the audience for online video ads in many cases is as large as that for syndicated TV shows.[7]

Given the pros and cons of the Internet versus mass media, marketers must use each medium for a specific purpose. Television and print can create awareness and start the brand-building process. Television can be effective in triggering the need, and can be very effective in creating an emotional response from consumers. The Internet can engage, create interest, and drive action (i.e., purchase). The Internet is by far the most effective medium for information search and brand comparison.

Contemporary ad campaigns usually have a television component and an interactive component. The best campaigns use a combination of media for synergistic results. By understanding the characteristics of each medium, marketers can design integrated marketing campaigns that take advantage of multiple media, including the Web. The next time you see an interesting TV or print ad, go to the Internet and see how the marketer is using the Web.

Here are some questions to ponder: Is Internet advertising better suited for some products than others? Why? When using multiple media in an advertising campaign, what are the possible pitfalls that marketers should avoid?

Go to: www.mcgrawhill.ca/college/wong
to apply this Insite in an exciting Internet exercise.

**publicity**
Any unpaid form of nonpersonal presentation of ideas, goods, or services

**Publicity** is any *unpaid* form of nonpersonal presentation of ideas, goods, or services. Of course, publicity people are paid. But they try to attract attention to the firm and its offerings without having to pay media costs. For example, movie studios try to get celebrities on TV talk shows because this generates a lot of interest and sells tickets to new movies without the studio paying for TV time. Marketing Demo 13-1 shows the power these efforts can have.

If a firm has a really new message, publicity may be more effective than advertising. Trade magazines, for example, may carry articles featuring the newsworthy products of regular advertisers—in part because they *are* regular advertisers. The firm's publicity people write the basic copy and then try to convince magazine editors to print it. Each year, magazines print photos and stories about new cars—and often the source of the information is the auto producers. A consumer might not pay any attention to an ad but might carefully read a long magazine story with the same information.

**sales promotion**
Promotion activities (other than advertising, publicity, and personal selling) that stimulate interest, trial, or purchase by final customers or others in the channel

**Sales promotion** refers to promotion activities—other than advertising, publicity, and personal selling—that stimulate interest, trial, or purchase by final customers or others in the channel. Sales promotion may be aimed at consumers, at intermediaries, or at a firm's own employees. Examples are listed in Exhibit 13-2. Relative to other promotion methods, sales promotion can usually be implemented quickly and get results sooner. In fact, most sales promotion efforts are designed to produce immediate results.

## Marketing Demo 13–1

### FANS GO CRAZY FOR AVRIL'S SHIRT

Canadian music artist Avril Lavigne recently demonstrated that publicity could also come as a pleasant surprise. During her appearance on *Saturday Night Live* in New York City, she wore an old hometown soccer T-shirt that read "Home Hardware Napanee." Afterwards, consumers from all over the country were walking into Home Hardware stores and asking about purchasing T-shirts. With that kind of exposure, Home Hardware had unexpectedly hit the jackpot. Lavigne was in front of the camera a total of seven minutes and 47 seconds. To buy that kind of advertising time on *Saturday Night Live* would have cost about 1,726,000 Canadian dollars. Since then, the Home Hardware store in Napanee, Ontario has produced and distributed a limited number of T-shirts and continues to enjoy being associated with one of Canada's most popular rising stars.[8]



We'll talk about individual promotion methods in more detail in the next two chapters. First, however, you need to understand the role of the whole promotion blend—personal selling, mass selling, and sales promotion combined—so you can see how promotion fits into the rest of the marketing mix.

### Who Is Involved in Integrated Marketing Communications?

Each promotion method has its own strengths and weaknesses. Each method also involves its own distinct activities and requires different types of expertise. As a result, it's usually the responsibility of specialists—such as sales managers, advertising managers, and promotion managers—to develop and implement the detailed plans for the various parts of the overall promotion blend.

**sales managers**
Managers concerned with personal selling

**advertising managers**
Managers concerned with their company's mass-selling effort (in television, newspapers, magazines, and other media)

**public relations**
Communication with non-customers, including labour, public interest groups, share-holders, and the government

**Types of promotion specialists** **Sales managers** are concerned with managing personal selling. Often the sales manager is responsible for building good distribution channels and implementing place policies. In smaller companies, the sales manager may also act as the marketing manager and be responsible for advertising and sales promotion.

**Advertising managers** manage their company's mass-selling effort—in television, newspapers, magazines, and other media. Their job is choosing the right media and developing the ads. Advertising departments within their own firms may help in these efforts, or they may use outside advertising agencies. The advertising manager may handle publicity, too. Or it may be handled by an outside agency or by whoever handles **public relations**—communication with noncustomers, including labour, public interest groups, shareholders, and the government.

Exhibit 13-2
Examples of sales-promotion activities.

| Aimed at final consumers or users | Aimed at intermediaries | Aimed at company's own salesforce |
|---|---|---|
| Contests | Price deals | Contests |
| Coupons | Promotion allowances | Bonuses |
| Aisle displays | Sales contests | Meetings |
| Samples | Calendars | Portfolios |
| Trade shows | Gifts | Displays |
| Point-of-purchase materials | Trade shows | Sales aids |
| Banners and streamers | Meetings | Training materials |
| Frequent-buyer programs | Catalogues | |
| Sponsored events | Merchandising aids | |

**sales promotion managers** Managers concerned with their company's sales promotion effort

**Sales promotion managers** manage their company's sales promotion effort. In some companies, a sales promotion manager has independent status and reports directly to the marketing manager. If a firm's sales promotion spending is substantial, it probably should have a specific sales promotion manager. Sometimes, however, the sales or advertising departments handle sales promotion efforts—or sales promotion is left as a responsibility of individual brand managers. Regardless of who the manager is, sales promotion activities vary so much that many firms use both inside and outside specialists.

**The role of the marketing manager** Although many specialists may be involved in planning for and implementing specific promotion methods, determining the blend of promotion methods is a strategy decision—and it is the responsibility of the marketing manager. The various promotion specialists tend to

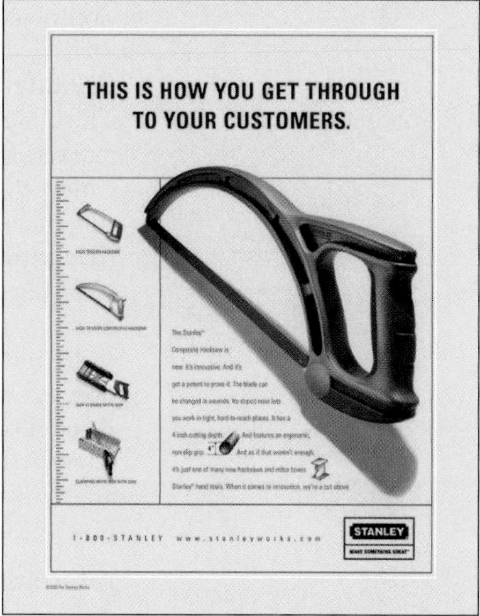

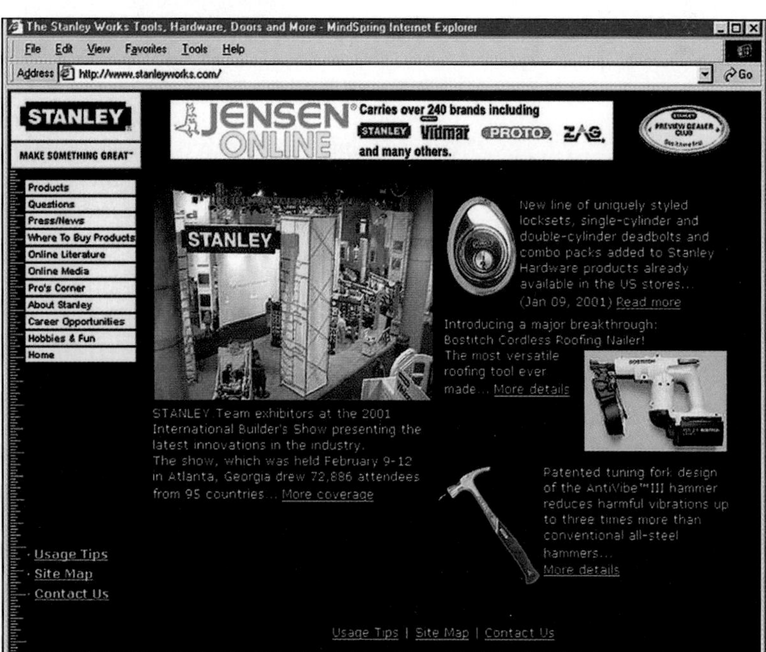


Stanley Works depends on a blend of integrated marketing communications, including sales presentations and product demonstration tours, trade ads focused on retailers, ads targeted at end-users, and a website that provides information on the whole line.

focus on what they know best and their own areas of responsibility. A creative Web page designer or advertising copywriter in Vancouver may have no idea what a salesperson does during a call on a wholesale distributor. In addition, because of differences in outlook and experience, the advertising, sales, and sales promotion managers often have trouble working with each other as partners. Too often they just view other promotion methods as using up budget money they want.

The marketing manager must weigh the pros and cons of the various promotion methods, then devise an effective promotion blend—fitting in the various departments and personalities and coordinating their efforts. Then the advertising, sales, and sales promotion managers should develop the details consistent with what the marketing manager wants to accomplish.

To get effective coordination, everyone involved with the promotion effort must clearly understand the plan for the overall marketing strategy. They all need to understand how each promotion method will contribute to achieve specific promotion objectives.[9]



## Specifying Promotion Objectives

The different promotion methods are all different forms of communication. But good marketing managers aren't interested in just communicating. They want communication that encourages customers to choose a *specific* product. They know that if they have a better offering, informed customers are more likely to buy. Therefore, they're interested in (1) reinforcing present attitudes or relationships that might lead to favourable behaviour, or (2) actually changing the attitudes and behaviour of the firm's target market.

In terms of demand curves, promotion may help the firm make its present demand curve more inelastic, or shift the demand curve to the right, or both. These possibilities are shown in Exhibit 13-3. The buyer behaviour model introduced in Chapter 6 showed the many influences on buying behaviour. You saw there that affecting buyer behaviour is a tough job—but that is exactly the objective of promotion.

**Alternative promotion objectives** A firm's promotion objectives must be clearly defined—because the right promotion blend depends on who the firm wants to reach and what the firm wants to accomplish with that target. In this regard, it's helpful to think of three basic promotion objectives: informing, persuading, and reminding target customers about the company and its marketing mix. All try to affect buyer behaviour by providing more information.

An *inform* objective focuses on educating the customer. The communication may be as simple as telling customers the product is available or as complex as explaining how it works and the various benefits it provides.

Exhibit 13-3
Promotion seeks to shift the demand curve.

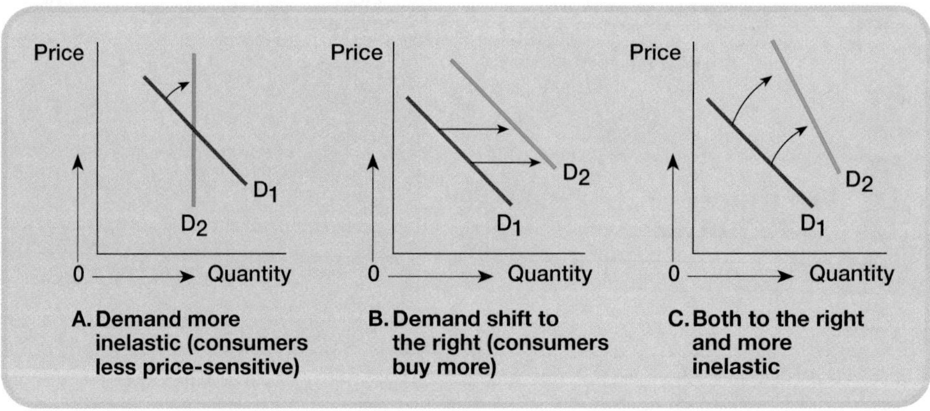

**Exhibit 13-4**
Relation of promotion objectives, adoption process, and AIDA model.

| Promotion Objectives | Adoption Process (Chapter 6) | AIDA Model |
|---|---|---|
| Informing | Awareness | Attention |
| | Interest | Interest |
| | Evaluation | Desire |
| Persuading | Trial | |
| | Decision | Action |
| Reminding | Confirmation | |

When competitors offer similar products, the firm must not only inform customers that its product is available but also persuade them to buy it. A *persuading* objective means the firm will try to develop a favourable set of attitudes so customers will buy, and keep buying, its product. A persuading objective often focuses on reasons why one brand is better than competing brands. To convince consumers to buy Tylenol rather than some other firm's brand, Johnson & Johnson's ads position Tylenol as the safe and effective pain-relief medicine that is typically used by hospitals.

If target customers already have positive attitudes about a firm's marketing mix—or a good relationship with a firm—a *reminding* objective might be suitable. This objective can be extremely important in some cases. Even though customers have been attracted and sold once, they are still targets for competitors' appeals. Reminding them of their past satisfaction may keep them from shifting to a competitor. Campbell realizes that most people know about its soup—so much of its advertising is intended to remind.

The reason for distinguishing among the different promotional objectives can best be understood in the context of how consumers choose to adopt a product. In Chapter 6, we looked at consumer buying as a problem-solving process in which buyers go through six steps—awareness, interest, evaluation, trial, decision, and confirmation—on the way to adopting (or rejecting) an idea or product. Now we see that the three basic promotion objectives relate to these six steps (see Exhibit 13-4). Informing and persuading may be needed to affect the potential customer's knowledge and attitudes about a product and then bring about its adoption. Later promotion can simply remind the customer about that favourable experience and confirm the adoption decision.

These ads appeared in the same issue of a leading Canadian business magazine. Using AIDA as your guide, which ad would you place on the magazine's back cover? the inside cover?

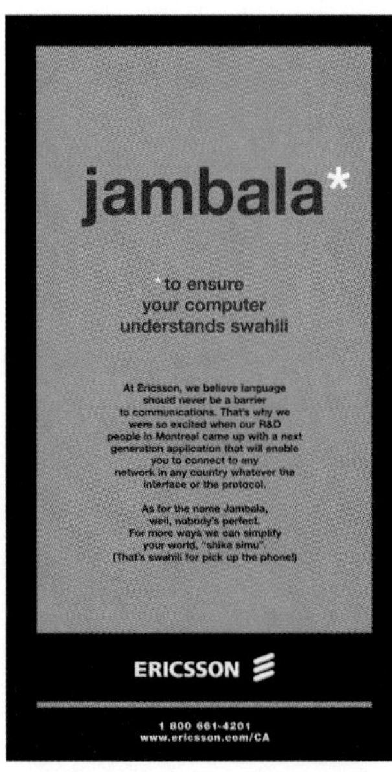


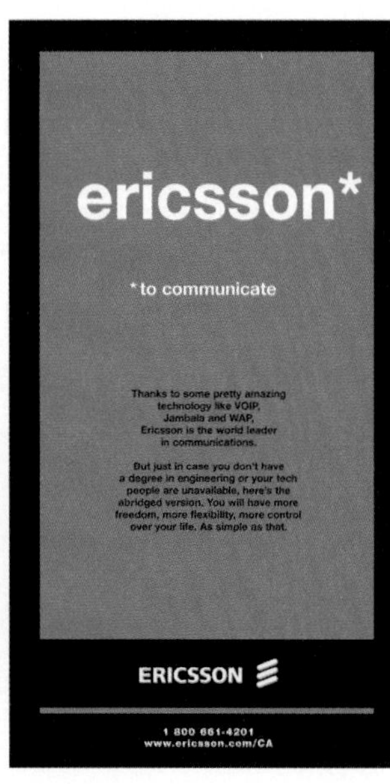


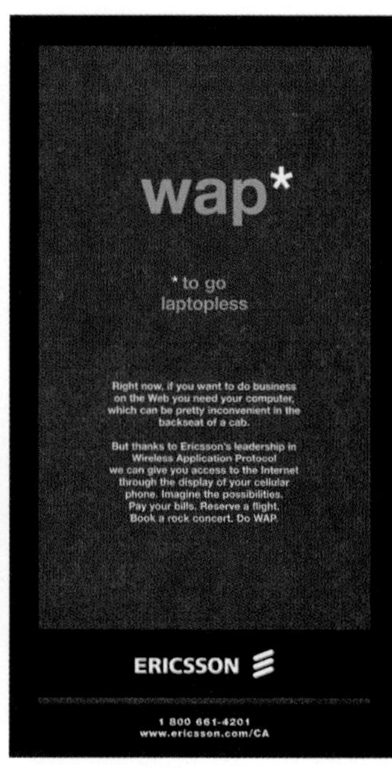

**How promotional objectives relate to consumer adoption** The basic promotion objectives and adoption process fit very neatly with another action-oriented model—called AIDA—that we will use in this and the next two chapters to guide some of our discussion. The **AIDA model** consists of four promotion jobs: (1) to get *attention*, (2) to hold *interest*, (3) to arouse *desire*, and (4) to obtain *action*.

**AIDA model**

Four promotion jobs: (1) to get *attention*, (2) to hold *interest*, (3) to arouse *desire*, and (4) to obtain *action*

Exhibit 13-4 shows the relationship of the adoption process to the AIDA jobs. Getting attention is necessary to make consumers aware of the company's offering. Holding interest gives the communication a chance to build the consumer's interest in the product. Arousing desire affects the evaluation process—perhaps building preference. And obtaining action includes gaining trial, which may lead to a purchase decision. Continuing promotion is needed to confirm the decision and encourage an ongoing relationship and additional purchases.

## Promotion as an Act of Communication



Promotion is wasted if it doesn't achieve its objectives. And that happens when it doesn't communicate effectively. There are many reasons why a promotion message can be misunderstood or not heard at all. To understand this, it's useful to think about how consumers receive and process information.

### The Communication Process

**communication process**

Occurs when a source tries to reach a receiver with a message

**source**

The sender of a message

**receiver**

A potential customer

The **communication process** means a source trying to reach a receiver with a message. Exhibit 13-5 shows the elements of the communication process. Here we see that a **source**—the sender of a message—is trying to deliver a message to a **receiver**—a potential customer. Research shows that customers evaluate not only the message but also the source of the message in terms of trustworthiness and credibility. For example, premium pet-food companies that have been certified by the Canadian Veterinary Medical Association will be sure to mention the endorsement in their promotion to help make their promotion messages credible.

The various promotion methods can be distinguished by the portion of the communications process they can affect. For example, a major advantage of personal selling is that the source—the seller—can get immediate feedback from the receiver. It's easier to judge how the message is being received and to change it if necessary. Mass sellers usually must depend on marketing research or total sales figures for feedback—and that can take too long. As we'll discuss later in this chapter, this has prompted many marketers to include toll-free telephone numbers and website addresses as ways of building direct-response feedback from consumers into their mass-selling efforts.

**noise**

Any distraction that reduces the effectiveness of the communication process

The **noise** (shown in Exhibit 13-5) is any distraction that reduces the effectiveness of the communication process. Conversations and snack-getting during TV ads

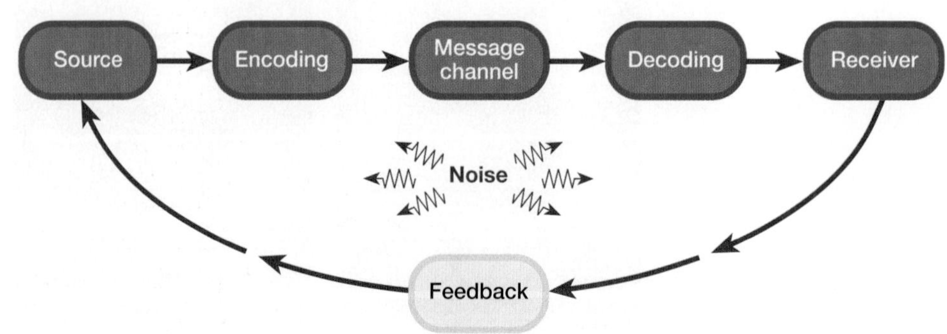


Exhibit 13-5
The traditional communication process.

are noise. The clutter of competing ads on the Internet is noise. Advertisers planning messages must recognize that many possible distractions—noise—can interfere with communications.

**encoding**
Occurs when the source decides what it wants to say and translates it into words or symbols that will have the same meaning to the receiver

**decoding**
Occurs when the receiver translates the message

**The message sent and the message received** The basic difficulty in the communication process occurs during encoding and decoding. **Encoding** is the source deciding what it wants to say and translating it into words or symbols that will have the same meaning to the receiver. **Decoding** is the receiver translating the message. This process can be very tricky. The meanings of various words and symbols may differ depending on the attitudes and experiences of the two groups. People need a common frame of reference to communicate effectively. See Exhibit 13-6.

**Exhibit 13-6**
The same message may be interpreted differently.

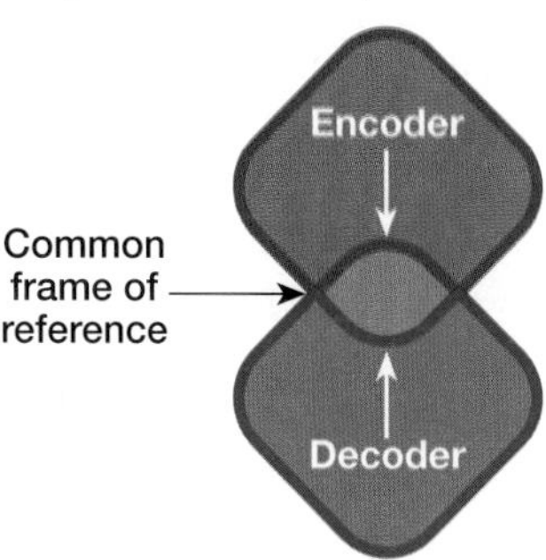


Maidenform encountered this problem with its promotion aimed at working women. The company ran a series of ads depicting women stockbrokers and doctors wearing Maidenform lingerie. The men in the ads were fully dressed. Maidenform was trying to show women in positions of authority, but some women felt the ad presented them as sex objects. In this case, the promotion people who encoded the message didn't understand the attitudes of the target market and how they would decode the message.[10]

Decoding problems often arise because different audiences may see the same message in different ways or interpret the same words differently. Such differences are common in international marketing when cultural differences or translation are problems. In Taiwan, the translation of the Pepsi slogan "Come alive with the Pepsi Generation" came out as "Pepsi will bring your ancestors back from the dead." When Frank Perdue said, "It takes a tough man to make a tender chicken," Spanish speakers heard "It takes a sexually stimulated man to make a chicken affectionate." Worse, a campaign for Schweppes Tonic Water in Italy translated the name into Schweppes Toilet Water. Many firms run into problems like this.[11]

Problems occur even when there is no translation. For example, a new children's cough syrup was advertised as "extra strength." The advertising people thought they were assuring parents that the product worked well. But moms and dads avoided the product because they feared that it might be too strong for their children.

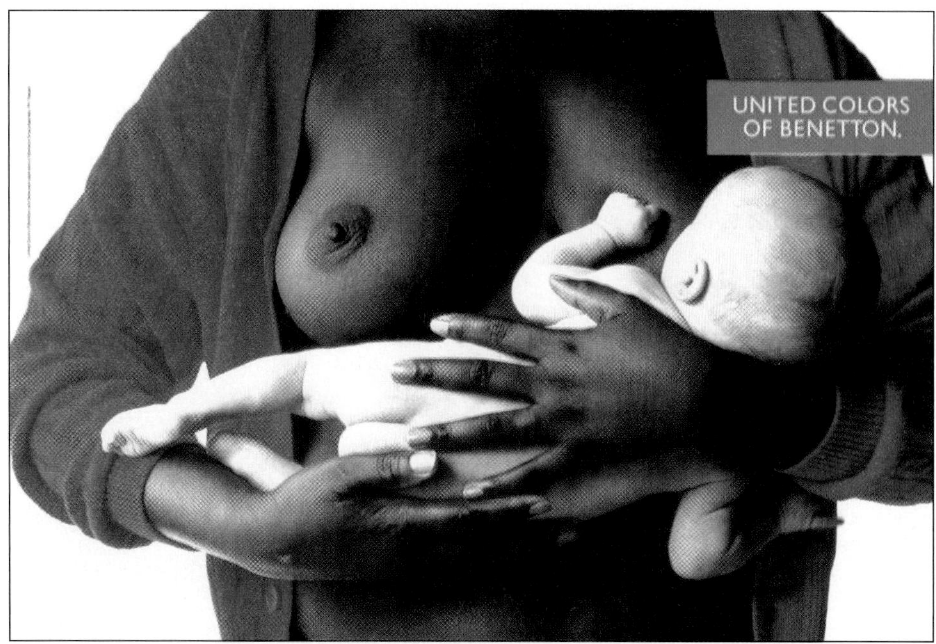


This Benetton ad was the most awarded in Benetton's history. However, the ad sparked unprecedented controversy and was subsequently banned in the United States given the historical connotations of slavery and racism. Other than history, what might prevent advertisers from having free creative control?

*Good Housekeeping* is building on consumer confidence in its seal and has developed a new program for website certification.

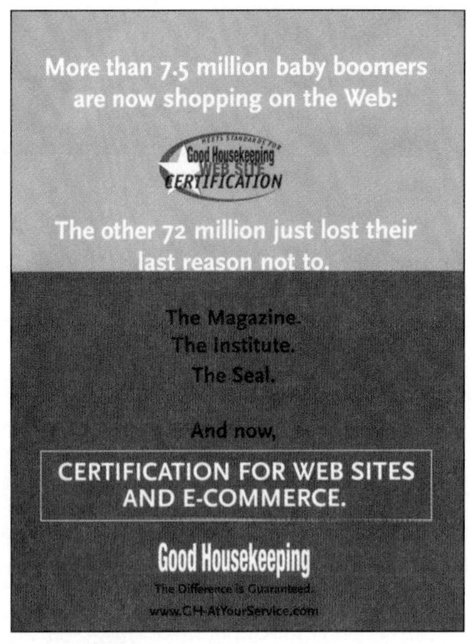
More than 7.5 million baby boomers are now shopping on the Web:
Good Housekeeping WEB SITE CERTIFICATION
The other 72 million just lost their last reason not to.
The Magazine.
The Institute.
The Seal.
And now,
CERTIFICATION FOR WEB SITES AND E-COMMERCE.
Good Housekeeping
The Difference is Guaranteed.
www.GH-AtYourService.com

**message channel**
The carrier of the message

**The effect of message channel** The communication process is complicated even more because the receiver knows the message is coming not only from a source but also through some **message channel**—the carrier of the message. A source can use many message channels to deliver a message. The salesperson does it in person with voice and action. Advertising must do it with magazines, newspapers, radio, and TV, or with media such as e-mail or websites. A particular message channel may enhance or detract from a message. A TV ad, for example, can *show* that Dawn

## Ethical Dimensions 13–1

### ETHICAL MARKETING COMMUNICATIONS

Promotion is one of the most often criticized areas of marketing, and many of the criticisms focus on whether communications are honest and fair. Marketers must sometimes make ethical judgments in considering these charges and in planning their promotion.

Video publicity releases provide an interesting example. When a TV news program broadcasts a video publicity release, consumers don't know it was prepared to achieve marketing objectives; they think the news staff is the source. That may make the message more credible, but is it fair? Many say yes—as long as the publicity information is truthful. But grey areas still remain. Consider, for example, a SmithKline Beecham video about a prescription heart attack drug. An estimated 27 million consumers saw the video on various TV news programs. The video included a laundry list of possible side effects and other warnings, just as is required for normal drug advertising. But there's never any guarantee that the warnings won't be edited out by local TV stations.

Critics raise similar concerns about the use of celebrities in advertisements. A person who plays the role of an honest and trustworthy person on a popular TV series may be a credible message source in an ad, but is using such a person misleading to consumers? Some critics believe it is. Others argue that consumers recognize advertising when they see it and know celebrities are paid for their endorsements.

The most common criticisms of promotion relate to promotional messages that make exaggerated claims. What does it mean for an ad or a salesperson to claim that a product is the "best available"? Is that the personal opinion of people in the firm, or should every statement—even very general ones—be backed up by objective proof? What type of proof should be required? Some promotional messages do misrepresent the benefits of a product. However, most marketing managers want to develop ongoing relationships with, and repeat purchases from, their customers. They realize that customers won't come back if the marketing mix doesn't deliver what the promotion promises. Further, consumers are becoming more skeptical about all the claims they hear and see. As a result, most marketing managers work to make promotion claims specific and believable.[12]

dishwashing detergent "Takes the grease away"; the same claim might not be very convincing—or might be resented—if it arrived in a consumer's e-mail. On the other hand, a receiver may attach value to a product if the message comes in a well-respected newspaper or magazine. Some consumers buy products advertised in *Good Housekeeping* magazine, for example, because they have faith in its seal, which carries a two-year limited warranty to replace a product (or refund the purchase price) if the product is defective.[13] See Ethical Dimensions 13-1 for some things to consider in undertaking ethical communications with customers.

### Customer-Initiated Communications

Traditional thinking about promotion—and for that matter about the communication process—has usually been based on the idea that it's the seller ("source") who initiates the communication. Of course, for decades consumers have been looking in the Yellow Pages for information or asking retail salespeople for help. Similarly, it's not news that organizational buyers contact potential vendors to ask questions or request bids.

Even so, marketers often think of the buyer as a more or less passive message receiver in the communication process—at least until the marketer has done something to stimulate attention, interest, and desire. That's one reason that targeting is so important—so that the promotion effort and expense isn't wasted on someone who isn't at all interested. Moreover, the need for a blend of promotion methods is built on the idea that at any given moment you can get a customer's attention and interest for only a few seconds—or a few minutes, if you're really lucky. Even with highly targeted direct-response promotion, the marketer typically has taken the first step with promotion to get the interaction started.

However, this is changing. In the information age, it is much easier for customers to search for information on their own. In fact, buyers can access a great deal of information and place an order without the seller having been directly involved at all. The new interactive information technologies enabling this change take many different forms, but some of the most important are websites, e-mail list-servers, caller-controlled fax-on-demand, computerized telephone voice-messaging systems, video kiosks in malls, CD-ROM and DVD drives on personal computers, and WebTV.

New variations on these interactive technologies are being developed all the time. For example, in England, where interactive cable TV systems have been operating for a decade, consumers have access to a system called Teletext. With Teletext, they can use their standard TV remote control unit to search through thousands of on-screen pages of information—ranging from the schedule for flights from London's airports and the current weather to advertising for automobiles and specials at the local supermarket. The benefits of Teletext are very similar to the benefits of the World Wide Web, but it uses a standard TV. Similar systems will become more available in other countries as government regulations change and as cable companies upgrade their equipment. See Marketing Demo 13-2 for more on interactive technologies.

Work is underway to develop broadcast systems in which icons will appear on-screen as consumers watch a program or movie. For example, an icon might appear on a jacket worn by a talk-show guest. A consumer who is interested in the product will be able to press a button on a remote control to get more information about the product or where to buy it—or even to place an order. The same concept is already implemented on DVDs for some movies. When this type of system is available via cable (or with streaming video over the Internet), it will provide a powerful new tool for marketers and, over time, reshape the way many marketing communications are handled.

## Marketing Demo 13–2

### WINK WINK...

Interactive television has been slow to catch on in the Canadian market, but the opportunities it presents could revolutionize the marketing scene. For marketers, one of the most attractive aspects of the iTV service is Enhanced TV, which was introduced to Canada by Toronto-based Rogers Cable in October 2001. Contrary to the popular notion about iTV, Enhanced TV won't enable Rogers' digital cable customers to buy that chi-chi little off-the-shoulder number worn by Rachel on *Friends*: Not yet anyway.

Using technology provided by Wink Communications, Rogers now offers roughly 300,000 digital cable subscribers in Ontario the ability to "interact" with selected content and commercials on seven channels, including MuchMusic, Citytv, SportsNet, and The Weather Network.

"Wink-ified" commercials allow viewers to receive everything from free samples to additional product information, with the simple click of a button. For example, when the Wink "i" appears on-screen during a Clorox Bleach commercial, viewers can hit "select" to call up an overlay that may ask if they'd like a $1-off coupon. Customers will have already registered personal information, like their name and mailing address, with the Wink system, so they can simply select "yes" to order, then sit back and wait for the coupon to arrive. Couponing without the dual hazards of scissors and paper cuts!

Although iTV has had difficulty gaining momentum among Canadian consumers and advertisers, Enhanced TV provides the opportunity to establish a more significant one-to-one relationship. This means that marketers will be able to get to know their customers better, as well as evaluate the performance of specific ads. A one-to-one relationship with customers is the Holy Grail for advertisers, and until the day that, say, Captain High Liner comes right to your home to cook up some fish sticks, interactive TV may be the next best thing.[14]



**How consumer-initiated communication works** This type of customer-initiated information search and/or communication represents a change that will become prevalent for more types of purchases in the future, so we should think about it in more detail. Let's start by contrasting the simple model of customer ("receiver")-initiated interactive communication shown in Exhibit 13-7. At first it doesn't seem very different from the traditional communication model we considered earlier (refer to Exhibit 13-5). However, the differences are significant.

**Consumers control the search process** In the model in Exhibit 13-7, a customer initiates the communication process with a decision to search for information in a particular message channel. The most far-reaching message chan-

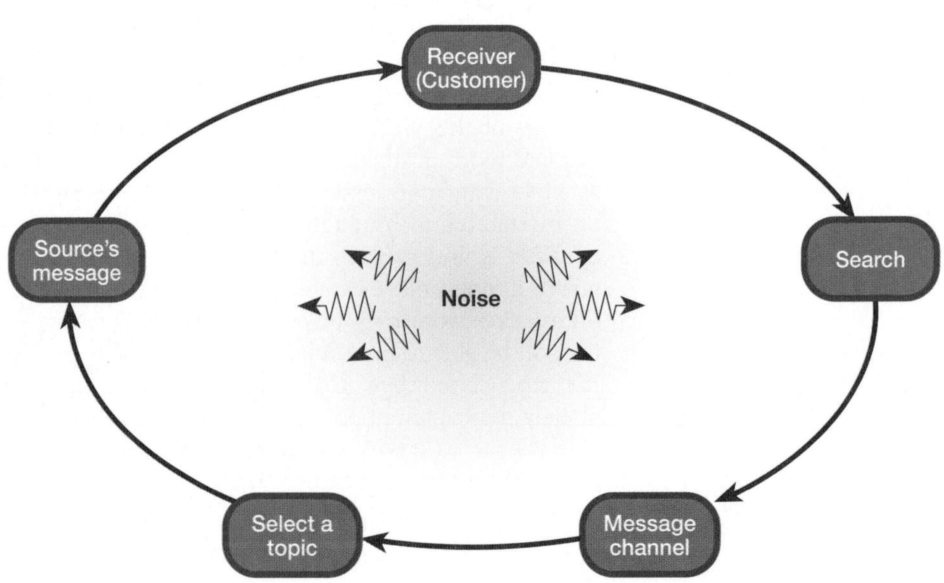


Exhibit 13-7
A model of customer-initiated interactive communication.

nel to search is the Internet. The message channel is still the carrier of the message, as was the case before, but "searchable" message channels usually feature an archive of existing messages on a number of topics. There may be many available topics—even millions.

In the next step, the consumer selects one specific topic on which to receive a message. Selecting a topic might be done in one of a variety of ways, depending on the message channel. The most typical approaches involve using a mouse, remote control device, or keypad to highlight a selection from an initial list (like a table of contents or index). Of course, other approaches are common. For example, many dial-up telephone systems are using voice-recognition systems. Or, in the case of the Internet, you might enter a word or phrase and have the computer search for a list of topics that include it.

**Interactivity opens new possibilities** Once a specific topic is selected, the message for that topic is displayed. Typically, the message is brief. But it may include a simple way to get more detailed information, select another related topic, return to the original selection process, or quit the search. Thus, after each message the consumer can decide whether to search further (say, to get more detail on an initial topic or to broaden the search to other topics). This interactive approach makes it easy for the consumer to conveniently get as much or little information as desired and to spend as much time searching as seems worthwhile. However, noise may still be a problem. For example, a consumer who wants information about a specific product may waste a lot of time and still not find what is needed—because it is not available on the message channel or it is too hard to find. So some firms offer consumers a website choice that establishes communication with a real person at a 24-hour-a-day service centre. Some of these systems, for example the one at Bell.ca, use instant messaging so that the consumer and a customer service person can chat online. With other systems, like AT&T's "Interactive Answers" approach, a person at the calling centre telephones the customer and provides the precise product information or help needed. Other firms are using variations of this approach, including live teleconferencing over the Internet. Many personal computers now come equipped with everything needed for this type of Internet teleconferencing.

Even without a voice link to a live salesperson, the action required to make a purchase by interactive media is usually very fast and easy—because one of the topics available for the customer to select is "how to buy." At many Internet sites, for example, a consumer can click on a selected item to place it in a virtual shopping cart, charge it to a credit card, and arrange for shipping by a service like UPS.

**Greater potential for customization** As you can see, the traditional principles of communication that we discussed earlier in the chapter are still important in customer-initiated interactive communication. At the same time, the interactive approach allows the marketer to customize communication to the needs and responses of the consumer. As new approaches develop in this arena, we are seeing more promotion targeted at single-person "segments."

Electronic media also allows many types of information—pictures, graphs, words, video, and sounds—to be used. As a result, a key advantage of the new electronic media is that all of the different promotional materials that a firm develops can be available in one place. This allows managers with different specialties to see how their materials work with the rest of the promotion blend—so there is even more incentive to develop integrated communications.[15]

## Direct-Response Communications

**direct marketing** Direct communication between a seller and an individual customer using a promotion method other than face-to-face personal selling

The challenge of developing promotions that reach *specific* target customers has prompted many firms to turn to **direct marketing**—direct communication between a seller and an individual customer using a promotion method other than face-to-face personal selling. Most direct marketing communications are designed to prompt immediate feedback—a direct response—by customers. That's why this type of communication is often called *direct-response promotion*.

Early efforts in the direct-response area focused on direct-mail advertising. A carefully selected mailing list—perhaps from the firm's customer relationship management (CRM) database—allowed advertisers to reach a specific target audience with specific interests. And direct-mail advertising proved to be very effective when the objective was to get a direct response from the customer.

Achieving a measurable, direct response from specific target customers is still the heart of direct promotion. But the promotion medium is evolving to include not just mail but also telephone, print, e-mail, a website, broadcast, and even interactive video. The customer's response may be a purchase (or donation), a question, or a request for more information. At a website, the response may be a simple mouse-click to link to more information, a click to put an item in a virtual shopping cart, or a click to purchase.

Often the customer responds by calling a toll-free telephone number or, in the case of business markets, by sending a fax or an e-mail. A knowledgeable salesperson talks with the customer on the phone and follows up. That might involve filling an order and having it shipped to the customer, or putting an interested prospect in touch with a salesperson who makes a personal visit. There are, however, many variations on this approach. For example, some firms route incoming information-request calls to a computerized answering system. The caller indicates what information is required by pushing a few buttons on the telephone keypad. Then the computer instantly sends requested information to the caller's fax machine.

Direct-response promotion is often an important component of integrated marketing communications programs and is closely tied to other elements of the marketing mix. However, what distinguishes this general approach is that the marketer targets more of its promotion effort at specific individuals who respond directly.[16]

A promotion campaign used by Universal Music Canada to sell more copies of the Tragically Hip's latest CD is a good example. Determined to combat the stream of free music downloaded from the Internet, Universal Music Canada was trying new ways to entice consumers to buy. The result was the "Hip Club" membership card, which provided access to two additional music tracks at the website, and advance information on concert tickets and special merchandise. Consumers were invited to join the club after purchasing a CD. The "Hip Club" members' database also allows Universal Music Canada to target Tragically Hip fans for future promotional efforts.[17]

As the Universal Music Canada example suggests, direct-response promotion usually relies on a customer (or prospect) database to target specific individuals. A computerized database includes customers' names and addresses (or telephone numbers) as well as past purchases and other segmenting characteristics. Individuals (or segments) who respond to direct promotion are the target for additional promotion. For example, a customer who buys lingerie from a catalogue or a website once is a good candidate for a follow-up. The follow up might extend to other types of clothing.

BMW and other car companies found that videotapes are a good way to provide consumers with a lot of information about a new model. However, it's too expensive to send tapes to everyone. To target the mailing, BMW first sends likely car buyers (high-income consumers who own a BMW or competing brand) personalized direct-mail ads that offer a free videotape. Interested consumers send back a return card. Then BMW sends the advertising tape and updates its database so a dealer will know to call the consumer. Ethical Dimensions 13-2 provides more information on the ethics of using such a targeted approach. Marketing Demo 13-3 discusses some new methods for this kind of database targeting as implemented by the Air Miles Reward Program.

## Ethical Dimensions 13–2

### DATABASE TARGETING

Direct-response promotion and customer relationship management database targeting have become an important part of many marketing mixes—and more and more customers find it very convenient. But not everyone is enthusiastic. Some critics argue that thousands of acres of trees are consumed each week just to make the paper for direct-response "junk mail" that consumers don't want. Most e-mail users also get uninvited messages, called spam. Other critics worry about privacy issues related to how a direct-response database might be used, especially if it includes detailed information about a consumer's purchases. Similarly, many consumers don't like getting direct promotion telephone solicitations at any time, but especially in the evening and at meal times, when they seem to be particularly frequent. Most states have passed laws prohibiting automatic calling systems that use pre-recorded messages rather than a live salesperson. There is also growing concern by computer users about receiving e-mail they don't want. Worse, some firms have been criticized for creating websites that secretly install programs on customers' computers. Then, unknown to the user, the program gathers information about other websites the user visits and sends it back to the firm over the Internet. Most firms that use direct-response promotion are very sensitive to these concerns and take steps to address them.[18]

## Marketing Demo 13–3

### NEW APPROACHES TO DIRECT MARKETING

**Bryan Pearson, President**
**Air Miles Reward Program**

The last 10 years have been a renaissance period for the marketing industry, with the emergence of new communications channels such as the Internet and advances in technology that have enabled significant capability en-hancements and cost improvements in the data-warehousing arena. This has created a renewed energy and focus behind techniques that for decades have been the relatively private domain of the professionals who made up the direct-marketing industry.

#### New Marketing Approaches

We are now seeing the adoption of these marketing approaches to the emerging challenge of managing consumer data, leveraging the data to create improved consumer facing programs, and then creating a customer experience that extends consistently across a multi-channel communications environment.

As one of the world's leading coalition loyalty programs, the Air Miles Reward Program in Canada has had the opportunity to work with many of the country's leading grocers, retailers, and credit card companies to bring a new approach to marketing activities. With more than 60 percent of Canadian households participating in the program, it provides an incredible data resource to help sponsor companies change their marketing approach by better understanding the underlying consumer dynamics of their business and then leveraging these insights to improve the profitability of their marketing activities.

#### The Evolution of Direct Marketing

Direct-marketing activities involve the use of consumer information to create targeted, direct-to-consumer communications that can be measured to determine the relative profitability of various activities. Traditionally, this type of marketing has involved the acquisition of mailing lists and development of a communication device that makes its way through the post office to the consumer's door.

However, the growth of devices such as loyalty cards and databases along with the development of new direct-to-consumer channels such as the Internet have significantly enlarged the scope of what direct marketers view as part of their industry. While the mass media continue to be an integral part of a marketer's toolkit, funds are increasingly being migrated to direct-marketing channels where a return on investment can be calculated and new marketing activities or incremental spending can be justified based on quantifiable results.

The rise of what can be called "measured marketing" is

central to the success of direct activities, and the desire to better understand consumer behaviour is one reason why the industry has experienced rapid growth in the area of loyalty programs. While the currency often associated with these programs can be a powerful motivator of consumer behaviour, the real asset they create is the database of consumer information that the organization can leverage to support its marketing activities.

## How the Data Are Used

For too long, many companies (and especially retailers) looked at their business in terms of *what* they were selling and this became the basis of the discipline of category management. Space planning for store shelves and direct product profitability were the key management tools to optimize profitability. With the introduction of consumer data related to purchasing activity, the question of *who* was buying could now bring an entirely new dimension to the marketing and profit equation.

These data are being used to create an entirely new way to market to a set of consumers. Understanding the total value of a customer to a business or a store and then aggregating these customers into groups based on common characteristics will result in creating different segments of consumers based on their actual behaviour. In turn, an organization can begin to target these segments to influence their spending behaviour over time so that their relative profitability increases either through improved revenues or a change of behaviour that makes them less costly to serve (e.g., migration to a less expensive channel such as the Internet). High-spending customers could be encouraged to continue to be loyal and maintain their spending over a longer period of time. Low-spending customers could be targeted with special offers to try new services or products in an effort to increase their total spending over time.

Let's consider a profile that is typical of what is experienced in the retail environment. In many cases, the top 30 percent of customers will represent 70 percent of sales volume at a chain of stores, and the best 5 percent of customers often represent as much as 20 percent of sales. Retaining the sales revenue from these top customers and finding ways to maintain their interest over a longer period of time is critical to the long-term success of the business.

By understanding who these customers are, the retailer can target specific communications not only to recognize them but also to provide them with relevant offers to hold or increase their interest in continuing to do business at the store. If an e-mail address is part of the customer information held by the organization, then the direct-marketing activities can use either the traditional mail channel or the Internet to communicate with each customer specifically regarding these special offers.

This is particularly important when the retailer decides that it wants to increase the spend levels of the other 70 percent of customers who represent only 30 percent of total sales. If a particularly rich offer is made to these customers as an incentive to increase the total business they do with the retailer, then the ability to target these offers to this segment will make the program more successful for the retailer. For one, the retailer can provide a richer offer since it knows it will be required to give the offer only to someone who actually demonstrates a change in behaviour. Secondly, the retailer doesn't have to worry about its best customers taking advantage of the offer since they will not receive it in the first place. This is significantly different from most pricing activity, such as sales, that provides equal access to all customers and must therefore be managed to account for product profitability first.

## How Air Miles Practises Direct Marketing

At the Air Miles Reward Program, we have been using these techniques for years to help our sponsors understand and manage their customers more effectively through a variety of direct-marketing techniques. These programs start with the insights derived from the database that is created when Collectors use their Air Miles cards at our participating sponsors. We track Collector behaviour over time and identify how they are migrating among segments based on the success of various targeted marketing initiatives. These can be executed via a statement mailing that reaches most Collectors four times a year, or via incremental stand-alone mailings that are sent based on seasonal shopping behaviour (e.g., back to school, pre-holiday).

The Internet is heavily leveraged on an inbound and outbound basis. Sponsors can send timely e-mail communication to Collectors as either a support to offline activities or as an independent marketing activity. Logging on to the Airmiles.ca website results in a stream of targeted content being served up to the Collector that is based on current activity in the reward program and the initiatives that various sponsors are intent on targeting to their customers. In specific cases, an Air Miles Collector will also encounter targeted communications when calling our customer care centre or when shopping at sponsors that are enabled at the point of sale (cash register) to deliver specific marketing messages. The key is managing the integration and interplay among these channels to ensure consistency and appropriate sequencing of the various messages and offers that the Collector receives.

In addition to traditional purchase-behaviour segmentation, many companies also have recognized that there are other applications where direct activities can be highly relevant and create a key point of leverage. Two key examples of this relate to what can be termed "life stage marketing."

The first example relates to finding common life stages among consumers and then recognizing when changes occur that indicate some migration into one of these events. Two periods in one's life when spending behaviour changes dramatically would be when someone has a new baby or decides to move homes. To find individuals who are moving through these life stages, databases are analyzed to look for changes in self-reported information (e.g., change of address) or by identifying changes in shopping behaviour over time.

The second example relates back to our sample retail chain. Most stores go through their own life stages. They are opened, business builds over time, and then they often need to be enlarged or renovated based on changes in strategy or merchandise mix. These periods provide similar opportunities to communicate directly with consumers provided the store has an understanding of who its customers are. A simple communication announcing a store renovation or thanking customers for their patience through the renovation and inviting them to the new store can build tremendous value into how that customer views their relationship with the retailer.

In both of these examples, using direct communication provides the most efficient way to ensure that relevant information about a marketing activity or program is provided to the individual customers who are most interested or affected by the life stage change. While the cost per contact may be higher than mass media devices, the message is relevant only to a subset of consumers, so it can be more cost-effective to execute a direct campaign. The ability to personalize the message to the individual customer is the added bonus that when properly leveraged can lead to improved customer activity and retention.

There is one other element of direct marketing that is becoming more common practice now that databases and advanced statistical analysis tools are establishing themselves as foundation tools for the marketing community. The ability to work through vast amounts of data to look for patterns means that the data can now be used to predict potential future activity from a group of consumers based on the past behaviour of another group of consumers.

Increasingly, companies are not waiting to see the actual behaviour change before they begin to target marketing activities to consumers. Instead, they are relying on underlying insights from the data to help define specific groups of consumers that will be targeted with offers or communication to prevent or augment the anticipated action.

For example, statistical models can be built to identify customers who have a high risk of decline in their spending. Before the customer has a chance to lower activity levels or to leave entirely, they are suddenly receiving special offers or phone calls from the company in question in an effort to ensure they are properly served and happy with the services provided.

In another case, a retailer may be opening a new store and can use the information from existing stores to create a variety of statistical models that will help to make the new store a success. First, it can model behaviour patterns from existing stores to understand the shape and size of the trading area for a typical store. This, in combination with specific customer demographic data, can help the chain determine where the best location would be for the new store. In addition, models can identify which customers would be more likely to shop at the new location, or the neighbourhoods where residents would be more likely to frequent the new store.

### Summary

Clearly, the use of information in combination with the evolving capabilities of our multi-channel communication networks is creating a new set of capabilities for today's marketing professional to be more relevant and targeted in the way they approach direct-to-consumer marketing. The ability to capitalize on this alternative approach to consumer marketing will be a powerful competitive differentiator for organizations that choose to make measured marketing the foundation of their marketing activities.

## How Typical Promotion Plans Are Blended and Integrated

There is no one *right* promotion blend for all situations. Each one must be developed as part of a marketing mix and should be designed to achieve the firm's promotion objectives in each marketing strategy. So let's take a closer look at different situations to see how a marketer might vary its promotional blend.

### Push-based Promotion—When Intermediaries Are Targeted

**pushing**

Using normal promotion effort (personal selling, advertising, and sales promotion) to help sell the whole marketing mix to possible channel members

When a channel of distribution involves intermediaries, their cooperation can be crucial to the success of the overall marketing strategy. **Pushing** (a product through a channel) means using normal promotion effort—personal selling, advertising, and sales promotion—to help sell the whole marketing mix to possible channel members. This approach emphasizes the importance of building a channel and securing the wholehearted cooperation of channel members to push the product down the channel to the final user.

Producers usually take on much of the responsibility for the pushing effort in the channel. However, most wholesalers also handle at least some of the promotion to retailers or other wholesalers farther down the channel. Similarly, retailers often

Barfly's ad stimulates consumer demand, while the Handeze ad targets retailers. Which one of these ads was designed using a push strategy? a pull strategy?

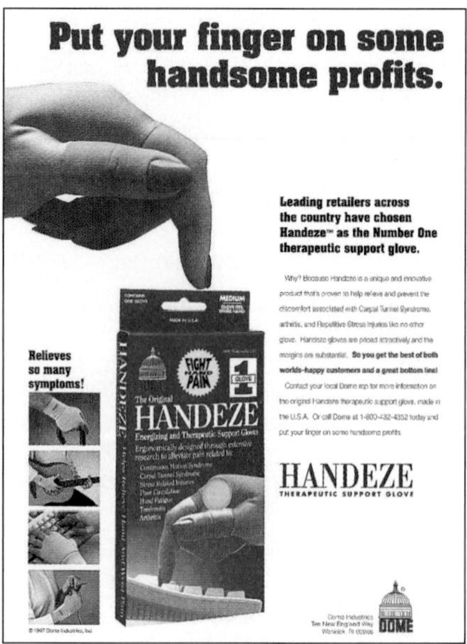


handle promotion in their local markets. The overall promotion effort is most likely to be effective when all of the individual messages are carefully integrated—that is, coordinated, consistent, and complete.

**Salespeople play a key role** Salespeople handle most of the important communication with intermediaries. Intermediaries don't want empty promises. They want to know what they can expect in return for their cooperation and help. A salesperson can answer questions about what promotion will be directed toward the final consumer, each channel member's part in marketing the product, and important details on pricing, markups, promotion assistance, and allowances.

A salesperson can help the firm determine when it should adjust its marketing mix from one intermediary to another. In highly competitive urban areas, for example, mixes may emphasize price.

When a number of suppliers offer similar products and compete for attention and shelf space, the wholesaler or retailer usually pays attention to the one with the best profit potential. In these situations, the sales rep must convince the intermediary that demand for the product exists and that making a profit will be easy. A firm can make the sales rep's job easier by targeting special sales promotions at intermediaries too.

## Profit-based Sales Incentives

Sales promotions targeted at intermediaries usually focus on short-term arrangements that will improve the intermediary's profits. For example, a soft-drink bottler might offer a convenience store a free case of drinks with each two cases it buys. The free case improves the store's profit margin on the whole purchase. Other types of sales promotions—such as contests that offer vacation trips for high-volume intermediaries—are also common.

**Informational advertising** Firms run ads in trade magazines to recruit new intermediaries or to inform channel members about a new offering. Trade ads usually encourage intermediaries to contact the supplier for more information, and then a salesperson takes over.

**The special case of internal marketing** Some firms emphasize promotion to their own employees—especially salespeople or others in contact with customers. This type of *internal marketing* effort is basically a variation on the pushing approach.

One objective of an annual sales meeting is to inform reps about important elements of the marketing strategy—so they'll work together as a team to implement it. Some firms use promotion to motivate employees to work harder at specific jobs—such as providing customer service or achieving higher sales. For example, many firms use sales contests and award free trips to big sellers.

Some companies design ads to communicate to employees and boost the employees' image. This is typical in services where the quality of the employees' efforts is a big part of the product. Some ads, for example, use the theme "we like to see you smile." The ads communicate to customers, but also remind employees that the service they provide is crucial to customer satisfaction.

## Pull-based Promotion—Targeting Consumers to Gain Push

Regardless of what promotion a firm uses to get help from channel members or employees in pushing a product, most producers focus a significant amount of promotion on customers at the end of the channel. This helps to stimulate demand and pull the product through the channel of distribution. **Pulling** means getting customers to ask intermediaries for the product.

**pulling**
Getting customers to ask intermediaries for a product

Pulling and pushing are usually used in combination (see Exhibit 13-8). However, if intermediaries won't work with a producer—perhaps because they're already carrying a competing brand—a producer may try to use a pulling approach by itself. This involves highly aggressive and expensive promotion to final consumers or users—perhaps using coupons or samples—temporarily bypassing intermediaries. If the promotion works, the intermediaries are forced to carry the product to satisfy customer requests. However, this approach is risky. An expensive promotion effort is wasted if customers lose interest before reluctant intermediaries make the product available. At minimum, intermediaries should be told about the planned pulling effort so they can be ready if the promotion succeeds.

Who handles promotion to final customers at the end of the channel varies in different channel systems—depending on the mix of pushing and pulling. Further, the promotion blend typically varies depending on whether customers are final consumers or business users.[19]

Exhibit 13-8
Promotion may encourage pushing by the channel, pulling by customers, or both.

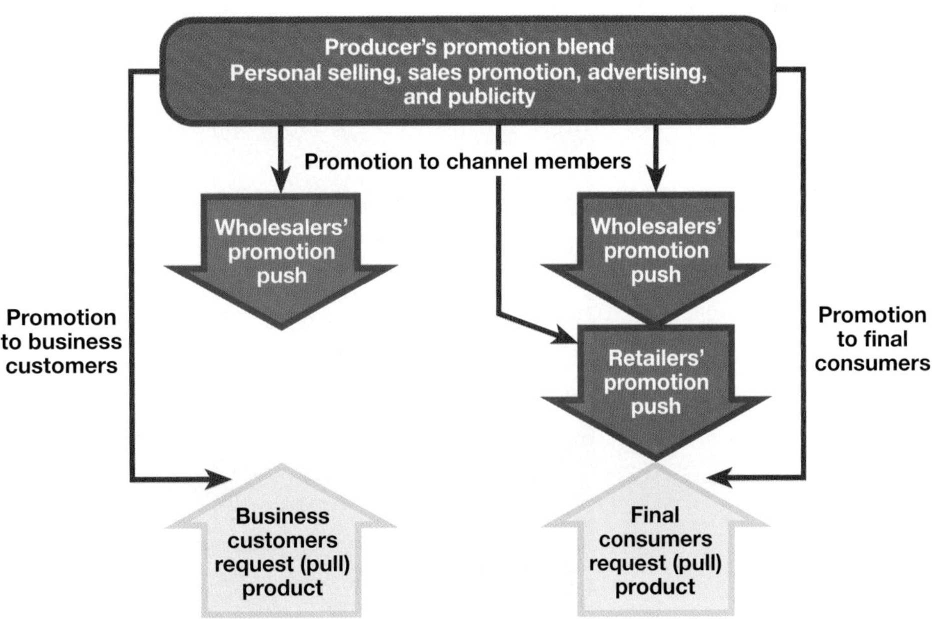

## Promotional Blends for Final Consumers

The large number of consumers almost forces producers of consumer products and retailers to emphasize advertising and sales promotion. Sales promotion—such as coupons, contests, or free samples—builds consumer interest and short-term sales of a product. Effective mass selling may build enough brand familiarity so that little personal selling is needed—as in self-service and discount operations.[20]

Some retailers—specialty shops in particular—rely heavily on well-informed salespeople. Technical products (like camcorders or computers) and personal services (like health care and estate planning) may also require personal selling. Direct-selling firms like Avon also rely on personal selling. But aggressive personal selling to final consumers usually is found in expensive channel systems, such as those for fashionable clothing, furniture, consumer electronics, and automobiles.

## Promotional Blends for Business Customers

Producers and wholesalers who target business customers often emphasize personal selling. This is practical because these customers are much less numerous than final consumers and their purchases are typically larger.

Moreover, business customers may have technical questions or need adjustments in the marketing mix. An extremely technical business product may require a heavy emphasis on personal selling—using technically trained salespeople. This is the only sure way to make the product understood and get feedback on how customers use it. The technical sales rep meets with engineers, production managers, purchasing agents, and top managers and can adjust the sales message to the needs of these various influences.

Sales reps can be more flexible in adjusting their companies' appeals to suit each customer—and personal contact is usually required to close a sale. A salesperson is also able to call back later to follow up with additional information, resolve any problems, and nurture the relationship with the customer.

While personal selling dominates in business markets, mass selling is necessary too. A typical sales call on a business customer costs about $200.[21] That's because salespeople spend less than half their time actually selling. The rest is consumed by such tasks as travelling, paperwork, sales meetings, and strictly service calls. So, it's seldom practical for salespeople to carry the whole promotion load.

This McGraw-Hill ad targets business consumers. What message is it trying to convey?

Ads in trade magazines or at a B2B e-commerce website, for instance, can inform potential customers that a product is available. Most trade ads give a toll-free telephone number, fax number, or website address to stimulate direct inquiries. Domestic and international trade shows also help identify prospects. Even so, most sellers who target business customers spend only a small percentage of their promotion budget on mass selling and sales promotion.

## The Adoption Process Can Guide Promotion Planning

Knowing what type of promotion is typically emphasized with different targets is useful in planning the promotion blend. But each unique market segment may need a separate marketing mix and a different promotion blend. Some mass-selling specialists miss this point. They think mainly in terms of mass marketing rather than target marketing. Aiming at large markets is desirable in some situations, but promotion aimed at everyone can end up hitting no one. In developing the promotion blend, you should be careful not to slip into a shotgun approach when what you really need is a rifle approach—with a more careful aim.

The AIDA and adoption processes look at individuals. This emphasis on individuals helps us understand how promotion affects the way that people behave. But it's also useful to look at markets as a whole. Different segments of customers within a market may behave differently—with some taking the lead in trying new products and, in turn, influencing others.

**adoption curve**
Shows when different groups accept ideas

Research on how markets accept new ideas has led to the **adoption curve** model. The adoption curve shows when different groups accept ideas. It shows the need to change the promotion effort as time passes. It also emphasizes the relations among groups and shows that individuals in some groups act as leaders in accepting a new idea.

Exhibit 13-9 shows the adoption curve for a typical successful product. Some of the important characteristics of each of these customer groups are discussed below. Which one are you?

**innovators**
Consumers who are the first to adopt a new product

**Innovators—The risk-takers** The **innovators** are the first to adopt. They are eager to try a new idea and willing to take risks. Innovators tend to be young and well educated. They are likely to be mobile and have many contacts outside their local social group and community. Business firms in the innovator group are often

Exhibit 13-9
The adoption curve.

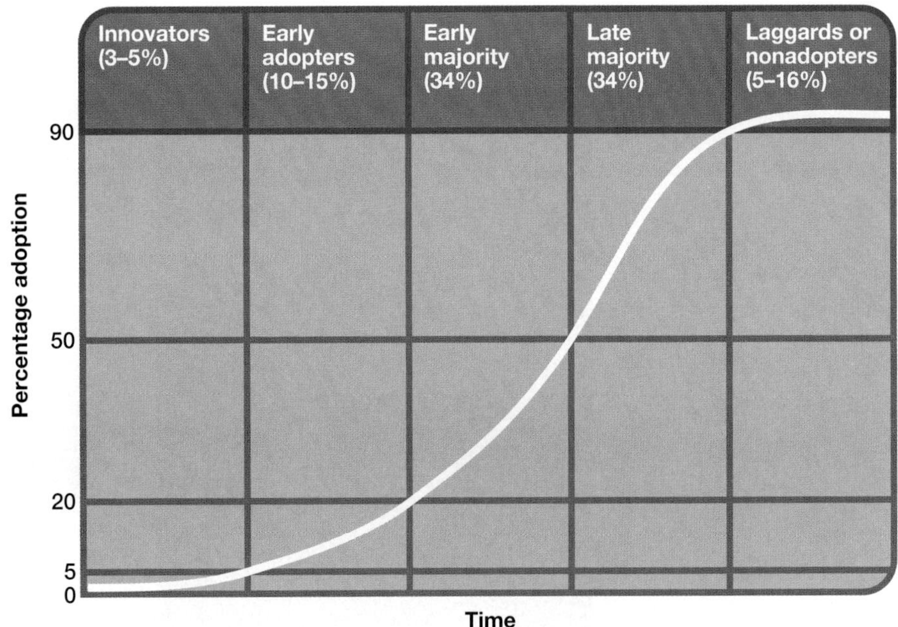

aggressive, small companies with an entrepreneurial view and willingness to take the risk of doing something new and different. However, large firms, especially specialized ones, may be in the innovator group.

An important characteristic of innovators is that they rely on impersonal and scientific information sources, or other innovators, rather than salespeople. They often search for information. For example, they might do a search on the Internet, read articles in technical publications, or look for informative ads in special-interest magazines.

**early adopters**

Consumers who are well respected by their peers; often opinion leaders

**Early adopters—The opinion leaders** **Early adopters** are well respected by their peers and often are opinion leaders. They tend to be younger, more mobile, and more creative than later adopters. But unlike innovators, they have fewer contacts outside their own social group or community. Business firms in this category also tend to be specialized.

Of all the groups, this one tends to have the greatest contact with salespeople. Mass media are important information sources too. Marketers should be very concerned with attracting and selling the early adopter group. Their acceptance is really important in reaching the next group, because the early majority look to the early adopters for guidance. The early adopters can help the promotion effort by spreading *word-of-mouth* information and advice among other consumers.

Marketers know the importance of personal conversations and recommendations by opinion leaders. If early groups reject the product, it may never get off the ground. For example, some moviegoers are the first to see new movies. If they think a movie is dull, they quickly tell their friends not to waste their time and money. Consumers are even more likely to talk about a negative experience than a positive experience.

But if opinion leaders accept a product, what they say about it can be very important. Such word-of-mouth publicity may do the real selling job—long before the customer ever walks into the retail store. That's why some companies try to target promotion to encourage opinion leadership and word-of-mouth publicity.

The Internet is also providing companies, even small ones, with a low-cost way to encourage word of mouth. An interesting Web page can attract attention—and customers can easily e-mail a copy to a friend, as illustrated in the Blue Light viral e-mail campaign described at the beginning of this chapter.

**early majority**

Consumers who avoid risk and wait to consider a new product after many early adopters have tried and liked it

**The early majority—The deliberate shoppers** The **early majority** avoid risk and wait to consider a new product after many early adopters have tried it—and

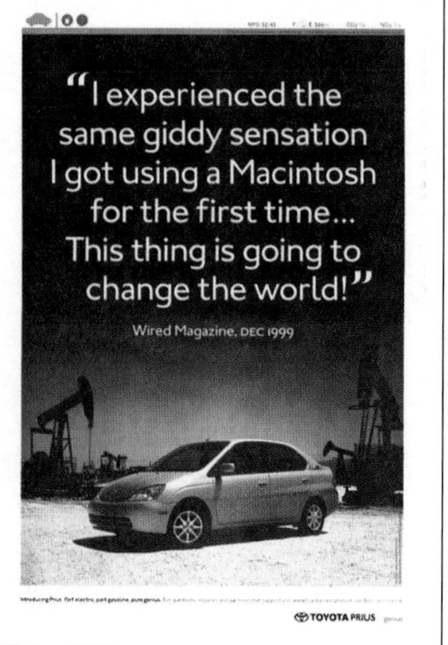


Compaq is targeting members of the late-majority group who just want a hassle-free way to use e-mail as part of their everyday life. On the other hand, Toyota's Prius ad targets innovators and early adopters. Describe how word-of-mouth advertising is important in targeting these different groups.

liked it. Average-sized business firms that are less specialized often fit in this category. If successful companies in their industry adopt the new idea, they will too.

The early majority have a great deal of contact with mass media, salespeople, and early-adopter opinion leaders. Members usually aren't opinion leaders themselves.

**late majority**
Consumers who are cautious about new ideas

**The late majority—The cautious shoppers** The **late majority** are cautious about new ideas. Often they are older than the early majority group and more set in their ways. So they are less likely to follow opinion leaders and early adopters. In fact, strong social pressure from their own peer group may be needed before they adopt a new product. Business firms in this group tend to be conservative, smaller-sized firms with little specialization.

The late majority make little use of marketing sources of information—mass media and salespeople. They tend to be oriented more toward other late adopters rather than outside sources they don't trust.

**laggards (nonadopters)**
Consumers who prefer to do things the way they've been done in the past and are very suspicious of new ideas

**Laggards—The traditionalists** **Laggards** or **nonadopters** prefer to do things the way they've been done in the past and are very suspicious of new ideas. They tend to be older and less well educated. The smallest businesses with the least specialization often fit this category. They cling to the status quo and think it's the safe way.

The main source of information for laggards is other laggards. This certainly is bad news for marketers who are trying to reach a whole market quickly or who want to use only one promotion method. In fact, it may not pay to bother with this group.[22]

## The Product Life Cycle Can Guide Promotion Planning

A new product concept seldom becomes a spectacular success overnight. The adoption curve helps explain why. Further, the adoption curve helps explain why a new product goes through the product life-cycle stages described in Chapter 10—market introduction, market growth, market maturity, and sales decline. During these stages, promotion blends may have to change to achieve different promotion objectives.

**primary demand**
Demand for a general product idea, not just for a company's own brand

**Market introduction—Focus on primary demand** During market introduction, the basic promotion objective is informing. If the product is a really new idea, the promotion must build **primary demand**—demand for the general product idea—not just for the company's own brand. Videophone service and electric cars are good examples of product concepts where primary demand is just beginning to grow. There may be few potential innovators during the introduction stage, and personal selling can help find them. Firms also need salespeople to find good channel members and persuade them to carry the new product. Sales promotion may be targeted at salespeople or channel members to get them interested in selling the new product. And sales promotion may also encourage customers to try it.

**selective demand**
Demand for a company's own brand

**Market growth—Focus on selective demand** In the market-growth stage, more competitors enter the market and promotion emphasis shifts from building primary demand to stimulating **selective demand**—demand for a company's own brand. The main job is to persuade customers to buy, and keep buying, the company's product.

Now that more potential customers are trying and adopting the product, mass selling may become more economical. But salespeople and personal selling must still work in the channels—expanding the number of outlets and cementing relationships with current channel members.

**Market maturity—Focus on persuasion and reminders** In the market-maturity stage, even more competitors have entered the market. Promotion becomes more persuasive. At this stage, mass selling and sales promotion may dominate the promotion blends of consumer products firms. Business products may require more

This Molson ad attempts to stimulate selective demand. With what stage of the product life cycle does this ad correspond?



aggressive personal selling—perhaps supplemented by more advertising. The total dollars allocated to promotion may rise as competition increases.

If a firm already has high sales—relative to competitors—it may have a real advantage in promotion at this stage. If, for example, Nabisco has twice the sales for a certain type of cookie as Keebler, its smaller competitor, and they both spend the same *percentage* of total sales on promotion, Nabisco will be spending twice as much and will probably communicate to more people. Nabisco may even get more than twice as much promotion because of economies of scale.

Firms that have strong brands can use reminder-type advertising at this stage. Similarly, many firms turn to various types of frequent-buyer promotions or newsletters targeted at current customers to strengthen the relationship and keep customers loyal. This may be less costly and more effective than efforts to win customers away from competitors.

**Sales decline—Focus on customer retention** During the sales-decline stage, the total amount spent on promotion usually decreases as firms try to cut costs to remain profitable. Since some people may still want the product, firms need more targeted promotion to reach these customers.

On the other hand, some firms may increase promotion to try to slow the cycle—at least temporarily. Crayola had almost all of the market for children's crayons, but sales were slowly declining as new kinds of markers came along. Crayola increased ad spending to urge parents to buy their kids a "fresh box."

### The Competitive Setting as a Guide for Promotion Planning

Firms in monopolistic competition may favour mass selling because they have differentiated their marketing mixes and have something to talk about. As a market tends toward pure competition, or oligopoly, it is difficult to predict what will happen. Competitors in some markets try to outpromote each other. The only way for a competitor to stay in this kind of market is to match rivals' promotion efforts—unless the whole marketing mix can be improved in some other way. We see a lot of such competitive advertising in our daily newspapers and in cents-off coupons at grocery store checkout counters.

In markets that are drifting toward pure competition, some companies resort to price-cutting. This *may* temporarily increase the number of units sold, but it may also reduce total revenue and the amount available for promotion *per unit*. And competitive retaliation, perhaps in the form of short-term sales promotions, may reduce the temporary sales gains and drag price levels down faster. As cash flowing into the business declines, spending may have to be cut back.[23]

## Setting the Promotion Budget

One of the hardest questions for any marketing manager to answer is "How much should we spend on promotion?" At issue is not just how much to spend but also how to divide those expenditures among various promotion methods. While the preceding discussion presents some of the factors that may influence what a firm will *want* to spend on each method, other factors may influence what the firm *can* spend.

For example, there are some economies of scale in promotion. An ad on national TV might cost less *per person* reached than an ad on local TV. Similarly, citywide radio, TV, and newspapers may be cheaper than neighbourhood newspapers or direct personal contact. But the *total cost* for some mass media may force small firms, or those with small promotion budgets, to use promotion alternatives that are more expensive per contact. Thus a small retailer might want to use local television but find that there is only enough money for a Web page, an ad in the Yellow Pages, and an occasional newspaper ad.

### Budgeting Methods

The most common method of budgeting for promotion expenditures is to compute a percentage of either past sales or sales expected in the future. The virtue of this method is its simplicity. A similar percentage can be used automatically each year—eliminating the need to keep evaluating the kind and amount of promotion effort needed and its probable cost. However, when a company's top managers have this attitude, they often get what they deserve—something less than the best results.

Just because budgeting a certain percentage of past or forecast sales is common doesn't mean that it's smart. This mechanical approach leads to expanding marketing expenditures when business is good and cutting back when business is poor. It may be desirable to increase marketing expenditures when business is good. But when business is poor, this approach may just make the problem worse—if weak promotion is the reason for declining sales. The most sensible approach may be to be *more*, not less, aggressive!

Other methods of budgeting for marketing expenditures are:

1. Match expenditures with competitors.
2. Set the budget as a certain number of cents or dollars per sales unit (by case, by thousand, or by tonne) using the past year or estimated year ahead as a base.
3. Base the budget on any uncommitted revenue, perhaps including budgeted profits. Companies with limited resources may use this approach. Or a firm may be willing to sacrifice some or all of its current profits for future sales—that is, it looks at promotion spending as an *investment* in future growth.
4. Base the budget on the job to be done. For example, the spending level might be based on the number of new customers desired and the percentage of current customers that the firm must retain to leverage investments in already-established relationships. This is called the **task method**—basing the budget on the job to be done.

**task method**
Basing the budget on the job to be done

In the light of our continuing focus on planning marketing strategies to reach objectives, the most sensible approach to budgeting promotion expenditures is the task method. In fact, this approach makes sense for *any* marketing expenditure, but here we'll focus on promotion.

A practical approach is to determine which promotion objectives are most important and which promotion methods are most economical and effective for the communication tasks relevant to each objective. There's never enough money to do all of the promotion that you might want to do. However, this approach helps you to set priorities so that the money you spend produces specific results.

The amount budgeted using the task method can be stated as a percentage of sales. But you should see that calculating the right amount is more involved than picking up a past percentage. It requires careful review of the specific promotion (and marketing) tasks to be accomplished and how each task fits with others to achieve the overall objectives. The costs of these tasks are then totalled to determine how much should be budgeted for promotion (just as money is allocated for other marketing activities required by the strategy). In other words, the firm can assemble its total promotion budget directly from detailed plans rather than by simply relying on historical patterns or ratios.

This method also helps to eliminate budget fights between different promotion areas. Such conflicts may occur if managers and specialists responsible for different promotion methods see themselves as pitted against each other for limited budget dollars. Instead, the task method of budgeting encourages everyone to focus on the overall strategy and what promotion objectives need to be achieved. The specialists may still make their own suggestions about how to perform tasks. But then the budget allocations are based on the most effective ways of getting things done, not on what the firm did last year, what some competitor does, or even on internal politics. With this approach, different promotion specialists are also more likely to recognize that they must all work together to achieve truly integrated marketing communications.[24]



## Chapter Summary

Promotion is an important part of any marketing mix. Most consumers and intermediate customers can choose from among many products. To be successful, a producer must not only offer a good product at a reasonable price but also inform potential customers about the product and where they can buy it. Further, producers must tell wholesalers and retailers in the channel about their product and their marketing mix. These intermediaries, in turn, must use promotion to reach their customers.

The promotion blend should fit logically into the strategy being developed to satisfy a particular target market. Strategy planning needs to state *what* should be communicated to them and *how*. The overall promotion objective is to affect buying behaviour, but the basic promotion objectives are informing, persuading, and reminding.

Three basic promotion methods can be used to reach these objectives. Behavioural-science findings can help firms combine various promotion methods for effective communication. In particular, what we know about the communication process and how individuals and groups adopt new products is important in planning promotion blends.

An action-oriented framework called AIDA can help marketing managers plan promotion blends. But the marketing manager has the final responsibility for combining the promotion methods into one integrated promotion blend for each marketing mix. A variety of factors must be considered in making these decisions. These include the relative emphasis on pull versus push in influencing intermediaries, the nature of final customers, the stage of the adoption process, and the life-cycle stage.

In this chapter, we considered some basic concepts that apply to all areas of promotion. In the next two chapters, we'll discuss personal selling, advertising, and sales promotion in more detail.

## Key Concepts

adoption curve, p. 403
advertising, p. 384
advertising managers, p. 386
AIDA model, p. 390
communication process, p. 390
decoding, p. 391
direct marketing, p. 395
early adopters, p. 404
early majority, p. 404

encoding, p. 391
innovators, p. 403
integrated marketing communications (IMC), p. 383
laggards (nonadopters), p. 405
late majority, p. 405
mass selling, p. 384
message channel, p. 392
noise, p. 390
personal selling, p. 383
primary demand, p. 405
promotion, p. 383
public relations, p. 386
publicity, p. 385
pulling, p. 401
pushing, p. 399
receiver, p. 390
sales managers, p. 386
sales promotion, p. 385
sales promotion managers, p. 387
selective demand, p. 405
source, p. 390
task method, p. 407

## Questions and Problems

1. Briefly explain the nature of the three basic promotion methods available to a marketing manager. What are the main strengths and limitations of each?

2. In your own words, discuss the integrated marketing communications concept. Explain what its emphasis on consistent and complete messages implies with respect to promotion blends.

3. Relate the three basic promotion objectives to the four jobs (AIDA) of promotion using a specific example.

4. Discuss the communication process in relation to a producer's promotion of an accessory product—say, a new electronic security system that businesses use to limit access to areas where they store confidential records.

5. If a company wants its promotion to appeal to a new group of target customers in a foreign country, how can it protect against its communications being misinterpreted?

6. Promotion has been the target of considerable criticism. What specific types of promotion are the probable objects of this criticism? Give a specific example that illustrates your thinking.

7. With direct-response promotion, customers provide feedback to marketing communications. How can a marketing manager use this feedback to improve the effectiveness of the overall promotion blend?

8. How can a promotion manager target a message to a certain target market with electronic media (like the Internet) when the customer initiates the communication? Give an example.

9. What promotion blend would be most appropriate for producers of the following established products? Assume average- to large-sized firms in each case and support your answer.

   a. Chocolate candy bar.
   b. Car batteries.
   c. Pantyhose.
   d. Castings for truck engines.
   e. A special computer used by manufacturers for control of production equipment.
   f. Inexpensive plastic rainhats.
   g. A digital tape recorder that has achieved specialty-product status.

10. A small company has developed an innovative new spray-on glass cleaner that prevents the buildup of electrostatic dust on computer screens and TVs. Give examples of some low-cost ways the firm might effectively promote its product. Be certain to consider both push and pull approaches.

11. Would promotion be successful in expanding the general demand for: *(a)* almonds, *(b)* air travel, *(c)* golf clubs, *(d)* walking shoes, *(e)* high-octane unleaded gasoline, *(f)* single-serving, frozen gourmet dinners, and *(g)* bricks? Explain why or why not in each case.

12. Explain how an understanding of the adoption process would help you develop a promotion blend for digital tape recorders, a new consumer electronics product that produces high-quality recordings. Explain why you might change the promotion blend during the course of the adoption process.

13. Explain how opinion leaders affect a firm's promotion planning.

14. Discuss how the adoption curve should be used to plan the promotion blend(s) for a new automobile accessory—an electronic radar system that alerts a driver if he or she is about to change lanes into the path of a car that is passing through a blind spot in the driver's mirrors.

15. If a marketing manager uses the task method to budget for marketing promotions, are competitors' promotion spending levels ignored? Explain your thinking and give an example that supports your point of view.

16. Discuss the potential conflict among the various promotion managers. How could this be reduced?

## Computer-Aided Problem 13

### Selecting a Communications Channel

Helen Troy, owner of three Sound Haus stereo equipment stores, is deciding what message channel (advertising medium) to use to promote her newest store. Her current promotion blend includes direct-mail ads that are effective for reaching her current customers. She also has knowledgeable salespeople who work well with consumers once they're in the store. However, a key objective in opening a new store is to attract new customers. Her best prospects are professionals in the 25–44 age range with incomes above $38,000 a year. But only some of the people in this group are audiophiles who want the top-of-the-line brands she carries. Troy has decided to use local advertising to reach new customers.

Troy narrowed her choice to two advertising media: an FM radio station and a biweekly magazine that focuses on entertainment in her city. Many of the magazine's readers are out-of-town visitors interested in concerts, plays, and restaurants. They usually buy stereo equipment at home. But the magazine's audience research shows that many local professionals do subscribe to the magazine. Troy doesn't think that the objective can be achieved with a single ad. However, she believes that ads in six issues will generate good local awareness with her target market. In addition, the magazine's colour format will let her present the prestige image she wants to convey in an ad. She thinks that will help convert aware prospects to buyers. Specialists at a local advertising agency will prepare a high-impact ad for $2,000, and then Troy will pay for the magazine space.

The FM radio station targets an audience similar to Troy's own target market. She knows repeated ads will be needed to be sure that most of her target audience is exposed to her ads. Troy thinks it will take daily ads for several months to create adequate awareness among her target market. The FM station will provide an announcer and prepare a tape of Troy's ad for a one-time fee of $200. All she has to do is tell the station what the message content for the ad should say.

Both the radio station and the magazine gave Troy reports summarizing recent audience research. She decides that comparing the two media in a spreadsheet will help her make a better decision.

a. *Based on the data displayed on the initial spreadsheet, which message channel (advertising medium) would you recommend to Troy? Why?*

b. *The agency that offered to prepare Troy's magazine ad will prepare a fully produced radio ad—including a musical jingle—for $2,500. The agency claims that its musical ad will have much more impact than the ad the radio station will create. The agency says its ad should produce the same results as the station ad, with 20 percent fewer insertions. If the agency claim is correct, would it be wise for Troy to pay the agency to produce the ad?*

c. *The agency will not guarantee that its custom-produced radio ad will reach Troy's objective—making 80 percent of the prospects aware of the new store. Troy wants to see how lower levels of awareness—between 50 percent and 70 percent—would affect the advertising cost per buyer and the cost per aware prospect. Use the feature analysis to vary the percentage of prospects who become aware. Prepare a table showing the effect on the two kinds of costs. What are the implications of your analysis?*

## Suggested Cases

To view the cases, go to www.mcgrawhill.ca/college/wong.

Interested in finding out what marketing looks like in the real world? *Marketing Magazine* is just a click away on your OLC! Visit www.mcgrawhill.ca/college/wong today.

When You Finish This Chapter, You Should

1. Understand the importance and nature of personal selling.

2. Know the three basic sales tasks and what the various kinds of salespeople can be expected to do.

3. Know how sales technology affects the way sales are performed.

4. Know what the sales manager must do—including selecting, training, and organizing salespeople—to carry out the personal-selling job.

5. Understand how the right compensation plan can help motivate and control salespeople.

6. Understand when and where to use the three types of sales presentations.

# Chapter Fourteen
# Personal Selling

## Empowering the Internet Generation

Cisco Systems, Inc., has enjoyed enormous growth by "empowering the Internet generation." In other words, what Cisco does is sell the backroom gear and systems that large and small businesses, government agencies, schools, and other organizations need to support their computer networks, websites, and e-commerce applications. Eighty percent of the traffic over the Internet runs on Cisco equipment.

Cisco takes care of customers with cutting-edge e-commerce technology at its website (www.cisco.com) whenever it can. Distributors also handle some needs. But Cisco's own salespeople handle the job of getting and keeping major accounts. Cisco's salesforce is as central to its success as its technology. Decisions to invest millions of dollars in information technology involve top management. Cisco's sales professionals, like Sue Bostrom, work with these executives to learn about their needs and then sell business solutions rather than "gear." Of course, a firm's IT specialists may also get in the

place price promotion produ

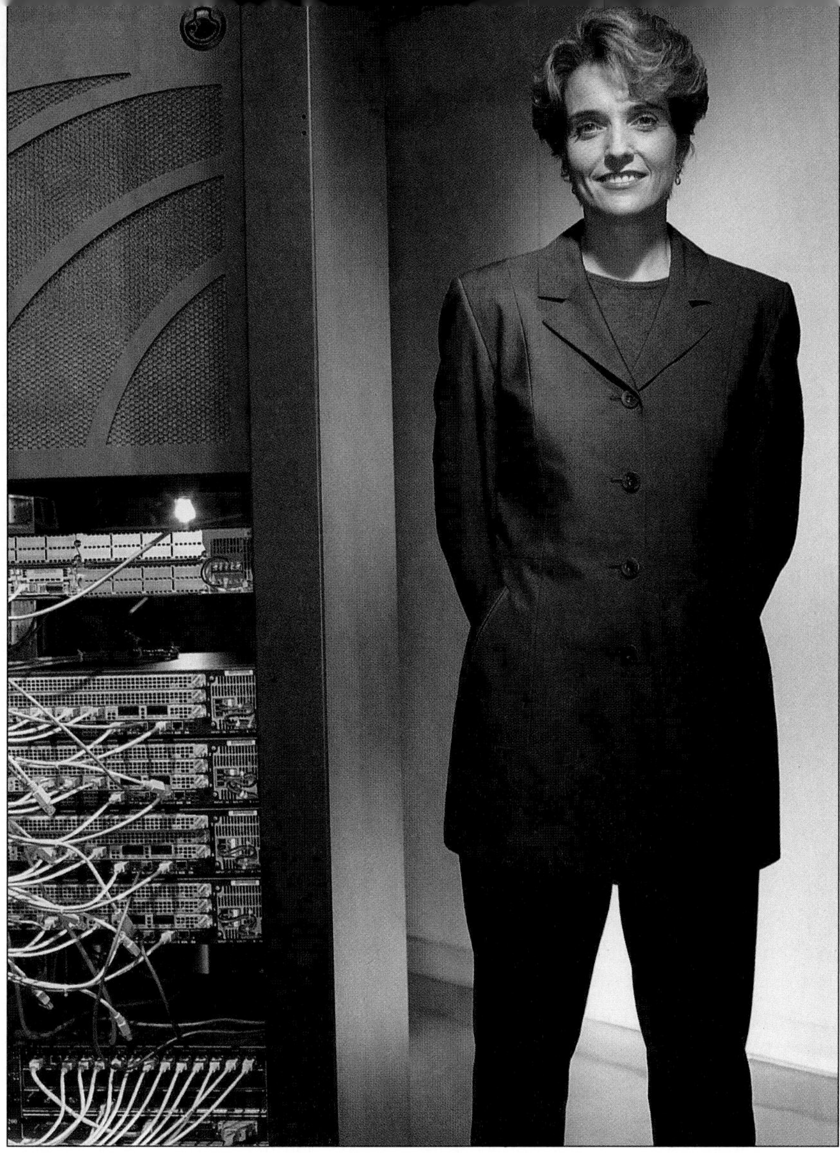

To be certain that these challenging jobs are done well, Cisco's sales managers recruit talented people using a wide variety of methods. For example, the Hot Jobs@Cisco section of its website collects job applicant profiles on an ongoing basis. When a position opens up, qualified candidates are notified. After the best people are selected, Cisco provides the sales training to make them even better. New people may need training to build professional problem-solving and sales presentation skills as well as technical knowledge. Even experienced sales reps need ongoing training. For example, Cisco gives its salespeople training in everything from the firm's policies on expenses to the latest developments in technology—with approaches ranging from traditional instructor-led workshops to cutting-edge e-learning opportunities.

act—and they want to know about technical details ("Will Cisco's router work with our system's security software?"). Technical specialists from Cisco's local sales office might handle some of these concerns as part of the sales team effort. And when the sales rep identifies a prospect that has the potential to become one of Cisco's "premier partners," Cisco's top brass may help cement a close relationship. Cisco faces tough competition, so even with all this help Cisco salespeople need real skill to get the order and close a deal. And to keep the relationship going, top-notch sales support is needed whenever a customer has a problem that can't be quickly handled online.

Cisco's salespeople have an array of different skills and experience. And Cisco has customers and sales offices all over the world. So Cisco must carefully match each salesperson to particular territories, industries, customers, and product lines. And to be sure that each salesperson is highly motivated, Cisco's sales managers must make certain that sales compensation arrangements and benefits reward salespeople for producing needed results.[1]

## In This Chapter

In this chapter, we will first focus on the importance and role of personal selling in companies. We will be able to see that personal selling requires a great deal of strategic thinking and decision making, as well as how a salesperson fits into the overall layout of the company. We'll discuss a number of frameworks and how-to approaches that guide these strategy decisions.

The discussion of personal selling's role will lead us into an assessment of what kinds of personal selling are needed. Three basic subdivisions of personal selling will be described. These are *order getters*, who develop new business relationships by establishing relationships with new customers; *order takers*, who nurture relationships to keep business flowing into the company by selling to established customers, completing most sales transactions, and maintaining relationships with their customers; and a *supporting salesforce* that informs and promotes in the channel while enhancing the relationship with the customer and getting sales in the long run.

Because there are many different roles for salespeople within a company it is crucial that a sales manager is able to organize the salesforce well, because the right structure helps assign responsibility. When organizing a salesforce it is useful for the sales manager to utilize available technology, because in many instances information technology can provide tools to do the job more efficiently and effectively. However, even the most advanced technology will not be able to compensate for a mediocre salesforce. That is why it is so important to ensure sound selection and training to build a salesforce. Once a salesforce is built, compensation and motivation are key factors in sales. Once all the logistics are dealt with, the salespeople are able to fully utilize all they have learned and demonstrate their personal-selling techniques though prospecting and presenting to potential customers.



## The Importance and Role of Personal Selling

Promotion is communicating with potential customers. As the Cisco case suggests, personal selling is often the best way to do it. Almost every company can benefit from personal selling. While face to face with prospects, salespeople can get more attention than an advertisement or a display. They can adjust what they say or do to take into consideration culture and other behavioural influences on the customer. They can ask questions to find out about a customer's specific interests. They can figure out ways to solve customer problems. If and when the prospect is ready to buy, the salesperson is there to ask for the order. And afterward, the salesperson is there to be certain that the customer is satisfied and that the relationship between the customer and the firm continues to be mutually beneficial.

However, this flexibility and comprehensiveness comes at a price. Relative to other promotional methods, personal selling is the most expensive on a cost-per-customer-reached basis. In fact, personal selling is often a company's largest single operating expense. And personal selling typically represents the largest number of

Exhibit 14-1
Strategic planning for personal selling.

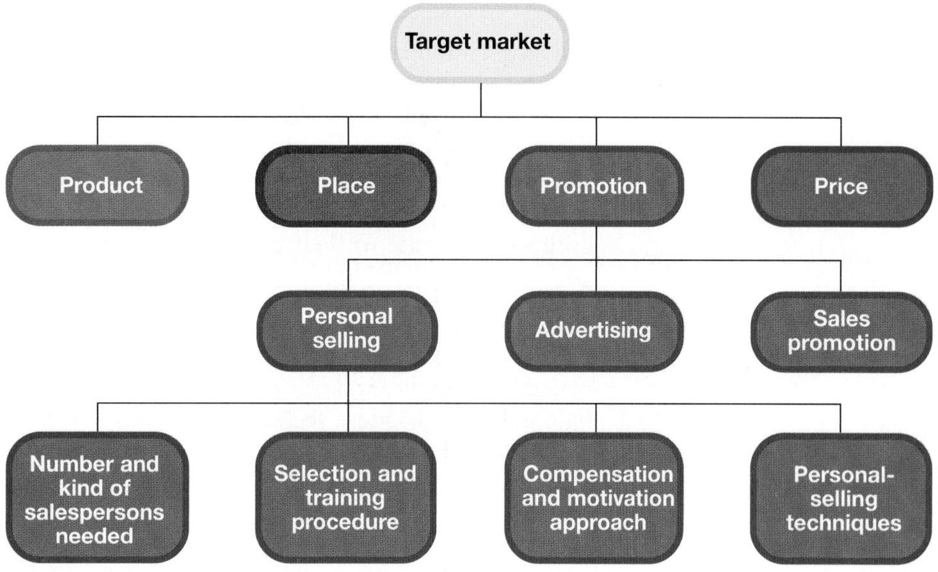


employees in marketing-related positions. In Canada, about 1.3 million people in the total labour force are involved in sales work.[2] That's about 20 times more people than are employed in Canada in advertising. Small wonder, then, that companies dedicate tremendous resources to the management of personal selling.

Marketing managers must decide how much, and what kind of, personal-selling effort each marketing mix needs. These strategy decisions are shown in Exhibit 14-1. Specifically, as part of their strategy planning, they must decide (1) how many salespeople they need, (2) what kind of salespeople they need, (3) what kind of sales technology support they need, (4) what kind of sales presentation to use, (5) how to select and train salespeople, and (6) how to supervise and motivate them. The sales manager provides input into these strategy decisions. Once made, it's the sales manager's job to implement the personal-selling part of a marketing strategy.

Because these decisions apply equally to domestic and international markets, we won't emphasize that distinction in this chapter. This does not mean, however, that personal-selling techniques don't vary from one country to another. To the contrary, in dealing with *any* customer, the salesperson must be very sensitive to cultural influences and other factors that might affect communication. For example, a Japanese customer and an Arab customer might respond differently to subtle aspects of a salesperson's behaviour.

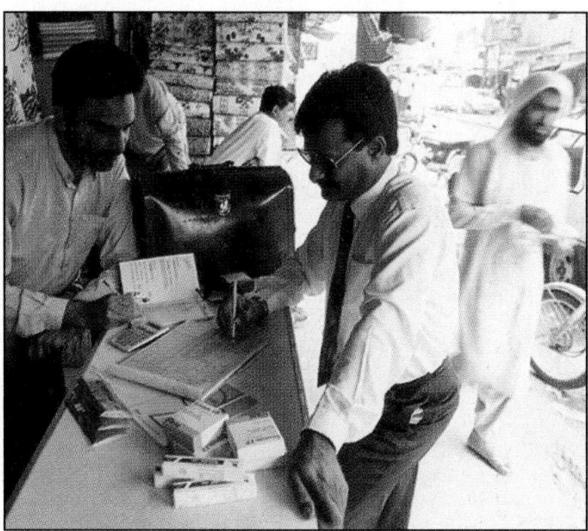

The Arab customer might expect to be physically close to a salesperson, perhaps less than a metre away, while they talk. The Japanese customer might consider that proximity rude. Similarly, what topics of discussion are considered sensitive, how messages are interpreted, and which negotiating styles are used vary from one country to another. A salesperson must know how to communicate effectively with each customer—wherever and whoever that customer is—but those details are beyond the strategy-planning focus of this text.[3]

## Three Key Roles of Personal Selling

Good salespeople don't just try to *sell* the customer. Rather, they try to *help the customer buy*—by understanding the customer's needs and presenting the advantages and disadvantages of their products. Such helpfulness results in satisfied customers and long-term relationships. And strong relationships often form the basis for a competitive advantage, especially for firms that target business markets.

You may think of personal selling in terms of an old-time stereotype of a salesperson: a bag of wind with no more to offer than a funny story, a big expense account, and an engaging grin. But that isn't true anymore. Old-time salespeople are being replaced by real professionals—problem solvers—who have something definite to contribute to their employers *and* their customers.

**A bridge between buyers and sellers** Increasingly, the salesperson is seen as a representative of the whole company—responsible for explaining its total effort to target customers rather than just pushing products. The salesperson may provide information about products, explain and interpret company policies, and even negotiate prices or diagnose technical problems when a product doesn't work well.

The sales rep is often the only link between the firm and its customers—especially if customers are far away. As you saw in Chapter 7, when a number of people from the firm are involved with the customer organization (which is increasingly common as more suppliers and customers form closer relationships) it is usually the sales rep who coordinates the relationship for his or her firm.

As this suggests, salespeople also represent their *customers* back inside their own firms. Recall that feedback is an essential part of both the communication process *and* the basic management process of planning, implementing, and control. For example, the sales rep is the likely one to explain to the production manager why a customer is unhappy with product performance or quality—or to the e-commerce specialist how better order status information available on the website could help the customer save money.

As evidence of these changing responsibilities, some companies give their salespeople such titles as field manager, sales consultant, market specialist, account representative, or sales engineer. For example, ProSlide Technology Inc. in Ottawa, which sells water rides to amusement parks, does not consider itself a fibreglass manufacturer. Instead, ProSlide's salespeople are "custom ride designers," and the company's mission is to design great rides.[4] Along the same lines, Toyota Canada has also discarded the term "salesperson" and replaced it with "product adviser."[5]

**A key source of information** The salesforce can aid in the marketing information function too. The sales rep may be the first to hear about a new competitor or



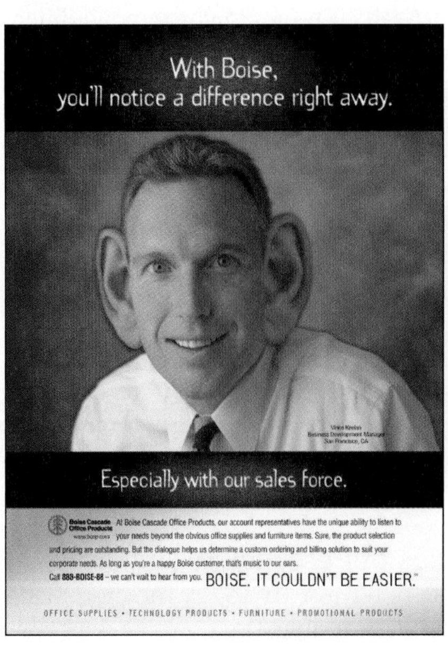

Good salespeople try to help the customer solve problems and meet needs—and often that requires both careful listening to really understand the customer and then effective service after the sale. What are some other important attributes good salespeople possess?

a competitor's new product or strategy. And, as the following example shows, sales reps who are well attuned to customers' needs can be a key source of ideas for new products.

Ballard Medical Products competes with international giants in the hospital-supply business. A key factor in Ballard's success is that its salespeople have a lot of say in what products the company produces and how they are designed. Ballard salespeople are trained as information specialists who seek and report on customer feedback. At each hospital, they work closely with the doctor and nurse specialists who use Ballard products. And when one of them says "we need a product that would solve this problem," the Ballard sales rep is right there to follow up with questions and invite suggestions. The rep quickly relays the customer's needs back to Ballard's new-products group.[6]

**A form of marketing manager** Some salespeople are expected to be marketing managers in their own territories. In fact, because top management in some firms make the error of not providing detailed strategy guidelines, these salespeople are the organization's only marketing managers.

The salesperson may have choices about (1) what target customers to aim at, (2) which particular products to emphasize, (3) which intermediaries to call on or to work with the hardest, (4) how to use promotion money, and (5) how to adjust prices. A salesperson who can put together profitable strategies and implement them well can rise very rapidly.

In some instances, especially in selling to businesses, the division of labour between marketing and sales is more a matter of different time horizons. Marketing managers assume responsibility for the long-term welfare and direction of the products. Sales representatives take responsibility for generating and meeting short-term sales targets. When responsibilities are split this way, it becomes essential that marketing and sales have some mechanism to coordinate their efforts. Otherwise, the salesforce may be doing things that run counter to the product's long-term best interests.

## What Kinds of Personal Selling Are Needed?

If a firm has too few salespeople, or the wrong kind, some important personal-selling tasks may not be completed. And having too many salespeople, or the wrong kind, wastes money. A sales manager needs to find a good balance—the right number and the right kind of salespeople. This balance may change over time with other changes in strategy or the market environment; that's why many firms have been restructuring their salesforces.

One of the difficulties of determining the right number and kind of salespeople is that every sales job is different. While an engineer or accountant can look forward to fairly specific duties, the salesperson's job changes constantly. However, there are three basic types of sales tasks. This gives us a starting point for understanding what selling tasks need to be done and how many people are needed to do them.

The three basic sales tasks are order getting, order taking, and supporting. For convenience, we'll describe salespeople by these terms referring to their primary task, although one person may do all three tasks in some situations.

**order getters**
Salespeople concerned with establishing relationships with new customers and developing new business

**order getting**
Seeking possible buyers with a well-organized sales presentation designed to sell a good, service, or idea

### Order Getters Develop New Business Relationships

**Order getters** are concerned with establishing relationships with new customers and developing new business. **Order getting** means seeking possible buyers with a well-organized sales presentation designed to sell a good, service, or idea.

Do salespeople in different industries or selling different products need to change their selling approaches when making a sale? If so, how? What qualities remain the same?

Order getters must know what they're talking about, not just be personal contacts. Order-getting salespeople work for producers, wholesalers, and retailers. They normally are well paid—many earn more than $80,000 a year.

**Order getting in manufacturing** Producers of all kinds of products, especially business products, have a great need for order getters. They use order getters to locate new prospects, open new accounts, see new opportunities, and help establish and build channel relationships.

Top-level customers are more interested in ways to save or make money than in technical details. Good order getters cater to this interest. They help the customer identify ways to solve problems; then they sell concepts and ideas, not just physical products. The goods and services they supply are merely the means of achieving the customer's end.

For example, Circadian, Inc., sells high-tech medical equipment. Changes in medicare rules mean that doctors can no longer routinely order expensive tests in hospitals because the costs can't be recovered easily. But the doctors *can* be paid for tests done in their offices—if they have the right equipment. When Circadian order getters call on doctors, they show how the firm's testing equipment can improve patient care and office profits. Reps can often get a $20,000 order on the spot because they can show that the equipment will pay for itself in the first year. The doctors don't care about technical details as long as the machines are accurate and easy to use.[7]

If competitors offer nearly the same product, the order getter's crucial selling job is to establish the relationship and get the company's name on the approved suppliers list. Keeping it there requires constant attention to the customer's needs, and doing whatever is necessary to maintain a mutually beneficial relationship between the supplier and customer firms.

**Order getting in professional service firms** Order getters for professional services—and other products where service is a crucial element of the marketing mix—face a special challenge. The customer usually can't inspect a service before deciding to buy. The order getter's communication and relationship with the customer may be the only basis on which to evaluate the quality of the supplier.

The importance of the timing of order getting is particularly important in professional service firms. Because services cannot be inventoried, orders must closely match the service-producing capabilities of a firm. For example, if a firm can provide 100 hours of service to customers, what happens if the order getters achieve only 50 hours of sales in one week but 150 hours of sales in the next? Even though the average is 100 hours per week, the firm's profitability severely suffers: in the first week, the firm operates at only 50 percent of its capacity, while in the next it has to turn down 50 hours of work.

## Marketing Demo 14–1

### PEDDLING FOR PROFIT

In today's sports-and-fitness-crazed society, selling bicycles shouldn't be an overwhelming challenge. But peddling bikes is an increasingly competitive business, and one that's in a current state of flux. Independent dealers, facing competition from mass-market sporting goods dealers, are experiencing flat revenues. They don't need salespeople to simply take orders—they need them to serve in a consulting capacity and help their businesses grow.

When Joe Shannon joined Raleigh USA Bicycle Company in 1997, he quickly realized this. "I inherited a very good salesforce," says Shannon, director of national sales for the Kent, Washington–based company. "But any salesforce, no matter how good, needs to evolve." Shannon's agenda for his reps: to make them the best and most consultative salespeople who walk through a dealer's door—period. Raleigh sells primarily to independent bike dealers, thus, "our salesforce needs not only to understand the technical side of a bicycle, but also to possess business acumen," he says. That means knowing everything about the bikes as well as knowing something about accounting and inventory—competencies that will help dealers run their businesses better and "create a value-added partnership between ourselves and our dealers."

Even with 18 years of experience in sales, Herb Hart, a top Raleigh rep based in New York, felt the training taught him to listen to the needs of his dealers better and ask more qualifying questions. "Joe was trying to invest in the salesforce—everyone benefits by that," he says. "When we came out of the training, as a company we were more focused."

Consider that a goal achieved. Since the training took place last February, Raleigh has doubled the number of dealers brought on board and increased sales 35 percent at a time when industry growth is 3 percent or less. Shannon credits training with the improvement, explaining, "nothing has really changed in terms of how good our bikes are." What has changed is the way his salespeople sell. "They took what they learned and applied it," he says. "Our dealers are sensing that there's a new salesforce walking through their doors."[8]

**Order getting in business markets** An order getter in business markets needs the know-how to help solve customers' problems. Often the order getter needs to understand a customer's whole business as well as technical details about the product and its applications. This is especially important for salespeople whose customers are producers. As shown in Marketing Demo 14-1, firms often give special training to business-trained post-secondary graduates in order to have technically competent order getters. Such salespeople can then work intelligently with their specialist customers. In fact, they may be more expert in their narrow specialty than anyone they encounter, so they provide a unique service. For example, a salesperson for automated manufacturing equipment must understand everything about a prospect's production process as well as the technical details of converting to computer-controlled equipment.

**Order getting in wholesale markets** Agent intermediaries often are order getters—particularly the more aggressive manufacturers' agents and brokers. They face the same tasks as producers' order getters. Unfortunately for them, once the order getting is done and the customers become established and loyal, producers may try to eliminate the agents and save money by using their own order takers.

Progressive merchant wholesaler sales reps are developing into consultants and store advisers rather than just order takers. Such order getters may become retailers' partners in the job of moving goods from the wholesale warehouse through the retail store to consumers. These order getters almost become a part of the retailer's staff. They help plan displays, write orders, and conduct demonstrations. In addition, working alongside the retailer, they often are involved in planning advertising, special promotions, and other retailing activities.

**Order getting in retail markets** Convincing consumers about the value of products they haven't seriously considered takes a high level of personal-selling ability.

Producers sometimes aid in the personal-selling effort by providing innovative displays that communicate not only the features but also the benefits of their products. To help salespeople explain the benefits of its new Profile washer and dryer, GE places this interactive display in dealers' stores.



Order getters for unsought products must help customers see how a new product can satisfy needs now being filled by something else. Early order getters for microwave ovens, for example, faced a tough job. They had to convince skeptical customers that this new kind of cooking was safe and that it would be more convenient than traditional approaches once the customer got used to it.

Without order getters, many of the products we now rely on—ranging from mutual funds to air conditioners—might have died in the market-introduction stage. The order getter helps bring products out of the introduction stage into the market-growth stage. Without sales and profits in the early stages, the product may fail—and never be offered again.

Order getters are also helpful for selling *heterogeneous* shopping products. Consumers shop for many of these items on the basis of price and quality. They welcome useful information. Thoughtful advice, based on an understanding of the consumer and a thorough knowledge of the product and its alternatives, may really help consumers and bring profits to the salesperson and retailer.

## Order Takers Nurture Relationships to Keep the Business Coming

**order takers**

Salespeople who sell to regular or established customers, complete most sales transactions, and maintain relationships with customers

**order taking**

The routine completion of sales made regularly to target customers

**Order takers** sell to regular or established customers, complete most sales transactions, and maintain relationships with their customers. After a customer becomes interested in a firm's products through an order getter or supporting salesperson, or through advertising or sales promotion, an order taker usually answers any final questions and completes the sale. **Order taking** is the routine completion of sales made regularly to the target customers. The routine completion of sales usually requires ongoing follow-up with the customer, to make certain that the customer is totally satisfied and that the relationship will continue in the future. Order-taking is extremely important. Many firms lose sales just because no one ever asks for the order and closes the sale.

**Order taking in manufacturing** Once industrial, wholesale, or retail accounts are established, regular follow-up is necessary. Order takers work on improving the whole relationship with the customer, not just on completing a single sale. Even if computers handle routine reorders, someone has to explain details, make adjustments, handle complaints, explain or negotiate new prices and terms, place sales

Good retail order takers can play an important role in building good relations with customers. What is the value of having a good relationship with a customer?

promotion materials, and keep customers informed of new developments. Someone may have to train customers' employees to use machines or products. In sales to intermediaries, someone may have to train wholesalers' or retailers' salespeople. All of these activities are part of the order taker's job. And a failure in meeting a customer's expectations on any of these activities might jeopardize the relationship and future sales.

Firms sometimes use order-taking jobs to train potential order getters and managers. Such jobs give them an opportunity to meet key customers and to better understand their needs. And, frequently, they run into some order-getting opportunities.

Order takers who are alert to order-getting opportunities can make the big difference in generating new sales. Bank of America recognizes the opportunities. At most banks, tellers are basically order takers and service providers. When a customer comes in to make a deposit or cash a cheque, the teller provides the needed service and that's it. In contrast, Bank of America encourages its tellers to help get new business. Its tellers are trained to ask customers if they have ever considered investing in one of the bank's guaranteed investment certificates or if they would like to learn more about a home equity loan. They give the interested customers sales literature about various financial services and ask if the customer would like to speak with a customer service representative.[9]

**Order taking in wholesaling** While producers' order takers usually handle relatively few items—and sometimes even a single item—wholesalers' order takers may sell 125,000 items or more. They have so many items that they can't possibly give aggressive sales effort to many—except perhaps newer or more profitable items. There are just too many items to single any out for special attention.

The wholesale order taker's main job is to maintain close contact with customers, perhaps once a week, and fill any needs that develop. Sometimes such order takers almost become part of the organization of the producer or retailer customers they serve. Some retailers leave it to the salesperson to decide how all of the brands in a product category, including those of competing producers, should be promoted. Obviously, this relationship of trust cannot be abused. The order taker normally checks to be sure the company fills the order promptly and accurately. The order taker also handles any adjustments or complaints and generally acts as a liaison between the company and its customers.

**Order taking in retail markets** Order-taking may be almost mechanical at the retail level—for example, at the supermarket checkout counter. Even so, retail order takers play a vital role in a retailer's marketing mix. Customers expect prompt and friendly service. They will find a new place to shop, or to do their banking or have their car serviced, rather than deal with a salesclerk who is rude or acts annoyed by having to complete a sale.

Some retail clerks are poor order takers because they aren't paid much—often only the minimum wage. But they may be paid little because they do little. In any case, order-taking at the retail level appears to be declining in quality. And there will probably be far fewer such jobs in the future as more marketers make adjustments in their mixes and turn to self-service selling. Checkout counters now have automated electronic scanning equipment that reads price codes directly from packages. Some supermarkets use systems where customers do their own scanning and then pay with a credit card. Other companies, such as Toronto-based Grocery Gateway (www.grocerygateway.com), have transferred grocery shopping into an online experience. This also eliminates the need for order takers on a retail level.



## Supporting Salesforce Informs and Promotes in the Channel

**supporting salespeople**
Salespeople who help the order-oriented salespeople but don't try to get orders themselves

**Supporting salespeople** help the order-oriented salespeople—but they don't try to get orders themselves. Their activities are aimed at enhancing the relationship with the customer and getting sales in the long run. For the short run, however, they are ambassadors of goodwill who may provide specialized services and information. Almost all supporting salespeople work for producers or intermediaries who do this supporting work for producers. There are two types of supporting salespeople: missionary salespeople and technical specialists.

**missionary salespeople**
Supporting salespeople who work for producers, calling on their intermediaries and their customers

**Missionary salespeople** **Missionary salespeople** are supporting salespeople who work for producers—calling on their intermediaries and their customers. They try to develop goodwill and stimulate demand, help the intermediaries train their salespeople, and often take orders for delivery by the intermediaries. Missionary salespeople are sometimes called merchandisers or detailers.

Producers who rely on merchant wholesalers or e-commerce to obtain widespread distribution often use missionary salespeople. The sales rep can give a promotion boost to a product that otherwise wouldn't get much attention because it's just one of many. A missionary salesperson for Vicks' cold-remedy products, for example, might visit pharmacists during the cold season and encourage them to use a special end-of-aisle display for Vicks' cough syrup—and then help set it up. The wholesaler that supplies the drugstore would benefit from any increased sales, but might not take the time to urge use of the special display.

An imaginative missionary salesperson can double or triple sales. Naturally, this doesn't go unnoticed. Missionary sales jobs are often a route to order-oriented jobs. In fact, this position is often used as a training ground for new salespeople. Recent college grads are often recruited for these positions.

**technical specialists**
Supporting salespeople who provide technical assistance to order-oriented salespeople

**Technical specialists** **Technical specialists** are supporting salespeople who provide technical assistance to order-oriented salespeople. Technical specialists usually are science or engineering graduates with the know-how to understand the customer's applications and explain the advantages of the company's product. They are usually more skilled in showing the technical details of their product than in trying to persuade customers to buy it. Before the specialist's visit, an order getter probably has stimulated

The Clorox sales team responsible for the launch of liquid bleach in the Brazilian market drew on people from R&D, marketing, and sales

interest. The technical specialist provides the details. The order getter usually completes the sale—but only after the customer's technical people give their approval.

### Team Selling

**team selling**

When different sales reps work together on a specific account

We have described three sales tasks—order getting, order taking, and supporting. However, a particular salesperson might be given two, or all three, of these tasks. Ten percent of a particular job may be order getting, 80 percent order taking, and the additional 10 percent supporting. Another company might have many different people handling the different sales tasks. This can lead to **team selling**—when different sales reps work together on a specific account. Sometimes one or more of the sales reps on a team may not be from the sales department at all. If improving the relationship with the customer calls for technical support from the quality control manager, then that person becomes a part of the team, at least temporarily.

Producers of high-ticket items often use team selling. AT&T uses team selling to sell office communications systems for a whole business. Different specialists handle different parts of the job, but the whole team coordinates its efforts to achieve the desired result.[10]

Strategy planners need to specify what types of selling tasks the salesforce will handle. Once the tasks are specified, the sales manager needs to assign responsibility for individual sales jobs so that the tasks are completed and the personal-selling objectives achieved.

## Factors Affecting Salesforce Structure and Organization

A sales manager must organize the salesforce so that all the necessary tasks are done well. A large organization might have different salespeople specializing by different selling tasks *and* by the target markets they serve.

Sales managers often divide salesforce responsibilities based on the type of customer involved. For example, Bigelow—a company that makes quality carpet for homes and office buildings—divided its salesforce into two groups of specialists. Some Bigelow salespeople call only on architects to help them choose the best type of carpet for new office buildings. These reps know all the technical details, such as how well a certain carpet fibre will wear or its effectiveness in reducing noise from office equipment. Often no selling is involved, because the architect only suggests specifications and doesn't actually buy the carpet. Other Bigelow salespeople call on retail carpet stores. These reps encourage the store manager to keep a variety of Bigelow carpets in stock. They also introduce new products, help train the store's salespeople, and try to solve any problems that occur.

It's up to sales and marketing management to be sure that salespeople know what they're supposed to do and how to do it. Hewlett-Packard Co. recently faced this problem. For years the company was organized into divisions based on different product lines—printers, network servers, and the like. However, sales reps who specialized in the products of one division often couldn't compete well against firms that could offer customers total solutions to computing problems. When a new top executive came in and reorganized the company, all sales reps needed a clear view of what their new responsibilities would be, how they would be organized, and what they should say to their customers about the benefits of the reorganization.[11]

## The Effect of Account Size

Very large customers often require special selling effort—and relationships with them are treated differently. Moen, a maker of plumbing fixtures, has a regular salesforce to call on building-material wholesalers and an elite **major accounts salesforce** that sells directly to large accounts.

**major accounts salesforce**
An elite salesforce that sells directly to large accounts

You can see why this sort of special attention is justified when you consider Procter & Gamble's relationship with Wal-Mart. Although P&G is an international powerhouse, its total sales in every country except the U.S. and Germany add up to less than its sales to Wal-Mart. That's why members of the P&G sales team that calls on Wal-Mart live in Bentonville, Arkansas, where Wal-Mart is based.[12]

While the sales volume represented by large accounts may justify a dedicated selling effort, the sales volume of smaller accounts can make even the cost of face-to-face visits impossible to absorb. Some firms have a group of salespeople who specialize in **telemarketing**—using the telephone to call on customers or prospects. A phone call has many of the benefits of a personal visit—including the ability to modify the message as feedback is received. The big advantage of telemarketing is that it saves time and money. Telemarketing is especially useful when customers are small or in hard-to-reach places.

**telemarketing**
Using the telephone to call on customers or prospects

Many firms are finding that a telemarketing salesforce can build profitable relationships with customers it might otherwise have to ignore altogether. Telemarketing is also important when many prospects have to be contacted to reach one that is actually interested in buying. In these situations, telemarketing may be the only economical approach. On the other hand, many people object to the growing number of uninvited solicitations. The high-pressure tactics of some telemarketers have resulted in the Canadian government proposing changes to the Competition Act to regulate this form of selling.

## The Effect of Customers' Geographical Location

Often, companies organize selling tasks on the basis of a **sales territory**—a geographic area that is the responsibility of one salesperson or several working together. A territory might be a region of a country, a province, or part of a city—depending on the market potential. An airplane manufacturer like Boeing might consider a whole country as *part* of a sales territory for one salesperson.

**sales territory**
A geographic area that is the responsibility of one salesperson or several working together

Carefully set territories can reduce travel time and the cost of sales calls. Assigning territories can also help reduce confusion about who has responsibility for a set of selling tasks. Consider the case of the Hyatt Hotel chain. Until recently, each hotel had its own salespeople to get bookings for big conferences and business meetings. That meant that professional associations and other prospects who had responsibility for selecting meeting locations might be called on by sales reps from 20 or 30 different Hyatt hotels in different parts of the world. Now, the Hyatt central office divides up responsibility for working with specific accounts; one rep calls on an account and then tries to sell space in the Hyatt facility that best meets the customer's needs.

### Taking Salesforce Workload into Account

Once the important selling tasks are specified and the responsibilities divided, the sales manager must decide how many salespeople are needed. The first step is estimating how much work can be done by one person in some time period. Then the sales manager can make an educated guess about how many people are required in total, as the following example shows.

For many years, the Parker Jewellery Company was very successful selling its silver jewellery to department and jewellery stores in Western Canada. But top managers wanted to expand into the big urban markets of Quebec and Ontario. They realized that most of the work for the first few years would require order getters. They believed that a salesperson would need to call on each account at least once a month to get a share of this competitive business. They estimated that a salesperson could make only five calls a day on prospective buyers and still allow time for travel, waiting, and follow-up on orders that came in. This meant that a sales rep who made calls 20 days a month could handle about 100 stores (5 stores a day × 20 days).

The managers used a personal computer and a CD-ROM database that included all of the telephone Yellow Pages listings for the country. Then they simply divided the total number of stores by 100 to estimate the number of salespeople needed. This also helped them set up territories—by defining areas that included about 100 stores for each salesperson. Obviously, managers might want to fine-tune this estimate for differences in territories—such as travel time. But the basic approach can be adapted to many different situations.[13]

When a company is starting a new salesforce, managers are concerned about its size. But many established firms ignore this problem. Some managers forget that over time the right number of salespeople may change as selling tasks change. Then when a problem becomes obvious, they try to change everything in a hurry—a big mistake. Consideration of what type of salespeople and how many are required should be ongoing. If the salesforce needs to be reduced, it doesn't make sense to let a lot of people go all at once—especially when that could be avoided with some planning.

### The Impact of Information Technology on Personal Selling

Like most areas in business, information technology is dramatically reshaping traditional practice. There are two avenues through which this impact is felt in personal selling (see Internet Insite 14-1). The first is the use of technology to perform sales tasks. The use of technology removes many of the logistical hurdles faced by salespeople and therefore affects the economics of dealing with accounts of different size and in different locations. The second is the use of information technology to support the salesforce. By providing more information in a more timely manner, the nature of the salesforce workload can be dramatically affected.

**Using information technology to sell** Marketing and sales managers in many firms are finding that some tasks that have traditionally been handled by a salesperson can now be handled effectively and at lower cost by information technology and e-commerce systems. For example, in business markets the nature of the selling situation that the firm faces may influence which approach makes the most sense and how many salespeople are really needed. See Exhibit 14-2.

A salesperson is likely to be required in important selling situations where there is a significant need to create and build relationships. Here the salesperson focuses on tasks like creative problem solving, persuading, coordinating among different people who do different jobs, and finding ways to support the customer. On the other hand, information technology is very effective and cost efficient in handling needs related to the recurring exchange of standardized information. For example, in discussing organizational buying (Chapter 7) and logistics (Chapter 11) we discussed how sellers use e-commerce to exchange information about inventory, orders,

# Internet Insite 14–1

## PERSONAL SELLING USING THE INTERNET

In Internet Insite 11-1 we saw how some companies may be trying to replace salespeople with the Internet. Here, we will explore how the Internet can make salespeople more effective in their roles.

The first aid available to salespeople is the intranet, which essentially is a website accessible only by authorized people within a company. The intranet can include daily news, corporate policies, and up-to-date product and pricing information. Salespeople on the road can easily access the information; in cases where a salesperson works for a long period from a remote location or without frequent interaction with colleagues, an intranet can be a valuable tool.

Intranets can also link salespeople to help them work more effectively as a team. Sales leads and competitive information can be posted and shared, and the company can use its intranet to keep its information on product, pricing, and availability current. The intranet can also be used in sales training. It can include product demonstrations (using multimedia tools), detailed online brochures, downloadable sales presentations, and other training materials.

Compaq (now part of Hewlett-Packard) used an intranet solution for its salespeople called Conjoin (see the exhibit below), which included product information and marketing content management, current events, competitor information, product literature, online reporting, and more. As Joe Batista, director of Internet and enterprise initiatives at Compaq, has said, "It (the intranet) collects, categorizes and assimilates the vital information that our salespeople use to close sales."[14] Compaq's internal studies showed that salespeople were 37 percent more efficient at responding to their clients' specific requests and the company was able to distribute new product or marketing information to salespeople 50 percent faster than before.[15]

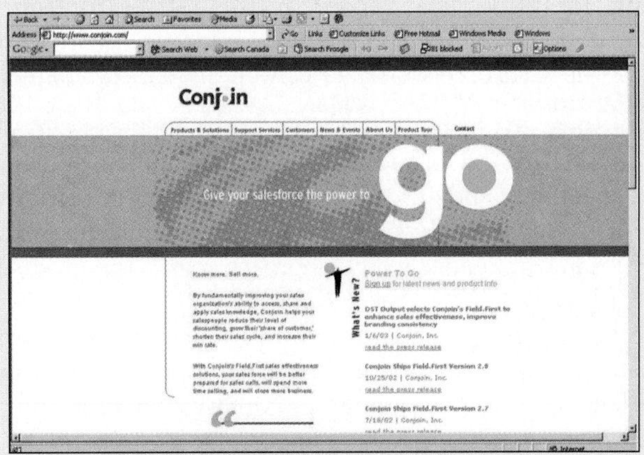


A second Internet tool available to salespeople is online sales leads. There are companies that specialize in providing e-mail lists of qualified buyers or contacts. Dun & Bradstreet (www.dnb.com) provides sales leads for business-to-business sales, with detailed information on prospects (see www.zapdata.com). Hoover's Online (www.hoovers.com) offers the ability to create lists based on user specified search criteria. Both Dun & Bradstreet and Hoover's cover a wide range of industries. There are also specialized firms such as Alansis (www.alansis.com), which provides sales leads for mortgage and insurance brokers. In addition to buying lists of potential buyers, salespeople can also visit the websites of potential customers to learn more about them.

A third Internet tool can be categorized as eCRM (where CRM stands for customer relationship management) and salesforce automation (SFA). At the low end, CRM and SFA tools include just contact management. More-sophisticated products include the ability to track customer history, share information among salespeople, assign sales leads to the right salesperson, and present up-to-date information on inventory levels and prices. Some popular products in this category where you can learn more about CRM and SFA include Goldmine (www.frontrange.com/goldmine), SalesLogix (www.saleslogix.com), Microsoft CRM (www. microsoft.com/BusinessSolutions/default.mspx), Salesforce (www.salesforce.com) and UpShot (www.upshot.com). These products are designed for small to mid-size companies. The current trend in the CRM industry is to provide information through mobile devices, which ensures current information flow to travelling salespeople.

CRM solutions can integrate the salespeople in the frontline with the call centres that also sell or provide support. That ensures that all parts of the organization have the same information and same view of the customer.

Investment in CRM solutions has skyrocketed in the last few years, with the size of the CRM industry estimated at $3 billion in the United States for 2002. Studies show that a big proportion of that investment is not being utilized. Salespeople are not using CRM solutions made available by their companies. According to one study 42 percent of the investment in CRM products is not utilized.[16] Why is this the case if all this technology is supposed to help salespeople?

Notice that many CRM and SFA products require information sharing and collaboration. Salespeople are often compensated based on individual quotas and performance, which works against collaboration. That means companies need to examine reward systems and incentives. Other reasons for poor utilization include inadequate training and resistance to change due to fear of technology. In some cases, CRM solutions are very technical and do not address the salesperson's needs.

In conclusion, there are a growing number of information technology tools available to salespeople. The sales process still involves understanding customer needs and finding effective solutions. Interpersonal skills and personal relationships cannot be replaced by technology. Technology, if used appropriately, can enhance the salesperson's effectiveness.

Here is a question to ponder: How can companies overcome resistance on the part of salespeople to the new information technology tools?

Go to: www.mcgrawhill.ca/college/wong
to apply this Insite in an exciting Internet exercise.

and delivery status. Similarly, basic information about the details of product specifications and prices can be organized at a website. Of course, even for these tasks there needs to be some way to provide good customer service when needs arise. A complex relationship that also involves standardized information might involve a mix of both approaches; using technology for standard information frees the sales rep to spend time on value-added communication.

When relationship building by a sales rep is not required and there is not a recurring need for routine information, a firm may be able to meet customer needs best by providing digital self-service. This is basically the role of ATMs for banks—to serve customers who don't want to wait until a teller is available. Similarly, Indigo.ca's virtual shopping carts play this role. But digital self-service can be more sophisticated. Some firms provide "intelligent agents" at their websites. An intelligent agent is a computer program that helps customers solve their own problems. At the L'Oreal Canada website (www.loreal.ca) and the Maybelline International website (www.maybelline.com) a customer interested in purchasing cosmetics can respond to a series of structured survey questions about the type of lipstick or eyeshadow colour or texture the customer prefers, and on what occasion the customer wishes to use the product. Upon completion of the questions, the intelligent agent (or "Beauty Advisor," as it is called on the sites), will recommend products that fit with the customer's needs. Similarly, a wholesaler's website might provide an agent to help retailers forecast demand for a new product based on information about their local market areas.

The total amount of personal-selling effort justified in any of these situations may depend on other factors, including how important the customer is. Further, we've focused on technology that substitutes for personal contact by a salesperson. But marketing managers also need to make decisions about providing sales technology support to help salespeople communicate more effectively (see Marketing Demo 14-2 for Fujifilm's solution).



Exhibit 14-2
Examples of possible personal-selling emphasis in some different business-market selling situations.

Standardized information exchanged on a recurring basis (orders, invoices, delivery status, product information, prices)

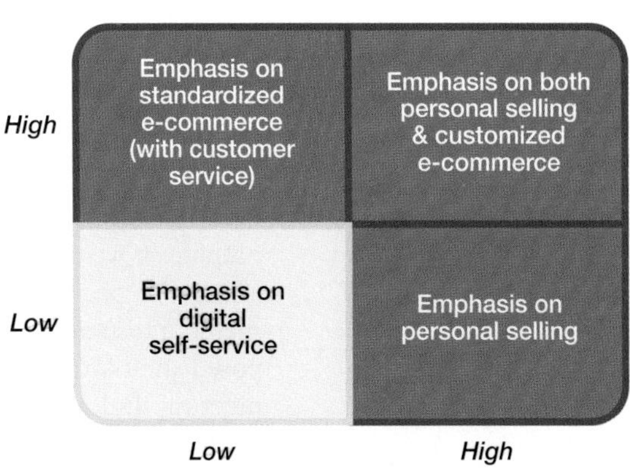


Relationship building required (problem solving, coordination, support, cooperation)

## Marketing Demo 14–2

### FUJIFILM

Lots of companies use websites to communicate with their end-users. But you can also use the Web to effectively provide information to your resellers and dealers for a lot less than the cost of traditional methods like mail, phone, and fax. Best of all, a sophisticated online program can often save your salespeople from travelling long distances.

Mississauga, Ontario–based Fujifilm recently developed two extranets, one for resellers and one for dealers. The extranets not only help these partners locate and contact Fujifilm salespeople, but also enable them to access content and build relationships online, all for a much lower end-cost to the company.

The reseller site, www.fujimediareseller.ca, offers downloadable product guides and online order forms for marketing materials like brochures and posters. In addition, pop-ups customized to each registered user present salespeople's contact information and photos. Sales reps can even customize the messages that appear with their photos.

The pop-ups mimic personal interaction and put faces with names, says Maria Carapina, assistant manager of marketing communications at Fujifilm. "Because Canada's such a large country, our reps can't physically get to all of our customers as often as they'd like," she says. The site provides one-on-one interaction and is convenient for customers who have questions or comments they want to share with their reps, she says.

Meanwhile, only select Fujifilm dealers can access the dealer extranet site ... via a login name and password. They can check for any new promotions or product information, or access information about Internet marketing and industry news. Dealers also can download product shots or logos for in-store flyers. Like resellers, they are greeted with customized salesperson pop-ups.

Fujifilm will monitor the activity on the extranet sites, counting unique and returning visitors, number of page views, time spent on the sites, times of heaviest use, and cities where users are based. "We will use the data to prove to management the value of the site," Carapina says. Calling it "a convenient resource," Cathy Lepiane, product manager at technology products reseller MicroWarehouse Canada in Mississauga, has been using FMm's reseller extranet since May to get product information and download pictures for brochures. She also uses it to quickly get in touch with customers and her Fujifilm sales rep. "There isn't as much personal interaction using the site, but it's a quicker avenue to get the information you're looking for," she says.[17]



**The support role of information technology** How sales tasks and responsibilities are planned and handled is changing in many companies because of the new sales-technology tools that are available. It is usually the sales manager's job—perhaps with help from specialists in technology—to decide what types of tools are needed and how they will be used.

To get a clearer sense of what is involved, consider a day in the life of a typical major accounts sales representative for a large consumer packaged goods firm. Over a hasty breakfast, she reviews the day's events on her laptop's organizer, logs on to the company network, and sorts through the dozen e-mail messages she finds there. One is from a buyer for a supermarket chain. He's worried that his store's sales in the paper-towel category are off 10 percent and wants to know if the rep can help. Working from her home PC, the rep dials in to an online database and downloads sales trend data for the chain and its competitors. A spreadsheet analysis of the data suggests that the chain is losing sales in the paper-towel category to new competition from warehouse clubs. Next, the rep places a conference call with a brand manager and a company sales promotion specialist to seek their advice. She then prepares a written recommendation for the buyer to include and frequently promote larger-size packages of both her company's and competitors' brands in the chain's merchandise mix. She also prepares a PowerPoint presentation, complete with a proposed shelf-space plan, that she will deliver to the buyer on her laptop PC at a later meeting. Before leaving home, the rep e-mails an advance copy of the report to the buyer and prints a colour copy for her manager.

This example uses a consumer-packaged-goods context, but the basic idea applies in all types of sales settings, especially in business markets. Many of today's sales

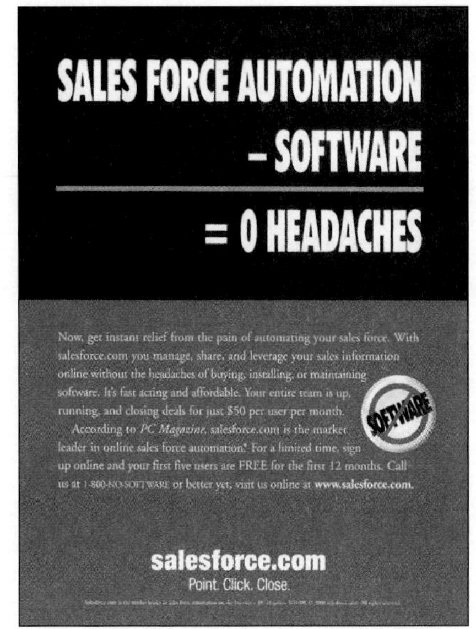

SALES FORCE AUTOMATION
– SOFTWARE
= 0 HEADACHES
Now, get instant relief from the pain of automating your sales force. With salesforce.com you manage, share, and leverage your sales information online without the headaches of buying, installing, or maintaining software. It's fast acting and affordable. Your entire team is up, running, and closing deals for just $50 per user per month.
According to PC Magazine, salesforce.com is the market leader in online sales force automation.* For a limited time, sign up online and your first five users are FREE for the first 12 months. Call us at 1-800-NO-SOFTWARE or better yet, visit us online at www.salesforce.com.
SOFTWARE
salesforce.com
Point. Click. Close.


New information technologies are making the modern salesforce more efficient and giving salespeople communication tools that are creating totally new ways to meet the needs of their customers while achieving the objectives of their jobs.

reps rely on an array of software and hardware that was hardly imaginable even a decade ago. For more, see Marketing Demo 14-3.

The information-technology explosion has put new software for spreadsheet analysis, electronic presentations, time management, sales forecasting, customer contact, and shelf-space management at the salesperson's fingertips. Still new but already commonplace hardware includes everything from wireless phones, fax machines, laptop computers, and pagers to personalized videoconferencing systems. In many situations these technologies are dramatically changing the ability of sales reps to meet the needs of their customers while achieving the objectives of their jobs.

However, the availability of these technologies does not change the basic nature of the sales tasks that need to be accomplished. What they do change is the way, and how well, the job is done. Yet this is not simply a matter of implementation that is best left to individual sales reps. A key reason is that many of these tools

Although technology is only one part in a sales pitch, there are many benefits that come with its use. How can a laptop help in securing a sales deal?

## Marketing Demo 14–3

### SALESPEOPLE WORK SMARTER—WITH THEIR FINGERTIPS

Laptop computers help more salespeople work smarter, not just harder. Salespeople use computers in many different ways.

Without a laptop, it was impossible for a wholesaler's salespeople to master Cincinnati Milacron's product line. Now a computer asks a series of questions and then helps the salesperson figure out which of 65,000 grinding wheels and hundreds of cutting fluids to sell to each metal shop. After adding this system, Milacron doubled its market share—without adding any new salespeople.

Laptops help keep salespeople for London Fog clothing up-to-date when they're on the road calling on accounts. Early each morning before leaving the hotel, the sales reps call into the company's central computer. It downloads to their laptops all the latest information about product availability, prices, customers' accounts, and the like. Later in the day, when a customer has a question about product delivery, the sales rep can answer it instantly—without scheduling another appointment or even calling the home office.

Salespeople for Metropolitan Life Insurance company use laptops to help customers analyze the financial implications of different investments. For example, when the manager of a pension fund wanted to see what would happen if she switched money from one investment to another, the salesperson used spreadsheet software on the laptop to do the analysis—on the spot. The customer was convinced, and the sales rep closed a $633,000 sale.

Herman Miller, the office equipment company, provides dealers who sell its furniture with software that allows their sales reps to do a better job in a variety of tasks ranging from competitor analysis to preparation of realistic three-dimensional graphics that show an arrangement of furniture in a customer's office space. The competitor database provides very useful information about the limitations of office furniture available from many other firms. For instance, a sales rep learned that a prospect was leaning toward buying a competitor's office cubicles. She got back on track when the database revealed that the cubicles had no electrical outlets.

Results like these explain why the number of companies equipping salespeople with laptops is growing so rapidly. New laptops that feature built-in DVD drives (to handle massive amounts of information, including full-motion video for demonstrations and presentations), wireless Internet access, and the power to handle e-commerce applications are attracting even more attention.[18]



may be necessary just to compete effectively. If competitors have the tools and they can do a better job of meeting customers' needs and providing service, a sales manager may have no choice. For example, if a customer expects a sales rep to access data on past sales and provide an updated sales forecast for the next three months, a sales organization that does not have this capability will be at a real disadvantage in getting or keeping that customer's business.

Moreover, many sales technologies must be in place for the whole sales organization in order for the system to work properly. For example, it doesn't do as much good for a salesperson to be able to use a laptop computer to dial in to the company if the data the rep needs are not available online and up-to-date in a format that makes it easy for the rep to analyze them.

On the other hand, these tools have associated costs. There is an obvious expense of buying the technology. But there is also the time cost of keeping everyone up-to-date on how to use it. Often that is not a simple matter. Some salespeople who have done the sales job well for a long time "the old-fashioned way" resent being told that they have to change what they are doing—even if it's what customers expect. And the flip side of that is that some customers don't want to deal with anything electronic. They don't want e-mail, spreadsheets, or faxes. They want personal attention. And to them, personal attention means a voice and face that they recognize. In some cases that means that the technology is a tool in the background. It is not seen or felt but its positive impact can be observed. Of course, if a firm expects salespeople to be able to use these technologies then that requirement needs to be included in selecting and training people for the job.[19]

## Salesforce Selection and Training

It is important to hire good, well-qualified salespeople. But the selection in many companies is a hit-or-miss affair—done without serious thought about exactly what kind of person the firm needs. Managers may hire friends and relations, or whoever is available, because they feel that the only qualifications for sales jobs are a friendly personality and nice appearance. This approach leads to poor sales and costly salesforce turnover.

Progressive companies are more careful. They constantly update a list of possible job candidates. They invite applications at the company's website. They schedule candidates for multiple interviews with various executives, do thorough background checks, and even use psychological tests. Unfortunately, such techniques can't guarantee success. But a systematic approach based on several different inputs results in a better salesforce.

### The Need for Detailed Job Descriptions

One problem in selecting salespeople is that two different sales jobs with identical titles may involve very different selling tasks and require different skills. A carefully prepared job description helps avoid this problem.

**job description**
A written statement of what a salesperson is expected to do

A **job description** is a written statement of what a salesperson is expected to do. It might list 10 to 20 specific tasks—as well as routine prospecting and sales-report writing. Each company must write its own job specifications, and it should provide clear guidelines about what selling tasks the job involves. This is critical to determine the kind of salespeople who should be selected—and later it provides a basis for seeing how they should be trained, how well they are performing, and how they should be paid.

### Are Good Salespeople Born or Made?

The idea that good salespeople are born may hold some truth—but it isn't the whole story. A salesperson needs to be taught about the company and its products, about giving effective sales presentations, and about building strong relationships with the firm's customers. A study of 100 of the U.K.'s most successful salespeople showed that their body language is significantly more "empathetic and sincere" than other people's; they are instinctively able to be "persuasive rather than pushy" when pursuing a sale; and their sense of timing is more acutely developed than that of their peers.[20]

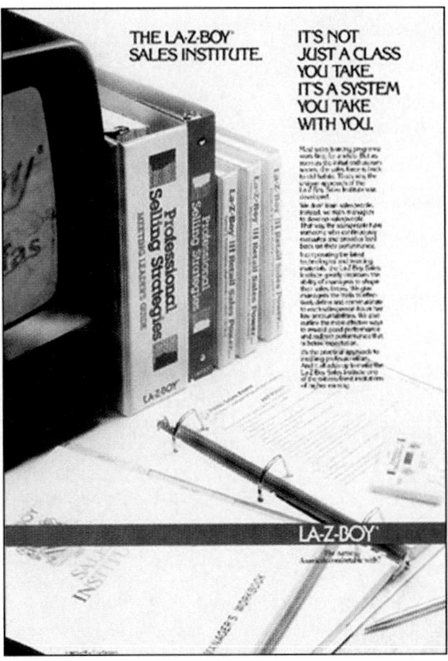


La-Z-Boy operates a sales training institute to help furniture retailers train their salespeople. When would online learning and training be more beneficial than in-house training?

Salespeople often need training to use the information technology that's relevant for their jobs. But this isn't always done. Many salespeople fail, or do a poor job, because they haven't had good training. Firms often hire new salespeople and immediately send them out on the road, or the retail selling floor, with no grounding in the basic selling steps and no information about the product or the customer. They just get a price list and a pat on the back. This isn't enough!

In other situations, salespeople may have some relevant selling experience or computer skills but need to know more about the firm's customers and their needs. Even a firm's own sales veterans may become set in their ways and profit greatly by—and often welcome the chance for—additional training.

### Types of Sales Training

The kind of initial sales training should be modified based on the experience and skills of the group involved. But the company's sales training program should cover at least the following areas: (1) company policies and practices, (2) product information, (3) building relationships with customer firms, and (4) professional selling skills.

Many companies spend the bulk of their training time on product information and company policy. They neglect training in selling techniques because they think selling is something anyone can do. More progressive companies know that training in selling skills can pay off. Estée Lauder, for example, has selling skills for the "beauty advisers" who sell its cosmetics down to a fine art—and its training manual and seminars cover every detail. Advisers who take the training seriously can immediately double their sales.[21] Training can help salespeople learn how to be more

## Marketing Demo 14–4

### TORONTO STARS—"STARS IN TRAINING"

When it comes to deciding whether to outsource training or develop and deliver it in-house, there isn't a definitive answer, says Jeffrey Goldstein, vice-president of Leadership and Sales Institute in Hartsdale, New York. One advantage of running a program yourself: You have the benefit of your leadership. Presumably, you have sales staff buy-in, Goldstein says. The *Toronto Star* managed to get that kind of buy-in by training its 80 salespeople with a combination of in-house and outsourced training. Pat O'Connor, the *Star*'s manager of training and development, and Frank Bourjot, director of advertising, wanted a program that would help reps increase revenue, lineage, and market share as well as establish closer relationships with clients, building a greater degree of commitment and trust. But they had neither the time nor the inclination to create such a program from scratch.

So the company looked to The Forum Corporation to develop a three-day sales training program. Together, the two companies pinpointed five major sales competencies in which *Star* reps needed training: knowledge base, customer-focused relationships, account management, teamwork, and partnership account relationships (building partnerships). During three days in the spring of 1997, reps were asked to develop target accounts; in the fall of 1998 a one-day follow-up session was held to reinforce the training and check on salespeople's progress on those accounts. "We were saying, we want you to build [the] skills that will help you get the business," O'Connor says. "Lots of people came back with success stories."

But what made the training different, and what made it especially successful, in O'Connor's opinion, was that it was delivered by four hand-picked *Star* employees—not by Forum trainers. "We felt [our own employees] would have a better sense of the salespeople's issues," O'Connor says. "Oftentimes an outside instructor doesn't have a sense of how those skills will be applied."

Jeff Fry, a salesperson who was promoted to advertising sales manager just before the training took place, was one of those chosen to teach his co-workers. The experience proved especially valuable for him, because in addition to requiring him to master the competencies he was teaching, it gave him the opportunity to strengthen his presentation, coaching, and mentoring skills—all of which would play a vital role in his success as a new manager. "I viewed it as a challenge," he says, "something I would be able to grow from."[22]

effective in cold calls on new prospects, in listening carefully to identify a customer's real objections, and in closing the sale. Training can also help a salesperson better analyze why present customers buy from the company, why former customers now buy from competitors, and why some prospects remain only prospects. Later in this chapter, we'll talk about some key ideas in this area—especially those related to different kinds of sales presentations.

Training on selling techniques often starts in the classroom with lectures, case studies, and videotaped trial presentations and demonstrations. But a complete training program adds on-the-job observation of effective salespeople and coaching from sales supervisors. Many companies also use weekly sales meetings or work sessions, annual conventions, and regular e-mail messages and newsletters, as well as ongoing training sessions, to keep salespeople up-to-date.[23] See Marketing Demo 14-4 for a description of an innovative training program undertaken at the *Toronto Star*.

## Compensating and Motivating Salespeople

To recruit and keep good salespeople, a firm has to develop an attractive compensation plan designed to motivate. Ideally, sales reps should be paid in such a way that what they want to do—for personal interest and gain—is in the company's interests too. Most companies focus on financial motivation—but public recognition, sales contests, and simple personal recognition for a job well done can be highly effective in encouraging greater sales effort.[24] Our main emphasis here, however, will be on financial motivation.[25]

Two basic decisions must be made in developing a compensation plan: (1) the level of compensation, and (2) the method of payment.

### What Drives the Level of Compensation?

Three factors influence the level of sales compensation: (1) the job being filled, (2) the skills needed, and (3) the competition for salespeople. These factors usually work in combination to determine what a salesperson should be paid or even whether the firm can afford to use personal selling.

To attract good salespeople, a company must pay at least the going market wage for different kinds of salespeople. To be sure it can afford a specific type of salesperson, the company should estimate—when the job description is written—how valuable such a salesperson will be. Depending upon the volume and dollar value of potential sales, a good order getter may be worth $50,000 to $100,000 to one company but only $15,000 to $25,000 to another. In such a case, the second company should rethink its job specifications, or completely change its promotion plans, because the going rate for order getters is much higher than $15,000 a year.

If a job requires extensive travel, aggressive pioneering, or contacts with difficult customers, the pay may have to be higher. But the salesperson's compensation level should compare, at least roughly, with the pay scale of the rest of the firm. Normally, salespeople earn more than the office or production force but less than top management.

### Method of Payment

Once a firm decides on the general level of compensation, it has to set the method of payment. There are three basic methods of payment: (1) straight salary, (2) straight commission, or (3) a combination plan. Straight salary normally supplies the most security for the salesperson—and straight commission the most incentive. These two represent extremes. Most companies want to offer their salespeople some balance between incentive and security, so the most popular method of payment is a combination plan that includes some salary and some commission. Bonuses, profit sharing, pensions, stock plans, insurance, and other fringe benefits may be included too. Still, some blend of salary and commission provides the basis for most combination plans.

What determines the choice of the pay plan? Four standards should be applied: control, incentive, flexibility, and simplicity.

**Exercising control** The proportion of a salesperson's compensation paid as salary affects how much *control* the sales manager has. It also affects how much supervision is required. A salesperson on straight salary earns the same amount regardless of how he or she spends time. So the salaried salesperson is expected to do what the sales manager asks—whether it is order taking, supporting sales activities, solving customer problems, or completing sales call reports. However, the sales manager maintains control *only* by close supervision. As a result, straight salary or a large salary element in the compensation plan increases the amount of sales supervision needed.

If such personal supervision would be difficult, a firm may get better control with a compensation plan that includes some commission, or even a straight commission plan with built-in direction. For example, if a company wants its salespeople to devote more time to developing new accounts, it can pay higher commissions for first orders from a new customer. However, a salesperson on a straight commission tends to be his or her own boss. The sales manager is less likely to get help on sales activities that won't increase the salesperson's earnings.

**Providing incentive** An *incentive* plan can range anywhere from an indirect incentive (a modest sharing of company profits) to a very direct incentive—where a salesperson's income is strictly commission on sales. The incentive should be large only if there is a direct relationship between the salesperson's effort and results.

When a company wants to expand sales rapidly, it usually offers strong incentives to order-getting salespeople. Strong incentives may also be sensible when the company's objectives are shifting or varied. In this way, the salesperson's activities and efforts can be directed and shifted as needed. One trucking company, for example, has a sales incentive plan that pays higher commissions on business needed to balance freight movements—depending on how heavily traffic has been moving in one direction or another.

An incentive compensation plan can help motivate salespeople, but you have to be certain that the incentives are really aligned with the firm's objectives. For example, some critics believe that IBM's sales commission plan resulted in IBM salespeople pushing customers to buy computers they didn't need; the sales reps got the sale and income, but then customers who were dissatisfied with what they'd purchased broke off their relationship with IBM and turned to other suppliers. Now IBM is trying to more carefully align its incentive plan with a customer orientation. For example, most IBM sales reps receive incentive pay that is based in part on customer satisfaction ratings they earn from their customers and in part on the profitability of the sales they get. Finding the right balance between these two criteria isn't easy. But many other firms use variations of this approach—because incentives that just focus on short-term or first-time sales may not be what is best to motivate sales reps to develop long-term, needs-satisfying relationships with their customers.

**Preserving flexibility** *Flexibility* is probably the most difficult aspect to achieve. One major reason that combination plans have become more popular is that they offer a way to meet varying situations. We'll consider four major kinds of flexibility.

*Flexibility in selling* costs is especially important for most small companies. With limited working capital and uncertain markets small companies like straight commission, or combination plans with a large commission element. When sales drop off, costs do too. Such flexibility is similar to using manufacturers' agents who get

Exhibit 14-3
Relation between personal-selling expenses and sales volume for three basic personal-selling compensation alternatives.

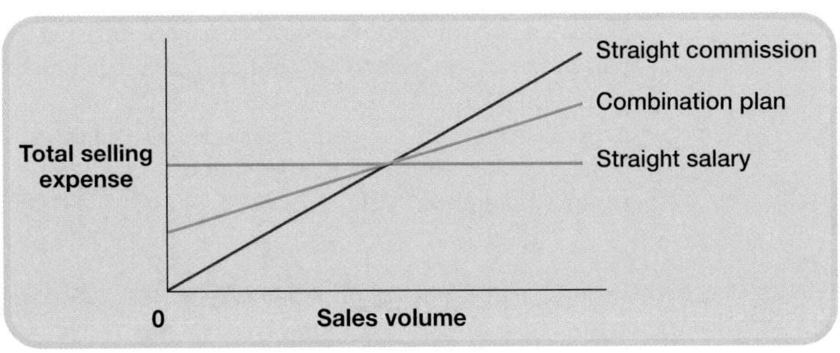


paid only if they deliver sales. This advantage often dominates in selecting a sales compensation method. Exhibit 14-3 shows the general relation between personal-selling expense and sales volume for each of the basic compensation alternatives.

Sales potential usually differs from one sales territory to another, so it is desirable for a compensation plan to offer *flexibility among territories*. Unless the pay plan allows for territory differences, the salesperson in a growing territory might have rapidly increasing earnings—while the sales rep in a poor area will have little to show for the same amount of work. Such a situation isn't fair—and it can lead to high turnover and much dissatisfaction. A sales manager can take such differences into consideration when setting a salesperson's **sales quota**—the specific sales or profit objective a salesperson is expected to achieve.

**sales quota**
The specific sales or profit objective a salesperson is expected to achieve

*Flexibility among people* is important because most companies' salespeople vary in their stage of professional development. Trainees and new salespeople usually require a special pay plan with emphasis on salary. This provides at least some stability of earnings.

*Flexibility among products* is desirable because most companies sell several different products with different profit potentials. Unless firms recognize this fact, the salespeople may push the products that sell best—ignoring overall company profit. A flexible commission system can more easily adjust to changing profit potentials.

**Maintaining simplicity** A final consideration is the need for *simplicity*. Complicated plans are hard for salespeople to understand. Salespeople become dissatisfied if they can't see a direct relationship between their effort and their income.

Simplicity is best achieved with straight salary. But in practice, it's usually better to sacrifice some simplicity to gain some incentive, flexibility, and control. The best combination of these factors depends on the job description and the company's objectives.

One way to increase flexibility and still make it faster and easier for a sales rep to see the relationship between effort and compensation is to provide that information online. For example, Oracle, a company that sells database systems, has developed sales compensation software so its own sales reps can check a website at any point and see how they are doing. As new sales results come in, the report at the website is updated. Sales managers can also make changes quickly—for example, by putting a higher commission on a product or more weight on customer satisfaction scores. The system works so well that Oracle has decided to offer it to customers—and now more than 150 firms use it. Some firms develop their own systems, or just give their sales reps a spreadsheet so that they can keep their own information up-to-date.[26]

## A Final Note on Salesforce Compensation

There are no easy answers to the compensation problem. It is up to the sales manager, together with the marketing manager, to develop a good compensation plan. The sales manager's efforts must be coordinated with the whole marketing mix because personal-selling objectives can be accomplished only if enough money is allocated for this job. Further, managers must regularly evaluate each salesperson's performance and be certain that all the needed tasks are being done well. The compensation plan may have to be changed if the pay and work are out of line. And by evaluating performance, firms can also identify areas that need more attention from the salesperson or management.[27] In Chapter 19, we'll talk more about controlling marketing activities.

## Personal-Selling Techniques—Prospecting, Qualifying, and Presenting

When we discussed the need for sales training programs, we stressed the importance of training in selling techniques. Now let's discuss these ideas in more detail so you understand the basic steps each salesperson should follow—including prospecting and selecting target customers, planning sales presentations, making sales presentations, and following up after the sale. Exhibit 14-4 shows the steps we'll consider. You can see that the salesperson is just carrying out a planned communication process—as we discussed in Chapter 13.[28]

### Prospecting

**prospecting**
Following all the leads in a target market to identify potential customers

Narrowing the personal-selling effort down to the right target requires constant, detailed analysis of markets and much prospecting. Basically, **prospecting** involves following all the leads in the target market to identify potential customers.

Finding live prospects who will help make the buying decision isn't as easy as it

Exhibit 14-4
Key steps in the personal-selling process.

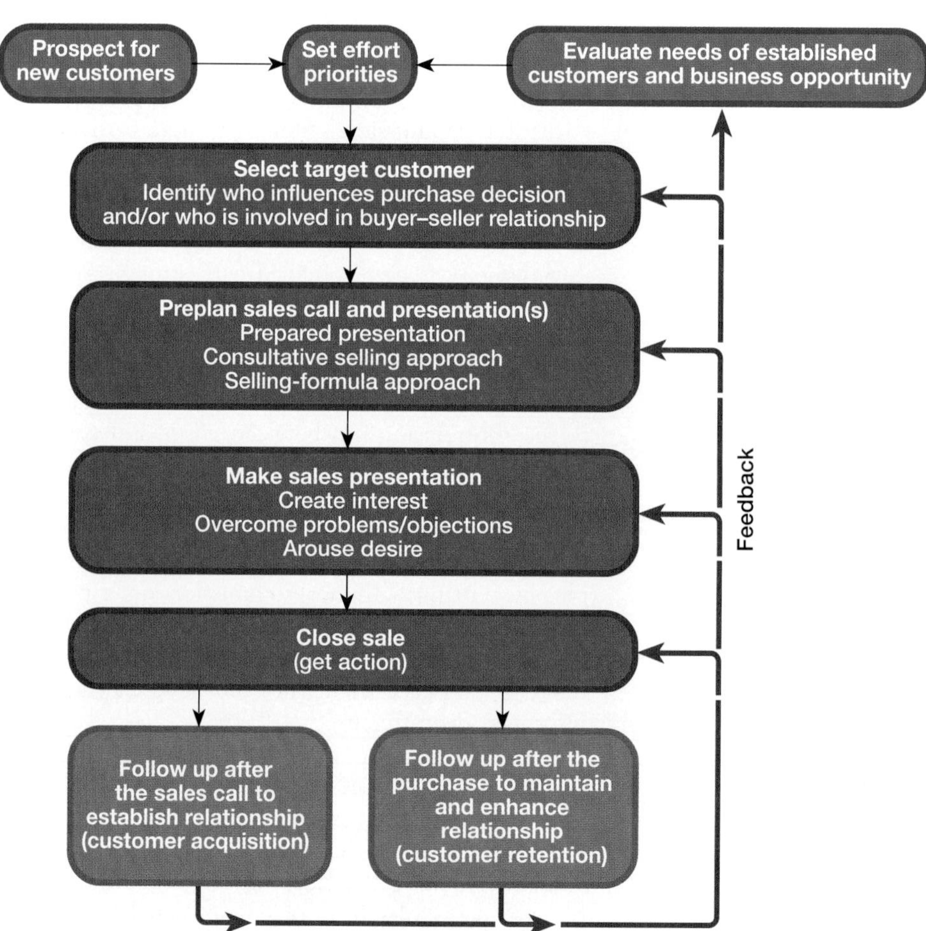

Sales managers are always looking for ways to make their salespeople more efficient and more effective. What are some ways they do this?

sounds. In business markets, for example, the salesperson may need to do some hard detective work to find the real purchase decision makers. Multiple buying influence is common, and companies regularly rearrange their organization structures and buying responsibilities.

Most salespeople use the telephone for much of their detective work. A phone call often saves the wasted expense of personal visits to prospects who are not interested—or it can provide much useful information for planning a follow-up sales visit. Some hot prospects can even be sold on the phone.

Some companies provide prospect lists to make this part of the selling job easier. Inquiries that come in at the firm's website or in response to an advertisement, for example, can be passed along to a sales rep for follow-up. In other instances, a more indirect approach may be required. For example, one insurance company checks the local newspaper for marriage announcements—then a salesperson calls to see if the new couple is interested in finding out more about life insurance.

### Qualifying Accounts

While prospecting focuses on identifying new customers, established customers require attention too. It's often time-consuming and expensive to establish a relationship with a customer, so once established it makes sense to keep the relationship healthy. That requires the rep to routinely review active accounts, rethink customers' needs, and re-evaluate each customer's long-term business potential. Some small accounts may have the potential to become big accounts, and some accounts that previously required a lot of costly attention may no longer warrant it. So a sales rep may need to set priorities both for new prospects and existing customers.

The salesperson usually makes these decisions by weighing the potential sales volume as well as the likelihood of a sale. This requires judgment. But well-organized salespeople usually develop some system because they have too many demands on their time—they can't wine and dine all of them.[29]

Many firms provide their reps with specially developed computer programs to help with this process. Most of them use some grading scheme. A sales rep might estimate how much each prospect is likely to purchase and the probability of getting and keeping the business given the competition. The computer then combines this information and grades each prospect. Attractive accounts may be labelled A—and the salesperson may plan to call on them weekly until the sale is made, the relationship is in good shape, or the customer is moved into a lower category. B customers might offer somewhat lower potential and be called on monthly. C accounts might be called on only once a year—unless they happen to contact the salesperson. And D accounts might be transferred to a telemarketing group or even ignored—unless the customer takes the initiative.[30]

## Sales Presentation

**sales presentation**
A salesperson's effort to make a sale or address a customer's problem

**prepared sales presentation**
A sales approach that uses a memorized presentation not adapted to each individual customer

**close**
The salesperson's request for an order

Once the salesperson selects a target customer, it's necessary to plan for the sales call. This pre-call planning usually involves preparing a **sales presentation**—a salesperson's effort to make a sale or address a customer's problem. But someone has to plan what kind of sales presentation to make. This is a strategy decision. The kind of presentation should be set before the sales rep goes calling. And in situations where the customer comes to the salesperson—in a retail store, for instance—planners have to make sure that prospects are brought together with salespeople.

A marketing manager can choose two basically different approaches to making sales presentations: the prepared approach, or the consultative selling approach. Another approach—the selling-formula approach—is a combination of the two. Each of these has its place.

**Prepared sales presentations** The **prepared sales presentation** approach uses a memorized presentation that is not adapted to each individual customer. A prepared (canned) presentation builds on the stimulus–response ideas discussed in Chapter 6. This model says that a customer faced with a particular stimulus will give the desired response—in this case, a yes answer to the salesperson's prepared statement, which includes a **close**, the salesperson's request for an order.

Exhibit 14-5
Prepared approach to sales presentations.

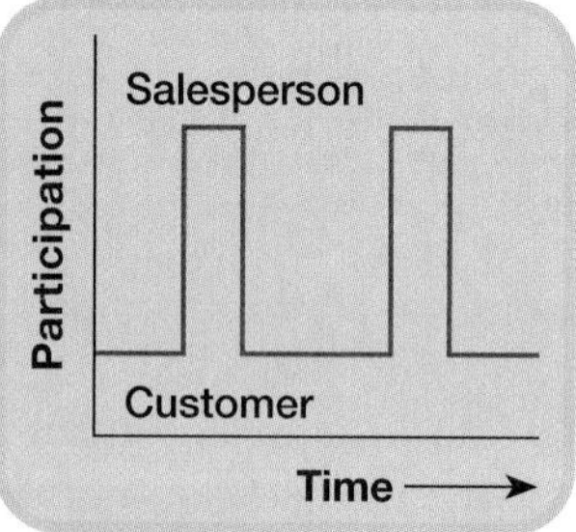


If one trial close doesn't work, the sales rep tries another prepared presentation and attempts another closing. This can go on for some time—until the salesperson runs out of material or the customer either buys or decides to leave. Exhibit 14-5 shows the relative participation of the salesperson and customer in the prepared approach. Note that the salesperson does most of the talking.

In modern selling, firms commonly use the canned approach when the prospective sale is low in value and only a short presentation is practical. It's also sensible when salespeople aren't very skilled. The company can control what they say and in what order. For example, Novartis uses missionary salespeople to tell doctors about new drugs when they're introduced. Doctors are busy, so they give the rep only a minute or two. That's just enough time to give a short, prepared pitch and leave some samples. To get the most out of the presentation, Novartis refines it based on feedback from doctors it pays to participate in focus groups.[31]

But a canned approach has a weakness: it treats all potential customers alike. It may work for some and not for others—and the salespeople probably won't know why or learn from experience. A prepared approach may be suitable for simple order-taking—but it is no longer considered good selling for complicated situations.

**consultative selling approach**
Sales approach that involves developing a good understanding of the individual customer's needs before trying to close the sale

**Consultative selling** The **consultative selling approach** involves developing a good understanding of the individual customer's needs before trying to close the sale. This name is used because the salesperson is acting almost as a consultant to help identify and solve the customer's problem. With this approach, the sales rep makes some general-benefit statements to get the customer's attention and interest. Then the salesperson asks questions and listens carefully to understand the customer's needs. Once they agree on needs, the seller tries to show the customer how the product fills those needs and to close the sale. This is a problem-solving approach—in which the customer and salesperson work together to satisfy the customer's needs. That's why it's sometimes called the needs-satisfaction approach. Exhibit 14-6 shows the participation of the customer and the salesperson during such a sales presentation.

Exhibit 14-6
Consultative approach to sales presentations.

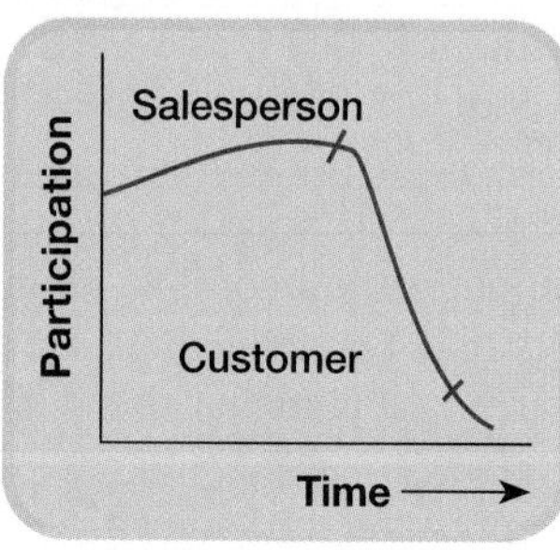


The consultative selling approach is most useful if there are many subtle differences among the customers in one target market. In the extreme, each customer may be thought of as a separate target market—with the salesperson trying to adapt to each one's needs and attitudes. This kind of selling takes more skill and time. The salesperson must be able to analyze what motivates a particular customer and show how the company's offering would help the customer satisfy those needs. An example of this is Mary Kay, a direct-to-home cosmetics company located in Mississauga, Ontario that uses personal consultants to make home or office consultations. According to Mary Kay, "The consultants are where the gold is, and they truly provide real value for the consumer today. Everybody is looking for people to help them maximize their time. To have a personal shopper look after your beauty needs when you barely have time to think of it yourself is a valuable service that makes us stand apart."[32]

The sales rep may even conclude that the customer's problem is really better solved with someone else's product. That might result in one lost sale, but it also is likely to build real trust and more sales opportunities over the life of the relationship with the customer. As you might expect, this is the kind of selling that is typical in business markets when a salesperson already has established a close relationship with a customer.

**selling-formula approach**

A sales approach that starts with a prepared presentation outline and leads the customer through some logical steps to a final close

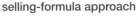

**The selling-formula approach** The **selling-formula approach** starts with a prepared presentation outline—much like the prepared approach—and leads the customer through some logical steps to a final close. The prepared steps are logical because we assume that we know something about the target customer's needs and attitudes.

Exhibit 14-7 shows the selling-formula approach. The salesperson does most of the talking at the beginning of the presentation—to communicate key points early. This part of the presentation may even have been prepared as part of the marketing strategy. As the sales presentation moves along, however, the salesperson brings the customer into the discussion to help clarify just what needs this customer has. The salesperson's job is to discover the needs of a particular customer to know how to proceed. Once it is clear what kind of customer this is, the salesperson comes back to show how the product satisfies this specific customer's needs and to close the sale.

This approach can be useful for both order-getting and order-taking situations—where potential customers are similar and firms must use relatively untrained salespeople. Some office equipment and computer producers use this approach. They know the kinds of situations their salespeople meet with and roughly what they want them to say. Using this approach speeds training and makes the salesforce productive sooner.

Exhibit 14-7
Selling-formula approach to sales presentations.

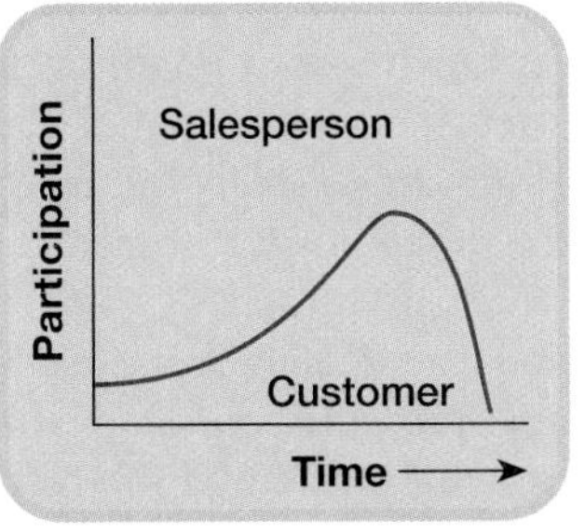

Keebler salespeople use an interactive tool called the Instant Data Evaluation Access (IDEA) Wizard on their laptop computers. It provides research data related to the marketing of cookies and crackers on topics such as shelf-space management and consumer purchase patterns. The sales rep can use the Wizard to support a consultative selling approach in working to develop closer relationships with retailers.

## Ethical Dimensions 14–1

### ETHICAL PERSONAL SELLING

As in every other area of marketing communications, ethical issues arise in the personal-selling area. The most basic issue, plain and simple, is whether a salesperson's presentation is honest and truthful. But addressing that issue is a no-brainer. No company is served well by a salesperson who lies or manipulates customers to get their business.

On the other hand, most sales reps sooner or later face a sales situation in which they must make more difficult ethical decisions about how to balance company interests, customer interests, and personal interests. Conflicts are less likely to arise if the firm's marketing mix really meets the needs of its target market. Similarly, they are less likely to arise when the firm sees the value of developing a longer-term relationship with the customer. Then the salesperson is arranging a happy marriage. By contrast, ethical conflicts are more likely when the sales rep's personal outcomes (such as commission income) or the selling firm's profits hinge on making sales to customers whose needs are only partially met by the firm's offering. But how close must the fit be between the firm's products and the customer's needs before it is appropriate for the salesperson to push for a sale?

Ideally, companies can avoid the whole problem by supporting their salespeople with a marketing mix that really offers target customers unique benefits. However, marketing managers and salespeople alike should recognize that the ideal may not exist in every sales call. Top executives, marketing managers, and sales managers set the tone for the ethical climate in which a salesperson operates. If they set impossible goals or project a "do-what-you-need-to-do" attitude, a desperate salesperson may yield to the pressure of the moment. When a firm clearly advocates ethical selling behaviour and makes it clear that manipulative selling techniques are not acceptable, the salesperson is not left trying to "swim against the flow."[33]



**Choosing the right presentation approach** Most sales presentations follow the AIDA sequence: attention, interest, desire, action. The how-to-do-it might even be set as part of the marketing strategy. The time a sales rep spends on each of the steps might vary depending on the situation and the selling approach being used. But it is still necessary to begin a presentation by getting the prospect's *attention* and, hopefully, to move the customer to *action* through a *close*.[34]

Each sales manager and salesperson needs to think about this sequence in deciding what sales approach to use and in evaluating a possible presentation. Does the presentation get the prospect's attention quickly? Will the presentation be interesting? Will the benefits be clear so that the prospect is moved to buy the product? Does the presentation consider likely objections and anticipate problems so the sales rep can act to close the sale when the time is right? These may seem like simple things, but too frequently they aren't done at all—and a sale is lost. See Ethical Dimensions 14-1 for an overview of the ethics of personal selling.

## Chapter Summary

In this chapter, we discussed the importance and nature of personal selling. Selling is much more than just getting rid of the product. In fact, a salesperson who is not given strategy guidelines may have to become the strategy planner for the market he or she serves. Ideally, however, the sales manager and marketing manager work together to set some strategy guidelines: the kind and number of salespersons needed, what sales technology support will be provided, the kind of sales presentation desired, and selection, training, and motivation approaches.

We discussed the three basic sales tasks: (1) order getting, (2) order taking, and (3) supporting. Most sales jobs combine at least two of these three tasks. Once a firm specifies the important tasks, it can decide on the structure of its sales organization and the number of salespeople it needs. The nature of the job and the level and method of compensation also depend on the blend of these tasks. Firms should develop a job description for each sales job. This, in turn, provides guidelines for selecting, training, and compensating salespeople.

Once the marketing manager agrees to the basic plan and sets the budget, the sales manager must implement the plan—including directing and controlling the salesforce. This includes assigning sales territories and controlling performance. You can see that the sales manager has more to do than jet across the country sipping martinis and entertaining customers. A sales manager is deeply involved with the basic management tasks of planning and control—as well as ongoing implementation of the personal-selling effort.

We also reviewed some basic selling techniques and identified three kinds of sales presentations. Each has its place—but the consultative selling approach seems best for higher-level sales jobs. In these kinds of jobs, personal selling is achieving a new, professional status because of the competence and level of personal responsibility required of the salesperson. The day of the old-time glad-hander is passing in favour of the specialist who is creative, industrious, persuasive, knowledgeable, highly trained, and therefore able to help the buyer. This type of salesperson always has been, and probably always will be, in short supply. And the demand for high-level salespeople is growing.

## Key Concepts

close, p. 438
consultative selling approach, p. 438
job description, p. 431
major accounts salesforce, p. 424
missionary salespeople, p. 422
order getters, p. 417
order getting, p. 417
order takers, p. 420
order taking, p. 420
prepared sales presentation, p. 438
prospecting, p. 436
sales presentation, p. 438
sales quota, p. 435
sales territory, p. 424
selling-formula approach, p. 439
supporting salespeople, p. 422
team selling, p. 422
technical specialists, p. 422
telemarketing, p. 424

## Questions and Problems

1. What strategy decisions are needed in the personal-selling area? Why should the marketing manager make these strategy decisions?
2. What kind of salesperson (or what blend of the basic sales tasks) is required to sell the following products? If there are several selling jobs in the channel for each product, indicate the kinds of salespeople required. Specify any assumptions necessary to give definite answers.
   a. Laundry detergent.
   b. Costume jewellery.
   c. Office furniture.
   d. Men's underwear.
   e. Mattresses.
   f. Corn.
   g. Life insurance.
3. Distinguish among the jobs of order-getting salespeople for producers, wholesalers, and retailers. If an order getter is needed, must all the salespeople in a channel be order getters? Illustrate.
4. Discuss the role of the manufacturers' agent in a marketing manager's promotion plans. What kind of salesperson is a manufacturers' agent? What type of compensation plan is used for a manufacturers' agent?
5. Discuss the future of the specialty shop if producers place greater emphasis on mass selling because of the inadequacy of retail order-taking.
6. Compare and contrast missionary salespeople and technical specialists.
7. How would a straight-commission plan provide flexibility in the sale of a line of women's clothing products that continually vary in profitability?
8. Explain how a compensation plan could be developed to provide incentives for experienced salespeople and yet make some provision for trainees who have not yet learned the job.
9. Cite an actual local example of each of the three kinds of sales presentations discussed in the chapter. Explain for each situation whether a different type of presentation would have been better.
10. Are the benefits and limitations of a canned presentation any different if it is supported with a slide show or videotape than if it is just a person talking? Why or why not?
11. Describe a consultative selling sales presentation that you experienced recently. How could it have been improved by fuller use of the AIDA framework?

12. How would our economy operate if personal salespeople were outlawed? Could the economy work? If so, how? If not, what is the minimum personal-selling effort necessary? Could this minimum personal-selling effort be controlled by law?

13. In selling, how can the customer have faith that the salesperson is selling them the best product and is not just concerned with personal commission?

## Computer-Aided Problem 14

### Sales Compensation

Franco Welles, sales manager for Nanek, Inc., is trying to decide whether to pay a sales rep for a new territory with straight commission or a combination plan. He wants to evaluate possible plans—to compare the compensation costs and profitability of each. Welles knows that sales reps in similar jobs at other firms make about $36,000 a year.

The sales rep will sell two products. Welles is planning a higher commission for Product B because he wants it to get extra effort. From experience with similar products, he has some rough estimates of expected sales volume under the different plans and various ideas about commission rates. The details are found in the spreadsheet. The program computes compensation and how much the sales rep will contribute to profit. "Profit contribution" is equal to the total revenue generated by the sales rep minus sales compensation costs and the costs of producing the units.

a. *For the initial values shown in the spreadsheet, which plan—commission or combination—would give the rep the highest compensation, and which plan would give the greatest profit contribution to Nanek, Inc.?*
b. *Welles thinks a sales rep might be motivated to work harder and sell 1,100 units of Product B if the commission rate (under the commission plan) were increased to 10 percent. If Welles is right (and everything else stays the same), would the higher commission rate be a good deal for Nanek? Explain your thinking.*
c. *A sales rep interested in the job is worried about making payments on her new car. She asks if Welles would consider paying her with a combination plan but with more guaranteed income (an $18,000 base salary) in return for taking a 3-percent commission on Products B and A. If this arrangement results in the same unit sales as Welles originally estimated for the combination plan, would Nanek, Inc., be better off or worse off under this arrangement?*
d. *Do you think the rep's proposal will meet Welles's goals for Product B? Explain your thinking.*

## Suggested Cases

To view the cases, go to www.mcgrawhill.ca/college/wong.

Interested in finding out what marketing looks like in the real world? *Marketing Magazine* is just a click away on your OLC! Visit **www.mcgrawhill.ca/college/wong** today.

# Chapter Fifteen

# Advertising and Sales Promotion

**When You Finish This Chapter, You Should**

1. Understand why a marketing manager sets specific objectives to guide the advertising effort.

2. Understand when the various kinds of advertising are needed.

3. Understand how to choose the best medium.

4. Understand the main ways that advertising on the Internet differs from advertising in other media.

5. Understand how to plan the best message—that is, the copy thrust.

6. Understand what advertising agencies do and how they are paid.

7. Understand how to advertise legally.

8. Understand the importance and nature of sales promotion.

9. Know the advantages and limitations of different types of sales promotion.

## BMW Films

Automotive companies do constant battle to capture an audience of eager players at the right moment in the purchasing funnel who are interested in driving off a lot with a new vehicle. We are all familiar with the commoditized "zero money down, zero percent APR financing" tactics that many traditional auto ads espouse; most every ad touts features and benefits that would sound alike in a blind taste test of vehicles. What then can be the differentiator across brands? Can it be possible for a marketing campaign to appeal to the more intangible and emotive side of a consumer and use nontraditional advertising to do it *well*?

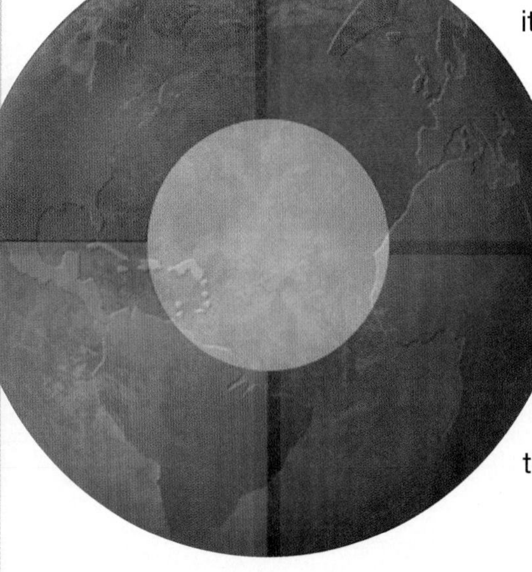

Such was the case in 2001, when the "Ultimate Driving Machine" became the ultimate interactive marketing campaign through BMW Films. Traditionally, BMW had always supported the release of a new vehicle with an advertising campaign designed to

place

price

promotion

produ

reinforce the brand promise of delivering the world's most exciting luxury cars. But in 2000, BMW had a window of opportunity when it could do something purely for the sake of branding—*sans release of a new vehicle*—to deliver a unique message in an increasingly crowded luxury/performance car market.

BMW knew that the average work-hard, play-hard customer was 46 years old, with a median income of about $150,000. Two-thirds were male, married, and had no children. As BMW sliced and diced its market further, an interesting statistic surfaced: Roughly 85 percent of BMW purchasers used the Internet before purchasing a BMW.

Led by Jim McDowell, VP of marketing for BMW North America, BMW embarked on a journey to develop a non-traditional concept to show consumers what makes a BMW a BMW. Combining the ideas of producing a series of short films and using the Internet in an advertising campaign, short films for the Internet were born with BMW Films.

BMW assembled a cast of A-list directors and actors, and developed scripts within the basic framework of having a central character who helped people through difficult circumstances using deft driving skills—in a BMW. The car became the star. Each director who chose a script was then given complete creative control over content and direction, something they would be hard-pressed to find in Hollywood, and something that BMW ordinarily wouldn't allow if filming a traditional advertisement. The result was a series of critically acclaimed films named "The Hire."

Supported with TV spots that mimicked movie trailers, print, and online advertising, the promotional campaign was designed explicitly to drive consumers to the BMW Films website for an entertainment experience found nowhere else.

Never before (or since) had

an automotive company taken such a strong stance to drive consumers to the Web, and the results are compelling. More than 10 million films have been viewed from bmwfilms.com. Nearly 2 million people registered on the site, with 60 percent of those registrants opting to receive more information via e-mail. An astonishing 94 percent of registrants recommended films to others, seeding the viral campaign, and more than 40,000 people voluntarily responded to a survey.

More recently, BMW extended its brand and wildly successful BMW Films effort to the big screen, as part of a promotional effort supporting Microsoft Corporation's new media format, Media 9 beta. BMW was the sponsor for a series of feature-length independent films, the "Digital Cinema Series." While these films present Microsoft with a major promotional opportunity, they also serve as a platform for BMW to show off new additions to its groundbreaking "The Hire" collection. For now, we all sit in eager anticipation for the next chapter of this truly effective integrated marketing campaign with measurable results.[1]



## In This Chapter

In this chapter we look at the tools of mass selling, with emphasis on the two most widely used tools—advertising and sales promotion. To provide you with a sense of how important these activities are to firms, we'll begin with a discussion of the scope of these activities—how much is spent, by whom, and on what media.

We'll then look at the decisions that must be made to develop an advertising campaign. Because many of these decisions must also be made for sales promotion programs, we'll examine these decisions in some detail. These decisions include setting advertising objectives, choosing the type of advertising, selecting media, developing the sales message, and deciding who will do the work. We'll also consider how to measure advertising effectiveness, and legal limits on advertising in an increasingly competitive environment.

Sales promotion will then be discussed. We'll consider how sales promotions affect sales, the various types of sales promotions, and the major problems in managing this important area. Finally, we'll look at the practice of publicity or public relations.

By the end of this chapter you should have a good sense of the issues involved in developing advertising, sales promotion, and public relations campaigns. In addition, you'll have a deeper appreciation of the challenges discussed in Chapter 13 in integrating mass marketing with personal selling.

Throughout the chapter we will be highlighting issues in performing these activities in international markets. While the major decisions do not change, the impact of culture and available media can require some significant adjustments.

## The Scope of Mass Selling in Canada

BMW's mass-selling effort—the carefully planned advertising and sales promotion—is an example of excellent promotion that leverages a great strategy. Indeed, mass selling is often a critical element in the success or failure of a strategy. It can be an inexpensive way—on a per-contact or per-sale basis—to inform, persuade, and activate customers. It can reach a large number of people very quickly and produce a combination of long- and short-term results. It often plays a central role in efforts to position a firm's marketing mix as the one that meets customers' needs and builds brand equity. It can help motivate channel members or a firm's own employees, as well as final customers. As you may recall from Chapter 13, the strengths and limits of advertising and sales promotion are different, but you can see why most promotion blends include them as well as personal selling and publicity.

## Mass-Selling Expenditures

In 2001, Canadian firms spent more than $11 billion on advertising alone. As shown in Exhibit 15-1, more than 25 percent of those funds were spent on television advertising, with just 20 percent being spent on non-classified newspaper ads. This probably is not a surprise. But it is interesting to note that direct mail and Yellow Pages advertising are on a par with radio and almost two times the level of spending in consumer magazines. And Internet advertising, which grew ten times in the period from 1997–2000, showed almost no change from 2000–2001.



Exhibit 15-1 Total advertising expenditures by medium.

**Total Advertising Expenditure by Medium**

| | | $ million | | | | | Percentage of total | | | | |
|---|---|---|---|---|---|---|---|---|---|---|---|
| | | **1997** | **1998** | **1999** | **2000** | **2001** | **1997** | **1998** | **1999** | **2000** | **2001** |
| Newspapers | Daily | 2,397 | 2,475 | 2,526 | 2,685 | – | 25.5 | 24.1 | 24.0 | 24.3 | – |
| | Community | 634 | 764 | 787 | 820 | – | 6.7 | 7.4 | 7.5 | 7.4 | – |
| | **Total** | **3,031** | **3,239** | **3,313** | **3,505** | **3,477** | **32.2** | **31.5** | **31.5** | **31.8** | **30.8** |
| | *of which display* | *1,951* | *2,085* | *2,132* | *2,256* | *2,238* | *20.7* | *20.3* | *20.3* | *20.4* | *19.8* |
| | *of which classified* | *1,080* | *1,154* | *1,181* | *1,249* | *1,239* | *11.5* | *11.2* | *11.2* | *11.3* | *11.0* |
| Magazines | Consumer | 408 | 531 | 541 | 605 | 636 | 4.3 | 5.2 | 5.1 | 5.5 | 5.6 |
| | Business | 344 | 375 | 382 | 397 | 384 | 3.7 | 3.7 | 3.6 | 3.6 | 3.4 |
| | **Total** | **752** | **906** | **923** | **1,002** | **1,020** | **8.0** | **8.8** | **8.8** | **9.1** | **9.0** |
| | *of which display* | *711* | *857* | *873* | *948* | *965* | *7.6* | *8.3* | *8.3* | *8.6* | *8.5* |
| | *of which classified* | *41* | *49* | *50* | *54* | *55* | *0.4* | *0.5* | *0.5* | *0.5* | *0.5* |
| Television | National | 1,290 | 1,423 | 1,425 | 1,448 | – | 13.7 | 13.9 | 13.6 | 13.1 | – |
| | Local | 388 | 398 | 407 | 384 | – | 4.1 | 3.9 | 3.9 | 3.5 | – |
| | Network | 498 | 532 | 528 | 522 | – | 5.3 | 5.2 | 5.0 | 4.7 | – |
| | Other[1] | 228 | 295 | 373 | 465 | – | 2.4 | 2.9 | 3.5 | 4.2 | – |
| | **Total** | **2,404** | **2,648** | **2,733** | **2,819** | **2,938** | **25.5** | **25.8** | **26.0** | **25.5** | **26.0** |
| Radio | National | 239 | 274 | 280 | 275 | – | 2.5 | 2.7 | 2.7 | 2.5 | – |
| | Local | 652 | 697 | 727 | 781 | – | 6.9 | 6.8 | 6.9 | 7.1 | – |
| | **Total** | **891** | **971** | **1,007** | **1,056** | **1,093** | **9.5** | **9.5** | **9.6** | **9.6** | **9.7** |
| Outdoor | | 259 | 294 | 317 | 345 | 362 | 2.8 | 2.9 | 3.0 | 3.1 | 3.2 |
| **TOTAL ABOVE** | | **7,337** | **8,058** | **8,293** | **8,727** | **8,890** | **77.9** | **78.5** | **78.9** | **79.1** | **78.7** |
| Internet | | 10 | 25 | 56 | 110 | 116 | 0.1 | 0.2 | 0.5 | 1.0 | 1.0 |
| Yellow Pages | | 899 | 935 | 975 | 1,000 | 1,040 | 9.5 | 9.1 | 9.3 | 9.1 | 9.2 |
| Direct Mail | | 1,168 | 1,251 | 1,190 | 1,200 | 1,250 | 12.4 | 12.2 | 11.3 | 10.9 | 11.1 |
| **TOTAL ADSPEND** | | **9,414** | **10,269** | **10,514** | **11,037** | **11,296** | **100.0** | **100.0** | **100.0** | **100.0** | **100.0** |

*Note(s):* [1]Includes Specialty and Infomercial advertising. Data for 2001 are estimates. All adspend data include agency commission but exclude production costs.

Exhibit 15-2 Advertising spending as percentage of sales for illustrative product categories.

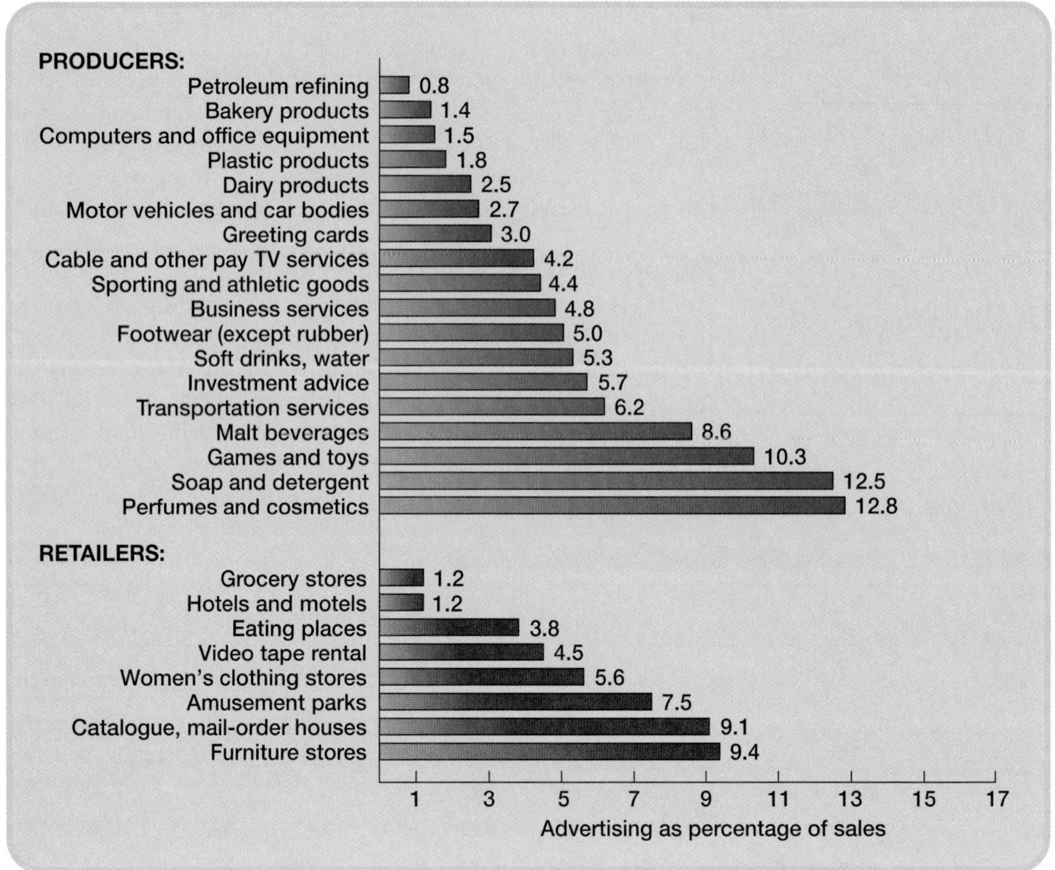




Exhibit 15-1 also shows that, at the national level, the breakdown of advertising expenditures by medium has not changed dramatically over the last five years. However, this does not mean that all firms use these media in equal proportions. As shown in Exhibits 15-2 and 15-3, both overall spending levels and the use of different media vary by industry. These differences do not occur by chance. Rather, they reflect differences in the marketing mixes of the firms in those industries and the strategic decisions of those firms with respect to the role of advertising.

This is perhaps best shown by looking at the expenditures of the top 25 advertisers in Canada (see Exhibit 15-4): a group that combined represents almost 25 percent of total spending. The 10 advertisers from the automotive sector vary greatly in how much they spend on different media. For example, while GM spent 61 percent of its advertising dollars on TV, Toyota spent only 33 percent on this medium but spent considerably more on newspaper and other forms of advertising.

Equivalent information on spending for sales promotions is not available, largely because sales promotion involves so many different activities that it is hard to measure accurately. However, even without hard numbers everyone seems to acknowledge that promotional spending exceeds advertising spending: estimates range from between 54 and 77 percent of communications budgets being spent on sales promotion!

**Why sales promotion spending is high** Companies that sell consumer products that are purchased frequently account for much of that increase. One reason is that they are often competing in mature markets: there's only so much soap, cereal, and deodorant that consumers want to buy, regardless of how many brands are vying for their dollars. There's also limited shelf space that retailers can allocate to a par-

Exhibit 15-3 Top advertising categories, 2001.

Top Advertising Categories, 2001

| | Total adspend | Share of total | | | | |
|---|---|---|---|---|---|---|
| | | TV | Radio | Newsp. | Mags. | Other |
| | $ 000s | % | % | % | % | % |
| 1 Retail | 997,250 | 32.0 | 8.3 | 53.6 | 3.3 | 2.8 |
| 2 Automotive | 918,069 | 34.7 | 2.7 | 56.9 | 3.6 | 2.1 |
| 3 Food | 368,193 | 75.9 | 3.8 | 2.0 | 9.0 | 9.2 |
| 4 Entertainment | 356,793 | 41.5 | 6.1 | 47.9 | 1.0 | 3.5 |
| 5 Financial/Insurance serv. | 319,020 | 39.4 | 7.6 | 39.2 | 8.3 | 5.4 |
| 6 Local automotive dealer advertising | 318,679 | 4.5 | 1.4 | 93.2 | 0.1 | 0.7 |
| 7 Travel & transportation | 241,495 | 15.8 | 4.2 | 68.3 | 7.8 | 4.0 |
| 8 Restaurants; catering services; night clubs | 232,650 | 72.2 | 13.8 | 4.7 | 0.3 | 9.1 |
| 9 Telecommunications | 212,000 | 29.6 | 6.8 | 49.4 | 4.6 | 9.6 |
| 10 Media | 202,271 | 26.9 | 8.0 | 39.4 | 11.8 | 14.0 |
| 11 Cosmetics & toiletries | 170,799 | 60.4 | 1.1 | 0.6 | 33.4 | 4.5 |
| 12 Computers/related products | 156,630 | 14.9 | 4.0 | 61.9 | 17.5 | 1.7 |
| 13 Alcohol & related beverages | 145,725 | 58.0 | 15.8 | 7.4 | 3.0 | 15.9 |
| 14 Government | 115,419 | 56.0 | 10.4 | 22.5 | 3.8 | 7.3 |
| 15 Drug products | 108,361 | 66.6 | 7.0 | 8.9 | 12.9 | 4.7 |
| 16 Internet related sites & services | 108,082 | 44.5 | 7.1 | 41.4 | 4.0 | 3.0 |
| 17 Entertainment equipment | 98,827 | 64.6 | 11.0 | 16.1 | 4.5 | 3.8 |
| 18 Petroleum products & services | 97,564 | 50.1 | 12.4 | 30.7 | 3.1 | 3.6 |
| 19 Lotteries | 88,727 | 50.5 | 11.2 | 31.2 | 0.3 | 6.8 |
| 20 Hair products | 74,280 | 61.0 | 0.5 | 3.3 | 27.1 | 8.0 |
| 21 Publishing | 67,064 | 29.5 | 7.6 | 43.5 | 10.6 | 8.8 |
| 22 Schools; correspondence courses; seminars | 54,502 | 34.2 | 5.5 | 49.5 | 4.1 | 6.7 |
| 23 Household supplies | 45,364 | 81.0 | 1.6 | 1.6 | 11.9 | 3.9 |
| 24 Sporting goods & recreational | 32,478 | 39.2 | 6.6 | 33.3 | 15.2 | 5.7 |
| 25 Personnel; management consultants; accountants | 28,337 | 28.1 | 7.0 | 49.9 | 6.5 | 8.5 |
| **Total 25** | **5,558,579** | **40.0** | **6.3** | **42.5** | **6.2** | **5.0** |
| **Total all categories** | **6,009,829** | **40.6** | **6.4** | **40.8** | **7.0** | **5.2** |



ticular product category.[2] The competitive situation is intensified by the growth of large, powerful retail chains. They have put more emphasis on their own dealer brands and are also demanding more sales promotion support for the manufacturer brands they do carry.

Perhaps in part because of this competition, many consumers have become more price-sensitive. Many sales promotions, such as coupons, have the effect of lowering the prices consumers pay. So, sales promotion helps overcome consumer price resistance.

Changes in technology have also made sales promotion more efficient. For example, with scanners at retail checkout counters it's possible to pinpoint instantly a customer who is the target for a particular coupon. If a customer buys a bottle of Kraft salad dressing, Kraft can have the retailer's computerized cash register print

Exhibit 15-4 Top advertisers, 2001.

| Top Advertisers, 2001 | | | | | | |
|---|---|---|---|---|---|---|
| | | Share of total | | | | |
| | **Total adspend $ 000s** | **TV %** | **Radio %** | **Newsp. %** | **Mags. %** | **Other %** |
| 1 BCE | 115,768 | 35.1 | 12.0 | 43.2 | 4.0 | 5.7 |
| 2 General Motors | 112,684 | 61.2 | 3.0 | 27.8 | 4.7 | 3.3 |
| 3 Government of Canada | 111,324 | 53.3 | 7.5 | 23.3 | 8.8 | 7.1 |
| 4 Procter & Gamble | 93,165 | 72.1 | 0.4 | 0.8 | 25.4 | 1.2 |
| 5 Hudson's Bay | 88,623 | 22.3 | 13.5 | 59.8 | 4.2 | 0.2 |
| 6 Chrysler Dodge Jeep Dealers Association | 88,136 | 20.8 | 2.4 | 76.7 | 0.1 | – |
| 7 GM Car Dealerships | 82,033 | 4.2 | 0.9 | 94.3 | 0.1 | 0.5 |
| 8 Rogers Communications | 75,522 | 34.7 | 13.5 | 39.4 | 6.7 | 5.7 |
| 9 Canwest Global Communications | 71,075 | 21.8 | 5.2 | 61.6 | 2.8 | 8.5 |
| 10 Chrysler Car Dealerships | 66,779 | 3.6 | 0.2 | 96.0 | 0.1 | 0.1 |
| 11 Sears Canada | 63,046 | 18.1 | 11.0 | 69.0 | 1.9 | – |
| 12 Viacom | 60,549 | 47.4 | 6.7 | 42.8 | 2.8 | 0.3 |
| 13 Pontiac Buick Cadillac | 60,349 | 8.3 | 0.9 | 90.7 | – | – |
| 14 Ford Dealers Association | 59,452 | 26.0 | 3.1 | 70.8 | – | – |
| 15 Chevrolet Oldsmobile Dealers Association | 57,409 | 7.8 | 1.1 | 90.6 | 0.3 | 0.2 |
| 16 Ontario Government | 56,475 | 50.5 | 18.3 | 21.7 | 1.1 | 8.4 |
| 17 Wendy's International | 52,165 | 75.5 | 11.0 | 2.5 | 0.8 | 10.3 |
| 18 Toyota Canada | 50,251 | 37.9 | 0.1 | 47.2 | 10.8 | 3.9 |
| 19 The Molson Companies | 50,087 | 64.2 | 12.9 | 8.2 | 0.4 | 14.3 |
| 20 DaimlerChrysler | 49,709 | 56.1 | 2.1 | 25.0 | 12.1 | 4.7 |
| 21 Ford Car Dealerships | 48,791 | 5.2 | 1.2 | 93.2 | 0.1 | 0.3 |
| 22 Telus Corporation | 48,397 | 32.8 | 4.4 | 40.1 | 1.3 | 21.4 |
| 23 IBM | 48,158 | 11.7 | 0.2 | 75.4 | 12.3 | 0.3 |
| 24 Interbrew | 48,035 | 59.8 | 19.4 | 5.7 | 1.1 | 14.0 |
| 25 McDonald's Restaurants | 46,657 | 76.1 | 6.6 | 2.4 | – | 14.9 |
| **Total 25** | **1,704,636** | **36.5** | **6.3** | **48.2** | **4.5** | **4.5** |
| **Total all advertisers** | **6,009,829** | **40.6** | **6.4** | **40.8** | **7.0** | **5.2** |



out a coupon—on the spot—to encourage the customer to buy Kraft again the next time.

Finally, the growth of sales promotion has also been fostered by the availability of more agencies and specialists who help plan and implement sales promotion programs. This trend should continue as the Internet makes it easier for suppliers and buyers of promotion-related services to work together on projects.

## The Special Case of International Mass Selling

The statistics presented so far apply to the Canadian marketplace. They should not assume that the same practices would be found in international markets. While the basic strategy planning decisions for advertising and sales promotion are the same regardless of where in the world the target market is located, the look and feel of advertising and sales promotion vary a lot in different countries. This is due in part

This Benetton ad was banned in Arab states because the tongues were viewed as pornographic. At the same time, it won awards of recognition in both Britain and Germany. What considerations need to be made prior to the launch of an international campaign to avoid cultural barriers?



because choices available to a marketing manager within each of the decision areas may vary dramatically from one country to another and in part because of the impact of different cultures on how mass-selling programs are viewed by target customers.

The target audience for advertising may be illiterate—making print ads useless. Commercial television may not be available. If it is, government rules or censors may place severe limits on the type of advertising permitted or when ads can be shown. Radio broadcasts in a market area may not be in the target market's language. Access to interactive media like the Internet may be nonexistent. Cultural, social, and behavioural influences may limit what type of ad messages can be communicated. Ad agencies who already know a nation's unique advertising environment may be unwilling to cooperate.

International dimensions may also have a significant impact on sales promotion alternatives. For example, in countries with a large number of very small retailers some types of trade promotion are difficult, or even impossible, to manage. A typical Japanese grocery retailer with only 250 square feet of space, for example, doesn't have room for *any* special end-of-aisle displays. Consumer promotions may be affected too. Polish consumers, for example, are skeptical about product samples; they don't have a lot of experience with sampling and they figure that if it's free something's amiss. In some developing nations samples can't be distributed through the mail—because they're routinely stolen from mailboxes before they ever get to the target customer. Similarly, coupons won't work unless consumers can redeem them, and in some regions there are no facilitators to help with that effort. Similarly, some countries ban consumer sweepstakes—because they see it as a form of gambling. Throughout this chapter we'll consider a number of these international promotion issues, but we'll focus on the array of choices available in Canada and other advanced, market-directed economies.[3]

## Basic Advertising Decisions

Exhibit 15-5 shows the basic decisions that every manager must make in connection with their advertising efforts. As the BMW case illustrates, marketing managers and the advertising agencies that work with them have important advertising decisions to make, including (1) who their target audience is, (2) what kind of advertising to use, (3) how to reach customers (via which types of media), (4) what to say to them (the copy thrust), and (5) who will do the work—the firm's own advertising department or outside agencies.

But perhaps the most fundamental decision is whether to use advertising or some other promotional method. In contrast to the flexibility and customized communication available through personal selling, mass-selling devices like advertising present a more or less standardized message and appeal to all who come in contact with it. In addition, while personal selling allows some degree of audience selection at the moment of message delivery, mass selling's ability to choose its audience is defined by the media it selects to carry its message.

These comments might suggest that advertising is an inferior communications vehicle. This is not so, provided we remember that every assessment of a marketing practice can be done only in the context of the target market.

For example, if appropriate market segmentation has been done, the target market's characteristics should be so homogeneous that a standardized message and a personal sales call would basically say the same things to the customer. In that instance, it becomes very significant that the cost per person reached of a sales call can be tens or even hundreds of times greater than the cost per reach of mass selling. In other words, while personal selling may be the ideal in effectiveness, advertising provides equivalent effectiveness at much greater efficiency under the right circumstances. This is the reason why Exhibit 15-5 shows the target market at the head of the chart and the target audience as the first of the five major advertising decisions.



Exhibit 15-5
Strategy planning for advertising.

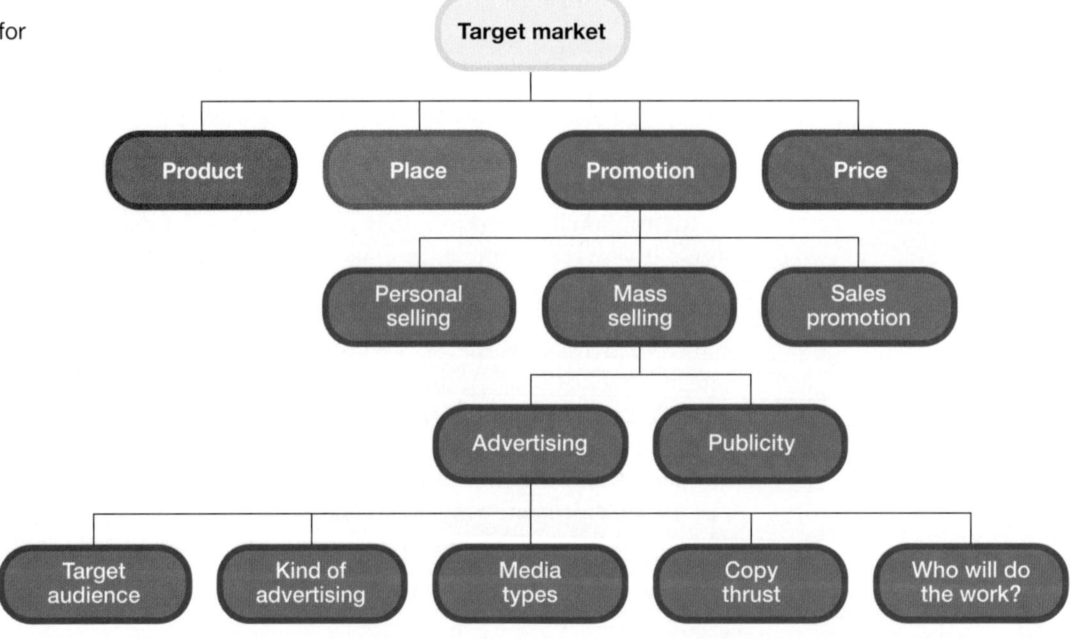

## Decision 1—Setting Advertising Objectives

Every ad and every advertising campaign should have clearly defined objectives. These should grow out of the firm's overall marketing strategy and the promotion jobs assigned to advertising. It isn't enough for the marketing manager to say "Promote the product." The marketing manager must decide exactly what advertising should do and the customer being targeted.

Advertising objectives should be more specific than personal-selling objectives. One of the advantages of personal selling is that salespeople can shift their presentations to meet customers' needs. Each ad, however, is a specific communication. It must be effective not for just one customer but for thousands, even millions, of them. This is why it is so important to know precisely who will be the audience for this communication.

Beyond the identity of the target market, the marketing manager might give the advertising manager one or more of the following specific objectives, along with the budget to accomplish them:

1. Help position the firm's brand or marketing mix by informing and persuading target customers or intermediaries about its benefits.
2. Help introduce new products to specific target markets.
3. Help obtain desirable outlets and tell customers where they can buy a product.
4. Provide ongoing contact with target customers—even when a salesperson isn't available.
5. Prepare the way for salespeople by presenting the company's name and the merits of its products.
6. Get immediate buying action.
7. Help to maintain relationships with satisfied customers, confirm their purchase decisions, and encourage more purchases.

The objectives listed above highlight that a balancing act may be required. The first objective is quite broad and relates to the basic decisions about how the marketing manager wants to differentiate and position the whole marketing mix. That should guide decisions about what other specific objectives are most important. In fact, some of the objectives listed are not as specific as they could be. If a marketing manager really wants specific results, they should be clearly stated. A general objective is "To help expand market share." This could be rephrased more specifically: "To increase shelf space in our cooperating retail outlets by 25 percent during the next three months." As more specific objectives are set—say, for each ad—it's still important that they are all consistent with the overall objectives.

The specific objectives obviously affect implementation. Advertising that might be right for encouraging consumers to switch from a competing brand might be all wrong for appealing to established customers with whom a firm already has a good relationship. Similarly, an ad that appeals to opinion leaders might not be what's needed to get repeat customers back into a retail store. As Exhibit 15-6 shows, the type of advertising that achieves objectives for one stage of the adoption process may be off-target for another. For example, most advertising for cameras in North America, Germany, and Japan focuses on foolproof pictures or state-of-the-art design, because most consumers in these countries already own *some* camera. In Africa, where only about 20 percent of the population owns a camera, ads must sell the whole concept of picture-taking.

Exhibit 15-6 Examples of different types of advertising over adoption-process stages.

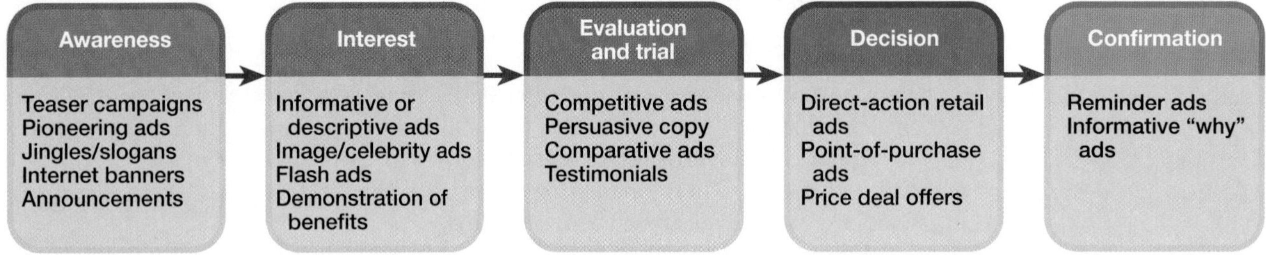


## Decision 2—The Kinds of Advertising Needed

There are two major types of advertising, distinguished by whether they focus on individual products or the overall organization. The selection of one over the other is largely determined by the advertising objectives that have been set.

**product advertising**
Advertising that tries to sell a product

**Product advertising** tries to sell a product. It may be aimed at final users or channel members. Companies that own a wide range of brands and products, for instance, must depend on product advertising. A good example of this is Procter & Gamble, whose products include well-known brands like Tide detergent and Folgers coffee. Each product is advertised individually.

**institutional advertising**
Advertising that tries to promote an organization's image, reputation, or ideas rather than a specific product

**Institutional advertising** tries to promote an organization's image, reputation, or ideas rather than a specific product. It is most widely used in companies branded at the corporate rather than the product level. Its basic objective is to develop goodwill or improve an organization's relations with various groups—not only customers but also current and prospective channel members, suppliers, shareholders, employees, and the general public. The British government, one of the top 50 advertisers in the world, uses institutional advertising to promote England as a place to do business.

### Product Advertising

Product advertising falls into three categories: pioneering, competitive, and reminder advertising. As a general rule, their use coincides with different stages of the product life cycle.

**pioneering advertising**
Advertising that tries to develop primary demand for a product category rather than demand for a specific brand

**Pioneering advertising—Builds primary demand** **Pioneering advertising** tries to develop primary demand for a product category rather than demand for a specific brand. Pioneering advertising is usually done in the early stages of the product life cycle; it informs potential customers about the new product and helps turn them into adopters. For example, Viagra's first advertising campaigns were unbranded public service announcements for erectile dysfunction. Then, with the emergence of copycat brands, Viagra turned to competitive advertising to attract new customers.[4]

**competitive advertising**
Advertising that tries to develop selective demand for a specific brand

**Competitive advertising—Emphasizes selective demand** **Competitive advertising** tries to develop selective demand for a specific brand. A firm is forced into competitive advertising as the product life cycle moves along—to hold its own against competitors.

Competitive advertising may be either direct or indirect. The direct type aims for immediate buying action. The indirect type points out product advantages to affect future buying decisions.

Most of the advertising for Internet access is of the direct competitive variety. Both telephone and cable companies use ads that show their superiority over the other on specific attributes like download speeds. By contrast, advertising for products such as coffee is usually of the indirect competitive type. Coffee makers lay claim to having the product with a better taste, more pleasing aroma, less bitterness, and the like—without ever mentioning the competitors' brands.

The United Way of Greater Toronto's current ad campaigns focus on illustrating real-life success stories. What is the United Way trying to promote here using institutional advertising, and how is the message different from that of a profit-generating context?

" I'm Rene. I had been living on the street for years, abusing alcohol and drugs
Because of the help of an agency funded by United Way, I got off the street ar
back into life. Now, I'm a successful artist with my own business. I'm marrie
and raising a son. I even have a mortgage. Thanks. Your money got to me. "

WITHOUT YOU, THERE WOULD BE NO WAY
WWW.UNITEDWAYTORONTO.COM 416-777-2001

**comparative advertising**
An extreme form of direct competitive advertising that involves making specific brand comparisons using actual product names

**Comparative advertising** is an extreme form of direct competitive advertising that involves making specific brand comparisons using actual product names. A comparative ad for Advil shows pictures of competing pain relievers; the ad copy makes specific superiority claims that it is longer lasting and easier on the stomach. In the same vein, battery ads often show thinly disguised competing brands running out of power while the advertiser's brand keeps running.

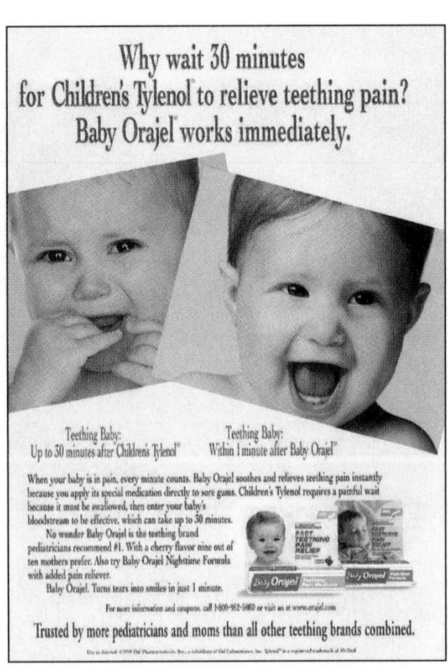

Comparative ads make direct comparisons with other brands using actual brand names. For example, the Baby Orajel ad touts its fast relief compared to Children's Tylenol. This Microsoft ad highlights the features of the Pocket PC compared to its rival, Palm. What are the strengths and weaknesses of comparative advertising?

Many countries forbid comparative advertising, but that situation is changing. For example, Japan banned comparative advertising until about 15 years ago, when the restrictions were relaxed. Japan's move followed an earlier change in the United States. The U.S. Federal Trade Commission decided to encourage comparative ads, after banning them for years—because it thought they would increase competition and provide consumers with more useful information. But this approach led to legal as well as ethical problems, and some advertisers and their agencies now back away from comparative advertising—even in countries like Canada, where it is allowed.

Superiority claims are supposed to be supported by research evidence—but the guidelines aren't clear. When P&G's Dryel did not fare well in independent test comparisons with stain removal by professional drycleaners, P&G changed its ad claims. However, some firms just keep running tests until they get the results they want. Others talk about minor differences that don't reflect a product's overall benefits. Some comparative ads leave consumers confused or even angry if the product they're using is criticized. Comparative ads can also backfire by calling attention to competing products that consumers had not previously considered.[5]

**reminder advertising**

Advertising that tries to keep the product's name before the public

**Reminder advertising—Reinforces a favourable relationship** **Reminder advertising** tries to keep the product's name before the public. It may be useful when the product has achieved brand preference or insistence—perhaps in the market-maturity or sales-decline stages. It is used primarily to reinforce previous promotion. Here, the advertiser may use soft-sell ads that just mention or show the name—as a reminder. Sunkist, for example, often relies on reminder ads because most consumers already know the brand name and, after years of promotion, associate it with high product quality.

### Institutional Advertising

Institutional advertising usually focuses on the name and prestige of an organization or industry. It may seek to inform, persuade, or remind.

Large companies with several divisions sometimes use a persuading kind of institutional advertising to link the divisions in customers' minds. Many Japanese firms, like Hitachi, emphasize institutional advertising, in part because they often use the company name as a brand name.

Companies sometimes rely on institutional advertising to present the company in a favourable light—perhaps to overcome image problems. Firestone, for example,

Buster Brown is a well-known brand with a hundred-year history; at back-to-school time, the company ran print and outdoor ads to remind parents of their positive feelings about Buster Brown shoes. Ads featured a toll-free number or website address so consumers could learn the location of the closest retailer.

relied on institutional advertising after discovering problems with its tires on Ford Explorers.

Some organizations use institutional advertising to advocate a specific cause or idea. Insurance companies and organizations like Mothers Against Drunk Driving, for example, use these advocacy ads to encourage people not to drink and drive.[6]

## The Special Case of Cooperative Advertising

Sometimes a producer knows that a promotion job or advertising job should be done but finds that it can be done more effectively or more economically by someone farther along in the channel. Alternatively, a large retail chain like the Future Shop may approach a manufacturer like Panasonic with a catalogue or ad program and tell them how much it will cost to participate. In either case, the producer may offer **advertising allowances**—price reductions to firms farther along in the channel to encourage them to advertise or otherwise promote the firm's products locally (see Ethical Dimensions 15-1 for more on using allowances).

**advertising allowances**

Price reductions given to firms in the channel to encourage them to advertise or otherwise promote the firm's products locally

**cooperative advertising**

Occurs when intermediaries and producers share in the cost of ads

**Cooperative advertising** involves intermediaries and producers sharing in the cost of ads. This helps wholesalers and retailers compete in their local markets. It also helps the producer get more promotion for their advertising dollars because media usually give local advertisers lower rates than national or international firms. In addition, a retailer or wholesaler that is paying a share of the cost is more likely to follow through.

Coordination and integration of ad messages in the channel is another reason for cooperative advertising. One big, well-planned, integrated advertising effort is often better than many different, perhaps inconsistent, local efforts. Many franchise operations like the idea of communicating with one voice. KFC, for example, encourages its franchisees to use a common advertising program. Before, many developed their own local ads—with themes like "Eight clucks for four bucks"—that didn't fit with the company's overall marketing strategy.

Producers often get this coordination, and reduce local intermediary costs, by providing a master of an ad on a videotape, cassette tape, website, or printed sheets. The intermediaries add their identification before turning the ad over to local media.

However, allowances and support materials alone don't ensure cooperation. When channel members don't agree with the advertising strategy, it can be a serious source of conflict. For example, Benetton, the Italian sportswear company, is known for its controversial ad campaigns, which often raised sensitive social issues

## Ethical Dimensions 15–1

### ALLOWANCE PROGRAMS

Ethical issues sometimes arise concerning advertising allowance programs. For example, a retailer may run one producer's ad to draw customers to the store but then sell them another brand. Is this unethical? Some producers think it is. A different view is that retailers are obligated to the producer to run the ad but obligated to consumers to sell them what they want, no matter whose brand it may be. A producer can often avoid the problem with a strategy decision—by setting the allowance amount as a percentage of the retailer's *actual purchases*. That way, a retailer who doesn't produce sales doesn't get the allowance.

Sometimes a retailer takes advertising allowance money but doesn't run the ads at all. Some producers close their eyes to this problem because they don't know what to do about intense competition from other suppliers for the retailer's attention. But there are also legal and ethical problems with that response. Basically, the allowance may have become a disguised price concession that results in price discrimination, which is illegal in Canada. Some firms pull back from cooperative advertising to avoid these problems. Smart producers insist on proof that the advertising was really done.[7]



through sometimes disturbing images. Many of its franchisees disagreed with the campaigns and stopped paying their franchise fees. A marketing manager should consider the likely reaction of other channel members before implementing any advertising program.[8]

## Decision 3—The Medium to Deliver the Message

What is the best advertising medium? There is no simple answer to this question. Effectiveness depends on how well the medium fits with the rest of a marketing strategy—that is, it depends on (1) your promotion objectives, (2) what target markets you want to reach, (3) the funds available for advertising, and (4) the nature of the media—including who they reach, with what frequency, with what impact, and at what cost.

Exhibit 15-7 shows some pros and cons of major kinds of media. However, some of the advantages noted in this table may not apply in all markets. In less-developed nations, for example, newspapers may *not* be timely. Placing an ad may require a long lead time if only a limited number of pages are available for ads. Direct mail may not be a flexible choice in a country with a weak postal system or high rate of illiteracy. Internet ads might be worthless if few target customers have access to the Internet. Similarly, TV audiences are often less selective and targeted, but a special-interest cable TV show may reach a very specific audience.[9]

### Consideration 1: Promotion Objectives

Before you can choose the best medium, you have to decide on your promotion objectives. If the objective is to increase interest and that requires demonstrating product benefits, TV may be the best alternative. If the objective is to inform—telling a long story with precise detail—and if pictures are needed, then Internet advertising might be right. Alternatively, with a broad target market, print media like magazines and newspapers may be better. For example, Jockey switched its advertising to magazines from television when it decided to show the variety of colours, patterns, and styles of its men's briefs. Jockey felt that it was too hard to show this in a 30-second TV spot. Further, Jockey felt that there were problems with modelling men's underwear on television. However, Jockey might have stayed

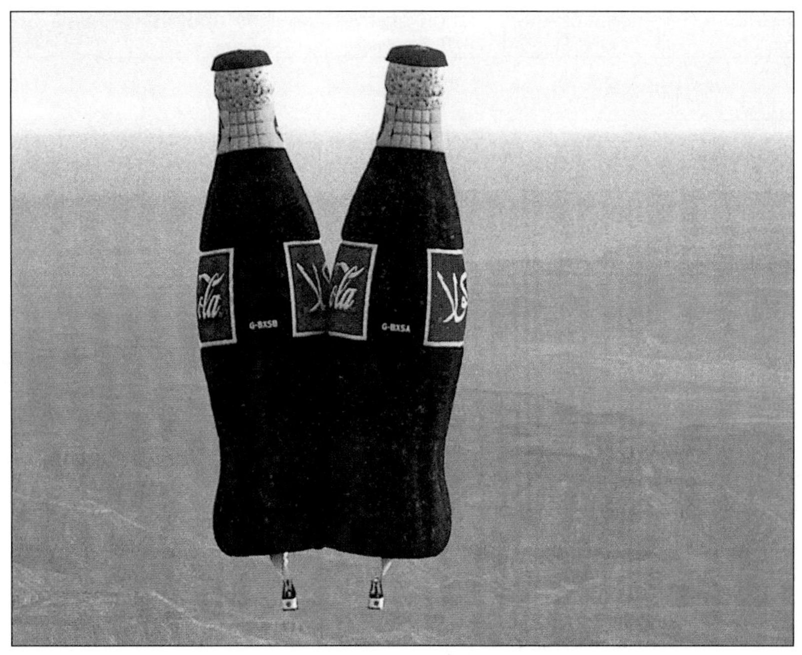

In North Africa and the Middle East, Coke uses hot-air balloons as an advertising medium. What are Coke's promotion objectives? Are they fulfilled through the use of this medium?

with TV if it had been targeting consumers in France or Brazil—where nudity in TV ads is common.[10]

### Consideration 2: The Target Market's Media Habits

To guarantee good media selection, the advertiser first must *clearly* specify its target market—a necessary step for all marketing strategy planning. Then the advertiser can choose media that are heard, read, or seen by those target customers.

The media available in a country may limit the choices. In less-developed nations, for example, radio is often the only way to reach a broad-based market of poor consumers who can't read or afford television.

In most cases, however, the major problem is to select media that effectively reach the target audience. Most of the major media use marketing research to develop profiles of the people who buy their publications or live in their broadcasting area. Generally, media research focuses on demographic characteristics rather than the segmenting dimensions specific to the planning needs of *each* different advertiser. The problem is even worse in some countries because available media don't provide any information—or they provide audience profiles that make the medium seem more attractive than it is.

Another problem is that the audience for media that *do* reach your target market may also include people who are *not* in the target group. But you pay for the whole audience the media delivers—including those who aren't potential customers. For example, Delta Faucet, a faucet manufacturer that wanted its ads to reach plumbers, placed ads on U.S. sports network ESPN's Saturday college football telecasts. Research showed that many plumbers watched the ESPN games. Yet plumbers are only a very small portion of the total college football audience—and the size of the total audience determined the cost of the advertising time.[11]

The cost of reaching the real target market goes up fastest when the irrelevant audience is very large. For example, the last episode of the wildly popular *Seinfeld* sitcom drew about 75 million viewers and NBC charged $1.5 million or more for a 30-second ad slot. It may have been worth that for Visa to reach such a large, mainly adult, audience; it serves a diverse group of customers.[12]

On the other hand, tiny Gardenburger, Inc. used borrowed money to buy an ad slot in a shoot-for-the-moon effort to turn the audience on to its veggie patties. This

Exhibit 15–7 Media characteristics—information on the strengths and weaknesses of media as advertising vehicles.

| | Newspapers | Consumer magazines | Radio | Television |
|---|---|---|---|---|
| Features | Broad information, life-style travel and entertainment, plus highly localized news of community activities through community weeklies. | Special interests and selective audiences. Usually high-quality reproduction. Long life. | Highly varied from hard rock to all talk, easy listening to country and western. A flexible medium. | Mass audience. Highly visible. Ubiquitous medium for instant exposure of pictures and ideas. High impact. |
| Audience | Broad: 60% of adults daily, 82% weekly. Higher among educated, older, affluent consumers. Total coverage with weeklies. | Selective, from hobbyists to investors, athletes to cooks. Also some general-interest magazines. | Varies by station and by time of day. Reaches 94% of Canadians weekly. Per capita listening: 21 hours weekly. Small audiences per program. | Broad; whole family. Varies by time of day but reaches 96% of Canadians weekly. 23 viewing hours weekly per capita. Large audiences per program. 78% of homes are equipped with VCRs, 76% cable penetration. |
| Location | Usually one daily per town; more in larger cities. Weeklies service target audiences, specific neighbourhoods, and suburban markets, and fill in holes not reached by dailies. | Most national, some regional. National magazines often have regional editors. Some are specific to one city. Many offer advertisers regional splits. | All markets. Major urban centres have up to 20 stations. Smallest cities usually have at least several. | Several TV stations in most cities. Many have more than four. Repeater stations and satellite ensure almost universal coverage. |
| Cost | Cost to cover 17 markets with 1/2-page ad in each of 18 dailies: $24,400. | Extreme variations, but a reasonable average is $3,500 for full-page four-colour for local publications. | To reach 40% of the Vancouver market an average of five times per week costs $11,000 to $13,000 weekly. | Costly for top-rated programs: $30,000 per week in Vancouver to reach 50% of the market four times per week. In B.C., $40,000 per week. Production costs can be $10,000 and more. |
| Best way to use | Local medium. Action and sales. Low costs (of media and production) for local advertisers. To convey information and for tie-ins with promotions. Maximum flexibility—size, timing. | Match specific products or product classes with editorial content. | Frequency medium. Selective exposure among pinpointed audiences. On-air personalities, short-term action, promotions. | Broad exposure. Product demonstration. Name identity. Awareness. Image. Lifestyle. High impact. Action. |
| Disadvantages | High cost for national campaigns. Non-selective audience. Limited appeal to young; reading patterns spotty. Short life. Limited readership data for weeklies. | Varies. Some are strong, some weak. Advertising clutter in some publications. Long lead times. Circulation patterns may not match product distribution. | Fragmented audience. Advertising and editorial clutter. Often used as background. | Cost may be prohibitive. Difficult to break through threshold of awareness and keep attention. Production can be extremely expensive. Clutter. Long lead times. |

| Outdoor | Transit | Direct mail | Yellow Pages |
|---|---|---|---|
| Many types, including billboards and backlit posters. Highly visible, good quality on backlits. Obtrusive. Limited applications for many companies. | Interior and exterior panels. Highly visible. Requires concise message. | Increasingly popular. Highly selective and personal. Efficient for narrow target audiences and both small and large advertisers. | Mass medium reaching most users and owners of telephones. Supported by phone company advertising. Readily accessible to consumers 24 hours per day, 365 days a year. |
| Very broad; anyone outdoors. Age, income, sex vary by location, but it's used to "cover the world." | Exterior reaches similar audience to outdoor billboards. Interior tends to cover students and a clerical/sales/technical audience versus business audience. | Completely controlled. Direct-mail lists available from internal and external sources to cover almost every conceivable market. | Qualified prospects searching for a specific product/service. |
| Billboards: anywhere there are cars and highways, especially in cities. Backlits: large urban centres. Restricted locations in B.C. | Anywhere there is a transit system. (In Vancouver, includes SkyTrain) | Controlled by the mailer. | There is a Yellow Pages directory in every market, in addition to specialized editions. |
| $40,000 to achieve a minimally effective billboard campaign for one month in B.C. (approx. 70 posters). Backlits: $8,000 per month in Vancouver for approximately five locations. | Exterior: $10,000–$20,000 to achieve a minimum one-month campaign in B.C.; $12,000 in Greater Vancouver. Interior: $3,000 for B.C.; $3,000 in Victoria. | Average cost to rent 1,000 names is $125. Costs of the entire mailing can run $300–$1,000 per 1,000 names. | Directories are published by different phone companies in different markets with varying standards and rates. Little or no production costs. |
| Broad awareness. Reinforce main campaign, name, and image. | Broad awareness. Simple, uncomplicated messages. | Personalized advertising effort. | Reaches consumers at information-search or vendor-identification use when looking to make a purchase, or visitors/new residents of area. |
| Limited ability to convey product information. Inability to narrow audience. Some local regulatory restrictions. Costly production. | Short exposure time. Difficult to target against a narrow audience. Limited copy detail available. | No editorial environment to attract and hold audience. Low response rate. "Junk mail" image. | More of a directional/ information medium versus creative. Must give full service details in ad to maximize value. |

was on the "creative theory" that the Gardenburger target market was primarily females age 25 to 54, that the final *Seinfeld* episode was like the Super Bowl for women, and that Gardenburger was just the ticket for their needs. Yet only about 8 percent of consumers have ever tasted a veggie burger. A 30-second ad, even a memorable one, isn't likely to change a basic mindset for most people. So in betting the farm on its *Seinfeld* ad, Gardenburger had to pay to reach a very large group of women, and men, who were not at all interested in what the company had to offer. Gardenburger is an extreme case, but research suggests that many of the firms that sponsor ads on such big-audience shows would get more for their money if they placed ads on shows that reached more targeted audiences.[13]

Because it's hard to pick the best media, media analysts often focus on comparing quantitative measures—such as cost per thousand of audience size or circulation. This may seem to be an objective approach, but advertisers preoccupied with keeping these costs down may ignore the relevant segmenting dimensions and slip into mass marketing.

### Consideration 3: The Availability of Specialized Media

Today the major media direct more attention to reaching smaller, more defined target markets. The most obvious evidence of this is in the growth of spending on direct-mail advertising to consumers in databases. However, other media—even traditional ones—are becoming more targeted as well.

TV is a good example. Cable TV channels—such as MuchMusic, CBC Newsworld, TSN, and YTV—are taking advertisers away from the networks because they target specific audiences. TSN, for example, has an audience heavily weighted toward affluent, male viewers. MuchMusic appeals most strongly to younger viewers while its sister business Much More Music appeals to older, more affluent viewers.

Infomercials—long commercials that are broadcast with a TV-show format—give a glimpse of how targeted cable TV will become when more consumers have access



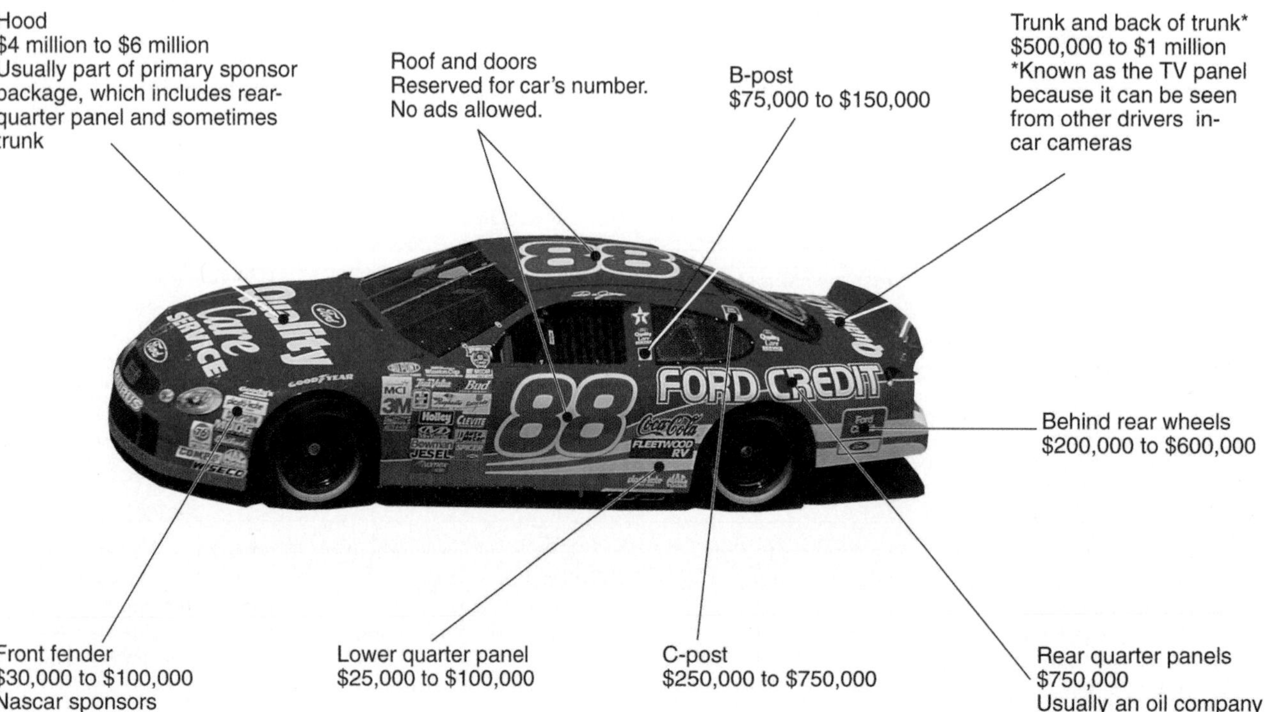


Advertising space on a racecar reaches racing fans and often benefits from extended TV coverage. But the cost for primary sponsors can be millions of dollars.

to hundreds, or perhaps even thousands, of TV channels. With many channels competing for attention, most will succeed only if they offer programs and commercials that are very specific to the interests and needs of smaller, more homogeneous target markets.

Radio has also become a more specialized medium. Some stations cater to particular ethnic and racial groups—such as Asians and French Canadians. Others aim at specific target markets with rock, country, or classical music. Religious programs and talk radio cater to people with specific attitudes and interests. Now that radio stations can get their programming to a larger number of consumers over the Internet and via satellite broadcast systems, expect even more targeting.

Many magazines serve only special-interest groups—such as soap opera fans, new parents, professional groups, and personal computer users. In fact, the most profitable magazines seem to be the ones aimed at clearly defined markets. Many specialty magazines also have international editions that help marketers reach consumers with similar interests in different parts of the world. *PC Magazine*, for example, offers European and Japanese editions.

There are trade magazines in many fields—such as chemical engineering, furniture retailing, electrical wholesaling, farming, and the aerospace market. *Canadian Advertising Rates and Data* provides a guide to the hundreds of magazines now available in Canada. Similar guides exist in most other countries.

Many of the national print media offer specialized editions. *Time* magazine, for example, offers not only several regional and metropolitan editions but also special editions for post-secondary students, educators, doctors, and business managers. Magazines like *Newsweek*, France's *Paris Match International*, and Germany's *Wirtschaftwoche* provide international editions.

The advertising media listed in Exhibit 15-7 are attracting the vast majority of advertising media budgets. But advertising specialists always look for cost-effective new media that will help advertisers reach their target markets. For example, one company successfully sells space for signs on bike racks that it places in front of 7-Eleven stores. In Eastern Europe, where major media are still limited, companies like Campbell's pay to put ads on bus shelters. Hotels and auto-rental companies buy space on advertising boards placed in the restrooms on airplanes. A new generation of ATMs—including ones placed in stores and shopping centres—is capable of showing video ads while customers are waiting to get their money. Some gas station pumps have similar displays.[14] See Marketing Demo 15-1 for more on creative venues for advertising.

## Marketing Demo 15–1

### HERE, THERE, AND EVERYWHERE

Is nothing sacred? It seems that anything is fair game as a venue for out-of-home advertising: bicycles, garbage cans, taxi hubcaps, urinals, office buildings, the CN Tower, mall food courts, golf course holes, parking lot boom gates, subway trains, grocery carts, and even apples and bananas in the produce section.

According to statistics from the Canadian Outdoor Management Bureau (COMB), the number of display faces across the country jumped from 30,418 in December 1995 to 42,303 as of July 1, 2001—or a 39 percent increase in less than six years.

Steve Conover, senior vice-president, executive creative director at Ambrose Carr Linton Carroll in Toronto says the allure of these new formats for advertisers is a combination of the "wow" factor and, in the case of a truly unique concept, the attendant media exposure.

"If you do it first, you're the guy who gets noticed," says Conover. "And to be the first out there means you not only get noticed, you often get residual PR and news stories, which is an absolute bonus."[15]

### Consideration 4: Budget

Selecting which media to use is still pretty much an art. The media buyer may start with a budgeted amount and try to buy the best blend to reach the target audience.

Some media are obvious "must-buys"—like the local newspaper for a retailer in a small or medium-sized town. Most firms serving local markets view a Yellow Pages listing as a must-buy. Website advertising is increasingly being seen as a must-buy. It may be the only medium for firms trying to reach business buyers in overseas markets. Must-buy ads may even use up the available funds.

For many firms, even national advertisers, the high cost of television may eliminate it from the media blend. The average cost just to produce a national TV ad is now about $250,000—and a big-impact ad can easily cost twice that. In the United States, a 30-second commercial on a popular prime-time show like *Friends* is well over $500,000. The price goes up rapidly for "big event" shows that attract the largest audiences. Thirty seconds of advertising on the 2001 Super Bowl cost sponsors about $2.3 million.[16]

## Advertising on the Internet: New Opportunities and New Challenges

Advertising on the Internet is growing rapidly as more mainstream advertisers join the quest for a more efficient way to reach target customers with promotion. The advertising messages take many forms, ranging from displays that basically look like traditional print ads to button and banner ads. A *banner ad* is a headline that appears on a Web page. Its purpose is to attract the interest of people in the advertiser's target market and encourage them to visit the advertiser's website for more information. A *button* is usually much smaller—perhaps just showing the advertiser's name or symbol.

Whatever specific form an ad takes, it is usually linked to the advertiser's website. When a viewer responds to an ad by clicking on it with a mouse, more detailed information appears. The information may include pictures, videos, sound, text, a product database, order-entry procedures, and much more.

Content on a website can be very different from traditional advertising. The advertiser can put up a great deal more information and allow viewers to self-direct to those pages that interest them the most. The website can also provide links to other outside sources of information. Or it can invite the viewer to e-mail or start a chat session for more detailed information on a particular topic. It can offer a sign-up for a weekly newsletter. The viewer may not buy right away and may not bookmark the website to come back to later. But if the viewer subscribes to the e-mail newsletter, all is not lost. The advertiser will have another chance to make a sale.

We talked about this sort of interactive communication in detail in Chapter 13. Now let's take a look at how the various types of online advertising and sales promotion tools (refer to Internet Insite 15-1) can be used to reach a target audience in the first place.

**Using the Internet to generate exposure** Some advertisers are primarily interested in placing ads on websites that will give their ads a lot of exposure—almost without regard to the content of the website or who visits it. Although there are millions of websites on the Internet, a small subset accounts for a large percentage of the potential audience. For example, many people see the Netscape, Microsoft, or Yahoo! website every time they use the Internet because by default their browser software starts at these websites. Some people refer to such websites as *portals* because they act like doorways to the Internet.

A few portal websites are becoming for the Internet what the major networks once were for television: *the* place where an advertiser is willing to pay high rates because they are uniquely able to reach a very large, broad market. For example, Dell might want its computer ads on the AOL or Yahoo! home page so they will be viewed by the large number of computer-user visitors. But what makes sense for

# Internet Insite 15–1

## ADVERTISING AND SALES PROMOTION ONLINE

The advantages of online advertising were discussed in Internet Insites 9-1 and 13-1. Here, we will first consider various forms of online advertising and discuss online sales promotional tools.

### Internet Advertising

Advertising on the Internet can take many forms. Let us examine two popular forms:

*Banner ads*: The most popular size for banner ads was 460×68 pixels. In the early days, ads were static. Then interactive ads were introduced, which allowed viewers to select their response on the banner ad. Now Flash and other technologies allow advertisers to use animation and sound in Internet ads. These ads are called rich-media ads. Flash remains the standard for rich-media ads, but we are seeing the emergence of full video ads on the Internet. With more consumers using broadband connections (cable modem or DSL), we are likely to see an increase in such ads. Ad sizes vary greatly, including skyscrapers (160×600) and rectangles. Pop-ups are the widely used ads that appear in a new window when browsing a site; the annoyance factor is likely to diminish their effectiveness. Interstitials, which appear between pages as the viewer moves from one Web page to the next, and floating ads, which float across the screen, can often grab attention. The Interactive Advertising Bureau (www.iab.net) sets voluntary standards and guidelines for Internet advertising.

Advertising networks, such as 24/7 Real Media (www.247realmedia.com) and DoubleClick (www.doubleclick.com), manage advertising space on behalf of publishers (or content sites). The space is typically sold to ad agencies, which work on behalf of advertisers. Advertising networks provide detailed measurement and reports. The number of times the ad was seen (or downloaded), click-throughs (percentages of viewers who clicked on the banner), unique visitors (number of identifiably unique persons/computers visiting a site), and other metrics are provided by these networks.

Online advertising is typically charged based on CPM (cost per thousand impressions). The rates can vary from $5 to $30 or more, depending on the stature of the site and whether it is a targeted audience. Some advertising networks, such as ValueClick (www.valueclick.com), charge based on click-throughs, where the advertiser pays a few cents for each click on the banner.

*E-mail advertising*: E-mail advertising was once seen as the saviour of direct marketing firms. Now consumers generally loathe such advertising due to the sheer volume of unsolicited ads (called spam) that reach their mailbox. It is easy to create e-mail lists containing thousands, if not millions, of e-mail addresses. If you've ever given your name to an online company or registered on a website with your e-mail address, chances are you are on several e-mail lists. New regulations in the U.S. have attempted to stop spam, but so far have failed to produce the desired result. Does this mean that e-mail advertising is not viable?

Not necessarily. Some firms do use e-mail advertising effectively. Canadian Tire (www.canadiantire.ca) asks consumers to sign up for weekly flyers called e-Flyers, where consumers can choose the categories where they would like to receive sale information. Such e-mail ads, based on consumers' consent and permission, are more effective than unsolicited ads. It is a good idea to seek consumers' permission and give them the opportunity to opt out if they no longer wish to receive the ads. Chapters (indigo.chapters.ca) sends ads to this author that are unsolicited but based on previous purchases, so they tend to be personally relevant. E-mail ads can include pictures, links, and interactive elements. They offer the benefit of measurability. If a consumer clicks on the links in the ad and visits the store, the clickstream can be tracked. However, it is hard to stand out in the clutter that is e-mail marketing. Permission-based marketing, advertising focused on providing value, and building trust with consumers are vital to successful e-mail advertising.

### Sales Promotion Online

Sales promotion on the Internet has remained on the sidelines while advertising on the Internet has garnered most of the media attention. Sales promotion focuses on immediate results, whereas advertising tries to build a connection between the brand and the consumer over a longer period. In its early days, the Web was seen as a direct marketer's dream for its potential for advertising special offers and sales where the consumer is only one click away from visiting the advertiser's store. Sales or coupons in newspapers or other media do not provide the same convenience to consumers.

Internet coupons are common. Sites likes Online-Coupons.com, Coupons.com, and eCoupons.com are just three of the dozens of coupon repository sites on the Internet. Some sites offer coupons for online stores only. These are called promotional codes. Other sites offer printable coupons that can be redeemed at a neighbourhood grocery store. There are no reliable studies on the redemption rates of such coupons.

Promotional codes must be entered during the checkout process in an online store. Consumers who do have a promotional code often abandon their shopping cart. A study of Internet coupon effectiveness found that the existence of a promotional code field in the checkout screen leads to a lower sense of price fairness and satisfaction among consumers.[17] Promotional codes, designed to boost sales, may have the opposite effect.

Coupons can also be delivered in real time, while the customer is shopping on the site. The offer on the coupon can be related to the items that the customer has in the shopping cart.[18] For instance, a customer who has selected a digital camera can be given offers on camera accessories. Such instant offers allow marketers to upsell or cross-sell products.

The most common sales promotions include direct discounts and free shipping. Amazon, Chapters Online, Buy.com, and many other major retailers use such promotions. Internet-only promotions are common for clicks-and-mortar operations, which means you get lower prices at times by shopping online. Experts have mixed reactions to such promotions. In the short run, such promotions do seem to increase sales, but their long-term impact is questionable.[19]

Here are some questions to ponder: When is e-mail marketing appropriate for a product or service? Given the advances in Internet advertising, do you see advertisers devoting more resources to the Internet medium relative to the mass media?

Go to: www.mcgrawhill.ca/college/wong to apply this Insite in an exciting Internet exercise.



Dell in that situation might not make sense for a different firm with a different target market and marketing mix. As with traditional media, getting lots of exposure for an Internet ad doesn't help if viewers are not in the firm's target market. At most websites, rates are set based on number of exposures, and you pay for an exposure regardless of who it reaches. Some advertisers don't see this distinction and have just transferred their old, untargeted shotgun approach to this new medium. That's especially wasteful on the Internet!

**Using the Internet to enhance targeting** Bristol-Myers Squibb's experiment with Web advertising is typical of what many other firms are trying to do—place ads on websites that attract the desired target market. In the middle of income-tax season, Bristol-Myers Squibb ran ads on financial websites extolling Excedrin as "the tax headache medicine." The ads offered a free sample of Excedrin. Within a month, more than 30,000 people clicked on the ad and typed their names into the firm's customer database. The cost of obtaining those names was half that of traditional methods. Now the firm can follow up the Excedrin samples with other database-directed promotions, either by e-mail or other methods.

**Context advertising** The Excedrin ads were quite targeted, but targeting on the Internet can be even more precise. For example, ads for Fragrance Counter (a cosmetics retailer) pop up when an Internet user does a search on a term such as *perfume* or *Estée Lauder*. This approach is called *context advertising*—monitoring the content a Net surfer is viewing and then serving up related ads. For example, if a consumer visits a website with information about cars, an ad for Amazon.com might appear and note that it carries books on buying a car. If the consumer clicks on the Amazon ad, a list of relevant books appears on screen and more detailed information on each title is a click away.

Another variation on the context theme allows noncompeting firms that have a similar target market to post ads on each other's websites. When Maytag introduced its Neptune high-efficiency washing machine, the Neptune website had a link to P&G's website for Tide HE, a new detergent designed for use in washers like the Neptune.

**Pointcasting** Another approach that offers more precise targeting is pointcasting. Pointcasting means displaying an ad *only* to an individual who meets certain qualifications. For instance, it might be a person who has previously expressed direct interest in the topic of the advertising. A pointcasting ad is usually included with other information that the customer wants and that a pointcasting service provides for free. An example shows how this works. A woman who is interested in financial planning might sign up with Time-Warner's Road Runner service and request that it routinely send her newly published articles on independent retirement accounts. When the service sends her that information over the Internet, it might include an ad from a mutual fund company. The pointcasting service matches ads to customer interests. Many advertisers like this concept but worry that pointcasting may overwhelm the recipient with clutter.

**Permission marketing** Permission marketing, like pointcasting, sends promotional messages only to qualified buyers. The difference is that permission marketing allows customers to specify whether they wish to receive promotional messages from the firm or related suppliers.

In addition, some websites offer people a benefit—like free e-mail or a chance to enter a contest—if they provide information about themselves and agree to view ads selected to match their interests. A look at Juno, a firm that offers a free e-mail service, shows how this works. When people sign up for e-mail accounts, they also provide detailed information for a database. The information might include demographics as well as interests, what products they use, where they shop, and where they live. Then, when a person checks for e-mail messages, ads are displayed. Each ad is selected specifically for that person based on characteristics in the database. For example, a cosmetics firm might specify that its ads be shown only to females who are 16 or older and who routinely wear nailpolish.

**Contingency billing** While the number of firms interested in putting ads on websites has grown, the number of websites that are chasing their ad dollars has grown at an even faster pace. Many websites charge advertisers a fee based on how frequently or how long an ad is shown. But there are still basic problems in getting good measures of how many people are exposed to an ad or pay any attention if they are exposed. One symptom of this is that many firms have sprung up to rate website traffic, but their ratings often don't agree.

This problem and competition for advertisers have pressed many websites to take a more novel approach. They display an ad for free and charge a fee only if the ad gets results. For example, the fee the advertiser pays is sometimes based on "click-through"—the number of people who actually click on the ad and link to the advertiser's website. Some websites set fees based on actual sales that result from the click-through. This is efficient for advertisers, and variations on this approach are becoming more common. This is a big shift from traditional media. Firms have to pay for their TV and print ads whether they work or not. A lot more firms will put ads on websites if there is a direct relationship between costs and results. Moreover, websites will then have more incentive to attract the type of viewers that some specific set of advertisers wants to reach.

Innovations like these make it clear that Internet advertising holds great promise. On the other hand, most Internet advertising does not yet provide the precise laser-accurate targeting that would be ideal. In fact, a lot of banner ads seem outright ineffective, and pop-ups can be obnoxious. Yet, as with other innovations, refinements to Internet advertising will take time. No one can yet be certain what it will be when it grows up, but it *is* growing.[20]

## Decision 4—Planning the Message: What to Communicate

**copy thrust**
What an advertisement's words and illustrations should communicate

Once you decide *how* the messages will reach the target audience, you have to decide on the **copy thrust**—what the words and illustrations should communicate. Carrying out the copy thrust is the job of advertising specialists and a full treatment of its intricacies would require at least one course in itself. But the advertising manager and the marketing manager need to understand the process to be sure that the job is done well.

### Using AIDA to Guide Message Planning

Basically, the overall marketing strategy should determine *what* the message should say. Then management judgment—perhaps aided by marketing research—can help decide how to encode this content so it will be decoded as intended. As a guide to message planning, we can use the AIDA concept: getting attention, holding interest, arousing desire, and obtaining action. These represent the four stages a message must move through en route to generating the desired result.

**Stage 1: Getting attention** Getting attention is an ad's first job. If an ad doesn't get attention, it doesn't matter how many people see or hear it. Many readers leaf through magazines and newspapers without paying attention to any of the ads. Many listeners or viewers do chores or get snacks during radio and TV commercials. When watching a program on videotape, they may zap past the commercial with a flick of the fast-forward button. On the Internet, they may click on the next website before the ad message finishes loading onto the screen.

Many attention-getting devices are available. A large headline, computer animations, newsy or shocking statements, attractive models, babies, animals, special effects—anything different or eye-catching—may do the trick. However, the attention-getting device can't detract from, and hopefully should lead to, the next step, holding interest.

**Stage 2: Holding interest** Holding interest is more difficult. A humorous ad, an unusual video effect, or a clever photo may get your attention—but once you've

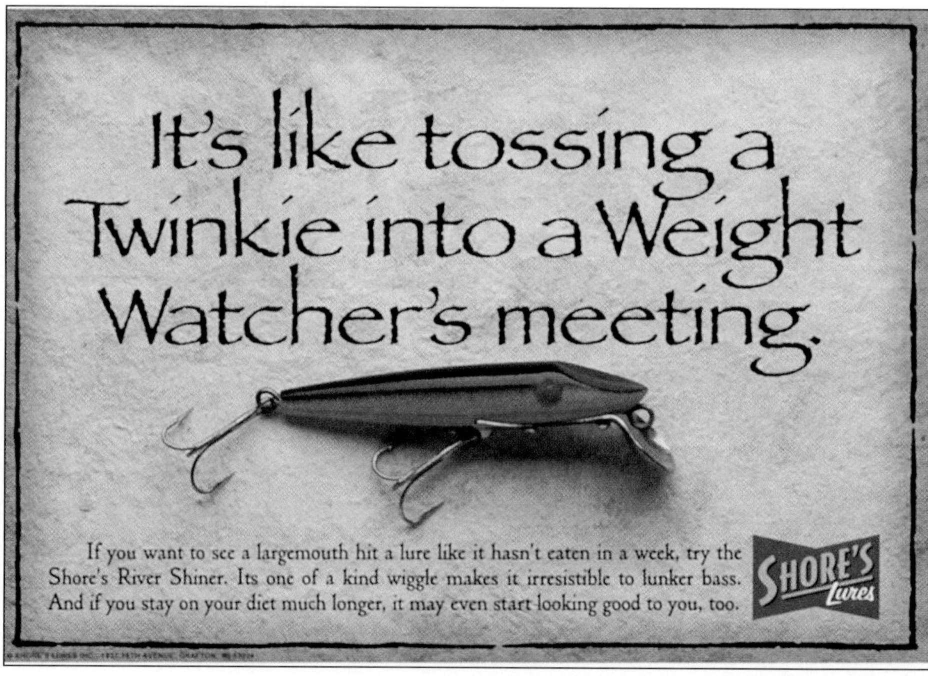

It's like tossing a Twinkie into a Weight Watcher's meeting.
If you want to see a largemouth hit a lure like it hasn't eaten in a week, try the Shore's River Shiner. Its one of a kind wiggle makes it irresistible to lunker bass. And if you stay on your diet much longer, it may even start looking good to you, too.
SHORE'S Lures


The right copy thrust helps an ad clearly communicate to its target market. How effective is this Shore's ad in each step of the AIDA concept?

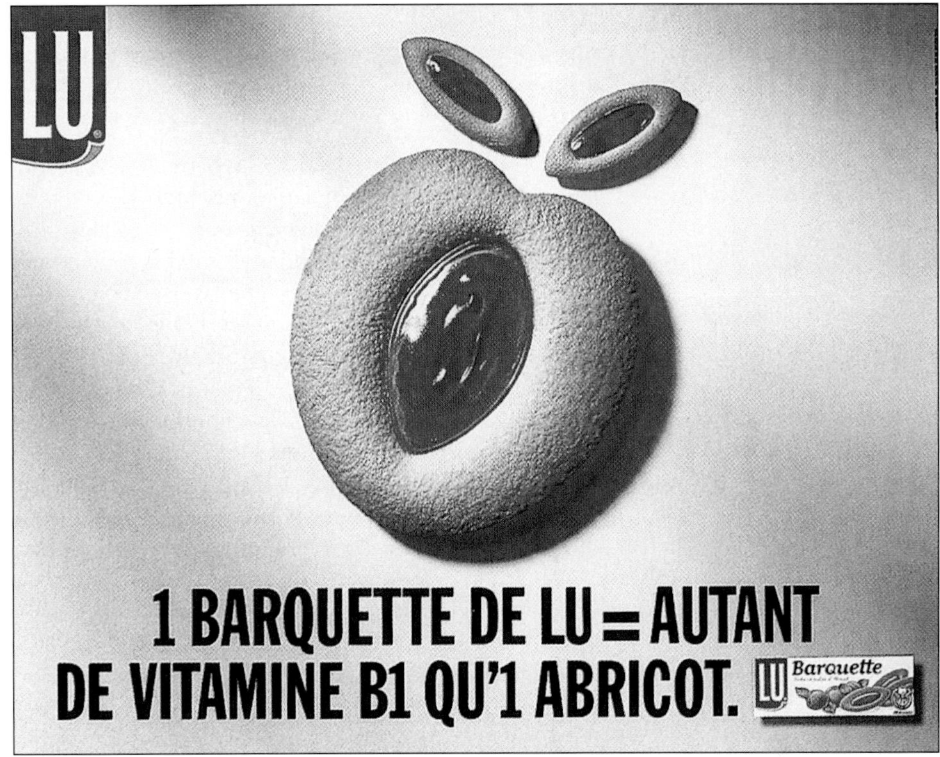


Ads that feature a unique selling proposition help consumers focus on what is different and better about a firm's marketing mix. LU wants health-conscious European consumers to know that its cookie has as much vitamin B1 as an apricot.

seen it, then what? If there is no relation between what got your attention and the marketing mix, you'll move on. To hold interest, the tone and language of the ad must fit with the experiences and attitudes of the target customers and their reference groups. As a result, many advertisers develop ads that relate to specific emotions. They hope that the good feeling about the ad will stick—even if its details are forgotten.

To hold interest, informative ads need to speak the target customer's language. Persuasive ads must provide evidence that convinces the customer. For example, TV ads often demonstrate a product's benefits.

Layouts for print ads should look right to the customer. Print illustrations and copy should be arranged to encourage the eye to move smoothly through the ad—perhaps from a headline that starts in the upper left corner to the illustration or body copy in the middle and finally to the lower right corner where the ad's "signature" usually gives the company or brand name, toll-free number, and website address. If all of the elements of the ad work together as a whole, they will help to hold interest and build recall.[21]

**Stage 3: Arousing desire** Arousing desire to buy a particular product is one of an ad's most difficult jobs. The ad must convince customers that the product can meet their needs. Testimonials may persuade a consumer that other people with similar needs like the product. Product comparisons may highlight the advantages of a particular brand.

Although products may satisfy certain emotional needs, many consumers find it necessary to justify their purchases on some logical basis. Snickers candy bar ads helped ease the guilt of calorie-conscious snackers by assuring them that "Snickers satisfies you when you need an afternoon energy break."

An ad should usually focus on a *unique selling proposition* that aims at an important unsatisfied need. This can help differentiate the firm's marketing mix and position its brand as offering superior value to the target market. For example,

Altoids' ads use humour to highlight the "curiously strong" flavour of its mints. Too many advertisers ignore the idea of a unique selling proposition. Rather than using an integrated blend of communications to tell the whole story, they cram too much into each ad—and then none of it has any impact.

**Stage 4: Obtaining action** Getting action is the final requirement—and not an easy one. From communication research, we now know that prospective customers must be led beyond considering how a product *might* fit into their lives to actually trying it or letting the company's sales rep demonstrate it.

Direct-response ads and interactive media can sometimes help promote action by encouraging interested consumers to do *something* that is less risky or demanding than actually making a purchase. For example, an ad that includes a toll-free telephone number might prompt some consumers who are not yet ready to buy to at least call for more information. Then follow-up brochures or a telephone salesperson can provide additional information and attempt to prompt another action—perhaps a visit to a store or a "satisfaction guaranteed" trial period. This approach seeks to get action one step at a time, where the first action suggested provides a "foot in the door" for subsequent communication efforts.

Whether or not some direct-response approach is used, to communicate more effectively ads might emphasize strongly felt customer needs. Careful research on attitudes in the target market may help uncover such strongly felt *unsatisfied* needs. Appealing to important needs can get more action and also provide the kind of information buyers need to confirm their decisions. Some customers seem to read more advertising *after* a purchase than before. The ad may reassure them about the correctness of their decision.

### Can Global Messages Work?

Many international consumer-products firms try to use one global advertising message all around the world. Of course, they translate the message or make other minor adjustments—but the focus is one global copy thrust. Some do it to cut the cost of developing different ads for each country. Others feel their customers' basic needs are the same, even in different countries. Some just do it because it's fashionable to "go global."

This approach works for some firms. Coca-Cola and IBM, for example, believe that the needs their products serve are very similar for customers around the world. They focus on the similarities among customers who make up their target market rather than the differences. However, most firms who use this approach experience terrible results. They may save money by developing fewer ads, but they lose sales because they don't develop advertising messages, and whole marketing mixes, aimed at specific target markets. They just try to appeal to a global "mass market."

Combining smaller market segments into a single, large target market makes sense if the different segments can be served with a single marketing mix. But when that is not the case, the marketing manager should treat them as different target markets and develop different marketing mixes for each target.[22]

## Decision 5—Who Will Do the Work?

An advertising manager manages a company's advertising effort. Many advertising managers—especially those working for large retailers—have their own advertising departments that plan specific advertising campaigns and carry out the details. Others turn over much of the advertising work to specialists—the advertising agencies.

**advertising agencies**
Specialists in planning and handling mass-selling details for advertisers

**Advertising agencies** are specialists in planning and handling mass-selling details for advertisers. Agencies play a useful role—because they are independent of the advertiser and have an outside viewpoint. They bring experience to an individual client's problems because they work for many other clients. As specialists they can often do the job more economically than a company's own department. And if an agency isn't doing a good job, the client can select another. However, ending a relationship with an agency is a serious decision. Too many marketing managers just use their advertising agency as a scapegoat. Whenever anything goes wrong, they blame the agency.

Some full-service agencies handle any activities related to advertising, publicity, or sales promotion. They may even handle overall marketing strategy planning as well as marketing research, product and package development, and sales promotion. Other agencies are more specialized. For example, in recent years there has been rapid growth of firms that specialize in developing websites and Internet banner ads. Similarly, creative specialists just handle the artistic elements of advertising but leave media scheduling and buying, research, and related services to other specialists or full-service agencies.

The vast majority of advertising agencies are small—with 10 or fewer employees. But the largest agencies account for most of the billings. Over the past decade many of the big agencies merged—creating mega-agencies with worldwide networks. Exhibit 15-8 shows a list of eight of the largest agency networks and examples of some of the products they advertise. Although their headquarters are located in different nations, they have offices worldwide. The move toward international marketing is a key reason behind the mergers.

Before the mergers, marketers in one country often had difficulty finding a capable, full-service agency in the country where they wanted to advertise. The mega-agency can offer varied services, wherever in the world a marketing manager needs them. This may be especially important for managers in large corporations—



Exhibit 15-8 Top eight advertising-agency supergroups and examples of products they advertise.

| Organization | Headquarters | Worldwide Gross Income, 2000 ($ millions) | Products |
|---|---|---|---|
| WPP Group | London | $7,971.0 | American Express, AT&T, Campbell's, Ford, IBM |
| Omnicom Group. | New York | 6,986.2 | Anheuser-Busch, DaimlerChrysler, McDonald's, PepsiCo, Visa |
| Interpublic Group of Cos. | New York | 6,595.9 | Coca-Cola, GM, Johnson & Johnson, Microsoft, UPS |
| Dentsu | Tokyo | 3,089.0 | Honda, Japan Air Lines, Kao, Matsushita, Toyota |
| Havas Advertising | Paris | 2,757.3 | Intel, Philips, PSA Peugeot-Citroen, Volkswagen, Worldcom |
| Publicis Groupe | Paris | 2,479.1 | BMW, British Airways, L'Oreal, Renault, Siemens |
| Bcom3 Group | Chicago | 2,215.9 | Canon, Delta, Hallmark, Heinz, Suzuki |
| Grey Advertising | New York | 1,863.2 | British American Tobacco, GlaxoSmithKline, Mars, Procter & Gamble, 3M |

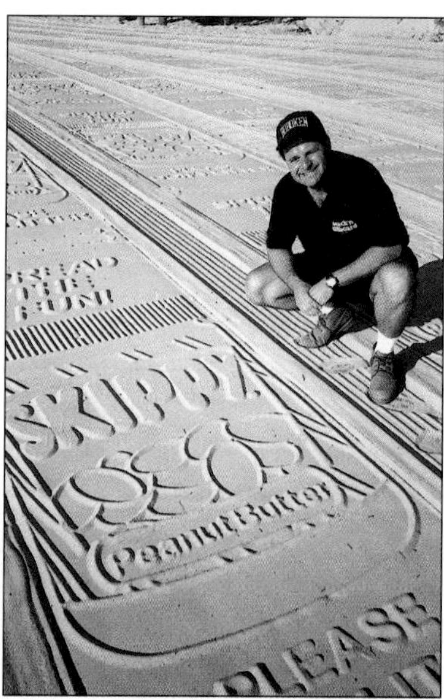


There are specialized advertising agencies that help advertisers with unique media—ranging from posters that cover a whole building to advertising messages pressed into the sand on public beaches. What are the advantages to using unique, and sometimes bizarre, media for advertising purposes?

like Toyota, Renault, Unilever, NEC, Philips, Procter & Gamble, Nestlé, and PepsiCo—that advertise worldwide.[23]

In spite of the growth of these very large agencies, smaller agencies will continue to play an important role. The really big agencies are less interested in smaller accounts. Smaller agencies will continue to appeal to customers who want more personal attention and a close relationship that is more attuned to their marketing needs.

### How Agencies Are Paid

Most advertising agencies are paid a commission of about 15 percent on media and production costs. Some are paid on a fee-for-service basis and a very small number on a fee-for-results basis. These are discussed below.

**Fixed-commission system** The fixed-commission system evolved because media usually have two prices: one for national advertisers and a lower rate for local advertisers, such as local retailers. The advertising agency gets a 15-percent commission on national rates but not on local rates. This makes it worthwhile for producers and intermediaries selling across Canada to use agencies. National advertisers have to pay the full media rate anyway, so it makes sense to let the agency experts do the work—and earn their commission. Local retailers—who are allowed the lower media rate—seldom use agencies.

There is growing resistance to the idea of paying agencies the same way regardless of the work performed or the results achieved. The commission approach also makes it hard for agencies to be completely objective about inexpensive media—or about promotion campaigns that use little space or time. Not all agencies are satisfied with the present arrangement either. Some would like to charge additional fees as their costs rise and as advertisers demand more services.

Canadian advertising budgets are, on the average, much smaller than American ones. And the rates charged by Canadian media reaching a more limited audience are, on a per-page or per-minute basis, far lower than American rates. On the other hand, the work Canadian agencies must do when planning campaigns and preparing effective advertisements isn't much different or less demanding, and the salaries they must pay aren't much lower. Because of these factors, the fee-for-service basis for agency compensation is well established and widely used in Canada.

## Ethical Dimensions 15–2

### CONFIDENTIAL INFORMATION

Ad agencies usually work closely with their clients, and they often have access to confidential information. This can create ethical conflicts if an agency is working with two or more competing clients. Most agencies are very sensitive to the potential problems and work hard to keep people and information from competing accounts completely separated. But many advertisers don't think that's enough—and they don't want to risk a problem. They refuse to work with an agency that handles any competing accounts, even when they're handled in different offices. For example, a top executive for the Budweiser brand ended a 79-year relationship with an agency when one of the agency's subsidiaries accepted an assignment to buy media space for a competing brand of beer.

This potential conflict of interest in handling competing products is a problem for some of the international mega-agencies. The worst case was years ago when the mergers had just started. Saatchi & Saatchi gained more than $300 million in billings through its mergers—but then quickly lost $462 million in billings when old clients departed because Saatchi's new clients included competitors.[24]

**Fee-for-results** A number of advertisers now "grade" the work done by their agencies—and the agencies' pay depends on the grade. Termed payment by results, or PBR, the approach seeks to tie compensation to the results generated by a campaign. For example, General Foods lowered its basic commission to about 13 percent. However, the company pays the agency a bonus of about 3 percent on campaigns that earn an A rating. If the agency earns only a B, it loses the bonus. If it earns a C, it must improve fast or General Foods removes the account.[25] Marketing Demo 15-2 discusses some of the issues both agencies and clients must resolve before the approach can become widespread.

Variations on this approach are becoming common. For example, Carnation directly links its agency's compensation with how well its ads score in market research tests. Gillette uses a sliding scale, and the percentage of compensation declines with increased advertising volume. And some agencies develop their own plans in which they guarantee to achieve the results expected or give the advertiser a partial refund. This approach forces the advertiser and agency to agree on very specific objectives for their ads and what they expect to achieve. It also reduces the likelihood of the creative people in an agency focusing on ads that will win artistic approval in their industry rather than ads that do what the firm needs done.[26] See Ethical Dimensions 15-2 for a discussion of some additional factors agencies have to be cognizant of.

## Measuring Advertising Effectiveness

The results that marketers actually achieve with mass selling are very uneven. It's often said that half of the money spent on these activities is wasted—but that too few managers know which half. Mass selling can be exciting and involving or it can be downright obnoxious. Sometimes it's based on careful analysis and research, yet much of it is created on the fly based on someone's crazy idea. The right creative idea may produce results beyond a manager's dreams, but the wrong one can be a colossal waste of money. It can stir deep emotions or go unnoticed. Some managers come up with mass-selling blends that are really innovative, but more often than not imitators will just copy the same idea and turn it into an overused fad.

# Marketing Demo 15–2

## PROBING PBR

On the evening of Sept. 13, anyone who happened to be passing by the offices of the Association of Canadian Advertisers on Toronto's Bloor Street might have seen a few unfamiliar faces trekking through the door. The ACA is keeping the identities of these people under wraps, but there are a few things we know for certain: None of them were marketing vice-presidents, packaged-goods company CEOs or advertising agency heads. Most of them weren't even ACA members.

Rather, they came from areas of the business world far removed from marketing or advertising. Their particular areas of expertise may well have run from information technology and finance to product distribution, auto-parts sourcing and beyond. All the ACA will reveal about its guests is that they had one thing in common: all use some form of payment by results (PBR) in their supplier relationships.

PBR, or pay for performance—whatever you choose to call it—is still rare in the marketing departments of Canadian companies. But the debate surrounding it has taken on a new urgency of late. The ACA's little information-gathering session—which was intended to further the association's understanding of performance-based compensation and how it works in other business functions—is just one facet of a new, in-depth study of PBR that promises to go far beyond the statistics of who's doing what. Susan Charles, the ACA's VP, member services and its resident expert on pay for performance, calls it an "intellectual analysis" that will be used to create a "roadmap" of sorts that its marketer-members and others can use to move forward on PBR.

"Success will be measured on our ability to provide some insight and guidance to the clients in such a way that the understanding on the agency side is such that they will also embrace this concept," Charles says. "Not embrace it in the sense of 'We will therefore do it,' but embrace it in terms of investigating the opportunity for it and to determine if it is correct."

The renewed buzz surrounding PBR stems partly from the fact that Procter & Gamble's much-discussed pay-for-performance plan took effect July 1. But there are other factors at play. For one thing, there's an increasing trend towards performance incentives at the level of individual employees, and with agencies viewed more and more as key partners, there's a desire to compensate all members of the marketing "team" in a similar fashion. Then there's the fact that marketers, in general, are becoming far better at financial cost-value analysis and quality management in areas like distribution. It's only natural they'd want to attempt to extend that to the marketing arena, too.

It's no simple task, though. Marketers have a tendency to fall in love with the idea of pay for performance. But they're often at a loss when it comes to, first, putting it into practice, and second, making it work in a way that doesn't put their relationships with their agencies—which they increasingly view as crucial to their marketing success—in jeopardy.

Hershey Canada, for instance, proposed the idea of PBR almost five years ago to its then-agency, Bozell Worldwide (which is now part of Harrod & Mirlin/FCB in Toronto). But it eventually gave up. Susan Skene, Hershey's VP marketing, recalls that Bozell was "really worried we'd be using it to hammer them. And it shouldn't be used that way. It should be an incentive... Finally, we thought, 'This is just terrorizing them too much.'"

While Skene doesn't rule out giving PBR another go at some point, she says Hershey's current fee-based arrangement with Toronto's Ambrose Carr Linton Carroll is working fine. "We've got a great agency relationship," she says, "and it doesn't worry me that we're not performance-based."

That statement probably applies to most Canadian marketers nowadays. Indeed, only one respondent to the ACA's 1999 agency-remuneration study indicated they were using a pay-for-performance system (while the names of the respondents aren't disclosed, chances are good this one uses the initials P and G). But there's no doubt there's growing interest.

"Most customers are inquiring more and more about how it could be worked into their agreement," says Stéfan Danis, president of Mandrake Management Consultants, a Toronto-based company whose services include acting as a consultant to marketers during their agency searches. "But very few of them that I've observed are making it happen that way."

There are a number of reasons for this. The most obvious one is agencies' nervousness about PBR, as illustrated in the Hershey case. But the essence of the debate surrounding PBR—and the central reason why more marketers aren't doing it—comes down to metrics. How do you measure performance, anyway? Is it brand awareness? Market share growth? The general state of the client-agency relationship? And how do you structure the agreement? How much should the reward be?

It's fine to reward an agency for a job well done. But will you also punish them if your brand share doesn't do as well as you'd hoped, even though there may be factors at play—from product performance to customer service to, let's be honest here, bad decisions by a client—that are far beyond the agency's control? And when times are tough, will a pay-for-performance setup alienate your agency at a time when, arguably, you need them most?

Unfortunately for marketers, there are no easy answers to

these questions. Unlike the 15% commission system of old, there's no one standardized model for PBR. Procter & Gamble's new system ties agency compensation to each brand's total annual sales, but this won't necessarily work in every situation.

As Jonathan Lace, the Allied Domecq Associate Professor in Advertising at Southampton Business School in the U.K. and the founder of the Advertising Research Consortium, wrote in the Aug. 21 issue of *Marketing* (p. 6), "with PBR tied solely to advertiser performance, P&G appears to be out of step with its peers." He noted that over half the PBR arrangements in the U.K. also take into account the performance of the advertising itself (in terms of brand awareness and so on) and the performance of the agency in the context of the client-agency relationship.

Meanwhile, earlier this year there were reports that Kraft—which already uses an incentive program to reward agencies for work that produces results, though their primary compensation comes from a flat media commission—was also considering a PBR plan. Given the obvious interest shown by these major packaged-goods marketers, it does appear that pay for performance is an unstoppable force that will eventually overtake the business.

In Canada, it isn't just marketers who are preparing for it. In addition to the study by the ACA—which hopes to have a preliminary report by the end of October, and follow that up with seminars on the subject—the Institute of Canadian Advertising, working with the U.K.'s Lace, has also recently wrapped up its own study on best practices in PBR. Citing the members-only nature of the effort, ICA president Rupert Brendon declined to offer any details.

One of the things the ACA says it is trying to change is the perception of pay for performance as a sort of "carrot" that can be held in front of an agency's face and jerked back at will. "We look at it very much as a strategic way of doing business," says ACA president and CEO Ron Lund. "Philosophically, there has to be an incredible amount of (trust). There's got to be a fundamental respect for each other. If that's not there, PBR is never going to work. You've fundamentally got to believe these guys are your partners."

That certainly seems to be the case with Enbridge Services and its agency of record, Grey Canada of Toronto. Ever since Markham, Ont.-based Enbridge hired Grey early this year, the two have been working with a compensation agreement that includes pay for performance, which is tied to the number of sales leads and brand awareness generated.

"If you're a member of the team, then you get compensated the way every other member of the team gets compensated," says David Strickland, who until late September was VP marketing at Enbridge (he's just taken the same position at Zellers). "You get a base that covers what it takes to keep you interested and, obviously, committed to the business enough to cover your costs and make a profit...and then you bonus (the agency) as you would bonus anybody else based on performance."

As with its individual employees, Strickland says Enbridge also sets objectives for Grey up front that are specific and measurable. It also sets checkpoints along the way in case anything changes that could drastically affect results or the resources the agency has to allocate to the business. In Enbridge's line of work, that could even mean a change in the weather: a warm winter, for instance, will almost certainly mean lower sales of heating fuel.

It's because of factors like the weather—and, for that matter, anything else beyond the control of ad agencies—that Strickland argues against using a 100% PBR plan. "I don't think moving people towards what might be called desperation when they're on a full performance plan is necessarily going to result in the right behaviour," he says. "That may result in very short-term thinking."

"Some of the extreme elements of pay for performance can set up an adversarial, almost, position," Strickland continues. "When times are tough is when you need to be the most together, and I think when you go too far on a pay-for-performance-type philosophy you start to actually see the relationship erode when the performance isn't where it needs to be." And that, he notes, "is exactly opposite to what you need to do in order to get yourself back on track."

John Clinton, president and CEO of Grey Canada, declines to discuss any specific PBR-type arrangements it has with its clients (in addition to Enbridge, Grey also does work for P&G). But it's clear he welcomes some form of PBR. "I think you have to go into this with a good-faith mentality that says, 'We're about helping build brands, and if we can find a way of measuring on that, then we'll both be successful,'" Clinton says.

Grey has no standard PBR model, negotiating each one on a case-by-case basis. And while Clinton expects that incentive-based pay for performance will grow dramatically, the punitive variety may prove "a lot trickier. Agencies, at the end of the day, still have to get paid for what they do. All you're in a position to gamble on is a percentage of your profit... Otherwise you're running the risk of going out of business."

He points out that you wouldn't sit down with an employee and tell them their salary is $50,000, but if they don't deliver they'll only get $30,000. Turn that around and offer an extra bit over and above the base in return for a stellar performance, and chances are they'll reach for the ring.

Ultimately, Clinton feels clients and agencies do want to develop incentive-based systems that work. "It makes sense to motivate people towards the same thing," he says. "It allows agencies more financial flexibility. It allows the clients to get more heavy lifting done. And I think it will help generate more ideas for clients."

*Source*: Lara Mills, *Marketing Magazine*, October 16, 2000.

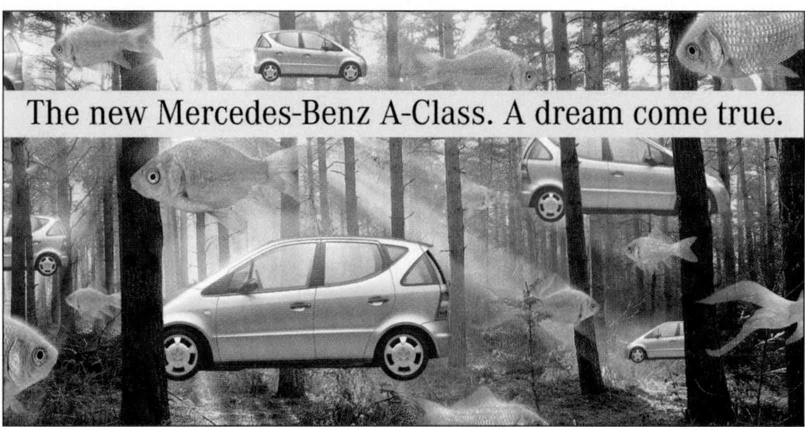

The new Mercedes-Benz A-Class. A dream come true.


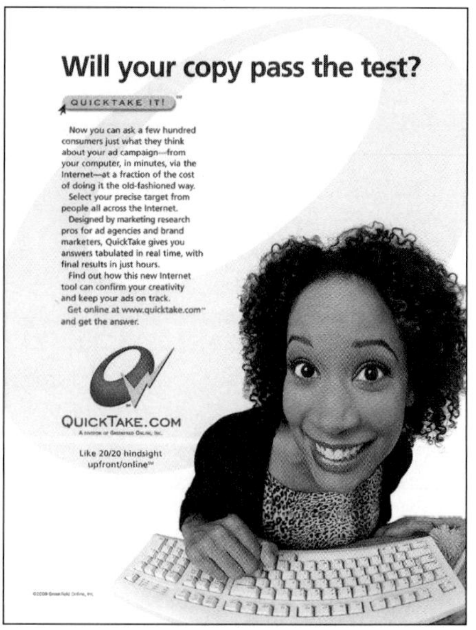


Mercedes used this ad to help introduce its new model and attract younger customers in Latin America. A bad economy dampened sales but the ad did pull the target market into showrooms—increasing the dealers' customer database used to target other promotions by 50 percent. Firms like QuickTake.com do research to help advertisers determine if a creative ad is also effective. More and more search is being done online.

It would be convenient if we could measure the results of advertising by looking at sales. Certainly some breakthrough ads do have a very direct effect on a company's sales—and the advertising literature is filled with success stories that "prove" advertising increases sales. Similarly, market-research firms like Information Resources can sometimes compare sales levels before and after, or during, the period of an ad campaign. Yet we usually can't measure advertising success just by looking at sales. The total marketing mix—not just promotion generally or advertising specifically—is responsible for the sales result. And sales results are also affected by what competitors do and by other changes in the external marketing environment. Only with direct-response advertising can a company make a direct link between advertising and sales results. Then, if an ad doesn't produce immediate results, it's considered a failure.

### Using Research and Testing

Ideally, advertisers should pre-test advertising before it runs rather than relying solely on their own guesses about how good an ad will be. The judgment of creative people or advertising experts may not help much. They often judge only on the basis of originality or cleverness of the copy and illustrations.

Many progressive advertisers now demand laboratory or market tests to evaluate an ad's effectiveness. For example, Molson Export's "Had Ex Today?" campaign was selected from a group of potential strategies, using focus-group interviews. Following the campaign, more tests were conducted to evaluate overall consumer response.

Split runs on cable TV systems in test markets are an important approach for testing ads in a normal viewing environment. Scanner sales data from retailers in those test markets can provide an estimate of how an ad is likely to affect sales. This approach will become even more powerful in the future as more cable systems and telephone companies add new interactive technology that allows viewers to provide immediate feedback to an ad as it appears on the TV.

After ads run, researchers may try to measure how much consumers recall about specific products or ads. Inquiries from customers may be used to measure the effectiveness of particular ads. The response to radio or television commercials or magazine readership can be estimated using various survey methods to check the size and composition of audiences (the Nielsen and Starch reports are examples). Similarly, most Internet advertisers use software that keeps track of how many hits on the firm's website come from ads placed at other websites.[27]

## Legal Issues in Advertising

In most countries, the government takes an active role in deciding what kinds of advertising are allowable, fair, and appropriate. For example, France and Japan limit the use of cartoon characters in advertising to children, and Quebec bans any advertising targeted directly at children. Greece and Sweden have had similar policies and want the rest of the European Union to adopt them. In Switzerland, an advertiser cannot use an actor to represent a consumer. New Zealand and Switzerland limit political ads on TV. In the United States, print ads must be identified so they aren't confused with editorial matter; in other countries ads and editorial copy can be intermixed. Most countries limit the number and length of commercials on broadcast media. Until recently, an Italian TV ad could be shown only 10 times a year.

What is seen as positioning in one country may be viewed as unfair or deceptive in another. For example, when Pepsi was advertising its cola as "the choice of the new generation" in most countries, Japan's Fair Trade Committee didn't allow it—because in Japan Pepsi was not "the choice."

Differences in rules mean that a marketing manager may face very specific limits in different countries, and local experts may be required to ensure that a firm doesn't waste money developing advertising programs that will never be shown or that consumers will think are deceptive.

Advertising abuses have been a favourite target of Canadian consumer activists. Their efforts, along with those of Consumer and Corporate Affairs Canada (now amalgamated with Industry Canada), have led to new legislation and to stricter enforcement of existing laws. Marketing Demo 15-3 lists the major provisions

## Marketing Demo 15–3

### THE COMPETITION ACT—MISLEADING ADVERTISING PROVISIONS

The following description of some of the misleading advertising provisions of the Competition Act is provided by the Bureau of Competition Policy, Industry Canada, for information purposes only and should not be taken to be a complete statement of the law. Provisions of the Competition Act more closely related to price, product, or place are discussed in other chapters of this text.

Section 52(1)(a): All representations, in any form whatever, that are false or misleading in a material respect are prohibited. This general provision prohibits all misleading representations not specifically prohibited elsewhere.

Section 52(1)(b): Any representation in the form of a statement, warranty, or guarantee of the performance, efficacy, or length of life of a product, not based on an adequate and proper test, is prohibited. The onus is on the one making the claim to prove that it is based on an adequate and proper test.

Section 52(1)(c): This paragraph covers any representation that purports to be a warranty or guarantee of a product, or a promise to replace, maintain, or repair an article, or any part of an article. Such representations are prohibited where their form is materially misleading or where there is no reasonable prospect that the warranty, guarantee, or promise will be carried out.

Section 52(1)(d): Any materially misleading representation as to the price at which a product is ordinarily sold is prohibited. Here, price means the price that the product ordinarily sells for in the market area, unless specified to be the advertiser's own selling price.

Section 57: Advertising a product at a bargain price that the advertiser does not have available for sale in reasonable quantities is prohibited. Liability will be avoided where the advertiser can establish that the nonavailability of the product was due to circumstances beyond its control, the quantity of the product obtained was reasonable, or the customer was offered a rain check when supplies were exhausted.

Section 58: The supply of any product at a price higher than the price currently being advertised is prohibited. This section does not apply where the price advertised was erroneous and immediately corrected, or where the seller is not a person engaged in the business of dealing in that product.

Section 59: Any contest that does not disclose the number and approximate value of prizes or important information relating to the chances of winning in the contest, that does not select participants or distribute prizes on the basis of skill or on a random basis, or in which the distribution of prizes is unduly delayed, is prohibited.

*Source*: Marketing Practices Branch, Bureau of Competition Policy, Industry Canada, "Misleading Advertising Bulletin," April 1–June 30, 1994, p. 21.

regarding misleading advertising in Canada. For up-to-date information on enforcement efforts, go to the Competition Bureau's website (http://cb-bc.gc.ca).

The stricter federal controls on advertising have their provincial counterparts. Such regulation is an especially prominent feature of the trade-practices laws that have been passed by many Canadian provinces. Conflicting provincial legislation can make it impossible for national advertisers to use the same campaign across Canada. Provincial differences are greatest in the advertising of liquor, beer, and wine. Some provinces ban such ads outright, while others place restrictions on what can be said, and still others limit the advertiser to specific media. Complying with all this legislation is no easy task.

The Canadian Radio-television and Telecommunications Commission (CRTC) controls the content of all radio and television commercials. The CRTC lets the Health Protection Branch of Health Canada regulate TV and radio advertising of drugs, cosmetics, and other health-related products. Similarly, the CRTC allows food commercials to be regulated by Agriculture Canada.

These government agencies don't have the same kind of advance veto power over print advertising. However, they can and do insist that print advertisements that violate existing regulations be corrected. Also, both advertisers and their agencies have been taken to court for violating the false-advertising provisions of the Competition Act or comparable provincial legislation.

Additional forms of regulation are imposed by the media themselves and by industry associations. The CBC and CTV television networks have their own codes of advertising acceptability. Advertising Standards Canada, in a process involving public representatives, administers a Code of Advertising Standards. More specific ASC codes govern advertisements directed toward children, the advertising of specific categories of products, and the use of potentially controversial practices such as comparative advertising. Guidelines to prevent advertising stereotyping also exist. As a way of giving teeth to its efforts at self-regulation, Advertising Standards Canada began in 1998 to make public the results of its investigations.

Despite such efforts at self-regulation, critics of the mass media continue to find much that they consider offensive, both in advertisements and the accompanying editorial or program content. That there is no effective way to control "spillover" American advertising obviously complicates Canadian efforts at self-regulation (see Ethical Dimensions 15-3).

Companies get no clear guidelines about how much research support they need to back up their ad claims. Unfortunately, there are many ways to lie with statistics, and unethical and/or desperate advertisers of me-too products try many of them. It only takes one such competitor in an industry to cause major shifts in market

## Ethical Dimensions 15–3

### UNFAIR OR DECEPTIVE ADVERTISING

What constitutes unfair and deceptive advertising is a difficult question and one that marketing managers will have to wrestle with for years to come. Sometimes the law provides guidelines, but in most situations the marketing manager must make personal judgments as well. The social and political environment is changing worldwide. Practices considered acceptable some years ago are now being questioned. Saying or even implying that your product is best may be viewed as deceptive.

share and affect the nature of competition in that market. As an old cliché says: One bad apple can spoil a whole barrel.[28]

It's really not hard to figure out how to avoid criticisms of being unfair and deceptive. A little puffing is acceptable—and probably always will be. But firms need to put a stop to the typical production-oriented approach of trying to use advertising to differentiate me-too products that are not different and don't offer customers better value.

## Stimulating Sales Using Sales Promotion

*Sales promotion* refers to those promotion activities—other than advertising, publicity, and personal selling—that stimulate interest, trial, or purchase by final customers or others in the channel. Refer to Exhibit 13-2 for examples of typical sales promotions targeted at final customers, channel members, or a firm's own employees.

Sales promotion is generally used to complement the other promotion methods. While advertising campaigns and salesforce strategy decisions tend to have longer-term effects, a particular sales promotion activity usually lasts for only a limited time period. But sales promotion can often be implemented quickly and get sales results sooner than advertising. Further, sales promotion objectives usually focus on prompting some short-term action. For an intermediary, such an action might be a decision to stock a product, provide a special display space, or give the product special emphasis in selling efforts to final customers. For a consumer, the desired action might be to try a new product, switch from another brand, buy more of a product, or perhaps buy earlier than would otherwise be the case. The desired action by an employee might be a special effort to satisfy customers or place more emphasis on selling a certain product.

### How Sales Promotions Affect Sales

There are many different types of sales promotion, but what type is appropriate depends on the situation and objectives. For example, Exhibit 15-9 shows some possible ways that a short-term promotion might affect sales. The sales pattern in the

Price-off coupons prompt consumers to try a product—and a consumer who is satisfied with the trial is likely to become a regular customer. What effect do you think these Soft Scrub coupons would have on sales during and after the promotion?

Exhibit 15-9 Some possible effects of a sales promotion on sales.

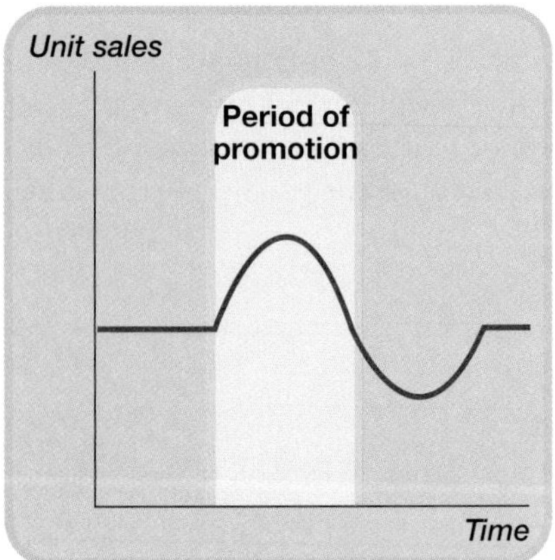


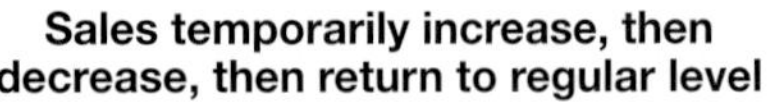
Sales temporarily increase, then decrease, then return to regular level

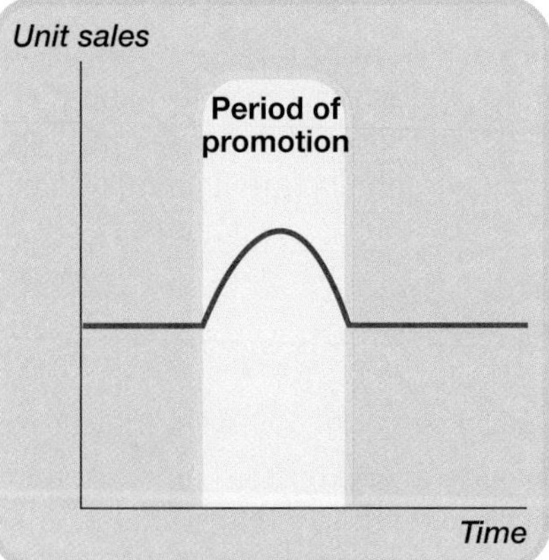

Sales temporarily increase and then return to regular level

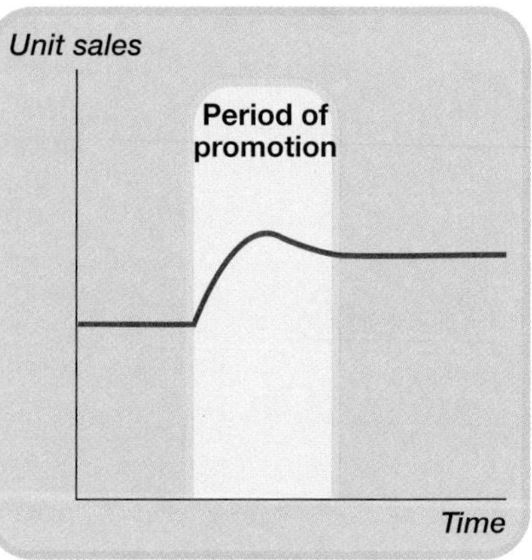

Sales increase and then remain at higher level



graph on the left might occur if Hellmann's issues coupons to help clear an excess mayonnaise inventory. Some consumers might buy earlier to take advantage of the coupon, but unless they use extra mayonnaise their next purchase will be delayed. In the centre graph, kids might convince parents to eat more Big Macs while McDonald's has a Disney promotion, but when it ends things go back to normal. The graph on the right shows a Burger King marketer's dream come true: free samples of a new style of french fries quickly pull in new customers who like what they try and keep coming back after the promotion ends. This is also the kind of long-term result that is the aim of effective advertising.

## Types of Sales Promotions

Earlier we said that sales promotions can be distinguished by the target of their efforts: final customers, channel members, or a firm's own employees. Let's consider each of these in turn.

**Consumer promotions** Much of the sales promotion aimed at final consumers or users tries to increase demand, perhaps temporarily, or speed up the time of purchase. Such promotion might involve developing materials to be displayed in retailers' stores—including banners, sample packages, calendars, and various point-of-purchase materials. The sales promotion people also might develop special displays for supermarkets. They might be responsible for sweepstakes contests as well as for coupons designed to get customers to buy a product by a certain date. Each year, about 300 billion coupons are distributed in North America—and consumers redeem enough of them to save, in total, nearly $4 billion.

All of these sales promotion efforts are aimed at specific objectives. For example, if customers already have a favourite brand, it may be hard to get them to try anything new. Or it may take a while for them to become accustomed to a different product. A free trial-sized bottle of mouthwash might be just what it takes to get cautious consumers to try, and like, the new product. Such samples might be distributed house to house, by mail, at stores, or attached to other products sold by the firm. In this type of situation, sales of the product might start to pick up as soon as customers try the product and find out that they like it. And sales will continue at the higher level after the promotion is over if satisfied customers make repeat purchases. Thus, the cost of the sales promotion in this situation might be viewed as a long-term investment.

When a product is already established, consumer sales promotion usually focuses on stimulating sales in the short term. Marketing managers must be careful to evaluate the cost of the promotion relative to the extra sales expected. If the increase in sales won't at least cover the cost of the promotion, it probably doesn't make sense to do it.

For example, after a price-off coupon for a soft drink is distributed, sales might temporarily pick up as customers take advantage of buying at a lower price. They may even consume more of the soft drink than would have otherwise been the case. However, once the coupon period is over, sales would return to the original level or they might even decline for a while. This is what happens if customers use a coupon to stock up on a product at the low price. Then it takes them longer than usual to buy the product again. As you can see, in instances like this the firm is "buying sales" at the cost of reduced profit.

Sales promotion directed at industrial customers might use the same kinds of ideas. In addition, the sales promotion people might set up and staff trade-show exhibits. Here, attractive models are often used to encourage buyers to look at a firm's product—especially when it is displayed near other similar products in a circus-like atmosphere. Trade shows are a cost-effective way to reach target customers and generate a list of "live" prospects for follow-up by sales reps. However, many firms handle these leads badly. A recent study says that 85 percent of the leads never get followed up by anybody.

Some sellers give promotion items—pen sets, watches, or clothing (perhaps with the firm's brand name on them)—to remind business customers of their products. This is common, but it can be a problem. Some companies do not allow buyers to take any gifts. They don't want the buyer's judgment to be influenced by who gives the best promotional items![29]

**Trade promotions** Sales promotion aimed at intermediaries—sometimes called *trade promotion*—emphasizes price-related matters. The objective may be to encourage intermediaries to stock new items, buy in larger quantity, buy early, or stress a product in their own promotion efforts.

The tools used here include price and/or merchandise allowances, promotion allowances, and perhaps sales contests to encourage retailers or wholesalers to sell specific items or the company's whole line. Offering to send contest winners to Hawaii, for example, may increase sales.

About half of the sales promotion spending targeted at intermediaries has the effect of reducing the price that they pay for merchandise from a supplier. Thus, it makes sense to think about trade promotions in the context of other price-related matters. So we'll go into more detail on different types of trade discounts and allowances in the next chapter.[30]

**Sales promotions for employees** Sales promotion aimed at the company's own salesforce might try to encourage providing better service, getting new customers, selling a new product, or selling the company's whole line. Depending on the objectives, the tools might be contests, bonuses on sales or number of new accounts, and holding sales meetings at fancy resorts to raise everyone's spirits.

*Ongoing* sales promotion work might also be aimed at the salesforce—to help sales management. Sales promotion might be responsible for preparing sales portfolios, videotapes on new products, displays, and other sales aids, as well as sales training material.

Service-oriented firms, such as hotels or restaurants, now use sales promotions targeted at their employees. Some, for example, give a monthly cash prize to the employee who provides the best service, and the employee's picture is displayed to give recognition.[31]

### Problems in Managing Sales Promotion

The planning of a sales promotion involves many of the same considerations as those outlined for advertising campaigns. However, there are also some distinct challenges and problems in the use of promotions.

**Problem 1: Overreliance and the loss of brand loyalty** Some experts think that marketing managers—especially those who deal with consumer packaged goods—put too much emphasis on sales promotions. They argue that the effect of most sales promotion is temporary and that money spent on advertising and personal selling helps the firm more over the long term. Their view is that most sales promotions don't help develop close relationships with consumers and instead erode brand loyalty.

There is heavy use of sales promotion in mature markets where competition for customers and attention from intermediaries is fierce. Moreover, if the total market is not growing, sales promotions may just encourage "deal-prone" customers (and intermediaries) to switch back and forth among brands. Here, all the expense of the sales promotions and the swapping around of customers simply contributes to lower profits for everyone. It also increases the prices that consumers pay because it increases selling costs—and ultimately it is consumers who pay for those selling costs.

However, once a marketing manager is in this situation there may be little choice other than to continue. At the mature stage of the product life cycle, frequent sales promotions may be needed just to offset the effects of competitors' promotions. One escape from this competitive rat race is for the marketing manager to seek new opportunities—with a strategy that doesn't rely solely on short-term sales promotions for competitive advantage.

Procter & Gamble is a company that changed its strategy, and promotion blend, to decrease its reliance on sales promotion targeted at intermediaries. It is offering intermediaries lower prices on many of its products and supporting those products with more advertising and promotion to final consumers. P&G believes that this approach builds its brand equity, serves consumers better, and leads to smoother-running relationships in its channels. Not all retailers are happy with P&G's changes. However, given concerns about the impact of trade promotion on brand loyalty, the number of producers who follow P&G's lead is likely to grow.

Firms are also experimenting with other approaches. For example, some reimburse intermediaries for promotion effort in proportion to their sales to final consumers. This supports intermediaries who actually increase sales to final consumers—which can be quite different from just giving sales promotion dollars to intermediaries who simply make the product available. Making the product available is a means to an end; but if making it available without producing sales is all that is accomplished, the sales promotion doesn't make sense.[32]

**Problem 2: Complex and costly to manage** Another problem in the sales promotion area is that it is easy to make big, costly mistakes. Because sales promotion includes a wide variety of activities—each of which may be custom-designed and used only once—it's difficult for the typical company to develop skill in this area. Mistakes caused by lack of experience can be very costly too. One promotion sponsored jointly by Polaroid and Trans World Airlines (TWA) proved to be a disaster. The promotion offered a coupon worth 25 percent off the price of any TWA ticket with the purchase of a $20 Polaroid camera. The companies intended to appeal to vacationers who take pictures when they travel. Instead, travel agents bought up many of the cameras. For the price of the $20 camera, they made an extra 25 percent on every TWA ticket they sold. And big companies bought thousands of the cameras to save on travel expenses. This is not an isolated example. Such problems are common.[33]

Sales promotion mistakes are likely to be worse when a company has no sales promotion manager. If the personal selling or advertising managers are responsible for sales promotion, they often treat it as a "stepchild." They allocate money to sales promotion if there is any left over—or if a crisis develops. Many companies, even some large ones, don't have a separate budget for sales promotion or even know what it costs in total.

Making sales promotion work is a learned skill, not a sideline for amateurs. That's why specialists in sales promotion have developed—both inside larger firms and as outside consultants. Some of these people are real experts and are willing to take over the whole sales promotion job. But it's the marketing manager's responsibility to set sales promotion objectives and policies that will fit in with the rest of each marketing strategy.[34]

## Chapter Summary

Theoretically, it may seem simple to develop an advertising campaign: just pick the medium and develop a message. But it's not that easy. Effectiveness depends on using the "best" available medium and the "best" message considering (1) promotion objectives, (2) the target markets, and (3) the funds available for advertising.

Specific advertising objectives determine what kind of advertising to use—product or institutional. If product advertising is needed, then the particular type must be decided—pioneering, competitive (direct or indirect), or reminder. And advertising allowances and cooperative advertising may be helpful.

Many technical details are involved in mass selling, and specialists—advertising agencies—handle some of these jobs. But specific objectives must be set for them, or their advertising may have little direction and be almost impossible to evaluate.

Effective advertising should affect sales. But the whole marketing mix affects sales—and the results of advertising usually can't be measured by sales changes alone. By contrast, sales promotion tends to be more action-oriented.

Sales promotion spending is big and growing. This approach is especially important in prompting action—by customers, intermediaries, or salespeople. There are many different types of sales promotion, and it is a problem area in many firms because it is difficult for a firm to develop expertise with all of the possibilities.

Advertising and sales promotion are often important parts of a promotion blend—but in most blends personal selling also plays an important role. Further, promotion is only a part of the total marketing mix a marketing manager must develop to satisfy target customers. So to broaden your understanding of the four Ps and how they fit together, in the next two chapters we'll go into more detail on the role of price in strategy decisions.



## Key Concepts

advertising agencies, p. 471
advertising allowances, p. 457
comparative advertising, p. 455
competitive advertising, p. 454
cooperative advertising, p. 457
copy thrust, p. 468
institutional advertising, p. 454
pioneering advertising, p. 454
product advertising, p. 454
reminder advertising, p. 456

## Questions and Problems

1. Identify the strategy decisions a marketing manager must make in the advertising area.
2. Discuss the relation of advertising objectives to marketing strategy planning and the kinds of advertising actually needed. Illustrate.
3. List several media that might be effective for reaching consumers in a developing nation with low per-capita income and a high level of illiteracy. Briefly discuss the limitations and advantages of each medium you suggest.
4. Give three examples where advertising to intermediaries might be necessary. What are the objective(s) of such advertising?

5. What does it mean to say that "money is invested in advertising"? Is all advertising an investment? Illustrate.
6. Find advertisements to final consumers that illustrate the following types of advertising: *(a)* institutional, *(b)* pioneering, *(c)* competitive, and *(d)* reminder. What objective(s) does each of these ads have? List the needs each ad appeals to.
7. Describe the type of media that might be most suitable for promoting: *(a)* tomato soup, *(b)* greeting cards, *(c)* a business component material, and *(d)* playground equipment. Specify any assumptions necessary to obtain a definite answer.
8. Briefly discuss some of the pros and cons an advertising manager for a producer of sports equipment might want to think about in deciding whether to advertise on the Internet.
9. Discuss the use of testimonials in advertising. Which of the four AIDA steps might testimonials accomplish? Are they suitable for all types of products? If not, for which types are they most suitable?
10. Find a magazine ad that you think does a particularly good job of communicating to the target audience. Would the ad communicate well to an audience in another country? Explain your thinking.
11. Johnson & Johnson sells its baby shampoo in many different countries. Do you think baby shampoo would be a good product for Johnson & Johnson to advertise with a single global message? Explain your thinking.
12. Discuss the future of smaller advertising agencies now that many of the largest are merging to form mega-agencies.
13. Does advertising cost too much? How can this be measured?
14. How would your local newspaper be affected if local supermarkets switched their weekly advertising to a service that delivered weekly, freestanding ads directly to each home?
15. Is it unfair to advertise to children? Is it unfair to advertise to less-educated or less-experienced people of any age? Is it unfair to advertise for "unnecessary" products? Is it unfair to criticize a competitor's product in an ad?
16. Explain why P&G and other consumer packaged goods firms are trying to cut back on some types of sales promotion like coupons for consumers and short-term trade promotions such as "buy a case and get a case free."
17. Discuss some ways that a firm can link its sales promotion activities to its advertising and personal-selling efforts so that all of its promotion efforts result in an integrated effort.
18. Indicate the type of sales promotion that a producer might use in each of the following situations and briefly explain your reasons:
    *a.* A firm has developed an improved razor blade and obtained distribution, but customers are not motivated to buy it.
    *b.* A competitor is about to do a test market for a new brand and wants to track sales in test-market areas to fine-tune its marketing mix.
    *c.* A big grocery chain won't stock a firm's new popcorn-based snack product because it doesn't think there will be much consumer demand.
19. Why wouldn't a producer of toothpaste just lower the price of its product rather than offer consumers a price-off coupon?
20. If sales promotion spending continues to grow—often at the expense of media advertising—how do you think this might affect the rates charged by mass media for advertising time or space? How do you think it might affect advertising agencies?



## Computer-Aided Problem 15

### Sales Promotion

As a community service, disc jockeys from radio station WMKT formed a basketball team to help raise money for local nonprofit organizations. The host organization finds or fields a competing team and charges $5 admission to the game. Money from ticket sales goes to the nonprofit organization.

Ticket sales were disappointing at recent games—averaging only about 300 people per game. When WMKT's marketing manager, Bruce Miller, heard about the problem, he suggested using sales promotion to improve ticket sales. The PTA for the local high school—the sponsor for the next game—is interested in the idea but is concerned that its budget doesn't include any promotion money. Miller tries to help them by reviewing his idea in more detail.

Specifically, he proposes that the PTA give a free T-shirt (printed with the school name and date of the game) to the first 500 ticket buyers. He thinks the T-shirt giveaway will create a lot of interest. In fact, he says he is almost certain the promotion would help the PTA sell 600 tickets—double the usual number. He speculates that the PTA might even have a sellout of all 900 seats in the school gym. Further, he notes that the T-shirts will more than pay for themselves if the PTA sells 600 tickets.

A local firm that specializes in sales promotion items agrees to supply the shirts and do the printing for $2.40 a shirt if the PTA places an order for at least 400 shirts. The PTA thinks the idea is interesting but wants to look at it more closely to see what will happen if the promotion doesn't increase ticket sales. To help the PTA evaluate the alternatives, Miller sets up a spreadsheet with the relevant information.

a. *Based on the data from the initial spreadsheet, does the T-shirt promotion look like a good idea? Explain your thinking.*

b. *The PTA treasurer worries about the upfront cost of printing the T-shirts and wants to know where they would stand if they ordered the T-shirts and still sold only 300 tickets. He suggests it might be safer to order the minimum number of T-shirts (400). Evaluate his suggestion.*

c. *The president of the PTA thinks the T-shirt promotion will increase sales but wonders if it wouldn't be better just to lower the price. She suggests $2.60 a ticket, which she arrives at by subtracting the $2.40 T-shirt cost from the usual $5.00 ticket price. How many tickets would the PTA have to sell at the lower price to match the money it would make if it used the T-shirt promotion and actually sold 600 tickets? (Hint: Change the selling price in the spreadsheet and then vary the quantity using the analysis feature.)*

## Suggested Cases

To view the cases, go to www.mcgrawhill.ca/college/wong.

Interested in finding out what marketing looks like in the real world? *Marketing Magazine* is just a click away on your OLC! Visit **www.mcgrawhill.ca/college/wong** today.

When You Finish This Chapter, You Should

1. Understand how pricing objectives should guide strategy planning for pricing decisions.

2. Understand choices the marketing manager must make about price flexibility.

3. Know what a marketing manager should consider when setting the price level for a product in the early stages of the product life cycle.

4. Understand the many possible variations of a price structure, including discounts, allowances, and who pays transportation costs.

5. Understand the value-pricing concept and its role in obtaining a competitive advantage and offering target customers superior value.

6. Understand the legality of price level and price flexibility policies.

# Chapter Sixteen

# Pricing Objectives and Policies

## IKEA's Attractive Price Tags

Sunday at IKEA, and there's a circus in the living room at the Swedish-origin furniture and home furnishings retailer's jam-packed store. Every chair has a potential buyer sitting in it, or prodding it, or circling it like a lion around a tethered goat.

The same scene is routinely played out across North America, where IKEA has launched 24 stores since 1985. The most powerful furniture retailer on planet Earth—with more than 180 stores in 32 countries—is about to get even bigger. By 2013, it expects to have 50 of the flag-festooned blue and yellow big-box furniture outlets open for business in North America.

Worldwide, the IKEA influence is even more dramatic. Though the company is privately held and doesn't release profit figures, its worldwide sales have grown by an estimated 20 percent a year for the past five years, and its

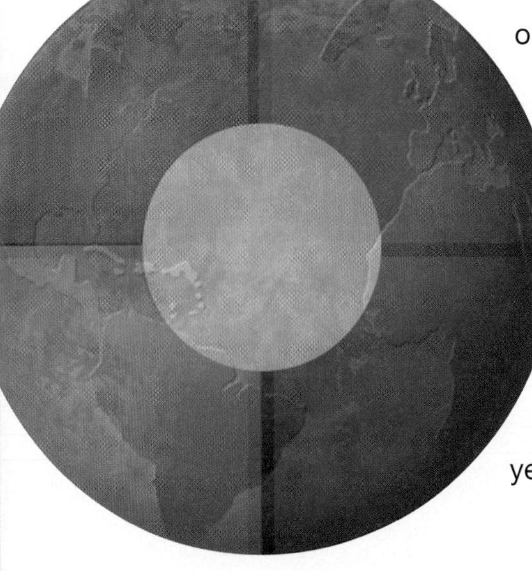

place price promotion produ

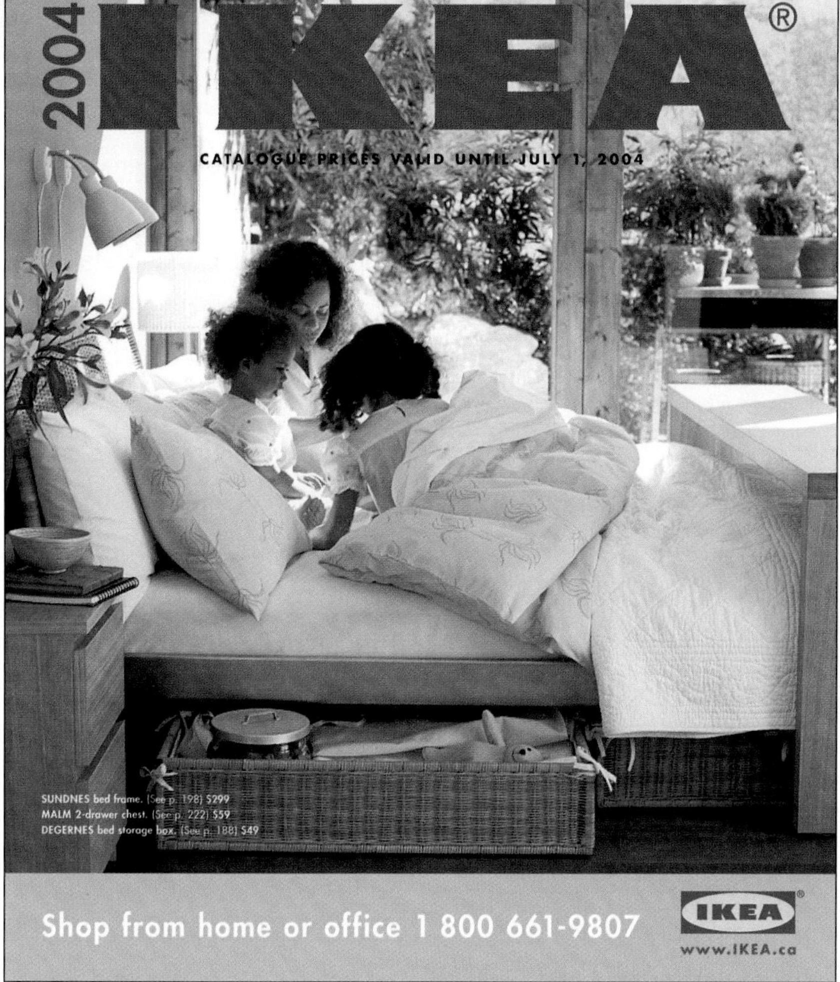


2003 revenues topped EUR 11 billion. Interbrand, a marketing research firm, recently ranked IKEA 44th on its list of the top 100 most valuable global brands, ahead of Pepsi, Harley-Davidson, and Apple.

So what's its secret? Much has been said about the quirks that make shopping at IKEA such a peculiar experience—the cavernous outlets; the conspicuously absent salespeople; the cafés that serve Swedish meatballs and lingonberry preserves; the heavy boxes that customers are expected to wrestle off towering racks; the complex furniture that they must assemble themselves.

But above all else, one factor accounts for IKEA's success: good quality at a low price. IKEA sells furniture that's cheap but not "cheapo," at prices that typically run 30 to 50 percent below the competition's. While the price of other companies' products tends to rise over time, IKEA says it has reduced its retail prices by a total of about 20 percent during the past four years.

At IKEA the process of driving down costs starts the moment a new item is conceived and continues relentlessly throughout its production run. The price of a basic Pöang chair, for example, has fallen from $149 in 2000 to $99 in 2001 to $79 today. IKEA expects the most recent price cut to increase Pöang sales by 30 to 50 percent.

IKEA's corporate mantra is "Low price with meaning." The goal is to make things less expensive without ever making customers feel cheap. Striking that balance demands a special kind of design, manufacturing, and distribution expertise. But IKEA pulls it off in its own distinctive way: tastefully, methodically, even cheerfully, and yet somehow differently than any other company anywhere.

Most manufacturers design a product, then try to figure out how to make it for a target price. At IKEA, the price literally comes first. Every product's

place price promotion product

sale price is set by a product developer like Per Carlsson, a large, bearded man who spends his days creating Volvo-style kitchens at Yugo prices. “Our goal,” he says, “is to solve problems.”

Typically, those “problems” are first identified in what IKEA calls its product-strategy council—a group of globe-trotting senior executives that monitors consumer trends and establishes priorities for IKEA’s product lineup. Think of the product-strategy council as a kind of central nervous system: It senses changes in the environment and relays them to subordinates such as Carlsson, the lead developer in the company’s kitchen department.

One “problem” recently identified by the council: Around the world, the kitchen has slowly replaced the living room as the social and entertaining center of the home. That means today’s kitchens need to project comfort and cleanliness to guests while also reflecting the gourmet aspirations of the host. But how do you do that globally? Comfort in Asia might be expressed in small, cozy appliances and spaces, while in North America, consumers aspire to own supersize glasses and giant refrigerators with names like Viking. Carlsson’s job is even more difficult when the council hands down directives that are broad, or even cryptic. He’s gotten instructions to “make more furniture for small spaces” and to “think cubic.”

After receiving a new set of instructions, Carlsson strolls up to the showroom on the third floor of IKEA’s headquarters, where each of the company’s kitchen items is marked with a large red-and-yellow price tag. Then he applies what IKEAns refer to as “the matrix.”

IKEA’s product managers use a price matrix to identify holes in the company’s product lineup—and how much to charge for a new product. Demonstrating how the matrix works, Carlsson draws a tic-tac-toe grid on a piece of paper, explaining that he can plot the price and style of any IKEA item within it. IKEA has three basic price ranges—high, medium, and low—and four basic styles: Scandinavian (sleek wood), modern (minimalist), country (neo-traditional), and young Swede (bare bones). To identify market opportunities, Carlsson takes a product council directive, plots his existing product lineup on the grid, and looks for empty spaces. Starting with the council’s small-spaces directive, for example, Carlsson found plenty of stand-alone kitchen islands at IKEA’s higher price points, but he noticed that he was missing an inexpensive kitchen unit suitable for use in studio apartments or offices. Carlsson surveys the competition to figure out how much the new product should cost, targets a price 30 to 50 percent lower than the rivals’, and voilá: An IKEA price point is born. This is the method Carlsson used to establish the target price for a low-end IKEA kitchen—complete with cabinets, sink, stove, and refrigerator—at $650.[1]

How successful is the IKEA concept? As of April 2004, Ingvar Kamprad, IKEA’s founder, was reportedly worth $53 billion compared to Bill Gates’ $47 billion, according to Veckans Affärer, a business weekly…and that’s a lot of bookcases!

## In This Chapter

This is the first of two chapters that deal with price. In this chapter we look at the strategic issues of price objectives and policies. Think of these as defining the "rules" for how managers should approach pricing decisions in their business. These rules will vary from firm to firm and even within the same firm for different products or at different points in time. In the next, we look at how firms actually set a price under those "rules."

These policies should explain (1) how flexible prices will be, (2) at what level they will be set over the product life cycle, (3) to whom and when discounts and allowances will be given, and (4) how transportation costs will be handled. See Exhibit 16-1. These price-related strategy decision areas are the focus of this chapter. After we've looked at specific decision areas, we will discuss how they combine to affect customer value as well as relevant laws.

## The Strategic Dimensions of Price

Price is one of the four major variables controlled by a marketing manager. Price-level decisions are especially important because they affect both the number of sales a firm makes and how much money it earns. From a customer's perspective, price is what must be given up to get the benefits offered by the rest of a firm's marketing mix, so it plays a direct role in shaping customer value.

Guided by the company's objectives, marketing managers must develop a set of pricing objectives and, based on those objectives, a set of pricing policies. These pricing policies spell out what price situations the firm will face and how it will handle them. These policies should explain (1) how flexible prices will be, (2) at what level they will be set over the product life cycle, (3) to whom and when discounts and allowances will be given, and (4) how transportation costs will be handled (see Exhibit 16-1). But before we consider the different objectives and policy alternatives available to managers, let's be certain we all understand what "price" really means: as you will see, it is much more than just a number on a sticker.

Exhibit 16-1 Strategy planning for price.

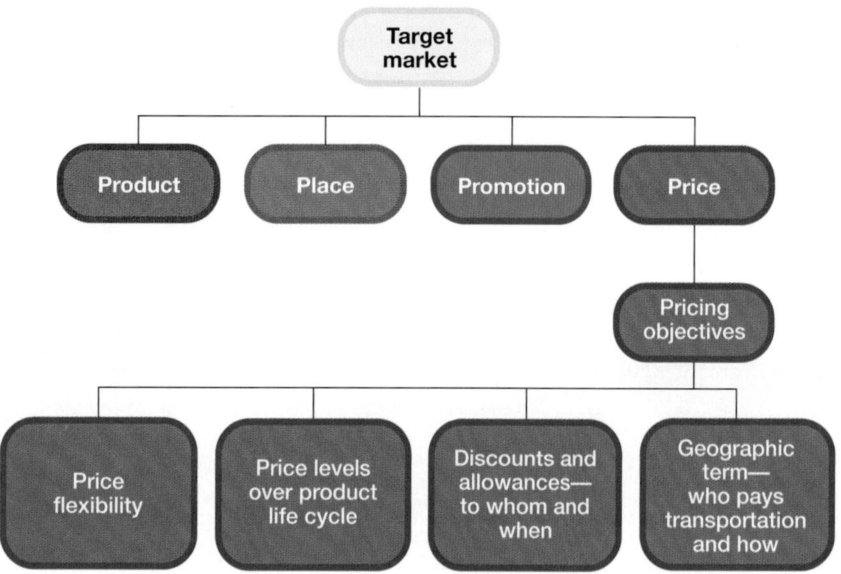

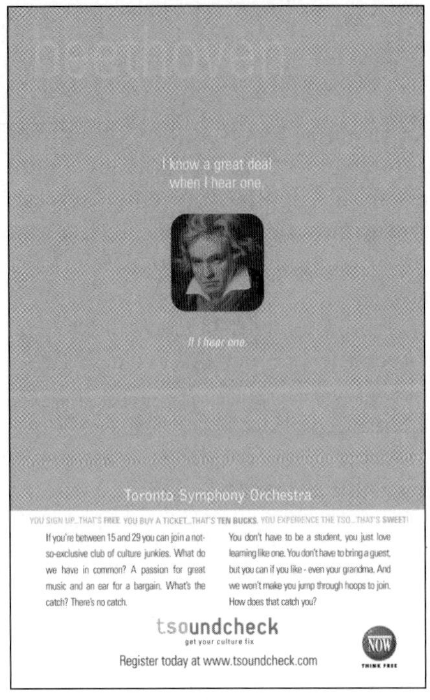


Since its existing customer base is aging, the Toronto Symphony Orchestra has introduced tsoundcheck as a way to attract young consumers by selling tickets that are cheaper than movie tickets.

## What Is a "Price"?

It's not easy to define price in real-life situations, because price reflects many dimensions and goes by many names. Universities call it tuition. Clubs call it dues. Hotels call it rates. Workers call it wages. Landlords call it rent. No matter what we call it, price always represents the same thing: the amount of money we expect the customer to give us in return for whatever we give them.

Logically, we might therefore expect that the more we give a customer, the higher the price we should receive. But this is not always the case. For example, suppose you were in your home on a typical day. How much would you pay for a glass of water? Likely, it is not very much. Now what if you had just spent two days in a dry hot desert and there was only one place to get refreshment. How much would you pay for that water now? How would that change if there were 10 places that could offer refreshment? Or consider this question: If all you could drink is one litre of water before filling up, how much extra would you pay for a second litre? A third? As you can see, prices aren't what we charge: prices are how much someone is willing to pay for something.

Exhibit 16-2
Price as seen by consumers or users.

| Price | Equals | Something of Value |
|---|---|---|
| *List Price*<br>Less: *Discounts*<br>Quantity<br>Seasonal<br>Cash<br>Temporary sales<br>Less: *Allowances*<br>Trade-ins<br>Damaged goods<br>Less: *Rebate and coupon value*<br>Plus: *Taxes* | equals | *Product*<br>Physical good<br>Service<br>Assurance of quality<br>Repair facilities<br>Packaging<br>Credit<br>Warranty<br>*Place of delivery or when available* |

Exhibit 16-3 Price as seen by channel members.

| Price | Equals | Something of Value |
|---|---|---|
| *List Price*<br>Less: *Discounts*<br>Quantity<br>Seasonal<br>Cash<br>Trade or functional<br>Temporary "deals"<br>Less: *Allowances*<br>Damaged goods<br>Advertising<br>Push money<br>Stocking<br>Plus: *Taxes and tariffs* | equals | *Product*<br>Branded—well known<br>Guaranteed<br>Warranteed<br>Service—repair facilities<br>Convenient packaging for handling<br>*Place*<br>Availability—when and where<br>*Price*<br>Price-level guarantee<br>Sufficient margin to allow chance for profit<br>*Promotion*<br>Promotion aimed at customers |

The "something" can be a physical product in various stages of completion, with or without supporting services, with or without quality guarantees, and so on. Or it could be a pure service—drycleaning, a lawyer's advice, or insurance on your car.

The nature and extent of this something determines the amount of money exchanged. Some customers pay list price. Others obtain large discounts or allowances because something is not provided. Exhibit 16-2 summarizes some possible variations for consumers or users, and Exhibit 16-3 does the same for channel members. These variations are discussed more fully below, and then we'll consider the customer value concept more fully—in terms of competitive advantage. But here it should be clear that price has many dimensions. How each of these dimensions is handled affects customer value. If a customer sees greater value in spending money in some other way, no exchange will occur. The thing to remember is that prices are affected not only by what is exchanged but also by the buyer's circumstances—the level of need, access to alternative ways of satisfying the need, the price of those alternatives, and so on.

## Decision 1—Pricing Objectives

Pricing objectives should flow from, and fit in with, company-level and marketing objectives. They should be explicitly stated and communicated, because they have a direct effect on pricing policies and on the methods used to set prices (see Chapter 18). Exhibit 16-4 shows the various types of pricing objectives we'll discuss.

Some of the distinctions between objectives may seem strange at first. After all, why do we need profit-oriented *and* sales-oriented objectives? Isn't one a direct result of the other? Why not just establish profit as the objective? The reason is that pricing often involves tradeoffs. For example, a business might reduce its price in order to sell more units, but if it lowers price too far it may find that those sales are unprofitable. Similarly, a firm might focus on the premium segment of the market and be highly profitable doing so: however, since premium segments are usually smaller in size, the number of units sold will not be large. Now, put yourself in the shoes of a salesperson who has been asked for a reduced price by a customer. As you can see, managers need to communicate the nature of the tradeoffs called for in their strategy to others who are involved in setting prices and giving discounts.

Exhibit 16-4 Possible pricing objectives.

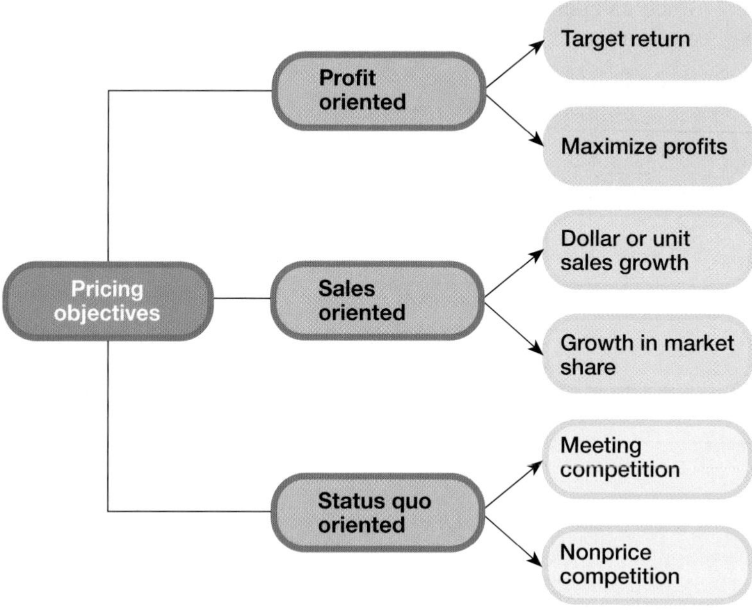




## Profit-Oriented Objectives

**target-return objective** An objective that states a specific level of profit

A **target-return objective** sets a specific level of profit as an objective. Often this amount is stated as a percentage of sales or of capital investment. A large manufacturer like Motorola might aim for a 15-percent return on investment. The target for Loblaw's and other grocery chains might be a 1-percent return on sales.

A target-return objective has administrative advantages in a large company, where the performance of many different businesses must be compared. The same target return can be set for the overall company or business-by-business depending upon their market and competitive environments. And some companies eliminate businesses or drop products if they fail to consistently meet the objective: even if they are profitable, the argument is that the company's resources could be put to more profitable use in businesses with a higher rate of return.

**profit-maximization objective** An objective that seeks to get as much profit as possible

**Profit maximization** A **profit-maximization** objective seeks to get as much profit as possible. It might be stated as a desire to earn a rapid return on investment—or, more bluntly, to charge all the traffic will bear.

Some people believe that anyone seeking a profit-maximization objective will charge high prices—prices that are not in the public interest. However, pricing to achieve profit maximization doesn't always lead to high prices. Low prices may expand the size of the market and result in greater sales and profits. For example, when prices of VCRs were very high, only innovators and wealthy people bought them. When producers lowered prices, nearly everyone bought one.

If a firm is earning a very large profit, other firms will try to copy or improve on what the company offers. Frequently, this leads to lower prices. IBM sold its original personal computer for about $4,500 in 1981. As Compaq, Dell, and other competitors started to copy IBM, it added more power and features and cut prices.

**When profit maximization isn't the target** Focusing on a target return does not always mean making as much money as possible. Some managers, for legitimate reasons, aim for only satisfactory returns. They just want returns that ensure the firm's survival and convince shareholders they're doing a good job. Similarly, some small family-run businesses aim for a profit that will provide a comfortable lifestyle.[2]

Some politicians want to control the prices of pharmaceuticals, but that may not be in the public interest if it reduces the incentive for firms to make the big investments required to develop innovative new medicines. That, in turn, would reduce consumer choices.

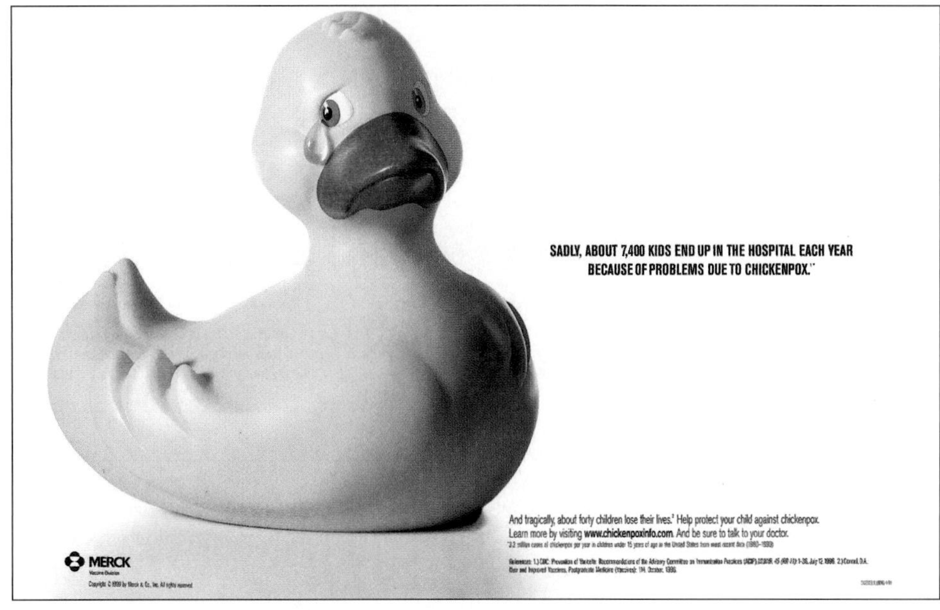

SADLY, ABOUT 7,400 KIDS END UP IN THE HOSPITAL EACH YEAR BECAUSE OF PROBLEMS DUE TO CHICKENPOX.
And tragically, about forty children lose their lives. Help protect your child against chickenpox.
Learn more by visiting www.chickenpoxinfo.com. And be sure to talk to your doctor.
MERCK


Many private and public nonprofit organizations set a price level that will just recover costs. In other words, their target-return figure is zero. For example, a government agency may charge motorists a toll for using a bridge but then drop the toll when the cost of the bridge is paid.

Companies that are leaders in their industries—like Blue Cross and Blue Shield (health insurance)—sometimes pursue only satisfactory long-run targets. They are well aware that their activities are in public view. The public and government officials expect them to follow policies that are in the public interest when they play the role of price leader or wage setter. Too large a return might invite government action. Similarly, firms that provide critical public services—including many utility and insurance companies, transportation firms, and defence contractors—often face public or government agencies that review and approve their prices.[3]

## Sales-Oriented Objectives

**sales-oriented objective**
Objective that seeks some level of unit sales, dollar sales, or share of market without referring to profit

A **sales-oriented objective** seeks some level of unit sales, dollar sales, or share of market—without referring to profit.

Some managers are more concerned about sales growth than profits. They think sales growth always leads to more profits. This kind of thinking causes problems when a firm's costs are growing faster than sales. Recently, many major corporations have had declining profits in spite of growth in sales. At the extreme, many dot-coms kept lowering prices to increase market share but never earned any profits. Pets.com had growing sales until it burned through investors' money and went bankrupt. Generally, however, business managers now pay more attention to profits, not just sales.[4]

Many firms seek to gain a specified share (percentage) of a market. If a company has a large market share, it may have better economies of scale than its competitors. While always important, scale economies are critical in industries like telecommunications, where the cost of establishing a network is the same regardless of the volume of traffic: in these cases, firms lose money until significant levels of sales are achieved. In addition, it's usually easier to measure a firm's market share than to determine if profits are being maximized and therefore easier to see whether objectives are being met.

A company with a longer-run view may decide that increasing market share is a sensible objective when the overall market is growing. The hope is that larger future

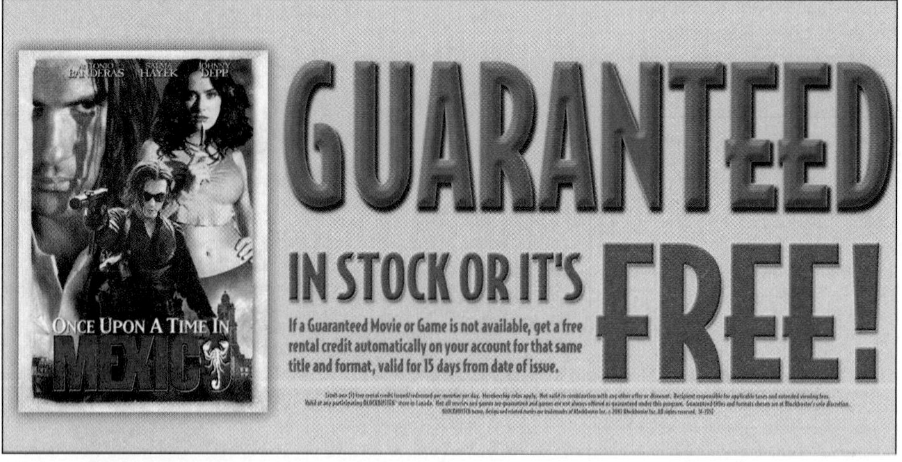


Blockbuster lures customers into its stores by guaranteeing that the latest movie releases will be available—it would rather provide a free rental than lose the long-term volume represented by each loyal customer.

volume will justify sacrificing some profit in the short run. In the early days of the Internet, Netscape took this approach with its browser software. And companies as diverse as 3M, Coca-Cola, and IBM look at opportunities in Eastern Europe this way. Later in this chapter we'll discuss the relative merits of charging low prices to build volume versus selling less but at higher prices.

Of course, objectives aimed at increasing market share have the same limitations as straight sales-growth objectives. A larger market share, if gained at too low a price, may lead to profitless "success."

### Status Quo Pricing Objectives

**status quo objectives**
Don't-rock-the-pricing-boat objectives

Managers satisfied with their current market share and profits sometimes adopt **status quo objectives**—don't-rock-the-pricing-boat objectives. Managers may say that they want to stabilize prices, or meet competition, or even avoid competition. This don't-rock-the-boat thinking is most common when the total market is not growing. Maintaining stable prices may discourage price competition and avoid the need for hard decisions.

**nonprice competition**
Aggressive action on one or more of the Ps other than price

A status quo pricing objective may be part of an aggressive overall marketing strategy focusing on **nonprice competition**—aggressive action on one or more of the Ps other than price. Fast-food chains like McDonald's, Wendy's, and Burger King experienced very profitable growth by sticking to nonprice competition for many years. However, when Taco Bell and others started to take away customers with price-cutting, the other chains also turned to price competition.[5]



## Decision 2—Price Flexibility

**administered prices**
Prices that are consciously set

Price policies usually lead to **administered prices**—consciously set prices. In other words, instead of letting daily market forces (or auctions) decide their prices, most firms set their own prices. They may hold prices steady for long periods of time or change them more frequently if that's what's required to meet objectives.

If a firm doesn't sell directly to final customers, it usually wants to administer both the price it receives from intermediaries and the price final customers pay. After all, the price customers pay will ultimately affect its sales. But it is often difficult—and sometimes illegal—to administer prices throughout the channel. Other channel members may also wish to administer prices to achieve their own objectives.

Some firms don't even try to administer prices. They just meet competition—or worse, mark up their costs with little thought of demand. They act as if they have no choice in selecting a price policy.

Remember that price has many dimensions. Managers do have many choices. They should administer their prices. And they should do it carefully because, ultimately, customers must be willing to pay these prices if the entire marketing mix is to succeed.

Having administered prices doesn't necessarily mean they are rigidly set for all occasions and all customers. Rather, managers must choose a level of price flexibility. Should the firm use a one-price or a flexible-price policy?

## Levels of Price Flexibility

**one-price policy**
Offering the same price to all customers who purchase products under essentially the same conditions and in the same quantities

A **one-price policy** means offering the same price to all customers who purchase products under essentially the same conditions and in the same quantities. The majority of Canadian firms use a one-price policy—mainly for administrative convenience and to maintain goodwill among customers.

A one-price policy makes pricing easier. But a marketing manager must be careful to avoid a rigid one-price policy. This can amount to broadcasting a price that competitors can undercut—especially if the price is somewhat high. One reason for the growth of mass-merchandisers like Wal-Mart is that conventional retailers rigidly applied traditional margins and stuck to them.

**flexible-price policy**
Offering the same product and quantities to different customers at different prices

A **flexible-price policy** means offering the same product and quantities to different customers at different prices.

Various forms of flexible pricing are more common now that most prices are maintained in a computer database. Frequent changes are easier. You see this when grocery chains give frequent-shopper club members reduced prices on weekly specials. They simply change the database in the central office. The checkout scanner reads the code on the package, then the computer looks up the club price or the regular price depending on whether a club card has been scanned.

Another twist on this is more recent. Some marketing managers have set up relationships with Internet companies whose ads invite customers to "set your own price." For example, Priceline operates a website at www.priceline.com. Visitors to the website specify their desired schedule for an airline flight and what price they're

## Internet Insite 16–1

### PRICING STRATEGIES FOR THE INTERNET

Retailers selling to consumers and businesses selling to other businesses (especially through catalogues) have in the past been constrained to charging published prices, even in the face of changing market conditions. A price printed in a catalogue or advertised in a newspaper leaves little room for change even when demand far exceeds supply. The Internet offers marketers greater flexibility in pricing while offering consumers the chance to find competitive prices. Dynamic and real-time pricing is possible online, which allows marketers to respond to market conditions. Let us examine a few of the pricing strategies available to marketers online.

**Auctions:** In an ideal world, marketers would like to see prices increase as demand increases and not fall below a floor price when demand decreases. Auctions allow marketers to set a floor price and sell the product to the highest bidder. The greater the demand, the higher the price under this pricing model.

The auction model is applicable to both consumer markets and business markets. On the consumer side, eBay is one of the best known sites, connecting millions of buyers and sellers worldwide. Each day there are thousands of products bought and sold on eBay through the auction process. Buyers can decide how much they wish to pay for a product and when they want to stop bidding. Buyers know the bidding history and the seller's rating. And it is no longer only individuals trying to sell used products through auctions. Larger firms and retailers participate in eBay as "power sellers" under eBay Stores. Consumers can buy new, unused products at very competitive prices.

**Reverse auctions:** The reverse auction model was popularized by Priceline.com. Under this model, consumers can choose dates and locations and then name the price they are willing to pay for services such as airline tickets, hotels, and rental cars. Priceline will relay the request to its service partners to find a service provider that matches or comes close to the price. In this case, the sellers bid for the buyer's business, which is the reverse of the traditional auction. From a consumer standpoint, in order for this model to work well awareness of prices for various services is essential.

Airlines, hotels, and car rentals are willing to participate in Priceline's reverse auction for a simple reason: a vacant seat on a flight or an empty room in a hotel is perishable and cannot be kept in inventory. If the sale is not made by the time the flight takes off, then that revenue opportunity is lost. Instead of losing the opportunity entirely, marketers are willing to accept a lower price to recoup their costs, or in some cases make a smaller profit than normal.

On the business side, several business-to-business (B2B) marketplaces have incorporated flexible pricing. Covisint, a B2B site created by General Motors, Ford, and DaimlerChrysler, has an auction feature where suppliers can submit bids. Buyers (major automobile manufacturers) can post a Request for Quote (RFQ) and then watch suppliers bid. Covisint allows for private online negotiation between the buyer and seller.

Reverse auctions tend to lower prices. In the case of airlines or hotels that do not want to keep a seat or room empty, last-minute reverse auctioning may make sense. Some experts suggest that the brand value and image may be diminished by offering products at a very low price through reverse auctions.[6]

**Aggregate pricing:** Aggregate buying involves a group of consumers joining to buy a product, leading to volume discounts for all. Costco offers lower prices based on volume purchases. Aggregate selling sites use the same approach. In the late 1990s, aggregate pricing was considered to be the next wave of e-commerce, with several high-profile players such as Accompany.com and Mercata.com vying to be the industry leader.

In the business-to-consumer category the aggregate buying model did not catch on. Start-ups Accompany and Mercata failed. In order for the aggregate buying model to work, consumers have to sign on to buy a product and then wait for more people to join so that the price can be lowered. Letusbuyit.com, with operations in several European countries, is the only large aggregate buyer currently operating. On the B2B side there are a few examples of aggregate buying, including ecmarket.com, which focuses on the food and beverage industry.

**Micro pricing and micro payments:** Here, the idea is that digitizable products, such as newspaper articles, songs, one-time-use software, pictures, or cartoons, can be priced as low as a few cents and can be sold to interested consumers. Someone doing research on a certain company may not mind paying a small amount for an old newspaper article on that company. Using credit cards for such transactions is not economical because the merchant has to pay a processing fee for transactions that can be more than the value of the transaction. Software solutions such as Millicent (owned by Digital and then Compaq), Digicash, and Cybercash failed to attract merchants who wanted to use micro pricing. Now a company called NewGenPay (www.newgenpay.com) provides a solution called Valuto. Micro pricing allows marketers to unbundle products and price them individually as well as in a bundle. For instance, a CD with 12 songs may be priced at $14.95, but to listen to a song once, the price may be $0.25. Problems with the technology and lack of a uniform standard that is acceptable to all banks, credit card companies, and merchants have hampered the acceptance of micro payments. Micro pricing has a future but it has yet to be exploited by marketers.

**Real-time pricing:** In the energy sector, energy companies can now monitor energy-consumption levels through Internet-based technologies and can adjust prices on a real-time basis by matching demand and supply. In the U.S., Washington-based Puget Sound Energy is one of the companies experimenting with such a pricing model.[7] Under this pricing scheme, the price per unit of energy will vary depending on the time of day and total demand for energy. Under such a pricing model, consumers can shift their consumption to a lower-priced time. Real-time pricing is not yet commonplace in the utility or other industries.

All of the pricing methods discussed here—the auction, reverse auction, aggregate pricing, micro pricing and real-time pricing—allow marketers greater flexibility. Pricing can be dynamic and responsive to demand and market conditions, as opposed to being fixed for long periods of time. At the end of the day, whatever pricing method is chosen should enable the firm to achieve long-term profitability.

Some consumers see the auction sites and aggregate buying sites as a place to get good deals. At the same time, such dynamic pricing models lead to different prices for different consumers. Research shows that consumers react strongly when they find out there is price discrimination.[8] Amazon.com tried charging different prices to different customers for the same DVD, which led to an uproar from customers and a hasty apology from the company.[9] While the flexibility of the Internet-based dynamic pricing tools is very attractive to marketers, consumer response to such pricing strategies must also be considered.

Here are some questions to ponder: As a consumer, what pros and cons do you see in the reverse-auction pricing model? Why hasn't micro pricing become a great success?

Go to: www.mcgrawhill.ca/college/wong
to apply this Insite in an exciting Internet exercise.

willing to pay. Priceline electronically forwards the information to airlines, and if one accepts the offer the consumer is notified. Priceline has a similar service for new cars and other products such as home mortgages, hotel rooms, rental cars, and long-distance rates. Internet Insite 16-1 shows a number of other ways that the Internet is being applied to developing new approaches to flexible pricing.

It may appear that these marketing managers have given up on administering prices. Just the opposite is true. They are carefully administering a flexible price. Most airlines, for example, set a very high list price. Not many people pay it. Travellers who plan ahead or who accept off-peak flights get a discount. Business travellers who want high-demand flights on short notice pay the higher prices. However, it doesn't make sense to stick to a high price and fly the plane half empty. So the airline continually adjusts the price on the basis of how many seats are left to fill. If seats are still empty at the last minute, the website offers a rock-bottom fare. Other firms, especially service businesses, use this approach when they have excess capacity.[10] (See Marketing Demo 16-1.)

Flexible pricing is most common in the channels, in direct sales of business products, and at retail for expensive items and homogeneous shopping products. Retail shopkeepers in less-developed economies typically use flexible pricing. These situations usually involve personal selling, not mass selling. The advantage of flexible

## Marketing Demo 16–1

### TORONTO GEARS TICKET PRICES TO CALENDAR

The Toronto Blue Jays will put their own touch on a growing trend in North American professional sports when they announce ... that they are pricing single-game tickets in accordance with the month and day of the week.

The concept, which the Blue Jays' marketing department is referring to as "dynamic pricing," borrows from the entertainment and travel industry, according to the club's senior vice-president of marketing and sales, Paul Allamby.

"It's a wakeup call for us to recognize that in April, May and the first part of June, our product isn't worth the same to the consumer as the product in July," Allamby said. "It doesn't mean the baseball part isn't the same. It means the entertainment product doesn't have the same ambient flavour."

The Blue Jays will have three price groupings, including seven premium games set around marquee events. That means the Blue Jays will not follow the lead of most clubs and fix the ticket prices to the drawing power of opponents.

The premium games will be opening day against the New York Yankees, Father's Day Sleepover Weekend against the Chicago Cubs, Yankees Summer Weekend, and Alumni Weekend against the Oakland Athletics.

In addition, the Blue Jays have designated 26 value games (weekday games in April and May and Monday through Thursday in June) in addition to 48 regular games (all Saturday and Sunday games, Friday games from June through September, and all weekday games in July, August, and September).

Allamby stressed that season subscribers will still come out at least 20 percent ahead, even with the value games factored in, and added that seats in the 200 level Family Zone, Lower SkyDeck and Upper SkyDeck will not fluctuate.

Ticket prices for the three most expensive seat sections in the SkyDome will not change for the 26 value games or regular games. For example, it will still cost $180 to sit in the "action" seats behind home plate, $49 for premium dugout seats, and $46 for field level infield seats, but they will rise to $186, $57, and $52, respectively, for premium games.

"In reality, the games in the early part of the season aren't the ones we make money on," Allamby said. "We want to make sure we have a lot of sampling going on in those early games."

European soccer clubs have used variable pricing for some time, and hockey and baseball clubs have started to get on board.

The Colorado Rockies had four tiers of games, charging more for "classic games" against interleague opponents such as the Yankees and Cleveland Indians. Last year, the Pittsburgh Penguins began charging $5 more for weekend and holiday games, bringing in an extra $1-million in revenue. And this year, the Vancouver Canucks raised prices for games against the Colorado Avalanche, New York Rangers, and Stanley Cup champion Detroit Red Wings.

Allamby said the club is committed to the pricing scheme beyond 2003, although the proportion of games in each category could change.

"This is our learning year," Allamby said. "It's where we find out what works and what doesn't."[11]

To reach its objectives, Carnival uses flexible pricing—including discounts for retired people. By contrast, *Professional Carwashing & Detailing,* a trade magazine, wants advertisers to know that it charges everyone the same price for ad space.

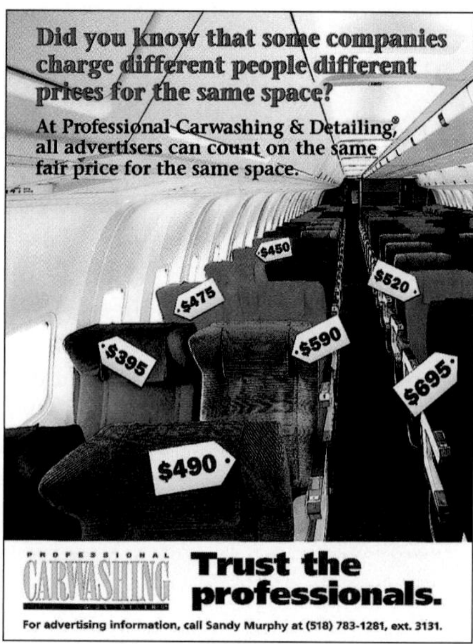


pricing is that the salesperson can make price adjustments—considering prices charged by competitors, the relationship with the customer, and the customer's bargaining ability. Flexible-price policies often specify a range in which the actual price charged must fall.[12]

Most auto dealers use flexible pricing. The producer suggests a list price, but the dealers bargain for what they can get. Their salespeople negotiate prices every day. Inexperienced consumers, reluctant to bargain, often pay hundreds of dollars more than the dealer is willing to accept. By contrast, however, Saturn dealers have earned high customer-satisfaction ratings by offering haggle-weary consumers a one-price policy.

Flexible pricing does have disadvantages. A customer who finds that others paid lower prices for the same marketing mix will be unhappy. Also, some sales reps let price-cutting become a habit. This reduces the role of price as a competitive tool and leads to a lower price level.



## Decision 3—Price-Level Policies over the Product Life Cycle

When marketing managers administer prices, they must consciously set a price-level policy. As they enter the market, they have to set introductory prices that may have long-run effects. They must consider where the product life cycle is and how fast it's moving. And they must decide if their prices should be above, below, or somewhere in between relative to the market.

Let's look for a moment at a new product in the market introduction stage of its product life cycle. Assuming that there are few direct competitors, the price-level decision should focus first on the nature of market demand. A high price may lead to higher profit from each sale but also to fewer units sold. A lower price might appeal to more potential customers. With this in mind, should the firm set a high or a low price?

**skimming price policy**

A policy that tries to sell to the top of a market at a high price before aiming at more price-sensitive customers

### Skimming Price Policies

A **skimming price policy** tries to sell the top (skim the cream) of a market—the top of the demand curve—at a high price before aiming at more price-sensitive customers.

Exhibit 16-5 Alternative introductory pricing policies.

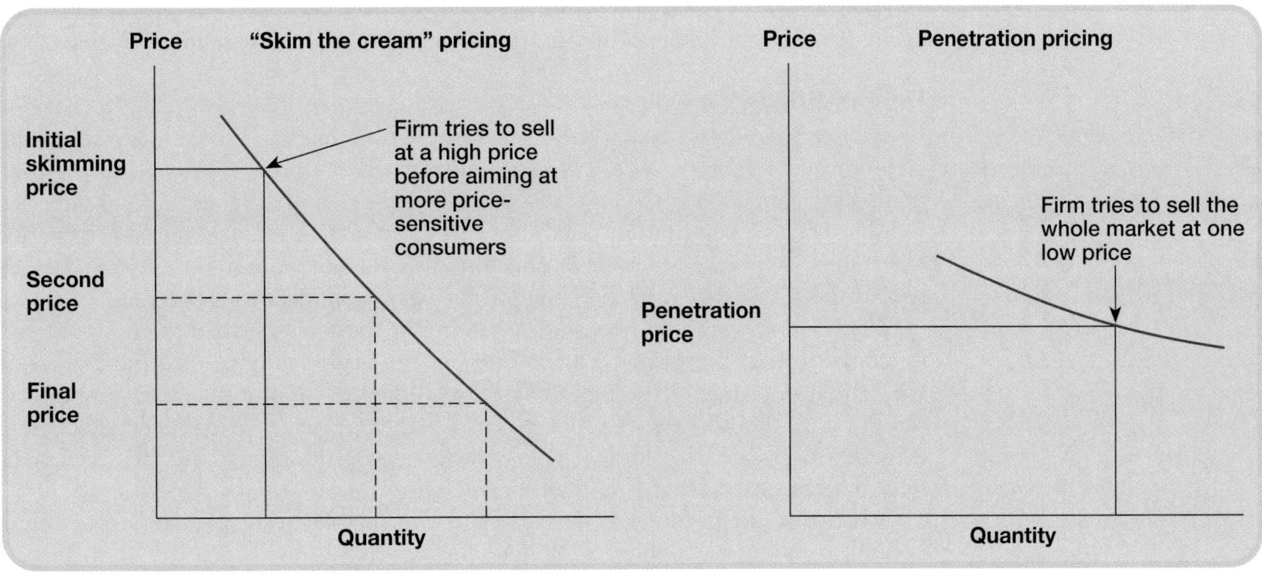


Skimming may maximize profits in the market-introduction stage for an innovation, especially if there is little competition. Competitor analysis may help clarify whether barriers will prevent or discourage competitors from entering. Skimming is also useful when you don't know very much about the shape of the demand curve. It's sometimes safer to start with a high price that customers can refuse and then reduce it if necessary.[13]

A skimming policy usually involves a slow reduction in price over time (see Exhibit 16-5). Note that as price is reduced new target markets are probably being sought. So, as the price level steps down the demand curve, new place, product, and promotion policies may be needed as well. Therefore, firms using this approach should identify a particular sequence of market entries as a means of determining when to make subsequent price cuts and other modifications to their marketing mix.

When Hewlett-Packard (HP) introduced its laser printer for personal computers, it initially set a high price—around $4,000. HP had a good head start on competitors, and no close substitute was available. HP sold the high-priced printers mainly to computer professionals and to business users with serious desktop-publishing needs. When other firms entered the market with similar printers, HP added features and lowered its price. It also did more advertising and added mail-order intermediaries to reach new target markets. Then, just as competitors were entering the market to go after budget-oriented buyers, HP introduced a new model at a lower price and added office-supply warehouse stores, like Office Depot, to the dis-

## Ethical Dimensions 16–1

### CRITICISMS OF SKIMMING

Some critics argue that for new products that have important social consequences, firms should not try to maximize profits by using a skimming policy. A patent-protected, life-saving drug, or a genetic technique that increases crop yields, is likely to have an inelastic demand curve. Yet many of those who need the product may not have the money to buy it. This is a serious concern. However, it's also a serious problem if firms don't have any incentive to take the risks required to develop breakthroughs in the first place.[14]

tribution channel. This is very typical of skimming, which involves dropping prices through a series of marketing-strategy changes over the course of the product life cycle. See Ethical Dimensions 16-1 for some criticisms of skimming policies.

## Penetration Price Policy

**penetration pricing policy**
A policy that tries to sell to the whole market at one low price

A **penetration pricing policy** tries to sell the whole market at one low price. Such an approach might be wise when the elite market—those willing to pay a high price—is small. This is the case when the whole demand curve is fairly elastic. See Exhibit 16-5. A penetration policy is even more attractive if selling larger quantities results in lower costs because of economies of scale. Penetration pricing may be wise if the firm expects strong competition very soon after introduction.

When a company uses penetration pricing in these circumstances, the result can be market ownership or dominance. Because the firm is the first into the market, it wins the lion's share of the rapidly developed market. By the time the competition has entered, the firm possesses large cost advantages tied to experience effects and economies of scale. In addition, it may have tied up the primary distribution channels. The result is a higher cost of market entry for potential competitors.

When the first version of the PalmPilot was introduced, competitors were close behind. In addition, Apple had failed when it tried to introduce the Newton personal information manager at a skimming price of $1,000. Most customers just didn't think it was worth it. So the focus for Palm was on a combination of features and price that would be a good value and help penetrate the market quickly. The initial price of about $250 resulted in sales of a million units in 24 months. Once Palm had a large base of users it worked at keeping them. For example, current owners could get $75 for trading in their old units on a new model, or they could upgrade for $129.[15]

Palm certainly faces competition in this market now, but its initial price probably kept some firms from jumping into the fray. That's why a low penetration price is sometimes called a stay-out price. It discourages competitors from entering the market.

The great risk in penetration pricing is that the cost–volume assumptions are not realized. For example, if the firm overestimated market potential or the speed with which customers would try the innovation—regardless of price—they may find themselves selling at a price that cannot be supported at their current cost. In addition, new competitors who realize the pioneering firm's advantages may seek out an alternative and more efficient way of producing the product that has fundamentally lower costs at a given level of volume. Thus the competition would not face the barriers to entry that were anticipated. Finally, the competition may find it possible to learn from the pioneer's experiences and thereby secure lower costs in areas like operations, distribution, and selling, even though their volume is not as great.

## Introductory Price Dealing

**introductory price dealing**
Temporary price cuts used to speed new products into a market or to gain some of the volume-building benefits of penetration pricing

Low prices do attract customers. Therefore, marketers often use **introductory price dealing**—temporary price cuts—to speed new products into a market or as a means of gaining some of the volume-building benefits of penetration pricing without giving up all of the margin gained in skimming pricing. Introductory price dealing may be used to get customers to try a new product concept as part of the pioneering effort or to attract customers to a new brand entry later in the life cycle. However, don't confuse these *temporary* price cuts with low penetration prices. The plan here is to raise prices as soon as the introductory offer is over. By then, hopefully, target customers will have tried the product and decided it was worth buying again at the regular price.

Established competitors often choose not to meet introductory price dealing—as long as the introductory period is not too long or too successful. However, some

Marketers often use introductory price dealing—in the form of temporary price cuts or introductory coupons—to speed new products into a market.

competitors quickly match introductory price deals with their own short-term sale prices; they want to discourage their established customers from shopping around.

Introductory price deals can also be offered to channel members. In these cases, a manufacturer may set different price-level policies for different levels in the channel. For example, a producer of a slightly better product might set a price level that is low relative to competitors when selling to retailers, while suggesting an above-the-market retail price. This encourages retailers to carry the product, and to emphasize it in their marketing mix, because it yields higher profits.

### Pricing in Mature Markets

Regardless of their introductory pricing policy, most firms face competition sooner or later in the product life cycle. When that happens, prices must be set relative not only to the market's demand curve but also to the prices charged by competitors. Firms that are not able to differentiate their products at a reasonable cost become commodity-like and may have few options other than to match competitors' prices. We'll discuss some of these options, and more importantly how to prevent this situation in the first place, in the next chapter.



## Decision 4—Discounts and Allowances: To Whom and When

**basic list prices**

The prices final customers or users are normally asked to pay for products

Most price structures are built around a base price schedule or price list. **Basic list prices** are the prices final customers or users are normally asked to pay for products. In this book, unless noted otherwise, list price refers to basic list price. In the next chapter, we discuss how firms set these list prices. For now, however, we'll consider the policy of whether and when to allow variations from list price and why they are made.

**discounts**

Reductions from list price given by a seller to buyers who either give up some marketing function or provide the function themselves

### Discount Policies—Reductions from List Prices

**Discounts** are reductions from list price given by a seller to buyers who either give up some marketing function or provide the function themselves. Discounts can be useful in marketing strategy planning. In the following discussion, think about what function the buyers are giving up, or providing, when they get each of these discounts. (Hint: recall Exhibits 16-2 and 16-3.)

**quantity discounts**
Discounts offered to encourage customers to buy in larger amounts

**Discounts based on quantity purchase** **Quantity discounts** are discounts offered to encourage customers to buy in larger amounts. This lets a seller get more of a buyer's business, or shifts some of the storing function to the buyer, or reduces shipping and selling costs—or all of these. Such discounts are of two kinds: cumulative and noncumulative.

**cumulative quantity discounts**
Discounts that apply to purchases over a given period; usually increase as the amount purchased increases

**Cumulative quantity discounts** apply to purchases over a given period—such as a year—and the discount usually increases as the amount purchased increases. Cumulative discounts are intended to encourage repeat buying by a single customer by reducing the customer's cost for additional purchases. This is a way to develop closer, ongoing relationships with customers. A cumulative quantity discount is often attractive to business customers who don't want to run up their inventory costs. They are rewarded for buying large quantities, even though individual orders may be smaller.

**noncumulative quantity discounts**
Discounts that apply only to individual orders

**Noncumulative quantity discounts** apply only to individual orders. Such discounts encourage larger orders but do not tie a buyer to the seller after that one purchase. The larger orders may reduce the seller's need for warehousing and may lead to lower shipping and handling costs.

While quantity discounts are usually given as price cuts, sometimes they are given as free or bonus products. Airline frequent-flyer programs use this approach.

Quantity discounts can be a very useful tool for the marketing manager. Some customers are eager to get them. But marketing managers must use quantity discounts carefully. Ideally, the quantity discount is "paid for" by the cost savings generated by whatever actions the customer must take to qualify: for example, buying more often or in larger orders. Thus, cost-volume relationships must be analyzed. This is especially true in business markets, where they must offer such discounts to all customers on equal terms to avoid price discrimination.

**seasonal discounts**
Discounts offered to encourage buyers to buy earlier than present demand requires

**Discounts based on seasonality and time of purchase** **Seasonal discounts** are discounts offered to encourage buyers to buy earlier than present demand requires. If used by a manufacturer, this discount tends to shift the storing function further along in the channel. It also tends to even out sales over the year. For example, a manufacturer of bedroom furniture might offer wholesalers a lower price if they buy in the fall—when sales are slow. The wholesalers can then offer a seasonal discount to retailers—who may try to sell the furniture during a special fall sale.

Discounts are also used to sell excess inventories when their season of use has passed. For example, a manufacturer of snow shovels might hold a sale near the end of winter. Since each sale reduces the cost of carrying inventory over the summer, the savings can be passed on to the customer. Firms selling products that are sensitive to fashion trends may also offer end-of-season discounts. For example, the Gap offers large discounts on their winter clothes right before they start stocking the spring line.



The Elixir nightclub advertises half-price entry on Wednesdays to drive traffic on a traditionally slow night.

Service firms that face irregular demand or capacity constraints often use seasonal discounts. For example, some telephone companies offer a discount for night-time calls when the load of business calls is low. Bars and clubs offer deals such as cheaper drinks during the week to supplement their busy weekends. The logic is the same for "Tuesday-night specials" at movie theatres.

**Discounts based on payment terms** Most sales to businesses are made on credit. The seller sends a bill (invoice) by mail or electronically, and the buyer's accounting department processes it for payment. Some firms depend on their suppliers for temporary working capital (credit). Therefore, it is very important for both sides to clearly state the terms of payment—including the availability of cash discounts—and to understand the commonly used payment terms.

**net**

An invoice term meaning that payment for the face value of the invoice is due immediately

**cash discounts**

Reductions in price to encourage buyers to pay their bills quickly

**2/10, net 30**

An invoice term meaning that the buyer can take a 2-percent discount off the face value of the invoice if the invoice is paid within 10 days; otherwise, the full face value is due within 30 days

**Net** means that payment for the face value of the invoice is due immediately. These terms are sometimes changed to net 10 or net 30—which means payment is due within 10 or 30 days of the date on the invoice.

**Cash discounts** are reductions in price to encourage buyers to pay their bills quickly. The terms for a cash discount usually modify the net terms. **2/10, net 30** means the buyer can take a 2-percent discount off the face value of the invoice if the invoice is paid within 10 days. Otherwise, the full face value is due within 30 days. And it usually is stated or understood that an interest charge will be added after the 30-day free-credit period.

Smart buyers carefully evaluate cash discounts. A discount of 2/10, net 30 may not look like much at first. But the buyer earns a 2-percent discount for paying the invoice just 20 days sooner than it should be paid anyway. By not taking the discount, the company in effect is borrowing at an annual rate of 36 percent. That is, assuming a 360-day year and dividing by 20 days, there are 18 periods during which the company could earn 2 percent—and 18 times 2 equals 36 percent a year.

Credit sales are also important to retailers. Some stores have their own credit systems. But most retailers use credit card services, such as Visa or MasterCard. The retailers pay a percentage of the revenue from each credit sale for this service—from 1 to 7 percent depending on the card company and the store's sales volume. For this reason, some retailers offer discounts to consumers who pay cash, and some credit card companies offer rebates and other rewards for card usage.

**trade (functional) discount**

A list price reduction given to channel members for the job they are going to do, such as storing, transporting, or selling

**Trade and functional discounts** A **trade (functional) discount** is a list price reduction given to channel members for the job they are going to do, such as storing, transporting, or selling. For example, a manufacturer might allow retailers a 30-percent trade discount from the suggested retail list price to cover the cost of the retailing function and their profit.

Sometimes manufacturers suggest a *chain* discount when selling through wholesalers. The manufacturer specifies what they feel is the appropriate discount for retailers to receive from wholesalers and what they are paying the wholesaler. For example, a firm might offer wholesalers a chain discount of 30 percent and 10 percent off the suggested retail price. In this case, the wholesalers would be expected to pass the 30-percent discount on to retailers and retain 10 percent for themselves.[16]

**sale price**

A temporary discount from the list price

**Special sales** A **sale price** is a temporary discount from the list price. Sale-price discounts encourage immediate buying. In other words, to get the sale price, customers give up the convenience of buying when they want to buy and instead buy when the seller wants to sell.

Special sales provide a marketing manager with a quick way to respond to changing market conditions—without changing the basic marketing strategy. For example, a retailer might use a sale to help clear extra inventory or to meet a competing store's price. Or a producer might offer an intermediary a special deal—in addition to the normal trade discount—that makes it more profitable for the intermediary to push the product. Retailers often pass some of the savings along to consumers.

In recent years, sale prices and deals have become much more common. At first it may seem that consumers benefit from all this. But prices that change constantly may confuse customers and erode brand loyalty.

**everyday low pricing (EDLP)** Setting a low list price rather than relying on a high list price that frequently changes with various discounts or allowances

To avoid these problems, some firms that sell consumer convenience products offer **everyday low pricing (EDLP)**—setting a low list price rather than relying on a high list price that frequently changes with various discounts or allowances. The notion is that there is a cost, beyond the reduced revenue, to promoting and holding a sale; EDLP avoids those costs and passes them onto the consumer.

Sale prices should be used carefully, consistent with well-thought-out pricing objectives and policies. A marketing manager who constantly uses temporary sales to adjust the price level probably has not done a good job setting the normal price.[17]

**allowances**

Reductions in price given to final consumers, customers, or channel members for doing something or accepting less of something

## Allowance Policies—Off-List Prices

**Allowances**, like discounts, are given to final consumers, customers, or channel members for doing something or accepting less of something.

**advertising allowances**

Price reductions given to firms in the channel to encourage them to advertise or otherwise promote the firm's products locally

**Advertising allowances** are price reductions given to firms in the channel to encourage them to advertise or otherwise promote the supplier's products locally. For example, General Electric gave an allowance (1.5 percent of sales) to its wholesalers of housewares and radios. They in turn were expected to spend the allowance on local advertising.

**stocking allowances (slotting allowances)**

Reductions in price given to an intermediary to get shelf space ("slots") for a product

**Stocking allowances**—sometimes called slotting allowances—are given to an intermediary to get shelf space ("slots") for a product. For example, a producer might offer a retailer cash or free merchandise to stock a new item. Stocking allowances are used mainly to get supermarket chains to handle new products. Supermarkets don't have enough slots on their shelves to handle all of the available new products. They're more willing to give space to a new product if the supplier will offset their handling costs—like making space in the warehouse, adding information on computer systems, and redesigning store shelves, for example.

There is controversy about stocking allowances. Critics say that retailer demands for big stocking allowances slow new-product introductions and make it hard for small producers to compete. Some producers feel that retailers' demands are unethical—just a different form of extortion. Retailers, on the other hand, point out that the fees protect them from producers that simply want to push more and more me-too products onto their shelves.

**push money (or prize money) allowances**

Price reductions given to retailers by manufacturers or wholesalers to pass on to the retailers' salesclerks for aggressively selling certain items

**Push money (or prize money) allowances**—sometimes called PMs or spiffs—are given to retailers by manufacturers or wholesalers to pass on to the retailers' salesclerks for aggressively selling certain items. PM allowances are used for new items, slower-moving items, or higher-margin items. They are often used for pushing furniture, clothing, consumer electronics, and cosmetics. A salesclerk, for example, might earn an additional $5 for each new-model Pansonic DVD player sold.

**trade-in allowance**

A price reduction given for used products when similar new products are bought

A **trade-in allowance** is a price reduction given for used products when similar new products are bought. Trade-ins give the marketing manager an easy way to lower the effective price without reducing list price and are particularly important in the case of durable goods like cars and appliances. They perform the task of disposing of the old unit for the consumer while offering the seller the potential of reselling the used item.

## The Special Case of Coupons and Rebates

Many producers and retailers offer discounts (or free items) through coupons distributed in packages, mailings, print ads, or at the store. By presenting a coupon to a retailer, the consumer is given a discount off list price. This is especially common in the consumer packaged goods business—but the use of price-off coupons is growing in other lines of business too.

Retailers are willing to redeem producers' coupons because it increases their sales—and they usually are paid for the trouble of handling the coupon. For example, a retailer who redeems a 50-cents-off coupon might be repaid 75 cents. In effect, the coupon increases the functional discount and makes it more attractive to sell the couponed product.

**rebates**

Refunds paid to consumers after a purchase

Some producers offer **rebates**—refunds paid to consumers after a purchase. Sometimes the rebate may be very large. Some automakers offer rebates of $500 to $2,500 to promote sales of slow-moving models. Rebates are used on lower-priced items too—ranging from Duracell batteries to Paul Masson wines.

Rebates give the producer a way to be certain that final consumers actually get the price reduction. If the rebate amount were just taken off the price charged intermediaries, they might not pass the savings along to consumers. In addition, many consumers buy because the price looks lower with the rebate—but then they don't request the refund.[18]

## Decision 5—Geographic Pricing Policies



Retail list prices sometimes include free delivery. Or free delivery may be offered to some customers as an aid to closing the sale. But deciding who pays the freight charge is more important on sales to business customers than to final consumers because more money is involved. There are many possible variations for an imaginative marketing manager, and some specialized terms have developed.

**F.O.B.**

A transportation term meaning free on board some vehicle at some place

A commonly used transportation term is **F.O.B.**—which means free on board some vehicle at some place. Typically, F.O.B. pricing names the place—often the location of the seller's factory or warehouse—as in F.O.B. Taiwan or F.O.B. mill. This means that the seller pays the cost of loading the products onto some vehicle, then title to the products passes to the buyer. The buyer pays the freight and takes responsibility for damage in transit.

F.O.B. shipping-point pricing simplifies the seller's pricing—but it may narrow the market. Since the delivered cost varies depending on the buyer's location, a customer located farther from the seller must pay more and might buy from closer suppliers. To simplify matters, companies break down F.O.B. pricing even further with zone and uniform delivered pricing.

**zone pricing**

Making an average freight charge to all buyers within specific geographic areas

**Zone pricing** means making an average freight charge to all buyers within specific geographic areas. The seller pays the actual freight charges and bills each customer for an average charge. For example, a company in Canada might divide the United States into seven zones, then bill all customers in the same zone the same amount for freight even though actual shipping costs might vary.

Zone pricing reduces the wide variation in delivered prices that results from an F.O.B. shipping-point pricing policy. It also simplifies transportation charges.

**uniform delivered pricing**

Making an average freight charge to all buyers

**Uniform delivered pricing** means making an average freight charge to all buyers. It is a kind of zone pricing—an entire country may be considered as one zone—that includes the average cost of delivery in the price. Uniform delivered pricing is most often used when (1) transportation costs are relatively low and (2) the seller wishes to sell in all geographic areas at one price—perhaps a nationally advertised price.

When all firms in an industry use F.O.B. shipping-point pricing, a firm usually competes well near its shipping point but not farther away. As sales reps look for business farther away, delivered prices rise and the firm finds itself priced out of the market.

**freight-absorption pricing**

Absorbing freight cost so that a firm's delivered price meets the nearest competitor's

This problem can be reduced with **freight-absorption pricing**—which means absorbing freight cost so that a firm's delivered price meets the nearest competitor's. This amounts to cutting list price to appeal to new market segments. Some firms look at international markets this way; they just figure that any profit from export sales is a bonus.

## Customer Value—Integrating Price in the Marketing Mix

We've discussed the details of pricing policies separately so far to emphasize that a manager should make *intentional* decisions in each of the areas of pricing policy. Overlooking any of them can be serious because ultimately they all combine to have an impact on customer value and whether or not the firm has a competitive advantage.

Ever since Chapter 2, we've emphasized that customer value is based on the benefits that a customer sees in a firm's marketing mix and all of the costs. This value is relative to competitors' ways of meeting a need. From the customer's view, price is usually the main contributor to the cost part of the value equation.

That means that when we talk about price we are really talking about the whole set of price policies that define the real price level. Second, it's important to keep firmly in mind that superior value isn't just based on having a lower price than some competitor but rather on the whole marketing mix.



### Value Pricing

Smart marketers look for the combination of price decisions that result in value pricing. Value pricing means setting a fair price level for a marketing mix that really gives the target market superior customer value.

**value pricing**
Setting a fair price level for a marketing mix that really gives the target market superior customer value

**Value pricing** doesn't necessarily mean cheap if cheap means bare-bones or low-grade (recall the IKEA vignette at the start of this chapter). Nor does it mean high prestige either, if the prestige is not accompanied by the right quality goods and services. Rather, the focus is on the customer's requirements and how the whole marketing mix meets those needs.

Toyota is a good example of a firm that has been effective with value pricing. It has different marketing mixes for different target markets. But from the low-price Tercel to the $40,000 Avalon, the Japanese automaker consistently offers better quality and lower prices than its competitors. Among discount retailers, Wal-Mart is a value pricing leader. Its motto, "The low price on the brands you trust," says it all.

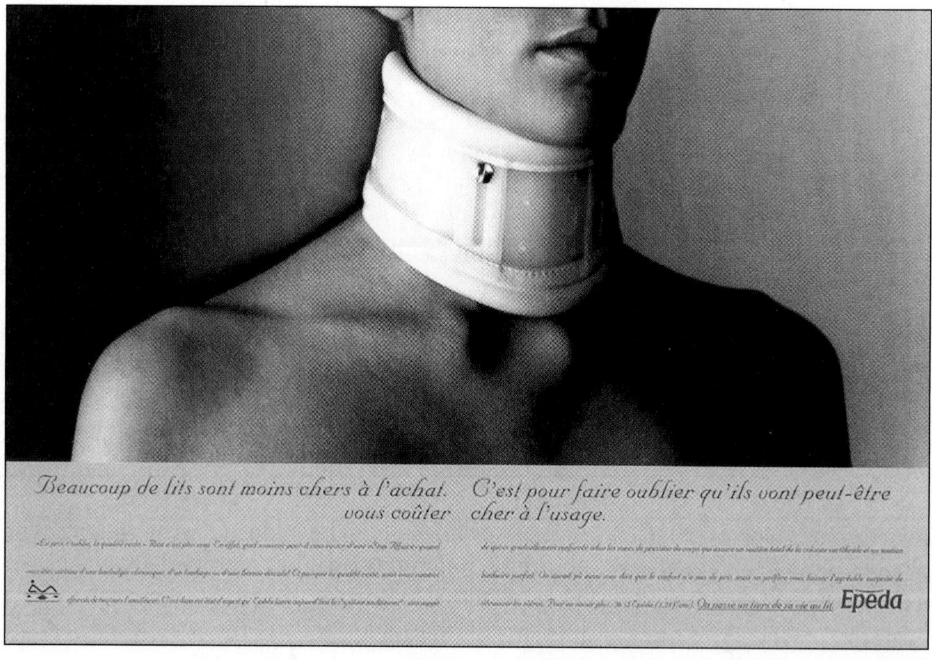


Epeda sells high-quality mattresses and wants customers to know that its higher price is worth it. This ad says, "Lots of mattresses are cheap to buy. The reason is to make you forget how much sleeping on them is going to cost you."

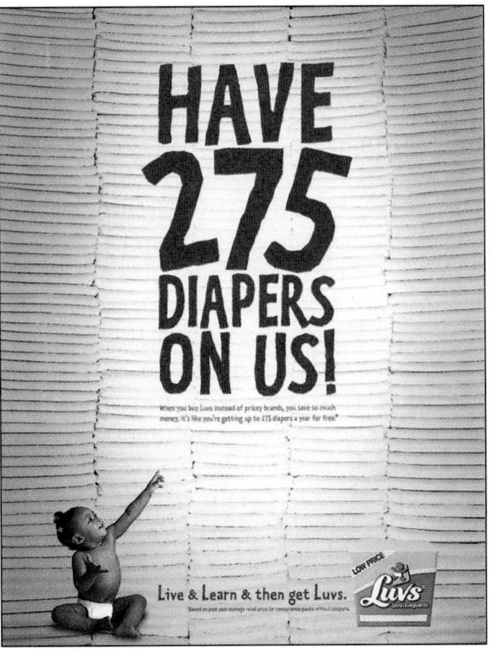


Marketers for Luvs diapers want consumers to know that compared to the pricey brands Luvs' value price is equivalent to getting 275 diapers a year for free.

These companies deliver on their promises. They try to give the consumer pleasant surprises—like an unexpected service—because it increases value and builds customer loyalty. They return the price if the customer isn't completely satisfied. They avoid unrealistic price levels—prices that are high only because consumers already know the brand name. They build relationships so customers will come back time and again.

### Price *and* Quality Define Value

Some marketing managers miss the advantages of value pricing. They think that in mature markets there is no alternative but to set a price level that is the same as or lower than that of competitors. These managers forget that value is measured not by price alone but by how much quality is provided at that price.

At one extreme, some firms are clearly above the market—they may even brag about it. Tiffany's is well known as one of the most expensive jewellery stores in the world. Other firms emphasize below-the-market prices in their marketing mixes. Prices offered by discounters and mass-merchandisers such as Wal-Mart, Future Shop, and Business Depot illustrate this approach. They may even promote their pricing policy with catchy slogans like "everyday low prices" or "we'll beat any advertised price."

### Value Is in the Eyes of the Target Segment

Do these various strategies promote prices that are above or below the market—or are there really different prices for different target markets or different marketing mixes? In making price decisions and using value pricing, it is important to clearly define the relevant target market and competitors when making price comparisons.

Consider Wal-Mart prices again from this view. Wal-Mart may have lower camera prices than conventional camera retailers, but it offers less help in the store, less selection, and it won't take old cameras in trade. Wal-Mart may be appealing to budget-oriented shoppers who compare prices and value among different mass-merchandisers. But a specialty camera store may be trying to appeal to different customers and not even be a direct competitor! Thus, it may be better to think of Wal-Mart's price as part of a different marketing mix for a different target market—not as a below-the-market price.

A camera producer with this point of view might develop different strategies for the Wal-Mart channel and the specialty-store channel. In particular, the producer might offer the specialty store one or more models that are not available to Wal-Mart—to ensure that customers don't view the two stores as direct competitors with price the only difference.

Further, the specialty store needs to communicate clearly to its target market how it offers superior value. Wal-Mart is certainly going to communicate that it offers a discount from some list price. If that's all customers hear, it's no wonder that they just focus on price. The specialty retailer has to be certain that consumers understand that price is not the only thing of value that is different. This same logic applies to comparisons between Internet sellers and bricks-and-mortar competitors. Each may have advantages or disadvantages that relate to value.

There will be times when a marketing manager's hands are tied and there is little that can be done to differentiate the marketing mix. However, most marketing managers do have choices—many choices. They can vary strategy decisions with respect to all of the marketing-mix variables, not just price, to offer target customers superior value. And when a marketer's hands are really tied, it's time to look for new opportunities that offer more promise.

So when you stop to think about it, value pricing is simply the best pricing approach for the type of market-oriented strategy planning we've been discussing throughout this whole text. To build profits and customer satisfaction, the whole marketing mix—including the price level—must meet target customers' needs and offer superior value.



## Legal Issues in Pricing

The Competition Act provides a framework for business conducted in Canada and encourages competition. Among its purposes are to ensure that small and medium-sized enterprises have an equitable opportunity to participate in the Canadian economy and to provide consumers with competitive prices and product choices. Some pricing policies are subject to the rules of the Competition Act, and you should be aware of these rules.

### Price Fixing

Except in the case of prices charged in regulated industries, the prices firms charge in Canada don't need government approval. Businesses can charge what they want—even outrageously high prices—provided these prices are not fixed with competitors. Difficulties with pricing, and violations of the Competition Act, usually occur when competing marketing mixes are quite similar. When the success of an entire marketing strategy depends on price, there's pressure (and temptation) to make agreements (conspire) with competitors. **Price fixing**—competitors getting together to raise, lower, or stabilize prices—is relatively easy. *But it is also completely illegal.* To discourage price fixing, the Competition Act provides that both companies and individual managers can be held responsible.

**price fixing**
Competitors getting together to raise, lower, or stabilize prices

### Price Discrimination

Trade or functional discounts can contravene the price discrimination provisions of the Competition Act. These provisions have to be considered whenever price differentials occur, such as discounts, rebates, allowances, price concessions, or other advantages. But price discrimination on the basis of the quantities of goods purchased is legal in Canada. For example, a manufacturer can legally use a quantity discount structure that favours large customers.

*Promotional allowances*—that is, price reductions granted by sellers as payment for promotional services performed by buyers—are also subject to the price discrimination provisions of the Competition Act, requiring that promotional allowances be granted proportionately to all competing customers. For example, a small customer purchasing half as much as a larger competitor must receive a promotional allowance equal to half of what was offered to the larger firm.

### Predatory Pricing

To give you an example of predatory pricing, imagine that a dominant firm charges low prices over a long enough period of time so as to drive a competitor from the market, or to deter others from entering the market, or both, and then the dominant firm raises its prices to recoup its losses. Section 50(1)(c) of the Competition Act provides that:

> Every one engaged in a business who . . . engages in a policy of selling products [goods and services] at prices unreasonably low, having the effect or tendency of substantially lessening competition or eliminating a competitor, or designed to have such effect, is guilty of an indictable offence and is liable to imprisonment for two years.

### Resale Price Maintenance

Some manufacturers would like to control the resale prices that retailers charge for their products. However, Section 50 of the Competition Act prohibits a manufacturer or supplier from requiring or inducing a retailer to sell a product [goods and services] at a particular price, or not below a particular price. A "suggested retail price" is allowed under the rules of Section 50 only if it is made clear to the retailer that the retailer can sell below the suggested price and that the retailer will not be discriminated against in any way if the product [goods and services] is sold at a lower price.

## Chapter Summary

The price variable offers an alert marketing manager many possibilities for varying marketing mixes. What pricing policies should be used depends on the pricing objectives. We looked at profit-oriented, sales-oriented, and status quo-oriented objectives.

A marketing manager must set policies about price flexibility, price levels over the product life cycle, who will pay the freight, and who will get discounts and allowances. While doing this, the manager should be aware of legislation that affects pricing policies.

In most cases, a marketing manager must set prices—that is, administer prices. Starting with a list price, a variety of discounts and allowances may be offered to adjust for the something of value being offered in the marketing mix.

Throughout this chapter, we talk about what may be included or excluded in the something of value and what objectives a firm might set to guide its pricing policies. We discuss how pricing policies combine to affect customer value. Price setting itself is not discussed. It will be covered in the next chapter—where we show ways to carry out the various pricing objectives and policies.

## Key Concepts

administered prices, p. 494
advertising allowances, p. 504
allowances, p. 504
basic list prices, p. 501
cash discounts, p. 503
cumulative quantity discounts, p. 502
discounts, p. 501
everyday low pricing, p. 504
flexible-price policy, p. 495
F.O.B., p. 505
freight-absorption pricing, p. 505
introductory price dealing, p. 500
net, p. 503
noncumulative quantity discounts, p. 502
nonprice competition, p. 494
one-price policy, p. 495
penetration pricing policy, p. 500
price fixing, p. 508
profit-maximization objective, p. 492
push money (or prize money) allowances, p. 504
quantity discounts, p. 502
rebates, p. 505
sale price, p. 503
sales-oriented objective, p. 493
seasonal discounts, p. 502
skimming price policy, p. 498
status quo objectives, p. 494
stocking allowances, p. 504
target-return objective, p. 492
trade (functional) discount, p. 503
trade-in allowances, p. 504
2/10 net 30, p. 503
uniform delivered pricing, p. 505
value pricing, p. 506
zone pricing, p. 505



## Questions and Problems

1. Identify the strategy decisions a marketing manager must make in the price area. Illustrate your answer for a local retailer.
2. How should the acceptance of a profit-oriented, a sales-oriented, or a status quo-oriented pricing objective affect the development of a company's marketing strategy? Illustrate for each.
3. Distinguish between one-price and flexible-price policies. Which is most appropriate for a hardware store? Why?
4. What pricing objective(s) is a skimming pricing policy most likely implementing? Is the same true for a penetration pricing policy? Which policy is probably most appropriate for each of the following products: *(a)* a new type of home lawn-sprinkling system, *(b)* a skin patch drug to help smokers quit, *(c)* a DVD of a best-selling movie, and *(d)* a new children's toy?
5. Are seasonal discounts appropriate in agricultural businesses (which are certainly seasonal)?
6. Do stocking allowances increase or reduce conflict in a channel of distribution? Explain your thinking.
7. Why would a manufacturer offer a rebate instead of lowering the suggested list price?
8. How can a marketing manager change a firm's F.O.B. terms to make an otherwise competitive marketing mix more attractive?
9. What type of geographic pricing policy is most appropriate for the following products (specify any assumptions necessary to obtain a definite answer): *(a)* a chemical by-product, *(b)* nationally advertised chocolate bars, *(c)* rebuilt auto parts, and *(d)* tricycles?
10. How would a ban on freight absorption (that is, requiring F.O.B. factory pricing) affect a producer with substantial economies of scale in production?
11. Give an example of a marketing mix that has a high price level but that you see as a good value. Briefly explain what makes it a good value.
12. Think about a business from which you regularly make purchases even though there are competing firms with similar prices. Explain what the firm offers that improves value and keeps you coming back.
13. Cite two examples of continuously selling above the market price. Describe the situations.
14. Explain the types of competitive situations that might lead to a meeting-competition pricing policy.
15. How would our marketing system change if manufacturers were required to set fixed prices on *all* products sold at retail and *all* retailers were required to use these prices? Would a manufacturer's marketing mix be easier to develop? What kind of an operation would retailing be in this situation? Would consumers receive more or less service?
16. Is price discrimination involved if a large oil company sells gasoline to taxicab associations for resale to individual taxicab operators for 2.5 cents per litre less than the price charged to retail service stations? What happens if the cab associations resell gasoline not only to taxicab operators but also to the general public?

## Computer-Aided Problem 16

### Cash Discounts

Joe Tulkin owns Tulkin Wholesale Co. He sells paper, tape, file folders, and other office supplies to about 120 retailers in nearby cities. His average retailer customer spends about $900 a month. When Tulkin started business in 1991, competing wholesalers were giving retailers invoice terms of 3/10, net 30. Tulkin never gave the issue much thought—he just used the same invoice terms when he billed customers. At that time, about half of his customers took the discount. Recently, he noticed a change in the way his customers were paying their bills. Checking his records, he found that 90 percent of the retailers were taking the cash discount. With so many retailers taking the cash discount, it seems to have become a price reduction. In addition, Tulkin learned that other wholesalers were changing their invoice terms.

Tulkin decides he should rethink his invoice terms. He knows he could change the percentage rate on the cash discount, the number of days the discount is offered, or the number of days before the face amount is due. Changing any of these, or any combination, will change the interest rate at which a buyer is, in effect, borrowing money if he does not take the discount. Tulkin decides that it will be easier to evaluate the effect of different invoice terms if he sets up a spreadsheet to let him change the terms and quickly see the effective interest rate for each change.

a. *With 90 percent of Tulkin's customers now taking the discount, what is the total monthly cash discount amount?*
b. *If Tulkin changes his invoice terms to 1/5, net 20, what interest rate is each buyer paying by not taking the cash discount? With these terms, would fewer buyers be likely to take the discount? Why?*
c. *Tulkin thinks 10 customers will switch to other wholesalers if he changes his invoice terms to 2/10, net 30, while 60 percent of the remaining customers will take the discount. What interest rate does a buyer pay by not taking this cash discount? For this situation, what will the total gross sales (total invoice) amount be? The total cash discount? The total net sales receipts after the total cash discount? Compare Tulkin's current situation with what will happen if he changes his invoice terms to 2/10, net 30.*

## Suggested Cases

To view the cases, go to www.mcgrawhill.ca/college/wong.

Interested in finding out what marketing looks like in the real world? *Marketing Magazine* is just a click away on your OLC! Visit **www.mcgrawhill.ca/college/wong** today.

# Chapter Seventeen

# Price Setting in the Business World

When You Finish This Chapter, You Should

1. Understand how most wholesalers and retailers set their prices—using markups.

2. Understand why turnover is so important in pricing.

3. Understand the advantages and disadvantages of average-cost pricing.

4. Know how to use break-even analysis to evaluate possible prices.

5. Understand the advantages of marginal analysis and how to use it for price setting.

6. Understand the various factors that influence customer price sensitivity.

7. Know the many ways that price setters use demand estimates in their pricing.

## Wal-Mart's Arrival in Canada

Wal-Mart came to Canada in 1994. At that time, Kmart was one of Canada's leading retailers. Less than a decade later, Wal-Mart is a recognized leader in sales and retail practice. Kmart no longer operates in Canada. What explains the big difference in growth and profits when the two chains are in many ways similar?

Part of the answer is that Wal-Mart has more sales volume in each store. Wal-Mart's sales revenue per square foot is more than twice that at Kmart. Wal-Mart's lower prices on similar products increases demand in its stores. But it also reduces its fixed operating costs as a percentage of sales. That means it can add a smaller markup, still cover its operating expenses, and make a larger profit. And as lower prices pull in more and more customers, its percentage of overhead costs to sales continues to drop—from about 20.2 percent in 1980 to about 16 percent now.

place price promotion produ

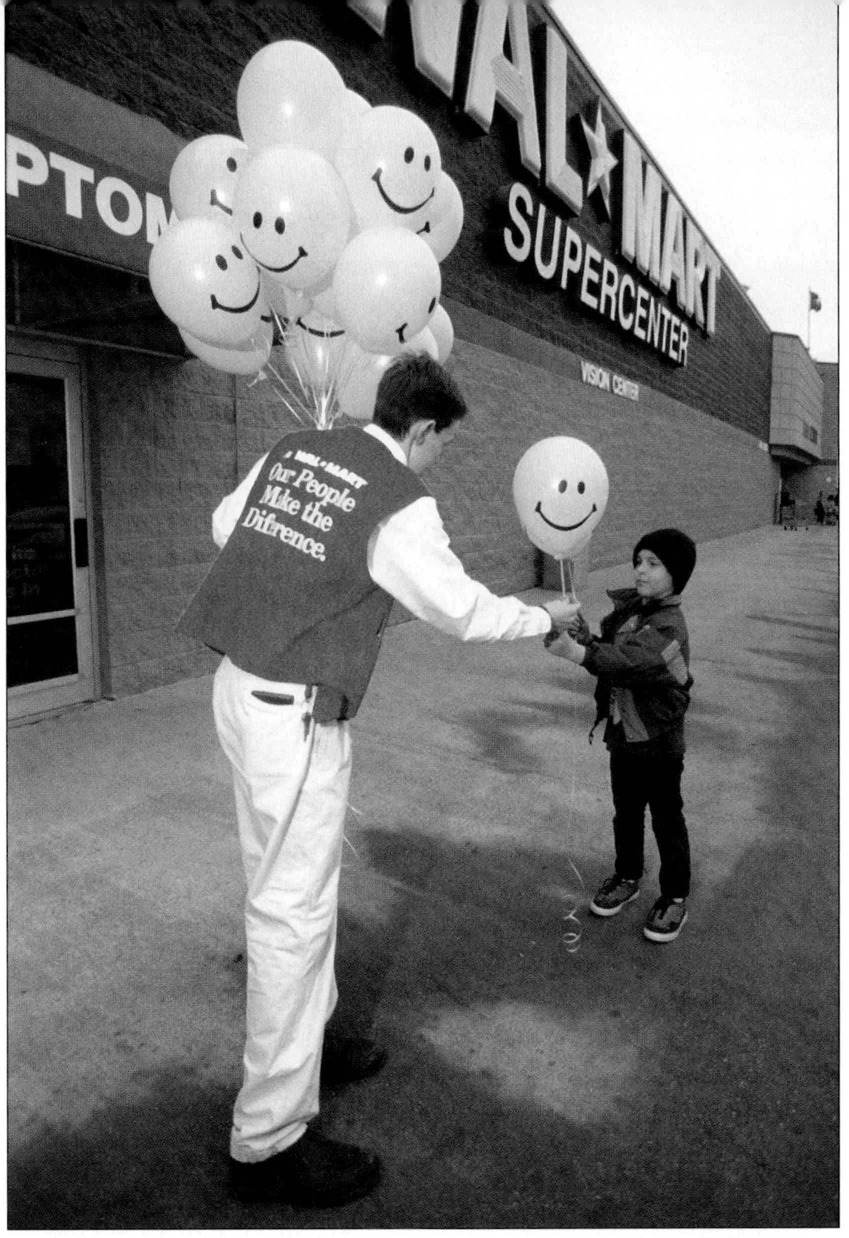


In the past few years, Wal-Mart has also improved profits by cutting unnecessary inventory by more than $2 billion, thereby saving $150 million in carrying cost and reducing markdowns. Wal-Mart also has lower costs for the goods it sells. Its buyers are tough in negotiating the best prices from suppliers—to be able to offer Wal-Mart customers the brands they want at low prices. But Wal-Mart also works closely with producers to reduce costs in the channel. For example, Wal-Mart was one of the first major retailers to insist that all orders be placed by computer; that helps to reduce stock-outs on store shelves and lost sales at the checkout counter. Wal-Mart also works with vendors to create private-label brands that sell for much less than national brands. These private-label products don't have big profit margins, but when customers come in to buy them they also pick up other, more profitable products.

Even with its lower costs, Wal-Mart isn't content to take the convenient route to price setting by just adding a standard percentage markup on different items. The company was one of the first retailers to give managers in every department in every store frequent, detailed information about what is selling and what isn't. They drop items that are collecting dust and roll back prices on the ones with the fastest turnover and highest margins. That not only increases stockturn but also puts the effort behind products with the most potential. For example, every department manager in every Wal-Mart store has a list of

place price promotion product

special VPIs (volume producing items). They give VPIs special attention and display space—to get a bigger sales and profit boost. For instance, Wal-Mart's analysis of checkout-scanner sales data revealed that parents often pick up more than one kids' video at a time. So now they are certain that special displays feature several videos and that the rest of the selection is close by.

Wal-Mart was the first major retailer to move to online selling (www.walmart.com). Its online sales still account for only a small percentage of its total sales, so there's lots of room to grow there too. Further, Wal-Mart is aggressively taking its low-price approach to other countries—ranging from Mexico to China. Here in Canada, Wal-Mart is contemplating the sale of more grocery products, retail gas, and other products lines, and may even enter the financial-services business. With its advantages in sales volume, unit costs, and margins it isn't hard to see why even the possibility of competing against Wal-Mart can cause a retail sector to take a long hard look at its pricing and related practices.[1]



## In This Chapter

In the previous chapter, we discussed the idea that pricing objectives and policies should guide pricing decisions. We accepted the idea of a list price and went on to discuss variations from list and how they combine to affect customer value. Now we'll see how the basic list price is set in the first place—based on information about costs, demand, and profit margins.

There are many ways to set list prices. But for simplicity they can be reduced to two basic approaches: *cost-oriented* and *demand-oriented* price-setting. We'll begin by looking at the cost-oriented approaches and the two key management tasks associated with their use: estimating costs and selecting an appropriate markup. We'll also discuss two key tools in cost-based pricing: break-even analysis and marginal analysis.

Our review of demand-oriented pricing will begin by identifying the factors that affect customers' price sensitivity and discussing how customers make price comparisons. With this background in place, we'll then look at a variety of demand-based pricing methods.

Once we have the essentials of price setting for an individual product, we'll consider two other special circumstances: pricing an entire product line and bid pricing.

## Price Setting Is a Key Strategy Decision

Many firms set a price by just adding a standard markup to the average cost of the products they sell. But this is changing. More managers are realizing that they should set prices by evaluating the effect of a price decision not only on profit margin for a given item but also on demand and therefore on sales volume, costs, and total profit.

In Wal-Mart's very competitive markets, this approach often leads to low prices that increase profits *and* at the same time reduce customers' costs. For other firms in different market situations, careful price setting leads to a premium price for a marketing mix that offers customers unique benefits and value. But these firms commonly focus on setting prices that earn attractive profits—as part of an overall marketing strategy that satisfies customers' needs.

With such variations in pricing approach, it should not be surprising that, on any given day, the same product may sell for a different price depending on who is selling, who is buying, and where and when the product is being bought and sold. For this reason, it may be easiest to think of a potential list price less as a specific number and more as a *range* of possible numbers.

The high end of the range, sometimes called a *price ceiling*, reflects the maximum someone would pay for what is offered. For example, if we were selling a new machine that promised to save 10 hours of labour per month for one year, the most we might expect someone to pay is the dollar value of 120 hours of labour. The low end of the range, sometimes called the *price floor*, is defined by a firm's costs—since any price below that cost would threaten the solvency of the business. Where the actual price will fall within that range depends on a host of market and competitive factors and the firm's overall marketing strategy (see Exhibit 17-1).

As you might imagine, there are many ways to set a list price within that range. However, for simplicity, they can be reduced to two basic approaches: cost-oriented and demand-oriented price setting. *Cost-oriented approaches* work price up from the price floor (i.e., cost). They start with the questions "What does it cost to produce this product?" and "How much can I add to my costs and still make the sale?" *Demand-oriented approaches* start at the price ceiling. They ask the questions "How much is this worth to someone?" and "By how much do we reduce that amount to deal with market and competitive conditions?"

One might expect that either approach will yield the same result. This is rarely



Exhibit 17-1 Key factors that influence price setting.

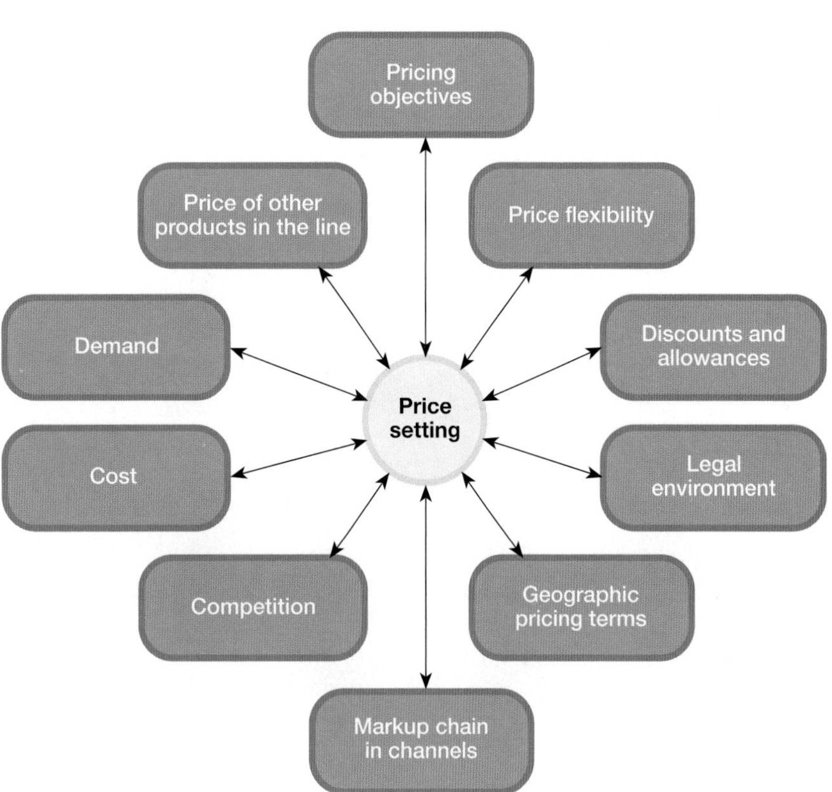

the case. Each has a particular set of factors to which it is sensitive and insensitive. Thus, most managers consider both approaches.

## Cost-Oriented Price Setting

**markup**
The amount added to the cost of products to get the selling price

Cost-oriented price setting is sometimes referred to as "cost-plus pricing": we estimate our costs then add an appropriate **markup**—the amount added to the cost of products to get the selling price. But while this would appear a fairly simple approach, a large number of factors must be considered to determine the "right" cost and markup numbers to use. Let's look at how markups are set and then review some important cost-related issues that affect pricing practices.

### Markups: What They Are and How They Are Set

Markups are usually stated as percentages of the final selling price rather than dollar amounts, unless otherwise noted. For example, a firm that buys a product for $2 and sells it for $3 is making a markup of 33-1/3 percent, or $1 out of $3. Markups are related to selling price for convenience in calculations. There's nothing wrong with the idea of markup on cost, but one must be careful to state which is being used. The calculations to change a markup on cost to one based on selling price, or vice versa, are simple. (See the section on markup conversion in the appendix on marketing arithmetic. The appendixes follow Chapter 19.)[2]

**Standard markups** Many intermediaries select a single, standard markup percentage and then apply it to all their products. This makes pricing easier. When you think of the large number of items the average retailer and wholesaler carry—and the small sales volume of any one item—this approach may make sense. Spending the time to find the best price to charge on every item in stock (day to day or week to week) might not pay.

Moreover, different companies in the same line of business often use the same markup percentage. Businesses adopting these industry-standard markups assume that all of the businesses have similar operating expenses. In these cases, the

Specialized products that rely on selective distribution and sell in smaller volume usually offer retailers higher markups, in part to offset the retailer's higher carrying costs and marketing expenses.

Exhibit 17-2 Examples of a markup chain and channel pricing.

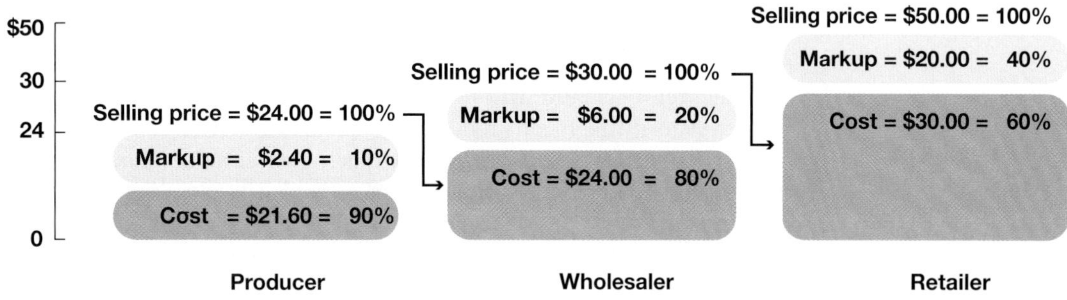


industry-standard markup should allow the firm to cover all of its operating expenses and provide a reasonable profit.

**Markup chains** The use of industry-standard markups applies to a particular stage in the distribution channel or chain. Different firms in a channel often use different markups because, for example, wholesalers and retailers usually have different operating expenses. A **markup chain**—the sequence of markups that firms use at different levels in a channel—determines the price structure in the whole channel. The markup is figured on the *selling price* at each level of the channel.

**markup chain**

The sequence of markups that firms use at different levels in a channel

Exhibit 17-2 illustrates the markup chain for an electric drill at each level of the channel system. The production (factory) cost of the drill is $21.60. In this case, the producer takes a 10-percent markup and sells the product for $24. The markup is 10 percent of $24, or $2.40. The producer's selling price now becomes the wholesaler's cost—$24. If the wholesaler is used to taking a 20-percent markup on selling price, the markup is $6—and the wholesaler's selling price becomes $30. The $30 now becomes the cost for the hardware retailer. And a retailer who is used to a 40-percent markup adds $20, which means consumers are faced with a retail selling price of $50. This final price is 131 percent more than the cost of manufacturing, showing that the greater the number of intermediaries, the greater the price. This is why consumers are so interested in "cutting out the middleman."

**Selecting the standard markup** How does a manager decide on a standard markup in the first place? A standard markup is often set close to the firm's *gross margin*. Managers regularly see gross margins on their operating (profit and loss) statements. The gross margin is the amount left—after subtracting the cost of sales (cost of goods sold) from net sales—to cover the expenses of selling products and operating the business. (See the appendix on marketing arithmetic if you are unfamiliar with these ideas.) For example, a firm earning a 33-percent gross margin would likely charge a price based on a 33-percent markup.

Producers pay attention to the gross margins and standard markups of intermediaries in their channel in order to estimate the retail price that will be charged after applying the markup chain. Because intermediaries will tend to set their markups based on their own gross margins, the intermediary's gross margin is a good guide to trade (functional) discounts that intermediaries expect.

**The markup–volume tradeoff** Setting markups equal to gross margin is a convenient guideline. However, there are occasions where a firm might apply a higher or lower markup, depending upon how much demand exists for their products and competitive practices.

Some people, including many conventional retailers, think high markups mean big profits. Often this isn't true. A high markup may result in a price that's too high—a price at which few customers will buy. You can't earn much if you don't sell much, no matter how high your markup. But many retailers and wholesalers seem more concerned with the size of their markup on a single item than with their total profit. And their high markups may lead to low profits or even losses.

Some retailers and wholesalers, however, try to speed turnover to increase profit—even if this means reducing their markups. They realize that a business runs up costs over time. If they can sell a much greater amount in the same time period, they may be able to take a lower markup and still earn higher profits at the end of the period.

This raises a very important question: will a business have greater profits selling a large volume of product at low prices, or would it be better to have higher prices even if it means selling less? As you will see later in this chapter, the correct answer depends on many factors. At this time, the important thing to remember is that we should never assume, without detailed investigation, that setting prices higher or lower is necessarily better.

**stockturn rate**
The number of times the average inventory is sold in a year

An important idea here is the **stockturn rate**—the number of times the average inventory is sold in a year. Various methods of figuring stockturn rates can be used (see the section "Computing the Stockturn Rate" in Appendix C). A low stockturn rate may be bad for profits.

At the very least, a low stockturn increases inventory carrying cost and ties up working capital. If a firm with a stockturn of 1 (once per year) sells products that cost it $100,000, it has that much tied up in inventory all the time. But a stockturn of 5 requires only $20,000 worth of inventory ($100,000 cost divided by 5 turnovers a year). If annual inventory carrying cost is about 20 percent of the inventory value, that reduces costs by $16,000 a year. That's a big difference on $100,000 in sales!

Whether a stockturn rate is high or low depends on the industry and the product involved. An autoparts wholesaler may expect an annual rate of 1—while a supermarket might expect 20 to 30 stockturns for soaps and detergents and 70 to 80 stockturns for fresh fruits and vegetables.

Channel intermediaries that use the same standard markup percentage on all their products ignore the importance of fast turnover. Mass-merchandisers know this. They put low markups on fast-selling items and higher markups on items that

This trade ad, targeted at retailers, emphasizes faster stockturn—which, together with markups, impacts the retailer's profitability.

Exhibit 17-3 Results of average-cost pricing.

| A. CALCULATION OF PLANNED PROFIT IF 40,000 ITEMS ARE SOLD | | B. CALCULATION OF ACTUAL PROFIT IF ONLY 20,000 ITEMS ARE SOLD | |
|---|---|---|---|
| **Calculation of costs:** | | **Calculation of costs:** | |
| Fixed overhead expenses | $30,000 | Fixed overhead expenses | $30,000 |
| Labour and materials ($.80 a unit) | 32,000 | Labour and materials ($.80 a unit) | 16,000 |
| Total costs | $62,000 | Total costs | $46,000 |
| "Planned" profit | 18,000 | | |
| Total costs and planned profit | $80,000 | | |
| **Calculation of profit (or loss):** | | **Calculation of profit (or loss):** | |
| Actual unit sales 3 price ($2.00*) | $80,000 | Actual unit sales 3 price ($2.00*) | $40,000 |
| Minus: total costs | 62,000 | Minus: total costs | 46,000 |
| Profit (loss) | $18,000 | Profit (loss) | ($6,000) |
| **Result:** | | **Result:** | |
| Planned profit of $18,000 is earned if 40,000 items are sold at $2.00 each. | | Planned profit of $18,000 is not earned. Instead, $6,000 loss results if 20,000 items are sold at $2.00 each. | |

*Calculation of "reasonable price": $\frac{\text{Expected total costs and planned profit}}{\text{Planned number of items to be sold}} = \frac{\$80,000}{\$40,000} = \$2.00$

sell less frequently. For example, Wal-Mart may put a small markup on fast-selling health and beauty aids (like toothpaste or shampoo) but higher markups on appliances and clothing.

## Calculating Costs—More Than Meets the Eye

**average-cost pricing** Adding a reasonable markup to the average cost of a product to arrive at the price

**Average-cost pricing** means adding a reasonable markup to the *average cost* of a product to arrive at the price. A manager usually finds the average cost per unit by studying past records. Dividing the total cost for the last year by all the units produced and sold in that period gives an estimate of the average cost per unit for the next year. If the cost was $32,000 for all labour and materials and $30,000 for fixed overhead expenses—such as selling expenses, rent, and manager salaries—then the total cost is $62,000. If the company produced 40,000 items in that time period, the average cost is $62,000 divided by 40,000 units, or $1.55 per unit.

To get the price, the producer decides how much profit per unit to add to the average cost per unit. If the company considers 45 cents a reasonable profit for each unit, it sets the new price at $2.00. Exhibit 17-3A shows that this approach produces the desired profit—if the company sells 40,000 units.

Sound simple? It is. But average-cost pricing can also be dangerous. It's easy to lose money with average-cost pricing. To see why, let's follow this example further. First, remember that the average cost of $2.00 per unit was based on output of 40,000 units. But if the firm is able to produce and sell only 20,000 units in the next year, it may be in trouble. Twenty thousand units sold at $2.00 each ($1.55 cost plus 45 cents for expected profit) yield a total revenue of only $40,000. The overhead is still fixed at $30,000, and the variable material and labour cost drops by half to $16,000—for a total cost of $46,000. This means a loss of $6,000, or 30 cents a unit. The method that was supposed to allow a profit of 45 cents a unit actually causes a loss of 30 cents a unit! (see Exhibit 17-3B).

The basic problem with the average-cost approach is that it does not adequately account for cost variations at different levels of output. This is because, in a typical situation, costs are high at low levels of output. But as output increases, economies of scale set in and some costs start to fall. As a result, the average cost per unit drops. This is why mass production and mass distribution often make sense.

It's also why it's important to develop a better understanding of the different types of costs a marketing manager should consider when setting a price.

This shortcoming can be particularly severe in markets where consumers see little difference among competing products. In these cases the consumer buys the product with the lowest price. The firm with the greatest volume likely has the lowest costs and therefore the lowest prices. As consumers purchase their product, costs fall even more and prices can be further reduced, which attracts even more consumers. This continues until the potential scale economies are used up.

## Understanding Volume–Cost Relationships

The problem with average-cost pricing exists because there are a variety of costs—and each changes in a *different* way as output changes. Any pricing method that uses cost must consider these changes. To understand why, we need to define six types of costs.

**total fixed cost**
The sum of those costs that are fixed in total—no matter how much is produced

**total variable cost**
The sum of those changing expenses that are closely related to output

1. **Total fixed cost** is the sum of those costs that are fixed in total—no matter how much is produced. Among these fixed costs are rent, depreciation, managers' salaries, property taxes, and insurance. Such costs stay the same even if production stops temporarily.
2. **Total variable cost**, on the other hand, is the sum of those changing expenses that are closely related to output—expenses for parts, wages, packaging materials, outgoing freight, and sales commissions.

At zero output, total variable cost is zero. As output increases, so do variable costs. If Levi's doubles its output of jeans in a year, its total cost for denim cloth also (roughly) doubles.

**total cost**
The sum of total fixed and total variable costs

3. **Total cost** is the sum of total fixed and total variable costs. Changes in total cost depend on variations in total variable cost—since total fixed cost stays the same.

**average cost**
Obtained by dividing total cost by the related quantity

**average fixed cost**
Obtained by dividing total fixed cost by the related quantity

**average variable cost**
Obtained by dividing total variable cost by the related quantity

The pricing manager usually is more interested in cost per unit than total cost because prices are usually quoted per unit.

1. **Average cost** (per unit) is obtained by dividing total cost by the related quantity (that is, the total quantity that causes the total cost).
2. **Average fixed cost** (per unit) is obtained by dividing total fixed cost by the related quantity.
3. **Average variable cost** (per unit) is obtained by dividing total variable cost by the related quantity.

Average fixed costs are lower when a larger quantity is produced.

Exhibit 17-4 Cost structure of a firm.

| QUANTITY (Q) | TOTAL FIXED COSTS (TFC) | AVERAGE FIXED COSTS (AFC) | AVERAGE VARIABLE COSTS (AVC) | TOTAL VARIABLE COSTS (TVC) | TOTAL COST (TC) | AVERAGE COST (AC) |
|---|---|---|---|---|---|---|
| 0 | $30,000 | — | — | — | $30,000 | — |
| 10,000 | 30,000 | $3.00 | $0.80 | $8,000 | 38,000 | $3.80 |
| 20,000 | 30,000 | 1.50 | 0.80 | 16,000 | 46,000 | 2.30 |
| 30,000 | 30,000 | 1.00 | 0.80 | 24,000 | 54,000 | 1.80 |
| 40,000 | 30,000 | 0.75 | 0.80 | 32,000 | 62,000 | 1.55 |
| 50,000 | 30,000 | 0.60 | 0.80 | 40,000 | 70,000 | 1.40 |
| 60,000 | 30,000 | 0.50 | 0.80 | 48,000 | 78,000 | 1.30 |
| 70,000 | 30,000 | 0.43 | 0.80 | 56,000 | 86,000 | 1.23 |
| 80,000 | 30,000 | 0.38 | 0.80 | 64,000 | 94,000 | 1.18 |
| 90,000 | 30,000 | 0.33 | 0.80 | 72,000 | 102,000 | 1.13 |
| 100,000 | 30,000 | 0.30 | 0.80 | 80,000 | 110,000 | 1.10 |

110,000 (TC)<br>−80,000 (TVC)<br>30,000 (TVD)

0.30 (AFC)<br>(Q)100,000 ⟌ 30,000 (TFC)

0.80 (AVC)

100,000 (Q)<br>× 0.80 (AVC)<br>80,000 (TVC)

30,000 (TFC)<br>+ 80,000 (TVC)<br>110,000 (TC)

1.10 (AC)<br>(Q)100,000 ⟌ 110,000 (TC)

A good way to get a feel for these different types of costs is to extend our example of average-cost pricing (Exhibit 17-3A). Exhibit 17-4 shows the six types of cost and how they vary at different levels of output. The line for 40,000 units is highlighted because that was the expected level of sales in our average-cost-pricing example. For simplicity, we assume that average variable cost is the same for each unit. Notice, however, that total variable cost increases when quantity increases. Exhibit 17-5 shows the three average-cost curves from Exhibit 17-4. To summarize, as the quantity produced increases:

- Average fixed costs go down
- Average variable costs stay the same
- Average total costs go down

With these relations in mind, let's reconsider the problem with average-cost pricing.

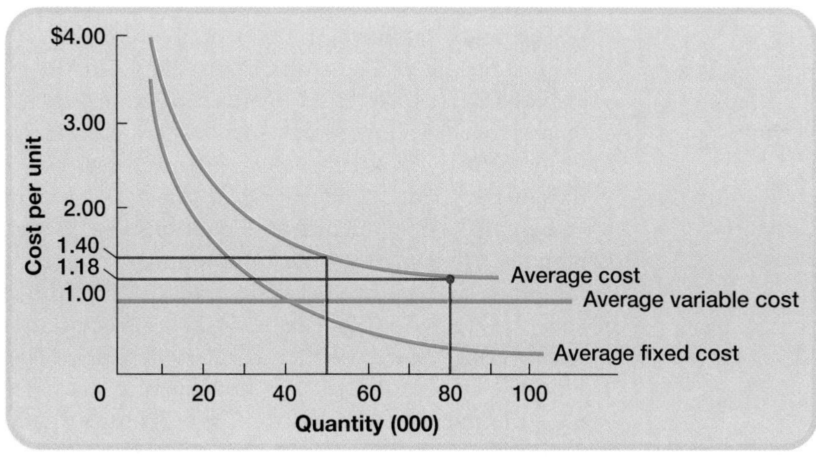


Exhibit 17-5 Typical shape of cost (per unit) when average variable cost per unit is consistent.

Exhibit 17-6 Evaluation of various prices along a firm's demand curve.

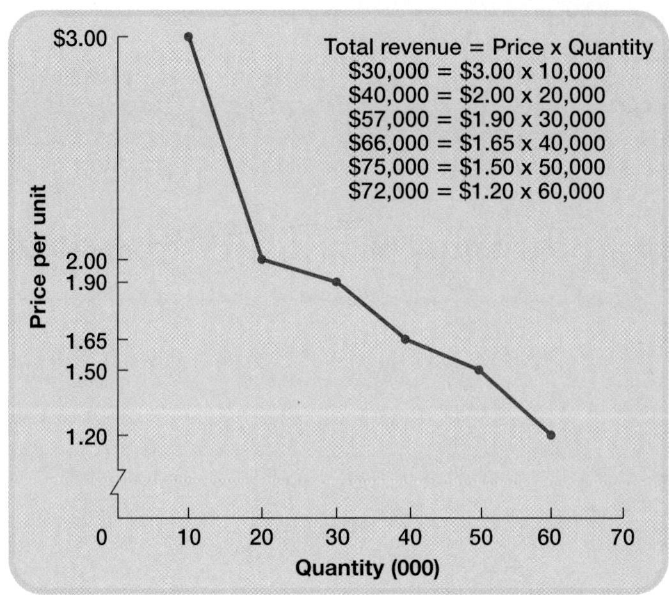




Average-cost pricing works well if the firm actually sells the quantity it used to set the average-cost price. Losses may result, however, if actual sales are much lower than expected. On the other hand, if sales are much higher than expected, then profits may be very good. But this will happen only by luck—because the firm's demand is much larger than expected.

To use average-cost pricing, a marketing manager must make *some* estimate of the quantity to be sold in the coming period. Without a quantity estimate, it isn't possible to compute average cost. But unless this quantity is related to price—that is, unless the firm's demand curve is considered—the marketing manager may set a price that doesn't even cover a firm's total cost! You saw this happen in Exhibit 17-3B, when the firm's price of $2.00 resulted in demand for only 20,000 units and a loss of $6,000.

The demand curve is still important even if management doesn't take time to think about it. For example, Exhibit 17-6 shows the demand curve for the firm we're discussing.

This demand curve shows *why* the firm lost money when it tried to use average-cost pricing. At the $2.00 price, quantity demanded is only 20,000. With this demand curve and the costs in Exhibit 17-4, the firm will incur a loss whether management sets the price at a high $3 or a low $1.20. At $3, the firm will sell only 10,000 units for a total revenue of $30,000. But total cost will be $38,000—for a loss of $8,000. At the $1.20 price, it will sell 60,000 units—at a loss of $6,000. However, the curve suggests that at a price of $1.65 consumers will demand about 40,000 units, producing a profit of about $4,000.

In short, average-cost pricing is simple in theory but often fails in practice. In stable situations, prices set by this method may yield profits, but not necessarily *maximum* profits. And note that such cost-based prices may be higher than a price that would be more profitable for the firm, as shown in Exhibit 17-6. When demand conditions are changing, average-cost pricing is even more risky.

Exhibit 17-7 summarizes the relationships discussed above. Cost-oriented pricing requires an estimate of the total number of units to be sold. That estimate determines the average fixed cost per unit and thus the *average* total cost. Then the firm adds the desired profit per unit to the average total cost to get the cost-oriented selling price. How customers react to that price determines the actual quantity the firm will be able to sell. But that quantity may not be the quantity used to compute the average cost! Further, the quantity the firm actually sells (times price)

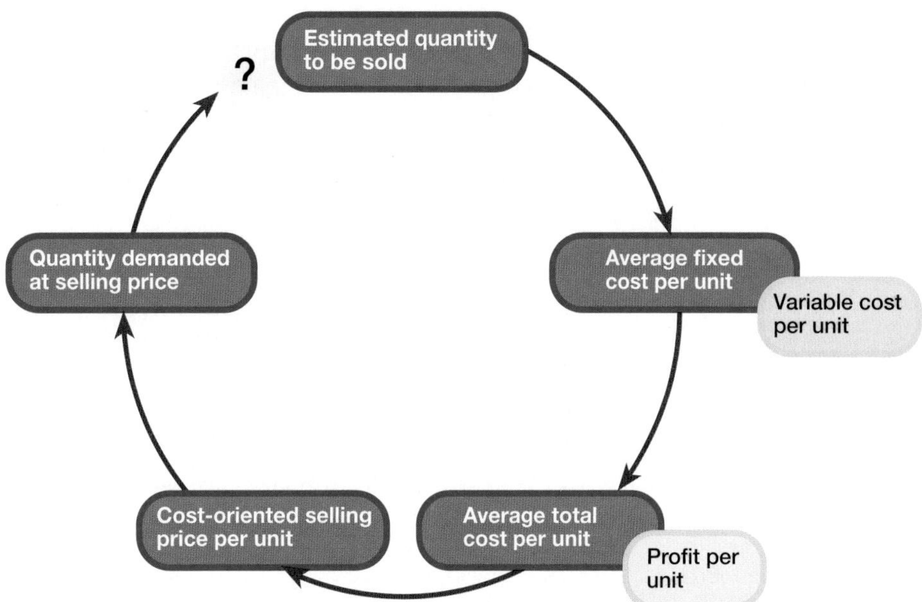


Exhibit 17-7 Summary of relationships among quantity, cost, and price using cost-oriented pricing.

determines total revenue (and total profit or loss). A decision made in one area affects each of the others, directly or indirectly. Average-cost pricing does not consider these effects.[3] A manager who forgets this can make serious pricing mistakes.

## Experience-Curve Pricing

**experience-curve pricing**

Average-cost pricing using an estimate of *future* average costs

Some aggressive firms use a variation of average-cost pricing called experience-curve pricing. **Experience-curve pricing** is average-cost pricing using an estimate of *future* average costs. This approach is based on the observation that over time—as an industry gains experience in certain kinds of production—managers learn new ways to reduce costs. In some industries, costs decrease about 15 to 20 percent each time cumulative production volume (experience) doubles. So a firm might set average-cost prices based on where it expects costs to be when products are sold in the future—not where costs actually are when the strategy is set. This approach is more common in rapidly growing markets, because cumulative production volume (experience) grows faster.

If costs drop as expected, this approach works. But it has the same risks as regular average-cost pricing. The price setter has to estimate what quantity will be sold to be able to read the right price from the experience-based average-cost curve.[4]

## Target-Return Pricing

**target-return pricing**

Adding a target return to the cost of a product

**Target-return pricing**—adding a target return to the cost of a product—is another form of cost-based pricing that has become popular in recent years. With this approach, the price setter seeks to earn (1) a percentage return (say, 10 percent per year) on the investment or (2) a specific total dollar return.

This method is a variation of the average-cost method since the desired target return is added into total cost. As a simple example, if a company had $180,000 invested and wanted to make a 10-percent return on investment, it would add $18,000 to its annual total costs in setting prices.

This approach has the same weakness as other average-cost pricing methods. If the quantity actually sold is less than the quantity used to set the price, then the company doesn't earn its target return—even though the target return seems to be part of the price structure. In fact, we saw this in Exhibit 17-3. Remember that we added $18,000 as an expected profit, or target return. But the return was much lower when the expected quantity was not sold. (It could be higher too—but only if the quantity sold is much larger than expected.) Target-return pricing clearly does not guarantee that a firm will hit the target.

**long-run target-return pricing**
Adding a long-run average target return to the cost of a product

Managers in some larger firms who want to achieve a long-run target return objective use another cost-oriented pricing approach—**long-run target-return pricing**—adding a long-run average target return to the cost of a product. Instead of estimating the quantity they expect to produce in any one year, they assume that during several years' time their plants will produce at, say, 80 percent of capacity. They use this quantity when setting their prices.

## Tools for Cost-Oriented Price-Setting

Taking into account the relationships between volume and costs and between volume and demand can be complicated. However, two tools—break-even analysis and marginal analysis—can make it easier to understand these relationships and discuss the available options.

**break-even analysis**
Evaluates whether the firm will be able to break even (i.e., cover all its costs) with a particular price

**break-even point (BEP)**
The quantity where the firm's total cost will just equal its total revenue

**Break-even analysis** Some price setters use break-even analysis in their pricing. **Break-even analysis** evaluates whether the firm will be able to break even—that is, cover all its costs—with a particular price. This is important because a firm must cover all costs in the long run or there is not much point being in business. This method focuses on the **break-even point (BEP)**—the quantity where the firm's total cost will just equal its total revenue.

***How it works*** To understand how break-even analysis works, look at Exhibit 17-8, an example of the typical break-even chart. The chart is based on a particular selling price—in this case, $1.20 a unit. The chart has lines that show total costs (total variable plus total fixed costs) and total revenues at different levels of production. The break-even point on the chart is at 75,000 units—where the total cost and total revenue lines intersect. At that production level, total cost and total revenue are the same—$90,000.

The difference between the total revenue and total cost at a given quantity is the profit—or loss! The chart shows that below the break-even point, total cost is higher than total revenue and the firm incurs a loss. The firm would make a profit above the break-even point. However, the firm would reach the break-even point, or get beyond it into the profit area, only *if* it could sell at least 75,000 units at the $1.20 price.

Break-even analysis can be very helpful if used properly, so let's look at this approach more closely.

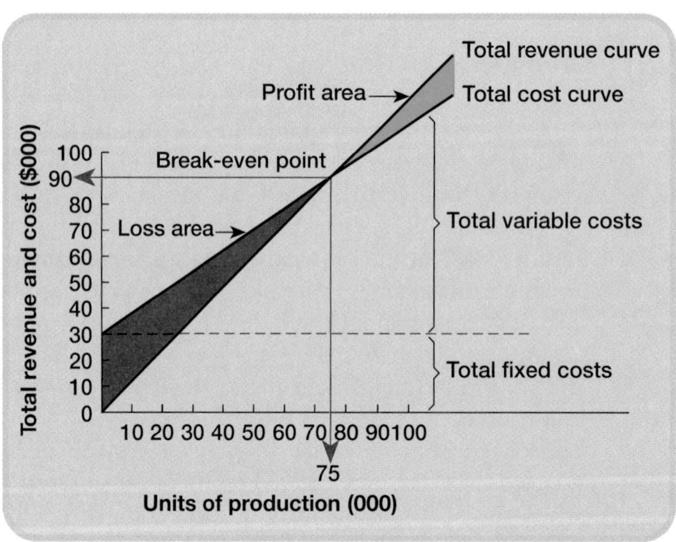


Exhibit 17-8 Break-even chart for a particular situation.

A break-even chart is an easy-to-understand visual aid, but it's also useful to be able to compute the break-even point.

**fixed-cost (FC) contribution per unit**

The assumed selling price per unit minus the variable cost per unit

The BEP, in units, can be found by dividing total fixed costs (TFC) by the **fixed-cost (FC) contribution per unit**—the assumed selling price per unit minus the variable cost per unit. This can be stated as a simple formula:

$$\text{BEP (in units)} = \frac{\text{Total fixed cost}}{\text{Fixed cost contribution per unit}}$$

This formula makes sense when we think about it. To break even, we must cover total fixed costs. Therefore, we must figure the contribution each unit will make to covering the total fixed costs (after paying for the variable costs to produce the item). When we divide this per-unit contribution into the total fixed costs that must be covered, we have the BEP (in units).

To illustrate the formula, let's use the cost and price information in Exhibit 17-8. The price per unit is $1.20. The average variable cost per unit is 80 cents. So the FC contribution per unit is 40 cents ($1.20280 cents). The total fixed cost is $30,000 (see Exhibit 17-8). Substituting in the formula:

$$\text{BEP} = \frac{\$30{,}000}{.40} = \quad 75{,}000 \text{ units}$$

From this, you can see that if this firm sells 75,000 units it will exactly cover all its fixed and variable costs. If it sells even one more unit, it will begin to show a profit—in this case, 40 cents per unit. Note that once the fixed costs are covered, the part of revenue formerly going to cover fixed costs is now *all profit.*

The BEP can also be figured in dollars. The easiest way is to compute the BEP in units and then multiply by the assumed per-unit price. If you multiply the selling price ($1.20) by the BEP in units (75,000) you get $90,000—the BEP in dollars.

We can gain further insights from break-even analysis by modifying our assumptions about profit targets, variable costs, and fixed costs. For example, it's useful to compute the break-even point for each of several possible prices and then compare the BEP for each price to likely demand at that price. The marketing manager can quickly reject some price possibilities when the expected quantity demanded at a given price is way below the break-even point for that price.

A second extended use of break-even analysis is in target return pricing. Just as we can find the quantity at which total revenue equals total cost—where profit is zero—we can also vary this approach to see what quantity is required to earn a certain level of profit. The analysis is the same as described above for the break-even point in units, but the amount of target profit is added to the total fixed cost. Then when we divide the total fixed cost plus profit figure by the contribution from each unit, we get the quantity that will earn the target profit.

A third use of break-even analysis is in assessing the sensitivity of profits to cost reductions. Indeed, break-even analysis makes it clear why managers must constantly look for effective new ways to get jobs done at lower costs. For example, if a manager can reduce the firm's total fixed costs—perhaps by using computer systems to cut out excess inventory carrying costs—the break-even point will be lower and profits will start to build sooner. Similarly, if the variable cost to produce and sell an item can be reduced, the fixed-cost contribution per unit increases; that too lowers the break-even point, and profit accumulates faster for each product sold beyond the break-even point.

Despite these insights, break-even analysis does have its limitations. For example, beyond the BEP, profits seem to be growing continually. And the graph—with its straight-line total-revenue curve—makes it seem that any quantity can be sold at the assumed price. But this usually isn't true. It is the same as assuming a perfectly horizontal demand curve at that price. In fact, most managers face down-sloping demand situations. And their total revenue curves do not keep going up.

The firm and costs we discussed in the average-cost pricing example earlier in this chapter illustrate this point. You can confirm from Exhibit 17-4 that the total fixed cost ($30,000) and average variable cost (80 cents) for that firm are the same ones shown in the break-even chart (Exhibit 17-8). So this break-even chart is the one we would draw for that firm assuming a price of $1.20 a unit. But the demand curve for that case showed that the firm could sell only 60,000 units at a price of $1.20. So that firm would never reach the 75,000 unit break-even point at a $1.20 price. It would sell only 60,000 units, and it would lose $6,000! A firm with a different demand curve—say, one where the firm could sell 80,000 units at a price of $1.20—would in fact break even at 75,000 units.

Break-even analysis is a useful tool for analyzing costs and evaluating what might happen to profits in different market environments. But it is a cost-oriented approach and suffers the same limitation as other cost-oriented approaches. Specifically, it does not consider the effect of price on the quantity that consumers will want—that is, the demand curve.

So to really zero in on the most profitable price, marketers are better off estimating the demand curve itself and then using marginal analysis, which we'll discuss next.[5]

**marginal analysis**

Focuses on the changes in total revenue and total cost from selling one more unit to find the most profitable price and quantity

**Marginal analysis** The best pricing tool marketers have for looking at costs and revenue (demand) at the same time is marginal analysis. **Marginal analysis** focuses on the changes in total revenue and total cost from selling one more unit to find the most profitable price and quantity. Marginal analysis shows how profit changes at different prices. Thus, it can help to find the price that maximizes profit. You can also see the effect of other price levels. Even if you adjust to pursue objectives other than profit maximization, you know how much profit you're giving up!

***How it works*** To explain how marginal analysis works, we'll use an example based on a firm with the specific cost and demand numbers in Exhibit 17-9. This example uses simple numbers to ensure that the explanations are easy to follow. However, the approach we cover is the same one that managers use.

A marketing manager often doesn't know the exact shape of the demand curve.

Exhibit 17-9 Revenue, cost, and profit at different prices for a firm.

| (1) Quantity (Q) | (2) Price (P) | (3) Total Revenue (TR) | (4) Total Variable Cost (TVC) | (5) Total Cost (TC) | (6) Profit (TR − TC) | (7) Marginal Revenue (MR) | (8) Marginal Cost (MC) | (9) Marginal Profit (MR − MC) |
|---|---|---|---|---|---|---|---|---|
| 0 | $150 | $ 0 | $ 0 | $200 | $ − 200 | | | |
| 1 | 140 | 140 | 96 | 296 | − 156 | $140 | $96 | $ + 44 |
| 2 | 130 | 260 | 116 | 316 | − 56 | 120 | 20 | +100 |
| 3 | 117 | 351 | 131 | 331 | + 20 | 91 | 15 | + 76 |
| 4 | 105 | 420 | 144 | 344 | + 76 | 69 | 13 | + 56 |
| 5 | 92 | 460 | 155 | 355 | + 105 | 40 | 11 | + 29 |
| 6 | 79 | 474 | 168 | 368 | + 106 | 14 | 13 | + 1 |
| 7 | 66 | 462 | 183 | 383 | + 79 | −12 | 15 | − 27 |
| 8 | 53 | 424 | 223 | 423 | + 1 | −38 | 40 | − 78 |
| 9 | 42 | 378 | 307 | 507 | − 129 | −46 | 84 | −130 |
| 10 | 31 | 310 | 510 | 710 | − 400 | −68 | 203 | −271 |

A practical way to start, though, is to think about a price that appears to be extremely high and one that is too low. Then, for prices at a number of points along the range between these two extremes, the manager can make an estimate of what quantity it might be possible to sell. The first two columns of Exhibit 17-9 show the price and quantity-demanded combinations for our example firm; multiplying them together gives the firm's total revenue at each specific price.

Plotting price and quantity gives a picture of the firm's demand curve. Thus, it's useful to think of a demand curve as an if–then curve—*if* a price is selected, *then* what is the related quantity that will be sold? Before the marketing manager sets the actual price, all these *if–then* combinations can be evaluated for profitability using marginal analysis.

This firm faces a demand curve that slopes down. That means that the marketer can expect to increase sales volume by lowering the price. Yet selling a larger quantity at a lower price may or may not increase total revenue. Similarly, profits may go up or down. Therefore, it's important to evaluate the likely effect of alternative prices on total revenue (and profit). The way to do this is to look at marginal revenue.

**Assessing impacts on marginal revenue** If demand grows as prices fall, and costs fall with increased output, it is tempting to jump to the conclusion that we should keep cutting prices until we have 100 percent of the market. A look at how marginal revenue changes at different levels of output can show why this is rarely done.

**marginal revenue**

The change in total revenue that results from the sale of one more unit of a product

**Marginal revenue** is the change in total revenue that results from the sale of one more unit of a product. At a price of $105, the firm in this example can sell four units for total revenue of $420. By cutting the price to $92, it can sell five units for total revenue of $460. Thus, the marginal revenue for the fifth unit is $460 – $420, or $40. Considering only revenue, it would be desirable to sell this extra unit. But will revenue continue to rise if the firm sells more units at lower prices? Exhibit 17-9 shows that marginal revenue is negative at price levels lower than $79. In other words, total revenue goes down. Obviously, this is not good for the firm! Note in the table that total revenue obtained is positive across the range of price cuts, but the marginal revenue—the extra revenue gained—may be positive or negative.

**Assessing impacts on marginal costs** We've already shown that different kinds of costs behave differently at different quantities. Exhibit 17-9 shows the total cost increasing as quantity increases. Remember that total cost is the sum of fixed cost (in this example, $200) and total variable cost. The fixed cost does not change over the entire range of output. However, total variable costs increase continually as more and more units are produced. So it's the increases in variable cost that explain the increase in total cost.

**marginal cost**

The change in total cost that results from producing one more unit

There is another kind of cost that is vital to marginal analysis. **Marginal cost** is the change in total cost that results from producing one more unit. In Exhibit 17-9, you can see that it costs $355 to produce five units of a product but only $344 to produce four units. Thus the marginal cost for the fifth unit is $11. In other words, marginal cost is the additional cost of producing one more *specific unit.* By contrast, average cost is the average for *all units.*

**Assessing impacts on marginal profit** The marginal-cost column in Exhibit 17-9 shows what each extra unit costs. This suggests the *minimum* extra revenue we would like to get for that additional unit. Usually, however, we're not interested in just covering costs—we're shooting for a profit.

**rule for maximizing profit**

The highest profit is earned at the price where marginal cost is just less than or equal to marginal revenue

In fact, to maximize profit a manager generally wants to lower the price and sell more units, as long as the marginal revenue from selling them is at least equal to the marginal cost of the extra units. From this we get the following **rule for maximizing profit**: the highest profit is earned at the price where marginal cost is just less than or equal to marginal revenue. (Note that this rule applies in the typical situations where the curves are shaped similarly to those discussed here. As a technical matter, however, we should add the following to the rule for maximizing profit: The marginal cost must be increasing, at a lesser rate than marginal revenue.)

You can see this rule operating in Exhibit 17-9. As the price is cut from $140 down to $79, the quantity sold increases to six units and the profit increases to its maximum level, $106. At that point, marginal revenue and marginal cost are about equal. However, beyond that point further price cuts result in lower profits, even though a larger quantity is sold. Note, for example, that at a price of $53, which would be required to sell eight units, the profit almost disappears. Below that price there would be losses.

**marginal profit**
The extra profit on the last unit sold

The key point is that total profit is at a maximum at the point where marginal revenue (MR) equals marginal cost (MC). However, **marginal profit**—the extra profit on the last unit—is near zero. Marginal analysis shows that when a firm is looking for the best price to charge, it should lower the price—to increase the quantity it will sell—as long as the last unit it sells will yield *extra* profit.

You can see the effect of all of these relationships clearly in Exhibit 17-10. It graphs the total-revenue, total-cost, and total-profit relationships for the numbers we've been working with in Exhibit 17-9. The highest point on the total profit curve is at a quantity of six units. This is also the quantity where we find the greatest vertical distance between the total-revenue curve and the total-cost curve. Exhibit 17-9 shows that it is the $79 price that results in selling six units, so $79 is the price that leads to the highest profit.

A price lower than $79 would result in a higher sales volume. But you can see that the total-profit curve declines beyond a quantity of 6 units. So a profit-maximizing marketing manager would not be interested in setting a lower price.

In Exhibit 17-10, note that there are two different points where total revenue equals total cost. These two break-even points show there is a *range of profit* around the price that produces maximum profit. The highest profit is for a price of $79, but this firm's strategy would be profitable all the way from a price of $53 to $117.

The implication of this is important. Marginal analysis seeks to identify the best



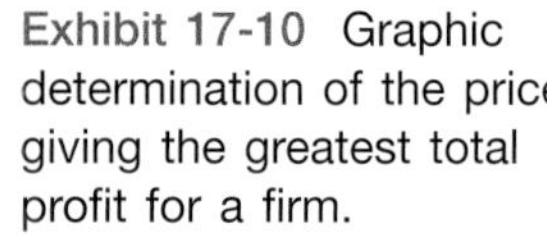
Exhibit 17-10 Graphic determination of the price giving the greatest total profit for a firm.

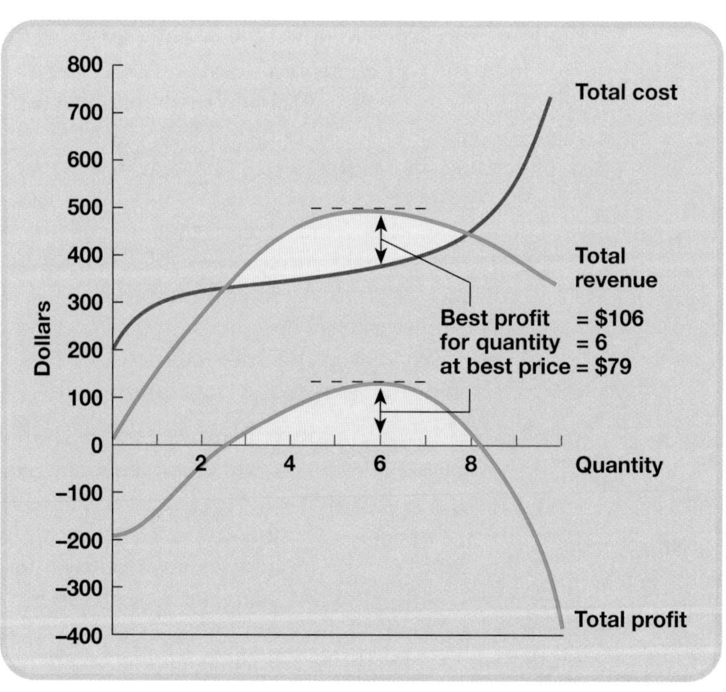

price, the price that maximizes profits. This is perhaps an ideal rather than what is usually achieved in practice. After all, few managers know the exact shape of the demand curve. However, the range of profit around the ideal price means that the price and quantity estimates don't have to be exact to be useful. They still help us get close to the ideal price even if we don't hit it exactly.

**A final note on marginal analysis** In this section we've shown that marginal analysis is a flexible and useful tool for marketing managers. Some managers don't take advantage of it because they think they can't determine the exact shape of the demand curve. But that view misses the point of marginal analysis.

Marginal analysis encourages managers to think very carefully about what they *do know* about costs and demand. Only rarely is either type of information exact. So in practical applications the focus of marginal analysis is not on finding the precise price that will maximize profit. Rather, the focus is on getting an estimate of how profit might vary across a range of relevant prices. Further, a number of practical demand-oriented approaches can help a marketing manager do a better job of understanding the likely shape of the demand curve for a target market (see Marketing Demo 17-1). We'll discuss these approaches next.

## Demand-Oriented Approaches for Setting Prices

Unlike cost-oriented pricing, which asks the question "How much can we add to costs?" demand-oriented pricing asks "How much will someone pay?" To determine

## Marketing Demo 17–1

### ANALYZING THE PSYCHOLOGY OF PRICING

Is your company leaving significant sums of money on the table due to badly planned pricing? Most likely it is, if you're practising cost–plus pricing. All too often, companies simply take their costs, add on a markup, and—presto!—that becomes the selling price of their product or service.

But there's a psychological component to consumers' perception of prices, which many organizations—to their detriment—do not consider. By sharpening price points, marketers can add a substantial amount to the bottom line.

For example, one educational institution that sells night-school and continuing-education courses—some $25 million worth—had always practised cost–plus pricing. Consequently, it had many different price points. Some courses were priced at $57, some at $65, some at $74, and so on. However, research revealed that, when it comes to less than $10 increments, people do not tend to distinguish between, say, $54 and $59. These are so-called "dead zones," where consumers don't discriminate between the higher and lower price points. So why charge $54 when you can charge $59 with no change in demand? In fact, studies have shown that prices ending in "9" can be more attractive to prospective buyers than lower numbers within the same range. After a review of the institution's price points, it was calculated that a whopping $1.8 million was left on the table.

In another instance, a brewery had a price point of $15.85. Research showed that an increase to $15.95 would have made no difference to the consumer. Not so for the company. As a result of having had the lower $15.85 price point in place for a year, it took a $4.1-million hit.

Some companies—IKEA and Compaq Computer Corp., for example—even follow a pricing philosophy called "design to price." They figure out the price point consumers are willing to pay to buy a particular item. Then they build the best product they can to meet that price point and achieve their profit objectives. In the case of Compaq, it had determined that under $2,000 was a key price point for personal computers. So it designed its computers accordingly, cutting back on some options and specifications to meet that price point and capture that share of the market.

Once you have decided to increase your prices and go for a price point, take a deep breath and go the distance—gain the extra profit. You may lose some customers, but those who stay with you will do so whether you exceed the threshold by a little or a lot. As the adage goes, in for a penny, in for a pound!

# Internet Insite 17–1

## ARE PRICES LOWER ONLINE?

There is a widespread belief that one can find great deals on the Internet. Are prices really lower on the Internet compared to the bricks-and-mortar stores? Let us examine some of the evidence and explore the factors driving online prices.

Companies like Buy.com and Amazon.com have at times engaged in price wars. When Amazon offered free shipping on all items above $49, Buy.com went one step further and offered free shipping on all products. Buy.com then went on to announce that it would sell books at 10 percent below Amazon's prices, which in many cases are already discounted.[6]

From airline tickets to consumer electronics and automobiles, there appear to be very low-priced offers all over the Internet. In Canada, Chapters Online (now chapters.indigo.ca) advertises massive savings on books and free shipping to boot.

A study of automobile prices showed that online consumers paid 1.2 percent less than offline consumers and Autobytel, a referral service that provides consumers competing quotes from several car dealers, enabled consumers to save as much as 2.2 percent.[7] In a study of prices in one homogeneous product category, DVDs, it was found that prices on the Internet were lower online compared to bricks-and-mortar stores.[8] Another study using 8,500 price observations in two product categories, books and CDs, concluded that Internet prices were lower by 9–16 percent.[9]

Other researchers have argued that Internet prices are not really lower. Marketers avoid lowering prices by focusing on niche markets or creating brand image and trust as well as versioning and bundling.[10] The use of branding, auctions (where the highest bidder gets the product), and bundling (ensuring that consumers buy two related products, rather than just one) are common strategies to ensure high prices and margins.[11]

Clearly, the evidence regarding lower prices on the Net is mixed. Since 2000, many Internet firms that competed aggressively on price have failed. The surviving firms, with a few exceptions, are much more sensitive to the issue of profitability. A comparison of prices in 2000 and 2001 (before and after the so-called dot-com meltdown) revealed that average prices were higher in 2001, compared to a year earlier for the same set of products.[12]

The cost of doing business online was supposed to be lower than the cost of operating a bricks-and-mortar operation. There is also some evidence that the transaction processing costs are much lower online. The expectation was that this would translate to lower prices online. However, most Internet retailers have found out that the cost of marketing (to draw traffic), the cost of building and maintaining a highly interactive site, and the cost of providing customer support means that operating online may not be all that inexpensive. Add to this the fact that many online firms have a smaller customer base, which means they cannot afford to have perennially low prices.

Consumers can compare prices of different brands and prices offered by different retailers using popular price-comparison sites (e.g., mySimon, BizRate, shopper.cnet.com, and NexTag). The easy access to price-comparison search engines, or so-called searchbots (or intelligent search agents or ISAs) should, in theory, enable competitors to know each other's prices quickly and adjust their prices accordingly. In other words, price dispersion (or difference between competitors' prices) should be very low on the Internet. However, in practice, that is not the case. Price dispersion on the Internet is high. One study reported a 33 percent price difference for books and a 25 percent price difference for CDs.[13] There is some evidence that prices in bricks-and-mortar stores are more dispersed than in online stores.[14]

Some retailers have joined the price-comparison sites in the hope that at least some of the price-comparison shoppers will visit their store through the link from the comparison site. Other retailers have blocked these searchbots from collecting price information from their sites,[15] which means the price information available at these comparison sites is not complete. Consumers should be aware that a site listed on top in the search result may have paid a fee for the top listing.

It is likely that consumers perceive prices to be lower online. Marketers do face immense price pressure online. But, so do they offline. Many marketers and scholars believe that the emphasis on reverse auctions and price-comparison search engines will damage brand image and reduce margins on products. Marketers who want to avoid this "commodity trap" must focus on building the brand, providing superior value, and building relationships with customers.

Some questions to ponder: Go to a price-comparison site and see the extent of price dispersion. If price comparison is so easy, why do some retailers charge more for the same product? How can marketers prevent the erosion of profit margins on the Internet?

Go to: www.mcgrawhill.ca/college/wong
to apply this Insite in an exciting Internet exercise.

that figure, demand-oriented pricing requires that we understand both the factors influencing customers' price sensitivity and how customers "think" about prices.

### Factors Influencing Customers' Price Sensitivity

A manager who knows what influences target customers' price sensitivity can do a better job estimating the demand curve that the firm faces. Marketing researchers have identified a number of factors that influence price sensitivity across many different market situations.

**Availability of substitutes** The first is the most basic. When customers have substitute ways of meeting a need, they are likely to be more price-sensitive. A cook who wants a cappuccino maker to be able to serve something distinctive to guests at a dinner party may be willing to pay a high price. However, if different machines are available and our cook sees them as pretty similar, price sensitivity will be greater. It's important not to ignore dissimilar alternatives if the customer sees them as substitutes. If a machine for espresso were much less expensive than one for cappuccino, our cook might decide that an espresso machine would meet her needs just as well.

**Ease of price comparison** The impact of substitutes on price sensitivity is greatest when it is easy for customers to *compare prices*. For example, unit prices make it easier for our cook to compare the prices of espresso and cappuccino grinds on the grocery-store shelf. Many people believe that the ease of comparing prices on the Internet will increase price sensitivity and ultimately bring down prices (see Internet Insite 17-1). If nothing else, it may make sellers more aware of competing prices.

**Cost sharing** People tend to be less price sensitive when someone else pays the bill or shares the cost. Perhaps this is just human nature. Insurance companies think that consumers would reject high medical fees if they were paying all of their own bills. And executives might plan longer in advance to get better discounts on airline flights if their companies weren't footing the bills.

**Amount spent** Customers tend to be more price sensitive the greater the total expenditure. Sometimes a big expenditure can be broken into smaller pieces. Mercedes knows this. When its ads focused on the cost of a monthly lease rather than the total price of the car, more consumers got interested in biting the bullet.

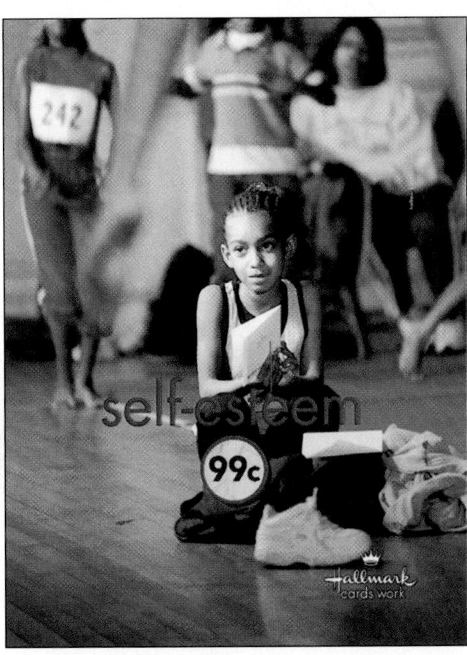

**Significance of the end benefit** Customers are less price sensitive the greater the significance of the end benefit of the purchase. Computer makers will pay more to get Intel processors if they believe that having an "Intel inside" sells more machines. Positioning efforts often focus on emotional benefits of a purchase to increase the significance of a benefit. Ads for L'Oreal hair colour, for example, show closeups of beautiful hair while popular endorsers like Portia de Rossi tell women to buy it "Because you're worth it." A consumer who cares about the price of a bottle of hair colour might still have no question that she's worth the difference in price.

**Sunk investments** Customers are sometimes less price sensitive if they already have a sunk investment that is related to the purchase. This is especially relevant with business customers. For example, once managers of a firm have invested to train employees to use Microsoft Excel, they are less likely to resist the high price of a new version of that software.

These factors apply in many different purchase situations, so it makes sense for a marketing manager to consider each of them in refining estimates of how customers might respond at different prices.[16]

## How Buyers Think About Price and Value

Some people don't devote much thought to what they pay for the products they buy—including some frequently purchased goods and services. But most consumers have a **reference price**—the price they expect to pay—for many of the products they purchase. And different customers may have different reference prices for the same basic type of purchase. For example, a person who really enjoys reading might have a higher reference price for a popular paperback book than another person who is only an occasional reader. Marketing research can sometimes identify different segments with different reference prices.[17]

**reference price**
The price consumers expect to pay for a product

If a firm's price is lower than a customer's reference price, customers may view the product as a better value and demand may increase (see Exhibit 17-11). Sometimes a firm will try to position the benefits of its product in such a way that consumers compare it with a product that has a higher reference price. PBS TV stations do this when they ask viewers to make donations that match what they pay for "just one month of cable service."

**Value-in-use** Organizational buyers think about how a purchase will affect their total costs. Many marketers who aim at business markets keep this in mind when estimating demand and setting prices. They use **value-in-use pricing**—which means

**value-in-use pricing**
Setting prices that will capture some of what customers will save by substituting the firm's product for the one currently being used

If the price of a product is set higher than the target market's reference price, there is not likely to be much demand.

Exhibit 17-11 How the customer's reference price influences perceived value (for a marketing mix with a given set of benefits and costs).

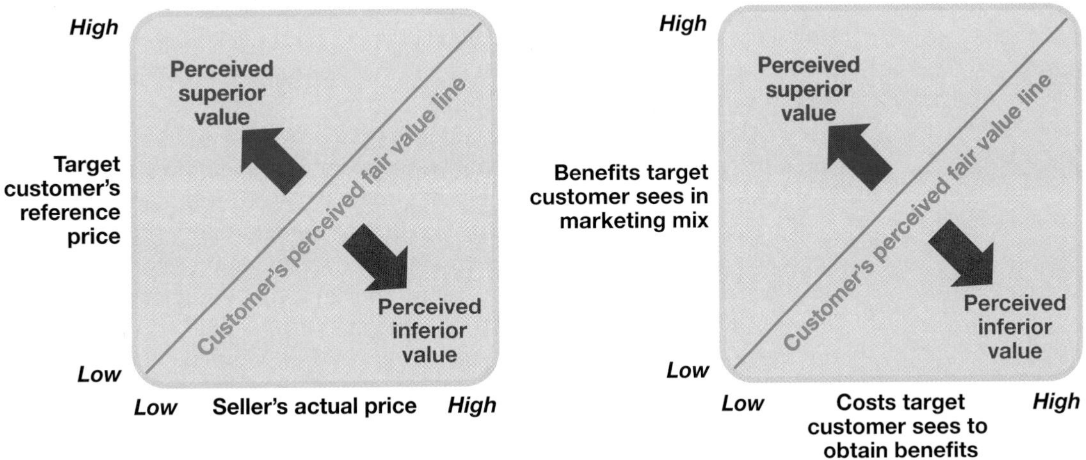




setting prices that will capture some of what customers will save by substituting the firm's product for the one currently being used.

For example, a producer of computer-controlled machines used to assemble cars knows that the machine doesn't just replace a standard machine. It also reduces labour costs, quality control costs, and—after the car is sold—costs of warranty repairs. The potential savings (value in use) might be different for different customers, because they have different operations and costs. However, the marketer can estimate what each auto producer will save by using the machine—and then set a price that makes it less expensive for the auto producer to buy the computerized machine than to stick with the old methods. The number of customers who have different levels of potential savings also provides some idea about the shape of the demand curve.

Creating a "better mousetrap" that could save customers money in the long run isn't any guarantee that customers will be willing to pay a higher price. To capture the value created, the seller must convince buyers of the savings—and buyers are likely to be skeptical. A salesperson needs to be able to show proof of the claims.[18]

## Alternative Demand-based Pricing Methods

There are several different ways to carry out demand-based pricing. Each of these methods seeks not only to respond to demand but also to shape it. Let's consider the most commonly used variations.

leader pricing

Setting some very low prices to get customers into retail stores

### Leader and bait pricing

**Leader pricing** means setting some very low prices—real bargains—to get customers into retail stores. The idea is not only to sell large quantities of the leader items but also to get customers into the store to buy other products. Certain products are picked for their promotion value and are priced low—but above cost. In food stores, the leader prices are the "specials" that are advertised regularly to give an image of low prices. Leader items are usually well-known, widely used items that customers don't stock heavily—paper towels, laundry detergent, ice cream, or coffee—but on which they will recognize a real price cut. In other words, leader pricing is normally used with products for which consumers do have a specific reference price.

Leader pricing may try to appeal to customers who normally shop elsewhere. But it can backfire if customers buy only the low-priced leaders. To avoid hurting profits, managers often select leader items that aren't directly competitive with major lines—as when bargain-priced videotapes are a leader for an electronics store.[19]

**bait pricing**
Setting some very low prices to attract customers, but then trying to sell more expensive models or brands once the customer is in the store

Leader pricing should not be confused with **bait pricing**. Bait pricing involves setting some very low prices to attract customers, but then trying to sell more expensive models or brands once the customer is in the store. For example, a furniture store may advertise a colour TV for $199. But once bargain hunters come to the store, salesclerks point out the disadvantages of the low-price TV and try to convince them to trade up to a better (and more expensive) set. Bait pricing is something like leader pricing. But here the seller doesn't plan to sell many at the low price.

If bait pricing is successful, the demand for higher-quality products expands. This approach may be a sensible part of a strategy to trade-up customers. And customers may be well served if, once in the store, they find that a higher-priced product offers better value, perhaps because its features are better suited to their needs. But bait pricing is generally viewed as unethical, and in Canada it can contravene the misleading-advertising rules of the Competition Act.

**psychological pricing**
Setting prices that have special appeal to target customers

**Psychological pricing** **Psychological pricing** means setting prices that have special appeal to target customers. Some people think there are whole ranges of prices that potential customers see as the same, so price cuts in these ranges do not increase the quantity sold. But just below this range, customers may buy more. Then, at even lower prices, the quantity demanded stays the same again—and so on. Exhibit 17-12 shows the kind of demand curve that leads to psychological pricing. Vertical drops mark the price ranges that customers see as the same. Pricing research (see Marketing Demo 17-2) shows that there are such demand curves.[20]

**odd-even pricing**
Setting prices that end in certain numbers

**Odd-even pricing** is setting prices that end in certain numbers. For example, products selling below $50 often end in the number 5 or the number 9—such as $24.95, or 49 cents. Prices for higher-priced products are often $1 or $2 below the next even dollar figure—such as $99 rather than $100.

Some marketers use odd-even pricing because they think consumers react better to these prices—perhaps seeing them as "substantially" lower than the next highest even price. Marketers using these prices seem to assume that they have a rather jagged demand curve—that slightly higher prices will substantially reduce the quantity demanded.

**price lining**
Setting a few price levels for a product line and then marking all items at these prices

**Price lining** **Price lining** is setting a few price levels for a product line and then marking all items at these prices. This approach assumes that customers have a certain reference price in mind that they expect to pay for a product. For example, many neckties are priced between $20 and $50. In price lining, there are only a few prices within this range. Ties will not be priced at $20, $21, $22, $23, and so on. They might be priced at four levels—$20, $30, $40, and $50.

Price lining has advantages other than just matching prices to what consumers expect to pay. The main advantage is simplicity—for both salespeople and customers. It is less confusing than having many prices. Some customers may consider items in only one price class. Their big decision, then, is which item(s) to choose at that price.

For retailers, price lining has several advantages. Sales may increase because (1) they can offer a bigger variety in each price class, and (2) it's easier to get customers to make decisions within one price class. Stock planning is simpler because demand is larger at the relatively few prices. Price lining can also reduce costs because inventory needs are lower.

Exhibit 17-12 Demand curve when psychological pricing is appropriate.

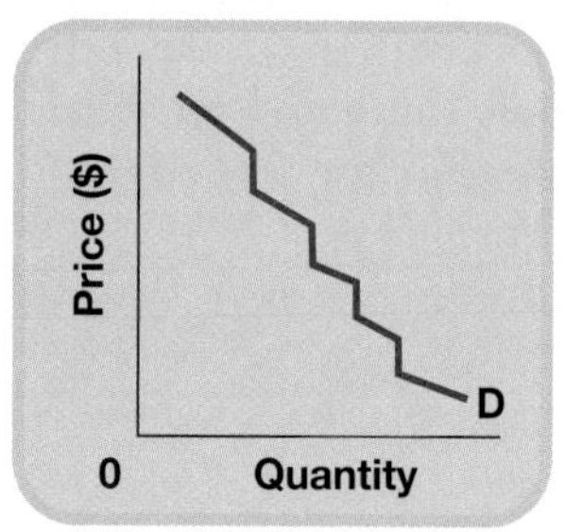

Prestige pricing is often used with luxury products like jewellery and high-end consumer electronics to suggest high quality. But Paradigm wants consumers to view its low price as a sign of good quality and good value, not as a signal of low quality.

## Marketing Demo 17–2

### PRICING RESEARCH

How do you know when your pricing is right? Many companies are turning to pricing research to optimize their profit.

And with good reason—it's a science that is proving to be increasingly accurate when used in the appropriate way. Considering the impact of pricing on profitability, this is a tool that companies cannot afford to ignore.

Take, for example, one well-known consumer products company that was mired in a key pricing threshold of 99¢ for one of its products. Since the company wasn't making money on the product at that price, executives wondered what would happen if they were to raise the price beyond that threshold. And how high should they go—$1.02, $1.09, $1.20? We did pricing research which accurately predicted that, once the $1 threshold was surpassed, volume did not change significantly until the price hit $1.29. Consequently, the company raised its price to $1.29, and made a lot more money.

Yet many organizations still shy away from pricing research, citing the cost and what they perceive as an inherent bias for customers to lie about pricing preferences. In many cases, their skepticism is well-founded, because there have been research methods used over the years that were not good at predicting price sensitivity or value.

The good news is that there are many new developments in pricing research, and its accuracy has been proven time and again in studies. So if you've decided you want to benefit from pricing research, here are some general guidelines to keep in mind:

- When it comes to new products, it's a good idea to do pricing research early in the development process. That way, you can practice a "design-to-price" philosophy, delivering the most value-added elements of a product. Pricing research will help you understand what your customers are willing to pay up front, and you can make more profitable design decisions.
- Never ask customers: "What would you be willing to pay?" Direct methods that explicitly ask customers what they are willing to pay feed into the inherent bias to lie. Most people underestimate what they would be willing to pay; others, by contrast, consider it a test of their loyalty, and overestimate. Indirect methods that focus on other issues, besides price, are more effective.
- Pricing research data should help you decide which segments of the market you are going to target and, perhaps more importantly, which ones you are *not* going to pursue.
- Once your pricing strategy has been set, the results of the research should be fed to the salesforce, so they can use it to help them sell at the recommended price. If they have access to the research, they will know which customers you want to target, and which ones you don't—and why. Although companies usually provide their sales representatives with product education, that information seldom relates to what customers are willing to pay. As a result, salespeople often claim prices are too high. So if you want to reduce your stress, share your pricing research with your salesforce.

Pricing research has been proven to be highly valuable in helping many companies determine when the price is right. And when the price is right, profit soars.[21]

**demand-backward pricing**
Setting an acceptable final consumer price and working backward to what a producer can charge

**Demand-backward pricing** **Demand-backward pricing** is setting an acceptable final consumer price and working backward to what a producer can charge. It is commonly used by producers of consumer products—especially shopping products such as women's clothing and appliances. It is also used with gift items for which customers will spend a specific amount—because they are seeking a $10 or a $15 gift. Here a reverse cost-plus pricing process is used. This method has been called market-minus pricing.

The producer starts with the retail (reference) price for a particular item and then works backward—subtracting the typical margins that channel members expect. This gives the approximate price the producer can charge. Then the average or planned marketing expenses can be subtracted from this price to find how much can be spent producing the item. Candy companies do this. They alter the size of the candy bar to keep the bar at the expected price.

Demand estimates are needed for demand-backward pricing to be successful. The quantity that will be demanded affects production costs—that is, where the firm will be on its average-cost curve. Also, since competitors can be expected to make the best product possible, it is important to know customer needs to set the best amount to spend on manufacturing costs. By increasing costs a little, the value may be so improved in consumers' eyes that the firm will sell many more units.

Exhibit 17-13 Demand curve showing a prestige pricing situation.

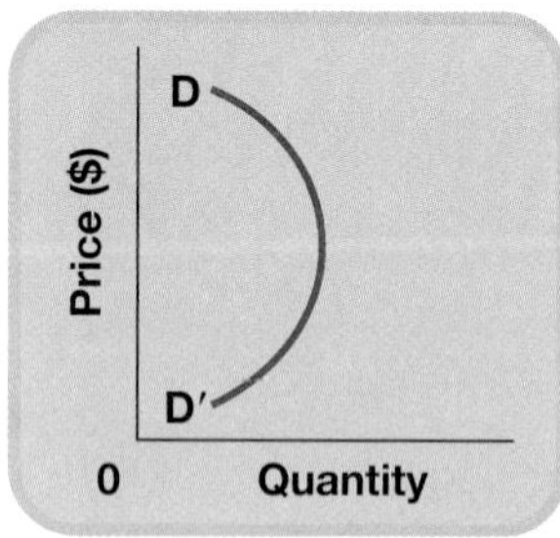


**prestige pricing**
Setting a rather high price to suggest high quality or high status

**Prestige pricing** **Prestige pricing** is setting a rather high price to suggest high quality or high status. Some target customers want the best, so they will buy at a high price. But if the price seems cheap, they worry about quality and don't buy. Prestige pricing is most common for luxury products such as furs, jewellery, and perfume.

It is also common in service industries, where the customer can't see the product in advance and relies on price to judge its quality. Target customers who respond to prestige pricing give the marketing manager an unusual demand curve. Instead of a normal down-sloping curve, the curve goes down for a while and then bends back to the left again.[22] See Exhibit 17-13.



## Pricing the Full Product Line

Our emphasis has been, and will continue to be, on the problem of pricing an individual product, mainly because this makes our discussion clearer. But most marketing managers are responsible for more than one product. In fact, their "product" may be the whole company line! So we'll discuss this matter briefly.

### Full-line Pricing

**full-line pricing**
Setting prices for a whole line of products

**Full-line pricing** is setting prices for a whole line of products. How to do this depends on which of two basic situations a firm is facing.

In one case, all products in the company's line are aimed at the same general target market, which makes it important for all prices and value to be logically related. This is a common approach with shopping products. A producer of TV sets might offer several models with different features at different prices to give its target customers some choice. The difference among the prices and benefits should appear reasonable when the target customers are evaluating them. Customer perceptions can be important here. A low-priced item, even one that is a good value at that price, may drag down the image of the higher end of the line. Alternatively, one item that consumers do not see as a good value may spill over to how they judge other products in the line.

In other cases, the different products in the line are aimed at entirely different

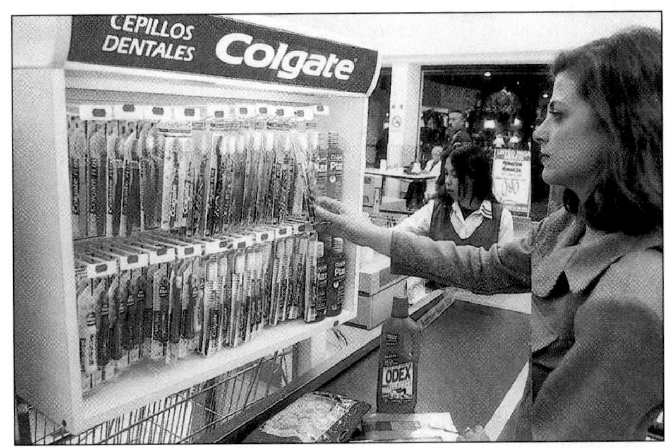


Colgate offers different lines of toothbrushes, with "good," better," and "best" quality, at different price levels to meet the needs of different market segments.

target markets so there doesn't have to be any relation between the various prices. A chemical producer of a wide variety of products with several target markets, for example, probably should price each product separately.

The marketing manager must try to recover all costs on the whole line—perhaps by pricing quite low on more competitive items and much higher on ones with unique benefits. However, estimating costs for each product is a challenge because there is no single right way to assign a company's fixed costs to each of the products; we'll address this topic in more detail in Chapter 18. Regardless of how costs are allocated, any cost-oriented pricing method that doesn't consider demand can lead to very unrealistic prices. To avoid mistakes, the marketing manager should judge demand for the whole line as well as demand for each individual product in each target market.

## Complementary Product Pricing

**complementary product pricing**
Setting prices on several products as a group

**Complementary product pricing** is setting prices on several products as a group. This may lead to one product being priced very low so that the profits from another product will increase, thus increasing the product group's total profits. A new Gillette shaver, for example, may be priced low to sell the blades, which must be replaced regularly.

Complementary product pricing differs from full-line pricing because different production facilities may be involved—so there's no cost allocation problem. Instead, the problem is really understanding the target market and the demand curves for each of the complementary products. Then various combinations of prices can be tried to see what set will be best for reaching the company's pricing objectives.

## Product-bundle Pricing

**product-bundle pricing**
Setting one price for a set of products

A firm that offers its target market several different products may use **product-bundle pricing**—setting one price for a set of products. Firms that use product-bundle pricing usually set the overall price so that it's cheaper for the customer to buy the products at the same time than separately. Drugstores sometimes bundle the cost of a roll of film and the cost of the processing. A bank may offer a product-bundle price for a safe-deposit box, traveller's cheques, and a savings account. Bundling encourages customers to spend more and buy products that they might not otherwise buy—because the added cost of the extras is not as high as it would normally be, so the value is better.

Most firms that use product-bundle pricing also set individual prices for the unbundled products. This may increase demand by attracting customers who want one item in a product assortment but don't want the extras. Many firms treat services this way. A software company may have a product-bundle price for its software and access to a toll-free telephone assistance service. However, customers who don't need help can pay a lower price and get just the software.[23]

## Bid Pricing and Negotiated Pricing

**bid pricing**

Offering a specific price for each possible job rather than setting a price that applies for all customers



We introduced the issue of competitive bidding and reverse auctions in Chapter 7. But now let's take a closer look at bid pricing. **Bid pricing** means offering a specific price for each possible job rather than setting a price that applies for all customers. In an e-commerce reverse auction for a standardized product, this may just require that the manager decide the firm's lowest acceptable selling price. But in many situations bid pricing is more complicated. For example, building contractors usually must bid on possible projects. And many companies selling services (like cleaning or data processing) must submit bids for jobs they would like to have.

A big problem in bid pricing on a complicated job is estimating all of the costs that will apply. This may sound easy, but a complicated bid may involve thousands of cost components. Further, management must include an overhead charge and a charge for profit.

Because many firms use an e-mail distribution list or website to solicit bids, the process is fast and easy for the buyer. But a seller has to be geared up to set a price and respond quickly. However, this system does allow the seller to set a price based on the precise situation and what marginal costs and marginal revenue are involved.

Sometimes it isn't possible to figure out specs or costs in advance. This may lead to a negotiated contract where the customer agrees to pay the supplier's total cost plus an agreed-on profit figure (say, 10 percent of costs or a dollar amount)—after the job is finished. See Ethical Dimensions 17-1 for an additional note on using cost-plus pricing.

Competition must be considered when adding in overhead and profit for a bid price. Usually, the customer will get several bids and accept the lowest one. So, unthinking addition of typical overhead and profit rates should be avoided. Some bidders use the same overhead and profit rates on all jobs, regardless of competition, and then are surprised when they don't get some jobs.

Because bidding can be expensive, marketing managers may want to be selective about which jobs to bid on and choose those where they believe they have the greatest chance of success. Firms can spend thousands, or even millions, of dollars just developing bids for large business or government customers.[24]

Some buying situations, including much government buying, require the use of bids—and the purchasing agent must take the lowest bid. In other cases, however,

### Ethical Dimensions 17–1

**COST-PLUS BID PRICING**

Some unethical sellers give bid prices based on cost-plus contracts a bad reputation by faking their records to make costs seem higher than they really are. In other cases, there may be honest debate about what costs should be allowed. We've already considered, for instance, the difficulties in allocating fixed costs.

the customer asks for bids and then singles out the company that submits the most attractive bid, not necessarily the lowest, for further bargaining.

The list price or bidding price the seller would like to charge is sometimes only the starting point for discussions with individual customers. What a customer will buy—if the customer buys at all—depends on the **negotiated price**, a price set based on bargaining between the buyer and seller.

**negotiated price**
A price set based on bargaining between the buyer and seller

As with simple bid pricing, negotiated pricing is most common in situations where the marketing mix is adjusted for each customer—so bargaining may involve the whole marketing mix, not just the price level. For example, a firm that produces machine tools used by other manufacturers to make their products might use this approach. Each customer may need custom-designed machines and different types of installation service. Through the bargaining process, the seller tries to determine what aspects of the marketing mix are most important to the customer. For one customer, selling price may be most important. Then the seller might try to find ways to reduce costs of other elements of the marketing mix—consistent with the customer's needs—in order to earn a profit. Another customer might want more of some other element of the marketing mix—like more technical help after the sale—and be less sensitive to price.

Sellers must know their costs to negotiate prices effectively. However, negotiated pricing is a demand-oriented approach. Here the seller analyzes very carefully a particular customer's position on a demand curve, or on different possible demand curves based on different offerings, rather than the overall demand curve for a group of customers.

## Chapter Summary

In this chapter, we discussed cost-based and demand-based approaches to price setting.

Cost-based approaches start with an estimate of costs and add a desired markup to arrive at the final price. Some businesses use the same markups for all their items. Others find that varying the markups increases turnover and profit. In other words, they consider demand and competition.

Many firms use average-cost pricing to help set their prices. But this approach sometimes ignores demand completely. A more realistic approach to average-cost pricing requires a sales forecast—maybe just assuming that sales in the next period will be roughly the same as in the last period. This approach does enable the marketing manager to set a price—but the price may or may not cover all costs and earn the desired profit.

Break-even analysis is useful for evaluating possible prices. It provides a rough-and-ready tool for eliminating unworkable prices. But management must estimate demand to evaluate the chance of reaching these possible break-even points.

Demand-based approaches seek to establish prices that reflect what customers value, regardless of what it costs to make the product. The major difficulty with demand-oriented pricing is estimating the demand curve. But experienced managers, aided perhaps by marketing research, can estimate the nature of demand for their products. Such estimates are useful even if they aren't exact. They get you thinking in the right ballpark. Sometimes, when all you need is a decision about raising or lowering price, even rough demand estimates can be very revealing. Further, a firm's demand curve does not cease to exist simply because it's ignored. Some information is better than none at all. And marketers should consider demand in their pricing. We see this with value-in-use pricing, online auctions, leader pricing, bait pricing, odd-even pricing, psychological pricing, full-line pricing, and even bid pricing. Understanding the factors that influence price sensitivity can make these approaches more effective.

Throughout the book, we stress that firms must consider the customer before they do anything. This certainly applies to pricing. It means that when managers are setting a price, they have to consider what customers will be willing to pay. This isn't always easy. But it's nice to know that there is a profit range around the best price. Therefore, even rough estimates about what potential customers will buy at various prices will probably lead to a better price than mechanical use of traditional markups or cost-oriented formulas.

While our focus in this chapter is on price setting, it's clear that pricing decisions must consider the cost of offering the whole marketing mix. Smart marketers don't just accept costs as a given. Target marketers always look for ways to be more efficient—to reduce costs while improving the value that they offer customers. Improved coordination of physical distribution, for example, may improve customer service and reduce costs. Carefully defined target markets may make promotion spending more efficient. Products that really meet customers' needs reduce costly new-product failures. Channel members can shift and share functions—so that the cost of performing needed marketing activities is as low as possible. Marketers should set prices based on demand as well as on costs. But creative marketers also look for ways to reduce costs—because costs affect profit.



## Key Concepts

average cost, p. 520
average fixed cost, p. 520
average variable cost, p. 520
average-cost pricing, p. 519
bait pricing, p. 534
bid pricing, p. 538
break-even analysis, p. 524
break-even point (BEP), p. 524
complementary product pricing, p. 537
demand-backward pricing, p. 536
experience-curve pricing, p. 523
fixed-cost (FC) contribution per unit, p. 525
full-line pricing, p. 536
leader pricing, p. 533
long-run target-return pricing, p. 524
marginal analysis, p. 526
marginal cost, p. 527
marginal profit, p. 528
marginal revenue, p. 527
markup, p. 516
markup chain, p. 517
negotiated price, p. 539
odd-even pricing, p. 534
prestige pricing, p. 536
price lining, p. 534
product-bundle pricing, p. 537
psychological pricing, p. 534
reference price, p. 532
rule for maximizing profit, p. 527
stockturn rate, p. 518
target-return pricing, p. 523
total cost, p. 520
total fixed cost, p. 520
total variable cost, p. 520
value-in-use pricing, p. 532

## Questions and Problems

1. Why do many department stores seek a markup of about 40 percent when some discount houses operate on a 20-percent markup?
2. A producer distributed its riding lawn mowers through wholesalers and retailers. The retail selling price was \$800, and the manufacturing cost to the company was \$312. The retail markup was 35 percent and the wholesale markup 20 percent. *(a)* What was the cost to the wholesaler? To the retailer? *(b)* What percentage markup did the producer take?
3. Relate the concept of stock turnover to the growth of mass-merchandising. Use a simple example in your answer.
4. If total fixed costs are \$200,000 and total variable costs are \$100,000 at the output of 20,000 units, what are the probable total fixed costs and total variable costs at an output of 10,000 units? What are the average fixed costs, average variable costs, and average costs at these two output levels? Explain what additional information you would want to determine what price should be charged.
5. Explain how experience-curve pricing differs from average-cost pricing.
6. Construct an example showing that mechanical use of a very large or a very small markup might still lead to unprofitable operation while some intermediate price would be profitable. Draw a graph and show the break-even point(s).
7. The Davis Company's fixed costs for the year are estimated at \$200,000. Its product sells for \$250. The variable cost per unit is \$200. Sales for the coming

year are expected to reach $1,250,000. What is the break-even point? Expected profit? If sales are forecast at only $875,000, should the Davis Company shut down operations? Why?

8. Discuss the idea of drawing separate demand curves for different market segments. It seems logical because each target market should have its own marketing mix. But won't this lead to many demand curves and possible prices? And what will this mean with respect to functional discounts and varying prices in the marketplace? Will it be legal? Will it be practical?

9. Distinguish between leader pricing and bait pricing. What do they have in common? How can their use affect a marketing mix?

10. Cite a local example of psychological pricing and evaluate whether it makes sense.

11. Cite a local example of odd-even pricing and evaluate whether it makes sense.

12. How does a prestige pricing policy fit into a marketing mix? Would exclusive distribution be necessary?

13. Is a full-line pricing policy available only to producers? Cite local examples of full-line pricing. Why is full-line pricing important?

## Computer-Aided Problem 17

### Break-Even/Profit Analysis

This problem lets you see the dynamics of break-even analysis. The starting values (costs, revenues, etc.) for this problem are from the break-even analysis example in this chapter (see Exhibit 17-8).

The first column computes a break-even point. You can change costs and prices to figure new break-even points (in units and dollars). The second column goes further. There you can specify target profit level, and the unit and dollar sales needed to achieve your target profit level will be computed. You can also estimate possible sales quantities, and the program will compute costs, sales, and profits. Use this spreadsheet to address the following issues.

a. *Vary the selling price between $1.00 and $1.40. Prepare a table showing how the break-even point (in units and dollars) changes at the different price levels.*

b. *If you hope to earn a target profit of $15,000, how many units would you have to sell? What would total cost be? Total sales dollars? (Note: Use the right-hand ["profit analysis"] column in the spreadsheet.)*

c. *Using the "profit analysis" column (column 2), allow your estimate of the sale quantity to vary between 64,000 and 96,000. Prepare a table that shows, for each quantity level, what happens to average cost per unit and profit. Explain why average cost changes as it does over the different quantity values.*

## Suggested Cases

To view the cases, go to www.mcgrawhill.ca/college/wong.

Interested in finding out what marketing looks like in the real world? *Marketing Magazine* is just a click away on your OLC! Visit www.mcgrawhill.ca/college/wong today.

# Chapter Eighteen

# Developing Innovative Marketing Plans

**When You Finish This Chapter, You Should**

1. Know the content of and differences among strategies, marketing plans, and a marketing program.
2. Understand, in detail, all of the elements of the marketing strategy planning process and the strategy decisions for the four Ps.
3. Understand why the product classes and typical mixes should be considered when developing a marketing plan.
4. Understand ways the marketing strategy and marketing plan is likely to need to change at different stages of the product life cycle.
5. Understand the basic forecasting approaches and why they are used to evaluate the profitability of potential strategies.
6. Know what is involved in preparing a marketing plan, including estimates of costs and revenue and specification of other time-related details.
7. Understand the different ways a firm can plan to become involved in international marketing.

## "Handraising" to Introduce the PT Cruiser

The launch of the Chrysler PT Cruiser was extremely important to DaimlerChrysler Canada. After the initial preview of the PT Cruiser at the North American Auto show in Detroit in January 1999, they felt they had a breakthrough product that would attract consumers to the Chrysler brand franchises: consumers who most likely never would have considered visiting one of their dealerships.

To take advantage of this excitement, they launched a "handraiser" campaign in which Chrysler traded product information for some personal consumer information. An outdoor and magazine campaign invited consumers to reach Chrysler through its website or a toll-free number. The URL,

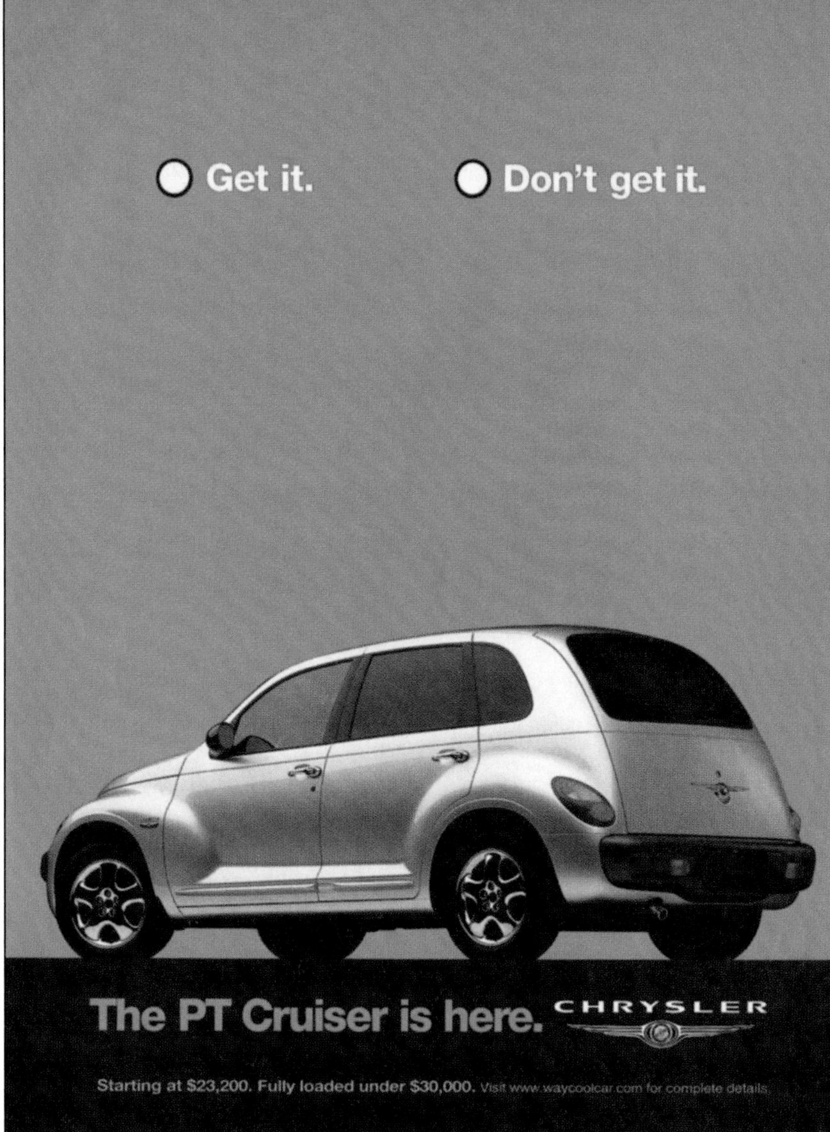


www.justyouraveragecar.com/yeahright, made a statement on its own.

Get it.
Don't get it.
The PT Cruiser is here.
CHRYSLER
Starting at $23,200. Fully loaded under $30,000. Visit www.waycoolcar.com for complete details.

As a result of this campaign, they approached the official launch of the PT Cruiser with the benefit of consumer data as well as information gathered from focus groups. Chrysler learned the PT Cruiser appealed to a wide range of consumers who could not be categorized into any traditional demographic or psychographic segment. It really was a state of mind, an emotional response to a totally new vehicle in the marketplace. The retro, yet modern, design appealed to the young, who viewed it as the coolest thing they'd ever seen, and to the older consumer who loved the vehicle as it reminded them of the cars their parents once had.

The other interesting thing they discovered is that there's a group of people who truly did not like the vehicle. The emotional reaction, at times, was extremely negative. But it was still a strong emotional response.

The common threads that bound this wide group of consumers were their passion for the vehicle and their desire to be individuals. The consumers did not want to be categorized and they did not agree on how this car should be categorized. The vehicle evoked a strong emotional response among a wide range of consumers, an ability to attract new customers to the franchise, and excitement in the marketplace that Chrysler had not seen since it created the minivan segment in 1983.

Chrysler developed some clear objectives for this launch. They didn't want to be traditional—the advertising had to be different, as this was no ordinary vehicle. Also, the

PT Cruiser makes a strong statement and so Chrysler did not want to miss the opportunity to say something about the Chrysler brand and bring some of that excitement to the whole franchise. Finally, they wanted to continue the excitement and "buzz" in the marketplace.

To pull this all together, Chrysler also had two underlying insights: First, the car makes the statement and the advertising should get out of the way; and second, the PT Cruiser evokes an emotional response, whether it's negative or positive.

The resulting campaign was as innovative as the product being launched. The outdoor and magazine creative executions themselves were very simple, with the vehicle in the forefront and a challenge to the consumer to react to the Chrysler PT Cruiser. The challenges were adapted to the media they were in. For example, in Internet publications the concept of "Get it" or "Don't get it" changed to "Add to shopping basket" or "Delete." The concept was robust and flexible.

The broadcast campaign played off this idea and highlighted consumers' reactions to the vehicle, where they either "Got it" or they "Didn't." They were also able to stretch the broadcast executions further with creative that played on the concept of "Who makes it?", with the response being Chrysler. Still another execution highlighted the fact that the Chrysler brand has fun "making up new cars." Both brand executions made strong statements about the daring and cutting-edge direction the Chrysler brand is now taking.

Overall, the launch was a great success. The press played back Chrysler's advertising concepts in articles, and even newspaper and magazine editorial cartoons were using the concept. And, the true measure of a great launch, the demand for the Chrysler PT Cruiser was unprecedented.[1]



## In This Chapter

By this stage in the book you have seen all of the elements that make up a marketing campaign and learned a great deal about how customers respond to those elements in a variety of situations. All of that material is intended to assist you in making the kinds of decisions made by marketing managers.

However, at some point, all of these individual decisions must be assembled into a complete marketing plan and, ultimately, that plan must be executed in the field. The two final chapters of this book explore these issues.

In this chapter we'll focus on the development of marketing plans. We'll start with a review of the many variables that must be considered in the marketing strategy planning process. You'll recognize that most of these are highlighted in the PT Cruiser vignette. Next we'll look at some of the key ways a marketing manager can identify the right marketing mix for an innovative strategy. Then we'll discuss how these ideas come together in a marketing plan. Given the managerial focus throughout this book, you'll find this discussion gives a good review of some key themes we've discussed.

We'll also discuss ways to forecast target market potential and sales, which is important not only in evaluating opportunities but also in developing the time-related details for a plan. Of course, plans must ultimately be blended into an overall program—and we'll suggest ways to approach that task. Planning strategies for international markets presents some special challenges, so we'll conclude the chapter by describing the different ways a marketer can address these challenges. Chapter 19 will then focus on issues related to the implementation and execution of marketing plans.

## The Art and Science of Marketing Planning

The PT Cruiser case shows that developing a successful marketing plan is a creative process, but it is also a logical process. And the logic that leads to a sound strategy may need to change as the market environment and target customers change.

Even so, the strategy planning process is guided by basic principles. The marketing concept emphasizes that all of a firm's activities should focus on its target markets. Further, a firm should try to find a competitive advantage in meeting the needs of some target market(s) that it can satisfy very well. If it can do that, it provides target customers with superior value. The target market(s) should be large enough to support the firm's efforts and yield a profit. And, ideally, the strategy should take advantage of trends in the external market, not buck them.

As we explained in Chapter 3, the marketing strategy planning process involves narrowing down from a broad set of possible marketing opportunities to a specific strategy the firm will pursue. A marketing *strategy* consists of a target market and a marketing mix; it specifies what a firm will do in some target market. A marketing *plan* includes the time-related details—including expected costs and revenues—for that strategy. In most firms, the marketing manager must ultimately combine the different marketing plans into an overall marketing *program*. Let's review some of the principles put forth in earlier chapters to guide these efforts.

### Select the "Right" Target Market

Developing a good marketing strategy and turning the strategy into a marketing plan requires blending the ideas we've discussed throughout this text. Exhibit 18-1

3M plans and develops different marketing mixes—including different products, promotion, and pricing—for different target markets around the world. Here are two examples of the diverse mixes that 3M implements.

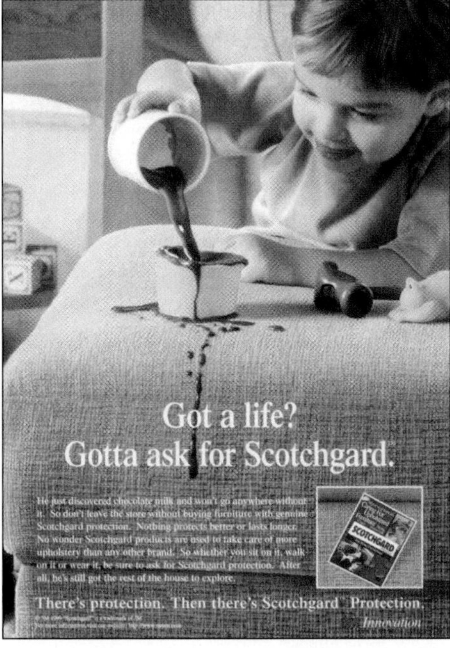


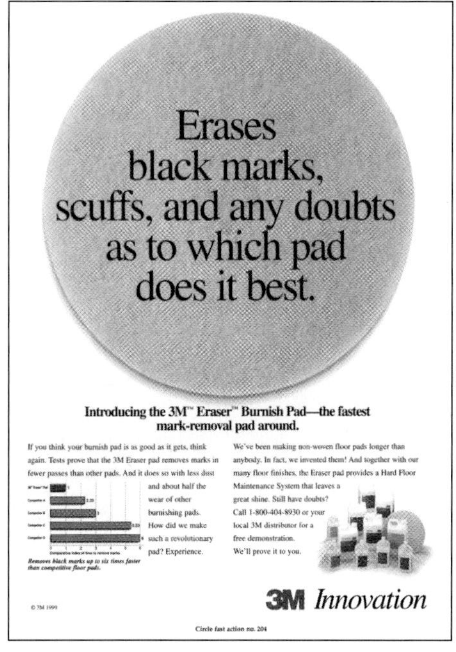

Exhibit 18-1
Overview of the marketing strategy planning process.

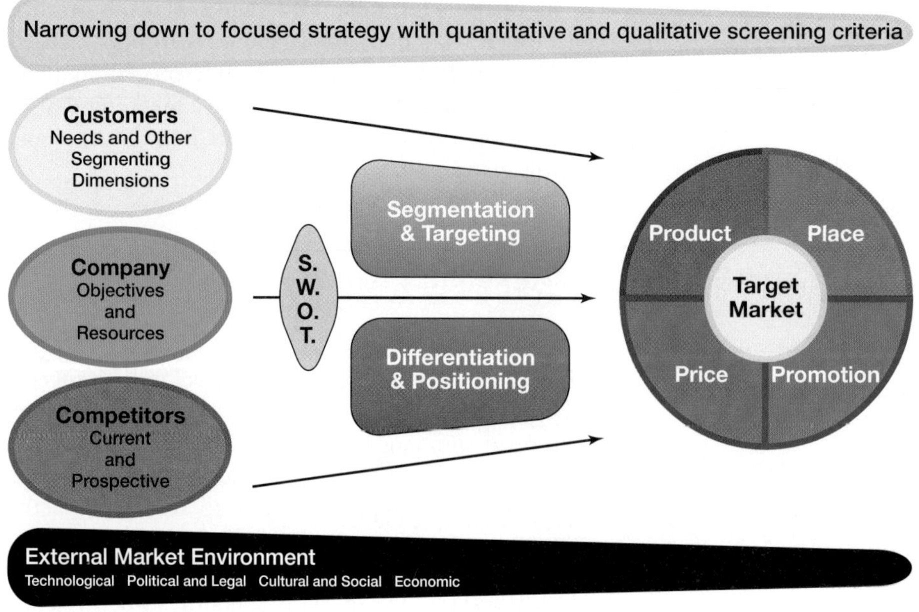




provides a broad overview of the major areas we've been talking about. You saw this before, in Chapter 3—before you learned what's really involved in each idea. Now we must integrate ideas about these different areas to narrow down to logical marketing mixes, marketing strategies, marketing plans—and a marketing program.

As suggested in Exhibit 18-1, developing an effective marketing strategy involves a process of narrowing down to a specific target market and marketing mix that represents a real opportunity. This narrowing-down process requires a thorough understanding of the market. That understanding is enhanced by careful analysis of customers' needs, current or prospective competitors, and the firm's own objectives and resources. Similarly, favourable or unfavourable factors and trends in the external market environment may make a potential opportunity more or less attractive.

There are usually more different strategy possibilities than a firm can pursue. Each possible strategy usually has a number of different potential advantages and disadvantages. This can make it difficult to zero in on the best target market and marketing mix. However, as we discussed in Chapter 4, developing a set of specific qualitative and quantitative screening criteria—to define what business and markets the firm wants to compete in—can help eliminate potential strategies that are not well suited for the firm.

**S.W.O.T. analysis**
Identifies and lists the firm's strengths and weaknesses and its opportunities and threats

**S.W.O.T analysis** Another useful aid for zeroing in on a feasible strategy is **S.W.O.T. analysis**—which identifies and lists the firm's strengths and weaknesses, and its opportunities and threats. A good S.W.O.T. analysis helps the manager focus on a strategy that takes advantage of the firm's opportunities and strengths while avoiding its weaknesses and the threats to its success. These can be compared with the pros and cons of strategies that are considered. For example, if a firm is considering a strategy that focuses on a target market that is already being served by several strong competitors, success will usually hinge on some sort of competitive advantage. Such a competitive advantage might be based on a better marketing mix—perhaps an innovative new product (like the PT Cruiser), improved distribution, more effective promotion, or a better price. Just offering a marketing mix that is like what is available from competitors usually doesn't provide superior value—or any real basis for the firm to position or differentiate its marketing mix as better for customers.

Vancouver-based Rethink launched a brand-new beer in 1999, fully aware that the company was just a small fish in the big sea of beer companies (see

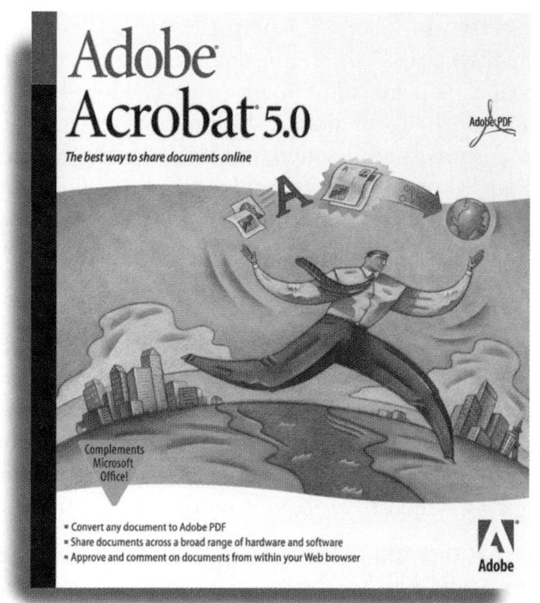


Adobe's Acrobat software allows users to save time by making it quick and easy to obtain digital signatures. Documents converted to Adobe's PDF format can be transferred through e-mail or the Internet. Adobe alleviates the time it takes to walk around and obtain signatures, and also keeps documents neat and organized.

www.rethinkbeer.com). Hence, it needed a feature that would separate Rethink from other beers. By using S.W.O.T analysis to analyze its market stance, Rethink came to create the first beer with an herbal charge. This energy boost contains ginseng, ginkgo, and tribulus. Having set the physical product apart as the first herbal-charged lager, the company's next challenge came in innovating the packaging. Rethink came to a clear decision that cardboard was out—and recycled plastic was in. From there, it designed a multi-use case that consumers could use for practical purposes around the house or for different crafts. Currently, the company is running several contests where customers can send in their new craft ideas about the case and receive Rethink prizes for the most interesting designs. Rethink is available only in British Columbia, but the company is constantly using S.W.O.T analysis to inquire about new markets and expansion.

### Focus Your Mix on the Target Market

Ideally, the ingredients of a good marketing mix flow logically from all the relevant dimensions of a target market. The market definition and segmenting approaches

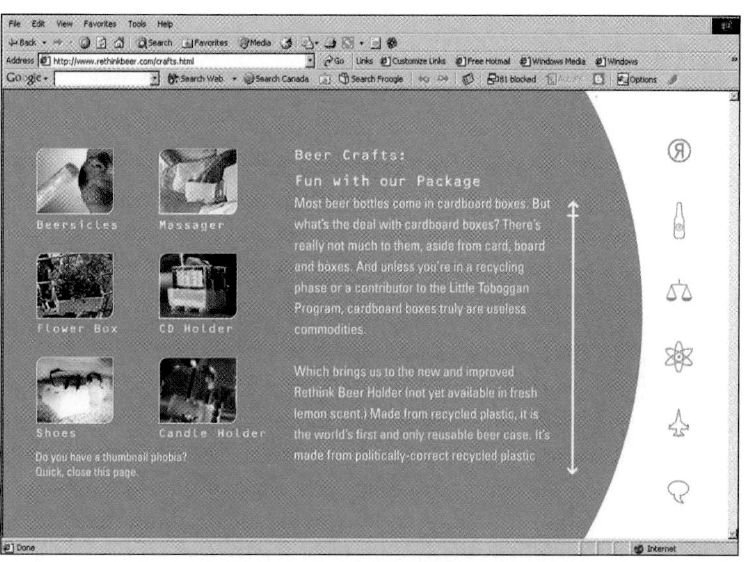


When Rethink Beer was launched, its makers wanted to set their product apart from that of other beer companies. Rethink's innovative marketers came up with packaging for this energy-boosted lager that can be reused for many practical (and some impractical) purposes.

we discussed in Chapter 3 help the marketing manager identify which dimensions are qualifying and which are determining in customers' choices.

Product benefits must match needs. How—and whether—customers search for information helps to define the promotion blend. Demographic dimensions reveal where customers are located and if they have the income to buy the product. Where customers shop for or buy products helps define channel alternatives. The value of the whole marketing mix and the urgency of customer needs, combined with an understanding of what customers see as substitute ways of meeting needs, helps companies estimate price sensitivity.

It would seem that if we fully understand the needs and attitudes of a target market, then combining the four Ps should be easy. Yet there are three important gaps in this line of reasoning. (1) We don't always know as much as we would like to about the needs and attitudes of our target markets, (2) competitors are also trying to satisfy these or similar needs—and their efforts may force a firm to shift its marketing mix, and (3) the other dimensions of the marketing environment may be changing—which may require more changes in marketing mixes.

**Use product classes to find a baseline mix** Even if you don't or can't know all you would like to about a potential target market, you usually know enough to decide whether the product is a consumer product or a business product and which product class is most relevant (refer to Exhibit 9-5 for a summary of the consumer product classes; Exhibit 9-6 summarizes the business product classes).

Identifying the proper product class helps because it suggests how a typical product should be distributed and promoted. So if you don't know as much as you'd like to about potential customers' needs and attitudes, at least knowing how they would view the company's product can give you a head start on developing a marketing mix. A convenience product—say, a new type of candy bar—usually needs more intensive distribution, and the producer usually takes on more responsibility for promotion. A specialty product, such as a minidisc player, needs a clear brand identity—which may require a more extensive positioning effort. A new unsought product, like the PT Cruiser, will need a mix that leads customers through the adoption process.

It's reassuring to see that product classes do summarize some of what you would like to know about target markets and what marketing mixes are relevant. After all, knowing what others have done in similar situations can serve as a guide to get started. From that base you may see a better way to meet needs that is not typical and that provides a competitive advantage.

**Use market knowledge to break away from the typical** The typical marketing mix for a given product class is not necessarily right for all situations. To the contrary, some marketing mixes are profitable because they depart from the typical—to satisfy some target markets better.

A marketing manager may have to develop a mix that is *not* typical because of various market realities—including special characteristics of the product or target market, the competitive environment, and each firm's capabilities and limitations. In fact, it is often through differentiation of the firm's product and/or other elements of the marketing mix that the marketing manager can offer target customers unique value.

When marketing managers fully understand their target markets, they may be able to develop marketing mixes that are superior to competitors' mixes. Such understanding may provide breakthrough opportunities. Taking advantage of these opportunities can lead to large sales and profitable growth. This is why we stress the importance of looking for breakthrough opportunities rather than just trying to imitate competitors' offerings. Marketing Demo 18-1 presents a good example of a firm that translated its knowledge of the target market into a distinctive marketing mix within a highly competitive environment.

## Marketing Demo 18–1

### BRAS WITH ATTITUDE

Recently, Montreal based Canadelle—makers of the Wonderbra—decided it needed to change its reputation to appeal to the younger, hipper, and more fashion-conscious crowd. According to *Marketing Magazine*'s Tracey Arial, "Bras and panties account for over 85 percent of Canada's intimate apparel sales." Therefore, Canadelle realized that it was missing out on a huge portion of the sales by having the reputation of being "my grandmother's bra." The solution? Designs by Wonderbra—a new line of underwear geared strictly at a more youthful customer. Claudette Groody, the national business manager of women's innerwear for Sears Canada, states that Canadelle's change has come at the perfect time, just when these younger shoppers have become more involved in the intimate apparel industry, and have helped to fuel this immense growth over the past five years.

To promote the new product Canadelle has also changed its advertising stance, and infiltrated its ads with an attractive young model with a hint of attitude and individualism. Canadelle noted that the advertising campaign is "all about attitude." It's hoping that with these daring and bold ads, it will attract target customers as a result. This fits perfectly into the new image of intimate apparel shoppers who prefer to be different and distinctive. These shoppers are known to follow current trends very quickly, and hence the market needs to stay active and innovative, to keep up with and cater to the ever-wanting needs of a very particular clientele.

When trying to revamp a company like Wonderbra's image, many obstacles can stand in the way. However, a huge bonus in this case was that the company had built a spectacular brand association based on excellent quality. Wonderbra kept the association, but also distanced itself with the new Designs collection, so as to shake the "grandmother's bra" image. This is a common technique used by companies who want to maintain an aspect of their current image, all while changing the product or introducing a new one.

Thus far, initial sales of the Designs collection have been good in the product's early stages of its life cycle. The numbers are expected to increase even further as more people become aware of the product—and as youthful shoppers are able to mentally shake the previous image and fill their minds with what Designs is all about.[2]

### Manage the Entire Mix

Exhibit 18-2 reviews the major marketing strategy decision areas organized by the four Ps. Each of these requires careful decision making. Yet marketing planning involves much more than just independent decisions and assembling the parts into a marketing mix. The four Ps must be creatively *blended*—so the firm develops the best mix for its target market. This is true whether one uses more traditional tools or newer technologies to execute the plan (see Internet Insite 18-1). In other words, each decision must work well with all of the others to make a logical whole.

Throughout the text, we've given the job of integrating the four Ps strategy decisions to the marketing manager. The title of that person might vary, but now you

Exhibit 18-2
Strategy decision areas organized by the four Ps.

| Product | Place | Promotion | Price |
|---|---|---|---|
| Physical good<br>Service<br>Features<br>Benefits<br>Quality level<br>Accessories<br>Installation<br>Instructions<br>Warranty<br>Product lines<br>Packaging<br>Branding | Objectives<br>Channel type<br>Market exposure<br>Kinds of intermediaries<br>Kinds and locations of stores<br>How to handle transporting and storing<br>Service levels<br>Recruiting intermediaries<br>Managing channels | Objectives<br>Promotion blend<br>Salespeople<br>Kind<br>Number<br>Selection<br>Training<br>Motivation<br>Advertising<br>Targets<br>Kinds of ads<br>Media type<br>Copy thrust<br>Prepared by whom<br>Sales promotion<br>Publicity | Objectives<br>Flexibility<br>Level over product life cycle<br>Geographic terms<br>Discounts<br>Allowances |

# Internet Insite 18–1

## THE INTERNET'S ROLE IN MARKETING PLANNING

The Internet is a great resource when developing a marketing plan—be it focused on the domestic market or on international markets. Internet Insites 4-1 and 8-2 provide many useful resources that can be used for industry and competitive analysis, for understanding trends, and for developing forecasts. The Internet strategy and overall business strategy can no longer be treated separately. They need to be integrated.

Many new Internet companies in the mid to late 1990s started without sound marketing and business plans. Hundreds of these companies are now bankrupt. Some prominent examples include Boo.com (more than $200 million invested), Egghead.com, Flooz.com, HomeGrocer, Chemdex, and Mercata.com. You can see a long list of dot-com failures at Ghostsites (www.disobey.com/ghostsites).

What were some common causes of the failures?

- Lack of critical mass of customers online
- No competitive advantage (too much competition)
- Very low prices (intended to grab market share) that were not sustainable
- Very high advertising and customer-acquisition costs (relative to the low revenues)
- Customers unprepared to shop and spend online (due to privacy/security concerns as well as drastic changes needed in consumer behaviour)
- Customer service and reverse-channel issues (returns and exchanges) not properly implemented, leading to low customer satisfaction
- Lack of management experience

Home delivery of groceries is an example. Typically, consumers shop for groceries in a store near their home or work. Most consumers like to inspect the perishable items, and some like to compare prices or learn about new products. Online grocery-delivery services such as HomeGrocer (which later became part of Webvan) spent tens of millions of dollars building warehouses, computer systems, and delivery systems, but grossly underestimated the challenge of changing consumer behaviour. Consumers did not flock to the online grocery-delivery services to save time as anticipated. The customer-acquisition costs and capital investments were huge relative to their sales revenues. The failure of companies like HomeGrocer (Webvan) highlights the importance of developing good forecasts of sales and understanding consumer behaviour.

The British grocery chain Tesco (www.tesco.co.uk) took a different approach to delivery. Tesco was already in the grocery business (unlike HomeGrocer, which was a new company). Instead of pouring millions of pounds into building new warehouses, they decided that they would home-deliver groceries from the local store. Customers use a membership card and so are recognized as the same person whether shopping online or offline. Products available online and offline are identical. The trust that consumers have in Tesco (through years of shopping in its stores) has led to a lower resistance to online shopping. Tesco also gives consumers a choice of two channels for shopping. This well-thought-out marketing strategy has paid off handsomely for Tesco.

In other industries, established companies have made drastic changes to their marketing activities and the way they reach customers, thanks to the Internet. Encyclopedia Britannica was in the business of packaging knowledge and publishing books. In the 1990s, competition from Encarta (a CD-ROM–based encyclopedia from Microsoft), which was given away free with most new PCs, changed Britannica's world forever. Soon the Internet made a lot of current and archived content available to the public from major magazine and newspaper publishers, often for free. Demand for hard-copy encyclopedias plummeted. Encyclopedia Britannica's response was to go online (www.britannica.com). It created a portal site with a lot of free information as well as access to full encyclopedia content for subscribers. In addition, the site has an online store, which sells not only encyclopedias (in print and CD format) but also other books, software, educational video and audio, and gift items. Britannica's business model (how the company delivers value and generates revenue) has changed drastically in the last few years. It is no longer a stodgy old publishing company.

Britannica is now able to reach a younger and more technically savvy global market, penetrate schools that have Internet access, and sell its many new products and services. The company no longer needs the hundreds of salespeople who once sold its encyclopedia sets door-to-door. There are many other companies like Britannica that have undergone drastic transformations to survive in the new economy.

The Internet could have a profound impact on a company or industry, or it could have a minor effect. Regardless of the extent of impact, the marketing planning process should carefully evaluate the role and impact of the Internet in different areas of marketing and, indeed, different areas of the business. The Internet can:

- Enable firms to reach previously inaccessible or prohibitively expensive global markets.
- Enable firms to sell products and services directly online, thereby developing a new sales channel (see Internet Insites 11-1 and 12-1)
- Enable firms to lower prices (see Internet Insite 17-1).
- Enable firms to understand customer needs better (see Internet Insites 6-1 and 8-1)

- Build stronger relationships with customers by providing customization and faster and better service (see Internet Insite 14-1)
- Build and enhance a brand image by using appropriate images, content, and interactive tools on a website (see Internet Insite 9-1)
- Bring new products to market faster through virtual product development (see Internet Insite 10-1) and direct selling online
- Measure marketing performance and monitor implementation more effectively (see Internet Insite 19-1)

It no longer makes sense to consider Internet operations as a separate part of the business. The Internet enables firms to more effectively perform two essential functions—communicating to consumers and selling products/services. In some cases it supports existing business practices, and in other cases it opens new possibilities.

Go to: www.mcgrawhill.ca/college/wong
to apply this Insite in an exciting Internet exercise.

should see the need for this integrating role. It is easy for specialists to focus on their own areas and expect the rest of the company to work for or around them. This is especially true in larger firms like DaimlerChrysler, where specialists are needed just because the size of the whole marketing job is too big for one person. Yet the ideas of the product manager, the advertising manager, the sales manager, the logistics manager, and whoever makes pricing decisions may have to be adjusted to improve the whole mix. It's critical that each marketing-mix decision work well with all of the others. A breakdown in any one decision area may doom the whole strategy to failure.

## Plan for Change

Careful consideration of where a firm's offering fits in the product life cycle can also be a big help in evaluating the best marketing mix. The concept for Exhibit 18-3 was introduced in Chapter 10 to summarize how marketing-mix variables typically change over the product life cycle. Now you can see that this exhibit is a good review of many topics we've discussed throughout the text. Certainly, the pioneering effort required for a really new product concept is different from the job of taking market share away from an established competitor late in the market-growth stage.

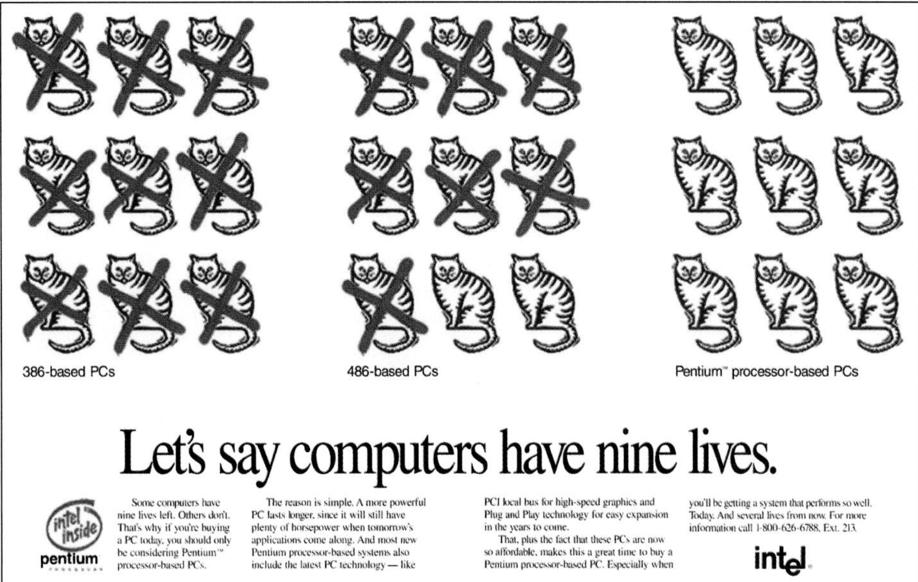


Intel could plan a marketing strategy—and forecast likely sales—for its updated Pentium processors based on the stage in the product life cycle and the success it had with its earlier processors.

Exhibit 18-3
Typical changes in marketing variables over the product life cycle.

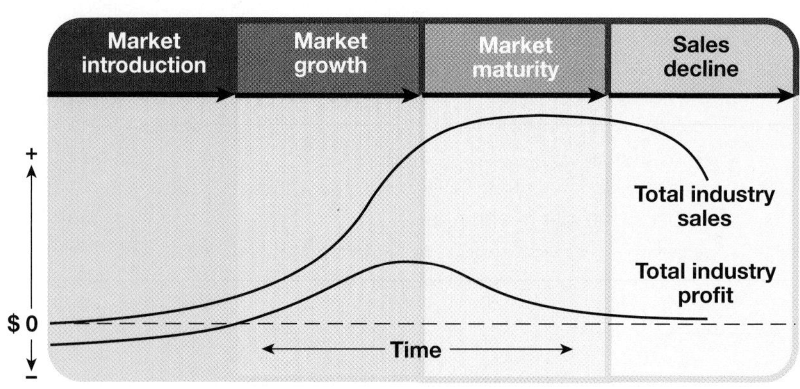


| | Market introduction | Market growth | Market maturity | Sales decline |
|---|---|---|---|---|
| **Competitive situation** | Monopoly or monopolistic competition | Monopolistic competition or oligopoly | Monopolistic competition or oligopoly heading toward pure competition → | |
| **Product** | One or few | Variety—try to find best product<br><br>Build brand familiarity | All "same"<br>Battle of brands | Some drop out |
| **Place** | Build channels<br><br>Maybe selective distribution → | | Move toward more intensive distribution → | |
| **Promotion** | Build primary demand<br><br>Pioneering-informing | Build selective demand →<br><br>Informing/Persuading → Persuading/Reminding (frantically competitive) | | |
| **Price** | Skimming or penetration | Meet competition (especially in oligopoly) →<br>or<br>Price dealing and price cutting → | | |

Further, when you're thinking about the product life cycle don't forget that markets change continually. This means you must plan strategies that can adjust to changing conditions. The original marketing plan for a new strategy may even include details about what adjustments in the marketing mix or target market will be required as the nature of competition and the adoption process evolve.[3]

## Forecasting Target-Market Potential and Sales

**target-market potential**
What a whole market segment might buy

**sales forecast**
An estimate of how much an industry or firm hopes to sell to a market segment

Effective strategy planning and developing a marketing plan require estimates of future sales, costs, and profits. Without such information, it's hard to know if a strategy is potentially profitable.

The marketing manager's estimates of sales, costs, and profits are usually based on a forecast (estimate) of **target-market potential**—what a whole market segment might buy—and a **sales forecast**—an estimate of how much an industry or firm hopes to sell to a market segment. Usually we must try to judge market potential before we can estimate what share a particular firm may be able to win with its particular marketing mix.

## Three Levels of Forecasting

We're interested in forecasting the potential in specific market segments. However, the developments in any one segment are affected by industry-wide developments—which, in turn, are affected by economy-wide developments. Thus, it helps to make three levels of forecasts: segment, industry, and economy.

This practice is especially important if you are selling internationally. Some economic conditions affect the entire global economy. Others may influence only one country or a particular industry. And some may affect only one company or one product's sales potential. For this reason, a common top-down approach to forecasting is to

1. Develop a *national income forecast* (for each country in which the firm operates) and use this to
2. Develop an *industry sales forecast*, which then is used to
3. Develop forecasts for a *specific company*, its *specific products*, and the *segments* it targets.

Generally, a marketing manager doesn't have to make forecasts for a national economy or the broad industry. This kind of forecasting—basically, trend projecting—is a specialty in itself. Such forecasts are available in business and government publications, and large companies often have their own technical specialists. Managers can use just one source's forecast or combine several. Unfortunately, however, the more targeted the marketing manager's earlier segmenting efforts have been, the less likely that industry forecasts will match the firm's product-markets. So managers have to move directly to estimating potential for their own companies and for their specific products.

## Two Types of Forecasts

Many methods are used to forecast market potential and sales, but they can all be grouped into two basic approaches: extending past behaviour and predicting future behaviour. The large number of methods may seem confusing at first, but this variety has an advantage. Forecasts are so important that managers often develop forecasts in two or three different ways and then compare the differences before preparing a final forecast.

When we forecast for existing products, we usually have some past data to go on. The basic approach—called **trend extension**—extends past experience into the future. With existing products, for example, the past trend of actual sales may be extended into the future (see Exhibit 18-4).

**trend extension**
Extending past experience into the future

Ideally, when extending past sales behaviour, we should decide why sales vary. This is the difficult and time-consuming part of sales forecasting. Usually we can gather a lot of data about the product or market or about changes in the marketing environment. But unless we know the *reason* for past sales variations, it's hard to predict in what direction, and by how much, sales will move. Graphing the data and statistical techniques—including correlation and regression analysis—can be useful here. (These techniques, which are beyond our scope, are discussed in beginning statistics courses.)

Exhibit 18-4
Straight-line trend projection—extends past sales into future.

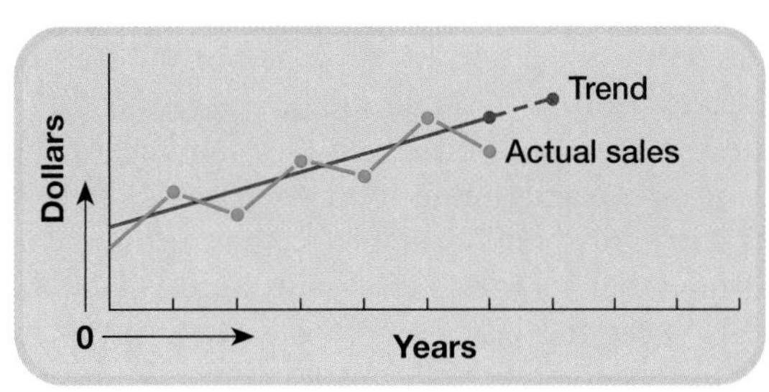

Once we know why sales vary, we can usually develop a specific forecast. For example, sales may be moving directly up as population grows in a specific market segment, so from there we can just estimate how population is expected to grow and project the effect on sales.

The weakness of the trend-extension method is that it assumes past conditions will continue unchanged into the future. In fact, the future isn't always like the past. For example, Chapters and Indigo bookstores were on a steady growth path, but the development of the Internet and e-commerce changed their structural framework—and that of the entire industry. Now, the Chapters Indigo website allows consumers to shop for their favourite books from the comfort of home, thus increasing sales and allowing the company to expand into other products. Aside from books, Chapters Indigo now offers its cybercustomers a wide variety of videos, DVDs, and domestic giftware (www.chapters.indigo.ca).

As another example, for years the trend in sales of disposable diapers moved closely with the number of new births. However, as the number of women in the workforce increased and as more women returned to jobs after babies were born, use of disposable diapers increased, and the trend changed. As in these examples, trend-extension estimates will be wrong whenever big changes occur. For this reason—although they may extend past behaviour for one estimate—most managers look for another way to help them forecast sharp market changes.

When we try to predict what will happen in the future, instead of just extending the past, we have to use other methods and add more judgment. Some of these methods (to be discussed later) include juries of executive opinion, salespeople's estimates, surveys, panels, and market tests.

### Techniques for Forecasting Based on Past Behaviour

While it may be difficult to forecast overall market conditions, at the very least a marketing manager ought to know what the firm's present markets look like and what the firm has sold to them in the past. A detailed sales analysis for products and geographic areas helps to project future results. Just extending past sales into the future may not seem like much of a forecasting method. But it's better than just assuming that next year's total sales will be the same as this year's.

**The factor method** A simple extension of past sales gives one forecast. But it's usually desirable to tie future sales to something more than the passage of time. The **factor method** tries to do this. The factor method tries to forecast sales by finding a relation between the company's sales and some other factor (or factors). The basic formula is this: something (past sales, industry sales, etc.) *times* some factor *equals* sales forecast. A **factor** is a variable that shows the relation of some other variable to the item being forecast. For instance, in our example above, both the birthrate and the number of working mothers are factors related to sales of disposable diapers.

**factor method**

A method to forecast sales by finding a relation between the company's sales and some other factor

**factor**

A variable that shows the relation of some other variable to the item being forecast

**Using the factor method for consumer products** The following example—about a bread producer—shows how firms can make forecasts for many geographic market segments using the factor method and available data. This general approach can be useful for any firm—producer, wholesaler, or retailer.

Analysis of past sales relationships showed that a bread manufacturer regularly sold one-tenth of 0.5 percent (0.005) of the total retail food sales in its various target markets. This is a single factor. By using this single factor, a manager could estimate the producer's sales in a new market for the coming period by multiplying a forecast of expected retail food sales by 0.005.

Let's carry this bread example further, using data for Victoria, British Columbia. Let's assume that Victoria's food sales were $400,000,000 for the previous year. Start by simply accepting last year's food sales as an estimate of the current year's sales. Then multiply the food sales estimate for Victoria by the 0.005 factor (the firm's usual share in such markets). The manager now has an estimate of the current year's bread sales in Victoria. That is, last year's food sales estimate ($400,000,000) times 0.005 equals this year's bread sales estimate of $2,000,000.

Going further, let's assume that the marketing manager expects an especially aggressive promotion campaign would increase the firm's share by 10 percent. The single factor is increased from 0.005 to 0.0055 and then multiplied by the food sales estimate for Victoria to obtain an estimate for the firm's Victoria bread sales.

The factor method isn't limited to the use of just one factor. Two or more factors can be used together. The most widely used source of information about market size and importance is *Canadian Markets*, published annually by the *Financial Post*. In its 1996 report, *Canadian Markets* revealed that 2.83 percent of all Canadian households were to be found within Calgary. However, the retail market in Calgary, an area of higher-than-average incomes, accounted for 3.61 percent of total retail sales in Canada.[4] Suppose we wished to construct an index giving equal weight to the number of households and the percentage of total retail sales. So we add 2.83 and 3.61 (= 6.44), and then divide by 2 (i.e., we weight the two factors equally). This leaves Calgary with a weighted value of 3.22.

We could, of course, easily adjust our weights for luxury products—giving, for example, Calgary's percentage of total retail sales a weight of 2 and its number of households a weight of 1. Doing this would leave Calgary with a weighted value of 3.35 (3.61 + 3.61 + 2.83 = 10.05/3 = 3.35) for this type of product. For every million dollars of industry sales of luxury products throughout Canada, we would expect $33,500 (3.35 percent) to be made in Calgary. Assuming that the company's marketing effort was as effective in Calgary as it was, on average, across the country, then 3.35 percent of company sales should be made in Calgary. If actual company sales are either higher or lower, the reasons why this is so should be determined.

The factor method, using either single or multiple factors, can also be used to estimate the sales potential of a new product. Let's assume that a retailer is interested in estimating the potential for sets of novelty beer mugs in the Winnipeg area. If about 5 percent of the target market could be expected to buy a $25 set within a one-year period, and if that target consisted of just about every household, the appropriate numbers could be multiplied to get the following forecast. The example shows that 13,125 buying households, each spending $25, would generate a total sales potential of $328,125.

**Using the factor method for business products** Exhibit 18-5 shows how one manufacturer estimated the market for fibre boxes for a particular CMA (Census Metropolitan Area). This approach could be used in each CMA to estimate the potential in many geographic target markets.

Here, SIC (Standard Industrial Classification) code data are used. This is common in the industrial sector because SIC code data are readily available and often very relevant. In this case, the value of box shipments by SIC code was collected by a trade association, but the rest of the data were available from government sources.

Basically, the approach involves calculating national consumption per employee for each SIC industry group and then multiplying by the number of employees in the particular CMA to estimate market potential for that group. Then the sum of these estimates becomes the total market potential in that CMA. A firm considering going into that market would need to estimate the share it could get with its own marketing mix.

Note that this approach can also aid management's control job. If the firm were already in this industry, it could compare its actual sales (by SIC code) with the potential and see how it's doing. If its typical market share is 10 percent of the market and it's obtaining only 2 to 5 percent of the market in various SIC submarkets, then some marketing-mix changes may be in order.

Exhibit 18-5 Estimated market for corrugated boxes and cartons (by industry groups for a target CMA).

| | (1) | (2) | (3) | (4) | (5) |
|---|---|---|---|---|---|
| | | | | A TARGET CMA | |
| Industry | Value of box shipments (by end use) ($000) | Production workers (by industry group) | Consumption per worker (1) ÷ (2) (dollars) | Production workers (by industry group) | Estimated size of the market (3) × (4) ($000) |
| Food and beverage | $316,752 | 159,703 | $1,983 | 24,343 | $48,272 |
| Tobacco products | 6,100 | 5,606 | 1,088 | — | — |
| Rubber and plastics products | 35,375 | 45,681 | 774 | 12,546 | 9,711 |
| Leather | 6,450 | 22,577 | 286 | 3,986 | 1,140 |
| Textile | 19,504 | 53,073 | 367 | 7,195 | 2,641 |
| Knitting mills | 3,140 | 17,851 | 179 | 3,288 | 589 |
| Clothing | 10,670 | 83,418 | 128 | 13,467 | 1,724 |
| Wood | 4,694 | 94,328 | 48 | 3,499 | 168 |
| Furniture and fixtures | 30,968 | 44,328 | 699 | 13,780 | 9,632 |
| Paper | 51,785 | 99,491 | 520 | 12,824 | 6,668 |
| Printing and publishing | 9,492 | 63,964 | 148 | 19,020 | 2,815 |
| Primary metal | 2,916 | 92,337 | 32 | — | — |
| Metal fabricating | 38,895 | 120,450 | 323 | 30,024 | 9,698 |
| Machinery | 9,883 | 70,784 | 140 | 14,238 | 1,993 |
| Transportation equipment | 11,905 | 136,102 | 87 | 25,899 | 2,253 |
| Electrical products | 40,856 | 84,282 | 485 | 26,834 | 13,014 |
| Nonmetallic mineral products | 40,294 | 40,145 | 1,004 | 5,919 | 5,943 |
| Petroleum and coal products | 3,800 | 8,457 | 449 | — | — |
| Chemical and chemical products | 50,176 | 46,398 | 1,081 | 11,600 | 12,540 |
| Miscellaneous manufacturing | 25,292 | 48,354 | 523 | 19,263 | 10,075 |
| TOTAL | $718,947 | | | | $138,876 |



**time series**

Historical records of the fluctuations in economic variables

**leading series**

A time series that changes in the same direction *but ahead of* the series to be forecast

**indices**

Statistical combinations of several time series in an effort to find some time series that will lead the series they're trying to forecast

**Time series and leading series analysis** Not all past economic or sales behaviour can be neatly extended with a straight line or some manipulation. Economic activity has ups and downs, and other uncontrollable factors change. To cope with such variation, statisticians have developed techniques for time series analysis. **Time series** are historical records of the fluctuations in economic variables. We can't give a detailed discussion of these techniques here, but note that there *are* techniques to handle daily, weekly, monthly, seasonal, and annual variations.[5]

All forecasters dream of finding an accurate **leading series**—a time series that changes in the same direction *but ahead of* the series to be forecast. For example, car producers watch trends in the Index of Consumer Sentiment, which is based on regular surveys of consumers' attitudes about their likely future financial security. People are less likely to buy a car or other big-ticket item if they are worried about their future income. As this suggests, a drop in the index usually "leads" a drop in car sales. It is important that there be some logical relation between the leading series and what is being forecast.

No single series has yet been found that leads GNP or other national figures. Lacking such a series, forecasters develop **indices**—statistical combinations of several time series—in an effort to find some time series that will lead the series they're trying to forecast. Government agencies publish some indices of this type. And business publications, like *Canadian Business*, publish their own indices.

## Techniques for Predicting Future Behaviour

Forecasts using past-extending methods use quantitative data—projecting past experience into the future and assuming that the future will be like the past. But this is a risky assumption in competitive markets. Usually, it's desirable to add some judgment to other forecasts before making the final forecast yourself. Let's look at some techniques that can be used to improve the quality of our judgment.

**jury of executive opinion**

A method of forecasting that combines the opinions of experienced executives

**Jury of executive opinion** One of the oldest and simplest methods of forecasting—the **jury of executive opinion**—combines the opinions of experienced executives, perhaps from marketing, production, finance, purchasing, and top management. Each executive estimates market potential and sales for the coming years. Then they try to work out a consensus.

The main advantage of the jury approach is that it can be done quickly and easily. On the other hand, the results may not be very good. There may be too much extending of the past. Some of the executives may have little contact with outside market influences. But their estimates could point to major shifts in customer demand or competition.

**Salesforce estimates** Using salespeople's estimates to forecast is like the jury approach. But salespeople are more likely than home office managers to be familiar with customer reactions and what competitors are doing. Their estimates are especially useful in some business markets where the few customers may be well known to the salespeople. But this approach may be useful in any type of market.

However, managers who use estimates from salespeople should be aware of the limitations. For example, new salespeople may not know much about their markets. Even experienced salespeople may not be aware of possible changes in the economic climate or the firm's other environments. And if salespeople think the manager is going to use the estimates to set sales quotas, the estimates may be low!

**Market research** Special surveys of final buyers, retailers, and/or wholesalers can show what's happening in different market segments. Some firms use panels of stores—or final consumers—to keep track of buying behaviour and to decide when just extending past behaviour isn't enough.

Surveys are sometimes combined with market tests when the company wants to estimate customers' reactions to possible changes in its marketing mix. A market

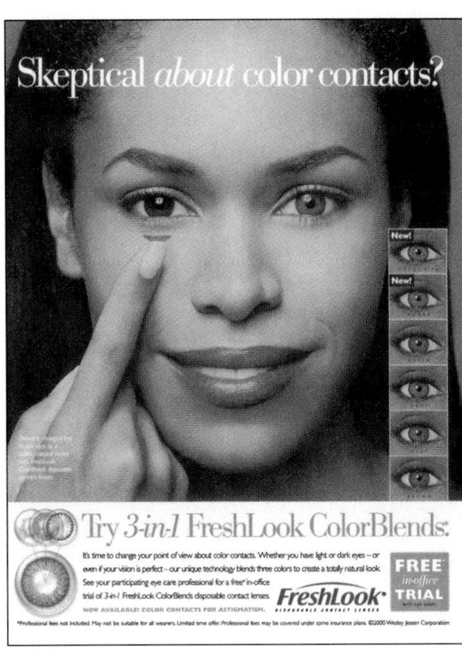


A marketing plan spells out the detailed costs of different marketing activities in the strategy. For example, FreshLook's plan for its new colour contact lenses might include estimates of the cost of each ad as well as the cost of the whole promotion blend.

test might show that a product increased its share of the market by 10 percent when its price was dropped 1 cent below competition. But this extra business might be quickly lost if the price were increased 1 cent above competition. Such market experiments help the marketing manager make good estimates of future sales when one or more of the four Ps is changed.

## Selecting the Right Marketing Mix

Once a manager has narrowed down to a few reasonable marketing mixes and the relevant forecasts, comparing the sales, costs, and profitability of the different alternatives helps in selecting the marketing mix the firm will implement. Three major tasks to be performed in this regard are estimating the cost of marketing activities, comparing the profitability of alternative strategies, and performing sensitivity analyses.



### Estimate the Costs of Marketing Activities

As we saw in the discussion of product costs in Chapter 17, estimating the costs of the marketing activities for a strategy may be easy or hard depending on the situation. Sometimes the accounting department can help with information about what average costs for similar activities have been in the past. Or sometimes estimates of competitors' costs—perhaps pulled out of annual reports or investor information posted on the Internet—can provide some guidance. However, in general the best approach for estimating costs is to use the task method.

We recommended this approach in Chapter 15 when we focused on promotion costs and budgets. However, the same ideas apply to any area of marketing activity. The estimated cost and budget for each activity is based on the job to be done—perhaps the number of salespeople needed to call on new customers or the amount of inventory required to provide some distribution customer-service level. The costs of these individual tasks are then totalled to determine how much should be budgeted for the overall plan. With this detailed approach, the firm can subsequently assemble its overall marketing budget directly from individual plans rather than just relying on historical patterns or ratios.

### Compare the Profitability of Alternative Strategies

Once costs and revenues for possible strategies are estimated, it makes sense to compare them with respect to overall profitability. Exhibit 18-6 shows such a comparison for a small appliance currently selling for $15—Mix A in the example. Here the marketing manager simply estimates the costs and likely results of four reasonable alternatives. And assuming profit is the objective *and* there are adequate resources to consider each of the alternatives, Mix C is obviously the best alternative.

Comparing the alternatives in Exhibit 18-6 is quite simple. But sometimes marketing managers need much more detail to evaluate a plan. Hundreds of calculations may be required to see how specific marketing resources relate to expected outcomes—like total costs, expected sales, and profit. To make that part of the planning job simpler and faster, marketing managers often use spreadsheet analysis. With **spreadsheet analysis**, costs, sales, and other information related to a problem are organized into a data table—a spreadsheet—to show how changing the value of one or more of the numbers affects the other numbers. This is possible because the relationships among the variables are programmed in the computer software. The table in Exhibit 18-6 was prepared using Excel, Microsoft's widely used spreadsheet program. (If you have never used Excel before, you should familiarize yourself with the program, as it is used in many aspects of business, and in various departments within companies. Go to http://lteu.cant.ac.uk for a quick Excel tutorial.)

**spreadsheet analysis**
Costs, sales, and other information related to a problem are organized into a data table (spreadsheet) to show how changing the value of one or more of the numbers affects the others

Exhibit 18-6 A spreadsheet comparing the estimated sales, costs, and profits of four "reasonable alternative" marketing mixes.

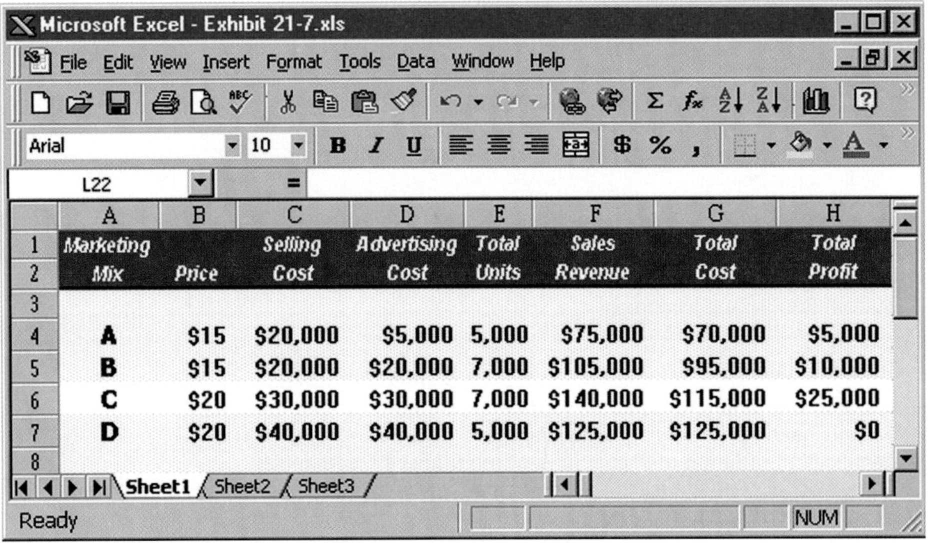

Microsoft Excel - Exhibit 21-7.xls

| Marketing Mix | Price | Selling Cost | Advertising Cost | Total Units | Sales Revenue | Total Cost | Total Profit |
|---|---|---|---|---|---|---|---|
| A | $15 | $20,000 | $5,000 | 5,000 | $75,000 | $70,000 | $5,000 |
| B | $15 | $20,000 | $20,000 | 7,000 | $105,000 | $95,000 | $10,000 |
| C | $20 | $30,000 | $30,000 | 7,000 | $140,000 | $115,000 | $25,000 |
| D | $20 | $40,000 | $40,000 | 5,000 | $125,000 | $125,000 | $0 |

## Perform Sensitivity Analysis

Spreadsheet analysis allows the marketing manager to evaluate what-if questions. For example, a marketing manager might be interested in the question "What if I charge a higher price and the number of units sold stays the same? What will happen to profit?" To look at how a spreadsheet program might be used to help answer this what-if question, let's take a closer look at Mix C in Exhibit 18-6.

The table involves a number of relationships. For example, price times total units equals sales revenue; and total revenue minus total cost equals total profit. If these relationships are programmed into the spreadsheet, a marketing manager can ask questions like: "What if I raise the price to $20.20 and still sell 7,000 units? What will happen to profit?" To get the answer, all the manager needs to do is type the new price into the spreadsheet and the program computes the new profit—$26,400.

Exhibit 18-7 A spreadsheet analysis showing how a change in price affects sales revenue and profit.

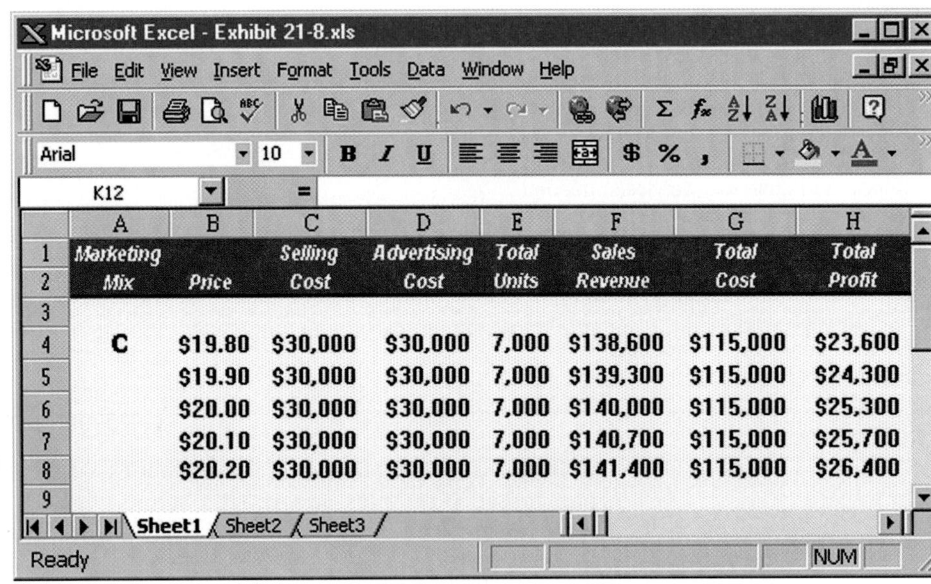

Microsoft Excel - Exhibit 21-8.xls

| Marketing Mix | Price | Selling Cost | Advertising Cost | Total Units | Sales Revenue | Total Cost | Total Profit |
|---|---|---|---|---|---|---|---|
| C | $19.80 | $30,000 | $30,000 | 7,000 | $138,600 | $115,000 | $23,600 |
| | $19.90 | $30,000 | $30,000 | 7,000 | $139,300 | $115,000 | $24,300 |
| | $20.00 | $30,000 | $30,000 | 7,000 | $140,000 | $115,000 | $25,300 |
| | $20.10 | $30,000 | $30,000 | 7,000 | $140,700 | $115,000 | $25,700 |
| | $20.20 | $30,000 | $30,000 | 7,000 | $141,400 | $115,000 | $26,400 |

Exhibit 18-8 Summary outline of different sections of a marketing plan.

**Name of Product-Market**

Major screening criteria relevant to product-market opportunity selected
- Quantitative (ROI, profitability, risk level, etc.)
- Qualitative (nature of business preferred, social responsibility, etc.)
- Major constraints

**Analysis of Other Aspects of External Market Environment (favourable and unfavourable factors and trends)**

Economic environment
Technological environment
Political and legal environment
Cultural and social environment

**Customer Analysis (organizational and/or final consumer)**

Possible segmenting dimensions (customer needs, other characteristics)
- Identification of qualifying dimensions and determining dimensions

Identification of target market(s) (one or more specific segments)
- Operational characteristics (demographics, geographic locations, etc.)
- Potential size (number of people, dollar purchase potential, etc.) and likely growth

Key psychological and social influences on buying
Type of buying situation
Nature of relationship with customers

**Competitor Analysis**

Nature of current/likely competition
Current and prospective competitors (and/or rivals)
- Current strategies and likely responses to plan

Competitive barriers to overcome and sources of potential competitive advantage

**Company Analysis**

Company objectives and overall marketing objectives
Company resources
*S.W.O.T.*: Identification of major *s*trengths, *w*eaknesses, *o*pportunities, and *t*hreats (based on above analyses of company resources, customers, competitors, and other aspects of external market environment)

**Marketing Information Requirements**

Marketing research needs (with respect to customers, marketing-mix effectiveness, external environment, etc.)
Secondary data and primary data needs
Marketing information system needs, models to be used, etc.

**Product**

Product class (type of consumer or business product)
Current product life cycle stage
New-product development requirements (people, dollars, time, etc.)
- Product liability, safety, and social responsibility considerations

Specification of core physical good and/or service
- Features, quality, etc.

Supporting customer service(s) needed
Warranty (what is covered, timing, who will support, etc.)
Branding (manufacturer versus dealer, family brand versus individual brand, etc.)
Packaging
- Promotion and labelling needs
- Protection needs

Cultural sensitivity of product
Fit with product line



In addition, the manager may also want to do many what-if analyses—for example, to see how sales and profit change over a range of prices. Computerized spreadsheet analysis does this quickly and easily. If the manager wants to see what happens to total revenue as the price varies between some minimum (say, $19.80) and a maximum (say, $20.20), the program can show the total revenue and profit for a number of price levels in the range from $19.80 to $20.20. The results are shown in the Excel spreadsheet table in Exhibit 18-7.

**Place**

Objectives
- Degree of market exposure required
- Distribution customer service level required

Type of channel (direct, indirect)
- Other channel members and/or facilitators required
  - Type/number of wholesalers (agent, merchant, etc.)
  - Type/number of retailers
- How discrepancies and separations will be handled
- How marketing functions will be shared

Coordination needed in company, channel, and supply chain
- Information requirements (EDI, the Internet, e-mail, etc.)

Transportation requirements
Inventory product-handling requirements
Facilities required (warehousing, distribution centres, etc.)
Reverse channels (for returns, recalls, etc.)

**Promotion**

Objectives
Major message theme(s) for integrated marketing communications (desired "positioning")
Promotion blend
- Advertising (type, media, copy thrust, etc.)
- Personal selling (type and number of salespeople, how compensated, how effort will be allocated, etc.)
- Sales promotion (for channel members, customers, employees)
- Publicity
- Interactive media

Mix of push and pull required
Who will do the work?

**Price**

Nature of demand (price sensitivity, price of substitutes)
Demand and cost analyses (marginal analysis)
Markup chain in channel
Price flexibility
Price level(s) (under what conditions) and impact on customer value
Adjustments to list price (geographic terms, discounts, allowances, etc.)

**Special Implementation Problems to Be Overcome**

People required
Manufacturing, financial, and other resources needed

**Control**

Marketing information system needs
Criterion measures comparison with objectives (customer satisfaction, sales, cost, performance analysis, etc.)

**Forecasts and Estimates**

Costs (all elements in plan, over time)
Sales (by market, over time, etc.)
Estimated operating statement *(pro forma)*

**Timing**

Specific sequence of activities and events, etc.
Likely changes over the product life cycle

In a problem like this, the marketing manager might be able to do the same calculations quickly by hand. But with more complicated problems the spreadsheet program can be a big help—making it very convenient to more carefully analyze different alternatives.

## Writing the Marketing Plan

Once the manager has selected the target market, decided on the (integrated) marketing mix to meet that target market's needs, and developed estimates of the costs and revenue for that strategy, it's time to put it all together in the marketing plan. The plan basically serves as a blueprint for what the firm will do.

### A Typical Plan Outline

Exhibit 18-8 provides a summary outline of the different sections of a complete marketing plan. You can see that this outline is basically an abridged overview of the topics we've covered throughout the text and highlighted in this chapter. Thus, you can flesh out your thinking for any portion of a marketing plan by reviewing the section of the book where that topic is discussed in more detail. The PT Cruiser case at the beginning of this chapter also gives you a real example of the types of thinking and detail that are included.

### Good Plans Address Timing Issues

Some time schedule is implicit in any strategy. A marketing plan simply spells out this time period and the time-related details. Usually, we think in terms of some reasonable length of time—such as six months, a year, or a few years. But it might be only a month or two in some cases—especially when rapid changes in fashion or technology are important. Or a strategy might be implemented over several years—perhaps the length of a product life cycle, or at least the early stages of the product's life.

Although the outline in Exhibit 18-8 does not explicitly show a place for the time frame for the plan or the specific costs for each decision area, these should be included in the plan—along with expected estimates of sales and profit—so that the plan can be compared with actual performance in the future. In other words, the plan not only makes it clear to everyone what is to be accomplished and how, but also provides a basis for the control process after the plan is implemented. See Marketing Demo 18-2 for a look at the value of getting outside help with the plan.

**Tools for setting time-related details** Figuring out and planning the time-related details and schedules for all of the activities in the marketing plan can be a challenge—especially if the plan involves a big start-from-scratch effort. To do a better job in this area, many managers have turned to flowcharting techniques such as CPM (critical path method) or PERT (program evaluation and review technique). These methods were originally developed as part of the U.S. space program (NASA) to ensure that the various contractors and subcontractors stayed on schedule and reached their goals as planned. PERT, CPM, and other similar project-management approaches are even more popular now since inexpensive programs for personal computers make them easier and faster to use. Updating is easier too.

The computer programs develop detailed flowcharts to show which marketing activities must be done in sequence and which can be done concurrently. These charts also show the time needed for various activities. Totalling the time allotments along the various chart paths shows the most critical (the longest) path—as well as the best starting and ending dates for the various activities.

Flowcharting is not complicated. Basically, it requires that all the activities—which have to be performed anyway—be identified ahead of time and their probable duration and sequence shown on one diagram. (It uses nothing more than addition and subtraction.) Working with such information should be part of the planning function anyway. Then the chart can be used later to guide implementation and control.[6]

# Marketing Demo 18–2

## PAYING FOR PLANNING

It's clear enough that planning is increasingly important these days among the services that marketers buy from their ad agencies. As research techniques become more sophisticated, media options more numerous, and consumers themselves more complex, planning is playing a larger role as a crucial first step toward creating a successful campaign.

What's less clear is how marketers should pay for it. There's no standard formula in this area. The way agencies bill for planning varies according to their own preferences and priorities and those of their clients. Planning might be done for free to start, or billed on an hourly, monthly, or yearly fee and/or on commission, but the method of compensation must satisfy both parties to ensure an effective, trusted relationship.

"There's a very different understanding of planning in different agencies," says Michael Fyshe, president and CEO of BBDO Canada in Toronto, the country's second-largest agency by revenues. "There's always been a traditional research role that agencies have played.... Now planning is an added value we've brought to our clients that basically is somewhere between account management and creative."

Fyshe's agency bills both on a commission and a fee basis. "We do charge for it, (but) it's like we don't charge for account management or media or creative—it's part of our labour," he says. "In essence, our fee to the client includes the cost of planning."

Frank Palmer, Vancouver-based president and CEO of Palmer Jarvis DDB and chair of DDB Group Canada, says planning is part of the total package provided by his agency. Its model of compensation involves an estimate of the hours needed for planning, which is all built into the monthly or yearly fee. About 90 percent of Palmer Jarvis DDB's clients are charged on a fee basis, says Palmer, but the commission is usually rebated back to the client on straight hours.

Billing for planning varies from client to client, says Richard Emberley, president of Bristol Communications in Halifax. His agency charges on an hourly fee basis or predetermined project contract or project fee basis. Some clients place a lot of value on front-end strategy and planning, so they're more than willing to compensate from the start, he says, while others pay once the campaigns and programs are implemented.

"I prefer the former, only because it's a heck of a lot more transparent," he says. "Why disguise or bury, in my judgment at least, one of the most valuable things that the agency should be doing for the client, which is making sure that they've got their strategy and planning nailed down before you start producing pretty pictures."

Emberley says providing planning for free is a considerable risk because the agency will have to recoup the cost somewhere. "If I know I'm getting paid for that, I don't have to concern myself to a large extent with what the strategy works into in terms of the campaign later on."

Ken Christoffel, president and CEO of Brown Communications in Regina, also says that billing arrangements differ among clients. "Fee-based is the route to go because there are so many different elements to the planning. It would be hard to come up with some kind of fair compensation system based only on commissions because it depends on what kind of depth of planning they want and what aspect of the plan they want to cover."

Brown Communications tries to avoid doing spec strategy, says Christoffel. "We feel that we have to convince the client that there's value in those services we provide and that they should be paying as they go through the process.... All that work is a major investment upfront," he says.

Marketers do seem to value the service. Chuck Thompson, director of television promotion at the CBC in Toronto, says the network outsourced planning because "the agency can help us to maximize our dollars in a very efficient way." He says an agency's wealth of resources is a big advantage. "They do this for a living all day long. That's where their area of expertise is, and we wanted to exploit it and capitalize on it for our own purposes." He says billing for planning is part of the total package, and the CBC pays a monthly fee and then commission on top of that.

Bos and Microcell Solutions, both based in Montreal, work closely together when they're doing the strategic planning for Fido, says Patrick Hadsipantelis, director of marketing communications at Microcell. "Every time we have determined we're going to go to market with a specific product or campaign, we bring them in very early in the process to ensure they can bring in that consumer perspective at the front of the plan," he says. "We're both very involved, and we feel that's the way we should be doing this."

The billing varies, but with Bos is fee-based on a retainer. And that's a comfortable approach, says Hadsipantelis. "It would be less to our advantage to go on a commission basis, because with the level of hours of work that they bring to the table, I think we benefit from that approach. It all depends on the relationship."

Anthony Partipilo, vice-president of marketing for RadioShack Canada in Barrie, Ont., says planners are important because they see the big picture. "They have the ability to look at what may appear to be quite a complex series of decisions and melt it all down to one common denominator, which in the end is one simple concept."

RadioShack pays for planning through hourly fees along with a bonus component tied to the success of the company. "The bonus factor is what really impacts them in a big way at the end of the year. That's ultimately what they work towards," says Partipilo. "Their paycheques are very much tied into the success of this company. And they like it that way, and we certainly like it that way."

As for believing the agency has the client's best interests at heart, Partipilo says the agency is held accountable from the standpoint of the agreement. "If we do well as a business, they also do well, and conversely the opposite is true," he says. "They don't just try to sell us more; more is not it. There's got to be a return on that investment. Selling us more has a double-edged sword because there's a risk factor."

PJ DDB's Palmer says trust is crucial between client and agency, and "our whole model is totally built on the trust factor. When you're working on a model fee and a performance bonus, then you're basically out for their best interest, you want to build their business. If you're building their share and you're being compensated for the performance that you built for their brand, then you're in it together."

Christoffel says trust is not necessarily an issue if planning is kept separate from execution. "If the agency is only getting its revenue from the media buy or the creative development, I suppose there could be that temptation to do things in the planning that would generate more work later on. But by separating the two ... there is no vested interest in the outcome, it's just a matter of doing a good-quality plan to start off with."

Ultimately, the results of an advertising campaign depend upon its beginnings. Thorough planning means developing effective solutions and strategy to satisfy both client and agency objectives. And compensation should reflect the importance of planning as an integral first step toward marketing success.[7]



### Good Plans Specify *Both* "What" and "Why"

The plan outline shown in Exhibit 18-8 is quite complete. It doesn't just provide information about marketing-mix decisions—it also includes information about customers (including segmenting dimensions), competitors' strategies, other aspects of the marketing environment, and the company's objectives and resources. This material provides important background relevant to the "why" of the marketing-mix and target-market decisions.

Too often, managers do not include this information; their plans just lay out the details of the target market and the marketing-mix strategy decisions. This shortcut approach is more common when the plan is really just an update of a strategy that has been in place for some time. However, that approach can be risky.

Managers too often make the mistake of casually updating plans in minor ways—perhaps just changing some costs or sales forecasts—but otherwise sticking with what was done in the past. A big problem with this approach is that it's easy to lose sight of why those strategy decisions were made in the first place. When the market situation changes, the original reasons may no longer apply. Yet if the logic for those strategy decisions is not retained, it's easy to miss changes taking place that should result in a plan being reconsidered. For example, a plan that was established in the growth stage of the product life cycle may have been very successful for a number of years. But a marketing manager can't be complacent and assume that success will continue forever. When market maturity hits, the firm may be in for big trouble—unless the basic strategy and plan are modified. If a plan spells out the details of the market analysis and logic for the marketing mix and target market selected, then it is a simple matter to routinely check and update it. Remember: The idea is for all of the analysis and strategy decisions to fit together as an integrated whole. Thus, as some of the elements of the plan or marketing environment change, the whole plan may need a fresh approach.

## Moving from Marketing Plans to a Marketing Program

**marketing program**
Blends all of a firm's marketing plans into one big plan

Most companies implement more than one marketing plan at the same time. A **marketing program** blends all of a firm's marketing plans into one big plan.

When the various plans in the company's program are different, managers may be less concerned with how well the plans fit together—except as they compete for the firm's usually limited financial resources.

When the plans are more similar, however, the same salesforce may be expected to carry out several plans. Or, the firm's advertising department may develop the publicity and advertising for several plans. In these cases, product managers try to get enough of the common resources—say, salespeople's time—for their own plans.

Since a company's resources are usually limited, the marketing manager must make hard choices. You can't launch plans to pursue every promising opportunity. Instead, limited resources force you to choose among alternative plans—while you develop the program.

How do you find the best program? There is no one best way to compare various plans. Managers usually rely on evaluation tools like those discussed in Chapter 4. Even so, much management judgment is usually required. Some calculations are helpful too. If a five-year planning horizon seems realistic for the firm's markets, managers can compare expected profits over the five-year period for each plan. This can be seen with the example of WestJet Airlines in the introduction to Chapter 19. Here, WestJet has built a steadily growing and profitable airline based on careful market research. WestJet is always looking to expand its service into new markets; the company evaluates all options through this research first, and makes a decision based on which plans will be the most profitable and beneficial in the long run.

Assuming the company has a profit-oriented objective, managers can evaluate the more profitable plans first—in terms of both potential profit and resources required. They also need to evaluate a plan's impact on the entire program. One profitable-looking alternative might be a poor first choice if it eats up all the company's resources and sidetracks several plans that together would be more profitable and spread the risks.

Some juggling among the various plans—comparing profitability versus resources needed and available—moves the company toward the most profitable program. This is another area where spreadsheet analysis can help the manager evaluate a large number of alternatives.[8]

## Planning for Involvement in International Marketing

When developing a plan for international markets, marketing managers must decide how involved the firm will be. We will discuss six basic kinds of involvement:

Pepsi's billboard is only one element in a comprehensive market plan, but it cleverly reinforces Pepsi's "The Joy of Cola" positioning.

exporting, licensing, contract manufacturing, management contracting, joint venturing, and wholly owned subsidiaries.

## Exporting

**exporting**
Selling some of what the firm produces to foreign markets

Some companies get into international marketing just by **exporting**—selling some of what the firm produces to foreign markets. Some firms start exporting just to get rid of surplus output. For others, exporting comes from a real effort to look for new opportunities.

Some firms try exporting without doing much planning. They don't change the product or even the service or instruction manuals! As a result, some early efforts are not very satisfying—to buyers or sellers.[9] When Toyota first exported cars to the United States, the effort was a failure. Americans just weren't interested in the Toyota model that sold well in Japan. Toyota tried again three years later with a new design and a new marketing mix. Obviously, Toyota's second effort was a real success.

Exporting does require knowledge about the foreign market. But managers who don't have enough knowledge to plan the details of a program can often get expert help from intermediary specialists. As we discussed in Chapter 13, export agents can handle the arrangements as products are shipped outside the country. Then agents or merchant wholesalers can handle the importing details. Even large producers with many foreign operations turn to international intermediaries for some products or markets. Such intermediaries know how to handle the sometimes confusing formalities and specialized functions. A manager trying to develop a plan alone can make a small mistake that ties products up at national borders for days or months.[10]

Exporting doesn't have to involve permanent relationships. Of course, channel relationships take time to build and shouldn't be treated lightly—sales reps' contacts in foreign countries are investments. But it's relatively easy to cut back on these relationships, or even drop them, if the plan doesn't work.

Some firms, on the other hand, plan more formal and permanent relationships with nationals in foreign countries. The relationships might involve licensing, contract manufacturing, management contracting, and joint venturing.

## Licensing

**licensing**
Selling the right to use some process, trademark, patent, or other right for a fee or royalty

Licensing is a relatively easy way to enter foreign markets. **Licensing** means selling the right to use some process, trademark, patent, or other right for a fee or royalty. The licensee takes most of the risk because it must invest some capital to use the right. Further, the licensee usually does most of the planning for the markets it is licensed to serve. If good partners are available, this can be an effective way to enter a market. Gerber baby food entered the Japanese market this way but exports to other countries.[11]

## Contract Manufacturing

**contract manufacturing**
Turning over production to others while retaining the marketing process

**Contract manufacturing** means turning over production to others while retaining the marketing process. Sears used this approach when it opened stores in Latin America and Spain. This approach doesn't make it any easier to plan the marketing program, but it may make it a lot easier to implement.

For example, this approach can be especially desirable where labour relations are difficult or where there are problems obtaining supplies or government cooperation. Growing nationalistic feelings may make this approach more attractive in the future.

## Management Contracting

**management contracting**
The seller provides only management skills and others own the production and distribution facilities

**Management contracting** means the seller provides only management skills—others own the production and distribution facilities. Some mines and oil refineries are operated this way—and Hilton Hotels operates all over the world catering to local owners. This is a relatively low-risk approach to international marketing. The company makes no commitment to fixed facilities—which can be taken over or damaged in riots or wars. If conditions get too bad, key management people can fly off on the next plane and leave the nationals to manage the operation.

## Joint Venturing

**joint venturing**
A domestic firm entering into a partnership with a foreign firm

**Joint venturing** means a domestic firm entering into a partnership with a foreign firm. As with any partnership, there can be honest disagreements over objectives—for example, how much profit is desired and how fast it should be paid out—as well as operating policies. Where a close working relationship can be developed—perhaps based on one firm's technical and marketing know-how and the foreign partner's knowledge of the local market and political connections—this approach can be very attractive to both parties.

In some situations, a joint venture is the only type of involvement possible. For example, in the 1980s IBM wanted to increase its 2-percent share of what business customers in Brazil spent on data processing services. But a Brazilian law severely limited expansion by foreign computer companies. To grow, IBM had to develop a joint venture with a Brazilian firm. Because of Brazilian laws, IBM could own only a 30-percent interest in the joint venture. But IBM decided it was better to have a 30-percent share of a business and be able to pursue new market opportunities than to stand by and watch competitors take the market.[12]

A joint venture usually requires a big commitment from both parties—and they both must agree on a joint plan. When the relationship doesn't work out well, the ensuing nightmare can make the manager wish that the venture had been planned as a wholly owned operation. But the terms of the joint venture may block this for years.[13]

## Wholly Owned Subsidiary

**wholly owned subsidiary**
A separate firm owned by a parent company

When a firm thinks a foreign market looks really promising, it may want to take the final step. A **wholly owned subsidiary** is a separate firm—owned by a parent company. This gives the firm complete control of the marketing plan and operations, and also helps a foreign branch work more easily with the rest of the company. If a firm has too much capacity in a country with low production costs, for example, it can move some production there from other plants and then export to countries with higher production costs.

WHEREVER YOU DO BUSINESS AROUND THE WORLD, WE'RE PART OF THE LOCAL FABRIC. At the AIG Companies, our business takes us from the canyons of Wall Street to the marketplaces of East Asia to the bazaars of the Middle East. But there's more to being global providers of insurance than just being a long way from home. AIG traces its roots to Shanghai in 1919, and today our network stretches across 130 countries and jurisdictions. We hire local managers who understand the business practices and needs of their own markets. If you're a multinational company doing business in today's fast-changing world, you need our unique global reach and global experience.
AIG
WORLD LEADERS IN INSURANCE AND FINANCIAL SERVICES.
American International Group, Inc., Dept. A, 70 Pine Street, New York, NY 10270.


AIG, an international financial services firm, relies on local managers who understand their own markets to develop marketing plans that meet the needs of local clients.

## Going Multinational

**multinational corporations**
Have a direct investment in several countries and run their businesses depending on the choices available anywhere in the world

As firms become more involved in international marketing, some begin to see themselves as worldwide businesses that transcend national boundaries. These **multinational corporations** have a direct investment in several countries and run their businesses depending on the choices available anywhere in the world. Well-known U.S.–based multinational firms include Coca-Cola, Eastman Kodak, Goodyear, Ford, and IBM. They regularly earn more than one-third of their total sales or profits abroad. And well-known foreign-based multinationals—such as Nestlé, Shell (Royal Dutch Shell), Unilever, Sony, and Honda—have well-accepted brands all around the world.

These multinational operations no longer just export or import. They hire local workers and build local plants. They have relationships with local businesses and politicians. These powerful organizations learn to plan marketing strategies that deal with nationalistic feelings and typical border barriers—treating them simply as part of the marketing environment. We don't yet have one world politically—but business is moving in that direction. We may have to develop new kinds of corporations and laws to govern multinational operations. In the future, it will make less and less sense for business and politics to be limited by national boundaries.

## A Final Note on Planning for International Markets

Usually marketing managers must plan the firm's overall marketing program so it's flexible enough to be adapted for differences in various countries. When the differences are significant, top management should delegate a great deal of responsibility for strategy planning to local managers (or even intermediaries). In many cases, it's not possible to develop a detailed plan without a local feel. In extreme cases, local managers may not even be able to fully explain some parts of their plans because they're based on subtle cultural differences. Then plans must be judged only by their results. The organizational setup should give these managers a great deal of freedom in their planning but ensure tight control against the plans they develop. Top management can simply insist that managers stick to their budgets and meet the plans that they themselves create. When a firm reaches this stage, it is being managed like a well-organized domestic corporation—which insists that its managers (of divisions and territories) meet their own plans so that the whole company's program works as intended.[14]



## Chapter Summary

In this chapter, we stressed the importance of developing whole marketing mixes—not just developing policies for the individual four Ps and hoping they will fit together into some logical whole. The marketing manager is responsible for developing a workable blend—integrating all of a firm's efforts into a coordinated whole that makes effective use of the firm's resources and guides it toward its objectives.

As a starting place for developing new marketing mixes, a marketing manager can use the product classes that have been a common thread through this text. Even if the manager can't fully describe the needs and attitudes of target markets, it is usually possible to select the appropriate product class for a particular product. This, in turn, will help set place and promotion policies. It may also clarify what type of marketing mix is typical for the product. However, just doing what is typical may not give a firm any competitive advantage. Creative strategies are often the ones that identify new and better ways of uniquely giving target customers what they want or need. Similarly, seeing where a firm's offering fits in the product life cycle helps to clarify how current marketing mixes are likely to change in the future.

Developing and evaluating marketing strategies and

plans usually requires that the manager use some approach to forecasting. We talked about two basic approaches to forecasting market potential and sales: (1) extending past behaviour and (2) predicting future behaviour. The most common approach is to extend past behaviour into the future. This gives reasonably good results if market conditions are fairly stable. Methods here include extension of past sales data and the factor method. We saw that projecting the past into the future is risky when big market changes are likely. To make up for this possible weakness, marketers predict future behaviour using their own experience and judgment. They also bring in the judgment of others—using the jury of executive opinion method and salespeople's estimates. And they may use surveys, panels, and market tests. Of course, any sales forecast depends on the marketing mix the firm actually selects.

Once forecasts of the expected sales and estimates of the associated costs for possible strategies are available, alternatives can be compared on potential profitability. Spreadsheet analysis software is an important tool for such comparisons. In the same vein, project planning approaches such as CPM and PERT can help the marketing manager do a better job in planning the time-related details for the strategy that is selected.

Throughout the text, we've emphasized the importance of marketing strategy planning. In this chapter, we went on to show that the marketing manager must develop a marketing plan for carrying out each strategy and then merge a set of plans into a marketing program.

Finally, we discussed different approaches that are helpful in planning strategies to enter international markets. The different approaches have different strengths and weaknesses.

## Key Concepts

contract manufacturing, p. 566
exporting, p. 566
factor, p. 554
factor method, p. 554
indices, p. 556
joint venturing, p. 567
jury of executive opinion, p. 557
leading series, p. 556
licensing, p. 566
management contracting, p. 566
marketing program, p. 564
multinational corporations, p. 568
sales forecast, p. 552
spreadsheet analysis, p. 558
S.W.O.T. analysis, p. 546
target-market potential, p. 552
time series, p. 556
trend extension, p. 553
wholly owned subsidiary, p. 567

## Questions and Problems

1. Distinguish clearly among a marketing strategy, a marketing plan, and a marketing program.
2. Discuss how a marketing manager could go about choosing among several possible marketing plans, given that choices must be made because of limited resources. Would the job be easier in the consumer-product or in the business-product area? Why?
3. Explain how understanding the product classes can help a marketing manager develop a marketing strategy for a really new product that is unlike anything currently available.
4. Distinguish between competitive marketing mixes and superior mixes that lead to breakthrough opportunities.
5. Explain the difference between a forecast of market potential and a sales forecast.
6. Suggest a plausible explanation for sales fluctuations for *(a)* computers, *(b)* ice cream, *(c)* washing machines, *(d)* tennis rackets, *(e)* oats, *(f)* disposable diapers, and *(g)* latex for rubber-based paint.
7. Explain the factor method of forecasting. Illustrate your answer.
8. Why is spreadsheet analysis a popular tool for marketing strategy planning?
9. In your own words, explain how a project-management technique such as PERT or CPM can help a marketing manager develop a better marketing plan.
10. Why should a complete marketing plan include details concerning the reasons for the marketing strategy decisions and not just the marketing activities central to the four Ps?
11. Consider how the marketing manager's job becomes more complex when it's necessary to develop and

plan *several* strategies as part of a marketing program. Be sure to discuss how the manager might have to handle different strategies at different stages in the product life cycle. To make your discussion more concrete, consider the job of a marketing manager for a sporting products manufacturer.

12. How would marketing planning be different for a firm that has entered foreign marketing with a joint venture and a firm that has set up a wholly owned subsidiary?
13. How can a firm set the details of its marketing plan when it has little information about a foreign market it wants to enter?
14. Review the PT Cruiser case at the beginning of this chapter and the outline of a marketing plan in Exhibit 18-8. Indicate which sections of the plan would probably require the most change as the competition responds to the Cruiser's innovative design. Briefly explain your thinking.

## Suggested Cases

To view the cases, go to www.mcgrawhill.ca/college/wong.

Interested in finding out what marketing looks like in the real world? *Marketing Magazine* is just a click away on your OLC! Visit www.mcgrawhill.ca/college/wong today.

When You Finish This Chapter, You Should

1. Understand how information technology is speeding up feedback for better implementation and control.

2. Know why effective implementation is critical to customer satisfaction and profits.

3. Know how total quality management can improve implementation—including implementation of service quality.

4. Understand how sales analysis can aid in marketing strategy planning.

5. Understand the differences in sales analysis, performance analysis, and performance analysis using performance indexes.

6. Understand the difference between the full-cost approach and the contribution-margin approach.

7. Understand how planning and control can be combined to improve the marketing-management process.

8. Understand what a marketing audit is and when and where it should be used.

# Chapter Nineteen

# Implementing and Controlling Marketing Plans: Evolution and Revolution

## Plane Crazy

"Hello everyone. We're going to be beginning our descent into Calgary in a few minutes, so I'd like to remind you to fasten your seat belts. I'd also like to remind you that this aircraft is equipped with special technology that allows us to determine if everyone is wearing his or her seat belt. So, if we find that anyone isn't buckled up, we'll have to return to Vancouver and try again, until we all get it right." This is an example of the typical humour that you will find when flying Canada's most successful discount airline, WestJet.

Until WestJet came on the scene, U.S. carrier Southwest Airlines had been the premier

place price promotion produ

discount no-frills airline in North America—the company turned a profit for 26 straight years, including during the recession years that plagued other airlines. Southwest saw its shares rise from $11 in June 1971 to $3,200 in October 1999. Between 1992 and 1997, Southwest beat all other major airlines in the U.S. for best on-time-arrival performance, best baggage handling, and fewest customer complaints. It was said by many experts that this track record of profitability and performance could not be replicated to the same degree. A consultant with Global Aviation Associates in Washington, D.C. stated that "others have tried to make themselves in the image of Southwest. There are no survivors." This may be true in the U.S., but not in Canada—where Calgary-based WestJet Airlines has taken the market by storm with its discount prices and no-frills approach. WestJet, which first took off in 1996, "is exactly rivet-for-rivet, stitch-for-stitch identical to Southwest," claims Julius Maldutis, an airline analyst for CIBC World Markets Corporation in New York.

WestJet was created by Calgary real estate developer Clive Beddoe in 1994. After spending thousands of dollars a month in fares to fly executives around Western Canada for business ventures, Beddoe and three business partners were so fed up with the costs they decided to start their own airline based on the model of Southwest and Morris Air (another discount airline). When it started flying, WestJet had five destinations, with fares comparable to bus

place price promotion product




www.mcgrawhill.ca/college/wong

tickets between the cities. A one-way ticket between Calgary and Edmonton would cost $29, but changing prices have allowed the company to stay profitable. WestJet now services 22 cities across Canada—not only Toronto, Montreal, Winnipeg, and Vancouver, but also secondary airports in places like Thunder Bay, Moncton, and Kelowna. Following the Southwest model, WestJet uses only one type of aircraft—the Boeing 737—which minimizes training time and costs for pilots.

WestJet bases its entire marketing strategy on being a low-cost discount airline, but what makes this airline—which doesn't even serve meals on its flights—so popular? It starts from the top with charismatic leadership, but overall it is known as the WestJet Spirit. According to www.westjet.ca, the company prides itself on creating "internal magic and external wow." This type of marketing philosophy is what brings in new customers and keeps the old ones hooked. It encompasses success on the ground and in the air, the commitment to great service, and the special attention paid to guests and employees. By referring to passengers as "guests," the company makes customers feel comfortable and welcome. This "external wow" is not just a figure of speech for the airline, however—statistics show that it really is wowing its guests. In 2001, 77.6 percent of WestJet's flights arrived on time. Further, its flight cancellation percentage was only .83 percent, as opposed to 1.7 percent for all other flights. While WestJet's on-time service is well above the market average, its internal service is just as good—in 2001, it had only six complaints out of 1,850,000 to the aviation committee.

A typical flight on WestJet is vastly different than on other commercial airlines—the airline has marketed itself based on personality and commitment to great service, highlighting the welcome feeling that passengers get when they fly with WestJet. While customers don't receive the perks that passengers of, say, Air Canada get, they are met with unique personal service in a laid-back atmosphere. WestJet team members add to the relaxed atmosphere by wearing khaki pants and denim shirts rather than formal uniforms. They are also encouraged to joke around with the guests and entertain them with humour rather than a movie. WestJet's marketing plan—which strictly follows the Southwest model—has been drawn perfectly, helping it become one of Canada's dominant airlines. In 2003, WestJet only improved its numbers from previous years, and continues to strive to be the best in all of its existing and new markets. A continuing emphasis on success has been the ultimate key to Southwest's impeccable reputation, and is now being adapted—like many other things from the company—to WestJet's formula in Canada.[1]

## In This Chapter

Throughout this book we have focused on making decisions and developing policies and plans that dictate marketing activities. Sooner or later, these decisions and plans must be executed and their performance monitored.

We've discussed some specific opportunities and challenges with respect to implementation and control as we introduced each of the marketing strategy decision areas, and in the previous chapter we looked at developing marketing plans and programs. In this chapter, we'll go into more depth on concepts and how-to approaches for making implementation and control more effective. We'll start with a discussion of how dramatic improvements in information technology and e-commerce are resulting in changes not only in implementation and control, but also in the whole strategy planning process. For many firms, these changes are critically important. They offer revolutionary new ways to meet customer needs. Next, we'll highlight some of the new approaches, including total quality management, that are improving marketing implementation. Then we'll explain how marketing managers use control-related tools, such as sales and performance analysis, to improve the quality of planning and implementation decisions. We'll conclude with a discussion of what a marketing audit is, and why it is sometimes necessary.



## The Importance of "Implementation" and "Control"

There is a good reason why our primary emphasis in this book is on the strategy planning part of the marketing manager's job. The one-time strategy decisions—those that decide what business the company is in and the strategies it will follow—set the firm on a course toward either profitable opportunities or, alternatively, costly failure. If a marketing manager makes an error with these basic decisions, there may never be a second chance to set things straight. In contrast, if good strategies and plans are developed, the marketing manager—and everyone else in the organization—knows what needs to be done. Thus, good marketing plans set the framework for effective implementation and control.

A manager's job does not stop with the development of a plan. Plans suggest what the business could achieve: in a sense, they are statements of business potential. Whether that potential is realized depends upon the quality of the plan's execution. That is, developing a potentially profitable plan does not ensure either satisfied customers or profit for the firm. Achieving the outcomes envisioned in the plan requires that the whole marketing-management process work well. As you learned in Chapter 2, the marketing-management process includes not only marketing strategy planning but also implementation and control (refer to Exhibit 2-5). In fact, in today's highly competitive markets customer satisfaction often hinges on skilful implementation. Further, the ongoing success of the firm is often dependent on **control**—the feedback process that helps the marketing manager learn (1) how ongoing plans and implementation are working and (2) how to plan for the future.

**control**
The feedback process that helps marketing managers learn how ongoing plans and implementation are working and how to plan for the future

## How Information Technology Can Help

Not long ago, marketing managers planned their strategies and put them into action—and then waited a long time before they got feedback to know if the strat-

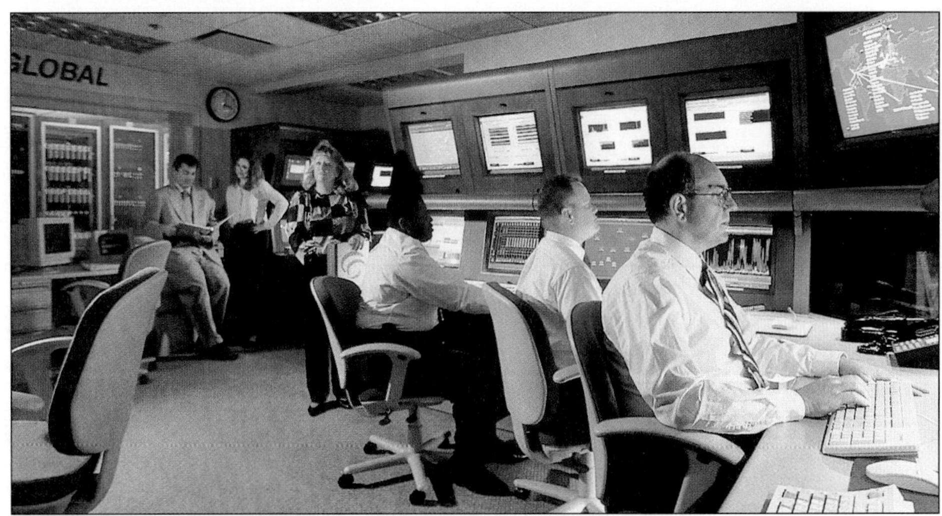


This state-of-the-art information centre has replaced more than 25 individual processing centres worldwide and allows Colgate managers to monitor activities across the entire supply chain—all of which brings products to consumers faster and more efficiently than ever before.



egy and implementation were really working as intended. For example, a marketing manager might not have much feedback on what was happening with sales, expenses, and profits until financial summaries were available—and that sometimes took months or even longer. Further, summary data weren't very useful in pinpointing which specific aspects of the plan were working and which were not. In that environment, the feedback was so general and took so long that there often wasn't anything the manager could do about a problem except start over.

That situation has now changed dramatically in many types of business. In Chapter 8, we discussed how firms are using intranets, databases, and marketing information systems to track sales and cost details day-by-day and week-by-week. Throughout the book, you've seen examples of how marketers get more information faster and use it quickly to improve a strategy or its implementation. For example, scanner data from a consumer panel can provide a marketing manager with almost immediate feedback on whether a new consumer product is selling at the expected level in each specific store—and whether it is actually selling to the intended target market rather than some other group. Similarly, e-commerce order systems can feed into real-time sales reports for each product.

### Information as a Competitive Advantage

Marketing managers who can get faster feedback on their decisions can often take advantage of it to develop a competitive advantage. They can quickly fine-tune a smooth-running implementation to make it work even better. If there are potential problems, they can often spot them early and keep them from turning into big problems.

For example, a manager who gets detailed daily reports that compare actual sales results in different cities with sales forecasts in the plan is able to see very quickly if there is a problem in a specific city. Then the manager can track down the cause of the problem. If sales are going slowly because the new salesperson in that city is inexperienced, then the sales manager might immediately spend more time working with that rep. On the other hand, if the problem is that a chain of retail stores in that particular city isn't willing to allocate much shelf space for the firm's product, then the salesperson might need to develop a special analysis to show the buyers for that specific chain how the product could improve the chain's profits.

When information is slow coming in and there is less detail, making implementation changes is usually more difficult. By the time the need for a change is obvious, a bigger change is required for it to have any effect.

The basic strategy planning concepts we've emphasized throughout the text are enduring and will always be at the heart of marketing. Yet the fast pace that is now

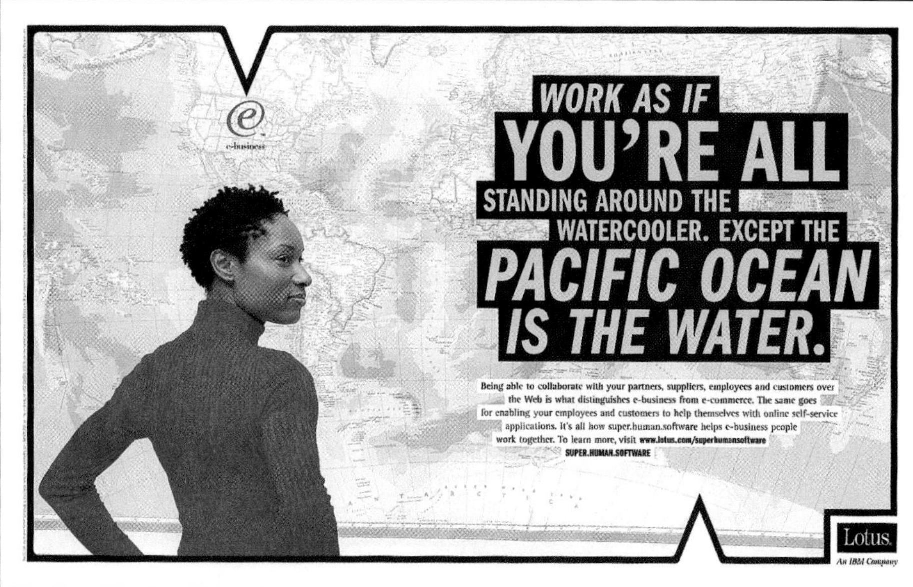


Lotus software allows managers in different locations, including different countries, to quickly share information, which helps to make implementation and control faster and more effective.

possible with e-commerce in getting information for control is resulting in fundamental changes in how many managers work, make decisions, plan, and implement their plans. Managers who can quickly adjust the details of their efforts to better solve customer problems or respond to changes in the market can do a better job for their firms—because they can make certain that their plans are really performing as expected.

### The Role of the Marketing Manager

Fast feedback improves implementation and control. And computers now take the drudgery out of analyzing data. But this kind of analysis is not possible unless the data are in machine-processible form—so they can be sorted and analyzed quickly. Here the creative marketing manager plays a crucial role by insisting that the necessary data be collected. If the data he or she wants to analyze are not captured as they come in, information will be difficult, if not impossible, to get later.

A marketing manager may need many different types of information to improve implementation efforts or to develop new strategies. In the past, this has often caused delays—even if the information was in a machine-processible form. In a large company, for example, it could take days or even weeks for a marketing manager to find out how to get needed information from another department. Imagine how long it could take for a marketing manager to get needed sales data from sales offices in different countries around the world.

### How New Technologies Have Changed How We Do Things

New approaches for electronic communication such as the Internet, fibre-optic telephone lines, and satellite transmission systems are already helping to solve these problems. For example, many companies are using these tools to immediately transfer data from a computer at one location to another. A sales manager with a laptop can pull data from the firm's network server from anywhere in the world. And marketing managers working on different aspects of a strategy can use e-mail messaging or online video conferencing to communicate. A marketing manager needs just a simple PC, the Internet, and software such as LapLink to make it possible to work at a computer on the other side of the world just as though he or she were sitting in front of it, which makes accessing and analyzing data quick and efficient.

This type of electronic pipeline makes data available instantly. A report—such as one that summarizes sales by product, salesperson, or type of customer—that in

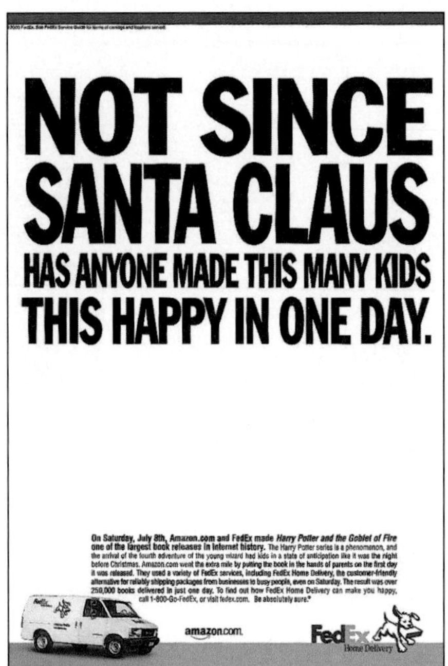


the past was done once a month now might be created weekly, daily, or whenever an online user wants it. Software can be programmed to search for and flag results that indicate a problem of some sort. Programs like Microsoft Excel can link to the new flow of data and instantly create graphs that make the information vivid and easy to interpret. Then the manager can allocate more time to resolving whatever particular problems show up.

Of course, many firms don't consider or use these types of approaches. But they are becoming increasingly common—especially as marketing managers find that they are losing out to more nimble competitors who get information more quickly and adjust their implementation and strategies more often.[2]

## Making Implementation More Effective

When a marketing manager has developed a good marketing plan, the challenge of implementing it often involves hundreds, or thousands, of operational decisions and activities. In a small company, these may all be handled by a few people, or even by a single person. In a large corporation, literally hundreds of different people may be involved in implementation, requiring a massive amount of careful coordination and communication. Either way, when operational decisions and activities are executed well, customers get what is intended. And if the original plan is good, customers will be satisfied and come back the next time the need arises. However, even a great plan can leave customers unhappy—and switching to someone else's offering—if implementation is poor.

Implementation is especially critical in mature and highly competitive markets. When several firms are following basically the same strategy—quickly imitating competitors' ideas—customers are often won or lost based on differences in the quality of implementation. Consider the rental-car business. Hertz has a strategy that targets business travellers with a choice of quality cars, convenient online reservations, fast pick-up and drop-off, accessories like cell phones, availability at most major airports, and a premium price. Hertz is extremely successful with this strategy even though there is little to prevent other companies from trying the same approach. But a major part of Hertz's success is due to implementation. Customers keep coming back because the Hertz service is both reliable and pain-free.

When a Hertz #1 Club Gold customer calls to make a reservation, the company already has the standard information about that customer in a computer database. At the airport, the customer skips over the line at the Hertz counter and instead just picks up an already-completed rental contract and goes straight to the Hertz bus. The driver gets the customer's name and radios ahead to have someone start the specific car that customer will drive. That way the air conditioner or heater is already doing its job when the bus driver delivers the customer right to the parking slot for his or her car. Customers are certain they're at the right place because there's an electronic sign beside each car with the customer's name on it. When the customer returns the car, an agent comes to the car, scans the customer's contract with a handheld computer, and prints the receipt.

The whole process is very smooth. Making this work—day in and day out, customer after customer—isn't easy. But Hertz has set up systems to make it all easier because that's what it takes to implement its plan and to keep customers loyal.[3]

As the Hertz example illustrates, marketing implementation usually involves decisions and activities related to both internal and external matters. Figuring out how the correct car will end up in the right parking slot, how the Hertz bus driver will contact the office, and who will coordinate getting the message to the person that starts the car are all internal matters. They are invisible to the customer—as long as they work as planned. On the other hand, some implementation issues are external and involve the customer. For example, the contract must be completed correctly and be in the right spot when the rental customer comes to pick it up, and someone needs to have filled the car with gas and cleaned it.

## The Objectives of Implementation Efforts

Whether implementation decisions and activities are internal or external, they all must be consistent with the objectives of the overall strategy and with the other details of the plan. However, there are also three general objectives that apply to all implementation efforts. Other things equal, the manager wants to get each implementation job done:

- Better, so customers really get superior value as planned.
- Faster, to avoid delays that cause customers problems.
- At lower cost, without wasting money on things that don't add value for the customer.

The ideal of doing things better, faster, and at lower cost is easy to accept, but in practice implementation is often complicated by tradeoffs among the three objectives. For example, doing a job better may take longer or cost more, but if implemented correctly the rewards will be greater than the costs. So just as a marketing manager should constantly look for new strategy opportunities, it's important to be creative in looking for better solutions to implementation problems. That may require finding ways to better coordinate the efforts of the different people involved, setting up standard operating procedures to deal with recurring problems, or juggling priorities to deal with the unexpected. When the Hertz bus driver is sick, someone still has to be there to pick up the customers and deliver them to their cars.

## Approaches to Improving Implementation Efforts

Sometimes the implementation effort can be improved by approaching the task in a new or different way. Marketing Demo 19-1 and Exhibit 19-1 each show some of the ways that firms are using information technology to improve specific implementation jobs. Note that some of the examples in Exhibit 19-1 focus on internal matters and some on external, customer-oriented matters.

**Total quality management** As we've shown throughout this book, even people with the best intentions sometimes lapse into a production orientation. When the pressure is on to get a job done, they forget about satisfying the customer—let alone consider working together! When the product manager is screaming for a budget report, the accountant may view a customer's concerns about a billing error as something a salesperson can smooth over—alone.

There are many different ways to improve implementation in each of the four Ps decision areas, but here we will focus on total quality management, which you can use to improve *any* implementation effort. With **total quality management (TQM)**, everyone in the organization is concerned about quality, throughout all of the firm's activities, to better serve customer needs.

**total quality management (TQM)**
A management approach in which everyone in the organization is concerned about quality, throughout all of the firm's activities, to better serve customer needs

In Chapter 9 we explained that product quality means the ability of a product to satisfy a customers' needs or requirements. Now we'll expand that idea and think about the quality of the whole marketing mix and how it is implemented to meet customer requirements.

Most of the early attention in quality management focused on reducing defects in goods produced in factories. Reliable goods are important, but there's usually a lot more to marketing implementation than that. Yet if we start by considering product defects, you'll see how the total quality management idea has evolved and how it applies to implementing a marketing program.

At one time, most firms assumed defects were an inevitable part of mass production. They assumed the cost of replacing defective parts or goods was just a cost of doing business—an insignificant one compared to the advantages of mass production. However, many firms were forced to rethink this assumption when Japanese

Exhibit 19-1 Examples of approaches to overcome specific marketing implementation problems.

| Marketing-Mix Decision Area | Operational Problem | Implementation Approach |
|---|---|---|
| **Product** | Develop design of a new product as rapidly as possible without errors | Use 3-D computer-aided design software |
| | Pretest consumer response to different versions of a label | Prepare sample labels with PC graphics software and test on Internet |
| **Place** | Coordinate inventory levels with intermediaries to avoid stock-outs | Use bar code scanner, EDI, and computerized reorder system |
| | Get franchisee's inputs and cooperation on a new program | Set up a televideo conference |
| **Promotion** | Quickly distribute TV ad to local stations in many different markets | Distribute final video version of the ad via satellite link |
| | Answer final consumers' questions about how to use a product | Put a toll-free telephone number and website address on product label |
| **Price** | Identify frequent customers for a quantity discount | Create a "favoured customer" club with an ID card |
| | Figure out if price sensitivity impacts demand for a product; make it easier for customers to compare prices | Show unit prices (for example, per 100 g) on shelf markers; set different prices in similar markets and track sales, including sales of competing products |

## Marketing Demo 19–1

### THE BLOGGING REVOLUTION

One of the most fascinating trends popping up in the marketing world is the creation of blogs on company websites. "Blogs," or weblogs, have been around for some time, and have mostly been used for personal use—individuals could publish their thoughts and opinions for a public audience with the click of a mouse. Blogs are used not only on the macro level for all to see (especially for political issues), but also on the micro level where only an invited group of friends or working partners can access the information. Blogs usually contain short notes or notices, often with links to interesting websites or articles. Many blogs are simply a daily diary of a person's life, and hence are not very interesting to the general public. Why, then, is blogging becoming a hot trend in marketing?

Creative marketers who have studied the blog phenomenon see the potential for these sites to become a spectacular way to handle customer relations. Macromedia, the maker of software such as Flash, Shockwave, and Dreamweaver, has created weblogs for its current products. The blogs were launched in tandem with four new products, and were based on the speculation that customers would have a multitude of questions regarding how the products work. Macromedia implemented what it calls the "blog strategy." Each blog keeps a continuous log of current news, tips, hints, links to pertinent sites, and customer feedback. Several staff members in various departments maintain blogs for the products they work with, which allows for quick response to problems that consumers may be having with the new software. For example, Matt Brown, the community manager for Dreamweaver MX, has a blog at http://radio.weblogs.com/0106884. It contains news and information about the product, and consumers are allotted space to give their opinions and feedback on each new entry from Brown. Each Macromedia blog is updated with customers in mind.

In contrast, there are also many unofficial blogs that have been set up by customers of a certain product to give their personal feedback among other consumers. A very popular type of weblog is for new-car owners who like to gather online and share their comments and experiences. Specific blogs have been set up for different companies and even different models. These sites are an excellent resource for marketing managers to consider when evaluating the launch of a new product.

The overwhelming positive response to existing corporate blogs has led other companies to explore their options in the "blogosphere." For example, the Harley-Davidson Motorcycle Company could make use of a blog to feature new-product releases and highlight customers who are using Harleys for charity events. As blogs become more integrated into the business world, their horizons will drastically expand. These examples are just the beginning of the integration between the corporate business world and the blogging world. While blogs are only in the introductory stage, many marketing managers are familiarizing themselves with the software and its possibilities for their company in the near future.[4]

While finding new approaches helps with some implementation problems, getting better implementation often depends on being vigilant in improving what the firm and its people are already doing. So let's take a closer look at some important ways that managers can improve the quality of their implementation efforts.[5]

producers of cars, electronics, and cameras showed that defects weren't inevitable. And their success in taking customers away from established competitors made it clear that the cost of defects wasn't just the cost of replacement!

**The cost of customer dissatisfaction** From the customer's point of view, getting a defective product and having to complain about it is a big headache. The customer can't use the defective product and suffers the inconvenience of waiting for someone to fix the problem—*if* someone gets around to it. It certainly doesn't deliver superior value. Rather, it erodes goodwill and leaves customers dissatisfied. The big cost of poor quality is the cost of lost customers.

In fact, one study reported that two-thirds of all customers who change suppliers do so due to dissatisfaction with their current supplier as opposed to being attracted to a superior offering from a competitor. That same study also noted that it costs six to eight times more to acquire a new account than it does to retain an existing account.[6] It isn't hard to see how marketing budgets, and overall profitability, are affected when quality problems exist.

Much to the surprise of some production-oriented managers, the Japanese experience showed that it is less expensive to do something right the first time than to pay to do it poorly and then pay again to fix problems. And quality wasn't just a matter of adding more assembly-line inspections. Products had to be designed to meet customer needs from the start. One defective part in 10,000 may not seem like much, but if that part keeps a completed car from cranking at the end of the automaker's production line, finding the problem is a costly nightmare.

Firms that adopted TQM methods to reduce manufacturing defects soon used the same approaches to overcome many other implementation problems. Their success brought attention to what is possible with TQM—whether the implementation problem concerns unreliable delivery schedules, poor customer service, advertising that appears on the wrong TV show, or salespeople who can't answer customers' questions.

**Continuous improvement** The idea of doing things right the first time seems obvious, but it's easier said than done. Problems always come up, and it's not always clear what isn't being done as well as it could be. Most people tend to ignore problems that don't pose an immediate crisis. But firms that adopt TQM always look for ways to improve implementation with **continuous improvement**—a commitment to constantly make things better one step at a time. Once you accept the idea that there may be a better way to do something, and you look for it, you may just find it! The place to start is to clearly define "defects" in the implementation process, from the customer's point of view. Because continuous improvement hinges on employee involvement and communication, many companies display all suggestions for improvements where employees can see them.

**continuous improvement**
A commitment to constantly make things better one step at a time

**The total quality process—An example** Managers who use the TQM approach think of quality improvement as a sorting process—a sorting out of things gone right and things gone wrong. The sorting process calls for detailed measurements related to a problem. Then managers use a set of statistical tools to analyze the measurements and identify the problem areas that are the best candidates for fixing. The statistical details are beyond our focus here, but it's useful to get a feel for how managers use the tools.

Let's consider the case of a restaurant that does well during the evening hours but wants to improve its lunch business. The restaurant develops a strategy that targets local businesspeople with an attractive luncheon buffet. The restaurant decides on a buffet because research shows that target customers want a choice of good healthy food and are willing to pay reasonable prices for it—as long as they can eat quickly and get back to work on time.

As the restaurant implements its new strategy, the manager wants a measure of how things are going. So she encourages customers to fill out comment cards that ask "How did we do today?" After several months of operation, things seem to be going reasonably well—although business is not as brisk as it was at first. The manager reads the comment cards and divides the ones with complaints into categories—to count up different reasons why customers weren't satisfied.

***Step 1: Pareto charts help find the problems*** This seemingly simple act presents a powerful message when the manager creates a graph showing a frequency distribution for the different types of complaints. Quality people call this a **Pareto chart**—a graph that shows the number of times a problem cause occurs, with problem causes ordered from most frequent to least frequent. The manager's Pareto chart, shown in Exhibit 19-2, reveals that customers complain most frequently that they have to wait for a seat. There were other common complaints—the buffet was not well organized, the table was not clean, and so on. However, the first complaint is much more common than the next most frequent.

**Pareto chart**
A graph that shows the number of times a problem cause occurs, with problem causes ordered from most frequent to least frequent

This type of pattern is typical. The worst problems often occur over and over again. This focuses the manager's attention on which implementation problem to fix first. A rule of quality management is to slay the dragons first—which simply means start with the biggest problem. After removing that problem, the battle

Exhibit 19-2
Pareto chart showing frequency of different complaints.

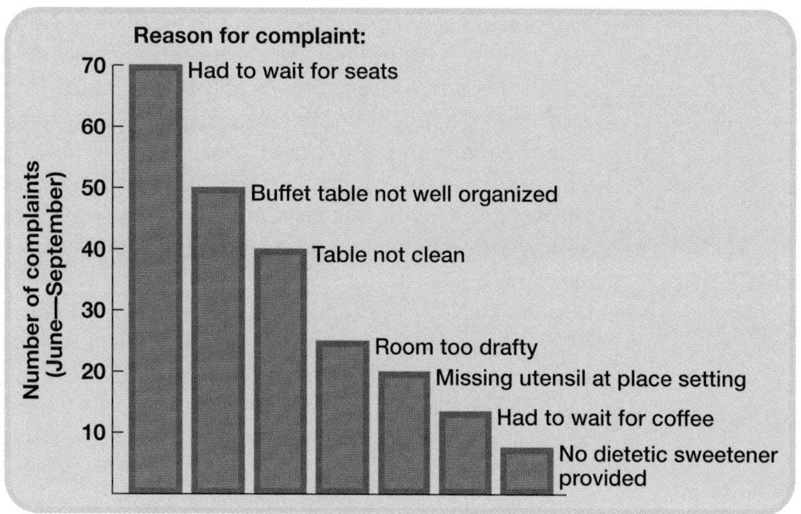


moves on to the next most frequent problem. If you do this *continuously*, you solve a lot of problems—and you don't just satisfy customers, you delight them.

**fishbone diagram**

A visual aid that helps organize cause-and-effect relationships for things gone wrong

***Step 2: Fishbone diagrams help figure out what went wrong*** So far, our manager has only identified the problem. To solve it, she creates a **fishbone diagram**—a visual aid that helps organize cause-and-effect relationships for "things gone wrong."

Our restaurant manager, for example, discovers that customers wait to be seated because tables aren't cleared soon enough. In fact, the Pareto chart (Exhibit 19-2) shows that customers also complain frequently about tables not being clean. So the two implementation problems may be related.

The manager's fishbone diagram (Exhibit 19-3) summarizes the various causes for tables not being cleaned quickly. There are different basic categories of causes—

Exhibit 19-3 Fishbone diagram showing cause and effect for "why tables are not cleared quickly."

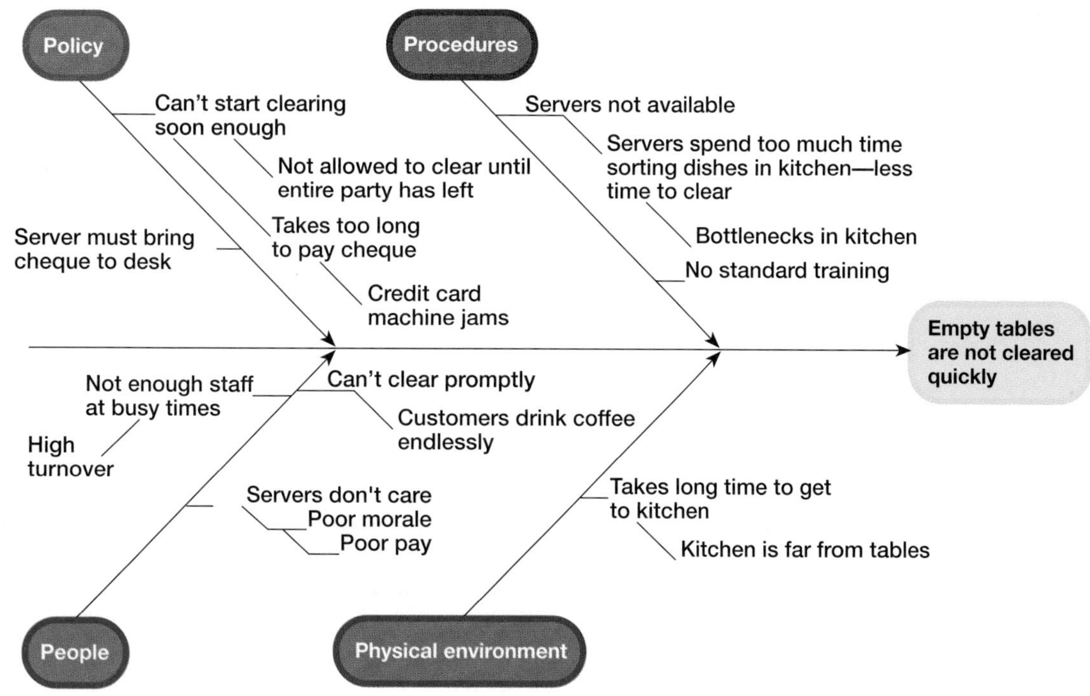

restaurant policy, procedures, people problems, and the physical environment. With this overview of different ways the service operation is going wrong, the manager can decide what to fix. She establishes different formal measures. For example, she counts how frequently different causes delay customers from being seated. She finds that the cashier's faulty credit card scanning machine holds up cheque processing. The fishbone diagram shows that restaurant policy is to clear the table after the entire party leaves. But customers have to wait at their tables while the staff deals with the faulty credit card machine, and cleaning is delayed. With the credit card machine replaced, the staff can clear the tables sooner—and because they're not so hurried, they do a better cleaning job. Two dragons are on the way to being slayed!

Our case shows that people in different areas of the restaurant affect customer satisfaction. The waitperson could not do what was needed to satisfy customers because the cashier had trouble with the credit card machine. The TQM approach helps everyone see and understand how their job affects what others do and the customer's satisfaction.[7] It also serves as an indicator for employees to see how their job affects the entire restaurant as a whole.



## Building Quality into Services

The restaurant case illustrates how a firm can improve implementation with TQM approaches. We used a service example because providing customer service is often a difficult area of implementation. Recently, marketers in service businesses have been paying a lot of attention to improving service quality.

But some people seem to forget that almost every firm must implement service quality as part of its plan—whether its product is primarily a service, primarily a physical good, or a blend of both. For example, a manufacturer of ball bearings isn't just providing wholesalers or producers with round pieces of steel. Customers need information about deliveries, they need orders filled properly, and they may have questions to ask the firm's accountant, receptionist, or engineers. Because almost every firm must manage the service it provides customers, let's focus on some of the special concerns of implementing quality service.

**Quality service comes from quality people** Quality gurus like to say that the firm has only one job: to give customers exactly what they want, when they want it, and where they want it. Marketing managers have been saying that for some time too. But customer service is hard to implement, because the server is inseparable from the service. A person doing a specific service job may perform one specific task correctly but still annoy the customer in a host of other ways. Customers will not be satisfied if employees are rude or inattentive—even if they "solve the customer's problem." There are two keys to improving how people implement quality service: (1) training, and (2) empowerment.

Firms that commit to customer satisfaction realize that all employees who have any contact with customers need training—many firms see 40 hours a year of training as a minimum. Simply showing customer-contact employees around the rest of the business—so that they learn how their contribution fits in the total effort—can be very effective. Good training usually includes role-playing on handling different types of customer requests and problems. This is not just sales training! A rental-car attendant who is rude when a customer is trying to turn in a car may leave the customer dissatisfied—even if the rental car was perfect. How employees treat a customer is as important as whether they perform the task correctly.

Companies can't afford an army of managers to inspect how each employee implements a strategy—and such a system usually doesn't work anyway. Quality cannot be "inspected in." It must come from the people who do the service jobs. So, firms that commit to service quality empower employees to satisfy customers' needs. Empowerment involves managers sharing their power with lower-ranked employees and encouraging their decision making and implementation authority.[8] For exam-

Saturn is just one of many companies that empowers its employees. By allowing them to shut the production line down to solve problems immediately, Saturn gives employees freedom to make mistakes and correct them on their own. What other implications does such a strategy yield? Disney prides itself on superior customer service and satisfaction. Aside from posting signs to show waiting times, what other techniques or strategies might Disney impose to decrease the frustration of waiting in lineups?



ple, in the Saturn car manufacturing plant, employees can stop the assembly line manually to correct a problem rather than passing it down the line.

**Manage expectations *and* performance** The implementation effort sometimes leaves customers dissatisfied because they expect much more than it is possible for the firm to deliver. Some firms react to this by shrugging their shoulders and faulting customers for being unreasonable. Research in the service quality area, however, suggests that the problems often go away if marketers clearly communicate what they are offering. Customers are satisfied when the service matches their expectations, and careful communication leads to reasonable expectations. Sometimes the solution is simple. At Disney World, for example, waiting in line for a popular ride can be very tiring. Disney found, however, that posting signs that show how long the wait will likely be reduced customer frustration. And it allowed people to pick another ride with less waiting time if they chose to do so.

Customers often tolerate a delay and remain satisfied with the service when they are given a full explanation. Most airline passengers seethe at the announcement of a takeoff delay but are happy to wait and stay safe if they know the delay is caused by a thunderstorm high over the airport.

**Separate the routine and plan for the special** Implementation usually involves some routine services and some that require special attention. Customer satisfaction increases when the two types of service encounters are separated. For example, banks set up special windows for commercial deposits, and supermarkets have cash-only lines. In developing the marketing plan, it's important to analyze the types of service customers will need and plan for all types of situations. In some cases, completely different strategies may be required.

Increasingly, firms try to use computers and other equipment to handle routine services. ATMs are quick and convenient for dispensing cash. Air Canada allows its customers to check flight arrival and departure times via its website. Similarly, passengers can also check for lost luggage on the site (www.aircanada.com). In the same way, the UPS website (www.ups.com) makes it easy for customers to check the status of a delivery with the click of a mouse.

Firms that study special service requests can use training so that even unusual customer requests become routine to the staff. Every day, hotel guests lose their keys, bank customers run out of cheques, and supermarket shoppers leave their wallets at home. A well-run service operation anticipates these special events so service providers can respond in a way that satisfies customers' needs.

**Managers must manage the quality effort** Quality implementation—whether in a service activity or in another activity—doesn't just happen by itself. Managers must show that they are committed to doing things right to satisfy customers and that quality is everyone's job. Without top-level support, some people won't get beyond their business-as-usual attitude—and TQM won't work. The top executive at American Express had his board of directors give him the title "chief quality officer" so that everyone in the company would know he was personally involved in the TQM effort.

Statements like those made in the preceding paragraph seem so obvious that many people never really take steps to ensure that managers are managing quality. But firms that are successful with quality programs usually go to the effort to clearly specify and write out exactly what tasks need to be done, how, and by whom. This may seem unnecessary. After all, most people know, in general, what they're supposed to do. However, if the tasks are clearly specified, it's easier to see what criteria should be used to measure performance.

Once criteria are established, there needs to be some basis on which to evaluate the job being done. In our restaurant example, one part of the job specification for the cashier is to process credit card payments. In that case, relevant criteria might include the amount of time that it takes and the number of people waiting in line to pay. If the restaurant manager had seen a record of how long it was taking to process credit cards, she would have known that for many customers it was taking too long. Without the measure, the precise nature of the problem was hidden.

**benchmarking**

Picking a basis of comparison for evaluating how well a job is being done

That takes us to the issue of **benchmarking**—picking a basis of comparison for evaluating how well a job is being done. For example, consider a case in which a firm asks each of its customers to rate their satisfaction with their sales rep. Then the company might benchmark each sales rep against other sales reps on the basis of average customer satisfaction. But if the firm's sales reps as a group are weak, that isn't a sensible approach. The ones that stink the least would look good on a relative basis. Many firms, however, try to benchmark against some external standard. For example, a sales manager might want to benchmark against a competitor's sales reps. Or, even better, the manager might identify firms in which sales reps earn superlative customer satisfaction ratings, regardless of their industry, and benchmark against them. That approach can also reveal job specifications—things that should be done—that the sales manager had not considered or measured in the first place. For example, salespeople at Saturn dealers earn high customer satisfaction ratings. Office Depot doesn't sell cars, but it might benchmark against Saturn's sales reps to find ways to improve its office equipment sales effort.

**Managers must champion the quality effort** While the cost of poor quality is lost customers, keep in mind that the types of quality efforts we've been discussing also result in costs. It takes time and energy to keep records, analyze the details of implementation efforts, and search for ways to reduce whatever type of defects might appear. It's important to find the right balance between quality in the implementation effort and what it costs to achieve it. This means that managers must "sell" the notion of quality management within their firm.

Getting every customer's order exactly correct is a challenge, but it's a basic ingredient of high-quality service for a drive-through restaurant. To improve order accuracy, McDonald's has added computerized displays so customers can confirm their order. With tires, quality means safety and durability, so Goodyear has continued to improve these features with its new design for the Aquatred tire.

**Managers must have a balanced view** However, at the same time, marketing managers must not become so obsessed with quality they forget that the objective of programs like TQM is to enhance profitability. Those who lose sight of the balance have often created quality programs that cost more than they're worth. It's easy to fall into the trap of running up unnecessary costs trying to improve some facet of implementation that really isn't that important to customer satisfaction or customer retention. When that happens, customers may still be satisfied, but the firm can't make a profit because of the extra costs. In other words, there isn't a financial return on the money spent to improve the quality of the implementation effort. Remember that getting everyone to work together to satisfy customers should be the route to profits. If the firm is spending money on quality efforts that don't really provide the customer with superior value—that cost more to provide than customers will ultimately be willing to pay—then someone has lost sight of the marketing concept.

As this suggests, TQM is not a cure-all. Further, it is not the only method for improving marketing implementation, but it is an important approach. Some firms don't yet use TQM; they may be missing an opportunity. Other firms apply some quality methods but act like they are the private property of a handful of "quality specialists" who want to control things. That's not good either. Everyone must own a TQM effort and keep a balanced view of how it improves customer satisfaction and what it costs.

As more marketing managers see the benefits of TQM, it will become a more important part of marketing thinking, especially marketing implementation. And when managers really understand implementation, they can do a better job of developing strategies and plans in the first place.[9]

## The Tools of Control—Providing Feedback on Plans and Implementation

We've said that computers and other types of information technology are speeding up the flow of feedback and prompting a revolution by allowing managers to improve plans and implementation quickly and continuously. This is especially true when plans involve the use of e-commerce (see Internet Insite 19-1). On the other hand, the basic questions that a modern marketing manager wants to answer to make better implementation and strategy decisions are pretty similar to what they've always been.

A good manager wants to know which products' sales are highest and why, which products are profitable, what is selling where, and how much the marketing process is costing. Managers need to know what's happening, in detail, to improve the bottom line.

Unfortunately, traditional accounting reports are usually too general to be much help in answering these questions. A company may be showing a profit, while 80 percent of its business comes from only 20 percent of its products—or customers.

## Internet Insite 19–1

### METRICS FOR JUDGING E-PERFORMANCE

Online marketers need to evaluate the impact of their marketing efforts. Marketers like to measure online performance for a variety of reasons, such as:

- To know if the targeted audience is responding to the ad campaign
- To know if a site redesign is attracting new visitors or repeat visits
- To know if a television or print campaign is driving traffic to the website
- To develop profiles of customers for use in segmenting the market
- To compute return on investment (ROI)
- To gauge customer satisfaction and retention

Luckily, there is no shortage of metrics for evaluating performance. The Internet is considered the most measurable of all media. Television and radio depend on sampling techniques to estimate the audience for a show; on the Web, it is possible to compute the audience size based on actual visitors without resorting to sampling.

#### Ad-Centric Metrics

Advertising metrics are typically provided by advertising networks, which are companies that manage the ad campaign (see Internet Insite 15-1 for an explanation of advertising networks). They can track the number of times an ad on a Web page is downloaded, the number of clicks on the ad, and so on. A typical Internet advertising campaign may involve purchase of ad space on a number of websites. The ad is downloaded each time from the advertising network's server, which facilitates tracking. Advertising networks like DoubleClick (www.doubleclick.com) report the results to advertisers to give them an indication of the effectiveness of the ad campaign. Typical ad-centric measures include:

- Ad impressions—The number of times an ad is requested. For instance, if the main page on Yahoo! carries an ad for Dell, each time the page is downloaded the Dell ad will be requested from the advertising network's server.
- Click-throughs—A click-through is the measurement of the user-initiated action of clicking on an ad element, causing a re-direct to another Web location.

Using tracking programs (see the NetTracker exhibit below), marketers can see if online ads placed on different sites are driving traffic to the online store. They can also find out what percentage of such visitors actually bought the advertised product.

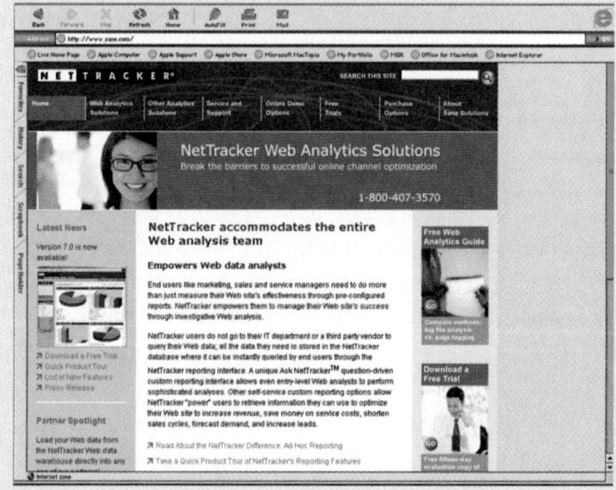


#### Site-Centric Metrics

Site-centric metrics can be developed by analyzing log files that record the activity on the Web server (such as number and names of pages downloaded, number of requests made for a page, identity of computers requesting the pages, and so on). Log files can contain data on click-throughs, page views, and unique visitors.[10] Log files contain information on every file that was requested from a Web server.[11] They include complete data on all visits to a site, which means that the metrics produced are accurate indicators of activity and are not estimates. Typical site-centric measures include:

- Page views—The number of times a Web page is requested from the server
- Entry and exit pages—The page on the website where the browser entered the site and exited the site
- Time spent on the site or on a page
- Number of pages viewed (or requested) per visit
- Top pages (in terms of page views)
- Time of visit

By studying these metrics, marketers can refine the website. Popular pages can be designed to download fast. Efforts can be made to increase the time spent on the site.

**User-Centric Metrics**

User-centric measures allow marketers to understand their current and potential customers. Customer preferences can be studied. Customer profiles can be developed, leading to more targeted marketing efforts. Typical user-centric metrics include:

- Number of visitors
- Number of unique visitors
- Number of repeat visitors and repeat rate
- Average amount of time spent on the site per visit
- Configuration of user's computer (browser type, operating system, etc.)
- User's location
- Profile of frequent visitors
- Buyer conversion rate: the number of browsing consumers who became paying customers.

The time spent on a page (say, a page featuring a particular product) can be an indication of the interest level in that product. If a person comes back again and again to look at a page, that could be seen as strong interest. Now the marketer should consider ways in which the interest could be converted to action or purchase. Certainly, some of the data from log files can offer insights into consumer motivation and interest.[12]

The user-centric measures captured through site logs do not indicate the demographics of the user (age, gender, and income) or their lifestyle. Marketers must resort to other means for capturing such data. Asking users to register on the site (for something in return) or allowing users to create a customized page (which can be accessed by using a username/password), the site can now obtain more information about the visitors to the site. Matching real and accurate demographic data with site-visit statistics is challenging.

Cookie files (small text files placed by a Web server on the user's computer for future identification purposes) can also help in identifying repeat visitors as well as user preferences. Chapters.Indigo.ca uses cookies and explains their use in its section on privacy.

Internet metrics are not perfect. The accuracy of the data must be checked carefully before drawing conclusions. Just because a page is requested, it does not mean that the ad in the page was viewed. If a visitor is coming back to the same page several times during a day, the page may be downloaded from the computer's cache (or memory) without the Web server being notified. This means the number of visits can be underestimated. Discussion of other technical flaws in the metrics is beyond scope of our discussion.

Compared to mass media such as television and print, the Internet offers greater measurability. As a retail channel, transactions conducted on a site can be monitored, aggregated, and analyzed for patterns. Each time a product is bought online, the vendor gathers credit card and address information. In bricks-and-mortar stores, cash transactions cannot be traced back to individual customers.

One cannot assume that just because so many metrics are available all firms are using such data effectively. Log files and cookie files can quickly add up to a huge mass of data. Data-mining techniques are employed to analyze and make sense out of these data. Many marketers do not understand and do not invest resources to benefit from the data.

The Internet does offer great measurability, but it also comes with a cost. Consumer privacy is often threatened by such data capture at every stage. Just as Chapters.Indigo.ca does, firms must post their policies clearly in simple language that consumers can understand. More importantly, they need to abide by their own policies.

Here are some questions to ponder: Canadian consumers are quite concerned about privacy on the Internet. How can marketers online balance the need to understand their customers with privacy concerns? What will you do to educate marketers about the nature and importance of log file data?

Go to: www.mcgrawhill.ca/college/wong
to apply this Insite in an exciting Internet exercise.

The other 80 percent may be unprofitable, but without special analyses managers won't know it. This 80/20 relationship is fairly common, and is often referred to as the *80/20 rule*.

What happened with Ben & Jerry's Peace Pops premium ice-cream bars is a good example. The initial plan called for intensive distribution of boxes of Peace Pops in supermarket freezer cases—to compete with competitors like Dove Bar and Häagen-Dazs. But after six months total sales were 50 percent lower than expected. However, detailed sales analysis by package and channel revealed a bright spot: individual Peace Pops were selling very well in local delis. After further work to better understand the reasons for this focused success, Ben & Jerry's marketing people realized that most of their target customers saw the premium-price Peace Pop as an impulse product rather than as a staple they were willing to heap into a shopping cart. So Ben & Jerry's revised the strategy to better reach impulse buyers at convenience stores. Within a year, the revised strategy worked. Sales increased 60 percent, and sales analysis showed that 70 percent of the sales were at convenience stores. A few years later, however, sales analysis showed that sales were slowly trending down. Rather than wait for a painful death of the product, they replaced it with a new item.[13]

As the Ben & Jerry's example shows, it *is* possible for marketing managers to get detailed information about how marketing plans are working—but only if they ask for and help develop the necessary data. In this section, we'll discuss the kinds of information that can be available and how to use it. The techniques are not really complicated. They basically require only simple arithmetic—and of course computers quickly and easily take care of that when a large volume of sorting, adding, and subtracting is required.



## Sales Analysis Shows What's Happening

**sales analysis**
A detailed breakdown of a company's sales records

**Sales analysis**—a detailed breakdown of a company's sales records—can be very informative. Detailed data can keep marketing executives in touch with what's happening in the market. In addition, routine sales analyses prepared each week or month may show trends and allow managers to check their hypotheses and assumptions.[14]

Some managers resist sales analysis, or any analysis for that matter, because they don't appreciate how valuable it can be. One top executive in a large firm made no attempt to analyze company sales, even by geographic area. When asked why, the executive replied: "Why should we? We're making money!"

But today's profit is no guarantee that you'll make money tomorrow. In fact, ignoring sales analysis can lead not only to poor sales forecasting but also to poor decisions in general. One manufacturer did much national advertising on the assumption that the firm was selling all over the country. But a simple sales analysis showed that most present customers were located within a 100-kilometre radius of the factory! In other words, the firm didn't know who and where its customers were—and it wasted most of the money it spent on national advertising.

Today, with computer networks and organized marketing information systems, effective sales analysis can be done easily and at a relatively small cost—if marketing managers decide they want it done. In fact, the desired information can be obtained as a by-product of basic billing and accounts-receivable procedures. The manager simply must make sure the company captures identifying information on important dimensions such as territory, sales reps, product models, customers, and so forth. Then computers can easily run sales analyses and simple trend projections.

**Frequently used sales breakdowns** There is no one best way to analyze sales data. Several breakdowns may be useful—depending on the nature of the company and product and what dimensions are relevant. Typical breakdowns include:

Information Resources, Inc. developed its DataServer Analyzer software to perform sales analysis and produce graphs that make it easy to see patterns that might otherwise be hidden in a table of numbers.

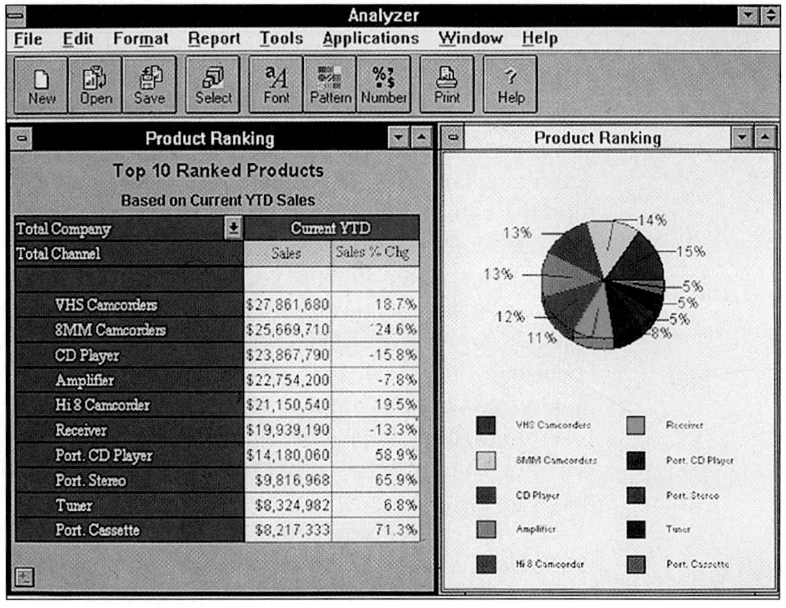


1. Geographic region—country, province, county, city, sales rep's territory.
2. Product, package size, grade, colour.
3. Customer size.
4. Customer type or class of trade.
5. Price or discount class.
6. Method of sale—online, telephone, or sales rep.
7. Financial arrangement—cash or charge.
8. Size of order.
9. Commission class.

While some sales analysis is better than none—or better than getting data too late for action—sales breakdowns that are too detailed can drown a manager in reports. Computers can spew out data faster than any manager can read. So, wise managers ask for only those breakdowns that will help them make decisions. Further, they use software that generates graphs and figures to make it easy to see patterns that otherwise might be hidden while scrolling through online tables with a browser. But to avoid coping with mountains of data—much of which may be irrelevant—most managers move on to *performance analysis*.

## Performance Analysis Looks for Differences

**performance analysis** Analysis that looks for exceptions or variations from planned performance

**Performance analysis** looks for exceptions or variations from planned performance. In simple sales analysis, the figures are merely listed or graphed—they aren't compared against standards. In performance analysis, managers make comparisons. They might compare one territory against another, against the same territory's performance last year, or against expected performance.

The purpose of performance analysis is to improve operations. The salesperson, territory, or other factors showing poor performance can be identified and singled out for detailed analysis and corrective action. Or, outstanding performances can be analyzed to see if the successes can be explained and made the general rule.

Performance analysis doesn't have to be limited to sales. Other data can be analyzed too. These data may include inventory required, number of calls made, number of orders, or the cost of various tasks.

A performance analysis can be quite revealing, as shown in the following example.

**An illustration** A manufacturer of business products sells to wholesalers through five sales reps, each serving a separate territory. Total net sales for the year amount to $2,386,000. Salesforce compensation and expenses come to $198,000, yielding a direct-selling expense ratio of 8.3 percent—that is, $198,000 ÷ $2,386,000 × 100.

This information—taken from a profit and loss statement—is interesting, but it doesn't explain what's happening from one territory to another. To get a clearer picture, the manager compares the sales results with other data from each territory (see Exhibits 19-4 and 19-5). Keep in mind that exhibits like these and others that follow in this chapter are now very easy to generate. Common computer packages like Microsoft Office make it easy to apply the ideas discussed here. Larger companies make such analysis available on an intranet so the manager can sort out whatever is needed.

The reps in sales areas D and E aren't doing well. Sales are low and marketing costs are high. Perhaps more aggressive sales reps could do a better job, but the number of customers suggests that sales potential might be low. Perhaps the whole plan needs revision.

The figures themselves, of course, don't provide the answers. But they do reveal the areas that need improvement. This is the main value of performance analysis. It's up to management to find the remedy, either by revising or changing the marketing plan.

## Performance Indexes Simplify Human Analysis

With a straight performance analysis, the marketing manager can evaluate the variations among sales reps to try to explain the "why." But this takes time. And poor performances are sometimes due to problems that bare sales figures don't reveal. Some uncontrollable factors in a particular territory—tougher competitors or inef-

Exhibit 19-4 Comparative performance of sales reps.

| Sales Area | Total Calls | Total Orders | Order–Call Ratio | Sales by Sales Rep | Average Sales-Rep Order | Total Customers |
|---|---|---|---|---|---|---|
| A | 1,900 | 1,140 | 60.0% | $ 912,000 | $800 | 195 |
| B | 1,500 | 1,000 | 66.7 | 720,000 | 720 | 160 |
| C | 1,400 | 700 | 50.0 | 560,000 | 800 | 140 |
| D | 1,030 | 279 | 27.1 | 132,000 | 478 | 60 |
| E | 820 | 165 | 20.1 | 62,000 | 374 | 50 |
| Total | 6,650 | 3,284 | 49.3% | $2,386,000 | $634 | 605 |

Exhibit 19-5 Comparative cost of sales reps.

| Sales Area | Annual Compensation | Expense Payments | Total Sales Rep Cost | Sales Produced | Cost–Sales Ratio |
|---|---|---|---|---|---|
| A | $ 22,800 | $11,200 | $ 34,000 | $ 912,000 | 3.7% |
| B | 21,600 | 14,400 | 36,000 | 720,000 | 5.0 |
| C | 20,400 | 11,600 | 32,000 | 560,000 | 5.7 |
| D | 19,200 | 24,800 | 44,000 | 132,000 | 33.3 |
| E | 20,000 | 32,000 | 52,000 | 62,000 | 83.8 |
| Total | $104,000 | $94,000 | $198,000 | $2,386,000 | 8.3% |

fective intermediaries—may lower the sales potential. Or, a territory just may not have much potential.

To get a better check on performance effectiveness, the marketing manager compares what did happen with what ought to have happened. This involves the use of performance indexes.

**Performance indexes** When a manager sets standards—that is, quantitative measures of what ought to happen—it's relatively simple to compute a **performance index**—a number, like a baseball batting average, that shows the relation of one value to another.

performance index
A number that shows the relation of one value to another

Baseball batting averages are computed by dividing the actual number of hits by the number of times at bat (the possible number of times the batter could have had a hit) and then multiplying the result by 100 to get rid of decimal points. A sales performance index is computed the same way—by dividing actual sales by expected sales for the area (or sales rep, product, etc.) and then multiplying by 100. If a sales rep is batting 82 percent, the index is 82.

The computation and use of a performance index is shown in the following example. Exhibit 19-6 breaks down Canada's population by regions as a percentage of the total population. The regions are the Atlantic provinces; Quebec; Ontario; the Prairies; and British Columbia, the Yukon, and the Northwest Territories. If we assume population is an effective measure of sales potential, then we would expect the distribution of the company's sales to reflect the distribution of the population. Thus, we could expect 7.8 percent of sales to come from the Atlantic provinces, 24.5 percent from Quebec, and so on.

Let's assume that a firm with $1 million in sales now wants to evaluate performance in each region. Column 2 shows the actual sales of $1 million broken down in proportion to the population in the five regions. This is what sales should have been if population were a good measure of future performance. Column 3 in Exhibit 19-6 shows the actual sales for the year for each region. Column 4 shows measures of performance (performance indexes): column 3 divided by column 2 × 100.

As you can see, the B.C., Yukon, and N.W.T. region isn't doing as well as expected. It has 13.3 percent of the total population, and expected sales (based on population) are $133,000. Actual sales, however, are only $105,000. This means that this region's performance index is only 79, calculated as (105,000 ÷ 133,000) × 100, because actual sales are much lower than expected on the basis of population. If population is a good basis for measuring expected sales (an important if), poor sales performance should be analyzed further. Perhaps sales reps in the B.C., Yukon, and N.W.T. region aren't working as hard as they should be. Perhaps pro-



Exhibit 19-6 Development of a measure of sales performance by region.

| Regions | (1) Population as percentage of Canada—1997 | (2) Expected distribution of sales based on population | (3) Actual sales | (4) Performance index |
|---|---|---|---|---|
| Atlantic | 7.8% | 78,000 | 75,000 | 96 |
| Quebec | 24.5 | 245,000 | 250,000 | 102 |
| Ontario | 37.8 | 378,000 | 390,000 | 103 |
| Prairies | 16.6 | 166,000 | 180,000 | 108 |
| British Columbia, Yukon, and N.W.T. | 13.3 | 133,000 | 105,000 | 79 |
| Total | 100% | $1,000,000 | $1,000,000 | |

motion there isn't as effective as it is elsewhere. Or competitive products may have entered the market. Whatever the cause, it's clear that performance analysis doesn't solve problems—it only points out potential problems.

**Using a series of performance analyses may find the real problem** Performance analysis helps a marketing manager see if the firm's marketing plans are working properly. If they aren't, it can lead to solutions to the problems. But this may require a series of performance analyses, as the following example shows. To get a feel for how performance analysis can be part of a problem-solving process, follow this example carefully, one exhibit at a time. Try to anticipate the marketing manager's decision.

***The case of Stereo, Inc.*** Stereo's sales manager found that sales for the Ontario region were $130,000 below the quota of $14,500,000 (that is, actual sales were $14,370,000) for the January to June period. The quota was based on sales forecasts for the various types of stereo equipment that the company sells. Specifically, the quota was based on forecasts for each product type in each store in each sales rep's territory.

Pam Dexter, the sales manager, felt that this difference was not too large (1.52 percent) and was inclined to forget the matter, especially since forecasts are usually in error to some extent. But she thought about e-mailing a letter aimed at stimulating sales effort to all sales reps and district supervisors in the region.

Exhibit 19-7 shows the overall story of what is happening to Stereo's sales in Ontario. What do you think the manager should do?

The Hamilton district had the poorest performance, but it wasn't too bad. Before sending a "let's get with it" letter to Hamilton and then relaxing, the sales manager decided to analyze the performance of the four sales reps in the Hamilton district. Exhibit 19-8 breaks down Hamilton's figures by sales rep. What conclusion or action do you suggest now?

Since Ted Smith previously had been top sales rep, the sales manager wondered if Smith was having trouble with some of his larger customers. Before making a drastic move, she obtained an analysis of Smith's sales to the five largest customers (see Exhibit 19-9). What action could the sales manager take now? Should Smith be fired?

Smith's sales in all the large stores were down significantly, although his sales in many small stores were holding up well. Smith's problem seemed to be general. Per-



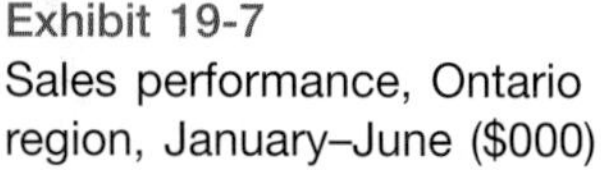
Exhibit 19-7
Sales performance, Ontario region, January–June ($000)

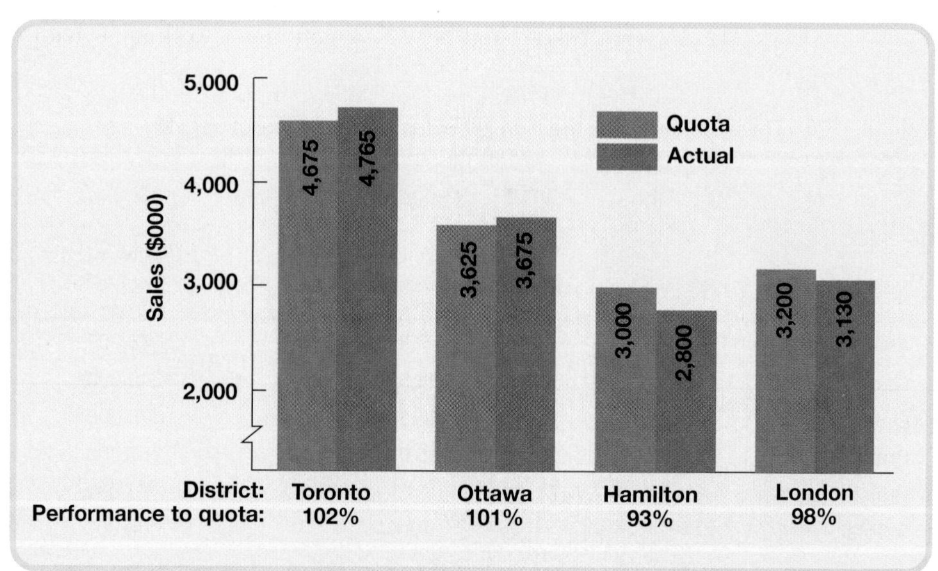

Exhibit 19-8
Sales performance, Hamilton district, January–June ($000)

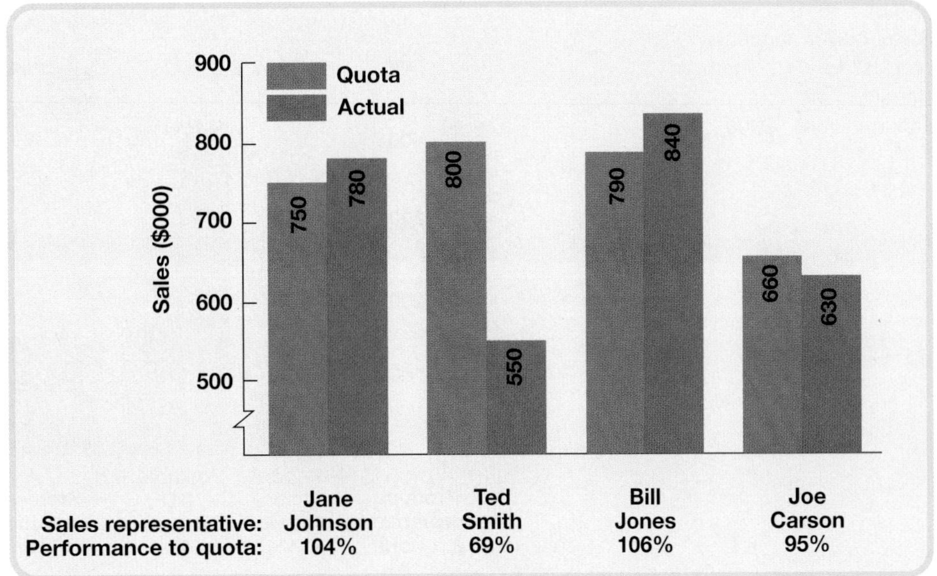


Exhibit 19-9
Sales performance, selected stores of Ted Smith, in Hamilton District, January–June ($000).

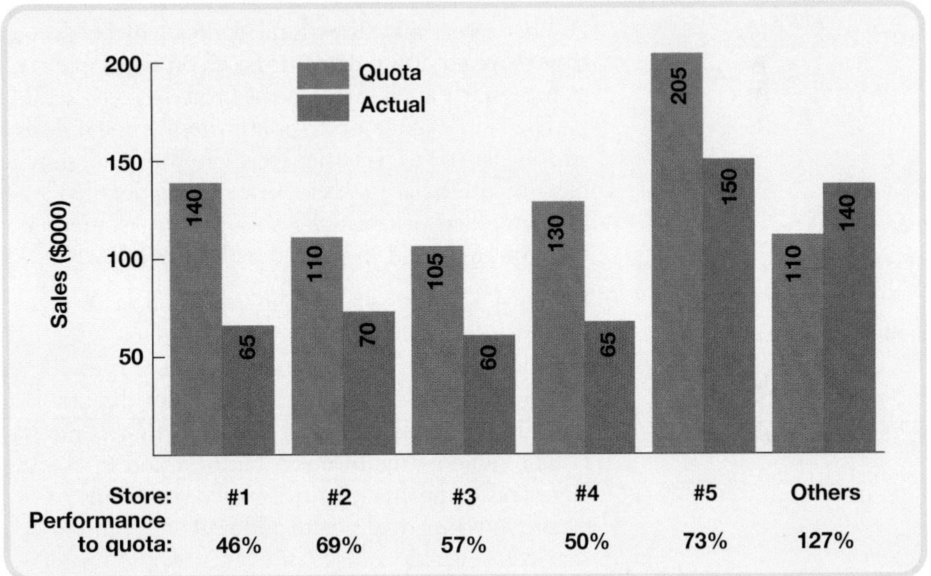




haps he just wasn't working very hard. Before calling him, the sales manager decided to look at Smith's sales of the four major products, as Exhibit 19-10 shows. What action is indicated now?

Smith is having real trouble with portable CD players. Is the problem Smith or the players?

Further analysis by product for the entire region showed that everyone in Ontario was having trouble with portable CD players because a regional competitor was cutting prices. But higher sales on other products had hidden this fact. Since portable CD player sales had been doing fine nationally, the problem was only now showing up. You can see that this is the major problem.

Since overall company sales were going fairly well, many sales managers wouldn't have bothered with this analysis. They might merely have traced the problem to Smith. And without detailed sales records and performance analysis, the natural human reaction for Smith would have been to blame business conditions or aggressive competition, or make some other handy excuse.

Exhibit 19-10
Sales performance, by product for Ted Smith, in Hamilton District, January–June ($000).

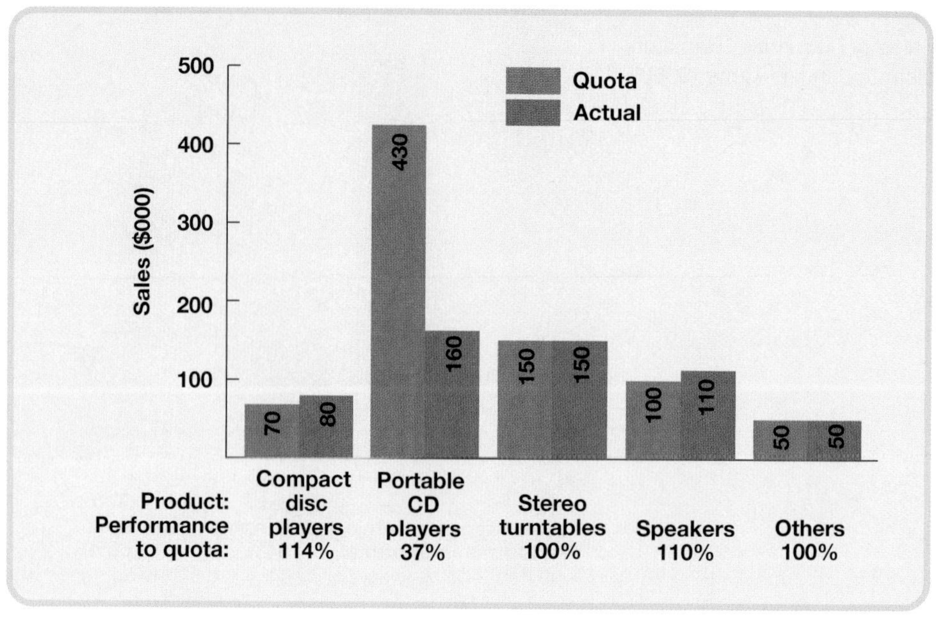


This case shows that total figures can be deceiving. Marketing managers need facts to avoid rash judgments based on incomplete information. Some students want to fire Smith after they see the store-by-store data (Exhibit 19-9).

The home office or computer network should have the records to isolate problem areas—managers then rely on the field staff for explanations and help with locating the exact problem. Continuing detailed analysis usually gives better insights into problems, as this case shows. With computers, managers can obtain information routinely and in great detail, *provided they ask for it.*



**iceberg principle**
The idea that much good information is hidden in summary data

**Beware of "icebergs"** One of the most interesting conclusions from the Stereo illustration is the **iceberg principle**—much good information is hidden in summary data. Icebergs show only about 10 percent of their mass above water level. The other 90 percent is below water level, and not directly below, either. The submerged portion almost seems to search out ships that come too near.

The same is true of much business and marketing data. Since total sales may be large and company activities varied, problems in one area may hide below the surface. Everything looks calm and peaceful. But closer analysis may reveal jagged edges that can severely damage or even sink the business. The 90:10 ratio—or the 80/20 rule we mentioned earlier—must not be ignored. Averaging and summarizing data are helpful, but be sure summaries don't hide more than they reveal.

## Marketing Cost Analysis—Controlling Costs Too

So far we have emphasized sales analysis. But sales come at a cost. And costs can and should be analyzed and controlled too. You can see why in the case of Watanake Packaging, Ltd. (WPL). WPL developed a new strategy to target the packaging needs of producers of high-tech electronic equipment. WPL designed unique Styrofoam inserts to protect electronic equipment during shipping. It assigned order getters to develop new accounts and recruited agent intermediaries to develop overseas markets. The whole marketing mix was well received—and the firm's skimming price led to good profits. But over time competing suppliers entered the market. When marketing managers at WPL analyzed costs, they realized their once-successful strategy was slipping. Personal-selling expense as a percentage of sales had doubled because it took longer to find and sell new accounts. It was costly to design special products for the many customers who purchased only small quantities. Profit margins were falling too because of increased price competition. In contrast, the analysis showed that online sales of ordinary cardboard shipping boxes for agricultural products were very profitable. So WPL stopped calling on small electronics firms and developed a new plan to improve its website and build the firm's share of the less glamorous, but more profitable, cardboard-box business.

Detailed cost analysis is very useful in understanding production costs—but much less is done with marketing cost analysis.[15] One reason is that many accountants show little interest in their firm's marketing process—or they don't understand the different marketing activities. They just treat marketing as overhead and forget about it. The problems with that approach are beyond the scope of this text. For now, however, you should see that careful analysis of most marketing costs shows that the money is spent for a specific purpose—for example, to develop or promote a particular product or to serve particular customers.

Let's reconsider Exhibit 19-5 from this perspective. It shows that the company's spending on sales compensation and sales expenses varies by salesperson and market area. By breaking out and comparing the costs of different sales reps, the marketing manager has a much better idea of what it is costing to implement the strategy in each sales area. In this example, it's clear not only that the sales reps in sales areas D and especially E are falling short in sales, but also that their costs are high relative to other reps who are getting more results. The table shows that the difference isn't due to annual compensation; that's lower. Rather, these reps have expenses that are two or three times the average. The smaller number of total customers in these sales areas (Exhibit 19-4) might explain the lower levels of sales, but it probably doesn't explain the higher expenses. Perhaps the customers are more spread out and require more travel to reach. Here again, the cost analysis doesn't explain *why* the results are as they are—but it does direct the manager's attention to a specific area that needs improvement. A more detailed breakdown of costs may help pinpoint the specific cause.

**Allocating marketing costs** Because marketing costs have a purpose, it usually makes sense to allocate costs to specific market segments, or customers, or to specific products. In some situations, companies allocate costs directly to the various geographical market segments they serve. This may let managers directly analyze the profitability of the firm's target markets. In other cases, companies allocate costs to specific customers or specific products and then add these costs for market segments depending on how much of which products each customer buys.

So far we've discussed general principles. But allocating costs is tricky. Some costs are likely to be fixed for the near future, regardless of what decision is made. And some costs are likely to be common to several products or customers, making allocation difficult.

Two basic approaches to handling this allocating problem are possible—the full-cost approach, and the contribution-margin approach.

**full-cost approach**
A marketing approach where all costs are allocated to products, customers, or other categories

***Full-cost approach*** In the **full-cost approach**, all costs are allocated to products, customers, or other categories. Even fixed costs and common costs are allocated in some way. Because all costs are allocated, we can subtract costs from sales and find the profitability of various customers, products, and so on. This is of interest to some managers.

The full-cost approach requires that difficult-to-allocate costs be split on some basis. Here the managers assume that the work done for those costs is equally beneficial to customers, to products, or to whatever group they are allocated. Sometimes this allocation is done mechanically. But often logic can support the allocation—if we accept the idea that marketing costs are incurred for a purpose. For example, advertising costs not directly related to specific customers or products might be allocated to *all* customers based on their purchases, on the theory that advertising helps bring in the sales.

**contribution-margin approach**
A marketing approach where all costs are not allocated in *all* situations

**Contribution-margin approach** When we use the **contribution-margin approach**, all costs are not allocated in all situations. Why?

When we compare various alternatives, it may be more meaningful to consider only the costs directly related to specific alternatives. Variable costs are relevant here.

The contribution-margin approach focuses attention on variable costs rather than on total costs. Total costs may include some fixed costs that do not change in the short run and can safely be ignored or some common costs that are more difficult to allocate.[16]

**Contrasting full-cost and contribution-margin approaches—An example** The difference between the full-cost approach and the contribution-margin approach is important. The two approaches may suggest different decisions, as we'll see in the following example.

***Full-cost example*** Exhibit 19-11 shows a profit and loss statement, using the full-cost approach, for a department store with three operating departments. (These could be market segments or customers or products.)

The administrative expenses, which are the only fixed costs in this case, have been allocated to departments based on the sales volume of each department. This is a typical method of allocation. In this case, some managers argued that Department 1 was clearly unprofitable and should be eliminated because it showed a net loss of $500. Were they right?

To find out, see Exhibit 19-12, which shows what would happen if Department 1 were eliminated.

Several facts become clear right away. The overall profit of the store would be reduced if Department 1 were dropped. Fixed costs of $3,000, now being charged to Department 1, would have to be allocated to the other departments. This would reduce net profit by $2,500, since Department 1 previously covered $2,500 of the

**Exhibit 19-11** Profit and loss statement by department.

| | Totals | Dept. 1 | Dept. 2 | Dept. 3 |
|---|---|---|---|---|
| Sales | $100,000 | $50,000 | $30,000 | $20,000 |
| Cost of sales | 80,000 | 45,000 | 25,000 | 10,000 |
| Gross margin | 20,000 | 5,000 | 5,000 | 10,000 |
| Other expenses: | | | | |
| Selling expenses | 5,000 | 2,500 | 1,500 | 1,000 |
| Administrative expenses | 6,000 | 3,000 | 1,800 | 1,200 |
| Total other expenses | 11,000 | 5,500 | 3,300 | 2,200 |
| Net profit or (loss) | $ 9,000 | $ (500) | $ 1,700 | $ 7,800 |

**Exhibit 19-12** Profit and loss statement by department if Department 1 were eliminated.

| | Totals | Dept. 2 | Dept. 3 |
|---|---|---|---|
| Sales | $50,000 | $30,000 | $20,000 |
| Cost of sales | 35,000 | 25,000 | 10,000 |
| Gross margin | 15,000 | 5,000 | 10,000 |
| Other expenses: | | | |
| Selling expenses | 2,500 | 1,500 | 1,000 |
| Administrative expenses | 6,000 | 3,600 | 2,400 |
| Total other expenses | 8,500 | 5,100 | 3,400 |
| Net profit or (loss) | $ 6,500 | $ (100) | $ 6,600 |

$3,000 in fixed costs. Such shifting of costs would then make Department 2 look unprofitable!

**Contribution-margin example** Exhibit 19-13 shows a contribution-margin income statement for the same department store. Note that each department has a positive contribution margin. Here the Department 1 contribution of $2,500 stands out better. This actually is the amount that would be lost if Department 1 were dropped. (Our simple example assumes that the fixed administrative expenses are *truly* fixed—that none of them would be eliminated if this department were dropped.)

A contribution-margin income statement shows the contribution of each department more clearly, including its contribution to both fixed costs and profit. As long as a department has some contribution margin, and as long as there is no better use for the resources it uses, the department should be retained.

**Comparing the two answers** Using the full-cost approach often leads to arguments within a company. Any method of allocation can make some products or customers appear less profitable.

For example, it's logical to assign all common advertising costs to customers based on their purchases. But this approach can be criticized on the grounds that it may make large-volume customers appear less profitable than they really are—especially if the marketing mix aimed at the larger customers emphasizes price more than advertising.

Those in the company who want the smaller customers to look more profitable usually argue *for* this allocation method on the grounds that general advertising helps build good customers because it affects the overall image of the company and its products.

Arguments over allocation methods can be serious. The method used may reflect on the performance of various managers—and it may affect their salaries and bonuses. Product managers, for example, are especially interested in how the various fixed and common costs are allocated to their products. Each, in turn, might like to have costs shifted to others' products.

Arbitrary allocation of costs also may have a direct impact on sales reps' morale. If they see their variable costs loaded with additional common or fixed costs over which they have no control, they may wonder what's the use.

To avoid these problems, firms often use the contribution-margin approach. It's especially useful for evaluating alternatives and for showing operating managers and salespeople how they're doing. The contribution-margin approach shows what they've actually contributed to covering general overhead and profit.

Top management, on the other hand, often finds full-cost analysis more useful. In the long run, some products, departments, or customers must pay for the fixed costs. Full-cost analysis has its place too.



Exhibit 19-13 Contribution-margin statement by departments.

| | Totals | Dept. 1 | Dept. 2 | Dept. 3 |
|---|---|---|---|---|
| Sales | $100,000 | $50,000 | $30,000 | $20,000 |
| Variable costs: | | | | |
| Cost of sales | 80,000 | 45,000 | 25,000 | 10,000 |
| Selling expenses | 5,000 | 2,500 | 1,500 | 1,000 |
| Total variable costs | 85,000 | 47,500 | 26,500 | 11,000 |
| Contribution margin | 15,000 | $ 2,500 | $ 3,500 | $ 9,000 |
| Fixed costs | | | | |
| Administrative expenses | 6,000 | | | |
| Net profit | $ 9,000 | | | |

## Planning and Control Combined

We've been treating sales and cost analyses separately up to this point. But management often combines them to keep a running check on its activities—to be sure the plans are working—and to see when and where new strategies are needed.

Let's see how this works at Cindy's Fashions, a small-town apparel retailer. This firm netted $155,000 last year. Cindy Reve, the owner, expects no basic change in competition and slightly better local business conditions. So she sets this year's profit objective at $163,000—an increase of about 5 percent.

Next, she develops tentative plans to show how she can make this higher profit. She estimates the sales volumes, gross margins, and expenses—broken down by months and by departments in her store—that she would need to net $163,000.

Exhibit 19-14 is a planning and control chart Reve developed to show the contribution each department should make each month. At the bottom of Exhibit 19-14, the plan for the year is summarized. Note that space is provided to insert the actual performance and a measure of variation. So this chart can be used to do both planning and control.

Exhibit 19-14 shows that Reve is focusing on the monthly contribution to overhead and profit by each department. The purpose of monthly estimates is to get more frequent feedback and allow faster adjustment of plans. Generally, the shorter the planning and control period, the easier it is to correct problems before they become emergencies.

In this example, Reve uses a modified contribution-margin approach—some of the fixed costs can be allocated logically to particular departments. On this chart, the balance left after direct fixed and variable costs are charged to departments is called Contribution to Store. The idea is that each department will contribute to covering general store expenses—such as top-management salaries and holiday decorations—and to net profits.



Exhibit 19-14 Planning and control chart for Cindy's Fashions.

| | Contribution to Store | | | | | | | |
|---|---|---|---|---|---|---|---|---|
| | Dept. A | Dept. B | Dept. C | Dept. D* | Total | Store Expense | Operating Profit | Cumulative Operating Profit |
| **January** | | | | | | | | |
| Planned | 27,000 | 9,000 | 4,000 | −1,000 | 39,000 | 24,000 | 15,000 | 15,000 |
| Actual | | | | | | | | |
| Variation | | | | | | | | |
| **February** | | | | | | | | |
| Planned | 20,000 | 6,500 | 2,500 | −1,000 | 28,000 | 24,000 | 4,000 | 19,000 |
| Actual | | | | | | | | |
| Variation | | | | | | | | |
| **November** | | | | | | | | |
| Planned | 32,000 | 7,500 | 2,500 | 0 | 42,000 | 24,000 | 18,000 | 106,500 |
| Actual | | | | | | | | |
| Variation | | | | | | | | |
| **December** | | | | | | | | |
| Planned | 63,000 | 12,500 | 4,000 | 9,000 | 88,500 | 32,000 | 56,500 | 163,000 |
| Actual | | | | | | | | |
| Variation | | | | | | | | |
| **Total** | | | | | | | | |
| Planned | 316,000 | 70,000 | 69,000 | −4,000 | 453,000 | 288,000 | 163,000 | 163,000 |
| Actual | | | | | | | | |
| Variation | | | | | | | | |

*The objective of minus $4,000 for this department was established on the same basis as the objectives for the other departments—that is, it represents the same percentage gain over last year when Department D's loss was $4,200. Plans call for discontinuance of the department unless it shows marked improvement by the end of the year.

In Exhibit 19-14, we see that the whole operation is brought together when Reve computes the monthly operating profit. She totals the contribution from each of the four departments, then subtracts general store expenses to obtain the operating profit for each month.

As time passes, Reve can compare actual sales with what's projected. If actual sales were less than projected, corrective action could take either of two courses: improving implementation efforts or developing new, more realistic strategies.

## The Marketing Audit

The analyses we've discussed so far are designed to help a firm plan and control its operations. They can help a marketing manager do a better job. Often, however, the control process tends to look at only a few critical elements, such as sales variations by product in different territories. It misses such things as the effectiveness of present and possible marketing strategies and mixes.

The marketing manager usually is responsible for day-to-day implementing as well as planning and control and may not have the time to evaluate the effectiveness of the firm's efforts. Sometimes crises pop up in several places at the same time. Attention must focus on adjusting marketing mixes or on shifting strategies in the short run.

To make sure that the whole marketing program is evaluated regularly, not just in times of crisis, marketing specialists developed the marketing audit. A marketing audit is similar to an accounting audit or a personnel audit, which businesses have used for some time.

**marketing audit**

A systematic, critical, and unbiased review and appraisal of the basic objectives and policies of the marketing function and of the organization, methods, procedures, and people employed to implement the policies

The **marketing audit** is a systematic, critical, and unbiased review and appraisal of the basic objectives and policies of the marketing function and of the organization, methods, procedures, and people employed to implement the policies.[17]

A marketing audit requires a detailed look at the company's current marketing plans to see if they are still the best plans the firm can offer. Customers' needs and attitudes change—and competitors continually develop new and better plans. Plans more than a year or two old may be outdated or even obsolete. Sometimes marketing managers are so close to the trees that they can't see the forest. An outsider can help the firm see whether it really focuses on some unsatisfied needs and offers appropriate marketing mixes. Basically, the auditor uses our strategy planning framework. But instead of developing plans, the auditor works backward and evaluates the plans being implemented. The consultant-auditor also evaluates the quality of the effort—looking at who is doing what and how well. This means interviewing customers, competitors, channel members, and employees. A marketing audit can be a big job. But if it helps ensure that the company's strategies are on the right track and being implemented properly, it can be well worth the effort.

A marketing audit takes a big view of the business—and it evaluates the whole marketing program. It might be done by a separate department within the company, perhaps by a marketing controller. But to get both expert and objective evaluation, it's probably better to use an outside organization such as a marketing consulting firm.

Ideally, a marketing audit should not be necessary. Good managers do their best in planning, implementing, and control—and they should continually evaluate the effectiveness of the operation. In practice, however, managers often become identified with certain strategies, and pursue them blindly when other strategies might be more effective. Since an outside view can give needed perspective, marketing audits may become more common in the future.

## Chapter Summary

In this chapter, we've focused on the important role of implementation and control in satisfying customers and the firm's ongoing success. We explained how improvements in information technology are playing a critical role in revolutionizing these areas. Managers should seek new and creative ways to improve implementation, which can often give a firm a competitive advantage in building stronger relationships with customers, even in highly competitive mature markets.

We also went into some detail on how total quality management can help the firm get the type of implementation it needs—implementation that continuously improves and does a better job of meeting customers' needs and at lower cost.

A marketing program must also be controlled. Good control helps the marketing manager locate and correct weak spots and at the same time find strengths that may be applied throughout the marketing program. Control works hand in hand with planning.

Simple sales analysis just gives a picture of what happened. But when sales forecasts or other data showing expected results are brought into the analysis, we can evaluate performance—using performance indexes.

Cost analysis also can be useful. There are two basic approaches to cost analysis—full-cost and contribution-margin. Using the full-cost approach, all costs are allocated in some way. Using the contribution-margin approach, only the variable costs are allocated. Both methods have their advantages and special uses.

Ideally, the marketing manager should arrange for a constant flow of data that can be analyzed routinely, preferably by computer, to help control present plans and plan new strategies. A marketing audit can help this ongoing effort. Either a separate department within the company or an outside organization may conduct this audit.



## Key Concepts

benchmarking, p. 586
continuous improvement, p. 582
contribution-margin approach, p. 598
control, p. 575
fishbone diagram, p. 583
full-cost approach, p. 597
iceberg principle, p. 596
marketing audit, p. 601
Pareto chart, p. 582
performance analysis, p. 591
performance index, p. 593
sales analysis, p. 590
total quality management (TQM), p. 580

## Questions and Problems

1. Using any product that you routinely buy or use, give an example of how a firm could use information technology to improve its marketing implementation and do a better job of meeting your needs.

2. Should marketing managers leave it to the accountants to develop reports that the marketing manager will use to improve implementation and control? Why or why not?

3. Give an example of a firm that has a competitive advantage because of the excellent job it does with the implementation of activities that directly affect customer satisfaction. Explain why you think your example is a good one.

4. What are the major advantages of total quality management as an approach for improving implementation of marketing plans? What limitations can you think of?

5. If you were asked to recommend a firm you've dealt with as a benchmark for good customer service after the sale, what firm would you recommend? What does this firm do that other firms do not do as well?

6. Various breakdowns can be used for sales analysis depending on the nature of the company and its products. Describe a situation (one for each) where each of the following breakdowns would yield useful information. Explain why.
   a. By geographic region.
   b. By product.
   c. By customer.
   d. By size of order.
   e. By size of sales rep commission on each product or product group.

7. Distinguish between a sales analysis and a performance analysis.

8. Carefully explain what the iceberg principle should mean to the marketing manager.
9. Explain the meaning of the comparative performance and comparative cost data in Exhibits 19-4 and 19-5. Why does it appear that eliminating sales areas D and E would be profitable?
10. Most sales forecasting is subject to some error (perhaps 5 to 10 percent). Should we then expect variations in sales performance of 5 to 10 percent above or below quota? If so, how should we treat such variations in evaluating performance?
11. Why is there controversy between the advocates of the full-cost and the contribution-margin approaches to cost analysis?
12. The June profit and loss statement for the Browning Company is shown. If competitive conditions make price increases impossible and management has cut costs as much as possible, should the Browning Company stop selling to hospitals and schools? Why?

Browning Company Statement

| | Retailers | Hospitals and Schools | Total |
|---|---|---|---|
| Sales: | | | |
| 80,000 units at $0.70 | $56,000 | | $56,000 |
| 20,000 units at $0.60 | | $12,000 | 12,000 |
| Total | 56,000 | 12,000 | 68,000 |
| Cost of sales | 40,000 | 10,000 | 50,000 |
| Gross margin | 16,000 | 2,000 | 18,000 |
| Sales and administrative expenses: | | | |
| Variable | 6,000 | 1,500 | 7,500 |
| Fixed | 5,600 | 900 | 6,500 |
| Total | 11,600 | 2,400 | 14,000 |
| Net profit (loss) | $ 4,400 | $ (400) | $ 4,000 |

13. Explain why a marketing audit might be desirable, even in a well-run company. Who or what kind of organization would be best to conduct a marketing audit? Would a marketing research firm be good? Would the present CPA firms be most suitable? Why?

## Computer-Aided Problem 19

### Marketing Cost Analysis

This problem emphasizes the differences between the full-cost approach and the contribution-margin approach to marketing cost analysis.

Tapco, Inc. currently sells two products. Sales commissions and unit costs vary with the quantity of each product sold. With the full-cost approach, Tapco's administrative and advertising costs are allocated to each product based on its share of total sales dollars. Details of Tapco's costs and other data are given in the spreadsheet. The first column shows a cost analysis based on the full-cost approach. The second column shows an analysis based on the contribution-margin approach.

a. *If the number of Product A units sold were to increase by 1,000 units, what would happen to the allocated administrative expense for Product A? How would the change in sales of Product A affect the allocated administrative expense for Product B? Briefly discuss why the changes you observe might cause conflict between the product managers of the two different products.*

b. *What would happen to total profits if Tapco stopped selling Product A but continued to sell 4,000 units of Product B? What happens to total profits if the firm stops selling Product B but continues to sell 5,000 units of Product A? (Hint: To stop selling a product means that the quantity sold would be zero.)*

c. *If the firm dropped Product B and increased the price of Product A by $2.00, what quantity of Product A would it have to sell to earn a total profit as large as it was originally earning with both products? (Hint: Change values in the spreadsheet to reflect the changes the firm is considering, and then use what-if analysis to vary the quantity of Product A sold and display what happens to total profit.)*

## Suggested Cases

To view the cases, go to www.mcgrawhill.ca/college/wong.

Interested in finding out what marketing looks like in the real world? *Marketing Magazine* is just a click away on your OLC! Visit **www.mcgrawhill.ca/college/wong** today.

# Marketing "YOU INC."—Preparing a Personal Marketing Plan*

**When You Finish This Appendix, You Should**

1. Understand the process of preparing a personal marketing plan.

2. Know how to identify personal payoffs and values, establish priorities, and construct a personal mission statement.

3. Know how to develop and write specific career goals.

4. Know how to prepare a personal and industry situation (S.W.O.T.) analysis.

5. Know how to identify and evaluate alternative career strategies.

6. Know how to prepare an action plan.

*This material was prepared by Deborah Lawton of The University College of the Cariboo for *Basic Marketing*.

## "Can People Find Satisfaction and Happiness in a Job?"

This is one of the big questions both young and not so young job seekers ask. Sal Divita, in an article in *Marketing News*, answers: "Absolutely. Both are achieved when the individual's personality profile is consistent with the demands of the job."[1]

Determining consistency in job fit is not a task taken lightly and can lead to unanticipated conclusions. Take this statement from a student who recently prepared a Personal Marketing Plan as a course requirement for an Introductory Marketing class.

> This paper turned out a lot different than I had originally thought that it would have. I started out with the idea of starting life with a comfortable salary to feed my family in Canada, and after I had evaluated all of the above, I then realized that many opportunities awaited me in Australia also. I wanted to finish my Bachelors Degree here in Kamloops . . ., and then perhaps get a job with a public relations firm. By writing this paper, it has made me re-evaluate my life, and the choices I will be facing in the very immediate future.[2]



## Why a Personal Marketing Plan?

All marketing has the single purpose of helping companies and individuals address and manage change. Companies plan their marketing strategies but, unfortunately, many individuals have no plan at all. Yet nothing is more important than a plan for managing the inevitable changes that life brings.

A Personal Marketing Plan is vital if we are to harness and manage change. This textbook teaches the fundamentals of marketing: how to market goods and services and develop an effective marketing plan for a business organization. Many of the tools and techniques presented in the text have been proven to improve business profits, efficiency, and effectiveness. These principles can be adapted to market the most important product in your life: You. They are equally effective for an individual embarking on a career or a person in mid-life dealing with any inevitable job change.

In a complex world of changing technology, uncertain economic conditions, increasing competition, and information overload, change is constant. Employees no longer have the luxury of counting on the "golden handshake" after a lifetime of dedication to one company. Today, the average worker can expect to change careers at least three times. Most will work for more than six companies throughout their career.

## Understanding the Personal Marketing Planning Process

> This is the first time I have ever had to seriously delve into the uncharted waters of myself, and actually try and figure out what motivates me and what is important as well. . . . I preferred to swim happily along, oblivious to such information. I have (now) discovered . . . a great deal about my wants, needs, values and behaviour . . . Needless to say that in addition to completing a requirement of this course, I have also learned a lot about myself.[3]

### The Most Important Investment You Can Make in Yourself

Think of yourself as a business: "YOU INC." To achieve career success, you must market yourself by offering your unique selling proposition and competitive advantage to the right target employer, at the right income or price, with the right blend of tools to promote your individual skills, education, and experience.

### A Planning Framework Provides Direction and Focus

This appendix is designed to help you write a personal marketing plan for "YOU INC." Exhibit A–1 summarizes the process. It presents a framework of marketing principles and outlines a series of independent but interrelated steps to follow in developing your own personal marketing plan. The process incorporates a systematic approach to making key life and career decisions. A planned approach to developing a personal marketing strategy will help you review progress and make revisions for effective execution.

Exhibit A–1 A Personal Marketing Planning Framework

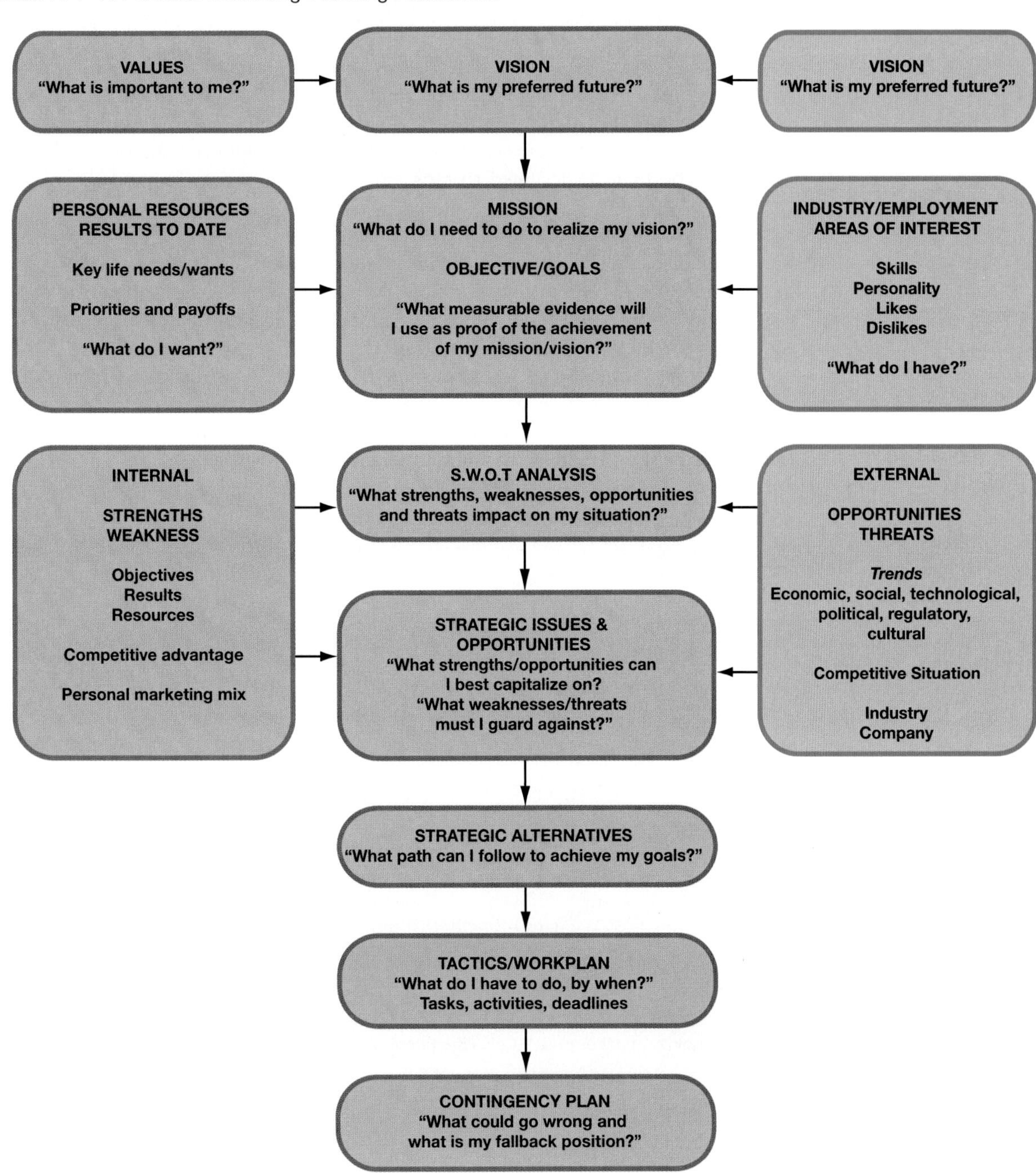

## Establishing an Overall Career Direction

To achieve a fulfilling career, we all must identify and define our own measure of success. This involves an honest self-appraisal, which includes the following:

1. Identifying your own wants, needs, values, dreams, strengths, and weaknesses.
2. Judging the "fit" of your unique skills and resources against the often uncontrollable environmental variables.
3. Establishing and keeping focused on your most critical life priorities.

### Priorities Keep Us Focused

We face many choices in life. We may naturally gravitate to one choice or another, but sometimes we need to make hard decisions. Our resources are limited. As options increase, we find it more difficult to allocate our resources. Setting priorities helps us sort out choices and keeps us focused on our most valuable payoffs.

A highly developed sense of priorities is an important planning skill and often marks the difference between an effective and an ineffective manager. A clear concept of priorities helps guard against a treadmill-like life. Exhibit A–2 illustrates a priority grid.[4] This tool helps sort out alternatives and identify the one with which to begin. The table is designed to rank ten items, but can be expanded.

### Values Underlie Our Concept of Success

*Values* are attitudes and beliefs that form the foundation of our personal ethics. They are often culturally determined, having been passed down from generation to generation. They determine our choices and actions, and ultimately, our concept of success. They influence all we say and do.

Values relate to both preferred consequences—what you want to happen—and modes of conduct—how you will behave to accomplish what you want. They influence our vision and guide our actions to realize it. To ensure career fulfilment we must be conscious of the most important values in our life, as compromising them will lead to personal tension. Awareness of our values enables us to make informed and satisfying career decisions.



**Exhibit A–2** Prioritizing Grid Worksheet

Make a list of items and number them. Start with the top line of the grid. Compare items 1 and 2 on your list. Which one is more important to you? Ask yourself, *"Of all the things I could do with my time, which would bring me the best overall payoff?"* Circle your choice, then compare the other pairs.

| | | | | | | | | |
|---|---|---|---|---|---|---|---|---|
| 1 2 | | | | | | | | |
| 1 3 | 2 3 | | | | | | | |
| 1. 4 | 2 4 | 3 4 | | | | | | |
| 1. 5 | 2 5 | 3 5 | 4 5 | | | | | |
| 1 6 | 2 6 | 3 6 | 4 6 | 5 6 | | | | |
| 1 7 | 2 7 | 3 7 | 4 7 | 5 7 | 6 7 | | | |
| 1 8 | 2 8 | 3 8 | 4 8 | 5 8 | 6 8 | 7 8 | | |
| 1 9 | 2 9 | 3 9 | 4 9 | 5 9 | 6 9 | 7 9 | 8 9 | |
| 1 10 | 2. 10 | 3 10 | 4 10 | 5 10 | 6 10 | 7 10 | 8 10 | 9 10 |

Total times each number got circled.

1__ 2__ 3__ 4__ 5__ 6__ 7__ 8__ 9__ 10__

Priority order—highest # of circles = highest priority etc.

1__ 2__ 3__ 4__ 5__ 6__ 7__ 8__ 9__ 10__

Rewrite your list beginning with the item that got the most circles. This is your prioritized list.

Note: In the case of a tie, look back to see what you circled when you compared those two numbers. This should break the tie.

SOURCE: Adapted from R.N. Bolles, *What Color is Your Parachute,* Ten Speed Press.

**Exhibit A–3** Instrumental and Terminal Values

| Instrumental/Being Values (preferred modes of conduct) | Terminal/End State Values (preferred end states) |
|---|---|
| **Personal** | **Physical** |
| Ambitious | Attractive |
| Analytical | Healthy |
| Courageous | Strong |
| Creative | Well-groomed |
| Decisive | |
| Flexible | **Security** |
| Imaginative | At peace |
| Independent | Comfortable |
| Organized | Free |
| Practical | Safe |
| Realistic | |
| Self-reliant | **Belonging** |
| Traditional | Loved, loving, intimate |
| True friendship | |
| **Interpersonal** | |
| Caring | **Self-esteem** |
| Cheerful | Accomplished |
| Compassionate | Contented |
| Courteous | Equal |
| Empathetic | Happy |
| Forgiving | Integrated |
| Helpful | Recognized |
| Honest | Self-respecting |
| Objective | Sense of accomplishment |
| Outgoing | |
| Principled | **Self-actualization** |
| Reliable | Beauty (nature and arts) |
| Reserved | Inner harmony |
| Respectful | Spiritual peace |
| Responsible | Understanding |
| Self-controlled | Wisdom |
| Sincere | |
| Sympathetic | |

For example, if you identify your core values as independence, creativity, equality, honesty, and ambition, you need to find an industry and company that reflects these values if you are to experience personal integrity. As Sal Divita says, "The value systems between employees and employers . . . must be compatible in order to form a 'perfect job.' "[5]

## Your Core Values Are Reflected in Your Dreams and Vision

Exhibit A–3 provides a framework for considering your values. To identify your core values, select the ten most important from the examples in Exhibit A–3. Add/reword any until they feel comfortable. Then rank them using the priority grid in Exhibit A–2. Write out your list. Your list should reflect your most cherished values.

Your core values are the basis of your dreams and goals. Living a life according to your personal values is critical to achieving an overall sense of well-being and fulfillment.

## Clarifying Vision—Creating a Picture of Your Preferred Future

Once you have prioritized your values, you will have a clear understanding of the beliefs and attitudes that drive your actions and behaviours. Now you need to have a clear picture or vision of your values in action.

Entrepreneurs have a vision of the company they want to create. Artists have a picture in mind of their finished product. Their respective visions guide their decisions and actions. So, too, each individual must have a vision of a personal future. Initially, the vision may be hazy and incomplete, but knowledge of personal values helps one to refine and clarify it. Visualizing your values in action will help you clarify the future you want to create for yourself.

### Vision Gives Life Meaning and Purpose

*Vision* acts as a catalyst giving life meaning and purpose. Vision keeps us from just going through the motions. It gives meaning to everyday activities. A comfortable home, a happy family, challenging work, and public recognition may be the ultimate payoffs of your vision. But to realize these, you must fashion your daily activities—going to school, completing assignments, working in a less than satisfying job—as steps designed to take you to where you want to go. When you see how your daily activities link to your vision, you will have the motivation to get through the tough and tedious steps.

What you see in life is what you get, so construct an appropriate vision of your preferred future and plan the steps to make it come true.



## Constructing a Personal Mission Statement

Businesses express their values and vision in the form of mission statements designed to guide the development of operational plans. They guide what a company will do and how they will accomplish it. Mission statements act as context for objectives, strategies, and tactics.

Every organization/person has a mission or purpose, although some may not have written down their mission statement or intentionally developed a strategy to execute their vision.

A mission statement creates boundaries on what is done. It also sets the tone for the overall direction and coordination of efforts and resources. Like businesses, individuals need a mission statement to guide what they want to be and how they will make it happen.

### Mission Statements Reflect Vision and Values

A personal mission statement expresses both your vision and your values. It suggests how you will take action on them. As Exhibit A–4 shows, a mission statement should address your values, your vision, and key markets, as well as how you will use your competitive advantage to benefit important areas of society.

Exhibit A–4 Characteristics of a Personal Mission Statement

1. It communicates your overall values and vision.
2. It expresses a picture of your preferred future—what you want to accomplish and for whom.
3. It clearly identifies the resources and skills you can provide.
4. It clearly identifies the industry/occupation you are interested in.
5. It briefly identifies your target market.

For example, a marketer's mission statement may be:

> I am an intelligent, ambitious person who takes pride in integrity, responsibility, personal growth, and lifelong learning. I will fulfill my vision and dreams by creating exceptional results for a medium- to large-sized, marketing-oriented company. I will embrace challenge and pursue excellence throughout a career in consumer goods marketing.

### Mission Statements Are Not Cast in Stone

Strategic decision making does not necessarily follow an orderly pattern. There is no one formula that can be applied in every situation. Business strategy is often formulated using a fluid process of identifying past success patterns and using them as a basis for creating new strategies.

Writing a personal mission statement may feel awkward. This feeling is normal. Companies often struggle with developing a mission statement and routinely take their senior executives "off site" for a few days to develop or reaffirm their mission.

Constructing a mission statement is not an exercise done once. People as well as businesses evolve and grow. A mission statement should be reviewed at regular intervals (once per year minimum) or whenever significant change occurs.



## Setting Goals—Making Your Vision Come True

Values and vision are the guiding principles expressed in your mission statement. Goals and objectives are the specific results needed to keep you on track to ensure that your values are preserved and that your visions are realized.

Goal setting acts as a framework for making your vision a reality. How you conceptualize your vision influences the goals you set and the strategies you implement. Goals help outline problems, clarify opportunities, and understand threats.

Goals are the practical side, the individual stepping stones of visions. A goal is a conscious decision based on logical analysis of the circumstances leading to your vision or dream. Goals give focus and direction, while vision provides purpose and energy.

### Goals Are the Practical Side of Vision

For example, your mission statement may reflect a long-term dream of self-employment. On the other hand, your goals will lay out the specific results you will achieve as personal evidence of your vision in action. These may vary from saving a specific amount of money to writing a business plan by a certain date or maintaining an A1 credit rating.

A goal must be written, as writing reflects commitment and makes the goal visible. It must have a deadline reinforcing the commitment.

## Making Goals "Smart"

Goals must be
**S**pecific
**M**easurable
**A**ttainable
**R**ealistic
**T**rue

The techniques for ensuring that goals turn into results can be summed up by the acronym SMART. For a goal to be truly actionable, it must be Specific, Measurable, Attainable, Realistic, and True. Exhibit A–5 summarizes the meaning of each letter.

To ensure that your goal is *specific*, you must state unambiguously what you want to accomplish—the results you are striving to achieve. Your goal must express results in terms of specific and concrete evidence of accomplishment. For example, many

**Exhibit A–5** Making Goals "SMART"

In order to turn a problem or opportunity into a goal, the end condition or result of solving the problem must be clearly identified.

**EVERY TIME YOU SET A GOAL, CHECK THAT IT IS "SMART."**

| | |
|---|---|
| S–SPECIFIC | **WHAT IS TO BE ACHIEVED?** Focus on specific, unambiguous, concrete key result areas or performance conditions. The goal must suggest action and leave no doubt as to its attainment. |
| M–MEASURABLE | **HOW WILL YOU MEASURE IT?** That is, know it is achieved? Put goals into numbers—how many, how big, how often, how much, when. Set specific, quantitative conditions. Set a deadline. |
| A–ACHIEVABLE | **DO YOU REALLY BELIEVE YOU CAN ACHIEVE IT?** Compared to other situations/conditions and with the resources on hand at this time. |
| R–REALISTIC | **DO YOU FEEL YOU HAVE A 60 TO 85 PERCENT CHANCE OF SUCCESS?** Can you do it during this time, with the resources you have if nothing else changes? Have you ever done this before? Is there any room for error or obstacles? What is the minimum you need to accomplish? The ideal? |
| T–TRUE | **WILL THIS UNQUESTIONABLY DELIVER A PERSONAL PAYOFF?** Does this represent an important change of routine, solution, or opportunity to you? Is it really worthwhile? Is it of value to you, to the people it will impact? How will you feel if it isn't achieved? Is it worth the time, effort, and money to reach this goal? Is there an easier way that will give the same feeling of success? |



of us want to be "better organized." This, however, is not clear or specific enough to be a goal. Furthermore, getting organized is highly subjective. To one person, being organized may mean maintaining an up-to-date personal calendar. To another, it may mean having a clean desktop and all papers filed. Thus, a goal must suggest a clear course of action and specify the results that will be used as proof of its successful completion.

Besides identifying the specific evidence of accomplishment, a goal must be *measurable*. A goal must include specific quantitative measures and deadlines—actual dates and timing. This reinforces and seals commitment.

## Attaining Goals Should Be a Challenge, But Routine

To make goals *attainable* and *realistic*, think of them in terms of the likelihood of accomplishment. What is the probability of achieving a goal if current circumstances, resources, and skills remain the same? Achieving goals should be the norm. Some might suggest setting a very challenging goal, with a low probability of success. They see this as motivation for people to reach beyond their means. But setting overly difficult goals can set up a situation of failure and disappointment. Evaluate your likelihood of success. To be attainable and realistic, while providing motivation or "stretch," goals should reflect a success probability of between 60 and 85 percent. Anything less than 60 percent courts failure, and thus can be discouraging and demotivating. On the other hand, anything above 85 percent does not have enough challenge. Such a goal is too easy to accomplish. Create a goal that stretches you to accomplish something you may not normally achieve without extra effort. If necessary, revise the goal until it reflects a challenging but realistic probability of success.

Finally, ensure that your goals are true. They must be important enough to warrant focus and unquestionably deliver a positive, personal payoff for you. Confirm that they are worth the time and effort to achieve.

## Establishing Goal Hierarchies and Time Frames

The time frame of goals can vary depending on the clarity of your long-term mission. Short-term goals are set to support longer-term visions. Daily, weekly, or monthly goals keep your everyday activities focused and on track to realizing annual or longer-term objectives. Goals are directional to keep you focused. They should be reviewed and, if necessary, revised frequently. Continually ask yourself, does this goal keep me moving in the right direction?

Goals should be viewed within the context of your mission in terms of both complexity and time. The more complex the vision and the longer the time frame, the more difficult it is to make the goal "SMART." To ensure that it is may involve constructing a goal hierarchy, often through trial and error. It is important to always keep your long-term vision in mind.

## Set Goals Using a "Top Down" or "Bottom Up" Planning Approach

You can set goals using a "top-down approach" by breaking your long-term vision into more manageable steps. Or you can use a "bottom-up approach" by executing small steps to explore your long-term dream.

For example, you may know you want to be a chartered accountant. A short-term goal of a high grade-point average in a finance course would support your longer-term vision. On the other hand, you may be unsure of what specific career you want but know that you like mathematics. In this situation, a more general goal, such as taking an accounting course, may be set as your first step. As you accomplish a sequence of goals, you will sort through your capabilities and specific interests and set more specific goals to support a longer-term vision.

## Avoiding the Pitfalls in Goal Setting

Goal setting requires precision of thought, forecasting ability, and the fortitude to make commitments. Goal execution requires discipline and a concerted effort to avoid being thrown off course. Three key principles regarding goal setting should be kept in mind:

1. ***Define and clarify your payoffs.*** Payoffs (especially internal, subjective ones) must be clearly thought through. Hasty identification of payoffs can result in a loss of interest in a goal. The motivational power of the payoff must be strong enough to maintain the activities necessary to ensure success. Clarifying payoffs requires concerted self-examination.

Exhibit A–6 Conducting a S.W.O.T. Appraisal

| Internal Appraisal | External Appraisal |
|---|---|
| **Strengths** | **Opportunities** |
| • What is my present position? | • What favourable environmental trends exist? |
| • What am I good at? | • How is my industry of choice developing? |
| • What major resources/expertise do I have? | • In what areas could I achieve success? |
| **Weaknesses** | **Threats** |
| • What is my present position? | • What unfortunate environmental trends exist? |
| • What are the major problems I face? | • How are my competitors developing? |
| • What am I poor at doing? | • Where is my performance likely to suffer? |
| • What major resources/expertise deficiencies do I have? | |

2. ***Prioritize to avoid goal conflicts.*** Sometimes two goals work against each other. For example, we often attempt to accomplish two goals simultaneously, such as:
   1. To get an "A" in a particular semester, and
   2. To earn $5,000 from part-time work during the semester.

   Unless you have above-average skills and resources, the probability of achieving both at the same time is low. That is why it is important to establish priorities and focus your goal-setting efforts on your highest priority. Be willing to compromise on your lower priorities.
3. ***Review your goals often.*** Sticking to goals is difficult. Many uncontrollable variables in the external environment can distract and throw us off track. Be aware of distractions, review your goals daily, and resolve to accomplish small steps on a regular basis.



## Conducting a Career-Oriented Situation Analysis

A *S.W.O.T. analysis* is a technique designed to identify strengths, weaknesses, opportunities, and threats and ensure that internal and external variables are consistent. Think of strengths and weaknesses in terms of internal or personal aspects, and opportunities and threats in terms of external, environmental conditions. Naturally, we have more control over the former than the latter. Exhibit A–6 outlines questions you need to ask yourself when conducting a S.W.O.T. analysis.

## Identifying External Opportunities and Threats

As with any corporate marketing plan, a thorough analysis of uncontrollable variables is necessary in order to identify opportunities and threats in the external environment. This step ensures that your vision and mission are viable. Use the framework in Exhibit A–7 as a checklist for your external analysis. Plan to conduct research as if preparing a situation analysis for a company.

### Conducting an Environmental Analysis

Research your career interests and analyze the external or environmental trends that influence your chosen career or employment area. Consider current and forecasted economic conditions. Examine legal, professional, and regulatory issues. What are the key technological, social, and cultural trends affecting your chosen area? Are there any location or mobility issues or opportunities? What external resources are available to assist you?

### Choosing an Occupation/Employment Area/Industry

Your written mission statement should give you a sense of career direction to help you identify potential industries and/or employment areas.

If you have minimal experience in the workforce, choosing an industry may be difficult. Begin by considering areas of interest. Ask yourself what kinds of jobs are available in these areas. If you have numerous areas of interest, use the priority grid to rank them. If you are considering starting your own business, you may first need to identify a market for investment sources, business advisers, and mentors. Begin with your highest-priority area, and gather information on your chosen career area.

Exhibit A–7 Conducting a Personal Marketing Plan Situation (S.W.O.T.) Analysis for YOU INC.: A Marketing Framework

External (Environmental) Analysis—Opportunities and Threats

| Environment Checklist | Industry/Target Market Checklist | Competitive Checklist |
|---|---|---|
| Economic conditions/trends | Industry size and growth | Intensity |
| Industry overview/considerations | Industry/life cycle position | Skills |
| Legal/regulatory/professional issues | Geographic scope | Strengths/weaknesses |
| Resource trends | Seasonality | Location |
| Societal & cultural issues/trends | Industry structure/segmentation | Contact modes |
| Technological trends | Employment rate/factors | Objectives |
| Economic trends | Segments, size, and accessability | Resources |
| Location/mobility trends | Target market(s) | |
| | Industries | Implications |
| Implications | Companies | Opportunities |
| Opportunities | Hiring practices | Threats |
| Threats | Decision makers, influencers, buyers, users | |
| | Needs/benefits/information wanted | |
| | Mobility/promotion issues/opportunities | |
| | | |
| | Implications | |
| | Opportunities | |
| | Threats | |

## Segmenting and Identifying Target Markets

Once you have narrowed your choice to a key industry, segment the industry and define potential target markets. For the industry and key market segments, collect data to assess market size, life cycle, growth trends, seasonality, and any other factors important to your identification of opportunities.

## Conducting a Company Analysis

Choose a target market with the best potential of employment, and then research individual companies to establish a contact list for your job search. Research employment trends, turnover, and promotion opportunities. How would you describe the climate and culture of your listed companies?

Constantly evaluate the fit of your findings against your mission statement and goals. Do not be discouraged if your research results in a false start or causes you to change direction. A trial-and-error approach is a natural part of the process. As long as you keep in mind your mission statement and values you will find yourself selecting the appropriate tools for a successful job search.

If you continue to experience positive signals, research the key decision makers. Determine the needs and the benefits they expect when employing a person with your skills and experience. Sal Divita recommends, "When competition is intense, you have to provide the prospective employer with compelling evidence and rationale supporting your claim that you're the best candidate for the position." He further describes that compelling evidence as "something that clearly and logically demonstrates that you offer the best solution to a need . . ., it's what you can do for the employer."[6]

## Assessing Competition

Research your competition. Consider graduation rates in your academic program or speciality and labour market conditions, as well as the skills, resources, strategies, strengths, and weaknesses of other people vying for the same positions. How will you differentiate yourself? As Philip Kitchen comments, "in a world of competitive job rivalry, differentiation and focus seem to be the best strategies to deploy."[7] Identify your competitive advantage and unique selling proposition.

### Summarizing Opportunities and Threats

Summarize your key findings and the implications they have for your career path. Prioritize the best opportunities and relevant threats. What overall strategic direction does your analysis suggest for the next two to five years? Product development? . . . Market development? . . . Market penetration? . . . Diversification?

## Conducting an Internal or Personal Analysis

A S.W.O.T. analysis must also address internal or personal variables. A thorough self-analysis will help develop an effective personal marketing plan for YOU INC. As Sal Divita explains, "It's entirely possible that someone will hold the right job, but be unhappy with the work. This happens when the dominant personality of the company does not mesh with that of the person."[8]

Personal success demands that we lead from strengths and minimize weaknesses. A self-analysis enables you to do this by examining past and current objectives, resources, and results. Avoid any self-deception when conducting a personal analysis.

You can organize your self-analysis into three areas:

1. What you want.
2. What you have.
3. The results you have achieved to date.

Exhibit A–8 provides a framework to assist in your self-analysis.



**Exhibit A–8** Conducting a Personal Marketing Plan Situation (S.W.O.T.) Analysis for YOU INC.: A Marketing Framework

**1. Internal (Personal) Analysis—Strengths and Weaknesses**

| Objectives Checklist | Resources Checklist | Results Checklist |
|---|---|---|
| Dreams | Personality | Milestones/life happenings |
| Values | Social style | Successes/disappointments |
| Likes/dislikes | Support network | Growth potential |
| Industries/jobs of interest | Contacts | Strategies/tactics |
| Decision criteria/priorities | Reference/peer groups | Product positioning |
| Wants/needs/goals | Financial | Product |
| Key life categories | Education | Price |
| Priorities | Assets | Place |
| | Energy level | Promotion |
| | Health | Competitive advantage |
| | Experience | Unique selling proposition (USP) |
| | Skills | Opportunities lost |
| | | Costs |
| | | Obstacles |
| | | Risks |
| | | Payoffs |
| | | Lessons learned |

Exhibit A–9 Dream List—Key Life Categories: Worksheet

Brainstorm your wants and needs for each of the categories below. Let your imagination soar. Do not edit your reactions, trust your instincts. Prioritize when completed.

| FAMILY | SOCIAL |
|---|---|
| ______ | ______ |
| ______ | ______ |
| ______ | ______ |
| ______ | ______ |
| **CAREER/WORK** | **FINANCIAL** |
| ______ | ______ |
| ______ | ______ |
| ______ | ______ |
| ______ | ______ |
| **HOME/LIVING/LOCATION** | **EDUCATIONAL** |
| ______ | ______ |
| ______ | ______ |
| ______ | ______ |
| ______ | ______ |
| **PERSONAL DEVELOPMENT/SPIRITUAL** | **PHYSICAL** |
| ______ | ______ |
| ______ | ______ |
| ______ | ______ |
| ______ | ______ |

## Assessing Objectives: "What You Want"

A clear definition of your values, a statement of mission, a review of wants and needs in all key life categories, and a clear sense of priorities will help clarify what you want. Any career decision will affect multiple areas of your life, so it is important to consider your career in the context of other areas of your life.

Exhibit A–9 presents a model for your "dream list"—eight life categories that interact with one another. Completing this exercise can help capture your wants and dreams as they relate to family, career, home, social, financial, educational, health, and personal development interests. Record your dreams and wants in each category that is relevant.

Prioritize your wants and needs from your "dream list." Confirm or adjust them based on the information you have collected regarding your potential employment area. Regularly review progress in each of the life areas to ensure that career goals support other important life goals.

## Assessing Resources: "What You Have"

What you have is your own unique personal attributes and experiences. Your "tools" for self-analysis include your prioritized values list, an unbiased assessment of your strengths and weaknesses, and information regarding your interests, likes, and dislikes. In addition, consider such factors as health and energy level as well as education and experience.

Understanding your assets and liabilities will help you prepare a personal profile indicating how you will compete in the marketplace. To identify your personal resources and limitations, develop a list of your strengths and weaknesses, skills, interests, likes, and dislikes. Many analytical tools exist to help organize a personal profile. Be ready and willing to use personality tests such as Myers-Briggs, management/leadership profiles, skills inventories, and school and employment records.

Career counsellors, friends, and relatives may contribute to your analysis. Include support networks and mentors. As with all tools, the better they are, the better the results will be.

Be tough and honest to present a realistic picture. The future is the culmination of what you do today. An honest self-appraisal will help clarify and refine your vision.

### Assessing Results: "What You Have Done"

A self-analysis involves reviewing life "happenings." Each milestone in your personal history has contributed to your present position in life. Think in terms of life successes and disappointments rather than failures. Adopt the perspective that "failure" is simply a learning experience to get you back on track. A helpful exercise follows.

Draw a line representing your life. On the appropriate spots, mark the date you were born and the current date. In the area to the left of the current date indicate key successes, disappointments, and life happenings that reflect milestones in your life and that have contributed to where you are today.

Then, in the area to the right of the current date, fill in some of the dreams and visions you have of your future. With what will you fill the remaining space in your "cup of life"? A personal lifeline will help put your life into perspective.

### Documenting "Lessons Learned"

Look at the strategies and tactics you have implemented and the results you have achieved to date. How would you describe your past activities? Have they been successful? If not, what needs to change?

Evaluate your results and your level of satisfaction with them. What lessons have you learned? In what direction do these lessons point?

When you have completed your situation analysis, you need to make sure your marketing mix reflects your career and personal priorities, will deliver high payoffs, and is consistent with the industry or employment area you have selected.

### Developing Strategies—Generating Broad Marketing Alternatives

In business, as well as in your personal life, there are many ways of allocating resources—that is, the time, energy, and money needed to accomplish goals. Brainstorm various strategies for effectively using your resources.

For example, if your goal is to earn your Chartered Accountant designation by December 2006, you must acquire certain education and experience. This suggests an overall "product development" strategy, but the method and order of accomplishing it may vary depending on your strengths and weaknesses and on the marketing mix area that is most important to plan. If your strengths lie in achieving high grades—the product area—you may select an "educational" product strategy. If, however, your key resources lie in work experience, you may focus on an "employment" place strategy, supplemented by night courses over time to fulfill the CA requirements.

When brainstorming strategies, keep your goal clearly in mind. Once you have generated a number of alternative ways to reach your goals, check to make sure that all alternatives will deliver a high, positive payoff. This will ensure equal motivation to execute each option.

## Establishing Your Personal Marketing Mix

As with any business, whether by choice or chance you are still making marketing and transaction decisions for YOU INC. In order to ensure the best match between

Exhibit A–10 Personal Marketing Mix—Strategy Decision Areas

**Product ("You Inc.")**
Vision
Mission
Values
Skills
Resources
Results
Competitive Advantage
Objectives
  Short-term
  Long-term
Strategies
Tactics
Priorities
Payoffs

**Place (Desired Location)**
Objectives
Strategies
Environment
  Work
  Living
  Leisure
Relocation
Tactics
Priorities

**Promotion (Contact Strategy)**
Objectives
  Inform
  Persuade,
  Remind
Strategies
USP
Features/Benefits
Positioning
Tactics
  Résume
  Networking
  Contact plan
  Interview plan

**Price (Income)**
Objectives
Expectations
  Short-term
  Long-term
Types of Compensation
Benefits
Constraints
Strategies
Flexibility
Tactics

your personal resources and objectives and the external environment, you need to plan and execute a personal marketing mix.

### Target Market

Your target market is an industry or employment area and those companies that you want your marketing mix to appeal to. This includes the people who have the power to hire you.

You may have identified a single, specific target market or a number of attractive segments. Thus you may develop marketing strategies to appeal to one narrow market. On the other hand, you may be considering a broader, combined market or multiple target markets. Whatever approach you choose, a clear concept of your target markets will help you determine the best ways to appeal to each one.

Exhibit A–10 shows how you might adapt the traditional "4 Ps" of marketing to reflect your personal marketing plan. For each element of the marketing mix, you will need to develop objectives, strategies, and tactics.

### Product

The product is YOU INC.: your personal goals, resources, strategies, and results. As quoted in a recent news story on personal marketing planning, Tom Peters wrote, "To be in business today, our most important job is to be head marketer for the brand called You."[9]

Write a concise and objective statement of product strategy outlining your features and benefits, key competitive advantage, and the image you want to project.

### Place

Place is your preferred working location. As with any element of the marketing mix, you need to set objectives to guide your strategy. Assess what YOU, the product, needs in terms of your work, home, and leisure environments. Identify your preferred geographic location. Include other potential influences such as company culture, preferred working environment, and mobility factors. Will you implement an extensive, selective, or exclusive distribution strategy? Do you require "intermediaries" to assist you?

### Price

Price is the income you want to receive. Again, objectives set the tone for your short- and long-term expectations. Are you profit, sales, or status quo oriented? How flexible can you be? Will you price yourself higher, or lower, or equal to the competition? What type of compensation plan is most appropriate for you? What benefits do you expect?

### Promotion

Promotion is how you communicate your benefits to the target market. Should you strive to inform, persuade, remind? Is your goal to attract attention, arouse interest, create desire, or achieve action? Which promotion area will be your priority—Mass Selling? Personal Selling?

Your promotion strategy should outline the broad "how" of creating your message and reaching your target. How will you position yourself relative to your competition? How best can you communicate your competitive advantage? How will you best reach your target audience? What blend of tactics will you use—résumés, networking, interviews, direct mail, cold calling?



## Evaluating Alternatives

The alternative you should first take action on should be the one that is the easiest to implement in terms of avoiding obstacles and minimizing costs and risks. Your text outlines a number of ways to evaluate and select the best alternative.

One quick and simple method, the *CORP method*, outlines key decision criteria and enables you to objectively evaluate each alternative.

**Costs** reflect your resources and values. Costs fall into three categories—time, money, and energy or emotional costs. Consider each alternative in terms of the level of resources needed.

**Exhibit A–11** The "CORP" Evaluation—Worksheet

| **Alternative 1** | **High** | **Medium** | **Low** |
|---|---|---|---|
| Net Cost (Time, $, Energy) | ________ | ________ | ________ |
| Key Obstacles | ________ | ________ | ________ |
| Risk Potential | ________ | ________ | ________ |
| Payoff Potential | ________ | ________ | ________ |
| **Alternative 2** | **High** | **Medium** | **Low** |
| Net Cost (Time, $, Energy) | ________ | ________ | ________ |
| Key Obstacles | ________ | ________ | ________ |
| Risk Potential | ________ | ________ | ________ |
| Payoff Potential | ________ | ________ | ________ |
| **Alternative 3** | **High** | **Medium** | **Low** |
| Net Cost (Time, $, Energy) | ________ | ________ | ________ |
| Key Obstacles | ________ | ________ | ________ |
| Risk Potential | ________ | ________ | ________ |
| Payoff Potential | ________ | ________ | ________ |

Selection: (Lowest Cost, Obstacles, Risk, Highest Payoff)

________________________________________

**Resources:** ________________________________________

Available ________________________________________

Required ________________________________________

**Obstacles** represent the barriers you are likely to encounter while implementing the strategy. These can be internal or external. For example, your strategy may require you to change a habit in order to reach your goal. Or there may be external problems, such as high local unemployment rates or strong competition, to be overcome. Often, identifying obstacles leads to the development of sub-steps that must be executed before or simultaneously with your main strategy.

**Risks** are the opportunities forgone by focusing on one particular strategy. Risk assessment makes it easier for you to consider the implications of taking an unproductive or dead-end route.

Finally, assessment of the payoffs for each option enables us to focus on the relative rewards of each strategy. For maximum motivational power, every alternative should carry a high payoff. If your first assessment does not result in a high payoff, rework the strategy until it does, or, alternatively, abandon it and replace it with a higher-payoff alternative.

### Applying CORP Criteria

Exhibit A–11 provides a framework for choosing the easiest yet highest-payoff strategy. When you apply CORP criteria to strategies, you consider both positive and negative implications. For each criterion, specify whether the expected outcome is high, medium, or low.

When first choosing outcomes, trust your instincts. An intuitive reaction results in better "truth." Often the "computer" of your mind can process complex data more efficiently than a conscious, calculated approach, so trust your initial instincts. As with any kind of screening method, both qualitative and quantitative criteria are valuable.

## Putting It All Together—Preparing an Action Plan

Action plans are the heart of accomplishing your goals and ultimately your vision. Exhibit A–12 provides a format for summarizing the necessary information into a plan of action.

### Tactics Are Specific Action Steps

Tactics are the specific and detailed steps needed to carry out your strategy. They must be clear and in chronological order. Deadlines should be set for each activity. This process helps reaffirm the appropriateness of your overall deadline by scheduling the steps needed. Your "Plan of Action" is really a series of short-term goals (daily or weekly) to keep you on track.

### Schedule Your Tactics

Consider the elements in your personal marketing mix to develop your plan of action. What do you have to do to define and access your target market? What product actions are necessary to accomplish your goals? What place, price, and promotion activities have to be coordinated to bring all the pieces together? As with any marketing mix, the individual elements must work in tandem.

Marketing Demo A–1 contains an executive summary from a personal marketing plan prepared by a student taking an introductory marketing course. It shows how one person, with a vision of becoming a marketing manager for a large retail chain, integrated the steps in the personal marketing plan process to produce a personal marketing plan.

**Exhibit A–12** Plan of Action—Worksheet

Date: ____________________

**"SMART" Goal:** (Change of Routine, Problem, or Opportunity)

______________________________________________

______________________________________________

______________________________________________

**Probability:**

Of Accomplishment with Current Resources? _____%

**Payoffs:** (Concrete & Personal)

1. ______________________________________________
2. ______________________________________________
3. ______________________________________________

**Alternatives** Must Accomplish the Goal and Deliver Payoffs

1. ______________________________________________
2. ______________________________________________
3. ______________________________________________

| Action Steps | Est. Hours | Deadline |
|---|---|---|
| | | |
| | | |
| | | |

| Key Performance Measurement | Source | Review |
|---|---|---|
| | | |

Date to Begin ____________________ Date Completed ____________________

Signed ____________________ Partner ____________________



## Staying On Track—Planning Contingencies

Before you rush off to implement your personal marketing plan, one last step in the process must be taken—the preparation of a contingency plan. This plan examines the "what ifs"—the key assumptions that underpin your career plan. Contingency planning also helps you develop broad strategies for revising your plan in the event that your assumptions do not materialize.

For example, you may have assumed that the economy would continue to strengthen and that opportunities for your chosen industry would open up. What if this assumption is incorrect? What if the economy plunges back into a recession? What is your fall-back plan? Marketing mix assumptions must also be scrutinized and backed up. You may have based your plan on passing a critical test or relocating easily to a new location. However, life circumstances change, and the more we consider and embrace potential change, the better prepared we are to adapt.

A contingency plan acknowledges that no forecast is 100 percent accurate. It prepares you to be aware of and adjust to early warning signals that things may be moving off course.

## Making It Happen

Now that your plan is researched, written, and ready to execute, take a deep breath—the fun is just beginning. Now it is time to get out there and make things happen.

In an article in *Marketing News*, Sal Divita says that "there are four major problems" facing a job searcher:[10]

1. Not knowing how and where to start.
2. Lacking in direction and focus.
3. Imagining personal barriers [and allowing them] to contribute to a low sense of self-worth.
4. Lacking confidence in managing the future.

The preparation of a personal marketing plan will go a long way toward alleviating these problems. As Mr. Divita proclaims, "Is there a perfect job for you? You bet."[11] Effective self-marketing helps you identify it. A propensity for action ensures that you will find it.

## Marketing Demo A-1

### PERSONAL MARKETING PLAN EXECUTIVE SUMMARY

The purpose of this report is to write a clear, concise plan for my career. My external analysis focused on evaluating the Canadian economic, social, and cultural climate as well as technological trends affecting the retail clothing industry. More specifically, I looked at the opportunities and threats that large retail clothing chain stores face in Canada. I chose this field as my area of career interest because of my past experience working in retail sales and my desire to continue working in this field after graduation.

My external analysis discovered a growing, but changing, retail sector due to advances in technology, a weak economic climate, and penetration of U.S. retailers into many Canadian markets. This analysis pointed to some strong opportunities for a career in the retail sector, especially with large established retailers.

I also conducted an internal analysis of my strengths and weaknesses, prioritized my values and formulated a personal mission statement in order to best judge the fit of my own personal resources with the retail clothing environment. I found my key strengths are my outgoing, "Expressive" social style and my ability to juggle part-time work and school demands while still realizing respectable grades. My weaknesses are my inconsistent organization skills and my tendency to procrastinate.

My analysis of some individual retail chains resulted in my awareness that there is a strong need for educated and experienced individuals to be groomed for top marketing positions within large retail firms. However, I also discovered that many companies prefer advanced degrees (MBA's), particularly with merchandising and marketing concentrations. I concluded that my biggest strategic issue was the need for education beyond a general business degree. Thus, the implication is that a continued "Product Development" strategy would be my best course of action for the next five years.

The goal I set for myself is to receive my MBA by June, 2005. The key threats to this are the lack of financial resources and the strong competition I face to get accepted into a good MBA program. With this in mind, I came up with three alternatives that I felt would best help me achieve my goal. They are:

1. Reduce my current working hours and apply for a student loan to help finance my undergraduate education and ultimately my MBA.
2. Reduce my current working hours and focus my efforts on getting high grades to attract a scholarship.
3. Take two years off school when I finish my BBA and work to save enough money to finance post-graduate education.

By applying the CORP evaluation criteria, I discovered that Alternative 2 would provide me with the highest payoff (no debt), with the least cost, obstacles and risks.

Some steps I will take to implement my plan are:

1. Research scholarship opportunities.
2. Discuss workload and career possibilities with my store supervisor.
3. Develop a study schedule and stick to it!

Receiving my MBA would be a major accomplishment for me and would significantly improve my chances of securing a good retail marketing position.

Appendix B

# Economics Fundamentals

**When You Finish This Appendix, You Should**

1. Understand the "law of diminishing demand."
2. Understand demand and supply curves and how they set the size of a market and its price level.
3. Know about elasticity of demand and supply.
4. Know why demand elasticity can be affected by availability of substitutes.
5. Know the different kinds of competitive situations and understand why they are important to marketing managers.
6. Recognize the important new terms (shown in red).

A good marketing manager should be an expert on markets and the nature of competition in markets. The economist's traditional analysis of demand and supply is a useful tool for analyzing markets. In particular, you should master the concepts of a demand curve and demand elasticity. A firm's demand curve shows how the target customers view the firm's Product—really its whole marketing mix. And the interaction of demand and supply curves helps set the size of a market and the market price. The interaction of supply and demand also determines the nature of the competitive environment, which has an important effect on strategy planning. These ideas are discussed more fully in the following sections.

## Products and Markets as Seen by Customers and Potential Customers

### Economists Provide Useful Insights

How potential customers (not the firm) see a firm's product (marketing mix) affects how much they are willing to pay for it, where it should be made available, and how eager they are for it—if they want it at all. In other words, their view has a very direct bearing on marketing strategy planning.

Economists have been concerned with market behavior for years. Their analytical tools can be quite helpful in summarizing how customers view products and how markets behave.

### Economists See Individual Customers Choosing Among Alternatives

Economics is sometimes called the dismal science—because it says that most customers have a limited income and simply cannot buy everything they want. They must balance their needs and the prices of various products.

Economists usually assume that customers have a fairly definite set of preferences and that they evaluate alternatives in terms of whether the alternatives will make them feel better (or worse) or in some way improve (or change) their situation.

But what exactly is the nature of a customer's desire for a particular product?

Usually economists answer this question in terms of the extra utility the customer can obtain by buying more of a particular product—or how much utility would be lost if the customer had less of the product. (Students who wish further discussion of this approach should refer to indifference curve analysis in any standard economics text.)

It is easier to understand the idea of utility if we look at what happens when the price of one of the customer's usual purchases changes.

### The Law of Diminishing Demand

Suppose that consumers buy potatoes in 10-pound bags at the same time they buy other foods such as bread and rice. If the consumers are mainly interested in buying a certain amount of food and the price of the potatoes drops, it seems reasonable to expect that they will switch some of their food money to potatoes and away from some other foods. But if the price of potatoes rises, you expect our consumers to buy fewer potatoes and more of other foods.

The general relationship between price and quantity demanded illustrated by this food example is called the **law of diminishing demand**—which says that if the price of a product is raised, a smaller quantity will be demanded and if the price of a product is lowered, a greater quantity will be demanded. Experience supports this relationship between prices and total demand in a market, especially for broad product categories or commodities such as potatoes.

The relationship between price and quantity demanded in a market is what economists call a "demand schedule." An example is shown in Exhibit B-1. For each

Exhibit B-1
Demand Schedule for Potatoes (10-pound bags)

| Point | (1) Price of Potatoes per Bag (P) | (2) Quantity Demanded (bags per month) (Q) | (3) Total Revenue per Month (P × Q = TR) |
|---|---|---|---|
| A | $1.60 | 8,000,000 | $12,800,000 |
| B | 1.30 | 9,000,000 | ________ |
| C | 1.00 | 11,000,000 | 11,000,000 |
| D | 0.70 | 14,000,000 | ________ |
| E | 0.40 | 19,000,000 | ________ |

row in the table, Column 2 shows the quantity consumers will want (demand) if they have to pay the price given in Column 1. The third column shows that the total revenue (sales) in the potato market is equal to the quantity demanded at a given price times that price. Note that as prices drop, the total *unit* quantity increases, yet the total *revenue* decreases. Fill in the blank lines in the third column and observe the behavior of total revenue—an important number for the marketing manager. We will explain what you should have noticed, and why, a little later.

## The Demand Curve—Usually Down-Sloping

If your only interest is seeing at which price the company will earn the greatest total revenue, the demand schedule may be adequate. But a demand curve shows more. A **demand curve** is a graph of the relationship between price and quantity demanded in a market—assuming that all other things stay the same. Exhibit B-2 shows the demand curve for potatoes—really just a plotting of the demand schedule in Exhibit B-1. It shows how many potatoes potential customers will demand at various possible prices. This is a "down-sloping demand curve."

Most demand curves are down-sloping. This just means that if prices are decreased, the quantity customers demand will increase.

Demand curves always show the price on the vertical axis and the quantity demanded on the horizontal axis. In Exhibit B-2, we have shown the price in dollars. For consistency, we will use dollars in other examples. However, keep in mind that these same ideas hold regardless of what money unit (dollars, yen, francs, pounds, etc.) is used to represent price. Even at this early point, you should keep in mind that markets are not necessarily limited by national boundaries—or by one type of money.

Note that the demand curve only shows how customers will react to various possible prices. In a market, we see only one price at a time, not all of these prices. The curve, however, shows what quantities will be demanded—depending on what price is set.

Exhibit B-2
Demand Curve for Potatoes (10-pound bags)

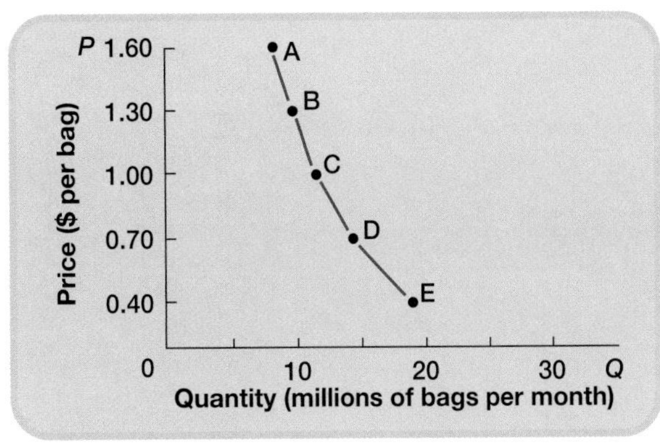

Exhibit B-3
Demand Schedule for 1-Cubic-Foot Microwave Ovens

| Point | (1) Price per Microwave Oven (P) | (2) Quantity Demanded per Year (Q) | (3) Total Revenue (TR) per Year (P × Q = TR) |
|---|---|---|---|
| A | $300 | 20,000 | $6,000,000 |
| B | 250 | 70,000 | 15,500,000 |
| C | 200 | 130,000 | 26,000,000 |
| D | 150 | 210,000 | 31,500,000 |
| E | 100 | 310,000 | 31,000,000 |

You probably think that most businesspeople would like to set a price that would result in a large sales revenue. Before discussing this, however, we should consider the demand schedule and curve for another product to get a more complete picture of demand-curve analysis.

### Microwave Oven Demand Curve Looks Different

A different demand schedule is the one for standard 1-cubic-foot microwave ovens shown in Exhibit B-3. Column (3) shows the total revenue that will be obtained at various possible prices and quantities. Again, as the price goes down, the quantity demanded goes up. But here, unlike the potato example, total revenue increases as prices go down—at least until the price drops to $150.

### Every Market Has a Demand Curve—for Some Time Period

These general demand relationships are typical for all products. But each product has its own demand schedule and curve in each potential market—no matter how small the market. In other words, a particular demand curve has meaning only for a particular market. We can think of demand curves for individuals, groups of individuals who form a target market, regions, and even countries. And the time period covered really should be specified—although this is often neglected because we usually think of monthly or yearly periods.

### The Difference Between Elastic and Inelastic

The demand curve for microwave ovens (see Exhibit B-4) is down-sloping—but note that it is flatter than the curve for potatoes. It is important to understand what this flatness means.

Exhibit B-4
Demand Curve for 1-Cubic-Foot Microwave Ovens

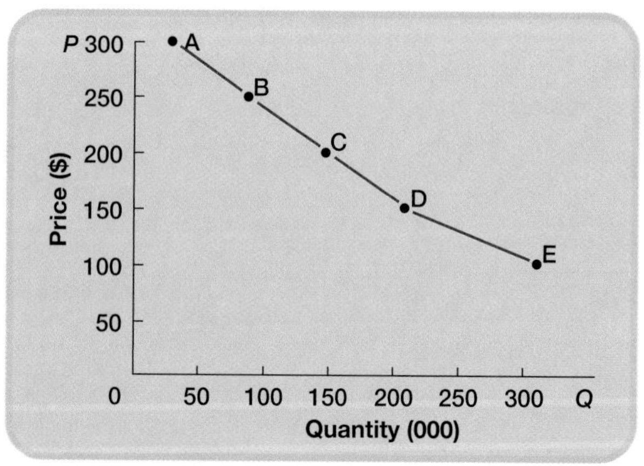

We will consider the flatness in terms of total revenue—since this is what interests business managers.*

When you filled in the total revenue column for potatoes, you should have noticed that total revenue drops continually if the price is reduced. This looks undesirable for sellers and illustrates inelastic demand. **Inelastic demand** means that although the quantity demanded increases if the price is decreased, the quantity demanded will not "stretch" enough—that is, it is not elastic enough—to avoid a decrease in total revenue.

In contrast, **elastic demand** means that if prices are dropped, the quantity demanded will stretch (increase) enough to increase total revenue. The upper part of the microwave oven demand curve is an example of elastic demand.

But note that if the microwave oven price is dropped from $150 to $100, total revenue will decrease. We can say, therefore, that between $150 and $100, demand is inelastic—that is, total revenue will decrease if price is lowered from $150 to $100.

Thus, elasticity can be defined in terms of changes in total revenue. *If total revenue will increase if price is lowered, then demand is elastic. If total revenue will decrease if price is lowered, then demand is inelastic.* (Note: A special case known as "unitary elasticity of demand" occurs if total revenue stays the same when prices change.)

### Total Revenue May Increase If Price Is Raised

A point often missed in discussions of demand is what happens when prices are raised instead of lowered. With elastic demand, total revenue will *decrease* if the price is *raised*. With inelastic demand, however, total revenue will *increase* if the price is *raised*.

The possibility of raising price and increasing dollar sales (total revenue) at the same time is attractive to managers. This only occurs if the demand curve is inelastic. Here total revenue will increase if price is raised, but total costs probably will not increase—and may actually go down—with smaller quantities. Keep in mind that profit is equal to total revenue minus total costs. So when demand is inelastic, profit will increase as price is increased!

Exhibit B-5
Changes in Total Revenue as Prices Increase

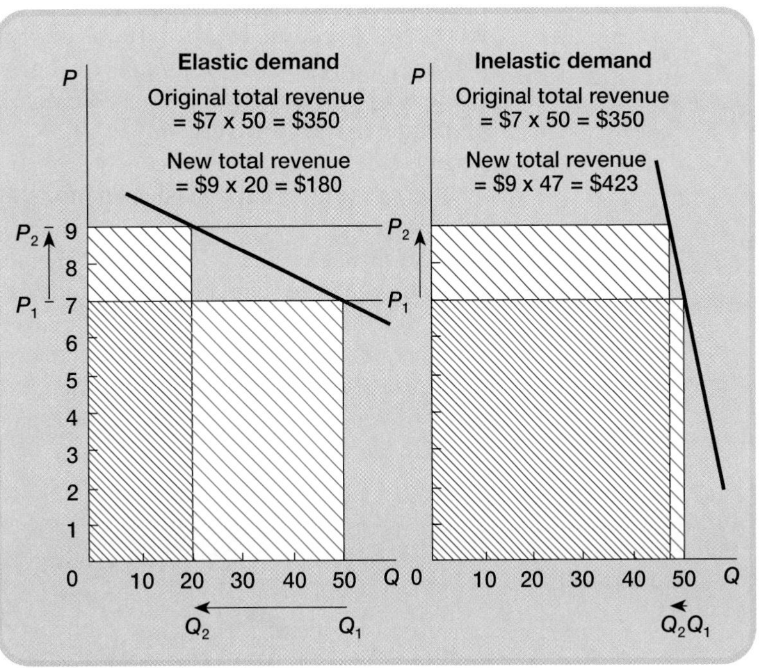


*Strictly speaking, two curves should not be compared for flatness if the graph scales are different, but for our purposes now we will do so to illustrate the idea of "elasticity of demand." Actually, it would be more accurate to compare two curves for one product—on the same graph. Then both the shape of the demand curve and its position on the graph would be important.

The ways total revenue changes as prices are raised are shown in Exhibit B-5. Here total revenue is the rectangular area formed by a price and its related quantity. The larger the rectangular area, the greater the total revenue.

$P_1$ is the original price here, and the total potential revenue with this original price is shown by the area with blue shading. The area with red shading shows the total revenue with the new price, $P_2$. There is some overlap in the total revenue areas, so the important areas are those with only one colour. Note that in the left-hand figure—where demand is elastic—the revenue added (the red-only area) when the price is increased is less than the revenue lost (the blue-only area). Now let's contrast this to the right-hand figure, when demand is inelastic. Only a small blue revenue area is given up for a much larger (red) one when price is raised.

## An Entire Curve Is Not Elastic or Inelastic

It is important to see that it is *wrong to refer to a whole demand curve as elastic or inelastic*. Rather, elasticity for a particular demand curve refers to the change in total revenue between two points on the curve, not along the whole curve. You saw the change from elastic to inelastic in the microwave oven example. Generally, however, nearby points are either elastic or inelastic—so it is common to refer to a whole curve by the degree of elasticity in the price range that normally is of interest—the *relevant range*.

## Demand Elasticities Affected by Availability of Substitutes and Urgency of Need

At first, it may be difficult to see why one product has an elastic demand and another an inelastic demand. Many factors affect elasticity—such as the availability of substitutes, the importance of the item in the customer's budget, and the urgency of the customer's need and its relation to other needs. By looking more closely at one of these factors—the availability of substitutes—you will better understand why demand elasticities vary.

**Substitutes** are products that offer the buyer a choice. For example, many consumers see grapefruit as a substitute for oranges and hot dogs as a substitute for hamburgers. The greater the number of "good" substitutes available, the greater will be the elasticity of demand. From the consumer's perspective, products are "good" substitutes if they are very similar (homogeneous). If consumers see products as extremely different, or heterogeneous, then a particular need cannot easily be satisfied by substitutes. And the demand for the most satisfactory product may be quite inelastic.

As an example, if the price of hamburger is lowered (and other prices stay the same), the quantity demanded will increase a lot—as will total revenue. The reason is that not only will regular hamburger users buy more hamburger, but some consumers who formerly bought hot dogs or steaks probably will buy hamburger too. But if the price of hamburger is raised, the quantity demanded will decrease—perhaps sharply. Still consumers will buy some hamburger—depending on how much the price has risen, their individual tastes, and what their guests expect (see Exhibit B-6).

Exhibit B-6
Demand Curve for Hamburger (a product with many substitutes)

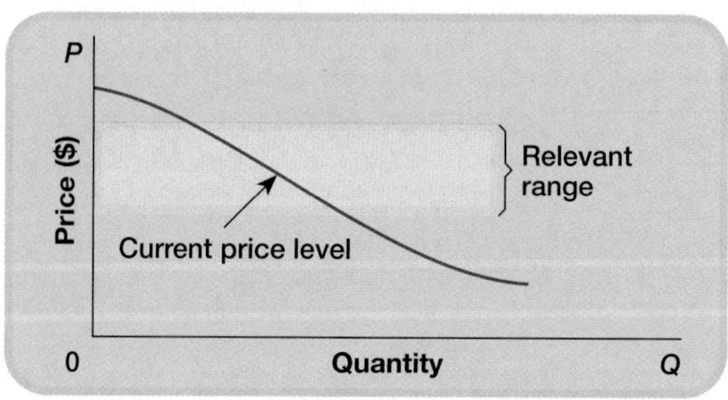

Exhibit B-7
Demand Curve for Motor Oil (a product with few substitutes)

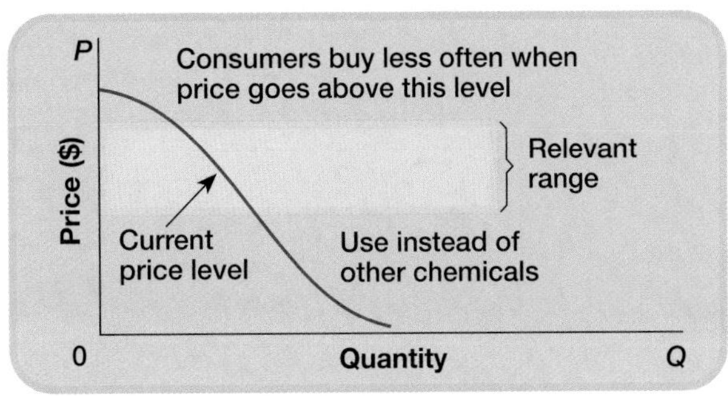


In contrast to a product with many "substitutes"—such as hamburger—consider a product with few or no substitutes. Its demand curve will tend to be inelastic. Motor oil is a good example. Motor oil is needed to keep cars running. Yet no one person or family uses great quantities of motor oil. So it is not likely that the quantity of motor oil purchased will change much as long as price changes are *within a reasonable range*. Of course, if the price is raised to a staggering figure, many people will buy less oil (change their oil less frequently). If the price is dropped to an extremely low level, manufacturers may buy more—say, as a lower-cost substitute for other chemicals typically used in making plastic (Exhibit B-7). But these extremes are outside the relevant range.

Demand curves are introduced here because the degree of elasticity of demand shows how potential customers feel about a product—and especially whether they see substitutes for the product. But to get a better understanding of markets, we must extend this economic analysis.



## Markets as Seen by Suppliers

Customers may want some product—but if suppliers are not willing to supply it, then there is no market. So we'll study the economist's analysis of supply. And then we'll bring supply and demand together for a more complete understanding of markets.

Economists often use the kind of analysis we are discussing here to explain pricing in the marketplace. But that is not our intention. Here we are interested in how and why markets work and the interaction of customers and potential suppliers. Later in this appendix we will review how competition affects prices, but how individual firms set prices, or should set prices, was discussed fully in Chapters 17 and 18.

### Supply Curves Reflect Supplier Thinking

Generally speaking, suppliers' costs affect the quantity of products they are willing to offer in a market during any period. In other words, their costs affect their supply schedules and supply curves. While a demand curve shows the quantity of products customers will be willing to buy at various prices, a **supply curve** shows the quantity of products that will be supplied at various possible prices. Eventually, only one quantity will be offered and purchased. So a supply curve is really a hypothetical (what-if) description of what will be offered at various prices. It is, however, a very important curve. Together with a demand curve, it summarizes the attitudes and probable behavior of buyers and sellers about a particular product in a particular market—that is, in a product-market.

Exhibit B-8
Supply Schedule for Potatoes (10-pound bags)

| Point | Possible Market Price per 10-lb. Bag | Number of Bags Sellers Will Supply per Month at Each Possible Market Price |
|---|---|---|
| A | $1.60 | 17,000,000 |
| B | 1.30 | 14,000,000 |
| C | 1.00 | 11,000,000 |
| D | 0.70 | 8,000,000 |
| E | 0.40 | 3,000,000 |

Note: This supply curve is for a month to emphasize that farmers might have some control over when they deliver their potatoes. There would be a different curve for each month.



## Some Supply Curves Are Vertical

We usually assume that supply curves tend to slope upward—that is, suppliers will be willing to offer greater quantities at higher prices. If a product's market price is very high, it seems only reasonable that producers will be anxious to produce more of the product and even put workers on overtime or perhaps hire more workers to increase the quantity they can offer. Going further, it seems likely that producers of other products will switch their resources (farms, factories, labor, or retail facilities) to the product that is in great demand.

On the other hand, if consumers are only willing to pay a very low price for a particular product, it's reasonable to expect that producers will switch to other products—thus reducing supply. A supply schedule (Exhibit B-8) and a supply curve (Exhibit B-9) for potatoes illustrate these ideas. This supply curve shows how many potatoes would be produced and offered for sale at each possible market price in a given month.

In the very short run (say, over a few hours, a day, or a week), a supplier may not be able to change the supply at all. In this situation, we would see a vertical supply curve. This situation is often relevant in the market for fresh produce. Fresh strawberries, for example, continue to ripen, and a supplier wants to sell them quickly—preferably at a higher price—but in any case, they must be sold.

If the product is a service, it may not be easy to expand the supply in the short run. Additional barbers or medical doctors are not quickly trained and licensed, and they only have so much time to give each day. Further, the prospect of much higher prices in the near future cannot easily expand the supply of many services. For example, a hit play or an "in" restaurant or nightclub is limited in the amount of "product" it can offer at a particular time.

## Elasticity of Supply

The term *elasticity* also is used to describe supply curves. An extremely steep or almost vertical supply curve, often found in the short run, is called **inelastic supply** because the quantity supplied does not stretch much (if at all) if the price is raised.

Exhibit B-9
Supply Curve for Potatoes (10-pound bags)

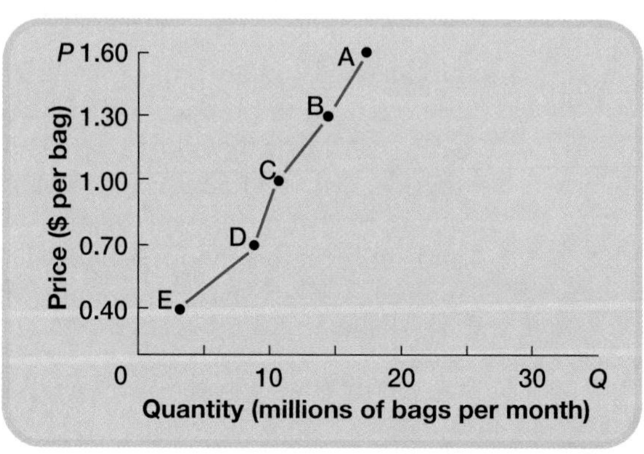

A flatter curve is called **elastic supply** because the quantity supplied does stretch more if the price is raised. A slightly up-sloping supply curve is typical in longer-run market situations. Given more time, suppliers have a chance to adjust their offerings, and competitors may enter or leave the market.

## Demand and Supply Interact to Determine the Size of the Market and Price Level

We have treated market demand and supply forces separately. Now we must bring them together to show their interaction. The *intersection* of these two forces determines the size of the market and the market price—at which point (price and quantity) the market is said to be in *equilibrium*.

The intersection of demand and supply is shown for the potato data discussed above. In Exhibit B-10, the demand curve for potatoes is now graphed against the supply curve in Exhibit B-9.

In this potato market, demand is inelastic—the total revenue of all the potato producers would be greater at higher prices. But the market price is at the **equilibrium point**—where the quantity and the price sellers are willing to offer are equal to the quantity and price that buyers are willing to accept. The $1.00 equilibrium price for potatoes yields a smaller *total revenue* to potato producers than a higher price would. This lower equilibrium price comes about because the many producers are willing to supply enough potatoes at the lower price. *Demand is not the only determiner of price level. Cost also must be considered—via the supply curve.*

### Some Consumers Get a Surplus

Presumably, a sale takes place only if both buyer and seller feel they will be better off after the sale. But sometimes the price a consumer pays in a sales transaction is less than what he or she would be willing to pay.

The reason for this is that demand curves are typically down-sloping, and some of the demand curve is above the equilibrium price. This is simply another way of showing that some customers would have been willing to pay more than the equilibrium price—if they had to. In effect, some of them are getting a bargain by being able to buy at the equilibrium price. Economists have traditionally called these bargains the **consumer surplus**—that is, the difference to consumers between the value of a purchase and the price they pay.

Some business critics assume that consumers do badly in any business transaction. In fact, sales take place only if consumers feel they are at least getting their money's worth. As we can see here, some are willing to pay much more than the market price.



Exhibit B-10
Equilibrium of Supply and Demand for Potatoes (10-pound bags)

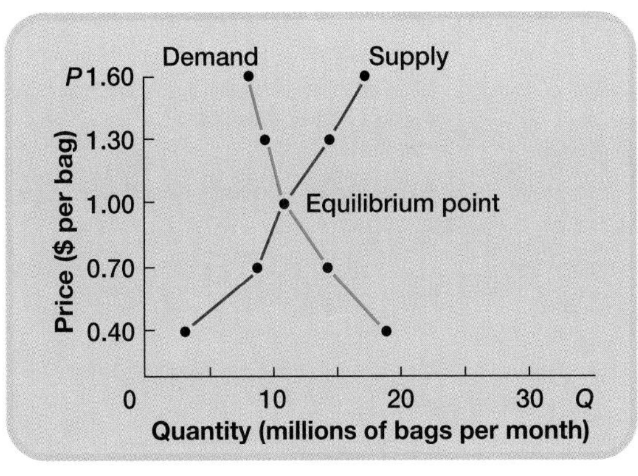

## Demand and Supply Help Us Understand the Nature of Competition

The elasticity of demand and supply curves and their interaction help predict the nature of competition a marketing manager is likely to face. For example, an extremely inelastic demand curve means that the manager will have much choice in strategy planning, especially price setting. Apparently customers like the product and see few substitutes. They are willing to pay higher prices before cutting back much on their purchases.

Clearly, the elasticity of a firm's demand curves makes a big difference in strategy planning, but other factors also affect the nature of competition. Among these are the number and size of competitors and the uniqueness of each firm's marketing mix. Understanding these market situations is important because the freedom of a marketing manager, especially control over price, is greatly reduced in some situations.

A marketing manager operates in one of four kinds of market situations. We'll discuss three kinds: pure competition, oligopoly, and monopolistic competition. The fourth kind, monopoly, isn't found very often and is like monopolistic competition. The important dimensions of these situations are shown in Exhibit B-11.

### When Competition Is Pure

**Many competitors offer about the same thing** **Pure competition** is a market situation that develops when a market has

1. Homogeneous (similar) products.
2. Many buyers and sellers who have full knowledge of the market.
3. Ease of entry for buyers and sellers; that is, new firms have little difficulty starting in business—and new customers can easily come into the market.

More or less pure competition is found in many agricultural markets. In the potato market, for example, there are thousands of small producers—and they are in pure competition. Let's look more closely at these producers.

Although the potato market as a whole has a down-sloping demand curve, each of the many small producers in the industry is in pure competition, and each of them faces a flat demand curve at the equilibrium price. This is shown in Exhibit B-12.



**Exhibit B-11**
Some Important Dimensions Regarding Market Situations

| | Types of Situations | | | |
|---|---|---|---|---|
| Important Dimensions | Pure Competition | Oligopoly | Monopolistic Competition | Monopoly |
| Uniqueness of each firm's product | None | None | Some | Unique |
| Number of competitors | Many | Few | Few to many | None |
| Size of competitors (compared to size of market) | Small | Large | Large to small | None |
| Elasticity of demand facing firm | Completely elastic | Kinked demand curve (elastic and inelastic) | Either | Either |
| Elasticity of industry demand | Either | Inelastic | Either | Either |
| Control of price by firm | None | Some (with care) | Some | Complete |

Exhibit B-12 Interaction of Demand and Supply in the Potato Industry and the Resulting Demand Curve Facing Individual Potato Producers

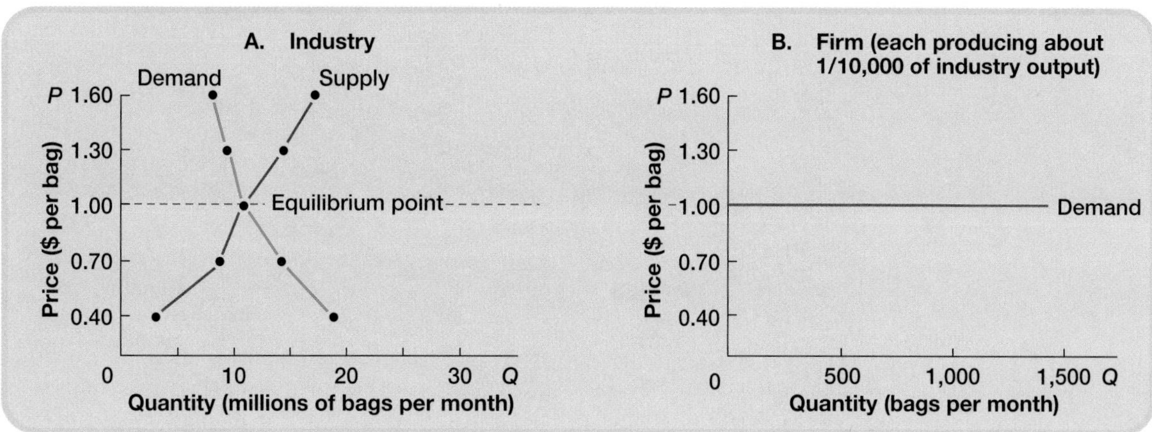


As shown at the right of Exhibit B-12, an individual producer can sell as many bags of potatoes as he chooses at $1—the market equilibrium price. The equilibrium price is determined by the quantity that all producers choose to sell given the demand curve they face.

But a small producer has little effect on overall supply (or on the equilibrium price). If this individual farmer raises 1/10,000th of the quantity offered in the market, for example, you can see that there will be little effect if the farmer goes out of business—or doubles production.

The reason an individual producer's demand curve is flat is that the farmer probably couldn't sell any potatoes above the market price. And there is no point in selling below the market price! So in effect, the individual producer has no control over price.

## Markets Tend to Become More Competitive

Not many markets are *purely* competitive. But many are close enough so we can talk about "almost" pure competition situations—those in which the marketing manager has to accept the going price.

Such highly competitive situations aren't limited to agriculture. Wherever *many* competitors sell *homogeneous* products—such as textiles, lumber, coal, printing, and laundry services—the demand curve seen by *each producer* tends to be flat.

Markets tend to become more competitive, moving toward pure competition (except in oligopolies—see below). On the way to pure competition, prices and profits are pushed down until some competitors are forced out of business. Eventually, in long-run equilibrium, the price level is only high enough to keep the survivors in business. No one makes any profit—they just cover costs. It's tough to be a marketing manager in this situation!

## When Competition Is Oligopolistic

**A few competitors offer similar things** Not all markets move toward pure competition. Some become oligopolies.

**Oligopoly** situations are special market situations that develop when a market has

1. Essentially homogeneous products—such as basic industrial chemicals or gasoline.
2. Relatively few sellers—or a few large firms and many smaller ones who follow the lead of the larger ones.
3. Fairly inelastic industry demand curves.

Exhibit B-13
Oligopoly—Kinked Demand Curve—Situation

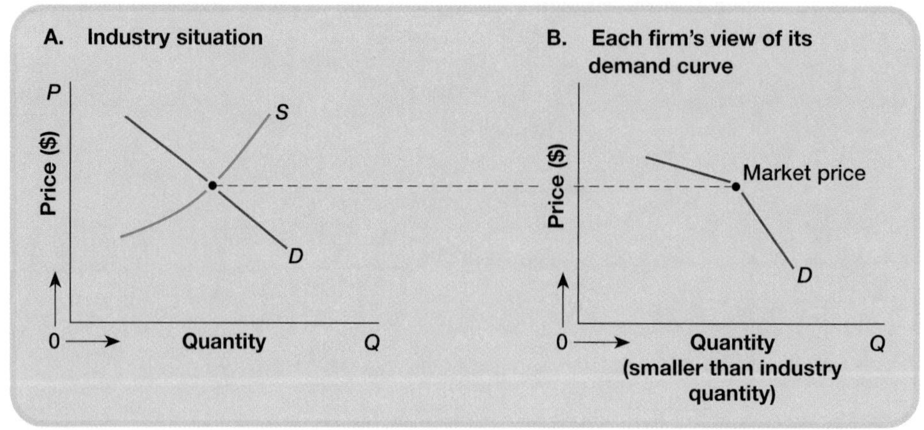




The demand curve facing each firm is unusual in an oligopoly situation. Although the industry demand curve is inelastic throughout the relevant range, the demand curve facing each competitor looks "kinked." See Exhibit B-13. The current market price is at the kink.

There is a market price because the competing firms watch each other carefully—and they know it's wise to be at the kink. Each firm must expect that raising its own price above the market price will cause a big loss in sales. Few, if any, competitors will follow the price increase. So the firm's demand curve is relatively flat above the market price. If the firm lowers its price, it must expect competitors to follow. Given inelastic industry demand, the firm's own demand curve is inelastic at lower prices—assuming it keeps its share of this market at lower prices. Since lowering prices along such a curve will drop total revenue, the firm should leave its price at the kink—the market price.

Actually, however, there are price fluctuations in oligopolistic markets. Sometimes this is caused by firms that don't understand the market situation and cut their prices to get business. In other cases, big increases in demand or supply change the basic nature of the situation and lead to price cutting. Price cuts can be drastic—such as Du Pont's price cut of 25 percent for Dacron. This happened when Du Pont decided that industry production capacity already exceeded demand, and more plants were due to start production.

It's important to keep in mind that oligopoly situations don't just apply to whole industries and national markets. Competitors who are focusing on the same local target market often face oligopoly situations. A suburban community might have several gas stations—all of which provide essentially the same product. In this case, the "industry" consists of the gas stations competing with each other in the local product-market.

As in pure competition, oligopolists face a long-run trend toward an equilibrium level—with profits driven toward zero. This may not happen immediately—and a marketing manager may try to delay price competition by relying more on other elements in the marketing mix.

## When Competition Is Monopolistic

**A price must be set** You can see why marketing managers want to avoid pure competition or oligopoly situations. They prefer a market in which they have more control. **Monopolistic competition** is a market situation that develops when a market has

1. Different (heterogeneous) products—in the eyes of some customers.
2. Sellers who feel they do have some competition in this market.

The word *monopolistic* means that each firm is trying to get control in its own little market. But the word *competition* means that there are still substitutes. The vigorous competition of a purely competitive market is reduced. Each firm has its own down-sloping demand curve. But the shape of the curve depends on the similarity of competitors' products and marketing mixes. Each monopolistic competitor has freedom—but not complete freedom—in its own market.

**Judging elasticity will help set the price** Since a firm in monopolistic competition has its own down-sloping demand curve, it must make a decision about price level as part of its marketing strategy planning. Here, estimating the elasticity of the firm's own demand curve is helpful. If it is highly inelastic, the firm may decide to raise prices to increase total revenue. But if demand is highly elastic, this may mean many competitors with acceptable substitutes. Then the price may have to be set near that of the competition. And the marketing manager probably should try to develop a better marketing mix.

## Conclusion

The economist's traditional demand and supply analysis provides a useful tool for analyzing the nature of demand and competition. It is especially important that you master the concepts of a demand curve and demand elasticity. How demand and supply interact helps determine the size of a market and its price level. The interaction of supply and demand also helps explain the nature of competition in different market situations. We discuss three competitive situations: pure competition, oligopoly, and monopolistic competition. The fourth kind, monopoly, isn't found very often and is like monopolistic competition.

The nature of supply and demand—and competition—is very important in marketing strategy planning. We discuss these topics more fully in Chapters 3 and 4 and then build on them throughout the text. This appendix provides a good foundation on these topics.

## Questions and Problems

1. Explain in your own words how economists look at markets and arrive at the "law of diminishing demand."
2. Explain what a demand curve is and why it is usually down-sloping. Then give an example of a product for which the demand curve might not be down-sloping over some possible price ranges. Explain the reason for your choice.
3. What is the length of life of the typical demand curve? Illustrate your answer.
4. If the general market demand for men's shoes is fairly elastic, how does the demand for men's dress shoes compare to it? How does the demand curve for women's shoes compare to the demand curve for men's shoes?
5. If the demand for perfume is inelastic above and below the present price, should the price be raised? Why or why not?
6. If the demand for shrimp is highly elastic below the present price, should the price be lowered?
7. Discuss what factors lead to inelastic demand and supply curves. Are they likely to be found together in the same situation?
8. Why would a marketing manager prefer to sell a product that has no close substitutes? Are high profits almost guaranteed?
9. If a manufacturer's well-known product is sold at the same price by many retailers in the same community, is this an example of pure competition? When a community has many small grocery stores, are they in pure competition? What characteristics are needed to have a purely competitive market?
10. List three products that are sold in purely competitive markets and three that are sold in monopolistically competitive markets. Do any of these products have anything in common? Can any generalizations be made about competitive situations and marketing mix planning?
11. Cite a local example of an oligopoly—explaining why it is an oligopoly.

Appendix C

# Marketing Arithmetic

**When You Finish This Appendix, You Should**

1. Understand the components of an operating statement (profit and loss statement).

2. Know how to compute the stockturn rate.

3. Understand how operating ratios can help analyze a business.

4. Understand how to calculate markups and markdowns.

5. Understand how to calculate return on investment (ROI) and return on assets (ROA).

6. Understand the important new terms (shown in red).

Marketing students must become familiar with the essentials of the language of business. Businesspeople commonly use accounting terms when talking about costs, prices, and profit. And using accounting data is a practical tool in analyzing marketing problems.

## The Operating Statement

An **operating statement** is a simple summary of the financial results of a company's operations over a specified period of time. Some beginning students may feel that the operating statement is complex, but as we'll soon see, this really isn't true. *The main purpose of the operating statement is determining the net profit figure and presenting data to support that figure.* This is why the operating statement is often referred to as the *profit and loss statement.*

Exhibit C-1 shows an operating statement for a wholesale or retail business. The statement is complete and detailed so you will see the framework throughout the

Exhibit C-1 An Operating Statement (profit and loss statement)

**Smith Company**
Operating Statement
For the Year Ended December 31, 200X

| | | | |
|---|---|---|---|
| Gross sales | | | $540,000 |
| Less: Returns and allowances | | | 40,000 |
| Net sales | | | $500,000 |
| Cost of sales: | | | |
| Beginning inventory at cost | | $ 80,000 | |
| Purchases at billed cost | $310,000 | | |
| Less: Purchase discounts | 40,000 | | |
| Purchases at net cost | 270,000 | | |
| Plus: freight-in | 20,000 | | |
| Net cost of delivered purchases | | 290,000 | |
| Cost of goods available for sale | | 370,000 | |
| Less: Ending inventory at cost | | 70,000 | |
| Cost of sales | | | 300,000 |
| Gross margin (gross profit) | | | 200,000 |
| Expenses: | | | |
| Selling expenses: | | | |
| Sales salaries | 60,000 | | |
| Advertising expense | 20,000 | | |
| Website updates | 10,000 | | |
| Delivery expense | 10,000 | | |
| Total selling expense | | 100,000 | |
| Administrative expense: | | | |
| Office salaries | 30,000 | | |
| Office supplies | 10,000 | | |
| Miscellaneous administrative expense | 5,000 | | |
| Total administrative expense | | 45,000 | |
| General expense: | | | |
| Rent expense | 10,000 | | |
| Miscellaneous general expenses | 5,000 | | |
| Total general expense | | 15,000 | |
| Total expenses | | | 160,000 |
| Net profit from operation | | | $ 40,000 |

discussion, but the amount of detail on an operating statement is *not* standardized. Many companies use financial statements with much less detail than this one. They emphasize clarity and readability rather than detail. To really understand an operating statement, however, you must know about its components.

## Only Three Basic Components

The basic components of an operating statement are *sales*—which come from the sale of goods and services; *costs*—which come from the making and selling process; and the balance—called *profit or loss*—which is just the difference between sales and costs. So there are only three basic components in the statement: sales, costs, and profit (or loss). Other items on an operating statement are there only to provide supporting details.

## Time Period Covered May Vary

There is no one time period an operating statement covers. Rather, statements are prepared to satisfy the needs of a particular business. This may be at the end of each day or at the end of each week. Usually, however, an operating statement summarizes results for one month, three months, six months, or a full year. Since the time period does vary, this information is included in the heading of the statement as follows:

**Smith Company**
Operating Statement
For the (Period) Ended (Date)

Also, see Exhibit C-1.

## Management Uses of Operating Statements

Before going on to a more detailed discussion of the components of our operating statement, let's think about some of the uses for such a statement. Exhibit C-1 shows that a lot of information is presented in a clear and concise manner. With this information, a manager can easily find the relation of net sales to the cost of sales, the gross margin, expenses, and net profit. Opening and closing inventory figures are available—as is the amount spent during the period for the purchase of goods for resale. Total expenses are listed to make it easier to compare them with previous statements and to help control these expenses.

All this information is important to a company's managers. Assume that a particular company prepares monthly operating statements. A series of these statements is a valuable tool for directing and controlling the business. By comparing results from one month to the next, managers can uncover unfavorable trends in the sales, costs, or profit areas of the business and take any needed action.

## A Skeleton Statement Gets Down to Essential Details

Let's refer to Exhibit C-1 and begin to analyze this seemingly detailed statement to get first-hand knowledge of the components of the operating statement.

As a first step, suppose we take all the items that have dollar amounts extended to the third, or right-hand, column. Using these items only, the operating statement looks like this:

| | |
|---|---:|
| Gross sales | $540,000 |
| Less: Returns and allowances | 40,000 |
| Net sales | 500,000 |
| Less: Cost of sales | 300,000 |
| Gross margin | 200,000 |
| Less: Total expenses | 160,000 |
| Net profit (loss) | $ 40,000 |

Is this a complete operating statement? The answer is *yes*. This skeleton statement differs from Exhibit C-1 only in supporting detail. All the basic components are included. In fact, the only items we must list to have a complete operating statement are

| | |
|---|---|
| Net sales | $500,000 |
| Less: Costs | 460,000 |
| Net profit (loss) | $ 40,000 |

These three items are the essentials of an operating statement. All other subdivisions or details are just useful additions.

## Meaning of Sales

Now let's define the meaning of the terms in the skeleton statement.

The first item is sales. What do we mean by sales? The term **gross sales** is the total amount charged to all customers during some time period. However, there is always some customer dissatisfaction or just plain errors in ordering and shipping goods. This results in returns and allowances—which reduce gross sales.

A **return** occurs when a customer sends back purchased products. The company either refunds the purchase price or allows the customer dollar credit on other purchases.

An **allowance** occurs when a customer is not satisfied with a purchase for some reason. The company gives a price reduction on the original invoice (bill), but the customer keeps the goods and services.

These refunds and price reductions must be considered when the firm computes its net sales figure for the period. Really, we're only interested in the revenue the company manages to keep. This is **net sales**—the actual sales dollars the company receives. Therefore, all reductions, refunds, cancellations, and so forth made because of returns and allowances are deducted from the original total (gross sales) to get net sales. This is shown below.

| | |
|---|---|
| Gross sales | $540,000 |
| Less: Returns and allowances | 40,000 |
| Net sales | $500,000 |

## Meaning of Cost of Sales

The next item in the operating statement—**cost of sales**—is the total value (at cost) of the sales during the period. We'll discuss this computation later. Meanwhile, note that after we obtain the cost of sales figure, we subtract it from the net sales figure to get the gross margin.

## Meaning of Gross Margin and Expenses

**Gross margin (gross profit)** is the money left to cover the expenses of selling the products and operating the business. Firms hope that a profit will be left after subtracting these expenses.

Selling expense is commonly the major expense below the gross margin. Note that in Exhibit C-1, **expenses** are all the remaining costs subtracted from the gross margin to get the net profit. The expenses in this case are the selling, administrative, and general expenses. (Note that the cost of purchases and cost of sales are not included in this total expense figure—they were subtracted from net sales earlier to get the gross margin. Note, also, that some accountants refer to cost of sales as cost of goods sold.)

**Net profit**—at the bottom of the statement—is what the company earned from its operations during a particular period. It is the amount left after the cost of sales and the expenses are subtracted from net sales. *Net sales and net profit are not the same*. Many firms have large sales and no profits—they may even have losses! That's why understanding costs, and controlling them, is important.

## Detailed Analysis of Sections of the Operating Statement

### Cost of Sales for a Wholesale or Retail Company

The cost of sales section includes details that are used to find the cost of sales ($300,000 in our example).

In Exhibit C-1, you can see that beginning and ending inventory, purchases, purchase discounts, and freight-in are all necessary to calculate costs of sales. If we pull the cost of sales section from the operating statement, it looks like this:

| Cost of sales: | | | |
|---|---|---|---|
| Beginning inventory at cost .......... | | $ 80,000 | |
| Purchases at billed cost .............. | $310,000 | | |
| Less: Purchase discounts .......... | 40,000 | | |
| Purchases at net cost .............. | 270,000 | | |
| Plus: Freight-in .................. | 20,000 | | |
| Net cost of delivered purchases .... | | 290,000 | |
| Cost of goods available for sale ....... | | 370,000 | |
| Less: Ending inventory at cost ....... | | 70,000 | |
| Cost of sales .................. | | | $300,000 |

Cost of sales is the cost value of what is *sold*, not the cost of goods on hand at any given time.

Inventory figures merely show the cost of goods on hand at the beginning and end of the period the statement covers. These figures may be obtained by physically counting goods on hand on these dates or estimated from perpetual inventory records that show the inventory balance at any given time. The methods used to determine the inventory should be as accurate as possible because these figures affect the cost of sales during the period and net profit.

The net cost of delivered purchases must include freight charges and purchase discounts received since these items affect the money actually spent to buy goods and bring them to the place of business. A **purchase discount** is a reduction of the original invoice amount for some business reason. For example, a cash discount may be given for prompt payment of the amount due. We subtract the total of such discounts from the original invoice cost of purchases to get the *net* cost of purchases. To this figure we add the freight charges for bringing the goods to the place of business. This gives the net cost of *delivered* purchases. When we add the net cost of delivered purchases to the beginning inventory at cost, we have the total cost of goods available for sale during the period. If we now subtract the ending inventory at cost from the cost of the goods available for sale, we get the cost of sales.

One important point should be noted about cost of sales. The way the value of inventory is calculated varies from one company to another—and it can cause big differences in the cost of sales and the operating statement. (See any basic accounting textbook for how the various inventory valuation methods work.)

Exhibit C-2 Cost of Sales Section of an Operating Statement for a Manufacturing Firm

| | | | |
|---|---|---|---|
| Cost of sales: | | | |
| Finished products inventory (beginning) . . . . . | | $ 20,000 | |
| Cost of production (Schedule 1) . . . . . . . . . . | | 100,000 | |
| Total cost of finished products available for sale | | 120,000 | |
| Less: Finished products inventory (ending) . . | | 30,000 | |
| Cost of sales . . . . . . . . . . . . . . . . . . . . | | | $ 90,000 |
| Schedule 1, Schedule of cost of production | | | |
| Beginning work in process inventory . . . . . . . . . | | | 15,000 |
| Raw materials: | | | |
| Beginning raw materials inventory . . . . . . . . . | | 10,000 | |
| Net cost of delivered purchases . . . . . . . . . . | | 80,000 | |
| Total cost of materials available for use . . . . . | | 90,000 | |
| Less: Ending raw materials inventory . . . . . | | 15,000 | |
| Cost of materials placed in production . . . . | | 75,000 | |
| Direct labor . . . . . . . . . . . . . . . . . . . . . . . . . | | 20,000 | |
| Manufacturing expenses: | | | |
| Indirect labor . . . . . . . . . . . . . . . . . . . . . . . | $4,000 | | |
| Maintenance and repairs . . . . . . . . . . . . . . . | 3,000 | | |
| Factory supplies . . . . . . . . . . . . . . . . . . . . . | 1,000 | | |
| Heat, light, and power . . . . . . . . . . . . . . . . . | 2,000 | | |
| Total manufacturing expenses . . . . . . . . . . | | 10,000 | |
| Total manufacturing costs . . . . . . . . . . . . . . . . | | | 105,000 |
| Total work in process during period . . . . . . . . . | | | 120,000 |
| Less: Ending work in process inventory . . . . . | | | 20,000 |
| Cost of production . . . . . . . . . . . . . . . . . . | | | $100,000 |

## Cost of Sales for A Manufacturing Company

Exhibit C-1 shows the way the manager of a wholesale or retail business arrives at his cost of sales. Such a business *purchases* finished products and resells them. In a manufacturing company, the purchases section of this operating statement is replaced by a section called cost of production. This section includes purchases of raw materials and parts, direct and indirect labor costs, and factory overhead charges (such as heat, light, and power) that are necessary to produce finished products. The cost of production is added to the beginning finished products inventory to arrive at the cost of products available for sale. Often, a separate cost of production statement is prepared, and only the total cost of production is shown in the operating statement. See Exhibit C-2 for an illustration of the cost of sales section of an operating statement for a manufacturing company.

## Expenses

Expenses go below the gross margin. They usually include the costs of selling and the costs of administering the business. They do not include the cost of sales—either purchased or produced.

There is no right method for classifying the expense accounts or arranging them on the operating statement. They can just as easily be arranged alphabetically or according to amount, with the largest placed at the top and so on down the line. In a business of any size, though, it is clearer to group the expenses in some way and use subtotals by groups for analysis and control purposes. This was done in Exhibit C-1.

## Summary on Operating Statements

The statement presented in Exhibit C-1 contains all the major categories in an operating statement—together with a normal amount of supporting detail. Further detail can be added to the statement under any of the major categories without changing the nature of the statement. The amount of detail normally is determined by how the statement will be used. A stockholder may be given a sketchy operating statement—while the one prepared for internal company use may have a lot of detail.

## Computing the Stockturn Rate

A detailed operating statement can provide the data needed to compute the **stockturn rate**—a measure of the number of times the average inventory is sold during a year. Note that the stockturn rate is related to the *turnover during a year,* not the length of time covered by a particular operating statement.

The stockturn rate is a very important measure because it shows how rapidly the firm's inventory is moving. Some businesses typically have slower turnover than others. But a drop in turnover in a particular business can be very alarming. It may mean that the firm's assortment of products is no longer as attractive as it was. Also, it may mean that the firm will need more working capital to handle the same volume of sales. Most businesses pay a lot of attention to the stockturn rate—trying to get faster turnover (and lower inventory costs).

Three methods—all basically similar—can be used to compute the stockturn rate. Which method is used depends on the data available. These three methods, which usually give approximately the same results, are shown below.*

(1) $$\frac{\text{Cost of sales}}{\text{Average inventory at cost}}$$

(2) $$\frac{\text{Net sales}}{\text{Average inventory at selling price}}$$

(3) $$\frac{\text{Sales in units}}{\text{Average inventory in units}}$$

Computing the stockturn rate will be illustrated only for Formula 1, since all are similar. The only difference is that the cost figures used in Formula 1 are changed to a selling price or numerical count basis in Formulas 2 and 3. Note: Regardless of the method used, you must have both the numerator and denominator of the formula in the same terms.

If the inventory level varies a lot during the year, you may need detailed information about the inventory level at different times to compute the average inventory. If it stays at about the same level during the year, however, it's easy to get an estimate. For example, using Formula 1, the average inventory at cost is computed by adding the beginning and ending inventories at cost and dividing by 2. This average inventory figure is then divided into the cost of sales (in cost terms) to get the stockturn rate.

For example, suppose that the cost of sales for one year was $1,000,000. Beginning inventory was $250,000 and ending inventory $150,000. Adding the two inventory figures and dividing by 2, we get an average inventory of $200,000. We next divide the cost of sales by the average inventory ($1,000,000 ÷ $200,000) and get a stockturn rate of 5. The stockturn rate is covered further in Chapter 18.

*Differences occur because of varied markups and nonhomogeneous product assortments. In an assortment of tires, for example, those with low markups might have sold much better than those with high markups. But with Formula 3, all tires would be treated equally.

## Operating Ratios Help Analyze the Business

Many businesspeople use the operating statement to calculate **operating ratios**—the ratio of items on the operating statement to net sales—and to compare these ratios from one time period to another. They can also compare their own operating ratios with those of competitors. Such competitive data is often available through trade associations. Each firm may report its results to a trade association, which then distributes summary results to its members. These ratios help managers control their operations. If some expense ratios are rising, for example, those particular costs are singled out for special attention.

Operating ratios are computed by dividing net sales into the various operating statement items that appear below the net sales level in the operating statement. The net sales is used as the denominator in the operating ratio because it shows the sales the firm actually won.

We can see the relation of operating ratios to the operating statement if we think of there being another column to the right of the dollar figures in an operating statement. This column contains percentage figures—using net sales as 100 percent. This approach can be seen below.

| | | |
|---|---|---|
| Gross sales | $540,000 | |
| Less: Returns and allowances | 40,000 | |
| Net sales | 500,000 | 100% |
| Less: Cost of sales | 300,000 | 60 |
| Gross margin | 200,000 | 40 |
| Less: Total Expenses | 160,000 | 32 |
| Net profit | $ 40,000 | 8% |

The 40 percent ratio of gross margin to net sales in the above example shows that 40 percent of the net sales dollar is available to cover sales expenses and administering the business and provide a profit. Note that the ratio of expenses to sales added to the ratio of profit to sales equals the 40 percent gross margin ratio. The net profit ratio of 8 percent shows that 8 percent of the net sales dollar is left for profit.

The value of percentage ratios should be obvious. The percentages are easily figured and much easier to compare than large dollar figures.

Note that because these operating statement categories are interrelated, only a few pieces of information are needed to figure the others. In this case, for example, knowing the gross margin percent and net profit percent makes it possible to figure the expenses and cost of sales percentages. Further, knowing just one dollar amount and the percentages lets you figure all the other dollar amounts.

## Markups

A **markup** is the dollar amount added to the cost of sales to get the selling price. The markup usually is similar to the firm's gross margin because the markup amount added onto the unit cost of a product by a retailer or wholesaler is expected to cover the selling and administrative expenses and to provide a profit.

The markup approach to pricing is discussed in Chapter 18, so it will not be discussed at length here. But a simple example illustrates the idea. If a retailer buys an article that costs $1 when delivered to his store, he must sell it for more than this cost if he hopes to make a profit. So he might add 50 cents onto the cost of the article to cover his selling and other costs and, hopefully, to provide a profit. The 50 cents is the markup.

The 50 cents is also the gross margin or gross profit from that item *if* it is sold. But note that it is *not* the net profit. Selling expenses may amount to 35 cents, 45 cents, or even 55 cents. In other words, there is no guarantee the markup will cover costs. Further, there is no guarantee customers will buy at the marked-up price. This may require markdowns, which are discussed later in this appendix.

## Markup Conversions

Often it is convenient to use markups as percentages rather than focusing on the actual dollar amounts. But markups can be figured as a percent of cost or selling price. To have some agreement, *markup (percent)* will mean percentage of selling price unless stated otherwise. So the 50-cent markup on the $1.50 selling price is a markup of 33⅓ percent. On the other hand, the 50-cent markup is a 50 percent markup on cost.

Some retailers and wholesalers use markup conversion tables or spreadsheets to easily convert from cost to selling price—depending on the markup on selling price they want. To see the interrelation, look at the two formulas below. They can be used to convert either type of markup to the other.

$$\text{(4)} \qquad \text{Percent markup on selling price} = \frac{\text{Percent markup on cost}}{100\% + \text{Percent markup on cost}}$$

$$\text{(5)} \qquad \text{Percent markup on cost} = \frac{\text{Percent markup on selling price}}{100\% - \text{Percent markup on selling price}}$$

In the previous example, we had a cost of $1, a markup of 50 cents, and a selling price of $1.50. We saw that the markup on selling price was 33⅓ percent—and on cost, it was 50 percent. Let's substitute these percentage figures—in Formulas 4 and 5—to see how to convert from one basis to the other. Assume first of all that we only know the markup on selling price and want to convert to markup on cost. Using Formula 5, we get

$$\text{Percent markup on cost} = \frac{33\tfrac{1}{3}\%}{100\% - 33\tfrac{1}{3}\%} = \frac{33\tfrac{1}{3}\%}{66\tfrac{2}{3}\%} = 50\%$$

On the other hand, if we know only the percent markup on cost, we can convert to markup on selling price as follows:

$$\text{Percent markup on selling price} = \frac{50\%}{100\% + 50\%} = \frac{50\%}{150\%} = 33\tfrac{1}{3}\%$$

These results can be proved and summarized as follows:

| | | |
|---|---|---|
| Markup $0.50 | = | 50% of cost, or 33⅓% of selling price |
| + Cost $1.00 | = | 100% of cost, or 66⅔% of selling price |
| Selling price $1.50 | = | 150% of cost, or 100% of selling price |

Note that when the selling price ($1.50) is the base for a markup calculation, the markup percent (33⅓ percent = $.50/$1.50) must be less than 100 percent. As you can see, that's because the markup percent and the cost percent (66⅔ percent = $1.00/$1.50) sums to exactly 100 percent. So if you see a reference to a markup percent that is greater than 100 percent, it could not be based on the selling price and instead must be based on cost.

## Markdown Ratios Help Control Retail Operations

The ratios we discussed above were concerned with figures on the operating statement. Another important ratio, the **markdown ratio,** is a tool many retailers use to measure the efficiency of various departments and their whole business. But note that it is *not directly related to the operating statement*. It requires special calculations.

A **markdown** is a retail price reduction required because customers won't buy some item at the originally marked-up price. This refusal to buy may be due to a variety of reasons—soiling, style changes, fading, damage caused by handling, or an original price that was too high. To get rid of these products, the retailer offers them at a lower price.

Markdowns are generally considered to be due to business errors—perhaps because of poor buying, original markups that are too high, and other reasons. (Note, however, that some retailers use markdowns as a way of doing business rather than a way to correct errors. For example, a store that buys out overstocked fashions from other retailers may start by marking each item with a high price and then reduce the price each week until it sells.) Regardless of the reason, however, markdowns are reductions in the original price—and they are important to managers who want to measure the effectiveness of their operations.

Markdowns are similar to allowances because price reductions are made. Thus, in computing a markdown ratio, markdowns and allowances are usually added together and then divided by net sales. The markdown ratio is computed as follows:

$$\text{Markdown } \% = \frac{\$ \text{ Markdowns} + \$ \text{ Allowances}}{\$ \text{ Net sales}} \times 100$$

The 100 is multiplied by the fraction to get rid of decimal points.

Returns are *not* included when figuring the markdown ratio. Returns are treated as consumer errors, not business errors, and therefore are not included in this measure of business efficiency.

Retailers who use markdown ratios usually keep a record of the amount of markdowns and allowances in each department and then divide the total by the net sales in each department. Over a period of time, these ratios give management one measure of the efficiency of buyers and salespeople in various departments.

It should be stressed again that the markdown ratio is not calculated directly from data on the operating statement since the markdowns take place before the products are sold. In fact, some products may be marked down and still not sold. Even if the marked-down items are not sold, the markdowns—that is, the reevaluations of their value—are included in the calculations in the time period when they are taken.

The markdown ratio is calculated for a whole department (or profit center), *not* individual items. What we are seeking is a measure of the effectiveness of a whole department, not how well the department did on individual items.

## Return on Investment (ROI) Reflects Asset Use

Another off-the-operating-statement ratio is **return on investment (ROI)**—the ratio of net profit (after taxes) to the investment used to make the net profit, multiplied by 100 to get rid of decimals. Investment is not shown on the operating statement. But it is on the **balance sheet** (statement of financial condition), another accounting statement, which shows a company's assets, liabilities, and net worth. It may take some digging or special analysis, however, to find the right investment number.

Investment means the dollar resources the firm has invested in a project or business. For example, a new product may require $4 million in new money—for inventory, accounts receivable, promotion, and so on—and its attractiveness may be judged by its likely ROI. If the net profit (after taxes) for this new product is expected to be $1 million in the first year, then the ROI is 25 percent—that is, ($1 million ÷ $4 million) × 100.

There are two ways to figure ROI. The *direct* way is

$$\text{ROI (in \%)} = \frac{\text{Net profit (after taxes)}}{\text{Investment}} \times 100$$

The *indirect* way is

$$\text{ROI (in \%)} = \frac{\text{Net profit (after taxes)}}{\text{Sales}} = \frac{\text{Sales}}{\text{Investment}} \times 100$$

This way is concerned with net profit margin and turnover—that is

$$\text{ROI (in \%)} = \text{Net profit margin} \times \text{Turnover} \times 100$$

This indirect way makes it clearer how to *increase* ROI. There are three ways:

1. Increase profit margin (with lower costs or a higher price).
2. Increase sales.
3. Decrease investment.

Effective marketing strategy planning and implementation can increase profit margins and/or sales. And careful asset management can decrease investment.

ROI is a revealing measure of how well managers are doing. Most companies have alternative uses for their funds. If the returns in a business aren't at least as high as outside uses, then the money probably should be shifted to the more profitable uses.

Some firms borrow more than others to make investments. In other words, they invest less of their own money to acquire assets—what we called *investments*. If ROI calculations use only the firm's own investment, this gives higher ROI figures to those who borrow a lot—which is called *leveraging*. To adjust for different borrowing proportions—to make comparisons among projects, departments, divisions, and companies easier—another ratio has come into use. **Return on assets (ROA)** is the ratio of net profit (after taxes) to the assets used to make the net profit—times 100. Both ROI and ROA measures are trying to get at the same thing—how effectively the company is using resources. These measures became increasingly popular as profit rates dropped and it became more obvious that increasing sales volume doesn't necessarily lead to higher profits—or ROI or ROA. Inflation and higher costs for borrowed funds also force more concern for ROI and ROA. Marketers must include these measures in their thinking or top managers are likely to ignore their plans and requests for financial resources.

## Questions and Problems

1. Distinguish between the following pairs of items that appear on operating statements: *(a)* gross sales and net sales, and *(b)* purchases at billed cost and purchases at net cost.
2. How does gross margin differ from gross profit? From net profit?
3. Explain the similarity between markups and gross margin. What connection do markdowns have with the operating statement?
4. Compute the net profit for a company with the following data:

| | |
|---|---|
| Beginning inventory (cost) | $ 150,000 |
| Purchases at billed cost | 330,000 |
| Sales returns and allowances | 250,000 |
| Rent | 60,000 |
| Salaries | 400,000 |
| Heat and light | 180,000 |
| Ending inventory (cost) | 250,000 |
| Freight cost (inbound) | 80,000 |
| Gross sales | 1,300,000 |

5. Construct an operating statement from the following data:

| | |
|---|---|
| Returns and allowances | $150,000 |
| Expenses | 20% |
| Closing inventory at cost | 600,000 |
| Markdowns | 2% |
| Inward transportation | 30,000 |
| Purchases | 1,000,000 |
| Net profit (5%) | 300,000 |

6. Compute net sales and percent of markdowns for the data given below:

| | |
|---|---|
| Markdowns | $ 40,000 |
| Gross sales | 400,000 |
| Returns | 32,000 |
| Allowances | 48,000 |

7. *(a)* What percentage markups on cost are equivalent to the following percentage markups on selling price: 20, 37½, 50, and 66⅔? *(b)* What percentage markups on selling price are equivalent to the following percentage markups on cost: 33⅓, 20, 40, and 50?
8. What net sales volume is required to obtain a stockturn rate of 20 times a year on an average inventory at cost of $100,000 with a gross margin of 25 percent?
9. Explain how the general manager of a department store might use the markdown ratios computed for her various departments. Is this a fair measure? Of what?
10. Compare and contrast return on investment (ROI) and return on assets (ROA) measures. Which would be best for a retailer with no bank borrowing or other outside sources of funds; that is, the retailer has put up all the money that the business needs?

# Notes

## Chapter 1

**1.** Charles R. Weiser, "Championing the Customer," *Harvard Business Review*, November 1995–December 1995, pp. 113–16; Stanley F. Slater and John C. Narver, "Market Orientation and the Learning Organization," *Journal of Marketing*, July 1995, pp. 63–74; Regina F. Maruca, "Getting Marketing's Voice Heard," *Harvard Business Review*, January–February 1998, pp. 10–11; Vikas Mittal, "Driving Customer Equity: How Customer Lifetime Value Is Reshaping Corporate Strategy," *Journal of Marketing*, April 2001, pp. 107–110; Christine Steinman, "Beyond Market Orientation: When Customers and Suppliers Disagree," *Journal of the Academy of Marketing Science*, Winter 2000, pp. 109–120; Francis J. Gouillart and Frederick D. Sturdivant, "Spend a Day in the Life of Your Customers," *Harvard Business Review*, January 1994–February 1994, pp. 116–20ff; George S. Day, "The Capabilities of Market-Driven Organizations," *Journal of Marketing*, October 1994, pp. 37–52; R.W. Ruekert, "Developing a Market Orientation: An Organizational Strategy Perspective," *International Journal of Research in Marketing*, August 1992, pp. 225–46; J. David Lichtenthal and David T. Wilson, "Becoming Market Oriented," *Journal of Business Research*, May 1992, pp. 191–208; George J. Avlonitis and Spiros P. Gounaris, "Marketing Orientation and Company Performance: Industrial Vs. Consumer Goods Companies," *Industrial Marketing Management*, September 1997, pp. 385–402; Bernard J. Jaworski and Ajay K. Kohli, "Market Orientation: Antecedents and Consequences," *Journal of Marketing*, July 1993, pp. 53–70. See also "The Marketing Revolution at Procter & Gamble," *Business Week*, July 25, 1988, pp. 72–73ff.; Frederick E. Webster, Jr., "The Changing Role of Marketing in the Corporation," *Journal of Marketing*, October 1992, pp. 1–17; Franklin S. Houston, "The Marketing Concept: What It Is and What It Is Not," *Journal of Marketing*, April 1986, pp. 81–87; George S. Day, "The Capabilities of Market-Driven Organizations," *Journal of Marketing*, October 1994, pp. 37–52.

**2.** "With the Telecom Industry on Hold, Nextel Sends Out a Different Signal," *Investor's Business Daily*, March 2, 2001, p. A1; "Keep 'Em Coming Back," *Business Week E. Biz*, May 15, 2000, p. EB20; "Marketers Put a Price on Your Life," *USA Today*, July 7, 1999, p. 3B.

**3.** "Remedies for an Economic Hangover," *Fortune*, June 25, 2001, pp. 130–39; "The Best Little Grocery Store in America," *Inc.*, June 2001, pp. 54–61; "Fanatics!" *Inc.*, April 2001, pp. 36–48; "Internet Nirvana," *Ecompany*, December 2000, pp. 99–108; "The *Inc.* Web Awards," *Inc.* Tech, No. 4, 2000, pp. 45–86; "The Bride Wore Swag," *Ecompany*, October 2000, pp. 201–202; "Why Women Find Lauder Mesmerizing," *Fortune*, May 25, 1998, pp. 96–106; "Smart Managing: The Power of Reflection," *Fortune*, November 24, 1997, pp. 291–96; "Why Some Customers Are More Equal than Others," *Fortune*, September 19, 1994, pp. 215–24; Stanley F. Slater and John C. Narver, "Market Orientation, Customer Value, and Superior Performance," *Business Horizons*, March–April 1994, pp. 22–28; "Relationships: Six Steps to Success," *Sales & Marketing Management*, April 1992, pp. 50–58; Stanley F. Slater, "Developing a Customer Value-Based Theory of the Firm," *Journal of the Academy of Marketing Science*, Spring 1997, pp. 162–67; Sharon E. Beatty, "Keeping Customers," *Journal of Marketing*, April 1994, pp. 124–25; Thomas W. Gruen, "Relationship Marketing: The Route to Marketing Efficiency and Effectiveness," *Business Horizons*, November–December 1997, pp. 32–38; A. Parasuraman, "Reflections on Gaining Competitive Advantage Through Customer Value," *Journal of the Academy of Marketing Science*, Spring 1997, pp. 154–61; Alan W. H. Grant and Leonard A. Schlesinger, "Realize Your Customers' Full Profit Potential," *Harvard Business Review*, September–October 1995, pp. 59–72; Diana L. Deadrick, R. B. McAfee, and Myron Glassman, "'Customers for Life': Does It Fit Your Culture?" *Business Horizons*, July–August 1997, pp. 11–16; Robert B. Woodruff, "Customer Value: The Next Source for Competitive Advantage," *Journal of the Academy of Marketing Science*, Spring 1997, pp. 139–53; Robert M. Morgan, "Aftermarketing: How to Keep Customers for Life Through Relationship Marketing," *Journal of the Academy of Marketing Science*, Winter 1997, pp. 92–93.

**4.** Available from World Wide Web: <http://www.llbean.com>; "Here's the Maine Store for the Great Outdoors," *The Blade*, (Toledo, Ohio), August 26, 1990; "L.L. Bean Scales Back Expansion Goals to Ensure Pride in Its Service Is Valid," *The Wall Street Journal*, July 31, 1989, p. B3; "Training at L.L. Bean," *TRAINING, The Magazine of Human Resources Development*, October 1988; "Using the Old (L.L.) Bean," *The Reader's Digest*, June 1986.

**5.** "Dot-Com Decline Turns into Lift for the Dot-Orgs," *The Wall Street Journal*, March 12, 2001, p. B1ff.; "With Recruiting Slow, the Air Force Seeks a New Ad Campaign," *The Wall Street Journal*, February 14, 2001, p. A1ff.; "Big Retailers Cutting into Nonprofits' Tree Sales," *The Wall Street Journal*, December 19, 2000, p. B1ff.; "Dot-Coop, Dot-Museum, Dot-Pro? Enter Domain of New Web Names," *Investor's Business Daily*, November 21, 2000, p. A10; "Uncle Sam Wants You—and So Does Pepsi," *Business Week*, September 4, 2000, p. 52; "When Nonprofits Go After Profits," *Business Week*, June 26, 2000, pp. 173–78; "Army Enlists Net to Be All It Can Be," *USA Today*, April 19, 2000, p. 10B; "Uncle Sam Wants You . . . to Have Fun!" *Business Week*, February 21, 2000, pp. 98–101; "Modern Marketing Helps Sell Life as a Nun," *The Wall Street Journal*, May 11, 1999, p. B1ff.; "This Exhibit Is Brought to You by . . . ," *Business Week*, November 10, 1997, pp. 91–94; "In Funding Squeeze, PBS Cozies Up to Madison Avenue 'Sponsors,'" *The Wall Street Journal*, July 3, 1996, p. B1ff.; "Non-Profits Get Market-Savvy," *Advertising Age*, May 29, 1995, p. 1ff.; William G. Bowen, "When a Business Leader Joins a Nonprofit Board," *Harvard Business Review*, September–October 1994, pp. 38–44; "Charities Draw Younger Donors with Hip Events and Door Prizes," *The Wall Street Journal*, April 25, 1994, p. B1; "Nonprofits Dig into Databases for Big Donors," *The Wall Street Journal*, September 8, 1992, p. B1ff.; William A. Sutton, "Sports Marketing: Competitive Business Strategies for Sports," *Journal of the Academy of Marketing Science*, Spring 1996, pp. 176–77; Russell W. Jones, Carolyn Marshall, and Thomas P. Bergman, "Can a Marketing Campaign Be Used to Achieve Public Policy Goals?" *Journal of Public Policy & Marketing*, Spring 1996, pp. 98–107; J. G. Dees, "Enterprising Nonprofits," *Harvard Business Review*, January–February 1998, pp. 55–67; W. C. Kim and Renee Mauborgne, "Value Innovation: The Strategic Logic of High Growth," *Harvard Business Review*, January–February 1997, pp. 102–12; Gerald E. Smith and Paul D. Berger, "The Impact of Direct Marketing Appeals on Charitable Marketing Effectiveness," *Journal of the Academy of Marketing Science*, Summer 1996, pp. 219–31; Shohreh A. Kaynama, "Fundraising for Non-Profits," *Journal of the Academy of Marketing Science*, Spring 1997, p.173; C. Scott Greene and Paul Miesing, "Public Policy, Technology, and Ethics: Marketing Decisions for NASA's Space Shuttle," *Journal of Marketing*, Summer 1984, pp. 56–67; Alan R. Andreasen, "Nonprofits: Check Your Attention to Customers," *Harvard Business Review*, May–June 1982, pp. 105–10.

**6.** Edward J. O'Boyle and Lyndon E. Dawson, Jr., "The American Marketing Association Code of Ethics: Instructions for Marketers," *Journal of Business Ethics*, December 1992, pp. 921–30; Ellen J. Kennedy and Leigh Lawton, "Ethics and Services Marketing," *Journal of Business Ethics*, October 1993, pp. 785–96; Michael R. Hyman, Robert Skipper, and Richard Tansey, "Ethical Codes Are Not Enough," *Business Horizons*,

March/April, 1990, pp. 15–22; John Tsalikis and David J. Fritzsche, "Business Ethics: A Literature Review with a Focus on Marketing Ethics," *Journal of Business Ethics*, September, 1989, pp. 695–702; G. R. Laczniak, R. F. Lusch, and P. E. Murphy, "Social Marketing: Its Ethical Dimensions," *Journal of Marketing*, Spring 1979, pp. 29–36.

## Chapter 2

**1.** Available from World Wide Web: <http://www.dell.com>; "The Mother of All Price Wars," *Business Week*, July 20, 2001, pp. 32–35; "Why Dell Isn't Dumb," *Fortune*, July 9, 2001, pp. 134–36; "Automate or Die," *Ecompany*, July 2001, pp. 60–67; "How Dell Fine-Tunes Its PC Pricing to Gain Edge in a Slow Market," *The Wall Street Journal*, June 8, 2001, p. A1ff.; "How Dell Keeps from Stumbling," *Business Week*, May 14, 2001, pp. 38B–D; "How Dell, Starwood and Teva Fight, Win in Commodity-Priced Business," *Investor's Business Daily*, May 4, 2001, p. A1; "Dell Dethrones Compaq as Global PC Sales Leader," *Investor's Business Daily*, April 23, 2001, p. A6; "Dell, Gateway Seen Turning Up the Heat in PC Price Wars," *Investor's Business Daily*, March 28, 2001, p. A7; "Price War Squeezes PC Makers," *The Wall Street Journal*, March 26, 2001, p. B1ff.; "Thinking Outside the Beige PC Box," *Investor's Business Daily*, March 6, 2001, p. A1; "Be like Mike," *Ecompany*, December 2000, pp. 85–86; "How a Low-Cost Provider like Dell also Delivers Best Customer Service," *Investor's Business Daily*, November 13, 2000, p. A1; "Going Digital? Think First," *Fortune*, November 13, 2000, pp. 190–98; "Can Michael Dell Escape the Box?" *Fortune*, October 16, 2000, pp. 92–120; "Dell's Second Web Revolution," *Business Week E.Biz*, September 18, 2000, pp. EB62–EB63; "Dell Looks for Ways to Rekindle the Fire It Had as an Upstart," *The Wall Street Journal*, August 31, 2000, p. A1ff.; "Direct PC Seller Dell Computer Aims to Sell Its Web Expertise," *Investor's Business Daily*, April 13, 2000, p. A6; "Dell to Offer Hosting of Small-Business Web Sites," *The Wall Street Journal*, February 22, 2000, p. B23; "Dell's Big New Act," *Fortune*, December 6, 1999, pp. 152–56; "Dell Cracks China," *Fortune*, June 21, 1999, pp. 120–24; "Nine Ways to Win on the Web," *Fortune*, May 24, 1999, pp. 112–25; "Dell Builds an Electronics Superstore on the Web," *The Wall Street Journal*, March 3, 1999, p. B1ff.; "The Internet: Leading the PC Pack," *The Wall Street Journal Reports*, December 7, 1998, p. R27; "Michael Dell Rocks," *Fortune*, May 11, 1998, pp. 58–70; "No Big Deal: Why Michael Dell Isn't Afraid of The New Compaq," *Fortune*, March 2, 1998, pp. 189–92; "Dell's Profit Leaps 52% as Asian Sales Soar," *The Wall Street Journal*, February 19, 1998, p. B20; "Asia: Why Business Is Still Bullish," *Fortune*, October 27, 1997, pp. 139–42; "And Give Me an Extra-Fast Modem with That, Please," *Business Week*, September 29, 1997, p. 38; "Now Everyone in PCs Wants to Be like Mike," *Fortune*, September 8, 1997, pp. 91–92; "Michael Dell Turns the PC World Inside Out," *Fortune*, September 8, 1997, pp. 76–86; "Dell Fights PC Wars by Emphasizing Customer Service," *The Wall Street Journal*, August 15, 1997, p. B4; Joan Magretta, "The Power of Virtual Integration: An Interview With Dell Computer's Michael Dell," *Harvard Business Review*, March–April 1998, pp. 72–84.

**2.** Mary Anne Raymond and Hiram C. Barksdale, "Corporate Strategic Planning and Corporate Marketing: Toward an Interface," *Business Horizons*, September/October, 1989, pp. 41–48; George S. Day, "Marketing's Contribution to the Strategy Dialogue," *Journal of the Academy of Marketing Science*, Fall 1992, pp. 323–30; P. Rajan Varadarajan and Terry Clark, "Delineating the Scope of Corporate, Business, and Marketing Strategy," *Journal of Business Research*, October–November 1994, pp. 93–106.

**3.** Available from World Wide Web: <http://www.learningco.com>; "Broderbund: Identify an Need, Turn a Profit," *Fortune*, November 30, 1992, pp. 78–79.

**4.** "Genesco Names New Executive of Children's Footwear Division," *Press Release*, Genesco, July 15, 1994; "Toddler University Ends Up in Westport," *Westport News*, March 8, 1991, p. A13; "Whiz Kid," *Connecticut*, August 1989, pp. 56–57; "The Young and the Restless," *Children's Business*, May 1989, p. 29; "Making the Grade," *Young Fashions Magazine*, February 1989.

**5.** *2000 Annual Report*, Gillette Company.

**6.** "For the Wrist that Has Everything," *Newsweek*, June 25, 2001, p. 80; "Now That's Good Timing," *Business Week Small Biz*, April 23, 2001, p. 14; "You Can Be a New-Product Dynamo: Medtronic, Pizza Hut, ADT Tell How," *Investor's Business Daily*, April 9, 2001, p. A1; "Movado Winds Up Lifestyle Effort, Expanded Line, with $15M in Print," *Brandweek*, April 2, 2001, p. 4; "Catching Up to Dick Tracy," *Business Week*, February 12, 2001, p. 100E4; "Timex Pursues Hip, Younger Set in Ads for Its New iControl Watch," *The Wall Street Journal*, May 19, 2000, p. B2; "Swatch: Ready for Net Time," *Business Week*, February 14, 2000, p. 61; "Timex Puts 'Iron' into TV with $5M," *Brandweek*, September 22, 1997, p. 6; "Timex Lines Goes for Museum-Goers," *Brandweek*, July 21, 1997, p. 8; "Timex Back to Basics to Retro-fit Gen X," *Brandweek*, August 5, 1996, p. 3; "Swatch Adds Metal Watch," *Advertising Age*, November 7, 1994, p. 60; Benetton Readies Watch Campaign," *Brandweek*, August 8, 1994, p. 5; "Indiglo Watch Lights Up Better Times for Timex," *Brandweek*, April 25, 1994, pp. 30–32.

**7.** Available from World Wide Web: <http://www.cyberatlas.com>; Michael Pastore, "IT Helps Nonprofits Increase Productivity," December 20, 2001.

**8.** Available from World Wide Web: <http://www.nua.ie>; "Aussie Charities Must Work Harder on the Web," June 18, 2001.

**9.** Available from World Wide Web: <http://www.nua.ie>; "Most Job Seekers Stay Faithful to One Website," May 7, 2002.

**10.** Available from World Wide Web: <http://www.cyberatlas.com>; Robyn Greenspan, "Direct Mail Best for Charity Awareness," August 15, 2003.

## Chapter 3

**1.** Beverly Cramp, "Reinventing Cool," *Profit*, December 2001, p. 41.

**2.** For more on Coleman, see "Events Light Coleman's Fire," *Advertising Age*, June 18, 2001, p. 61; "Growing to Match Its Brand Name," *Fortune*, June 13, 1994, p. 114; "Coleman's Familiar Name Is Both Help and Hindrance," *The Wall Street Journal*, May 17, 1990, p. B2.

**3.** For more on McDonald's, see "Disney Orders McDonald's Burger Joint for New Park," *USA Today*, January 15, 2001, p. 1B; "For East German Pair, McDonald's Serves Up an Economic Parable," *The Wall Street Journal*, November 8, 1999, p. A1ff.; "Fast-food Icon Wants Shine Restored to Golden Arches," *USA Today*, May 1, 1998, p. 1Bff.; "McD's Eyes Rollout of Loyalty Card," *Advertising Age*, April 27, 1998, p. 3; "A Really Big Mac," *Newsweek*, November 17, 1997, pp. 56–58; "Why You Won't Find Any Egg McMuffins for Breakfast in Brazil," *The Wall Street Journal*, October 23, 1997, p. A1ff.; "Burger Wars Sizzle as McDonald's Clones the Whopper," *The Wall Street Journal*, "September 17, 1997, p. B1ff.; "Toilet Paper and a Big Mac," *American Demographics*, July 1996, p. 15–16; "McDonald's Conquers the World," *Fortune*, October 17, 1994, pp. 103–16.

**4.** For more on Heinz EZ Squirt, see "Heinz Picks Purple as New EZ Squirt Color," *Brandweek*, June 25, 2001, p. 7; "Kids Salivate for New, Yucky, Weirdly Colored Food," *USA Today*, April 23, 2001, p. 7B; "Do E-Ads Have a Future?" *Business Week E.Biz*, January 22, 2001, pp. EB46–EB50; "Squeezing New from Old," *USA Today*, January 4, 2001, p. 1Bff.; "Bottled Up," *Fortune*, September 18, 2000, pp. 194–206; "EZ Being Green: Kids Line Is Latest Heinz Innovation," *Advertising Age*, July 10, 2000, p. 3ff.; *2000 Annual Report*, Heinz. For more on ski resorts, see "It's All Downhill: Sugar Mountain Opens Slopes to Mountain Bikers," *Raleigh News & Observer*, July 25, 1999, p. 1Hff.; "Bikers Give Ski

Resorts Summer Time Lift," *The Wall Street Journal*, July 7, 1994, p. B1ff. For more on Nike, see "Nike Puts Its Swoosh on MP3 Players, Walkie-Talkies, Heart Monitors," *The Wall Street Journal*, May 10, 2000, p. B1ff.; *2000 Annual Report*, Nike; "It's Not Just about Shoes," *Newsweek*, May 18, 1998, pp. 50–51.

**5.** Mark B. Houston, "Competing for the Future: Breakthrough Strategies for Seizing Control of Your Industry and Creating the Markets of Tomorrow," *Journal of the Academy of Marketing Science*, Winter 1996, pp. 77–79; George S. Day and Robin Wensley, "Assessing Advantage: A Framework for Diagnosing Competitive Superiority," *Journal of Marketing*, April 1988, pp. 1–20; Kevin P. Coyne, "Sustainable Competitive Advantage—What It Is, What It Isn't," *Business Horizons*, January/February 1986, pp. 54–61; Michael E. Porter, *Competitive Advantage—Creating and Sustaining Superior Performance* (New York: Free Press, MacMillan, 1986).

**6.** "GM Warms Up Its Branding Iron," *Business Week*, April 16, 2001, pp. 56–58; "GM Still Pushing Lame-Duck Oldsmobiles," *USA Today*, February 19, 2001, p. 4B; "One Last Look at Oldsmobile," *Brandweek*, Janary 8, 2001, pp. 28–32; "GM: 'Out with the Olds' Is Just the Start," *Business Week*, December 25, 2000, p. 57; "In Order to Grow, GM Finds that the Order of the Day Is Cutbacks," *The Wall Street Journal*, December 18, 2000, p. A1ff.; "How to Sell a Dying Brand," *Advertising Age*, December 18, 2000, p. 4ff.; "After Decades of Brand Bodywork, GM Parks Oldsmobile—for Good," *The Wall Street Journal*, December 13, 2000, p. B1ff.; "GM Decides to Shutter Oldsmobile," *USA Today*, December 13, 2000, p. 3B; "Oldsmobile to Go as GM Outlines Cost-Cutting Steps," *Investor's Business Daily*, December 13, 2000, p. A13.

**7.** "Taking On Procter & Gamble," *Inc.*, October 2000, pp. 66–71.

**8.** Shelby D. Hunt and Robert M. Morgan, "Resource-Advantage Theory: A Snake Swallowing Its Tail or a General Theory of Competition?" *Journal of Marketing*, October 1997, pp. 74–82; Stavros P. Kalafatis and Vicki Cheston, "Normative Models and Practical Applications of Segmentation in Business Markets," *Industrial Marketing Management*, November 1997, pp. 519–30; Lisa R. Adam, "Nichecraft: Using Your Specialness to Focus Your Business, Corner Your Market, and Make Customers Seek You Out," *Journal of the Academy of Marketing Science*, Summer 1997, pp. 259–60; S. Ratneshwar, Cornelia Pechmann, and Allan D. Shocker, "Goal-Derived Categories and the Antecedents of Across-Category Consideration," *Journal of Consumer Research*, December 1996, pp. 240–50; George S. Day, A. D. Shocker, and R. K. Srivastava, "Customer-Oriented Approaches to Identifying Product-Markets," *Journal of Marketing*, Fall 1979, pp. 8–19; Rajendra K. Srivastava, Mark I. Alpert, and Allan D. Shocker, "A Customer-Oriented Approach for Determining Market Structures," *Journal of Marketing*, Spring 1984, pp. 32–45.

**9.** Available from World Wide Web: <http://www.hallmark.com>; *2000 Annual Report*, Hallmark; "American Greetings Thinks Time for 'Anytime' Is Now," *The Wall Street Journal*, March 24, 1998, p. B9; "American Greeting, Hallmark's Cards Will Send an Earful," *The Wall Street Journal*, November 5, 1993, p. B10B; "Old-Fashioned Sentiments Go High-Tech," *The Wall Street Journal*, November 9, 1992, p. B1ff.

**10.** Terry Elrod and Russell S. Winer, "An Empirical Evaluation of Aggregation Approaches for Developing Market Segments," *Journal of Marketing*, Fall 1982, pp. 32–34; Frederick W. Winter, "A Cost-Benefit Approach to Market Segmentation," *Journal of Marketing*, Fall 1979, pp. 103–11; Andrew Hilton, "Mythology, Markets, and the Emerging Europe," *Harvard Business Review*, November–December 1992, pp. 50–127.

**11.** Philip A. Dover, "Segmentation and Positioning for Strategic Marketing Decisions," *Journal of the Academy of Marketing Science*, Summer 2000, pp. 438–41; John Hogan, "Defining Your Market: Winning Strategies for High-Tech, Industrial, and Service Firms," *Journal of the Academy of Marketing Science*, Summer 2000, pp. 442–4; Hershey H. Friedman and Linda W. Friedman, "Reducing the 'Wait' in Waiting-Line Systems: Waiting Line Segmentation," *Business Horizons*, July–August 1997, pp. 54–58; Alex Chernev, "The Effect of Common Features on Brand Choice: Moderating Role of Attribute Importance," *Journal of Consumer Research*, March 1997, pp. 304–11; Dianne S.P. Cermak, Karen Maru File, and Russ Alan Prince, "A Benefit Segmentation of the Major Donor Market," *Journal of Business Research*, February 1994, pp. 121–30; Robert L. Armacost and Jamshid C. Hosseini, "Identification of Determinant Attributes Using the Analytic Hierarchy Process," *Journal of the Academy of Marketing Science*, Fall 1994, pp. 383–92; Joel S. Dubow, "Occasion-based vs. User-based Benefit Segmentation, A Case Study," *Journal of Advertising Research*, March/April 1992, pp. 11–19; Peter R. Dickson and James L. Ginter, "Market Segmentation, Product Differentiation, and Marketing Strategy," *Journal of Marketing*, April 1987, pp. 1–10; Russell I. Haley, "Benefit Segmentation—20 Years Later," *Journal of Consumer Marketing* 1, no. 2 (1984), pp. 5–14.

**12.** Elizabeth Adams, "Eating Up a Brand New Category," *Marketing Magazine*, December 22, 1997.

**13.** For more on wired hotels, see "New at the Inn: Remote-Control Curtains," *The Wall Street Journal*, April 27, 2001, p. W9; "Find Wired Hotels at Bargain Prices," *Investor's Business Daily*, September 15, 2000, p. A1; "Hotels Add Fast Internet to Room Services," *Investor's Business Daily*, July 5, 2000, p. A8; "Hotels Target Generation X," *USA Today*, February 10, 2000, p. 1Bff.; "Hotels Fired Up to Get Wired Up," *USA Today*, September 2, 1999, p. 1Bff.; "For Hotel Guests with Glitches, High-Tech Room Service," *The Wall Street Journal*, August 30, 1999, p. B1ff.

**14.** "Marketers Find 'Tweens' Too Hot to Ignore," *USA Today*, July 10, 2001, p. 13A; "Yamada Card Gives Credit to Struggling Brazilians," *The Wall Street Journal*, March 27, 2001, p. B1ff.; "Grown-Up Drinks for Tender Taste Buds," *Business Week*, March 5, 2001, p. 96; "Boosting Diageo's Spirits," *The Wall Street Journal*, February 12, 2001, p. B1ff.; "Soda Pop That Packs a Punch," *Newsweek*, February 19, 2001, p. 45; "New Web Sites Let Kids Shop, Like, Without Credit Cards," *The Wall Street Journal*, June 14, 1999, p. B1ff.; "How Big Liquor Takes Aim at Teens," *Business Week*, May 19, 1997, p. 92; "How 'Medicaid Moms' Became a Hot Market for Health Industry," *The Wall Street Journal*, May 1, 1997, p. A1ff.; Suzeanne Benet, Robert E. Pitts, and Michael LaTour, "The Appropriateness of Fear Appeal Use for Health Care Marketing to the Elderly: Is It OK to Scare Granny?" *Journal of Business Ethics*, January 1993, pp. 45–56; "New Converse Shoe Named Run 'N Gun Is Angering Critics," *The Wall Street Journal*, February 8, 1993, p. B5; "'Black Death' Becomes 'Black Hat' so that Vodka Can Stay on Shelves," *The Wall Street Journal*, May 12, 1992, p. B6; "Malt Liquor Makers Find Lucrative Market in the Urban Young," *The Wall Street Journal*, March 9, 1992, p. A1ff.; Richard W. Pollay, S. Siddarth, Michael Siegel, Anne Haddix et al., "The Last Straw? Cigarette Advertising and Realized Market Shares Among Youths and Adults, 1979–1993," *Journal of Marketing*, April 1996, pp. 1–16; N. C. Smith and Elizabeth Cooper-Martin, "Ethics and Target Marketing: The Role of Product Harm and Consumer Vulnerability," *Journal of Marketing*, July 1997, pp. 1–20.

**15.** Girish Punj and David W. Stewart, "Cluster Analysis in Marketing Research: Review and Suggestions for Application," *Journal of Marketing Research*, May 1983, pp. 134–48; Fernando Robles and Ravi Sarathy, "Segmenting the Computer Aircraft Market with Cluster Analysis," *Industrial Marketing Management*, February 1986, pp. 1–12.

**16.** For more on CRM, see Chapter 8, footnote #5. For more on Amazon, see "This Race Isn't Even Close," *Business Week*, December 18, 2000, pp. 208–10; "Amazon: King of the On-Line Jungle, Master of All Domains," *DSNRetailing Today*, November 20, 2000, pp. 18–22; "The Amazon Way Is Still the Best Model for Web Shopping," *The Wall Street Journal*, September 21, 2000, p. B1; "Amazon: Creative Coddling, Great Word of Mouth," *Business Week E. Biz*, September 16, 2000; "E-Commerce: At Your Service," *Wall Street Journal Reports*, April 17, 2000,

p. R12ff.; "Secrets of the New Brand Builders," *Fortune*, June 22, 1998, pp. 167–70. For more on privacy, see Chapter 8, footnote #4 and Chapter 22, footnote #18.

**17.** David A. Aaker and J. Gary Shansby, "Positioning Your Product," *Business Horizons*, May/June, 1982, pp. 56–62; Al Ries and Jack Trout, *Positioning: The Battle for Your Mind* (New York: McGraw-Hill, 1981), p. 53. For some current examples of positioning, see "Getting Corian Out of the Kitchen," *The Wall Street Journal*, December 12, 2000, p. B1ff.; "Corian Refashions," *Advertising Age*, September 18, 2000, pp. 74–76; "Pie in the Sky," *Brandweek*, December 16, 1996, pp. 23–24; "From the Horse's Mouth: Try a Little Hoof Fix on Your Nails," *The Wall Street Journal*, July 29, 1994, p. B1ff.; Hans Muhlbacher, Angelika Dreher, and Angelika Gabriel-Ritter, "MIPS-Managing Industrial Positioning Strategies," *Industrial Marketing Management*, October 1994, pp. 287–98.

**18.** Alice M. Tybout and Brian Sternthal, "Brand Positioning," chapter 2 in *Kellogg on Marketing* (John Wiley & Sons, 2001), p. 51-54.

## Chapter 4

**1.** Philip Siekman, "The Smart Car is Looking More So," *Fortune*, April 4, 2002.

**2.** Micheline Maynard, "Get Smart," *Fortune*, April 18, 2001.

**3.** Available from World Wide Web: <http://www.unesco.org/courier/1998_12/uk/dossier/txt.26htm>; Rene Lefort, "A Philosophy on Four Wheels," 1998.

**4.** Available from World Wide Web: <http://www.unesco.org/courier/1998_12/uk/dossier/txt.26htm>; Rene Lefort, "A Philosophy on Four Wheels," 1998.

**5.** Warren Keegan and Mark Green, *Global Marketing: Third Edition* (Prentice Hall, 2003), p. 441.

**6.** Available from World Wide Web: <http://www.smart.com>; "Smart Receives Industry Accolades," 2002.

**7.** Dr. Remko Van Hoek, *Smart (Car) and Smart Logistics* (Belgium: University of Ghent), 1997, p. 17.

**8.** Available from World Wide Web: <http://www.smart.com>; "Sales of the City-Coupe and Cabrio Rise by More Than Six Percent," 2002.

**9.** Philip Siekman, "eMotion Imports a Smart Idea," *Fortune*, April 15, 2002.

**10.** Jack Ewing and Marsha Johnston, "The Smart Car's Not So Dumb," *BusinessWeek*, September 20, 1999, p. 22.

**11.** See Peter F. Drucker, *Management: Tasks, Responsibilities, Practices, and Plans* (New York: Harper and Row, 1973); Sev K. Keil, "The Impact of Business Objectives and the Time Horizon of Performance Evaluation on Pricing Behavior," *International Journal of Research in Marketing*, June 2001, p. 67; Kenneth E. Clow, "Marketing Strategy: The Challenge of the External Environment," *Journal of the Academy of Marketing Science*, Summer 2000, pp. 437–9.

**12.** Lance Leuthesser and Chiranjeev Kohli, "Corporate Identity: The Role of Mission Statements," *Business Horizons*, May–June 1997, pp. 59–66; Christopher K. Bart, "Sex, Lies, and Mission Statements," *Business Horizons*, November–December 1997, pp. 9–18; Christopher K. Bart, "Industrial Firms and the Power of Mission," *Industrial Marketing Management*, July 1997, pp. 371–83.

**13.** "Why Inflation Is Not Inevitable," *Fortune*, September 12, 1988, pp. 117–24.

**14.** "Behind Cisco's Woes Are Some Wounds of Its Own Making," *The Wall Street Journal*, April 18, 2001, p. A1ff.; Robert Jacobson and David A. Aaker, "Is Market Share All That It's Cracked Up to Be?" *Journal of Marketing*, Fall 1985, pp. 11–22; Carolyn Y. Woo, "Market-Share Leadership—Not Always So Good," *Harvard Business Review*, January–February 1984, pp. 50–55; "Reichhold Chemicals: Now the Emphasis Is on Profits Rather than Volume," *Business Week*, June 20, 1983, pp. 178–79.

**15.** Available from World Wide Web: <http://www.harley-davidson.com>; "Harley Davidson's Jeffrey Bleustein: Communication Focus Keeps His Company Roaring," *Investor's Business Daily*, February 28, 2001, p. A4; *2000 Annual Report*, Harley-Davidson; "Motorcycle Madness Revvs Up Ad Budgets," *Advertising Age*, November 8, 1999, p. 38; "Gearing Up for the Cruiser Wars," *Fortune*, August 3, 1998, pp. 128B–L; "Motorcycle Maker Caters to the Continent," *USA Today*, April 22, 1998, p. 8B; "That Vroom! You Hear May Not Be a Harley," *Business Week*, October 20, 1997, pp. 159–60; "Have Brands, Will Travel," *Brandweek*, October 6, 1997, pp. 22–26; "Japan's Bikers: The Tame Ones," *Business Week*, October 6, 1997, pp. 30D-F; "Killer Strategies that Make Shareholders Rich," *Fortune*, June 23, 1997, pp. 70–84; "Aided by Research, Harley Goes Whole Hog," *Marketing News*, December 2, 1996, pp. 16–17; "Tune-Up Time for Harley," *Business Week*, April 8, 1996, pp. 90–94; "The Rumble Heard Round the World," *Business Week*, May 24, 1993, p. 58–60; "Put to the Test," *Adweek*, December 7, 1992, pp. 28–32; "Yuppies Help Fuel Demand," *USA Today*, July 22, 1991, p. 1Bff.; "Harley-Davidson's U-Turn," *USA Today*, March 2, 1990, p. 1Bff.; "How Harley Beat Back the Japanese," *Fortune*, September 25, 1989, pp. 155–64.

**16.** For more on patents, see "Would You Buy a Patent License from This Man?" *Ecompany*, April 2001, pp. 104–10; "PrilosecTime Is Just About Up," *Business Week*, January 8, 2001, p. 47; "Eli Lilly Loses Prozac Patent-Protection Battle," *The Wall Street Journal*, August 10, 2000, p. A3ff.; "Businesses Battle over Intellectual Property," *USA Today*, August 2, 2000, p. 1Bff.; "Qualcomm Hits the Big Time," *Fortune*, May 15, 2000, pp. 213–29; "New Teeth for Old Patents," *Business Week*, November 30, 1998, pp. 92–95; "What's Next—A Patent for the 401(K)?" *Business Week*, October 26, 1998, pp. 104–107; "Drug Pirates," *Fortune*, October 12, 1998, pp. 146–48.

**17.** For more on Microsoft's Xbox, see "This Game's Not Over Yet," *Fortune*, July 9, 2001, p. 164; ". . . Games," *The Wall Street Journal Reports*, June 25, 2001, p. R6; "Game Wars 5.0," *Newsweek*, May 28, 2001, pp. 65–66; "Let the Game-System War Begin," *USA Today*, May 21, 2001, p. 3D; "The Battle of Seattle," *Time*, May 21, 2001, pp. 58–59; "Sony, AOL Join Up to Link PlayStation 2 to Internet in Move to Outflank Microsoft," *The Wall Street Journal*, May 15, 2001, p. A3; "Xbox Marks the Spot for Launch of Microsoft's Game," *USA Today*, April 23, 2001, p. 1B; "As Microsoft's Xbox Debut Nears, Fan Sites Get Cocky, Rivals—Wary," *The Wall Street Journal*, April 12, 2001, p. B1ff.; "How Microsoft Hopes to Win with Xbox," *The Wall Street Journal*, January 31, 2001, p. B1ff.; "Game Wars," *Time*, March 20, 2000, pp. 44–45; "How Four Renegades Persuaded Microsoft to Make a Game Machine," *The Wall Street Journal*, March 10, 2000, p. B1ff.

**18.** Excerpted from Scott Gardiner, "In Praise of Saint Timmy," *Marketing Magazine*, August 21, 2000, p. 10.

**19.** Peter J. Williamson, "Asia's New Competitive Game," *Harvard Business Review*, September–October 1997, pp. 55–67; David J. Collis and Cynthia A. Montgomery, "Competing on Resources: Strategy in the 1990s," *Harvard Business Review*, July–August 1995, pp. 118–28; "How Goodyear Forecast a Great Decade," *American Demographics*, March 1995, p. 39; "Firms Analyze Rivals to Help Fix Themselves," *The Wall Street Journal*, May 3, 1994, p. B1ff.; Thomas S. Gruca and D Sudharshan, "A Framework for Entry Deterrence Strategy: The Competitive Environment, Choices, and Consequences," *Journal of Marketing*, July 1995, pp. 44–55; Venkatram Ramaswamy, Hubert Gatignon, and David J. Reibstein, "Competitive Marketing Behavior in Industrial Markets," *Journal of Marketing*, April 1994, pp. 45–55; Z. S. Deligonul and S. T. Cavusgil, "Does the Comparative Advantage Theory of Competition

Really Replace the Neoclassical Theory of Perfect Competition?" *Journal of Marketing*, October 1997, pp. 65–73; J. S. Armstrong, "Co-Opetition," *Journal of Marketing*, April 1997, pp. 92–95; John L. Haverty and Myroslaw J. Kyj, "What Happens when New Competitors Enter an Industry," *Industrial Marketing Management* 20, no. 1 (1991), pp. 73–80; Arch G. Woodside and Elizabeth J. Wilson, "Diagnosing Customer Comparisons of Competitors' Marketing Mix Strategies," *Journal of Business Research*, October–November 1994, pp. 133–44; David W. Cravens and Shannon H. Shipp, "Market-Driven Strategies for Competitive Advantage," *Business Horizons*, January/February, 1991, pp. 53–61; William W. Keep, Glenn S. Omura, and Roger J. Calantone, "What Managers Should Know about Their Competitors' Patented Technologies," *Industrial Marketing Management*, July 1994, pp. 257–64.

**20.** *Kao* (Cambridge, MA: Harvard Business School Press, 1984); Bruce R. Klemz, "Managerial Assessment of Potential Entrants: Processes and Pitfalls," *International Journal of Research in Marketing*, June 2001, p. 37.

**21.** For more on P&G, see "P&G Wins Lawsuit, Loses Market," *Advertising Age*, September 18, 1989, p. 72. For more on corporate spying, see "More Firms Hire Sleuths to Avoid Nasty Surprises," *USA Today*, June 26, 2001, p. 1Bff.; "Your Employees Love IM. Should You Worry?" *Ecompany*, June 2001, pp. 102–106; "Spooked: Is That Salesman Really a Spy?" *Fortune*, January 8, 2001, p. 192; Adam L. Penenberg and Marc Barry, *Spooked: Espionage in Corporate America* (New York: HarperCollins, 2000); "Hey, It's Not Prying; It's Competitive Intelligence," *Raleigh News & Observer*, August 6, 2000, p. 14E; "Call It Mission Impossible *Inc.*—Corporate-Spying Firms Thrive," *The Wall Street Journal*, July 3, 2000, p. B1ff.; "Protecting Corporate Secrets: Does Your Company Own What You Know?" *USA Today*, January 19, 2000, p. 1Aff.; "Eyeing the Competition," *Time*, March 22, 1999, pp. 58–60; "How Safe Are Your Secrets?" *Fortune*, September 8, 1997, pp. 114–20; "High-Tech Tools Usher in Stolen-Information Age," *USA Today*, April 10, 1997, p. 1Bff. For more on the Oracle/Microsoft case, see "Oracle Case Shines Light on Corporate Spying," *Investor's Business Daily*, June 30, 2000, p. A7; "Oracle-Style Investigations Common, Experts Say," *USA Today*, June 29, 2000, p. 3B; "How Piles of Trash Became Latest Focus in Bitter Software Feud," *The Wall Street Journal*, June 29, 2000, p. A1ff.; "Oracle Hired Firm to Probe Microsoft Allies, *The Wall Street Journal*, June 28, 2000, p. A3ff. For more on other specific cases, see "System Breach Is Stirring Up Airline Rivalry," *The Wall Street Journal*, June 27, 2000, p. B1ff.; "China's Spies Target Corporate America," *Fortune*, March 30, 1998, pp. 118–22; "In the Debris of a Failed Merger: Trade Secrets," *The Wall Street Journal*, March 10, 1998, p. B1ff.; "Ex-Kodak Manager Is Sentenced to Jail; Company Sues Scherer," *The Wall Street Journal*, November 17, 1997, p. B17. See also Shaker A. Zahra, "Unethical Practices in Competitive Analysis: Patterns, Causes and Effects," *Journal of Business Ethics*, January 1994, pp. 53–62.

**22.** Helen P. Burwell, Online Competitive Intelligence (Tempe, Arizona: Facts on Demand Press), 1999.

**23.** "Devaluation's Downbeat Start," *The Economist*, January 10, 2002, p. 34-35.

**24.** Rajdeep Grewal, "Building Organizational Capabilities for Managing Economic Crisis: The Role of Market Orientation and Strategic Flexibility," *Journal of Marketing*, April 2001, pp. 67–81; "Gas Prices May Level Off—Until Next Summer," *USA Today*, May 22, 2001, p. 1Aff.; "Daimler Thinks Small: With Gas Prices Soaring, Will Americans Get 'Smart'?" *Newsweek*, May 21, 2001, p. 48; "Europeans Unmoved by USA's Energy Plight," *USA Today*, May 17, 2001, p. 8A; "Diesel-Sippers Win Fans as Gas Prices Soar," *USA Today*, Mary 15, 2001, p. 1B; "Shock at the Wheel: Wonder Why Gas Prices Suddenly Got So High?" *The Wall Street Journal*, May 14, 2001, p. A1ff.; "Wary Consumers Watch as Inflation Nudges Prices Up," *USA Today*, April 30, 2001, p. 1Bff.; "Time for a Reality Check," *Business Week*, December 2, 1996, pp. 58–67; "Industry Covets Potential of Pacific Rim," *USA Today*, June 17, 1996, p. 1Bff.; "Biggest Show of Force in a Decade Halts Slide of the Dollar—for Now," *The Wall Street Journal*, May 5, 1994, p. A1ff.; "Demand for Wood Leads to Building Panic," *USA Today*, March 17, 1993, p. 1Bff.

**25.** Michael Hitt et al., *Strategic Management Concepts: First Canadian Edition* (Nelson Thompson Learning, 2002), p. 175.

**26.** "New Frontiers: A New Brand of Tech Cities," *Newsweek*, April 30, 2001, pp. 44–70; "Technology: The Era of Living Wirelessly," *USA Today Bonus*, June 26, 2001; "Technology: What's Ahead," *The Wall Street Journal Reports*, June 25, 2001; "tough Times in Techland," *The Wall Street Journal*, December 28, 2000, p. B1ff.; "Tech Extra: Consumer Electronics," *Investor's Business Daily*, December 8, 2000; "Technology: How Technology Has Changed the Way We . . . ," *The Wall Street Journal Reports*, November 13, 2000; "Telecommunications: Untangling the Cord," *The Wall Street Journal Reports*, September 18, 2000; "Tech Extra: The Web Goes Wireless," *Investor's Business Daily*, September 15, 2000; "Gadget Envy," *The Wall Street Journal*, August 3, 2000, p. B1ff.; "Special Report: Wireless in Cyberspace," *Business Week*, May 29, 2000, pp. 136–64; "Special Report: Digital Wheels," *Business Week*, April 10, 2000, pp. 114–24; "Entertainment + Technology: Together at Last," *The Wall Street Journal Reports*, March 20, 2000; "Technology: Cleaning Out Your Desk," *The Wall Street Journal Reports*, November 15, 1999; "The Internet Age," *Business Week*, October 4, 1999, pp. 69–98; "Beyond the PC," *Business Week*, March 8, 1999, pp. 79–88; "Technology: Thinking about Tomorrow," *The Wall Street Journal Reports*, November 16, 1998; "Digital D-Day," *Business Week*, October 26, 1998, pp. 144–58; "Technology: In the Chips," *The Wall Street Journal Reports*, June 15, 1998; Robert A. Peterson, Sridhar Balasubramanian, and Bart J. Bronnenberg, "Exploring the Implications of the Internet for Consumer Marketing," *Journal of the Academy of Marketing Science*, Fall 1997, pp. 329–46; John Deighton, "Commentary on 'Exploring the Implications of the Internet for Consumer Marketing'," *Journal of the Academy of Marketing Science*, Fall 1997, pp. 347–51; D L. Andrus, "Inside the Tornado: Marketing Strategies From Silicon Valley's Cutting Edge," *Journal of Marketing*, April 1997, pp. 97–99; Kim Schatzel, "The Dynamics of Technological Innovation: The Evolution and Development of Information Technology," *Journal of Product Innovation Management*, January 1998, pp. 103–04; Karen A. Graziano, "The Innovator's Dilemma: When New Technologies Cause Great Firms to Fail," *Journal of Product Innovation Management*, January 1998, pp. 95–97; Thomas Kiely, "Obeying the Laws of Cyberspace," *Harvard Business Review*, September–October 1997, pp. 12–13; Edward McDonough, "Strategic Management of Technology and Innovation," *Journal of Product Innovation Management*, November 1997, pp. 533–34.

**27.** "Chips: Breaking the Light Barrier," *Business Week*, April 16, 2001, pp. 74–75; "Handhelds That Do It All," *Business Week*, February 12, 2001, pp. 98–99; "Will Light Bulbs Go the Way of the Victrola?" *Business Week*, January 22, 2001, p. 94H; "Dick Tracy, Meet '3G,'" *The Wall Street Journal*, January 18, 2001, p. B1ff.; "Raft of New Wireless Technologies Could Lead to Airwave Gridlock," *The Wall Street Journal*, January 8, 2001, p. B1ff.; "Drive-by-Wire Technology Promises Simpler and Safer Car Control," *The Wall Street Journal*, January 12, 2001, p. B1ff.; "Wireless Telephones Shed Keypads to Make Way for Bigger Screens," *The Wall Street Journal*, January 11, 2001, p. B1ff.; "GSM, CDMA, TDMA Make for a Wireless Tower of Babel," *Investor's Business Daily*, December 28, 2000, p. A5; "High-Tech Applications Transform Old Economy," *USA Today*, September 7, 2000, p, 3B; "In Dot-Com World, the Hot New Thing Is the Old Telephone," *The Wall Street Journal*, June 30, 2000, p. A1ff.; "In Japan, the World Goes Flat," *The Wall Street Journal*, June 29, 2000, p. B1ff.; "The World Is Your Office," *Fortune*, June 12, 2000, pp. 227–34; "Wireless Summer," *Time*, May 29, 2000, pp. 58–66; "Wireless Gets Easier and Faster," *Business Week*, May 29, 2000, p. 34; "An Efficiency Drive: Fast-Food Lanes Are Getting Even Faster," *The Wall Street Journal*, May 18, 2000, p. A1ff.; "E-Novel Approach Promises New Chapter for Book Lovers," *USA Today*, May 9, 2000, p. 1Bff.; "Chips for the Post-PC Era," *Business Week*, March 27, 2000, pp. 96–104; "Welcome to 2010," *Business Week*, March 6, 2000, pp. 102–12; "Wireless Option Opens Door to a New E-World," *USA Today*, February 18, 2000, p. 1Aff.; "Wireless Takes to the High Wire," *Business Week*, February 14, 2000, pp. 68–70; "This Frame Fetches Photos from the Net, Staging a Slide Show," *The Wall Street Journal*, February 3, 2000, p. B1; "The Soul of a New Refrigerator," *Business Week*, January 17, 2000, p. 42; "Driving a Stick," *Brandweek*, January 10, 2000, pp. 28–33; "Will the Future Be Written in E-Ink?" *The Wall Street Journal*, January 4, 2000, p. B1ff.; "Made in Japan," *Fortune*, December 6, 1999, pp. 190–202; "GM Will Connect Drivers to the World Wide Web," *The Wall Street Journal*, November 3, 1999, p. B1ff.; "Here Come Smart Phones," *Business Week*, October 25, 1999, pp. 167–94; "Here Come PVRs: Is Network TV Doomed?" *Time*, September 27, 1999, pp. 62–63; "So Many Megabytes, So Little Space," *The Wall Street Journal*, September 3, 1999, p. B1ff.; "Battle of the Batteries," *Business Week*, August 9, 1999, pp. 87–88; "Forget Microwaves: 'Speed Cookers' Also Crisp and Brown," *The Wall Street Journal*, June 30, 1999, p. B1ff.; "Evolutionary Wars," *Brandweek*, January 11, 1999, pp. 20–25; "A PC in Your Car? Why?" *Fortune*, September 7, 1998, pp. 113–15; "In HDTV Age, Successor to VCR Is a Long Way Off," *The Wall Street Journal*, April 8, 1998, p. B1ff.; "The Automakers' Big-Time Bet on Fuel Cells," *Fortune*, March 30, 1998, pp. 122C-P; "Take the Internet with You in a Phone, Watch or Shoe," *USA Today*, March 19, 1998, p. 1Bff.; "Detroit's Impossible Dream," *Business Week*, March 2, 1998, pp. 66–68; "Computer Industry Races to Conquer the Automobile," *The Wall Street Journal*, February 23, 1998, p. B1ff.; "Let's Talk: Speech Technology," *Business Week*, February 23, 1998, pp. 61–80; "Technology, Not Fashion, Now Seen as Crucial to Selling Athletic Shoes," *Brandweek*, February 16, 1998, p. 16; "How Smart Sensors Keep Factories Humming," *Fortune*, March 17, 1997, pp. 144A-H; "In Digital Dorm, Click on Return for Soda," *The Wall Street Journal*, January 23, 1997, p. B1ff.; Noel Capon and Rashi Glazer, "Marketing and Technology: A Strategic Coalignment," *Journal of Marketing*, July 1987, pp. 1–14.

**28.** Jeremy Glunt, "Canada Ratifies Kyoto Protocol: All Eyes on Russia Next," *Oxy-Fuel News*, December 23, 2002, p. 1.

**29.** "Corporate America's Woes, Continued—Enron: One Year On," *The Economist*, November 30, 2002, p. 59-61.

**30.** Ann Cavoukian, *The Privacy Payoff* (McGraw-Hill, 2002).

**31.** Available from World Wide Web: <http://www.privcom.gc.ca>; Privacy Commission of Canada web site.

**32.** John Gustavon, "Telemarketing's Bad Apples," *Marketing Magazine*, November 5, 2001.

**33.** Seymour Lipset, *Continental Divide: The Values and Institutions of the United States and Canada* (New York: Routledge, 1990).

**34.** For more on the changing nature of families, see "In 24-Hour Workplace, Day Care Is Moving to the Night Shift," *The Wall Street Journal*, July 6, 2001, p. A1ff.; Rebecca Gardyn, "Granddaughters of Feminism," *American Demographics*, April 2001, pp. 42–47; "High-Tech List for India's Women," *The Wall Street Journal*, November 1, 2000, p. B1ff.; "Net Lets Japanese Women Join Work Force at Home," *The Wall Street Journal*, February 29, 2000, p. B1ff.; "The New Debate Over Working Moms," *Business Week*, September 18, 2000, pp. 102–16; "Mommy, Do You Love Your Company More Than Me?" *Business Week*, December 20, 1999, p. 175; "More Dads Raise Families without Mom," *The Wall Street Journal*, October 3, 1997, p. B1ff.; "Ads that Portray Women," *USA Today*, September 9, 1996, p. 4B; "In Fitful Pursuit of American Women," *Advertising Age*, January 8, 1996, P. S4ff.; "Narrowcast in Past, Women Earn Revised Role in Advertising," *Advertising Age*, October 4, 1993, p. S1ff.; "Stay-at-Home Moms Are Fashionable Again in Many Communities," *The Wall Street Journal*, July 23, 1993, p. A1ff. For more on changing food habits, see "Skip the Tofu—More Americans Tear into Steaks," *The Wall Street Journal*, March 8, 2001, p. B1ff.; "Food Industry Battles for Moms Who Want to Cook—Just a Little," *The Wall Street Journal*, March 7, 2001, p. A1ff.; "Personal Chefs Are No Longer Just for the Rich," *USA Today*, February 9, 2001, p. 1Aff.; "Can Tyson Fight 'Chicken Fatigue' with Pork, Beef?" *The Wall Street Journal*, January 10, 2001, p. B1ff.; "Takeout Turkey on More Tables as Cooks Relax," *The Wall Street Journal*, November 24, 2000, p. A11ff.; "Bring on the Junk Food," *Newsweek*, July 10, 2000, p. 44; "Breakfast Eats Time, So Workers Gobble at the Office," *USA Today*, June 22, 2000, p. 6B; "Stewing in a Tough Market: Beef Industry Hopes New Ideas . . . ," *USA Today*, July 8, 1999, p. 1Bff.; "On the Run," *Advertising Age*, August 24, 1998, p. 1ff. For more on poverty of time, see "Can Workplace Stress Get Worse?" *The Wall Street Journal*, January 16, 2001, pp. B1ff.; "Telecommuters' Lament," *The Wall Street Journal*, October 31, 2000, p. B1ff.; "The Price of Speed," *USA Today*, August 3, 2000, p. 10D; "Why Everyone Is So Short-Tempered," *USA Today*, July 18, 2000, p. 1Aff.; "The End of Leisure," *American Demographics*, July 2000, pp. 50–56; "Home Is Where the Office Is," *American Demographics*, June 2000, pp. 54–60; "Surviving Commuting," *American Demographics*, July 1998, pp. 51–55. See also Eric Panitz, "Marketing in a Multicultural World: Ethnicity, Nationalism and Cultural Identity," *Journal of the Academy of Marketing Science*, Spring 1997, pp. 169–71; Victoria D. Bush and Thomas Ingram, "Adapting to Diverse Customers: A Training Matrix for International Marketers," *Industrial Marketing Management*, September 1996, pp. 373–83.

**35.** Frank R. Bacon, Jr., and Thomas W. Butler, Jr., *Planned Innovation*, rev. ed. (Ann Arbor: Institute of Science and Technology, University of Michigan, 1980).

**36.** Paul F. Anderson, "Marketing, Strategic Planning and the Theory of the Firm," *Journal of Marketing*, Spring 1982, pp. 15–26; George S. Day, "Analytical Approaches to Strategic Market Planning," in *Review of Marketing 1981*, ed. Ben M. Enis and Kenneth J. Roering (Chicago: American Marketing Association, 1981), pp. 89–105; Ronnie Silverblatt and Pradeep Korgaonkar, "Strategic Market Planning in a Turbulent Business Environment," *Journal of Business Research*, August 1987, pp. 339–58.

**37.** Richard N. Cardozo and David K. Smith, Jr., "Applying Financial Portfolio Theory to Product Portfolio Decisions: An Empirical Study," *Journal of Marketing*, Spring 1983, pp. 110–19; Yoram Wind, Vijay Mahajan, and Donald J. Swire, "An Empirical Comparison of Standardized Portfolio Models," *Journal of Marketing*, Spring 1983, pp. 89–99; Philippe Haspeslagh, "Portfolio Planning: Uses and Limits," *Harvard Business Review*, January–February 1982, pp. 58–73.

**38.** Keith B. Murray and Edward T. Popper, "Competing under Regulatory Uncertainty: A U.S. Perspective on Advertising in the Emerging European Market," *Journal of Macromarketing*, Fall 1992, pp. 38–54; "Inside Russia—Business Most Unusual," *UPS International Update*, Spring 1994, p. 1ff.; "Freighted with Difficulties," *The Wall Street Journal*, December 10, 1993, p. R4; "Russia Snickers after Mars Invades," *The Wall Street Journal*, July 13, 1993, p. B1ff.; Michael G. Harvey and James T. Rothe, "The Foreign Corrupt Practices Act: The Good, the Bad and the Future," in *1983 American Marketing Association Educators' Proceedings*, ed. P. E. Murphy et al. (Chicago: American Marketing Association, 1983), pp. 374–79.

**39.** "Sensitive Export: Seeking New Markets for Tampons, P&G Faces Cultural Barriers," *The Wall Street Journal*, December 8, 2000, p. A1ff.; "Pizza Queen of Japan Turns Web Auctioneer," *The Wall Street Journal*, March 6, 2000, p. B1ff.; "What Makes Italy Easier?" *Going Global—Italy* (supplement to *Inc.*), 1994; "Jean Cloning," *Brandweek*, May 30, 1994, pp. 15–22; "Double Entendre: The Life and the Life of Pepsi Max," *Brandweek*, April 18, 1994, p. 40; "Global Ad Campaigns, After Many Missteps, Finally Pay Dividends," *The Wall Street Journal*, August 27, 1992, p. A1ff.; Kamran Kashani, "Beware the Pitfalls of Global Marketing," *Harvard Business Review*, September–October 1989, pp. 91–98.

## Chapter 5

**1.** Eve Lazarus, "Building Better Relationships," *Marketing Magazine*, May 19, 2003.

**2.** Based on U.S. Census data and United Nations statistical data including *World Population Prospects: The 1999 Revision of the UN Population Division* (New York: United Nations, 2000); World Bank data including, *World Development Indicators: 2000* (Washington, DC: International Bank for Reconstruction and Development/The World Bank, 2000) and available from World Wide Web: <http://www.worldbank.org/data/wdi2000> and <http://devdata.worldbank.org/data-query>; Central Intelligence Agency data and available from World Wide Web: <http://www.odci.gov/cia/publications/factbook>; Population Reference Bureau data, including *2000 World Population Data Sheet* (Washington, DC: Population Reference Bureau, 2000) and available from World Wide Web: <http://www.prb.org/pubs/wpds2000>; and CountryWatch, available from World Wide Web: <http://www.countrywatch.com>; "How Rich Nations Can Defuse the Population Bomb," *Business Week*, May 28, 2001, p. 28; "China Tries Easing Once-Brutal Approach to Family Planning," *The Wall Street Journal*, February 2, 2001, p. A1ff.; "These Oldies Look Golden to Japan Inc.," *Business Week*, August 7, 2000, p. 59; "Rough Translation: 'No English, No Job'—A Reality Many of Asia's Workers Face," *USA Today*, July 21, 2000, p. 1Bff.; "The Big Crunch," *Time* (Special Issue), April–May 2000, pp. 44–47; "On the Move," *The Wall Street Journal*, January 1, 2000, p. R42ff.; Michel J. Weiss, *The Cluttered World* (Little, Brown and Company, 2000); "Parallel Universe," *American Demographics*, October 1999, pp. 58–63; "Six Billion Served," *American Demographics*, June 1999, pp. 14–16; Tamer S. Cavusgil, "Measuring the Potential of Emerging Markets: An Indexing Approach," *Business Horizons*, January–February 1997, pp. 87–91; E. B. Keehn, "A Yen to Spend," *Harvard Business Review*, March–April 1996, pp. 154–59; Tarun Khanna and Krishna Palepu, "Why Focused Strategies May Be Wrong for Emerging Markets," *Harvard Business Review*, July–August 1997, pp. 41–51.

**3.** Based on World Bank GNP and GDP data and available from World Wide Web: <http://www.worldbank.org/data/wdi>; and Central Intelligence Agency GDP data available from World Wide Web: <http://www.odci.gov/cia/publications/factbook>. Discussion of difference in GNP/GDP available from World Wide Web: <http://www.cyberus.ca/choose.sustain/Question/GDP-GNP.html>.

**4.** "World Bank Seeks to Give Poor More Clout," *Investor's Business Daily*, September 13, 2000, p. A10; and World Bank statistical data available from World Wide Web: <http://www.worldbank.org/data/wdi2000/worldview>.

**5.** Available from World Wide Web: <http://www.nua.ie>; "UNCTAD: Global Internet Population Reaches New High," November 19, 2002.

**6.** "RIP: The Online Consumer, 1998 to 2003," Forrester Research, July 25, 2003.

**7.** "Internet Use in Canada," *The Daily*, Statistics Canada, July 25, 2002.

**8.** Available from World Wide Web: <http://www.nua.ie>; "eMarketer: Worldwide B2B Revenues to Pass One Trillion," April 1, 2003.

**9.** Ramesh Venkat, "A Study on the Impact of Business-to-Business e-Commerce in Canada," *Proceedings of the PMAC Annual Conference*, June 7-8, 2001.

**10.** Available from World Wide Web: <http://www.statcan.ca/Daily/English/020926/d020926b.htm>.

**11.** Adapted from World Wide Web: <http://www.statcan.ca/english/Pgdb/demo02.htm>.

**12.** Available from World Wide Web: <http://www12.statcan.ca/english/census01/Products/Analytic/companion/etoimm/canada.cfm>.

**13.** Based on Statistics Canada data and *The American Marketplace* (1999); "A Slow Fade for the Echo Boom," *American Demographics*, July 1994, p. 15; "The Baby Boomlet May End with a Blizzard," *American Demographics*, March 1994, p. 16.

**14.** Available from World Wide Web: <http://www12.statcan.ca/english/census01/Products/Analytic/companion/age/canada.cfm>.

**15.** Anita Lahey, "Gluttons for media," *Marketing Online*, September 1, 1997; Anita Lahey, "Looking the Other Way," *Marketing Online*, September 1, 1997; Anita Lahey, "Looking Forward," *Marketing Online*, September 23, 1996; John Straiton, "Persuading the Skeptical Consumer," *Marketing Online*, September 23, 1996.

**16.** Available from World Wide Web: <http://www12.statcan.ca/english/census01/Products/Analytic/companion/fam/canada.cfm>.

**17.** Available from World Wide Web: <http://www12.statcan.ca/english/census01/Products/Analytic/companion/fam/canada.cfm>.

**18.** Available from World Wide Web: <http://www.statcan.ca/Daily/English/021202/d021202f.htm>.

**19.** Available from World Wide Web: <http://www12.statcan.ca/english/census01/Products/Analytic/companion/fam/canada.cfm>.

**20.** Available from World Wide Web: <http://www12.statcan.ca/english/census01/Products/Analytic/companion/fam/canada.cfm>.

**21.** Statistics Canada, *Dictionary of the 1971 Census Terms*, Cat. 12–540 (Ottawa: Information Canada, December 1972).

**22.** Available from World Wide Web: <http://www12.statcan.ca/english/census01/Products/Analytic/companion/mob/canada.cfm>.

**23.** "Going Where the Grass Is Greener," *Brandweek*, August 22, 1994, pp. 20–21; "Census Finds Fewer People Are on the Move," *The Wall Street Journal*, November 17, 1992, p. A5; "Mobility of U.S. Society Turns Small Cities into Giants," *The Wall Street Journal*, February 8, 1991, p. B1ff.; "Americans on the Move," *American Demographics*, June 1990, pp. 46–49; James R. Lumpkin and James B. Hunt, "Mobility as an Influence on Retail Patronage Behavior of the Elderly: Testing Conventional Wisdom," *Journal of the Academy of Marketing Science*, Winter 1989, pp. 1–12.

**24.** From StatsCan Catalogue #75-202 XIE.

**25.** From StatsCan Catalogue #75-202 XIE.

**26.** From StatsCan Catalogue #75-202 XIE.

**27.** Statistics Canada, *The Daily*, Thursday, September 14, 2000, "Women in Canada."

**28.** Jan Larson, "The New Face of Homemakers," *American Demographics*, September 1997, pp. 45–50; "Work & Family" (Special Section), *The Wall Street Journal*, March 31, 1997, pp. 1–20; "Family Values: Some Surprises," *USA Today*, March 11, 1997, P. 6D; Margaret K. Ambry, "Receipts from a Marriage," *American Demographics*, February 1993, pp. 30–37; "A Snapshot of Younger Lifestage Group Purchases," *American Demographics*, November 9, 1992, p. 28; Patrick E. Murphy and William A. Staples, "A Modernized Family Life Cycle," *Journal of Consumer Research*, June 1979, pp. 12–22.

**29.** Based on U.S. Census data and Joan Raymond, "The Ex-Files," *American Demographics*, February 2001, pp. 60–64; "The Ties that Bind," *Time*, August 18, 1997, pp. 48–50; "Mobility Mangles Marriage," *USA Today*, September 11, 1996, p. 15A; Frank F. Fustenberg, Jr., "The Future of Marriage," *American Demographics*, June 1996, pp. 34–40.

**30.** Based on U.S. Census data and "Just How Deep Are Those Teen Pockets?" *Business Week*, July 30, 2001, p. 39; "Special Report: Teen

Marketing," *Advertising Age*, June 25, 2001, pp. S1–12; "Marketers Have a Crush on Teens," *USA Today*, November 27, 2000, p. 10B; "To Reach the Unreachable Teen," *Business Week*, September 18, 2000, pp. 78–80; "Rushing to Cash In on the New Baby Boom," *The Wall Street Journal*, August 9, 2000, p. B1ff.; "Stores Roll Out Welcome Mat for Mall Rats," *The Wall Street Journal*, August 9, 2000. P. B1ff.; "My, You've Grown: The Teen Economy Is Like Totally Awesome," *The Wall Street Journal*, June 28, 2000, p. S3; "The Six Value Segments of Global Youth," *Brandweek*, May 22, 2000, pp. 38–50; "Can Levi's Be Cool Again?" *Business Week*, March 13, 2000, pp. 144–48; Elissa Moses, *The $100 Billion Allowance: Accessing the Global Teen Market* (John Wiley & Sons, 2000); Jeff Brazil, "Play Dough," *American Demographics*, December 1999, pp. 56–61; "Generation Y," *Business Week*, February 15, 1999, pp. 80–88; "Teen Retailing: The Underground Tastemakers," *The Wall Street Journal*, December 9, 1998, p. B1ff.; "Teen-Magazine Boom: Beauty, Fashion, Stars and Sex," *The Wall Street Journal*, December 7, 1998, p. B1ff.; "Apartments Replace the Dorm," *The Wall Street Journal*, October 28, 1998, p. B18; "Generation Y: Boomers' Kids a Booming Market," *USA Today*, October 6, 1998, p. 1Aff.; "The Boom Tube," *Adweek*, May 18, 1998, pp. 44–52; "Girl Power," *Fortune*, December 8, 1997, pp. 132–40; "In Developing Nations, Many Youths Splurge, Mainly on U.S. Goods," *The Wall Street Journal*, June 26, 1997, p. A1ff.; Soyeon Shim, "Adolescent Consumer Decision-Making Styles: The Consumer Socialization Perspective," *Psychology & Marketing*, September 1996, pp. 547–69.

**31.** Based on U.S. Census data and Joan Raymond, "The Joy of Empty Nesting," *American Demographics*, May 2000, pp. 48–54; "Take My Stuff, Please!" *The Wall Street Journal*, March 31, 2000, P.W1ff.; "The Big House Backlash," *The Wall Street Journal*, March 17, 2000, p. W1ff.; "Big Footprints: Hey, Baby Boomers Need Their Space, OK? Look at All Their Stuff," *The Wall Street Journal*, January 7, 2000, p. A1ff.; "Extreme Nesting," *The Wall Street Journal*, January 7, 2000, p. W1ff.; Don Fost, "Growing Older, But Not Up," *American Demographics*, September 1998, pp. 59–65.

**32.** Available from World Wide Web: <http://www12.statcan.ca/english/census01/Products/Analytic/companion/age/canada.cfm#senior_men_gaining>.

**33.** Based on Census data, including "The Older Population in the United States: March 1999, P20–532"; "Senior Theses," *Brandweek*, August 4, 1997, pp. 22–27; "The Ungraying of America," *American Demographics*, July 1997, pp. 12–15; Linda J. Barton, "A Shoulder to Lean On: Assisted Living in the U.S.," *American Demographics*, July 1997, pp. 45–51; "Real-Estate Innovator Sees Future in Catering to Needs of the Elderly," *The Wall Street Journal*, June 30, 1997, p. A1ff.; "Brave Old World," *Newsweek*, June 30, 1997, p. 63; "WebTV Finds a Following among Net-Surging Seniors," *The Wall Street Journal*, April 8, 1997, p. B1ff.; "For One 73-Year-Old, Punching Time Clock Isn't a Labor of Love," *The Wall Street Journal*, March 31, 1997, p. A1ff.; "High-Class Hospital Food," *Brandweek*, September 2, 1996, pp. 31–32; George P. Moschis, "Life Stages of the Mature Market," *American Demographics*, September 1996, pp. 44–50; Paco Underhill, "Seniors in Stores," *American Demographics*, April 1996, pp. 44–48.

**34.** Available from World Wide Web: <http://www12.statcan.ca/english/census01/Products/Analytic/companion/etoimm/canada.cfm>.

**35.** Available from World Wide Web: <http://www12.statcan.ca/english/census01/Products/Analytic/companion/etoimm/canada.cfm#threefold_increase>.

**36.** Available from World Wide Web: <http://www12.statcan.ca/english/census01/Products/Analytic/companion/lang/canada.cfm>.

**37.** Available from World Wide Web: <http://www.statcan.ca/english/Pgdb/demo18a.htm>.

**38.** Available from World Wide Web: <http://www12.statcan.ca/english/census01/Products/Analytic/companion/lang/canada.cfm>.

**39.** Barbara Passmore, "Understanding the Game of Life," PMB '95, pp. 13–14.

**40.** Francois Vary, "Quebec Consumer Has Unique Buying Habits," *Marketing*, March 23, 1992, p. 28.

**41.** This section is drawn, almost verbatim, from Jennifer Lynn, "Approaching Diversity," *Marketing*, July 3–10, 1995, p. 11.

**42.** P.C. Lefrancois and Giles Chatel, "The French-Canadian Consumer: Fact and Fancy," in *New Ideas for Successful Marketing, Proceedings of the 1966 World Congress*, ed. J. S. Wright and J. L. Goldstucker (Chicago: American Marketing Association, 1966), p. 706.

**43.** Available from World Wide Web: <http://www12.statcan.ca/english/census01/Products/Analytic/companion/lang/canada.cfm>.

**44.** Available from World Wide Web: <http://www12.statcan.ca/english/census01/Products/Analytic/companion/lang/provs.cfm>.

**45.** See also Michael Laroche, Chung K. Kim, and Madeleine Clarke, "The Effects of Ethnicity Factors on Consumer Deal Interests: An Empirical Study of French- and English-Canadians," *Journal of Marketing Theory & Practice*, Winter 1997, pp. 100–12.

## Chapter 6

**1.** Hollie Shaw, "Skip the Chevy—Buy Yourself a Beemer," *Financial*, July 10, 2003.

**2.** "What Works for One Works for All," *Business Week*, April 20, 1992, pp. 112–13.

**3.** For more on Ben & Jerry's, see "Ben & Jerry's Keeps Its Folksy Focus," *Advertising Age*, February 12, 2001, p. 4ff. See also Jennifer Gregan-Paxton and Deborah R. John, "Consumer Learning by Analogy: A Model of Internal Knowledge Transfer," *Journal of Consumer Research*, December 1997, pp. 266–84; M. C. Macklin, "Preschoolers' Learning of Brand Names From Visual Cues," *Journal of Consumer Research*, December 1996, pp. 251–61; Jaideep Sengupta, Ronald C. Goodstein, and David S. Boninger, "All Cues Are Not Created Equal: Obtaining Attitude Persistence Under Low-Involvement Conditions," *Journal of Consumer Research*, March 1997, pp. 351–61; John Kim, Jeen-Su Lim, and Mukesh Bhargava, "The Role of Affect in Attitude Formation: A Classical Conditioning Approach," *Journal of the Academy of Marketing Science*, Spring 1998, pp. 143–52; Paul S. Speck and Michael T. Elliott, "Predictors of Advertising Avoidance in Print and Broadcast Media," *Journal of Advertising*, Fall 1997, pp. 61–76; Frances K. McSweeney and Calvin Bierley, "Recent Developments in Classical Conditioning," *Journal of Consumer Research*, September 1984, pp. 619–31; Scott A. Hawkins and Stephen J. Hoch, "Low-Involvement Learning: Memory without Evaluation," *Journal of Consumer Research*, September 1992, pp. 212–25.

**4.** "Purina Dog Chow: Grand Effie Winner, Pet Care/Gold Winner," *Brandweek*, (Special Effies Winner Supplement), 1997. See also Edward Rosbergen, Rik Pieters, and Michel Wedel, "Visual Attention to Advertising: A Segment-Level Analysis," *Journal of Consumer Research*, December 1997, pp. 305–14; Gavan J. Fitzsimons and Vicki G. Morwitz, "The Effect of Measuring Intent on Brand-Level Purchase Behavior," *Journal of Consumer Research*, June 1996, pp. 1–11; Ellen C. Garbarino and Julie A. Edell, "Cognitive Effort, Affect, and Choice," *Journal of Consumer Research*, September 1997, pp. 147–58.

**5.** Vikas Mittal, William T. Ross, and Patrick M. Baldasare, "The Asymmetric Impact of Negative and Positive Attribute-Level Performance on Overall Satisfaction and Repurchase Intentions," *Journal of Marketing*, January 1998, pp. 33–47; Mary F. Luce, "Choosing to Avoid: Coping With Negatively Emotion-Laden Consumer Decisions," *Journal of Consumer Research*, March 1998, pp. 409–33; Calvin P. Duncan and Richard W. Olshavsky, "External Search: The Role of Consumer Beliefs,"

Journal of Marketing Research, February 1982, pp. 32–43; M. Joseph Sirgy, "Self-Concept in Consumer Behavior: A Critical Review," *Journal of Consumer Research*, December 1982, pp. 287–300.

**6.** "The Dirt on At-Home Dry Cleaning," *The Wall Street Journal*, September 15, 2000, p. W14; "Does P&G Still Matter?" *Advertising Age*, September 25, 2000, pp. 48–54; "P&G Shifts Strategy for Dryel," *Advertising Age*, January 24, 2000, p. 4; "Novel P&G Product Brings Dry Cleaning Home," *The Wall Street Journal*, November 19, 1997, p. B1ff.

**7.** For more on Van Heusen, see "Men Are Taking a Cotton to Wrinkle-Free Pants," *USA Today*, June 16, 1994, p. 5D; "'Wrinkle-Free' Shirts Don't Live Up to the Name," *The Wall Street Journal*, May 11, 1994, p. B1ff. See also "Rogaine Urges the Nonbald to Use Ounces of Prevention," *The Wall Street Journal*, September 20, 1999, p. B1ff. For more on service quality, see Chapter 9, footnote #2. For more on service expectations, see "Customer Service with a :-)," *USA Today*, December 6, 2000, p. 1Eff.; "Spotty Service Irks Cellphone Users," *USA Today*, November 6, 2000, p. 1Aff.; "Why Service Stinks," *Business Week*, October 23, 2000, pp. 118–28; "Cliff-Hanger Christmas," *Business Week E.Biz*, October 23, 2000, pp. 30–38; "It's the People, Stupid," *Business Week E.Biz*, October 23, 2000, p. EB138; "Service, Please," *Business Week E.Biz*, October 23, 2000, pp. EB48–EB50; "Seller of Suits Loosens Collar, Breathes Easier," *Investor's Business Daily*, October 19, 2000, p. A12; "On a Power Trip, They Arrive with Grating Expectations," *USA Today*, September 22, 2000, p. 1Dff.; "Customer Service: Rewriting the Rules of the Road," *Business Week E.Biz*, September 18, 2000, p. EB86; "How to Lose a Customer in a Matter of Seconds," *Fortune*, June 12, 2000, p. 326; "Special Report: E-Tailing," *Business Week E.Biz*, May 15, 2000, pp. EB103–EB118; "It's the Service, Stupid," *Business Week E.Biz*, April 3, 2000, p. EB118; "Just Another Medium," *Business Week E.Biz*, September 27, 1999, p. EB78; "Internet Businesses Customize to Survive," *Investor's Business Daily*, April 27, 2000, p. A8; "You'll Wanna Hold Their Hands," *Business Week E.Biz*, March 22, 1999, pp. EB30–EB31; "Online with the Operator," *American Demographics*, February 1999, pp. 36–39. See also A. Parasuraman, Valarie A. Zeithaml, and Leonard L. Berry, "Reassessment of Expectations As a Comparison Standard in Measuring Service Quality: Implications for Further Research," *Journal of Marketing*, January 1994, pp. 111–24; Alain Genestre and Paul Herbig, "Service Expectations and Perceptions Revisited: Adding Product Quality to SERVQUAL," *Journal of Marketing Theory & Practice*, Fall 1996, pp. 72–82; Valarie A. Zeithaml, Leonard L. Berry, and A. Parasuraman, "The Nature and Determinants of Customer Expectations of Service," *Journal of the Academy of Marketing Science*, Winter 1993, pp. 1–12.

**8.** Angela Kryhul, *Marketing Magazine*, October 8, 2001.

**9.** Leslie Young, "Unilever's Axe Makes Its Mark," *Marketing Magazine*, July 29, 2002.

**10.** Statistics Canada, *Dictionary of the 1971 Census Terms*, Cat. 12–540 (Ottawa: Information Canada, December 1972).

**11.** "Going Where the Grass Is Greener," Brandweek, August 22, 1994, pp. 20–21; "Census Finds Fewer People Are on the Move," *The Wall Street Journal*, November 17, 1992, p. A5; "Mobility of U.S. Society Turns Small Cities into Giants," *The Wall Street Journal*, February 8, 1991, p. B1ff.; "Americans on the Move," *American Demographics*, June 1990, pp. 46–49; James R. Lumpkin and James B. Hunt, "Mobility as an Influence on Retail Patronage Behavior of the Elderly: Testing Conventional Wisdom," *Journal of the Academy of Marketing Science*, Winter 1989, pp. 1–12.

**12.** "Generation Next," *Advertising Age*, January 15, 2001, pp. 14–16; "Head Trips," *American Demographics*, October 2000, pp. 38–40; "Label-Crazy Marketers Have Got You Pegged," *USA Today*, August 1, 2000, p. 1Bff.; "Simple Sells," *USA Today*, June 1, 2000, p. 1Aff.; "Make Room for Daddy," *American Demographics*, June 2000, pp. 34–36; "Join the Club," *Brandweek*, February 15, 1999, pp. 26–32; Annetta Miller, "The Millennial Mind-Set," *American Demographics*, January 1999, pp. 60–65; Rebecca Piirto Heath, "The Frontier of Psychographics," *American Demographics*, July 1996, pp. 38–43; "Making Generational Marketing Come of Age," *Fortune*, June 26, 1995, pp. 110–13; Robert A. Mittelstaedt, "Economics, Psychology, and the Literature of the Subdiscipline of Consumer Behavior," *Journal of the Academy of Marketing Science*, Fall, 1990, pp. 303–12; W. D. Wells, "Psychographics: A Critical Review," *Journal of Marketing Research*, May 1975, pp. 196–213.

**13.** For more on kids' influence in purchase decisions, see James U. McNeal, "Tapping the Three Kids' Markets," *American Demographics*, April 1998, pp. 37–41; "Software Firms Coddle a Growing Market: The Preschool Crowd," *The Wall Street Journal*, April 2, 1998, p. A1ff.; "Not All Approve of Barbie's MasterCard," *USA Today*, March 30, 1998, p. 6B; "More than Play Dough," *Brandweek*, November 24, 1997, pp. 18–19; "Kodak Focuses on Putting Kids behind a Camera," *The Wall Street Journal*, May 6, 1997, p. B8; "Cybergiants See the Future—and It's Jack and Jill," April 14, 1997, p. 44; "Special Report: Reaching Kids," Advertising Age, February 10, 1997, pp. 25–28; "The Rise of the Net-Generation," *Advertising Age*, October 14, 1996, p. 31ff.; Sharon E. Beatty and Salil Talpade, "Adolescent Influence in Family Decision Making: A Replication with Extension," *Journal of Consumer Research*, September 1994, pp. 332–41. See also Ugur Yavas, Emin Babakus, and Nejdet Delener, "Family Purchasing Roles in Saudi Arabia: Perspectives from Saudi Wives," *Journal of Business Research*, September 1994, pp. 75–86; Rosemary Polegato and Judith L. Zaichkowsky, "Family Food Shopping: Strategies Used by Husbands and Wives," *Journal of Consumer Affairs*, Winter 1994, pp. 278–99; Eric H. Shaw and Stephen F. I. Pirog, "A Systems Model of Household Behavior," *Journal of Marketing Theory & Practice*, Summer 1997, pp. 17–30; Kay M. Palan and Robert E. Wilkes, "Adolescent-Parent Interaction in Family Decision Making," *Journal of Consumer Research*, September 1997, pp. 159–69; Mary C. Gilly, John L. Graham, Mary F. Wolfinbarger, and Laura J. Yale, "A Dyadic Study of Interpersonal Information Search," *Journal of the Academy of Marketing Science*, Spring 1998, pp. 83–100; Conway L. Lackman, David P. Hanson, and John M. Lanasa, "Social Relations in Culture and Marketing," *Journal of Marketing Theory & Practice*, Winter 1997, pp. 144–52; Ellen R. Foxman, Patriya S. Tansuhaj, and Karin M. Ekstrom, "Adolescents' Influence in Family Purchase Decisions: A SocializationPerspective," *Journal of Business Research*, March 1989, pp. 159–72; C. Lackman and J.M. Lanasa, "Family Decision-Making Theory: An Overview and Assessment," *Psychology & Marketing*, March/April 1993, pp. 81–94.

**14.** See Gurprit S. Kindra, Michel LaRoche, and Thomas C. Muller, *Consumer Behaviour in Canada* (Scarborough, Ont.: Nelson Canada, 1989), pp. 301–40.

**15.** "Luxury for the Masses," *Brandweek*, June 25, 2001, pp. 16–34; "Special Report: Luxury Marketing," *Advertising Age*, June 11, 2001, pp. S1–14; "Which Is Luxury?" *USA Today*, May 4, 2001, p. 1Bff.; Hassan Fattah, "The Rising Tide," *American Demographics*, April 2001, pp. 48–53; "Despite Downturn, Japanese Are Still Having Fits for Luxury Goods," *The Wall Street Journal*, April 24, 2001, p. B1ff.; "The Rise of the Comfortable," *Advertising Age*, October 16, 2000, pp. 60–62; "90s Luxury Beyond Top of the Line," *USA Today*, July 6, 1999, p. 1Aff.; Debra Goldman, "Paradox of Pleasure," *American Demographics*, May 1999, pp. 50–53; "Culture Class: How America's Youth Defines Luxury," *Brandweek*, April 19, 1999, pp. 67–76; Rebecca Piirto Heath, "The New Working Class," *American Demographics*, January 1998, pp. 51–55; "Education Marks a Widening Income Divide," *The Wall Street Journal*, June 28, 1996, p. R2; "Class in America," *Fortune*, February 7, 1994, pp. 114–26; Basil G. Englis and Michael R. Solomon, "To Be and Not to Be: Lifestyle Imagery, Reference Groups, and the Clustering of America," *Journal of Advertising*, Spring 1995, pp. 13–28; Greg J. Duncan, Timothy M. Smeeding, and Willard Rodgers, "The Incredible Shrinking Middle Class," *American Demographics*, May 1992, pp. 34–38; Dennis L. Rosen and Richard W. Olshavsky, "The Dual Role of Informational Social Influence: Implications for Marketing Management," *Journal of Business Research*, April 1987, pp. 123–44; Terry L. Childers and Akshay R. Rao, "The Influence of Familial and Peer-based Reference Groups on Consumer Decisions," *Journal of Consumer Research*, September 1992, pp. 198–211; Basil G. Englis and Michael R. Solomon, "To Be and Not to Be: Lifestyle Imagery, Reference Groups, and The Clustering of America," *Journal of Advertising*, Spring 1995, pp. 13–28.

**16.** "Auto Makers Find They Don't Want to Avoid Collisions in Movies," *The Wall Street Journal*, July 5, 2001, p. B1ff.; "Small Wonder," *The Wall Street Journal*, June 25, 2001, p. R; Rebecca Gardyn, "Granddaughters of Feminism," *American Demographics*, April 2001, pp. 43–47; "A Wide Web of Advice," *Business Week E.Biz*, January 22, 2001, pp. EB18–EB20; "How to Generate Buzz to Sell Your Product," *Investor's Business Daily*, October 3, 2000, p. A1; "Word of Mouth in the Digital Age: Marketers Win when Friends Hit 'Send,'" *Brandweek*, October 2, 2000, pp. 24–26; "Ebola. Smallpox. Christina Aguilera." *Ecompany*, October 2000, pp. 48–52; "Steering to the Right Sites for the Best Buy," *Time Digital*, May 2000, p. 92; "Marketing Superstars: Aki Maita, Tamagotchi," *Advertising Age International*, December 1997, p. 10; James H. Myers and Thomas S. Robertson, "Dimensions of Opinion Leadership," *Journal of Marketing Research*, February 1972, pp. 41–46.

**17.** "Art of Noise," *Brandweek*, November 1, 1999, p. 78.

**18.** "Overcoming the Stigma of Dishwashers in Japan," *The Wall Street Journal*, May 19, 2000, p. B1ff.; Sydney Roslow, "International Consumer Behavior: Its Impact on Marketing Strategy Development," *Journal of the Academy of Marketing Science*, Summer 1996, pp. 278–79; R. Mead, "Where is the Culture of Thailand?" *International Journal of Research in Marketing*, September 1994, pp. 401–04.

**19.** John L. Graham, "How Culture Works," *Journal of Marketing*, April 1996, pp. 134–35; Gary D. Gregory and James M. Munch, "Cultural Values in International Advertising: An Examination of Familial Norms and Roles in Mexico," *Psychology & Marketing*, March 1997, pp. 99–119; Shiretta F. Ownbey and Patricia E. Horridge, "Acculturation Levels and Shopping Orientations of Asian-American Consumers," *Psychology & Marketing*, January 1997, pp. 1–18; Jennifer L. Aaker and Durairaj Maheswaran, "The Effect of Cultural Orientation on Persuasion," *Journal of Consumer Research*, December 1997, pp. 315–28; Grant McCracken, "Culture and Consumption: A Theoretical Account of the Structure and Movement of the Cultural Meaning of Consumer Goods," *Journal of Consumer Research*, June 1986, pp. 71–84.

**20.** "No More Shoppus Interruptus," *American Demographics*, May 2001, pp. 39–40; "No Buy? Then Bye-Bye," *Business Week E.Biz*, April 16, 2001, p. EB6; "Ok, Forget the Whole Damn Thing," *Ecompany*, December 2000, pp. 185–88; "Clinching the Holiday E-Sale," *The Wall Street Journal*, October 9, 2000, p. B1ff.; "A New Cure for Shoppus Interruptus," *American Demographics*, August 2000, pp. 44–47; "Special Report: E-Tailing," *Business Week E.Biz*, May 15, 2000, pp. EB103–EB118; "Many Web Shoppers Abandon Virtual Carts," *Investor's Business Daily*, May 11, 2000, p. A8; Charles S. Areni, Pamela Kiecker, and Kay M. Palan, "Is It Better to Give Than to Receive? Exploring Gender Differences in the Meaning of Memorable Gifts," *Psychology & Marketing*, January 1998, pp. 81–109; Russell W. Belk, "Situational Variables and Consumer Behavior," *Journal of Consumer Research* 2, 1975, pp. 157–64; John F. Sherry, Jr., "Gift Giving in Anthropological Perspective," *Journal of Consumer Research*, September 1983, pp. 157–68.

**21.** Adapted and updated from James H. Myers and William H. Reynolds, *Consumer Behavior and Marketing Management* (Boston: Houghton Mifflin, 1967), p. 49. See also Ronald E. Goldsmith, "A Theory of Shopping," *Journal of the Academy of Marketing Science*, Fall 2000, pp. 541–4; Judith Lynne Zaichkowsky, "Consumer Behavior: Yesterday, Today, and Tomorrow," *Business Horizons*, May/June 1991, pp. 51–58.

**22.** William Cunnings and Mark Venkatesan, "Cognitive Dissonance and Consumer Behavior: A Review of the Evidence," *Journal of Marketing Research*, August 1976, pp. 303–8; Sarah Fisher Gardial et al., "Comparing Consumers' Recall of Prepurchase and Postpurchase Product Evaluation Experience," *Journal of Consumer Research*, March 1994, pp. 548–60.

**23.** Cele Otnes, Tina M. Lowrey, and L J. Shrum, "Toward an Understanding of Consumer Ambivalence," *Journal of Consumer Research*, June 1997, pp. 80–93; Ronald E. Goldsmith, "Consumer Involvement: Concepts and Research," *Journal of the Academy of Marketing Science*, Summer 1996, pp. 281–83; Jeffrey B. Schmidt and Richard A. Spreng, "A Proposed Model of External Consumer Information Search," *Journal of the Academy of Marketing Science*, Summer 1996, pp. 246–56; Judith L. Zaichkowsky, "The Personal Involvement Inventory: Reduction, Revision, and Application to Advertising," *Journal of Advertising*, December 1994, pp. 59–70; Raj Arora, "Consumer Involvement—What It Offers to Advertising Strategy," *International Journal of Advertising* 4, no. 2 (1985), pp. 119–30; J. Brock Smith and Julia M. Bristor, "Uncertainty Orientation: Explaining Differences in Purchase Involvement and External Search," *Psychology & Marketing*, November/December 1994, pp. 587 608; Don R. Rahtz and David L. Moore, "Product Class Involvement and Purchase Intent," *Psychology and Marketing*, Summer 1989, pp. 113–28.

**24.** Ravi Dhar and Steven J. Sherman, "The Effect of Common and Unique Features in Consumer Choice," *Journal of Consumer Research*, December 1996, pp. 193–203; Victor V. Cordell, "Consumer Knowledge Measures As Predictors in Product Evaluation," *Psychology & Marketing*, May 1997, pp. 241–60; John V. Petrof and Naoufel Daghfous, "Evoked Set: Myth or Reality?" *Business Horizons*, May–June 1996, pp. 72–77; Wayne D. Hoyer, "An Examination of Consumer Decision Making for a Common Repeat Purchase Product," *Journal of Consumer Research*, December 1984, pp. 822–29; James R. Bettman, *An Information Processing Theory of Consumer Choice* (Reading, Mass.: Addison-Wesley Publishing, 1979); Richard W. Olshavsky and Donald H. Granbois, "Consumer Decision Making-Fact or Fiction?" *Journal of Consumer Research*, September 1979, pp. 93–100.

**25.** Available from World Wide Web: <http://www.cyberatlas.com>; Robyn Greenspan, "Searching for Satisfaction," *CyberAtlas*, February 4, 2003.

**26.** Available from World Wide Web: <http://www.cyberatlas.internet.com>; Michael Pastore, "Niche Travel Sites Keeping Customers Satisfied," December 5, 2000 and Michael Pastore, "Online Travel Consumers Seeking More Options," January 13, 2000.

**27.** Available from World Wide Web: <http://www.internetnews.com/IAR/>; Christopher Saunders, "Study: Multi-channel Shoppers Actually Not So Hot," *Internet Advertising Report*, August 1, 2002.

**28.** Adapted from E. M. Rogers with F. Shoemaker, *Communication of Innovation: A Cross Cultural Approach* (New York: Free Press, 1968). For some sampling (trial examples), see "The Cookie Queen," *The Wall Street Journal*, March 30, 1998, p. 6; "Brand Builders: Progresso Warriors," *Brandweek*, June 23, 1997, pp. 20–22; "Read This. It's Free," *Brandweek*, June 16, 1997, p. 42.

**29.** "PepsiCo Tries to Clarify Pepsi One's Image," *The Wall Street Journal*, February 25, 2000, p. B7.

**30.** Robert M. March, *The Honourable Customer: Marketing and Selling to the Japanese in the 1990s* (Melbourne, Vic.: Longman Professional, 1990); Robert Gottliebsen, "Japan's Stark Choices," *Business Review Weekly*, October 16, 1992.

## Chapter 7

**1.** "Outsourcing Is More than Cost Cutting," *Fortune*, October 26,

1998, pp. 238C–V; 2000 *Annual Report*, Deere & Company; *1999 Annual Report*, Deere & Company.

**2.** "The Push to Streamline Supply Chains," *Fortune*, March 3, 1997, pp. 108C–R; P. F. Johnson, Michiel R. Leenders, and Harold E. Fearon, "Evolving Roles and Responsibilities of Purchasing Organizations," *International Journal of Purchasing & Materials Management*, Winter 1998, pp. 2–11; "Purchasing's New Muscle," *Fortune*, February 20, 1995, pp. 75–83; Harry R. Page, "Revolution in Purchasing: Building Competitive Power Through Proactive Purchasing," *International Journal of Purchasing & Materials Management*, Fall 1996, p. 56; Joseph R. Carter and Ram Narasimhan, "Purchasing and Supply Management: Future Directions and Trends," *International Journal of Purchasing & Materials Management*, Fall 1996, pp. 2–12; Joseph R. Carter and Ram Narasimhan, "A Comparison of North American and European Future Purchasing Trends," *International Journal of Purchasing & Materials Management*, Spring 1996, pp. 12–22.

**3.** Jeffrey E. Lewin, "The Effects of Downsizing on Organizational Buying Behavior: An Empirical Investigation," *Journal of the Academy of Marketing Science*, Spring 2001, pp. 151–165; Larry C. Giunipero and Judith F. Vogt, "Empowering the Purchasing Function: Moving to Team Decisions," *International Journal of Purchasing & Materials Management*, Winter 1997, pp. 8–15; Jerome M. Katrichis, "Exploring Departmental Level Interaction Patterns in Organizational Purchasing Decisions," *Industrial Marketing Management*, March 1998, pp. 135–46; Robert D. McWilliams, Earl Naumann, and Stan Scott, "Determining Buying Center Size," *Industrial Marketing Management*, February 1992, pp. 43–50; Ajay Kohli, "Determinants of Influence in Organizational Buying: A Contingency Approach," *Journal of Marketing*, July 1989, pp. 50–65; Melvin R. Mattson, "How to Determine the Composition and Influence of a Buying Center," *Industrial Marketing Management*, August 1988, pp. 205–14.

**4.** "Detroit to Suppliers: Quality or Else," *Fortune*, September 30, 1996, p. 134Cff.; G. M. Naidu, V. K. Prasad, and Arno Kleimenhagen, "Purchasing's Preparedness for ISO 9000 International Quality Standards," *International Journal of Purchasing & Materials Management*, Fall 1996, pp. 46–53; Wade Ferguson, "Impact of the ISO 9000 Series Standards on Industrial Marketing," *Industrial Marketing Management*, July 1996, pp. 305–10.

**5.** H. L. Brossard, "Information Sources Used by an Organization During a Complex Decision Process: An Exploratory Study," *Industrial Marketing Management*, January 1998, pp. 41–50; Michele D. Bunn, "Taxonomy of Buying Decision Approaches," *Journal of Marketing*, January 1993, pp. 38–56; Patricia M. Doney and Gary M. Armstrong, "Effects of Accountability on Symbolic Information Search and Information Analysis by Organizational Buyers," *Journal of the Academy of Marketing Science*, Winter 1996, pp. 57–65; Thomas G. Ponzurick, "International Buyers Perspective Toward Trade Shows and Other Promotional Methods," *Journal of Marketing Theory & Practice*, Winter 1996, pp. 9–19; Mark A. Farrell and Bill Schroder, "Influence Strategies in Organizational Buying Decisions," *Industrial Marketing Management*, July 1996, pp. 293–303; R. Venkatesh, Ajay K. Kohli, and Gerald Zaltman, "Influence Strategies in Buying Centers," *Journal of Marketing*, October 1995, pp. 71–82; Richard G. Newman, "Monitoring Price Increases With Economic Data: A Practical Approach," *International Journal of Purchasing & Materials Management*, Fall 1997, pp. 35–40; Barbara Kline and Janet Wagner, "Information Sources and Retailer Buyer Decision-Making: The Effect of Product-Specific Buying Experience," *Journal of Retailing*, Spring 1994, p. 75; Ellen Day and Hiram C. Barksdale, Jr., "How Firms Select Professional Services," *Industrial Marketing Management*, May 1992, pp. 85–92; H. Michael Hayes and Steven W. Hartley, "How Buyers View Industrial Salespeople," *Industrial Marketing Management* 18, no. 2 (1989), pp. 73–80; Peter Banting et al., "Similarities in Industrial Procurement Across Four Countries," *Industrial Marketing Management*, May 1985, pp. 133–44; Edward F. Fern and James R. Brown, "The Industrial/Consumer Marketing Dichotomy: A Case of Insufficient Justification," *Journal of Marketing*, Spring 1984, pp. 68–77; Rowland T. Moriarty, Jr. and Robert E. Spekman, "An Empirical Investigation of the Information Sources Used During the Industrial Buying Process," *Journal of Marketing Research*, May 1984, pp. 137–47.

**6.** "Strong Brands Lure Web Buyers," *Investor's Business Daily*, May 30, 2001, p. A5; "With Promise of Big Savings, Net Bill Paying Could Soon Win Fans among U.S. Businesses," *Investor's Business Daily*, February 26, 2001, p. A7; "How Baxter, PNC, Pratt & Whitney Make the Internet Work for Them," *Investor's Business Daily*, February 12, 2001, p. A1; "Look, Ma, No Humans," *Business Week E.Biz*, November 20, 2000, p. EB132; "Hewlett-Packard's Slick Procurement System," *Ecompany*, November 2000, pp. 236–38; "Schools Are Buying Online; The Savings Could Add Up," *Investor's Business Daily*, July 7, 2000, p. A4; "E-Purchasing Saves Businesses Billions," *USA Today*, February 7, 2000, p. 1Bff.; "Supply Side," *The Wall Street Journal*, November 15, 1999, p. R22; "Purchasing in Packs," *Business Week E.Biz*, November 1, 1999, pp. EB32–EB38; "From Regineering to E-Engineering," *Business Week E.Biz*, March 22, 1999, pp. EB14–EB18; "Setting Standards for Corporate Purchasing on the Internet," *Fortune*, September 8, 1997, pp. 156–58; "Invoice? What's an Invoice?" *Business Week*, June 10, 1996, pp. 110–12; "On-Line Service Offers Fast Lane to Small Businesses," *The Wall Street Journal*, October 11, 1994, p. B2; Earl D. Honeycutt, Theresa B. Flaherty, and Ken Benassi, "Marketing Industrial Products on the Internet," *Industrial Marketing Management*, January 1998, pp. 63–72; A. C. Samli, James R. Wills, and Paul Herbig, "The Information Superhighway Goes International: Implications for Industrial Sales Transactions," *Industrial Marketing Management*, January 1997, pp. 51–58; Barbara C. Perdue, "The Size and Composition of the Buying Firm's Negotiation Team in Rebuys of Component Parts," *Journal of the Academy of Marketing Science*, Spring 1989, pp. 121–28.

**7.** W. E. I. Patton, "Use of Human Judgment Models in Industrial Buyers' Vendor Selection Decisions," *Industrial Marketing Management*, March 1996, pp. 135–49; Minette E. Drumwright, "Socially Responsible Organizational Buying: Environmental Concern As a Noneconomic Buying Criterion," *Journal of Marketing*, July 1994, pp. 1–19; Lisa M. Ellram, "A Structured Method for Applying Purchasing Cost Management Tools," *International Journal of Purchasing & Materials Management*, Winter 1996, pp. 11–19; Morgan P. Miles, Linda S. Munilla, and Gregory R. Russell, "Marketing and Environmental Registration/Certification: What Industrial Marketers Should Understand About ISO 14000," *Industrial Marketing Management*, July 1997, pp. 363–70; Morry Ghingold and Bruce Johnson, "Technical Knowledge As Value Added in Business Markets," *Industrial Marketing Management*, May 1997, pp. 271–80; Sime Curkovic and Robert Handfield, "Use of ISO 9000 and Baldrige Award Criteria in Supplier Quality Evaluation," *International Journal of Purchasing & Materials Management*, Spring 1996, pp. 2–11; M. Bixby Cooper, Cornelia Droge, and Patricia J. Daugherty, "How Buyers and Operations Personnel Evaluate Service," *Industrial Marketing Management* 20, no. 1 (1991), pp. 81–90.

**8.** Jeanette J. Arbuthnot, "Identifying Ethical Problems Confronting Small Retail Buyers During the Merchandise Buying Process," *Journal of Business Ethics*, May 1997, pp. 745–55; Gail K. McCracken and Thomas J. Callahan, "Is There Such a Thing As a Free Lunch?" *International Journal of Purchasing & Materials Management*, Winter 1996, pp. 44–50; Robert W. Cooper, Garry L. Frank, and Robert A. Kemp, "The Ethical Environment Facing the Profession of Purchasing and Materials Management," *International Journal of Purchasing & Materials Management*, Spring 1997, pp. 2–11; I. Frederick Trawick, John E. Swan, Gail W. McGee, and David R. Rink, "Influence of Buyer Ethics and Salesperson Behavior on Intention to Choose a Supplier," *Journal of the Academy of Marketing Science*, Winter 1991, pp. 17–24; Michael J. Dorsch and Scott W. Kelley, "An Investigation into the Intentions of Purchasing Executives to Reciprocate Vendor Gifts," *Journal of the Academy of Marketing Science*, Fall 1994, pp. 315–327; J. A. Badenhorst, "Unethical Behaviour in Procurement: A Perspective on Causes and Solutions," *Journal of Business Ethics*, September 1994, pp. 739–46.

**9.** "The New Golden Rule of Business," *Fortune*, February 21, 1994, pp. 60–64; Janet L. Hartley and Thomas Y. Choi, "Supplier Development: Customers As a Catalyst of Process Change," *Business Horizons*, July–August 1996, pp. 37–44; Theodore P. Stank, Margaret A. Emmelhainz, and Patricia J. Daugherty, "The Impact of Information on Supplier Performance," *Journal of Marketing Theory & Practice*, Fall 1996, pp. 94–105.

**10.** "The Push to Streamline Supply Chains," *Fortune*, March 3, 1997, pp. 108C-R; "Push from Above," *The Wall Street Journal*, May 23, 1996, p. R24; "The New Golden Rule of Business," *Fortune*, February 21, 1994, pp. 60–64.

**11.** Much of the discussion in this section is based on research reported in Joseph P. Cannon and William D. Perreault, Jr., "Buyer-Seller Relationships in Business Markets," *Journal of Marketing Research*, November 1999; Joseph P. Cannon, "Buyer-Supplier Relationships and Customer Firm Costs," *Journal of Marketing*, January 2001, pp. 29–44; Alexandra J. Campbell, "What Affects Expectations of Mutuality in Business Relationships?" *Journal of Marketing Theory & Practice*, Fall 1997, pp. 1–11; James C. Anderson, Hakan Hakansson, and Jan Johanson, "Dyadic Business Relationships Within a Business Network Context," *Journal of Marketing*, October 1994, pp. 1–15; Patricia M. Doney and Joseph P. Cannon, "An Examination of the Nature of Trust in Buyer-Seller Relationships," *Journal of Marketing*, April 1997, pp. 35–51; James M. Comer and B.J. Zirger, "Building a Supplier-Customer Relationship Using Joint New Product Development," *Industrial Marketing Management*, March 1997, pp. 203–11; Arun Sharma and Jagdish N. Sheth, "Supplier Relationships: Emerging Issues and Challenges," *Industrial Marketing Management*, March 1997, pp. 91–100; William W. Keep, Stanley C. Hollander, and Roger Dickinson, "Forces Impinging on Long-Term Business-to-Business Relationships in the United States: An Historical Perspective," *Journal of Marketing*, April 1998, pp. 31–45.

**12.** "Purchasing's New Muscle," *Fortune*, February 20, 1995, pp. 75–83; Rosemary P. Ramsey and Ravipreet S. Sohi, "Listening to Your Customers: The Impact of Perceived Salesperson Listening Behavior on Relationship Outcomes," *Journal of the Academy of Marketing Science*, Spring 1997, pp. 127–37.

**13.** For more on outsourcing, see "Why Some Sony Gear Is Made in Japan—by Another Company," *The Wall Street Journal*, June 14, 2001, p. A1ff.; "Inside Out-Sourcing," *Fortune*/CNET Technology Review, Summer 2001, pp. 85–92; "Taiwan Goes after the World's Chip Business," *Fortune*, May 14, 2001, pp. 216T–HH; "Outsourcing as a Strategic Option: It's about More than Saving Money," *Investor's Business Daily*, May 7, 2001, p. A1; "The Tech Slump's Next Victim?" *Business Week*, March 5, 2001, pp. 104–105; "Solectron, All Along the Chain Except the Ends," *Fortune*, October 30, 2000, pp. T208T–Z; "You Order It, They'll Make It," *Business Week*, May 29, 2000, pp. 218D–J; "The Low-Tech King of High Tech," *Fortune*, October 25, 1999, pp. 339–43; "New Saturn Is Heavy on Outsourcing," *USA Today*, July 5, 1996, p. 1Bff. For more on supplier speeds and costs, see "When Cool Heads Prevail," *Business Week*, June 11, 2001, p. 114; "Should Suppliers Be Partners?" *Business Week*, June 4, 2001, pp. 30B–D; "Machete Time," *Business Week*, April 9, 2001, pp. 42–43; "Can Chrysler Get Blood from a Supplier?" *Business Week*, December 25, 2000, p. 56; "Chrysler's Checks to Suppliers, Shoppers to Shrink," *The Wall Street Journal*, December 8, 2000, p. B4; "Firms Boost Suppliers' Speeds, Win Investors' Hearts," *The Wall Street Journal*, April 6, 1998, p. A20; "Stores' Demands Squeeze Apparel Companies," *The Wall Street Journal*, July 15, 1997, p. B1ff.; "Hardball Is Still GM's Game," *Business Week*, August 8, 1994, p. 26; "Big Customers' Late Bills Choke Small Suppliers," *The Wall Street Journal*, June 22, 1994, p. B1. For more on JIT, see "As Christmas Approaches, Parts Shortages Plague Electronic Makers," *TheWall Street Journal*, October 10, 2000, p. B1ff.; "Parts Shortages Hamper Electronics Makers," *The Wall Street Journal*, July 7, 2000, p. B5. For some excellent examples, see "The Web at Work: Clorox Co." *The Wall Street Journal*, October 9, 2000, p. B21; "Kimberly-Clark Keeps Costco in Diapers, Absorbing Costs Itself," *The Wall Street Journal*, September 7, 2000, p. A1ff.; "At Ford, E-Commerce Is Job 1," *Business Week*, February 28, 2000, pp. 74–78; "Where 'Build to Order' Works Best," *Fortune*, April 26, 1999, pp. 160C-V. See also John Ramsay, "The Case Against Purchasing Partnerships," *International Journal of Purchasing & Materials Management*, Fall 1996, pp. 13–19; George S. Day, "Managing Market Relationships," *Journal of the Academy of Marketing Science*, Winter 2000, pp. 24–31; John V. Petrof, "Relationship Marketing—the Emperor in Used Clothes," *Business Horizons*, March–April 1998, pp. 79–82; Shankar Ganesan, "Determinants of Long-Term Orientation in Buyer-Seller Relationships," *Journal of Marketing*, April 1994, pp. 1–19; Brian K. H. Low, "Long-Term Relationship in Industrial Marketing: Reality or Rhetoric?" *Industrial Marketing Management*, January 1996, pp. 23–35; Allan J. Magrath and Kenneth G. Hardy, "Building Customer Partnerships," *Business Horizons*, January–February 1994, pp. 24–28; Paul Dion, Debbie Easterling, and Shirley Jo Miller, "What is Really Necessary in Successful Buyer/Seller Relationships?" *Industrial Marketing Management*, January 1995, pp. 1–10.

**14.** For another example of a Toyota partnership, see "Why Toyota Wins Such High Marks on Quality Surveys," *The Wall Street Journal*, March 15, 2001, p. A1ff. See also "Japanese Auto Makers Help U.S. Suppliers Become More Efficient," *The Wall Street Journal*, September 9, 1991, p. A1ff.; David L. Blenkhorn and A. Hamid Noori, "What It Takes to Supply Japanese OEMs," *Industrial Marketing Management*, February, 1990, pp. 21–30.

**15.** For other examples of big/small partnerships, see "A Fruitful Relationship," *Business Week E.Biz*, November 20, 2000, pp. EB94–EB96; "Automating an Automaker," *Inc. Tech 2000*, No. 4, p. 86. See also "Polaroid Corp. Is Selling Its Technique for Limiting Supplier Price Increases," *The Wall Street Journal*, February 13, 1985, p. 36; "Making Honda Parts, Ohio Company Finds, Can Be Road to Ruin," *The Wall Street Journal*, October 5, 1990, p. A1ff.; "Toshiba Official Finds Giving Work to Firms in U.S. Can Be Tricky," *The Wall Street Journal*, March 20, 1987, p. 1ff.

**16.** "A Blaze in Albuquerque Sets Off Major Crisis for Cell-Phone Giants," *The Wall Street Journal*, January 29, 2001, p. A1ff.; "Toyota's Fast Rebound after Fire at Supplier Shows Why It Is Tough," *The Wall Street Journal*, May 8, 1997, p. A1ff.; Larry R. Smeltzer and Sue P. Siferd, "Proactive Supply Management: The Management of Risk," *International Journal of Purchasing & Materials Management*, Winter 1998, pp. 38–45; Paul D. Larson and Jack D. Kulchitsky, "Single Sourcing and Supplier Certification: Performance and Relationship Implications," *Industrial Marketing Management*, January 1998, pp. 73–81; Rasmus F. Olsen and Lisa M. Ellram, "A Portfolio Approach to Supplier Relationships," *Industrial Marketing Management*, March 1997, pp. 101–13; Cathy Owens Swift, "Preferences for Single Sourcing and Supplier Selection," *Journal of Business Research*, February 1995, pp. 105–12.

**17.** "You Buy My Widgets, I'll Buy Your Debt," *Business Week*, August 1, 1988, p. 85; Robert E. Weigand, "The Problems of Managing Reciprocity," *California Management Review*, Fall 1973, pp. 40–48.

**18.** Available from World Wide Web: <http://www.nua.ie/surveys>; "Worldwide B2B Revenues to Pass One Trillion," April 1, 2003.

**19.** Available from World Wide Web: <http://www.nua.ie/surveys>; "B2C Holiday Sales to Grow," October 29, 2002.

**20.** Ramesh Venkat, "A Study on the Impact of Business-to-Business e-Commerce in Canada," *Proceedings of the PMAC Annual Conference*, June 7-8, 2001.

**21.** Available from World Wide Web: <http://www.ComputerWeekly.com>; Hazel Ward, "B2B Exchanges Fail to Deliver," November 29, 2001.

**22.** Available from World Wide Web: <http://www.national.com>. See also "Web Masters," *Sales & Marketing Management*, 2000 and 2001.

**23.** Available from World Wide Web: <http://www.naics.com>. See also "Classified Information," *American Demographics*, July 1999, p. 16; "SIC: The System Explained," *Sales and Marketing Management*, April 22, 1985, pp. 52–113; "Enhancement of SIC System Being Developed," *Marketing News Collegiate Edition*, May 1988, p. 4.

## Chapter 8

**1.** Available from World Wide Web: <http://www.lenscrafters.com>; "LensCrafters Hits One Billion in Sales," *Business Wire*, February 3, 1998; "LensCrafters Polishes Image with Style," *Chain Store Age Executive*, October 1996, p. 144ff.; "'SuperOpticals' Edge out the Corner Optician," *Adweek's Marketing Week*, October 1, 1990, p. 36; "LensCrafters Takes the High Road," *Adweek's Marketing Week*, April 30, 1990, pp. 26–27.

**2.** "How an Intranet Opened Up the Door to Profits," *Business Week E. Biz*, July 26, 1999, pp. EB32–EB38; "Here Comes the Intranet," *Business Week*, February 26, 1996, pp. 76–84.

**3.** "Virtual Management," *Business Week*, September 21, 1998, pp. 80–82; John T. Mentzer and Nimish Gandhi, "Expert Systems in Marketing: Guidelines for Development," *Journal of the Academy of Marketing Science*, Winter, 1992, pp. 73–80; William D. Perreault, Jr., "The Shifting Paradigm in Marketing Research," *Journal of the Academy of Marketing Science*, Fall 1992, pp. 367–76; J.M. McCann, W.G. Lahti, and J. Hill, "The Brand Manager's Assistant: A Knowledge-Based System Approach to Brand Management," *International Journal of Research in Marketing*, April 1991, pp. 51–74.

**4.** For more on CRM, see Chapter 3, footnote #16. "Marketers Hone Targeting," *Advertising Age*, June 18, 2001, p. T16; "Data Miners Reel after Wal-Mart Snub," *Brandweek*, May 21, 2001, p. 9; "Closer Than Ever," *Business Week Small Biz*, May 21, 2001, pp. 14–15; "CRM: Shooting Holes in the Hype," *Advertising Age*, April 16, 2001, p. 1ff.; "Firms See Value of CRM Software, but Adoption Can Be Costly," *Investor's Business Daily*, April 4, 2001, p. A7; "A Singular Sensation," *Brandweek*, February 28, 2001, pp. 32–38; "Product by Design," *American Demographics*, February 2001, pp. 38–41; "CRM Firms Adjust to Downturn," *Investor's Business Daily*, December 28, 2000, p. A4; "The New Software Whizzes," *Business Week E.Biz*, December 11, 2000, pp. EB30–EB42; "Mystery Shoppers," *American Demographics*, December 2000, pp. 41–43; "Mountains to Mine," *American Demographics*, August 2000, pp. 40–44; "With All Companies Lured to Web, Enterprise Software Is a Must-Have," *Investor's Business Daily*, April 17, 2000, p. A10; "Mining Everyone's Business," *Brandweek*, February 28, 2000, pp. 32–56; "An Eagle Eye on Customers," *Business Week*, February 21, 2000, pp. 66–76; "The Information Gold Mine," *Business Week E.Biz*, July 26, 1999, pp. EB16–EB30; "Data Mining Digs In," *American Demographics*, July 1999, pp. 38–45; "Looking for Patterns," *The Wall Street Journal*, June 21, 1999, p. R16ff.; "Know Your Customer," *The Wall Street Journal*, June 21, 1999, p. R18. See also Siva K. Balasubramanian, "The New Marketing Research Systems—How to Use Strategic Database Information for Better Marketing Decisions," *Journal of the Academy of Marketing Science*, Spring 1996, pp. 179–81; John I. Hagel and Jeffrey F. Rayport, "The Coming Battle for Customer Information," *Harvard Business Review*, January–February 1997, pp. 53–65; "What's the Best Source of Market Research?" *Inc.*, June 1992, p. 108; James M. Sinkula, "Perceived Characteristics, Organizational Factors, and the Utilization of External Market Research Suppliers," *Journal of Business Research*, August, 1990, pp. 1–18.

**5.** Adapted from: Marlene Milczarek, "Database Diamond Mining," *Marketing Magazine*, August 13, 2001.

**6.** Linda I. Nowak, Paul D. Boughton, and Arun J. A. Pereira, "Relationships Between Businesses and Marketing Research Firms," *Industrial Marketing Management*, November 1997, pp. 487–95; Peter M. Chisnall, "The Effective Use of Market Research: A Guide for Management to Grow the Business," *International Journal of Market Research*, Summer 2000, Vol. 42, 3, p. 359; Seymour Sudman and Edward Blair, *Marketing Research: A Problem Solving Approach* (Burr Ridge, IL: Irwin/McGraw-Hill, 1998). See also Christine Moorman, Rohit Deshpande, and Gerald Zaltman, "Factors Affecting Trust in Market Research Relationships," *Journal of Marketing*, January 1993, pp. 81–101.

**7.** For a discussion of ethical issues in marketing research, see "How 'Tactical Research' Muddied Diaper Debate: a Case," *The Wall Street Journal*, May 17, 1994, p. B1ff.; John R. Sparks and Shelby D. Hunt, "Marketing Researcher Ethical Sensitivity: Conceptualization, Measurement, and Exploratory Investigation," *Journal of Marketing*, April 1998, pp. 92–109; Naresh K. Malhotra and Gina L. Miller, "An Integrated Model for Ethical Decisions in Marketing Research," *Journal of Business Ethics*, February 1998, pp. 263–80; Stephen B. Castleberry, Warren French and Barbara A. Carlin, "The Ethical Framework of Advertising and Marketing Research Practitioners: A Moral Development Perspective," *Journal of Advertising*, June 1993, pp. 39–46; Ishmael P. Akaah, "Attitudes of Marketing Professionals toward Ethics in Marketing Research: A Cross-National Comparison," *Journal of Business Ethics*, January, 1990, pp. 45–54.

**8.** From ARF position paper, "Phony or Misleading Polls," *Journal of Advertising Research*, Special Issue 26, January 1987, p. RC3-RC8; and George S. Day, "The Threats to Marketing Research," *Journal of Marketing Research 12*, November 1975, p. 462-467. Taken From David A. Aaker and George S. Day, eds., *Marketing Research*, 4th ed. (New York: John Wiley & Sons), p. 217, 218.

**9.** "Special Report: 2001 David Ogilvy Research Awards," *American Demographics*, March 2001, pp. S1–21; "Special Report: 2000 David Ogilvy Research Awards," *American Demographics*, March 2000, pp. S1–22; "What Consumer Research Won't Tell You," *Brandweek*, November 1, 1999, pp. 40–48; "Intelligence Agents," *American Demographics*, March 1999, pp. 52–60; "Grandma Got Run Over by Bad Research," *Inc.*, January 1998, p. 27.

**10.** For more detail on data analysis techniques, see William R. Dillon, Thomas J. Madden, and Neil H. Firtle, *Marketing Research in a Marketing Environment*, 3rd ed. (Burr Ridge, IL: Irwin/McGraw-Hill, 1993) or other current marketing research texts. See also "Merry Maids Clean Up Territories with MapInfo System," *Investor's Business Daily*, February 20, 2001, p. A8; Michael D. Johnson and Elania J. Hudson, "On the Perceived Usefulness of Scaling Techniques in Market Analysis," *Psychology & Marketing*, October 1996, pp. 653–75; Milton D. Rosenau, "Graphing Statistics and Data: Creating Better Charts," *Journal of Product Innovation Management*, March 1997, p. 144.

**11.** "Careful What You Ask For," *American Demographics*, July 1998, pp. 8–15; See also John G. Keane, "Questionable Statistics," *American Demographics*, June 1985, pp. 18–21. Detailed treatment of confidence intervals is beyond the scope of this text, but it is covered in most marketing research texts, such as Donald R. Lehmann, *Analysis for Marketing Planning* 4th ed. (Burr Ridge, IL: Irwin/McGraw-Hill, 1997).

**12.** Justin Smallbridge, "Toyota Micro-targets Through Time," *Marketing*, January 26, 1998, vol. 103, no. 3., p.3.

**13.** E. Jerome McCarthy et al., *Basic Marketing: A Managerial Approach*, 1st Australasian ed. (Richard D. Irwin: Burr Ridge, IL, 1994), pp. 128–29.

**14.** "Eyes and Ears of Business: Marketing Research is Taking On Even More Importance in Helping Companies Grow," *Marketing*, May 17, 1999, vol. 104, no. 19, p. 18; and Patrick Lejtenyi, "Underlying Differences," *Marketing Magazine*, June 5, 2000.

**15.** Alan R. Andreasen, "Cost-Conscious Marketing Research," *Harvard Business Review*, July–August, 1983, pp. 74–81; A. Parasuraman, "Research's Place in the Marketing Budget," *Business Horizons*, March/April 1983, pp. 25–29; Jack J. Honomichl, "Point of View: Why Marketing Information Should Have Top Executive Status," *Journal of Advertising Research*, November/December 1994, pp. 61–66; Jim Bessen, "Riding the Marketing Information Wave," *Harvard Business Review*, September–October 1993, pp. 150–61.

**16.** Allyson L. Stewart-Allen, "Do your International Homework First," *Marketing News* (Chicago), January 4, 1999, vol. 33, p. 25, ISSN: 00253790.

**17.** This material was prepared by Dr. Stanley J. Shapiro, with guidance from Ms. Elaine Fairey, Business and Economics Librarian at Simon Fraser University. Materials downloaded from the libraries of Queen's University and Simon Fraser University have been used in its preparation.

**18.** Available from World Wide Web: <http://www.burke.com/ice/online>; "Heinz Picks Purple as New EZ Squirt Color," *Brandweek*, June 25, 2001, p. 7; "Web Enhances Market Research," *Advertising Age*, June 18, 2001, p. T18; "Marketers Call on Kids to Help Design Web Sites," *USA Today*, June 5, 2001, p. 1Bff.; "Speaking Up: One Focus Group Revealed," *The Wall Street Journal*, November 27, 2000, p. B21; "Double Play," *Business Week E.Biz*, October 23, 2000, pp. EB42–EB46; "More Marketers Bypass Focus Groups," *USA Today*, August 23, 1999, p. 6B. See also William J. McDonald, "Focus Group Research Dynamics and Reporting: An Examination of Research Objectives and Moderator Influences," *Journal of the Academy of Marketing Science*, Spring 1993, pp. 161; Thomas Kiely, "Wired Focus Groups," *Harvard Business Review*, January–February 1998, pp. 12–16.

**19.** "Selling Sibelius Isn't Easy," *American Demographics*, The 1994 Directory, pp. 24–25; "Symphony Strikes a Note for Research as It Prepares to Launch a New Season," *Marketing News*, August 29, 1988, p. 12.

**20.** Doug Saunders, "Getting Into Focus—Groups, That Is," *The Globe and Mail*, January 10, 1998, p. C1.

**21.** Norma Ramage, "TacoTime Dreams Grande," *Marketing Magazine*, March 3, 2003.

**22.** "CBC Radio Feeds the Curious: a CD Sampler Strikes a Chord with the Broadcaster's Desire 'Cultural Creative' Target," *Marketing*, August 19, 2002, vol. 107, no. 33, p. 11.

**23.** Carey Toane, "Smells Like Teen Research," Digital Marketing Report, *Marketing Magazine*, July 24, 2000.

**24.** "P&G Checks Out Real Life," *The Wall Street Journal*, May 17, 2001, p. B1ff.; "Research on a Shoestring," *American Demographics*, April 2001, pp. 38–39; "Consumers in the Mist," *Business Week*, February 26, 2001, pp. 92–94; "Under the Lens," *American Demographics*, September 2000, pp. 42–45; "O&M Turns Reality TV into Research Tool," *Advertising Age*, July 10, 2000, p. 6; "How Do You Like Your Beef?" *American Demographics*, January 2000, pp. 35–37; "Attention Shoppers: This Man Is Watching You," *Fortune*, July 19, 1999, pp. 131–34; "What Shoppers Want," *Inc.*, July 1999, pp. 72–82; "New Ways to Get into Our Heads," *USA Today*, March 2, 1999, p. 1Bff.; "The New Market Research," *Inc.*, July 1998, pp. 87–94. See also Stephen J. Grove and Raymond P. Fisk, "Observational Data Collection Methods for Services Marketing: An Overview," *Journal of the Academy of Marketing Science*, Summer 1992, pp. 217–24; "Coupon Clippers, Save Your Scissors," *Business Week*, June 20, 1994, pp. 164–66; Magid M. Abraham and Leonard M. Lodish, "An Implemented System for Improving Promotion Productivity Using Store Scanner Data," *Marketing Science*, Summer 1993, pp. 248–69; "The Nitty-Gritty of ECR Systems: How One Company Makes It Pay," *Advertising Age*, May 2, 1994, pp. S1ff.; Peter J. Danaher and Terence W. Beed, "A Coincidental Survey of People Meter Panelists: Comparing What People Say with What They Do," *Journal of Advertising Research*, January/February 1993, p. 86.

**25.** "Only in Canada? Not For Long If Research Pays Off," *Marketing*, October 30, 2000, vol. 105, no. 43, p. 14; and "Sink or Swim? Test Markets Allow a Company to Evaluate Whether a New Product will Float Before Taking the Plunge into a National Rollout," *Marketing*, October 30, 2000, vol. 105, no. 43, p. 13-15.

**26.** "Will Your Web Business Work? Take It for a Test Drive," *Ecompany*, May 2001, pp. 101–104; "Ads Awaken to Fathers' New Role in Family Life," *Advertising Age*, January 10, 1994, p. S8; "AT&T's Secret MultiMedia Trials Offer Clues to Capturing Interactive Audiences," *The Wall Street Journal*, July 28, 1993, p. B1ff.; "Experimenting in the U.K.: Phone, Cable Deals Let U.S. Test Future," *USA Today*, June 28, 1993, p. 1Bff. See also Raymond R. Burke, "Virtual Shopping: Breakthrough in Marketing Research," *Harvard Business Review*, March–April 1996, pp. 120–31; Glen L. Urban, Bruce D. Weinberg, and John R. Hauser, "Premarket Forecasting of Really-New Products," *Journal of Marketing*, January 1996, pp. 47–60; "Bar Wars: Hershey Bites Mars," *Fortune*, July 8, 1985, pp. 52–57.

**27.** "Nielsen Plans New Pricing as Part of Bid to Double People Meters," *The Wall Street Journal*, June 29, 2001, p. B6; "Confessions of a Nielsen Household," *American Demographics*, May 2001; "Trying to Clean Up Sweeps," *American Demographics*, May 2001, pp. 42–49; "The Metrics System," *Brandweek*, November 13, 2000, pp. 106–10; "Special Report: Top 25 Global Research Organizations," *Advertising Age*, August 24, 2000; "We're Being Watched," *American Demographics*, October 1998, pp. 52–58; "Special Report: 100 Leading Research Companies," *Advertising Age*, May 19, 1997; "Rivals Duel Bitterly for Job of Supplying Market Information, *The Wall Street Journal*, November 15, 1993, p. A1ff.

## Chapter 9

**1.** Available from World Wide Web: <http://www.kodak.com>; "Price Wars, Shift to Digital Photos Leaving Kodak Out of the Picture," *Investor's Business Daily*, March 19, 2001, p. A1; "Will Kodak's Carp Miss His Photo Op?" *Business Week*, October 9, 2000, p. 52; "Kodak Hires Web Guru to Develop Its Digital Plans," *The Wall Street Journal*, October 9, 2000, p. B1ff.; "With Polaroid Film, You're Seconds from Digital Fun," *USA Today*, September 20, 2000, p. 3D; "Affordable Digital Cameras Arrive, Bringing Decent Quality under $150," *Investor's Business Daily*, September 8, 2000, p. A4; "Digital Video Cameras Give Amateurs Entree to Real Movie-Making," *The Wall Street Journal*, August 31, 2000, p. B1; "Shutterbugs Ditch 35mm Gear for Digital Cameras, Computer Printers," *The Wall Street Journal*, May 8, 2000, p. B1ff.; "Businesses Prove the Focus of Big Digital Camera Sales," *Investor's Business Daily*, April 25, 2000, p. A6; "Wall Street Left to Wonder Whether Kodak's Getting the Digital Picture," *Investor's Business Daily*, April 11, 2000, p. A1; "Eastman Kodak Splits Focus Between Old, New Film Worlds," *USA Today*, February 14, 2000, p. 5B; "Fuji: Beyond Film," *Business Week*, November 22, 1999, pp. 132–38; "Film vs. Digital: Can Kodak Build a Bridge?" *Business Week*, August 2, 1999, pp. 66–69; "Shutter Snaps on Fisher's Leadership at Kodak," *The Wall Street Journal*, June 10, 1999, p. B1ff.; "Momentous Shifts," *Brandweek*, June 1, 1998, pp. 26–30; "For New Film, a Brighter Picture," *The Wall Street Journal*, May 5, 1998, p. B1ff.; "For Kodak's Advantix, Double Exposure as Company Relaunches Camera System," *The Wall Street Journal*, April 23, 1997, p. B1ff.; "APS Camera Brands Make Picture-Imperfect Debut," *Ad Age International*, January 1997, p. 12ff.; "Camera System Is Developed but Not Delivered," *The Wall Street Journal*, August 7, 1996, p. B1ff.

**2.** For more on service expectations, see Chapter 6, footnote #7. For more on service quality, see Leonard L. Berry, "Cultivating Service Brand Equity," *Journal of the Academy of Marketing Science*, Winter 2000, pp. 128–138; Dwayne D. Gremler, "Discovering the Soul of Service: The Nine Drivers of Sustainable Business Success," *Journal of the Academy of Marketing Science*, Spring 2000, pp. 311–13; *2000 Annual Report*, MCI; *2000 Annual Report*, Merrill Lynch; "Air Service Faces Heat from Fliers,"

USA Today, June 1, 2000, p. 3B; "Airlines and Airwaves: Services Take Off," *Advertising Age*, May 1, 2000, pp. 18–20; "The Death of the Bellman," *The Wall Street Journal*, March 10, 2000, p. W11; "Avis to Try Even Harder with Ads Touting High Quality of Service," *The Wall Street Journal*, February 18, 2000, p. B9; "Better Service or Lip Service?" *USA Today*, December 16, 1999, p. 1Bff.; "How Does Low Unemployment Affect Service?" *Raleigh News & Observer*, December 5, 1999, pp. 27A–28A; "Price Isn't Everything," *The Wall Street Journal*, July 12, 1999, p. R20; "Only Extra Nice Will Suffice," *The Wall Street Journal*, June 14, 1999, p. 16ff.; "Buckling Up the Business Traveler," *American Demographics*, December 1998, pp. 48–52; "Service Is Everybody's Business," *Fortune*, June 27, 1994, pp. 48–60; James Golleher, "Value-Added Customer Service," *Journal of Personal Selling & Sales Management*, Spring 1997, p.71; James Reardon, Chip Miller, Ronald Hasty, and Blaise J. Waguespack, "A Comparison of Alternative Theories of Services Marketing," *Journal of Marketing Theory & Practice*, Fall 1996, pp. 61–71; Kirk Smith, "Service Aspects of Industrial Products Lead to Future Product Purchase Intentions," *Industrial Marketing Management*, January 1998, pp. 83–93; James C. Anderson and James A. Narus, "Capturing the Value of Supplementary Services," *Harvard Business Review*, January 1995–February 1995, pp. 75–83; Banwari Mittal and Walfried M. Lassar, "The Role of Personalization in Service Encounters," *Journal of Retailing*, Spring 1996, pp. 95–109; Barry J. Babin and James S. Boles, "Employee Behavior in a Service Environment: A Model and Test of Potential Differences Between Men and Women," *Journal of Marketing*, April 1998, pp. 77–91; Mary Jo Bitner, Bernard H. Booms, and Lois A. Mohr, "Critical Service Encounters: The Employee's Viewpoint," *Journal of Marketing*, October 1994, pp. 95–106; Leonard L. Berry, A. Parasuraman, and Valarie A. Zeithaml, "The Service-Quality Puzzle," *Business Horizons*, September/October 1988, pp. 35–43; Leonard L. Berry, "Services Marketing Is Different," in Christopher H. Lovelock, *Services Marketing* (Englewood Cliffs, NJ: Prentice-Hall, 1984), pp. 29–37.

**3.** *2000 Annual Report*, Sara Lee; *2000 Annual Report*, Enterprise; *2000 Annual Report*, 3M; Edward M. Tauber, "Why Do People Shop?" *Journal of Marketing*, October 1972, pp. 46–49; Christopher H. Lovelock, "Classifying Services to Gain Strategic Marketing Insights," *Journal of Marketing*, Summer 1983, pp. 9–20.Tom Boyt and Michael Harvey, "Classification of Industrial Services," *Industrial Marketing Management*, July 1997, pp. 291–300.

**4.** Dennis W. Rook, "The Buying Impulse," *Journal of Consumer Research*, September 1987, pp. 189–99; Cathy J. Cobb and Wayne D. Hoyer, "Planned Versus Impulse Purchase Behavior," *Journal of Retailing*, Winter 1986, pp. 384–409.

**5.** For example, see "Russian Maneuvers Are Making Palladium Ever More Precious," *The Wall Street Journal*, March 6, 2000, p. A1ff. See also William S. Bishop, John L. Graham, and Michael H. Jones, "Volatility of Derived Demand in Industrial Markets and Its Management Implications," *Journal of Marketing*, Fall 1984, pp. 95–103.

**6.** William B. Wagner and Patricia K. Hall, "Equipment Lease Accounting in Industrial Marketing Strategy," *Industrial Marketing Management* 20, no. 4 (1991), pp. 305–10; Robert S. Eckley, "Caterpillar's Ordeal: Foreign Competition in Capital Goods," *Business Horizons*, March/April 1989, pp. 80–86; M. Manley, "To Buy or Not to Buy," *Inc.*, November 1987, pp. 189–90.

**7.** P. Matthyssens and W. Faes, "OEM Buying Process for New Components: Purchasing and Marketing Implications," *Industrial Marketing Management*, August 1985, pp. 145–57; Paul A. Herbig and Frederick Palumbo, "Serving the Aftermarket in Japan and the United States," *Industrial Marketing Management*, November 1993, pp. 339–46; Ralph W. Jackson and Philip D. Cooper, "Unique Aspects of Marketing Industrial Services," *Industrial Marketing Management*, May 1988, pp. 111–18; Timothy L. Wilson and Frank E. Smith, "Business Services 1982–1992: Growth, Industry Characteristics, Financial Performance," *Industrial Marketing Management*, March 1996, pp. 162–71.

**8.** Ruth H. Krieger and Jack R. Meredith, "Emergency and Routine MRO Part Buying," *Industrial Marketing Management*, November 1985, pp. 277–82; Warren A. French et al., "MRO Parts Service in the Machine Tool Industry," *Industrial Marketing Management*, November 1985, pp. 283–88. See also "The Web's New Plumbers," *Ecompany*, March 2001, pp. 126–28.

**9.** For more on Starbucks' Frappuccino, see "Starbucks Cultivates Caffeine Rush," *USA Today*, April 30, 1998, p. 1Bff.; "All Things Starbucks," *Brandweek*, December 1, 1997, p. 1ff.; "Starbucks Gives Vitamin Jolt to Frappuccino Drink," *Advertising Age*, September 15, 1997, p. 82; "Starbucks Does Not Live by Coffee Alone," *Business Week*, August 5, 1996, p. 76; "Starbucks Readies Supermarket Invasion," *Advertising Age*, June 9, 1997, p. 1ff. For more on brand extensions, see "Cookie Makers Bake Up New Twists," *USA Today*, March 27, 2001, p. 3B; "Much about History," *Brandweek*, March 12, 2001, pp. 19–20; "Watershed Crystal," *Brandweek*, October 30, 2000, pp. 22–25; "Reposition: Simplifying the Customer's Brandscape," *Brandweek*, October 2, 2000, pp. 36–48; "The Joy of Laundry," *Business Week*, July 17, 2000, p. 8; "Crackers Say Cheese," *Advertising Age*, April 24, 2000, p. 32; "M&M/Mars Ice Cream Sees Red for Its Debut," *Advertising Age*, March 13, 2000, p. 33; "Clorox Tries Formula 409 for Carpets," *Advertising Age*, March 10, 1997, p. 6; "Can Betty Crocker Heat Up General Mills' Cereal Sales?" *The Wall Street Journal*, July 19, 1996, p. B1ff.; "Nabisco to Bring Top Cookie Brands to Breakfast Line," *The Wall Street Journal*, February 23, 1994, p. B5; "Multiple Varieties of Established Brands Muddle Consumers, Make Retailers Mad," *The Wall Street Journal*, January 24, 1992, p. B1ff. For more on brand equity and brand value, see "When Designers Attack!" *Ecompany*, June 2001, pp. 45–46; "Designated Shopper," *Brandweek*, May 28, 2001, p. 40; "Brand Building: Chairman of the Board," *Business Week*, May 28, 2001, p. 96; "In the Movie 'Foodfight,' Mr. Clean Plays Bit Part That Worries His Agent," *The Wall Street Journal*, April 30, 2001, p. A1ff.; "Mission, Message and Monitoring: How the Best Build, Nurture Brands," *Investor's Business Daily*, March 12, 2001, p. A1; David F. D'Alessandro, *Brand Warfare: 10 Rules for Building the Killer Brand* (2001); "Making the Emotional Connection," *Brandweek*, January 29, 2001, pp. 23–27; "What to Do with a Brand Gone Bland?" *The Wall Street Journal*, December 14, 2000, p. B14; "Pledge of Allegiance," *American Demographics*, November 2000, pp. 40–42; Marc Gob, *Emotional Branding: The New Paradigm for Connecting Brands to People* (New York: Watson-Gruptill, 2000); Marc Braunstein and Edward H. Levine, *Deep Branding on the Internet* (2000); "Making Your Mark Online," *Advertising Age*, October 9, 2000, pp. 46–48; "A Word of Advice to Body Shop: Don't Undermine Your Fine Branding with an Inconsistent Internet Effort," *Brandweek*, September 25, 2000, pp. 34–36; "Brands in a Bind," *Business Week*, August 28, 2000, pp. 234–38; "Branded Blooms Find Fertile Market," *Advertising Age*, January 24, 2000, p. 16; "Two Ways to Destroy a Valuable Brand," *Brandweek*, November 15, 1999, p. 26; "Creating the New Gold Standard," *Brandweek*, July 27, 1998, pp. 27–30. See also Elise K. Prosser, "Brand Marketing: Building Winning Brand Strategies That Deliver Value and Customer Satisfaction," *Journal of the Academy of Marketing Science*, Winter 1996, pp. 86–87; David A. Aaker, "Should You Take Your Brand to Where the Action Is?" *Harvard Business Review*, September–October 1997, pp. 135–43; Richard C. Leventhal, "Branding Strategy," *Business Horizons*, September–October 1996, pp. 17–23; Deborah R. John, Barbara Loken, and Christopher Joiner, "The Negative Impact of Extensions: Can Flagship Products Be Diluted?" *Journal of Marketing*, January 1998, pp. 19–32; Cathy J. Cobb-Walgren, Cynthia A. Ruble, and Naveen Donthu, "Brand Equity, Brand Preference, and Purchase Intent," *Journal of Advertising*, Fall 1995, pp. 25–40; Vijay Vishwanath and Jonathan Mark, "Your Brand's Best Strategy," *Harvard Business Review*, May–June 1997, pp. 123–29; Michael A. Kamins and Nancy A. Frost, "A 'Brand' New Language," *Journal of Marketing*, April 1994, pp. 129–30; John A. Quelch and David Kenny, "Extend Profits, Not Product Lines," *Harvard Business Review*, September 1994–October 1994, pp. 153–60; Linda B. Samuels and Samuels Jeffery M, "Famous Marks Now Federally

Protected Against Dilution," *Journal of Public Policy & Marketing*, Fall 1996, pp. 307–10; Pamela W. Henderson and Joseph A. Cote, "Guidelines for Selecting or Modifying Logos," *Journal of Marketing*, April 1998, pp. 14–30; Erich Joachimsthaler and David A. Aaker, "Building Brands Without Mass Media," *Harvard Business Review*, January–February 1997, pp. 39–50; Kevin Lane Keller, "Conceptualizing, Measuring, and Managing Customer-Based Brand Equity," *Journal of Marketing*, January 1993, pp. 1–22.

**10.** Available from World Wide Web: <http://www.atalink.co.uk/iaa2000/html/p064.htm>; Allen Rosenshine, "The Agency of the Not-too-distant Future," *Technology and World of International Marketing Communications*, International Advertising Association, April 2000.

**11.** Bob Tedeschi, "Brand Building on the Internet," *The New York Times*, August 25, 2003.

**12.** Sarah L. Roberts-Witt, "Branded," *PC Magazine*, April 17, 2001.

**13.** Bruce Horowitz, "Marketers Call on Kids to Design Web Sites," *BizReport*, June 6, 2001.

**14.** Charles H. Schwepker, "Trademark Problems and How to Avoid Them," *Journal of the Academy of Marketing Science*, Winter 1997, pp. 89–90; Lee B. Burgunder, "Trademark Protection of Product Characteristics: A Predictive Model," *Journal of Public Policy & Marketing*, Fall 1997, pp. 277–88; Itamar Simonson, "Trademark Infringement from the Buyer Perspective: Conceptual Analysis and Measurement Implications," *Journal of Public Policy & Marketing*, Fall 1994, pp. 181–99; "Asian Trademark Litigation Continues," *The Wall Street Journal*, February 16, 1994, p. B8.

**15.** "China's CD Pirates Find a New Hangout," *Business Week*, December 15, 1997, p. 138F; "Busting Bogus Merchandise Peddlers with the Logo Cops," *The Wall Street Journal*, October 24, 1997, p. B1ff.; "Reebok Tussles with Venezuelan Company over Name, Designs," *Ad Age International*, September 1997, p. 138; "CD Piracy Flourishes in China, and West Supplies Equipment," *The Wall Street Journal*, April 24, 1997, p. A1ff.; "A Pirate under Every Rock," *Business Week*, June 17, 1996, pp. 50–51; "Hackers Put Pirated Software on Internet," *The Wall Street Journal*, October 31, 1994, p. B5; Janeen E. Olsen and Kent L. Granzin, "Using Channels Constructs to Explain Dealers' Willingness to Help Manufacturers Combat Counterfeiting," *Journal of Business Research*, June 1993, pp. 147–70; Ronald F. Bush, Peter H. Bloch, and Scott Dawson, "Remedies for Product Counterfeiting," *Business Horizons*, January–February 1989, pp. 59–65; Alexander Nill and Clifford J. Clifford J II, "The Scourge of Global Counterfeiting," *Business Horizons*, November–December 1996, pp. 37–42.

**16.** For a detailed discussion of a recent Canadian trademark controversy, see Eric Swetsky, "Wool-Mart Versus Wal-Mart," *Marketing Magazine* (June 24, 1996), p. 20; Brian Banks and David North "Ticked Off: Wal-Mart's Infuriating Ways," *Canadian Business* (January 1996), pp. 23–24.

**17.** "Global Products Require Name-Finders," *The Wall Street Journal*, April 11, 1996, p. B8; Martin S. Roth, "Effects of Global Market Conditions on Brand Image Customization and Brand Performance," *Journal of Advertising*, Winter 1995, pp. 55–75.

**18.** Available from World Wide Web: <http://www.yahoo.com>; "Coterie of Early Hires Made Yahoo! A Hit but an Insular Place," *The Wall Street Journal*, March 9, 2001, p. A1ff.; "Yahoo Drops Bomb with Koogle's Exit," *USA Today*, March 8, 2001, p. 1Bff.; "Voulez-vous Yahoo Avec Moi?" *Fortune*, October 16, 2000, pp. 245–54; "Yahoo's Grand Vision for Web Advertising Takes Some Hard Hits," *The Wall Street Journal*, September 1, 2000, p. A1ff.; "Yahoo Stands Alone in Web Wars," *USA Today*, August 24, 2000, p. 1Bff.; "Surprise! Yahoo Goes Broadband," *Fortune*, May 29, 2000, pp. 182–92; "The Two Grown-Ups behind Yahoo!'s Surge," *The Wall Street Journal*, April 10, 1998, p. B1ff.; "Yahoo! Challenges AOL as a Portal to World Wide Web," *The Wall Street Journal*, March 19, 1998, p. B1; "How Yahoo! Won the Search Wars," *Fortune*, March 2, 1998, pp. 148–54; "*Brandweek's* Marketers of the Year: Yahoo!, Karen Edwards," *Superbrands '98*, October 20, 1997, pp. 70–74; "What Hath Yahoo Wrought?" *Business Week*, February 12, 1996, pp. 88–89.

**19.** "Highway Safety: Time for Tougher Cops," *Business Week*, July 2, 2001, p. 42; "Firestone Plans to Close Troubled Decatur Factory," *The Wall Street Journal*, June 28, 2001, p. A3ff.; "First, Crunch Time for Jac," *Fortune*, June 25, 2001, pp. 34–35; "Ford: Why It's Worse than You Think," *Business Week*, June 25, 2001, pp. 80–89; "Ford: Other Firestone Tires Fail, Too," *USA Today*, June 14, 2001, p. 1B; "Firestone: Is This Brand beyond Repair?" *Business Week*, June 11, 2001, p. 48; "Ford Vs. Firestone: A Corporate Whodunit," *Business Week*, June 11, 2001, pp. 46–47; "Ford's Gamble: Will It Backfire?" *Business Week*, June 4, 2001, pp. 40–41; "Tired of Each Other," *Time*, June 4, 2001, pp. 50–56; "Ford Has Big Problem Beyond the Tire Mess: Making Quality Cars," *The Wall Street Journal*, May 25, 2001, p. A1ff.; "Confused Drivers May Have Trouble Trusting Either Firm," *USA Today*, May 23, 2001, p. 1Bff.; "Ford to Replace Up to 13 Million Firestone Tires," *Investor's Business Daily*, May 23, 2001, p. A9; "Firestone Quits as Tire Supplier to Ford," *The Wall Street Journal*, May 22, 2001, p. A3ff.; "Meet the New Face of Firestone," *Business Week*, April 30, 2001, pp. 64–66; "Facing or Fearing a Publicity Crisis? Right Steps to Get Past the Trouble," *Investor's Business Daily*, April 23, 2001, p. A1; "After Tireless Efforts, Ford Launches All-New Explorer," *USA Today*, March 29, 2001, p. 1Bff.; "Under Glare of Recall, Tire Makers Are Giving New Technology a Spin," *The Wall Street Journal*, March 23, 2001, p. A1ff.; "Industry Report: Tires," *Investor's Business Daily*, February 12, 2001, p. B22; "More Firestone Tires Peel," *USA Today*, February 8, 2001, p. 1Bff.; "What Japan's CEOs Can Learn from Bridgestone," *Business Week*, January 29, 2001, p. 50; "Firestone Leaves an Indelible Mark," *USA Today*, December 26, 2000, p. 1Bff.; "Cost Hinders Wider Use of Nylon to Make Steel-Belted Tires Safer," *The Wall Street Journal*, December 20, 2000, p. A8; "Firestone Admits Manufacturing Problems But Also Scrutinizes Tire-Inflation Levels," *The Wall Street Journal*, December 20, 2000, p. A3ff; "Firestone Recall Fuels Interest in 'Smart' Tires," *The Wall Street Journal*, November 22, 2000, p. B1ff.; "Drivers Complained of Tread Problems Years before Recall," *USA Today*, November 15, 2000, p. 1Bff.; "Firestone Dealers Step Up to Defend Tiremaker," *USA Today*, November 10, 2000, p. 10B; "Can Courts' Cloak of Secrecy Be Deadly?" *USA Today*, October 16, 2000, p. 1Bff.; "The Tire Flap: Behind the Feeding Frenzy," *Business Week*, October 16, 2000, pp. 126–28; "Firestone Team Faces Challenge of Steering Company Past Crisis," *The Wall Street Journal*, October11, 2000, p. A1ff.; "Squabbles between Ford and Firestone May Hurt Their Legal Defense," *The Wall Street Journal*, October 9, 2000, p. B1ff.; "Documents Imply Firestone Knew of Tire Trouble in '94," *USA Today*, October 4, 2000, p. 1Bff.; "Would You Buy One?" *Business Week*, September 25, 2000, pp. 46–47; "Jac Nasser's Biggest Test," *Fortune*, September 18, 2000, pp. 123–28; "Ford: A Crisis of Confidence," *Business Week*, September 18, 2000, pp. 40–42; "Answers Still Elusive in Tire Crisis," *The Wall Street Journal*, September 15, 2000, p. B1ff.; "Anatomy of a Recall," *Time*, September 11, 2000, pp. 28–32; "How Ford, Firestone Let the Warnings Slide By as Debacle Developed," *The Wall Street Journal*, September 6, 2000, p. A1ff.; "Tension between Ford and Firestone Mounts amid Recall Efforts," *The Wall Street Journal*, August 28, 2000, p. A1ff.; "More People Die Despite Recall," *USA Today*, August 22, 2000, p. 1Bff.; "Ford CEO Takes Recall Reins as More Questions Arise," *USA Today*, August 17, 2000, p. 1Bff.; "What You Don't Know about Your Tires," *USA Today*, August 11, 2000, p. 1Bff.; "Bridgestone/Firestone Handling of Recall Results in Consumer Confusion, Chaos," *The Wall Street Journal*, August 11, 2000, p. A3ff.; "How the Tire Problem Turned into a Crisis for Firestone and Ford," *The Wall Street Journal*, August 10, 2000, p. A1ff.; "Could $1 Worth of Nylon Have Saved People's Lives?" *USA Today*, August 9, 2000, p. 1Bff.; "A Blowout Blindsides Bridgestone," *The Wall Street Journal*, August 7, 2000, p. A8ff.

**20.** For more on licensing, see "Washed Up at Warnaco?" *Time*, June 25, 2001, pp. 36–37; "Jordan Leaps into Palm of Your Hand," *USA Today*, June 18, 2001, p. 4B; "Ford Buys Beanstalk for Licensing Magic," *The Wall Street Journal*, June 11, 2001, p. B6; "New Jeep Is Sure to Turn Heads, on the Playground," *The Wall Street Journal*, January 9, 2001, p. B1ff.; "Brand New Goods," *Time*, November 1, 1999; "Deals that Go Bump in the Night," *Business Week*, February 16, 1998, p. 84; "Brand Builders: Licensing, the Color of Money," *Brandweek*, September 15, 1997, pp. 22–23; "Toy Makers Offer the Moon for New 'Star Wars' Licenses," *The Wall Street Journal*, August 19, 1997, p. B1ff.; "Arm & Hammer's Owner Looks at Licensing to Freshen Results," *The Wall Street Journal*, August 6, 1997, p. B2.

**21.** Amitabh Mungale, "Managing Product Families," *Journal of Product Innovation Management*, January 1998, pp. 102–03; Gloria Barczak, "Product Management," *Journal of Product Innovation Management*, September 1997, pp. 425–26; "Brand Managing's New Accent," *Adweek's Marketing Week*, April 15, 1991, pp. 18–22; "Brand Managers: 90s Dinosaurs?" *Advertising Age*, December 19, 1988, p. 19.

**22.** "Ten Years May Be Generic Lifetime," *Advertising Age*, March 23, 1987, p. 76; Brian F. Harris and Roger A. Strang, "Marketing Strategies in the Age of Generics," *Journal of Marketing*, Fall 1985, pp. 70–81.

**23.** "Dr. Pop and Frisk Help a Grocery Chain Grow," *The Wall Street Journal*, April 13, 1998, p. B1ff.; Marcia Mogelonsky, "When Stores Become Brands," *American Demographics*, February 1995, pp. 32–38; "Big Firms Come Out Fighting, Slow Sales of Private-Label Rivals," *The Wall Street Journal*, July 7, 1994, p. B8; "Exposing the Five Myths of Private Label Brands," *Brandweek*, June 20, 1994, p. 17; R. Sethuraman and J. Mittelstaedt, "Coupons and Private Labels: A Cross-Category Analysis of Grocery Products," *Psychology & Marketing*, November/December 1992, pp. 487–500; "Store-Brand Sales Have Their Ups and Downs as Buying Habits Shift," *The Wall Street Journal*, May 12, 1994, p. B6; John A. Quelch and David Harding, "Brands Versus Private Labels: Fighting to Win," *Harvard Business Review*, January–February 1996, pp. 99–109.

**24.** "Getting a Grip on Consumer Tastes," *Business Week*, July 16, 2001, p. 12; "Color Me Popular: Marketers Shape Up Packaging," *USA Today*, February 8, 2001, p. 7B; "See-Through Stuff Sells Big," *USA Today*, December 26, 2000, p. 6B; "This Potion's Power Is in Its Packaging," *The Wall Street Journal*, December 21, 2000, p. B12; "APPEX Show Features Top Auto Products," *DSN Retailing Today*, November 20, 2000, p. 4ff.; "Heinz Puts Squeeze on Places Refilling Its Ketchup Bottles," *The Wall Street Journal*, June 22, 2000, p. A1ff.; "Online Sales Pack a Crunch," *USA Today*, December 6, 1999, p. 1Dff.; "Hefty's Plastic Zipper Bag Is Rapping Rivals," *The Wall Street Journal*, April 16, 1999, p. B1ff.; "Excedrin Is Upfront about New Package," *The Wall Street Journal*, April 8, 1998, p. B8; "Quaker, Coca-Cola Introduce Colorful Drink Contenders," *Advertising Age*, January 26, 1998, p. 52; "What's Foiling the Aluminum Can," *Business Week*, October 6, 1997, pp. 106–8; "Breakthrough Bottles," *Brandweek*, May 20, 1996, pp. 32–52; "If Your Brand's Number Two, Get with the Package Program," *Brandweek*, June 27, 1994, pp. 26–27; Brian Wansink, "Can Package Size Accelerate Usage Volume?" *Journal of Marketing*, July 1996, pp. 1–14.

**25.** "UPC Registers Retailing Impact," *Advertising Age*, April 7, 1986, p. 3ff.; "Bar Codes: Beyond the Checkout Counter," *Business Week*, April 8, 1985, p. 90; Ronald C. Goodstein, "UPC Scanner Pricing Systems: Are They Accurate?" *Journal of Marketing*, April 1994, pp. 20–30; "Firms Line Up to Check Out Bar Codes," *USA Today*, December 4, 1985, pp. B1–2.

**26.** Paula Fitzgerald, Bone Corey, and Robert J. Corey, "Ethical Dilemmas in Packaging: Beliefs of Packaging Professionals," *Journal of Macromarketing*, Spring 1992, pp. 45–54. For more on downsizing, see "Big Trend: Smaller Packaging," USA Today, April 1, 1993, p. 1Bff.; "State AGs Attack Downsized Brands," *Advertising Age*, February 18, 1991, p. 1ff.; "Critics Call Cuts in Package Size Deceptive Move," *The Wall Street Journal*, February 5, 1991, p. B1ff. For more discussion on disposable products, see "Disposing of the Green Myth," *Adweek's Marketing Week*, April 13, 1992, pp. 20–21; "The Waste Land," *Adweek*, November 11, 1991, p. 26; "Ridding the Nation of Polystyrene Peanuts," *Adweek's Marketing Week*, October 22, 1990, p. 17.

**27.** J. E. Russo, "The Value of Unit Price Information," *Journal of Marketing Research*, May 1977, pp. 193–201; David A. Aaker and Gary T. Ford, "Unit Pricing Ten Years Later: A Replication," *Journal of Marketing*, Winter 1983, pp. 118–22.

**28.** Sections 52(1)(b), 52(1)(c), and 52(1)(a) of the *Competition Act*.

**29.** For more on service guarantees, see "Got a Gripe? Amtrak Patrons Get Free Ride," *USA Today*, July 7, 2000, p. 2B; "Amtrak Rolls Out Service Guarantee, New Logo," *Investor's Business Daily*, July 7, 2000, p. A7; "Biztravel.com Promises Money Back for Flight Delays," *USA Today*, May 23, 2000, p. 1Bff.; "It's Service in a Box from Hewlett-Packard," *Advertising Age*, May 10, 1993, p. 5; "More Firms Pledge Guaranteed Service," *The Wall Street Journal*, July 17, 1991, p. B1ff. For more on warranties, see M. E. Blair and Daniel E. Innis, "The Effects of Product Knowledge on the Evaluation of Warranteed Brands," *Psychology & Marketing*, August 1996, pp. 445–56; Ellen M. Moore and F. Kelly Shuptrine, "Warranties: Continued Readability Problems After the 1975 Magnuson-Moss Warranty Act," *Journal of Consumer Affairs*, Summer 1993, pp. 23–36; M.A.J. Menezes and I.S. Currim, "An Approach for Determination of Warranty Length," *International Journal of Research in Marketing*, May 1992, pp. 177–96; "Service Dealers Complain about Warranty Business," *The Wall Street Journal*, February 20, 1992, p. B2.

## Chapter 10

**1.** Available from World Wide Web: <http://www.palm.com>; "Palm Slips to No. 2 in Revenue as iPaq Grabs the Top Spot," *Investor's Business Daily*, June 19, 2001, p. A6; "Jordan Leaps into Palm of Your Hand," *USA Today*, June 18, 2001, p. 4B; "Palm's Fortune Take a Tumble, Pressuring CEO," *The Wall Street Journal*, June 4, 2001, p. B1ff.; "The 411 on PDAs," *Ecompany*, June 2001, pp. 133–35; "Has Palm Lost Its Grip?" *Fortune*, May 28, 2001, pp. 104–108; "Palm Shares Sink as One-Time Star Says Sales Fading," *Investor's Business Daily*, May 21, 2001, p. A6; "HandEra's Hand-Held Puts Some New Twists on the Usual Formula," *The Wall Street Journal*, May 10, 2001, p. B1; "Hand-Helds that Are Less of a Handful," *Business Week*, April 9, 2001, p. 18; "PDA Wars: Round 2," *Time*, April 2, 2001, pp. 40–41; "No Cartwheels for Handspring," *Business Week*, April 2, 2001, pp. 56–58; "Palm and Handspring Offer Welcome Updates to Hand-Held Models," *The Wall Street Journal*, March 29, 2001, p. B1; "New Devices Shrink Difference in Price for Palm, Pocket PC," *Investor's Business Daily*, March 21, 2001, p. A6; "Palm and Handspring Lead a Sector that Hardly Had to Sweat," *Investor's Business Daily*, January 2, 2001, p. A6; "Palm, Microsoft Extend Rivalry to Wireless Arena," *Investor's Business Daily*, November 20, 2000, p. A6; "Seeding Demand for Handspring," *Advertising Age*, November 6, 2000, p. S36; "Palm Hopes to Blaze a New Image in Major Campaign," *The Wall Street Journal*, November 1, 2000, p. B10; "Hard Cell," *Fortune*, October 30, 2000, pp. 305–308; "Hand-Held Makers Spring Free from Parent," *Investor's Business Daily*, October 4, 2000, p. A12; "Palm and Handspring Go Hand to Hand," *Fortune*, September 18, 2000, pp. 319–20; "Palm Puts Up Its Fists as Microsoft Attacks Hand-Held PC Market," *The Wall Street Journal*, August 8, 2000, p. A1ff.; "Army of Programmers Helps Palm Keep Its Edge," *The Wall Street Journal*, June 1, 2000, p. B1ff.; "Improved Hand-Helds Still Don't Capture the Magic of Palms," *The Wall Street Journal*, May 4, 2000, p. B1; "If at First You Don't Succeed . . . ," *Business Week*, April 24, 2000, pp. 120–30; "Palm Gets Ready for New Hands," *The Wall Street Journal*, February 28, 2000, p. B1ff.; "3Com Tries to Solve Its Palm Problem," *Fortune*, October 11, 1999, pp. 167–68; "Palm Has the Whole World in Its Hand," *USA Today*, September 14, 1999, p. 1Bff.; "Putting Fluff over Function," *Fortune*, March 15, 1999, pp. 163–65; "The Palm Pilot Sequel Is a Hit," *Fortune*, April 13, 1998, pp. 154–56; "3Com Again Changes Name of Hot-Selling PalmPilot," *Advertising Age*, March 9, 1998, p. 4; "Apple Drops Newton, an Idea Ahead of Its Time," *The Wall Street Journal*,

March 2, 1998, p. B1ff.; "What's in a Name? Ask 3Com," *Business Week*, January 26, 1998, p. 6; "Little Computers, Big New Marketing Battle," *The Wall Street Journal*, November 17, 1997, p. B1ff.; "A Rocket in Its Pocket," *Business Week*, September 9, 1996, pp. 111–14; "How Palm Computing Became an Architect," *Harvard Business Review*, September–October 1997, p. 89.

**2.** Lee G. Cooper, "Strategic Marketing Planning for Radically New Products," *Journal of Marketing*, January 2000, pp. 1–16; Robert W. Veryzer, "Key Factors Affecting Customer Evaluation of Discontinuous New Products," *Journal of Product Innovation Management*, March 1998, pp. 136–50; Laura Birou, Stanley E. Fawcett, and Gregory M. Magnan, "Integrating Product Life Cycle and Purchasing Strategies," *International Journal of Purchasing & Materials Management*, Winter 1997, pp. 23–31; Frank H. Alpert and Michael A. Kamins, "An Empirical Investigation of Consumer Memory, Attitude and Perceptions Toward Pioneer and Follower Brands," *Journal of Marketing*, October 1995, pp. 34–45; Neil A. Morgan, "Managing Imitation Strategies: How Later Entrants Seize Market Share From Pioneers," *Journal of Marketing*, October 1995, pp. 104–06; David M. Szymanski, Lisa C. Troy, and Sundar G. Bharadwaj, "Order of Entry and Business Performance: An Empirical Synthesis and Reexamination," *Journal of Marketing*, October 1995, pp. 17–33; George Day, "The Product Life Cycle: Analysis and Applications Issues," *Journal of Marketing*, Fall 1981, pp. 60–67; John E. Swan and David R. Rink, "Fitting Marketing Strategy to Varying Product Life Cycles," *Business Horizons*, January/February 1982, pp. 72–76; Igal Ayal, "International Product Life Cycle: A Reassessment and Product Policy Implications," *Journal of Marketing*, Fall 1981, pp. 91–96; Edward T. Popper and Bruce D. Buskirk, "Technology Life Cycles in Industrial Markets," *Industrial Marketing Management*, February 1992, pp. 23–32; Vijay Mahajan, Subhash Sharma, and Robert D. Buzzell, "Assessing the Impact of Competitive Entry on Market Expansion and Incumbent Sales," *Journal of Marketing*, July 1993, pp. 39–52; Mary Lambkin and George S. Day, "Evolutionary Processes in Competitive Markets: Beyond the Product Life Cycle," *Journal of Marketing*, July 1989, pp. 4–20.

**3.** Jorge Alberto Sousa De Vasconcellos, "Key Success Factors in Marketing Mature Products," *Industrial Marketing Management* 20, no. 4 (1991), pp. 263–78; Paul C.N. Michell, Peter Quinn, and Edward Percival, "Marketing Strategies for Mature Industrial Products," *Industrial Marketing Management* 20, no. 3 (1991), pp. 201–6; "Computers Become a Kind of Commodity, to Dismay of Makers," *The Wall Street Journal*, September 5, 1991, p. A1ff.; Peter N. Golder and Gerard J. Tellis, "Pioneer Advantage: Marketing Logic or Marketing Legend?" *Journal of Marketing Research*, May 1993, pp. 158–70; "As Once Bright Market for CAT Scanners Dims, Smaller Makers of the X-Ray Devices Fade Out," *The Wall Street Journal*, May 6, 1980, p. 40.

**4.** Adrian Mello, "Solving the Product Development Puzzle," *ZDNet*, April 1, 2003.

**5.** Jeff Goodwin, "World Wide Web: Engineers' Indispensable Tool," *Test & Measurement Worldwide*, vol. 23 (6), June 2003, W1.

**6.** "Pioneer, Panasonic Drive toward Recordable DVD," *Investor's Business Daily*, June 26, 2001, p. A7; "Blockbuster Tests Postvideo Future," *The Wall Street Journal*, June 18, 2001, p. B1ff.; "DVDs Aren't Ready for Home Movies Yet," *Business Week*, May 7, 2001, p. 28; "DVDs' Popularity Gives Studio Earnings Much-Needed Spin," *USA Today*, April 30, 2001, p. 4B; "Vivastar's DVD System Is Affordable, Recordable," *Investor's Business Daily*, April 20, 2001, p. A4; "Apple and Compaq Give a Sneak Preview of DVD Recording," *The Wall Street Journal*, April 5, 2001, p. B1; "Is It Time to Hop on the DVD Bandwagon?" *Ecompany*, March 2001, pp. 162–64; "Sales of DVD Players Boom, but Makers Record Little Profit," *Investor's Business Daily*, January 22, 2001, p. A6; "DVD Makers Battle over Recording Standard," *The Wall Street Journal*, November 9, 2000, p. B6ff.; "To DVD—or Not to DVD?" *The Wall Street Journal*, November 3, 2000, p. W1ff.; "Those Great DVD Sets Are Hitting the Market, but Don't Buy One Yet," *The Wall Street Journal*, August 24, 2000, p. B1ff.; "DVD Sales Energize Home Video Market," *USA Today*, April 30, 2000, p. 3B; "Don't Throw Away Those CDs Yet, Recordable DVDs a Long Way Off," *Investor's Business Daily*, April 13, 2000, p. A6; "DVD Players: Don't Toss That VCR Yet," *Business Week*, March 6, 2000, p. 160H; "As Prices Tumble, Sales of DVD Players Explode for the Holidays," *The Wall Street Journal*, December 9, 1999, p. B1ff.; "Thou Shalt Buy DVD," *Fortune*, November 8, 1999, pp. 201–208; "DVD Acceptance Picks Up Pace," *Discount Store News*, August 9, 1999, pp. 29–34; "With a Clear Path Ahead, DVD Readies for Mass Rule," *Discount Store News*, July 12, 1999, pp. 29–44; "DVD and Conquer: Why One Technology Prevailed," *Business Week*, July 5, 1999, p. 34; "Divx: The Video Technology That Geeks Love to Hate," *Fortune*, June 21, 1999, p. 177; "Circuit City Pulls the Plug on Its Divx Videodisk Venture," *The Wall Street Journal*, June 17, 1999, p. B10; "8–Tracks, Betamax—and Divx?" *Business Week*, November 9, 1998, pp. 108–10; "DVDs Catch On (but Don't Junk the VCR Yet)," *The Wall Street Journal*, September 8, 1998, p. B1ff.; "A New Spin," *Time*, August 24, 1998, pp. 60–61.

**7.** "Video Games Win Respect as Researchers Adapt Features for Computer Programs," *The Wall Street Journal*, August 29, 1991, p. B1ff.; "Multimedia Goes Mainstream," *Business Marketing*, June 1991, pp. 20–22; "A New Spin on Videodiscs," *Newsweek*, June 5, 1989, pp. 68–69.

**8.** *2000 Annual Report*, RJR Nabisco; "Oreo, Ritz Join Nabisco's Low-Fat Feast," *Advertising Age*, April 4, 1994, p. 3ff.; "They're Not Crying in Their Crackers at Nabisco," *Business Week*, August 30, 1993, p. 61; "Nabisco Unleashes a New Batch of Teddies," *Adweek's Marketing Week*, September 24, 1990, p. 18.

**9.** For more on Tide, see *2000 Annual Report*, Procter & Gamble; "Detergent Tablets of the '70s Make a Comeback," *USA Today*, July 27, 2000, p. 9B; "Boom in Liquid Detergents Has P&G Scrambling," *The Wall Street Journal*, September 25, 1997, p. B1ff.; "Ultra-Clean—Retail Cheers Still More P&G Concentrates," *Advertising Age*, August 22, 1994, p. 1ff.; "Detergent Industry Spins into New Cycle," *The Wall Street Journal*, January 5, 1993, p. B1ff.; "P&G Unleashes Flood of New Tide Products," *Advertising Age*, June 16, 1986, p. 3ff. For more on rescuing products online, see "How the Web Rescued Quisp from a Cereal Killing," *The Wall Street Journal*, April 24, 2000, p. B1ff.; "Oh, Heavenly Tastes: We Miss You Back on Earth," *USA Today*, March 24, 2000, p. 5D. See also "The Hard Life of Orphan Brands," *The Wall Street Journal*, April 13, 2001, p. B1ff.; "Orphan Relief," *Advertising Age*, March 19, 2001, p. 3ff.

**10.** For more on rejuvenating mature products, see "Dawn Gets Grease Out of Traffic's Way after Tanker Truck Spill," *Raleigh News & Observer*, May 6, 1998, p. 1Aff.; Brian Wansink, "Making Old Brands New," *American Demographics*, December 1997, pp. 53–58; "Classic Roller Skates Return as Safety Fears Dull Blades," *The Wall Street Journal*, October 24, 1997, p. B1ff.; "Dusting Off the *Britannica*," *Business Week*, October 20, 1997, pp. 143–46; "Never Say 'Old and Lousy,'" *Fortune*, October 13, 1997, p. 40; "At Du Pont, Time to Both Sow and Reap," *Business Week*, September 29, 1997, pp. 107–8; "A Boring Brand Can Be Beautiful," *Fortune*, November 18, 1991, pp. 169–77; "Teflon Is 50 Years Old, but Du Pont Is Still Finding New Uses for Invention," *The Wall Street Journal*, April 7, 1988, p. 34; Stephen W. Miller, "Managing Imitation Strategies: How Later Entrants Seize Markets From Pioneers," *Journal of the Academy of Marketing Science*, Summer 1996, pp. 277–78; Richard E. Anderson, "Phased Product Development Friend or Foe?" *Business Horizons*, November–December 1996, pp. 30–36; Regina Fazio Maruca and Amy L. Halliday, "When New Products and Customer Loyalty Collide," *Harvard Business Review*, November–December 1993, pp. 22–36.

**11.** Available from World Wide Web: <http://www.statcan.ca/english/Pgdb/famil09b.htm>.

**12.** "Netscape's Plan: Survive, Thrive—New Focus Is on Digital Economy," *USA Today*, April 21, 1998, p. 1Bff.; "Netscape to Share Browser Program Code," *The Wall Street Journal*, January 23, 1998, p. B6; "Special Report: The Internet," *The Wall Street Journal*, December 8, 1997, pp. R1–32; "Netspeed at Netscape," *Business Week*, February 10, 1997, pp. 78–86; "A Sea Change for Netscape: Internet Upstart Shows Muscle on the Web," *USA Today*, February 6, 1996, p. 1Bff.

**13.** "Would You Buy a Patent License from This Man?" *Ecompany*,

April 2001, pp. 104–10; "Businesses Battle Over Intellectual Property," *USA Today*, August 2, 2000, p. 1Bff.; "Rivals Square Off Toe to Toe," *USA Today*, August 24, 1993, p. 1Bff.; "The Patent Pirates Are Finally Walking the Plank," *Business Week*, February 17, 1992, pp. 125–27; "Is It Time to Reinvent the Patent System?" *Business Week*, December 2, 1991, pp. 110–15; C. C. Baughn, Michael Bixby, and L S. Woods, "Patent Laws and the Public Good: IPR Protection in Japan and the United States," *Business Horizons*, July–August 1997, pp. 59–65; Karen Bronikowski, "Speeding New Products to Market," *The Journal of Business Strategy*, September/October 1990, pp. 34–37.

**14.** For more on Zara, see "Just-in-Time Fashion," *The Wall Street Journal*, May 18, 2001, p. B1ff.; "The Fashion Cycle Hits High Gear," *Business Week E.Biz*, September 18, 2000, p. EB66; "Zara Has a Made-to-Order Plan for Success," *Fortune*, September 4, 2000, p. 80; "The Mark of Zara," *Business Week*, May 29, 2000, pp. 98–100.

**15.** "Retailers Seek Higher Profits in Low-Rise Jeans," *The Wall Street Journal*, June 28, 2001, p. B1ff.; "Recipe for a Fashion Brand?" *The Wall Street Journal*, June 25, 2001, p. B1ff.; "Dusting Off Fashion's Old Bags," *Time* (Special Issue: Your Business), June 2001, pp. Y2–Y4; "Retailers' Holiday Leather Fetish," *The Wall Street Journal*, November 29, 2000, p. B1ff.; "Designers Howl for Fur," *The Wall Street Journal*, September 22, 2000, p. B1ff.; "Goose Bumps Define the Height of Fashion as Fall Tinges the Air," *The Wall Street Journal*, September 12, 2000, p. A1ff.; "More Teens Get Hung Up on Cellphones," *USA Today*, July 18, 2000, p. 3B; "Like, Be Hip or Be Gone in Teen Clothes Market," *USA Today*, July 5, 2000, p. 8B; "To Track Fickle Fashion, Apparel Firms Go Online," *The Wall Street Journal*, May 11, 2000, p. B1ff.; "Blue Collar No More," *Time*, May 8, 2000, p. 80; "Frilly and Full," *USA Today*, April 10, 2000, p. 8D; "Claiborne Patches Together an Empire," *The Wall Street Journal*, February 2, 2000, p. B1ff.; "Pokemon Makes a Monster Splash," *USA Today*, December 7, 1999, p. 1Dff.; "Forget the Clothes—Fashion Fortunes Turn on Heels and Purses," *The Wall Street Journal*, November 23, 1999, p. A1ff.; "Pokemon Poised to Stomp Elmo, Furby," *USA Today*, November 10, 1999, p. 1Bff.; "True Grit, or How Sights Denim Makes Money in Dirty Jeans," *The Wall Street Journal*, October 12, 1999, p. A1ff.; "Beanie Brouhaha," *Advertising Age*, September 6, 1999, p. 1ff.; "The Latest Trend in Newfangled Bangles," *The Wall Street Journal*, September 2, 1999, p. B1ff.; "It's Lustrous, It's Chic, It's Plastic," *The Wall Street Journal*, September 1, 1999, p. B1ff.; "Nokia Shoots for the Stars with New Phone," *The Wall Street Journal*, August 24, 1999, p. B7; "Fashion Coup at Dawson's Creek," *The Wall Street Journal*, June 22, 1999, p. B1ff.; "Sheer Marketing: Bare Pantyhose," *The Wall Street Journal*, May 24, 1999, p. B1ff.; "Banana Republic's Answer to Khaki Overdose: Chino!" *The Wall Street Journal*, March 26, 1999, p. B1ff.; "Fashion Understatement: That's So 5 Minutes Ago," *USA Today*, March 23, 1999, p. 1Dff.; "A Fad Flames Out, and Retailers Get Burned," *The Wall Street Journal*, January 21, 1999, p. B1ff.; "Urban Wear Goes Suburban," *Fortune*, December 21, 1998, pp. 169–72; "Despite Hype, There Are No Endangered Furbies," *USA Today*, December 15, 1998, p. 1D; "Army Pants with Pouchy Pockets Storm Fashion World," *The Wall Street Journal*, July 9, 1998, p. B1ff.; "At McDonald's, a Case of Mass Beaniemania," *The Wall Street Journal*, June 5, 1998, p. B1ff.; "Fidel Meets Naomi," *The Wall Street Journal*, March 2, 1998, p. B1ff.; "Updating a Classic: The Man in the Gray Spandex Suit," *The Wall Street Journal*, January 27, 1998, p. B1ff.; "Teletubbies Are Coming: Brit Hit Sets U.S. Invasion," *Advertising Age*, January 19, 1998, p. 12; "Rural Kids Like Hip Clothes, Too, Hot Chain Discovers," *The Wall Street Journal*, January 15, 1998, p. B1ff.; "A Grumpy Old Lady Becomes a Big Hit for Hallmark," *The Wall Street Journal*, December 24, 1997, p. B1ff.; "How Belgian Engineer Created a Global Backpack Trend," *The Wall Street Journal*, December 10, 1997, p. B1ff.; "Will Working Women Wear This Stuff?" *The Wall Street Journal*, October 8, 1997, p. B1ff.; "Virtual Pets Are Some Campers' Best Friends," *USA Today*, July 29, 1997, p. 1D; "The Beanie Factor," *Brandweek*, June 16, 1997, pp. 22–27. See also Martin G. Letscher, "How to Tell Fads from Trends," *American Demographics*, December 1994, pp. 38–45; R.E. Goldsmith, J.B. Freiden, and J.C. Kilsheimer, "Social Values and Female Fashion Leadership: A Cross-Cultural Study," *Psychology & Marketing*, September/October 1993, pp. 399–412; "Special Report: Fashion Marketing," *Advertising Age*, August 22, 1994, pp. 23–28; Craig J. Thompson and Diana L. Haytko, "Speaking of Fashion: Consumers' Uses of Fashion Discourses and the Appropriation of Countervailing Cultural Meanings," *Journal of Consumer Research*, June 1997, pp. 15–42.

**16.** "Betamax Wars All Over Again," *Business Week*, September 29, 1997, pp. 35–36; "The Next Great Gadget," *Time*, January 20, 1997, p. 66; "Sony Isn't Mourning the 'Death' of Betamax," *Business Week*, January 25, 1988, p. 37; Sigvald J. Harryson, "How Canon and Sony Drive Product Innovation Through Networking and Application-Focused R&D," *Journal of Product Innovation Management*, July 1997, pp. 288–95; M. Lambkin, "Pioneering New Markets: A Comparison of Market Share Winners and Losers," *International Journal of Research in Marketing*, March 1992, pp. 5–22.

**17.** "Novel P&G Product Brings Dry Cleaning Home," *The Wall Street Journal*, November 19, 1997, p. B1ff.; "Colgate Places a Huge Bet on a Germ-Fighter," *The Wall Street Journal*, December 29, 1997, p. B1ff.; "Smart Toothbrush," *Fortune*, November 4, 1991, p. 168.

**18.** "Too Many Choices," *The Wall Street Journal*, April 20, 2001, p. B1ff.; "Reposition: Simplifying the Customer's Brandscape," *Brandweek*, October 2, 2000, pp. 36–48; "Consumers to GM: You Talking to Me?" *Business Week*, June 19, 2000, pp. 213–16; "How Growth Destroys Differentiation," *Brandweek*, April 24, 2000, pp. 42–50; "P&G, Seeing Shoppers Were Being Confused, Overhauls Marketing," *The Wall Street Journal*, January 15, 1997, P. A1ff.; "Make It Simple," *Business Week*, September 9, 1996, pp. 96–104; "Diaper Firms Fight to Stay on the Bottom," *The Wall Street Journal*, March 23, 1993, p. B1ff.; "Multiple Varieties of Established Brands Muddle Consumers, Make Retailers Mad," *The Wall Street Journal*, January 24, 1992, p. B1ff.

**19.** Available from World Wide Web: <http://www.productscan.com/index.cfm?nid=5>.

**20.** "Too Many Choices," *The Wall Street Journal*, April 20, 2001, p. B1ff.; "Special Report: New Products," *Ad Age International*, April 13, 1998, pp. 17–20; "The Ghastliest Product Launches," *Fortune*, March 16, 1998, p. 44; "New and Improved," *American Demographics*, March 1998, p. 32; "Seems the Only Problem with New Products Is That They're New," *Brandweek*, August 22, 1994, pp. 36–40; "Flops: Too Many New Products Fail. Here's Why—and How to Do Better," *Business Week*, August 16, 1993, pp. 76–82; Brian D. Ottum and William L. Moore, "The Role of Market Information in New Product Success/Failure," *Journal of Product Innovation Management*, July 1997, pp. 258–73.

**21.** "Makers of Chicken Tonight Find Many Cooks Say, 'Not Tonight,'" *The Wall Street Journal*, May 17, 1994, p. B1ff.; "Failure of Its Oven Lovin' Cookie Dough Shows Pillsbury Pitfalls of New Products," *The Wall Street Journal*, June 17, 1993, p. B1ff.; Sharad Sarin and Gour M. Kapur, "Lessons From New Product Failures: Five Case Studies," *Industrial Marketing Management*, November 1990, pp. 301–14.

**22.** "How Top Software Firms Dominate," *Investor's Business Daily*, June 12, 2001, p. A1; "Opening the Spigot," *Business Week E.Biz*, June 4, 2001, pp. EB16–Eb20; "Digital Workflow Speeds Time to Shelf," *Brand Packaging*, March/April 2001, pp. 24–26; "Shelf Life Is Short for Innovations: How to Speed Products to Market," *Investor's Business Daily*, February 26, 2001, p. A1; "How the Web Is Retooling Detroit," *Business Week*, November 27, 2000, pp. 194B–D; "How Fast Can This Baby Go?" *Business Week*, April 10, 2000, pp. 38–40; Kathleen M. Eisenhardt and Shona L. Brown, "Time Pacing: Competing in Markets That Won't Stand Still," *Harvard Business Review*, March–April 1998, pp. 59–69; Marco Iansiti and Alan MacCormack, "Developing Product on Internet Time," *Harvard Business Review*, September–October 1997, pp. 108–17; Bryan Lilly and Rockney Walters, "Toward a Model of New Product Preannouncement Timing," *Journal of Product Innovation Management*, January 1997, pp. 4–20; Richard Bauhaus, "Developing Products in Half the Time," *Journal of Product Innovation Management*, January 1997, pp. 68–69; "Fast-Selling Software that Hurries Products to Market," *For-*

*tune*, April 29, 1996, p. 150Cff.; Joseph T. Vesey, "Time-to-Market: Put Speed in Product Development," *Industrial Marketing Management*, May 1992, pp. 151–58. For more on P&G's efforts to bring products to market faster, see "Brands in a Bind," *Business Week*, August 28, 2000, pp. 234–238; "Warm and Fuzzy Won't Save Procter & Gamble," *Business Week*, June 26, 2000, pp. 48–50; "Is P&G's Makeover Only Skin-Deep?" *Business Week*, November 15, 1999, p. 52; "P&G and Unilever's Giant Headaches," *Advertising Age*, May 24, 1999, pp. 22–28.

**23.** "How Burger King Got Burned in Quest to Make the Perfect Fry," *The Wall Street Journal*, January 16, 2001, p. A1ff.; "Tailoring World's Cars to U.S. Tastes," *The Wall Street Journal*, January 15, 2001, p. B1ff.; "From Research Dollars to Riches," *Investor's Business Daily*, December 5, 2000, p. A1ff; "Look Who's Doing R&D," *Fortune*, November 27, 2000, pp. 232C-Z; "Why Dow Chemical Finds Slime Sublime," *The Wall Street Journal*, November 15, 1999, p. B1ff.; "Product Development Is Always Difficult; Consider the Frito Pie," *The Wall Street Journal*, October 25, 1999, p. A1ff.; Robert Polk, Richard E. Plank, and David A. Reid, "Technical Risk and New Product Success: An Empirical Test in High Technology Business Markets," *Industrial Marketing Management*, November 1996, pp. 531–43; X. M. Song and Mark E. Parry, "A Cross-National Comparative Study of New Product Development Processes: Japan and the United States," *Journal of Marketing*, April 1997, pp. 1–18; Robert G. Cooper, "Overhauling the New Product Process," *Industrial Marketing Management*, November 1996, pp. 465–82; Jeffrey B. Schmidt and Roger J. Calantone, "Are Really New Product Development Projects Harder to Shut Down?" *Journal of Product Innovation Management*, March 1998, pp. 111–23; S. N. Wasti and Jeffrey K. Liker, "Risky Business or Competitive Power? Supplier Involvement in Japanese Product Design," *Journal of Product Innovation Management*, September 1997, pp. 337–55; Cheryl Nakata and K Sivakumar, "National Culture and New Product Development: An Integrative Review," *Journal of Marketing*, January 1996, pp. 61–72; William H. Murphy and Linda Gorchels, "How to Improve Product Management Effectiveness," *Industrial Marketing Management*, January 1996, pp. 47–58; Gary S. Lynn, Joseph G. Morone, and Albert S. Paulson, "Marketing and Discontinuous Innovation: The Probe and Learn Process," *California Management Review*, Spring 1996, pp. 8–37; Dorothy Leonard and Jeffrey F. Rayport, "Spark Innovation Through Empathic Design," *Harvard Business Review*, November–December 1997, pp. 102–8ff.; Gary L. Ragatz, Robert B. Handfield, and Thomas V. Scannell, "Success Factors for Integrating Suppliers into New Product Development," *Journal of Product Innovation Management*, May 1997, pp. 190–202; X. M. Song and Mitzi M. Montoya-Weiss, "Critical Development Activities for Really New Versus Incremental Products," *Journal of Product Innovation Management*, March 1998, pp. 124–35.

**24.** "Hallmark Hits the Mark," *USA Today*, June 14, 2001, p. 1Dff.; "Pickups Get Women's Touch," *USA Today*, June 13, 2001 p. 1Bff.; "Windstar's Designing Women," *USA Today*, July 19, 1999, p. 3B; "Where Great Ideas Come From," *Inc.*, April 1998, pp. 76–94; Ari-Pekka Hameri and Jukka Nihtila, "Distributed New Product Development Project Based on Internet and World-Wide Web: A Case Study," *Journal of Product Innovation Management*, March 1997, pp. 77–87; "Seeing the Future First," *Fortune*, September 5, 1994, pp. 64–70; "Detroit's New Strategy to Beat Back Japanese Is to Copy Their Ideas," *The Wall Street Journal*, October 1, 1992, p. A1ff.

**25.** "It Was a Hit in Buenos Aires—So Why Not Boise?" *Business Week*, September 7, 1998, pp. 56–58; Don R. Graber, "How to Manage a Global Product Development Process," *Industrial Marketing Management*, November 1996, pp. 483–89; "U.S. Companies Shop Abroad for Product Ideas," *The Wall Street Journal*, March 14, 1990, p. B1ff.

**26.** Eric von Hippel, *The Sources of Innovation* (New York: Oxford University Press, 1988).

**27.** "Gun Makers to Push Use of Gun Locks," *The Wall Street Journal*, May 9, 2001, p. B12; "U.S. Recalls Millions of Evenflo 'Joyride' Infant Seats, Carriers," *The Wall Street Journal*, May 2, 2001, p. B6; "Cosco's History Reads Like Recipe for Recalls," *USA Today*, April 4, 2001, p. 1Bff.; "Stand Up and Fight," *Business Week*, September 11, 2000, pp. 54–55; "Why One Jury Dealt a Big Blow to Chrysler in Minivan-Latch Case," *The Wall Street Journal*, November 19, 1997, p. A1ff.; "Chinese Discover Product-Liability Suits," *The Wall Street Journal*, November 13, 1997, p. B1ff.; Paula Mergenhagen, "Product Liability: Who Sues?" *American Demographics*, June 1995, pp. 48–55; "How a Jury Decided that a Coffee Spill Is Worth $2.9 Million," *The Wall Street Journal*, September 1, 1994, p. A1ff.; Paul A. Herbig and James E. Golden, "Innovation and Product Liability," *Industrial Marketing Management*, July 1994, pp. 245–56; Robert N. Mayer and Debra L. Scammon, "Caution: Weak Product Warnings May Be Hazardous to Corporate Health," *Journal of Business Research*, June 1992, pp. 347–60; Thomas V. Greer, "Product Liability in the European Community: The Legislative History," *Journal of Consumer Affairs*, Summer 1992, pp. 159–76.

**28.** "Want Shelf Space at the Supermarket? Ante Up," *Business Week*, August 7, 1989, pp. 60–61; "Grocer 'Fee' Hampers New-Product Launches," *Advertising Age*, August 3, 1987, p. 1ff; Frank H. Alpert, Michael A. Kamins, and John L. Graham, "An Examination of Reseller Buyer Attitudes Toward Order of Brand Entry," *Journal of Marketing*, July 1992, pp. 25–37.

**29.** "This Bright Idea Could Make GE a Billion," *Business Week*, December 4, 1989, p. 120.

**30.** Fred Langerak, Ed Peelen, and Harry Commandeur, "Organizing for Effective New Product Development," *Industrial Marketing Management*, May 1997, pp. 281–89; Keith Goffin, "Evaluating Customer Support During New Product Development—An Exploratory Study," *Journal of Product Innovation Management*, January 1998, pp. 42–56; Paul S. Adler, Avi Mandelbaum, Vien Nguyen, and Elizabeth Schwerer, "Getting the Most Out of Your Product Development Process," *Harvard Business Review*, March–April 1996, pp. 134–52; Frank R. Bacon, Jr., and Thomas W. Butler, Jr., *Planned Innovation*, rev. ed. (Ann Arbor: Institute of Science and Technology, University of Michigan, 1980); Christer Karlsson and Par Ahlstrom, "Perspective: Changing Product Development Strategy—A Managerial Challenge," *Journal of Product Innovation Management*, November 1997, pp. 473–84.

**31.** "Torture Testing," *Fortune*, October 2, 2000, pp. 244B–X; "Industry's Amazing New Instant Prototypes," *Fortune*, January 12, 1998, pp. 120E–L; "Secrets of Product Testing," *Fortune*, November 28, 1994, pp. 166–72; "A Smarter Way to Manufacture," *Business Week*, April 30, 1990, pp. 110–17; "Oops! Marketers Blunder Their Way through the 'Herb Decade,'" *Advertising Age*, February 13, 1989, p. 3ff.

**32.** For more on Gillette's razor costs, see "Gillette's Edge," *Brandweek*, May 28, 2001, p. 5; "No New CEO, but Gillette Does Have a New Product," *Advertising Age*, November 6, 2000, p. 25; "Brands in a Bind," *Business Week*, August 28, 2000, pp. 234–38; "Gillette Loses Face," *Fortune*, November 8, 1999, pp. 147–52; "Everything's at a Premium," *Advertising Age*, August 2, 1999, pp. 12–15; "Would You Spend $1.50 for a Razor Blade?" *Business Week*, April 27, 1998, p. 46; "The Men Who Broke Mach3," *Time*, April 27, 1998, p. 4; "Gillette Puts $300 Mil behind Its Mach3 Shaver," *Advertising Age*, April 20, 1998, p. 6; "How Gillette Brought Its MACH3 to Market," *The Wall Street Journal*, April 15, 1998, p. B1ff.; "Gillette Finally Reveals Its Vision of the Future, and It Has 3 Blades," *The Wall Street Journal*, April 14, 1998, p. A1ff. For more on Gillette's toothbrush costs, see "All About Gadgets and Gizmosity," *Fortune*, February 19, 2001, p. 264; "Gillette Lines Up Oral-B Ad Push," *Advertising Age*, December 4, 2000, p. 22; "Fashionable Mouths Bristle at the Ordinary," *USA Today*, May 10, 2000, p. 5D; "Oral-B Hopes New Toothbrush Scrubs the Competition," *USA Today*, January 4, 1999, p. 10B; "New Toothbrush Is Big-Ticket Item," *The Wall Street Journal*, October 27, 1998, p. B1ff.

**33.** "Oops! Marketers Blunder Their Way Through the 'Herb Decade,'" *Advertising Age*, February 13, 1989, p. 3ff.

**34.** Available from World Wide Web: <http://www.marketingmag.ca>; Astrid Van Den Broek, "Kellogg Markets 'Tasty' Soy Cereal," April 23, 2001.

**35.** "An Rx for Drug Trials," *Business Week E.Biz*, December 11, 2000, pp. EB66–EB68; "Web Sites Give Retailers Better Way to Test-Market Products," *USA Today*, August 29, 2000, p. 3B; "Can Procter & Gamble Change Its Culture, Protect Its Market Share, and Find the Next Tide?" *Fortune*, April 26, 1999, pp. 146–52; "To Test or Not to Test . . . ," *American Demographics*, June 1998, p. 64; John R. Dickinson and Carolyn P. Wilby, "Concept Testing With and Without Product Trial," *Journal of Product Innovation Management*, March 1997, pp. 117–25; "Born to Be a Little Too Wild," *Business Week*, December 18, 2000, pp. 69–70.

**36.** William E. Souder, David Buisson, and Tony Garrett, "Success Through Customer-Driven New Product Development: A Comparison of U.S. and New Zealand Small Entrepreneurial High Technology Firms," *Journal of Product Innovation Management*, November 1997, pp. 459–72; Artemis March, "Usability: The New Dimension of Product Design," *Harvard Business Review*, September 1994–October 1994, pp. 144–49; Peter H. Bloch, "Seeking the Ideal Form: Product Design and Consumer Response," *Journal of Marketing*, July 1995, pp. 16–29; Roger J. Calantone, "Engines of Innovation: U.S. Industrial Research at the End of an Era," *Journal of Product Innovation Management*, July 1997, pp. 315–17; George M. Chryssochoidis and Veronica Wong, "Rolling Out New Products Across Country Markets: An Empirical Study of Causes of Delays," *Journal of Product Innovation Management*, January 1998, pp. 16–41; Erik J. Hultink, Abbie Griffin, Susan Hart, and Henry S. Robben, "Industrial New Product Launch Strategies and Product Development Performance," *Journal of Product Innovation Management*, July 1997, pp. 243–57; Alan Flaschner, "Technology Fountainheads: The Management Challenge of R&D Consortia," *Journal of Product Innovation Management*, July 1997, pp. 309–12; William Q. Judge, Gerald E. Fryxell, and Robert S. Dooley, "The New Task of R&D Management: Creating Goal-Directed Communities for Innovation," *California Management Review*, Spring 1997, pp. 72–85; John P. Workman, Jr., "Marketing's Limited Role in New Product Development in One Computer Systems Firm," *Journal of Marketing Research*, November 1993, pp. 405–21.

**37.** Available from World Wide Web: <http://www.marketingmag.ca>; Sarah Smith, "Heinz Kickers Target Adult Taste Buds," June 3, 2002.

**38.** "Brands at Work," *Brandweek*, April 13, 1998, pp. 27–35; "Special Report: Auto Marketing & Brand Management," *Advertising Age*, April 6, 1998, pp. S1–28; "P&G Redefines the Brand Manager," *Advertising Age*, October 13, 1997, p1ff.; Don Frey, "Learning the Ropes: My Life as a Product Champion," *Harvard Business Review*, September/October 1991, pp. 46–57; Stephen K. Markham, "New Products Management," *Journal of Product Innovation Management*, July 1997, pp. 312–14; Manfred F. Maute and William B. Locander, "Innovation as a Socio-Political Process: An Empirical Analysis of Influence Behavior among New Product Managers," *Journal of Business Research*, June 1994, pp. 161–74.

**39.** Available from World Wide Web: <http://www.3m.com>; *2000 Annual Report*, 3M; "How to Get the Most Out of R&D: Balance Funds against Risk, Timing" *Investor's Business Daily*, May 11, 2001, p. A1; "3M: Glued to the Web," *Business Week E.Biz*, November 20, 2000, pp. EB65–EB70; "3M's Big Cleanup," *Business Week*, June 5, 2000, pp. 96–98; "3M: The Heat Is on the Boss," *Business Week*, March 15, 1999, pp. 82–84; "Steel Wool Dino Roars a Powerful Message," *Advertising Age*, September 16, 1996, p. 55; "3M Eyes Retail Software with E-Post-it Notes," *Brandweek*, March 11, 1996, p. 12; "How 3M, by Tiptoeing into Foreign Markets, Became a Big Exporter," *The Wall Street Journal*, March 29, 1991, p. A1ff.

## Chapter 11

**1.** "Coca-Cola Gets Hip to the 'Net," *Advertising Age*, July 2, 2001, p. 21; "Coke and Pepsi Escalate Their Water Fight," *The Wall Street Journal*, May 18, 2001, p. B8; "Sports Drinks Refresh Rivalry for Coke, Pepsi," *The Wall Street Journal*, May 8, 2001, p. B1ff.; "Will Coke.net Be the Real Thing to Put Fizz into Fountain Sales?" *Investor's Business Daily*, May 4, 2001, p. A5; "Coke Hopes to Add Fizz to Future with New Structure, Management," *Investor's Business Daily*, April 18, 2001, p. A1; "Why Coke Indulges (the Few) Fans of Tab," *The Wall Street Journal*, April 13, 2001, p. B1ff.; "Guess Who's Winning the Cola Wars," *Fortune*, April 2, 2001, pp. 164–65; "Coca-Cola Readies Global Assault," *Advertising Age*, April 2, 2001, p. 1ff.; "Repairing the Coke Machine," *Business Week*, March 19, 2001, pp. 86–88; "Coke and P&G's Shotgun Wedding," *Ad Age Global*, March 2001, p. 6; "Coke's 'Think Local' Strategy Has Yet to Prove Itself," *The Wall Street Journal*, March 1, 2001, p. B6; "Is Coke Getting as Good as It Gives in P&G Partnership?" *The Wall Street Journal*, February 22, 2001, p. B4; "Coke and P&G Plan to Create $4.2 Billion Juice and Snack Company," *The Wall Street Journal*, February 21, 2001, p. B1ff.; "Coke Retains Top Spot in U.S. Soda Sales," *The Wall Street Journal*, February 16, 2001, p. B8; "Coke Shifts Strategy as Surge Fizzles," *Advertising Age*, February 12, 2001, p. 1ff.; "Coke to Acquire Maker of Coffee, Bottled Drinks," *The Wall Street Journal*, January 12, 2001, p. B4; "Tea Is a Hit for Coke," *Ad Age Global*, January 2001, p. 5; "Pepsi, Coke Still at War, but on Different Fronts," *Advertising Age*, December 11, 2000, p. 4; "Coke and Pepsi Do Battle on the Web," *Ad Age Global*, November 2000, p. 48; "Pepsi, Coke Duke It Out in India, China," *Ad Age Global*, October 2000, p. 6; "Consumers Lose Some Appetite for Fizzy Drinks," *The Wall Street Journal*, September 19, 2000, p. B1ff.; "Brands in a Bind," *Business Week*, August 28, 2000, pp. 234–38; "Coca-Cola Light Employs Local Edge," *Advertising Age*, August 21, 2000, p. 18ff.; "For Coke, Local Is It," *Business Week*, July 3, 2000, p. 122; "To Fix Coca-Cola, Daft Sets Out to Get Relationships Right," *The Wall Street Journal*, June 23, 2000, p. A1ff.; "Coke Looses Ad Reins," *Ad Age International*, April 2000, p. 1ff.; "Now, Coke Is No Longer It," *Business Week*, February 28, 2000, pp. 148–51; "Guess Who Wants to Make a Splash in Water," *Business Week*, March 1, 1999, p. 36; "The China Card," *Fortune*, May 25, 1998, p. 82; "For Pepsi, a Battle to Capture Coke's Fountain Sales," *The Wall Street Journal*, May 11, 1998, p. B1ff.; "Pepsi Hits Coca-Cola with an Antitrust Lawsuit," *The Wall Street Journal*, May 8, 1998, p. A3ff.; "For Coke in India, Thums Up Is the Real Thing," *The Wall Street Journal*, April 29, 1998, p. B1ff.; "I'd Like the World to Buy a Coke," *Business Week*, April 13, 1998, pp. 70–76; "If You Can't Beat 'Em, Copy 'Em," *Business Week*, November 17, 1997, p. 50; "Where Coke Goes from Here," *Fortune*, October 13, 1997, pp. 88–91; "Advertising Breezes along the Nile River with Signs for Sails," *The Wall Street Journal*, July 18, 1997, p. A1ff.; "Coke Recruits Paraplegics to Help Fight PepsiCo in Soda War in India," *The Wall Street Journal*, June 10, 1997, p. B9; "A Coke and a Perm? Soda Giant Is Pushing into Unusual Locales," *The Wall Street Journal*, May 8, 1997, p. A1ff.; "For Coca-Cola in Japan, Things Go Better with Milk," *The Wall Street Journal*, January 20, 1997, p. B1ff.; "Coke Pours into Asia," *Business Week*, October 28, 1996, p. 72ff.; "Coke's Soda Fountain for Offices Fizzles, Dashing High Hopes," *The Wall Street Journal*, June 14, 1993, p. A1ff.; "The World's Best Brand," *Fortune*, May 31, 1993, pp. 44–54. For more on Pepsi's distribution, see "Playing for Time," *Brandweek*, June 11, 2001, p. 4; "Beverage Marketers See Refreshing Distribution Possibilities," *The Wall Street Journal*, May 29, 2001, p. B2; "FTC Could Try to Block Pepsi-Quaker Merger," *USA Today*, May 10, 2001, p. 1B.; "Necessity and Invention," *Brandweek*, February 19, 2001, pp. 22–25; "Done Duo," *Brandweek*, January 15, 2001, p. 1ff.; "Quaker Accepts Pepsi's $13.4B Bid," *USA Today*, December 5, 2000, p. 3B; "Race to Buy Gatorade Stirs Up Drink Market," *Investor's Business Daily*, December 4, 2000, p. A10; "Regulators to Keep Close Eye on PepsiCo after Deal," *USA Today*, December 4, 2000, p. 14A; "PepsiCo Hopes to Feast on Profits from Quaker Snacks," *The Wall Street Journal*, December 4, 2000, p. B4; "Behind the Coke Board's Refusal to Let CEO Daft Buy Quaker Oats," *The Wall Street Journal*, November 30, 2000, p. B1ff.; "Gotta Get That Gator," *Business Week*, November 27, 2000, pp. 91–94; "Cadbury's Snapple Testing Out Bottled Beer," *Advertising Age*, November 27, 2000, p. 26; "New Age Dawns as Soda Giants Go Alternative," *Advertising Age*, November 6, 2000, p. 96; "Pepsi Edges Past Coke, and It Has Nothing to Do with Cola," *The Wall Street Journal*, November 6, 2000, p. A1ff.;

"Pepsi Edges Coke in Deal to Buy New Age SoBe," *The Wall Street Journal*, October 30, 2000, p. B1ff.; "Pucker Up! Pepsi's Latest Weapon Is Lemon-Lime," *The Wall Street Journal*, October 13, 2000, p. B1ff.; "Snapple vs. SoBe," *Brandweek*, July 10, 2000, p. 1ff.; "PepsiCo's New Formula: How Roger Enrico Is Remaking the Company . . . and Himself," *Business Week*, April 10, 2000, pp. 172–84; "Lizard Wizards," *Brandweek*, November 22, 1999, pp. 30–32; "A Fruity Kind of Cola War," *USA Today*, August 3, 1999, p. 1Bff.; "Between Coke and a Hard Place," *Brandweek*, June 22, 1998, pp. 34–38; "Pepsi Gets Back in the Game," *Time*, April 26, 1999, pp. 44–46; "Herbal-Tonic Bottler Has Healthy Start," *Inc.*, June 1999, pp. 21–22.

**2.** William Mcinnes, "A Conceptual Approach to Marketing," in *Theory in Marketing*, second series, ed. Reavis Cox, Wroe Alderson, and Stanley J. Shapiro (Homewood, IL: Richard D. Irwin, 1964), pp. 51–67.

**3.** For more on Coke and Pepsi's attempt to sell more in different locales in U.S., see "For Pepsi, a Battle to Capture Coke's Fountain Sales," *The Wall Street Journal*, May 11, 1998, p. B1ff.; "Pepsi Hits Coca-Cola with an Antitrust Lawsuit," *The Wall Street Journal*, May 8, 1998, p. A3ff.; "A Coke and a Perm? Soda Giant Is Pushing into Unusual Locales," *The Wall Street Journal*, May 8, 1997, p. A1ff. For a classic discussion of the discrepancy concepts, see Wroe Alderson, "Factors Governing the Development of Marketing Channels," in *Marketing Channels for Manufactured Goods*, ed. Richard M. Clewett (Homewood, IL: Richard D. Irwin, 1954), pp. 7–9.

**4.** For some examples on how channels change to adjust discrepancies, see "How Magazines Arrive on Shelves, and Why Some Soon May Not," *The Wall Street Journal*, February 26, 1998, p. A1ff.; "Blockbuster Seeks a New Deal with Hollywood," *The Wall Street Journal*, March 25, 1998, p. B1ff.; Robert A. Mittelstaedt and Robert E. Stassen, "Structural Changes in the Phonograph Record Industry and Its Channels of Distribution, 1946–1966," *Journal of Macromarketing*, Spring 1994, pp. 31–44; Arun Sharma and Luis V. Dominguez, "Channel Evolution: A Framework for Analysis," *Journal of the Academy of Marketing Science*, Winter 1992, pp. 1–16.

**5.** "Cellular Carriers Bypass Dealers, Creating Static," *The Wall Street Journal*, March 9, 1998, p. B1ff.

**6.** *2000 Annual Report*, Colgate-Palmolive; *2000 Annual Report*, Procter & Gamble; "After Gobbling Up Iams, P&G Finds People Who Have Bones to Pick," *The Wall Street Journal*, June 14, 2000, p. B1ff.; "For Online Pet Stores, It's Dog-Eat-Dog," *Business Week*, March 6, 2000, pp. 78–80; "P&G Is Out to Fetch Distribution Gains for Iams Pet Food," *The Wall Street Journal*, January 6, 2000, p. A6; "Pet Supplies: Pure-Plays Teach Old Dogs New Tricks," *Discount Store News*, December 13, 1999, p. 49; "Big Pet-Supply Retailers Try to Tame the Competition," *The Wall Street Journal*, August 20, 1999, p. B4; "P&G to Buy Iams: Will Pet-Food Fight Follow?" *The Wall Street Journal*, August 12, 1999, p. B1ff.; "A Web Surfer's Best Friend," *The Wall Street Journal*, July 12, 1999, p. R45; "It's Becoming a Dogfight for the $15 Billion Pet Supply Market," *Raleigh News & Observer*, September 25, 1994, p. 5F; "Pet Superstores Collar Customers from Supermarkets, Small Shops," *The Wall Street Journal*, November 18, 1993, p. B12.

**7.** For a discussion of the advantages and disadvantages of direct channel systems, see Donald Bowersox and M. Bixby Cooper, *Strategic Marketing Channel Management*, 2nd ed. (Burr Ridge, IL: Irwin/McGraw-Hill, 1992). See also David Shipley, Colin Egan, and Scott Edgett, "Meeting Source Selection Criteria: Direct versus Distributor Channels," *Industrial Marketing Management* 20, no. 4 (1991), pp. 297–304; Thomas L. Powers, "Industrial Distribution Options: Trade-Offs to Consider," *Industrial Marketing Management* 18, no. 3 (1989), pp. 155–62.

**8.** "Sears Says Stores Won't Sell Makeup, a Setback for Avon's New Line," *The Wall Street Journal*, July 11, 2001, p. B1ff.; "Avon Thinks Younger, Wealthier," *Advertising Age*, October 2, 2000, p. 69; "Avon Expects Boutiques in Sears, Penneys to Break Even by 2002," *The Wall Street Journal*, September 28, 2000, p. B14; "Avon: The New Calling," *Business Week*, September 18, 2000, pp. 136–48; "Avon Goes Store to Store," *The Wall Street Journal*, September 18, 2000, p. B1ff.; "Avon's Calling Beyond In-House," *Advertising Age*, June 19, 2000, p. 1ff.; "Tour de Face," *Brandweek*, May 29, 2000, pp. 34–36; *2000 Annual Report*, Avon; "Ding-Dong, Avon Calling (on the Web, Not Your Door)," *The Wall Street Journal*, December 28, 1999, p. B4; "Deck the Mall with Kiosks," *Business Week*, December 13, 1999, pp. 86–88; "Is the Bell Tolling for Door-to-Door Selling?" *Business Week E.Biz*, November 1, 1999, pp. EB58–EB60; "Not Your Mother's Avon," *Fortune*, May 24, 1999, pp. 44–46; *1999 Annual Report*, Avon; "Avon Malling," *American Demographics*, April 1999, pp. 38–40; "Avon Is Calling with a New Way to Make a Sale," *The Wall Street Journal*, October 27, 1997, p. B1ff.; "Avon's New Calling: Sell Barbie in China," *The Wall Street Journal*, May 1, 1997, p. B1ff.

**9.** Edward L. Nash, *Direct Marketing* (New York: McGraw-Hill, 1986).

**10.** "Apple Gambles with Retail Plan," *Advertising Age*, June 4, 2001, p. 45; "Sorry, Steve: Here's Why It Won't Work," *Business Week*, May 21, 2001, pp. 44–45; "Apple to Open 25 Retail Stores This Year in a Bid to Reach Out to New Customers," *The Wall Street Journal*, May 16, 2001, p. B8; "Mac Sales Coming to Mall Near You," *USA Today*, May 16, 2001, p. 3D.

**11.** For a discussion of indirect channel systems, see Richard Parker and G. R. Funkhouser, "The Consumer as an Active Member of the Channel: Implications for Relationship Marketing," *Journal of Marketing Theory & Practice*, Spring 1997, pp. 72–79; Gordon C. Bruner, "Cyberspace: The Marketing Frontier," *Journal of Marketing*, January 1997, pp. 112–13; Lou E. Pelton, David Strutton, and James R. Lumpkin, Marketing Channels: A Relationship Management Approach (Burr Ridge, IL: Irwin/McGraw-Hill, 1997). See also Bert Rosenbloom and Trina L. Larsen, "How Foreign Firms View Their U.S. Distributors," *Industrial Marketing Management*, May 1992, pp. 93–102; Frank Lynn, "The Changing Economics of Industrial Distribution," *Industrial Marketing Management*, November 1992, pp. 355–60. For more on intermediaries and their functions, see Richard Greene, "Wholesaling," *Forbes*, January 2, 1984, pp. 226–28; James D. Hlavacek and Tommy J. McCuistion, "Industrial Distributors—When, Who, and How?" *Harvard Business Review*, January–February 1983, pp. 96–101; Elizabeth J. Wilson and Arch G. Woodside, "Marketing New Products with Distributors," *Industrial Marketing Management*, February 1992, pp. 15–22; W. Benoy et al., "How Industrial Distributors View Distributor–Supplier Partnership Arrangements," *Industrial Marketing Management*, January 1995, pp. 27–36.

**12.** "What's Wrong with Selling Used CDs?" *Business Week*, July 26, 1993, p. 38.

**13.** Alorie Gilbert and Beth Bacheldor, "The Big Squeeze," *Information Week*, March 17, 2000.

**14.** "The Multi-Channel Imperative," *Global Online Retailing*, Ernst & Young, 2001.

**15.** Available from World Wide Web: <http://www.baselinemag.com/article2/0,3959,656177,00.asp>; Mary Jo Foley and Tom Steinert-Threlkeld, "The Ultimate CRM Machine," October 29, 2001.

**16.** Alorie Gilbert and Beth Bacheldor, "The Big Squeeze," *Information Week*, March 17, 2000.

**17.** Alorie Gilbert and Beth Bacheldor, "The Big Squeeze," *Information Week*, March 17, 2000.

**18.** Jakki J. Mohr, Robert J. Fisher, and John R. Nevin, "Collaborative Communication in Interfirm Relationships: Moderating Effects of Integration and Control," *Journal of Marketing*, July 1996, pp. 103–15; Joseph P. Cannon, "Contracts, Norms, and Plural Form Governance," *Journal of the Academy of Marketing Science*, Spring 2000, pp. 180–195; Amy E. Cox and Orville C. Walker, "Reactions to Disappointing Performance in Manufacturer-Distributor Relationships: The Role of Escalation and Resource Commitments," *Psychology & Marketing*, December 1997, pp. 791–821; Rajiv P. Dant and Patrick L. Schul, "Conflict Resolution Processes in Contractual Channels of Distribution," *Journal of Marketing*, January 1992, pp. 38–54.

**19.** "Get Great Results from Salespeople by Finding What Really Moves Them," *Investor's Business Daily*, July 2, 2001, p. A1.

**20.** "Kimberly-Clark Keeps Costco in Diapers, Absorbing Costs Itself," *The Wall Street Journal*, September 7, 2000, p. A1ff.

**21.** "For Two Tire Makers, a Flat-Out Pitch for Safer Wheels," *The Wall Street Journal*, July 3, 1997, p. B4; "Bridgestone Takes on Goodyear in Aggressive Campaign," *The Wall Street Journal*, April 16, 1997, p. B2; "Goodyear Revs Image," *Brandweek*, February 10, 1997, p. 12; "Goodyear Wins Court Dispute with Dealers," *The Wall Street Journal*, July 2, 1996, p. B6; "Stan Gault's Designated Driver," *Business Week*, April 8, 1996, pp. 128–30; "Goodyear Drives Home Lifetime Promise," *The Wall Street Journal*, March 7, 1996, p. B8; "Goodyear Expands Just Tires by Converting Full Service Centers," *Discount Store News*, May 16, 1994, p. 6; "Goodyear Plans to Sell Its Tires at Sears Stores," *The Wall Street Journal*, March 3, 1992, p. B1ff.; Thomas L. Baker, "Leaders in Selling and Sales Management: An Analysis of the Impact of Sales and Marketing Principles on the Career of Stanley C. Gault," *Journal of Personal Selling & Sales Management*, Spring 1993, pp. 91–94; Wujin Chu and Paul R. Messinger, "Information and Channel Profits," *Journal of Retailing*, Winter 1997, pp. 487–99; Donald V. Fites, "Make Your Dealers Your Partners," *Harvard Business Review*, March–April 1996, pp. 84–95; John F. Tanner, Rick E. Ridnour, and Stephen B. Castleberry, "Types of Vertical Exchange Relationships: An Empirical Re-Examination of the Cadre/Hired-Hand Distinction," *Journal of Marketing Theory & Practice*, Summer 1997, pp. 109–25; Zhan G. Li and Rajiv P. Dant, "An Exploratory Study of Exclusive Dealing in Channel Relationships," *Journal of the Academy of Marketing Science*, Summer 1997, pp. 201–13.

**22.** "Making the Middleman an Endangered Species," *Business Week*, June 6, 1994, pp. 114–15; Jule B. Gassenheimer et al., "Models of Channel Maintenance: What Is the Weaker Party to Do?" *Journal of Business Research*, July 1994, pp. 225–36; Gregory T. Gundlach, Ravi S. Achrol, and John T. Mentzer, "The Structure of Commitment in Exchange," *Journal of Marketing*, January 1995, pp. 78–92; Jan B. Heide, "Interorganizational Governance in Marketing Channels," *Journal of Marketing*, January 1994, pp. 71–85; Jean L. Johnson et al., "The Exercise of Interfirm Power and Its Repercussions in U.S.-Japanese Channel Relationships," *Journal of Marketing*, April 1993, pp. 1–10.

**23.** Ravi S. Achrol, "Changes in the Theory of Interorganizational Relations in Marketing: toward a Network Paradigm," *Journal of the Academy of Marketing Science*, Winter 1997, pp. 56–71; Aric Rindfleisch and Jan B. Heide, "Transaction Cost Analysis: Past, Present, and Future Applications," *Journal of Marketing*, October 1997, pp. 30–54; Robert F. Lusch and James R. Brown, "Interdependency, Contracting, and Relational Behavior in Marketing Channels," *Journal of Marketing*, October 1996, pp. 19–38; Robert D. Buzzell, "Is Vertical Integration Profitable?" *Harvard Business Review*, January–February 1983, pp. 92–102; Michael Etgar and Aharon Valency, "Determinants of the Use of Contracts in Conventional Marketing Channels," *Journal of Retailing*, Winter 1983, pp. 81–92; Louis W. Stern and Torger Reve, "Distribution Channels as Political Economies: A Framework for Comparative Analysis," *Journal of Marketing*, Summer 1980, pp. 52–64.

**24.** Angela Kryhul, *Marketing Magazine*, December 20/27, 1999.

**25.** "Special Report: Partners," *Business Week*, October 25, 1999, pp, 106–30.

**26.** "A Talk with the Man Who Got Rayovac All Charged Up," *Business Week*, February 21, 2000, pp. 32F–32H.

**27.** "Esprit's Spirited Style Is Hot Seller," *USA Today*, March 25, 1986, p. B5; "Apparel Firm Makes Profits, Takes Risks by Flouting Tradition," *The Wall Street Journal*, June 11, 1985, p. 1ff; David Rylander, David Strutton, and Lou E. Pelton, "Toward a Synthesized Framework of Relational Commitment: Implications for Marketing Channel Theory and Practice," *Journal of Marketing Theory & Practice*, Spring 1997, pp. 58–71; Gary L. Frazier and Walfried M. Lassar, "Determinants of Distribution Intensity," *Journal of Marketing*, October 1996, pp. 39–51; Adam J. Fein and Erin Anderson, "Patterns of Credible Commitments: Territory and Brand Selectivity in Industrial Distribution Channels," *Journal of Marketing*, April 1997, pp. 19–34.

**28.** For more on Reebok, see *2000 Annual Report*, Reebok; "Reebok's Direct Sales Spark a Retail Revolt," *Adweek's Marketing Week*, December 2, 1991, p. 7. See also Saul Sands and Robert J. Posch, Jr., "A Checklist of Questions for Firms Considering a Vertical Territorial Distribution Plan," *Journal of Marketing*, Summer 1982, pp. 38–43; Debra L. Scammon and Mary Jane Sheffet, "Legal Issues in Channels Modification Decisions: The Question of Refusals to Deal," *Journal of Public Policy and Marketing* 5 (1986), pp. 82–96. For more on VW Beetle sales online, see "Volkswagen Drives Some Beetle Sales Online," *Investor's Business Daily*, June 21, 2000, p. A8; "VW Rides a Hot Streak," *Newsweek*, May 22, 2000, pp. 48–50; "VW Targets Web-Savvy with Online Beetle Offer," *Advertising Age*, May 8, 2000, p. 18. For more on Volvo sales online, see "Driving through the Clutter," *Brandweek*, November 27, 2000, pp. IQ34–IQ36; "Volvo Plans Online Ad Campaign for Latest Launch," *The Wall Street Journal*, September 25, 2000, p. B1ff.; "Volvo, Seeking Younger Buyers, Tries to Create a Sexier Image," *The Wall Street Journal*, August 26, 1999, p. B1ff.

**29.** Gregory T. Gundlach and Patrick E. Murphy, "Ethical and Legal Foundations of Relational Marketing Exchanges," *Journal of Marketing*, October 1993, pp. 35–46; Craig B. Barkacs, "Multilevel Marketing and Antifraud Statutes: Legal Enterprises or Pyramid Schemes?" *Journal of the Academy of Marketing Science*, Spring 1997, pp. 176–77; Robert A. Robicheaux and James E. Coleman, "The Structure of Marketing Channel Relationships," *Journal of the Academy of Marketing Science*, Winter 1994, pp. 38–51; Brett A. Boyle and F. Robert Dwyer, "Power, Bureaucracy, Influence and Performance: Their Relationships in Industrial Distribution Channels," *Journal of Business Research*, March 1995, pp. 189–200.

**30.** "It's Getting Easier to Return Items Bought on the Web," *Investor's Business Daily*, Mary 1, 2001, p. A8; "Returning Gifts Bought Online Presents Fewer Problems," *Investor's Business Daily*, January 22, 2001, p. A8.

**31.** See, for example, "P&G to Stores: Keep the Dented Crisco Cans," *The Wall Street Journal*, March 21, 1997, p. B1ff.; "Turning Trash into Cash," *Traffic Management*, October 1993, pp. 46–48; Harvey Alter, "Cost of Recycling Municipal Solid Waste With and Without a Concurrent Beverage Container Deposit Law," *Journal of Consumer Affairs*, Summer 1993, pp. 166–86.

**32.** Available from World Wide Web: <http://www.transora.com> and <http://www.fmi.org/media/bg/ecr1>; "How to Make a Frozen Lasagna (with Just $250 Million)," *Fortune*, April 30, 2001, pp. 149–54; "Delivering the Goods," *Fortune*, November 28, 1994, pp. 64–78; "Making the Middleman an Endangered Species," *Business Week*, June 6, 1994, pp. 114–15; "The Nitty-Gritty of ECR Systems: How One Company Makes It Pay," *Advertising Age*, May 2, 1994, pp. S1ff.; "Behind the Tumult at P&G," *Fortune*, March 7, 1994, pp. 74–82.

**33.** Daniel J. Flint, "Logiticians as Marketers: Their Role When Customers' Desired Value Changes," *Journal of Business Logistics*, 2000, Vol. 21, 2, pp. 19–46; "Logistics Gets a Little Respect," *Business Week E.Biz*, November 20, 2000, pp. EB112–EB116; "One Smart Cookie," *Business Week E.Biz*, November 20, 2000, p. EB120; "A Cereal Maker Hitches Its Wagons to the Web," *Business Week E.Biz*, September 18, 2000, p. EB80; "Costs Too High? Bring in the Logistics Experts," *Fortune*, November 10, 1997, pp. 200C–T; "Ryder Sees the Logic of Logistics," *Business Week*, August 5, 1996, p. 56; Carol J. Emerson and Curtis M. Grimm, "The Relative Importance of Logistics and Marketing Customer Service: A Strategic Perspective," *Journal of Business Logistics*, 1998, pp. 17–32; Edward A. Morash, Cornelia L. M. Droge, and Shawnee K. Vickery,

"Strategic Logistics Capabilities for Competitive Advantage and Firm Success," *Journal of Business Logistics*, 1996, pp. 1–22; John L. Kent and Daniel J. Flint, "Perspectives on the Evolution of Logistics Thought," *Journal of Business Logistics*, 1997, pp. 15–29; Jonathan W. Kohn and Michael A. McGinnis, "Logistics Strategy: A Longitudinal Study," *Journal of Business Logistics*, 1997, pp. 1–14; Steven R. Clinton and David J. Closs, "Logistics Strategy: Does It Exist?" *Journal of Business Logistics*, 1997, pp. 19–44; Prabir K. Bagchi and Helge Virum, "Logistical Alliances: Trends and Prospects in Integrated Europe," *Journal of Business Logistics*, 1998, pp. 191–213.

**34.** For more on Clorox, see *2000 Annual Report*, Clorox; "The Web @ Work/Clorox Co.," *The Wall Street Journal*, October 9, 2000, p. B21; also available from World Wide Web: <http://www.clorox.com>. See also Forrest E. Harding, "Logistics Service Provider Quality: Private Measurement, Evaluation, and Improvement," *Journal of Business Logistics*, 1998, pp. 103–20; Carol C. Bienstock, John T. Mentzer, and Monroe M. Bird, "Measuring Physical Distribution Service Quality," *Journal of the Academy of Marketing Science*, Winter 1997, pp. 31–44; G. T. M. Hult, "Measuring Cycle Time of the Global Procurement Process," *Industrial Marketing Management*, September 1997, pp. 403–12; R. Mohan Pisharodi, "Preference for Supplier When Supplier and Customer Perceptions of Customer Service Levels Differ," *The Logistics and Transportation Review*, March 1994, pp. 31–54; Benson P. Shapiro, V.K. Rangan, and J.J. Sviokla, "Staple Yourself to an Order," *Harvard Business Review*, July–August, 1992, pp. 113–22; J.B. Fuller, J. O'Conor, and R. Rawlinson, "Tailored Logistics: The Next Advantage," *Harvard Business Review*, May–June 1993, pp. 87–98.

**35.** "Compaq Stumbles as PCs Weather New Blow," *The Wall Street Journal*, March 9, 1998, p. B1ff.; "At What Profit Price?" *Brandweek*, June 23, 1997, pp. 24–28; "Delivering the Goods," *Fortune*, November 28, 1994, pp. 64–78; Brian F. O'Neil and Jon L. Iveson, "Strategically Managing the Logistics Function," *The Logistics and Transportation Review*, December 1991, pp. 359–78; Lloyd M. Rinehart, M. Bixby Cooper, and George D. Wagenheim, "Furthering the Integration of Marketing and Logistics Through Customer Service in the Channel," *Journal of the Academy of Marketing Science*, Winter 1989, pp. 63–72; Philip B. Schary, "A Concept of Customer Service," *The Logistics and Transportation Review*, December 1992, pp. 341–52; Edward A. Morash and John Ozment, "Toward Management of Transportation Service Quality," *The Logistics and Transportation Review*, June 1994, pp. 115–40; Michael H. Morris and Duane L. Davis, "Measuring and Managing Customer Service in Industrial Firms," *Industrial Marketing Management*, November 1992, pp. 343–54; Gary L. Frazier, Robert E. Spekman, and Charles R. O'Neal, "Just-In-Time Exchange Relationships in Industrial Markets," *Journal of Marketing*, October 1988, pp. 52–67; William D. Perreault, Jr., and Frederick A. Russ, "Physical Distribution Service in Industrial Purchase Decisions," *Journal of Marketing*, April 1976, pp. 3–10.

**36.** Cornelia Droge, "The Relationship of Electronic Data Interchange with Inventory and Financial Performance," *Journal of Business Logistics*, 2000, Vol. 21, 2, pp. 209–31; Lisa R. Williams, Avril Nibbs, Dimples Irby, and Terence Finley, "Logistics Integration: The Effect of Information Technology, Team Composition, and Corporate Competitve Positioning," *Journal of Business Logistics*, 1997, pp. 31–41; Paul R. Murphy and James M. Daley, "International Freight Forwarder Perspectives on Electronic Data Interchange and Information Management Issues," *Journal of Business Logistics*, 1996, pp. 63–84; Kenneth B. Kahn and John T. Mentzer, "EDI and EDI Alliances: Implications for the Sales Forecasting Function," *Journal of Marketing Theory & Practice*, Spring 1996, pp. 72–78; Ira Lewis and Alexander Talalayevsky, "Logistics and Information Technology: A Coordination Perspective," *Journal of Business Logistics*, 1997, pp. 141–57.

**37.** "A Smart Cookie at Pepperidge," *Fortune*, December 22, 1986, pp. 67–74.

## Chapter 12

**1.** Adapted from: Marina Strauss, "The Best Bet for Your Bottom Dollar," *Globe and Mail*, Saturday, August 2, 2003, p. B1.

**2.** Joel R. Evans, Barry Berman, and William J. Wellington, *Marketing Essentials* (Scarborough, Ont.: Prentice Hall Canada, Inc., 1998) p. 272.

**3.** "Remedies for an Economic Hangover," *Fortune*, June 25, 2001, pp. 130–39; "Outlet Centers Go Upmarket with Amenities," *The Wall Street Journal*, June 6, 2001, p. B12; "Designer Stores, in Extra Large," *The Wall Street Journal*, June 6, 2001, p. B1ff.; "Special Report: The New Leaders," *DSN Retailing Today*, May 8, 2000, pp. 37–130; "Feisty Mom-and-Pops of Gotham Strike Back at Drugstore Chains," *The Wall Street Journal*, March 20, 2000, p. A1ff.; "Making Malls (Gasp!) Convenient," *The Wall Street Journal*, February 8, 2000, p. B1ff.; "Look Who's Thinking Small," *Business Week*, May 17, 1999, pp. 66–70; "Revolution in the Showroom," *Business Week*, February 19, 1996, pp. 70–76; "The Future of Retailing," *American Demographics*, September 1995, p. 26ff.

**4.** "99 Cents Only Stores: So You Think It's Funny? Well, Come On In," *Investor's Business Daily*, July 13, 2001, p. A6; "Family Dollar Uses 'Hardline' Stance to Get a Leg Up in Discount Battles," *Investor's Business Daily*, May 23, 2001, p. A1; "Family Dollar's Howard Levine: Information Helps Him Keep His Company on Top," *Investor's Business Daily*, May 18, 2001, p. A3; "Cheap Thrills for Shoppers," *Newsweek*, April 16, 2001, p. 45; "Dollar General Hits Milestone," *DSN Retailing Today*, February 19, 2001, p. 1ff.; "In ModestTimes, 'Dollar' Stores Remain Upbeat," *The Wall Street Journal*, December 22, 2000, p. B1ff.; "The Buck Stops Here," *Advertising Age*, November 6, 2000, p. 1ff.; "Penny Pinchers Propel a Retail Star," *The Wall Street Journal*, March 20, 1998, p. B1ff.; "The Best Retailer You've Never Heard Of," *Fortune*, March 16, 1998, pp. 110–12; "For You, Toto, 10% Off on the Lamp," *Fortune*, February 2, 1998, pp. 148D–F; "Ikea's New Game Plan," *Business Week*, October 6, 1997, pp. 99–102; "Beyond the Database: Sales and Service on a First-Name Basis," *Colloguy*, No. 1, 1997, pp. 8–9; "Neiman Marcus, Saks Wage Expensive Battle for Upscale Shoppers," *The Wall Street Journal*, November 21, 1996, p. A1ff.; Eric R. Spangenberg, Ayn E. Crowley, and Pamela W. Henderson, "Improving the Store Environment: Do Olfactory Cues Affect Evaluations and Behaviors?" *Journal of Marketing*, April 1996, pp. 67–80; Richard L. Oliver, Roland T. Rust, and Sajeev Varki, "Customer Delight: Foundations, Findings, and Managerial Insight," *Journal of Retailing*, Fall 1997, pp. 311–36; William R. Darden and Barry J. Babin, "Exploring the Concept of Affective Quality: Expanding the Concept of Retail Personality," *Journal of Business Research*, February 1994, pp. 101–10; Jeffrey S. Conant, Denise T. Smart, and Roberto Solano-Mendez, "Generic Retailing Types, Distinctive Marketing Competencies, and Competitive Advantage," *Journal of Retailing*, Fall, 1993, pp. 254–79; Robert J. Donovan et al., "Store Atmosphere and Purchasing Behavior," *Journal of Retailing*, Fall 1994, p. 283; John P. Dickson and Douglas L. MacLachlan, "Social Distance and Shopping Behavior," *Journal of the Academy of Marketing Science*, Spring 1990, pp. 153–62.

**5.** "Store Chains Put Squeeze on Suppliers," Financial Post, November 26–28, 1994, p. 13; "Suppliers Don't Like New Sears Policies," Montreal Gazette, December 6, 1994, pp. C1–C2; "Drugs in a Big Box (Will Mass Merchandisers Upset Quebec's Market?)" Marketing, April 10, 1995, p. 12; "West Meets East (Albert Cohen is Looking for Ways to Grow his Retail Empire)," Marketing, June 12, 1995, pp. 27–28.

**6.** "Career Choices: A Study of Career Choices among College and University Students in Ontario," John C. Williams Consultants, Limited, March 1995 (Ontario Retail Sector Strategy, Human Resources Group).

**7.** "Evolve to Survive Retailers Warned," Toronto Star, November 12, 1994, P. C1; "Measuring Up: Knowing Your Core Market and How to Find New Customers Key to Small Retailers," Calgary Herald, January

16, 1995, p. C1; "The Ladies Who Lunch Have All Gone to Florida (Ira Berg Store Changes with the Times)," Toronto Life, March 1995, pp. 68–70ff.

**8.** "All in Stride for Brown's (the 32-Store Footwear Chain's Success Is the Result of Gutsy Buying, Smooth Merchandising and Careful Staffing)," This Week in Business, September 6, 1991, pp. C8–C9ff.; "Special Report: Premiums and Incentives; Retailers Are Getting into the Game," Strategy, April 17, 1995, pp. 31–34.

**9.** "Why Subway Is 'The Biggest Problem in Franchising,'" Fortune, March 16, 1998, pp. 126–34; "Fast-Food Fight," Business Week, June 2, 1997, pp. 34–36; "Rattling the Chains," Brandweek, April 21, 1997, pp. 28–40; "Lawsuit Spoils the Party at Tupperware," The Wall Street Journal, November 29, 1996, p. B1ff.; "Court Decides Franchisees Get Elbow Room," The Wall Street Journal, August 14, 1996, p. B1ff.; "Chicken and Burgers Create Hot New Class: Powerful Franchisees," The Wall Street Journal, May 21, 1996, p. A1ff.; "Some Franchisees Say Moves by McDonald's Hurt Their Operations," The Wall Street Journal, April 17, 1996, p. A1ff.; Robert Dahlstom, "Franchising: Contemporary Issues and Research," Journal of Public Policy & Marketing, Spring 1996, pp. 159–61; Surinder Tikoo, "Assessing the Franchise Option," Business Horizons, May–June 1996, pp. 78–82; Rajiv P. Dant, Audhesh K. Paswan, and Patrick J. Kaufman, "What We Know About Ownership Redirection in Franchising: A Meta-Analysis," Journal of Retailing, Winter 1996, pp. 429–44; Alessandro Baroncelli and Angelo Manaresi, "Franchising As a Form of Divestment: An Italian Study," Industrial Marketing Management, May 1997, pp. 223–35; Roger D. Blair and Jill B. Herndon, "Franchise Supply Agreements: Quality Control or Illegal Tying?" Journal of the Academy of Marketing Science, Spring 1997, pp. 177–78; Richard C. Hoffman and John F. Preble, "Franchising into the Twenty-First Century," Business Horizons, November–December 1993, pp. 35–43; "Trouble in Franchise Nation," Fortune, March 6, 1995, pp. 115–29; Francine Lafontaine and Patrick J. Kaufmann, "The Evolution of Ownership Patterns in Franchise Systems," Journal of Retailing, Summer 1994, pp. 97–114; "The Franchise Hall of Fame," Inc., April 1994, pp. 86–95.

**10.** "Small Retailers Outfox Big Rivals," *Investor's Business Daily*, November 28, 2000, p. A1; "Urban Rarity: Stores Offering Spiffy Service," *The Wall Street Journal*, July 25, 1996, p. B1ff.; "Airports: New Destination for Specialty Retailers," *USA Today*, January 11, 1996, p. 5B; "Buoyant Shoppers Boost Specialty Sales," *The Wall Street Journal*, December 15, 1992, p. B1ff.; Sharon E. Beatty, Morris Mayer, James E. Coleman, Kristy E. Reynolds, and Jungki Lee, "Customer-Sales Associate Retail Relationships," *Journal of Retailing*, Fall 1996, pp. 223–47.

**11.** "Department Stores and Designer Tenants Jockey Over Real Estate," *The Wall Street Journal*, October 31, 2000, p. A1ff.; "They Tried to Save It, but This Penney Store Is Set to Close Forever," *The Wall Street Journal*, March 31, 1998, p. A1ff.; "Bright Lights, Big Store," *Business Week*, March 17, 1997, p. 43; "Reinventing Sears," *Time*, December 23, 1996, pp. 53–55; "Department Stores, Seemingly Outmoded, Are Perking Up Again," *The Wall Street Journal*, January 4, 1994, p. A1ff.; Richard A. Rauch, "Retailing's Dinosaurs: Department Stores and Supermarkets," *Business Horizons*, September/October 1991, pp. 21–25.

**12.** David Appel, "The Supermarket: Early Development of an Institutional Innovation," *Journal of Retailing*, Spring 1972, pp. 39–53.

**13.** "How Growth Destroys Differentiation," *Brandweek*, April 24, 2000, pp. 42–50.

**14.** "Catalog Showrooms Revamp to Keep Their Identity," *Business Week*, Industrial/Technology Edition, June 10, 1985, pp. 117–20; Pradeep K. Korgaonkar, "Consumer Preferences for Catalog Showrooms and Discount Stores," *Journal of Retailing*, Fall 1982, pp. 76–88.

**15.** For more on Wal-Mart and Kmart, see Chapter 17, footnote #1. See also James Reardon, Ron Hasty, and Barbara Coe, "The Effect of Information Technology on Productivity in Retailing," *Journal of Retailing*, Winter 1996, pp. 445–61; Christopher D. Norek, "Mass Merchant Discounters: Drivers of Logistics Change," *Journal of Business Logistics*, 1997, pp. 1–17.

**16.** George H. Condon, *Canadian Grocer*, April 2000.

**17.** "Warehouse Clubs: When the Going Gets Tough . . . ," *Business Week*, July 16, 2001, p. 60; "BJ's Wholesale Club: Exclusive Club Has Retailer Raising the Stakes," *Investor's Business Daily*, February 28, 2001, p. A12; "Costco's In-Store Foodservice Operations Add Relish to the Company's Overall Sales," *DSN Retailing Today*, January 22, 2001, p. 24; "Gasoline Fuels Heavier Traffic at Clubs," *DSN Retailing Today*, January 1, 2001, p. 7; "Costco Cooks Up Factory Concept," *DSN Retailing Today*, November 6, 2000, p. 3ff.; "Costco to Bridge Coastal Presence with Aggressive 3-Year Plan," *DSN Retailing Today*, October 23, 2000, p. 1ff.; "Sharpening Its Razor-Thin Margins Is Costco's Way of Doing Business," *Investor's Business Daily*, April 13, 2000, p. A1; "Inside the Cult of Costco," *Fortune*, September 6, 1999, pp. 184–90; "Why Sam's Wants Businesses to Join the Club," *Business Week*, June 27, 1994, p. 48; "Warehouse-Club War Leaves Few Standing, and They Are Bruised," *The Wall Street Journal*, November 18, 1993, p. A1ff.

**18.** "Category Killers Go from Lethal to Lame in the Space of a Decade," *The Wall Street Journal*, March 9, 2000, p. A1ff.; "U.S. Superstores Find Japanese Are a Hard Sell," *The Wall Street Journal*, February 14, 2000, p. B1ff.; "Look Who's Thinking Small," *Business Week*, May 17, 1999, pp. 66–70; "Office-Supply Superstores Find Bounty in the Boonies," *The Wall Street Journal*, September 1, 1998, p. B1ff.; "Health-Care Superstores Experience Growing Pains," *The Wall Street Journal*, May 12, 1997, p. B1ff.; "New Sneaker Superstores Aim to Step on Their Competition," *The Wall Street Journal*, March 19, 1997, p. B1ff.; "Bridal Superstores Woo Couples with Miles of Gowns and Tuxes," *The Wall Street Journal*, February 14, 1996, p. B1ff.; "Superstore Sells Every Necessity for Reading, 'Riting, 'Rithmetic," *The Wall Street Journal*, May 16, 1994, p. B1ff.; "This Do-It-Yourself Store Is Really Doing It," *Business Week*, May 2, 1994, p. 108; "Pet Superstores Collar Customers from Supermarkets, Small Shops," *The Wall Street Journal*, November 18, 1993, p. B12.

**19.** For more on 7-Eleven in Japan, see "From Convenience Store to Online Behemoth?" *Business Week*, April 10, 2000, p. 64; "Japan Goes Web Crazy," *Fortune*, February 7, 2000, pp. 115–18; "Seven-Eleven Japan, Sony Set E-Commerce Plan," *The Wall Street Journal*, January 7, 2000, p. A13; "In Japan, the Hub of E-Commerce Is a 7-Eleven," *The Wall Street Journal*, November 1, 1999, p. B1ff. For more on 7-Eleven in the U.S., see "New Banking Hours: From 7 a.m. to 11 p.m.," *Newsweek*, May 7, 2001, p. 79; "7-Eleven Kiosk Program Banks on Shifts in Strategy," *DSN Retailing Today*, March 19, 2001, p. 2; "Mobile Phone with That Slurpee? Holiday Shoppers Buy on the Run," *USA Today*, December 15, 2000, p. 1B; "Now at 7-Eleven: Gas, Food and Christmas Shopping," *The Wall Street Journal*, November 28, 2000, p. B1ff.; "New 7-Eleven Kiosks Bring On-Line Transactions Home," *Discount Store News*, February 21, 2000, p. 2ff.; "7-Eleven Stores Face Fresh Food Showdown," *Brandweek*, February 28, 1994, p. 1ff.

**20.** "Push-Button Lover," *The Economist*, November 16, 1991, p. 88; "Machines Start New Fast-Food Era," *USA Today*, July 19, 1991, pp. 1B-2B; "High-Tech Vending Machines Cook Up a New Menu of Hot Fast-Food Entrees," *The Wall Street Journal*, May 13, 1991, p. B1ff.

**21.** "New Page in E-Retailing: Catalogs," *The Wall Street Journal*, November 30, 2000, p. B1ff.; "Beyond Mail Order: Catalogs Now Sell Image, Advice," *The Wall Street Journal*, July 29, 1997, p. B1ff.; "Catalogers Expand in Asia," *USA Today*, October 18, 1996, p. 4B; "Spiegel's Book Is a Real Page-Turner," *Business Week*, September 12, 1994, pp. 74–76; "U.S. Catalogers Test International Waters," *The Wall Street Journal*, April 19, 1994, p. B1; C.R. Jasper and P.N.R. Lan, "Apparel Catalog Patronage: Demographic, Lifestyle, and Motivational Factors," *Psychology & Marketing*, July/August 1992, pp. 275–96; "Shoppers Seem to Prefer Mail over Mall," *USA Today*, August 12, 1993, p. 4B.

**22.** "Is There a Future for the TV Mall?" *Brandweek*, March 25, 1996, pp. 24–26; "QVC Draws Wares from Everywhere," *USA Today*, November 1, 1994, p. 1Dff.; "Battling for Buck$," *Profiles*, November 1994, pp. 49–52; "MTV Home Shopping Picks Model Host," *The Wall Street Journal*, July 18, 1994, p. B5; "TV or Not TV," *Inc.*, June 1994, pp. 63–68; "Purchasing Power," *U.S. News & World Report*, January 31, 1994, pp. 56–59; "Home Shoppers to Be Given Yet Another Service," *The Wall Street Journal*, January 14, 1994, p. B1ff.

**23.** "Etoys to Close Up Shop This Spring," *DSN Retailing Today*, February 19, 2001, p. 6ff.; "The eToys Saga: Costs Kept Rising But Sales Slowed," *The Wall Street Journal*, January 22, 2001, p. B1ff.; "Bridging the Loyalty Gap," *Business Week E.Biz*, January 22, 2001, p. EB10; "Etoys' Disappointing Holiday Spells Disaster for Pure-Players," *DSN Retailing Today*, January 1, 2001, p. 11ff.; "Toy Stores Make Their Own Hits," *The Wall Street Journal*, December 20, 2000, p. B1ff.; "Etoys' Disappointing Forecast Prompts Hard Look at Rest of E-Commerce Sector," *The Wall Street Journal*, December 18, 2000, p. A3ff.; "E-Tailers Alter Marketing Plans, Invest New Dollars in Old Medium," *DSN Retailing Today*, December 11, 2000, p. 6ff.; "Santa's Middleman Takes Stock," *The Wall Street Journal*, December 8, 2000, p. B1ff.; "Etoys Isn't Playing Around in Strategy," *USA Today*, November 24, 2000, p. 5B; "Toby Lenk," *Brandweek*, October 30, 2000, pp. IQ36–46; "The Last e-Store on the Block," *Fortune*, September 18, 2000, pp. 214–20; "He's Not Playing," *Business Week E.Biz*, July 24, 2000, pp. EB92–EB96; "Etoys' Strategy to Stay in the Game," *The Wall Street Journal*, April 25, 2000, p. B1ff.; "Stocking a Giant Toybox," *USA Today*, November 24, 1999, p. 1Bff.; "Amazon, Etoys Make Big, Opposing Bets; Which One Is Right?" *The Wall Street Journal*, November 2, 1999, p. A1ff.; "On the Internet, Toys R Us Plays Catch-Up," *The Wall Street Journal*, August 19, 1999, p. B1ff.; "This Toy War Is No Game," *Business Week*, August 9, 1999, p. 86ff.; "Etoys Story," *The Wall Street Journal*, July 12, 1999, p. R38.

**24.** Eve Lazarus, *Marketing Magazine*, September 10, 2001.

**25.** Available from World Wide Web: <http://www.shop.org>; "Multi-Channel Retailing Report," 2001.

**26.** Available from World Wide Web: <http://www.cyberatlas.com>; Robyn Greenspan, "Shoppers Utilize Multichannel Choices," March 5, 2003.

**27.** Available from World Wide Web: <http://www.shop.org>; "The State of Retailing Online 5.0," 2002.

**28.** "The Multi-Channel Imperative," *Global Online Retailing*, Ernst & Young, 2001.

**29.** Available from World Wide Web: <http://www.retail-merchandiser.com>; Debby Garbato Stankevich, "Sears Adds New Tools to Multi-Channel Strategy," June 1, 2002.

**30.** "Beyond Mail Order: Catalogs Now Sell Image, Advice," *The Wall Street Journal*, July 29, 1997, p. B1ff.; "Catalogers Expand in Asia," *USA Today*, October 18, 1996, p. 4B; "Spiegel's Book Is a Real Page-Turner," *Business Week*, September 12, 1994, pp. 74–76; "U.S. Catalogers Test International Waters," *The Wall Street Journal*, April 19, 1994, p. B1; C.R. Jasper and P.N.R. Lan, "Apparel Catalog Patronage: Demographic, Lifestyle, and Motivational Factors," *Psychology & Marketing*, July/August 1992, pp. 275–96; "Shoppers Seem to Prefer Mail over Mall," *USA Today*, August 12, 1993, p. 4B.

**31.** Foo N. Ho, Beng S. Ong, and Seonsu Lee, "A Multicultural Comparison of Shopping Patterns Among Asian Consumers," *Journal of Marketing Theory & Practice*, Winter 1997, pp. 42–51.

**32.** Philip R. Cateora, *International Marketing*, 10th ed. (Burr Ridge, IL: Irwin/McGraw-Hill, 1999); Saeed Samiee, "Retailing and Channel Considerations in Developing Countries: A Review and Research Propositions," *Journal of Business Research*, June 1993, pp. 103–30; "In Guam, Shopping Sprees Are Replacing Tanning," *The Wall Street Journal*, August 23, 1996, p. B4; "How's This for a Cultural Revolution? Chinese Are Getting Home Shopping," *The Wall Street Journal*, January 4, 1996, p. A6; "Retailers Go Global," *Fortune*, February 20, 1995, pp. 102–8; "Russians Say 'Ja' to Swedish Shops," *Advertising Age*, November 7, 1994, p. 47; "A Different World," *The Wall Street Journal*, October 28, 1994, p. R6; "Wal-Mart Is Slowed by Problems of Price and Culture in Mexico," *The Wall Street Journal*, July 29, 1994, p. A1ff.; "A Bargain Basement Called Japan," *Business Week*, June 27, 1994, pp. 42–43; "From Men's Suits to Sake, Discounting Booms in Japan," *Advertising Age International*, March 21, 1994, p. I1ff.; "Europe's Smaller Food Shops Face Finis," *The Wall Street Journal*, May 12, 1993, p. B1ff.

**33.** Wendy Evans and Steven Cox, *Retail Border Wars III: Case Studies of International Retailers Operating in Canada*, CSCA Research Report #10, 1997 (Centre for the Study of Commercial Activity at Ryerson Polytechnic University).

**34.** Wendy Evans, *Retail Border Wars II: Canadian Cases in International Retailing*, CSCA Research Report #8, 1997 (Centre for the Study of Commercial Activity at Ryerson Polytechnic University).

**35.** For a detailed discussion of wholesaling within a channels context, see Louis W. Stern, Adel L. El-Ansary and James R. Brown, *Management in Marketing Channels* (Englewood Cliffs, N.J.: Prentice Hall, 1989).

**36.** "Why the Web Can't Kill the Middleman," *Ecompany*, April 2001, p. 75; "Not Dead Yet," *Inc. Tech*, No. 1, 2001, pp. 58–59; "Electronics Distributors Are Reporting Record Profits," *The Wall Street Journal*, July 13, 2000, p. B4; "Chow (On)Line," *Business Week E.Biz*, June 5, 2000, pp. EB84–EB90; "Why Online Distributors—Once Written Off—May Thrive," *Fortune*, September 6, 1999, pp. 270–72; "Middlemen Find Ways to Survive Cyberspace Shopping," *The Wall Street Journal*, December 12, 1996, p. B6; "Invoice? What's an Invoice?" *Business Week*, June 10, 1996, pp. 110–12; "Computer Wholesalers Face Shakeout and Consolidation," *The Wall Street Journal*, August 26, 1994, p. B4; "Electric Power Brokers Create New Breed of Business," *The Wall Street Journal*, August 2, 1994, p. B4; Allan J. Magrath, "The Hidden Clout of Marketing Middlemen," *Journal of Business Strategy*, March/April 1990, pp. 38–41; Paul Herbig and Bradley S. O'Hara, "Industrial Distributors in the Twenty-First Century," *Industrial Marketing Management*, July 1994, pp. 199–204.

**37.** "Cold War: Amana Refrigeration Fights Tiny Distributor," *The Wall Street Journal*, February 26, 1992, p. B2. For another example, see "Quickie-Divorce Curbs Sought By Manufacturers' Distributors," *The Wall Street Journal*, July 13, 1987, p. 27; "Merger of Two Bakers Teaches Distributors a Costly Lesson (3–parts)," *The Wall Street Journal*, September 14, 1987, p. 29; October 19, 1987, p. 35; November 11, 1987, p. 33.

**38.** "Why Manufacturers Are Doubling as Distributors," *Business Week*, January 17, 1983, p. 41. See also "Who Is Bob Kierlin—and Why Is He So Successful?" *Fortune*, December 8, 1997, pp. 245–48; Robert F. Lusch, Deborah S. Coykendall, and James M. Kenderdine, *Wholesaling in Transition: An Executive Chart Book* (Norman, OK: Distribution Research Program, University of Oklahoma, 1990).

**39.** "Revolution in Japanese Retailing," *Fortune*, February 7, 1994, pp. 143–46; Arieh Goldman, "Evaluating the Performance of the Japanese Distribution System," *Journal of Retailing*, Spring 1992, pp. 11–39; "Japan Begins to Open the Door to Foreigners, a Little," *Brandweek*, August 2, 1993, pp. 14–16.

**40.** Available from World Wide Web: <http://www.rell.com>; "Richardson Electronics Ltd.: Maker of Ancient Tech Finds a Way to Prosper," *Investor's Business Daily*, June 27, 2000, p. A12; *2000 Annual Report*, Richardson Electronics.

**41.** Available from World Wide Web: <http://www.inmac.com> and <http://www.grainger.com>; "B2B: Yesterday's Darling," *The Wall Street Journal*, October 23, 2000, p. R8; "W.W. Grainger's Web Investments: Money Well Spent? Don't Ask Street," *Investor's Business Daily*, September 19, 2000, p. A1; "Junk That Catalog and Get On the Web," *Business Week*, June 26, 2000, pp. 28B–D.

**42.** For more on manufacturers' agents being squeezed, see "Wal-Mart

Draws Fire: Reps, Brokers Protest Being Shut Out by New Policy," *Advertising Age*, January 13, 1992, p. 3ff.; Patrick R. Mehr, "Identifying Independent Reps," *Industrial Marketing Management*, November 1992, pp. 319–22; "Independent Sales Reps Are Squeezed by the Recession," *The Wall Street Journal*, December 27, 1991, p. B1. For more discussion on wholesaling abroad, see "Japan Rises to P&G's No. 3 Market," *Advertising Age*, December 10, 1990, p. 42; "'Papa-Mama' Stores in Japan Wield Power to Hold Back Imports," *The Wall Street Journal*, November 14, 1988, p. 1ff.; Yoo S. Yang, Robert P. Leone, and Dana L. Alden, "A Market Expansion Ability Approach to Identify Potential Exporters," *Journal of Marketing*, January 1992, pp. 84–96; Daniel C. Bello and Ritu Lohtia, "The Export Channel Design: The Use of Foreign Distributors and Agents," *Journal of the Academy of Marketing Science*, Spring 1995, pp. 83–93; Jim Gibbons, "Selling Abroad with Manufacturers' Agents," *Sales & Marketing Management*, September 9, 1985, pp. 67–69; Evelyn A. Thomchick and Lisa Rosenbaum, "The Role of U.S. Export Trading Companies in International Logistics," *Journal of Business Logistics*, September 1984, pp. 85–105; D. Steven White, "Behind the Success and Failure of U.S. Export Intermediaries: Transactions, Agents and Resources," *Journal of the Academy of Marketing Science*, Summer 2001, pp. 18–20.

**43.** "Keep the Excess Moving," *Business Week E.Biz*, November 20, 2000, pp. EB78–EB82; "Good-Bye to Fixed Pricing?" *Business Week*, May 4, 1998, pp. 71–84; "Sales Are Clicking on Manufacturing's Internet Mart," *Fortune*, July 7, 1997, pp. 136C–T.

**44.** "Sick of Checkout Lines? These Guys Can Help," *Investor's Business Daily*, July 9, 2001, p. A7; "What's Ahead for Retailing," *The Wall Street Journal*, June 25, 2001, p. R16; "Digital ID Cards," *The Wall Street Journal*, June 25, 2001, p. R16; "Get Smart: Target Will Be First Among Big Stores to Issue Cards," *The Wall Street Journal*, June 20, 2001, p. B6; "Now, Harried Shoppers Can Take Control at Supermarkets," *USA Today*, June 7, 2001, p. 1Aff.; "Leave It in the Box," *Business Week E.Biz*, December 11, 2000, pp. EB82–EB83; "Master Plan," *Brandweek*, October 18, 1999, pp. 52–54.

## Chapter 13

**1.** Available from World Wide Web: <http://www.marketingmag.ca>; adapted from: Steve Silverstone, "The Joy of Free Time," *Marketing Magazine*: Out of Home Report, November 19, 2001.

**2.** Available from World Wide Web: <http://www.nua.ie/surveys>; "Net Displaces Offline Communication Channels," October 15, 2002.

**3.** Available from World Wide Web: <http://www.sciencedaily.com>; "Internet Takes a Toll on Television Viewing," November 30, 2001.

**4.** Available from World Wide Web: <http://www.cyberatlas.com>; Michael Pastore, "Young, Sophisticated Net Users Find TV Expendable," February 5, 2001.

**5.** Available from World Wide Web: <http://www.ChannelSeven.com>; Zachary Rodgers,"CokeMusic.com's Viral Explosion," May 14, 2003.

**6.** Available from World Wide Web: <http://www.ChannelSeven.com>; Zachary Rodgers, "Rich Media Acts Locally," December 11, 2002.

**7.** Available from World Wide Web: <http://www.ChannelSeven.com>; Zachary Rodgers, "Aging of Rich Media," July 9, 2003.

**8.** Available from World Wide Web: <http://www.thestar.com>; adapted from: Kate Harries, "Fans Go Crazy for Avril's Shirt," January 17, 2002.

**9.** "Small Wonder," *The Wall Street Journal*, June 25, 2001, p. R; "Minute Maid Opens Juicy Site to Promote New Drink," *Brandweek*, April 30, 2001, p. B; "PMA Reggie Awards 2001," *Brandweek* (Supplement), March 12, 2001, pp. R1–R22; "Mystery Shoppers," *American Demographics*, December 2000, pp. 41–43; "Sweet Deals," *Inc. Tech*, No. 4, 2000, pp. 98–109; "Hot Wheels," *American Demographics*, August 2000, pp. 48–49; "Calling All Car Worms," *Brandweek*, March 6, 2000, pp. 22–23; "Sharp Curves Ahead for Car Marketers," *Brandweek*, January 3, 2000, pp. 18–19; "Talbots Mounting Its Biggest Integrated Marketing Push," *Advertising Age*, August 11, 1997, p. 29; "Olds' Intrigue Stars in Web Game Based on NBC TV Show," *Advertising Age*, July 28, 1997, p. 16ff.; "Product Program Flea Control," *Advertising Age*, Special Issue, 1997, p. E8; "Promotion Marketing," *Brandweek*, March 4, 1996, pp. 22–26; J. R. Shannon, "The New Promotions Mix: A Proposed Paradigm, Process, and Application," *Journal of Marketing Theory & Practice*, Winter 1996, pp. 56–68; Kathleen J. Kelly, "Integrated Marketing Communication: Putting It Together & Making It Work," *Journal of the Academy of Marketing Science*, Winter 1997, pp. 83–85.

**10.** "High-Tech Branding: Pushing Digital PCS," *Brandweek*, August 4, 1997, pp. 30–34; "Brand Builders: Delivery Guy Chic," *Brandweek*, June 30, 1997, pp. 18–19; "Eye-Catching Logos All Too Often Leave Fuzzy Images in Minds of Consumers," *The Wall Street Journal*, December 5, 1991, p. B1ff.; David I. Gilliland and Wesley J. Johnston, "Toward a Model of Business-to-Business Marketing Communications Effects," *Industrial Marketing Management*, January 1997, pp. 15–29; Michel T. Pham and Gita V. Johar, "Contingent Processes of Source Identification," *Journal of Consumer Research*, December 1997, pp. 249–65; Louisa Ha and Barry R. Litman, "Does Advertising Clutter Have Diminishing and Negative Returns?" *Journal of Advertising*, Spring 1997, pp. 31–42; Barbara B. Stern, "A Revised Communication Model for Advertising: Multiple Dimensions of the Source, the Message, and the Recipient," *Journal of Advertising*, June 1994, pp. 5–15; Ronald E. Dulek, John S. Fielden, and John S. Hill, "International Communication: An Executive Primer," *Business Horizons*, January/February 1991, pp. 20–25; Kaylene C. Williams, Rosann L. Spiro, and Leslie M. Fine, "The Customer-Salesperson Dyad: An Interaction/Communication Model and Review," *Journal of Personal Selling and Sales Management*, Summer 1990, pp. 29–44; Susan Mitchell, "How to Talk to Young Adults," *American Demographics*, April 1993, p. 50; Richard F. Beltramini and Edwin R. Stafford, "Comprehension and Perceived Believability of Seals of Approval Information in Advertising," *Journal of Advertising*, September 1993, pp. 3–14; Jacob Jacoby and Wayne D. Hoyer, "The Comprehension/Miscomprehension of Print Communication: Selected Findings," *Journal of Consumer Research*, March 1989, pp. 434–43.

**11.** "Global Branding: Same, But Different," *Brandweek*, April 9, 2001, p. 25; "When You Translate 'Got Milk' for Latinos, What Do You Get?" *The Wall Street Journal*, June 3, 1999, p. A1ff.; "Cash, Cache, Cachet: All 3 Seem to Matter When You Buy a PC," *The Wall Street Journal*, December 18, 1998, p. A1ff.; "Hey, #!@*% Amigo, Can You Translate the Word 'Gaffe'?" *The Wall Street Journal*, July 8, 1996, p. B2; "Lost in Translation: How to 'Empower Women' in Chinese," *The Wall Street Journal*, September 13, 1994, p. A1ff.; "In World Cup Games, Words Get Lost and Gained in Translation," *The Wall Street Journal*, July 14, 1994, p. B1ff.; "Too Many Computer Names Confuse Too Many Buyers," *The Wall Street Journal*, June 29, 1994, p. B1ff.; "Go Ask Alice," *Adweek*, January 17, 1994, p. 32.

**12.** "The Corruption of TV Health News," *Business Week*, February 28, 2000, pp. 66–68; "Collagen Corp.'s Video Uses News Format," *The Wall Street Journal*," March 29, 1994, p. B8; "Totally Hidden Video," *Inside PR*, August 1990, pp. 11–13; "'News' Videos That Pitch Drugs Provoke Outcry for Regulations," *The Wall Street Journal*, February 8, 1990, p. B6; Thomas H. Bivins, "Public Relations, Professionalism, and the Public Interest," *Journal of Business Ethics*, February 1993, pp. 117–26; Siva K. Balasubramanian, "Beyond Advertising and Publicity: Hybrid Messages and Public Policy Issues," *Journal of Advertising*, December 1994, pp. 47–58.

**13.** "Good Housekeeping Unveils Web Site Review Program," *Brandweek*, May 29, 2000, p. 52; "Good Housekeeping to Offer 'Seal' to Autos," *Advertising Age*, June 29, 1998, p. 18; "Marketing in Which We Bash a Baby Seal," *Fortune*, September 8, 1997, p. 36ff; Jagdish Agrawal and Wagner A. Kamakura, "The Economic Worth of Celebrity Endorsers: An Event Study Analysis," *Journal of Marketing*, July 1995, pp. 56–62; David J. Moore, John C. Mowen, and Richard Reardon,

"Multiple Sources in Advertising Appeals: When Product Endorsers Are Paid by the Advertising Sponsor," *Journal of the Academy of Marketing Science*, Summer 1994, pp. 234–43.

**14.** Available from World Wide Web: <http://www.marketingmag.ca>; adapted from: Chris Powell, "Giving Wink a Nudge," *Marketing Magazine*: Report on Television, December 9, 2002; Chris Powell, "The Flashing 'i'," *Marketing Magazine*: Report on Television, December 10, 2001.

**15.** Donna L. Hoffman and Thomas P. Novak, "Marketing in Hypermedia Computer-Mediated Environments: Conceptual Foundations," *Journal of Marketing*, July 1996, pp. 50–68; Gregory C. Mosier and James M. Jackman, "Personal Jurisdiction: Is Internet Presence Enough?" *Journal of the Academy of Marketing Science*, Spring 1998, p.164; Pierre Berthon, Leyland Pitt, and Richard T. Watson, "Marketing Communication and the World Wide Web," *Business Horizons*, September–October 1996, pp. 24–32.

**16.** "Escalade Got Game," *Advertising Age*, June 11, 2001, p. 42; "All Juiced Up," *American Demographics*, January 2001, pp. 42–44; Albert Schofield, "Alternative Reply Vehicles in Direct-Response Advertising," *Journal of Advertising Research*, September/October 1994, pp. 28–34. For an electronic direct mail example, see "Web Slice," *Brandweek*, May 26, 1997, pp. 22–23; Judy F. Davis, "Maintaining Customer Relationships Through Effective Database Marketing: A Perspective for Small Retailers," *Journal of Marketing Theory & Practice*, Spring 1997, pp. 31–42; Craig A. Conrad, "Response! The Complete Guide to Direct Marketing," *Journal of the Academy of Marketing Science*, Winter 1998, pp. 70–71; Kapil Bawa, "Influences on Consumer Response to Direct Mail Coupons: An Integrative Review," *Psychology & Marketing*, March 1996, pp. 129–56; William J. Carner, "Direct Marketing Through Broadcast Media: TV, Radio, Cable, Infomercials, Home Shopping, and More," *Journal of the Academy of Marketing Science*, Winter 1997, pp. 86–87.

**17.** Available from World Wide Web: <http://www.marketingmag.ca>; Sarah Smith, "Universal Music Gets Hip to the Web," *Marketing Magazine:* National News, June 17, 2002.

**18.** "Why Those Companies Are So Eager to Get Your E-Mail Address," *The Wall Street Journal*, February 12, 2001, p. B1; "Direct Mail That Really Sells Hinges on Data Smarts and Clever Content," *The Wall Street Journal*, January 22, 2001, p. A1; "When E-Mail Ads Aren't Spam," *Business Week*, October 16, 2000, pp. 112–14; "Special Report: Direct and Database Marketing," *Advertising Age*, October 16, 2000, pp. S1–22; "Jupiter Projects E-Mail Marketing Will Jump to $7.3 Billion by 2005," *Advertising Age*, May 8, 2000, p. 80ff.; "E-Mail Direct," *Brandweek*, April 10, 2000, pp. 108–12; "You've Got Snail Mail!" *American Demographics*, March 2000, pp. 54–56; "Special Report: Direct and Database Marketing," *Advertising Age*, October 18, 1999, pp. S1–8; "Special Report: Direct Marketing," *Advertising Age*, October 12, 1998, pp. S1–8; "Customers Are Eager, Infrastructure Lags," *Advertising Age*, October 5, 1998, p. 12; George R. Milne and Mary Ellen Gordon, "Direct Mail Privacy-Efficiency Trade-Offs Within an Implied Social Contract Framework," *Journal of Public Policy & Marketing*, Fall 1993, pp. 206–15.

**19.** See, for example, "Campaign for Prozac Targets Consumers," *The Wall Street Journal*, July 1, 1997, p. B1ff.; "Branding Fever Strikes among Prescription Drugs," *Advertising Age*, November 22, 1993, p. 12; "New Contraceptive Targets the Pill," *USA Today*, November 15, 1993, p. 3B; "TV Ads Boost Nestle's Infant Formula," *The Wall Street Journal*, March 30, 1993, p. B1ff.; "Drug Ads: A Prescription for Controversy," *Business Week*, January 18, 1993, pp. 58–60; "Kellogg Shifts Strategy to Pull Consumers In," *The Wall Street Journal*, January 22, 1990, p. B1ff.; Steven W. Kopp and Mary J. Sheffet, "The Effect of Direct-to-Consumer Advertising of Prescription Drugs on Retail Gross Margins: Empirical Evidence and Public Policy Implications," *Journal of Public Policy & Marketing*, Fall 1997, pp. 270–76; Mary C. Gilly and Mary Wolfinbarger, "Advertising's Internal Audience," *Journal of Marketing*, January 1998, pp. 69–88; S.A. Erdem and L.J. Harrison-Walker, "Managing Channel Relationships: Toward an Identification of Effective Promotional Strategies in Vertical Marketing Systems," *Journal of Marketing Theory & Practice*, Spring 1997, pp. 80–87; Michael Levy, John Webster, and Roger Kerin, "Formulating Push Marketing Strategies: A Method and Application," *Journal of Marketing*, Winter 1983, pp. 25–34.

**20.** "Decker Scores with Sweepstakes to Promote Days Inn," *USA Today*, November 6, 1997, p. B10; "Biore: The Nose Knew at Lilith Fair," *Brandweek*, September 15, 1997, p. 28; "Brand Builders: Progresso Warriors," *Brandweek*, June 23, 1997, pp. 20–22; "Advertisers Often Cheer the Loudest," *USA Today*, March 27, 1997, p. 1Aff.; "Crossing the Border," *Brandweek*, December 16, 1996, pp. 17–22; "Brand Builders: Pie in the Sky," *Brandweek*, December 16, 1996, pp. 23–24; "Tractor Dealers Get Down in the Dirt Promoting Machines," *The Wall Street Journal*, July 16, 1996, p. A1ff.; "Pepsi Cancels an Ad Campaign as Customers Clamor for Stuff," *The Wall Street Journal*, June 27, 1996, p. B1ff.

**21.** "Compensation and Expenses," *Sales & Marketing Management*, June 28, 1993, p. 65; "The Cost of Selling Is Going Up," *Boardroom Reports*, December 15, 1991, p. 15; "An In-House Sales School," *Inc.*, May 1991, pp. 85–86.

**22.** Meera P. Venkatraman, "Opinion Leaders, Adopters, and Communicative Adopters: A Role Analysis," *Psychology and Marketing*, Spring 1989, pp. 51–68; S. Ram and Hyung-Shik Jung, "Innovativeness in Product Usage: A Comparison of Early Adopters and Early Majority," *Psychology & Marketing*, January/February 1994, pp. 57–68; Robert J. Fisher and Linda L. Price, "An Investigation into the Social Context of Early Adoption Behavior," *Journal of Consumer Research*, December 1992, p. 477; Leisa R. Flynn, Ronald E. Goldsmith, and Jacqueline K. Eastman, "Opinion Leaders and Opinion Seekers: Two New Measurement Scales," *Journal of the Academy of Marketing Science*, Spring 1996, pp. 137–47; Everett M. Rogers and F. Floyd Shoemaker, *Communication of Innovations: A Cross-Cultural Approach* (New York: Free Press, 1971), pp. 203–9.

**23.** Kusum L. Ailawadi, Paul W. Farris and Mark E. Parry, "Share and Growth Are Not Good Predictors of the Advertising and Promotion/Sales Ratio," *Journal of Marketing*, January 1994, pp. 86–97.

**24.** Deborah Utter, "Marketing on a Budget," *Journal of the Academy of Marketing Science*, Summer 2000, pp. 441–3; Kim P. Corfman and Donald R. Lehmann, "The Prisoner's Dilemma and the Role of Information in Setting Advertising Budgets," *Journal of Advertising*, June 1994, pp. 35–48; C.L. Hung and Douglas West, "Advertising Budgeting Methods in Canada, the UK and the USA," *International Journal of Advertising* 10, no. 3 (1991), pp. 239–50; Pierre Filiatrault and Jean-Charles Chebat, "How Service Firms Set Their Marketing Budgets," *Industrial Marketing Management*, February 1990, pp. 63–68; James E. Lynch and Graham J. Hooley, "Industrial Advertising Budget Approaches in the U.K.," *Industrial Marketing Management* 18, no. 4 (1989), pp. 265–70; "Beat the Budgeting Blues," *Business Marketing*, July 1989, pp. 48–57; Douglas J. Dalrymple and Hans B. Thorelli, "Sales Force Budgeting," *Business Horizons*, July/August 1984, pp. 31–36; Peter J. Danaher and Roland T. Rust, "Determining the Optimal Level of Media Spending," *Journal of Advertising Research*, January/February 1994, pp. 28–34.

## Chapter 14

**1.** Available from World Wide Web: <http://www.cisco.com>; "Cisco Fractures Its Own Fairy Tale," *Fortune*, May 14, 2001, pp. 105–12; "Tech Consultants: You'll Need One Sooner or Later—So Get It Right," *Investor's Business Daily*, March 5, 2001, p. A1; "How Cisco Makes Takeovers Work with Rules, Focus on Client Needs," *Investor's Business Daily*, November 20, 2000, p. A1; "Going Digital? Think First," *Fortune*, November 13, 2000, pp. 190—98; "Cisco Not the Top Choice of Every Network Builder," *Investor's Business Daily*, November 13, 2000, p. A6; "Cisco Keeps Growing, But Exactly How Fast Is Becoming an Issue," *The Wall Street Journal*, November 3, 2000, p. A1ff.; "Accelerating Natural

Contagion," *Brandweek*, October 30, 2000, pp. 31–38; "Factory Marks New Optical Era for Cisco," *Investor's Business Daily*, October 4, 2000, p. A8; "At Cisco, Executives Accumulate Stakes in Clients, Suppliers," *The Wall Street Journal*, October 3, 2000, p. A1ff.; "The World's Most Admired Companies," *Fortune*, October 2, 2000, pp. 183–89; "Cisco: A Web-Profit Prophet Spreads the Word," *Business Week E.Biz*, September 18, 2000, p. EB68; "Spread the Web: Cisco Reaches Beyond Techies," *The Wall Street Journal*, June 13, 2000, p. B1ff.; "Cisco High," *Business Week E.Biz*, June 5, 2000, pp. EB102–EB104; "How to Drive an Express Train," *The Wall Street Journal*, June 1, 2000, p. B1ff.; "How Cisco and Alcoa Make Real Time Work," *Fortune*, May 29, 2000, pp. 284–86; "There's Something About Cisco," *Fortune*, May 15, 2000, pp. 114–38; "Eating Their Own Dog Food," *The Wall Street Journal*, April 19, 2000, p. B1ff.; "Ford, Cisco Team Up to Speed Wiring of 40,000 Suppliers and Dealers for Web," *The Wall Street Journal*, February 10, 2000, p. A5; "Do You Know Cisco?" *Time*, January 17, 2000, pp. 72–74; "Customers Move Into the Driver's Seat," *Business Week*, October 4, 1999, pp. 103–106; "Mr. Internet," *Business Week*, September 13, 1999, pp. 128–40; "The Corporation of the Future," *Business Week*, August 31, 1998, pp. 102–106; "The New Economy Is Still Being Driven by the Old Hard Sell," *The Wall Street Journal*, August 13, 1999, p. B1.

**2.** Joel R. Evans, Barry Berman, and William J. Wellington, *Marketing Essentials*, (Scarborough Ont.: Prentice Hall Canada, 1998) p. 326.

**3.** "The Seoul Answer to Selling," *Going Global* (supplement to *Inc.*), March 1994; "AIG Sells Insurance in Shanghai, Testing Service Firms' Role," *The Wall Street Journal*, July 21, 1993, p. A1ff.; "Hungarians Seeking to Find a New Way Find Instead Amway," *The Wall Street Journal*, January 15, 1993, p. A1ff.; "The Secret to Northern's Japanese Success: When in Tokyo . . . ," *Business Week*, July 27, 1992, p. 57; "U.S. Companies in China Find Patience, Persistence and Salesmanship Pay Off," *The Wall Street Journal*, April 3, 1992, p. B1ff.; Paul A. Herbig and Hugh E. Kramer, "Do's and Don'ts of Cross-Cultural Negotiations," *Industrial Marketing Management*, November 1992, pp. 287–98; Alan J. Dubinsky et al., "Differences in Motivational Perceptions among U.S., Japanese, and Korean Sales Personnel," *Journal of Business Research*, June 1994, pp. 175–86; Carl R. Ruthstrom and Ken Matejka, "The Meanings of 'YES' in the Far East," *Industrial Marketing Management*, August 1990, pp. 191–92.

**4.** Chad Kaydo, "Selling a Product That's All Wet," *Sales and Marketing Management*, June 1999, vol. 151, issue 6, p. 18.

**5.** Judy Waytiuk, "No Hassle, No Haggle," *Marketing Magazine*, August 28, 2000.

**6.** Tom Richman, "Seducing the Customer: Dale Ballard's Perfect Selling Machine," *Inc.*, April, 1988, pp. 96–104; *1987 Annual Report*, Ballard Medical Products.

**7.** "Pushing Doctors to Buy High Tech for the Office," *Business Week*, September 2, 1985, pp. 84–85.

**8.** Erika Rasmusson, "Getting Schooled in Outsourcing," *Sales and Marketing Management*, January 1999, vol. 151, issue 1, p. 48.

**9.** "NationsBank Asks Tellers to Branch Out," *Raleigh News & Observer*, September 12, 1993, p. 1Fff.

**10.** Mark A. Moon and Susan F. Gupta, "Examining the Formation of Selling Centers: A Conceptual Framework," *Journal of Personal Selling & Sales Management*, Spring 1997, pp. 31–41; S. Joe Puri and Pradeep Korgaonkar, "Couple the Buying and Selling Teams," *Industrial Marketing Management* 20, no. 4 (1991), pp. 311–18; "P&G Rolls Out Retailer Sales Teams," *Advertising Age*, May 21, 1990, p. 18.

**11.** "Fiorina Whips H-P into Fighting Shape," *USA Today*, June 5, 2001, p. 3B; "H-P Profit Drops 66% But Tops Forecast," *The Wall Street Journal*, May 17, 2000, p. A3ff.; "H-P Woes Are Deeper Than the Downturn," *Business Week*, May 7, 2001, p. 48; "The Radical: Carly Fiorina's Bold Management Experiment at HP," *Business Week*, February 19, 2001, pp. 68–80; "The Boss," *Business Week*, August 2, 1999, pp. 76–84.

**12.** Dan C. Weilbaker and William A. Weeks, "The Evolution of National Account Management: A Literature Perspective," *Journal of Personal Selling & Sales Management*, Fall 1997, pp. 49–59; C. J. Lambe and Robert E. Spekman, "National Account Management: Large Account Selling or Buyer-Supplier Alliance?" *Journal of Personal Selling & Sales Management*, Fall 1997, pp. 61–74; Catherine Pardo, "Key Account Management in the Business to Business Field: The Key Account's Point of View," *Journal of Personal Selling & Sales Management*, Fall 1997, pp. 17–26; Sanjit Sengupta, Robert E. Krapfel, and Michael A. Pusateri, "Switching Costs in Key Account Relationships," *Journal of Personal Selling & Sales Management*, Fall 1997, pp. 9–16; Paul Dishman and Philip S. Nitse, "National Accounts Revisited: New Lessons From Recent Investigations," *Industrial Marketing Management*, January 1998, pp. 1–9.

**13.** "How to Remake Your Sales Force," *Fortune*, May 4, 1992, pp. 98–103; "What Flexible Workers Can Do," *Fortune*, February 13, 1989, pp. 62–64; "Apparel Makers Play Bigger Part on Sales Floor," *The Wall Street Journal*, March 2, 1988, p. 31; Ravipreet S. Sohi, Daniel C. Smith, and Neil M. Ford, "How Does Sharing a Sales Force Between Multiple Divisions Affect Salespeople?" *Journal of the Academy of Marketing Science*, Summer 1996, pp. 195–207; David W. Cravens and Raymond W. LaForge, "Salesforce Deployment Analysis," *Industrial Marketing Management*, July 1983, pp. 179–92; Michael S. Herschel, "Effective Sales Territory Development," *Journal of Marketing*, April 1977, pp. 39–43.

**14.** Available from World Wide Web: <http://www.intranetjournal.com>; Compaq Intranet Case Study, Conjoin: A Sales & Marketing Solution, *Intranet Journal*.

**15.** Available from World Wide Web: <http://www.cio.com>; Alison Bass, "Customer Care: The Shelfware Boondoggle," August 11, 2003.

**16.** Available from World Wide Web: <http://www.crmdaily.com >; Erika Morphy, "Report: 42% of CRM Goes Unused," CRM Daily, March 7, 2003.

**17.** Jennifer Gilbert, "Resellers, Click Here," *Sales and Marketing Management*, September 2002, vol. 154, issue 9, p. 25.

**18.** "Salespeople Say Automation Software Still Lacking," *Investor's Business Daily*, January 18, 2001, p. A4; "MarketSoft Tailors Products to Solve Problems," *The Wall Street Journal*, November 30, 2000, p. B8; "New Software's Payoff? Happier Salespeople," *Investor's Business Daily*, May 23, 2000, p. A8; "Making the Sale," *The Wall Street Journal*, November 15, 1999, p. R16; "Free Software from Anywhere?" *Business Week*, September 13, 1999, pp. 37–38; "Offices Goin' Mobile," *USA Today*, May 17, 1999, p. 3B; "Bob Schmonsees Has a Tool for Better Sales and It Ignores Excuses," *The Wall Street Journal*, March 26, 1999, p. B1; "Companies Sold on the Latest Technology for the Sales Force," *Chicago Tribune*, November 8, 1992, Sect. 19, p. 5; "New Software Is Helping Reps Fill Custom Orders without Glitches," *The Wall Street Journal*, August 11, 1992, p. B6; "Salespeople on Road Use Laptops to Keep in Touch," *The Wall Street Journal*, April 25, 1991, p. B1.

**19.** "Supercharged Sell," *Inc. Tech*, No. 2, 1997, pp. 42–51; Mary Jo Bitner, "Technology Infusion in Service Encounters," *Journal of the Academy of Marketing Science*, Winter 2000, pp. 138–150; Allan J. Magrath, "From the Practitioner's Desk: A Comment on 'Personal Selling and Sales Management in the New Millennium'," *Journal of Personal Selling & Sales Management*, Winter 1997, pp. 45–47; Michael J. Swenson and Adilson Parrella, "Sales Technology Applications: Cellular Telephones and the National Sales Force," *Journal of Personal Selling & Sales Management*, Fall 1992, pp. 67–74; Paul Dishman and Kregg Aytes, "Exploring Group Support Systems in Sales Management Applications," *Journal of Personal Selling & Sales Management*, Winter 1996, pp. 65–77.

**20.** Virginia Matthews, "What Makes a Sales Superhero?" *Marketing Magazine*, November 27, 2000.

**21.** "The Art of the Sale," *The Wall Street Journal,* January 11, 2001, p. B1ff.

**22.** Erika Rasmusson, "Getting Schooled in Outsourcing," *Sales and Marketing Management,* January 1999, vol. 151, issue 1, p. 48.

**23.** Ellen B. Pullins, Leslie M. Fine, and Wendy L. Warren, "Identifying Peer Mentors in the Sales Force: An Exploratory Investigation of Willingness and Ability," *Journal of the Academy of Marketing Science,* Spring 1996, pp. 125–36; Alan J. Dubinsky, "Some Assumptions About the Effectiveness of Sales Training," *Journal of Personal Selling & Sales Management,* Summer 1996, pp. 67–76; Earl D. Honeycutt, Ashraf M. Attia, and Angela R. D Auria, "Sales Certification Programs," *Journal of Personal Selling & Sales Management,* Summer 1996, pp. 59–65; "Systematizing Salesperson Selection," *Sales and Marketing Management,* February 1992, pp. 65–68; "The Faxable International Sales-Rep Application," *Inc.,* November 1993, pp. 95–97; Patrick L. Schul and Brent M. Wren, "The Emerging Role of Women in Industrial Selling: A Decade of Change," *Journal of Marketing,* July 1992, pp. 38–54; William A. Weeks and Carl G. Stevens, "National Account Management Sales Training and Directions for Improvement: A Focus on Skills/Abilities," *Industrial Marketing Management,* September 1997, pp. 423–31; Earl D. Honeycutt, Jr., John B. Ford, and John F. Tanner, Jr., "Who Trains Salespeople? The Role of Sales Trainers and Sales Managers," *Industrial Marketing Management,* February 1994, pp. 65–70; Jeffrey K. Sager, "Recruiting and Retaining Committed Salespeople," *Industrial Marketing Management* 20, no. 2 (1991), pp. 99–104; S. Joe Puri, "Where Industrial Sales Training Is Weak," *Industrial Marketing Management,* May 1993, pp. 101–8.

**24.** Douglas M. Lambert, Arun Sharma, and Michael Levy, "What Information Can Relationship Marketers Obtain From Customer Evaluations of Salespeople?" *Industrial Marketing Management,* March 1997, pp. 177–87; Erin Anderson and Thomas S. Robertson, "Inducing Multiline Salespeople to Adopt House Brands," *Journal of Marketing,* April 1995, pp. 16–31; Stephen B. Knouse and David Strutton, "Molding a Total Quality Salesforce Through Managing Empowerment, Evaluation, and Reward and Recognition Processes," *Journal of Marketing Theory & Practice,* Summer 1996, pp. 24–35; Ajay K. Kolhi and Bernard J. Jaworksi, "The Influence of Coworker Feedback on Salespeople," *Journal of Marketing,* October 1994, pp. 82–94; "Fire Up Your Sales Force," *Business Marketing,* July 1990, pp. 52–55; William L. Cron, Alan J. Dubinsky, and Ronald E. Michaels, "The Influence of Career Stages on Components of Salesperson Motivation," *Journal of Marketing,* January 1988, pp. 78–92.

**25.** Goutam Ghallagalla, "Supervisory Orientations and Salesperson Work Outcomes: the Moderating Effect of Salesperson Location," *The Journal of Personal Selling & Sales Management,* Summer 2000, pp. 161–172; "Creating Incentives Down in Ranks: Marriott Ties Pay to Guest Replies," *Investor's Business Daily,* July 6, 2001, p. A1; "Get Great Results from Salespeople by Finding What Really Moves Them," *Investor's Business Daily,* July 2, 2001, p. A1; "Medical Gear Sales Force Works on Commission," *Investor's Business Daily,* July 25, 2000, p. A14; Rene Y. Darmon, "Selecting Appropriate Sales Quota Plan Structures and Quota-Setting Procedures," *Journal of Personal Selling & Sales Management,* Winter 1997, pp. 1–16; Thomas E. Tice, "Managing Compensation Caps in Key Accounts," *Journal of Personal Selling & Sales Management,* Fall 1997, pp. 41–47; Kissan Joseph and Manohar U. Kalwani, "The Role of Bonus Pay in Salesforce Compensation Plans," *Industrial Marketing Management,* March 1998, pp. 147–59; Russell Abratt and Michael R. Smythe, "A Survey of Sales Incentive Programs," *Industrial Marketing Management,* August 1989, pp. 209–14; "Incentive Pay Isn't Good for Your Company," *Inc.,* September 1994, pp. 23–24; "The Few, the True, the Blue," *Business Week,* May 30, 1994, pp. 124–26; Arun Sharma, "Customer Satisfaction-Based Incentive Systems: Some Managerial and Salesperson Considerations," *Journal of Personal Selling & Sales Management,* Spring 1997, pp. 61–70; William Strahle and Rosann L. Spiro, "Linking Market Share Strategies to Salesforce Objectives, Activities, and Compensation Policies," *Journal of Personal Selling and Sales Management,* August 1986, pp. 11–18.

**26.** "New Software's Payoff? Happier Salespeople," *Investor's Business Daily,* May 23, 2000, p. A8.

**27.** Richard L. Oliver and Erin Anderson, "An Empirical Test of the Consequences of Behavior- and Outcome-Based Sales Control Systems," *Journal of Marketing,* October 1994, pp. 53–67; Susan K. DelVecchio, "The Salesperson's Operating Freedom: A Matter of Perception," *Industrial Marketing Management,* January 1998, pp. 31–40; Vlasis Stathakopoulos, "Sales Force Control: A Synthesis of Three Theories," *Journal of Personal Selling & Sales Management,* Spring 1996, pp. 1–12; Gregory A. Rich, "The Constructs of Sales Coaching: Supervisory Feedback, Role Modeling and Trust," *Journal of Personal Selling & Sales Management,* Winter 1998, pp. 53–63; Goutam N. Challagalla and Tasadduq A. Shervani, "Dimensions and Types of Supervisory Control: Effects on Salesperson Performance and Satisfaction," *Journal of Marketing,* January 1996, pp. 89–105; Steven P. Brown and Robert A. Peterson, "The Effect of Effort on Sales Performance and Job Satisfaction," *Journal of Marketing,* April 1994, pp. 70–80; Paul A. Dion, Debbie Easterling, and Raj Javalgi, "Women in the Business-to-Business Salesforce: Some Differences in Performance Factors," *Industrial Marketing Management,* September 1997, pp. 447–57; Frederick A. Russ, Kevin M. McNeilly, and James M. Comer, "Leadership, Decision Making and Performance of Sales Managers: A Multi-Level Approach," *Journal of Personal Selling & Sales Management,* Summer 1996, pp. 1–15; Jhinuk Chowdhury, "The Motivational Impact of Sales Quotas on Effort," *Journal of Marketing Research,* February 1993, pp. 28–41; Alan J. Dubinsky, Francis J. Yammarino, and Marvin A. Jolson, "Closeness of Supervision and Salesperson Work Outcomes: An Alternate Perspective," *Journal of Business Research,* March 1994, pp. 225–38; David W. Cravens et al., "Behavior-Based and Outcome-Based Salesforce Control Systems," *Journal of Marketing,* October 1993, pp. 47–59; Daniel A. Sauers, James B. Hunt, and Ken Bass, "Behavioral Self-Management as a Supplement to External Sales Force Controls," *Journal of Personal Selling and Sales Management,* Summer 1990, pp. 17–28; Douglas N. Behrman and William D. Perreault, Jr., "A Role Stress Model of the Performance and Satisfaction of Industrial Salespersons," *Journal of Marketing,* Fall 1984, pp. 9–21; Richard T. Hise and Edward L. Reid, "Improving the Performance of the Industrial Sales Force in the 1990s," *Industrial Marketing Management,* October 1994, pp. 273–80.

**28.** "Chief Executives Are Increasingly Chief Salesmen," *The Wall Street Journal,* August 6, 1991, p. B1ff.; Joe F. Alexander, Patrick L. Schul, and Emin Babakus, "Analyzing Interpersonal Communications in Industrial Marketing Negotiations," *Journal of the Academy of Marketing Science,* Spring 1991, pp. 129–40.

**29.** Andris A. Zoltners, "Sales Territory Alignment: An Overlooked Productivity Tool," *The Journal of Personal Selling & Sales Management,* Summer 2000, pp. 139–151; Sanjit Sengupta, "An Empirical Investigation of Key Account Salesperson Effectiveness," *The Journal of Personal Selling & Sales Management,* Fall 2000, pp. 253–62; Ken Grant, "The Role of Satisfaction with Territory Design on the Motivation, Attitudes, and Work Outcomes of Salespeople," *Journal of the Academy of Marketing Science,* Spring 2001, pp. 165–179; William C. Moncrief, et al., "Examining the Roles of Telemarketing in Selling Strategy," *Journal of Personal Selling and Sales Management,* Fall 1989, pp. 1–12; J. David Lichtenthal, Saameer Sikri, and Karl Folk, "Teleprospecting: An Approach for Qualifying Accounts," *Industrial Marketing Management,* February 1989, pp. 11–18.

**30.** "When Should I Give Up on a Sales Prospect?" *Inc.,* May 1998, p. 129; "Downloading Their Dream Cars," *Business Week,* March 9, 1998, pp. 93–94; "The New Wave of Sales Automation," *Business Marketing,* June 1991, pp. 12–16; L. Brent Manssen, "Using PCs to Automate and Innovate Marketing Activities," *Industrial Marketing Management,* August 1990, pp. 209–14; Doris C. Van Doren and Thomas A. Stickney, "How to Develop a Database for Sales Leads," *Industrial Marketing Management,* August 1990, pp. 201–8.

**31.** "Novartis' Marketing Doctor," *Business Week,* March 5, 2001, p. 56.

**32.** Mikala Folb, "Finding New Ways to Sell Beauty," *Marketing Magazine*: Marketing Direct, May 3, 1999.

**33.** For more on pharmaceutical company selling tactics, see "Doctors Step Out; Drug Salesmen Step In," *USA Today*, July 5, 2001, p. 11A; "Why Some Dialysis Patients Take $12-a-Day Drug Instead of Tums," *The Wall Street Journal,* June 26, 2001, p. B1ff.; "Sales Pitch: Drug Firms Use Perks to Push Pills," *USA Today*, May 16, 2001, p. 1Bff.; "Drug Database for Doctors Sells Ads to Sponsors," *The Wall Street Journal,* June 19, 2000, p. B1ff.; "Who's Teaching the Doctors?" *USA Today*, March 9, 2000, p. 1Dff.; "Web Links Give Drug Reps Foot in Doctors' Door," *The Wall Street Journal,* May 18, 1999, p. B1ff.; "In Marketing of Drugs, Genentech Tests Limits of What Is Acceptable," *The Wall Street Journal*, January 10, 1995, p. A1ff.; "Pharmacy Chain's Successful Sales Pitch Dismays Some Doctors and Drug Firms," *The Wall Street Journal*, February 26, 1993, p. B1ff. For more on Sears' selling tactics, see "Did Sears Take Other Customers for a Ride?" *Business Week*, August 3, 1992, pp. 24–25. See also Barry J. Babin, " Representing the Perceived Ethical Work Climate among Marketing Employees," *Journal of the Academy of Marketing Science*, Summer 2000, pp. 345–359; Bulent Menguc, "Organizational Consequences, Marketing Ethics and Salesforce Supervision: Further Empirical Evidence," *Journal of Business Ethics*, March 1998, pp. 333–52; David Strutton, J. B. I. Hamilton, and James R. Lumpkin, "An Essay on When to Fully Disclose in Sales Relationships: Applying Two Practical Guidelines for Addressing Truth-Telling Problems," *Journal of Business Ethics*, April 1997, pp. 545–60; Lawrence B. Chonko, John F. Tanner, and William A. Weeks, "Ethics in Salesperson Decision Making: A Synthesis of Research Approaches and an Extension of the Scenario Method," *Journal of Personal Selling & Sales Management*, Winter 1996, pp. 35–52; Alan J. Dubinsky, Marvin A. Jolson, Masaaki Kotabe, and Chae Un Lim, "A Cross-National Investigation of Industrial Salespeople's Ethical Perceptions," *Journal of International Business Studies*, Winter 1991, pp. 651–70.

**34.** For more on sales presentation approaches, see "Advise and Conquer," *Brandweek*, May 14, 2001, p. 1ff.; "Rick Francolini, TV Guide," *Brandweek*, October 25, 1999, p. 22; "The 60-Second Sales Pitch," *Inc.*, October 1994, pp. 87–89; David M. Szymanski, "Modality and Offering Effects in Sales Presentations for a Good Versus a Service," *Journal of the Academy of Marketing Science*, Spring 2001, pp. 179–190; Cathy Waters, "Customer Centered Selling: Eight Steps to Success from the World's Best Sales Force," *Journal of the Academy of Marketing Science*, Fall 2000, pp. 546–8; Jon M. Hawes, James T. Strong, and Bernard S. Winick, "Do Closing Techniques Diminish Prospect Trust?" *Industrial Marketing Management*, September 1996, pp. 349–60; Stephen B. Castleberry and C. David Shepherd, "Effective Interpersonal Listening and Personal Selling," *Journal of Personal Selling & Sales Management*, Winter 1993, pp. 35–50; Morgan P. Miles, Danny R. Arnold, and Henry W. Nash, "Adaptive Communication: The Adaption of the Seller's Interpersonal Style to the Stage of the Dyad's Relationship and the Buyer's Communication Style," *Journal of Personal Selling and Sales Management*, Winter 1990, pp. 21–28; Harish Sujan, Barton A. Weitz, and Nirmalya Kumar, "Learning Orientation, Working Smart, and Effective Selling," *Journal of Marketing*, July 1994, pp. 39–52.

## Chapter 15

**1.** Available from World Wide Web: <http://www.imediaconnection.com/content/features/071002b.asp>; adapted from Tim McHale, Tom Hespos, and Eric Porres, "BMW Films: The Ultimate Marketing Scheme," July 10, 2002. Available from World Wide Web: <http://www.Internetnews.com/IAR/article.php/1457171>; adapted from Christopher Saunders, "BMW Films Hit Hollywood, Courtesy of Microsoft," September 5, 2002.

**2.** "Events & Promotions," *Advertising Age*, March 17, 1997, pp. S1–6; "Special Report: Promotional Marketing," *Advertising Age*, March 21, 1994, pp. S1–14; "Special Report: Sales Promotion," *Advertising Age*, May 4, 1992, pp. 29–36; "More Marketers Leaving a (Prepaid) Calling Card," *The Wall Street Journal*, July 25, 1994, p. B1; "Beyond the Plastic Swizzle Stick," *Adweek's Marketing Week*, May 13, 1991, p. 20; K. Sivakumar, "Tradeoff Between Frequency and Depth of Price Promotions: Implications for High- and Low-Priced Brands," *Journal of Marketing Theory & Practice*, Winter 1996, pp. 1–8.

**3.** "Special Report: U.S. Multinationals," *Ad Age International*, January 1998, pp. 17–26; "Colgate-Palmolive Is Really Cleaning Up in Poland," *Business Week*, March 15, 1993, pp. 54–56; Charles R. Taylor, Gordon E. Miracle, and R. D. Wilson, "The Impact of Information Level on the Effectiveness of U.S. and Korean Television Commercials," *Journal of Advertising*, Spring 1997, pp. 1–18; Ann M. Barry, "Advertising and Culture: Theoretical Perspectives," *Journal of the Academy of Marketing Science*, Winter 1998, pp. 67–68; Siew M. Leong, Sween H. Ang, and Leng L. Tham, "Increasing Brand Name Recall in Print Advertising Among Asian Consumers," *Journal of Advertising*, Summer 1996, pp. 65–81; Ronald E. Taylor, Mariea G. Hoy, and Eric Haley, "How French Advertising Professionals Develop Creative Strategy," *Journal of Advertising*, Spring 1996, pp. 1–14; Nan Zhou and Mervin Y. T. Chen, "A Content Analysis of Men and Women in Canadian Consumer Magazine Advertising: Today's Portrayal, Yesterday's Image?" *Journal of Business Ethics*, April 1997, pp. 485–95; Johny K. Johansson, "The Sense of 'Nonsense': Japanese TV Advertising," *Journal of Advertising*, March 1994, pp. 17–26; Yong Zhang and Betsy D. Gelb, "Matching Advertising Appeals to Culture: The Influence of Products' Use Conditions," *Journal of Advertising*, Fall 1996, pp. 29–46; John L. Graham, Michael A. Kamins and Djoko S. Oetomo, "Content Analysis of German and Japanese Advertising in Print Media from Indonesia, Spain, and the United States," *Journal of Advertising*, June 1993, pp. 5–16; Bob D. Cutler and Rajshekhar G. Javalgi, "A Cross-Cultural Analysis of the Visual Components of Print Advertising: The United States and the European Community," *Journal of Advertising Research*, January/February 1992, p.71; Terence Nevett, "Differences Between American and British Television Advertising: Explanations and Implications," *Journal of Advertising*, December 1992, pp. 61–72; Bob D. Cutler and Rajshekhar G. Javalgi, "Comparison of Business-to-Business Advertising: The United States and the United Kingdom," *Industrial Marketing Management*, April 1994, pp. 117–24.

**4.** Available from World Wide Web: <http://www.marketingmag.ca>; Lesley Young, "Viagra's Wake-Up Call," *Marketing Magazine*: Feature, April 1, 2002.

**5.** For more on Dryel, see "The Dirt on At-Home Dry Cleaning," *The Wall Street Journal*, September 15, 2000, p. W14. See also "Sour Dough: Pizza Hut v. Papa John's," *Brandweek*, May 21, 2001, pp. 26–30; Kenneth C. Manning, "Understanding the Mental Representations Created by Comparative Advertising," *Journal of Advertising*, Summer 2001, pp. 27–40; "Irate Firms Take Comparisons to Court," *The Wall Street Journal*, December 22, 1999, p. B8; "Survey: Comparative Ads Can Dent Car's Credibility," *Advertising Age*, May 4, 1998, p. 26; "Rivals Take the Gloves Off as Taste-Test Wars Heat Up," *The Wall Street Journal*, March 30, 1998, p. B10; "Industry Panel Refers FedEx Case to FTC," *The Wall Street Journal*, April 11, 1997, p. B6; Diana L. Haytko, "Great Advertising Campaigns: Goals and Accomplishments," *Journal of Marketing*, April 1995, pp. 113–15; Carolyn Tripp, "Services Advertising: An Overview and Summary of Research, 1980–1995," *Journal of Advertising*, Winter 1997, pp. 21–38; Dhruv Grewal, Sukumar Kavanoor, Edward F. Fern, Carolyn Costley, and James Barnes, "Comparative Versus Noncomparative Advertising: A Meta-Analysis," *Journal of Marketing*, October 1997, pp. 1–15; Marla R. Stafford and Ellen Day, "Retail Services Advertising: The Effects of Appeal, Medium, and Service," *Journal of Advertising*, Spring 1995, pp. 57–71; For more on AT&T, MCI, and Sprint's comparative ads, see "Best Phone Discounts Go to Hardest Bargainers," *The Wall Street Journal*, February 13, 1997, p. B1ff.; "Fighting for Customers Gets Louder," *USA Today*, January 9, 1995, p. 1Bff.; "Discount War Can Be Confusing," *USA Today*, September 23, 1994, p. 1Bff.; "AT&T Tweaks MCI's 'Friends,'" *Advertising Age*, March 2, 1992, p. 4.

For other examples of comparative advertising, see "Allergy Drugs Wage a Bitter War of the Noses," *The Wall Street Journal*, May 23, 1996, p. B1ff.; "New Drug Ads Give Doctors Heartburn," *The Wall Street Journal*, April 25, 1996, p. B9; "Bitter Ads to Swallow," *Time*, April 1, 1996, pp. 48–49; "More Heartburn Relief Unsettles Market," *The Wall Street Journal*, February 7, 1996, p. B6; "New Ammo for Comparative Ads," *Advertising Age*, February 14, 1994, p. 26; Thomas E. Barry, "Comparative Advertising: What Have We Learned in Two Decades?" *Journal of Advertising Research*, March/April 1993, pp. 19–29; Naveen Donthu, "Comparative Advertising Intensity," *Journal of Advertising Research*, November/December 1992, pp. 53–58.

**6.** "Brawl Erupts Over Do-Good Advertising," *The Wall Street Journal*, September 29, 1997, p. B1ff.; "Cause and Effects Marketing," *Brandweek*, April 22, 1996, pp. 38–40; "Are Good Causes Good Marketing?" *Business Week*, March 21, 1994, pp. 64–66; "Chemical Firms Press Campaigns to Dispel Their 'Bad Guy' Image," *The Wall Street Journal*, September 20, 1988, p. 1ff.; "Spiffing up the Corporate Image," *Fortune*, July 21, 1986, pp. 68–72; Minette E. Drumwright, "Company Advertising With a Social Dimension: The Role of Noneconomic Criteria," *Journal of Marketing*, October 1996, pp. 71–87; Eric Haley, "Exploring the Construct of Organization As Source: Consumer's Understandings of Organizational Sponsorship of Advocacy Advertising," *Journal of Advertising*, Summer 1996, pp. 19–35; John K. Ross III, Larry T. Patterson, and Mary Ann Stutts, "Consumer Perceptions of Organizations That Use Cause-Related Marketing," *Journal of the Academy of Marketing Science*, Winter 1992, pp. 93–98.

**7.** For more on co-op ads, see "Big Blue Offers Solutions with $60 Mil Co-op Effort," *Advertising Age*, April 30, 2001, p. 8; "Revlon Plans Another Makeover," *The Wall Street Journal*, November 21, 2000, p. B1ff.; "Retailers Open Doors Wide for Co-op," *Advertising Age*, August 1, 1994, p. 30; John P. Murry and Jan B. Heide, "Managing Promotion Program Participation Within Manufacturer-Retailer Relationships," *Journal of Marketing*, January 1998, pp. 58–68. For more on joint promotions, see "Joint Marketing with Retailers Spreads," *The Wall Street Journal*, October 24, 1996, p. B6; "Joint Promotions Spawn Data Swap," *Advertising Age*, October 7, 1991, p. 44; "H&R Block, Excedrin Discover Joint Promotions Can Be Painless," *The Wall Street Journal*, February 28, 1991, p. B3.

**8.** For more on Benetton, see "Store Owners Rip into Benetton," *Advertising Age*, February 6, 1995, p. 1; "Benetton, German Retailers Squabble," *Advertising Age*, February 6, 1995, p. 46; "Benetton Brouhaha," *Advertising Age*, February 17, 1992, p. 62. For more on Intel, see "Intel Inside at 10," *Advertising Age*, April 30. 2001, p. 4ff.; "Co-op Crossroads," *Advertising Age*, November 15, 1999, p. 1ff.; "Intel Will Help Pay Costs of PC Makers' Web Ads," *USA Today*, August 5, 1997, p. 1B; "Changes to Intel's Co-Op Program Could Boost Web Advertising 40%," *The Wall Street Journal*, August 5, 1997, p. B7; "Intel Co-op Could Bring $150 Million to the Web," *Advertising Age*, July 28, 1997, p. 16; "How Strong Is the Case Against Intel?" *Business Week*, June 22, 1998, p. 42; "Intel Proposal Is Angering Web Publishers," *The Wall Street Journal*, January 16, 1998, p. B1ff.; "Trade Bait," *Brandweek*, December 1, 1997, pp. 36–44; "Intel's Amazing Profit Machine," *Fortune*, February 17, 1997, pp. 60–72. For more on GM, see "Still Pulling the Strings, But Locally, Too," *Brandweek*, April 17, 2000, pp. 34–42; "GM Dealers Rebel Against Local Ad Structure," *Advertising Age*, January 24, 2000, p. 3ff.; "GM Dealers Aren't Buying It," *Business Week*, February 8, 1999, pp. 46–50.

**9.** *Standard Rate and Data*, 2000; "Special Report: Media Outlook 2001," *Adweek*, September 25, 2000. For more on the Yellow Pages medium, see "Print Yellow Pages Are Still Profitable," *The Wall Street Journal*, May 22, 2000, p. B16; "The Truth About Yellow Pages: Making Them Work for You," *Journal of the Academy of Marketing Science*, Winter 1998, pp. 71–72; "'Sleeping Giant,' the Yellow Pages, Tries to Waken Madison Avenue," *The Wall Street Journal*, August 19, 1993, p. B6. For more on videotape medium, see "Are Spots on Home Video Badvertising?" *Brandweek*, January 29, 1996, p. 40; "Special Report: Direct Marketing," *Advertising Age*, October 28, 1996, pp. S1–6; "Direct Marketers Press Fast-Forward on Videotape Use," *The Wall Street Journal*, October 31, 1994, p. B8B. For more on the outdoor medium, see "A Market on the Move," *Ad Age Global*, April 2001, p. 38; "Billboards Help Media Firms Weather Slowdown," *USA Today*, December 12, 2000, p. 6B; "New Technology, Improved Image Draw Companies to Billboard Ads," *The Wall Street Journal*, July 31, 2000, p. B10; "Look Up! Seeing Is Believing," *Advertising Age*, August 2, 1999, p. S2; "The Great Outdoors," *Fortune*, March 1, 1999, pp. 150–57; "Billboards Aren't Boring Anymore," *Business Week*, September 21, 1998, pp. 86–90. See also Charles R. Taylor and John C. Taylor, "Regulatory Issues in Ourdoor Advertising: A Content Analysis of Billboards," *Journal of Public Policy & Marketing*, Spring 1994, pp. 97–107. For more on the radio medium, see "Old Media Get a Web Windfall," *The Wall Street Journal*, September 17, 1999, p. B1ff.; "TV Commercials Turn Obscure Songs into Radio Hits," *The Wall Street Journal*, October 9, 1998, p. B1ff.; "Radio's New Spin on an Oldie: Pay-for-Play," *The Wall Street Journal*, March 16, 1998, p. B1ff. See also Darryl W. Miller and Lawrence J. Marks, "Mental Imagery and Sound Effects in Radio Commercials," *Journal of Advertising*, December 1992, pp. 83–94. For more on the newspaper medium, see "Special Report: Newspaper Industry," *Advertising Age*, April 30, 2001, pp. S1–7; "Special Report: Newspapers," *Adweek*, April 30, 2001, pp. SR1–14; "Special Report: Newspapers," *Advertising Age*, May 8, 2000, pp. S1–20; "Publish or Perish?" *Fortune*, January 10, 2000, pp. 140–54; "Special Report: Newspapers," *Adweek*, April 26, 1999, pp. 1–28; "Newspapers," *Advertising Age*, April 26, 1999, pp. S1–22. See also Lawrence C. Soley and Robert L. Craig, "Advertising Pressures on Newspapers: A Survey," *Journal of Advertising*, December 1992, pp. 1–10; Srini S. Srinivasan, Robert P. Leone, and Francis J. Mulhern, "The Advertising Exposure Effect of Free Standing Inserts," *Journal of Advertising*, Spring 1995, pp. 29–40; Karen W. King, Leonard N. Reid, and Margaret Morrison, "Large-Agency Media Specialists' Opinions on Newspaper Advertising for National Accounts," *Journal of Advertising*, Summer 1997, pp. 1–17. For more on the magazine medium, see "To Sell Ad Pages, Magazines Offer Extra Services," *The Wall Street Journal*, July 9, 2001, p. B1ff.; "O Sister, Where Art Thou? Buying O," *USA Today*, January 18, 2001, p. 10D; "Special Report: Magazine Forecast," *Advertising Age*, October 23, 2000, pp. S1–36; "Magazines Think Outside the Rack," *USA Today*, November 15, 1999, p. 1Bf.; "Special Report: Magazines," *Advertising Age*, October 25, 1999, pp. S1–28. For more on the television and cable medium, see "MTV Networks Chief Juggles Expectations," *USA Today*, June 11, 2001, p. 1Bff.; "Special Report: TV's Upfront," *Advertising Age*, May 14, 2001, pp. S1–54; "Special Report: Cable TV," *Ad Age Global*, May 1, 2001, pp. 25–38; "Special Report: Cable TV," *Advertising Age*, April 16, 2001, pp. S1–28; "Special Report: TV's Upfront," *Advertising Age*, May 15, 2000, pp. S1–60; "Special Report: Cable TV Convergence," *Advertising Age*, April 10, 2000, pp. S1–38; "Special Report: Cable TV," *Advertising Age*, December 6, 1999, pp. S1–28. See also Jean L. Rogers, "Mail Advertising and Consumer Behavior," *Psychology & Marketing*, March 1996, pp. 211–33; Elizabeth C. Hirschman and Craig J. Thompson, "Why Media Matter: Toward a Richer Understanding of Consumers' Relationships With Advertising and Mass Media," *Journal of Advertising*, Spring 1997, pp. 43–60; Richard J. Fox and Gary L. Geissler, "Crisis in Advertising?" *Journal of Advertising*, December 1994, pp. 79–84; Roland T. Rust and Richard W. Oliver, "The Death of Advertising," *Journal of Advertising*, December 1994, pp. 71–77.

**10.** "Sex-Themed Ads Often Don't Travel Well," *The Wall Street Journal*, March 31, 2000, p. B7; "U.S. Admakers Cover It Up; Others Don't Give a Fig Leaf," *USA Today*, June 27, 1997, p. 1Bff.; "Mars Inc. Dips into Sex to Lure Consumers into Arms of M&M's," *The Wall Street Journal*, January 21, 1997, p. B9; "Underwear Ads Caught in Bind over Sex Appeal," *Advertising Age*, July 8, 1996, p. 27; "No Sexy Sales Ads, Please—We're Brits and Swedes," *Fortune*, October 21, 1991, p. 13.

**11.** "Looking for Mr. Plumber," *MediaWeek*, June 27, 1994, p. 7ff.; "Those Really Big Shows Are Often Disappointing to Those Who

Advertise," *The Wall Street Journal*, June 14, 1994, p. B1ff.

**12.** "Yech and Yada in 'Seinfeld' Ads," *Advertising Age*, May 18, 1998, p. 63; "'Seinfeld' Finale Advertisers Put on Game Faces," *USA Today*, April 29, 1998, p. 1B; "NBC May Get Only $1.5 Million for Ad Spots on 'Seinfeld' Finale," *The Wall Street Journal*, March 4, 1998, p. B6.

**13.** "Gardenburger's Ad May Help Its Rival," *The Wall Street Journal*, May 20, 1998, p. B8; "Gardenburger Bets the (Soybean) Farm on the Last 'Seinfeld,'" *The Wall Street Journal*, April 13, 1998, p. A1ff..

**14.** For more on ATM ads, see "Ads on Automated Teller Machines Multiply as Technology Improves," *Investor's Business Daily*, October 5, 2000, p. A6; "ATMs Are Latest Place-Based Medium," *Advertising Age*, November 24, 1997, p. 1ff. For more on Nascar ads, see "Revved-Up Prices Stall Fox Nascar Spots," *The Wall Street Journal*, March 26, 2001, p. B8; "On-Track Tragedy May Create Hazard for Future Nascar Sponsorships," *Brandweek*, February 26, 2001, p. 8; "Nascar's New Deal: Will Street Ride Along?" *Investor's Business Daily*, February 16, 2001, p. A8; "Forget Football," *American Demographics*, February 2001, pp. 34–36; "Start the Engines!" *Brandweek*, October 9, 2000, p. 1ff.; "Speed Sells," *Fortune*, April 12, 1999, pp. 56–70; "Babes, Bordeaux, and Billy Bobs," *Time*, May 31, 1999, pp. 70–76; "Sports Marketing: Stock Rising," *Brandweek*, March 22, 1999, pp. 24–26; "The Green Flag Is Up," *American Demographics*, April 1999, pp. 33–36; "Smile, You're a Winner!" *Time* June 15, 1998, pp. 42–43; "Speed Sells," *Business Week*, August 11, 1997, pp. 86–90; "New Breed of Sponsors Race to NASCAR," *USA Today*, April 5, 1996, p. 1Bff. See also Alan J. Greco and Linda E. Swayne, "Sales Response of Elderly Consumers to Point-of-Purchase Advertising," *Journal of Advertising Research*, September/October 1992, pp. 43–53.

**15.** Available from World Wide Web: <http://www.marketingmag.ca>; extracted from Chris Powell, "Here, There and Everywhere," *Marketing Magazine*: Out of Home Report, November 19, 2001.

**16.** "Ads Held Viewers the Super Bowl Bored," *The Wall Street Journal*, February 2, 2001, p. B6; "Super Bowl Ad Meter," *USA Today*, January 29, 2001, p. 8Bff.; "Super Bowl Accepts No Half-Hearted Effort," *USA Today*, January 26, 2001, p. 1Bff.; "Super Bowl's 30-Second Ad Rush," *The Wall Street Journal*, January 26, 2001, p. B1ff.; "No Gain," *Advertising Age*, January 25, 2001, p. 1ff.; "Diageo Designs Sneak Ad Play for Super Bowl," *The Wall Street Journal*, January 15, 2001, p. B1ff.; "CBS Eyes Windfall from Record Rates for 'Survivor' Ads," *The Wall Street Journal*, January 12, 2001, p. B4; "Edgy Spots Stir Controversy, and Results," *The Wall Street Journal*, January 11, 2001, p. B13; "Super Bowl Ads Are Latest Victim of Downturn," *The Wall Street Journal*, January 9, 2001, p. B1ff.; "Firms Pick Super Bowl as Prime Time for Kickoff Ads," *USA Today*, January 2, 2001, p. 1B; "VW + XXXV = $uper Bowl $trategy," *USA Today*, December 20, 2000, p. 2B; "ER Tops Price Charts, Regis Wears the Crown," *Advertising Age*, October 2, 2000, p. 1ff.; "ABC Tally for Oscar: $62.4 Mil," *Advertising Age*, March 20, 2000, pp. 40–42.

**17.** Deena M. Amato-McCoy, "On-Line Promotion Codes May Alienate e-Shoppers," *Stores*, vol. 85 (5), May 2003, p. 107.

**18.** Available from World Wide Web: <http://www.isoc.org>; Rangachari Anand, Manoj Kumar, Anant Jhingran, "Distributing e-Coupons on the Internet," INET 1999 Proceedings, Internet Society.

**19.** Ann Meyer, "Promotion Commotion," *Catalog Age*, vol. 20(7), June 2003, p. 82.

**20.** Kim Bartel Sheehan, "Re-Weaving the Web: Integrating Print and Online Communications," *Journal of Interactive Marketing*, Spring 2001, p. 47; Lee Sherman, "Banner Advertising: Measuring Effectiveness and Optimizing Placement," *Journal of Interactive Marketing*, Spring 2001, p. 60; "Behind the Wheel Driving the Web," *Advertising Age*, July 23, 2001, pp. 10–12; "Web Ads Getting in Your Way? Try Blocking Software," *Investor's Business Daily*, July 12, 2001, p. A6; "Aggressive Web Ads Push Ahead," *Investor's Business Daily*, July 3, 2001, p. A5; "The Bright Future of Web Advertising," *Ecompany*, June 2001, pp. 51–60; "Can You Say 'Cheese'? Intrusive Web Ads Could Drive Us Nuts," *The Wall Street Journal*, May 21, 2001, p. B1; "Choices, Choices . . . Web Advertising," *The Wall Street Journal*, April 23, 2001, p. R12; "Ad Nauseam," *The Wall Street Journal*, April 23, 2001, p. R8ff.; "Advertisers Have a Banner Year," *Investor's Business Daily*, March 9, 2001, p. A4; "Web's Next Phase Will Weave Through Your Life," *USA Today*, March 2, 2001, p. 1Bff.; "Looking Beyond Banners to Revive Web Advertising," *The Wall Street Journal*, February 26, 2001, p. B1ff.; "Dot-Com Rarity: NextCard Finds Online Ads Work," *The Wall Street Journal*, January 29, 2001, p. B1f.; "Do e-Ads Have a Future?" *Business Week E.Biz*, January 22, 2001, pp. EB46–EB50; "Beyond the Banner Ad," *Business Week E.Biz.*, December 11, 2000, p. EB16; "As Ads Fail to Heat Up, Sites Turning to Paid Subscribers," *Investor's Business Daily*, December 11, 2000, p. A8; "Content on Web Is Under Fire for Losing Cash," *The Wall Street Journal*, October 9, 2000, p. B1ff.; "Web Sites Toot Their Horns Amid Ad Chill," *The Wall Street Journal*, June 27, 2000, p. B1ff.; "Online Ads Turn to Hand-Held Devices," *The Wall Street Journal*, February 4, 2000, p. B6; "The Silicon Alley Heart of Internet Advertising," *Fortune*, December 6, 1999, pp. 166–68; "Banner Ads Are Driving Web Purchases," *The Wall Street Journal*, November 24, 1999, p. B9ff.; "Now It's Time for a Commercial," *The Wall Street Journal*, November 22, 1999, p. R28ff.; "Internet Waves Hit Asia Shores," *Ad Age International*, November 1999, p. 43ff.; "The Net Chases the Networks," *Fortune*, October 11, 1999, p. 296; "Humor Is Used to Slow Down Web Surfers," *The Wall Street Journal*, August 17, 1999, p. B9; "P&G Lathers On-Line Ad Revolution," *USA Today*, July 15, 1999, p. 3B; "Getting Noticed," *The Wall Street Journal*, July 12, 1999, p. R16ff.; "Online Persuaders," *The Wall Street Journal*, July 12, 1999, p. R12ff.; "Wacky Internet Ads Ride Creative Wave," *USA Today*, June 9, 1999, p. 1Bff.; "The Trouble with Web Advertising," *Fortune*, April 12, 1999, pp. 147–48; "Clicks for Free," *American Demographics*, February 1999, pp. 54–55; "Ads Click for Net Retailers," *USA Today*, January 28, 1999, p. 3B; "Your Message Here," *Inc. Tech*, No. 1, 1999, pp. 76–80; "Web Sites Say: Your Ad Sells or It's on Us," *The Wall Street Journal*, June 27, 1997, p. B9; "How Net Is Becoming More Like Television to Draw Advertisers," *The Wall Street Journal*, December 13, 1996, p. A1ff.; Richard T. Watson, Sigmund Akselsen, and Leyland F. Pitt, "Attractors: Building Mountains in the Flat Landscape of the World Wide Web," *California Management Review*, Winter 1998, pp. 36–56; W W. Kassaye, "Global Advertising and the World Wide Web," *Business Horizons*, May–June 1997, pp. 33–42.

**21.** See "Subaru's Forester Takes Female Athletes on a New $18M Ad Ride," *Brandweek*, April 30, 2001, p. 16; "Why Sports Should Fear the Hand that Feeds It," *Ad Age Global*, October 2000, p. 29; "Holly Wired," *Time Digital*, May 2000, pp. 78–81; "Meet Lycra's New Face," *Brandweek*, April 24, 2000, p. 1ff.; "Kwan Spins Silver into Gold," *USA Today*, February 9, 2000, p. 1Bff.; "Battle of the Golf Shirts," *The Wall Street Journal*, January 6, 2000, p. B1ff.; "Golfing with Troy, and Other Perks," *The Wall Street Journal*, October 4, 1999, p. B1ff.; "Sports Bra's Flash Could Cash In," *USA Today*, July 13, 1999, p. 1Aff.; "Show Me the Money," *The Wall Street Journal*, May 17, 1999, p. B1ff.; "Home-Run Heroes Bring In Few Endorsements," *The Wall Street Journal*, October 21, 1998, p. B1ff.; "In the NBA, Shoe Money Is No Longer a Slam-Dunk," *The Wall Street Journal*, May 14, 1998, p. B1ff. See also "Dip Ad Stirs Church Ire," *Advertising Age*, July 2, 2001, p., 8ff.; "Ghosts of Cannes," *Advertising Age*, June 11, 2001, p. 1ff.; "Duck Ads Have New Customers," *USA Today*, September 18, 2000, p. 13B; "Cough Syrup Touts 'Awful' Taste in U.S.," *The Wall Street Journal*, December 15, 1999, p. B10; "Honda Hopes Mr. Clean Helps to Make Its Image Sparkle," *The Wall Street Journal*, September 26, 1997, p. B20; "Madison Avenue Picks an Average Joe as '90s Pitchman," *The Wall Street Journal*, September 11, 1996, p. B1ff. See also Erik L. Olson, "How Magazine Articles Portrayed Advertising From 1900 to 1940," *Journal of Advertising*, Fall 1995, pp. 41–54; Audhesh K. Paswan, "Marketing to the Mind: Right Brain Strategies for Advertising and Marketing," *Journal of the Academy of Marketing Science*, Winter 1998, pp. 68–69; Avery M. Abernethy and George R. Franke, "The Information Content of Advertising: A Meta-Analysis," *Journal of Adver-*

*tising*, Summer 1996, pp. 1–17; James H. Leigh, "The Use of Figures of Speech in Print Ad Headlines," *Journal of Advertising*, June 1994, pp. 17–33; Bruce A. Huhmann and Timothy P. Brotherton, "A Content Analysis of Guilt Appeals in Popular Magazine Advertisements," *Journal of Advertising*, Summer 1997, pp. 35–45; Margaret F. Callcott a nd Wei-Na Lee, "A Content Analysis of Animation and Animated Spokes-Characters in Television Commercials," *Journal of Advertising*, December 1994, pp. 1–12; Alan J. Bush and Victoria D. Bush, "The Narrative Paradigm As a Perspective for Improving Ethical Evaluations of Advertisements," *Journal of Advertising*, September 1994, pp. 31–41; L. W. Turley and Scott W. Kelley, "A Comparison of Advertising Content: Business to Business Versus Consumer Services," *Journal of Advertising*, Winter 1997, pp. 39–48; Eleonora Curlo and Robert Chamblee, "Ad Processing and Persuasion: The Role of Brand Identification," *Psychology & Marketing*, May 1998, pp. 279–99; V. C. Broach, Thomas J. Page, and R. D. Wilson, "Television Programming and Its Influence on Viewers' Perceptions of Commercials: The Role of Program Arousal and Pleasantness," *Journal of Advertising*, Winter 1995, pp. 45–54; Laurie A. Babin and Alvin C. Burns, "Effects of Print Ad Pictures and Copy Containing Instructions to Imagine on Mental Imagery That Mediates Attitudes," *Journal of Advertising*, Fall 1997, pp. 33–44; Noel M. Murray and Sandra B. Murray, "Music and Lyrics in Commercials: A Cross-Cultural Comparison Between Commercials Run in the Dominican Republic and in the United States," *Journal of Advertising*, Summer 1996, pp. 51–63; Barbara B. Stern, "Advertising Intimacy: Relationship Marketing and the Services Consumer," *Journal of Advertising*, Winter 1997, pp. 7–19; Baba Shiv, Julie A. Edell, and John W. Payne, "Factors Affecting the Impact of Negatively and Positively Framed Ad Messages," *Journal of Consumer Research*, December 1997, pp. 285–94; Harlan E. Spotts, Marc G. Weinberger, and Amy L. Parsons, "Assessing the Use and Impact of Humor on Advertising Effectiveness: A Contingency Approach," *Journal of Advertising*, Fall 1997, pp. 17–32; Martha Rogers and Kirk H. Smith, "Public Perceptions of Subliminal Advertising: Why Practitioners Shouldn't Ignore This Issue," *Journal of Advertising Research*, March/April 1993, pp. 10–18; Kathryn T. Theus, "Subliminal Advertising and the Psychology of Processing Unconscious Stimuli: A Review of Research," *Psychology & Marketing*, May/June 1994, pp. 271–90; Carolyn A. Lin, "Cultural Differences in Message Strategies: A Comparison between American and Japanese TV Commercials," *Journal of Advertising Research*, July/August 1993, pp. 40–49; Robert Chamblee and Dennis M. Sandler, "Business-to-Business Advertising: Which Layout Style Works Best?" *Journal of Advertising Research*, November/December 1992, pp. 39–46.

**22.** Fahad S. Al-Olayan, "A Content Analysis of Magazine Advertisements from the United States and the Arab World," *Journal of Advertising*, Fall 2000, pp. 69–83; "Exxon Centralizes New Global Campaign," *The Wall Street Journal*, July 11, 2001, p. B6; "McCann Finds Global a Tough Sell in Japan," *The Wall Street Journal*, June 19, 1997, p. B2; "Microsoft Global Image Campaign Is Dizzying without a Hard Sell," *The Wall Street Journal*, November 11, 1994, p. B7; Fred Zandpour et al., "Global Reach and Local Touch: Achieving Cultural Fitness in TV Advertising," *Journal of Advertising Research*, September/October 1994, pp. 35–63; Michael G. Harvey, "A Model to Determine Standardization of the Advertising Process in International Markets," *Journal of Advertising Research*, July/August 1993, pp. 57–64; Barbara Mueller, "Standardization vs. Specialization: An Examination of Westernization in Japanese Advertising," *Journal of Advertising Research*, January/February 1992, pp. 15–24; Dana L. Alden, Wayne D. Hoyer, and Chol Lee, "Identifying Global and Culture-Specific Dimensions of Humor in Advertising: A Multinational Analysis," *Journal of Marketing*, April 1993, pp. 64–75; "International Special Report: Global Media," *Advertising Age International*, July 18, 1994, p. I11–16; Ali Kanso, "International Advertising Strategies: Global Commitment to Local Vision," *Journal of Advertising Research*, January/February 1992, pp. 10–14; "Professor Stands by His Theory on Global Advertising," *The Wall Street Journal*, October 13, 1992, p. B10; Theodore Levitt, "The Globalization of Markets," *Harvard Business Review*, May–June 1983, pp. 92–102; Kamran Kashani, "Beware the Pitfalls of Global Marketing," *Harvard Business Review*, September/October 1989, pp. 91–98; Ludmilla G. Wells, "Western Concepts, Russian Perspectives: Meanings of Advertising in the Former Soviet Union," *Journal of Advertising*, March 1994, pp. 83–95; William L. Shanklin and David A. Griffith, "Crafting Strategies for Global Marketing in the New Millennium," *Business Horizons*, September–October 1996, pp. 11–16.

**23.** "Will Ad Agencies Survive Slowdown?" *Investor's Business Daily*, May 8, 2001, p. A1; "IBD Corporate Leaders: Advertising Agencies," *Investor's Business Daily*, May 8, 2001, p. B20; "Agency Report," *Advertising Age*, April 23, 2001, pp. S1–36; "Interpublic Still Faces Hurdles in True North Deal," *Advertising Age*, March 26, 2001, p. 3fff.; "Slim Selection Is Seen for Takeover Targets," *The Wall Street Journal*, March 21, 2001, p. B14; "Slow Ad Period Likely to Spur More Deals," *The Wall Street Journal*, March 20, 2001, p. B2; "A Chill Hits Madison Avenue," *The Wall Street Journal*, March 19, 2001, p. B1ff.; "Culture Shock," *Advertising Age*, January 8, 2001, p. 1ff.; "How the Internet Gave Big Edge to Tiny Ad Firm," *The Wall Street Journal*, June 22, 2000, p. B1ff.; "Road Less Traveled Leads Cappelli to Success," *USA Today*, May 11, 2000, p. 3B; "Agencies Teach Skill Building," *Advertising Age*, May 1, 2000, p. 12; "Agencies Form Group to Help Set Guidelines for Ads on the Web," *The Wall Street Journal*, April 19, 2000, p. B7; "Special Report: Interactive," *Advertising Age*, March 6, 2000, pp. S1–48; "It's Splitsville When Dot-Coms Irk Ad Agencies," *The Wall Street Journal*, December 8, 1999, p. B1ff.; "Agencies Left in Cold as Marketers Expand Online," *Advertising Age*, July 26, 1999, pp. S26–30; "The Old Order Blurreth," *Brandweek*, April 19, 1999, pp. 54–64; "Agencies Centralize Web Ad Serving," *Advertising Age*, March 1, 1999, pp. S1–12; "IQ's Leading Agencies," *Brandweek*, January 18, 1999, pp. IQ20–41; "The Race to Inter-Activity," *Advertising Age*, January 4, 1999, p. 1ff. See also Louise Ripley, "Why Industrial Advertising is Often Done in House," *Industrial Marketing Management*, November 1992, pp. 331–34; Murray Young and Charles Steilen, "Strategy-Based Advertising Agency Selection: An Alternative to 'Spec' Presentations," *Business Horizons*, November–December 1996, pp. 77–80; Douglas C. West, "Purchasing Professional Services: The Case of Advertising Agencies," *International Journal of Purchasing & Materials Management*, Summer 1997, pp. 2–9; Douglas W. LaBahn and Chiranjeev Kohli, "Maintaining Client Commitment in Advertising Agency-Client Relationships," *Industrial Marketing Management*, November 1997, pp. 497–508; Alan T. Shao and John S. Hill, "Executing Transnational Advertising Campaigns: Do U.S. Agencies Have the Overseas Talent?" *Journal of Advertising Research*, January/February 1992, pp. 49–58.

**24.** "Can An Agency Be Guilty of Malpractice?" *Advertising Age*, January 31, 2000, pp. 24–25; "Bowl Postmortem: Tadpoles, Ad Polls," *Advertising Age*, February 6, 1995, p. 44; "Why A-B Bounced Bud," *Advertising Age*, November 21, 1994, p. 1ff.; "Ties that Bind Agency, Client Unravel," *The Wall Street Journal*, November 16, 1994, p. B9; Paul C.N. Mitchell, Harold Cataquet, and Stephen Hague, "Establishing the Causes of Disaffection in Agency-Client Relations," *Journal of Advertising Research*, March/April 1992, pp. 41–48.

**25.** "Becoming Strategic Partners in the 1990s," *Advertising Age*, June 8, 1998, p. 28; "P&G Poised to Rewrite Ad Agency Pay Policies," *Advertising Age*, February 16, 1998, p. 1ff.; "Blame-the-Messenger Mentality Leaves Scars on Madison Avenue," *The Wall Street Journal*, November 20, 1991, p. B4; R. Susan Ellis and Lester W. Johnson, "Agency Theory as a Framework for *Advertising* Agency Compensation Decisions," *Journal of Advertising Research*, September/October 1993, p. 76; Thorolf Helgesen, "Advertising Awards and Advertising Agency Performance Criteria," *Journal of Advertising Research*, July/August 1994, pp. 43–53.

**26.** "Feeling the Squeeze," *Advertising Age*, June 4, 2001, p.1ff.; "Unilever Reviews the Way It Pays for Ads," *The Wall Street Journal*, April 27, 2001, p. B6; "Kraft Folds $800 Million into Starcom," *Advertis-*

ing Age, December 18, 2000, p. 1ff.; "Agencies, Beware a Downturn," *Advertising Age*, July 10, 2000, p. 30; "Performance Pays," *Advertising Age*, February 28, 2000, pp. S14–S16; "Agencies Get Dot-Com Stock for Hot Spots," *The Wall Street Journal*, February 8, 2000, p. B1ff.; "Dot-Compensation: Ad Agencies Feel Net Effect," *Advertising Age*, February 7, 2000, p. 1ff.; "P&G Expands Its Program to Tie Agency Pay to Brand Performance," *The Wall Street Journal*, September 16, 1999, p. B12; "Nissan Ties TBWA's Pay to Car Sales," *Advertising Age*, June 7, 1999, p. 1ff.; "Incentive Compensation: A Trend or a Tsunami?" *Advertising Age*, March 1, 1999, p. 26; "P&G to Test Ad-Agency Pay Tied to Sales," *The Wall Street Journal*, November 9, 1998, p. B10; "Price Becomes Prime Issue," *Advertising Age*, September 14, 1998, p. 24; "ANA Survey: Under 50% Pay Agency Commissions," *Advertising Age*, June 15, 1998, p. 18; "Becoming Strategic Partners in the 1990s," *Advertising Age*, June 8, 1998, p. 28; "P&G Poised to Rewrite Ad Agency Pay Policies," *Advertising Age*, February 16, 1998, p. 1ff. See also R. Susan Ellis and Lester W. Johnson, "Agency Theory as a Framework for Advertising Agency Compensation Decisions," *Journal of Advertising Research*, September/October 1993, p. 76; Thorolf Helgesen, "Advertising Awards and Advertising Agency Performance Criteria," *Journal of Advertising Research*, July/August 1994, pp. 43–53.

**27.** Ann Marie Barry, "How Advertising Works: The Role of Research," *Journal of the Academy of Marketing Science*, Winter 2001, p.1036. For one specific example, see "Dog-Gone Days: FCB Creates Ads for Taco Bell Acc't," *Advertising Age*, July 24, 2000, p. 4; "Taco Bell Drops the Chihuahua in Management Shuffle," *USA Today*, July 19, 2000, p. 1B; "Taco Bell Fences in Chihuahua for Ads," *Advertising Age*, July 3, 2000, p. 32; "Chihuahua Gets Muzzled as Taco Bell Pushes Value," *Advertising Age*, November 29, 1999, p. 26; "Taco Bell Ads to Focus on Food, Not Dog," *The Wall Street Journal*, October 11, 1999, p. B10; "Say Bark in Hindi!" *Advertising Age*, January 11, 1999, p. 1ff.; "Taco Bell Finds a Dog's Life Quite Fetching," *USA Today*, October 22, 1998, p. 1Bff.; "Chiat's New Day," *Newsweek*, August 3, 1998. See also "How Terrific Ads Propelled Colgate, Dethroned Longtime Leader P&G," *Investor's Business Daily*, April 20, 2001, p. A1ff.; "MasterCard Learns Ads Can Be Tricky," *The Wall Street Journal*, February 23, 2001, p. B8; "Measuring Up," *Advertising Age*, February 5, 2001, p. 1ff.; "Does Creativity Count?" *Brandweek*, December 11, 2000, pp. 32–44; "The Metrics System," *Brandweek*, November 13, 2000, pp. 106–10; "Protests Let Air Out of Nike Ads," *USA Today*, November 13, 2000, p. 6B; "Nike Rescinds Ad, Apologizes to Disabled People," *The Wall Street Journal*, October 26, 2000, p. B20; "Hard Selling on the Net," *Advertising Age*, October 23, 2000, pp. 48–52; "Jazzy Sprint Ads Fail to Connect," *USA Today*, August 28, 2000, p. 5B; "Uncle Sam Wants Who? New Report Calls Military's Ads Off Target," *The Wall Street Journal*, July 6, 2000, p. B1ff.; "Where Have All the Gerbils Gone?" *The Wall Street Journal*, March 30, 2000, p. B1ff.; "Shock Treatment," *Newsweek*, November 1, 1999, pp. 58–59; "Omnicom Group to Measure How Ads Do," *The Wall Street Journal*, October 21, 1999, p. B16; "Glamour Sets Out to Prove Its Ads Work," *The Wall Street Journal*, August 26, 1999, p. B8; "Where's the Commercial?" *USA Today*, June 25, 1999, p. 1Bff.; "I'd Like to Teach the World to Sell," *Business Week*, June 7, 1999, p. 59; "Traditional Marketing Is Dead," *Advertising Age*, May 31, 1999, pp. 24–26; "ADKnowledge Goes Beyond Clicks to Measurable Results," *Advertising Age*, March 1, 1999, p. S14 "Nissan's Crisis Was Made in the U.S.A.," *The Wall Street Journal*, November 25, 1998, p. B1ff.; "Great Ad! What's It For?" *Business Week*, July 20, 1998, pp. 118–20; "When Ads Get Creative, Some Click, Some Bomb," *USA Today*, December 15, 1997, p. 1Bff. See also Gerald J. Tellis and Doyle L. Weiss, "Does TV Advertising Really Affect Sales? The Role of Measures, Models, and Data Aggregation," *Journal of Advertising*, Fall 1995, pp. 1–12; John H. Holmes, "When Ads Work," *Journal of the Academy of Marketing Science*, Winter 1997, pp. 88–89; Karen Whitehill King, John D. Pehrson, and Leonard N. Reid, "Pretesting TV Commercials: Methods, Measures, and Changing Agency Roles," *Journal of Advertising*, September 1993, p. 85; "Researchers Probe Ad Effectiveness Globally," *Marketing News*, August 29, 1994, pp. 6–7. See also Erik du Plessis, "Recognition versus Recall," *Journal of Advertising Research*, May/June 1994, pp. 75–91.

**28.** Ivan L. Preston, "Regulatory Positions Toward Advertising Puffery of the Uniform Commercial Code and the Federal Trade Commission," *Journal of Public Policy & Marketing*, Fall 1997, pp. 336–44; Claude R. Martin, Jr., "Ethical Advertising Research Standards: Three Case Studies," *Journal of Advertising*, September 1994, pp. 17–30; William K. Darley and Robert E. Smith, "Advertising Claim Objectivity: Antecedents and Effects," *Journal of Marketing*, October 1993, pp. 100–13; George M. Zinkhan, "Advertising Ethics: Emerging Methods and Trends," *Journal of Advertising*, September 1994, pp. 1–4; Alexander Simonson and Morris B. Holbrook, "Permissible Puffery Versus Actionable Warranty in Advertising and Salestalk: An Empirical Investigation," *Journal of Public Policy & Marketing*, Fall 1993, pp. 216–33.

**29.** "The Cyber-Show Must Go On," *Trade Media*, May 7, 2001, pp. SR3–4; "Getting the Most from a Trade-Show Booth," *Investor's Business Daily*, April 25, 2000, p. 1; Marnik G. Dekimpe, Pierre Francois, Srinath Gopalakrishna, Gary L. Lilien, and Christophe Van den Bulte, "Generalizing About Trade Show Effectiveness: A Cross-National Comparison," *Journal of Marketing*, October 1997, pp. 55–64; Scott Barlass, "How to Get the Most Out of Trade Shows," *Journal of Product Innovation Management*, September 1997, pp. 423–24; Srinath Gopalakrishna, Gary L. Lilien, Jerome D. Williams, and Ian K. Sequeira, "Do Trade Shows Pay Off?" *Journal of Marketing*, July 1995, pp. 75–83; Ronald C. Curhan and Robert J. Kopp, "Obtaining Retailer Support for Trade Deals: Key Success Factors," *Journal of Advertising Research*, December 1987–January 1988, pp. 51–60; Donald W. Jackson, Janet E. Keith, and Richard K. Burdick, "The Relative Importance of Various Promotional Elements in Different Industrial Purchase Situations," *Journal of Advertising* 16, no. 4 (1987), pp. 25–33.

**30.** "Trade Promotion Rises," *Advertising Age*, April 3, 2000, p. 24; "Getting Tough on Trade," *Adweek*, April 13, 1992, pp. 20–30; "A Shift in Direction?" *Adweek's Marketing Week*, April 13, 1992, pp. 26–27; Mary A. Raymond and Jong W. Lim, "Promotion and Trade Mix Considerations for Entering and Competing in the Korean Market," *Journal of Marketing Theory & Practice*, Winter 1996, pp. 44–55; Sunil Gupta, "Impact of Sales Promotions on When, What, and How Much to Buy," *Journal of Marketing Research*, November 1988, pp. 342–55.

**31.** "Creating Incentives Down in Ranks: Marriott Ties Pay to Guest Replies," *Investor's Business Daily*, July 6, 2001, p. A1; "Get Great Results from Salespeople by Finding What Really Moves Them," *Investor's Business Daily*, July 2, 2001, p. A1.

**32.** "Too Many Choices," *The Wall Street Journal*, April 20, 2001, p. B1ff.; "Reposition: Simplifying the Customer's Brandscape," *Brandweek*, October 2, 2000, pp. 36–48; "Make It Simple," *Business Week*, September 9, 1996, pp. 96–104; "Pay for Performance Picking Up Speed," *Advertising Age*, August 9, 1993, p. 19; Donald R. Lichtenstein, Scot Burton, and Richard G. Netemeyer, "An Examination of Deal Proneness Across Sales Promotion Types: A Consumer Segmentation Perspective," *Journal of Retailing*, Summer 1997, pp. 283–97; Donald R. Glover, "Distributor Attitudes Toward Manufacturer-Sponsored Promotions," *Industrial Marketing Management* 20, no. 3 (1991), pp. 241–50; A.S.C. Ehrenberg, Kathy Hammond, and G.J. Goodhardt, "The After-Effects of Price-related Consumer Promotions," *Journal of Advertising Research*, July/August 1994, pp. 11–21; Jean J. Boddewyn and Monica Leardi, "Sales Promotions: Practice, Regulation and Self-Regulation Around the World," *International Journal of Advertising* 8, no. 4 (1989), pp. 363–74.

**33.** For another example, see "Shopper Turns Lots of Pudding into Free Miles," *The Wall Street Journal*, January 24, 2000, p. B1ff.; "The Pudding Guy Flies Again (and Again) Over Latin America," *The Wall Street Journal*, March 16, 2000, p. B1. See also P. Rajan Varadarajan, "Horizontal Cooperative Sales Promotion: A Framework for Classification and Additional Perspectives," *Journal of Marketing*, April, 1986 pp. 61–73.

34. J. F. Engel, M. R. Warshaw, and T. C. Kinnear, *Promotional Strategy* (Homewood, IL: Richard D. Irwin, 1988).

## Chapter 16

1. Adapted from: Lisa Margonelli, "How IKEA Designs Its Sexy Price Tags," *Business 2.0*, October 2002.

2. Alfred Rappaport, "Executive Incentives versus Corporate Growth," *Harvard Business Review*, July–August 1978, pp. 81–88; David M. Szymanski, Sundar G. Bharadwaj, and P. Rajan Varadarajan, "An Analysis of the Market Share-Profitability Relationship," *Journal of Marketing*, July 1993, pp. 1–18.

3. Pricing "in the public interest" is often an issue in pricing government services; for an interesting example, see "Price Policy on Space Shuttle's Commercial Use Could Launch—or Ground—NASA's Rockets," *The Wall Street Journal*, March 21, 1985, p. 64.

4. "Applying Old Pricing Lessons to a New Investing World," *The Wall Street Journal*, May 21, 2001, p. C1ff.; Stephen E. Frank, *Net Worth* (2001); "E-Assets for Sale," *Business Week E.Biz*, May 14, 2001, pp. EB20–EB22; "Last Guys Finish First," *Ecompany*, May 2001, pp. 93–97; "After the Wild Ride," *Business Week E.Biz*, April 16, 2001, pp. EB29–EB30; "Study: Net Start-Ups Ignored Economics 101," *Investor's Business Daily*, March 2, 2001, p. A8; "12 Months When the Dot Turned into a Dark Period," *Investor's Business Daily*, January 2, 2001, p. A6; "We're Heading into Something Big—but What?" *USA Today*, December 29, 2000, p. 1Bff.; "What Detonated Dot-Bombs?" *USA Today*, December 4, 2000, p. 1Bff.; "Dot-Bombs," *Brandweek*, November 27, 2000, pp. IQ16–IQ20; "Pets.com's Demise: Too Much Litter, Too Few Funds," *The Wall Street Journal*, November 8, 2000, p. B1ff.; "Dot-Coms, What Have We Learned?" *Fortune*, October 30, 2000, pp. 82–137; "Sock Dogma," *Brandweek*, June 5, 2000, pp. IQ28–IQ34; "Shakeout E-Tailers," *Business Week E.Biz*, May 15, 2000, pp. EB102–EB118; "E-Tail Gets Derailed: How Web Upstarts Misjudged the Game," *The Wall Street Journal*, April 5, 2000, p. A1ff.

5. "What Are Price Wars Good For? Absolutely Nothing," *Fortune*, May 12, 1997, p. 156; "Price Wars," *Adweek's Marketing Week*, June 8, 1992, pp. 18–22; "A Remarkable Gamble in an Industry Slump Pays Off Fast for Agco," *The Wall Street Journal*, August 19, 1997, p. A1ff.; "Why the Price Wars Never End," *Fortune*, March 23, 1992, pp. 68–78; "Avis, Sidestepping Price Wars, Focuses on the Drive Itself," *Adweek's Marketing Week*, February 12, 1990, p. 24.

6. Jacques Chevron, "Online Reverse Auctions are Brand Killers," *Brand Week*, December 4, 2000, vol. 41(47), p. 32.

7. . Jane Bryant Quinn, "Buying Power Per Hour," *Newsweek*, vol. 137(18), April 30, 2001, p. 39.

8. Ellen Garbarino and Olivia F. Lee, "Dynamic Pricing in Internet Retail: Effects on Consumer Trust," *Psychology and Marketing*, vol. 20(6), June 2003, p. 495.

9. Available from World Wide Web: <http://www.ecommercetimes.com>; Lori Enos, "Amazon Apologizes for Pricing Blunder," September 28, 2000.

10. For more on Priceline, see "Fasten Your Seat Belt!" *Time* Digital, 2001; "Inside Jay Walker's House of Cards," *Fortune*, November 13, 2000, pp. 127–38; "Live Long and Prosper?" *The Wall Street Journal*, October 23, 2000, p. R22ff.; "How Jay Walker Built WebHouse on a Theory that He Couldn't Prove," *The Wall Street Journal*, October 16, 2000, p. 1Aff.; "Letting the Masses Name Their Price," *Business Week E.Biz*, September 18, 2000, p. EB44; "Be Yor Own Barcode," *Time*, July 10, 2000, pp. 96–97; "Name Your Price—for Everything?" *Business Week*, April 17, 2000, pp. 72–78; "The Hype Is Big, Really Big, at Priceline," *Fortune*, September 6, 1999, pp. 193–202. For more on other online travel sites, see "Orbitz Doesn't Soar," *Business Week E.Biz*, July 9, 2001, p. EB8; "Southwest Limits Most Travel Data to Own Web Site," *USA Today*, July 6, 2001, p. 3B; "Your Family May Be Too Big for Orbitz," *USA Today*, June 29, 2001, p. 5D; "Airlines Jettison Incentives for Making Reservations Over the Internet," *The Wall Street Journal*, June 25, 2001, p. B1; "Hotel Reservation Network: Travel Site Enjoys Solid Profits," *Investor's Business Daily*, June 20, 2001, p. A5; "Good Fares Await Travelers Buying Tickets Online," *Investor's Business Daily*, June 12, 2001, p. A8; "Where the Net Delivers: Travel," *Business Week*, June 11, 2001, pp. 142–44; "Southwest Pushes Its Online Booking, Says Internet Rivals Come Up Short," *Brandweek*, June 11, 2001, p. 16; "Orbitz Puts New Spin on Airfares," *USA Today*, June 8, 2001, p. 8D; "Big Airlines Officially Open Online Outlet," *USA Today*, June 4, 2001, p. 1Bff.; "Airlines to Offer Cheap Tickets on the Internet," *The Wall Street Journal*, June 29, 2000, p. B1ff.

11. Stephen P. Bradley, "Ebay, Inc.," *Journal of Interactive Marketing*, Autumn 2000, p. 73; "Ebay Allows Sellers to Set Up 'Storefronts' Online in Bid to Expand Beyond Auctions," *The Wall Street Journal*, June 12, 2001, p. B8; "Corporate Sellers Put the Online Auctioneer on Even Faster Track," *The Wall Street Journal*, June 1, 2001, p. A1ff.; "One Man's Economic Gotterdammerung Is Another's Clearance Sale," *Ecompany*, May 2001, pp. 106–108; "Ebay's Bid to Conquer All," *Time*, February 5, 2001, pp. 48–51; "A Revolution in Pricing? Not Quite," *Business Week*, November 20, 2000, pp. 48–49; "Will Auction Frenzy Cool?" *Business Week E. Biz*, September 18, 2000, p. EB140; "Going, Going, Gone," *Business Week*, April 12, 1999, pp. 30–32; "Good-Bye to Fixed Pricing," *Business Week*, May 4, 1998, pp. 71–84; "One-Price Deals Save Time, Hassles, but Not Money," *USA Today*, March 11, 1998, p. 1Bff; "Airlines Raise Their Class Consciousness," *Business Week*, February 23, 1998, p. 40; "Haggling in Cyberspace Transforms Car Sales," *The Wall Street Journal*, December 30, 1997, p. B1ff.; "Car Hagglers May Still Drive Best Car Deals," *The Wall Street Journal*, October 12, 1994, p. B1ff. See also Eric Matson, "Customizing Prices," *Harvard Business Review*, November–December 1995, pp. 13–14; Sanjay K. Dhar and Stephen J. Hoch, "Price Discrimination Using in-Store Merchandising," *Journal of Marketing*, January 1996, pp. 17–30; Michael H. Morris, "Separate Prices as a Marketing Tool," *Industrial Marketing Management*, May 1987, pp. 79–86; P. Ronald Stephenson, William L. Cron, and Gary L. Frazier, "Delegating Pricing Authority to the Sales Force: The Effects on Sales and Profit Performance," *Journal of Marketing*, Spring 1979, pp. 21–24.

12. Jeff Blair, *Globe and Mail*, Thursday, January 9, 2003, p. S2.

13. "Mobile Warfare," *Time*, May 26, 1997, pp. 52–54; "Motorola Goes for the Hard Cell," *Business Week*, September 23, 1996, p. 39; "Why Motorola Has Nonworking Numbers," *Business Week*, July 22, 1996, p. 39; "Cell-Phone Service May Be Getting Cheaper," *The Wall Street Journal*, January 11, 1996, p. B1ff.; Alan Reynolds, "A Kind Word for 'Cream Skimming,'" *Harvard Business Review*, November–December 1974, pp. 113–20.

14. "AZT Price Cut for Third World Mothers-to-Be," The Wall Street Journal, March 5, 1998, p. B1ff.; "Breakthrough in Birth Control May Elude Poor," *The Wall Street Journal*, March 4, 1991, p. B1ff; "Burroughs Wellcome Reaps Profits, Outrage from Its AIDS Drug," *The Wall Street Journal*, September 15, 1989, p. A1ff.; Richard A. Spinello, "Ethics, Pricing and the Pharmaceutical Industry," *Journal of Business Ethics*, August 1992, pp. 617–26; Dhruv Grewal and Larry D. Compeau, "Comparative Price Advertising: Informative or Deceptive?" *Journal of Public Policy & Marketing*, Spring 1992, pp. 52–62.

15. For more on Palm, see Chapter 10, footnote #1. See also "A Best Seller Gets Better," *Newsweek*, March 16, 1998, p. 79; "Apple Drops Newton, an Idea Ahead of Its Time," *The Wall Street Journal*, March 2, 1998, p. B1ff.; "A Rocket in Its Pocket," *Business Week*, September 9, 1996, pp. 111–14.

16. "Discounts Follow Dip in Business Travel," *USA Today*, June 21, 2001, p. 1Bff.; "Sailing on Sale: Travelers Ride a Wave of Discounts on Cruise Ships," *The Wall Street Journal*, July 17, 2000, p. B1ff.; "Compet-

ing Online, Drugstore Chains Virtually Undersell Themselves," *The Wall Street Journal*, January 10, 2000, p. B1ff.; "Prescription: Cash Only, Some Doctors Offer Discounts," *USA Today*, December 22, 1999, p. 1Bff.; "Printer Wars: Toner Discount Incites Rivals," *The Wall Street Journal*, April 10, 1998, p. B1ff.; "Snaring Cheap Fares on the Internet," *The Wall Street Journal*, October 10, 1997, p. B10; "Ask and It Shall Be Discounted," *Business Week*, October 6, 1997, pp. 116–18; "The Latest Weapon in the Price Wars," *Fortune*, July 7, 1997, p. 200; "Owens Corning: Back from the Dead," *Fortune*, May 26, 1997, pp. 118–26; "Travelers Take Internet Route for Discounts," *USA Today*, January 13, 1997, p. 3B; Douglas D. Davis and Charles A. Holt, "List Prices and Discounts: The Interrelationship Between Consumer Shopping Patterns and Profitable Marketing Strategies," *Psychology & Marketing*, July 1996, pp. 341–63; David W. Arnesen, C. P. Fleenor, and Rex S. Toh, "The Ethical Dimensions of Airline Frequent Flier Programs," *Business Horizons*, January–February 1997, pp. 47–56; K.J. Blois, "Discounts in Business Marketing Management," *Industrial Marketing Management*, April 1994, pp. 93–100; James B. Wilcox et al., "Price Quantity Discounts: Some Implications for Buyers and Sellers," *Journal of Marketing*, July 1987, pp. 60–70; Mark T. Spriggs and John R. Nevin, "The Legal Status of Trade and Functional Price Discounts," *Journal of Public Policy & Marketing*, Spring 1994, pp. 61–75; Judith Waldrop, "The Seasons of Business," *American Demographics*, May 1992, pp. 40–45; "Cash Discounts," *Electrical Wholesaling*, May 1989, pp. 90–96.

**17.** For more on P&G's everyday low pricing, see "P&G, Others Try New Uses for Coupon-Heavy Media," *Advertising Age*, September 22, 1997, p. 20; "Move to Drop Coupons Puts Procter & Gamble in Sticky PR Situation," *The Wall Street Journal*, April 17, 1997, p. A1ff.; "Zeroing In on Zero Coupons," *Brandweek*, June 3, 1996, pp. 30–36; "Company Makes Big Cuts to Stay Fit," *USA Today*, July 16, 1993, p. 1Bff.; "P&G Plays Pied Piper on Pricing," *Advertising Age*, March 9, 1992, p. 6; Stephen J. Hoch, Xavier Dreze, and Mary E. Purk, "EDLP, Hi-Lo, and Margin Arithmetic," *Journal of Marketing*, October 1994, pp. 16–27; George S. Bobinski, Dena Cox, and Anthony Cox, "Retail 'Sale' Advertising, Perceived Retailer Credibility, and Price Rationale," *Journal of Retailing*, Fall 1996, pp. 291–306; Francis J. Mulhern and Daniel T. Padgett, "The Relationship Between Retail Price Promotions and Regular Price Purchases," *Journal of Marketing*, October 1995, pp. 83–90.

**18.** For more on coupons on the Web, see "Penny-Pinchers' Paradise," *Business Week E.Biz*, January 22, 2001, p. EB12; "E-Tailers Missing the Mark with Flood of Web Coupons," *Advertising Age*, September 25, 2000, p. 104. For more on rebates on the Web, see "Free-with-Rebate Costs Web Buyers Some Big Bucks," *The Wall Street Journal*, May 18, 2001, p. B1ff.; "One Web Retailer's Watchword: 'Free after Rebate,'" *The Wall Street Journal*, March 5, 2001, p. B1ff. For more on rebates on green cars, see "How to Get Green Cars on the Road," *Business Week*, November 20, 2000, p. 89; "If You Paid Half Price for That New SUV, You Must Be in Arizona," *The Wall Street Journal*, October 26, 2000, p. A1ff. See also William D. Diamond, "Just What Is a 'Dollar's Worth'? Consumer Reactions to Price Discounts vs. Extra Product Promotions," *Journal of Retailing*, Fall 1992, pp. 254–70; Kenneth A. Hunt and Susan M. Keaveney, "A Process Model of the Effects of Price Promotions on Brand Image," *Psychology & Marketing*, November/December 1994, pp. 511–32; "Coupon Scams Are Clipping Companies," *Business Week*, June 15, 1992, pp. 110–11; "Rebates' Secret Appeal to Manufacturers: Few Consumers Actually Redeem Them," *The Wall Street Journal*, February 10, 1998, p. B1ff.; Peter K. Tat, "Rebate Usage: A Motivational Perspective," *Psychology & Marketing*, January/February 1994, pp. 15–26; Abdul Ali, Marvin A. Jolson, and Rene Y. Darmon, "A Model for Optimizing the Refund Value in Rebate Promotions," *Journal of Business Research*, March 1994, pp. 239–46.

## Chapter 17

**1.** For more on Wal-Mart International, see "Wal*Mart International, the Division that Defines the Future," *DSN Retailing Today* (Special Issue), June 2001; "Wal-Mart Gets Aggressive about Brazil," *The Wall Street Journal*, May 25, 2001, p. A8ff.; "Wal-Mart to Add Japan to Global Lineup," *DSN Retailing Today*, January 22, 2001, p. 1ff.; "Wal-Mart de Mexico to Grow Stores by 10%," *DSN Retailing Today*, March 19, 2001, p. 3ff.; "Wal-Mart Fumes at Argentine Legislation," *The Wall Street Journal*, November 28, 2000, p. A23; "Stores Told to Lift Prices in Germany," *The Wall Street Journal*, September 11, 2000, p. A27ff.; "Wal-Mart Girds for Major German Expansion," *The Wall Street Journal*, July 20, 2000, p. A21ff.; "Who's Afraid of Wal-Mart," *Fortune*, June 26, 2000, pp. 186–96; "With ASDA in Tow, Wal-Mart Shakes Up Supermarket World," *Ad Age International*, February 2000, p. 4; "Wal-Mart's Not-So-Secret British Weapon," *Business Week*, January 24, 2000, p. 132; "As Wal-Mart Invades Europe, Rivals Rush to Match Its Formula," *The Wall Street Journal*, October 6, 1999, p. A1ff.; "For French Retailers, a Weapon against Wal-Mart," *The Wall Street Journal*, September 27, 1999, p. B1ff.; "En Garde, Wal-Mart," *Business Week*, September 13, 1999, pp. 54–55; "French Retailers Create New Wal-Mart Rival," *The Wall Street Journal*, August 31, 1999, p. A14; "Wal-Mart Rocks European Retailing as It Rolls into United Kingdom," *Discount Store News*, July 12, 1999, p. 1ff.; "Watch Out: Here Comes Wal-Mart," *Business Week*, June 28, 1999, pp. 48–49; "Wal-Mart Goes Shopping in Europe," *Fortune*, June 7, 1999, pp. 105–12; "Wal-Mart Ends Speculation with Euro Entry, Acquires German Chain," *Discount Store News*, January 5, 1998, p. 1ff.; "The Wal-Mart Way Sometimes Gets Lost in Translation Overseas," *The Wall Street Journal*, October 8, 1997, p. A1ff.; "Wal-Mart Spoken Here," *Business Week*, June 23, 1997, pp. 138–44; "Wal-Mart International Reshapes the World Retailing Order," *Discount Store News*, January 20, 1997, pp. 21–28. For more on Wal-Mart's Neighborhood Markets, see "Neighborhood Market Redefines Convenience," *DSN Retailing Today*, February 5, 2001, p. 5ff.; "Store Distinctions Blur at Wal-Mart," *Discount Store News*, February 7, 2000, p. 6ff; "Wal-Mart Upgrades Neighborhood Market," *Discount Store News*, November 22, 1999, p. 1ff.; "Wal-Mart's 'Small-Marts' May Make It Biggest Grocer," *The Wall Street Journal*, June 21, 1999, p. B4; "Wal-Mart Goes Express with 'Market' Concept," *Discount Store News*, February 22, 1999, p. 1ff.; "Look Out, Supermarkets—Wal-Mart Is Hungry," *Business Week*, September 14, 1998, pp. 98–100. For more on Wal-Mart on the Web, see "Amazon + Wal-Mart = Win/Win," *Business Week*, March 19, 2001, p. 42; "Walmart.com Purchases Garden.com Content Assets," *DSN Retailing Today*, February 5, 2001, p. 8; "Will Walmart.com Get It Right This Time?" *Business Week*, November 6, 2000, pp. 104–12; "Wal-Mart Launches Web Site a Third Time, This Time Emphasizing Speed and Ease," *The Wall Street Journal*, October 31, 2000, p. B12; "Preparing for Net-Speed, Walmart.com Names CEO," *Discount Store News*, March 20, 2000, p. 1ff.; "A Matchmaker for 'Bricks' and 'Clicks,'" *The Wall Street Journal*, March 13, 2000, p. B1ff.; "Overhauling Its Web Site, Wal-Mart Will Push Toys and Electronics," *The Wall Street Journal*, October 1, 1999, p. B1ff.; "Wal-Mart's Goal: To Reign over Web," *Advertising Age*, July 5, 1999, p. 1ff.; "When Wal-Mart Flexes Its Cybermuscles . . . ," *Business Week*, July 26, 1999, pp. 82–85; "As Web Retailing Surges, Where's Wal-Mart?" *The Wall Street Journal*, May 17, 1999, p. B1ff. For more on Wal-Mart in the U.S., see "Kmart, Wal-Mart Face Off in Price-Cutting Fight," *USA Today*, *USA Today*, June 8, 2001, p. 1B; "How Wal-Mart Transfers Power," *The Wall Street Journal*, March 27, 2001, p. B1ff.; "After Legendary Sprint to the Top, Wal-Mart Finally Hits Speed Bump," *Investor's Business Daily*, March 14, 2001, p. A1; "Super Stores: Land for Plenty," *Raleigh News & Observer*, March 3, 2001, p. 1Dff.; "Wal-Mart Wows with Growth Plan," *DSN Retailing Today*, October 23, 2000, p. 3ff.; "Big Three Redirect Efforts, Let Spoils Go to Regionals, Smaller-Format Chains," *DSN Retailing Today*, August 7, 2000, pp. 31–32; "Wal-Mart 'Imagines' Even Greater Growth," *DSN Retailing Today*, June 19, 2000, p. 1ff.; "Sam Would Be Proud," *Fortune*, April 17, 2000, pp. 130–44; "Wal-Mart Wins Reversal in Trademark Lawsuit," *The Wall Street Journal*, March 23, 2000, p. A3ff.; "Bankers Assail Mint for Deal with Wal-Mart," *The Wall Street Journal*, February 9, 2000, p. B1ff.; "Someday, Lee, This May All Be Yours," *Business Week*, November 15, 1999, pp. 84–92; *2000 Annual Report*, Wal-Mart; "Wal*Mart, Retailer of the Century," *Discount Store*

*News* (Special Issue), October 1999; "Wal-Mart Sets Computer Doctor Centers," *The Wall Street Journal*, September 20, 1999, p. A3; "Power Retailer: Wal-Mart," *Discount Store News*, June 7, 1999, pp. 81–147; "Logistics Whiz Rises at Wal-Mart," *The Wall Street Journal*, March 11, 1999, p. B1ff.; "An Unstoppable Marketing Force," *USA Today*, November 6, 1998, p. 1Bff.; "Wal-Mart's Garth-Quake May Spur Sales," *The Wall Street Journal*, November 2, 1998, p. B1ff. See also Norman W. Hawker, "Wal-Mart and the Divergence of State and Federal Predatory Pricing Law," *Journal of Public Policy & Marketing*, Spring 1996, pp. 141–47. For more on Kmart Bluelight, see "Battle-Tested Rules of Online Retail," *Ecompany*, April 2001; "No Bluelight Special as Kmart Is Forced into Free ISP Field," *Investor's Business Daily*, December 5, 2000, p. A6; "Going for Gold at BlueLight," *Business Week E.Biz*, November 20, 2000, pp. EB43–EB46; "Attention Kmart Bashers," *Fortune*, November 13, 2000, pp. 213–22; "BlueLight, Green Light," *Brandweek*, October 2, 2000, pp. 21–22; "Kmart Gives Green Light to Bluelight Business Model," *DSN Retailing Today*, July 24, 2000, p. 18ff.; "BlueLight.com Aims to Coax Kmart Shoppers Online," *The Wall Street Journal*, June 19, 2000, p. B4; "It's All Net," *Brandweek*, May 1, 2000, pp. IQ18–IQ22. For more on Kmart, see "CEO Rings Up Plan to Restore Kmart," *USA Today*, June 27, 2001, p. 3B; "Turning Up the Intensity on a Storied Turnaround," *DSN Retailing Today*, May 21, 2001, pp. 17–18; "Super K Showcases the Future," *DSN Retailing Today*, May 21, 2001, p. 1ff.; "Kmart's Bright Idea," *Business Week*, April 19, 2001, pp. 50–52; "Kmart Turns to Blue Light to Boost Image," *DSN Retailing Today*, April 16, 2001, p. 1ff.; "Code Blue," *Advertising Age*, April 9, 2001, p. 1ff.; "Kmart: On the Threshold of a New Era," *DSN Retailing Today*, March 5, 2001, pp. 33–68; "Kmart Targets Target as It Taps TBWA for Ads," *Advertising Age*, October 2, 2000, p. 20; "A Kmart Special: Better Service," *Business Week*, September 4, 2000, pp. 80–84; "Kmart's New CEO Outlines Plans for Fast Changes," *The Wall Street Journal*, July 27, 2000, p. B4; "Attention, Kmart Investors: Retailer Is Likely to Be Second Fiddle Awhile," *Investor's Business Daily*, May 2, 2000, p. 1; "Ms. Stewart's Advice for How to Improve Kmart: Ask Martha," *The Wall Street Journal*, May 1, 2000, p. A1ff.; "Power Retailer: Kmart," *Discount Store News*, March 6, 2000, pp. 49–81; "Kmart Food Supply Deal Whets Retailer's Appetite," *Discount Store News*, August 9, 1999, p. 1ff.; "Power Retailer: Kmart," *Discount Store News*, March 22, 1999, pp. 21–71.

**2.** Marvin A. Jolson, "A Diagrammatic Model for Merchandising Calculations," *Journal of Retailing*, Summer 1975, pp. 3–9; C. Davis Fogg and Kent H. Kohnken, "Price-Cost Planning," *Journal of Marketing*, April 1978, pp. 97–106.

**3.** "The Little Extras That Count (Up)," *The Wall Street Journal*, July 12, 2001, p. B1ff.; "CEO Rings Up Plan to Restore Kmart," *USA Today*, June 27, 2001, p. 3B; "Battle-Tested Rules of Online Retail," *Ecompany*, April 2001; "The Return of Pricing Power," *Business Week*, May 8, 2000, pp. 50–51; "The Power of Smart Pricing," *Business Week*, April 10, 2000, pp. 160–64. See also Mary L. Hatten, "Don't Get Caught with Your Prices Down: Pricing in Inflationary Times," *Business Horizons*, March 1982, pp. 23–28; Douglas G. Brooks, "Cost Oriented Pricing: A Realistic Solution to a Complicated Problem," *Journal of Marketing*, April 1975, pp. 72–74; Steven M.Shugan, "Retail Product-Line Pricing Strategy When Costs and Products Change," *Journal of Retailing*, Spring 2001, Vol. 77, 1, p. 17.

**4.** William W. Alberts, "The Experience Curve Doctrine Reconsidered," *Journal of Marketing*, July, 1989, pp. 36–49; G. Dean Kortge et al., "Linking Experience, Product Life Cycle, and Learning Curves: Calculating the Perceived Value Price Range," *Industrial Marketing Management*, July 1994, pp. 221–28.

**5.** G. Dean Kortge, "Inverted Breakeven Analysis for Profitable Marketing Decisions," *Industrial Marketing Management*, October 1984, pp. 219–24; Thomas L. Powers, "Breakeven Analysis with Semifixed Costs," *Industrial Marketing Management*, February 1987, pp. 35–42.

**6.** Available from World Wide Web: <http://www.nwfusion.com/news>; Scarlet Pruitt, "Buy.com Launches Price War Against Amazon," Nework-WorldFusion, June 25, 2002.

**7.** Florian Zettelmeyer, Fiona M. Scott Morton, and Jorge Silva Risso, "Cowboys or Cowards: Why are Internet Car Prices Lower?" Marketing Working Paper 01-1, Haas School, UC Berkeley.

**8.** Ramesh Venkat and Vanitha Thurairajah, "A Study of Internet Pricing Strategies for Homogeneous Products," Marketing Working Paper, Sobey School of Business, Saint Mary's University, 2002.

**9.** Erik Brynjolfsson and Michael D. Smith, "Frictionless Commerce? A Comparison of Internet and Conventional Retailers," *Management Science*, vol. 46(4), April 2000, p. 563-585.

**10.** Hernan Riquelme, "An Empirical Review of Price Behaviour on the Internet," *Electronic Markets*, vol. 11(4), 2001, p. 263-272.

**11.** James V. Koch, "Are Internet Prices Lower? Not Always!" *Business Horizons*, January/February 2003, p. 47-52.

**12.** Ramesh Venkat and Vanitha Thurairajah, "A Study of Internet Pricing Strategies for Homogeneous Products," Marketing Working Paper, Sobey School of Business, Saint Mary's University, 2002.

**13.** Erik Brynjolfsson and Michael D. Smith, "Frictionless Commerce? A Comparison of Internet and Conventional Retailers," *Management Science*, vol. 46(4), April 2000, p. 563-585.

**14.** Ramesh Venkat and Vanitha Thurairajah, "A Study of Internet Pricing Strategies for Homogeneous Products," Marketing Working Paper, Sobey School of Business, Saint Mary's University, 2002.

**15.** Ganesh Iyer and Amit Pazgel, "Internet Shopping Agents: Virtual Co-Location and Competition," *Marketing Science*, Winter issue, vol. 22(1), p. 85-106.

**16.** "Latest Supermarket Special—Gasoline," *The Wall Street Journal*, April 30, 2001, p. B1ff.; "Who Really Needs a Pentium 4?" *Fortune*, January 8, 2001, pp. 217–18; "Extra $75 a Month Helps the Medicine Go Down," *USA Today*, October 30, 2000, p. 1Bff.; "Marriott International: A Hotel That Clicks with Guests," *Business Week E.Biz*, September 18, 2000, p. EB58; "The Paradox of Value," *Brandweek*, June 5, 2000, pp. 40–56; Watts Wacker and Jim Taylor, *The Visionary's Handbook: Nine Paradoxes That Will Shape the Future of Your Business* (HarperCollins, 2000); "Selling Pears at $5 a Pound," *USA Today*, December 3, 1999, p. 1Bff.; "How Low Should They Go?" *The Wall Street Journal*, November 22, 1999, p. R20ff.; "Your Room Costs $250 . . . No! $200 . . . No . . . ," *The Wall Street Journal*, May 5, 1999, p. B1ff. See also Dhruv Grewal, Kent B. Monroe, and R. Krishnan, "The Effects of Price-Comparison Advertising on Buyers' Perceptions of Acquisition Value, Transaction Value, and Behavioral Intentions," *Journal of Marketing*, April 1998, pp. 46–59; John T. Gourville, "Pennies-a-Day: The Effect of Temporal Reframing on Transaction Evaluation," *Journal of Consumer Research*, March 1998, pp. 395–408; Joel E. Urbany, Rosemary Kalapurakal, and Peter R. Dickson, "Price Search in the Retail Grocery Market," *Journal of Marketing*, April 1996, pp. 91–104; Venkatesh Shankar and Lakshman Krishnamurthi, "Relating Price Sensitivity to Retailer Promotional Variables and Pricing Policy: An Empirical Analysis," *Journal of Retailing*, Fall 1996, pp. 249–72; Chakravarthi Narasimhan, Scott A. Neslin, and Subrata K. Sen, "Promotional Elasticities and Category Characteristics," *Journal of Marketing*, April 1996, pp. 17–30; K. Sivakumar and S. P. Raj, "Quality Tier Competition: How Price Change Influences Brand Choice and Category Choice," *Journal of Marketing*, July 1997, pp. 71–84.

**17.** Thomas T. Nagle, *The Strategy and Tactics of Pricing* (Englewood Cliffs, NJ: Prentice-Hall, 2001), pp. 249–55; Hooman Estelami, "The Impact of Research Design on Consumer Price Recall Accuracy: An Integrative Review," *Journal of the Academy of Marketing Science*, Winter 2001, pp. 36–50; Richard A. Briesch, Lakshman Krishnamurthi, Tridib Mazumdar, and S. P. Raj, "A Comparative Analysis of Reference Price Models," *Journal of Consumer Research*, September 1997, pp. 202–14;

Tracy A. Suter and Scot Burton, "Believability and Consumer Perceptions of Implausible Reference Prices in Retail Advertisements," *Psychology & Marketing*, January 1996, pp. 37–54; K. N. Rajendran and Gerard J. Tellis, "Contextual and Temporal Components of Reference Price," *Journal of Marketing*, January 1994, pp. 22–34; Abhijit Biswas, Elizabeth J. Wilson, and Jane W. Licata, "Reference Pricing Studies in Marketing: A Synthesis of Research Results," *Journal of Business Research*, July 1993, pp. 239–56; Daniel S. Putler, "Incorporating Reference Price Effects into a Theory of Consumer Choice," *Marketing Science*, Summer 1992, pp. 287–309; Kristina D. Frankenberger and Ruiming Liu, "Does Consumer Knowledge Affect Consumer Responses to Advertised Reference Price Claims?" *Psychology & Marketing*, May/June 1994, pp. 235–52; Tridib Mazumdar and Kent B. Monroe, "Effects of Inter-store and In-store Price Comparison on Price Recall Accuracy and Confidence," *Journal of Retailing*, Spring 1992, pp. 66–89.

**18.** "Fram Pays Up Now," *Brandweek*, July 20, 1998, pp. 16–17; "New Long-Life Bulbs May Lose Brilliance in a Crowded Market," *The Wall Street Journal*, June 2, 1992, p. B4; Benson P. Shapiro and Barbara P. Jackson, "Industrial Pricing to Meet Customer Needs," *Harvard Business Review*, November–December 1978, pp. 119–27; "The Race to the $10 Light Bulb," *Business Week*, May 19, 1980, p. 124; see also Michael H. Morris and Donald A. Fuller, "Pricing an Industrial Service," *Industrial Marketing Management*, May 1989, pp. 139–46.

**19.** For an example applied to a high-price item, see "Sale of Mink Coats Strays a Fur Piece from the Expected," *The Wall Street Journal*, March 21, 1980, p. 30.

**20.** Noel M. Noel and Nessim Hanna, "Benchmarking Consumer Perceptions of Product Quality With Price: An Exploration," *Psychology & Marketing*, September 1996, pp. 591–604; Niraj Dawar and Philip Parker, "Marketing Universals: Consumers' Use of Brand Name, Price, Physical Appearance, and Retailer Reputation As Signals of Product Quality," *Journal of Marketing*, April 1994, pp. 81–95; Tung-Zong Chang and Albert R. Wildt, "Impact of Product Information on the Use of Price As a Quality Cue," *Psychology & Marketing*, January 1996, pp. 55–75; B. P. Shapiro, "The Psychology of Pricing," *Harvard Business Review*, July–August 1968, pp. 14–24; Lutz Hildebrandt, "The Analysis of Price Competition Between Corporate Brands," *International Journal of Research in Marketing*, June 2001, p. 139.

**21.** Paul Hunt, *Marketing Magazine*, "The Price is Right," October 21, 2002.

**22.** "Keeping the Cachet," *The Wall Street Journal*, April 23, 2001, p. R28; "Luxury Sites Get Scrappy," *The Wall Street Journal*, December 4, 2000, p. B1ff.; "Online Luxury Has Limits," *Business Week E.Biz*, September 18, 2000, p. EB24; "Special Report: Luxury Marketing," *Advertising Age*, August 14, 2000, pp. S1–14; "The Galloping Gourmet Chocolate," *Brandweek*, July 31, 2000, pp. 32–37. See also Rebecca Piirto Heath, "Life on Easy Street," *American Demographics*, April 1997, pp. 33–38; K. M. Monroe and S. Petroshius, "Buyers' Subjective Perceptions of Price: An Update of the Evidence," in *Perspectives in Consumer Behavior*, ed. T. Robertson and H. Kassarjian (Glenview, IL: Scott Foresman, 1981), pp. 43–55; G. Dean Kortge and Patrick A. Okonkwo, "Perceived Value Approach to Pricing," *Industrial Marketing Management*, May 1993, pp. 133–40; Valarie A. Zeithaml, "Consumer Perceptions of Price, Quality, And Value: A Means-End Model and Synthesis of Evidence," *Journal of Marketing*, July 1988, pp. 2–22.

**23.** "Combatting a Fading Signal," *Brandweek*, November 27, 2000, pp. 37–42; "Why 'Bundling' Its Consumer Services Hasn't Benefited AT&T," *The Wall Street Journal*, October 24, 2000, p. B1ff.; "Soda Marketers Pour Out Fast-Feeding Frenzy of Ads," *Advertising Age*, September 11, 2000, p. 14; "PeoplePC Taps 9-Year-Old to Front $40 Mil Campaign," *Advertising Age*, May 8, 2000, p. 1ff.; Andrea Ovans, "Make a Bundle Bundling," *Harvard Business Review*, November–December 1997, pp. 18–20; Preyas S. Desai and Kannan Srinivasan, "Aggregate Versus Product-Specific Pricing: Implications for Franchise and Traditional Channels," *Journal of Retailing*, Winter 1996, pp. 357–82; Manjit S. Yadav and Kent B. Monroe, "How Buyers Perceive Savings in a Bundle Price: An Examination of a Bundle's Transaction Value," *Journal of Marketing Research*, August 1993, pp. 350–58; Dorothy Paun, "When to Bundle or Unbundle Products," *Industrial Marketing Management*, February 1993, pp. 29–34.

**24.** Peter E. Connor and Robert K. Hopkins, "Cost Plus What? The Importance of Accurate Profit Calculations in Cost-Plus Agreements," *International Journal of Purchasing & Materials Management*, Spring 1997, pp. 35–40; Daniel T. Ostas, "Ethics of Contract Pricing," *Journal of Business Ethics*, February 1992, pp. 137–46; J. Steve Davis, "Ethical Problems in Competitive Bidding: The Paradyne Case," *Business and Professional Ethics Journal*, 7, no. 2 (1988), pp. 3–26; David T. Levy, "Guaranteed Pricing in Industrial Purchases: Making Use of Markets in Contractual Relations," *Industrial Marketing Management*, October 1994, pp. 307–14; Akintola Akintoye and Martin Skitmore, "Pricing Approaches in the Construction Industry," *Industrial Marketing Management*, November 1992, pp. 311–18.

## Chapter 18

**1.** Adapted from: Pearl Davies, "Love It or Leave It," *Marketing Magazine*, October 9, 2000.

**2.** Arial Tracey, "Bras with Attitude," *Marketing Magazine*, February 3, 2003.

**3.** "Good Product. Sound Plans. No Sure Thing," *The New York Times*, January 18, 1998, Sect. 3, p. 1ff.; John E. Smallwood, "The Product Life Cycle: A Key to Strategic Marketing Planning," *MSU Business Topics*, Winter 1973, pp. 29–35; Richard F. Savach and Laurence A. Thompson, "Resource Allocation within the Product Life Cycle," *MSU Business Topics*, Autumn 1978, pp. 35–44; Peter F. Kaminski and David R. Rink, "PLC: The Missing Link between Physical Distribution and Marketing Planning," *International Journal of Physical Distribution and Materials Management* 14, no. 6 (1984), pp. 77–92.

**4.** 1996 Canadian Markets published by *The Financial Post*. Estimated population and retail spending. Reproduced in Media Digest 1997–98. Prepared by the Canadian Media Directors' Council and published by *Marketing Magazine*.

**5.** See most basic statistics textbooks under time series analysis.

**6.** Gloria Barczak, "Analysis for Marketing Planning," *Journal of Product Innovation Management*, September 1997, pp. 424–25; William A. Sahlman, "How to Write a Great Business Plan," *Harvard Business Review*, July–August 1997, pp. 98–108; Paul Boughton, "The 1-Day Marketing Plan: Organizing and Completing the Plan That Works," *Journal of the Academy of Marketing Science*, Summer 1996, pp. 275–76; William Sandy, "Avoid the Breakdowns Between Planning and Implementation," *The Journal of Business Strategy*, September/October 1991, pp. 30–33; Michael MacInnis and Louise A. Heslop, "Market Planning in a High-Tech Environment," *Industrial Marketing Management*, May 1990, pp. 107–16; David Strutton, "Marketing Strategies: New Approaches, New Techniques," *Journal of the Academy of Marketing Science*, Summer 1997, pp. 261–62; Rita G. McGrath and Ian C. MacMillan, "Discovery-Driven Planning," *Harvard Business Review*, July 1995–August 1995, pp. 44–54; Jeffrey Elton and Justin Roe, "Bringing Discipline to Project Management," *Harvard Business Review*, March–April 1998, pp. 153–58; Tridib Mazumdar, K Sivakumar, and David Wilemon, "Launching New Products With Cannibalization Potential: An Optimal Timing Framework," *Journal of Marketing Theory & Practice*, Fall 1996, pp. 83–93; Andrew Campbell and Marcus Alexander, "What's Wrong With Strategy?" *Harvard Business Review*, November–December 1997, pp. 42–51; "Marketing Software Review: Project Management Made Easy," *Business Marketing*, February 1989, pp. 20–27.

**7.** Sarah Smith, *Marketing Magazine*, November 29, 1999.

**8.** For further discussion on evaluating and selecting alternative plans, see Francis Buttle, "The Marketing Strategy Worksheet—A Practical

Planning Tool," *Long Range Planning*, August 1985, pp. 80–88; Douglas A. Schellinck, "Effect of Time on a Marketing Strategy," *Industrial Marketing Management*, April 1983, pp. 83–88; George S. Day and Liam Fahey, "Valuing Market Strategies," *Journal of Marketing*, July 1988, pp. 45–57.

**9.** Sam C. Okoroafo, "Modes of Entering Foreign Markets," *Industrial Marketing Management* 20, no. 4 (1991), pp. 341–46; Mike Van Horn, "Market-Entry Approaches for the Pacific Rim," *The Journal of Business Strategy*, March/April 1990, pp. 14–19; Refik Culpan, "Export Behavior of Firms: Relevance of Firm Size," *Journal of Business Research*, May, 1989, pp. 207–18; Anthony C. Koh and Robert A. Robicheaux, "Variations in Export Performance Due to Differences in Export Marketing Strategy: Implications for Industrial Marketers," *Journal of Business Research*, November 1988, pp. 249–58; S. Tamer Cavusgil, Shaoming Zou, and G.M. Naidu, "Product and Promotion Adaptation in Export Ventures: An Empirical Investigation," *Journal of International Business Studies*, Third Quarter 1993, pp. 479–506; Camille P. Schuster and Charles D. Bodkin, "Market Segmentation Practices of Exporting Companies," *Industrial Marketing Management*, May 1987, pp. 95–102.

**10.** Constantine S. Katsikeas and Neil M. Morgan, "Firm-Level Export Performance Assessment: Review, Evaluation, and Development," *Journal of the Academy of Marketing Science*, Fall 2000, pp. 493–512; "For U.S. Marketers, the Russian Front Is No Bowl of 'Vishnyas,'" *Adweek's Marketing Week*, March 5, 1990; "Learning the Exporting Ropes," *Business Marketing*, May 1989, pp. 80–85; "'Papa-Mama' Stores in Japan Wield Power to Hold Back Imports," *The Wall Street Journal*, November 14, 1988, p. A1ff.; Jerry Haar and Marta Ortiz-Buonafina, "The Internationalization Process and Marketing Activities: The Case of Brazilian Export Firms," *Journal of Business Research*, February 1995, pp. 175–82; "U.S. Concerns Trying to Do Business in Japan Face Government, Market, Cultural Barriers," *The Wall Street Journal*, July 8, 1985, p. 16; Robert E. Morgan and Constantine S. Katsikeas, "Exporting Problems of Industrial Manufacturers," *Industrial Marketing Management*, March 1998, pp. 161–76.

**11.** Masaaki Kotabe, Arvind Sahay, and Preet S. Aulakh, "Emerging Role of Technology Licensing in the Development of Global Product Strategy: Conceptual Framework and Research Propositions," *Journal of Marketing*, January 1996, pp. 73–88; John A. Quelch, "How to Build a Product Licensing Program," *Harvard Business Review*, May–June 1985, p. 186ff.

**12.** "The Steel Deal That Could Boost Big Blue in Brazil," *Business Week*, May 19, 1986, p. 66. See also Robert Porter Lynch, "Building Alliances to Penetrate European Markets," *The Journal of Business Strategy*, March/April 1990, pp. 4–9; D. Robert Webster, "International Joint Ventures with Pacific Rim Partners," *Business Horizons*, March/April 1989, pp. 65–71; Kenichi Ohmae, "The Global Logic of Strategic Alliances," *Harvard Business Review*, March/April 1989, pp. 143–54.

**13.** "Top U.S. Companies Move into Russia," *Fortune*, July 31, 1989, pp. 165–71; "When U.S. Joint Ventures with Japan Go Sour," *Business Week*, July 24, 1989, pp. 30–31; Ashish Nanda and Peter J. Williamson, "Use Joint Ventures to Ease the Pain of Restructuring," *Harvard Business Review*, November 1995–December 1995, pp. 119–28; Paul Lawrence and Charalambos Vlachoutsicos, "Joint Ventures in Russia: Put the Locals in Charge," *Harvard Business Review*, January–February 1993, pp. 44–55; F. Kingston Berlew, "The Joint Venture—A Way into Foreign Markets," *Harvard Business Review*, July–August 1984, pp. 48–55.

**14.** "Place vs. Product: It's Tough to Choose a Management Model," *The Wall Street Journal*, June 27, 2001, p. A1ff.; "Distractions Make Global Manager a Difficult Role," *The Wall Street Journal*, November 21, 2000, p. B1ff.; "How to Project Power Around the World," *The Wall Street Journal*, November 13, 2000, p. A23ff.; "New CEO Preaches Rebellion for P&G's Cult," *The Wall Street Journal*, December 11, 1998, p. B1ff.; "Young Managers Learn Global Skills," *The Wall Street Journal*, March 31, 1992, p. B1; "As Costs of Overseas Assignments Climb, Firms Select Expatriates More Carefully," *The Wall Street Journal*, January 9, 1992, p. B1ff.; Regina F. Maruca, "The Right Way to Go Global: An Interview With Whirlpool CEO David Whitwam," *Harvard Business Review*, March 1994–April 1994, pp. 134–45; Tevfik Dalgic, "Multinational Companies in United States International Trade: A Statistical and Analytical Sourcebook," *Journal of the Academy of Marketing Science*, Spring 1997, pp. 172–73; Keith Cerny, "Making Local Knowledge Global," *Harvard Business Review*, May–June 1996, pp. 22–26; Chi-fai Chan and Neil B. Holbert, "Whose Empire Is This, Anyway? Reflections on the Empire State of Multi-National Corporations," *Business Horizons*, July–August 1994, pp. 51–54; Syed H. Akhter and Yusuf A. Choudhry, "Forced Withdrawal from a Country Market: Managing Political Risk," *Business Horizons*, May–June 1993, pp. 47–54; M. Krishna Erramilli and C.P. Rao, "Service Firms' International Entry-Mode Choice: A Modified Transaction-Cost Analysis Approach," *Journal of Marketing*, July 1993, pp. 19–38.

## Chapter 19

**1.** Ann Walmsley, "Plane Crazy," *Report on Business Magazine*, December 1999, p. 62-71. See also World Wide Web: <http://www.westjet.com>.

**2.** For more on Weyerhaeuser as an example, see "How Fast Can This Baby Go?" *Business Week*, April 10, 2000, pp. 38–40; Garold Lantz, "Clockspeed Winning Industry Control in the Age of Temporary Advantage," *Journal of the Academy of Marketing Science*, Summer 2000, pp. 443–5; Peter R. Dickson, "Dynamic Strategic Thinking," *Journal of the Academy of Marketing Science*, Summer 2001, p. 216–38; "Weblining," *Business Week E.Biz*, April 3, 2000, pp. EB26–EB34; "How an Intranet Opened Up the Door to Profits," *Business Week E.Biz*, July 26, 1999, pp. EB32–EB38. For more on Pillsbury as an example, see "Pillsbury: Saving Dough with NetStat," *Business Week E.Biz*, September 18, 2000, p. EB94; "A Digital Doughboy," *Business Week E.Biz*, April 3, 2000, pp. EB78–EB86. For more on Utz as an example, see "Using the Net to Stay Crisp," *Business Week E.Biz*, April 16, 2001, pp. EB34–EB36. For more on Nestle as an example, see "Nestle: An Elephant Dances," *Business Week E.Biz*, December 11, 2000, pp. EB44–EB48. For more on Webcor as an example, see "Wired at Webcor," *Business Week E.Biz*, November 20, 2000, pp. EB58–EB62. For more on Kaiser as an example, see "Kaiser Takes the Cyber Cure," *Business Week E.Biz*, February 7, 2000, pp. EB80–EB86. For more on Office Depot as an example, see "Empire Builders: Office Depot," *Business Week E.Biz*, May 14, 2001, p. EB28; "Why Office Depot Loves the Net," *Business Week E.Biz*, September 27, 1999, pp. EB66–EB68. For more on Cemex as an example, see "Cemex Unit to Form E-Commerce Portal for Latin America," *The Wall Street Journal*, December 12, 2000, p. A23; "Going Digital? Think First," *Fortune*, November 13, 2000, pp. 190–98; "Cemex Loves Its 'Ants' but Wants More," *The Wall Street Journal*, October 2, 2000, p. A22. See also Kevin Rollins, "Using Information to Speed Execution," *Harvard Business Review*, March–April 1998, p.81; Clayton M. Christensen, "Making Strategy: Learning by Doing," *Harvard Business Review*, November–December 1997, pp. 141–56; Ram Charan, "How Networks Reshape Organizations—For Results," *Harvard Business Review*, September/October 1991, pp. 104–15; William J. Bruns, Jr., and W. Warren McFarlan, "Information Technology Puts Power in Control Systems," *Harvard Business Review*, September–October, 1987, pp. 89–94.

**3.** Available from World Wide Web: <http://www.hertz.com>; *2000 Annual Report*, Hertz; "How Market Leaders Keep Their Edge," *Fortune*, February 6, 1995, pp. 88–98.

**4.** Jim Carroll, "Jumping On the Corporate Blog Wagon," *Marketing Magazine*, September 30, 2002.

**5.** Available from World Wide Web: <http://www.wired.com/news/culture/0.1284,52380,00.html>; Farhad Manjoo, "Flash—Blogging Goes Corporate," May 9, 2002.

**6.** Available from World Wide Web: <http://www.pillsbury.com>; Available from World Wide Web: <http://www.bettycrocker.com>; "Pillsbury's Telephones Ring with Peeves, Praise," *The Wall Street Journal*, April 20, 1994, p. B1ff.; "'Do Call Us': More Companies Install 1-800

Phone Lines," *The Wall Street Journal*, April 20, 1994, p. B1ff; "Your Pet Iguana Swallowed a Staple? Computerized Help Desk Will Try to Help," *The Wall Street Journal*, November 3, 1993, p. B1ff.

**7.** The restaurant case is adapted from Marie Gaudard, Roland Coates and Liz Freeman, "Accelerating Improvement," *Quality Progress*, October 1991, pp. 81–88. For more on quality management and control, see "Miller Brewing: Beer with a Good Head on Its Shoulders," *Business Week E.Biz*, September 18, 2000, p. EB64; "How to Bring Out Better Products Faster," *Fortune*, November 23, 1998, pp. 238B–T. See also Roland T. Rust, Anthony J. Zahorik, and Timothy L. Keiningham, "Return on Quality (ROQ): Making Service Quality Financially Accountable," *Journal of Marketing*, April 1995, pp. 58–70; "TQM: More than a Dying Fad?" *Fortune*, October 18, 1993, pp. 66–72; "Quality Control from Mars," *The Wall Street Journal*, January 27, 1992, p. A12; William B. Locander and Daniel J. Goebel, "The Quality Train Is Leaving and Marketers Are Nodding Off in the Club Car," *Journal of Marketing Theory & Practice*, Summer 1996, pp. 1–10; William C. LaFief, "Total Quality Marketing: The Key to Regaining Market Shares," *Journal of the Academy of Marketing Science*, Fall 1996, pp. 377–78; David W. Finn, Julie Baker, Greg W. Marshall, and Roy Anderson, "Total Quality Management and Internal Customers: Measuring Internal Service Quality," *Journal of Marketing Theory & Practice*, Summer 1996, pp. 36–51; Robert F. Hurley, Melissa T. Gropper, and Gianpaolo Roma, "The Role of TQM in Advertising: A Conceptualization and a Framework for Application," *Journal of Marketing Theory & Practice*, Summer 1996, pp. 11–23; Teresa A. Swartz, "Why TQM Fails and What to Do About It," *Journal of the Academy of Marketing Science*, Fall 1996, pp. 380–81; Iris Mohr-Jackson, "Managing a Total Quality Orientation: Factors Affecting Customer Satisfaction," *Industrial Marketing Management*, March 1998, pp. 109–25; Cengiz Haksever, "Total Quality Management in the Small Business Environment," *Business Horizons*, March–April 1996, pp. 33–40; Michael P. Bigwood, "Total Quality Management at Work: Development of an Effective Competitive Analysis Process," *Industrial Marketing Management*, September 1997, pp. 459–66.

**8.** Afsaneh Nahavandi, *The Art and Science of Leadership* (New Jersey: Prentice Hall, 2000).

**9.** For examples of empowerment, see "Whole Foods Vs. Wild Oats Markets: A Study in Culture, Vision, Execution," *Investor's Business Daily*, June 29, 2001, p. A1; "Glass Act: How a Window Maker Rebuilt Itself," *Fortune*, November 13, 2000, pp. 384BiV. See also Roland T. Rust, Anthony J. Zahorik, and Timothy L. Keiningham, *Return on Quality* (Chicago: Probus, 1994); Valarie A. Zeithaml, "Service Quality, Profitability, and the Economic Worth of Customers: What We Know and What We Need to Learn," *Journal of the Academy of Marketing Science*, Winter 2000, pp. 67–86; Warren S. Martin and Wendy K. Martin, "The Application of Benchmarking to Marketing," *Journal of Marketing Theory & Practice*, Summer 1996, pp. 52–59; J. J. Cronin and Steven A. Taylor, "SERVPERF Versus SERVQUAL: Reconciling Performance-Based and Perceptions-Minus-Expectations Measurement of Service Quality," *Journal of Marketing*, January 1994, pp. 125–31; Timothy C. Johnston and Molly A. Hewa, "Fixing Service Failures," *Industrial Marketing Management*, September 1997, pp. 467–73; Shirley Taylor, "Waiting for Service: The Relationship Between Delays and Evaluations of Service," *Journal of Marketing*, April 1994, pp. 56–69; Mary J. Bitner, Bernard H. Booms, and Lois A. Mohr, "Critical Service Encounters: The Employee's Viewpoint," *Journal of Marketing*, October 1994, pp. 95–106; G T. M. Hult, "Service Quality: New Directions in Theory and Practice," *Journal of the Academy of Marketing Science*, Summer 1997, pp. 264–65; Scott W. Kelley, Timothy Longfellow, and Jack Malehorn, "Organizational Determinants of Service Employees' Exercise of Routine, Creative, and Deviant Discretion," *Journal of Retailing*, Summer 1996, pp. 135–57; Pierre Filiatrault, Jean Harvey, and Jean-Charles Chebat, "Service Quality and Service Productivity Management Practices," *Industrial Marketing Management*, May 1996, pp. 243–55; Joseph H. Foegen, "Are Managers Losing Control?" *Business Horizons*, March–April 1998, pp. 2–5; Robert Simons, "Control in an Age of Empowerment," *Harvard Business Review*, March 1995–April 1995, pp. 80–88; "Finding, Training & Keeping the Best Service Workers," *Fortune*, October 3, 1994, pp. 110–22; Timothy L. Keiningham, Roland T. Rust, and M. Marshall Weems, "The Bottom Line on Quality," *Financial Executive*, September/October 1994, pp. 50–52.

**10.** *2000 Annual Report*, Ben & Jerry's; "Ben & Jerry's: Surviving the Big Squeeze," *Food Business*, May 6, 1991, pp. 10–12; "The Peace Pop Puzzle," *Inc.*, March 1990, p. 25. See also William C. Taylor, "Control in an Age of Chaos," *Harvard Business Review*, November–December 1994, pp. 64–90; Bernard J. Jaworski, Vlasis Stathakopoulos, and H. Shanker Krishnan, "Control Combinations in Marketing: Conceptual Framework and Empirical Evidence," *Journal of Marketing*, January 1993, pp. 57–69; Subhash Sharma and Dale D. Achabal, "STEMCOM: An Analytical Model for Marketing Control," *Journal of Marketing*, Spring 1982, pp. 104–13; Kenneth A. Merchant, "Progressing Toward a Theory of Marketing Control: A Comment," *Journal of Marketing*, July 1988, pp. 40–44.

**11.** Ed Weymes, "A Different Approach to Retail Sales Analysis," *Business Horizons*, March/April 1982, pp. 66–74; Robert H. Collins, Regan F. Carey, and Rebecca F. Mauritson, "Microcomputer Applications: Maps on a Micro—Applications in Sales and Marketing Management," *Journal of Personal Selling and Sales Management*, November 1987, p. 83ff.

**12.** Jill Corso McNabb, "Measurement on the Internet," Darden case UVA-M-0608, University of Virginia, 1999.

**13.** Available from World Wide Web: <http://www.wdvl.internet.com>; Charlie Morris, "How Log Files Work," Web Developer's Virtual Library, August 2, 1999.

**14.** Rodney Fuller and Johannes J. de Graafe, "Measuring User Motivation from Server Log Files," Conference Presentation for Designing for the Web: Empirical Studies, Microsoft Corporation, October 1996.

**15.** "The Numbers Game," *Business Week*, May 14, 2001, pp. 100–110; "Accounting Gets Radical," *Fortune*, April 16, 2001, pp. 184–94; "Kmart's Bright Idea," *Business Week*, April 9, 2001, pp. 50–52; "Manufacturing Masters Its ABCs," *Business Week*, August 7, 2000, p. 86J; Robin Cooper and W. B. Chew, "Control Tomorrow's Costs Through Today's Designs," *Harvard Business Review*, January–February 1996, pp. 88–97; Robin Cooper and Robert S. Kaplan, "Profit Priorities From Activity-Based Costing," *Harvard Business Review*, May/June 1991, pp. 130–37; Douglas M. Lambert and Jay U. Sterling, "What Types of Profitability Reports Do Marketing Managers Receive?" *Industrial Marketing Management*, November, 1987, pp. 295–304; Nigel F. Piercy, "The Marketing Budgeting Process: Marketing Management Implications," *Journal of Marketing*, October 1987, pp. 45–59; Michael J. Sandretto, "What Kind of Cost System Do You Need?" *Harvard Business Review*, January–February 1985, pp. 110–18; Patrick M. Dunne and Harry I. Wolk, "Marketing Cost Analysis: A Modularized Contribution Approach," *Journal of Marketing*, July 1977, pp. 83–94.

**16.** Technically, a distinction should be made between variable and direct costs, but we will use these terms interchangeably. Similarly, not all costs that are common to several products are fixed costs, and vice versa. But the important point here is to recognize that some costs are fairly easy to allocate, and other costs are not. See Stewart A. Washburn, "Establishing Strategy and Determining Costs in the Pricing Decision," *Business Marketing*, July 1985, pp. 64–78.

**17.** James T. Rothe, Michael G. Harvey, and Candice E. Jackson, "The Marketing Audit: Five Decades Later," *Journal of Marketing Theory & Practice*, Summer 1997, pp. 1–16; Douglas Brownlie, "The Conduct of Marketing Audits," *Industrial Marketing Management*, January 1996, pp. 11–22; Leonard L. Berry, Jeffrey S. Conant, and A. Parasuraman, "A Framework for Conducting a Services Marketing Audit," *Journal of the Academy of Marketing Science*, Summer 1991, pp. 255–68; John F. Grashof, "Conducting and Using a Marketing Audit," in *Readings in Basic Marketing*, ed. E. J. McCarthy, J. J. Grashof, and A. A. Brogowicz (Homewood, IL: Richard D. Irwin, 1984).

# Illustration Credits

## Chapter 1

**Exhibits:** *P.* 11, E1-3, Adapted from R.F. Vizza, T.E. Chambers, and E.J. Cook, *Adoption of the Marketing Concept—Fact or Fiction* (New York: Sales Executive Club, Inc., 1967), pp. 13–15. *P.* 19, E1-5, Adapted from discussions of an American Marketing Association Strategic Planning Committee.

**Photos/ads:** *P.* 5, (trick bike) Alan Bailey/Rubberball Productions/Getty Images; (tandem bike) C Squared Studios/PhotoDisc Green/Getty Images; (camping gear) C Squared Studios/PhotoDisc Green/Getty Images. *P.* 12 (left), Courtesy Burst.com; (right), Courtesy The Valvoline Company. *P.* 16, Courtesy of L.L.Bean, Inc. *P.* 18 (top), Courtesy of Obata Design and Emerson Electric Co.; (bottom) Courtesy CMG Communications.

## Chapter 2

**Exhibits:** *P.* 39, E2-9, Copernicus: The Marketing Investment Strategy Group, Inc., 450 Lexington Street, Auburndale, MA 02166.

**Photos/ads:** *P.* 25, © Brian Coats, All Rights Reserved. *P.* 29, Courtesy of Spin Master Toys. *P.* 34 (left and right), Courtesy of Toddler University, Inc. *P.* 37, Courtesy Timex Corporation.

## Chapter 3

**Exhibits:** *P.* 43, Excerpts were taken from the following article: Beverly Cramp, "Reinventing Cool," *Profit*, Volume 20, Issue #8, p. 41, December 2001; *Marketing Magazine*, October 27, 1997; www.jonessoda.com. *P.* 45, E3-1, Igor Ansoff, Corporate Strategy (New York: McGraw-Hill, 1965). *P.* 71, E3-14, Russell I. Haley, "Benefit Segmentation: A Decision-Oriented Research Tool," *Journal of Marketing*, July 1968, p. 33.

**Photos/ads:** *P.* 43, Courtesy of Jones Soda. *P.* 46, Ilja C. Hendel/The Image Works. *P.* 47 (top), Courtesy of General Mills; (bottom), CP/AP Photo/Keith Srakocic. *P.* 49 (left), S.C. Johnson & Son, Inc.; (right), Crème Savers. *P.* 50, Limited use granted courtesy of Pfizer Canada Inc., Pfizer Consumer Healthcare division. *P.* 51, Used with permission of Yahoo! *P.* 52, Courtesy of Audi of Norway; Agency: Bates Reklamebyra/Oslo. *P.* 54 (left), Courtesy Olympus America, Inc.; (middle), Courtesy of Vivitar Corporation: Potter, Katz, Postal and Ferguson: MGI Software Inc.; (right), Courtesy of Sony Electronics Inc. *P.* 62, Made available courtesy of iVillage, Inc., www.ivillage.com, © 1999 iVillage, Inc. All rights reserved. *P.* 65, Photographer: Steve Bonini. *P.* 69, Courtesy Nabisco Brands, Inc. *P.* 70 (left), Used with permission of Volvo Cars of Canada; (right), Courtesy Grey Worldwide/Thailand.

## Chapter 4

**Exhibits:** *P.* 86, MD4-1, Excerpted from Scott Gardiner, "In Praise of Saint Timmy," *Marketing Magazine*, August 21, 2000, p.10. *P.* 94, E4-3a, "Canada's Merchandise Exports," Statistics Canada, Trade and Economic Analysis Division, www.dfait-maeci.gc.ca/eet, June 7, 2002. *P.* 94, E4-3b, "Provincial Pocket Facts," Statistics Canada, www.dfait-maeci.gc.ca/eet/menu-e.asp. *P.* 100, ED4-3, The OECD Code of Fair Information Practices, used with permission of Organization for Economic Co-operation and Development. *P.* 101, E4-4, Annual Report of the Commissioner of Competition for the Year Ending March 31, 2000, reproduced with the permission of the Minister of Public Works and Government Services, 2003. *P.* 104, E4-5, From *Marketing Strategy*, 1st edition, by Ferrell/Hartline/Lucas/Luck, ©1999, reprinted with permission of South-Western, a division of Thomson Learning, www.thomsonrights.com, fax 800-730-2215. *P.* 107, E4-8, Adapted from M.G. Allen, "Strategic Problems Facing Today's Corporate Planner," speech given at the Academy of Management, 36th Annual Meeting, Kansas City, Missouri, 1976.

**Photos/ads:** *P.* 80, www.smart.com. *P.* 84, Courtesy Harley-Davidson Motor Company. *P.* 86, Courtesy of BBDO/Detroit, photographer: Mark Preston. *P.* 87, © The Procter & Gamble Company. Used by permission. *P.* 91, Courtesy of Hoover's, Inc., www.hoovers.com. *P.* 93, Courtesy Smart Money, ad created by DiMassimo Brand Advertising, New York. *P.* 97, Courtesy Adero, Inc. *P.* 108 (left, middle, and right), Courtesy of American Honda Motor Co.

## Chapter 5

**Exhibits:** *P.* 115, Eve Lazarus, "Building Better Relationships," *Marketing Magazine*, May 19, 2003, used with permission. *P.* 126, E5-2, "Population of Canada by Province, 1982 and 2002 (in thousands)," adapted from the Statistics Canada website, http://www.statcan.ca/Daily/English/020926/d020926b.htm. *P.* 127, E5-3, "Changes in the Canadian Birthrate, 1930–2002," adapted from the Statistics Canada publication, "Annual Demographic Statistics 2002," Catalogue 91-213, March 2003, and from the Statistics Canada CANSIM database, http://cansim2.statcan.ca, Tables 051-001 and 051-0004. *P.* 128, E5-4, "Population Distribution (and Percentage Growth Rate) by Age Groups over a 10-Year Period," adapted from the Statistics Canada CANSIM database, http://cansim2.statcan.ca, Table 051-001. *P.* 129, MD5-1, Leslie Danis, "Straight Talk on Marketing to Women Over 50," *Marketing Magazine*, August 28, 2000. *P.* 131, E5-5, Total Population of Census Metropolitan Areas, 1981 and 2001 (in thousands), adapted from the Statistics Canada website, http://www12.statcan.ca/english/census01/products/standard/popdwell/Table-CMA-N.cfm?T=1&SR=1&S=3&O=D. *P.* 133, E5-6, "Percentage of Family Income Going to Different Income Groups, 2000," adapted from the Statistics Canada publication, "Income in Canada," Catalogue 72-202, November 2002. *P.* 134, E5-7, "Personal Income Geographic Distribution, 2001," adapted from the Statistics Canada publication, "Income in Canada 2001," Catalogue 75-202, June 2003. *P.* 136, E5-8, "Household Expenditures of Upper and Lower Quintile, Canada, 2000," adapted from the Statistics Canada publication, "Detailed average household expenditure by household income quintile for Canada and provinces 2002," Catalogue 62F0032, December 2003.

**Photos/ads:** *P.* 115, Used with permission of RONA. *P.* 118, Courtesy of W Network. *P.* 119 (left), Courtesy Delia's; (right), Courtesy Wieden & Kennedy/Amsterdam. *P.* 122 (left and right), Courtesy Colgate-Palmolive Company. *P.* 128, Courtesy of AARP. *P.* 135, Oasis International Group Limited.

## Chapter 6

**Exhibits:** *P.* 145, Hollie Shaw, "Skip the Chevy—Buy yourself a Beemer," *Financial Post*, July 10, 2003, material reprinted with the express permission of The National Post Company, a CanWest Partnership. *P.* 155, MD 6-2, Angela Kryhul, "Un-Fit Behaviour," *Marketing Magazine*, October 8, 2001, used with permission.

**Photos/ads:** *P.* 145, Alison Derry. *P.* 147 (left), © The Procter & Gamble Company. Used by permission; (right), Courtesy of ConAgra Foods. *P.* 150, Courtesy Ortho-McNeil Pharmaceutical. *P.* 151, Ad created for Lasik Vision by Wreglesworth Design Consultancy. *P.* 153, Used with permission of Procter & Gamble. *P.* 154 (left), Courtesy White Wave Inc.; (right), Courtesy PureTek Corporation. *P.* 157, Courtesy of General Mills. *P.* 158 (top), M. Hurby; (bottom left), Courtesy of GM; (bottom right), GM Yukon Ad: Advertising Agency MacLaren McCann. *P.* 160, © 2000 Jockey International, Inc. World rights reserved. *P.* 161, Courtesy Saltron, Inc. *P.* 162, Courtesy Discover Card. © 1999 Greenwood Trust Company. *P.* 169, Used with permission of Bizrate.com. *P.* 170 (left), Courtesy Colgate-Palmolive Company; (right), © John Abbott. *P.* 172 (left and right), Courtesy eTrade Group, Inc.

## Chapter 7

**Exhibits:** *P.* 182, E7-4, Frank B. Cespedes, "Concurrent Marketing," Boston, MA, 1995, reprinted by permission of Harvard Business School Press, copyright © 2004 by the Harvard Business School Publishing Corporation, all rights reserved.

**Photos/ads:** *P.* 177, © Sonia Katchian. *P.* 183, Courtesy of Microsoft Corporation. *P.* 185, Courtesy of Federal Express. *P.* 190, Courtesy Toyota Motor North America, Inc. *P.* 194, Covisint, L.L.C. *P.* 196, Courtesy National Semiconductor. *P.* 198, Contracts Canada website.

## Chapter 8

**Exhibits:** *P.* 210, MD8-1, Marlene Milczarek, "Marketers are increasingly turning to their customer information banks for research," adapted from "Database Diamond Mining," *Marketing Magazine*, August 13, 2001, used with permission. *P.* 212, ED8-1, ARF position paper, "Phony or misleading polls," *Journal of Advertising Research*, Special Issue 26 (January 1987), pp. RC3-RC8; and George S. Day, "The Threats to Marketing Research," *Journal of Marketing Research 12* (November 1975), pp. 462–467, taken from David A. Aaker and George S. Day, eds., *Marketing Research*, 4th ed. (New York: John Wiley & Sons), pp. 217, 218. *P.* 220, MD8-2, Based on "Eyes and ears of business: Marketing research is taking on even more importance in helping companies grow," *Marketing Magazine*, May 17, 1999, Vol. 104, No. 19, p. 18; "Underlying Differences," *Marketing Magazine*, Patrick Lejtenyi, June 5, 2000, used with permission. *P.* 222, MD8-3, Allyson L. Stewart-Allen, International Marketing Research Tips, "Do your international homework first," *Marketing News*, Vol. 33, p. 25, ISSN 00253790, Chicago, January 4, 1999, used with permission of the American Marketing Association. *P.* 227, E8-5, McDaniel and Gates, "Qualitative versus Quantitative Research," *Marketing Research*, 2002, p. 123. *P.* 228, MD8-4, Doug Saunders, "Getting into focus—groups, that is," *The Globe and Mail*, January 10, 1998, p. C1, reprinted with permission from *The Globe and Mail*. *P.* 229, MD8-5, Norma Ramage, "Taco-Time Dreams Grande," *Marketing Magazine Online*, March 3, 2003, used with permission. *P.* 231, MD8-6, "Using Incentives to Increase Response Rates, CBC Radio feeds the curious: a CD sampler strikes a chord with the broadcaster's desired 'cultural creative' target," *Marketing Magazine*, August 19, 2002, Vol. 107, No. 33, p. 11, used with permission. *P.* 233, ED8-2, Carey Toane, "Smells Like Teen Research," Digital Marketing Report, *Marketing Magazine*, July 24, 2000, used with permission.

**Photos/ads:** *P.* 205, © 1994 LensCrafters, Inc. *P.* 208 (left), Courtesy of Sun Microsystems, Inc., Agency: Lowe & Partners; (right), Courtesy of MapInfo. *P.* 211, *The Toronto Star*. *P.* 213, Courtesy Zero Knowledge Systems, Inc. *P.* 216, Agency: Renfer Mayr. *P.* 217 (left), Courtesy Survey Sampling, Inc.; (right), Courtesy Simmons Custom Research. *P.* 218 (left), Courtesy SPSS, Inc.; (right), Courtesy StarSoft. *P.* 221 (left), Courtesy P. Roberts & Partners; (right), Courtesy Quality Controlled Services, St. Louis, MO. *P.* 223 (left), Reprinted with permission from Northern Light Technology, Inc. Copyright 1999; (right), Courtesy Greenfield Online, Inc. *P.* 230, Courtesy Cetia, Inc. *P.* 231 (left and right), Courtesy Greenfield Online, Inc. *P.* 234 (left), Used with permission of Perseus Development Corporation; (right), Used with permission of www.surveysite.com. *P.* 235 (left), © John Harding; (right), Courtesy Information Resources, Inc. *P.* 236 (left and right), Courtesy Simmons Company.

## Chapter 9

**Photos:** *P.* 241, Alison Derry and Sandra de Ruiter, *P.* 244, Doctor's Associates Inc. (DAI)/Subway, *P.* 245, SNCF. *P.* 246, M&T Web Banking. *P.* 247, Courtesy 3M. *P.* 248 (left and right), Courtesy of Bridgestone Corporation, Tokyo, Japan. *P.* 251 (left), Used with permission of Yoplait USA; (right) © The Procter & Gamble Company. Used with permission. *P.* 252, Courtesy GE Plastics. *P.* 254 (left), Courtesy Provident Bank; (right), Courtesy Phillips Plastics Corporation™. *P.* 255, Courtesy Printnation.com. *P.* 262 (left), Courtesy Del Monte Fresh Produce N.A., Inc.; (right), Courtesy GE Lighting. *P.* 264, Courtesy of The Thomas Pigeon Design Group. *P.* 267, Used with permission of Dean's Food Company.

## Chapter 10

**Exhibits:** *P.* 296, MD10-1, Astrid Van Den Broek, "Kellogg markets 'tasty' soy cereal," www.marketingmag.com, April 23, 2001, used with permission. *P.* 299, MD10-2, Sarah Smith, "Heinz Kickers target adult taste buds," www.marketingmag.com, June 3, 2002, used with permission.

**Photos/ads:** *P.* 273, 3Com, the 3Com logo, and Graffiti are registered trademarks and HotSync, Palm OS, Palm Pilot logo are trademarks of 3Com Corporation or its subsidiaries. All other brands and product names are trademarks and registered trademarks of their respective holders. This product is not manufactured by Pilot Corporation or Pilot Corporation of America, manufacturers and distributors of writing instruments. *P.* 276, CLEO Photography, Whitby, Ontario. *P.* 282, Used with permission of Unilever Canada. Photography by Chris Gordancer. *P.* 283 (left and right), Courtesy of 3M. *P.* 284 (left and right), © The Procter & Gamble Company. Used by permission. *P.* 286 (left), Courtesy Leo Burnett, Singapore; (right), Courtesy of Nabisco Brands, Inc. *P.* 289, Courtesy E.I. Dupont De Nemours & Co. *P.* 293 (left), Courtesy E.I. Dupont De Nemours & Co.; (right), Courtesy Komatsu America. *P.* 294, Courtesy GE Company. *P.* 297, Courtesy Porsche Cars North America. *P.* 301, Courtesy Nabisco Brands, Inc.

## Chapter 11

**Exhibits:** *P.* 325, MD11-3, Angela Kryhul, "Bringing fashion to food," *Marketing Magazine*, December 20/27, 1999, used with permission.

**Photos/ads:** *P.* 305, © Fritz Hoffman. *P.* 309, Courtesy Office Depot. *P.* 313 (left and right), Mark Joseph Photography, Chicago. All other rights are reserved by Mark Joseph Photography except those specifically granted by this delivery memo. *P.* 314 (left and right), Courtesy Colgate-Palmolive. *P.* 315 (left, middle, and right), Courtesy Unilever P.L.C.; Photographer: Bill Prentice. *P.* 317, © 2001 *USA Today*. Reprinted with permission. *P.* 319, Forrester Research, Inc., 2000. *P.* 321 (left), © The Procter & Gamble Company. Used by permission; (right), Courtesy Leisure Concepts, Inc. *P.* 322, Courtesy The Goodyear Tire & Rubber Company. *P.* 323 (left), Courtesy Nyman; (right), Dave Nichols photo appeared in Angela Kryhul, "Bringing Fashion to Food," *Marketing Magazine*, December 20/27, 1999. Used with permission. *P.* 327, Tom Wagner/SABA. *P.* 328, Alain McLaughlin Photography. *P.* 331 (top), Courtesy Volkswagen of America, Inc.; (bottom), Courtesy Reebok International.

## Chapter 12

**Exhibits:** *P.* 341, Adapted from "The Best Bet for Your Bottom Dollar," Marina Strauss, *The Globe and Mail*, Saturday, August 2, 2003, p. B1, reprinted with permission from *The Globe and Mail*. *P.* 353, MD12-1, George H. Condon, *Canadian Grocer*, April 2000. P. 360, MD 12-3, Eve Lazarus, "Air Drugstore," *Marketing Magazine*, September 10, 2001, used with permission.

**Photos/ads:** *P.* 341, Marina Strauss, "The Best Bet for Your Bottom Dollar," *The Globe and Mail*, Saturday, August 2, 2003, p. B1. Photographer: Louie Palu. Reprinted with permission from *The Globe and Mail*. *P.* 344 (left), Courtesy Toys "R" Us; (middle), Courtesy Lands' End Inc.; (right), Courtesy of the Home Depot. *P.* 349 (left), Courtesy Colgate-Palmolive; (right), Tom Wagner/SABA. *P.* 350–351, Courtesy of Office Depot. *P.* 355, Speedpass photo courtesy of Imperial Oil. *P.* 359, © Canadian Tire Corporation, Limited. *P.* 361, Courtesy Jersey Gardens Outlet Mall. *P.* 363, © Canadian Tire Corporation, Limited, *P.* 365, Courtesy Tesco Stores, Ltd., Agency: Lowe-Howard Spink/London, Photographer: Tony Campbell. *P.* 366, Used with the permission of Inter IKEA Systems B.V. *P.* 367, Courtesy Cross Link, Inc. *P.* 368, © Ovak Arsianian. *P.* 370 (left), Courtesy Unilever, P.L.C.; (right), © 2000 by Reid Horn. *P.* 371, © Steve Niedorf. *P.* 373, Advance Bar Code Technology. *P.* 374, Courtesy Tradeout.com.

## Chapter 13

**Exhibits:** *P.* 381, Adapted from Steve Silverstone, "The Joy of Free Time," *Marketing Magazine: Out of Home Report*, Nov. 19, 2001, www.marketingmag.ca, 2002 Rogers Media Inc., February 25, 2003, used with permission. *P.* 386, MD13-1, Kate Harries, "Fans go crazy for Avril's shirt," *The Toronto Star*, Jan. 17, 2002, reprinted with permission from Torstar Syndication Services. *P.* 393, MD13-2, Wink Wink, adapted from Chris Powell, "Giving Wink a Nudge," *Marketing Magazine: Report on Television*, December 9, 2002; Chris Powell, "The Flashing 'i'," *Marketing Magazine: Report on Television*, December 10, 2001, used with permission. *P.* 397, MD13-3, New Approaches to Direct Marketing, Bryan Pearson, President, Air Miles.

**Photos/ads:** *P.* 381, Used with permission of Labatt Canada. *P.* 387 (all), Courtesy Stanley Works. *P.* 389 (left, middle, and right), Courtesy Ericsson. *P.* 391, © Copyright 1989 Benetton Group S.p.A., Photographer: O. Toscani. *P.* 392, Courtesy *Good Housekeeping*. *P.* 400 (left), Barfly, Creative Director: Glen Hunt, Artistic Director: Colin Brown; (right), Courtesy Dome Industries. *P.* 402, McGraw-Hill. *P.* 404 (left), Advertisement courtesy of Compaq Computer Corporation, photo courtesy of Brad Harris; (right), Courtesy Oasis The Campaign Agency. *P.* 406, © Molson Canada.

## Chapter 14

**Exhibits:** *P.* 419, MD14-1, Erika Rasmusson, "Getting schooled in outsourcing," Vol. 151, Issue 1, copyright 1999 by V N U BUS PUBNS USA, reproduced with permission of V N U BUS PUBNS USA in the format Other Book via Copyright Clearance Center. *P.* 428, MD14-2, Jennifer Gilbert, "Resellers, click here," Vol. 154, Issue 9, copyright 2002 by V N U BUS PUBNS USA, reproduced with permission of V N U BUS PUBNS USA in the format Other Book via Copyright Clearance Center. *P.* 432, MD14-4, Erika Rasmusson, "Getting schooled in outsourcing," Vol. 151, Issue 1, copyright 1999 by V N U BUS PUBNS USA, reproduced with permission of V N U BUS PUBNS USA in the format Other Book via Copyright Clearance Center.

**Photos/ads:** *P.* 413, © Timothy Archibald. *P.* 415, Photograph courtesy of Glaxo Holdings. *P.* 416 (left), Courtesy Boise Cascade Office Products; (right), Courtesy of Sauder Woodworking Company. *P.* 418 (left), Courtesy The Home Depot; (right), Courtesy Unisys. *P.* 420, Courtesy General Electric Company. Photo by Brownie Harris. *P.* 421, © 1996 Vickers & Beechler. *P.* 422, Courtesy Alcoa. Photo by Ropber Feldman. *P.* 423, Courtesy The Clorox Company. Photo by Lisa Papal. *P.* 426, Used with permission of www.conjoin.com. *P.* 429 (top), Courtesy salesforce.com; (bottom), Larry Dale Gordon/ Image Bank/Getty Images. *P.* 431, Courtesy Ross Roy Advertising Agency. *P.* 437 (left), Courtesy Experian; (right), Courtesy Eiki International, Inc. *P.* 439, Courtesy Keebler.

## Chapter 15

**Exhibits:** *P.* 445, Adapted from Tim McHale, Tom Hespos, and Eric Porres, "BMW Films: The Ultimate Marketing Scheme," Jul. 10, 2002, www.imediaconnection.com/content/features/071002b.asp, 2003 iMedia Communications Inc., February 2, 2003; Christopher Saunders, "BMW Films Hit Hollywood, Courtesy of Microsoft," September 5, 2002, www.Internetnews.com/IAR/article.php/1457171, 2003 Jupitermedia Corporation, February 20, 2003. *P.* 447, E15-1, Nielsen Media Research, *The Canadian Marketing Pocket Book 2004*, published by WARC, www.warc.com. *P.* 449, E15-3, Top Advertising Categories, 2001, Nielsen Media Research. *P.* 450, E15-4, Top Advertisers, 2001, Nielsen Media Research. *P.* 460, E15-7, Media Characteristics—Information on the Strengths and Weaknesses of Media as Advertising Vehicles, adapted from Wright, Winter, Zeigler, and O'Dea, *Advertising*, McGraw-Hill Ryerson Ltd., with research assistance from Palmer Jarvis Advertising, reproduced in the *Ad Pages*, 1995, pp. 4–5. *P.* 463, MD15-1, Chris Powell, "Here, There and Everywhere," *Marketing Magazine: Out of Home Report*, November 19, 2001, www.marketingmag.ca, 2002, used with permission. *P.* 473, MD15-2, "Proving PBR," Lara Mills, *Marketing Magazine*, October 16, 2000, used with permission. *P.* 477, MD15-3, "The Competition Act—Misleading Advertising Provisions," *Misleading Advertising Bulletin*, Marketing Practices Branch, Bureau of Competition Policy, Industry Canada, April 1–June 30, 1994, p. 21, reproduced with permission of the Minister of Public Works and Government Services Canada, 2003.

**Photos/ads:** *P.* 445, Used with permission of the BMW Group. *P.* 451, © Copyright 1991 Benetton Group S.p.A., Photographer: O. Toscani. *P.* 455, Used with permission of United Way of Greater Toronto. *P.* 456 (left), Courtesy Del Pharmaceuticals, Inc.; (right), © Microsoft Corporation. *P.* 457 (left and right), Courtesy of Brown Shoe Co., Inc. *P.* 459, Michael Goldwater/Network. *P.* 462, David Taylor/Allsport. *P.* 468, Courtesy Birdsall Voss & Kloppenburg. *P.* 469, Courtesy Euro RSCG. *P.* 472 (left), Lara Jo Regan/Gettysource Liaison Agency; (right), Patrick Dori/Beach 'n Billboard™. *P.* 476 (left), Courtesy Bates USA South/Miami; (right), Courtesy Greenfield Online, Inc. *P.* 479, Courtesy Act Media.

## Chapter 16

**Exhibits:** *P.* 487, Adapted from Lisa Margonelli, "How IKEA Designs Its Sexy Price Tags," *Business 2.0*, October 2002 Issue. *P.* 497, MD16-1, Jeff Blair, "Toronto gears ticket prices to calendar," Thursday, January 9, 2003, *The Globe and Mail*, p. S2. *P.* 499, Alternative Introductory Pricing Policies.

**Photos/ads:** *P.* 487, Used with the permission of Inter IKEA Systems B.V. *P.* 490, Courtesy of Toronto Symphony Orchestra. *P.* 493, Courtesy Merck Co, Inc. *P.* 494, Courtesy of Blockbuster Video. *P.* 498 (left), Courtesy Carnival Corporation; (right), Courtesy National Trade Publications, Inc. *P.* 501 (left), Courtesy 8 in 1 Pet Products, Inc.; (right), Courtesy H.J. Heinz Company. Used with permission. *P.* 502, H. Douglas Jones, Elixir Nightclub 2004. *P.* 506, Epeda. *P.* 507, © The Procter & Gamble Company. Used by permission.

## Chapter 17

**Exhibits:** *P.* 536, MD17-2, Paul Hunt, "Pricing Research," *Marketing Magazine*, used with permission.

**Photos/ads:** *P.* 513, © Brian Coats. All rights reserved. *P.* 516, Courtesy Kohler Co. *P.* 518, Anheuser-Busch Companies, St. Louis, MO. *P.* 520, Courtesy Colgate-Palmolive. *P.* 531, Courtesy Hallmark Cards, Inc., Agency: Leo Burnett/Chicago IL. *P.* 532, Courtesy of Devito/Verdi. *P.* 536 (left), Courtesy Dior, Photo: Albert Gordoan; (right), Courtesy Audio Stream. *P.* 537, Courtesy Colgate-Palmolive.

## Chapter 18

**Exhibits:** *P.* 543, Adapted from Pearl Davies, "Love It or Leave It," *Marketing Magazine*, October 9, 2000, used with permission. *P.* 549, MD18-1, Tracey Arial, "Bras with Attitude," *Marketing Magazine*, February 3, 2003, used with permission. *P.* 563, MD18-2, Sarah Smith, "Paying for Planning," *Marketing Magazine*, November 29, 1999, used with permission.

**Photos/ads:** *P.* 543, Chrysler. *P.* 545 (left and right), Courtesy 3M. *P.* 547 (top), Adobe Acrobat 5.0 box shot reprinted with permission from Adobe Systems Incorporated; (bottom), Used with permission of www.rethinkbeer.com. *P.* 551, © 1994 Intel Corporation. *P.* 557, Courtesy Wesley Jessen Corporation. *P.* 565, Courtesy Pepsi-Cola Canada, Ltd. *P.* 567, Courtesy of American International Group Inc.

## Chapter 19

**Exhibits:** *P.* 573, Based on Ann Walmsley, "Plane Crazy," *Report on Business Magazine*, December 1999, pp. 62–71; www.westjet.com. *P.* 581, MD19-1, Based on Jim Carroll, "Jumping on the corporate blog wagon," *Marketing Magazine*, September 30, 2002; "Flash—Blogging Goes Corporate," http://www.wired.com/news/culture/0,1284,52380,00.html, May 9, 2002. *P.* 593, E19-6, Adapted from "Quarterly Demographic Statistics," Statistics Canada, 1997, Catalogue No. 91-002, Volume 11, No. 2, p. 15.

**Photos/ads:** *P.* 573, CP/Adrian Wyld. *P.* 576, Courtesy Colgate-Palmolive. *P.* 577, Courtesy Lotus Development Corporation, and IBM company. *P.* 578, FedEx. *P.* 579, Courtesy The Hertz Corporation. *P.* 585 (left), CP/Richard Buchan; (right), AP Photo/Peter Cosgrove. *P.* 587 (left), Courtesy McDonald's Corporation, Photograph by Robert Mizono; (right), Courtesy Goodyear Tire & Rubber Company. *P.* 589, Used with permission of sane.com. *P.* 591, Courtesy Information Resources, Inc.

# Glossary

**Accessories** Short-lived capital items

**Accumulating** Collecting products from many small producers

**Administered channel systems** Systems in which the channel members informally agree to cooperate with each other

**Administered prices** Prices that are consciously set

**Adoption curve** Shows when different groups accept ideas

**Adoption process** The steps individuals go through on the way to accepting or rejecting a new idea

**Advertising** Any *paid* form of nonpersonal presentation of ideas, goods, or services by an identified sponsor

**Advertising agencies** Specialists in planning and handling mass-selling details for advertisers

**Advertising allowances** Price reductions to firms in the channel to encourage them to advertise or otherwise promote the firm's products locally

**Advertising managers** Managers concerned with their company's mass-selling effort (in television, newspapers, magazines, and other media)

**Agent intermediaries** Wholesalers who do not own the products they sell

**AIDA model** Four promotion jobs: (1) to get attention, (2) to hold interest, (3) to arouse desire, and (4) to obtain action

**Allowances** Reductions in price given to final consumers, customers, or channel members for doing something or accepting less of something

**Assorting** Putting together a variety of products to give a target market what it wants

**Attitude** A person's point of view toward something

**Auction companies** Companies that provide a place where buyers and sellers can come together and bid to complete a transaction

**Automatic vending** Selling and delivering products through vending machines

**Average cost** Obtained by dividing total cost by the related quantity

**Average-cost pricing** Adding a reasonable markup to the average cost of a product to arrive at the price

**Average fixed cost** Obtained by dividing total fixed cost by the related quantity

**Average variable cost** Obtained by dividing total variable cost by the related quantity

**Bait pricing** Setting some very low prices to attract customers, but then trying to sell more expensive models or brands once the customer is in the store

**Basic list prices** The prices final customers or users are normally asked to pay for products

**Battle of the brands** Competition between dealer brands and manufacturer brands

**Belief** A person's opinion about something

**Benchmarking** Picking a basis of comparison for evaluating how well a job is being done

**Bid pricing** Offering a specific price for each possible job rather than setting a price that applies for all customers

**Birthrate** The number of babies born per 1,000 people

**Brand equity** The value of a brand's overall strength in the market

**Brand familiarity** How well customers recognize and accept a company's brand

**Brand insistence (brand loyalty)** When customers insist on a firm's branded product and are willing to search for it

**Brand name** A word, letter, or group of words or letters

**Brand nonrecognition** When final consumers don't recognize a brand at all

**Brand preference** When target customers usually choose the brand over other brands

**Brand recognition** When customers remember a brand

**Brand rejection** When potential customers won't buy a brand unless its image is changed

**Branding** The use of a name, term, symbol, or design (or a combination of these) to identify a product

**Break-even analysis** Evaluates whether the firm will be able to break even (i.e., cover all its costs) with a particular price

**Break-even point (BEP)** The quantity where the firm's total cost will just equal its total revenue

**Breakthrough opportunities** Opportunities that help innovators develop hard-to-copy marketing strategies that will be profitable in the long term

**Brokers** Agents who bring buyers and sellers together

**Bulk-breaking** Dividing larger quantities into smaller quantities as products get closer to the final market

**Business and organizational customers** Any buyers who buy for resale or to produce other goods and services

**Business products** Products meant for use in producing other products

**Buyers** Those who make the actual purchase of the product or service

**Capital item** A long-lasting product that can be used and depreciated for many years

**Cash-and-carry wholesalers** Wholesalers that operate like service wholesalers, except the customer must pay cash

**Cash discounts** Reductions in price to encourage buyers to pay their bills quickly

**Catalogue showroom retailers** Retailers that sell several lines out of a catalogue and display showroom

**Catalogue wholesalers** Wholesalers that sell out of catalogues distributed widely to smaller industrial customers or retailers who might not be called on by other intermediaries

**Census Metropolitan Area (CMA)** The "main labour market area" of a continuous built-up area having a population of 100,000 or more

**Channel captain** A manager who helps direct the activities of a whole channel and tries to avoid or solve channel conflicts

**Channel of distribution** Any series of firms (or individuals) that participate in the flow of products from producer to final user or consumer

**Close** The salesperson's request for an order

**Co-branding** Combining both family and individual brand names

**Combination export manager** A blend of manufacturers' agent and selling agent who handles the entire export function for several producers of similar but non-competing lines

**Combined target market approach** Combining two or more submarkets into one larger target market as a basis for one strategy

**Communication process** Occurs when a source tries to reach a receiver with a message

**Comparative advertising** An extreme form of direct competitive advertising that involves making specific brand comparisons using actual product names

**Competitive advantage** A marketing mix that the target market sees as better than a competitor's mix

**Competitive advertising** Advertising that tries to develop selective demand for a specific brand

**Competitive barriers** Conditions that may make it difficult, or even impossible, for a firm to compete in a market

**Competitive bids** The terms of sale offered by different suppliers in response to purchase specifications posted by the buyer

**Competitive environment** Affects the number and types of competitors the marketing manager must face and how they may behave

**Competitive rivals** Firms that will be the closest competitors

**Competitor analysis** An organized approach for evaluating the strengths and weaknesses of current or potential competitors' marketing strategies

**Complementary product pricing** Setting prices on several products as a group

**Components** Processed expense items that become part of a finished product

**Concept testing** Getting reactions from customers about how well a new-product idea fits their needs

**Confidence intervals** The range on either side of an estimate that is likely to contain the true value for the whole population

**Consultative selling approach** Sales approach that involves developing a good understanding of the individual customer's needs before trying to close the sale

**Consumer panels** Groups of consumers who provide information on a continuing basis

**Consumer products** Products meant for the final consumer

**Consumerism** A social movement that seeks to increase the rights and powers of consumers in relation to sellers and the government

**Continuous improvement** A commitment to constantly make things better one step at a time

**Contract manufacturing** Turning over production to others while retaining the marketing process

**Contractual channel systems** Systems in which the channel members agree by contract to cooperate with each other

**Contribution-margin approach** A marketing approach where all costs are not allocated in *all* situations

**Control** The feedback process that helps marketing managers learn how ongoing plans and implementation are working and how to plan for the future

**Convenience products** Products a consumer needs but isn't willing to spend much time or effort shopping for

**Convenience (food) stores** A convenience-oriented variation on the conventional limited-line food stores

**Cooperative advertising** Occurs when intermediaries and producers share in the cost of ads

**Cooperative chains** Retailer-sponsored groups, formed by independent retailers, that run their own buying organizations and conduct joint promotion efforts

**Copy thrust** What an advertisement's words and illustrations should communicate

**Corporate chain** An organization operating four or more retail outlets in the same kind of business, under the same legal ownership

**Corporate channel systems** Systems that have corporate ownership all along the channel

**Coverage** The amount of the target market that is reached by the channels of distribution

**Cues** Products, signs, ads, and other stimuli in the environment

**Cultural and social environment** Affects how and why people live and behave as they do

**Culture** The whole set of beliefs, attitudes, and ways of doing things of a reasonably homogeneous set of people

**Cumulative quantity discounts** Discounts that apply to purchases over a given period; usually increase as the amount purchased increases

**Customer satisfaction** The extent to which a firm fulfills a customer's needs, desires, and expectations

**Customer service level** How rapidly and dependably a firm can deliver what its customers want

**Customer value** The difference between the benefits a customer sees from a market offering and the costs of obtaining those benefits

**Data warehouse** A place where databases are stored so that they are available when needed

**Dealer brands (private brands)** Brands created by intermediaries

**Deciders** Those who evaluate the alternatives that are identified by gatekeepers

**Decision support system (DSS)** A computer program that makes it easy for a marketing manager to get and use information *as he or she is making decisions*

**Decoding** Occurs when the receiver translates the message

**Demand-backward pricing** Setting an acceptable final consumer price and working backward to what a producer can charge

**Demographics** Information and trends about the size, location, and characteristics of target markets

**Department stores** Larger stores that are organized into many separate departments and offer many product lines

**Derived demand** The demand for business products derives from the demand for final consumer products

**Determining dimensions** Dimensions that actually affect the customer's purchase of a specific product or brand in a product-market

**Differentiation** When the marketing mix is distinct from and better than what is available from a competitor

**Direct marketing** Direct communication between a seller and an individual customer using a promotion method other than face-to-face personal selling

**Discounts** Reductions from list price given by a seller to buyers who either give up some marketing function or provide the function themselves

**Discrepancy of assortment** The difference between the lines a typical producer makes and the assortment final consumers or users want

**Discrepancy of quantity** The difference between the quantity of products it is economical for a producer to make and the quantity final users or consumers normally want

**Discretionary income** What is left of disposable income after paying for necessities

**Disposable income** Income remaining after paying taxes

**Dissonance** Tension caused by uncertainty about the rightness of a decision

**Distribution cost** The amount that is paid to members of the distribution channel in order to achieve the desired levels of coverage and promotional intensity

**Diversification** Moving into totally different lines of business

**Door-to-door selling** A selling approach where a salesperson goes directly to the consumer's home

**Drive** A strong stimulus that encourages action to reduce a need

**Drop-shippers** Wholesalers that own the products they sell but do not actually handle, stock, or deliver them

**Dual distribution** Occurs when a producer uses several competing channels to reach the same target market, perhaps using several intermediaries in addition to selling directly

**Early adopters** Consumer who are well respected by their peers; often opinion leaders

**Early majority** Consumers who avoid risk and wait to consider a new product after many early adopters have tried and liked it

**Economic and technological environments** Affect the way that firms—and the whole economy—use resources

**Economic buyers** People who know the facts and logically compare choices in terms of cost and value received to get the greatest satisfaction from spending their time and money

**Economic needs** Making the best use of a consumer's time and money

**Electronic data interchange (EDI)** An approach that puts information in a standardized format easily shared between different computer systems

**Emergency products** Products that are purchased immediately when the need is great

**Encoding** Occurs when the source decides what it wants to say and translates it into words or symbols that will have the same meaning to the receiver

**Everyday low pricing (EDLP)** Setting a low list price rather than relying on a high list price that frequently changes with various discounts or allowances

**Exchange rate** How much one country's money is worth in another country's currency

**Exclusive distribution** Selling through only one intermediary in a particular geographic area

**Expectation** An outcome or event that a person anticipates or looks forward to

**Expense item** A product whose total cost is treated as a business expense in the year it's purchased

**Experience-curve pricing** Average-cost pricing using an estimate of *future* average costs

**Experimental method** Method where researchers compare the responses of two (or more) groups that are similar except on the characteristic being tested

**Export and import brokers** Agents who operate like other brokers, but specialize in bringing together buyers and sellers from different countries

**Export or import agents** Manufacturers' agents who specialize in international trade

**Exporting** Selling some of what the firm produces to foreign markets

**Extensive problem solving** When consumers put effort into deciding how to satisfy a completely new or important need

**Facilitators** Those who provide one or more of the marketing functions other than buying or selling

**Factor** A variable that shows the relation of some other variable to the item being forecast

**Factor method** A method to forecast sales by finding a relation between the company's sales and some other factor

**Fad** An idea that is fashionable only to certain groups who are enthusiastic about it

**Family brand** Using the same brand name for several products

**Farm products** Products grown by farmers

**Fashion** The currently accepted or popular style

**Fishbone diagram** A visual aid that helps organize cause-and-effect relationships for things gone wrong

**Fixed-cost (FC) contribution per unit** The assumed selling price per unit minus the variable cost per unit

**Flexible-price policy** Offering the same product and quantities to different customers at different prices

**F.O.B.** A transportation term meaning free on board some vehicle at some place

**Focus-group interview** Involves interviewing 6 to 10 people in an informal group setting

**Form utility** Provided when someone produces something tangible

**Franchise operation** The franchiser develops a good marketing strategy, which the retail franchise holders then carry out in their own units

**Freight-absorption pricing** Absorbing freight cost so that a firm's delivered price meets the nearest competitor's

**Full-cost approach** A marketing approach where all costs are allocated to products, customers, or other categories

**Full-line pricing** Setting prices for a whole line of products

**General merchandise wholesalers** Service wholesalers who carry a wide variety of nonperishable items

**Generic market** A market with broadly similar needs

**Generic products** Products that have no brand at all other than identification of their contents and the manufacturer or intermediary

**Gross domestic product (GDP)** The total market value of goods and services produced by a country's economy in a year, including foreign income

**Gross national product (GNP)** The total market value of goods and services produced by a country's economy in a year

**Heterogeneous shopping products** Shopping products the customer sees as different and wants to inspect for quality and suitability

**Homogeneous shopping products** Shopping products the customer sees as basically the same and wants at the lowest price

**Hypotheses** Educated guesses about the relationships between things or about what will happen in the future

**Iceberg principle** The idea that much good information is hidden in summary data

**Ideal market exposure** Making a product available widely enough to satisfy target customers' needs but not exceed them

**Impulse products** Products that are bought quickly—as unplanned purchases—because of a strongly felt need

**Indices** Statistical combinations of several time series in an effort to find some time series that will lead the series they're trying to forecast

**Individual brands** Separate brand names for each product

**Individual product** A particular product within a product line

**Influencers (gatekeepers)** Those who define the specifications for what is bought and for gathering information on the alternative ways of meeting those specifications

**Initiators** Those who act as a catalyst for the buying process

**Innovators** Consumers who are the first to adopt a new product

**Installations** Important capital items

**Institutional advertising** Advertising that tries to promote an organization's image, reputation, or ideas rather than a specific product

**Integrated marketing communications** The intentional coordination of every communication from a firm to a target customer to convey a consistent and complete message

**Intranet** A system for linking computers within a company

**Introductory price dealing** Temporary price cuts used to speed new products into a market or to gain some of the volume-building benefits of penetration pricing

**Intensive distribution** Selling a product through all responsible and suitable wholesalers or retailers that will stock and/or sell the product

**Intermediary** Someone who specializes in trade rather than production

**ISO 9000** A way for a supplier to document its quality procedures according to internationally recognized standards

**Job description** A written statement of what a salesperson is expected to do

**Joint venturing** A domestic firm entering into a partnership with a foreign firm

**Jury of executive opinion** A method of forecasting that combines the opinions of experienced executives

**Just-in-time delivery** Reliably getting products to a customer's location just before the customer needs them

**Laggards (nonadopters)** Consumers who prefer to do things the way they've been done in the past and are very suspicious of new ideas

**Late majority** Consumers who are cautious about new ideas

**Leader pricing** Setting some very low prices to get customers into retail stores

**Leading series** A time series that changes in the same direction *but ahead of* the series to be forecast

**Learning** A change in a person's thought processes caused by prior experience

**Legal environment** Sets the basic rules for how a business can operate in society

**Licensed brand** A well-known brand that sellers pay a fee to use

**Licensing** Selling the right to use some process, trademark, patent, or other right for a fee or royalty

**Limited-function wholesalers** Wholesalers that provide only some wholesaling functions

**Limited problem solving** Used when consumers are willing to put some effort into deciding the best way to satisfy a need

**Logistics (physical distribution)** The transporting, storing, and handling of goods to match target customers' needs with a firm's marketing mix

**Long-run target-return pricing** Adding a long-run average target return to the cost of a product

**Low-involvement purchases** Purchases that have little importance or relevance for the customer

**Major accounts salesforce** An elite salesforce that sells directly to large accounts

**Management contracting** The seller provides only management skills and others own the production and distribution facilities

**Manufacturer brands (national brands)** Brands created by producers

**Manufacturers' agent** Agent who sells similar products for several non-competing producers, for a commission on what is actually sold

**Manufacturers' sales branches** Warehouses that producers set up at separate locations away from their factories

**Marginal analysis** Focuses on the changes in total revenue and total cost from selling one more unit to find the most profitable price and quantity

**Marginal cost** The change in total cost that results from producing one more unit

**Marginal profit** The extra profit on the last unit sold

**Marginal revenue** The change in total revenue that results from the sale of one more unit of a product

**Market** A group of potential customers with similar needs who are willing to exchange something of value with sellers offering various goods and/or services

**Market development** Trying to increase sales by selling current products in new markets

**Market growth** The product life cycle stage when industry sales grow fast and industry profits rise but then start falling

**Market introduction** The product life cycle stage when sales usually are low as a new idea is first introduced to a market

**Market maturity** The product life cycle stage when industry sales level off as the pool of potential users is exhausted

**Market-oriented firm** A firm that uses customers' needs to determine what is required to create customer satisfaction and then commits all of its efforts to those opportunities where it can profitably service those needs

**Market penetration** Trying to increase sales of a firm's present products in its present markets, usually through a more aggressive marketing mix

**Market segmentation** A technique used to identify and understand different subgroups

**Marketing audit** A systematic, critical, and unbiased review and appraisal of the basic objectives and policies of the marketing function and of the organization, methods, procedures, and people employed to implement the policies

**Marketing concept** A way of thinking about management that has an organization aiming all its efforts at satisfying its customers at a profit

**Marketing ethics** Moral standards that guide marketing decisions and actions

**Marketing information system (MIS)** An organized way of continually gathering, accessing, and analyzing the information that marketing managers need to make decisions

**Marketing management process** The process of (1) *planning* marketing activities, (2) directing the *implementation* of the plans, and (3) *controlling* these plans

**Marketing mix** The controllable variables the company puts together to satisfy this target group

**Marketing model** A statement of relationships among marketing variables

**Marketing orientation** Identifying and channelling all of an organization's efforts into profitably satisfying the customer's needs

**Marketing plan** A written statement of a marketing strategy and the time-related details for carrying out the strategy

**Marketing program** Program that blends all of the firm's marketing plans into one "big" plan

**Marketing research** Procedures to develop and analyze new information

**Marketing research process** A five-step application of the scientific method

**Marketing strategy** Specifies a target market and a related marketing mix; a big picture of what a firm will do in some market

**Markup** The amount added to the cost of products to get the selling price

**Markup chain**

The sequence of markups that firms use at different levels in a channel

**Mass marketing** Vaguely aims at everyone with the same marketing mix

**Mass selling** Communicating with large numbers of customers at the same time

**Mass-merchandisers** Large, self-service stores with many departments that emphasize "soft goods" and staples with lower margins for faster turnover

**Mass-merchandising concept** The idea that retailers should offer low prices to get faster turnover and greater sales volumes.

**Merchant wholesalers** Wholesalers that own (take title to) the products they sell

**Message channel** The carrier of the message

**Metropolitan areas** Urban areas attractive to marketers because of their large, concentrated populations

**Mission statement** Statement that sets out an organization's basic purpose for being

**Missionary salespeople** Supporting salespeople who work for producers, calling on their intermediaries and their customers

**Modified rebuy** The in-between process where some review of the buying situation is done

**Multinational corporations** Have a direct investment in several countries and run their businesses depending on the choices available anywhere in the world

**Multiple target-market approach** Segmenting the market and choosing two or more segments, then treating each as a separate target market needing a different marketing mix

**Natural products** Products that occur in nature

**Needs** The basic forces that motivate a person to do something

**Negotiated contract buying** Agreeing to a contract that allows for changes in the purchase arrangements

**Negotiated price** A price set based on bargaining between the buyer and seller

**Net** An invoice term meaning that payment for the face value of the invoice is due immediately

**New product** One that is new *in any way* for the company concerned

**New unsought products** Products offering really new ideas that potential customers don't know about yet

**New-task buying** Occurs when an organization has a new need and the customer wants a great deal of information

**Noise** Any distraction that reduces the effectiveness of the communication process

**Noncumulative quantity discounts** Discounts that apply only to individual orders

**Nonprice competition** Aggressive action on one or more of the Ps other than price

**Odd-even pricing** Setting prices that end in certain numbers

**One-price policy** Offering the same price to all customers who purchase products under essentially the same conditions and in the same quantities

**Opinion leader** A person who influences others

**Order getters** Salespeople concerned with establishing relationships with new customers and developing new business

**Order getting** Seeking possible buyers with a well-organized sales presentation designed to sell a good, service, or idea

**Order takers** Salespeople who sell to regular or established customers, complete most sales transactions, and maintain relationships with customers

**Order taking** The routine completion of sales made regularly to target customers

**Packaging** Involves promoting, protecting, and enhancing the product

**Pareto chart** A graph that shows the number of times a problem cause occurs, with problem causes ordered from most frequent to least frequent

**Penetration pricing policy** A policy that tries to sell to the whole market at one low price

**Perception** How we gather and interpret information from the world around us

**Performance analysis** Analysis that looks for exceptions or variations from planned performance

**Performance index** A number that shows the relation of one value to another

**Personal needs** An individual's need for personal satisfaction unrelated to what others think or do

**Personal selling** Direct spoken communication between sellers and potential customers

**Physiological needs** Biological needs including food, drink, rest, and sex

**Pioneering advertising** Advertising that tries to develop primary demand for a product category rather than demand for a specific brand

**Place** Making goods and services available in the right quantities and locations—when the customer wants them

**Place utility** Having the product available where the customer wants it

**Political environment** Affects opportunities at a local or international level

**Population** The total group marketers are interested in

**Portfolio management** Treats alternative products, divisions, or strategic business units (SBUs) as though they were stock investments, to be bought and sold using financial criteria

**Positioning** When the central idea is to narrow down all possible marketing mixes to one that is differentiated to meet target customers' needs in a superior way

**Positive reinforcement** Occurs when a response is followed by satisfaction

**Possession utility** Obtaining a good or service and having the right to use or consume it

**Prepared sales presentation** A sales approach that uses a memorized presentation not adapted to each individual customer

**Prestige pricing** Setting a rather high price to suggest high quality or high status

**Price** Everything the target group gives up to receive a product

**Price fixing** Competitors getting together to raise, lower, or stabilize prices

**Price lining** Setting a few price levels for a product line and then marking all items at these prices

**Primary data** Information collected to solve a current problem

**Primary demand** Demand for a general product idea, not just for a company's own brand

**Product** The need-satisfying offering of the firm

**Product advertising** Advertising that tries to sell a product

**Product assortment** The set of all product lines and individual products that a firm sells

**Product (brand) managers** Managers of specific products

**Product development** Offering new or improved products for current markets

**Product liability** The legal obligation of sellers to pay damages to individuals who are injured by defective or unsafe products

**Product life cycle** The stages a new-product idea goes through from beginning to end

**Product line** A set of individual products that are closely related

**Product-bundle pricing** Setting one price for a set of products

**Product-market** A market with very similar needs and sellers offering various close-substitute ways of satisfying those needs

**Production** Actually making goods or performing services

**Production orientation** When firms make whatever products they want to produce and then try to sell them

**Professional services** Specialized services that support a firm's operations

**Profit-maximization objective** An objective that seeks to get as much profit as possible

**Promotion** Communicating information between a seller and a potential buyer or others in the channel to influence attitudes and behaviour

**Promotional intensity** How much effort is expended by the other members of the channel in order to promote, sell, and service the product

**Prospecting** Following all the leads in a target market to identify potential customers

**Psychographics (lifestyle analysis)** The analysis of a person's day-to-day pattern of living as expressed in that person's activities, interests, and opinions

**Psychological pricing** Setting prices that have special appeal to target customers

**Public relations** Communication with noncustomers, including labour, public interest groups, shareholders, and the government

**Publicity or public relations** Any *unpaid* form of nonpersonal presentation of ideas, goods, or services

**Pulling** Getting customers to ask intermediaries for a product

**Purchasing specifications** A written description of what the firm wants to buy

**Push money (or prize money) allowances** Price reductions given to retailers by manufacturers or wholesalers to pass on to the retailers' salesclerks for aggressively selling certain items

**Pushing** Using normal promotion effort (personal selling, advertising, and sales promotion) to help sell the whole marketing mix to possible channel members

**Qualifying dimensions** Dimensions that are relevant to including a customer type in a product-market

**Qualitative research** Research that seeks in-depth, open-ended responses, not yes or no answers

**Quality** A total product's ability to satisfy a customer's needs or requirements

**Quantitative research** Research that seeks structured responses that can be summarized in numbers, like percentages, averages, or other statistics

**Quantity discounts** Discounts offered to encourage customers to buy in larger amounts

**Rack jobbers** Wholesalers that specialize in hard-to-handle assortments of products that a retailer doesn't want to manage, usually displayed on their own wire racks

**Random sampling** Each member of a population has the same chance of being included in the sample

**Raw materials** Unprocessed expense items that are moved to the next production process with little handling

**Reciprocity** Trading sales for sales

**Reference group** The people to whom an individual looks when forming attitudes about a particular topic

**Reference price** The price consumers expect to pay for a product

**Refusal to supply** Applies when a firm or individual is unable to obtain, on the usual terms, adequate supplies of an article or service not generally in short supply

**Regrouping activities** Adjust the quantities and/or assortments of products handled at each level in a channel of distribution

**Regularly unsought products** Products that stay unsought but not unbought forever

**Relative quality** How products measure up against the criteria used by consumers in making a purchase decision

**Reminder advertising** Advertising that tries to keep the product's name before the public

**Research proposal** A plan that specifies what information will be obtained and how

**Response** An effort to satisfy a drive

**Response rate** The percentage of people contacted who complete a questionnaire

**Retailing** All of the activities involved in the sale of products to final consumers

**Reverse channels** Channels used to retrieve products that customers no longer want

**Routinized response behaviour** Used by consumers when they regularly select a particular way of satisfying a need when it occurs

**Rule for maximizing profit** The highest profit is earned at the price where marginal cost is just less than or equal to marginal revenue

**Safety needs** Needs for protection and physical well-being (health, food, medicine, and exercise)

**Sale price** A temporary discount from the list price

**Sales analysis** A detailed breakdown of a company's sales records

**Sales decline** The product life cycle stage when new products replace the old

**Sales forecast** An estimate of how much an industry or firm hopes to sell to a market segment

**Sales managers** Managers concerned with personal selling

**Sales presentation** A salesperson's effort to make a sale or address a customer's problem

**Sales promotion** Those promotion activities, other than advertising, publicity, and personal selling, that stimulate interest, trial, or purchase by final customers or others in the channel

**Sales promotion managers** Managers concerned with their company's sales promotion effort

**Sales quota** The specific sales or profit objective a salesperson is expected to achieve

**Sales territory** A geographic area that is the responsibility of one salesperson or several working together

**Sales-oriented objective** Objective that seeks some level of unit sales, dollar sales, or share of market without referring to profit

**Sample** A part of the relevant population

**Scientific method** A decision-making approach that focuses on being objective and orderly in *testing* ideas before accepting them

**Scrambled merchandising** A retailer carrying any product line it thinks it can sell profitably

**Search engine** A computer program that helps a marketing manager find information that is needed

**Seasonal discounts** Discounts offered to encourage buyers to buy earlier than present demand requires

**Secondary data** Information that has already been collected and published

**Segmenting** An aggregating process of clustering people with similar needs into a market segment.

**Selective demand** Demand for a company's own brand

**Selective distribution** Selling through only those intermediaries who will give the product special attention

**Selective exposure** Our eyes and minds seek out and notice only information that interests us or is relevant to our life in some way

**Selective perception** We screen out or modify ideas, messages, and information that conflict with previously learned attitudes and beliefs

**Selective retention** We remember only what we want to remember

**Selling agents** Agents that take over the whole marketing job of producers, not just the selling function

**Selling-formula approach** A sales approach that starts with a prepared presentation outline and leads the customer through some logical steps to a final close

**Service** A deed performed by one party for another

**Service mark** The same as a trademark except that it refers to a service offering

**Service wholesalers** Merchant wholesalers who provide all of the wholesaling functions

**Shopping products** Products that a customer feels are worth the time and effort to compare with competing products

**Single target-market approach** Segmenting the market and choosing one of the homogeneous segments as the firm's target market

**Single-line (or general-line) wholesalers** Service wholesalers who carry a narrower line of merchandise than general merchandise wholesalers

**Single-line or limited-line stores** Stores that specialize in certain lines of related products rather than a wide assortment

**Situation analysis** An informal study of what information is already available in the problem area

**Skimming price policy** A policy that tries to sell to the top of a market at a high price before aiming at more price-sensitive customers

**Social class** A group of people who have approximately equal social position as viewed by others in the society

**Social needs** Needs that involve a person's interaction with others (love, friendship, status, and esteem)

**Social responsibility** A firm's obligation to improve its positive effects on society and reduce its negative effects

**Sorting** Separating products into grades and qualities desired by different target markets

**Specialty products** Consumer products that the customer really wants and makes a special effort to find

**Specialty shop** A type of conventional limited-line store

**Specialty wholesalers** Service wholesalers who carry a very narrow range of products and offer more information and service than other service wholesalers

**Spreadsheet analysis** Costs, sales, and other information related to a problem are organized into a data table (spreadsheet) to show how changing the value of one or more of the numbers affects the others

**Staples** Products that are bought often, routinely, and without much thought

**Statistical packages** Easy-to-use computer programs that analyze data

**Status quo objectives** Don't-rock-the-pricing-boat objectives

**Stocking allowances (slotting allowances)** Reductions in price given to an intermediary to get shelf space ("slots") for a product

**Stockturn rate** The number of times the average inventory is sold in a year

**Straight rebuy** A routine repurchase that may have been made many times before

**Strategic business unit (SBU)** An organizational unit (within a larger company) that focuses on some product-markets and is treated as a separate profit centre

**Strategic (management) planning** The managerial process of developing and maintaining a match between an organization's resources and its market opportunities

**Supercentres (hypermarkets)** Very large stores that try to carry not only food and drug items but also all goods and services that the consumer purchases routinely

**Supermarkets** Large stores specializing in groceries, with self-service and wide assortments

**Supplies** Expense items that do not become part of a finished product

**Supply chain** The complete set of firms and facilities and logistics activities that are involved in procuring materials, transforming them into intermediate or finished products, and distributing them to customers

**Supporting salespeople** Salespeople who help the order-oriented salespeople but don't try to get orders themselves

**S.W.O.T. analysis** A strategy that identifies and lists the firm's strengths and weaknesses, and its opportunities and threats

**Tactical or operational decisions** Short-run decisions about the specific activities required to implement a marketing plan

**Target market** A fairly homogeneous (similar) group of customers to which a company wishes to appeal

**Target marketing** Sees everyone as different and therefore requires a tailored marketing mix

**Target-market potential** What a whole market segment might buy

**Target-return objective** An objective that states a specific level of profit

**Target-return pricing** Adding a target return to the cost of a product

**Task method** Basing the budget on the job to be done

**Task utility** Provided when someone performs a task for someone else

**Team selling** When different sales reps work together on a specific account

**Technical specialists** Supporting salespeople who provide technical assistance to order-oriented salespeople

**Telemarketing** Using the telephone to call on customers or prospects

**Telephone and direct-mail retailing** Allow consumers to shop at home, placing orders by mail or a toll-free telephone call and charging the purchase to a credit card

**Time series** Historical records of the fluctuations in economic variables

**Time utility** Having the product available *when* the customer wants it

**Total cost** The sum of total fixed and total variable costs

**Total fixed cost** The sum of those costs that are fixed in total—no matter how much is produced

**Total quality management (TQM)** A management approach in which everyone in the organization is concerned about quality, throughout all of the firm's activities, to better serve customer needs

**Total variable cost** The sum of those changing expenses that are closely related to output

**Total-cost approach** Evaluating each possible PD system and identifying all of the costs of each alternative

**Trade (functional) discount** A list price reduction given to channel members for the job they are going to do, such as storing, transporting, or selling

**Trade-in allowance** A price reduction given for used products when similar new products are bought

**Trademark** Only those words, symbols, or marks that are legally registered for use by a single company

**Traditional channel systems** Systems where the various channel members buy and sell from each other but make little or no effort to cooperate

**Trend extension** Extending past experience into the future

**Truck wholesalers** Wholesalers that specialize in delivering products they stock in their own trucks

**2/10, net 30** An invoice term meaning that the buyer can take a 2-percent discount off the face value of the invoice if the invoice is paid within 10 days; otherwise, the full face value is due within 30 days

**Uniform delivered pricing** Making an average freight charge to all buyers

**Unique selling proposition** Tells its target audience why they should choose the given product over others in the market

**Unit pricing** Placing the price per 100 grams (or some other standard measure) on or near the product

**Universal functions of marketing** Buying, selling, transporting, storing, standardization and grading, financing, risk taking, and market information

**Universal product code (UPC)** Identifies each product with marks readable by electronic scanner

**Unsought products** Products that potential customers don't yet want or know they can buy

**Users** Those who actually use the product or service being bought

**Utility** The power to provide consumers with goods that satisfy their needs and wants

**Validity** The extent to which data measure what they are intended to measure

**Value pricing** Setting a fair price level for a marketing mix that really gives the target market superior customer value

**Value-in-use pricing** Setting prices that will capture some of what customers will save by substituting the firm's product for the one currently being used

**Vendor analysis** A formal rating of suppliers on all relevant areas of performance

**Vertical integration** The practice of acquiring firms at different levels of channel activity

**Vertical marketing systems** Systems in which the whole channel focuses on the same target market at the end of the channel

**Voluntary chains** Wholesaler-sponsored groups that work with independent retailers

**Wants** "Needs" that are learned during a person's life

**Warranty** Explains what the seller promises about its product

**Wheel of retailing theory** The idea that new types of retailers enter the market as low-status, low-margin, low-price operators and then evolve into more conventional retailers offering more services with higher operating costs and higher prices

**Wholly owned subsidiary** A separate firm owned by a parent company

**Zone pricing** Making an average freight charge to all buyers within specific geographic areas

# Name Index

# Subject Index

# Company Index